Business Information Management I:

Texas Edition

Andrea Mehaffie

Catherine Skintik

Teri Watanabe

Suzanne Weixel

Boston • Columbus • Indianapolis • New York • San Francisco
Amsterdam • Cape Town • Dubai • London • Madrid • Milan • Munich • Paris • Montréal • Toronto
Delhi • Mexico City • São Paulo • Sydney • Hong Kong • Seoul • Singapore • Taipei • Tokyo

Pearson

Pearson

330 Hudson Street, New York, NY 10013

Hardcover ISBN 10: 0-13-445717-X
Hardcover ISBN 13: 978-0-13-445717-8

1 16

Table of Contents

Microsoft Excel 2013

Microsoft Access 2013

Chapter 1 Getting Started with Microsoft Access 2013 646

Chapter 2 Working with Queries 714

Chapter 3 Working with Forms and Reports 774

Microsoft PowerPoint 2013

Chapter 1 Getting Started with Microsoft PowerPoint 2013 844

Chapter 2 Working with Lists and Graphics 904

Introduction

Microsoft Office 2013 is Microsoft's suite of application software. The Standard version includes Word, Excel, Outlook, and PowerPoint. Other editions may also include Access, Publisher, OneNote, and InfoPath. This book covers Word (the word processing tool), Excel (the spreadsheet tool), PowerPoint (the presentation tool), and Access (the database tool). Because Microsoft Office is an integrated suite, the components can all be used separately or together to create professional-looking documents and to manage data.

How the Book Is Organized

Business Information Management I is made up of five sections:

- **Basics.** This chapter introduces essential Microsoft Office 2013 skills—including starting Microsoft Office, using the mouse and keyboard, screen elements, and an overview of the applications. If you are completely new to the Office suite, you should start with this chapter.
- **Word 2013.** With Word you can create letters, memos, Web pages, newsletters, and more.
- **Excel 2013.** Excel, Microsoft's spreadsheet component, is used to organize and calculate data, track financial data, and create charts and graphs.
- **Access 2013.** Access is Microsoft's powerful database tool. Using Access you will learn to store, retrieve, and report on information.
- **PowerPoint 2013.** Create dynamic onscreen presentations with PowerPoint, the presentation graphics tool.

Chapters are comprised of short lessons designed for using Microsoft Office 2013 in real-life business settings. Each lesson is made up of six key elements:

- **What You Will Learn.** Each lesson starts with an overview of the learning objectives covered in the lesson.
- **Words to Know.** Key terms are included and defined at the start of each lesson, so you can quickly refer back to them. The terms are then highlighted in the text.
- **What You Can Do.** Concise notes for learning the computer concepts.
- **Try It.** Hands-on practice activities provide brief procedures to teach all necessary skills.
- **Practice.** These projects give students a chance to create documents, spreadsheets, database objects, and presentations by entering information. Steps provide all the how-to information needed to complete a project.
- **Apply.** Each lesson concludes with a project that challenges students to apply what they have learned through steps that tell them what to do, without all the how-to information. In the Apply projects, students must show they have mastered each skill set.
- Each chapter ends with two assessment projects: **Critical Thinking** and **Portfolio Builder**, which incorporate all the skills covered throughout the chapter.

Working with Data and Solution Files

As you work through the projects in this book, you'll be creating, opening, and saving files. You should keep the following instructions in mind:

- For many of the projects, you will use data files. Other projects will ask you to create new documents and files and then enter text and data into them, so you can master creating documents from scratch.
- The data files are used so that you can focus on the skills being introduced—not on keyboarding lengthy documents.
- When the project steps tell you to open a file name, you open the data file provided.
- All the projects instruct you to save the files created or to save the project files under a new name. This is to make the project file your own and to avoid over-writing the data file in the storage location. Throughout this book, when naming files and folders, replace *xx* with your name or initials as instructed by your teacher.
- Follow your instructor's directions for where to access and save the files on a network, local computer hard drive, or portable storage device such as a USB drive.
- Many of the projects also provide instructions for including your name in a header or footer. Again, this is to identify the project work as your own for grading and assessment purposes.
- Unless the book instructs otherwise, use the default settings for text size, margin size, and so on when creating a file. If someone has changed the default software settings for the computer you're using, your exercise files may not look the same as those shown in this book. In addition, the appearance of your files may look different if the system is set to a screen resolution other than 1024 × 768.

Navigating the Textbook and Supplemental Print Resources

Student Textbook

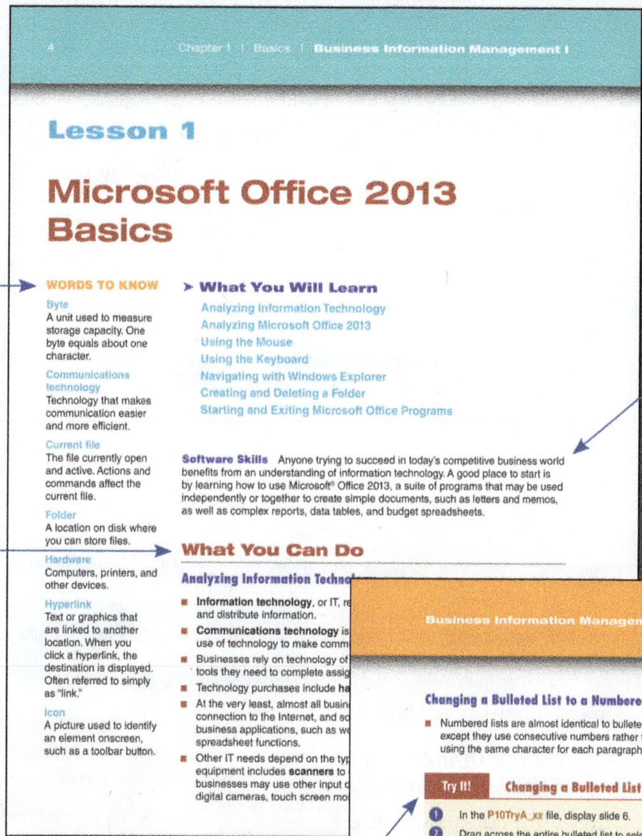

4 Chapter 1 | Basics | **Business Information Management I**

Lesson 1

Microsoft Office 2013 Basics

WORDS TO KNOW

Byte
A unit used to measure storage capacity. One byte equals about one character.

Communications technology
Technology that makes communication easier and more efficient.

Current file
The file currently open and active. Actions and commands affect the current file.

Folder
A location on disk where you can store files.

Hardware
Computers, printers, and other devices.

Hyperlink
Text or graphics that are linked to another location. When you click a hyperlink, the destination is displayed. Often referred to simply as "link."

Icon
A picture used to identify an element onscreen, such as a toolbar button.

➤ What You Will Learn

Analyzing Information Technology
Analyzing Microsoft Office 2013
Using the Mouse
Using the Keyboard
Navigating with Windows Explorer
Creating and Deleting a Folder
Starting and Exiting Microsoft Office Programs

Software Skills Anyone trying to succeed in today's competitive business world benefits from an understanding of information technology. A good place to start is by learning how to use Microsoft® Office 2013, a suite of programs that may be used independently or together to create simple documents, such as letters and memos, as well as complex reports, data tables, and budget spreadsheets.

What You Can Do

Analyzing Information Techno

- **Information technology**, or IT, re and distribute information.
- **Communications technology** is use of technology to make comm
- Businesses rely on technology of tools they need to complete assig
- Technology purchases include **ha**
- At the very least, almost all busin connection to the Internet, and so business applications, such as w spreadsheet functions.
- Other IT needs depend on the typ equipment includes **scanners** to businesses may use other input d digital cameras, touch screen mo

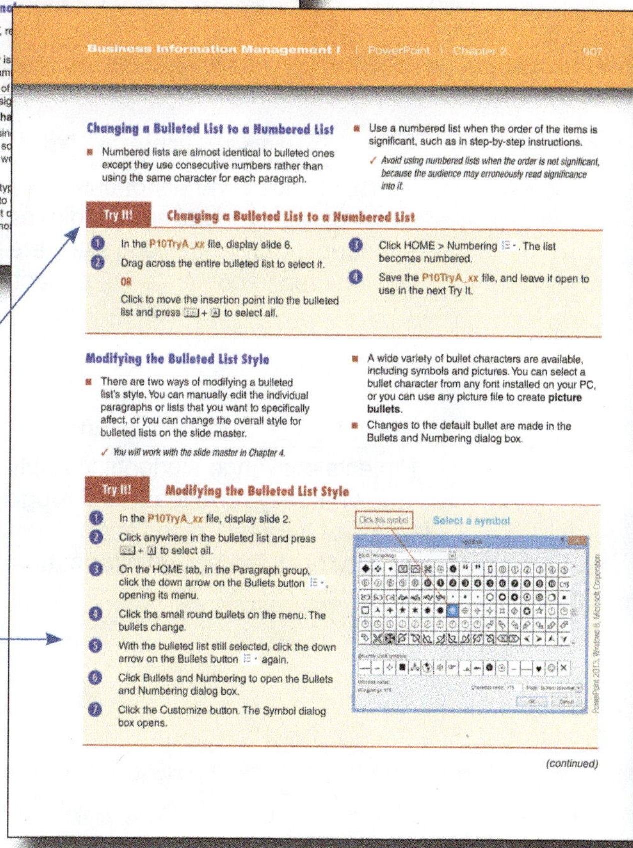

Business Information Management I | PowerPoint | Chapter 2 907

Changing a Bulleted List to a Numbered List

- Numbered lists are almost identical to bulleted ones except they use consecutive numbers rather than using the same character for each paragraph.
- Use a numbered list when the order of the items is significant, such as in step-by-step instructions.

✓ *Avoid using numbered lists when the order is not significant, because the audience may erroneously read significance into it.*

Try It! Changing a Bulleted List to a Numbered List

1. In the P10TryA_xx file, display slide 6.
2. Drag across the entire bulleted list to select it.
   OR
   Click to move the insertion point into the bulleted list and press Ctrl + A to select all.
3. Click HOME > Numbering. The list becomes numbered.
4. Save the P10TryA_xx file, and leave it open to use in the next Try It.

Modifying the Bulleted List Style

- There are two ways of modifying a bulleted list's style. You can manually edit the individual paragraphs or lists that you want to specifically affect, or you can change the overall style for bulleted lists on the slide master.

✓ *You will work with the slide master in Chapter 4.*

- A wide variety of bullet characters are available, including symbols and pictures. You can select a bullet character from any font installed on your PC, or you can use any picture file to create **picture bullets**.
- Changes to the default bullet are made in the Bullets and Numbering dialog box.

Try It! Modifying the Bulleted List Style

1. In the P10TryA_xx file, display slide 2.
2. Click anywhere in the bulleted list and press Ctrl + A to select all.
3. On the HOME tab, in the Paragraph group, click the down arrow on the Bullets button, opening its menu.
4. Click the small round bullets on the menu. The bullets change.
5. With the bulleted list still selected, click the down arrow on the Bullets button again.
6. Click Bullets and Numbering to open the Bullets and Numbering dialog box.
7. Click the Customize button. The Symbol dialog box opens.

(continued)

Words to Know

Vocabulary terms are listed at the start of each lesson for easy reference and appear in bold in the text on first use.

What You Can Do

The technology concepts are introduced and explained.

Software Skills

Each lesson begins with an introduction that highlights the computer skills that will be covered in the lesson.

Try It!

Short, hands-on activities give students the opportunity to practice the software features in a sample document.

Illustrations

Illustrations throughout the text can be used as guidelines for visual learners.

End-of-Lesson Projects

Each lesson includes two hands-on projects where students can use all of the skills that they have learned in the lesson.

End-Result Solutions

Students can refer to solution illustrations to make sure that his or her work is on track.

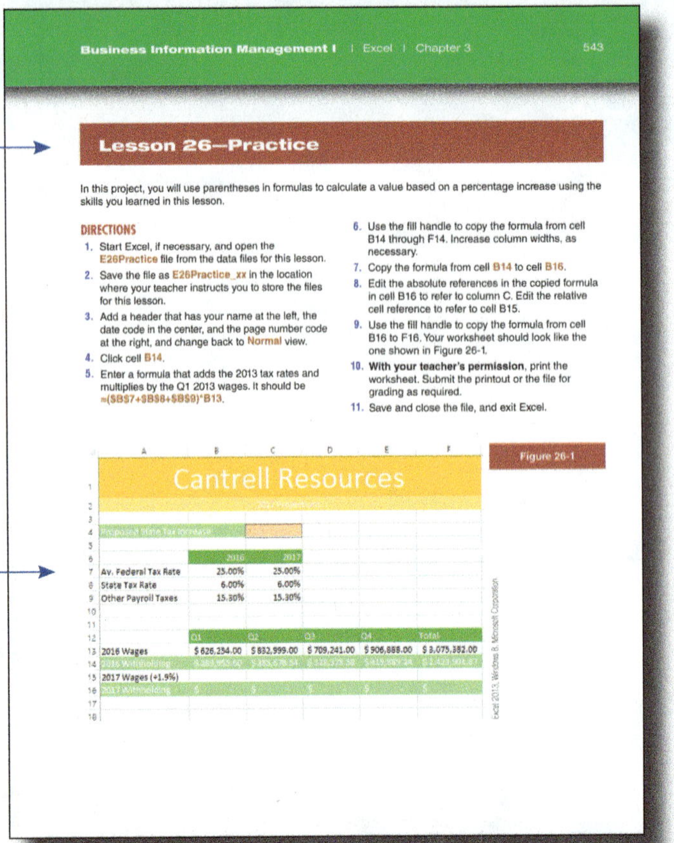

Business Information Management I | Excel | Chapter 3 543

Lesson 26—Practice

In this project, you will use parentheses in formulas to calculate a value based on a percentage increase using the skills you learned in this lesson.

DIRECTIONS

1. Start Excel, if necessary, and open the E26Practice file from the data files for this lesson.
2. Save the file as E26Practice_xx in the location where your teacher instructs you to store the files for this lesson.
3. Add a header that has your name at the left, the date code in the center, and the page number code at the right, and change back to Normal view.
4. Click cell B14.
5. Enter a formula that adds the 2013 tax rates and multiplies by the Q1 2013 wages. It should be =($B$7+$B$8+$B$9)*B13.
6. Use the fill handle to copy the formula from cell B14 through F14. Increase column widths, as necessary.
7. Copy the formula from cell B14 to cell B16.
8. Edit the absolute references in the copied formula in cell B16 to refer to column C. Edit the relative cell reference to refer to cell B15.
9. Use the fill handle to copy the formula from cell B16 to F16. Your worksheet should look like the one shown in Figure 26-1.
10. **With your teacher's permission**, print the worksheet. Submit the printout or the file for grading as required.
11. Save and close the file, and exit Excel.

Figure 26-1

End-of-Chapter Activities

Topics include a variety of business, career, and college-readiness scenarios. Critical-thinking skills are required to complete the project.

Directions

Projects challenge students to apply what they have learned through steps that tell what needs to be done, without all the how-to information.

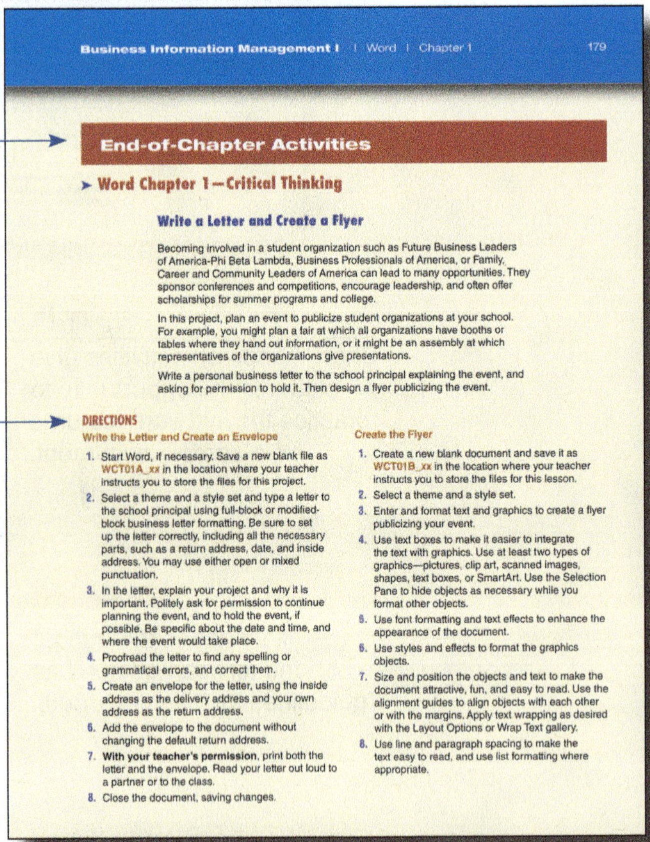

Business Information Management I | Word | Chapter 1 179

End-of-Chapter Activities

➤ **Word Chapter 1—Critical Thinking**

Write a Letter and Create a Flyer

Becoming involved in a student organization such as Future Business Leaders of America-Phi Beta Lambda, Business Professionals of America, or Family, Career and Community Leaders of America can lead to many opportunities. They sponsor conferences and competitions, encourage leadership, and often offer scholarships for summer programs and college.

In this project, plan an event to publicize student organizations at your school. For example, you might plan a fair at which all organizations have booths or tables where they hand out information, or it might be an assembly at which representatives of the organizations give presentations.

Write a personal business letter to the school principal explaining the event, and asking for permission to hold it. Then design a flyer publicizing the event.

DIRECTIONS

Write the Letter and Create an Envelope

1. Start Word, if necessary. Save a new blank file as WCT01A_xx in the location where your teacher instructs you to store the files for this project.
2. Select a theme and a style set and type a letter to the school principal using full-block or modified-block business letter formatting. Be sure to set up the letter correctly, including all the necessary parts, such as a return address, date, and inside address. You may use either open or mixed punctuation.
3. In the letter, explain your project and why it is important. Politely ask for permission to continue planning the event, and to hold the event, if possible. Be specific about the date and time, and where the event would take place.
4. Proofread the letter to find any spelling or grammatical errors, and correct them.
5. Create an envelope for the letter, using the inside address as the delivery address and your own address as the return address.
6. Add the envelope to the document without changing the default return address.
7. **With your teacher's permission**, print both the letter and the envelope. Read your letter out loud to a partner or to the class.
8. Close the document, saving changes.

Create the Flyer

1. Create a new blank document and save it as WCT01B_xx in the location where your teacher instructs you to store the files for this lesson.
2. Select a theme and a style set.
3. Enter and format text and graphics to create a flyer publicizing your event.
4. Use text boxes to make it easier to integrate the text with graphics. Use at least two types of graphics—pictures, clip art, scanned images, shapes, text boxes, or SmartArt. Use the Selection Pane to hide objects as necessary while you format other objects.
5. Use font formatting and text effects to enhance the appearance of the document.
6. Use styles and effects to format the graphics objects.
7. Size and position the objects and text to make the document attractive, fun, and easy to read. Use the alignment guides to align objects with each other or with the margins. Apply text wrapping as desired with the Layout Options or Wrap Text gallery.
8. Use line and paragraph spacing to make the text easy to read, and use list formatting where appropriate.

Teacher's Wraparound Edition

The Teacher's Wraparound Edition includes the entire student edition along with point-of-use teaching strategies, tips, and supplemental material.

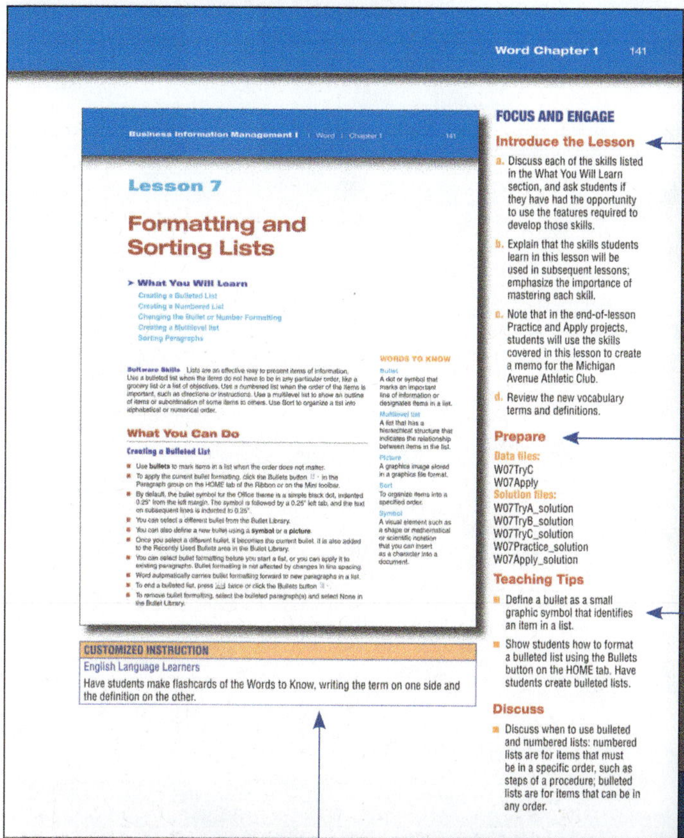

Introduce the Lesson

This provides the instructor with some basic information to get started on the lesson skills.

Prepare

These include a listing of all of the student data files and solution files needed to complete the activities in the lesson.

Teaching Tips

These items help explain the content and provide additional information for instructors to use in the classroom.

English Language Learners Customized Instruction

Support for English language learners is provided throughout.

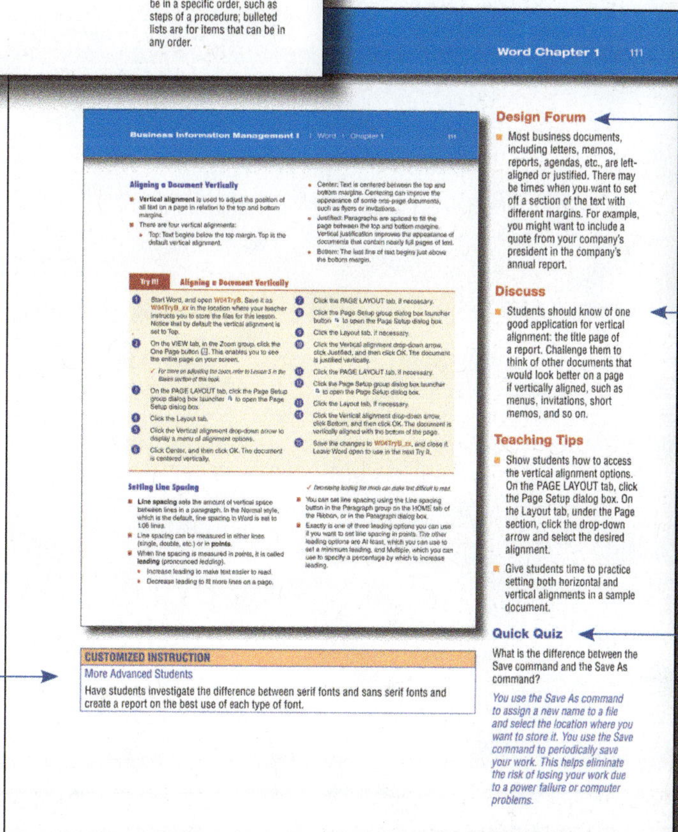

Skills Extensions

These provide additional material not covered in the student edition.

Discuss

These discussion topics relate directly and indirectly to the content on the current page.

Quick Quizzes

These provide questions to ask students. Sample answers are provided for the instructor.

Customized Instruction Boxes

These include adaptions and additional activities for More Advanced, Less Advanced, English Language Learners, and Special Needs Students.

Business Information Management I:

Texas Edition

Chapter 1

(Courtesy Goodluz/Shutterstock)

Using the Common Features of Microsoft Office 2013

Lesson 1
Microsoft Office 2013 Basics

- Analyzing Information Technology
- Analyzing Microsoft Office 2013
- Using the Mouse
- Using Touch Mode
- Using the Keyboard
- Analyzing Data Storage
- Navigating with Windows Explorer
- Creating and Deleting a Folder
- Starting a Microsoft Office Program, Creating a Blank File, and Exiting the Program

Lesson 2
Saving, Printing, and Closing Microsoft Office Files

- Identifying Common Microsoft Office Screen Elements
- Entering and Editing Text
- Correcting Errors
- Saving a File
- Printing a File
- Closing a File

Lesson 3
Working with Existing Files

- Opening an Existing File
- Saving a File with a New Name
- Viewing File Properties
- Using the Ribbon
- Using Access Keys
- Selecting Text
- Formatting Text

Lesson 4
Using Command Options

- Using the Quick Access Toolbar
- Using the Mini Toolbar
- Using Shortcut Menus
- Using Dialog Box Options
- Using Task Panes
- Formatting Pages

Lesson 5
Managing Program Windows

- Changing the View
- Using Window Controls
- Zooming
- Scrolling
- Using Multiple Windows
- Using the Microsoft Office Clipboard

Lesson 6
Using Microsoft Office Help

- Using Microsoft Office Help
- Searching for Help
- Using the Help Table of Contents
- Viewing Application Options
- Customizing the Ribbon
- Using AutoRecover and Autosave

Lesson 7
Managing Information Technology

- Copying Files and Folders
- Moving Files and Folders
- Compressing Files
- Recognizing Types of Business Documents
- Determining the Risks and Rewards of Developing an IT Strategy
- Identifying Needed Equipment and Supplies
- Establishing, Scheduling, and Following Maintenance Procedures
- Demonstrating Professional Standards of Behavior

End-of-Chapter Activities

Lesson 1

Microsoft Office 2013 Basics

➤ What You Will Learn

Analyzing Information Technology
Analyzing Microsoft Office 2013
Using the Mouse
Using the Keyboard
Navigating with Windows Explorer
Creating and Deleting a Folder
Starting and Exiting Microsoft Office Programs

WORDS TO KNOW

Byte
A unit used to measure storage capacity. One byte equals about one character.

Communications technology
Technology that makes communication easier and more efficient.

Current file
The file currently open and active. Actions and commands affect the current file.

Folder
A location on disk where you can store files.

Hardware
Computers, printers, and other devices.

Hyperlink
Text or graphics that are linked to another location. When you click a hyperlink, the destination is displayed. Often referred to simply as "link."

Icon
A picture used to identify an element onscreen, such as a toolbar button.

Software Skills Anyone trying to succeed in today's competitive business world benefits from an understanding of information technology. A good place to start is by learning how to use Microsoft® Office 2013, a suite of programs that may be used independently or together to create simple documents, such as letters and memos, as well as complex reports, data tables, and budget spreadsheets.

What You Can Do

Analyzing Information Technology

- **Information technology**, or IT, refers to the use of computers to collect, store, and distribute information.
- **Communications technology** is part of information technology. It refers to the use of technology to make communication easier and more efficient.
- Businesses rely on technology of many types to make sure employees have the tools they need to complete assignments, tasks, and other responsibilities.
- Technology purchases include **hardware** and **software**.
- At the very least, almost all businesses require a computer, a printer, a connection to the Internet, and software such as Microsoft Office for basic business applications, such as word processing, data management, and spreadsheet functions.
- Other IT needs depend on the type and size of business. Some common IT equipment includes **scanners** to convert printed material to digital format. Some businesses may use other input devices such as voice recognition software, digital cameras, touch screen monitors or tablet PCs, and microphones.

- Other technology a company might need includes projectors, bar code readers, cash registers, and video conferencing systems.
- Departments must evaluate the needs of each employee, research the available technologies and then purchase and install the appropriate systems. They must also be sure employees know how to use the new systems.
- Requirements vary from department to department and from company to company. For example, a large financial services company will have different technology needs than a small travel agency.
- When evaluating technology, consider the following:
  - Tasks you need to accomplish
  - Cost
  - Ease-of-use
  - Compatibility with existing systems
- You can learn more about hardware and software technology using the Internet, consulting a magazine or buyer's guide, or by visiting a retailer in your area to talk to a salesperson.

Analyzing Microsoft Office 2013

- Microsoft Office 2013 is a version of the popular Microsoft Office **software suite**.
- You use the Microsoft Office programs for many business tasks, including to create various types of documents, to communicate with co-workers and customers, and to store and manage information.
- The Microsoft Office 2013 software suite is available in different editions.
- Most editions include the following core Microsoft Office programs:
  - Microsoft® Word, a word processing program.
  - Microsoft® Excel®, a spreadsheet program.
  - Microsoft® PowerPoint®, a presentation graphics program.
  - Microsoft® Outlook®, a personal information manager and communications program.
- Some editions may include the following additional programs:
  - Microsoft® Access®, a database application.
  - Microsoft® Publisher, a desktop publishing program.
  - Microsoft® OneNote®, a note-taking and management program.
  - Microsoft® InfoPath™, an information gathering and management program.
- This book covers the most commonly used programs in the Microsoft Office 2013 suite: Word, Excel, Access, and PowerPoint.
- Microsoft Office 2013 runs with the Microsoft® Windows® 8 or Microsoft® Windows® 7 operating system.
- There may be slight differences in the programs depending on the operating system you are using.
- For example, features that involve browsing for storage locations are different depending on the operating system. This includes opening and saving a file, and selecting a file to insert.

Information technology (IT)
The use of computers to collect, store, and distribute information. Also the various technologies used in processing, storing, and communicating business and personal information.

Insertion point
The flashing vertical line that indicates where typed text will display.

Library
In Microsoft Windows 7 and above, a location where you can view files and folders that are actually stored in other locations on your computer system.

Menu
A list of commands or choices.

Mouse
A device that allows you to select items onscreen by pointing at them with the mouse pointer.

Mouse pad
A smooth, cushioned surface on which you slide a mouse.

Mouse pointer
A marker on your computer screen that shows you where the next mouse action will occur.

Object
Icon, menu, or other item that is part of an onscreen interface.

Random access memory (RAM)
Temporary memory a computer uses to store information while it is processing.

Read-only memory (ROM)
Fixed memory stored on a chip in a computer that provides startup and other system instructions.

Scanner
A device that converts printed documents into digital file formats.

Scroll
To page through a document in order to view contents that is not currently displayed.

Scroll wheel
A wheel on some mouse devices used to navigate through a document onscreen.

Software
Programs that provide the instructions for a computer or other hardware device.

- In addition, there may be some visual differences in the way the programs look onscreen.
- The procedures in this book assume you are using Microsoft Windows 8. Ask your teacher for information on procedures that may be different on systems using Windows 7.

Using the Mouse

- Use your **mouse** to point to and select commands and features of Microsoft Office 2013 programs.
- Most mouse devices work using light. Some older models work by sliding a tracking ball on your desk.
- Notebook computers may have a touchpad or trackball to move the pointer on the screen in place of a mouse.
- When you move the mouse on your desk, the **mouse pointer** moves onscreen. For example, when you move the mouse to the left, the mouse pointer moves to the left.
- Hovering the pointer over an **object** such as an **icon** or menu name usually displays a ScreenTip that identifies the object.
- When you click a mouse button, the program executes a command. For example, when you move the mouse pointer to the Save button and then click, the program saves the current document or file.
- Clicking a mouse button can also be used to move the **insertion point** to a new location.
- A mouse may have one, two, or three buttons. Unless otherwise noted, references in this book are to the use of the left mouse button.
- Your mouse might have a **scroll wheel**. Spin the scroll wheel to **scroll**—move—through the file open on your screen.

Table 1-1 Mouse Actions

Action	Description
Point to	Move mouse pointer to touch specified element.
Click	Point to element then press and release left mouse button.
Right-click	Point to element then press and release right mouse button.
Double-click	Point to element then press and release left mouse button twice in rapid succession.
Drag	Point to element, hold down left mouse button, then move mouse pointer to new location.
Drop	Release the mouse button after dragging.
Scroll	Rotate center wheel backward to scroll down, or forward to scroll up.
Pan	Press center wheel and drag up or down.
Auto-Scroll	Click center wheel to scroll down; move pointer up to scroll up.
Zoom	Hold down Ctrl and rotate center wheel.

- The mouse pointer changes shape depending on the program in use, the object being pointed to, and the action being performed. Common mouse pointer shapes include an arrow for selecting, an I-beam, and a hand with a pointing finger to indicate a **hyperlink**.
- You should use a mouse on a **mouse pad** that is designed specifically to make it easy to slide the mouse.
- You can move the mouse without moving the mouse pointer by picking it up. This is useful if you move the mouse too close to the edge of the mouse pad or desk.

Try It! Using the Mouse

1. Start your computer if it is not already on. Log in to your user account, if necessary.
   ✓ *Ask your teacher how to log in to your user account.*
2. Click the Desktop tile on the Windows 8 Start screen.
   ✓ *If you are using Windows 7, skip step 2.*
3. Move the mouse pointer to point at the Recycle Bin icon.
4. Right-click the Recycle Bin icon. A shortcut menu displays (see picture at right).
5. On the shortcut menu, click Open. The Recycle Bin window opens and displays files and folders that have been deleted.
6. Click the Close button in the upper-right corner of the Recycle Bin window.
7. Double-click the Recycle Bin icon. This is another method of opening an object.
   ✓ *Some systems are set to open objects with a single click.*
8. Click the Close button in the upper-right corner of the Recycle Bin window.

Right-click to display a shortcut menu

Windows 8, Microsoft Corporation

Software suite
A group of software programs sold as a single unit. Usually the programs have common features that make it easy to integrate and share data.

Storage
A computer device or component used to store data such as programs and files.

Stylus pen
A pen shaped device used to interact with a touch screen.

Subfolder
A folder stored within another folder.

Template
A document that contains formatting, styles, and sample text that you can use to create new documents.

Window
The area onscreen where a program or document is displayed.

Using a Touch Screen

- If you are using the Windows 8 operating system on a device with a touch screen, you can use touch mode.
- With touch mode, you use your fingers or a **stylus pen** instead of a mouse.
- The basic gestures for interacting with a touch screen are tap and swipe.
- Tap means to gently touch the screen and then lift straight up. A tap is similar to a mouse click.
- Swipe means to slide your finger or pen across the screen.
- See Table 1-2 on the next page for more information on touch screen gestures.

Table 1-2 Touch Gestures

Tap	Tap once on an item. This opens or selects the item that is tapped.
Press and hold	Press down and hold for a few seconds. This selects an item (such as an icon), displays a ScreenTip, or opens a shortcut menu.
Pinch or stretch	Touch with two or more fingers and move the fingers closer (pinch) or apart (stretch). This displays different levels of information or zooms in or out.
Swipe to scroll	Drag across the screen. This scrolls in the direction you drag.
Swipe to select	Quickly drag a short stroke in the opposite direction you would swipe to scroll. This selects an item.
Swipe from edge	Start on an edge and swipe in. Results vary depending on the edge.

Try It! Using a Touch Screen

1. Start your computer if it is not already on. Log into your user account, if necessary.

   ✓ *Ask your teacher how to log in to your user account.*
2. Swipe from right to left to scroll the Start screen.
3. Swipe from left to right to scroll back.
4. Tap the Desktop tile to display the desktop.
5. Press and hold the Recycle Bin icon.
6. Tap Open on the shortcut menu.
7. Tap the Close button [×] in the upper-right corner of the Recycle Bin window.

Using the Keyboard

- Use your keyboard to type characters, including letters, numbers, and symbols. The keyboard can also be used to access program commands and features.
- On a touch-enabled device, you can display a touch keyboard by tapping the Touch Keyboard button on the Taskbar.
- Function keys (F1–F12) often appear in a row above the numbers at the top of the keyboard. They can be used as shortcut keys to perform certain tasks.
- Modifier keys such as Shift [SHIFT], Alt [ALT], and Ctrl [CTRL] are used in combination with other keys or mouse actions to select certain commands or perform actions. In this book, key combinations are shown as: the modifier key followed by a plus sign followed by the other key or mouse action. For example, [CTRL] + [S] is the key combination for saving the **current file**.
- The 17-key keypad to the right of the main group of keyboard keys on an enhanced keyboard includes the numeric keys.
- Most notebook computers and portable devices integrate the numeric keys into the regular keyboard.
- When the Num Lock [NUM LOCK] feature is on, the keypad can be used to enter numbers. When the feature is off, the keys can be used as directional keys to move the insertion point in the current file.
- The Escape key [ESC] is used to cancel a command.
- Use the Enter key [ENTER] to execute a command or to start a new paragraph when typing text.
- Directional keys are used to move the insertion point.
- Editing keys such as Insert [INS], Delete [DEL], and Backspace [BACKSPACE] are used to insert or delete text.
- The Windows key [⊞] (sometimes called the Winkey or the Windows Logo key) is used alone to open the Windows Start **menu**, or in combination with other keys to execute certain Windows commands.
- The Application key [▤] is used alone to open a shortcut menu, or in combination with other keys to execute certain application commands.
- Some keyboards also have keys for opening shortcut menus, launching a Web browser, or opening an e-mail program.

Try It! Using the Keyboard

1. Press [Windows] on your keyboard to open the Start screen.

   ✓ *On a touch-enabled device, tap the Touch Keyboard button on the Taskbar to display the keyboard.*

2. Press [TAB] twice to select the first tile.

3. Press the up- down-, left-, and right-arrow keys to select different tiles; stop when the Calendar tile is selected.

4. Press [ENTER] to open the Calendar app window.

5. Press [ALT] + [F4] to close the window.

6. Press [ESC] to close the Start Screen and display the desktop.

Analyzing Data Storage

- Data **storage** is any device or component which can record and retain data, or information.
- Without storage, you would not be able to save files or access computer programs.
- Storage capacity is measured in bytes. One **byte** is equal to about one character.
- A typical hard disk drive today may have a capacity of 3 terabytes (TB) or more!
- The type of storage you have available depends on your computer system.
- Some common storage devices include the following:
  - Internal hard disk drive, which is a device mounted inside a computer, and used to store programs and data files.
  - External hard disk drive, which is similar to an internal hard disk drive except that it connects to the outside of the computer via a cable and a port, such as a Universal Serial Bus (USB).
  - Network drive, which is a hard disk drive attached to a network, Computers attached to the same network can access the information on the drive.
  - Flash drive, which is a small, portable device that can be attached to a USB port on the outside of a computer. A flash drive is convenient for transporting files from one computer to another.
  - Memory card, which is a small card that is usually inserted into a slot in a computer or other device, such as a digital camera or printer.
  - DVD, which is a disk that you insert into a DVD drive to record or read data. DVDs are often used for storing video, music, and pictures.
  - CD, which is an older form of storage disk.
  - Virtual drive, which is an area on a storage device that is identified as a separate drive.
  - Online storage, which allows you to save, access, and share data using storage space on the Internet. The data is protected from unauthorized access using a password. For example, SkyDrive, offered by Microsoft Corp., allows free access to up to 25 GB of online storage for saving and sharing files.
- Memory is also a type of storage. There are two types of computer memory:
  - **Read-only memory** (ROM) which is stored on a chip inside the computer. It provides the instructions your computer needs to start and begin operation, and it cannot be changed under normal circumstances,
  - **Random access memory** (RAM) is the temporary memory your computer uses to store information it is currently processing. Information stored in RAM is lost when then computer shuts down; you must save it on a storage device if you want to use it in the future.

Navigating with File Explorer

- You use File Explorer, a feature of the Windows 8 operating system, to navigate among your system components to find and use the information you need.

  ✓ *If you are using Windows 7, the navigation program is called Windows Explorer. The interface is slightly different. Ask your teacher for information on using Windows 7.*

- For example, you navigate to a storage device such as a disk drive to locate and open a file or program. You navigate to an output device such as a printer to perform maintenance, adjust settings, or use the device.

- Windows comes with built-in **folders** that organize your computer components to make it easier to find the object you need. When you open a folder in File Explorer, its contents display in a **window** on your monitor.
- For example, open the Computer folder window in File Explorer to display devices such as hard disk drives. Open the Libraries folder window to display **libraries** organized on your system. Open the Network window to display the devices connected to the same network as your system.
- To select an item displayed in a window, click it. To open an item, double-click it.

✓ *This book assumes your system is set to open an object using a double click. If your system is set to open an object on a single click, you will use that method instead.*

✓ *This book assumes you are using a mouse. If you are using a touch-enabled device, you will use your finger or a pen instead.*

- Every computer system has different components. For example, one system might have a DVD drive, and another system might not. One might connect to a networked printer, while another has a printer directly connected to a USB port. No matter what the system components might be, the methods for navigating are the same:
  - Use the Back and Forward buttons to move through windows you have opened recently.
  - Use the Recent Locations menu to go directly to a window you have opened recently.
  - Click a location in the Address bar to open it.
  - Click an arrow between locations in the Address bar to display a menu, then click a location on the menu to open it.
  - Each window displays a navigation pane which provides links to common locations. Click a location in the Navigation pane to display its contents in the window.

Try It! Navigating with File Explorer

1. If you have a removable storage device to use for storing your work in this class, connect it to your computer. For example, insert a removable disk in a drive, or connect a flash drive to a USB port.
2. If necessary, press ESC to switch from the Windows start screen to the desktop. Click the File Explorer icon on the Taskbar.
3. Click Computer in the Navigation pane of the File Explorer window to open the Computer window to view the storage devices that are part of your computer system.

   OR

   If you are storing your work for this class on a network location, click Network in the Navigation pane to open the Network window to view the components that are part of your computer network.

   ✓ *The Computer and Network components are specific to your system and may be different from those shown in the illustration.*
4. In the Content pane of the open window, double-click the location where you are storing your work for this class. For example, double-click the icon for the removable device you connected in step 1.
5. Click the Back button above the navigation pane to display the previous storage location.
6. Click the Forward button to move forward to the last window you had opened.
7. Click the Close button to close the window. If other windows are open, close them as well.

(continued)

Try It! Navigating with File Explorer *(continued)*

Navigate with File Explorer

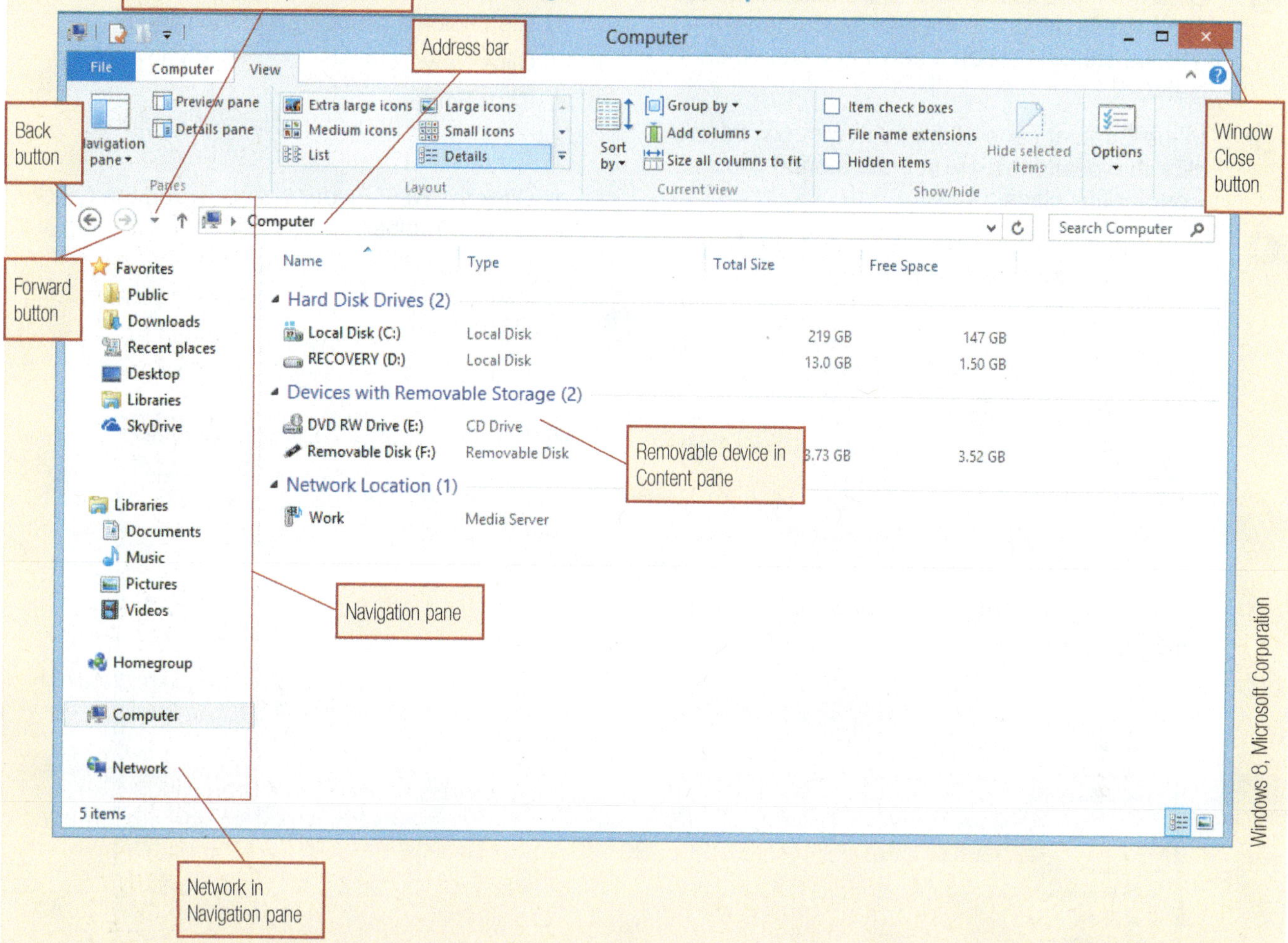

Windows 8, Microsoft Corporation

Creating and Deleting a Folder

- A folder is a named location on a storage device that you create using the Windows operating system.
- To create a folder, you specify where you want it on your computer system, and then give it a name.
- Folders help you keep your data organized, and make it easier to find the files you need when you need them.
- For example, you might store all the documents you use for planning a budget in a folder named Budget. You might store all the documents you use for a marketing project in a folder named Marketing Project.
- You can create a folder within an existing folder to set up layers of organization. A folder within another folder may be called a **subfolder**.
- You can delete a folder you no longer need. Deleting removes the folder from its current location and stores it in the Recycle Bin.

Try It! Creating a Folder

1. Click the File Explorer icon on the Taskbar, and then Computer in the Navigation pane. If you are storing files on a network location, click Network.
2. In the Content pane of the open window, double-click the location where you are storing your work for this class.
3. Click the Home tab on the Ribbon. In the New group, click the New Folder button .

   OR

   a. Right-click a blank area of the window.

   b. Click New.

   c. Click Folder.

   OR

   - Click the New Folder button on the Quick Access Toolbar.
4. Type **B01Try**.
5. Press ENTER .

Create a folder

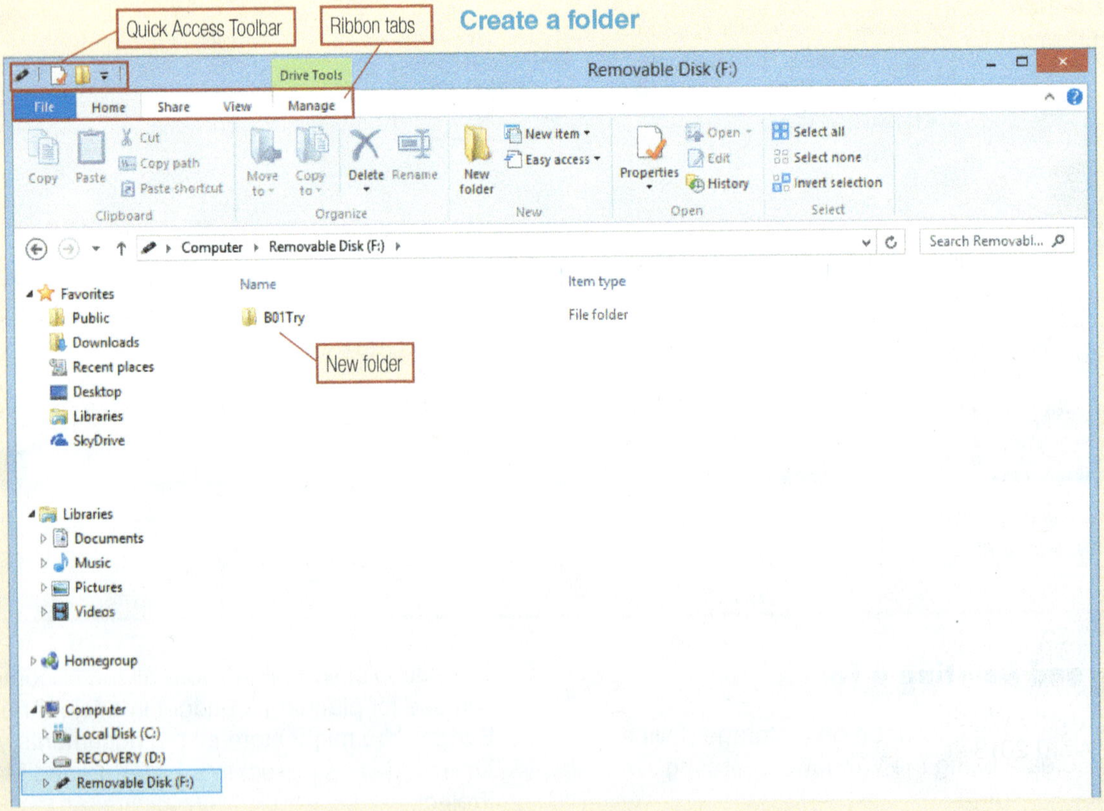

Windows 8, Microsoft Corporation

Try It! Deleting a Folder

1. Right-click the **B01Try** folder.
2. Click Delete on the shortcut menu.
3. Click Yes to move the folder to the Recycle Bin.
4. Click the Close button in the storage location window to close File Explorer.

Starting a Microsoft Office Program, Creating a Blank File, and Exiting the Program

- To use a Microsoft Office 2013 program you must first start it so it is running on your computer.
- Use Windows to start a Microsoft Office program.
- The way you start a Microsoft Office program depends on your system configuration.
  - You will usually find the program's tile on your Windows Start screen. Click the tile to start the program.
  - If the program shortcut icon displays on your Windows desktop, you can click the Desktop tile on the Start screen, and then double-click the program icon.
  - If the program icon has been added to the Taskbar, you can display the desktop and click the program icon on the Taskbar.
  - If the program is not available on the Start screen or the desktop, you will find it on the Apps screen. The Apps screen lists all installed apps and programs alphabetically. Scroll to locate the Microsoft Office 2013 programs, then click the name of the program you want to open.
- When you start a Microsoft Office 2013 program, it displays a list of recently-used files and a gallery of available **templates**.
- Each program has a Blank template; click the Blank template to create a new blank file.
- When you are done using a Microsoft Office program, close it to exit. If you have a file open, the program prompts you to save, or to exit without saving.

Try It! Starting a Microsoft Office Program and Creating a Blank File

1. From the Windows 8 Start screen, click the Word 2013 program tile:

Windows 8, Microsoft Corporation

✓ *Depending on the number of tiles displayed, you may have to scroll to the right to locate the tile.*

OR

a. From the Windows 8 Start screen, click the Desktop tile.
b. On the Windows desktop, double-click the Word 2013 shortcut icon.

OR

- On the Taskbar, click the Word 2013 icon.

OR

a. Right-click a blank area of the Windows 8 Start screen.
b. Click the All apps button.
c. Scroll to the Microsoft Office 2013 programs.
d. Click Word 2013.

2. Click the Blank document template.

Try It! Exiting a Microsoft Office Program

1. In the Microsoft Word program window, click the Close button × at the right end of the program's title bar.
2. If you have a file open, a dialog box displays. Click Save to save changes to the file and exit, or click Don't Save to exit without saving.

Lesson 1—Practice

You have just been hired as the office manager at Restoration Architecture, a growing firm that specializes in remodeling, redesign, and restoration of existing properties. In this project, you practice using your computer's operating system to create and name a folder. You also practice starting and exiting a Microsoft Office 2013 program.

DIRECTIONS

1. If you have a removable storage device to use for storing your work in this class, connect it to your computer. For example, insert a removable disk in a drive, or connect a flash drive to a USB port. (Close the AutoPlay dialog box without taking any action, if necessary.)
2. If necessary, press ESC to display the desktop. Click the **File Explorer** icon on the Windows Taskbar.
3. Click **Computer** in the navigation pane. The computer window opens. It displays the storage devices that are part of your computer system.
4. Follow your teacher's directions to navigate to and open the specific location where you will store the files and folders for this book.
5. Click the **View** tab on the Ribbon to display the commands on the View tab of the Ribbon.
6. In the Layout group, click **Medium icons** to select the way the items in the window display.
7. Click the Home tab and then click the **New folder** button to create a new folder.
8. Type **B01Practice_xx**.

   ✓ *Throughout this book, when naming files and folders, replace xx with your name or initials as instructed by your teacher.*

9. Press ENTER to name the new folder. The window should look similar to Figure 1-1 on the next page.
10. Double-click the new folder to open it.
11. Click the **Back** button above the navigation pane to display the previous storage location.
12. Click the **Forward** button to move forward to the **B01Practice_xx** folder window.
13. Click the **Close** button × to close the window.
14. Press the Windows key on your keyboard to display the Start screen.
15. Click the Excel 2013 tile:

    Windows 8, Microsoft Corporation

    OR

    a. Right-click a blank area of the Start screen and click the **All apps** button.
    b. Scroll to locate the Microsoft Office 2013 programs.
    c. Click **Excel 2013**.

    ✓ *A quick way to locate a program from the Start screen is just to start typing its name. Windows displays a list of matching programs.*

16. Click the **Blank workbook** template.
17. Click the **Close** button × to exit Excel. Click **Don't Save** if prompted, to exit without saving the file.

Figure 1-1

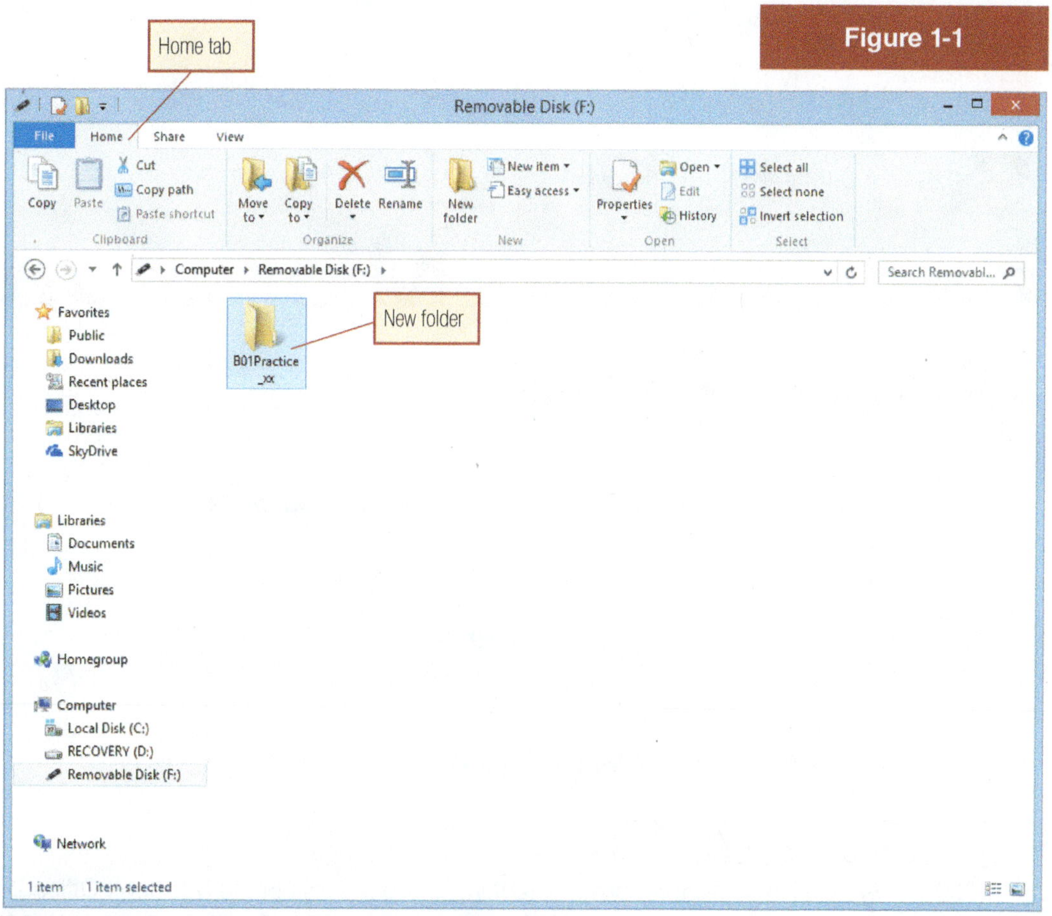

Windows 8, Microsoft Corporation

Lesson 1—Apply

In this project, you use your computer's operating system to navigate to a storage location where you create a subfolder. You then delete a subfolder and a folder and, finally, you practice starting and exiting Microsoft Office 2013 programs.

DIRECTIONS

1. Use File Explorer to navigate to and open the **B01Practice_xx** folder you created in Lesson 1—Practice
2. Create a new folder named **B01Apply_xx**.
3. Open the **B01Apply_xx** folder, then navigate back to the **B01Practice_xx** folder.
4. Navigate forward to the **B01Apply_xx** folder.
5. Navigate back to the **B01Practice_xx** folder.
6. Delete the **B01Apply_xx** folder.
7. Navigate back to the storage location where the **B01Practice_xx** folder is stored, and then delete the **B01Practice_xx** folder.
8. Close the File Explorer window.
9. Start Word 2013 and create a blank document.
10. Exit Word.
11. Start PowerPoint 2013 and create a blank presentation.
12. Exit PowerPoint.

Lesson 2

Saving, Printing, and Closing Microsoft Office Files

➤ What You Will Learn

Identifying Common Microsoft Office Screen Elements
Entering and Editing Text
Correcting Errors
Saving a File
Printing a File
Closing a File

WORDS TO KNOW

Backstage view
A feature of Microsoft Office 2013 from which you access file and program management commands.

Toolbar
A row of command buttons.

Software Skills The programs in the Microsoft Office 2013 suite share common elements. That means that once you learn to accomplish a task in one program, you can easily transfer that skill to a different program. For example, the steps for saving a file are the same, no matter which program you are using.

What You Can Do

Identifying Common Microsoft Office Screen Elements

- When a program is running, it is displayed in a window on your screen.
- The program windows for each of the Microsoft Office applications contain many common elements.
- You will find more information about the individual program windows in the other sections of this book.
- Refer to Figure 2-1 on the next page to locate and identify these common window elements:
  - Ribbon. Displays buttons for accessing features and commands.

    ✓ *Note that the way items display on the Ribbon may depend on the width of the program window. If your program window is wider than the one used in the figures, more or larger buttons may display. If your program window is narrower, fewer or smaller buttons may display. Refer to Lesson 3 for more information on using the Ribbon.*

- Ribbon tabs. Used to change the commands displayed on the Ribbon.
- Quick Access Toolbar. A **toolbar** that displays buttons for commonly used commands. You can customize the Quick Access Toolbar to display buttons you use frequently.
- Close button. Used to close the program window. It is one of three buttons used to control the size and position of the program window.
- Mouse pointer. Marks the location of the mouse on the screen.
- Scroll bar. Used with a mouse to shift the onscreen display up and down or left and right.
- Status bar. Displays information about the current document.
- Document area. The workspace where you enter text, graphics, and other data.

✓ *The appearance of the document area is different in each program.*

- ScreenTip. Displays information about the element on which the mouse pointer is resting.
- Title bar. Displays the program and file names.
- Zoom slider. Used to increase or decrease the size of the document onscreen.
- Help button. Used to start the program's Help system.
- View buttons. Used to change the document view.

Figure 2-1

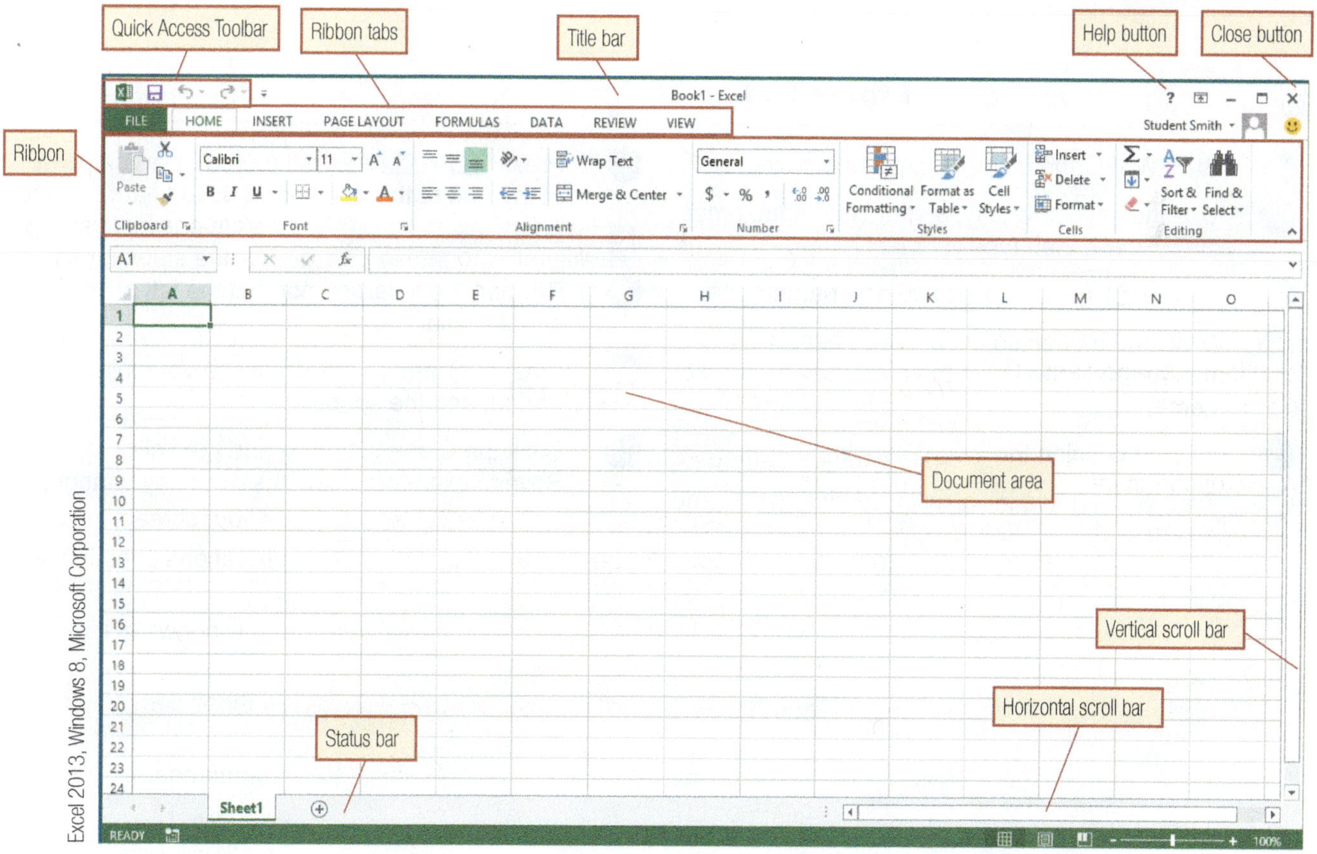

Excel 2013, Windows 8, Microsoft Corporation

Entering and Editing Text

- Use your keyboard to enter or edit text in a file.
- Characters you type are inserted to the left of the insertion point.
- You position the insertion point using your mouse, touch device, or the directional keys on your keyboard.
- Press BACKSPACE to delete the character to the left of the insertion point.
- Press DEL to delete the character to the right of the insertion point.

✓ *When you are working in a program such as Access or Excel, text is entered into the selected cell. You learn about entering information in specific programs in each section of this book.*

Table 2-1 Positioning the Insertion Point with the Keyboard

Movement	Keys	Movement	Keys
One character left	←	Up one paragraph	CTRL + ↑
One character right	→	Down one paragraph	CTRL + ↓
One line up	↑	Beginning of document	CTRL + HOME
One line down	↓	End of document	CTRL + END
Previous word	CTRL + ←	Beginning of line	HOME
Next word	CTRL + →	End of line	END

Try It! Entering and Editing Text

1. Start Word, and create a blank document.
2. Use the keyboard to type your first name, press SPACEBAR and then type your last name.
3. Press ENTER twice to start two new paragraphs.
4. Move the mouse so the pointer I-beam is positioned to the left of the first letter in your last name.
5. Click to position the insertion point.
6. Type your middle initial followed by a period and a space.
7. Press CTRL + END to position the insertion point at the end of the document.
8. Press BACKSPACE twice.
9. Position the insertion point to the left of your middle initial.
10. Press DEL three times to delete your initial, the period, and the space.
11. Click the Close button × and then click Don't Save to exit Word without saving any changes.

Correcting Errors

- Press ESC to cancel a command or close a menu or dialog box before the command affects the current file.
- Use the Undo button on the Quick Access Toolbar to reverse a single action made in error, such as deleting the wrong word.
- Use the Undo drop-down list to reverse a series of actions. The most recent action is listed at the top of the list; click an action to undo it and all actions above it.
- Use the Redo button on the Quick Access Toolbar to reinstate any actions that you reversed with Undo.
- If the Undo button is dimmed, there are no actions that can be undone.
- If the Redo button is dimmed, there are no actions that can be redone.
- Sometimes when there are no actions to redo, the Repeat button is available in place of Redo. Use Repeat to repeat the most recent action.

Try It! Correcting Errors

1. Start Excel, and create a blank workbook file.
2. Use the keyboard to type your first name in the first cell (the rectangular area in the upper-left corner) and then press ENTER.
3. Click the Undo button on the Quick Access Toolbar. The previous action—typing your first name—is undone.
4. Click the Redo button on the Quick Access Toolbar. The undone action is redone.
5. Press the down arrow key ↓ three times to select the cell in the fourth row of column A.
6. Type today's date and press ENTER.
7. Click the Undo drop-down arrow to display the Undo menu. It should list two actions you could undo.
8. Press ESC. The menu closes without any action taking place.
9. Click the Close button × and then click Don't Save to exit Excel without saving any changes.

Saving a File

- If you want to have a file available for future use, you must save it on a storage device.
- The first time you save a new file you must give it a name and select the location where you want to store it.
- Each Microsoft Office program is set to save files in a default storage location.
- You can select a different storage location on the Save As page in the program's Backstage view or in the Save As dialog box, or you can create and name a new folder using the New folder command on the menu bar in the Save As dialog box.
- After you save a file for the first time, you save changes to the file in order to make sure that you do not lose your work.
- Saving changes updates the previously saved version of the file with the most recent changes.

Try It! Saving a File

1. Start Word, and create a blank document.
2. Click Save on the Quick Access Toolbar.

   OR

   a. Click the FILE tab.

   b. Click Save.

   ✓ *If the Save As dialog box displays, your computer was modified to skip the Backstage view. Skip step 3.*
3. On the Save As page in the Backstage view, click Computer, and then under Computer, click Browse.

   ✓ *If the location where you want to store the file displays in the Backstage view, click it instead of clicking Browse.*
4. In the Save As dialog box, select the contents in the File name text box if it is not selected already.

   ✓ *To select the contents, drag across it with your mouse.*
5. Type **B02Try_xx**.

   ✓ *Remember to replace xx with your own name or initials, as instructed by your teacher. This will be the standard format for naming files throughout this book.*
6. Use the Navigation pane to navigate to the location where your teacher instructs you to store the files for this lesson. If necessary, click New folder on the menu bar to create and name a new folder.

   ✓ *If the Navigation pane is not displayed, click Browse Folders.*
7. Click Save or press ENTER.
8. Leave the **B02Try_xx** file open to use in the next Try It.

The Save As page in the Backstage view

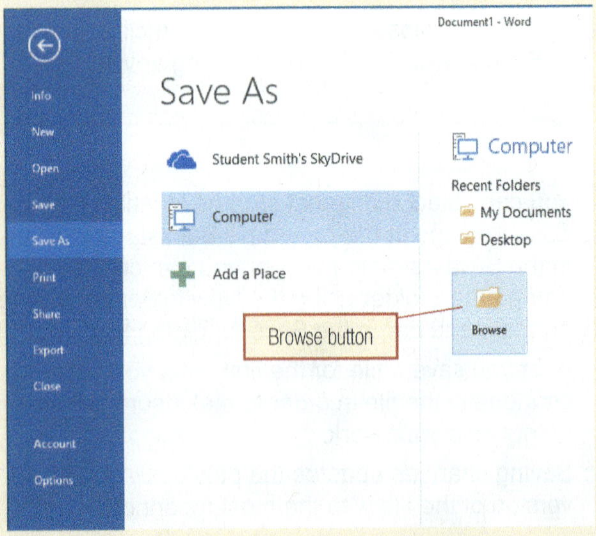

Word 2013, Windows 8, Microsoft Corporation

Save As dialog box

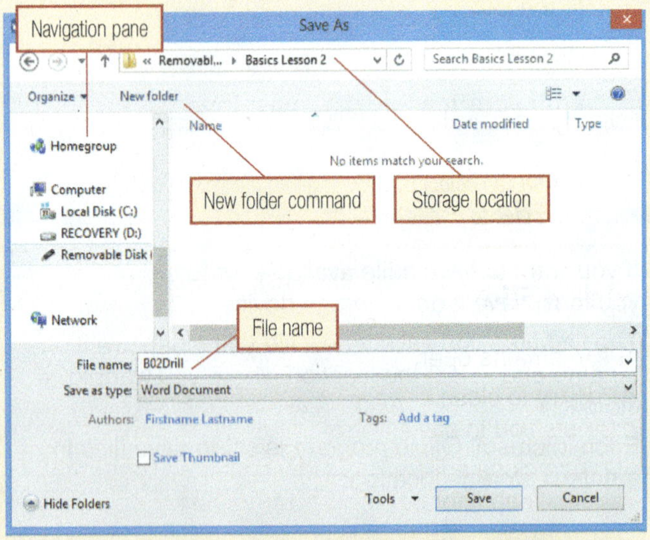

Word 2013, Windows 8, Microsoft Corporation

Try It! Saving Changes to a File

1. In the B02Try_xx file, type your first name, press SPACEBAR, type your last name, and then press ENTER.
2. Type today's date.
3. Click Save on the Quick Access Toolbar.

OR

a. Click FILE.

b. Click Save.

✓ *You can also press CTRL + S to save changes.*

4. Leave the B02Try_xx file open to use in the next Try It.

Printing a File

- Printing creates a hard copy version of a file on paper.
- In Microsoft Office 2013 programs you use the Print page in the **Backstage view** to preview and print a file.
- You can also select printer settings such as the number of copies to print and which printer to use.

✓ *Printer setting options vary depending on the system configuration.*

- Your computer must be connected to a printer loaded with paper and ink in order to print.
- Ask your teacher for permission before printing.

✓ *Steps for printing in Access are different from printing in the other Microsoft Office programs. You learn how to print in Access in the Access section of this book.*

Try It! Printing the Current File

1. In the B02Try_xx file, click FILE.
2. Click Print.
3. **With your teacher's permission,** click the Print button.

✓ *You can select settings such as the printer and number of copies to print before printing.*

4. Leave the B02Try_xx file open to use in the next Try It.

✓ *To return to the current file from the Backstage view, click the Back button in the upper-left of the page.*

Closing a File

- A file remains open onscreen until you close it.
- If you try to close a file without saving, the program prompts you to save.
- You can close a file without saving it if you do not want to keep it for future use.
- You can use the Close button to close the file and exit the program; if there are multiple files open, the program remains running.
- You can also use the FILE > Close command

✓ *In this book, the symbol > is used to indicate a series of steps. In this case, click the FILE tab and then click Close.*

Try It! Closing a File

1. With the B02Try_xx file open in Word, click the Close button ×.

OR

a. Click FILE.

b. Click Close.

✓ *If you have made changes since the last time you saved, click Save to save changes and close the file, or click Don't Save to close the file without saving. In Access, click Yes to save changes or click No to close without saving.*

Lesson 2—Practice

In this project, you practice the skills you have learned in this lesson to create, save, and print a file in Microsoft Word 2013.

DIRECTIONS

1. If you have a removable storage device to use for storing your work in this class, connect it to your computer. For example, insert a removable disk in a drive, or connect a flash drive to a USB port.
2. Start Word, and click the **Blank document template**.
3. Move the mouse pointer so it is resting on the **Save** button on the Quick Access Toolbar. The ScreenTip displays Save.
4. Point to the **Zoom** slider on the right end of the status bar.
5. Click the **INSERT** tab on the Ribbon.
6. Click the **FILE** tab.
7. Click **Save** > **Computer** > **Browse** to display the Save As dialog box.
8. Type **B02Practice_xx**.
9. Navigate to the location where your teacher instructs you to store the files for this lesson.

   ✓ *If necessary, create a new folder for storing the files.*
10. Click **Save** in the Save As dialog box to save the file.
11. In the new file, type your first name and your last name and press ENTER to start a new line.
12. Type today's date and press ENTER.
13. Type **Notes on using Microsoft Office 2013**.
14. Click the **Undo** button on the Quick Access Toolbar to undo the typing.
15. Click the **Redo** button to redo the action.
16. Click the **Save** button on the Quick Access Toolbar to save the changes to the file.
17. Click the **FILE** tab.
18. Click **Print**. Your screen should look similar to Figure 2-2.
19. **With your teacher's permission,** click the **Print** button to print the file.

   ✓ *If necessary, click the Printer drop-down arrow and select the printer your teacher wants you to use.*
20. Click the **FILE** tab, then click **Close** to close the file.
21. Exit Word.

Figure 2-2

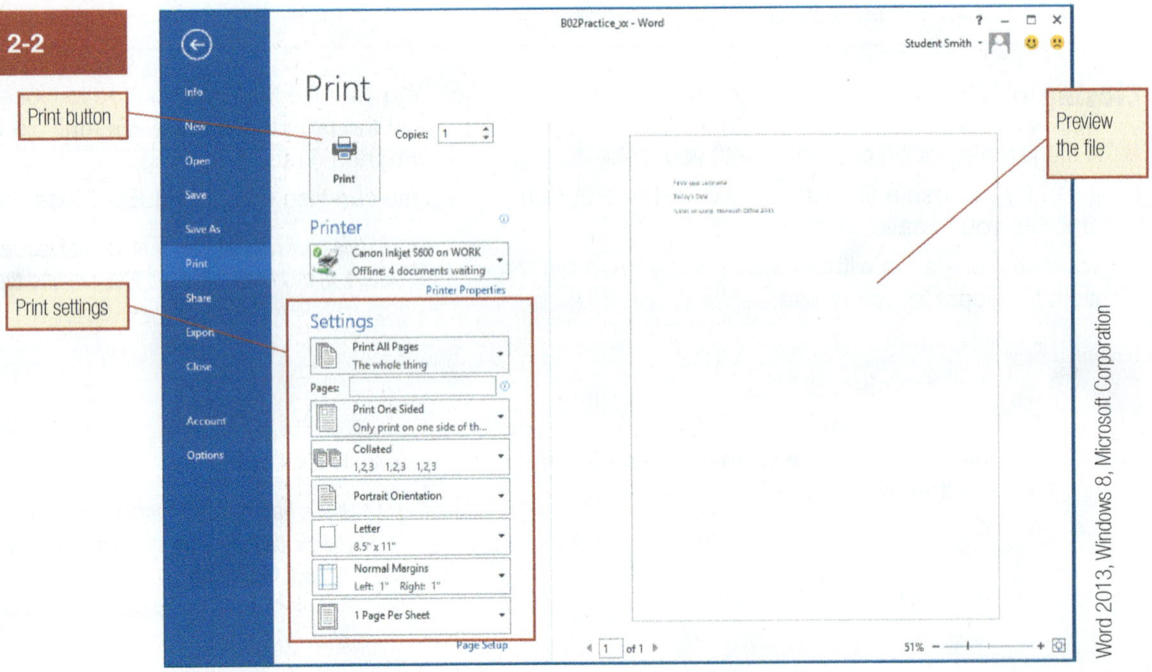

Word 2013, Windows 8, Microsoft Corporation

Lesson 2—Apply

As the new office manager at Restoration Architecture, you have been asked to analyze how the company might use Microsoft Office to achieve its business goals. In this project, you will use the skills you learned in this lesson to compare the Microsoft Office 2013 programs.

DIRECTIONS

1. Start Excel, and create a blank workbook.
2. Point to the following common elements in the Excel window: Zoom slider, Save button on the Quick Access Toolbar, View buttons, and the vertical scroll bar.
3. Click the **INSERT** tab on the Ribbon.
4. Click the **FILE** tab, and then click **Save**.
5. Click **Computer** > **Browse**, and then type **B02ApplyA_xx**.
6. Navigate to the location where your teacher instructs you to store the files for this lesson, and then click **Save** to save the file.
7. In the new file, type your first name and your last name and press ENTER.

   ✓ *In Excel, typing displays in the current, or selected, cell. Pressing ENTER enters the data in the cell and usually moves to the next cell down. If it does not move to the next cell down, press the down arrow key.*
8. Type today's date and press ENTER

   ✓ *Excel might apply date formatting to the entry. You learn more about formatting in a worksheet in the Excel section of this book.*
9. Click **Undo**.
10. Click **Undo** again.
11. Click **Redo** twice.
12. Click the **Save** button on the Quick Access Toolbar to save the changes to the file.
13. Click the **FILE** tab, and then click **Print**.
14. **With your teacher's permission,** print the file.
15. Click the **Close** button × to close the file and exit Excel.
16. Start PowerPoint, and create a blank presentation.
17. Point to the following common elements in the PowerPoint window: Zoom slider, Save button on the Quick Access Toolbar, View buttons, and the Close button.
18. Click the **INSERT** tab on the Ribbon.
19. Click the **FILE** tab, and then click **Save**.
20. Click **Computer** > **Browse** and then type **B02ApplyB_xx**.
21. Navigate to the location where your teacher instructs you to store the files for this lesson, and then click **Save** to save the file.
22. In the new file, type your first name and your last name and press ENTER. Type today's date.

    ✓ *In PowerPoint, typing displays in the current, or selected, placeholder. Pressing ENTER starts a new line.*
23. Click **Undo**.
24. Click **Redo**.
25. Click the **Save** button on the Quick Access Toolbar to save the changes to the file.
26. Click the **FILE** tab, and then click **Print**.
27. **With your teacher's permission,** print the file.
28. Click the **Close** button × to close the file and exit PowerPoint.

Lesson 3

Working with Existing Files

WORDS TO KNOW

Access keys
Keys you can use to select or execute a command.

Command
Input that tells the computer which task to execute.

Contextual tab
A Ribbon tab that is only available in a certain context or situation.

Contiguous
Adjacent or in a row.

Dialog box launcher
A button you click to open a dialog box.

File properties
Information about a file.

Font
A complete set of characters in a specific face, style, and size.

Font color
The color of characters in a font set.

Font size
The height of an uppercase letter in a font set.

Font style
The slant and weight of characters in a font set.

Format
To change the appearance of text or other elements.

➤ What You Will Learn

Opening an Existing File
Saving a File with a New Name
Viewing File Properties
Using the Ribbon
Using Access Keys
Selecting Text
Formatting Text

Software Skills You can open an existing file in the program used to create it. You can then use Microsoft Office program commands to save it with a new name so you can edit or format it, leaving the original file unchanged. Formatting improves the appearance and readability of text.

What You Can Do

Opening an Existing File

- To view or edit a file that has been saved and closed, open it again.
- Recently used files display when you first start a Microsoft Office program and on the Open page in the Backstage view; click a file to open it.
- You can use the Open dialog box to locate and open any file.

Try It! **Opening an Existing File**

1. Start Excel.
2. At the bottom of the Recent list on the left side of the page, click Open Other Workbooks.
3. Click Computer, and then click the location you want to open, or click the Browse button and navigate to the location where the data files for this lesson are stored.

(continued)

Try It! Opening an Existing File *(continued)*

4. Double-click **B03TryA** to open it.

   OR

   a. Click **B03TryA**.

   b. Click Open.

5. Click FILE > Close to close the file, but leave Excel open to use in the next Try It.

Open dialog box

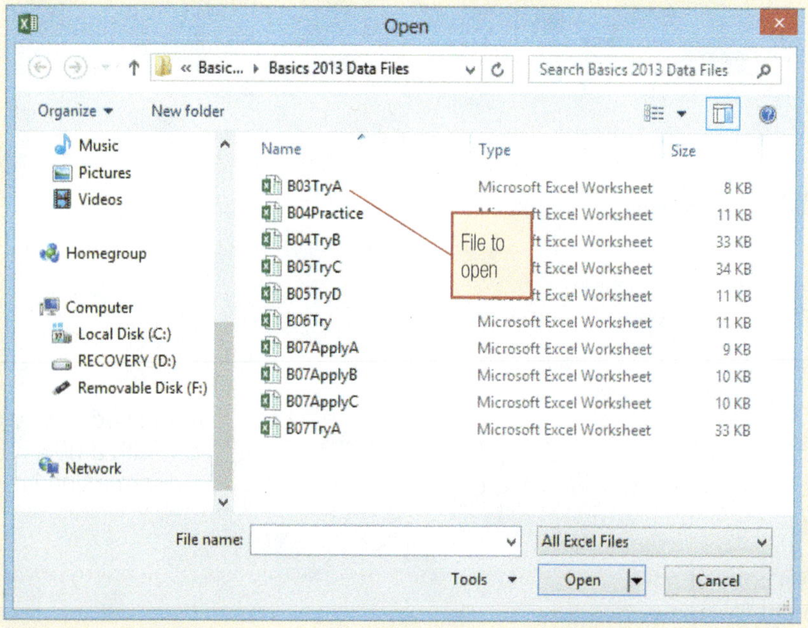

Excel 2013, Windows 8, Microsoft Corporation

Try It! Opening a Recently Opened Document

1. In Excel, click FILE.
2. In the list of Recent Workbooks, click **B03TryA**.
4. Leave the file open in Excel to use in the next Try It.

(continued)

Gallery
A menu that displays pictures instead of plain text options.

Highlighted
Marked with color to stand out from the surrounding text.

KeyTip
A pop-up letter that identifies the access key(s) for a command.

Live Preview
A feature of Microsoft Office that shows you how a command will affect the selection before you actually select the command.

Noncontiguous
Not adjacent.

Select
Mark text as the focus of the next action.

Selection bar
A narrow strip along the left margin of a page that automates selection of text. When the mouse pointer is in the selection area, the pointer changes to an arrow pointing up and to the right.

Toggle
A type of command that can be switched off or on.

Try It! Opening a Recently Opened Document *(continued)*

Open a Recent Workbook

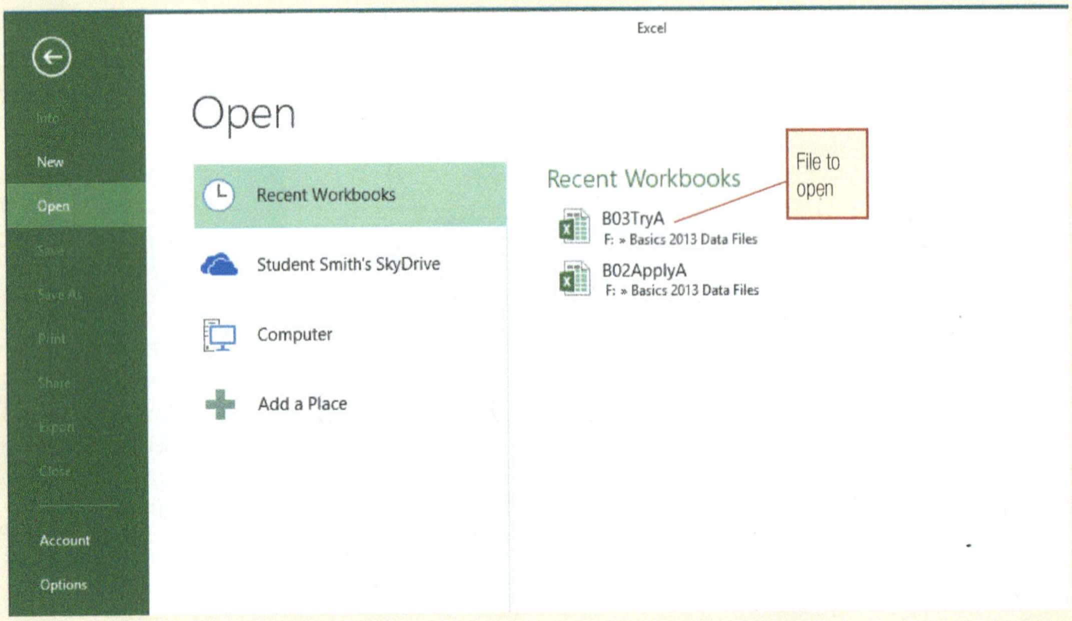

Excel 2013, Windows 8, Microsoft Corporation

Saving a File with a New Name

- Use the Save As command to save a copy of a file in a different location or with a different file name.
- The original file remains unchanged.

Try It! Saving a File with a New Name

1. In Excel, with the **B03TryA** file open, click FILE.
2. Click Save As.
3. Click Computer and then click the location where you want to store the file, or click the Browse button.
4. Type **B03TryB_xx** to rename the file.
5. Navigate to the location where your teacher instructs you to store the files for this lesson.
6. Click Save.
7. Close the file, and exit Excel.

Viewing File Properties

- You can view **file properties** on the Info tab in the Backstage view.
- File properties include information about the file, such as how big it is and when it was created or modified.

Try It! Viewing File Properties

1. Start PowerPoint.
2. Click Open Other Presentations.
3. Click Computer, then click the location you want to open, or click Browse and navigate to the location where the data files for this lesson are stored.
4. Double-click **B03TryB** to open it.
5. Click FILE. The Info page displays, with the Properties listed on the right.
6. Close the file, and exit PowerPoint.

Properties display on the Info page

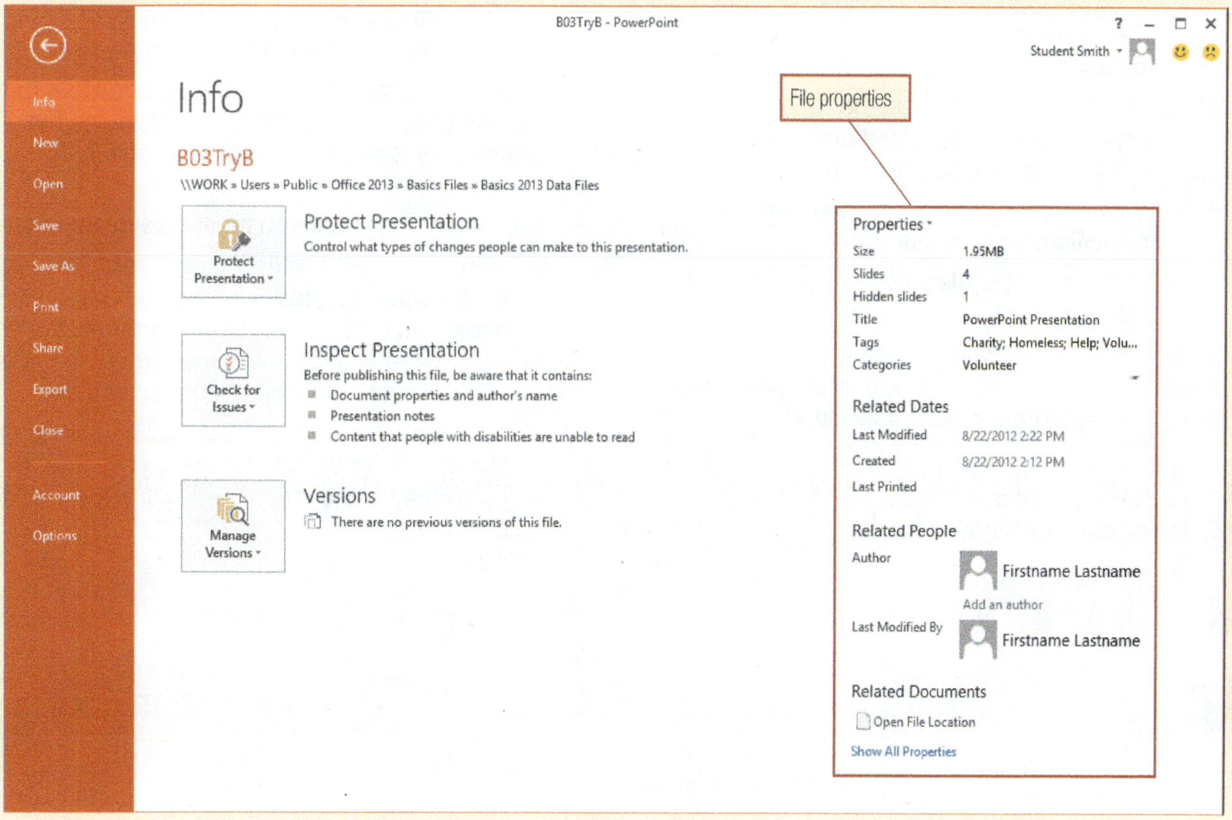

Using the Ribbon

- To accomplish a task in a Microsoft Office 2013 program, you execute **commands**. For example, Save is the command for saving a file.
- Most commands are available as buttons on the Ribbon. Refer to Figure 3-1 to identify parts of the HOME tab of the Ribbon.
- The Ribbon is organized into tabs based on activities, such as reviewing a file or inserting content. On each tab, commands are organized into groups.
- **Contextual tabs** are only available in certain situations. For example, if you select a picture, the PICTURE TOOLS tab becomes available. If you deselect the picture, the PICTURE TOOLS tab disappears.
- You can collapse the Ribbon to display only the tabs if you want to see more of a file, and expand it when you need to use the commands.
- In Word, Excel, and PowerPoint, you can change the Ribbon Display Options to Auto-hide the Ribbon, to show the Ribbon tabs only, or to show the tabs and the commands all the time (the default).
- When you point to a button on the Ribbon with the mouse, the button is highlighted and a ScreenTip displays information about the command.
- Buttons representing commands that are not currently available are dimmed.
- Some buttons are **toggles**; they appear highlighted when active, or "on."
- If there is a drop-down arrow on a button, it means that when you click the arrow, a menu or **gallery** displays so you can make a specific selection.

✓ *In this book, when it says "click the button" you should click the button; when it says "click the drop-down arrow" you should click the arrow on the button.*

- Sometimes, the entire first row of a gallery displays on the Ribbon.
- You can rest the mouse pointer on a gallery item to see a **Live Preview** of the way your document will look if you select that item.
- You can scroll a gallery on the Ribbon, or click the More button to view the entire gallery.
- Some Ribbon groups have a **dialog box launcher** button. Click the dialog box launcher to display a dialog box, task pane, or window where you can select additional options, or multiple options at the same time.
- Note that the way items display on the Ribbon may depend on the width of the program window.
  - If the window is wide enough, groups expand to display all items.
  - If the window is not wide enough, groups collapse to a single group button. Click the button to display a menu of commands in the group.
  - The size of icons in a group may vary depending on the width of the window.
- If your program window is narrower or wider than the one used in this book, the Ribbon on your screen may look different from the one in the figures.
- In addition, the steps you must take to complete a procedure may vary slightly.
  - If your screen is narrower than the one in this book, you may have to click a group button to display the commands in that group before you can complete the steps in the procedure.
  - If your screen is wider, you may be able to skip a step for selecting a group button and go directly to the step for selecting a specific command.

Figure 3-1

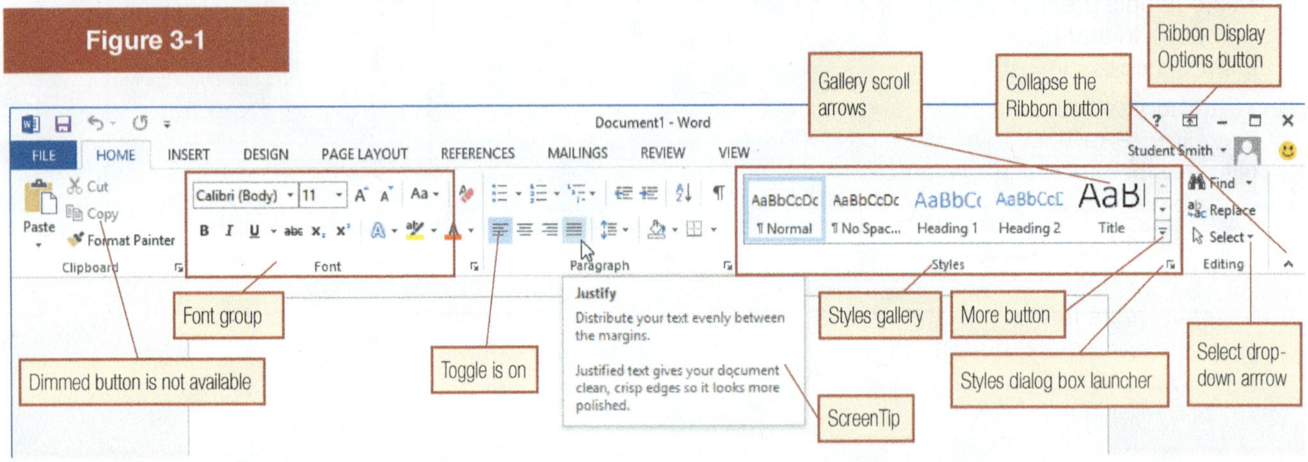

Word 2013, Windows 8, Microsoft Corporation

Try It! Using the Ribbon

1. Start Word, and create a blank document.
2. Save the file as **B03TryC_xx** in the location where your teacher instructs you to store files for this lesson.
3. Point to the Center button ≡ on the Ribbon. The ScreenTip displays the button name, shortcut keys, and a description.
4. Click the Center button ≡. The insertion point moves to the center of the current line.
5. Type your first name, press ENTER, and then type your last name.
6. Press CTRL + ENTER, the shortcut key combination for starting a new page, and type today's date.
7. Click the VIEW tab on the Ribbon to make it active.
8. Click the Multiple Pages button. This command changes the view to display two pages at the same time.
9. Click the One Page button. This command changes the view to display one page at a time.
10. Save the changes to **B03TryC_xx**, and keep it open to use in the next Try It.

Try It! Setting Ribbon Display Options

1. In **B03TryC_xx**, click the Collapse the Ribbon button ˄. The Ribbon is hidden.

   ✓ *CTRL + F1 is the shortcut key combination for unpinning/pinning the Ribbon.*

2. Click the INSERT tab. Clicking any tab expands the Ribbon temporarily so you can select a command.
3. Click the Pin the ribbon button to keep the Ribbon displayed.
4. Double-click the VIEW tab. Double-clicking any tab is an alternative way to collapse/pin the Ribbon.
5. Click the Ribbon Display Options button.
6. Click Show Tabs and Commands to expand the Ribbon and keep it displayed.
7. Save the changes to **B03TryC_xx**, and keep it open to use in the next Try It.

Using Access Keys

- Microsoft Office 2013 programs are designed primarily for use with a mouse or touch device.
- Some people prefer to select commands using the keyboard. In that case, you can press the Alt key to activate **access keys**.
- When access keys are active, **KeyTips** showing one or more keyboard letters display on the screen over any feature or command that can be selected using the keyboard.
- You press the letter(s) shown in the KeyTip to select the command or feature.
- If there is more than one access key for a command, you may press the keys in combination (at the same time) or consecutively (press the first key and then immediately press the next key).
- If a KeyTip is dimmed, the command is not available.
- The KeyTips remain active if you must press additional keys to complete a command.
- Once a command is executed, the KeyTips disappear.
- To continue using the keyboard, you must press the Alt key to activate the access keys again.

  ✓ *People accustomed to the shortcut key combinations in previous versions of Microsoft Office will be happy to know that they function in Microsoft Office 2013 programs as well. For example, you can still press CTRL + SHIFT + F to open the Font dialog box.*

Try It! Using Access Keys

1. With the **B03TryC_xx** file still displayed, press ALT. The KeyTips for the Ribbon tabs display.
2. Press W to make the VIEW tab active. The KeyTips for the VIEW tab display.
3. Press 2 to change to Two Page view.
4. Press ALT, W, 1 to change to One Page view.
5. Press ALT, W, J to change the view to show the file at 100% magnification.
6. Press ALT, H to make the HOME tab of the Ribbon active.
7. Press ESC twice to cancel the KeyTips.
8. Save the changes to **B03TryC_xx**, and keep it open to use in the next Try It.

KeyTips on the View tab

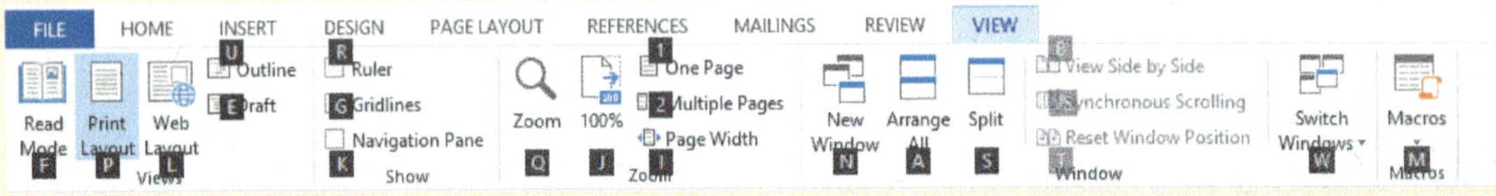

Word 2013, Windows 8, Microsoft Corporation

Selecting Text

- **Select** text in order to edit it or format it.
- You can select any amount of **contiguous** or **noncontiguous** text.
- You can also select non-text characters, such as symbols; nonprinting characters, such as paragraph marks; and graphics, such as pictures.
- By default, selected text appears **highlighted** onscreen.
- When you first select text, the Mini toolbar may display. Move the mouse pointer away from the selection to hide the Mini toolbar.
- When text is selected, any command or action affects the selection. For example, if text is selected and you press DEL, the selection is deleted.
- To select text on a touch device, tap in the text and drag the selection handle. Refer to Table 3-1 for keyboard selection commands. Refer to Table 3-2 on the next page for mouse selection commands.

Table 3-1 Keyboard Selection Commands

To Select	Press
One character right	SHIFT + →
One character left	SHIFT + ←
One line up	SHIFT + ↑
One line down	SHIFT + ↓
To end of line	SHIFT + END
To beginning of line	SHIFT + HOME
To end of document	SHIFT + CTRL + END
To beginning of document	SHIFT + CTRL + HOME
Entire document	CTRL + A

Table 3-2 Mouse Selection Commands

To Select	Do This
One word	Double-click word.
One sentence	CTRL + click in sentence.
One line	Click in **selection bar** to the left of the line.
One paragraph	Double-click in selection bar to the left of the paragraph.
Document	Triple-click in selection bar.
Noncontiguous text	Select first block, press and hold CTRL, then select additional block(s).

Try It! Selecting Text

1. In B03TryC_xx, press CTRL + HOME, the shortcut key combination to move the insertion point to the beginning of a Word document.
2. Position the mouse pointer to the left of the first character in your first name.
3. Hold down the left mouse button.
4. Drag the mouse across your first name to select it.
5. Click anywhere outside the selection to cancel it.
6. Double-click your last name to select it.
7. Press DEL. The selected text is deleted.
8. Save the changes to B03TryC_xx, and keep it open to use in the next Try It.

Formatting Text

- You can **format** text to change its appearance.
- Formatting can enhance and emphasize text, and set a tone or mood for a file.
- Microsoft Office 2013 programs offer many options for formatting text; you will learn more in the other sections of this book.
- Some common formatting options include:
  - **Font**
  - **Font size**
  - **Font style**
  - **Font color**
- You can change the formatting of selected text, or you can select formatting before you type new text.
- You can preview the way selected text will look with formatting by resting the mouse pointer on the formatting command on the Ribbon.

Try It! Formatting Selected Text

1. In **B03TryC_xx**, double-click your first name to select it.
2. On the HOME tab, in the Font group, click the Bold button **B**.
3. On the HOME tab, in the Font group, click the Font Size drop-down arrow [11 ▾] to display a list of font sizes, and rest the mouse pointer on the number 28 to preview the text with the formatting.
4. Click 16 on the Font size drop-down list to change the font size to 16 points.
5. On the HOME tab, in the Font group, click the Underline button U.
6. On the HOME tab, in the Font group click the Italic button *I*.
7. Click anywhere outside the selection in the document to deselect the text.
8. Save the changes to **B03TryC_xx**, and keep it open to use in the next Try It.

Try It! Formatting New Text

1. In **B03TryC_xx**, move the insertion point to the end of your first name and press ENTER to start a new line.
2. Type your middle name. (If you do not have a middle name, type any name.) Notice that the current formatting carries forward to the new line.
3. Press ENTER to start a new line. Click the Bold **B**, Italic *I*, and Underline U buttons to toggle those commands off.
4. Click the Font drop-down arrow [Calibri (Body) ▾] and click Arial on the list of available fonts.

   ✓ *The list of fonts is alphabetical. Scroll down to find Arial.*
5. Click the Font Color drop-down arrow A ▾ and click Green.
6. Type your last name. The text displays in green 16-point Arial, without bold, italic, or underline formatting.
7. Close **B03TryC_xx**, saving the changes, and exit Word.

Select a font color

Word 2013, Windows 8, Microsoft Corporation

Lesson 3—Practice

As a public relations assistant at Voyager Travel Adventures, you are responsible for preparing press releases. In this project, you will open an existing press release file in Word and save it with a new name. You will then enter, edit, and format text to prepare it for distribution.

DIRECTIONS

1. If you have a removable storage device to use for storing your work in this class, connect it to your computer. For example, insert a removable disk in a drive, or connect a flash drive to a USB port.
2. Start Word.
3. Click **Open Other Documents**.
4. Click **Computer**, then click the location you want to open, or click **Browse**, and navigate to the location where the data files for this lesson are stored.
5. Double-click the file **B03Practice** to open it.
6. Click the **FILE** tab, and then click **Save As**.
7. Click Computer, and then under **Computer**, click the **Browse** button.
8. Type **B03Practice_xx** in the File name box.
9. Navigate to the location where your teacher instructs you to store the files for this lesson.
10. Click **Save**.
11. Select the headline: *Voyager Travel Adventures Announces Exciting Summer Tours*.
12. Click the **Bold** button B.
13. Click the **Font Size** drop-down arrow 11 and click **14**.
14. Select the text *Denver, Colorado – Today's Date –* and then click the **Italic** button I.
15. Select the text *Today's Date*, press DEL to delete it, and then type the actual date.
16. Press CTRL + END to move the insertion point to the end of the document, and press ENTER to start a new line.
17. Click the **Font** drop-down arrow Calibri (Body) and click **Arial**.
18. Click the **Font Size** drop-down arrow 11 and click **12**.
19. Type **For more information contact:** and press ENTER.
20. Click the **Bold** button B.
21. Click the **Font Color** drop-down arrow A and click **Red**.
22. Type your full name. The file should look similar to Figure 3-2.
23. Save the changes to file.
24. Click the **FILE** tab. Click **Info**, if necessary, to view the file properties. Note the date and time the file was created and modified.
25. **With your teacher's permission**, print the file.
26. Close the file, saving changes, and exit Word.

FOR IMMEDIATE RELEASE:

Voyager Travel Adventures Announces Exciting Summer Tours

Denver, Colorado –Today's Actual Date– Voyager Travel Adventures, an adventure tour operator based in Denver, has announced three new travel opportunities for the coming summer months.

For more information contact:

Firstname Lastname

Figure 3-2

Word 2013, Windows 8, Microsoft Corporation

Lesson 3—Apply

In this project, you will open another press release and use the skills you have learned in this lesson to edit, format, and print the file.

DIRECTIONS

1. Start Word.
2. Open the file **B03Apply** from the location where the data files for this lesson are stored.
3. Save the file as **B03Apply_xx** in the location where your teacher instructs you to store the files for this lesson.
4. Change the font of the headline to Times New Roman and the font size to 16.
5. Replace the text *Today's Date* with the current date.
6. Position the insertion point at the end of the main paragraph and insert the paragraph shown in Figure 3-3, applying formatting as marked.
7. Move the insertion point to the end of the document, press ENTER, and type your full name in 12-point Times New Roman, bold, as shown in Figure 3-3.
8. Change the color of the first line of text to Light Blue and increase the font size to 12.

   ✓ *Use ScreenTips to identify the correct color.*
9. Save the changes.
10. **With your teacher's permission**, print the file.
11. Close the file, saving changes, and exit Word.

Figure 3-3

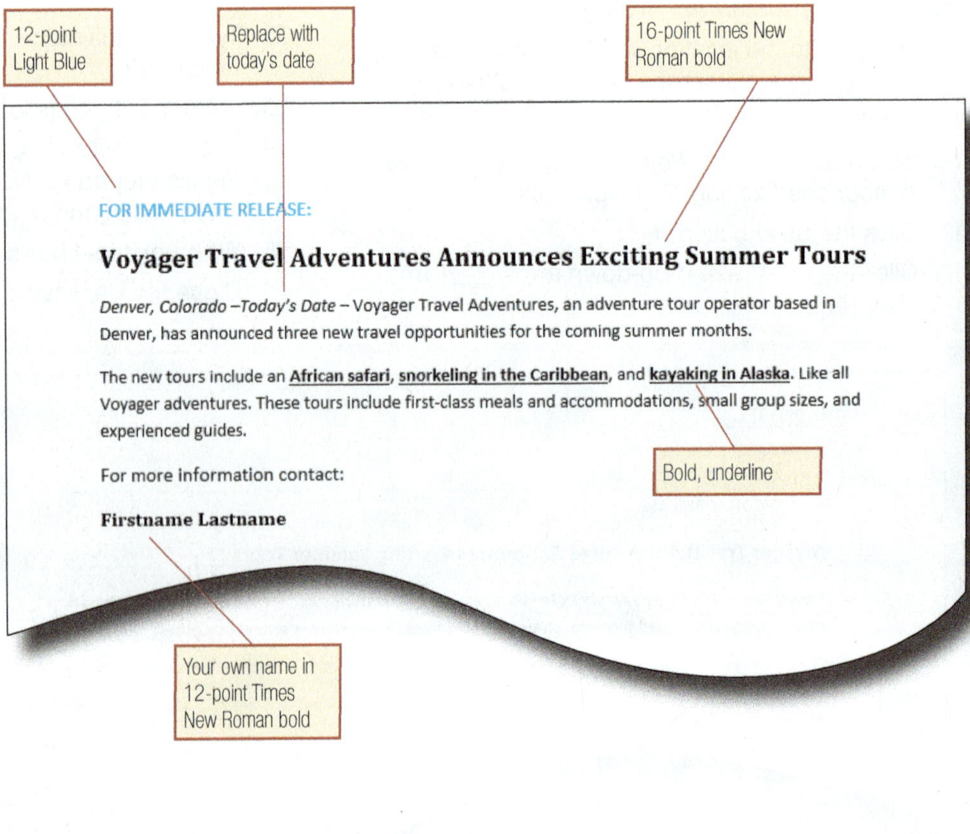

Word 2013, Windows 8, Microsoft Corporation

Lesson 4

Using Command Options

➤ What You Will Learn

Using the Quick Access Toolbar
Using the Mini Toolbar
Using Shortcut Menus
Using Dialog Box Options
Using Task Panes
Formatting Pages

Software Skills As you have learned, to accomplish a task in a Microsoft Office 2013 program, you must execute a command. Most commands are available on the Ribbon, but you may also use toolbars, menus, dialog boxes, or task panes. To prepare a file for printing or other types of distribution you may have to change the page formatting, such as adjusting the margin width, or selecting a page size.

What You Can Do

Using the Quick Access Toolbar

- The Quick Access Toolbar displays in the upper-left corner of the program window.
- To select a command from the Quick Access Toolbar, click its button.
- By default, there are three buttons on the Quick Access Toolbar: Save, Undo, and Repeat. The Repeat button changes to Redo once you use the Undo command.
- Use the Customize Quick Access Toolbar button ▾ to add or remove buttons for common commands, or use the Customize the Quick Access Toolbar options in the Word Options dialog box.
- The buttons on the Quick Access Toolbar are not available in the Backstage view.

WORDS TO KNOW

Dialog box
A window in which you select options that affect the way the program executes a command.

Landscape orientation
Rotating document text so it displays and prints horizontally across the longer side of a page.

Margins
The amount of white space between the text and the edge of the page on each side.

Portrait orientation
The default position for displaying and printing text horizontally across the shorter side of a page.

Scale
Adjust the size proportionately.

Shortcut menu
A menu of relevant commands that displays when you right-click an item. Also called a context menu.

Task pane
A small window that displays options and commands for certain features in a Microsoft Office program.

Try It! Adding and Removing Quick Access Toolbar Buttons

1. Start Word, create a blank document, and save it as **B04TryA_xx** in the location where your teacher instructs you to store the files for this lesson.
2. Click the Customize Quick Access Toolbar button to display a menu of common commands.

   ✓ *A check mark next to a command indicates it is already on the Quick Access Toolbar.*
3. Click Print Preview and Print on the menu. The button for Print Preview and Print is added to the Quick Access Toolbar.
4. Right-click the Paste button on the HOME tab of the Ribbon.
5. Click Add to Quick Access Toolbar.
6. Click the Customize Quick Access Toolbar button to display a menu of common commands.
7. Click Print Preview and Print. The button is removed from the Quick Access Toolbar.
8. Right-click the Paste button on the Quick Access Toolbar.
9. Click Customize Quick Access Toolbar.
10. In the list on the right side of the Word Options dialog box, click Paste to select it.
11. Click the Remove button « Remove, and then click OK.
12. Save the changes to **B04TryA_xx**, and keep it open to use in the next Try It.

Using the Mini Toolbar

- The Mini toolbar displays when the mouse pointer rests on selected text or data that can be formatted.
- Select a command from the Mini toolbar the same way you select a command from the Ribbon.

Try It! Using the Mini Toolbar

1. In the **B04TryA_xx** document, type your first name, and then select it. The Mini toolbar displays.
2. Click the Bold button **B** on the Mini toolbar.
3. Save the changes to **B04TryA_xx**, and leave it open to use in the next Try It.

Formatting with the Mini toolbar

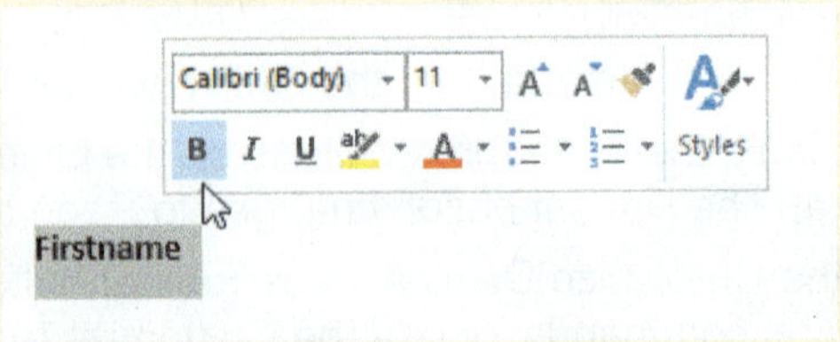

Word 2013, Windows 8, Microsoft Corporation

Using Shortcut Menus

- When you right-click almost any element on the screen in any Microsoft Office 2013 program, a **shortcut menu** displays.
- Shortcut menus include options relevant to the current item.

  ✓ *Shortcut menus are sometimes called context menus.*
- Click an option on the shortcut menu to select it.
- Alternatively, press the access key—the key that is underlined in the command name.

  ✓ *Sometimes, selecting an option on a shortcut menu opens a submenu, which is simply one menu that opens off another menu.*
- If you right-click selected data, the Mini toolbar may display in addition to the shortcut menu. The Mini toolbar disappears when you select an option on the menu.

Try It! Using a Shortcut Menu

1. In **B04TryA_xx**, click anywhere outside the selected text to deselect it.
2. Right-click the HOME tab of the Ribbon to display a shortcut menu.
3. Click Show Quick Access Toolbar Below the Ribbon on the shortcut menu. The Quick Access Toolbar moves below the Ribbon.
4. Right-click the status bar at the bottom of the Word window.
5. Click Zoom Slider on the shortcut menu to toggle the Zoom slider display off.
6. Click Zoom Slider on the shortcut menu again, to toggle the Zoom Slider display on.
7. Right-click the VIEW tab of the Ribbon to display a shortcut menu.
8. Click Show Quick Access Toolbar Above the Ribbon on the shortcut menu to move the toolbar back to its default position.
9. Leave the **B04TryA_xx** file open to use in the next Try It.

Use a shortcut menu to toggle screen elements off and on in Word

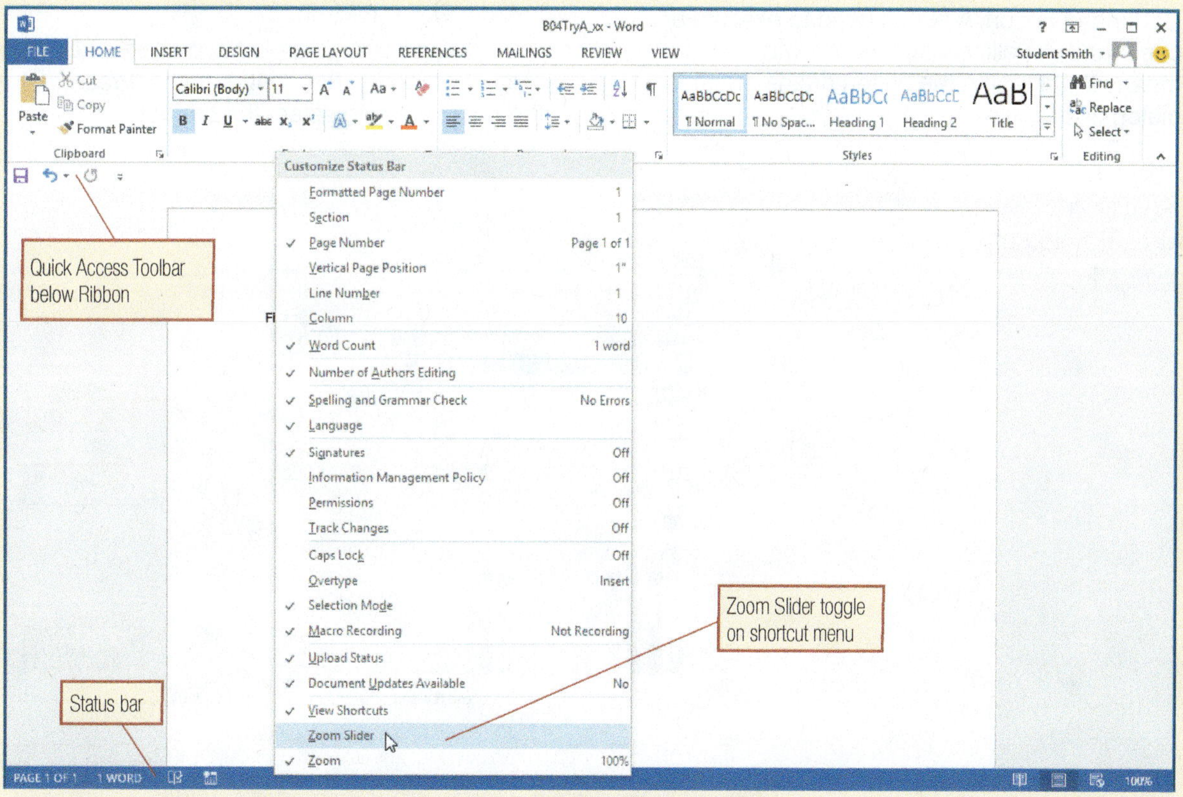

Using Dialog Box Options

- When you must provide additional information before executing a command, a **dialog box** displays.
- You enter information in a dialog box using a variety of controls (refer to Figures 4-1 and 4-2):
  - List box. A list of items from which selections can be made. If more items are available than can fit in the space, a scrollbar is displayed.
  - Palette. A display, such as colors or shapes, from which you can select an option.
  - Drop-down list box. A combination of text box and list box; type your selection in the box or click the drop-down arrow to display the list.
  - Check box. A square that you click to select or clear an option. A check mark in the box indicates that the option is selected.
  - Command button. A button used to execute a command. An ellipsis on a command button means that clicking the button opens another dialog box.
  - Tabs. Markers across the top of the dialog box that, when clicked, display additional pages of options within the dialog box.
  - Preview area. An area where you can preview the results of your selections before executing the commands.
  - Increment box. A space where you type a value, such as inches or numbers, or use increment arrows beside the box to increase or decrease the value with a mouse. Sometimes called a spin box.
  - Text box. A space where you type variable information, such as a file name.
  - Option buttons. A series of circles, only one of which can be selected at a time. Click the circle you want to select it.
- To move from one control to another in a dialog box you can click the control with the mouse, or press TAB.
- Some dialog box controls have access keys which are underlined in the control name. Press ALT and the access key to select the control.

Figure 4-1

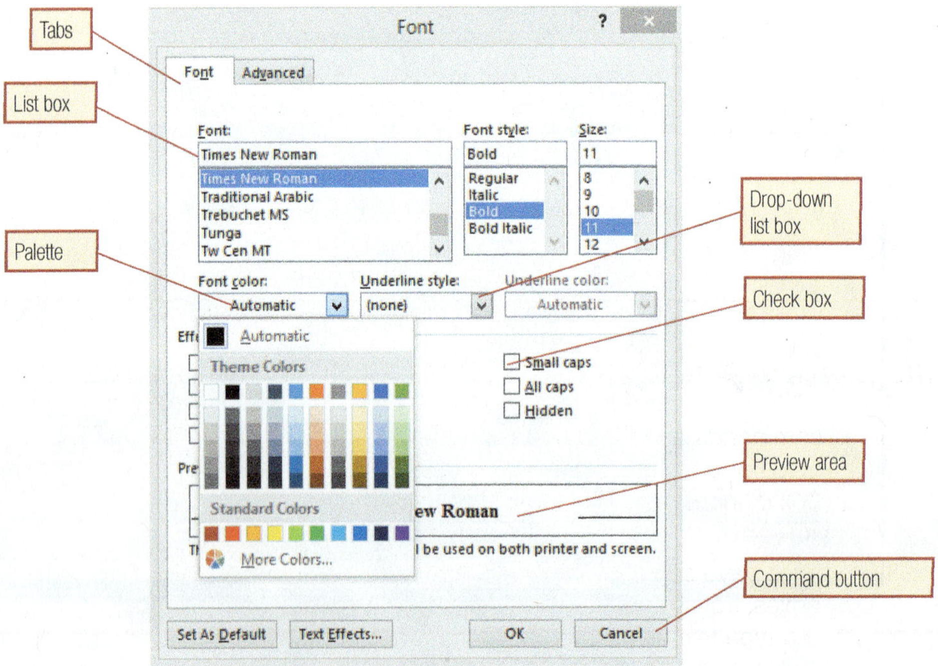

Word 2013, Windows 8, Microsoft Corporation

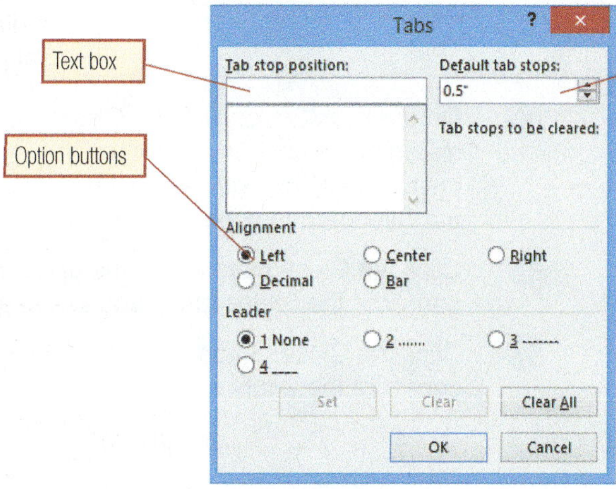

Word 2013, Windows 8, Microsoft Corporation

Figure 4-2

Try It! Using Dialog Box Options

1. In **B04TryA_xx**, select your first name.
2. On the HOME tab, click the Font group dialog box launcher to open the Font dialog box.

Font group on the Home tab

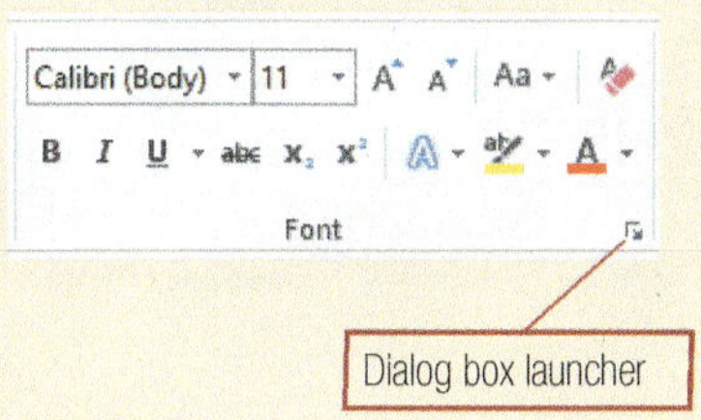

3. In the Font style list box, click Italic.
4. In the Size box, select 11 and then type **8**.
5. Click the Underline style drop-down arrow, and click the double underline that is second from the top.
6. In the Effects section, click the Small caps check box to select it.
7. Click the OK command button to apply the formatting to the selected text.
8. Deselect the text, then save the changes to **B04TryA_xx**, and leave it open to use in the next Try It.

Displaying Task Panes

- Some commands open a **task pane** instead of a dialog box. For example, if you click the Clipboard dialog box launcher, the Clipboard task pane displays.
- Task panes have some features in common with dialog boxes. For example, some have text boxes in which you type text as well as drop-down list boxes, check boxes, and options buttons.
- Unlike a dialog box, you can leave a task pane open while you work, move it, or close it to get it out of the way. You can also have more than one task pane open at the same time.

✓ *You learn how to accomplish tasks using task panes in the lesson in which that feature is covered. For example, in Basics Lesson 5 you learn how to use the Office Clipboard task pane to copy or move a selection.*

Try It! Displaying Task Panes

1. In the **B04TryA_xx** document, on the HOME tab, click the Styles group dialog box launcher ⧉ to open the Styles task pane.
2. In the document window, click to position the insertion point at the end of your name.
3. In the Styles task pane, click Clear All. This clears the formatting from the text.
4. Press ENTER to start a new line, and then type your last name.
5. On the HOME tab, click the Clipboard group dialog box launcher ⧉ to open the Clipboard task pane. Now, both the Styles task pane and the Clipboard task pane are open.
6. Click the Close button × in the upper-right corner of the Styles task pane to close it.
7. Click the Close button × in the upper-right corner of the Clipboard task pane to close it.
8. Close **B04TryA_xx**, saving changes, and exit Word.

Open multiple task panes

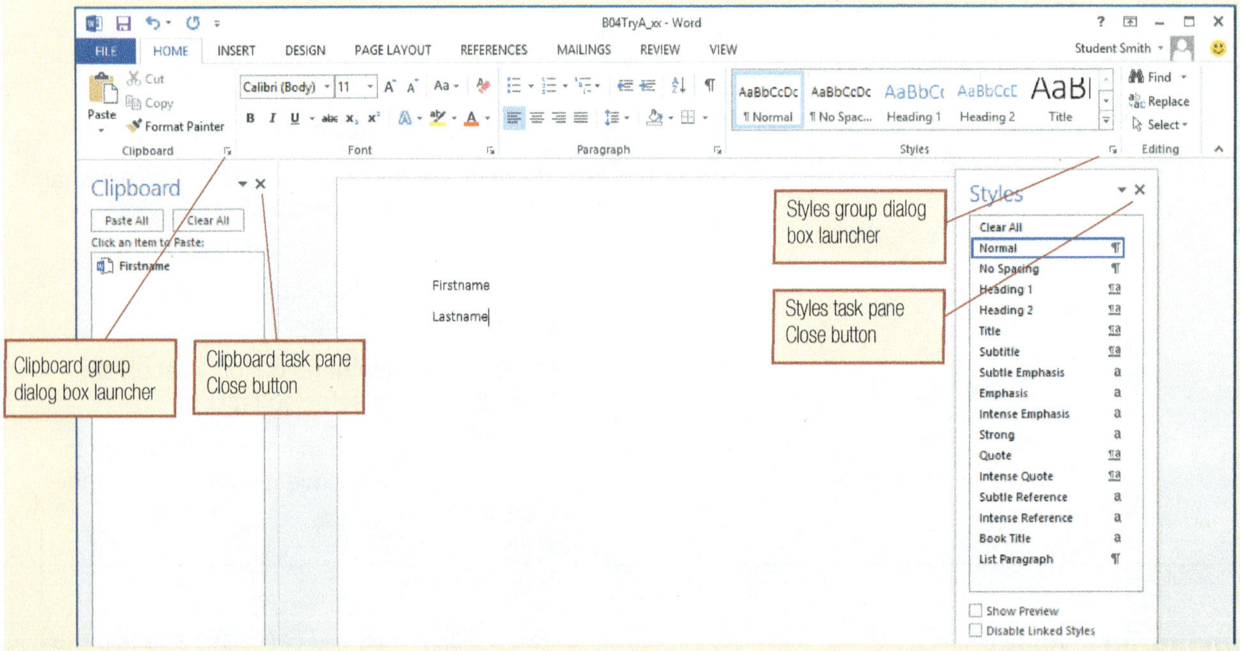

Word 2013, Windows 8, Microsoft Corporation

Formatting Pages

- Before you print or otherwise distribute a file, you may need to adjust the page formatting.
- Use the Print options in the Backstage view to select basic page formatting settings.
- In Access, use the options on the Print Preview tab.
- You can select an orientation, a paper size, and **margin** widths. You can also select to **scale** the file, if necessary, to fit on the selected paper size.
- Orientation is either portrait or landscape.
  - Select **Portrait orientation**—the default—when you want data displayed across the shorter length of a page.
  - Select **Landscape orientation** when you want data displayed across the wider length of a page.

✓ *You will learn about more advanced page formatting settings, such as setting custom margins and adjusting the alignment, in the program sections of this book.*

- You can select from a list of preset margins, including Normal, Wide, and Narrow. Margins are measured in inches.

Try It! Formatting Pages

1. Start Excel, and open **B04TryB** from the data files for this lesson. Save the file as **B04TryB_xx** in the location where your teacher instructs you to store the files for this lesson.
2. Click the FILE tab, and then click Print. In the preview, you see that not all columns fit on the first page.
3. Click the Margins down arrow and click Narrow on the menu. This changes the width of the margins to 0.75" on the top and bottom and 0.25" on the left and right. Now, only the Total column is still on page 2.
4. Click the Scaling down arrow and click Fit Sheet on One Page. Now all columns fit, but they are quite small.
5. Click the Orientation down arrow and click Landscape Orientation to provide more room across the page.
6. Click the Margins down arrow and click Normal to increase the width of the margins.
7. Close **B04TryB_xx**, saving changes, and exit Excel.

Formatting pages before printing

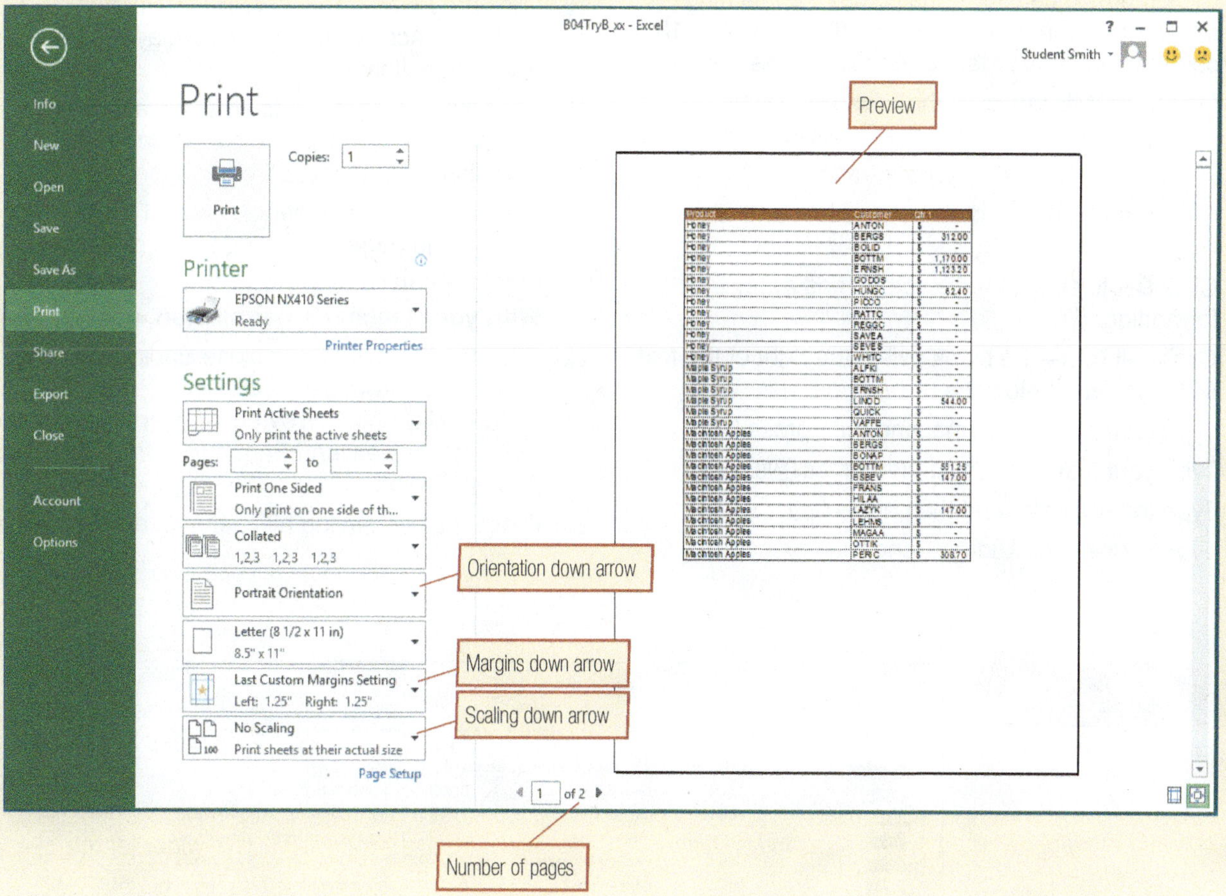

Excel 2013, Windows 8, Microsoft Corporation

Lesson 4—Practice

As the store manager for Whole Grains Bread, a bakery, you must prepare a contact list of your employees for the franchise owner. In this project, you will use Excel to complete and format the contact list.

DIRECTIONS

1. Start Excel, open the file **B04Practice** from the data files for this lesson, and save it as **B04Practice_xx** in the location where your teacher instructs you to store the files for this lesson.
2. Double-click on the word *Position* (in cell A2). This positions the insertion point in the cell.
3. Select the word *Position*. The Mini toolbar displays.
4. Cick the **Bold** button B on the Mini-toolbar.
5. Click the next cell down the column, containing the text *Clerk*, and drag down to the cell in row 12, containing the text *Manager*. This selects the cells.
6. On the HOME tab, click the **Font group dialog box launcher** to open the Font dialog box.
7. In the Font style list box, click **Italic**.
8. Click the **Underline** drop-down arrow and click **Double**.
9. Click **OK** to close the dialog box and apply the formatting.
10. Click cell **B12**—the blank cell to the right of the text *Manager* and below the text *Kevin*.
11. Type your own first name, and then press TAB.
12. Type your last name, and then press TAB.
13. Type today's date, and then press TAB.
14. Type your e-mail address, and then press TAB.
15. Right-click your e-mail address to display a shortcut menu
16. On the shortcut menu, click **Remove Hyperlink**. This removes the hyperlink formatting from your e-mail address. The data in your file should look similar to Figure 4-3.
17. Click the **Customize Quick Access Toolbar** button and click **Print Preview and Print** to add the Print Preview and Print button to the Quick Access Toolbar.
18. Click the **Print Preview and Print** button on the Quick Access Toolbar to display the Print tab in Backstage view.
19. Click the **Orientation** down arrow and click **Landscape Orientation** to change the page formatting to Landscape orientation.
20. Click the **Margins** down arrow and click **Normal** to change the page formatting to the default Normal margin widths.
21. **With your teacher's permission**, print the file.
22. Click the Back button to close Backstage view, click the **Customize Quick Access Toolbar** button , and click **Print Preview and Print** to remove the Print Preview and Print button from the Quick Access Toolbar
23. Close the file, saving all changes, and exit Excel.

Figure 4-3

E12 | student@school.edu

	A	B	C	D	E	F	G
1							
2	**Position**	First Name	Last Name	Date Hired	Email	Telephone	
3	*Clerk*	Karen	Smith	5/8/2014	karen.smith@wgbreads.net	555-555-5551	
4	*Clerk*	William	Brown	1/17/2014	william.brown@wgbreads.net	555-555-5552	
5	*Baker*	Jorge	Hernandez	9/22/2013	jorge.hernandez@wgbreads.net	555-555-5553	
6	*Baker*	Lisa	McAnn-Dinardo	10/11/2013	lisa.mcann.dinardo@wgbreads.net	555-555-5554	
7	*Baker*	Amil	Muhammed	6/1/2012	amil.muhammed@wgbreads.net	555-555-5555	
8	*Baker*	Peter	Shepherd	5/22/2012	peter.j.shepherd@wgbreads.net	555-555-5556	
9	*Stock*	Jackson	Little	7/13/2014	jackson.little@wgbreads.net	555-555-5557	
10	*Assistant Manager*	Angela	Greene	8/23/2003	angela.greene@wgbreads.net	555-555-5558	
11	*Assistant Manager*	Kevin	Duchesne	9/22/2012	kevin.duchesne@wgbreads.net	555-555-5559	
12	*Manager*	Firstname	Lastname	9/18/2015	student@school.edu	555-555-5560	
13							

Excel 2013, Windows 8, Microsoft Corporation

Lesson 4—Apply

The Whole Grains Bread franchise owner has asked for the employee list in a Word document. In this project, you will open an existing Word file and then revise, format, and print the document.

DIRECTIONS

1. Start Word.
2. Open the file **B04Apply** from the data files for this lesson, and save it as **B04Apply_xx** in the location where your teacher instructs you to store the files for this lesson.
3. Display the Print options in the Backstage view and change to Landscape Orientation.
4. Set the margins to Normal.
5. Close the Backstage view.
6. Select all data in the document, and use the Mini toolbar to increase the font size to **12** points.
7. Display the Quick Access Toolbar below the Ribbon.
8. Type your name, today's date, and your e-mail address into the appropriate cells in the document.
9. Use a shortcut menu to remove the hyperlink formatting from your e-mail address.
10. Select the line of text above the table, and use the Styles task pane to clear all formatting, then close the Styles task pane.
11. With the first line of text still selected, open the Font dialog box, and apply **Bold, Green, 14-point** formatting. When you deselect the text, your screen should look similar to Figure 4-4.
12. **With your teacher's permission**, print the file.
13. Return the Quick Access Toolbar to its position above the Ribbon.
14. Close the file, saving changes, and exit Word.

Figure 4-4

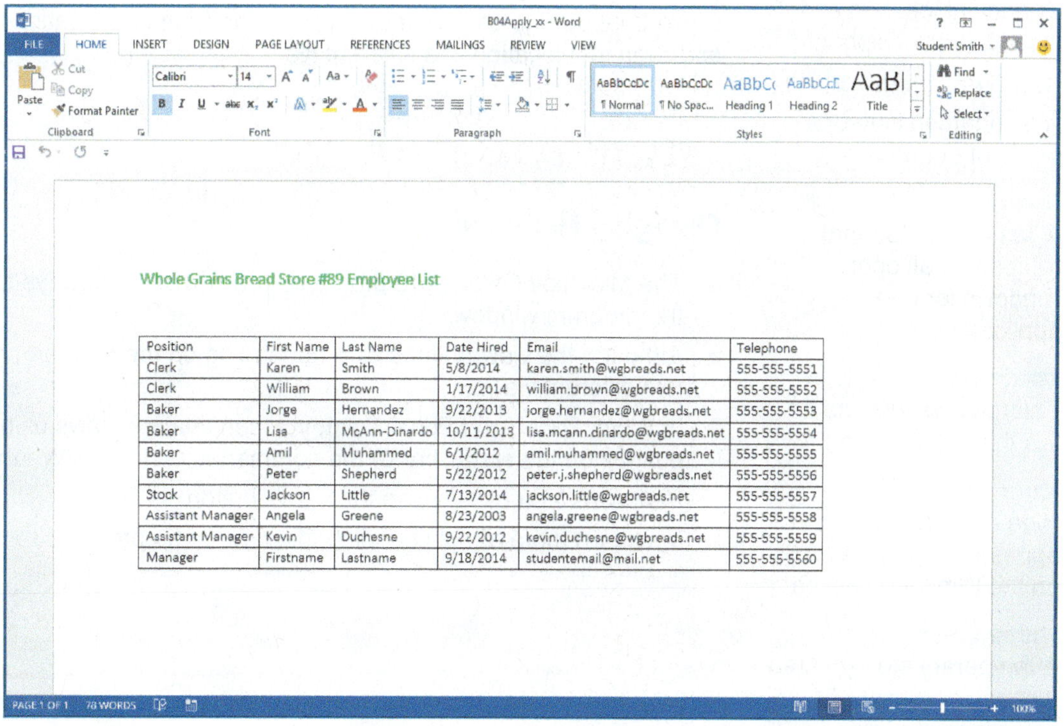

Whole Grains Bread Store #89 Employee List

Position	First Name	Last Name	Date Hired	Email	Telephone
Clerk	Karen	Smith	5/8/2014	karen.smith@wgbreads.net	555-555-5551
Clerk	William	Brown	1/17/2014	william.brown@wgbreads.net	555-555-5552
Baker	Jorge	Hernandez	9/22/2013	jorge.hernandez@wgbreads.net	555-555-5553
Baker	Lisa	McAnn-Dinardo	10/11/2013	lisa.mcann.dinardo@wgbreads.net	555-555-5554
Baker	Amil	Muhammed	6/1/2012	amil.muhammed@wgbreads.net	555-555-5555
Baker	Peter	Shepherd	5/22/2012	peter.j.shepherd@wgbreads.net	555-555-5556
Stock	Jackson	Little	7/13/2014	jackson.little@wgbreads.net	555-555-5557
Assistant Manager	Angela	Greene	8/23/2003	angela.greene@wgbreads.net	555-555-5558
Assistant Manager	Kevin	Duchesne	9/22/2012	kevin.duchesne@wgbreads.net	555-555-5559
Manager	Firstname	Lastname	9/18/2014	studentemail@mail.net	555-555-5560

Lesson 5

Managing Program Windows

WORDS TO KNOW

Active window
The window in which you are currently working.

Cascade
Arrange windows so they overlap, with the active window in front. Only the title bars of the nonactive windows are visible.

Copy
To duplicate a selection. The original remains unchanged.

Cut
To delete a selection from its original location and move it to the Clipboard.

Default
A standard setting or mode of operation.

Group button
A Taskbar button that represents all open windows for one application.

Maximize
Enlarge a window so it fills the entire screen.

Minimize
Hide a window so it appears only as a button on the Windows Taskbar.

Office Clipboard
A temporary storage area that can hold up to 24 selections at a time.

➤ What You Will Learn

Changing the View
Using Window Controls
Zooming
Scrolling
Using Multiple Windows
Using the Microsoft Office Clipboard

Software Skills Controlling the way Microsoft Office 2013 programs and documents are displayed on your computer monitor is a vital part of using the programs successfully. For example, you can control the size and position of the program window onscreen, and you can control the size a document is displayed. In addition, you can open more than one window onscreen at the same time, so that you can work with multiple documents and even multiple programs at once. Use the Office Clipboard to copy or move a selection from one location in a file to another, and even to a location in a different file.

What You Can Do

Changing the View

- The Microsoft Office 2013 programs provide different ways to view your data in the program window.
- Although the view options vary depending on the program, most offer at least two different views.
- In Word, Excel, and PowerPoint, you can change views using the View shortcut buttons on the status bar or the commands on the VIEW tab of the Ribbon.
- In Access, you usually use the Views button.
- You learn more about changing the view in the program sections of this book.

Try It! Changing the View

1. Start Excel and create a blank workbook file.
2. Click the VIEW tab.
3. In the Workbook Views group, click the Page Layout button to change from Normal view to Page Layout view. In Excel, Page Layout view displays the header and footer areas and rulers.
4. On the status bar, click the Normal view button.
5. Leave the file open to use in the next Try It.

Page Layout view in Excel

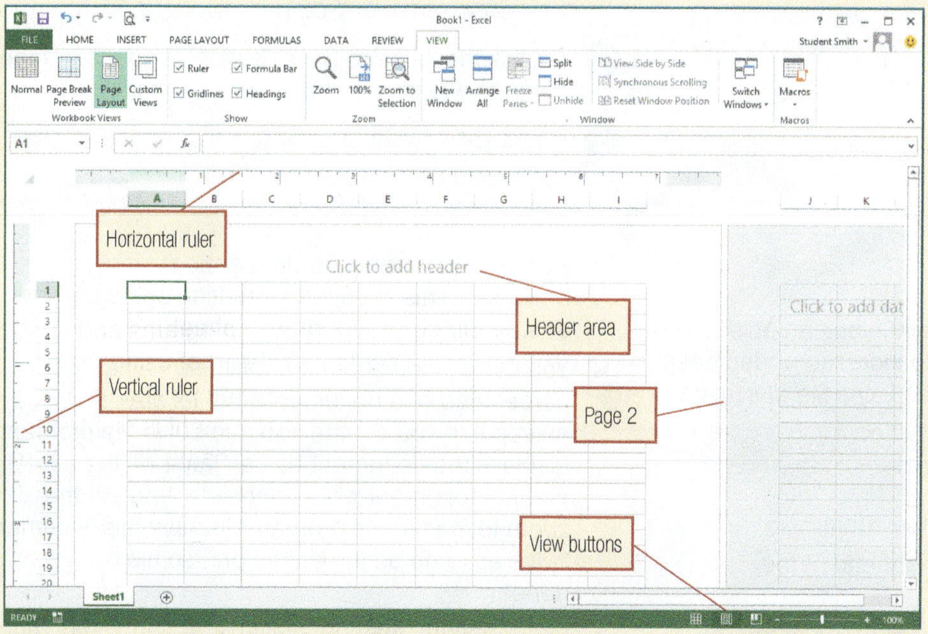

Excel 2013, Windows 8, Microsoft Corporation

Using Window Controls

- When you start a Microsoft Office 2013 program, it opens in a program window using **default** settings.
- You can control the size and position of the program window.
  - You can **maximize** the window to fill the screen.
  - You can **minimize** the window to a Taskbar button.
  - You can **restore** a minimized window to its previous size and position.
  - You can **restore down** a maximized window to its previous size and position.
  - In Word, Excel, and PowerPoint, you can Auto-hide the Ribbon to display the window in Full Screen Mode.

Paste
To insert a selection from the Clipboard into a document.

Restore
Return a minimized window to its previous size and position on the screen.

Restore down
Return a maximized window to its previous size and position on the screen.

Scroll
Shift the displayed area of the document up, down, left, or right.

Tile
Arrange windows so they do not overlap.

Zoom
Adjust the magnification of the content displayed on the screen. This does not affect the actual size of the printed document.

Zoom in
Increase the size of the document as it is displayed onscreen.

Zoom out
Decrease the size of the document as it is displayed onscreen.

- Use the Control buttons located on the right end of the title bar to control a program window.
  - Minimize
  - Maximize
  - Restore Down

✓ *Restore Down is only available in a maximized window.*

- You can also use the program's control menu to Maximize, Minimize, or Restore the window.

Try It! Using Window Controls

1. In the Excel window, click the Minimize button –. When the program window is minimized, it displays as a button on the Windows Taskbar.
2. Click the Excel program icon on the Windows Taskbar to restore the window to its previous size and position.
3. In the Excel window, click the Maximize button.

   ✓ *If the Maximize button is not displayed, the window is already maximized. Continue with step 4.*
4. Click the Restore Down button to restore the window to its previous size and position.
5. Exit Excel without saving any changes.

Zooming

- In Word, Excel, and PowerPoint, you can adjust the **zoom** magnification setting to increase or decrease the size a program uses to display a file onscreen.

✓ *The Zoom options may be different depending on the program you are using.*

- There are three ways to set the zoom:
  - The Zoom slider on the right end of the program's status bar
  - The commands in the Zoom group of the VIEW tab on the Ribbon
  - The Zoom dialog box
- **Zoom in** to make the data appear larger onscreen. This is useful for getting a close look at graphics, text, or data.

✓ *When you zoom in, only a small portion of the file will be visible onscreen at a time.*

- **Zoom out** to make the data appear smaller onscreen. This is useful for getting an overall look at a document, slide, or worksheet.
- You can set the zoom magnification as a percentage of a document's actual size. For example, if you set the zoom to 50%, the program displays the document half as large as the actual, printed document would appear. If you set the zoom to 200%, the program displays the document twice as large as the actual printed file would appear.
- Other options may be available depending on your program.
  - In Word, you can select from the following preset sizes:
    - Page Width. Word automatically sizes the document so that the width of the page matches the width of the screen. You see the left and right margins of the page.

- Text width. Word automatically sizes the document so that the width of the text on the page matches the width of the screen. The left and right margins may be hidden.
- One Page (or Whole page). Word automatically sizes the document so that one page is visible on the screen.
- Multiple Pages. Word automatically sizes the document so that multiple pages are visible on the screen.
- Many pages. Word automatically sizes the document so that the number of pages you select can all be seen onscreen.

✓ *Some options may not be available, depending on the current view. Options that are not available will appear dimmed.*

- In Excel you can Zoom to Selection, which adjusts the size of selected cells to fill the entire window.
- In PowerPoint you can Fit to Window, which adjusts the size of the current slide to fill the entire window.

Try It! Zooming Using the Slider

1. Start Word, and open **B05TryA** from the data files for this lesson. Save the file as **B05TryA_xx** in the location where your teacher instructs you to store the files for this lesson.
2. Drag the Zoom slider to the left to zoom out, or decrease the magnification. At 10% magnification, the document page is so small you cannot view the content.
3. Drag the Zoom slider to the right to zoom in, or increase the magnification. At 500% magnification, the document page is so large you can only view a small portion of the content.
4. Click the Zoom Out button at the left end of the Zoom slider. Each time you click, the magnification zooms out by 10%.
5. Click the Zoom In button at the right end of the Zoom slider. Each time you click, the magnification zooms in by 10%.
6. Leave the **B05TryA_xx** file open to use in the next Try It.

Zoom out to 10%

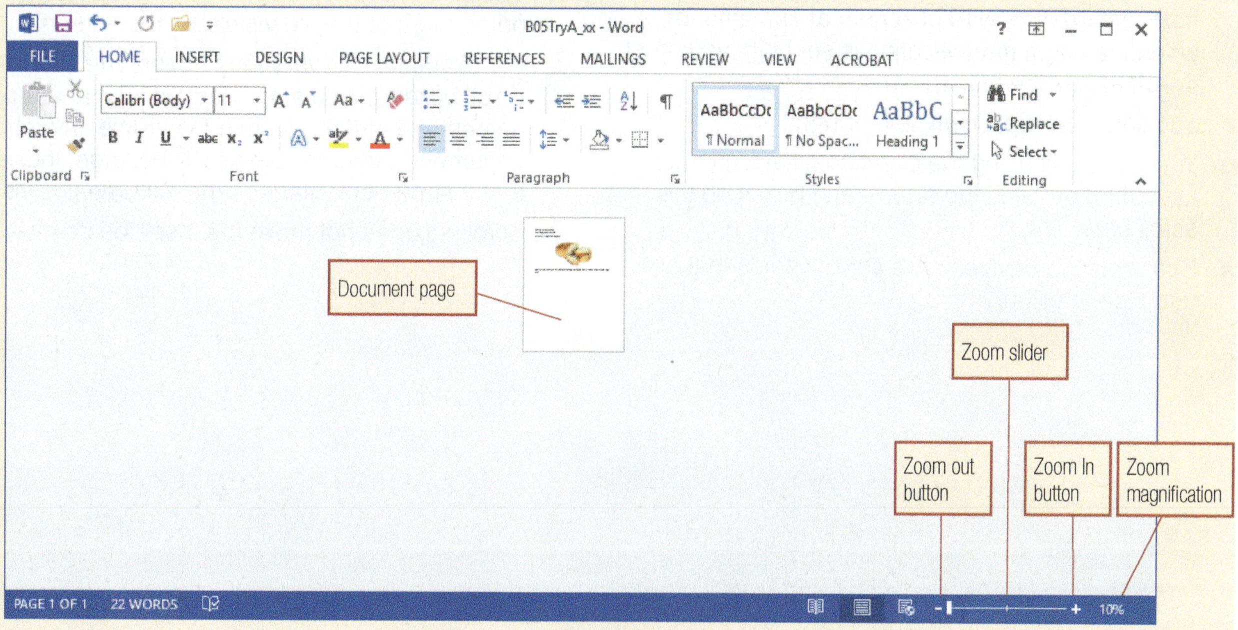

Word 2013, Windows 8, Microsoft Corporation

Try It! Zooming Using the View Tab

1. With the **B05TryA_xx** file open, click the VIEW tab on the Ribbon and locate the Zoom group of commands.
2. Click the 100% button in the Zoom group. The magnification adjusts to display the document at its actual size.
3. Click the Zoom button in the Zoom group to open the Zoom dialog box.
4. Click the 75% option button and then click OK to apply the change and close the dialog box.
5. Click the Zoom button in the Zoom group again, and use the Percent increment arrows to set the zoom magnification to 150%.

   ✓ *In Excel, set the percentage in the Custom box.*
6. Click OK.
7. Save the changes to **B05TryA_xx**, and leave it open to use in the next Try It.

Zoom using the Zoom group on the View tab

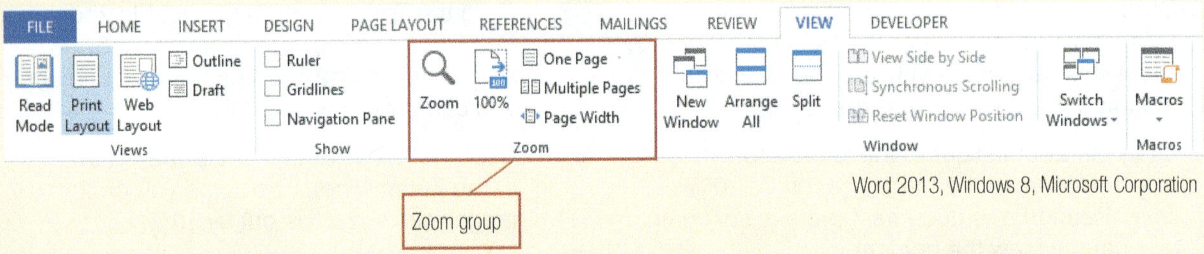

Word 2013, Windows 8, Microsoft Corporation

Scrolling

- When there is more data in a window or dialog box than can be displayed onscreen at one time, or when the zoom magnification is set high, you must **scroll** to see the hidden parts.
- You can scroll up, down, left, or right.
- You can scroll using the directional keys on the keyboard, or using the arrows and boxes on the scroll bars.
- Some mouse devices have scroll wheels that are used for scrolling.
- If you are using a touch device, you scroll by swiping left, right, up, or down.
- The size of the scroll boxes change to represent the percentage of the file visible on the screen.
- For example, in a very long document, the scroll boxes will be small, indicating that a small percentage of the document is visible. In a short document, the scroll boxes will be large, indicating that a large percentage of the document is visible.
- Scrolling does not move the insertion point.

Try It! Scrolling

1. In the **B05TryA_xx** file, click the down scroll arrow ▾ at the bottom of the vertical scroll bar on the right side of the window. The content in the window scrolls down.

   ✓ *If you have a wide screen, you may have to increase the zoom for the vertical scroll bar to display.*

2. Drag the vertical scroll box about halfway to the bottom of the scroll bar to scroll down in the file until you can see the line of text below the picture.

3. Click the right scroll arrow ▸ at the right end of the horizontal scroll bar above the status bar at the bottom of the window to scroll to the right so you can see the entire line of text.

4. Drag the vertical scroll box all the way to the top of the scroll bar to scroll to the top of the document page.

5. Save the changes to **B05TryA_xx**, and leave it open to use in the next Try It.

Tools for scrolling in a document

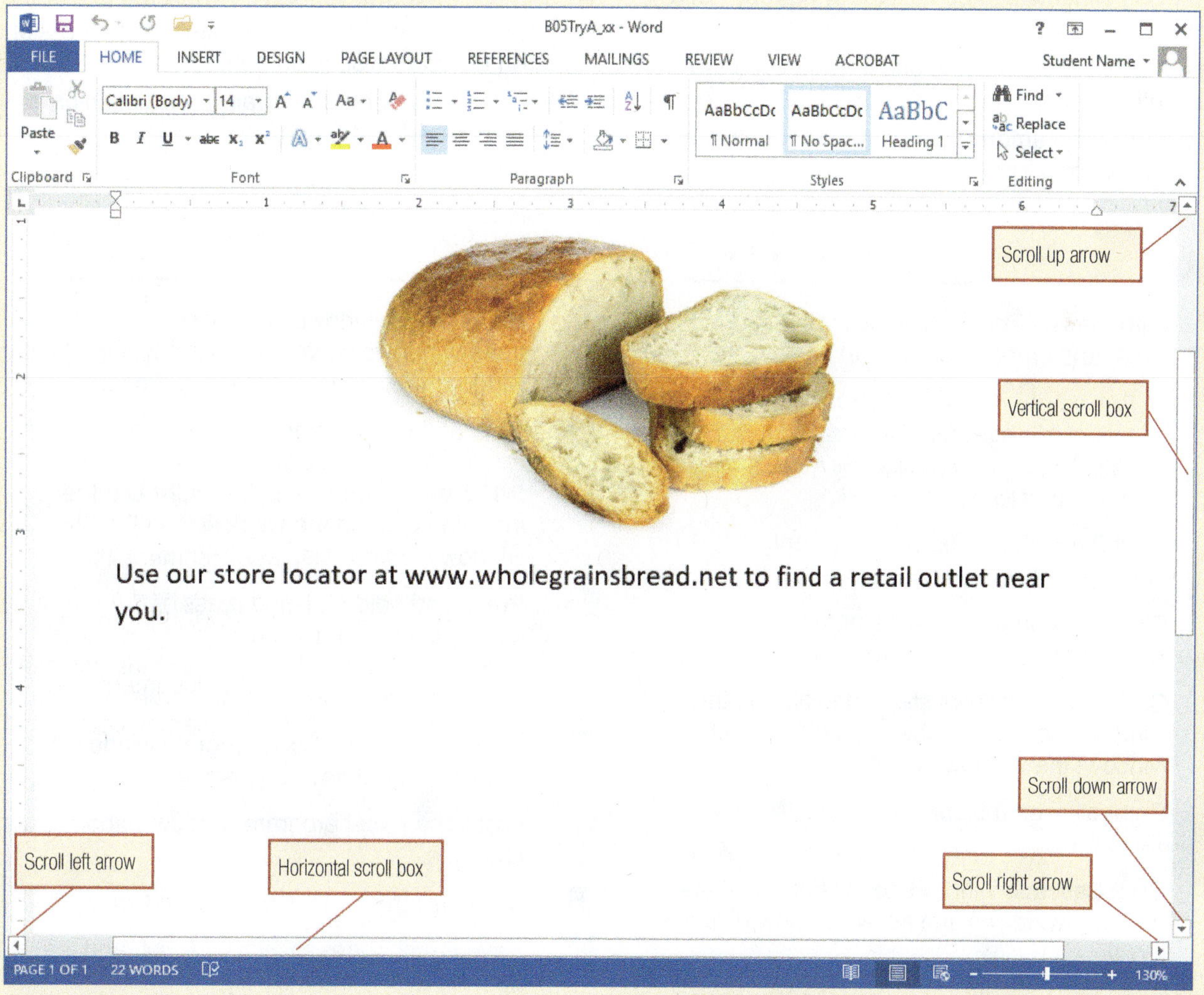

Word 2013, Windows 8, Microsoft Corporation

Using Multiple Windows

- You can open multiple program windows at the same time.
- You can also open multiple document windows in Word, PowerPoint, and Excel.
- Each open window is represented by a button on the Windows Taskbar.
- If there is not room on the Taskbar to display buttons for each open window, Windows displays a **group button**.

  ✓ *The Taskbar may not be visible onscreen if Windows is set to hide the Taskbar, or to display windows on top of the Taskbar. To see the Taskbar, move the mouse pointer to the edge of the screen where it usually displays.*

- Only one window can be active—or current—at a time.
- The **active window** is the one in which you are currently working.
- You can switch among open windows to make a different window active.
- You can **tile** windows if you want to see all of them at the same time. Tiled windows do not overlap; they are arranged side by side or stacked so you see the full width of each window across the screen. The active window has a brightly colored border.
- The more windows you have open, the smaller they display when tiled.
  - If necessary in smaller windows, the program may hide or condense common screen elements such as the Quick Access Toolbar and Ribbon and display only a program icon on the left end of the title bar.
  - You can click the program icon to display a shortcut menu of commands including Maximize, Minimize, and Close.
- You can **cascade** windows if you want to see the active window in its entirety, with the title bars of all open windows displayed behind it.
- You can also open and arrange multiple files in Word, PowerPoint, and Excel.

Try It! Using Multiple Program Windows

1. With the **B05TryA_xx** file still open in Word, start Excel and create a blank workbook.

   ✓ *To display the Windows desktop, move the mouse to the lower-right corner of the display, and click. To display the Windows 8 Start screen, move the mouse to the lower-left corner of the display and click.*

2. Start PowerPoint and create a blank presentation.
3. Right-click on a blank area of the Windows Taskbar to display a shortcut menu.
4. Click Show windows stacked to tile the three windows so you see the full width of each window; the window height is reduced.
5. Right-click on a blank area of the Windows Taskbar.
6. Click Cascade windows to overlap the three program windows; the active window displays on top.
7. Right-click on a blank area of the Windows Taskbar.
8. Click Show windows side by side to tile the three windows so you see the full height of each window; the window width is reduced.
9. Click at the beginning of the text in the **B05TryA_xx** document window. Now, the **B05TryA_xx** window is active. Notice the insertion point in the window, and that the window's border displays brighter.
10. Press and hold ALT and press TAB. A bar of icons representing open windows displays. Press TAB to move through the icons until the Excel window is selected, then release ALT.
11. Click in the PowerPoint program window and close it without saving changes.
12. Close the Excel program window without saving changes.
13. Maximize the Word program window.
14. Save the changes to **B05TryA_xx**, and leave it open to use in the next Try It.

(continued)

Try It! Using Multiple Program Windows *(continued)*

Arrange multiple windows side by side

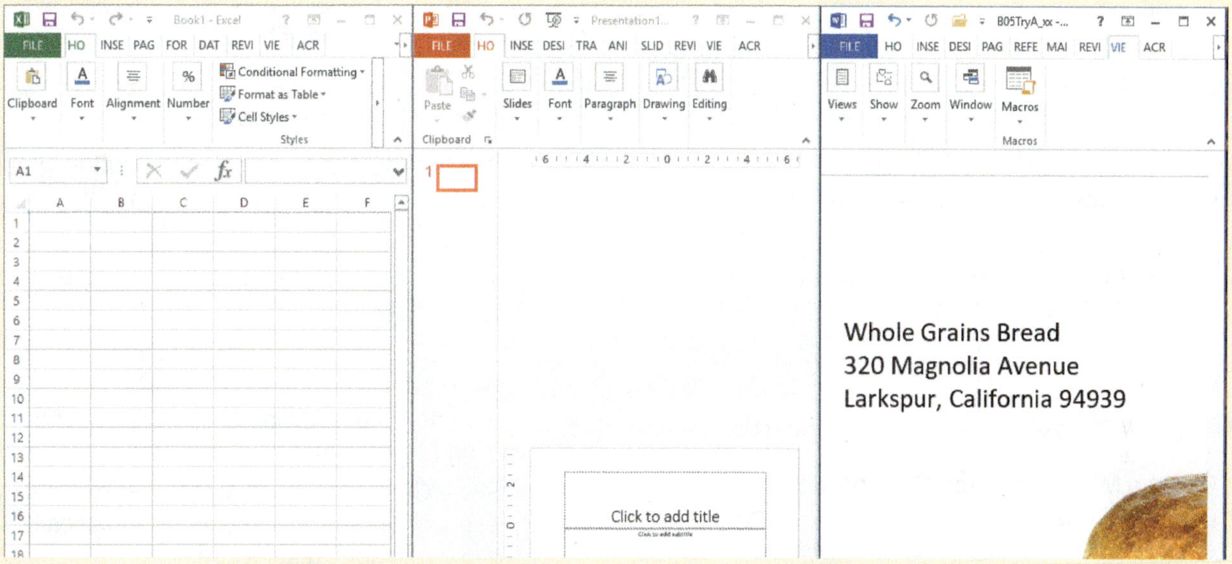

Excel 2013, Windows 8, Microsoft Corporation

Try It! Arranging Multiple Files in Word

1. With the **B05TryA_xx** window open, click FILE > Open.
2. Open **B05TryB** from the data files for this lesson. Now, both files are open in Word at the same time.
3. Rest the mouse pointer on the Word icon on the Taskbar to view thumbnails of all open Word files.
4. Click the **B05TryA_xx** thumbnail to make that window active.
5. Click the VIEW tab on the Ribbon.
6. In the Window group, click the Arrange All button. The two open files are tiled in the program window.

   ✓ *If nothing happens when you click Arrange All, you may have to Restore Down the B05TryA_xx window.*
7. Close both files, without saving any changes, and exit Word.

Try It! Arranging Multiple Files in Excel

1. Start Excel and maximize the window, if necessary. Open **B05TryC** from the data files for this lesson.
2. Click FILE > Open, and then open **B05TryD** from the data files for this lesson. Both files are now open in Excel.
3. Click the VIEW tab on the Ribbon.
4. In the Window group, click the Arrange All button. The Arrange Windows dialog box opens.
5. Click the Horizontal option button and then click OK to tile the open files one above the other (stacked).
6. Click in the **B05TryC** window to make it active.
7. Click VIEW > Arrange All again to open the dialog box, click the Vertical option button, and then click OK. The files are tiles side by side.
8. Close both files, without saving any changes, and exit Excel.

Try It! Arranging Multiple Files in PowerPoint

1. Start PowerPoint and maximize the window, if necessary. Open B05TryE from data files for this lesson.
2. Click FILE > Open, and then open B05TryF from the data files for this lesson. Both files are now open in PowerPoint.
3. Click the VIEW tab on the Ribbon.
4. In the Window group, click the Cascade button to overlap the windows with the active window on top.
5. In the Window group, click the Switch Windows button to display a list of open windows. A check mark displays beside the active window.
6. Click B05TryE on the Switch Windows drop-down list to make it active.
7. Click the VIEW tab, then, in the Window group, click the Arrange All button to tile the windows side by side.
8. Close both files, without saving changes, and exit PowerPoint.

Using the Microsoft Office Clipboard

- Use the Microsoft **Office Clipboard** with the Cut, Copy, and Paste commands to copy or move a selection from one location to another.
- The **Copy** command stores a duplicate of the selection on the Office Clipboard, leaving the original selection unchanged.
- The **Cut** command deletes the selection from its original location, and stores it on the Office Clipboard.
- You can then use the **Paste** command to paste the selection from the Office Clipboard to the insertion point location in the same file or a different file.
- By default, the last 24 items cut or copied display in the Office Clipboard task pane.
- You can paste or delete one or all of the items.
- You can turn the following Office Clipboard options off or on (a check mark indicates the option is on):
  - Show Office Clipboard Automatically. Sets the Clipboard task pane to open automatically when you cut or copy a selection.
  - Show Office Clipboard When Ctrl+C Pressed Twice. Sets Word to display the Clipboard task pane when you press and hold CTRL and then press C on the keyboard twice.
  - Collect Without Showing Office Clipboard. Sets the Clipboard task pane so it does not open automatically when you cut or copy data.
  - Show Office Clipboard Icon on Taskbar. Adds a Clipboard icon to the Show Hidden Icons group on the taskbar.
  - Show Status Near Taskbar When Copying. Displays a ScreenTip with the number of items on the Clipboard when you cut or copy a selection.

Try It! Using the Microsoft Office Clipboard

1. Start Word and maximize the window, if necessary. Open B05TryG from the location where the data files for this lesson are stored, and save it as B05TryG_xx in the location where your teacher instructs you to store the files for this lesson.
2. On the HOME tab click the Clipboard group dialog box launcher to display the Clipboard task pane.
3. In the document, select the text *Whole Grains Bread*.

(continued)

Try It! Using the Office Clipboard *(continued)*

4 Right-click the selection and click Copy. The selected text is copied to the Office Clipboard. Notice that it remains in its original location in the document, as well.

5 In the document window, click on the picture to select it. (A selection box displays around a selected picture.)

6 Right-click the selection and click Cut. The selection is deleted from the document, and displays in the Clipboard task pane.

7 In Word, open **B05TryH** from the location where the data files for this lesson are stored. The Clipboard task pane is still displayed.

8 Save the file as **B05TryH_xx** in the location where your teacher instructs you to store the files for this lesson. Make sure the insertion point is at the beginning of the document, and then press ENTER to insert a blank line. Press the up arrow key ↑ to move the insertion point to the blank line.

9 In the Clipboard task pane, click the picture of the bread. It is pasted into the document at the insertion point location. It also remains on the Clipboard so you can paste it again, if you want.

10 Right-click the picture of the runner in the document and click Copy to copy it to the Clipboard. Now, there are three selections stored on the Clipboard.

11 Save the changes to **B05TryH_xx**, and close it. **B05TryG_xx** is still open.

12 Position the insertion point at the end of the document and press ENTER to insert a new line.

13 Click the picture of the runner in the Clipboard task pane. It is pasted into the document. Even though the original file is closed, you can still paste a selection that is stored on the Clipboard. Save the changes to the file and leave it open to use in the next Try It.

Try It! Deleting Selections from the Office Clipboard

1 With **B05TryG_xx** still open, click the Options button at the bottom of the Clipboard task pane. A menu of settings that affect the Clipboard displays. A check mark indicates that an option is selected.

2 In the Clipboard task pane, rest the mouse pointer on the picture of the runner, and click the down arrow that displays.

3 Click Delete on the drop-down menu. The selection is removed from the Clipboard, but it remains in place in the document.

4 Rest the mouse pointer on the picture of the bread in the Clipboard task pane, click the down arrow that displays, and click Delete.

5 Rest the mouse pointer on the text *Whole Grains Bread*, click the down arrow, and click Delete. Now, the Office Clipboard is empty.

✓ *Click Clear All at the top of the Clipboard task pane to quickly delete all selections.*

6 Close the Clipboard task pane.

7 Close **B05TryG_xx**, saving changes, and exit Word.

Lesson 5—Practice

You are a marketing assistant at Voyager Travel Adventures, a tour group operator. In this project, you will practice managing program windows and using the Office Clipboard to copy a picture of kayaking from a PowerPoint presentation to a Word document.

DIRECTIONS

1. Start Word, and create a blank document.
2. Save the file as **B05PracticeA_xx** in the location where your instructor tells you to store the files for this lesson.
3. Click the **VIEW** tab.
4. In the Zoom group, click the **100%** button to set the zoom to 100% magnification.
5. On the first line of the document, type the text **Kayak in the Land of the Midnight Sun** and then press ENTER.
6. Click the **HOME** tab.
7. Select the text, and then change the font to Times New Roman and the font size to 28 points.
8. Move the insertion point to the end of the document, set the font size to 12 points, and type: **Join Voyager Travel Adventures on a 10-day sea kayaking trip in one of the most beautiful and exciting places on earth! Experience the thrill of seeing whales, bears, and other wildlife up close, while enjoying a comfortable base camp and first-class dining.**
9. Press ENTER and then save the changes.
10. Click the **VIEW** tab on the Ribbon, and then, in the Document Views group, click the **Read Mode** button to change to Read Mode view.
11. Click the **Print Layout** button on the status bar to change back to Print Layout view.
12. Click the **Zoom In** button on the Zoom slider as many times as necessary to increase the zoom magnification to 150%.
13. Save the changes to the file, and then click the **Minimize** button - to minimize the Word program window.
14. Start PowerPoint and maximize the window if necessary. Open the file **B05PracticeB** from the location where the data files for this lesson are stored.
15. Click the **Word** button on the Windows Taskbar to restore the Word program window.
16. Right-click a blank area of the Windows Taskbar and click **Show windows Side by Side** to view both the Word and PowerPoint windows.

   ✓ *If you have other windows open, they will be arranged as well. Minimize them, and then repeat step 16.*

17. Click the **Maximize** button in the PowerPoint window.
18. Click the **HOME** tab, if necessary, and then click the **Clipboard group dialog box launcher**.
19. In the list of slides on the left side of the PowerPoint window, right-click **slide 2**—Kayaking in Alaska.
20. Click **Copy** on the shortcut menu to copy the selection to the Clipboard.
21. Close the PowerPoint window without saving any changes.
22. Click the **Maximize** button in the Word window.
23. Click the **HOME** tab and then click the **Clipboard group dialog box launcher** to open the Clipboard task pane. The picture copied from the presentation in step 20 should display.
24. Make sure the insertion point is at the end of the **B05PracticeA_xx** document, and then click **Kayaking in Alaska** in the Clipboard task pane to paste the selection into the Word document.
25. Click the **Zoom Out** button on the Zoom slider until the magnification is set to 80%.
26. Rest the mouse pointer on the picture in the Clipboard task pane, click the **down arrow** that displays, and click **Delete**.
27. Click the **Close** button × in the Clipboard task pane.
28. **With your teacher's permission**, print the file.
29. Close the file, saving changes, and exit Word.

Lesson 5—Apply

In this project, you will use the skills you have learned in this lesson to cut a picture from a Word document and paste it into a PowerPoint presentation, and cut a picture from a PowerPoint presentation and paste it as an illustration in a Word document.

DIRECTIONS

1. Start Word, and open **B05ApplyA** from the data files for this lesson.
2. Save the file as **B05ApplyA_xx** in the location where your teacher instructs you to store the files for this lesson.
3. Zoom out to 80% so you can see all content in the document.
4. Display the Clipboard task pane.
5. Cut the picture from the document to the Clipboard.
6. Start PowerPoint and maximize the window, if necessary.
7. Open **B05ApplyB** from the location where the data files for this lesson are stored. Save it as **B05ApplyB_xx** in the location where your teacher instructs you to store the files for this lesson.
8. Display the Clipboard task pane, if necessary.
9. Click slide 3 in the list of slides to make that slide active. On the slide in the main area of the window, right-click the picture and click **Cut**.
10. Click the dotted line bordering the placeholder for content on the slide to select it, as shown in Figure 5-1 on the next page.
11. In the Clipboard task pane, click the picture you cut from the Word document to paste it on to the slide.
12. Close the Clipboard task pane and save the changes to the PowerPoint presentation.
13. Make the Word program window active, and then arrange the PowerPoint presentation and the Word document side by side.
14. Arrange them stacked.
15. Minimize the PowerPoint presentation window.
16. Maximize the Word window.
17. Paste the picture you copied from the PowerPoint presentation on to the last line of the Word document.
18. Close the Clipboard task pane and zoom out so you can see the entire document.
19. **With your teacher's permission**, print the file.
20. Close the file, saving all changes, and exit Word.
21. Maximize the PowerPoint window.
22. Close the file, saving changes, and exit PowerPoint.

Figure 5-1

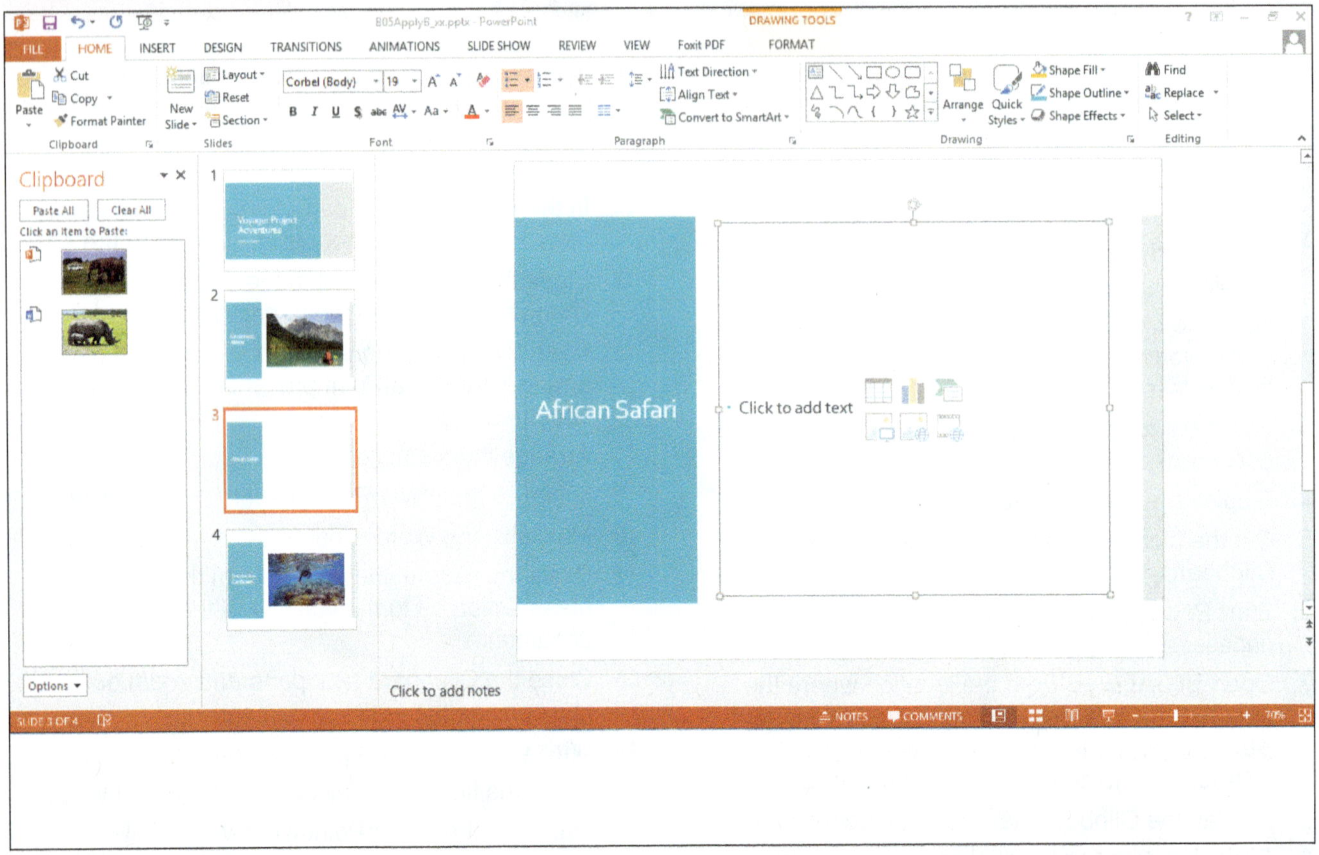

PowerPoint 2013, Windows 8, Microsoft Corporation

Lesson 6

Using Microsoft Office Help

➤ What You Will Learn

Using a Help Program
Searching for Help
Viewing Application Options
Customizing the Ribbon
Using AutoRecover and AutoSave

Software Skills Each Microsoft Office 2013 program comes with Help information that you can access and display in a window while you work. Use the Help program to get help about using a specific command, search for help topics, or link to additional resources on the Microsoft Office Web site. Each program also has optional settings you use to control how the program operates. For example, you can specify how often the program should automatically save an open file.

WORDS TO KNOW

AutoRecover
A feature in some Microsoft Office 2013 programs that automatically saves files at a set interval so that in the event of a system failure the files may be recovered.

Read-only mode
A mode in which the open file can be viewed but not edited.

What You Can Do

Using Microsoft Office Help

- Each Microsoft Office program has its own Help program.
- You can start Help by clicking the Help button ? which displays in the upper-right corner of the program window, or in a dialog box.
- Help opens in a window that you can keep open while you work.
- By default, the Help Home page displays links to popular searches and program basics.
- When the mouse pointer touches a link, it changes to a hand with a pointing finger.
- Click a link to display a list of related articles or specific Help information.
- Links may be graphics, or text. Text links are formatted in blue so they stand out from the surrounding text.

- Use the buttons on the Help window toolbar to control the Help display.
  - Back ⊖. Displays the previously viewed page.
  - Forward ⊖. Returns to a viewed page.
  - Home ⌂. Displays the Help Home page.
  - Print 🖶. Prints the current page.
  - Change Font Size A. Displays an option to change the size of the characters in the Help window.
  - Keep Help on Top. Sets the Help window to always display on top of other windows.
- At the bottom of most Help pages there is a question asking if you found the information helpful. If you are connected to the Internet, click Yes, No, or I don't know to display a text box where you can type information that you want to submit to Microsoft.
- Most Microsoft Office Help information is available online. If you do not have Internet access, you may not be able to take full advantage of the Help program.

Try It! Using Office Help

1. Start Access.
2. Click the Help button ? in the upper-right corner of the window
3. Click the first link under Popular searches.
4. Click the first link in the list that displays.
5. Click the Back button ⊖ on the toolbar to display the previously viewed page.
6. Click the Home button ⌂ on the toolbar to display the Help Home page.
7. Close the Help program window, and exit Access.

Searching for Help

- You can search for a Help topic from any Help page.
- Simply type the term or phrase for which you want to search in the Search box, and then click the Search button.
- A list of topics that contain the term or phrase displays in the Help window.
- Click a topic to display the Help information.

Try It! Searching for Help

1. Start PowerPoint.
2. Click the Help button ? to to start the Help program.
3. Click in the Search box, and type **Print**.
4. Click the Search button. A list of topics related to the term *Print* displays.
5. Click the topic Create and print handouts to display that article.
6. Close the Help window, and exit PowerPoint.

Viewing Application Options

- Each of the Microsoft Office programs has options for controlling program settings.
- The settings depend on the program, although some are the same for all of Microsoft Office. For example, you can enter a user name, set a default storage location for files, and control the way the programs open read-only files.
- You view and set program options in the program's Options dialog box, which is accessed from the Backstage view.

Try It! Viewing Application Options

1. Start Excel and create a blank workbook. Maximize the window, if necessary.
2. Click FILE and then click Options to open the Excel Options dialog box. The General options display. Note the options under Personalize your copy of Microsoft Office.
3. Click Save in the list on the left side of the dialog box to display the Save options. Locate the default local file location, which is where Office files are saved by default.
4. Click Proofing to display the Proofing options. This is where you select options for spelling, including foreign languages.
5. Click Cancel to close the dialog box without making any changes.
6. Leave Excel open to use in the next Try It.

Customizing the Ribbon

- In Microsoft Office 2013 applications, you can customize the Ribbon by adding commands you use frequently or removing commands you rarely use.
- You can create new groups on a Ribbon tab, and you can even create a completely new tab with new groups.
- Commands for customizing the Ribbon are on the Customize Ribbon tab of the Options dialog box in each application.

Try It! Customizing the Ribbon

1. In Excel right-click anywhere on the Ribbon and click Customize the Ribbon.
2. On the right side of the dialog box, under Main Tabs, click to clear the check mark to the left of Insert, then click OK to apply the change and close the Excel Options dialog box. Notice on the Ribbon that the Insert tab no longer displays.
3. Click FILE > Options to open the Excel Options dialog box.
4. Click Customize the Ribbon.
5. Under Main tabs, click to select Home and then click the New Tab button. Excel creates a new tab with one new group.
6. Click to select New Tab (Custom), click the Rename button, and type **WORKBOOK**. Click OK.
7. Click to select New Group (Custom), click the Rename button, and type **Management**. Click OK.
8. In the upper-left of the dialog box, click the Choose commands from drop-down arrow and click File Tab.

(continued)

Try It! Customizing the Ribbon *(continued)*

9 In the list of commands, click Close, and then click the Add button.

10 In the list of commands, click New, and then click the Add button.

11 In the list of commands, click Save As, and then click the Add button.

12 Click OK to close the Excel Options dialog box, then click the WORKBOOK tab on the Ribbon to view the new group of commands.

13 Right-click anywhere on the Ribbon and click Customize the Ribbon.

14 Click the Reset button and then click Reset all customizations.

15 Click Yes in the confirmation dialog box and then click OK. Leave Excel open to use in the next Try It.

Custom tab on the Ribbon

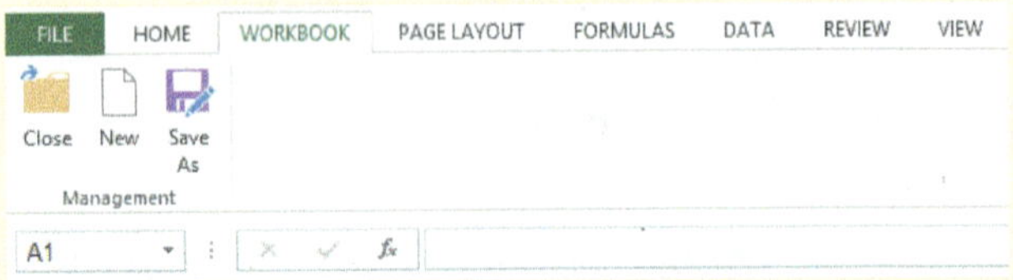

Excel 2013, Windows 8, Microsoft Corporation

Using AutoRecover and AutoSave

- By default the **AutoRecover** feature in Word, Excel, and PowerPoint is set to automatically save open files every ten minutes.
- If you close a file that has been autosaved without saving changes, the autosaved version will be available on the Info tab in the Backstage view.
  - If you were working in a new, unsaved file, click the Manage Versions button to recover a draft version from the UnsavedFiles folder.
  - If you were working in a file that had been saved, but not since your most recent changes, it will be listed under Versions; click a version to open it.
- An autosaved file opens in **read-only mode**, which means you must save it with a new name, or replace the existing file with the same name if you want to edit it.
- AutoRecovered files are stored for up to four days or until you edit the file, and then deleted.
- If a program closes unexpectedly due to a system failure or power outage, the Document Recovery task pane may display the next time you start the program.
- Up to three autosaved versions of the file(s) you were working on before the program closed are listed in the task pane. You may select the version you want to save, and delete the others.

Try It! Setting AutoRecover and AutoSave Options

1 In Excel, open **B06Try** from the location where the data files for this lesson are stored, and save it as **B06Try_xx** in the location where your teacher instructs you to store the files.

2 Click the FILE tab to display the Backstage view.

3 Click Options > Save to display the Save options in the Excel Options dialog box.

4 Use the Save AutoRecover information every increment arrows to set the time to 1 minute.

5 Verify that there is a check mark in the Keep the last autosaved version if I close without saving check box.

✓ *A check mark indicates the option is selected. If it is not, click the check box to select it.*

6 Verify that there is no check mark in the Disable AutoRecover for this workbook only check box.

7 Click OK to apply the changes and close the dialog box. Leave **B06Try_xx** open in Excel to use in the next Try It.

Try It! Opening an Autosaved File

1. In the **B06Try_xx** file, click on cell B6, where the total sales figure displays, if it is not already selected.
2. Press DEL to delete the information.
3. Wait at least one minute without saving the file.
4. Click FILE > Close > Don't Save.

   ✓ *Notice the text in the file delete confirmation dialog box indicating that a recent copy of the file will be temporarily available.*
5. Open the **B06Try_xx** file in Excel.
6. Click FILE > Info. Under Versions, a list of autosaved versions of the file displays including versions closed without saving.
7. Under Versions, click the file that was automatically saved when you closed without saving. Notice the information bar that indicates that it is a recovered file that is temporarily stored on your computer. Notice also that the contents of cell B6 has been deleted.
8. Close both versions of the file without saving changes. Leave Excel open to use in the next Try It.

Open an autosaved file

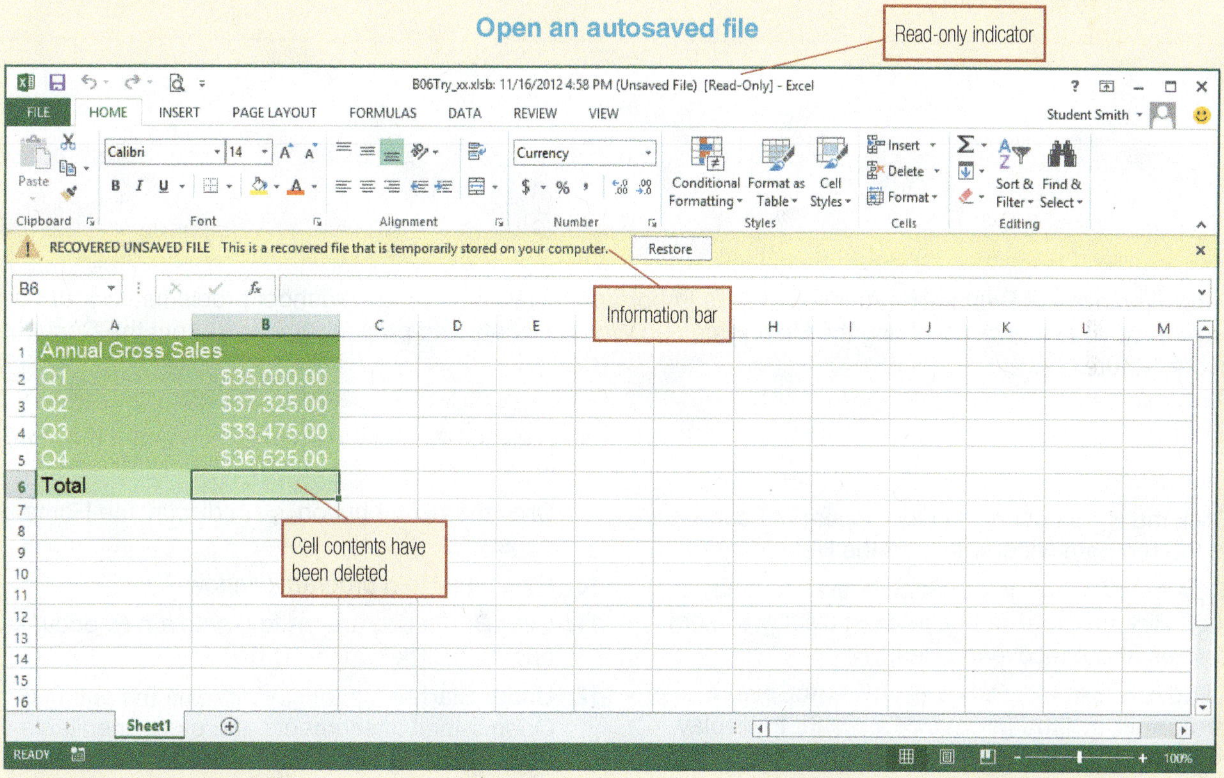

Try It! Opening a Draft Version of an Unsaved File

1. In Excel, create a new blank workbook. Maximize the window, if necessary.
2. Type your first name, press ENTER, type your last name, and press ENTER.
3. Wait at least a minute without saving the file.
4. Close the file without saving.
5. Click FILE to display the Open page in the Backstage view.
6. At the bottom of the Recent Workbooks list on the right side of the window, click Recover Unsaved Workbooks to display the contents of the UnsavedFiles folder in the Open dialog box.
7. Click the unsaved file at the bottom of the list, and then click Open to open it in Excel.
8. Close the file without saving the changes.
9. Click FILE > Options > Save to display the Save tab of the Excel Options dialog box.
10. Change the Save AutoRecover information setting back to 10 minutes.
11. Click OK to apply the changes and close the dialog box. Exit Excel.

Lesson 6—Practice

As a new employee at Restoration Architecture, it's important to learn how to troubleshoot problems on your own. In this project, you will practice using the Help system in Word to locate and print information about the Document Recovery feature.

DIRECTIONS

1. Start Word.
2. Click the **Help** button ? in the upper-right corner of the program window to start the Help program.
3. Type **autorecover** in the Search text box, and then click the **Search** button to display a list of articles about recovering files.
4. Click **Turn on AutoRecover and AutoSave to protect your files in case of a crash.** to display that article.
5. Maximize the **Help** window to make it easier to read the content.
6. Click the link to **My Office program did not open a recovered file** to display that article.
7. **With your teacher's permission**, click the **Print** button and print the article.
8. Click the **Back** button to display the previous page.
9. Click the **Home** button to display the Home page.
10. Close the Help program window.
11. Click **Blank document** to create a new document, and then click **FILE** > **Options**.
12. Under Start up options, verify that the option to Open e-mail attachments and other uneditable files in reading view is no selected. If it is selected, click the check box to deselect it.
13. Click **OK** to close the Word Options dialog box.
14. Exit Word.

Lesson 6—Apply

In this project, you will use the skills you have learned in this lesson to search the Help program in Word for information about formatting text with superscript and subscript.

DIRECTIONS

1. Start Word, and open the file **B06Apply** from the data files for this lesson.
2. Save the file as **B06Apply_xx** in the location where your teacher instructs you to store the files for this lesson.
3. Create a custom Ribbon tab named **DOCUMENT**, with a group named **Management**. Add the New, Close, Save As, and Print buttons to the group.
4. On the first line of the file, type your first name and last name. Press ENTER and type today's date, and then press ENTER to insert a blank line.
5. Start the Help program.
6. Search for information about how to format text with superscript and subscript.
7. Set the Help window to remain on top of other windows, and then use the information in the Help article to apply superscript to the *nd* and *rd* in the sentence.
8. Use the information in the Help article to apply subscript to the *2* in H_2O.
9. Close the Help program window. The **B06Apply_xx** document should look similar to Figure 6-1.
10. Save the changes to the document.
11. **With your teacher's permission**, print the file.
12. Reset all Ribbon customizations.
13. Close the file, saving changes, and exit Word.

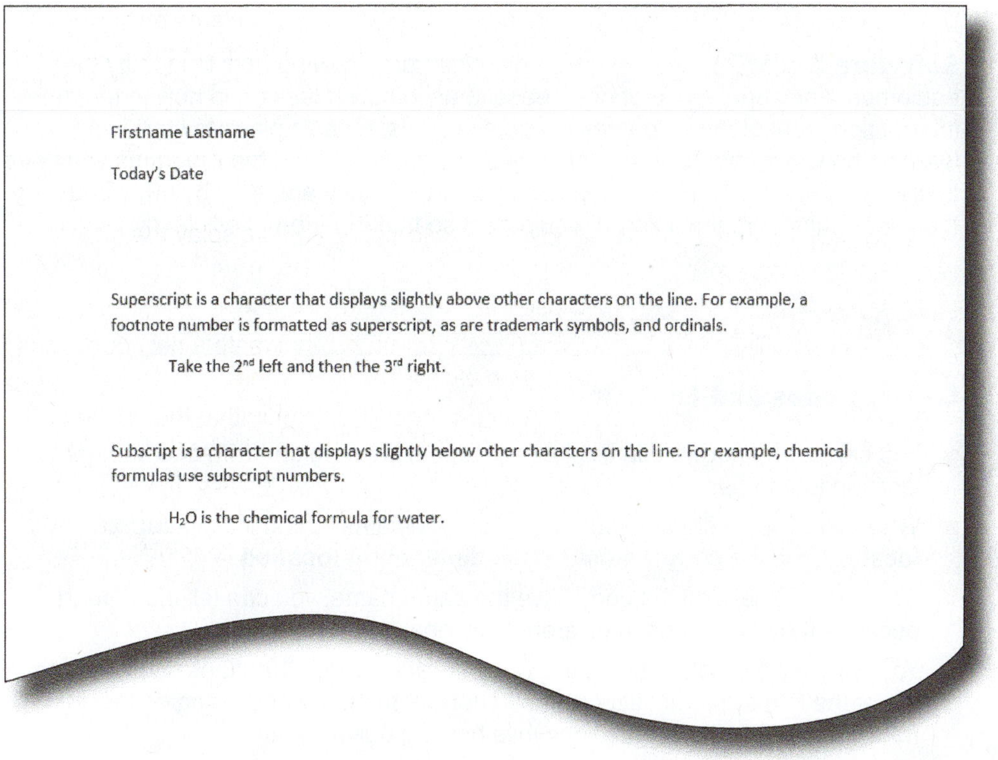

Firstname Lastname

Today's Date

Superscript is a character that displays slightly above other characters on the line. For example, a footnote number is formatted as superscript, as are trademark symbols, and ordinals.

Take the 2nd left and then the 3rd right.

Subscript is a character that displays slightly below other characters on the line. For example, chemical formulas use subscript numbers.

H_2O is the chemical formula for water.

Figure 6-1

Word 2013, Windows 8, Microsoft Corporation

Lesson 7

Managing Information Technology

WORDS TO KNOW

Business document
A professional document used to communicate information within a company, or between one company and another.

Compress
Minimize the file size.

Destination location
The location where a folder or file is stored after it is moved.

Ethical
Conforming to accepted standards of social or professional behavior.

Extract
Remove, or separate from.

Integrity
Adherence to a strict moral or ethical code.

IT strategy
A plan that identifies how information technology will be put in place over time to help an organization achieve its overall business goals.

Source location
The original location where a folder or file is stored.

Technology infrastructure
The computer systems, networking devices, software, and other technologies used to collect, store, and distribute information.

➤ What You Will Learn

Copying Files and Folders
Moving Files and Folders
Compressing Files
Recognizing Types of Business Documents
Determining the Risks and Rewards of Developing an IT Strategy
Identifying Needed Equipment and Supplies
Establishing, Scheduling, and Following Maintenance Procedures
Demonstrating Professional Standards of Behavior

Software Skills Every employee benefits from knowing how to identify the equipment and supplies he or she needs to accomplish tasks and how to manage information technology resources to achieve goals. A basic place to start is by learning how to recognize types of business documents and the programs you need to create, view, and edit them. You can also save money and time by understanding the importance of maintaining IT equipment so that it performs efficiently.

What You Can Do

Copying Files and Folders

- You can use Windows File Explorer to copy a file or folder from one storage location to another.
- When you copy a file or folder, the original remains stored in it its **source location** and the copy is stored in the **destination location**.
- Both the original and the copy have the same name; you can tell them apart because they are stored in different locations.
- You copy a file or folder using the Copy and Paste buttons on the Home tab of the File Explorer Ribbon or on shortcut menus, or by dragging the item from its source to its destination while holding down CTRL.
- You can also use the Copy to button on the Home tab of the Ribbon,
- When you copy a folder, all the items stored in the folder are copied as well.

- If you try to copy a folder or file to a location that already contains a folder or file with the same name, Windows offers three options:
  - Replace the file in the destination. Select this option to replace the existing file with the copy.
  - Skip this file. Select this option to cancel the command.
  - Compare info from both files. Select this option to display information about both files. You can choose to replace one file or to keep both.

Try It! Copying Files and Folders

1. From the Windows desktop, click the File Explorer button on the Taskbar and navigate to the location where your teacher instructs you to store the files for this lesson.
2. Create a new folder named **B07Try_Copy_xx**, and open it.
3. Without closing the File Explorer window, right-click the **File Explorer** button on the Taskbar and click **File Explorer** on the shortcut menu to open a second File Explorer window. In the second window, navigate to the location where the data files for this lesson are stored.
4. Click a blank area of the Windows Taskbar and click Show windows side by side to arrange the two windows so you can see the contents of both.
5. In the location where the data files are stored, right-click the Excel file named **B07TryA** and click Copy on the shortcut menu.
6. Right-click a blank area in the **B07Try_Copy_xx** folder and click Paste on the shortcut menu.
7. Press and hold CTRL and drag the **B07TryB** Word file from the data files storage location to the **B07Try_Copy_xx** folder.
8. Drop the file and release CTRL when the ScreenTip displays *Copy to B07Try_Copy_xx*.
9. On your screen, you can see the two copied files in the **B07Try_Copy_xx** folder. The originals are still in the original location.
10. Maximize the **B07Try_Copy_xx** folder, and click the Back button to return to the location where you are storing the files for this lesson.
11. Click the **B07Try_Copy_xx** folder to select it, and click Home > Copy to > Desktop.
12. Navigate to the desktop, locate the **B07Try_Copy_xx** folder, and open it.
13. Navigate back to the desktop and delete the **B07Try_Copy_xx** folder.
14. In File Explorer, navigate to the location where you are storing the files for this lesson. Notice that the original **B07Try_Copy_xx** folder is still there. Leave both File Explorer windows open to use in the next Try It.

(continued)

Try It! Copying Files and Folders *(continued)*

Copy by dragging

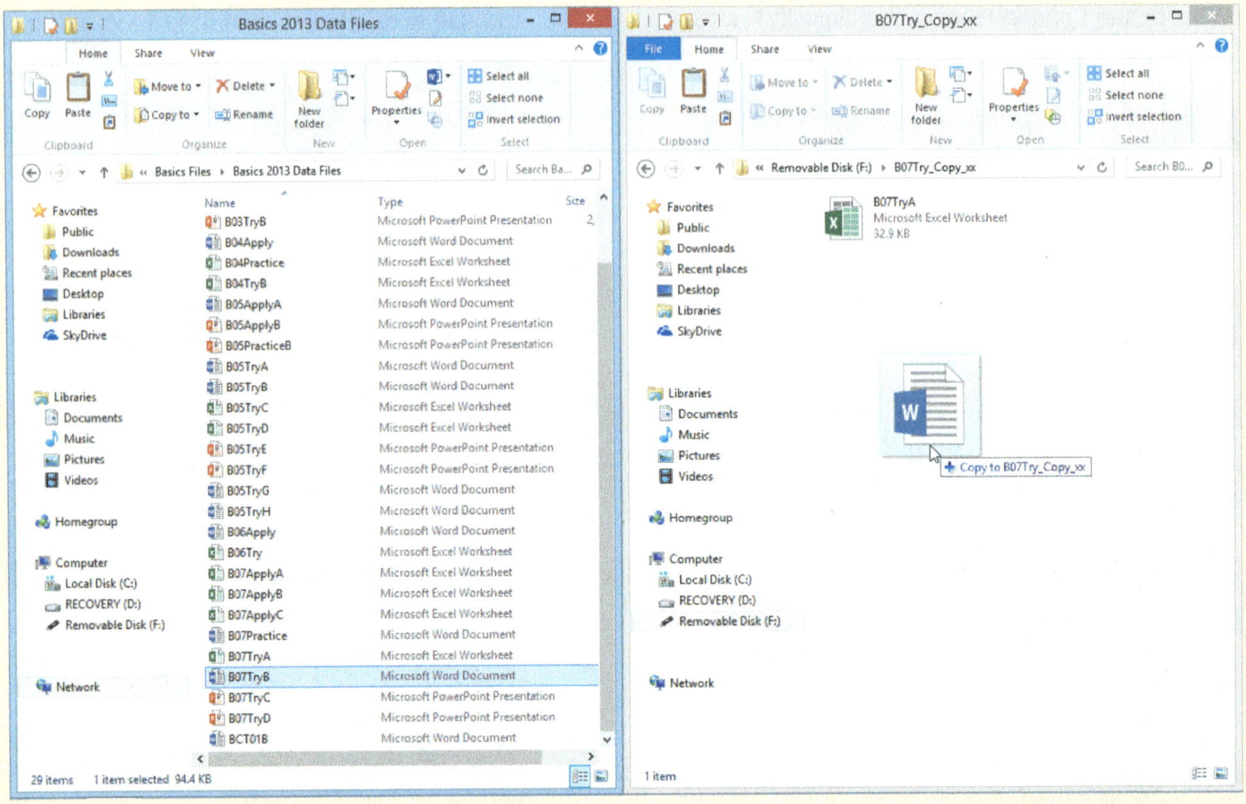

Windows 8, Microsoft Corporation

Moving Files and Folders

- You can move a file or folder from one storage location to another.
- When you move a file or folder, it is deleted from its source location and is stored in the destination location.
- You move a file or folder using the Cut and Paste buttons on the Home tab of the File Explorer Ribbon or on shortcut menus, or by dragging it to the destination.
- You can also use the Move to button on the Home tab of the Ribbon.
- When you move a folder, all the items stored in the folder are moved as well.
- If you try to move a folder or file to a location that already contains a folder or file with the same name, Windows offers three options:
  - Replace the file in the destination. Select this option to replace the existing file with the one you are moving.
  - Skip this file. Select this option to cancel the command.
  - Compare info for both files. Select this option to display information about both files. You can choose to replace one file or to keep both.

Try It! Moving Files and Folders

1. In the File Explorer window open the **B07Try_Copy_xx** folder.
2. Right-click the **B07TryA** file, and click Cut on the shortcut menu.
3. Click the Back button to display the location where you are storing the files for this lesson, right-click a blank area and click Paste on the shortcut menu. The file is deleted from its previous location and pasted into the new location.
4. In the current window, create a new folder named **B07Try_Move_xx**.
5. Drag the **B07TryA** file on to the **B07Try_Move_xx** folder.
6. Release the mouse button when the ScreenTip displays *Move to B07Try_Move_xx*.The file is deleted from its original location, and pasted into the **B07Try_Move_xx** folder.
7. Click the **B07Try_Move_xx** folder, and click Home > Move to > Desktop.
8. Navigate to the desktop and open the **B07Try_Move_xx** folder. Note that the file was moved as well.
9. Click the Back button , click to select the **B07Try_Move_xx** folder on the desktop, and click Home > Cut .
10. Navigate to the location where you are storing the files for this lesson, and click Home > Paste .
11. Open the **B07Try_Copy_xx** folder, and leave File Explorer open to use in the next Try It.

Compressing Files

- **Compress**, or zip, a file to minimize its size, making it easier to store or transmit.
- You use Windows to compress files.
- When you compress a file, you create a compressed, or zipped, folder in which the file is stored.
- By default, the compressed folder has the same name as the compressed file, but you can rename it, if you want.
- You can compress multiple files together into one folder.
- You can even compress entire folders.
- To use the compressed files, you must extract them from the folder.
- When you **extract** the files, you copy them from the compressed folder to a destination location. By default, the location is a new folder with the same name as the compressed folder, but you can select a different location.
- The Zip command is on on the Share tab of the File Explorer Ribbon and on shortcut menus; the Extract command is on the Compressed Folder Tools Extract tab of the Ribbon and on shortcut menus.

Try It! Compressing Files

1. Arrange the **B07Try_Copy_xx** window and the window for the location where the data files for this lesson are stored side by side.
2. Press and hold CTRL and drag the **B07TryC** file to copy it from the location where the data files are stored to the **B07Try_Copy_xx** folder.

(continued)

Try It! Compressing Files *(continued)*

3. In the **B07Try_Copy_xx** window, click to select the **B07TryC** file, then click Share > Zip on the Ribbon. Windows zips the file into a compressed folder. The new folder name is selected so you can type a new name.

4. Type **B07Try_compressed_xx**, and press ENTER. Notice that the compressed folder has fewer kilobytes (KB) than the original file. Kilobytes are a measurement of size.

5. In the location where the data files are stored, right-click the **B07TryD** file and click Copy on the shortcut menu.

6. Right-click the **B07Try_compressed_xx** folder and click Paste on the shortcut menu. This copies the **B07TryD** file into the compressed folder.

7. Double-click the **B07Try_compressed_xx** folder to open it and view its contents. It contains both the **B07TryC** and **B07TryD** files.

8. Click the Back button and maximize the File Explorer window in which the **B07Try_compressed_xx** folder is stored. Leave it open to use in the next Try It.

A compressed file is smaller than the original

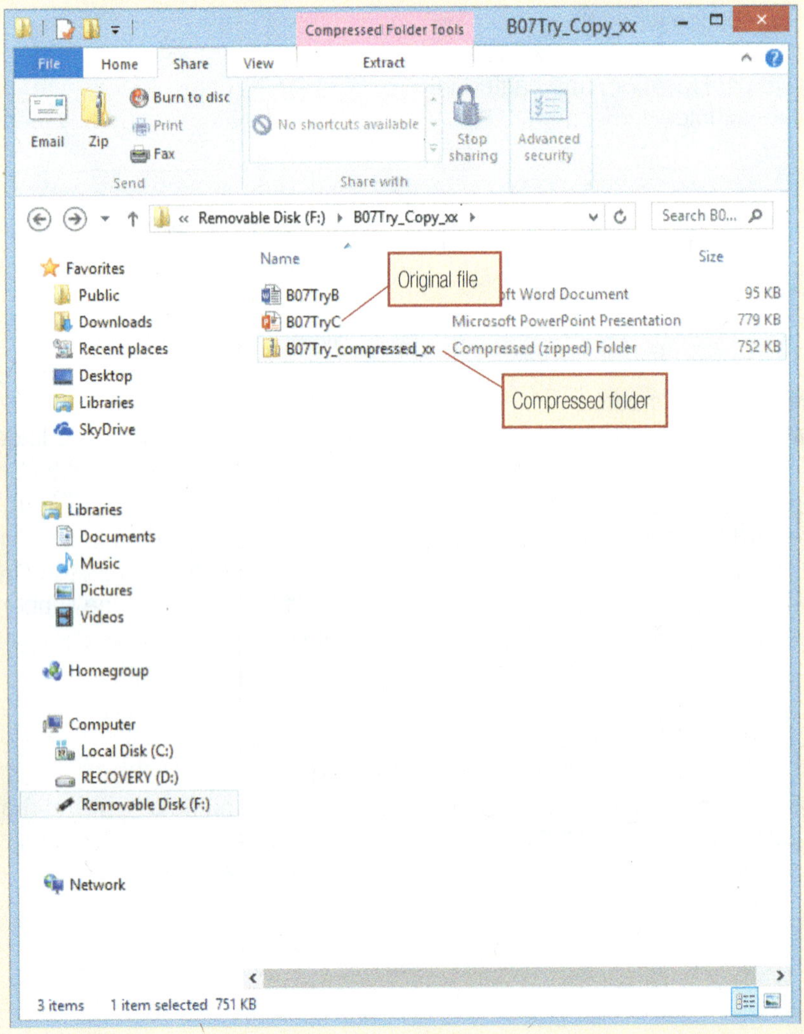

Windows 8, Microsoft Corporation

Try It! Extracting Compressed Files

1. In File Explorer, click to select the **B07Try_compressed_xx** folder, and then click Extract all on the Extract tab of the Ribbon. Windows displays the name of the default folder where it will store the extracted files.
2. Select just the text *compressed* in the folder name and then type **extracted** to change the name to **B07Try_extracted_xx**.
3. Click Extract. Windows creates a new folder in the current location and copies the files to it. By default, it opens the new folder in a separate window. You can see the extracted files.

   ✓ *If the window does not open by default, double-click the B07Try_extracted_xx folder to open it.*
4. Close all open File Explorer windows.

Recognizing Types of Business Documents

- Some common **business documents** used by most companies include letters, memos, fax covers, marketing presentations, training slide shows, invoices, purchase orders, press releases, agendas, reports, and newsletters.
- Certain businesses—or departments within a larger company—may have specialized documents. For example, a law office or legal department produces legal documents such as wills, contracts, and bills of sale.
- In additional, individuals create personal business documents such as letters, research papers, and resumes.
- Each Microsoft Office program is designed for creating specific types of business documents.
  - Microsoft Word is used for text-based documents, such as letters, memos, and reports.
  - Microsoft Excel is used for numeric or financial documents, such as invoices, sales reports, and graphic analysis.
  - Microsoft PowerPoint is used for slide shows and presentation graphics.
  - Microsoft Access is used to store and search data and create forms, tables, and reports based on that data.
- Most business documents have standard formats, which means each type of document includes similar parts.
- You will learn about the standard formats for different types of documents throughout the lessons in this book.

Determining the Risks and Rewards of Developing an IT Strategy

- Information systems and information communication technology play a strategic role in business. For example, they can help employees respond more quickly to customers, suppliers, and competitors, which can provide a competitive advantage. They can also help a company identify areas for improvement.
- An **IT strategy** is a road map or plan that identifies how information technology will be put in place over time to help an organization achieve its overall business goals.
- A successful IT strategy prepares a business for future growth and puts the technology in place that a company needs to make the best use of available resources, solve problems, and compete.
- Companies that take the time and make the effort to include IT in their overall business plans are more likely to implement successful IT strategies.
- Different businesses have different IT needs.
- Each business must address the issues involved in designing and developing systems for different environments.
  - A small business might require only a desktop computer, an all-in-one printer/scanner device, and an Internet connection.
  - A large business might require hundreds of desktop PCs, notebook and tablet computers, one or more internal networks, corporate servers, a telephone system, printers, scanners, and copier machines, projection systems, and more.

- Some businesses might require specialized IT tools.
    - A construction company might require rugged portable devices that can withstand extreme weather or rough conditions.
    - A design firm might require high-end computer-aided design software, while an investment firm requires high-end financial applications.
- A successful IT strategy takes into consideration factors such as the current needs of the company, how to best use systems currently in place, and how to implement new technologies that support the business.
- It also takes into consideration the cost of new equipment, maintenance, and training, as well as the physical environment in which IT will be installed. For example, a small business must consider if there is space to install new computer systems. A large company might need to install a climate control system for a new data center.
- There are two primary risks of locking in to a particular IT strategy: a plan that is too advanced, and a plan that is not advanced enough.
    - If a company puts a plan in place that is more advanced than it can support, it wastes money on unnecessary technology that employees do not know how to use.
    - If a company puts a plan in place that is not advanced enough, the company may lose ground to its competition or find that it has to spend money to upgrade systems sooner than expected.
- When an IT strategy balances the needs, costs, and corporate goals, the risks are minimized and the rewards are achievable.

Identifying Needed Equipment and Supplies

- Almost every business has a **technology infrastructure**, which is the computer systems, networking devices, software, and other technologies used to collect, store, and distribute information.
- No matter how large or small a business may be, it is vital that someone monitor, manage, and maintain the technology infrastructure in order to keep the business running.
    - In a small organization, each employee might be responsible for his or her own technology. That might mean changing the ink in a desktop printer, keeping a virus-protection program up-to-date, and backing up files regularly.
    - In larger organizations, the employees in the IT department are responsible for the IT systems.
- Performing an inventory of the current IT situation is a good first step in developing an IT strategy. Knowing what is already in place and how well it meets current needs helps define future needs.
- Researching and budgeting for an IT project is much like planning any project. You can check pricing online, get bids from various consultants and vendors, or use a combination of those techniques.
- When budgeting for IT systems, it is important to factor in the costs of ongoing support, maintenance, and training.

Establishing, Scheduling, and Following Maintenance Procedures

- Technology systems require maintenance to operate properly. In a large company, maintenance is a constant need. A dedicated staff of technicians responds to employee requests, services hardware, and upgrades software, or outside technicians are hired to provide service.
- In a small company, maintenance might be as basic as keeping a computer keyboard clean, installing a virus protection program, backing up files on a regular schedule, and changing the ink in the printer, when necessary.
- All systems will be more reliable and effective if maintenance is performed on a regular basis.
- Establishing maintenance schedules enables you to plan and perform maintenance appropriately, provide notice to users when maintenance is due, and budget for ongoing maintenance costs.
- Many maintenance tasks can be automated, including data backup, virus scans, and program updates.
- Manufacturers provide maintenance procedures for all equipment and programs. If the user does not follow the manufacturer's recommended maintenance procedures, warranties and service contracts become void, and the company becomes responsible for costs associated with damage and repair.
- In addition, qualified IT professionals are able to diagnose and solve problems individually and as a team to keep the systems running efficiently.

Demonstrating Professional Standards of Behavior

- Employees and employers should conduct themselves in a professional and **ethical** manner, with honesty and **integrity**, according to legal and corporate policies.
- Most companies and organizations establish corporate computer application policies or rules, as well as policies for using the Internet and e-mail.
- These policies address the legal and social aspects of computer use and are designed to protect privacy while respecting personal and corporate values and adhering to federal and local laws.
- As an employee of any company, you will also be expected to demonstrate a professional attitude by behaving in a way appropriate for your workplace; displaying a positive and productive work ethic; complying with the rules, laws, and regulations that are applicable in your workplace; and working efficiently by prioritizing tasks and following schedules.

Lesson 7—Practice

You have been hired by the Michigan Avenue Athletic Club to set up policies for purchasing and maintaining information technology equipment and supplies. In this project, you use Word to create a memo to the office manager asking him to conduct an inventory of hardware currently owned by the club, the software programs currently in use, and the current maintenance schedules. You also ask him to provide you with a list of needed equipment and supplies. You will create a folder and a compressed folder where you can store the related files.

DIRECTIONS

1. Start Word.
2. Open the file **B07Practice** from the data files for this lesson, and save it as **B07Practice_xx** in the location where your teacher instructs you to store the files for this lesson.
3. Replace the text *Student's Name* with your own first and last name.
4. Replace the text *Today's Date* with the current date.
5. Press CTRL + END to move the insertion point to the last line of the document and type the following paragraph:

   Tom, as a first step in developing policies for purchasing and maintaining the club's IT equipment and supplies, I need to know what we have and what we need. Please take an inventory of the hardware we currently own, the software we currently use, and the maintenance schedule currently in place. I would also like a list of any equipment and supplies we need.
6. Press ENTER and type the following paragraph:

   I would like to receive this information by the end of the week. Thanks so much for your assistance. Let me know if you have any questions.
7. Save the document. It should look similar to Figure 7-1 on the next page.
8. **With your teacher's permission**, print the file.
9. Close the file and exit Word.
10. Open File Explorer and navigate to the desktop.
11. Create a folder named **B07Practice_xx** on the desktop.
12. Right-click the **B07Practice_xx** folder and click **Cut** on the shortcut menu. This cuts the folder from the desktop and stores it on the Clipboard.
13. Navigate to the location where your teacher instructs you to store the files for this lesson.
14. Right-click a blank area of the window, and click **Paste** on the shortcut menu to paste the folder from the Clipboard into the selected storage location.
15. Right-click the **B07Practice_xx** Word file, and click **Copy** on the shortcut menu.
16. Right-click the **B07Practice_xx** folder, and click **Paste** on the shortcut menu. This copies the file into the folder. The original file remains stored in its current location.
17. Right-click the original **B07Practice_xx** Word file, click Send to, and then click Compressed (zipped) folder. The file is sent to a compressed folder with the default name **B07Practice_xx**.

18. Type **B07Practice_xx_compressed** to rename the folder, and press ENTER to rename the compressed folder.
19. Right-click the original **B07Practice_xx** Word file, and click **Delete** on the shortcut menu.
20. Click **Yes** to delete the file. Now, you have a regular folder named **B07Practice_xx**, which contains the Word memo file, and a compressed folder named **B07Practice_xx_compressed**, which contains a compressed version of the Word memo file.
21. Leave File Explorer open to use in the Apply project.

Figure 7-1

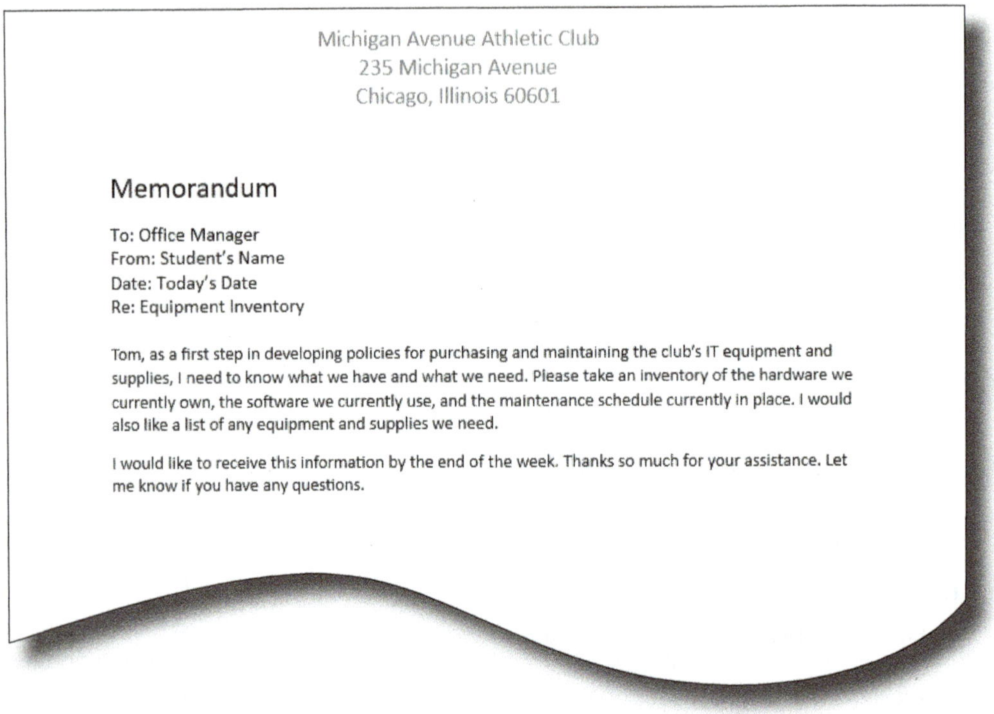

Michigan Avenue Athletic Club
235 Michigan Avenue
Chicago, Illinois 60601

Memorandum

To: Office Manager
From: Student's Name
Date: Today's Date
Re: Equipment Inventory

Tom, as a first step in developing policies for purchasing and maintaining the club's IT equipment and supplies, I need to know what we have and what we need. Please take an inventory of the hardware we currently own, the software we currently use, and the maintenance schedule currently in place. I would also like a list of any equipment and supplies we need.

I would like to receive this information by the end of the week. Thanks so much for your assistance. Let me know if you have any questions.

Word 2013, Windows 8, Microsoft Corporation

Lesson 7—Apply

In this project, you use the skills you learned in this lesson to copy, move, and compress files.

DIRECTIONS

1. In File Explorer, in the location where your teacher instructs you to store the files for this lesson, create a new folder named **B07Apply_xx**.
2. Copy **B07ApplyA** from the location where the data files for this lesson are stored to the **B07Apply_xx** folder.
3. Copy **B07ApplyB** from the location where the data files for this lesson are stored to the **B07Apply_xx** folder.
4. Copy **B07ApplyC** from the location where the data files for this lesson are stored to the **B07Apply_xx** folder.
5. Compress the **B07Apply_xx** folder and its contents into a compressed folder named **B07Apply_xx_compressed**.
6. Move the **B07Practice_xx** regular folder into the **B07Apply_xx_compressed** compressed folder.
7. Open the **B07Apply_xx_compressed** compressed folder.
8. Extract all files from **B07Apply_xx_compressed** into a folder named **B07Apply_xx_extracted**.
9. Close all open File Explorer windows.

End-of-Chapter Activities

➤ Basics Chapter 1—Critical Thinking

Create an IT Strategy

You are responsible for performing an analysis to determine ways a group, organization, or business might use Microsoft Office 2013 as part of a business plan and IT strategy. Start by selecting the group. It might be a club, team, or organization to which you belong, the place where you work, or any business of your choice. Research its goals, current IT infrastructure, and requirements, including the types of business documents it uses. You can do this by talking to the people responsible for the information technology and taking notes, and also by observing the information technology in use. Then, use Microsoft Office 2013 and the skills you have learned in this chapter to develop a list of how the group might use Microsoft Office as part of its business and IT strategy to meet its information management requirements and business needs. Then, write a paragraph explaining issues the group might face when designing and developing systems for its specific environment, with attention to the risks and rewards that result from developing the system.

DIRECTIONS

1. Create a folder named BCT01_xx in the location where your teacher instructs you to store the files for this chapter.
2. Start the Microsoft Office 2013 program you want to use to create the list. For example, you might use Word or Excel.
3. Create a blank file and save the file as BCT01A_xx in the BCT01_xx folder.
4. Type your name in the file.
5. Type the date in the file.
6. Type a title for your list and format the title using fonts, font styles, and font color.
7. Type the list of ways the group, organization, or business might use Microsoft Office 2013 as part of an IT strategy.
8. Save the changes to the file.
9. Start Word, if necessary, and open BCT01B. Save it as BCT01B_xx in the BCT01_xx folder.
10. Type your name on the first line of the file and the date on the second line. Then, move the insertion point to the blank line above the picture, and type a paragraph explaining the list you typed in step 7.
11. Save the changes to the file.
12. **With your teacher's permission**, print the file. If necessary, adjust page formatting such as orientation, scale, and margins so its fits on a single page. It should look similar to Illustration 1A on the next page.
13. Copy the picture in the file to the Clipboard, and then close the file, saving all changes.
14. Make the BCT01A_xx file active, and paste the picture at either the beginning or end of the file.
15. Save the changes, and, **with your teacher's permission**, print the file. If necessary, adjust page formatting such as orientation, scale, and margins so it fits on a single page. It should look similar to Illustration 1B.
16. Close the file, saving changes, and exit all programs.
17. Compress the BCT01_xx folder into a compressed folder named BCT01_xx_compressed.

Illustration 1A

Firstname Lastname

Today's Date

Issues Regarding Designing and Developing Systems for this Environment

I typed a list of business needs and information management requirements for the school marching band. I then proposed ways the band might use Microsoft Office to meet these needs and requirements. Every business, group, organization, or individual has unique business, IM, and systems needs. For the marching band, one issue is that it is run mostly by volunteers who have different levels of experience with information management and technology. These volunteers might work in the school but may need to access information while at home, as well. They may need to work on some projects by themselves but may need to collaborate on some projects. The band also needs to create a wide variety of document types, including letters, memos, reports, financial statements, brochures, presentations, and email messages.

I recommend using Microsoft Office because it can be installed locally or online and it comes with OneDrive cloud storage. The suite includes programs to create the types of documents that band requires. Because the programs are similar, the volunteers should be able to learn to use them quickly and easily. There will be a certain amount of risk involved in requiring use of a suite such as Microsoft Office, which will mean all volunteers will have to acquire and gain proficiency in the applications, but the rewards that will result in all users having access to the same tools will mean more sophisticated and consistent documents overall.

Word 2013, Windows 8, Microsoft Corporation

Illustration 1B

Firstname Lastname
Today's Date

Marching Band

Information Management Requirements and Business Needs

Business Needs	IM Requirements	MS Office Solution
Support Volunteer Efforts	Integrated set of programs with common features	Use Microsoft Office suite of programs.
Printed Communication	Flexible, text-based documents	Use Microsoft Word to create memos to band members, letters to parents, and fundraising letters to send to neighborhood businesses.
Financial Analysis	Automated, easy-to-use worksheets	Use Microsoft Excel to create worksheets tracking income and expenses, to create a budget, and to create graphs illustrating the data.
Data Storage and Analysis	Relational database	Use Microsoft Access to set up and maintain a database of members, parents, volunteers, and community supporters.
Marketing	Desktop publishing solution	Use Microsoft Publisher to create postcard mailings, flyers, and even brochures.
Community Outreach	Automated presentation program	Use Microsoft PowerPoint to create an informational presentation.
Electronic Communication	E-mail client with calendar, contacts, and scheduling support	Use Microsoft Outlook for communication.
Shared Resources	Cloud storage and online access	Use Microsoft Office suite of programs.

➤ Basics Chapter 1—Portfolio Builder

Create a Memo

Voyager Travel Adventures is opening a new office. You have been asked to make a list of IT equipment and supplies needed to get the office up and running. In this project, you will create a folder for storing your work. You will start Microsoft Office 2013 programs and create, save, and print files. You will also open and save existing files, use the Office Clipboard to copy a selection from one file to another, and prepare a file for distribution. Finally, you will compress the files. With your teacher's permission, you will set up a schedule to automate key maintenance tasks such as backing up data and running a virus scan.

DIRECTIONS

1. On the Windows desktop, create a new folder named **BPB01_xx**.
2. Move the folder to the location where your teacher instructs you to store the files for this chapter.
3. Start Microsoft Word, and create a new blank document. Save the file in the **BPB01_xx** folder with the name **BPB01A_xx**.
4. On the first line of the document, type today's date. Press ENTER and type your full name. Press ENTER and type the following:

   I recommend the following IT equipment to get the new Voyager Travel Adventures office up and running:
5. Press ENTER and type the following list, pressing ENTER at the end of each line to start a new line.

   4 personal computers running Microsoft Windows, with Microsoft Office installed

   2 notebook computers to be shared as necessary, also running Microsoft Windows, with online access to Microsoft Office

   2 tablet PCs to be shared as necessary, with online access to Microsoft Office

   Wireless network devices

   1 all-in-one printer/scanner/copier

   1 external hard drive for backing up data

   Internet telephone system
6. Save the changes to the document.
7. Format the date in bold and increase the font size to 14, then format your name in bold italic, and increase the font size to 12.
8. Start the Help program and locate information about how to format a bulleted list.
9. Use the Help information to apply bullet list formatting to the list of equipment.

   If you cannot find information about bullet list formatting, select the items in the list, and then click the Bullets button in the Paragraph group on the HOME tab of the Ribbon.
10. Save the changes to the file.
11. Start Microsoft Excel and open the file **BPB01B** from the data files for this chapter. Save the file in the **BPB01_xx** folder as **BPB01B_xx**.
12. Copy the picture in the Excel file to the Clipboard.
13. Arrange the Excel and Word windows side by side.
14. Make the Word window active and display the Clipboard task pane.
15. Exit Excel without saving any changes, and maximize the Word window.
16. Paste the picture on to the last line of the document, and then delete it from the Clipboard.
17. Close the Clipboard task pane.
18. Save the changes to the Word document.
19. Change the margins for the document to Wide.
20. **With your teacher's permission**, print the document. It should look similar to Illustration 1C on the next page.
21. Close the file, saving changes, and exit Word.
22. Navigate to the location where you are saving the files for this lesson.
23. Compress the entire **BPB01_xx** folder into a compressed folder named **BPB01_xx_compressed**.
24. **With your teacher's permission**, use Windows to set up an automatic schedule for downloading and installing updates, backing up important files, and running a virus scan.

25. **With your teacher's permission**, check the ink levels in a classroom printer.

26. If you have completed your session, close all open windows and log off your computer account.

Illustration 1C

Today's Date

Firstname Lastname

I recommend the following IT equipment to get the new Voyager Travel Adventures office up and running:

- 4 personal computers running Microsoft Windows, with Microsoft Office installed
- 2 notebook computers to be shared as necessary, also running Microsoft Windows with online access to Microsoft Office
- 2 tablet PCs to be shared as necessary, with online access to Microsoft Office
- Wireless network devices
- 1 all-in-one printer/scanner/copier
- 1 external hard drive for backing up data
- Internet telephone system

Chapter 1

(Courtesy Konstantin Chagin/Shutterstock)

Getting Started with Microsoft Word 2013

Lesson 1
Creating Word Documents with Headers and Footers

- Starting and Exiting Microsoft Word 2013
- Exploring the Microsoft Word 2013 Window
- Changing the Microsoft Word 2013 Window
- Showing or Hiding Nonprinting Characters
- Typing in a Document
- Typing in the Header or Footer
- Splitting a Word Window
- Saving a Document

Lesson 2
Formatting Documents with Themes and Styles

- Creating a New, Blank Document
- Closing a Document
- Using Click and Type
- Opening a Saved Document
- Saving a Document with a New Name
- Applying a Built-In Style
- Changing the Style Set
- Applying a Theme
- Analyzing a Press Release

Lesson 3
Editing and Correcting Documents

- Inserting Text
- Using Overtype Mode
- Selecting and Replacing Text
- Canceling a Command
- Using Undo, Redo, and Repeat

Lesson 4
Adjusting Alignment and Spacing

- Aligning Text Horizontally
- Aligning a Document Vertically
- Setting Line Spacing
- Setting Paragraph Spacing
- Analyzing Memos

Lesson 5
Creating Letters and Envelopes

- Indenting Text
- Setting and Modifying Tabs
- Inserting the Date and Time
- Inserting a Watermark
- Writing a Business Letter
- Creating an Envelope

Lesson 6
Formatting Text with Fonts and Effects

- Changing the Font
- Changing the Font Size
- Changing the Font Color
- Applying Font Styles and Effects
- Applying Underlines
- Clearing Formatting
- Editing a Built-In Style
- Writing a Personal Business Letter

Lesson 7
Formatting and Sorting Lists

- Creating a Bulleted List
- Creating a Numbered List
- Changing the Bullet or Number Formatting
- Creating a Multilevel List
- Sorting Paragraphs

Lesson 8
Inserting Pictures, Text Boxes, and Shapes

- Analyzing Objects
- Inserting Pictures
- Inserting a Text Box
- Inserting Shapes
- Selecting Objects
- Resizing and Deleting Objects
- Scanning Content to Insert in a Document

Lesson 9
Formatting Graphics Objects

- Wrapping Text Around an Object
- Moving and Positioning an Object
- Formatting Objects
- Modifying Pictures
- Modifying a Text Box
- Changing a Shape
- Adding Text to a Shape
- Inserting a Caption

Lesson 10
Working with SmartArt Graphics, Text Effects, and Page Borders

- Inserting a SmartArt Graphic
- Entering Text in a SmartArt Graphic
- Modifying the Design of a SmartArt Graphic
- Creating a SmartArt Graphic from a Picture
- Applying Text Effects and WordArt Styles
- Applying a Page Border

End-of-Chapter Activities

Lesson 1

Creating Word Documents with Headers and Footers

➤ What You Will Learn

- Starting and Exiting Microsoft Word 2013
- Exploring the Microsoft Word 2013 Window
- Changing the Microsoft Word Window
- Showing or Hiding Nonprinting Characters
- Typing in a Document
- Typing in the Header or Footer
- Splitting a Word Window
- Saving a Document

Software Skills Microsoft Word 2013 is the word processing application included in the Microsoft Office 2013 suite. You use Word to create text-based documents such as letters, memos, reports, flyers, and newsletters. The first step in mastering Word is learning how to start the program and create a document.

What You Can Do

Starting and Exiting Microsoft Word 2013

- To use Microsoft Word 2013, you must first start it so it is running on your computer.
- Use Microsoft Windows to start Word.
- When Word starts, it displays a list of recent files (if you have created any) and a gallery of templates you can choose to start a new document.

  ✓ *You learn more about templates in Lesson 2.*

- When you are done using Word, close it to exit.

WORDS TO KNOW

Active pane
The pane in which the insertion point is currently located.

Default
Standard.

Footer
Text or graphics printed at the bottom of all pages in a document.

Header
Text or graphics printed at the top of all pages in a document.

Insertion point
The flashing vertical line that indicates where the next action will occur.

Nonprinting characters
Characters such as paragraph marks and tab symbols that are not printed in a document but that can be displayed on the screen.

Paragraph mark
A nonprinting character inserted in a document to indicate where a paragraph ends.

Word wrap
A feature that causes text to move automatically from the end of one line to the beginning of the next line.

Try It! Starting and Exiting Microsoft Word 2013

Using Windows 8:

- From the Start screen, click the Word 2013 tile:

OR

- From the desktop, double-click the Word 2013 shortcut icon.

OR

- Click the Word icon on the Taskbar.

Using Windows 7 or earlier:

1. Click Start > All Programs. If necessary, scroll until you see the Microsoft Office 2013 folder icon.

   ✓ *In this book, the symbol > is used to indicate a series of steps. In this case, click Start and then click All Programs.*

2. Click the Microsoft Office 2013 folder icon.
3. Click Word 2013.

OR

1. Click Start.
2. Click Word 2013 in the list of recently used programs.

OR

- Double-click the Word 2013 shortcut icon on the desktop.

OR

- Click the Word icon on the Taskbar.

To start a new document:

- From the Word Welcome screen, click Blank document.

To exit Microsoft Word:

- Click the Close button × at the right end of the Word title bar.

  ✓ *If you have made changes to the open document, Word displays a dialog box. Click Save to save the changes and then exit, or click Don't Save to exit without saving.*

Word 2013 Welcome screen

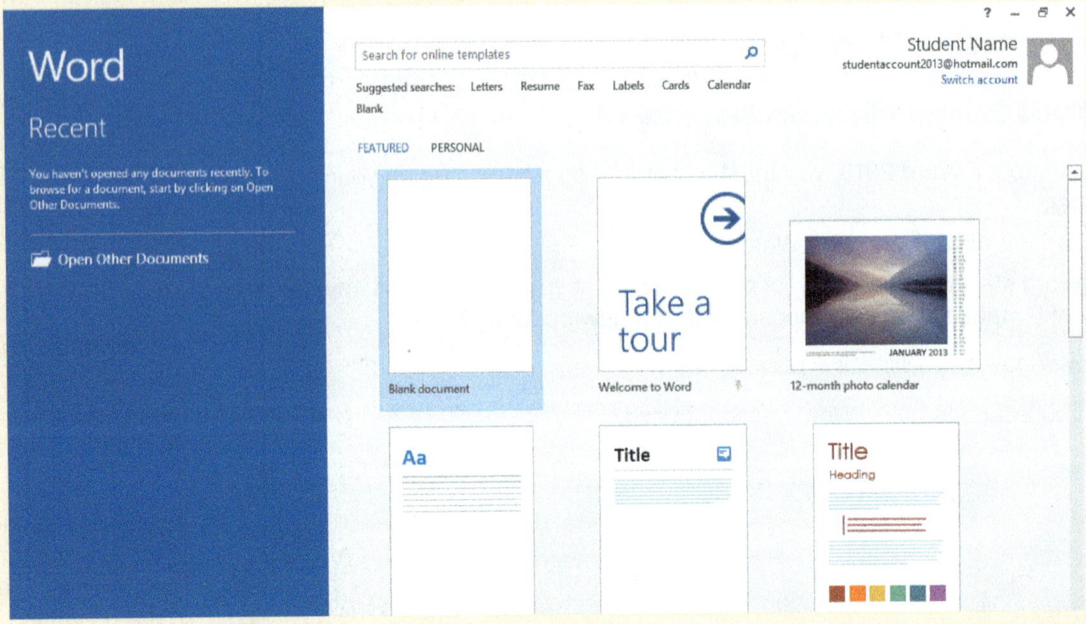

Word 2013, Windows 8, Microsoft Corporation

Exploring the Microsoft Word 2013 Window

- A new blank Word 2013 document uses standard, or **default**, settings. Default settings control features such as the margins, the line spacing, the character font, and the font size.

  ✓ *If the text [Compatibility Mode] displays on the Word title bar, it indicates that your software is set to open in a mode that is compatible with older versions of the program.*

- By default, the new document displays in Print Layout view, showing the most common tools you need to create, edit, format, and distribute a document.
- Many of the elements in the Word window are the same as those in other Microsoft Office 2013 programs, such as the Ribbon and the Quick Access Toolbar.
- Following are some of the typical elements you will see in the Word window:
  - Quick Access Toolbar. A toolbar that displays buttons for commonly used commands. You can customize the Quick Access Toolbar to display buttons you use frequently.
  - Ribbon. Displays buttons for accessing features and commands.

    ✓ *Note that the way items display on the Ribbon may depend on the width of the program window. If your program window is wider than the one used in the figures, more or larger buttons may display. If your program window is narrower, fewer or smaller buttons may display.*

  - Close button. Used to close the program window. It is one of three buttons used to control the size and position of the program window.
  - Title bar. Displays the program and document name.
  - Ribbon tabs. Used to change the commands displayed on the Ribbon.
  - Document area. The workspace where you enter text, graphics, and other data.
  - Rulers. The horizontal ruler measures the width of the document page; it displays information such as margins, tab stops, and indents. The vertical ruler measures the height of the document page.

    ✓ *The rulers may not display by default. You can click the Ruler check box in the Show group on the VIEW tab of the Ribbon to toggle them on or off.*

  - Insertion point. A blinking vertical line that displays to the right of the space where characters are inserted in a document.
  - Scroll bars. Used with a mouse to shift the onscreen display up and down or left and right.
  - Status bar. Displays information about the current document.
  - Zoom slider. Used to increase or decrease the size of the document onscreen.
  - Help button. Used to start the program's Help system.
  - View buttons. Used to change the document view.

Try It! Exploring the Microsoft Word 2013 Window

1. Start Microsoft Word 2013.
2. Click Blank document to open a new blank document.
3. Rest your mouse pointer on a window element to display a descriptive ScreenTip.

The Word window

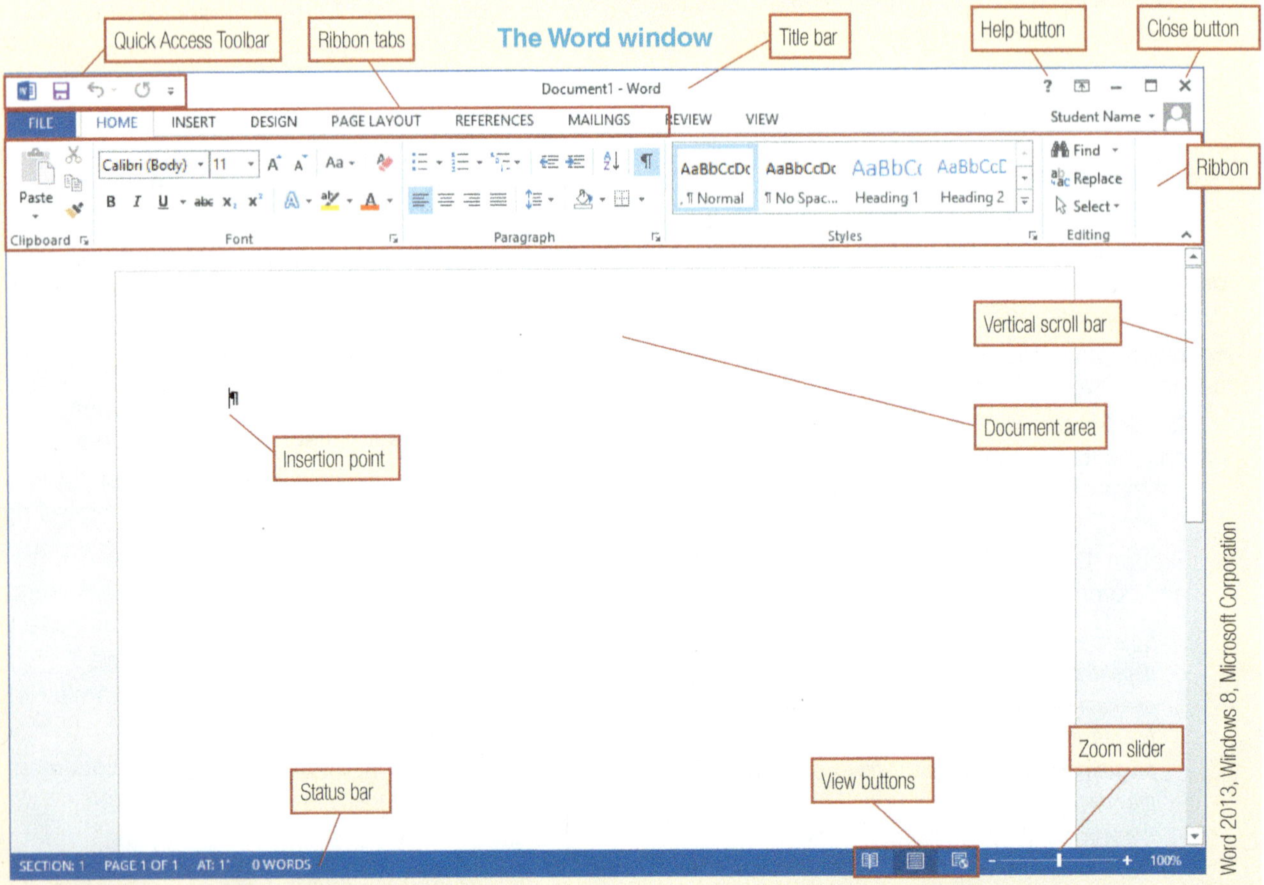

Word 2013, Windows 8, Microsoft Corporation

Changing the Microsoft Word Window

- You can control whether certain Word elements display while you work.
- You can show or hide rulers.
- You can change the Ribbon Display Options to Auto-hide the Ribbon, to show the Ribbon tabs only, or to show the tabs and the commands all the time (the default).
- You can change views using the View buttons on the status bar or the commands in the Views group on the VIEW tab of the Ribbon. Each view displays the tools you need to work in that view.
  - Print Layout view displays a document onscreen the way it will look when it is printed. It is the default view.
  - Web Layout view wraps text to fit the window, the way it would on a Web page document.
  - Outline view is used to create and edit outlines.
  - Read Mode adjusts the display of text to make it easier to read documents onscreen.
  - Draft view can be used for most typing, editing, and formatting, but some formatting does not show onscreen.

✓ *Outline view and Draft view are available only on the VIEW tab.*

Try It! Changing the Word Window

1. Start Word, if necessary, and create a new, blank document, or continue working in the open document.
2. Click the VIEW tab.
3. In the Show group, click to select the Ruler check box.

   ✓ *A check in the check box indicates the ruler is displayed.*
4. Click the Collapse the ribbon button ^ to show Ribbon tabs only.
5. Click any tab to expand the Ribbon to display tabs and commands, and then click the Pin the ribbon button ⇥ to show the Ribbon tabs and commands all the time.
6. Double-click any tab on the Ribbon. This is an alternative way to collapse the Ribbon.
7. Click the VIEW tab and then click the Pin the ribbon button ⇥ .
8. In the Views group, click the Draft button to change from Print Layout view to Draft view.
9. On the status bar, click the Read Mode button.
10. On the status bar, click the Web Layout button.
11. Click the VIEW tab and then click the Outline button.
12. On the status bar, click the Print Layout button.

Ruler check box

The Word 2013 VIEW tab

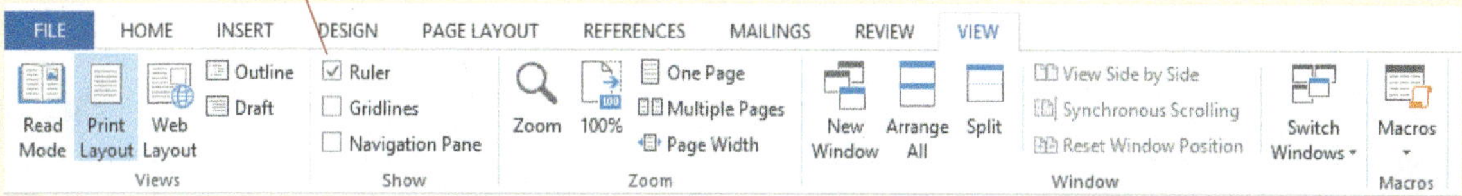

Word 2013, Windows 8, Microsoft Corporation

Showing or Hiding Nonprinting Characters

- When you type in Word you insert **nonprinting characters** such as spaces, tabs, and paragraph marks along with printing characters such as letters and numbers.
- Displaying nonprinting characters onscreen is helpful because you see where each paragraph ends and if there are extra spaces or unwanted tab characters.
- You can also easily see blank paragraphs in a document and remove them if they are not necessary.
- The command for showing and hiding nonprinting characters is a toggle; use it to turn the feature off and on.
- Onscreen, the most common nonprinting characters display as follows:
  - Space: dot (·)
  - Paragraph: paragraph symbol (¶)
  - Tab: right arrow (→)

✓ *Other nonprinting characters include optional hyphens, page breaks, and line breaks.*

Try It! Showing or Hiding Nonprinting Characters

1. Start Word, if necessary, and create a new, blank document, or continue working in the open document.
2. Click the HOME tab. In the Paragraph group, click Show/Hide ¶ ¶ .

   OR

   Press CTRL + SHIFT + *.

   ✓ *If the feature was already on, it is now toggled off. Repeat the steps to turn it back on.*
3. Press ENTER. Word starts a new paragraph. You can see the paragraph mark at the end of the previous line.
4. Press SPACE five times. You can see the space characters to the left of the insertion point.
5. Press TAB. You can see the tab character to the left of the insertion point.
6. Press ENTER to insert another new paragraph, and then press BACKSPACE to remove the blank paragraph.
7. Click Show/Hide ¶ ¶ to toggle off nonprinting characters. Leave the document open to use in the next Try It.

Display nonprinting characters in a document

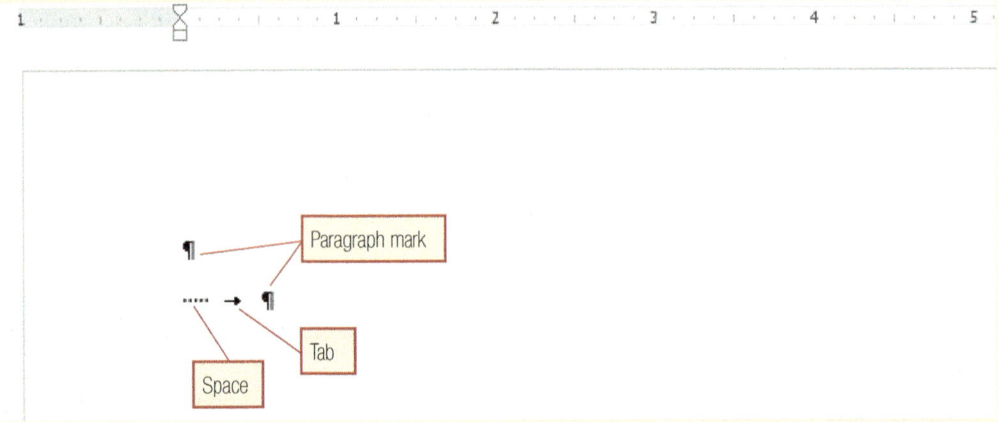

Word 2013, Windows 8, Microsoft Corporation

Typing in a Document

- The **insertion point** indicates where text will be inserted or deleted.
- By default, the insertion point is positioned at the beginning (left end) of the first line of a new document.
- You simply begin typing to insert new text.
- Characters you type are inserted to the left of the insertion point.
- Press BACKSPACE to delete the character to the left of the insertion point; press DEL to delete the character to the right of the insertion point.
- You can move the insertion point anywhere in the existing text with keystrokes or mouse clicks, or by tapping if you are using a touch screen.
- Scrolling to shift the document view does not move the insertion point.
- **Word wrap** automatically wraps the text at the end of a line to the beginning of the next line.
- When you press ENTER, Word inserts a **paragraph mark** and starts a new paragraph.
- After you type enough text to fill a page, Word automatically starts a new page.

✓ *Note that Word includes many features designed to make your work easier, such as a spelling checker. These features are often displayed automatically onscreen as colored underlines or buttons. Simply ignore these features for now; you learn to use them later in this book.*

Table 1-1 Keystrokes for Moving the Insertion Point

One character left	←	Up one paragraph	CTRL + ↑
One character right	→	Down one paragraph	CTRL + ↓
One line up	↑	Beginning of document	CTRL + HOME
One line down	↓	End of document	CTRL + END
Previous word	CTRL + ←	Beginning of line	HOME
Next word	CTRL + →	End of line	END

Try It! Typing in a Document

1. With the default Document1 file open in Word, click Show/Hide ¶ ¶ to toggle on nonprinting characters.
2. Press ENTER and then use the keyboard to type the following paragraph:

   Microsoft Word 2013 is the word processing program that comes with the Microsoft Office 2013 suite of programs. I can use it to create, edit, and format text-based documents such as letters, memos, and reports.
3. Press ENTER at the end of the paragraph.
4. Move the mouse so the pointer I-beam is positioned to the left of the first paragraph mark on the first line of the document.
5. Click to position the insertion point.
6. Type your first name, a space, and then your last name.
7. Press ENTER to start a new paragraph.
8. Press CTRL + HOME to position the insertion point at the beginning of the document.
9. Press DEL enough times to delete all the characters in your name but not the paragraph mark. Leave the document open to use in the next Try It.

Typing in the Header or Footer

- Type in a **header** when you want text to display at the top of every page of a document.
- Type in a **footer** when you want text to display at the bottom of every page of a document.
- For example, type your name in the header so it displays at the top of every page; insert page numbers in the footer so they display at the bottom of every page.
- The header area consists of the top 1 inch of the page. The footer area is the bottom 1 inch.
- To type in a header or footer, you first double-click in the area to make it active.
- When the header or footer is active, the main document area is not active, and the HEADER & FOOTER TOOLS DESIGN tab displays on the Ribbon.
- When you are finished working in the header or footer, the main document area is made active again.
- Headers and footers do not display in Draft view; use Print Layout view to see them on the screen.

Try It! Typing in the Header or Footer

1. With the default Document1 file open in Word, double-click in the header area—the white space between the first paragraph mark and the top of the page—to make the header active. Word moves the insertion point into the header.
2. Type your full name.
3. Double-click in the main document area to make it active. You can see the text in the header, but it is not active.

   OR

   On the HEADER & FOOTER TOOLS DESIGN tab of the Ribbon, in the Close group, click the Close Header and Footer button ☒.
4. Scroll down and position the mouse pointer on the bottom edge of the page and double-click to make the footer active.

   ✓ *For information on scrolling, refer to Basics, Lesson 5. If you have trouble making the footer area active, click the INSERT tab, then, in the Header & Footer group, click Footer, and then click Edit Footer.*
5. Type today's date.
6. On the HEADER & FOOTER TOOLS DESIGN tab, in the Navigation group, click the Go to Header button. The insertion point moves up to the header area.
7. Click the Go to Footer button. The insertion point moves to the footer.
8. Double-click in the main document area.

   OR

   On the HEADER & FOOTER TOOLS DESIGN tab of the Ribbon, in the Close group, click the Close Header and Footer button ☒.
9. Leave the file open to use in the next Try It.

Typing in the header

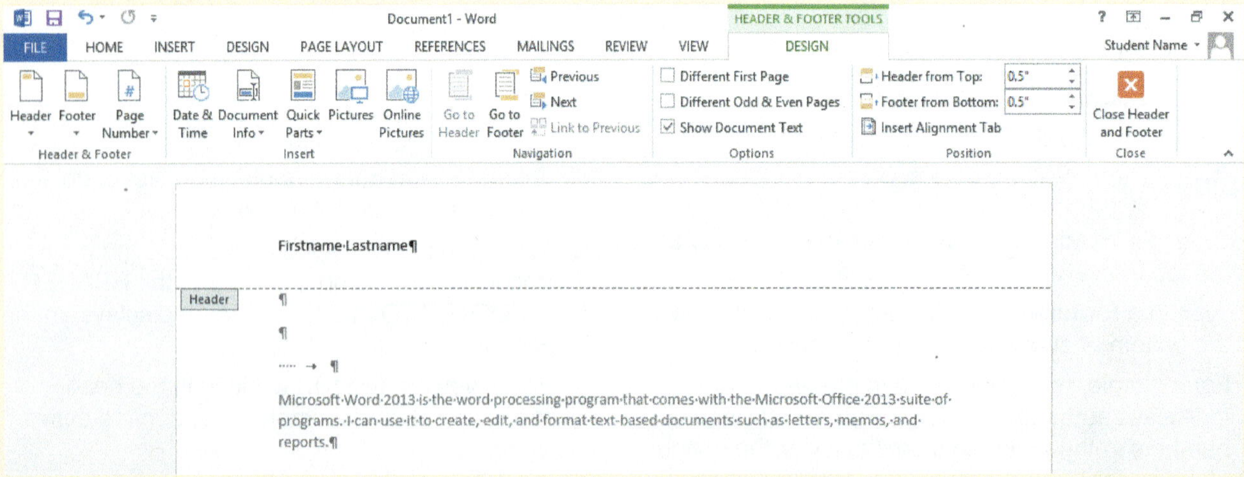

Word 2013, Windows 8, Microsoft Corporation

Splitting a Word Window

- Split the Word window into two panes so you can see and work in different sections of a single document.
- Word tiles the panes one above the other within the program window, separated by a split bar.
- Each pane has its own scroll bars so you can scroll each section independently from the other.
- Each pane also has its own rulers.
- There is only one menu bar, one title bar, and one Ribbon.
- Commands affect the **active pane**. For example, you can change the zoom in the top pane if it is active without affecting the inactive bottom pane.
- To switch from one pane to the other to make edits and formatting changes, simply click in the pane you want to make active.

Try It! Splitting a Word Window

1. In the default document, click the VIEW tab.
2. In the Window group, click the Split button . The window automatically splits in half horizontally.
3. Click in the document below the split bar to make that pane active, then click in the top pane again.
4. In the default document, click the VIEW tab.
5. In the Window group, click the Remove Split button .

   ✓ *You can also double-click the Split bar that divides the panes.*

Saving a Document

- If you want to have a Word file available for future use, you must save it on a storage device.
- The first time you save a new file you use the Save As dialog box to give it a name and select the location where you want to store it.
- If Microsoft Word 2013 is running in compatibility mode, it prompts you to confirm you want to save in the most current Word document format.
- After you save a file for the first time, you save changes to the file in order to make sure that you do not lose your work.
- Saving frequently ensures that no work will be lost if there is a power outage or you experience computer problems.

  ✓ *The AutoRecover feature also helps ensure that you won't lose your work. Refer to Basics Lesson 6 for more information on AutoRecover.*

- Saving changes updates the previously saved version of the file with the most recent changes.

Try It! Saving a Document

1. In the default document, click Save on the Quick Access Toolbar.

   OR

   a. Click FILE.

   b. Click Save.
2. On the Save As page, click Computer.
3. Click the Browse button in the right pane.
4. Select the File name text box if it is not selected already.
5. Type **W01Try_xx.**

   ✓ *Replace xx with your initials or full name, as instructed by your teacher.*

(continued)

Try It! Saving a Document *(continued)*

6. Use the Navigation pane to navigate to the location where your teacher instructs you to store the files for this lesson. Create a new folder, if necessary.

   ✓ *Refer to Lesson 1 of the Basics section of this book for information on navigating in Windows Explorer.*

7. Click Save or press ENTER.
8. If a confirmation dialog box displays, click OK.
9. On the first line of the **W01Try_xx** file, type your teacher's name and then press ENTER.
10. Type the period or class time.
11. Click the Save button on the Quick Access Toolbar.

    OR

    a. Click FILE.

    b. Click Save.

    ✓ *You can also press CTRL + S to save changes.*

12. Click the Close button × to close the document and exit Word.

Save As dialog box

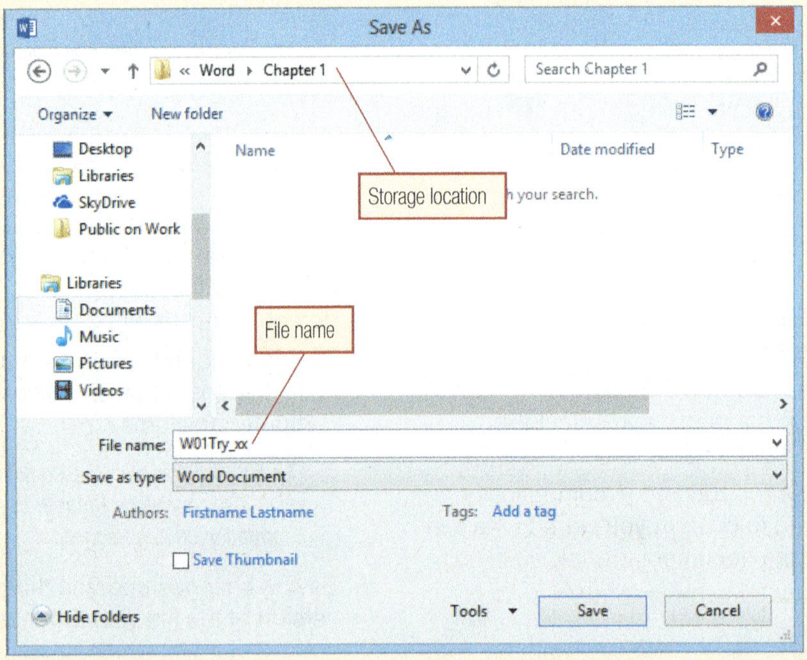

Word 2013, Windows 8, Microsoft Corporation

Lesson 1—Practice

You are the office manager at the Michigan Avenue Athletic Club in Chicago, Illinois. Two new employees have recently joined the staff. In this project, you will create and save a document and type a brief biography of a personal trainer that will be made available at the club and sent to members. When you are finished, you will exit Word.

DIRECTIONS

1. Start Word, and click **Blank document**.
2. Save the file as **W01Practice_xx** in the location where your teacher instructs you to store the files for this lesson.

   ✓ *Remember to replace the xx with your initials or full name, as instructed by your teacher.*

3. On the **VIEW** tab, in the Show group, click in the **Ruler** check box to display the rulers, if necessary.
4. On the **HOME** tab, in the Paragraph group, click the **Show/Hide ¶** button ¶ to display nonprinting characters. If nonprinting characters are already displayed, skip this step.
5. Type the following paragraph. Do not press ENTER at the end of each line. Word wrap automatically moves the text to the next line as necessary.

   Michigan Avenue Athletic Club is pleased to announce that David Fairmont has joined our staff. David is a licensed personal trainer with extensive experience in cardiovascular health. He holds a master's degree in health management from the University of Vermont in Burlington, Vermont. After graduation, he remained at UVM as an instructor. He recently moved to the Chicago area with his family.

   ✓ *If you make a typing error, press BACKSPACE to delete it, and then type the correct text.*

6. At the end of the paragraph, press ENTER to start a new paragraph.
7. Type the following paragraph:

   We are certain that David will be a valuable addition to our staff. His skills and experience make him highly qualified, and his attitude and personality make him a lot of fun to have around. David is available for private, semi-private, and group sessions. Please contact the club office for more information or to schedule an appointment.

8. Proofread the document, and correct any errors.

   ✓ *Word marks spelling errors with a red wavy underline, and grammatical errors with a blue wavy underline. If you see these lines in the document, proofread for errors.*

9. Click the **Save** button on the Quick Access Toolbar to save the changes to the document.
10. Click the **Web Layout** button on the status bar to change to Web Layout view.
11. On the **VIEW** tab, in the Views group, click the **Draft** button to change to **Draft** view.
12. On the **VIEW** tab, in the Views group, click the **Read Mode** button to change to Read Mode view.
13. On the status bar, click the **Print Layout** button to change to Print Layout view.
14. Click the **Collapse the Ribbon** button ^ in the upper-right corner of the window.
15. Double-click in the header area and type your full name. The document should look similar to Figure 1-1 on the next page.
16. Click the **HEADER & FOOTER TOOLS DESIGN** tab to expand the Ribbon, and then click the **Pin the ribbon** button .
17. On the **HEADER & FOOTER TOOLS DESIGN** tab, in the Navigation group, click the **Go to Footer** button to move the insertion point to the footer area.
18. Type today's date.
19. Double-click in the document area to make it active.
20. On the **VIEW** tab, in the Show group, click to deselect the **Ruler** check box. This hides the rulers.
21. On the **HOME** tab, in the Paragraph group, click the **Show/Hide ¶** button ¶ to turn off the display of nonprinting characters.
22. **With your teacher's permission**, print the document.

    ✓ *Refer to Lesson 2 of the Basics section of this book for information on printing a file.*

23. Close the document, saving changes, and exit Word.

Figure 1-1

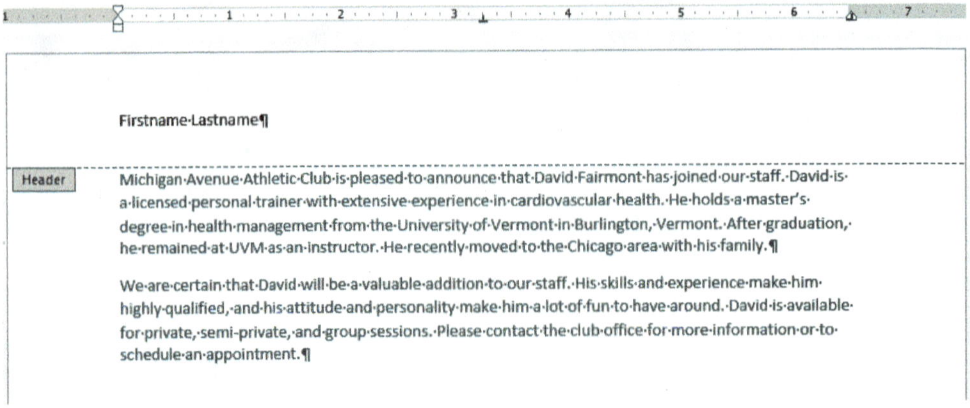
Header

Firstname·Lastname¶

Michigan·Avenue·Athletic·Club·is·pleased·to·announce·that·David·Fairmont·has·joined·our·staff.·David·is·a·licensed·personal·trainer·with·extensive·experience·in·cardiovascular·health.·He·holds·a·master's·degree·in·health·management·from·the·University·of·Vermont·in·Burlington,·Vermont.·After·graduation,·he·remained·at·UVM·as·an·instructor.·He·recently·moved·to·the·Chicago·area·with·his·family.¶

We·are·certain·that·David·will·be·a·valuable·addition·to·our·staff.·His·skills·and·experience·make·him·highly·qualified,·and·his·attitude·and·personality·make·him·a·lot·of·fun·to·have·around.·David·is·available·for·private,·semi-private,·and·group·sessions.·Please·contact·the·club·office·for·more·information·or·to·schedule·an·appointment.¶

Lesson 1—Apply

In this project, you will create a new document and type a biography of a nutritionist recently hired at the Michigan Avenue Athletic Club. When you are finished, you will exit Word.

DIRECTIONS

1. Start Word, and create a blank document.
2. Save the default Document1 file as **W01Apply_xx** in the location where your teacher instructs you to store the files for this lesson.
3. Display the rulers.
4. Display nonprinting characters.
5. Type the two paragraphs shown in Figure 1-2.
6. Type your name in the header area.
7. Type today's date in the footer area.
8. Save the changes to the document.
9. See how the document looks in Reading Mode view.
10. See how the document looks in Draft view.
11. Change back to Print Layout view.
12. Hide the rulers.
13. Hide nonprinting characters.
14. **With your teacher's permission**, print the document.
15. Close the document, saving changes, and exit Word.

Figure 1-2

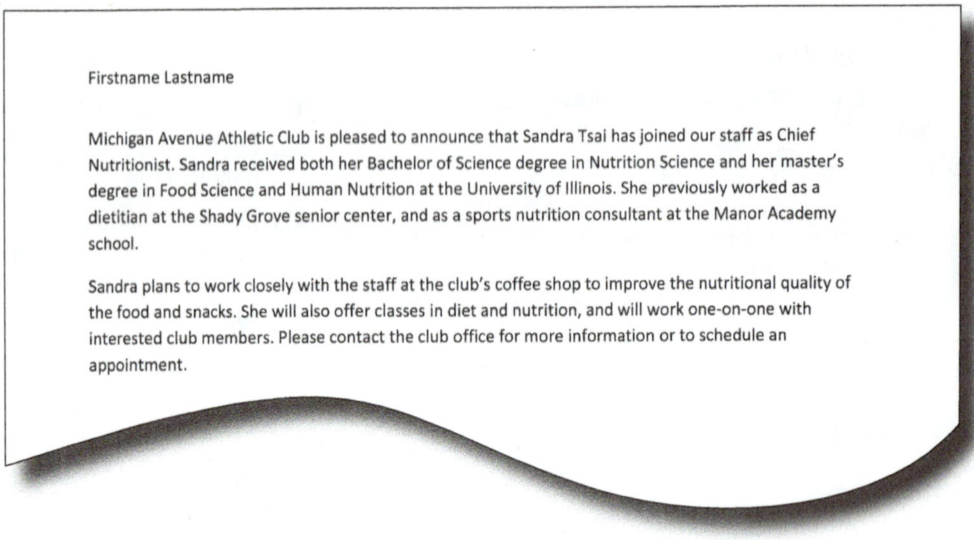
Firstname Lastname

Michigan Avenue Athletic Club is pleased to announce that Sandra Tsai has joined our staff as Chief Nutritionist. Sandra received both her Bachelor of Science degree in Nutrition Science and her master's degree in Food Science and Human Nutrition at the University of Illinois. She previously worked as a dietitian at the Shady Grove senior center, and as a sports nutrition consultant at the Manor Academy school.

Sandra plans to work closely with the staff at the club's coffee shop to improve the nutritional quality of the food and snacks. She will also offer classes in diet and nutrition, and will work one-on-one with interested club members. Please contact the club office for more information or to schedule an appointment.

Lesson 2

Formatting Documents with Themes and Styles

➤ What You Will Learn

Software Skills You can open a saved document to edit it or save it with a new name for editing, and you can create a new document at any time. The click and type feature makes it easy to position text in the center or right side of a line, and you can use themes and styles to give your documents a professional, consistent appearance.

WORDS TO KNOW

Horizontal alignment
The position of text in relation to the width of the page.

Style
A collection of formatting settings that can be applied to characters or paragraphs.

Style set
A collection of styles that have coordinated colors and fonts.

Template
A document that contains formatting, styles, and sample text that you can use to create new documents.

Theme
A set of coordinated colors, fonts, and effects that can be applied to Office 2013 documents.

What You Can Do

Creating a New, Blank Document

- As you learned in Lesson 1, when you start Word it opens and displays a gallery of different types of documents, including the default Blank document.
- You can create additional new documents without exiting and restarting Word.
- Each new document is based on a **template**, which is a file that includes settings for page and text formatting. For example, a calendar template is formatted in a grid to look like a calendar; a business card template is set to use a 2-inch high by 3.5-inch wide page size.

- Blank documents are based on the Normal template, which includes settings for creating typical business documents. For example, the Normal template page size is 8.5 inches by 11 inches.

  ✓ *Using other types of templates is covered in Word, Lesson 19.*

- Each new document is named using consecutive numbers, so the second document is Document2, the third is Document3, and so on. You give the document a different name when you save it.

Try It! Creating a New, Blank Document

1. Start Word. Click the Blank document template. The blank document file displays in the program window.
2. Click FILE to display the Backstage view.
3. Click New. The New tab displays in the Backstage view.
4. Click Blank document.
5. The new, blank document opens. It is named Document2. Document1 remains open until you close it.

✓ *The shortcut key combination for creating a new, blank document is* CTRL + N.

The New tab in the Backstage view

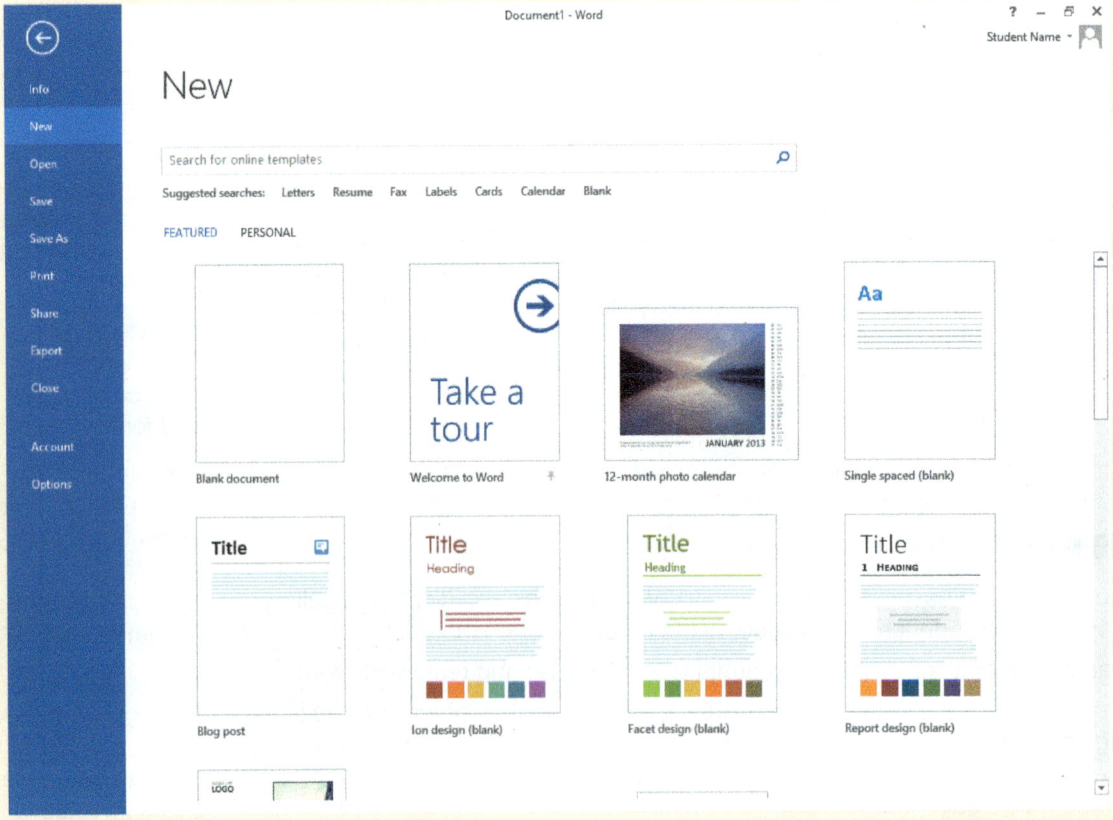

Word 2013, Windows 8, Microsoft Corporation

Closing a Document

- A file remains open onscreen until you close it.
- If you try to close a document without saving, the program prompts you to save.
- You can close a document without saving it if you do not want to keep it for future use.
- In Word you can use the Close button to close the document if there are multiple documents open.
- If there is one document open, use the Close button to close it and exit Word, or use the Close command in Backstage view to close the document and leave Word running.

Try It! Closing a Document

1. With the Document2 file open in Word, click the Close button ×.

   ✓ *If you have made any changes to the file, Word asks if you want to save it before closing. Click Save to save the changes or Don't Save to close it without saving.*

2. Word remains running, and the Document1 file remains open.
3. Click FILE to display the Backstage view.
4. Click Close. Word remains running, but there are no open documents.

   ✓ *Again, if you have made any changes to the file, Word asks if you want to save it before closing. Click Save to save the changes or Don't Save to close it without saving.*

Using Click and Type

- Use the click and type feature in Print Layout view to position the insertion point to begin typing.
- When click and type is active, the mouse pointer changes to indicate the **horizontal alignment** of the new text, as follows:
  - Text will be flush—even with—with the left margin.
  - Text will be centered.
  - Text will be flush with the right margin.
  - The first line of text will be indented 0.5".

✓ *Click and type is usually active by default. If it is not active on your system, you can turn it on by clicking FILE > Options. In the Word Options dialog box, click Advanced. Click to select the Enable click and type check box, and then click OK.*

Try It! Using Click and Type

1. With Word still running, click FILE > New > Blank document to open a new document.
2. Display nonprinting characters.
3. Position the mouse pointer in the center of the document area so it changes to look like this.
4. Double-click to position the insertion point, and type **Centered**.
5. Position the mouse pointer at the right side of the document area along the same line so it changes to look like this.
6. Double-click to position the insertion point, and type **Right**.
7. Position the mouse pointer down one or two lines along the left side of the document area so it changes to look like this.
8. Double-click to position the insertion point, and type **Left**.
9. Position the mouse pointer down one or two lines and about 0.5" in from the left margin, so it changes to look like this.
10. Double-click to position the insertion point, and type **Use click and type to indent the first line of text in a paragraph by one-half inch. The other lines remain flush left.**
11. Click the Close button ×, and then click Don't Save to close the file and exit Word without saving any changes.

Opening a Saved Document

- To view or edit a document that has been saved and closed, open it again.
- Word displays a list of recently used documents in the left pane of its opening screen, as well as the Open Other Documents option that launches the Open tab.
- The Open tab offers a list of recent documents and allows you to search for other documents on the OneDrive or your computer.

✓ *You can also use Windows to open a saved document. Use File Explorer to navigate to the location where the document is stored and then double-click the file name.*

Try It! Opening a Saved Document

1. Start Word.
2. Click Open Other Documents to display the Open tab in the Backstage view.
3. Click Computer, then click the Browse button and navigate to the location where the data files for this lesson are stored.
4. Double-click **W02TryA** to open it.

   OR

   a. Click **W02TryA**.

   b. Click Open.
5. Click FILE > Close to close the document without saving any changes, but leave Word open to use in the next Try It.

Try It! Opening a Recently Used Document

1. In Word, click FILE. The Open tab displays with Recent Documents selected.
2. Click **W02TryA** under Recent Documents on the right side of the screen.
3. Leave the **W02TryA** document open to use in the next Try It.

Saving a Document with a New Name

- Use the Save As command to save a copy of a file in a different location or with a different file name.
- The original file remains unchanged.

Try It! Saving a Document with a New Name

1. In Word, with the **W02TryA** file open, click FILE > Save As.
2. Click the Browse button and navigate to the location where your teacher instructs you to store the files for this lesson.
3. Type **W02TryA_xx**.
4. Click Save.
5. Close the document, and exit Word.

Applying a Built-In Style

- **Styles** make it easy to apply a collection of formatting settings to characters or paragraphs all at once.
- Word 2013 comes with built-in Quick Styles for formatting common document parts, such as titles, headings, and subheadings.

  ✓ *There are also Quick Styles for formatting other elements, such as pictures and tables. You learn how to use them later in this book.*

- The Quick Styles display in the Styles gallery in the Styles group on the HOME tab of the Ribbon, and in the Styles task pane.
- To apply a style to a paragraph, click anywhere within the paragraph, and then click the style name in the Styles gallery or task pane.
- To apply a style to text, select the text and then click the style name.
- You can also select a style before you type new text.
- The default style for new text is called Normal.
- Only one row of styles displays in the Styles gallery at a time, but you can scroll the gallery, or click the More button to display the entire gallery.
- You can preview how a style will affect text by resting the mouse pointer on the style in the Styles gallery.
- Paragraphs that have been formatted with built-in heading styles display small gray arrows to the left of the heading that you can use to hide all text under the heading. You will learn more about this collapse and expand feature later in the course.

Try It! Applying a Built-In Style

1. Start Word, and open the file W02TryB from the data files for this lesson.
2. Save the file as W02TryB_xx in the location where your teacher instructs you to store the files for this lesson.
3. Click anywhere within the first line of text.
4. On the HOME tab, in the Styles group, click the Heading 1 style in the Styles gallery. The Style is applied to the current paragraph—in this case, the first line.

   ✓ *Any amount of text followed by a paragraph mark is a paragraph in Word—even a single character.*

   ✓ *Move the mouse pointer over the text you just formatted with Heading 1 to see the collapse arrow to the left of the heading.*

5. Click the More button on the Styles gallery to display additional styles.
6. Click the Title style to apply it to the current paragraph.
7. Click the HOME tab and then click the Styles gallery dialog box launcher to display the Styles task pane.
8. Click anywhere within the second line of text.
9. Click the Subtitle style in the Styles task pane to apply it to the paragraph.
10. Select the text *Denver, Colorado*, and then click the Emphasis style in the Styles task pane to apply it to the selection.

    ✓ *For more on selecting, refer to Lesson 3 of the Basics section of this book.*

11. Close the Styles task pane.
12. Save the changes to the document, and keep it open to use in the next Try It.

Changing the Style Set

- The fonts used for Quick Styles depend on the current theme; formatting depends on the current **style set**.
- Select a style set from the Style Set gallery in the Document Formatting group on the DESIGN tab.

Try It! Changing the Style Set

1. With the W02TryB_xx file open, click the DESIGN tab.
2. In the Document Formatting group, rest the mouse pointer on the Basic (Elegant) style set to see how the change affects the document.

   ✓ *Rest the mouse pointer on a style set to display its name.*
3. Click Centered to change to the Centered style set.
4. Click the More button to display the entire Style Set gallery.
5. Click Reset to the Default Style Set to change back to the default style set.
6. Save the changes to the document, and keep it open to use in the next Try It.

Applying a Theme

- Office 2013 comes with built-in **themes** that you can apply to documents.
- Each theme includes a set of coordinated colors, fonts, styles, and effects.
- The default theme is Office.
- Click the Themes button on the DESIGN tab of the Ribbon to display the Themes gallery.
- To preview how a theme will affect the current document, rest your mouse pointer on it in the gallery.
- The same themes are available in other Microsoft Office 2013 programs.
- By using a theme, you can easily create different types of documents that have a consistent and professional appearance.

Try It! Applying a Theme

1. In the W02TryB_xx file, click the DESIGN tab.
2. In the Document Formatting group, click the Themes button to display the Themes gallery.
3. Rest the mouse pointer on the Facet theme in the gallery. Notice that the appearance of the text in the current document changes to show how it would look formatted with the Facet theme.
4. Rest the mouse pointer on the Ion theme in the gallery to see how the text changes.
5. Scroll down in the gallery and click the Wisp theme to apply it to the document.
6. Click the Themes button again and click the Office theme to change back to the default theme.
7. Close the W02TryB_xx file, saving changes, and exit Word.

Analyzing a Press Release

- Use a press release to announce information about your company to media outlets, such as Web sites, newspapers, and magazines.
- For example, you can issue a press release about new products, trends, developments, and even to provide tips or hints.
- The media outlet may provide you with publicity by reporting the information.
- A press release should be no more than one page in length. It should provide the basic facts, details that define why the content is newsworthy, and who to contact for more information.
- The basic parts of a press release include the following:
  - Contact information
  - Headline
  - Location
  - Lead paragraph
  - Additional information and details

Lesson 2—Practice

Voyager Travel Adventures wants to issue a press release announcing new tours on its winter schedule. In this project, you will create a new document and type the first press release. You will save and close the document, and open it to save with a new name. You will edit and format the documents using click and type, themes, and styles.

DIRECTIONS

1. Start Word, and click **Blank document** to start a new document.
2. Click **FILE** > **Close** to close the default Document1.
3. Click **FILE** > **New** to display the New tab in the Backstage view.
4. Click **Blank document** to create another new blank document.
5. Save the document as **W02PracticeA_xx** in the location where your teacher instructs you to store the files for this lesson.
6. Display nonprinting characters and the rulers.
7. On the first line of the document, type **For Immediate Release**.
8. Position the mouse pointer at the middle of the next line, and when the Center pointer icon displays, double-click to position the insertion point.
9. Type **Voyager Travel Adventures Announces New Winter Tours**.
10. Position the mouse pointer flush left on the next line and double-click to position the insertion point.
11. Type **Denver, Colorado**, and press Enter twice.
12. Type today's date, press Enter twice, and type **Voyager Travel Adventures, an adventure tour operator based in Denver, has announced its winter tour schedule, which includes exciting new offerings.**

    ✓ *Word's AutoCorrect feature replaces the double hyphens with an em dash character. You learn about AutoCorrect in Word, Lesson 18.*

13. Press ENTER to start a new paragraph and type **This winter, you have the option of joining Voyager Travel Adventures for cross-country ski touring in either Yellowstone National Park in Wyoming or the White Mountain National Forest in New Hampshire. For travelers who prefer warmer adventures, the company is also adding a tour of Central America. Highlights include a visit to the Costa Rican rain forest and a trip through the Panama Canal.**
14. Press ENTER and type **For more information contact:**.
15. Press ENTER and type your full name.
16. Save the changes to the document. It should look similar to Figure 2-1.

Figure 2-1

For Immediate Release

Voyager Travel Adventures Announces New Winter Tours

Denver, Colorado—Today's date—Voyager Travel Adventures, an adventure tour operator based in Denver, has announced its winter tour schedule, which includes exciting new offerings.

This winter, you have the option of joining Voyager Travel Adventures for cross-country ski touring in either Yellowstone National Park in Wyoming or the White Mountain National Forest in New Hampshire. For travelers who prefer warmer adventures, the company is also adding a tour of Central America. Highlights include a visit to the Costa Rican rain forest and a trip through the Panama Canal.

For more information contact:

Firstname Lastname

Word 2013, Windows 8, Microsoft Corporation

17. Click **FILE** > **Close** to close the document.
18. Click **FILE** > **Open** to display a list of recent documents.
19. Click **W02PracticeA_xx** to open it.
20. Click **FILE** > **Save As** to open the Save As tab.
21. Click the desired folder in the Computer list on the right side of the tab, and save the file with the name **W02PracticeB_xx**.
22. Click the **DESIGN** tab. Then, in the Document Formatting group, click the Themes button to display the **Themes** gallery.
23. Click **Facet** in the Themes gallery to apply the theme to the document.
24. Click anywhere in the first line of text, click the **HOME** tab, click the **More** button in the Styles gallery, and click the **Title** Quick Style to apply it to the paragraph.
25. Click anywhere in the second line of text and click the **Subtitle** Quick Style in the Styles gallery.
26. Select the text *Denver, Colorado*, and then click the **Emphasis** Quick Style in the Styles gallery.
27. Select today's date, and then click the **Emphasis** Quick Style in the Styles gallery.
28. On the **DESIGN** tab, in the Document Formatting group, click the **Lines (Distinctive)** style set.
29. Save the changes to the document.
30. **With your teacher's permission**, print the document. It should look similar to Figure 2-2.
31. Close the document, saving changes, and exit Word.

Figure 2-2

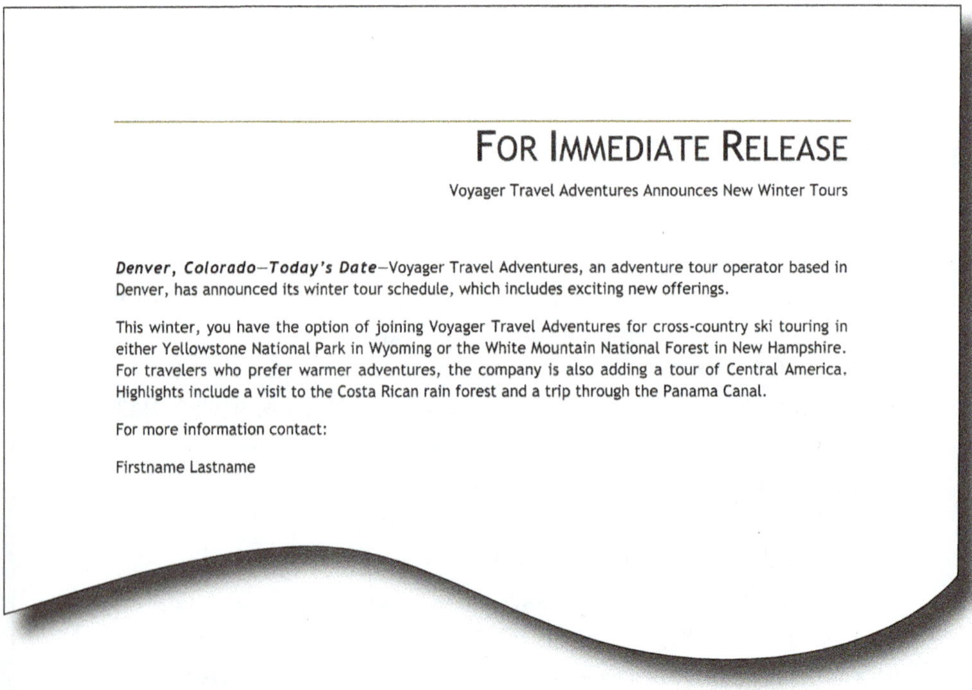
FOR IMMEDIATE RELEASE

Voyager Travel Adventures Announces New Winter Tours

Denver, Colorado—Today's Date—Voyager Travel Adventures, an adventure tour operator based in Denver, has announced its winter tour schedule, which includes exciting new offerings.

This winter, you have the option of joining Voyager Travel Adventures for cross-country ski touring in either Yellowstone National Park in Wyoming or the White Mountain National Forest in New Hampshire. For travelers who prefer warmer adventures, the company is also adding a tour of Central America. Highlights include a visit to the Costa Rican rain forest and a trip through the Panama Canal.

For more information contact:

Firstname Lastname

Word 2013, Windows 8, Microsoft Corporation

Lesson 2—Apply

In this project, you will open an existing press release for Voyager Travel Adventures and save it with a new name. Then, you will edit the document using skills you have learned in this lesson.

DIRECTIONS

1. Start Word.
2. Open the file **W02Apply** from the data files for this lesson.
3. Save the file as **W02Apply_xx** in the location where your teacher instructs you to store the files for this lesson.
4. Display the rulers and nonprinting characters if they are not already displayed.
5. Replace the sample text *Today's Date* with the actual date, and *Firstname Lastname* with your own first and last names.
6. Make the header area active, then position the mouse pointer on the right side of the header area so the Right pointer displays, and double-click to position the insertion point flush right in the header.
7. Type **Page 1 of 1**.
8. Close Header and Footer view to make the main document active.
9. Apply the **Heading 1** Quick Style to the first line of text.
10. Apply the **Subtitle** Quick Style to the second line of text.
11. Apply the **Intense Emphasis** Quick Style to the text *Denver, Colorado* and to today's date.
12. Apply the **Slice** theme to the document.
13. Change the style set to **Shaded**.
14. Save the changes to the document.
15. **With your teacher's permission**, print the document. It should look similar to Figure 2-3.
16. Close the document, saving changes, and exit Word.

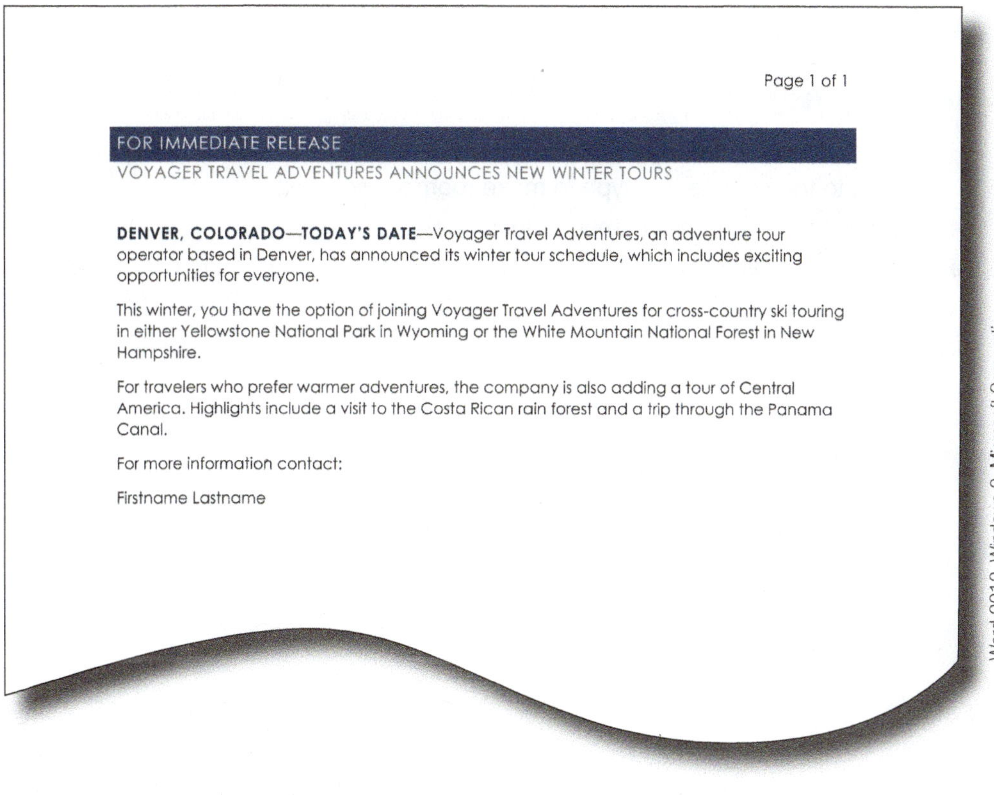

Page 1 of 1

FOR IMMEDIATE RELEASE

VOYAGER TRAVEL ADVENTURES ANNOUNCES NEW WINTER TOURS

DENVER, COLORADO—TODAY'S DATE—Voyager Travel Adventures, an adventure tour operator based in Denver, has announced its winter tour schedule, which includes exciting opportunities for everyone.

This winter, you have the option of joining Voyager Travel Adventures for cross-country ski touring in either Yellowstone National Park in Wyoming or the White Mountain National Forest in New Hampshire.

For travelers who prefer warmer adventures, the company is also adding a tour of Central America. Highlights include a visit to the Costa Rican rain forest and a trip through the Panama Canal.

For more information contact:

Firstname Lastname

Word 2013, Windows 8, Microsoft Corporation

Figure 2-3

Lesson 3

Editing and Correcting Documents

➤ What You Will Learn

Inserting Text
Using Overtype Mode
Selecting and Replacing Text
Canceling a Command
Using Undo, Redo, and Repeat

WORDS TO KNOW

Insert mode
The method of operation used for inserting new text within existing text in a document. Insert mode is the default.

Overtype mode
The method of operation used to replace existing text in a document with new text.

Software Skills Microsoft Word 2013 includes many tools for editing and correcting documents. You can easily insert and replace existing text. You can also undo actions and then redo them, if necessary. In some cases, you can use the Repeat command to repeat an action, which might save you time and keystrokes.

What You Can Do

Inserting Text

- By default, you insert new text in a document in **insert mode**. Existing text moves to the right as you type to make room for new text.
- You can insert text anywhere in a document.
- You can also insert nonprinting characters as you type, including paragraph marks to start a new paragraph (press ENTER), tabs (press TAB), and spaces (press SPACE).

Try It! Inserting Text

1. Open **W03Try** from the data files for this lesson, and save it as **W03Try_xx** in the location where your teacher instructs you to store the files for this lesson.
2. Position the insertion point to the right of the *R* in the word *FOR* on the first line.
3. Press SPACE and then type **IMMEDIATE**.
4. Save the changes to the document, and keep it open to use in the next Try It.

Using Overtype Mode

- To replace text as you type, use **overtype mode**.
- In overtype mode, existing characters do not shift right to make room for new characters. Instead, new characters delete existing characters as you type.
- Overtype mode is off by default. You can change Word options to make overtype mode active all the time, or to set the Insert key to toggle overtype mode off and on.
- Most editing should be done in insert mode, so you do not accidentally type over text that you need.
- You can customize the status bar with a typing mode indicator that displays Insert when you are working in insert mode or Overtype when you are working in overtype mode.

Try It! Using Overtype Mode

1. With the **W03Try_xx** document open, right-click the status bar to display a shortcut menu.
2. Click Overtype on the menu. The typing mode indicator displays near the left end of the status bar.

   ✓ *A check mark next to the command on the shortcut menu indicates that it is selected.*
3. Click Overtype on the menu again to hide the indicator.
4. Press ESC to close the menu.
5. Click FILE > Options to open the Word Options dialog box.
6. Click Advanced to display the advanced options.
7. Click to select the Use the Insert key to control overtype mode check box. A check mark indicates that the option is selected.
8. Click OK.
9. Position the insertion point to the left of the *I* in the word *Illinois*.

   ✓ *You can increase the zoom magnification to make it easier to position the insertion point, if you want.*
10. Press INS. This toggles on overtype mode.
11. Type **Colorado**. Each character that you type replaces an existing character in the document.
12. Press INS. This toggles off overtype mode.
13. Click FILE > Options.
14. Click Advanced to display the advanced options.
15. Click to clear the check mark from the Use the Insert key to control overtype mode check box.
16. Click OK.
17. Save the changes to the document, and leave it open to use in the next Try It.

Selecting and Replacing Text

- You select text in order to edit it or format it.

  ✓ *Refer to Lesson 3 of the Basics section of this book for more information on selecting and formatting text.*

- You can also select nontext characters, such as symbols; nonprinting characters, such as paragraph marks; and graphics, such as pictures.
- When text is selected, any command or action affects the selection.
- Press DEL to delete the selection.
- Type new text to replace the selection.
- To select on a touch screen, tap in the text and then drag the selection handle.
- Refer to Table 3-1 for keyboard selection commands. Refer to Table 3-2 for mouse selection commands.

Table 3-1 Keyboard Selection Commands

To Select	Press
One character right	SHIFT + →
One character left	SHIFT + ←
One line up	SHIFT + ↑
One line down	SHIFT + ↓
To end of line	SHIFT + END
To beginning of line	SHIFT + HOME
To end of document	SHIFT + CTRL + END
To beginning of document	SHIFT + CTRL + HOME
Entire document	CTRL + A

Table 3-2 Mouse Selection Commands

To Select	Do This
One word	Double-click word.
One sentence	CTRL + click in sentence.
One line	Click in selection bar to the left of the line.
One paragraph	Double-click in selection bar to the left of the paragraph.
Document	Triple-click in selection bar.
Noncontiguous text	Select first block, press and hold CTRL, select additional block(s).

Try It! Selecting and Replacing Text

1. In the **W03Try_xx** document, position the insertion point to the left of the date, then hold down the left mouse button.
2. Drag the mouse pointer across the date to select it.
3. Type today's date. The selected text is deleted and replaced with the text you type.
4. Double-click on the word *guides* at the end of the document to select it. Notice that the period is not selected.
5. Type the word **leaders** but do not type a period. The text you type replaces the selected text.
6. Save the changes to the document, and leave it open to use in the next Try It.

Canceling a Command

- Press ESC to cancel a command or close a menu or dialog box before the command affects the current file.
- You can also click anywhere outside a menu to close it without selecting a command.

Try It! Canceling a Command

1. In the **W03Try_xx** document, press CTRL + A, the shortcut key combination for selecting all text in a document.
2. Click anywhere in the document to cancel the selection.
3. Right-click the status bar to display the shortcut menu.
4. Press ESC to close the menu without making a selection.
5. On the HOME tab, click the Font group dialog box launcher to open the Font dialog box.
6. Press ESC to close the dialog box without changing any options.
7. On the HOME tab, in the Editing group, click the Select button to display the Select menu.
8. Click anywhere in the document outside the menu to close it without making a selection.
9. Leave the document open to use in the next Try It.

Using Undo, Redo, and Repeat

- Use the Undo button on the Quick Access Toolbar to reverse a single action made in error, such as deleting the wrong word.
- Use the Undo drop-down list to reverse a series of actions.
- The most recent action is listed at the top of the list; click an action to undo it and all actions above it.
- Use the Redo button on the Quick Access Toolbar to reinstate any actions that you reversed with Undo.
- If the Undo button is dimmed, there are no actions that can be undone.
- If the Redo button is dimmed, there are no actions that can be redone.
- Sometimes when there are no actions to redo, the Repeat button is available in place of Redo. Use Repeat to repeat the most recent action.

Try It! Using Undo, Redo, and Repeat

1. In the **W03Try_xx** document, press CTRL + A to select all text in the document.
2. Press DEL. The entire selection is deleted.
3. Click the Undo button on the Quick Access Toolbar. The previous action—deleting the selection—is undone.
4. Click the Redo button on the Quick Access Toolbar. The undone action is redone—the selection is deleted again.
5. Click the Undo button again to undo the deletion.

   ✓ *CTRL + Z is the shortcut key combination for undoing an action. CTRL + Y is the shortcut key combination for redoing an action.*

6. Select the second line of text and press DEL. The line is deleted from the document.
7. Position the insertion point in the first line of text and then click Heading 1 in the Styles gallery to apply the Quick Style.
8. Click the Undo down arrow on the Quick Access Toolbar. Both actions display on the Undo menu; the most recent action is at the top.
9. Click Clear on the Undo menu. All actions between the action you click and the top of the menu are undone.

Use the Undo menu to undo a series of actions

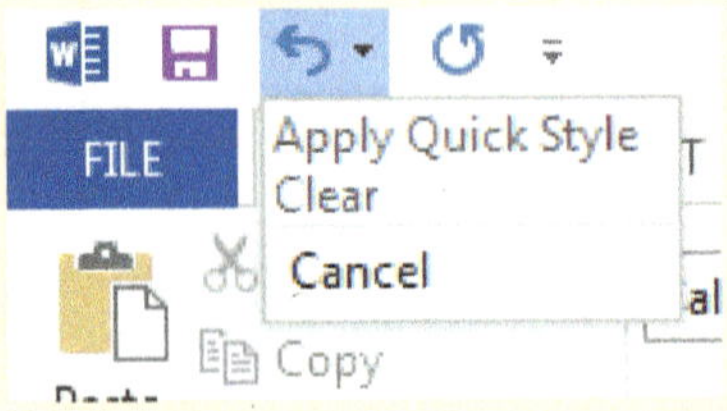

Word 2013, Windows 8, Microsoft Corporation

10. Position the insertion point in the first line of text.
11. On the HOME tab, in the Styles group, click Heading 1 in the Styles gallery to apply the Quick Style.
12. Position the insertion point anywhere in the second line of text and then click the Repeat button on the Quick Access Toolbar. Word repeats the most recent action—applying the Heading 1 Quick Style.

    ✓ *CTRL + Y is the shortcut key combination for repeating an action.*

13. Close the **W03Try_xx** document, saving changes, and exit Word.

Lesson 3—Practice

Voyager Travel Adventures wants you to make changes to a press release document. In this project, you will open the existing press release document so you can make edits and corrections.

DIRECTIONS

1. Start Word, if necessary, and open **W03Practice** from the data files for this lesson.
2. Save it as **W03Practice_xx** in the location where your teacher instructs you to store the files for this lesson.
3. Click **FILE** > **Options** to open the Word Options dialog box.
4. Click the **Advanced** tab to display the advanced options, and then click to select the **Use the Insert key to control overtype mode** check box.
5. Click **OK** to apply the setting and close the dialog box.
6. Right-click the status bar and click to select **Overtype** on the shortcut menu to display the indicator on the status bar.

7. Press ESC to close the shortcut menu.
8. Delete the first line of text, and then click the **Undo** button to reverse the delete action.
9. Click the **Redo** button to redo the action and delete the line.
10. Select *New Winter Tours* in the second line of text and type **Two Cross-Country Ski Adventures** to replace the selection.
11. Select the text *CO* and type **Colorado**, followed by two hyphens and today's date.
12. Press INS to make overtype mode active.
13. Position the insertion point to the left of the *e* in the word *exciting*, and type: **two amazing cross-country ski adventures.**
14. Press INS to make insert mode active.
15. Apply the **Title** style to the first line of the press release.
16. Position the insertion point in the second line of the press release and click the **Repeat** button on the Quick Access Toolbar to apply the Title style to the paragraph.
17. Click the **Undo** button on the Quick Access Toolbar to undo the action and remove the Title style.
18. Apply the Subtitle style to the second line.
19. Select the text *Denver, Colorado* and apply the **Intense Emphasis** style.
20. Select today's date and click the **Repeat** button on the Quick Access Toolbar to apply the **Intense Emphasis** style to the selection.
21. Click the **arrow** on the **Undo** button to display the Undo menu, and click the second action in the list—**Apply Quick Style**. The last two actions are undone.
22. Select the text *Denver, Colorado* and apply the **Emphasis** style.
23. Select today's date and click the **Repeat** button on the Quick Access Toolbar to apply the **Emphasis** style to the selection.
24. Move the insertion point to the end of the document, press ENTER to start a new paragraph and type your full name.
25. **With your teacher's permission,** print the document. It should look similar to Figure 3-1.
26. Click **FILE** > **Options** to open the Word Options dialog box.
27. Click the **Advanced** tab to display the Advanced options, and then click to clear the check mark from the **Use the Insert key to control overtype mode** check box.
28. Click **OK** to apply the setting and close the dialog box.
29. Right-click the status bar and click to deselect **Overtype** on the shortcut menu to hide the indicator on the status bar.
30. Click anywhere in the document area outside the shortcut menu to close it.
31. Close the document, saving changes, and exit Word.

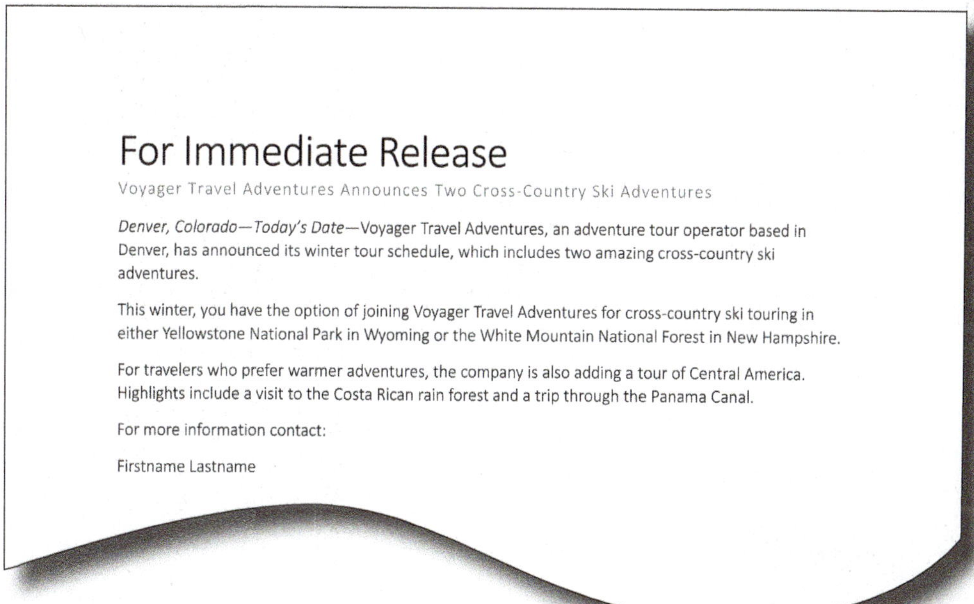

For Immediate Release

Voyager Travel Adventures Announces Two Cross-Country Ski Adventures

Denver, Colorado—Today's Date—Voyager Travel Adventures, an adventure tour operator based in Denver, has announced its winter tour schedule, which includes two amazing cross-country ski adventures.

This winter, you have the option of joining Voyager Travel Adventures for cross-country ski touring in either Yellowstone National Park in Wyoming or the White Mountain National Forest in New Hampshire.

For travelers who prefer warmer adventures, the company is also adding a tour of Central America. Highlights include a visit to the Costa Rican rain forest and a trip through the Panama Canal.

For more information contact:

Firstname Lastname

Word 2013, Windows 8, Microsoft Corporation

Figure 3-1

Lesson 3—Apply

Voyager Travel Adventures wants you to make changes to another press release. In this project, you will edit an existing document using the skills you have learned in this lesson.

DIRECTIONS

1. Start Word and open the file **W03Apply** from the data files for this lesson.
2. Save the file as **W03Apply_xx** in the location where your teacher instructs you to store the files for this lesson.
3. Open the Word Options dialog box and display the Advanced options.
4. Select the option to **Use the Insert key to control overtype mode** check box.
5. Click **OK** to apply the setting and close the dialog box.
6. Right-click the status bar and click to select **Overtype** on the shortcut menu; then close the shortcut menu.
7. Press INS to turn on overtype mode.
8. Position the insertion point to the left of *Announces Two Cross-Country Ski Adventures* in the second line of text and type **Adds a Central American Getaway to Its Winter Schedule**.
9. Undo the action, and then redo it.
10. Press INS to turn on insert mode.
11. Select the text *Costa Rica* and type **Denver, Colorado**, followed by two hyphens and today's date.
12. Select the text *This winter, you have the option of joining*, and type **For those who prefer colder weather,**.
13. Select the word *for* between *Adventures* and *cross-country* and type **is offering**.
14. Apply the **Subtitle** style to the first line, then undo the action and apply the **Title** style.
15. Apply the **Heading 3** style to the second line, and then repeat the action to apply it to the last line.

   ✓ *If the Heading 3 style does not display in the Style gallery, apply the Heading 2 style first. The Heading 3 style should then become available.*

16. Move the insertion point to the last line, press ENTER to start a new paragraph, and type your full name.
17. **With your teacher's permission**, print the document. It should look similar to Figure 3-2.
18. Open the Word Options dialog box, display the Advanced options, and clear the **Use the Insert key to control overtype mode** check box.
19. Click **OK** to apply the setting and close the dialog box.
20. Remove the overtype indicator from the status bar.
21. Close the document, saving changes, and exit Word.

Figure 3-2

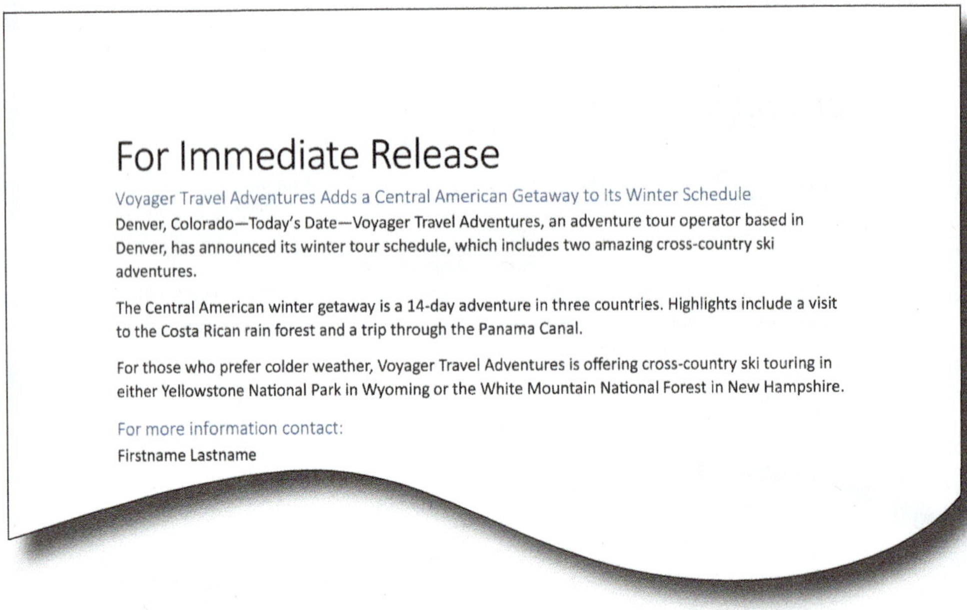

For Immediate Release

Voyager Travel Adventures Adds a Central American Getaway to Its Winter Schedule

Denver, Colorado—Today's Date—Voyager Travel Adventures, an adventure tour operator based in Denver, has announced its winter tour schedule, which includes two amazing cross-country ski adventures.

The Central American winter getaway is a 14-day adventure in three countries. Highlights include a visit to the Costa Rican rain forest and a trip through the Panama Canal.

For those who prefer colder weather, Voyager Travel Adventures is offering cross-country ski touring in either Yellowstone National Park in Wyoming or the White Mountain National Forest in New Hampshire.

For more information contact:

Firstname Lastname

Lesson 4

Adjusting Alignment and Spacing

➤ What You Will Learn

Aligning Text Horizontally
Aligning a Document Vertically
Setting Line Spacing
Setting Paragraph Spacing
Analyzing Memos

Software Skills Changing the horizontal and vertical alignment can improve the appearance of a document and make it easier to read. Format documents using the right amount of space between lines and paragraphs to make the pages look better and the text easier to read, and to achieve the standard page setup for documents such as memos and letters.

WORDS TO KNOW

Horizontal alignment
The position of text across a line in relation to the left and right margins.

Leading
Line spacing measured in points.

Line spacing
The amount of white space between lines of text in a paragraph.

Paragraph spacing
The amount of white space between paragraphs.

Point
A unit of measurement used in desktop publishing and graphic design.

Vertical alignment
The position of text in relation to the top and bottom page margins.

What You Can Do

Aligning Text Horizontally

- **Horizontal alignment** is used to adjust the position of paragraphs in relation to the left and right margins of a page.

  ✓ *You have already used click and type to align text horizontally in a document.*

- There are four horizontal alignments:
  - Left
    Text is flush with left margin. The text along the right side of the page is uneven (or ragged). Left is the default horizontal alignment.
  - Right
    Text is flush with right margin. The text along the left side of the page is uneven (or ragged).
  - Center
    Text is centered between margins.
  - Justify
    Text is spaced so it runs evenly along both the left and right margins.

- You can use different alignments in a document.
- Buttons for changing the alignment are available in the Paragraph group on the HOME tab of the Ribbon.
- You can also use shortcut key combinations:
  - Align Left .... CTRL + L
  - Center .... CTRL + E
  - Align Right .... CTRL + R
  - Justify .... CTRL + J

Try It! Aligning Text Horizontally

1. Open **W04TryA**, and save it as **W04TryA_xx** in the location where your teacher instructs you to store the files for this lesson.
2. Click anywhere in the first paragraph.
3. On the HOME tab, in the Paragraph group, click the Align Left button. The text, which was aligned right, is now aligned left.
4. Select the second and third paragraphs.
5. In the Paragraph group, click the Center button. Both paragraphs are centered.
6. Click in the fourth paragraph.
7. In the Paragraph group, click the Align Right button. The two lines in the paragraph are aligned flush with the right margin.
8. Click in the last paragraph.
9. In the Paragraph group, click the Justify button. Word adjusts the spacing between words so that both margins are even.
10. Save the changes to **W04TryA_xx**, and close it. Leave Word open to use in the next Try It.

Horizontal alignments

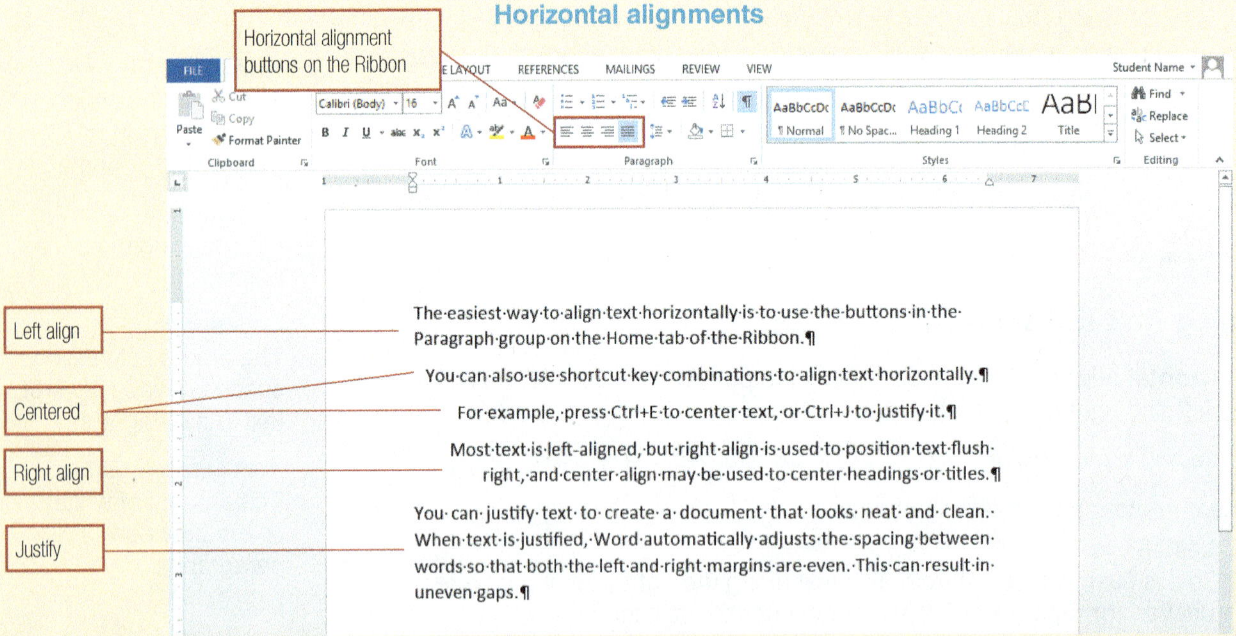

Word 2013, Windows 8, Microsoft Corporation

Aligning a Document Vertically

- **Vertical alignment** is used to adjust the position of all text on a page in relation to the top and bottom margins.
- There are four vertical alignments:
  - Top: Text begins below the top margin. Top is the default vertical alignment.
  - Center: Text is centered between the top and bottom margins. Centering can improve the appearance of some one-page documents, such as flyers or invitations.
  - Justified: Paragraphs are spaced to fill the page between the top and bottom margins. Vertical justification improves the appearance of documents that contain nearly full pages of text.
  - Bottom: The last line of text begins just above the bottom margin.

Try It! Aligning a Document Vertically

1. Start Word, and open **W04TryB**. Save it as **W04TryB_xx** in the location where your teacher instructs you to store the files for this lesson. Notice that by default the vertical alignment is set to Top.
2. On the VIEW tab, in the Zoom group, click the One Page button. This enables you to see the entire page on your screen.

   ✓ *For more on adjusting the zoom, refer to Lesson 5 in the Basics section of this book.*
3. On the PAGE LAYOUT tab, click the Page Setup group dialog box launcher to open the Page Setup dialog box.
4. Click the Layout tab.
5. Click the Vertical alignment drop-down arrow to display a menu of alignment options.
6. Click Center, and then click OK. The document is centered vertically.
7. Click the PAGE LAYOUT tab, if necessary.
8. Click the Page Setup group dialog box launcher button to open the Page Setup dialog box.
9. Click the Layout tab, if necessary.
10. Click the Vertical alignment drop-down arrow, click Justified, and then click OK. The document is justified vertically.
11. Click the PAGE LAYOUT tab, if necessary.
12. Click the Page Setup group dialog box launcher to open the Page Setup dialog box.
13. Click the Layout tab, if necessary.
14. Click the Vertical alignment drop-down arrow, click Bottom, and then click OK. The document is vertically aligned with the bottom of the page.
15. Save the changes to **W04TryB_xx**, and close it. Leave Word open to use in the next Try It.

Setting Line Spacing

- **Line spacing** sets the amount of vertical space between lines in a paragraph. In the Normal style, which is the default, line spacing in Word is set to 1.08 lines.
- Line spacing can be measured in either lines (single, double, etc.) or in **points**.
- When line spacing is measured in points, it is called **leading** (pronounced *ledding*).
  - Increase leading to make text easier to read.
  - Decrease leading to fit more lines on a page.

✓ *Decreasing leading too much can make text difficult to read.*

- You can set line spacing using the Line spacing button in the Paragraph group on the HOME tab of the Ribbon, or in the Paragraph dialog box.
- Exactly is one of three leading options you can use if you want to set line spacing in points. The other leading options are At least, which you can use to set a minimum leading, and Multiple, which you can use to specify a percentage by which to increase leading.

Try It! Setting Line Spacing

1. Start Word, and open **W04TryC** from the data files for this lesson. Save it as **W04TryC_xx** in the location where your teacher instructs you to store the files for this lesson.
2. Increase the zoom to 100%.
3. Position the insertion point in the first paragraph.
4. Click the HOME tab, then, in the Paragraph group, click the Line and Paragraph Spacing button.
5. Click 2.0 on the menu to change the line spacing to 2.0 lines. Notice that the line spacing in the other paragraphs is not affected.

   ✓ *The shortcut key combination to set line spacing to 2.0 lines is CTRL + 2. Use CTRL + 1 for single line spacing, or CTRL + 5 for 1.5 line spacing.*

6. Select the first and second paragraphs.
7. On the HOME tab, click the Paragraph group dialog box launcher to open the Paragraph dialog box.

   ✓ *You can also click the Line Spacing Options item on the Line and Paragraph Spacing menu to open the dialog box.*

8. If necessary, click the Indents and Spacing tab.
9. Click the Line spacing drop-down arrow to display a menu of line spacing options.
10. Click Single. This would set the line spacing to 1 line.
11. Click the Line spacing drop-down arrow again, and click Exactly.
12. Use the At box increment arrows to set the leading to 15 pts.
13. Click OK to apply the change to the selection.
14. Save the changes to the document, and leave it open to use in the next Try It.

Setting Paragraph Spacing

- **Paragraph spacing** affects space before and after paragraphs.
- The amount of space is usually specified in points. In the Normal style, paragraph spacing in Word is set to 8 points after each paragraph.
- You can set paragraph spacing in the Paragraph group on the PAGE LAYOUT tab of the Ribbon, or in the Paragraph dialog box.
- Use the Paragraph dialog box when you want to set multiple paragraph formatting options at the same time, such as line spacing and paragraph spacing.
- Use increased paragraph spacing in place of extra returns or blank lines.

  ✓ *To quickly remove all paragraph and line spacing, apply the No Spacing Quick Style.*

Try It! Setting Paragraph Spacing

1. In the **W04TryC_xx** document, click anywhere in the second paragraph.
2. Click the PAGE LAYOUT tab.
3. In the Paragraph group, use the Spacing Before box increment arrows to set the spacing before the paragraph to 24 pts.
4. Use the Spacing After box increment arrows to set the spacing after the paragraph to 36 pts.

(continued)

Try It! Setting Paragraph Spacing *(continued)*

5. On the PAGE LAYOUT tab, click the Paragraph group dialog box launcher to open the Paragraph dialog box.

   ✓ *You can also open the Paragraph dialog box by clicking the Paragraph dialog box launcher in the Paragraph group on the HOME tab.*

6. Under Spacing, click in the Before box and replace the 24 with 14.

7. Click in the After box and replace 36 with 16.

8. Click OK to apply the changes.

9. Make sure the insertion point is within the second paragraph.

10. Click the HOME tab, and then, in the Paragraph group, click the Line and Paragraph Spacing button.

11. Click Remove Space After Paragraph. All space after the paragraph is removed.

12. Click the Line and Paragraph Spacing button again.

    ✓ *Notice that now the Add Space After Paragraph command is available in place of Remove Space After Paragraph.*

13. Click Remove Space Before Paragraph to remove the space before the paragraph.

    ✓ *There is still space between the first and second paragraphs because there is space after the first paragraph.*

14. Close **W04TryC_xx**, saving changes, and exit Word.

Set paragraph spacing on the PAGE LAYOUT tab

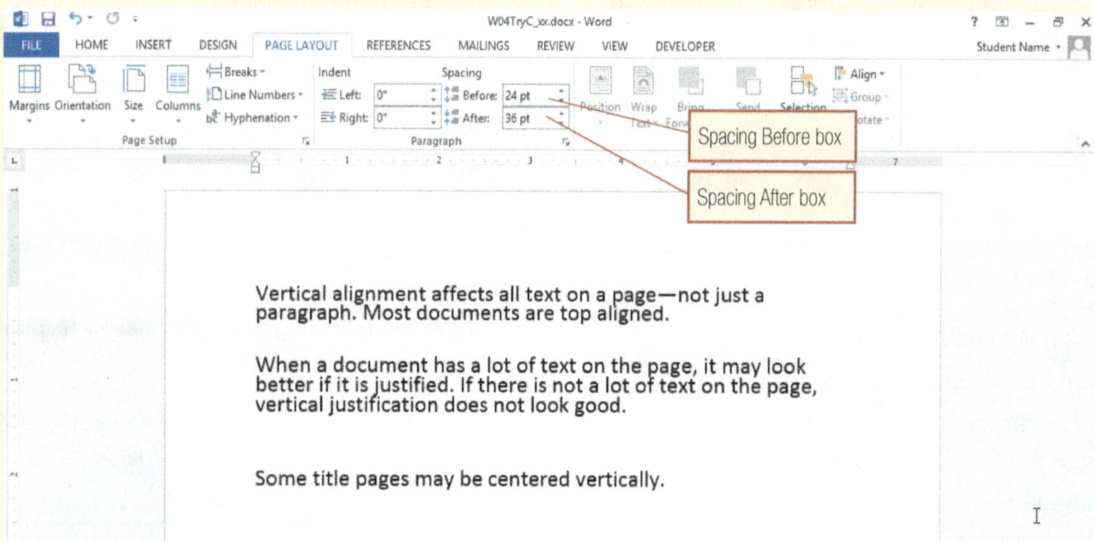

Word 2013, Windows 8, Microsoft Corporation

Analyzing Memos

- A memo, or memorandum, is a business document commonly used for communication within a company.
- Unlike a letter, a memo may or may not be addressed to a particular individual and does not include a formal closing.

  ✓ *Word Lesson 5 explains letter formatting.*

- Usually, a memo includes the company name, the word *memo*, the headings To:, From:, Date:, and Subject:, and the memo text.
- Line spacing in a memo is usually set to Single, so that no extra space is left between lines.
- One blank line, or spacing equal to one line, may be used to separate parts of a memo.
- The writer may include his or her name, title, and/or signature at the end of the memo text or it may be in the From line at the beginning of the memo.
- If someone other than the writer types the memo, that person's initials should be entered below the memo text. In addition, if there is an attachment or an enclosure, the word *Attachment* or *Enclosure* should be entered after the text (or the typist's initials).
- Some variations on this memo format include typing headings in all uppercase letters, typing the subject text in all uppercase letters, and leaving additional spacing between memo parts. Also, the word *memo* may be omitted.

Lesson 4—Practice

You are an assistant in the personnel department at Whole Grains Bread, a manufacturer of specialty breads and pastries based in Larkspur, California. In this project, your supervisor has asked you to type a memo to employees about a new automatic payroll deposit option.

DIRECTIONS

1. Start Word, if necessary, create a new blank document, and save it as **W04Practice_xx** in the location where your teacher instructs you to store the files for this lesson.
2. Display nonprinting characters.
3. Before you begin typing, on the **HOME** tab, click the **Paragraph** group dialog box launcher to open the Paragraph dialog box.
4. Click the **Indents and Spacing** tab, if necessary.
5. Click the **Line spacing** drop-down arrow and click **Single**.
6. Use the **After increment arrows** to set the spacing after paragraphs to **0**.
7. Click **OK** to apply the settings.
8. On the **HOME** tab, in the Paragraph group, click the **Center** button. Type **MEMO**, and press ENTER.
9. On the **HOME** tab, in the Paragraph group, click the **Align Left** button. Type **To: All Employees** and press ENTER.
10. Type **From: Human Resources**, and press ENTER.
11. Type **Date:**, press SPACE, type today's date, and then press ENTER.
12. Type **Subject: New Option**, and then press ENTER.
13. Save the changes.
14. Type the following paragraph: **We are pleased to offer a new automatic deposit option for all payroll checks. This new option provides security as well as convenience, because you do not run the risk of misplacing your paycheck.**
15. Press ENTER and type the following paragraph: **Additional information and enrollment forms will be available starting Monday at 9:00 a.m. in the human resources department.**
16. Press ENTER. On the **HOME** tab, in the Paragraph group, click the **Align Right** button and type your full name.
17. Press ENTER and type **Human Resources Assistant.**

18. Click the **PAGE LAYOUT** tab, and then click the **Page Setup** group dialog box launcher to open the Page Setup dialog box.
19. Click the **Layout** tab, if necessary.
20. Click the **Vertical alignment** drop-down arrow and click **Center**. Click **OK** to vertically center the document on the page.
21. **With your teacher's permission**, print the document. It should look similar to Figure 4-1.
22. Close the document, saving changes, and exit Word.

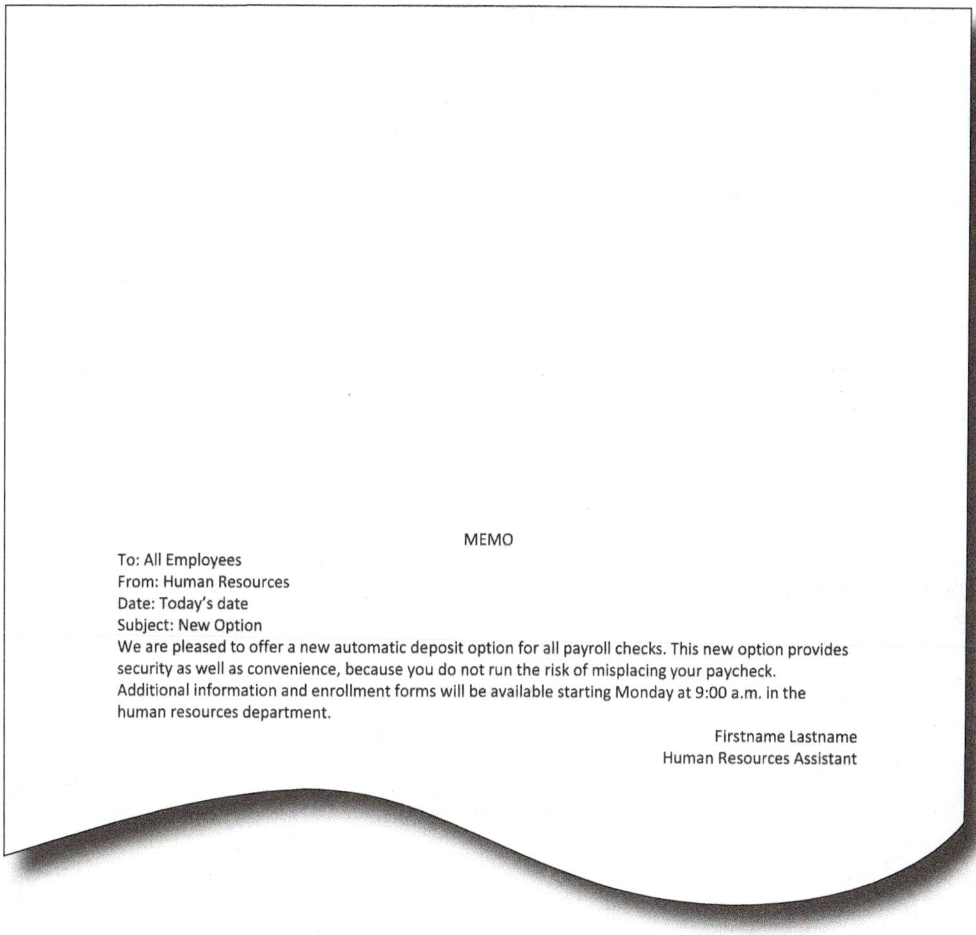

MEMO

To: All Employees
From: Human Resources
Date: Today's date
Subject: New Option
We are pleased to offer a new automatic deposit option for all payroll checks. This new option provides security as well as convenience, because you do not run the risk of misplacing your paycheck. Additional information and enrollment forms will be available starting Monday at 9:00 a.m. in the human resources department.

Firstname Lastname
Human Resources Assistant

Figure 4-1

Lesson 4—Apply

In this project, you will use the skills you have learned in this lesson to open and edit an existing memo for Whole Grains Bread.

DIRECTIONS

1. Start Word, and open **W04Apply** from the data files for this lesson.
2. Save it as **W04Apply_xx** in the location where your teacher instructs you to store the files for this lesson.
3. Replace the sample text *Today's Date* with the actual date, then double-click in the header area to make it active.
4. Type **Whole Grains Bread** and center the text.
5. Press ENTER and type **320 Magnolia Avenue, Larkspur, California**.
6. Make the main document active, and click the **PAGE LAYOUT** tab.
7. Click in the word *MEMO*, and set paragraph spacing **Before** to **24** points and paragraph spacing **After** to **36** points.
8. Click in the word *Subject* and set paragraph spacing **After** to **18** points.
9. Select the two paragraphs of text in the main body of the memo.
10. Open the Paragraph dialog box and set line spacing to **Exactly 18** points.
11. Set paragraph spacing **After** to **16** points.
12. Justify the selected paragraphs horizontally.
13. Move the insertion point to the end of the document and press ENTER to start a new line.
14. Set the horizontal alignment to **Right**, and then type your full name.
15. Remove the spacing after the paragraph.
16. Press ENTER and type **Human Resources Assistant**.
17. Open the Page Setup dialog box and set the vertical alignment to **Top**.
18. Save the changes to the document.
19. **With your teacher's permission**, print the document. It should look similar to Figure 4-2.
20. Close the document, saving changes, and exit Word.

Figure 4-2

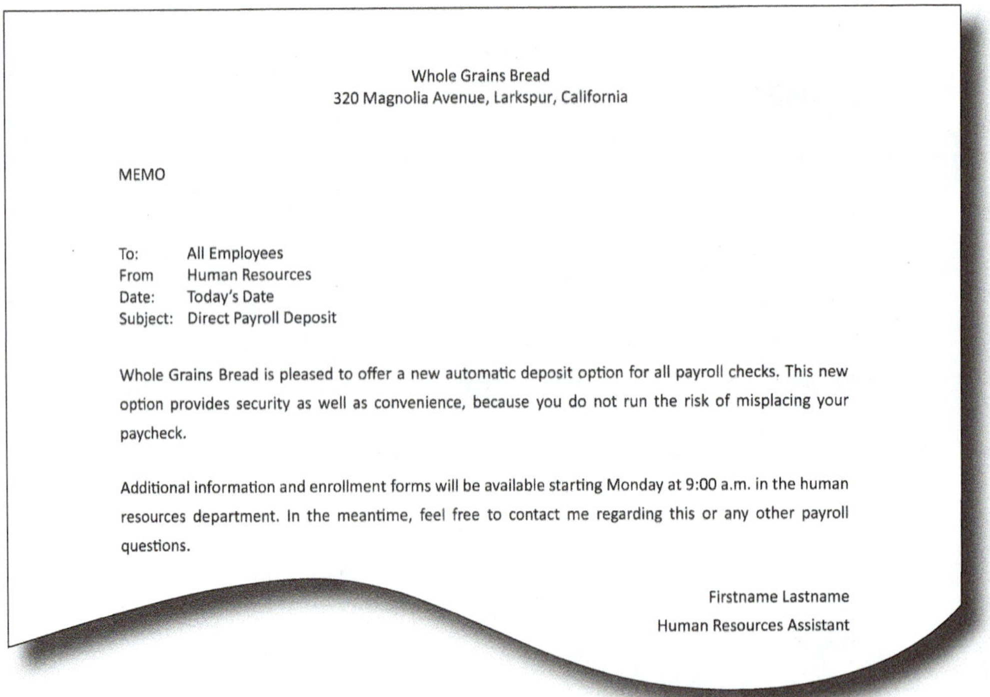

Whole Grains Bread
320 Magnolia Avenue, Larkspur, California

MEMO

To: All Employees
From Human Resources
Date: Today's Date
Subject: Direct Payroll Deposit

Whole Grains Bread is pleased to offer a new automatic deposit option for all payroll checks. This new option provides security as well as convenience, because you do not run the risk of misplacing your paycheck.

Additional information and enrollment forms will be available starting Monday at 9:00 a.m. in the human resources department. In the meantime, feel free to contact me regarding this or any other payroll questions.

Firstname Lastname
Human Resources Assistant

Lesson 5

Creating Letters and Envelopes

➤ What You Will Learn

Indenting Text
Setting and Modifying Tabs
Inserting the Date and Time
Inserting a Watermark
Writing a Business Letter
Creating an Envelope

Software Skills Write business letters as a representative of your employer to communicate with other businesses, such as clients or suppliers, or to communicate with individuals, such as prospective employees. You use tabs to position text along a line in a document and indents to call attention to a paragraph, to achieve a particular visual effect, or to leave white space along the margins for notes or illustrations. Place a watermark on a document to convey information about the document.

WORDS TO KNOW

Computer's clock
The clock/calendar built into your computer's main processor to keep track of the current date and time.

Delivery address
A recipient's address printed on the outside of an envelope.

Field
A placeholder for data that might change.

Full block
A style of letter in which all lines start flush with the left margin—that is, without indents.

Indent
A temporary left and/or right margin for lines or paragraphs.

Inside address
The recipient's address typed in the letter above the salutation.

Modified block
A style of letter in which some lines start at the center of the page.

Return address
The writer's address, typically appearing at the very top of the letter as well as in the upper-left corner of an envelope.

What You Can Do

Indenting Text

- There are four types of **indents**:
  - *Left* indents text from the left margin.
  - *Right* indents text from the right margin.
  - *First line* indents just the first line of a paragraph from the left margin.
  - *Hanging* indents all lines but the first line from the left margin.

  ✓ *You can also use the mirror indents option to set inside and outside indents for bound pages. Inside indents from the margin along the binding; outside indents from the margin opposite the binding.*

- To set any type of indent, use the Paragraph dialog box.
- You can also drag the indent markers on the horizontal ruler.

Salutation
The line at the start of a letter including the greeting and the recipient's name, such as Dear Mr. Doe.

Tab
The measurement of the space the insertion point advances when you press the Tab key.

Tab leader
A series of characters inserted along the line between the location of the insertion point when you press the Tab key and the tab stop.

Tab stop
The location on a horizontal line to which the insertion point advances when you press the Tab key.

Watermark
A pale or semitransparent graphics object positioned behind text in a document.

- Use the Increase Indent button in the Paragraph group on the HOME tab of the Ribbon to move the current left indent 0.5" to the right.
- Use the Decrease Indent button to move the current left indent 0.5" to the left.
- You can set precise left and/or right indents in the Paragraph group on the PAGE LAYOUT tab of the Ribbon.
- You can apply indents before you type new text, for the current existing paragraph, or for selected multiple paragraphs.
- Once you set indents, the formatting is carried forward each time you start a new paragraph.

Try It! Adjusting the Left Indent by 0.5"

1. Start Word, and open **W05TryA** from the data files for this lesson. Save the document as **W05TryA_xx** in the location where your teacher instructs you to store the files for this lesson.
2. Display the rulers, and then click anywhere in the second paragraph.
3. Click the HOME tab, if necessary, and then, in the Paragraph group, click the Increase Indent button to increase the left indent by 0.5".
4. Click the Increase Indent button again. Now, the left indent is set at 1.0" on the horizontal ruler.
5. In the Paragraph group, click the Decrease Indent button to decrease the left indent by 0.5". It is now set at 0.5" on the horizontal ruler.
6. Save the changes to the document, and leave it open to use in the next Try It.

Adjust the left indent

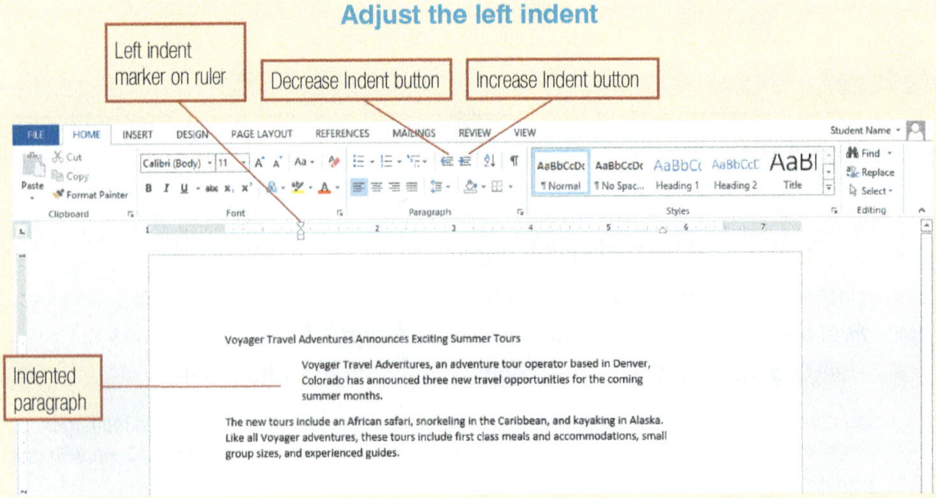

Word 2013, Windows 8, Microsoft Corporation

Try It! Setting a Left or Right Indent Precisely

1. In the **W05TryA_xx** document, select the first two paragraphs.
2. Click the PAGE LAYOUT tab.
3. In the Paragraph group, use the Left Indent increment arrows to set the left indent to 1.2".
4. Use the Right Indent increment arrows to set the right indent to 0.8".

   ✓ *When you indent a paragraph from both the left and right margins it is called a double indent.*

5. Save the changes to the document, and leave it open to use in the next Try It.

Set precise left and right indents

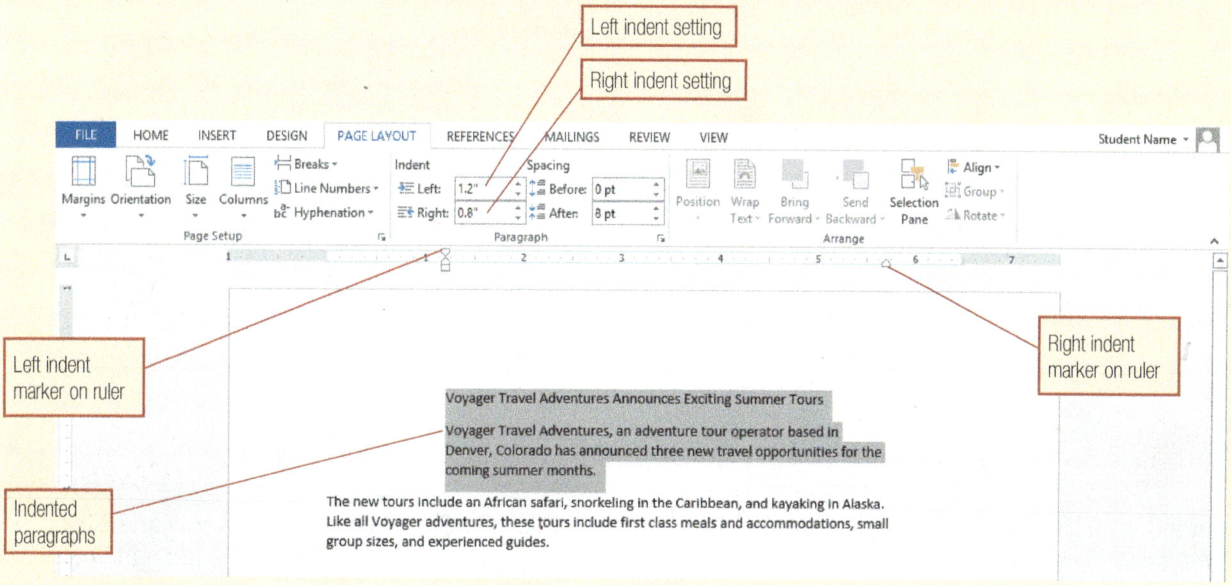

Word 2013, Windows 8, Microsoft Corporation

Try It! Setting Indents Using the Paragraph Dialog Box

1. In the **W05TryA_xx** document, click anywhere in the third paragraph.
2. On the PAGE LAYOUT tab, click the Paragraph group dialog box launcher ⊡.

   ✓ *You can use the Paragraph group dialog box launcher on the HOME tab or the PAGE LAYOUT tab.*

3. Click the Indents and Spacing tab, if necessary.
4. Under Indentation, use the Left increment arrows to set the left indent to 0.4".
5. Use the Right increment arrows to set the right indent to 0.6".

   ✓ *If you were setting indents for a bound publication, you could select the Mirror indents check box and set inside and outside indents instead of left and right indents.*

6. Click the Special drop-down arrow and click First line on the list. By default, the first line indent is set to 0.5".
7. Use the By increment arrows to set the first line indent to 0.8".

(continued)

Try It! Setting Indents Using the Paragraph Dialog Box

8 Click OK to apply the settings to the current paragraph.

✓ *To quickly apply a first line indent, press TAB at the beginning of a paragraph.*

9 Save the changes to the document, and leave it open to use in the next Try It.

Paragraph dialog box

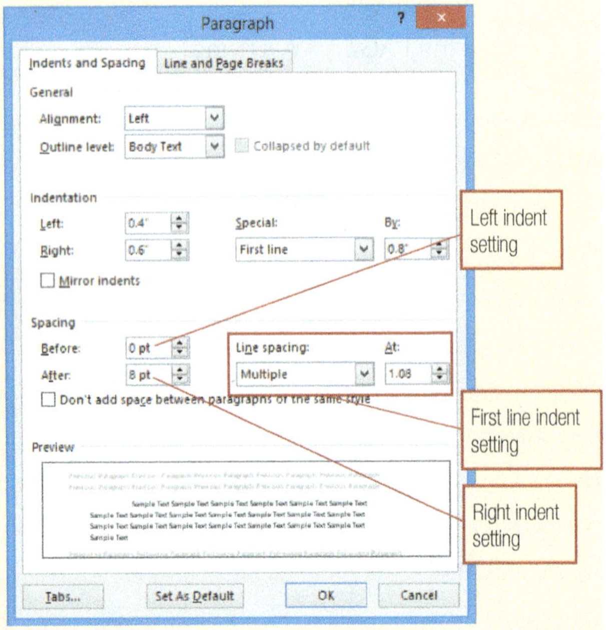

Word 2013, Windows 8, Microsoft Corporation

Try It! Setting a Hanging Indent Using the Paragraph Dialog Box

1 In the **W05TryA_xx** document, click anywhere in the second paragraph.

2 Click the Paragraph group dialog box launcher.

✓ *You can use the Paragraph group dialog box launcher on the HOME tab or the PAGE LAYOUT tab.*

3 Click the Indents and Spacing tab, if necessary.

4 Use the Left increment arrows to set the left indent to 0.4".

5 Click the Special drop-down arrow and click Hanging on the list. By default, the hanging indent is set to 0.5".

6 Use the By increment arrows to set the hanging indent to 0.8".

7 Click OK to apply the settings to the current paragraph.

8 Close the **W05TryA_xx** document, saving changes. Leave Word open to use in the next Try It.

Setting and Modifying Tabs

- **Tabs** are used to indent a single line of text.
- Each time you press the TAB key, the insertion point advances to the next set **tab stop**.
- There are five types of tab stops:
  - *Left*: Text starts flush left with the tab stop.
  - *Right*: Text ends flush right with the tab stop.
  - *Center*: Text is centered on the tab stop.
  - *Decimal*: Decimal points are aligned with the tab stop.
  - *Bar*: A vertical bar is displayed at the tab stop position.
- By default, left tab stops are set every 0.5" on the horizontal ruler.
- You can set any type of tab stop at any point along the ruler.

- To select a tab type, click the Tab selector box at the left end of the ruler until the tab you want to use displays.

  ✓ *Note that after the five tab types display on the Tab selector, the first line indent and hanging indent markers display.*

- You can use the Tabs dialog box to set precise tab stops.
- You can also select a **tab leader** in the Tabs dialog box.
- You can set tabs before you type new text, for the current paragraph, or for selected multiple paragraphs.
- Once you set tabs, the formatting is carried forward each time you press ENTER to start a new paragraph.

Try It! Setting Left and Center Tabs Using the Horizontal Ruler

1. Create a new document in Word. Save the document as **W05TryB_xx** in the location where your teacher instructs you to store the files for this lesson. Notice that by default, the Left Tab type displays in the Tab selector box.
2. Display nonprinting characters.
3. Click at the 1.0" mark on the horizontal ruler. This sets a left tab stop at that point.
4. Press TAB. The insertion point advances to the tab stop.
5. Type your first name.
6. Click the Tab selector box once to change the tab type to Center Tab.
7. Click at the 4.0" mark on the horizontal ruler.
8. Press TAB to advance the insertion point to the Center tab stop, and then type **Microsoft Word 2013**. The text is centered on the tab stop.
9. Press ENTER to start a new line. Notice that the tab settings carry forward to the new line.
10. Save the changes to the document, and leave it open to use in the next Try It.

Try It! Setting Right, Decimal, and Bar Tabs Using the Horizontal Ruler

1. In the **W05TryB_xx** document, click the Tab selector box once to change the tab type to Right Tab.
2. Click at the 3.0" mark on the horizontal ruler to set a right tab stop.
3. Press TAB. The insertion point advances to the left tab stop.
4. Press TAB again. The insertion point advances to the right tab stop. Type your last name.
5. Click the Tab selector box once to change the tab type to Decimal Tab.
6. Click at the 5.0" mark on the horizontal ruler to set a decimal tab stop.
7. Press TAB. The insertion point advances to the center tab stop.
8. Press TAB again. The insertion point advances to the decimal tab stop. Type **$123.75**. The decimal point in the dollar value aligns with the decimal tab stop.
9. Click the Tab selector box once to change the tab type to Bar Tab, then click at the 6.0" mark on the horizontal ruler to set a bar tab stop. A vertical bar displays at the tab stop location.
10. Save the changes to the document, and leave it open to use in the next Try It.

Set tabs on the horizontal ruler

Word 2013, Windows 8, Microsoft Corporation

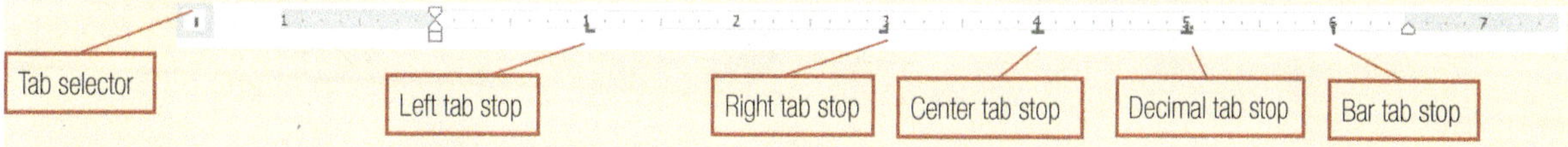

Try It! Setting Tabs in the Tabs Dialog Box

1. In the **W05TryB_xx** document, select the first line of text.
2. Click the HOME tab, if necessary, and then click the Paragraph group dialog box launcher.
3. Click the Tabs button in the lower left of the Paragraph dialog box to open the Tabs dialog box. Notice that the two tabs that are currently set in the selected text are listed under the Tab stop position box, and that the Left tab type is selected by default.
4. Click the Clear All button to remove all tabs from the selection.

   ✓ *To remove only one tab, select it in the Tab stop position list, and then click the Clear button.*

5. Type **.75** in the Tab stop position box, and then click the Set button. This sets a left tab stop at 0.75" on the horizontal ruler.

   ✓ *If you only want to set one tab stop, you can click OK instead of Set.*

6. Click the Center option button to change the tab type to Center tab, and then select the value in the Tab stop position box.
7. Type **3.0** and then click the Set button. This sets a Center tab stop at 3.0" on the horizontal ruler.
8. Click OK to apply the settings. In the document, the text adjusts to the new tab stop settings.
9. Save the changes to the document, and leave it open to use in the next Try It.

Tabs dialog box

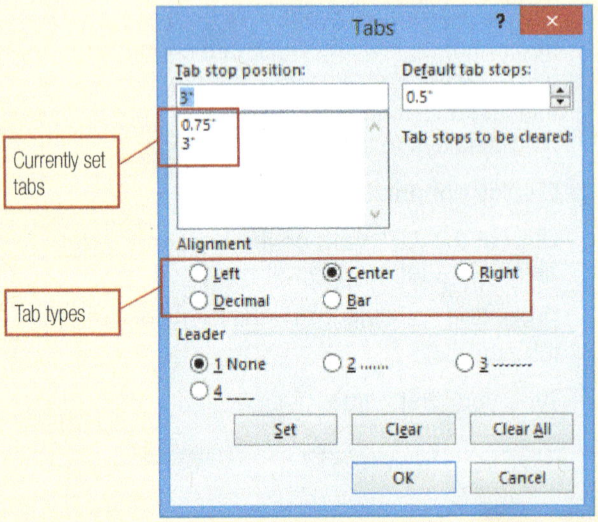

Word 2013, Windows 8, Microsoft Corporation

Try It! Using the Horizontal Ruler to Adjust and Clear Tab Stops

1. In the **W05TryB_xx** document, position the insertion point anywhere along the second line of text.
2. Drag the Bar Tab stop off the horizontal ruler. This is a quick method of removing a tab stop.
3. Drag the Right Tab stop from the 3.0" mark on the ruler to the 2.5" mark on the ruler. The text adjusts to the new tab stop position.
4. Save the changes to the document, and leave it open to use in the next Try It.

Try It! Selecting a Tab Leader

1. Move the insertion point to the end of the W05TryB_xx document, and press ENTER to start a new line.
2. Click the HOME tab, if necessary, and then click the Paragraph group dialog box launcher.
3. Click the Tabs button in the lower left of the Paragraph dialog box to open the Tabs dialog box.
4. In the Leader area, click option 2 to select a dotted line tab leader, and then click OK to apply the change.
5. In the document, press TAB to advance the insertion point to the first set tab stop. Word inserts the dotted tab leader.
6. Type your first name. The text begins after the tab leader.
7. Save the changes to W05TryB_xx, and leave it open to use in the next Try It.

Inserting the Date and Time

- Use the Insert Date & Time feature to automatically enter today's date and/or time into a document.
- The inserted date and time are based on your **computer's clock**. A variety of date and time formats are available.
- If you want, you can insert the date and/or time as a **field**, so that it updates automatically whenever you save or print the document.
- To quickly insert the current date, type the first four letters of the name of the current month. When Word displays the date in a ScreenTip, press ENTER. If the month has fewer than four characters, you do not have to press ENTER.

Try It! Inserting the Date and Time

1. In the W05TryB_xx document, position the insertion point at the end of the last line of text and press ENTER to start a new line.
2. Type Sept—the first four characters of the name of the month September. Word displays the text *September (Press ENTER to Insert)* in a ScreenTip.
3. Press ENTER.
4. Press ENTER to start a new line.
5. Click the INSERT tab, then, in the Text group, click the Date & Time button to open the Date and Time dialog box. The default format is mm/dd/yyyy.
6. Click the second format in the list of Available formats, and then click OK. Word inserts the date in the selected format.

   ✓ *Select the Update automatically check box if you want the date to update automatically every time you save or print the document.*

7. Press ENTER, then click the Date & Time button again.
8. Click the last format in the list of available formats, and then click OK to insert the time into the document.
9. Save the changes to W05TryB_xx, and leave it open to use in the next Try It.

Inserting a Watermark

- Insert a **watermark** to provide a background image for text-based documents.
- Word 2013 comes with built-in watermark styles that you can select from the Watermark gallery.
- Watermarks are usually inserted into the document header so that they automatically appear on every page and so that they are not affected by changes made to the document content.
- You can remove a watermark if desired.

Try It! Inserting a Watermark

1. In the W05TryB_xx document, adjust the zoom to display the entire page.
2. Click the DESIGN tab, then, in the Page Background group, click the Watermark button to display the Watermark gallery.
3. Click the CONFIDENTIAL 1 style. Word inserts the watermark on the page.
4. Click the Watermark button again, and click Remove Watermark.
5. Close W05TryB_xx, saving changes. Leave Word open to use in the next Try It.

Writing a Business Letter

- A business letter is written to communicate with other businesses, such as clients or suppliers, or to communicate with individuals, such as prospective employees. For example, a bank manager might write a business letter to a customer to explain changes in an account, or a marketing representative might write a business letter to an advertising agency requesting rates.
- Traditionally, business letters are printed and mailed, but in some circumstances they may be sent via e-mail.
- Refer to Figure 5-1 on the next page to identify the parts of a business letter.
  - **Return address (**may be omitted if the letter is printed on letterhead stationery)
  - Date
  - **Inside address**
  - **Salutation**
  - Body
  - Closing
  - Signature line
  - Job title line (the job title of the letter writer)
  - Reference initials (the initials of the person who wrote the letter, followed by a slash, followed by the initials of the person who typed the letter).
  - Special notations (included only when appropriate):
    - Mail service notation indicates a special delivery method. It is typed in all capital letters, two lines below the date. Typical mail service notations include CERTIFIED MAIL, REGISTERED MAIL, or BY HAND.
    - Subject notation identifies or summarizes the letter topic. The word Subject may be typed in all capital letters or with just an initial capital. It is placed two lines below the salutation.

    ✓ *The text Re (meaning with regard to) is sometimes used in place of the word Subject.*
  - Enclosure or Attachment notation indicates whether there are other items in the envelope. It is typed two lines below the reference initials in any of the following styles: ENC., Enc., Encl., Enclosure, Attachment. The name of the item(s) may be listed under the notation.

    ✓ *If there are multiple items, the number may be typed in parentheses following the notation.*
  - Copy notation indicates if any other people are receiving copies of the letter. It is typed two lines below either the enclosure notation, or reference initials, whichever is last. It may be typed as Copy to:, cc:, or pc: (photocopy) with the name(s) of the recipient(s) listed after the colon.

Figure 5-1

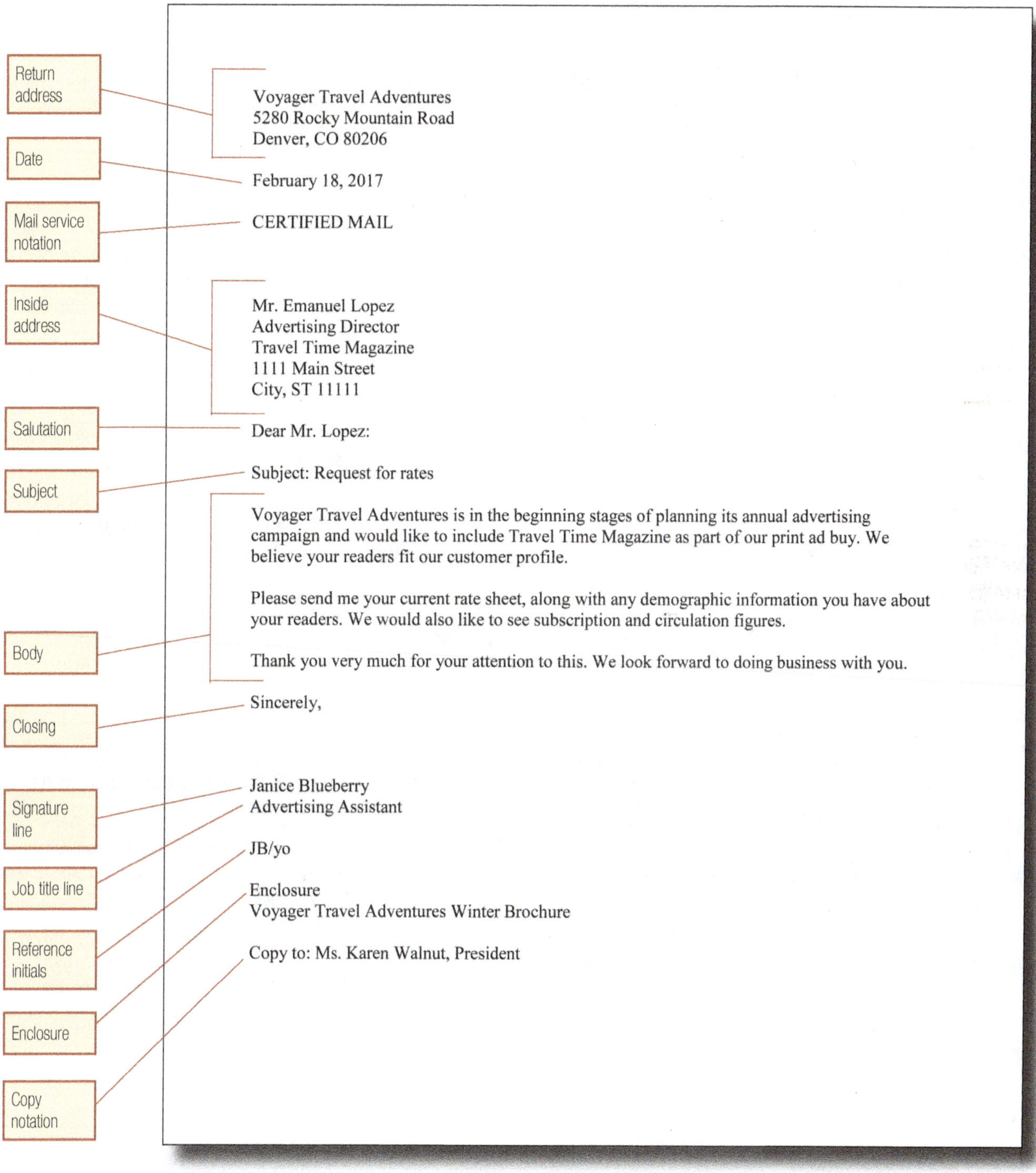

Voyager Travel Adventures
5280 Rocky Mountain Road
Denver, CO 80206

February 18, 2017

CERTIFIED MAIL

Mr. Emanuel Lopez
Advertising Director
Travel Time Magazine
1111 Main Street
City, ST 11111

Dear Mr. Lopez:

Subject: Request for rates

Voyager Travel Adventures is in the beginning stages of planning its annual advertising campaign and would like to include Travel Time Magazine as part of our print ad buy. We believe your readers fit our customer profile.

Please send me your current rate sheet, along with any demographic information you have about your readers. We would also like to see subscription and circulation figures.

Thank you very much for your attention to this. We look forward to doing business with you.

Sincerely,

Janice Blueberry
Advertising Assistant

JB/yo

Enclosure
Voyager Travel Adventures Winter Brochure

Copy to: Ms. Karen Walnut, President

Word 2013, Windows 8, Microsoft Corporation

- There are different styles of business letters. The most common are full block and modified block.
  - In a **full-block** business letter, all lines start flush with the left margin.
  - In a **modified-block** business letter, the return address, date, closing, signature, and job title lines begin at the center of the page at a left tab stop.
- The parts of a business letter are the same regardless of the style.
- Punctuation following the salutation and closing text can also differ in business letters. Business letter writers commonly use either mixed punctuation or open punctuation.
  - When using mixed punctuation, insert a colon following the salutation and a comma following the closing. You can see mixed punctuation in Figure 5-1 on the previous page.
  - When using open punctuation, omit any punctuation after both the salutation and the closing.

Creating an Envelope

- Use Word's Envelopes and Labels dialog box to set up an envelope for printing.
- If a letter document is open onscreen, Word may use the first address as a delivery address; you can select the inside address to identify it as the **delivery address**.
- Alternatively, you can type any delivery address you want.
- You can type a return address or select to omit the return address if you are printing on an envelope that has the return address pre-printed, or if you plan to use return address labels.
- If you type a return address, Word asks if you want to make it the default return address.
- Before printing an envelope, you should be certain the envelope is correctly inserted in your printer, and that the printer is set to print an envelope.
- Consult your printer's manual or ask your teacher for information on using the available printer to print envelopes.

  ✓ *For this lesson, your teacher may instruct you to print the envelope on standard paper.*

- You can print the envelope immediately or add it to the beginning of the open document and save it to print later.

Try It! Creating an Envelope

1. In Word, open **W05TryC** from the data files for this lesson. Save it as **W05TryC_xx** in the location where your teacher instructs you to store the files for this lesson.
2. On the MAILINGS tab, in the Create group, click the Envelopes button to open the Envelopes and Labels dialog box.
3. In the Delivery address box, type your name and address to replace the sample, using proper address formatting.

   ✓ *Refer to the following figure to see proper address formatting.*

4. Click to clear the Omit check box, if necessary, then click in the Return address box and type your school's address.

   ✓ *Click the Omit check box if there is a return address printed on your envelopes already, or if you plan to use return address labels.*

5. Follow your teacher's instructions to properly insert envelopes or paper into the printer.

(continued)

Try It! Creating an Envelope *(continued)*

6. **With your teacher's permission**, click the Print button to print the envelope.
7. Click No to continue without making the return address the default.
8. In the document, select the five lines of the inside address, beginning with *Mr. Emanuel Lopez*.
9. Click the MAILINGS tab on the Ribbon, then, in the Create group, click the Envelopes button to open the Envelopes and Labels dialog box.
10. Click in the Return address box and type your own address.
11. Click Add to Document.
12. Click No to continue without making the return address the default. Word inserts the envelope as the first page in the current document. Once you save the document, you can print the envelope by printing just the first page.
13. Close the document, saving changes, and exit Word.

Envelopes tab of the Envelopes and Labels dialog box

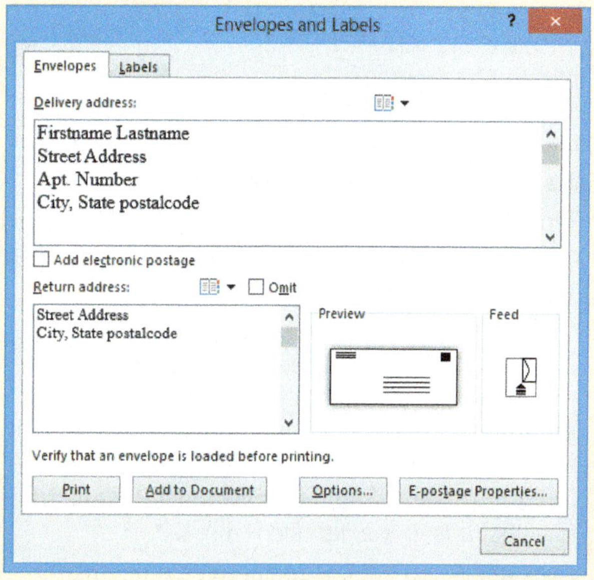

Word 2013, Windows 8, Microsoft Corporation

Lesson 5—Practice

You are the assistant to Mr. Frank Kaplan, the Franchise Manager for Whole Grains Bread. He has asked you to type letters to people interested in opening store franchises outside of California. The first letter will be in full-block format. You will create an envelope as well.

DIRECTIONS

1. Start Word, if necessary, create a new document, and save the document as **W05Practice_xx** in the location where your teacher instructs you to store the files for this lesson.
2. Display the rulers and nonprinting characters, if necessary.
3. Apply the **No Spacing** style to set the line spacing to single and the paragraph spacing to 0 points before and after.
4. Type the following return address, pressing ENTER after each line:

   Whole Grains Bread
   320 Magnolia Avenue
   Larkspur, CA 94939
5. Press ENTER to leave a blank line.
6. Click the **INSERT tab**, and then, in the Text group, click the **Date & Time** button to open the Date and Time dialog box.
7. Click the **third format** in the list and then click **OK** to insert the date.

8. Press ENTER twice, type **CERTIFIED MAIL**, and then press ENTER four times.
9. Type the following inside address, pressing ENTER after each line:

   Ms. Lindsey Parks
   Franchisee
   Whole Grains Bread
   456 Main Street
   Brentwood, CA 94513
10. Press ENTER to leave a blank line, then type **Dear Ms. Parks:** and press ENTER twice.
11. Type **Subject: New franchise opportunity** and press ENTER twice.
12. Type the following paragraph:

    Thanks for your interest in opening an additional franchise outside of California. In response to your question, I have enclosed a financing brochure. In general, we believe you will need the following funds:
13. Press ENTER twice, and then click the **Tab selector** to select a **Decimal** tab stop.
14. Click at **1.5"** on the horizontal ruler to set the tab stop, then press TAB to advance the insertion point.
15. Type **$125,500.00**, press ENTER, press TAB, and type **$21,250.00**. Press ENTER, press TAB, type **$5,400.00**, and press ENTER twice.
16. Drag the Decimal Tab stop off the horizontal ruler, and then type: **The challenges and rewards of starting a new Whole Grains Bread franchise can be summed up by the following quote from our founder:** and press ENTER twice.
17. Click the **PAGE LAYOUT** tab, then use the Left increment arrows to set the left indent to **1.5"** and the Right increment arrows to set the right indent to **1.5"**.
18. Type the following: **"Starting a new Whole Grains franchise is both expensive and difficult. However, when done properly, it brings financial rewards and a strong sense of personal satisfaction."**
19. Press ENTER, and use the Left increment arrows to set the left indent to **0"** and the Right increment arrows to set the right indent to **0"**.
20. Press ENTER, type **Sincerely,** and press ENTER four times.
21. Type your name, press ENTER, and type **Manager**.
22. Press ENTER twice, type **Enclosure**, press ENTER, and type **Financing brochure**.
23. Press ENTER twice and type **Copy to: Mr. Anthony Splendora, CEO**.
24. Save the changes to the document.
25. Select the **inside address**, and then click the **MAILINGS** tab on the Ribbon.
26. Click the **Envelopes** button in the Create group to open the Envelopes and Labels dialog box.
27. Click in the **Return address** box and type

    320 Magnolia Avenue
    Larkspur, CA 94939
28. Click **Add to Document** to add the envelope to the document.
29. Click **No** to continue without making the return address the default. Word inserts the envelope as the first page in the current document. The document should look similar to Figure 5-2 on the next page.
30. **With your teacher's permission**, print both the letter and the envelope.
31. Close the document, saving changes, and exit Word.

Figure 5-2

320 Magnolia Avenue
Larkspur, CA 94939

Ms. Lindsey Parks
Franchisee
Whole Grains Bread
456 Main Street
Brentwood, CA 94513

Whole Grains Bread
320 Magnolia Avenue
Larkspur, CA 94939

August 7, 2017

CERTIFIED MAIL

Ms. Lindsey Parks
Franchisee
Whole Grains Bread
456 Main Street
Brentwood, CA 94513

Dear Ms. Parks:

Subject: New franchise opportunity

Thanks for your interest in opening an additional franchise outside of California. In response to your question, I have enclosed a financing brochure. In general, we believe you will need the following funds:

$125,500.00
$21,250.00
$5,400.00

The challenges and rewards of starting a new Whole Grains Bread franchise can be summed up by the following quote from our founder:

> "Starting a new Whole Grains franchise is both expensive and difficult. However, when done properly, it brings financial rewards and a strong sense of personal satisfaction."

Sincerely,

Firstname Lastname
Manager

Enclosure
Financing brochure

Copy to: Mr. Anthony Splendora, CEO

Lesson 5—Apply

In this project, you will open and edit an existing document to create a modified block format business letter. You will also create an envelope for the letter.

DIRECTIONS

1. Start Word, if necessary, and open **W05Apply** from the data files for this lesson.
2. Save the file as **W05Apply_xx** in the location where your teacher instructs you to store the files for this lesson.
3. Display the rulers and nonprinting characters, if necessary.
4. Press CTRL + A to select all text in the document.
5. Open the Paragraph dialog box, and click the **Tabs** button to open the Tabs dialog box.
6. Verify that **Left** is the selected alignment, type **3.25** in the **Tab stop position** box, and then click **OK**. This sets a left tab stop in the center of the document page.
7. Position the insertion point at the beginning of the first line of the return address, and press TAB. The text on the line advances to the tab stop.
8. Tab the remaining two lines in the return address to the tab stop.
9. Delete the sample text **Today's Date**, and press TAB to advance the insertion point to the tab stop.
10. Insert the eighth format in the Available formats list in the Date and Time dialog box.
11. Select the inside address and replace it with the following:

    Mr. Cameron McGill
    Franchisee
    Whole Grains Bread
    222 Oak Hill Avenue
    Omaha, NE 68180
12. Edit the salutation line to **Dear Mr. McGill:**
13. Position the insertion point at the beginning of the Closing line (*Sincerely,*) and press TAB to advance the text.
14. Delete the sample text **Student's Name**, press TAB to advance the insertion point to the tab stop, and type your name.
15. Tab the Job Title line in to the tab stop.
16. Insert the **Confidential 1** watermark.
17. Save the changes to the document.
18. Create an envelope for the letter, using the inside address as the delivery address and **320 Magnolia Avenue, Larkspur, CA 94939** as the return address.
19. Add the envelope to the document without changing the default return address. To remove the watermark from the envelope, double-click in the header area of the envelope and then, on the **HEADER & FOOTER TOOLS DESIGN** tab, in the Options group, click **Different First Page**. The document should look similar to Figure 5-3 on the next page.
20. **With your teacher's permission**, print both the letter and the envelope.
21. Close the document, saving changes, and exit Word.

Figure 5-3

320 Magnolia Avenue
Larkspur, CA 94939

Mr. Cameron McGill
Franchisee
Whole Grains Bread
222 Oak Hill Avenue
Omaha, NE 68180

Word 2013, Windows 8, Microsoft Corporation

Whole Grains Bread
320 Magnolia Avenue
Larkspur, CA 94939

Aug. 7, 17

CERTIFIED MAIL

Mr. Cameron McGill
Franchisee
Whole Grains Bread
222 Oak Hill Avenue
Omaha, NE 68180

Dear Mr. McGill:

Subject: New franchise opportunity

Thanks for your interest in opening an additional franchise outside of California. In response to your question, I have enclosed a financing brochure. In general, we believe you will need the following funds:

$125,500.00
$21,250.00
$5,400.00

The challenges and rewards of starting a new Whole Grains Bread franchise can be summed up by the following quote from our founder:

> "Starting a new Whole Grains franchise is both expensive and difficult. However, when done properly, it brings financial rewards and a strong sense of personal satisfaction."

Sincerely,

Firstname Lastname
Manager

Enclosure
Financing brochure

Copy to: Mr. Anthony Splendora, CEO

Word 2013, Windows 8, Microsoft Corporation

Lesson 6

Formatting Text with Fonts and Effects

WORDS TO KNOW

Cover letter
A personal business letter that you send with your resume when you apply for a job.

Font
A complete set of characters in a specific design, style, and size.

Font color
The color of a font set.

Font effects
Enhancements applied to font characters.

Font size
The uppercase letter height in a font set.

Font style
The slant and weight of characters in a font set.

Sans serif
A font with straight edges.

Script
A font that looks like handwriting.

Serif
A font with curved or extended edges.

Thank-you letter
A letter you send after a job interview to thank the interviewer and review important points.

Theme fonts
The default font sets applied with a theme.

➤ What You Will Learn

Changing the Font
Changing the Font Size
Changing the Font Color
Applying Font Styles and Effects
Applying Underlines
Clearing Formatting
Editing a Built-In Style
Writing a Personal Business Letter

Software Skills Write personal business letters to communicate with businesses such as your bank or your insurance company, or to apply for a job. Fonts are a basic means of applying formatting to text and characters. They can set a mood, command attention, and convey a message.

What You Can Do

Changing the Font

- Microsoft Office 2013 comes with built-in **fonts**; you can install additional fonts.
- Each font set includes upper- and lowercase letters, numbers, and punctuation marks.
- There are three basic categories of fonts:
  - **Serif** fonts are easy to read and are often used for document text.
  - **Sans serif** fonts are often used for headings.
  - **Script** fonts are often used to simulate handwriting on invitations or announcements.
- A fourth font category includes decorative fonts that may have embellishments such as curlicues or double lines designed to dress up or enhance the characters.
- The current font name displays in the Font box on the HOME tab of the Ribbon.
- The default font for the Office theme Normal style is Calibri.

- Click the Font box drop-down arrow in the Font group or on the Mini toolbar to display a gallery of available fonts. The fonts display in alphabetical order, but **theme fonts** and recently used fonts are listed at the top.

  ✓ *Refer to Word, Lesson 2 for information about themes.*

- On a tablet, select the text you want to format, then tap it to display the Mini toolbar.
- You can also type the name of the font you want to use directly into the Font box or select a font in the Font dialog box.
- You can set the tone of a document by putting thought into the fonts you select.
- More than two or three fonts in one document look disjointed and unprofessional.
- You can change the font of existing text, or you can select a font before you type new text.
- To preview how selected text will look in a particular font, rest the mouse pointer on the font name in the Font list.

Try It! Changing the Font

1. Start Word, and open **W06Try** from the data files for this lesson. Save it as **W06Try_xx** in the location where your teacher instructs you to store the files for this lesson.
2. Select the text *African Safari*.
3. On the HOME tab, in the Font group, click the Font drop-down arrow [Calibri (Body)] to display a list of available fonts.
4. Scroll down the list and click Broadway to change the font of the selected text.

   ✓ *You can quickly scroll the list by typing the first character or two of a font name. For example, type* [B] [R] *to scroll to fonts beginning with the letters BR.*

5. Select the two full paragraphs of text.
6. In the Font group, click the Font drop-down arrow [Calibri (Body)], scroll down the list, and click Times New Roman.

   ✓ *The fonts installed on your system may not be the same as those shown in the figure.*

7. Save the changes to the document, and leave it open to use in the next Try It.

Change the font

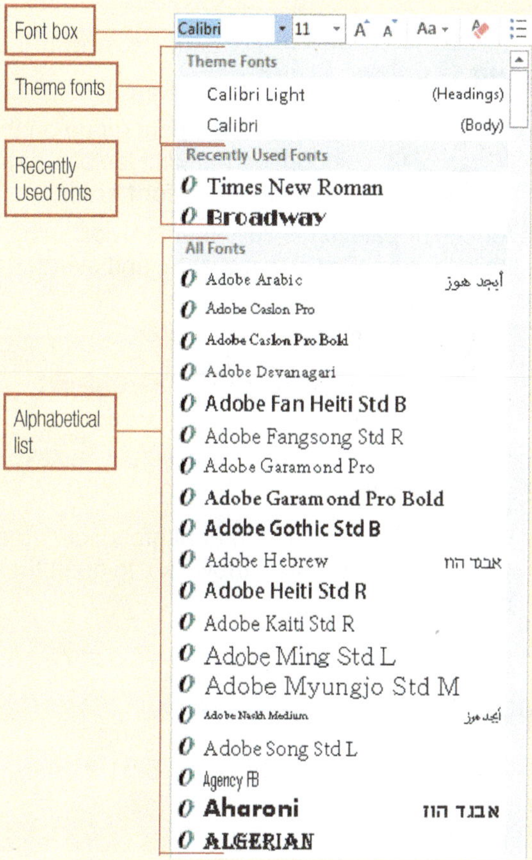

Word 2013, Windows 8, Microsoft Corporation

Changing the Font Size

- **Font size** is measured in points. There are 72 points in an inch.
- The default font size for the Office theme Normal style is 11 points.
- The current font size displays in the Font Size box on the HOME tab of the Ribbon.
- Click the Font Size drop-down arrow [11] in the Font group or on the Mini toolbar to display a gallery of font sizes.

- Alternatively, you can select a font size in the Font dialog box, or type a specific font size in the Font Size box.
- You can also use the Increase Font Size A and Decrease Font Size A buttons to adjust the font size by set increments.

Try It! Changing the Font Size

1. In the W06Try_xx document, select the text *African Safari*.
2. On the HOME tab, in the Font group, click the Font Size drop-down arrow 11 to display a list of font sizes.
3. Click 28 to change the font size of the selected text.
4. Select the two full paragraphs of text.
5. In the Font group, click the Decrease Font Size button A to reduce the font size by 1 point to 10 points.
6. In the Font group, click Increase Font Size A button twice to increase the font size by 2 points to 12 points.
7. Save the changes to the document, and leave it open to use in the next Try It.

Changing the Font Color

- Use the Font Color palette in the Font group on the HOME tab of the Ribbon, on the Mini toolbar, or in the Font dialog box to change the **font color**.
- The font color palette displays theme colors, which are the colors applied with a theme, and standard colors.
- When you select a font color, consider how people will be viewing the document. For example, will it be printed or displayed on a monitor?
- Also consider who will be viewing the document. For example, a business letter to a bank should not include pastel colors such as light blue or pink, or bold colors such as bright orange or yellow.

Try It! Changing the Font Color

1. In the W06Try_xx document, select the text *African Safari*.
2. On the HOME tab, in the Font group, click the Font Color drop-down arrow A to open the color palette.
3. Under Standard Colors, click Blue (third from right) to change the color of the selected text.
4. Save the changes to the document, and leave it open to use in the next Try It.

Applying Font Styles and Effects

- The most common **font styles** are bold **B** and italic *I* .
- When a font has no style applied, it is called regular.
- Font styles can be combined, such as bold italic.
- Font styles are available in the Font group on the HOME tab of the Ribbon, on the Mini toolbar, or in the Font dialog box.
- You can also use shortcut key combinations to apply font styles.
  - Bold **B** .... CTRL + B
  - Italic *I* .... CTRL + I
- **Font effects** include formatting options applied to regular font characters. Common font effects include strikethrough, superscript, and subscript.
- Some font effects are available in the Font group on the HOME tab of the Ribbon; they are all available in the Font dialog box.
- Font styles and effects are toggles; click the button once to apply the formatting, and then click it again to remove the formatting.

✓ *Font effects are not the same as text effects. Text effects are covered in Word, Lesson 10.*

Try It! Applying Font Styles and Effects

1. In the **W06Try_xx** document, select the text *Voyager Travel Adventures* in the first sentence.
2. On the HOME tab, in the Font group, click the Bold **B** button to apply the bold style to the selected text.
3. Click the Font group dialog box launcher to open the Font dialog box.
4. In the Effects area, click to select the Small caps check box.
5. Click OK to close the dialog box and apply the effect.
6. Save the changes to the document, and leave it open to use in the next Try It.

Font dialog box

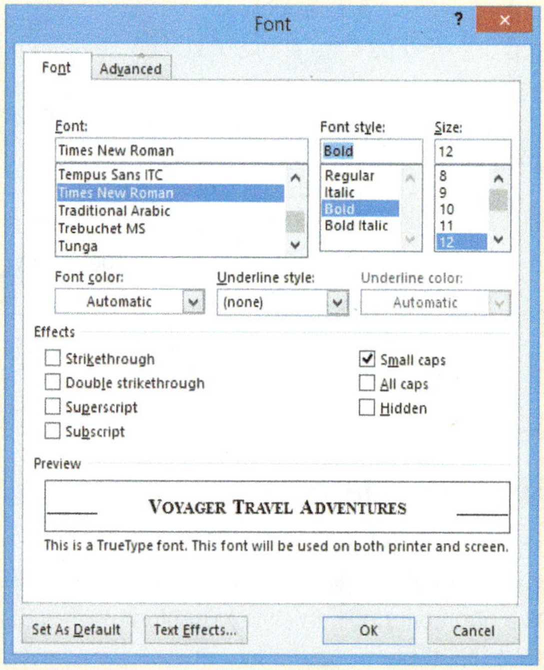

Word 2013, Windows 8, Microsoft Corporation

Applying Underlines

- There are 17 types of underline styles available in Word, which include:
  - Single (underlines all characters, including nonprinting characters such as spaces and tabs)
  - Words only
  - Double
  - Dotted
- Some underlines are available from the Underline gallery in the Font group on the HOME tab of the Ribbon, or you can select from the complete list in the Font dialog box.
- Press CTRL + U to apply the default single underline.
- By default, the underline color matches the current font color. You can select a different color from the Underline color palette off the Underline gallery or in the Font dialog box.

Try It! Applying Underlines

1. In the **W06Try_xx** document, select the text *African Safari*.
2. On the HOME tab, in the Font group, click the Underline **U** button to apply a single underline.
3. Click the Underline drop-down arrow **U** to display the gallery of underline styles and then click Wave underline to apply it to the text.
4. Click the Underline drop-down arrow **U** again and click Underline Color to display the underline color palette.
5. Under Standard Colors, click Dark Red (the first color on the left) to change the color of the underline.
6. Save the changes to the document, and leave it open to use in the next Try It.

Clearing Formatting

- Use the Clear All Formatting button in the Font group on the HOME tab of the Ribbon to remove all formatting from a selection.
- You can also use the shortcut key combination CTRL + SPACE.

Try It! Clearing Formatting

1. Select all text in the W06Try_xx document.
2. On the HOME tab, in the Font group, click the Clear All Formatting button to remove all formatting from the selection.
3. Save the changes to the document, and leave it open to use in the next Try It.

Editing a Built-In Style

- You learned in Lesson 2 how to apply a built-in style from the Styles gallery.
- You can edit a built-in style to customize formats for your document.
- When you modify a style that has already been applied to text in the document, the formatting is updated to reflect the changes to the style.
- If you modify a style and give it a new name, it becomes a new style; the original style remains unchanged.
- You can quickly modify a style by changing the formatting and then updating the style in the Quick Styles gallery.
- When you want to modify any or all of the style properties at the same time, you can use the Modify Style dialog box.

Try It! Editing a Built-In Style

1. In the W06Try_xx document, click in the first paragraph and then click Heading 1 in the Styles gallery.
2. Select the heading text, click the Font drop-down arrow, and select Times New Roman from the Recently Used Fonts list.
3. With the text still selected, click the Decrease Font Size button A one time to reduce font size to 14.
4. With the text still selected, click the Bold button **B** .
5. With the text still selected, right-click the Heading 1 style in the Styles gallery and click Update Heading 1 to Match Selection. Note that the Heading 1 style in the Styles gallery now shows the same formats that you applied to text.
6. Close W06Try_xx, saving changes, and exit Word.

Writing a Personal Business Letter

- A personal business letter is written on behalf of an individual instead of on behalf of another business.
- A personal business letter may be full block or modified block. It usually includes a return address and contact information such as telephone number or e-mail address—unless it is printed on paper that has a letterhead. It does not usually include a title line or reference initials.
- A **cover letter** is a personal business letter that you send with your resume when you apply for a job. You use a cover letter to introduce yourself and to highlight the qualities that make you suitable for the position.
- A cover letter should be short and to the point. You address it to the person who is responsible for hiring. If you do not know the person's name, title, and address, you should call the company and ask.
- Include the following in any cover letter:
  - The job title for the position you want.
  - Where you learned about the position.
  - The skills that qualify you for the position.
  - Your contact information.
- Be sure to thank the reader for his or her time and consideration, and to correct all spelling and grammatical errors.
- A well-written and well-organized cover letter helps you make a positive impression. It shows that you have taken the time to match your qualifications with a specific job.
- After a job interview, you can improve your chances of being hired by sending a **thank-you letter**.
- Use this letter to thank the interviewer and reiterate your interest in the job.
- You can also remind the interviewer of your strengths and how they may be of value in the job.
- If you feel you did not adequately describe your qualifications for the job during the interview, you can use the thank-you letter to deliver that information.

✓ *For information on writing other types of business letters, refer to Word, Lesson 5.*

Lesson 6—Practice

You are looking for a summer job in recreation management. In this project, you will write a personal business letter to Voyager Travel Adventures asking about job opportunities. You will try out different font and text formatting options to see how they affect the document.

DIRECTIONS

1. Start Word, if necessary, create a new document, and save the document as **W06Practice_xx** in the location where your teacher instructs you to store the files for this lesson.
2. Display the rulers and nonprinting characters, if necessary.
3. Apply the **No Spacing** style to set the line spacing to single and the paragraph spacing to 0 points before and after.
4. On the HOME tab, in the Font group, click the **Font** drop-down arrow Calibri (Body) and click **Times New Roman** to change the font.
5. Click the **Font Size** drop-down arrow 11 and click **12** to change the font size.
6. Type your own return address, pressing ENTER after each line.
7. Press ENTER to leave a blank line. Click the **INSERT** tab, then, in the Text group, click the **Date & Time** button to open the Date and Time dialog box.
8. Click today's date in the month day, year format (third from the top) and then click **OK** to insert the date.
9. Press ENTER four times to leave blank space, then type the following inside address, pressing ENTER after each line:

   Ms. Maria Sanchez
   Human Resources Manager
   Voyager Travel Adventures
   1635 Logan Street
   Denver, CO 80205

10. Press ENTER to leave a blank line, then type **Dear Ms. Sanchez:** and press ENTER twice.
11. Type the following paragraphs, pressing ENTER twice to leave space between them, as shown in Figure 6-1:

    I am writing to inquire about summer job opportunities or internships as a tour leader at Voyager Travel Adventures. My uncle, who traveled with your company to Costa Rica last year, suggested that I contact you.

    I am currently pursuing a degree in recreation management and I think a position at Voyager Travel Adventures would fit my interests and abilities. Last summer, I worked as a camp counselor. My responsibilities included leading groups of campers on backpacking and kayaking trips. I am also a certified lifeguard. I believe that my experience, education, and knowledge of nature and first aid make me uniquely qualified to work for you.

    I would appreciate the opportunity to meet with you to discuss possible employment options. I look forward to hearing from you.
12. Press ENTER twice, type **Sincerely,** and press ENTER four times.
13. Type your name, press ENTER, and type your phone number.
14. Press ENTER and type your e-mail address.
15. Select the text **Human Resources Manager** in the inside address.
16. Click the **HOME** tab, then, in the Font group, click the **Italic** button *I* to apply italic to the selection.
17. Click the **Italic** button *I* again to remove the style.

Figure 6-1

Student Street Address
City, State postalcode

Today's Date

Ms. Maria Sanchez
Human Resources Manager
VOYAGER TRAVEL ADVENTURES
1635 Logan Street
Denver, CO 80205

Dear Ms. Sanchez:

I am writing to inquire about summer job opportunities or internships as a tour leader at Voyager Travel Adventures. My uncle, who traveled with your company to Costa Rica last year, suggested that I contact you.

I am currently pursuing a degree in recreation management and I think a position at Voyager Travel Adventures would fit my interests and abilities. Last summer, I worked as a camp counselor. My responsibilities included leading groups of campers on backpacking and kayaking trips. I am also a certified lifeguard. I believe that my experience, education, and knowledge of nature and first aid make me uniquely qualified to work for you.

I would appreciate the opportunity to meet with you to discuss possible employment options. I look forward to hearing from you.

Sincerely,

Firstname Lastname
Phone number
Email address

18. Select the text *Voyager Travel Adventures* in the inside address.
19. Click the **Font** group dialog box launcher to open the Font dialog box.
20. Click to select the **Small caps** check box, and then click **OK** to apply the effect.
21. With the text still selected, click the **Bold** button **B** to apply bold to the selection.
22. With the text still selected, click the **Font Color** drop-down arrow to display the Font Color palette.
23. Under Standard Colors, click **Purple** (last color on the right) to apply it to the selection.
24. With the text still selected, click the **Underline** button arrow **U** to display the gallery of underline styles.
25. Click the **Thick underline** style (third in the list) to apply it to the selection.
26. **With your teacher's permission**, print the letter. It should look similar to Figure 6-1 on the previous page.
27. Close the document, saving changes, and exit Word.

Lesson 6—Apply

In this project, you will open an existing document and edit it to create a thank-you letter for a job interview at Michigan Avenue Athletic Club.

DIRECTIONS

1. Start Word, if necessary, and open **W06Apply** from the data files for this lesson.
2. Save the file as **W06Apply_xx** in the location where your teacher instructs you to store the files for this lesson.
3. Display the rulers and nonprinting characters, if necessary.
4. Press CTRL + A to select all text in the document.
5. Click the **Clear Formatting** button to remove all formatting in the document, and then apply the **No Spacing** style.
6. Right-click the **No Spacing style** in the Styles gallery, and then click **Modify**.
7. In the Modify Style dialog box, type **Arial** in the **Font** box, type **13** in the Size box, and then click **OK** to change the style formatting to 13-point Arial.
8. Replace the sample return address with your own address.
9. Replace the sample date with the current date.
10. Replace the first two lines of the inside address with the following:

    Ms. Jen Chu
    Assistant Personnel Director
11. Change the font of the company name to **Georgia** and increase the font size to **14** points.
12. Edit the salutation line to **Dear Ms. Chu:**
13. Edit the first paragraph of the letter body to the following:

    Thank you for taking the time to meet with me to discuss summer job opportunities at Michigan Avenue Athletic Club. I enjoyed meeting you and seeing the Athletic Club's state-of-the-art fitness facilities.
14. Edit the second paragraph of the letter body to the following:

    You mentioned that the Athletic Club plans to start youth day camps this summer. I believe I could be a strong asset in this program. When we talked, I did not have a chance to tell you that last summer, I worked as a camp counselor at Pine Acres Day Camp. My responsibilities included teaching swimming classes, organizing H2O Fun Day, and leading fitness sessions for campers and counselors of all ages. As I indicated when we talked, I am a certified lifeguard and have completed about half my coursework toward a degree in recreation management.
15. Select the text *Pine Acres Day Camp* and apply italic with a double underline.
16. Select the character *2* in H_2O and apply the subscript font effect.

17. Edit the third paragraph of the letter body to the following:

    Thank you again for speaking with me. I look forward to hearing from you soon and spending my summer at Michigan Avenue Athletic Club!

18. Replace the sample text *Student's Name* with your own name.
19. Replace the sample text *Telephone number* with your own number.
20. Replace the sample text *Email address* with your own e-mail address.
21. **With your teacher's permission**, print the letter. It should look similar to Figure 6-2.
22. Close the document, saving changes, and exit Word.

Figure 6-2

Street Address
City, State postal code

Today's Date

Ms. Jen Chu
Assistant Personnel Director
Michigan Avenue Athletic Club
235 Michigan Avenue
Chicago, IL 60601

Dear Ms. Chu:

Thank you for taking the time to meet with me to discuss summer job opportunities at Michigan Avenue Athletic Club. I enjoyed meeting you and seeing the Athletic Club's state-of-the-art fitness facilities.

You mentioned that the Athletic Club plans to start youth day camps this summer. I believe I could be a strong asset in this program. When we talked, I did not have a chance to tell you that last summer, I worked as a camp counselor at *Pine Acres Day Camp*. My responsibilities included teaching swimming classes, organizing H_2O Fun Day, and leading fitness sessions for campers and counselors of all ages. As I indicated when we talked, I am a certified lifeguard and have completed about half my coursework toward a degree in recreation management.

Thank you again for speaking with me. I look forward to hearing from you soon and spending my summer at Michigan Avenue Athletic Club!

Sincerely,

Firstname Lastname
Telephone number
Email address

Word 2013, Windows 8, Microsoft Corporation

Lesson 7

Formatting and Sorting Lists

➤ What You Will Learn

Creating a Bulleted List
Creating a Numbered List
Changing the Bullet or Number Formatting
Creating a Multilevel List
Sorting Paragraphs

Software Skills Lists are an effective way to present items of information. Use a bulleted list when the items do not have to be in any particular order, like a grocery list or a list of objectives. Use a numbered list when the order of the items is important, such as directions or instructions. Use a multilevel list to show an outline of items or subordination of some items to others. Use Sort to organize a list into alphabetical or numerical order.

WORDS TO KNOW

Bullet
A dot or symbol that marks an important line of information or designates items in a list.

Multilevel list
A list that has a hierarchical structure that indicates the relationship between items in the list.

Picture
A graphics image stored in a graphics file format.

Sort
To organize items into a specified order.

Symbol
A visual element such as a shape or mathematical or scientific notation that you can insert as a character into a document.

What You Can Do

Creating a Bulleted List

- Use **bullets** to mark items in a list when the order does not matter.
- To apply the current bullet formatting, click the Bullets button in the Paragraph group on the HOME tab of the Ribbon or on the Mini toolbar.
- By default, the bullet symbol for the Office theme is a simple black dot, indented 0.25" from the left margin. The symbol is followed by a 0.25" left tab, and the text on subsequent lines is indented to 0.25".
- You can select a different bullet from the Bullet Library.
- You can also define a new bullet using a **symbol** or a **picture**.
- Once you select a different bullet, it becomes the current bullet. It is also added to the Recently Used Bullets area in the Bullet Library.
- You can select bullet formatting before you start a list, or you can apply it to existing paragraphs. Bullet formatting is not affected by changes in line spacing.
- Word automatically carries bullet formatting forward to new paragraphs in a list.
- To end a bulleted list, press ENTER twice or click the Bullets button.
- To remove bullet formatting, select the bulleted paragraph(s) and select None in the Bullet Library.

Try It! Creating a Bulleted List

1. Start Word, and create a blank document. Save it as **W07TryA_xx**.
2. On the HOME tab, in the Paragraph group, click the Bullets button.
3. Type **Milk**, and then press ENTER.
4. Type **Orange juice**, and then press ENTER twice to turn off bullet formatting.
5. Select the two items in the bulleted list.
6. Click the Bullets drop-down arrow to open the Bullet Library.
7. Click the check mark bullet symbol.
8. With the two bulleted items still selected, click the Line and Paragraph Spacing button and click 2.0. Then click Undo to restore default line spacing.
9. With the two bulleted items still selected, click the Bullets drop-down arrow to open the Bullet Library.
10. Click Define New Bullet to open the Define New Bullet dialog box.
11. Click Symbol to open the Symbol dialog box. The characters that are part of the Wingdings font set display.

    ✓ *You can select a different font set from the Font drop-down list.*

12. Click the font drop-down arrow, scroll up, and click Symbol. Click the heart-shaped symbol and then click OK.
13. Click OK in the Define New Bullet dialog box to apply the symbol as the bullet.
14. With the two bulleted items still selected, click the Bullets drop-down arrow to open the Bullet Library.

Bullet Library

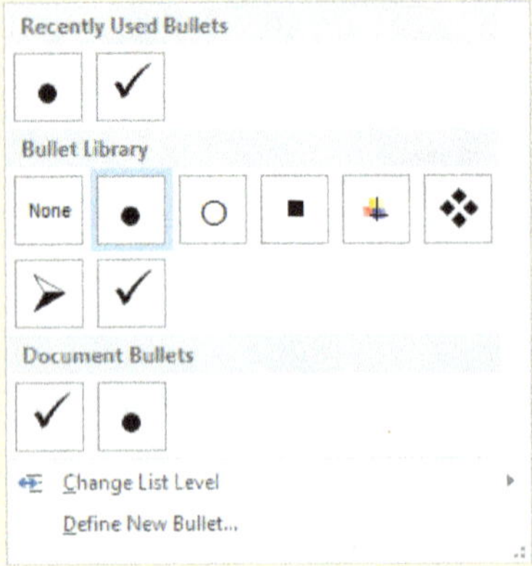

Word 2013, Windows 8, Microsoft Corporation

15. Click Define New Bullet to open the Define New Bullet dialog box.
16. Click Picture to open the Insert Pictures dialog box. You have the options of browsing for a picture on your computer, finding a picture on Office.com, or searching for a picture using Bing.

    ✓ *You learn more about working with pictures in Word, Lesson 8.*

17. Click Office.com Clip Art, and then, in the text box, type **bullet**.
18. Click the Search button. A gallery of pictures that match the search term bullet displays.
19. Click the right-pointing red arrow in the second row of search results (the ScreenTip says Red arrow bullet icon), and then click Insert.
20. Click OK in the Define New Bullet dialog box to apply the picture as the bullet.
21. Save the changes to the document, and leave it open to use in the next Try It.

Creating a Numbered List

- Use numbers to mark items in a list when the order matters, such as for directions or how-to steps.
- Word automatically renumbers a list when you add or delete items.
- By default, Word continues list numbering sequentially. You can select to restart numbering in the middle of a list, and you can set the numbering value if you want to start at a number other than 1.
- To apply the current number formatting, click the Numbering button in the Paragraph group on the HOME tab of the Ribbon.

- The default numbering style for the Office theme is an Arabic numeral followed by a period.
- You can select a different number format from the Numbering Library.
- Once you select a different number format, it becomes the current format. It is also added to the Recently Used Number Formats area in the Numbering Library.
- You can select number formatting before you start a list, or you can apply it to existing paragraphs.
- Word automatically carries numbering forward to new paragraphs in a list.
- To end a numbered list, press ENTER twice, or click the Numbering button.

Try It! Creating a Numbered List

1. In **W07TryA_xx**, move the insertion point to the end of the document and press ENTER.
2. On the HOME tab, in the Paragraph group click the Numbering button.
3. Type **Turn left on Main Street.** Press ENTER.
4. Type **Bear right at the fork.** Press ENTER.
5. Type **Go straight for 3 miles to destination.** Press ENTER.
6. Right-click the list number 4 to display a shortcut menu.
7. Click Restart at 1. Word changes the 4 to a 1.
8. Right-click the number 1 marking the fourth item in the list.
9. On the shortcut menu, click Continue Numbering. Word changes the 1 back to a 4.
10. Type **Park behind the building.** Press ENTER twice.
11. Right-click the number 1 marking the first item in the numbered list.
12. On the shortcut menu, click Set Numbering Value.
13. Use the Set value to increment arrows to enter 5 in the box, and then click OK. Word changes the first number to a 5, and renumbers the other items in the list accordingly.
14. Select all the lines in the numbered list.
15. In the Paragraph group, click the Numbering drop-down arrow to open the Numbering Library.
16. Click the list that uses lowercase letters followed by parentheses.
17. Save the changes to the document, and leave it open to use in the next Try It.

Changing the Bullet or Number Formatting

- You can create a customized bullet or number by changing the font and/or paragraph formatting.
- The commands for changing the font and paragraph formatting are the same as for changing the formatting of regular text.

Try It! Changing the Bullet or Number Formatting

1. In the **W07TryA_xx** document, right-click the first picture bullet and click Font on the shortcut menu to open the Font dialog box.
2. Type **14** in the Size box (or click 14 on the Size list).
3. Click OK to apply the formatting.
4. Right-click the first picture bullet and click Paragraph on the shortcut menu to open the Paragraph dialog box.
5. Select the value in the By text box and type **.75** to increase the Hanging indent setting to 0.75".
6. Click OK to apply the formatting. Notice that is applied to the current line only.
7. Right-click any of the numbers (the letters followed by parentheses) and click Font on the shortcut menu to open the Font dialog box.
8. Click Bold Italic in the Font style list.

(continued)

Try It! Changing the Bullet or Number Formatting *(continued)*

9. Click 18 on the Size list.
10. Click the Font color drop-down arrow and click Red under Standard Colors.
11. Click OK to apply the formatting.
12. Select all the lines in the numbered list.
13. Right-click the selection and click Paragraph on the shortcut menu to open the Paragraph dialog box.
14. Use the Left increment arrows to increase the left indent setting to 1.0".
15. Click OK to apply the formatting.
16. Save the changes to the document, and close it. Leave Word open to use in the next Try It.

Creating a Multilevel List

- Use Word's **multilevel list** styles to format items into a list that has more than one level.
- Each level in the list has different formatting so you can clearly see the relationship between items.
- To apply multilevel list formatting, select the list style from the gallery of Multilevel List styles, and then type the list.
- Decrease the level of an item by pressing TAB or by clicking the Increase Indent button on the HOME tab.
- Increase the level by pressing ENTER twice, by pressing SHIFT + TAB, or by clicking the Decrease Indent button.
- You can change the style of a multilevel list by selecting the list and clicking a different style in the List Library.

Try It! Creating a Multilevel List

1. Start Word, create a blank document, and save the document as **W07TryB_xx** in the location where your teacher instructs you to store the files for this lesson.
2. On the HOME tab, in the Paragraph group, click the Multilevel List button.
3. In the List Library, click the style in the middle of the first row.
4. Type **Microsoft Office 2013** and press ENTER.
5. Press TAB, type **Microsoft Word**, and press ENTER.
6. Click the Increase Indent button, type **Word processing**, and press ENTER.
7. Press SHIFT + TAB, type **Microsoft Excel**, and press ENTER.
8. Type **Microsoft PowerPoint** and press ENTER three times to end the list.
9. Select all list items, click the Multilevel List button, and click the first style on the third row.
10. Close **W07TryB_xx**, saving changes. Leave Word open to use in the next Try It.

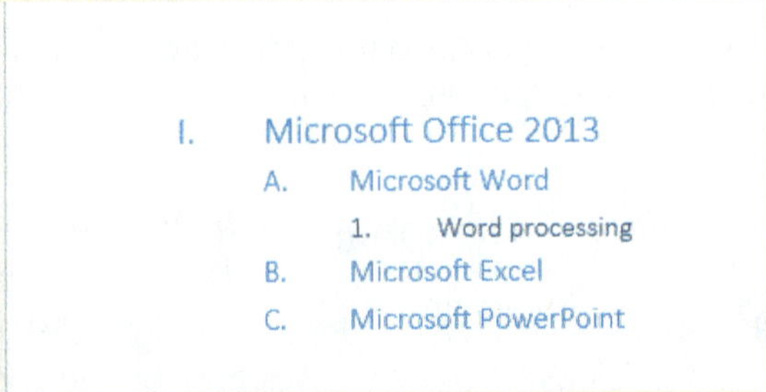

Word 2013, Windows 8, Microsoft Corporation

Sorting Paragraphs

- Use the Sort feature to **sort** paragraphs into alphabetical, numerical, or chronological order. Word identifies the type of sort automatically.
- A sort can be ascending (A to Z or 0 to 9) or descending (Z to A or 9 to 0).
- The default sort order is alphabetical ascending.

Try It! Sorting Paragraphs

1. Open **W07TryC** from the data files for this lesson. Save the file as **W07TryC_xx** in the location where your teacher instructs you to store the files for this lesson.
2. Select the items in the bulleted list.
3. On the HOME tab, in the Paragraph group, click the Sort button to open the Sort Text dialog box.
4. Click OK to sort the list in ascending alphabetical order.
5. Click the Sort button again to open the Sort Text dialog box.
6. Click the Descending option, then click OK to reverse the sort into descending alphabetical order.
7. Select the four numbers.
8. In the Paragraph group, click the Sort button to open the Sort Text dialog box. Notice that Word selects Number as the sort type. The sort order is still set to Descending, because that was the last option you used.
9. Click OK to sort the list into descending numerical order.
10. Click the Sort button again, click the Ascending option, and then click OK to reverse the sort into ascending numerical order.
11. Close the document, saving changes, and exit Word.

Lesson 7—Practice

As the customer service manager at the Michigan Avenue Athletic Club, you have recently received a number of complaints about the club's check-in policy for members who forget their ID badges. In this project, you will create a memo to employees about the proper check-in procedure. You will use a bulleted list and a numbered list, and you will sort the bulleted list into alphabetical order.

DIRECTIONS

1. Start Word, if necessary.
2. Create a new blank document, and save it as **W07Practice_xx** in the location where your teacher instructs you to store the files for this lesson.
3. Display the rulers and nonprinting characters, if necessary.
4. Set paragraph spacing **Before** to **24** points and paragraph spacing **After** to **36** points.
5. Type **MEMO**, and press ENTER.
6. Apply the **No Spacing** style, and set a left tab stop at **0.75"** on the horizontal ruler.
7. Type **To:**, press TAB, and type **Desk Management Associates**. Press ENTER.
8. Type **From:**, press TAB, and type your own name. Press ENTER.
9. Type **Date:**, press TAB, and type or insert today's date. Press ENTER.
10. Type **Subject:**, press TAB, and type **Check-in Procedures**. Press ENTER twice.
11. Apply the Normal style and type the following paragraph: **In an effort to reduce the wait at the reception desk for members who forget to bring their ID badges, we are implementing new procedures. Please review the following, and post this memo where you can refer to it as necessary.**
12. Press ENTER, then type **Check-in Procedure** and press ENTER.
13. On the **HOME** tab, in the Paragraph group, click the **Numbering** button to apply the default numbered list format—an Arabic numeral followed by a period—and then type the following four list items, pressing ENTER between each item:

Greet member politely.

Ask to see picture identification, such as a driver's license or school ID card.

Enter the member's name and the type of ID in the Forgotten Badge Log book.

Press buzzer to allow member to enter.

14. Press Enter twice to turn off numbering.
15. Type **Check-in Guidelines** and press Enter.
16. On the **HOME** tab, in the Paragraph group, click the **Bullets** drop-down arrow to display the Bullets Library.
17. Click the diamond pattern bullet (refer to Figure 7-1).
18. Type the following list items, pressing Enter between each item:

    Never let a member wait more than two minutes.

    Call a manager if there is a problem.

    Always be polite and patient.

    Remember that members take priority over telephone calls and co-workers.

19. Press Enter twice and type **Thank you for your cooperation.**
20. Select the items in the bulleted list. On the **HOME** tab, in the Paragraph group, click the **Sort** button to open the Sort Text dialog box.
21. Verify that the **Ascending** option is selected, and then click **OK** to sort the list into ascending alphabetical order.
22. **With your teacher's permission**, print the memo. It should look similar to Figure 7-1.
23. Close the document, saving changes, and exit Word.

Figure 7-1

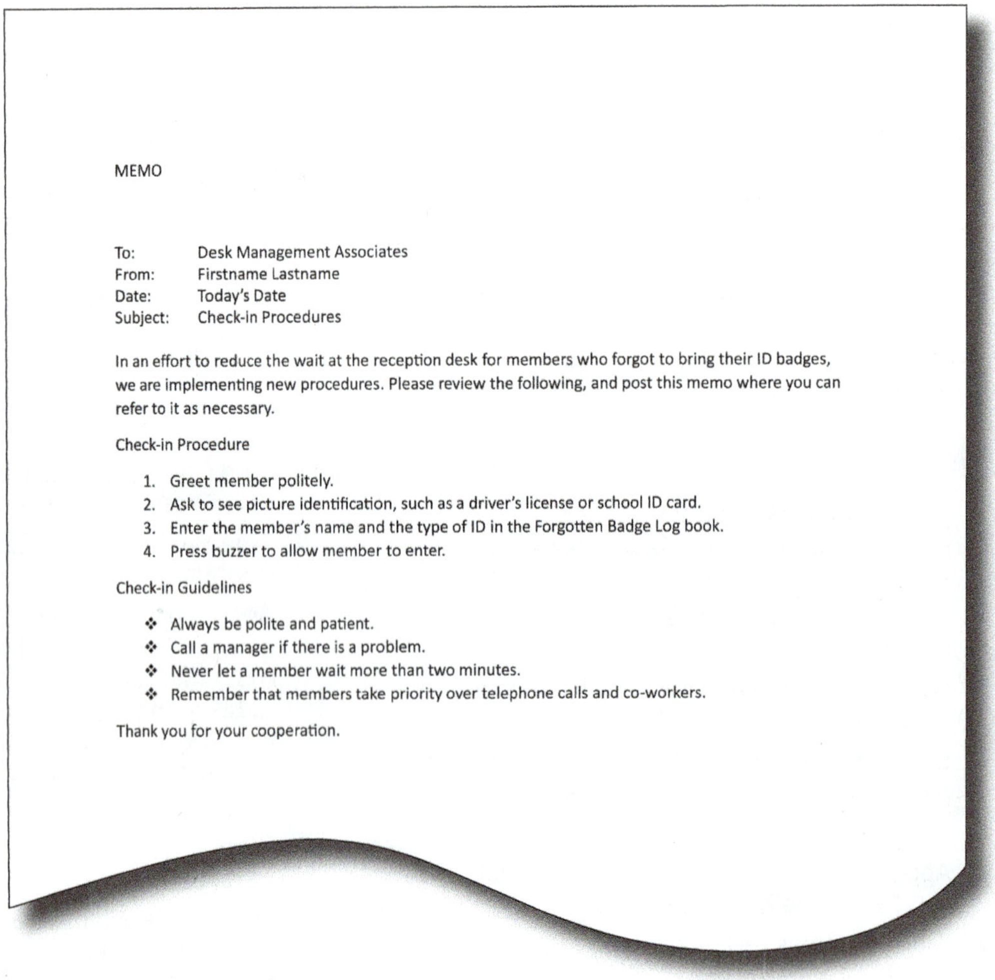

MEMO

To: Desk Management Associates
From: Firstname Lastname
Date: Today's Date
Subject: Check-in Procedures

In an effort to reduce the wait at the reception desk for members who forgot to bring their ID badges, we are implementing new procedures. Please review the following, and post this memo where you can refer to it as necessary.

Check-in Procedure

1. Greet member politely.
2. Ask to see picture identification, such as a driver's license or school ID card.
3. Enter the member's name and the type of ID in the Forgotten Badge Log book.
4. Press buzzer to allow member to enter.

Check-in Guidelines

- Always be polite and patient.
- Call a manager if there is a problem.
- Never let a member wait more than two minutes.
- Remember that members take priority over telephone calls and co-workers.

Thank you for your cooperation.

Word 2013, Windows 8, Microsoft Corporation

Lesson 7—Apply

In this project, you will revise an existing memo to Michigan Avenue Athletic Club employees so you can send it to club members.

DIRECTIONS

1. Start Word, if necessary, and open **W07Apply** from the data files for this lesson.
2. Save it as **W07Apply_xx** in the location where your teacher instructs you to store the files for this lesson.
3. Display the rulers and nonprinting characters, if necessary.
4. Select the text **MEMO** and change the font to **Calibri Light** and the font size to **24** points.
5. Replace the sample text *Student's Name* with your own name.
6. Replace the sample text *Today's Date* with the current date.
7. Select the text *If you forget your badge:* and apply the **Bold** font style and a **single, black underline**.
8. Select the next four lines and apply the numbering format that uses Arabic numbers followed by a parenthesis.
9. Select the four lines beginning with the word *Attend*.
10. Apply bullet list formatting using the check mark bullet symbol.
11. Sort the bulleted list into descending alphabetical order.
12. **With your teacher's permission**, print the memo. It should look similar to Figure 7-2.
13. Close the document, saving changes, and exit Word.

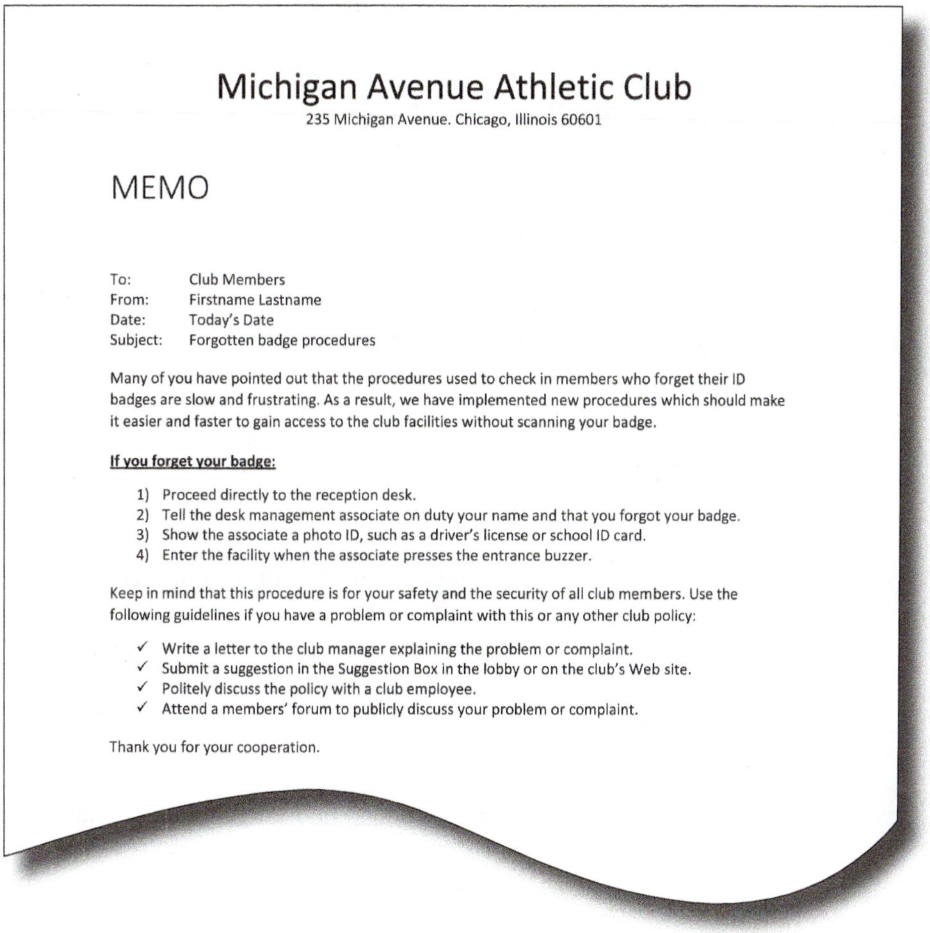

Michigan Avenue Athletic Club
235 Michigan Avenue. Chicago, Illinois 60601

MEMO

To: Club Members
From: Firstname Lastname
Date: Today's Date
Subject: Forgotten badge procedures

Many of you have pointed out that the procedures used to check in members who forget their ID badges are slow and frustrating. As a result, we have implemented new procedures which should make it easier and faster to gain access to the club facilities without scanning your badge.

If you forget your badge:

1) Proceed directly to the reception desk.
2) Tell the desk management associate on duty your name and that you forgot your badge.
3) Show the associate a photo ID, such as a driver's license or school ID card.
4) Enter the facility when the associate presses the entrance buzzer.

Keep in mind that this procedure is for your safety and the security of all club members. Use the following guidelines if you have a problem or complaint with this or any other club policy:

✓ Write a letter to the club manager explaining the problem or complaint.
✓ Submit a suggestion in the Suggestion Box in the lobby or on the club's Web site.
✓ Politely discuss the policy with a club employee.
✓ Attend a members' forum to publicly discuss your problem or complaint.

Thank you for your cooperation.

Figure 7-2

Word 2013, Windows 8, Microsoft Corporation

Lesson 8

Inserting Pictures, Text Boxes, and Shapes

➤ What You Will Learn

Analyzing Objects
Inserting Pictures
Inserting a Text Box
Inserting Shapes
Selecting Objects
Resizing and Deleting Objects
Scanning Content to Insert in a Document

WORDS TO KNOW

AutoShapes
Predrawn shapes that come with Word 2013.

Bounding box
A border that displays around the edges of a selected object.

Clip art
Predrawn pictures that you can insert in an Office document.

Device driver
A software program that provides the instructions your computer needs to communicate with a device, such as a scanner.

Floating object
An object that is positioned independently from the document text.

Software Skills Use graphics objects, such as pictures, shapes, and text boxes, to illustrate and add visual interest to a document. You can insert picture files from any storage location connected to your computer or from online sources. You can also use a scanner to convert a printed picture to a file. Once you insert an object, you can resize it to fit properly on the page. You can use the Selection Pane to select objects in a document.

What You Can Do

Analyzing Objects

- **Objects** are elements that can be selected, edited, resized, positioned, and formatted independently from the surrounding text.
- Common objects include pictures, shapes, text boxes, diagrams, charts, and tables.
- When you select an object in a Word document, a **bounding box** and **sizing handles** display around its borders (see Figure 8-1 on the next page).
- You will also see the Layout Options button near the upper-right corner of the object. This button offers wrapping and positioning options you can apply to the object.

✓ *You work with Layout Options in the next lesson.*

- In addition, tabs specifically for use in editing and formatting the object become available on the Ribbon.

- For example, when you select a picture, the PICTURE TOOLS FORMAT tab becomes available (see Figure 8-1); when you select a shape, the DRAWING TOOLS FORMAT tab becomes available.
- Many of the commands you use to edit or format one type of object are the same as or similar to those you use to edit or format other types of objects.

Figure 8-1

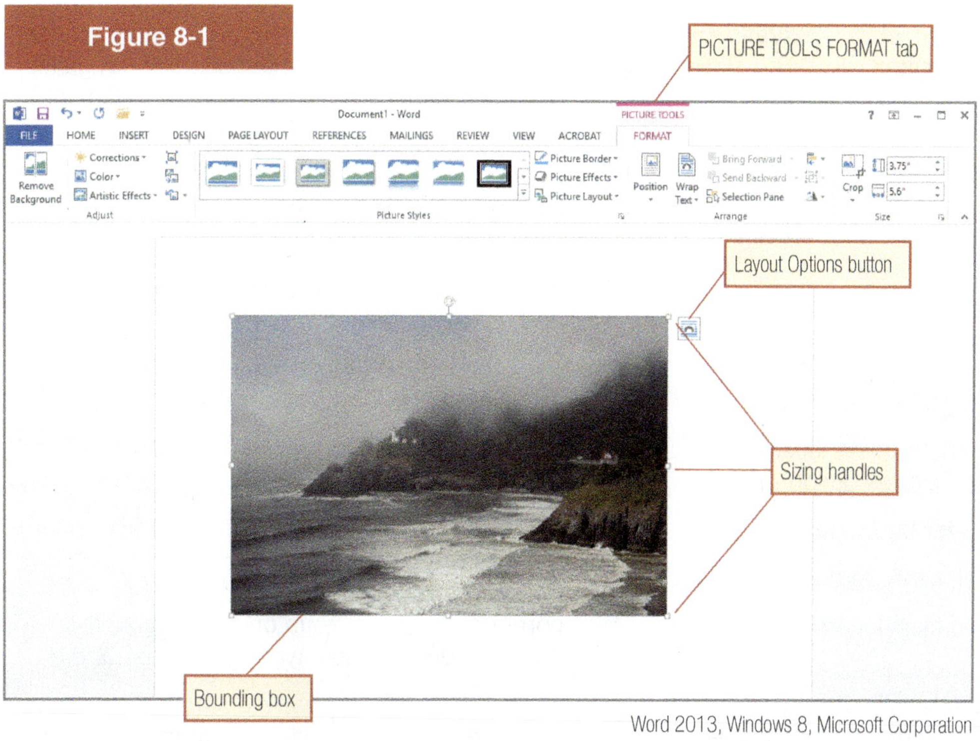

Word 2013, Windows 8, Microsoft Corporation

Inserting Pictures

- Pictures are graphics files that are inserted as objects in your Microsoft Office documents.
- Some pictures are the drawn illustrations called **clip art**, and some are photographs.
- You use the Pictures command to insert a picture file stored in a location that can be accessed from your computer.
- You use the Online Pictures command to search for an image using the Bing search engine.
- You can also insert a **screenshot** or **screen clipping** of any window currently open on your computer desktop.

Object
A graphic, picture, chart, shape, text box, or other element that can be inserted in a document.

Scanner
A device that converts printed documents into digital file formats.

Screenshot
A picture of the content currently displayed in a window open on your computer desktop.

Screen clipping
A picture of selected content currently displayed in a window open on your computer desktop.

Sizing handles
Small symbols around the edges of a selected object that you use to resize the object.

Text box
A rectangular drawing object in which text or graphics images can be inserted and positioned anywhere on a page.

USB
Universal Serial Bus. A type of connection used to attach devices such as flash drives, scanners, cameras, and printers to a computer.

Try It! Inserting Pictures

1. Start Word, create a new blank document, and save it as **W08TryA_xx** in the location where your teacher instructs you to store the files for this lesson.
2. Click the INSERT tab, then, in the Illustrations group, click the Pictures button.

   ✓ *The Insert Picture dialog box displays.*
3. Navigate to the location where the data files for this lesson are stored.
4. Click **W08TryA_picture**.
5. Click Insert.
6. With the picture still selected, press → once and then press ENTER twice to move the insertion point below the picture.
7. Click the INSERT tab, then, in the Illustrations group, click the Online Pictures button.
8. Click in the search box for Bing Image Search.
9. Type **computer** and click the Search button.
10. Click a picture and then click Insert to insert it in the document.
11. Click anywhere outside the clip art picture to deselect it, and then scroll up so you can see the top of the document on your screen. Select the HOME tab, if necessary.
12. Create a new blank document. Save the document as **W08TryB_xx** in the location where your teacher instructs you to store the files for this lesson.
13. Click the INSERT tab, then, in the Illustrations group, click the Screenshot button. A gallery of all windows currently open on your desktop displays.
14. In the gallery, click **W08TryA_xx** to insert a picture of that entire window into the current document.
15. In **W08TryB_xx**, move the insertion point to the end of the document and press ENTER twice.
16. Click the INSERT tab, then, in the Illustrations group, click the Screenshot button.
17. Click Screen Clipping. Word makes the **W08TryA_xx** document active in clipping mode. It appears dim, and the mouse pointer resembles a cross hair +.
18. Position the mouse pointer in the upper-left corner of the Font group on the Ribbon, then click and drag to the lower-right corner of the Font group.
19. Release the mouse button. Word inserts just the area you selected—the Font group—into the **W08TryB_xx** document.
20. Close both documents, saving changes. Leave Word open to use in the next Try It.

Inserting a Text Box

- Insert a **text box** to position several blocks of text on a page or to change the direction of the text.
- You can create a text box by selecting a text box style from the Text Box gallery and then typing text in the text box.
- The text box gallery includes styles for setting up quotes and sidebars, as well as for a simple text box.
- Alternatively, you can draw your own blank text box, or draw a text box around existing text.

Try It! Inserting a Text Box

1. Start Word, if necessary, and open **W08TryC**. Save the file as **W08TryC_xx** in the location where your teacher instructs you to store the files for this lesson.
2. Move the insertion point to the end of the document.
3. Click the INSERT tab, then, in the Text group, click the Text Box button.
4. Scroll down and click the Simple Quote text box style.

Text Box gallery

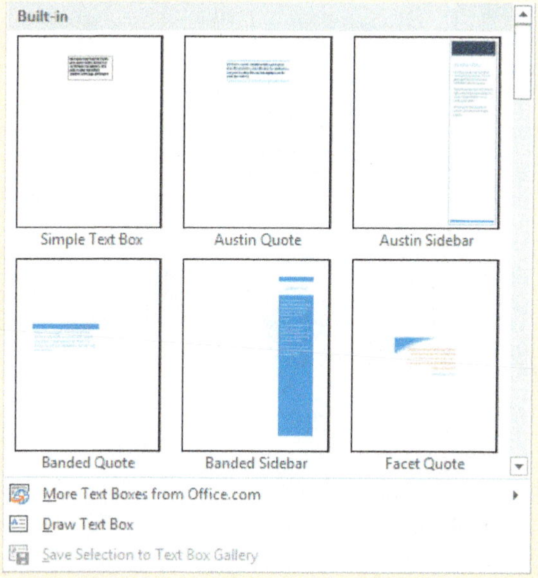

Word 2013, Windows 8, Microsoft Corporation

5. Type **"Martha's Vineyard is beautiful even when the ocean is raging and the clouds block the sun."**
6. Click outside the text box to deselect it.
7. Click the boundary, or edge, of the text box to select it.
8. Press DEL.

   ✓ *If the text box remains, you may have positioned the insertion point in the text box instead of selecting the text box. Click the boundary again and make certain the text box is selected before you press DEL.*

9. On the INSERT tab, in the Text group, click the Text Box button.
10. Click Draw Text Box. The mouse pointer changes to a crosshair +.
11. Click below the second paragraph of text, where you want to position a corner of the text box, then drag diagonally to draw the box.
12. Release the mouse button when the box is the size you want. The insertion point is inside the box.
13. Type **"Martha's Vineyard is beautiful even when the ocean is raging and the clouds block the sun."**
14. In the main document, select the text *Martha's Vineyard Beach Scene*.
15. Click the INSERT tab, then, in the Text group, click the Text Box button.
16. Click Draw Text Box.
17. Save the changes to the document, and close it. Leave Word open to use in the next Try It.

Inserting Shapes

- Shapes, like pictures and text boxes, are objects you insert into documents.
- You can insert closed shapes, such as ovals and rectangles; lines, such as curves and arrows; or **AutoShapes**, such as hearts, stars, and lightning bolts.
- When you click the Shapes button in the Illustrations group on the INSERT tab of the Ribbon, Word displays a gallery of shapes organized into palettes.

  ✓ *Rest the mouse pointer on a shape in the gallery to display a ScreenTip describing the shape.*

- Click a shape in the gallery to select it, and then click and drag in the document to insert the shape in the desired size.
- To insert a shape in the default size, select it and then click in the document.
- When you select an inserted shape, the Insert Shapes gallery becomes available on the DRAWING TOOLS FORMAT tab, so you can easily insert additional shapes.
- By default, Word inserts shapes as **floating objects** so they can be positioned anywhere on a page.
- You can insert a single shape, or combine multiple shapes to create a larger drawing.
- If you use multiple shapes, you can group them together so you can edit and format them as one.

Try It! Inserting Shapes

1. Create a new blank document in Word, and save it as W08TryD_xx in the location where your teacher instructs you to store the files for this lesson.
2. Click the INSERT tab, then, in the Illustrations group, click the Shapes button to display the Shapes gallery.
3. Under Basic Shapes, click the Oval—second from the left in the first row. The mouse pointer changes to a crosshair +.
4. Click and drag diagonally to draw the oval.

   ✓ *Press and hold SHIFT while you drag with the Oval tool to draw a circle. Use the same technique with the rectangle tool to draw a square.*
5. On the DRAWING TOOLS FORMAT tab, in the Insert Shapes group, click the 5-Point Star.
6. Click a blank area on the page. Word inserts the shape in the default size.
7. Click the INSERT tab, then, in the Illustrations group, click the Shapes button to display the Shapes gallery.
8. Under Lines, click the Line tool—first on the left. The mouse pointer changes to a crosshair +.

   ✓ *If a shape is selected in the document, you can click the Line tool on the DRAWING TOOLS FORMAT tab in the Insert Shapes gallery.*
9. Click and drag in the document below the other two shapes to draw the line.
10. Click INSERT > Shapes.
11. Under Lines, click the Curve tool—third from the right. The mouse pointer changes to a crosshair +.
12. Click a blank area of the document where you want the line to begin.
13. Click at the first point where you want the line to curve.

Shapes gallery

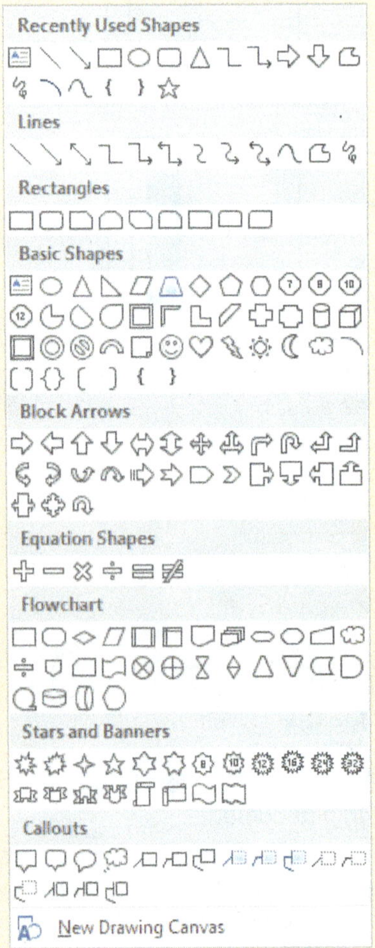

Word 2013, Windows 8, Microsoft Corporation

(continued)

Try It! Inserting Shapes *(continued)*

14 Click at the next point where you want the line to curve.

15 When you have created all the curves, double-click to end the line.

16 Click INSERT > Shapes.

17 Under Lines, click the Freeform tool—second from the right. The mouse pointer changes to a crosshair +.

18 Click and hold the mouse button in a blank area of the document where you want the line to begin, then drag to draw freehand as if you are using a pencil, or release the mouse button and click to draw straight lines.

19 When you are finished drawing, double-click to end the line.

20 Click INSERT > Shapes.

21 Under Lines, click the Scribble tool—last one on the right. The mouse pointer changes to a crosshair +.

22 Click and hold the mouse button in the area of the document where you want the line to begin. The mouse pointer changes to a pencil icon.

23 Drag to draw freehand as if you are using a pencil. For example, sign your name.

24 When you are finished drawing, release the mouse button to end the line.

25 Close **W08TryD_xx**, saving changes. Leave Word open to use in the next Try It.

Selecting Objects

- Before you can format or manipulate objects, you must first select them.
- Select an object by clicking it to display the object's bounding box and sizing handles.
- On a touchscreen, tap an object to select it.
- As you add objects to a document, some objects may obscure others. You can use the Selection Pane to see a list of all objects in the document.
- Use the Selection Pane to select any object, as well as hide objects from view. You can also use this pane to adjust layering, so that an object comes to the front or moves to the back of the stack of objects.

✓ *You learn more about layering in Word, Lesson 9.*

Try It! Selecting Objects

1 Start Word, if necessary, and open **W08TryE** from the data files for this lesson.

2 Save the document as **W08TryE_xx** in the location where your teacher instructs you to store the files for this lesson.

3 On the HOME tab, in the Editing group, click Select and then click Selection Pane. The Selection Pane lists the four objects in the current document.

4 In the Selection Pane, click the 5-Point Star 4 object to select it. The star's bounding box becomes active. This shape is currently hidden behind the oval shape.

5 Click on the star's bounding box and drag the shape to the right to move it away from the oval.

6 Click on the edge of the heart shape that is hidden behind the oval shape. The shape becomes selected in the document and in the Selection Pane.

(continued)

Try It! Selecting Objects *(continued)*

7. Drag the heart shape to the left to move it away from the oval.
8. In the Selection Pane, click the Straight Connector 5 object, and then click the visibility eye to hide the object.
9. Save the changes to **W08TryE_xx**, and leave it open to use in the next Try It.

Objects display in the Selection Pane

Word 2013, Windows 8, Microsoft Corporation

Resizing and Deleting Objects

- You can resize an object to make it larger or smaller.
- You can resize it evenly so the height and width remain proportional, or you can resize it unevenly, distorting the image.
- Drag the sizing handles to resize a picture using the mouse.
- Enter a precise size using the Shape Height and Shape Width boxes in the Size group on the FORMAT tab of the Ribbon.

Try It! Resizing and Deleting Objects

1. In the **W08TryE_xx** document, click the oval shape to select it.
2. Rest the mouse pointer over the sizing handle in the upper-right corner until the pointer resembles a diagonal double-headed arrow.
3. Drag the handle down and to the left to decrease the height and width of the shape at the same time. (When you press the left mouse button, the pointer changes to a crosshair +.)
4. Drag the sizing handle in the middle of the right side to the right to increase the width of the object. The height does not change.
5. Click the star shape to select it, and then click the DRAWING TOOLS FORMAT tab. In the Size group, use the Shape Height increment arrows to set the height to 1.8".

   ✓ *If the Height and Width tools are not visible, click the Size button.*

6. Use the Shape Width increment arrows to set the width of the shape to 2.0".

   ✓ *When you resize some objects, such as photographs, Word may automatically adjust the dimensions to keep the object in proportion.*

7. In the Selection Pane, click Show All, and then click the Straight Connector 5 object to select it.
8. Press DEL.
9. Save the changes to the document, and leave it open to use in the next Try It.

Scanning Content to Insert in a Document

- Use a **scanner** to convert printed documents or images into digital files.
- You can insert the scanned image into an Office file, such as a Word document, using the Pictures command on the INSERT tab.
- Other technologies are available for importing content into digital format, including digital cameras, digital video cameras, tablet PCs, and voice recognition devices.
- Before use, a scanner must be connected to the computer system. Most scanners connect via a **USB** cable.
- The first time the device is connected, Windows automatically installs the necessary **device driver** software. If Windows cannot find the correct driver, you may download the driver from the hardware manufacturer's Web site, or insert a driver installation CD that comes with the hardware.
- Use a program such as Windows Fax and Scan, one of the Windows Accessories, or the software that comes with your scanner to scan the image.

Try It! Scanning Content to Insert in a Document

1. Follow the manufacturer's instructions to install the scanner for use with your computer, if necessary.
2. Connect the scanner to your computer and turn it on.
3. Place a picture of your choice face down on the scanner surface.
4. Launch the scanner from a program on your computer or from the scanner itself.
5. If necessary, specify the area to scan.

   ✓ *Follow the prompts for your scanner to select resolution and other options.*
6. Save the scanned image as **W08TryE_picture_xx** in the location where your teacher instructs you to store the files for this lesson.
7. In **W08TryE_xx**, double-click below the shapes to position the insertion point at the left margin.
8. On the INSERT tab, click the Pictures button.
9. In the Insert Picture dialog box, navigate to the location where you stored **W08TryE_picture_xx**.
10. Select the picture and click Insert.
11. Close **W08TryE_xx**, saving changes, and exit Word and your scanner software if necessary.

Lesson 8—Practice

The Michigan Avenue Athletic Club has asked you to create a flyer announcing classes with a new trainer. In this project, you create a flyer using a picture, a shape, and a text box.

DIRECTIONS

1. Start Word, if necessary, create a blank document, and save the document as **W08Practice_xx** in the location where your teacher instructs you to store the files for this lesson.
2. Display the rulers and nonprinting characters, if necessary.
3. Press ENTER five times and type **Spin with David!**
4. Press ENTER to start a new line.
5. On the **HOME** tab, in the Font group, click the **Font Size** drop-down arrow and click **14** to increase the font size to 14 points.

6. Type the following paragraph: **David Fairmont, licensed personal trainer, is starting an early morning spinning class designed specifically to improve cardiovascular health. The 45-minute class will be held Monday through Friday beginning at 5:30 a.m.**
7. Press ENTER four times, click the **Font Size** drop-down arrow, and click **18** to increase the font size to 18 points.
8. Type the following paragraph: **David Fairmont is one of the club's new trainers. He holds a master's degree in health management from the University of Vermont in Burlington, Vermont, and specializes in fitness and cardiovascular health.**
9. Click the **INSERT** tab and then, in the Illustrations group, click the **Shapes** button to display the Shapes gallery.
10. Under Stars and Banners, click the **Explosion 1** AutoShape (the first shape on the left).
11. Position the mouse pointer over the first paragraph mark at the beginning of the document, then click and drag diagonally down and to the right to draw a shape about 1.0" high by 1.0" wide.
12. On the DRAWING TOOLS FORMAT tab, in the Size group, use the **Shape Height** increment arrows to set the height to **2.0"** and the **Shape Width** increment arrows to set the width to **2.0"**.
13. Click the **HOME** tab, click **Select**, and click **Selection Pane**.
14. In the Selection Pane, click **Explosion 1 1**, and then click the visibility eye to hide the shape temporarily.
15. Select the text **Spin with David!** Click the **HOME** tab and click **Heading 1** in the Styles gallery to apply the style.
16. In the Paragraph group, click the **Center** button to center the text.
17. Click the **Font Size** drop-down arrow and click **48** to increase the font size to 48 points.
18. Click the **Paragraph** group dialog box launcher to open the Paragraph dialog box.
19. Use the **Before** increment arrows to set the Before spacing to **36 pt**, and then click **OK**. Deselect the text.
20. In the Selection Pane, click **Show All**, and then close the pane.
21. Click the **INSERT** tab, then, in the Text group, click the **Text Box** button, and click **Draw Text Box**.
22. Position the crosshair on the blank line below the first full paragraph of text and about 1.0" in from the left margin.
23. Click and drag diagonally down and to the right to draw a text box approximately 0.75" high by 5.0" inches wide.
24. Click the **HOME** tab, then, in the Font group, click the **Font Size** drop-down arrow and click **24**.
25. Type **Class size is limited so sign up now!**
26. Position the insertion point at the end of the last paragraph of text in the document and press ENTER.
27. Click the **INSERT** tab and then in the Illustrations group, click the **Pictures** button to display the Insert Picture dialog box.
28. Navigate to the location where the data files for this lesson are stored.
29. Click **W08Practice_picture** and then click **Insert**.

    ✓ *You may use a scanned picture instead.*

30. On the **PICTURE TOOLS FORMAT** tab, in the Size group, use the **Shape Height** increment arrows to set the picture height to **2.0"**. The width should decrease automatically to keep the picture in proportion.
31. Double-click in the header area and type your first and last name. Press TAB twice to move to the right tab stop and type or insert today's date.
32. Close the header.
33. Save the changes to the document.
34. **With your teacher's permission**, print the document. It should look similar to Figure 8-2 on the next page.
35. Close the document, saving changes, and exit Word.

Figure 8-2

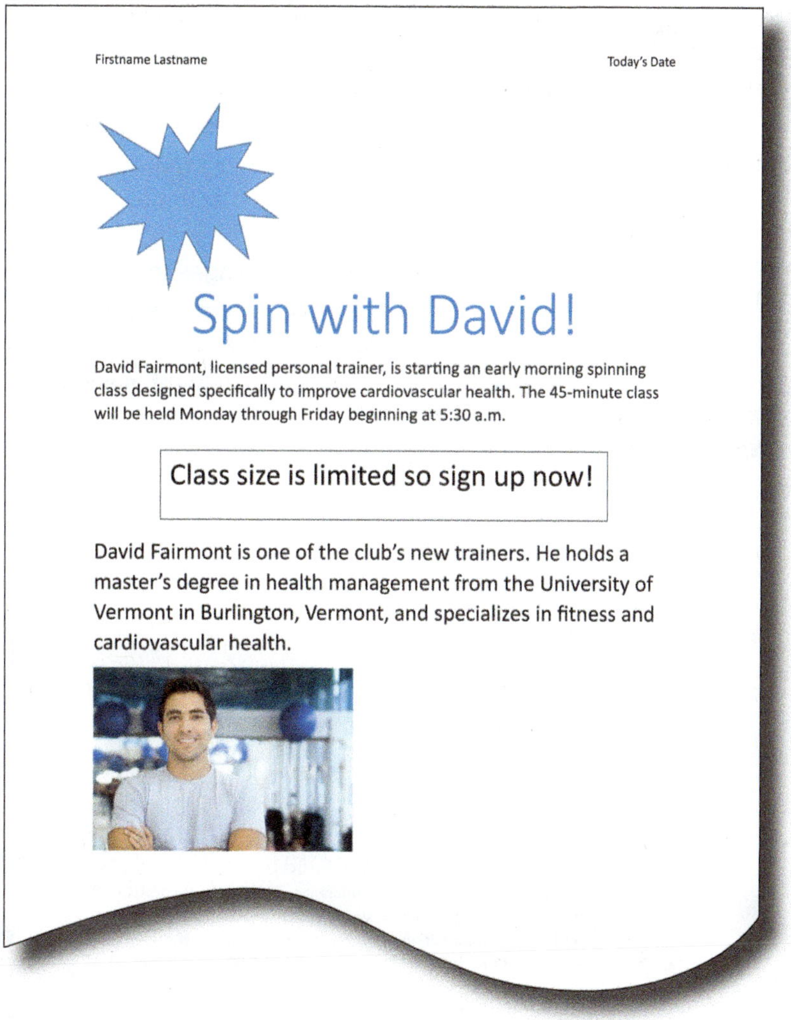
Firstname Lastname Today's Date

Spin with David!

David Fairmont, licensed personal trainer, is starting an early morning spinning class designed specifically to improve cardiovascular health. The 45-minute class will be held Monday through Friday beginning at 5:30 a.m.

Class size is limited so sign up now!

David Fairmont is one of the club's new trainers. He holds a master's degree in health management from the University of Vermont in Burlington, Vermont, and specializes in fitness and cardiovascular health.

Lesson 8—Apply

In this project, you will revise an existing flyer announcing classes with the new nutritionist to include a shape, text box, and other graphics.

DIRECTIONS

1. Start Word, if necessary, and open **W08Apply** from the data files for this lesson.
2. Save the file as **W08Apply_xx** in the location where your teacher instructs you to store the files for this lesson.
3. Display the rulers and nonprinting characters, if necessary.
4. Type your full name and today's date in the header.
5. Position the insertion point on the first line of the document and choose to insert an online picture.
6. Search for pictures using the search text **heart**, and insert an appropriate picture, such as the one shown in Figure 8-3 on the next page. Resize the picture to **1.5"** high.

7. Insert a Heart AutoShape in the upper-right corner of the page. Resize the shape to **2.0" × 2.0"**.
8. Apply the **Title** style to the text *Eat Heart Healthy with Sandra!*
9. Increase the font size of the first paragraph to **14 points**.
10. Increase the font size of the text *Class size is limited. Register now so you won't be left out!* to **24 points**, and center the text horizontally.
11. Draw a text box around the text.

    ✓ *If one line of text displays below the text box make sure the text box is selected, then press ↓ to nudge the text box down in the document so it displays below the paragraph.*

12. Increase the font size of the last paragraph to **14 points**.
13. Position the insertion point on the blank line below the last paragraph and insert the data file **W08Apply_picture**.

    ✓ *You may use a scanned picture instead.*

14. Resize the picture height to **2.5"**. The width should adjust automatically to keep the picture in proportion.
15. Save the changes to the document.
16. **With your teacher's permission**, print the document. It should look similar to Figure 8-3.
17. Close the document, saving changes, and exit Word.

Figure 8-3

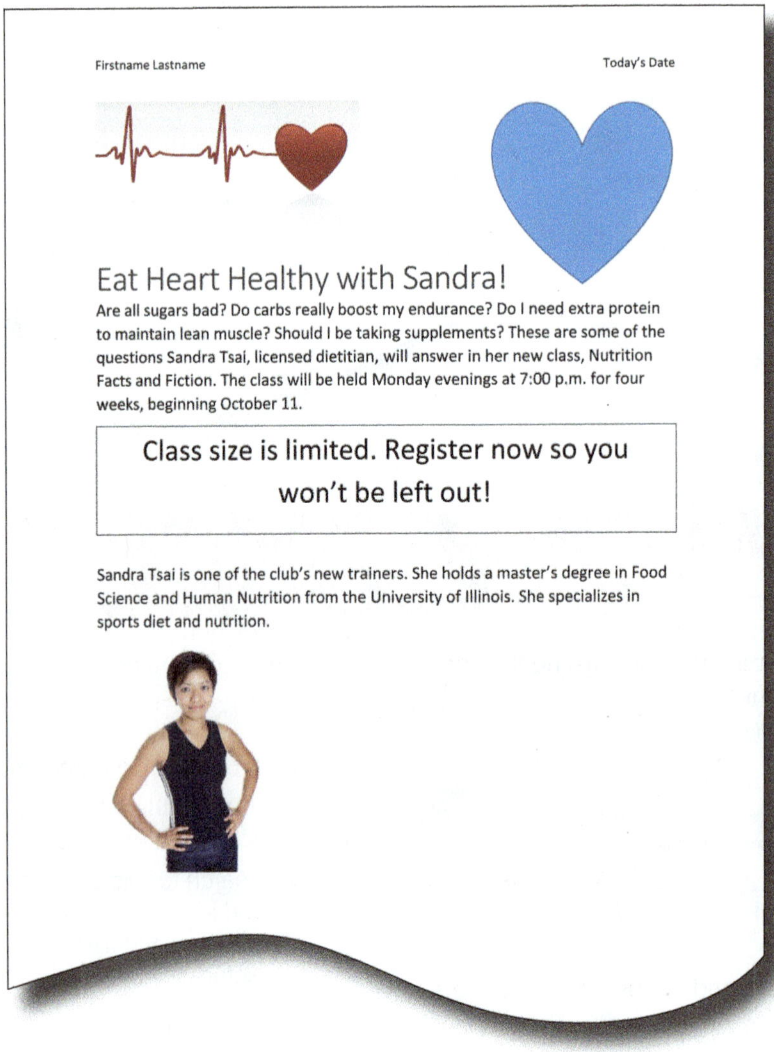

Firstname Lastname

Today's Date

Eat Heart Healthy with Sandra!

Are all sugars bad? Do carbs really boost my endurance? Do I need extra protein to maintain lean muscle? Should I be taking supplements? These are some of the questions Sandra Tsai, licensed dietitian, will answer in her new class, Nutrition Facts and Fiction. The class will be held Monday evenings at 7:00 p.m. for four weeks, beginning October 11.

Class size is limited. Register now so you won't be left out!

Sandra Tsai is one of the club's new trainers. She holds a master's degree in Food Science and Human Nutrition from the University of Illinois. She specializes in sports diet and nutrition.

Lesson 9

Formatting Graphics Objects

➤ What You Will Learn

Wrapping Text Around an Object
Moving and Positioning an Object
Formatting Objects
Modifying Pictures
Modifying a Text Box
Changing a Shape
Adding Text to a Shape
Inserting a Caption

Software Skills You can position and format objects to integrate them into a Word document, making the document easier to read and more interesting for the reader. For example, you can apply styles, or add effects such as shadows or borders. Add a caption to an object to make it easy to refer to in a document.

WORDS TO KNOW

3-D
A perspective added to give the appearance of three dimensions.

Brightness
The amount of white or black added to a color; sometimes called tint.

Caption
A text label that identifies an illustration such as a figure, table, or picture.

Contrast
The difference between color values in different parts of the same image.

Fill
The inside area of a shape or other object.

Outline
The border that defines the outer boundary of a shape or other object.

Saturation
The intensity or depth of a color.

Shadow
An effect designed to give the appearance of a shadow behind a border.

Tone
The amount of gray added to a color.

What You Can Do

Wrapping Text Around an Object

- You can change the wrapping style to affect the way a picture or any other object, such as a shape or text box, is integrated into the document text. Select from seven wrapping options:
  - In Line with Text: Picture is positioned on a line with text characters.
  - Square: Text is wrapped on the sides of the picture.
  - Tight: Text is wrapped to the contours of the image.
  - Through: Text runs through the picture.
  - Top and Bottom: Text is displayed above and below picture but not on the left or right sides.
  - Behind Text: Picture is layered behind the text.
  - In Front of Text: Picture is layered on top of the text.
- By default, pictures have In Line with Text wrapping.
- You can use the Layout Options button to quickly apply wrapping styles.
- You can also apply wrapping using the Wrap Text button on an object's FORMAT tab.

Try It! Wrapping Text Around an Object

1. Start Word, and open **W09Try**. Save the document as **W09Try_xx** in the location where your teacher instructs you to store the files for this lesson.
2. Display nonprinting characters and rulers.
3. Click the picture to select it.
4. Click the Layout Options button near the upper-right corner of the picture. The Layout Options gallery displays.
5. Click Square. The text wraps on the right and bottom of the picture.
6. Click Behind Text.
7. On the PICTURE TOOLS FORMAT tab, in the Arrange group, click the Wrap Text button and click In Line with Text. Click outside the picture to deselect it.
8. Save the changes to the document, and leave it open to use in the next Try It.

Square text wrapping

Word 2013, Windows 8, Microsoft Corporation

Moving and Positioning an Object

- You can drag an object to a new location.
- You can nudge an object that is not in line with text using the directional arrow keys on your keyboard.
- You can use the Cut and Paste commands to move an inline object the way you would move any character.
- You can position an object relative to the top, bottom, left, right, and middle of a page.
- Use alignment guides or Ribbon commands to align objects with each other or with specific locations such as the top of the page or the left or right margin.
- You can rotate an object around its center axis or flip it horizontally or vertically.
- Layer objects that overlap to designate which will be in front and which will be in back.
- Group multiple objects together so you can edit or format them as one.

Try It! Moving and Positioning an Object

1. In the W09Try_xx document, click the picture to select it, if necessary.
2. Position the mouse pointer over the selected picture until the mouse pointer changes to a four-headed arrow.
3. Drag the picture to the end of the first paragraph of text. As you drag, the Move pointer displays.
4. When the vertical bar in the move pointer displays between the period at the end of the paragraph and the paragraph mark, release the mouse button to move the picture.
5. Click the picture to select it, if necessary.
6. On the PICTURE TOOLS FORMAT tab, in the Arrange group, click the Position button.
7. Under With Text Wrapping, click the style on the right end of the top row—Position in Top Right with Square Text Wrapping.
8. With the picture still selected, on the PICTURE TOOLS FORMAT tab, in the Arrange group, click the Align Objects button.
9. Verify that the Align to Margin option is selected, and then click Align Left.

   ✓ *A check mark next to the option indicates it is selected. If Align to Page is selected, click Align to Margin, and then repeat steps 8 and 9.*

10. With the picture still selected, click on the picture, then hold down the mouse button until the green alignment guides display.

    ✓ *If the guides do not display, click the Align Objects button, click to select Use Alignment Guides, and then repeat step 10.*

11. Drag downward until the horizontal alignment guide indicates that the top of the picture is aligned with the top of the title text (see illustration on next page). Release the mouse button.
12. Scroll down if necessary and click the sun AutoShape to select it.
13. Click the Layout Options button, and choose Tight text wrapping.
14. With the shape still selected, drag upward until the horizontal alignment guide indicates the top of the shape is aligned with the top of the last paragraph of text. Make sure the left side of the shape is still aligned with the left margin. Release the mouse button.
15. Position the mouse pointer over the shape's rotation handle so it resembles a circular arrow.
16. Drag the handle about 1 inch to the right to rotate the object clockwise (to the right).
17. Drag the rotation handle about 0.5 inches to the left to rotate the picture counterclockwise (to the left).

    ✓ *The first word of the last paragraph may now be wrapped to the left of the sun shape.*

18. Press ↓ to nudge the shape downward until the first line of the paragraph no longer wraps around the shape.
19. Click the picture to select it.
20. Click the PICTURE TOOLS FORMAT tab, then, in the Arrange group, click the Rotate Objects button.
21. Click Flip Vertical.
22. Click the Rotate Objects button and click Flip Horizontal.
23. Click the Rotate Objects button and click Flip Vertical.
24. Save the changes to W09Try_xx, and leave it open to use in the next Try It.

(continued)

Try It! Moving and Positioning an Object *(continued)*

Use alignment guides to align an object and text

Word 2013, Windows 8, Microsoft Corporation

Try It! Layering and Grouping Objects

1. In the **W09Try_xx** document, click the sun shape to select it.
2. Click the DRAWING TOOLS FORMAT tab, then, in the Arrange group, click the Position button.
3. Click Position in Top Center with Square Text Wrapping.
4. With the shape still selected, in the Arrange group, click the Send Backward button to move the shape back behind the picture.
5. Click the Bring Forward button to move the shape forward in front of the picture.
6. Click the picture to select it.
7. Press and hold SHIFT.
8. Click the shape to select it, and then release SHIFT.
9. On the PICTURE TOOLS FORMAT tab, in the Arrange group, click the Group Objects button.

   ✓ *You can select any available FORMAT tab.*
10. Click Group.
11. Click the Layout Options button and choose Tight text wrapping.
12. Click the group to select it, if necessary.
13. On the PICTURE TOOLS FORMAT tab in the Arrange group, click the Group Objects button.

    ✓ *You can select any available FORMAT tab.*
14. Click Ungroup, then click anywhere outside the selected objects to deselect them.
15. Save the changes to the document, and leave it open to use in the next Try It.

(continued)

Try It! Layering and Grouping Objects *(continued)*

Grouped and layered objects

Formatting Objects

- When you select a graphics object, commands for editing and formatting become available on a FORMAT tab of the Ribbon.
- Each type of object has a gallery of styles you can use to apply a collection of formatting settings, such as **outlines** and **fills**.
- You can also apply outlines and fill settings independently.
- You can use effects such as **3-D** and **shadows** to format objects, as well.
- In Word 2013, right-clicking an object displays not only the shortcut menu but a small toolbar that offers formatting shortcuts.
- If you right-click a picture, for example, you will see options to apply a picture style or crop the picture. If you right-click a shape, you will see options for modifying shape style, fill, and outline.

Try It! Formatting Objects

1. In the W09Try_xx document, right-click the sun shape, click Style on the shortcut toolbar, and then click the third style from the right in the last row of gallery—Intense Effect - Gold, Accent 4.
2. Right-click the picture, click Style on the shortcut toolbar, and then click the last style in the gallery—Metal Oval.
3. Click the picture to select it, if necessary.
4. On the PICTURE TOOLS FORMAT tab, in the Picture Styles group, click the Picture Effects button .
5. Click Shadow to display a gallery of shadow styles.
6. Under Perspective, click the first style on the left—Perspective Diagonal Upper Left.
7. Click the AutoShape to select it.
8. On the DRAWING TOOLS FORMAT tab, in the Shape Styles group, click the Shape Fill drop-down arrow .

   ✓ *To quickly apply the color displayed on the button, click the button instead of the drop-down arrow.*
9. Under Theme Colors, click Orange, Accent 2.
10. Right-click the shape to display the shortcut toolbar.
11. Click the Outline button .
12. Under Theme Colors, click Blue, Accent 1.
13. Click the Outline button again, and click Weight to display a gallery of line weights.
14. Click 1½ pt.
15. Save the changes to the document, and leave it open to use in the next Try It.

Modifying Pictures

- Use the buttons in the Adjust group on the PICTURE TOOLS FORMAT tab to modify the appearance of a picture.
  - Use the Corrections gallery to sharpen or soften a picture, or adjust the **brightness** and **contrast**.
  - Use the Color gallery to change the color palette, **saturation**, or **tone** of the picture.
  - Use the Artistic Effects gallery to apply an effect to make a picture look more like a sketch, drawing, or painting.

Try It! Modifying Pictures

1. In the W09Try_xx document, click the picture to select it.
2. On the PICTURE TOOLS FORMAT tab, in the Adjust group, click the Corrections button .
3. Under Brightness/Contrast, click the middle style in the bottom row—Brightness: 0% (Normal) Contrast: +40%.

(continued)

Try It! Modifying Pictures *(continued)*

Corrections gallery

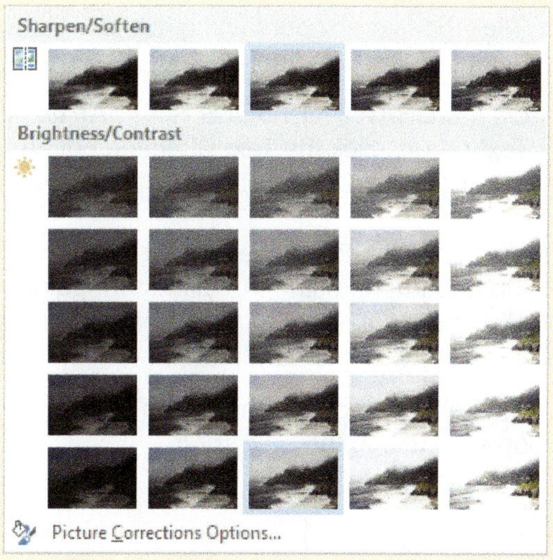

Word 2013, Windows 8, Microsoft Corporation

4. On the PICTURE TOOLS FORMAT tab, in the Adjust group, click the Color button.

5. Under Recolor, click the style second from the left end of the bottom row—Blue, Accent color 1 Light.

6. On the PICTURE TOOLS FORMAT tab, in the Adjust group, click the Reset Picture button.

   ✓ *To reset the picture formatting and size, click the Reset Picture drop-down arrow and click Reset Picture & Size.*

7. On the PICTURE TOOLS FORMAT tab, in the Adjust group, click the Artistic Effects button.

8. Rest the mouse pointer on any effect to preview what it does to the picture.

9. Click the style in the middle of the third row—Film Grain.

   ✓ *Zoom in to get a good look at the effects.*

Color gallery

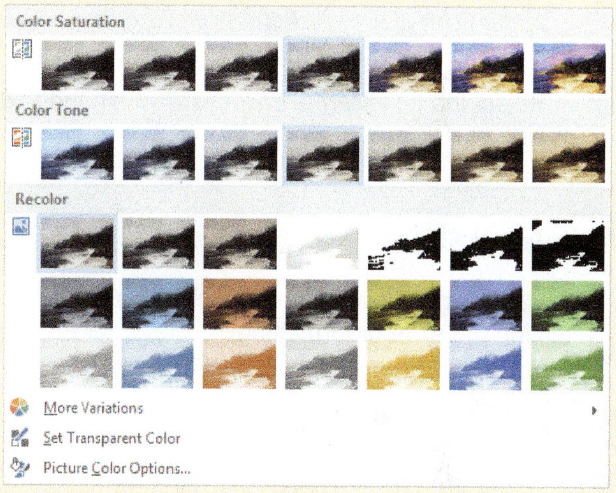

Word 2013, Windows 8, Microsoft Corporation

10. Save the changes to the document, and leave it open to use in the next Try It.

Modifying a Text Box

- You can format text within a text box using the same commands as you would to format regular text. For example, you can apply fonts and font styles, or change the font size.
  - Select the text box to apply formatting to all text within the box.
  - Select specific text to apply formatting to the selection.
- You can change the direction of text within a text box so it runs horizontally up or down.
  - Rotate the text 90° if you want it to run from the top of the box to the bottom.
  - Rotate the text 270° if you want it to run from the bottom of the box to the top.

Try It! Modifying a Text Box

1. In **W09Try_xx**, select the title, *Martha's Vineyard Beach Scene*.

   ✓ *To select the text without the objects, do not select the paragraph mark.*

2. Click the INSERT tab. In the Text group, click the Text Box button and click Draw Text Box.
3. Drag the text box below the last paragraph of text.
4. With the text box selected, click the HOME tab. In the Font group, click the Font Size drop-down arrow and click 18.
5. Select the text *Martha's Vineyard* within the text box.
6. Click the Italic button *I*.
7. Click the text box containing the text *Martha's Vineyard Beach Scene* to select it.
8. On the DRAWING TOOLS FORMAT tab, in the Text group, click the Text Direction button.
9. Click Rotate all text 270°.
10. Drag the text box to the upper-right corner of the document, using the alignment guides to align horizontally with the top of the picture and vertically with the right margin.
11. Save the changes to the document, and leave it open to use in the next Try It.

Changing a Shape

- You can change the shape of an object without affecting the style or formatting.
- For example, you can change a rectangular text box into an oval, or change a star shape into a moon.

Try It! Changing a Shape

1. In the **W09Try_xx** document, click the sun AutoShape to select it.
2. On the DRAWING TOOLS FORMAT tab, in the Insert Shapes group, click the Edit Shape button, then click Change Shape to display the Shapes gallery.
3. Under Basic Shapes, click the Heart.
4. On the DRAWING TOOLS FORMAT tab, in the Arrange group, click the Rotate Objects button.
5. Click Flip Horizontal.
6. Save the changes to the document, and leave it open to use in the next Try It.

Adding Text to a Shape

- You can add text to a shape by inserting a text box within the shape's boundaries.
- By default, the text box does not display borders, so it looks as if the text is inserted in the shape itself.

Try It! Adding Text to a Shape

1. In the **W09Try_xx** document, right-click the heart AutoShape.
2. Click Add Text on the shortcut menu.

   ✓ *If there is already text in the shape, the command is Edit Text.*

3. Type **Wow!**.
4. Select the text *Wow!* and increase the font size to 22 points.
5. Save the changes to the document, and leave it open to use in the next Try It.

Inserting a Caption

- Add a **caption** to an object so you can easily identify it and refer to the object in the text of a document.
- Word provides default captions for figures, tables, and equations.
- Each caption includes a text label and a number field.
- By default, captions for figures display below the object. You can change the caption position to display it above the object.
- You can also change the numbering format, create a new label for a particular kind of object, or exclude the label entirely.
- When the picture is floating—not in line with text—picture captions are inserted in a text box. Use standard commands and options to format or edit the caption in the text box. For example, you can change the font size.
- Word automatically updates the numbers for each caption entered; however, if you delete or move a caption, you must manually update the remaining captions.

Try It! Inserting a Caption

1. In the **W09Try_xx** file, click the picture to select it.
2. Click the REFERENCES tab, and then, in the Captions group, click the Insert Caption button to open the Caption dialog box.
3. Click the Position down arrow and select Above selected item.
4. Click in the Exclude label from caption check box to select it.
5. In the Caption box, press SPACEBAR once to insert a space after the default text (Figure 1).
6. Type **Beach on a Cloudy Day**.
7. Click OK to apply the caption to the picture.
8. Click Undo to remove the caption, and then click the Insert Caption button again.
9. Click the Position down arrow and select Below selected item.
10. Clear the check from the Exclude label from caption check box.
11. Click in the Caption box, press SPACEBAR, and then type **Beach on a Cloudy Day.** Click OK.
12. Select the text box that contains the caption, then right-click to display the shortcut menu and toolbar.
13. Click Fill, and then click Gray - 25%, Background 2 in the first row of Theme Colors.
14. Close **W09Try_xx**, saving changes, and exit Word.

Add a caption to a picture

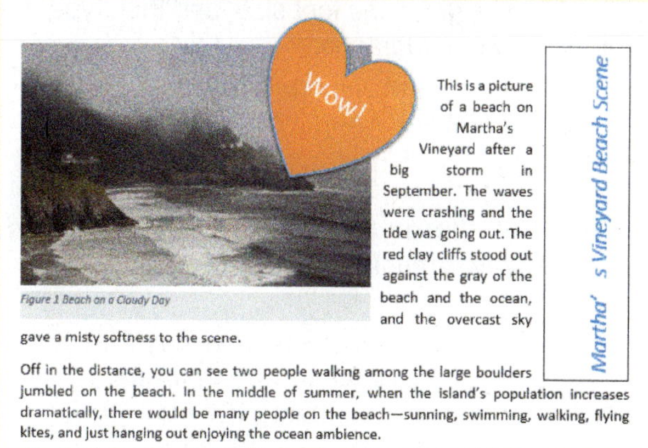

Word 2013, Windows 8, Microsoft Corporation

Lesson 9—Practice

Voyager Travel Adventures is preparing a booklet describing some of the wildlife travelers might encounter while on an African Safari. In this project, you will prepare a page describing lions, formatting pictures, shapes, and text boxes to illustrate the document.

DIRECTIONS

1. Start Word, if necessary, create a blank document, and save the document as **W09Practice_xx** in the location where your teacher instructs you to store the files for this lesson.
2. Display the rulers and nonprinting characters, if necessary.
3. Double-click in the header area and type your full name and today's date.
4. Move the insertion point to the first line of the document, type **Lion** and press ENTER.
5. Select the text *Lion* and click **Title** in the Styles gallery to format the text.
6. On the **HOME** tab, in the Paragraph group, click the **Center** button to center the selected text.
7. Move the insertion point to the blank line below the title. Click the **Font Size** drop-down arrow and click **18** to increase the font size, and then type the following two paragraphs:

   One of the most thrilling moments of a Voyager Travel Adventures African Safari is when you encounter a pride of lions. Lions are called the King of Beasts for a reason. They are majestic, huge, and dangerous. They are found in savannas, grasslands, dense bush, and woodlands.

   Lions generally sleep during the day and hunt at night. We often find them lounging on rock formations enjoying the sun. They live in groups called prides, so when we come across one lion there are likely to be others nearby. Usually, there is one male with multiple females. Viewing a pride with cubs is a particularly exciting event.
8. Click the **INSERT** tab and, in the Illustrations group, click the **Pictures** button to open the Insert Picture dialog box.
9. Navigate to the data files for this lesson and select **W09Practice_picture**.
10. Click **Insert** to insert the picture in the document.
11. On the **PICTURE TOOLS FORMAT** tab, in the Size group, use the **Height** increment arrows to set the picture height to 2.5". The width should adjust automatically.
12. Click the Layout Options button, and then click **Square** to apply the Square text wrapping style to the picture.
13. Drag the picture to the right side of the page and use the alignment guides to align it at the right with the right margin. Align the bottom of the picture as near the bottom of the first paragraph as you can, nudging it into place as necessary. Click anywhere outside the picture to deselect it.
14. Click at the beginning of the second paragraph. Click the **INSERT** tab and, in the Text group, click the **Text Box** button.
15. In the Text Box gallery, scroll down and click the **Austin Quote** style to insert it into the document.
16. Type **"Seeing a pride of lions was the highlight of my African Safari."**
17. Click the outside of the text box to select the text box. Right-click, click **Style** on the shortcut toolbar, and click the style that is third from the right in the fourth row—**Subtle Effect, Gold, Accent 4**.
18. Click the **INSERT** tab and then, in the Illustrations group, click the **Shapes** button to display the Shapes gallery.
19. Under Stars and Banners, click the **Explosion 1 AutoShape**.

   ✓ *The shape may also be available under Recently Used Shapes.*
20. Click to the right of the title text, *Lion*, and drag to draw a shape 2.0" high by 2.0" wide.

   ✓ *Use the Height and Width increment boxes in the Size group on the DRAWING TOOLS FORMAT tab to adjust the size, if necessary.*

21. On the **DRAWING TOOLS FORMAT** tab, click the **Shape Styles More** button and click the style at the end of the second row—**Colored Fill – Green, Accent 6**.
22. Right-click the shape and click **Add Text**.
23. Type **King of the Beasts!**
24. Select the text you just typed. Then, click the **HOME** tab. In the Font group, click the **Font Size** drop-down arrow and click **14** to increase the font size.
25. Click the **DRAWING TOOLS FORMAT** tab. In the Arrange group, click the **Position** button, and then click the style on the right end of the top row under With Text Wrapping – **Position in Top Right with Square Text Wrapping**. This positions the shape overlapping the lion picture (refer to Figure 9-1).
26. With the shape selected, press and hold SHIFT and click the picture to select it, too.
27. Click the **DRAWING TOOLS FORMAT** tab. In the Arrange group, click the **Group Objects** button. Click **Group** to group the two objects.
28. Click the **DRAWING TOOLS FORMAT** tab, then, in the Arrange group, click the **Position** button, and then click the style on the right end of the top row under With Text Wrapping – **Position in Top Right with Square Text Wrapping**. This moves the group to the top right.
29. With the group still selected, click the **REFERENCES** tab, and in the Captions group, click **Insert Caption**.
30. Press SPACEBAR once and type **Lions Resting at the End of the Day**. If necessary, select to position the caption below the group. Make sure the caption label appears with the caption.
31. Click **OK** to insert the caption.
32. Save the changes to the document.
33. **With your teacher's permission**, print the document. It should look similar to Figure 9-1.
34. Close the document, saving changes, and exit Word.

Figure 9-1

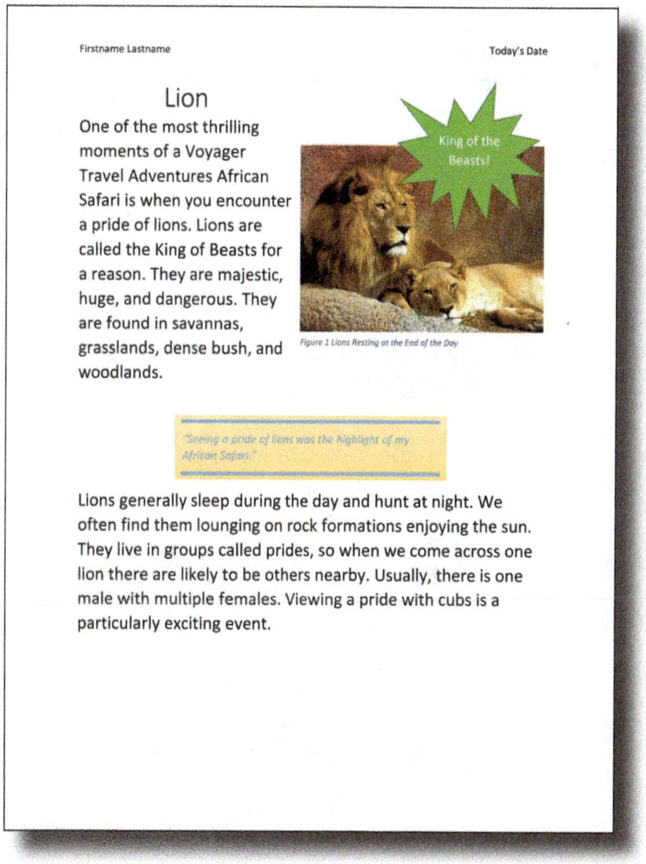
Firstname Lastname Today's Date

Lion

One of the most thrilling moments of a Voyager Travel Adventures African Safari is when you encounter a pride of lions. Lions are called the King of Beasts for a reason. They are majestic, huge, and dangerous. They are found in savannas, grasslands, dense bush, and woodlands.

King of the Beasts!

Figure 1 Lions Resting at the End of the Day

"Seeing a pride of lions was the highlight of my African Safari."

Lions generally sleep during the day and hunt at night. We often find them lounging on rock formations enjoying the sun. They live in groups called prides, so when we come across one lion there are likely to be others nearby. Usually, there is one male with multiple females. Viewing a pride with cubs is a particularly exciting event.

Lesson 9—Apply

In this project, you will prepare a page for the African Safari booklet on zebras. You will illustrate the page using a shape, picture, and a text box.

DIRECTIONS

1. Start Word, if necessary, and open **W09Apply** from the data files for this lesson.
2. Save the file as **W09Apply_xx** in the location where your teacher instructs you to store the files for this lesson.
3. Display the rulers and nonprinting characters, if necessary.
4. Type your full name and today's date in the header.
5. Resize the **Explosion 2** shape in the upper-left corner of the page to **2.0"** high by **2.5"** wide, and format it with the **Subtle Effect – Orange, Accent 2** shape style. Modify the shape outline to increase the outline weight to **3 points**.
6. Add the text **Zebras at the water hole** to the shape, setting the font size to **12 points**.
7. Position the shape in the bottom right of the page with square text wrapping.
8. Resize the **Explosion 1** shape in the upper-right corner of the page to **2.5"** high by **2.0"** wide.
9. Format it with the **Colored Fill – Orange, Accent 2** shape style. Modify the shape outline to increase the outline weight to **3 points**.
10. Position the shape in the bottom right of the page with square text wrapping, so it layers behind the Explosion 2 shape.
11. Group the two shapes.
12. Select the second sentence in the document and draw a text box around it. Rotate the text direction **270°** and resize the height of the text box to **4.5"**.
13. Apply the **Light 1 Outline, Colored Fill – Black, Dark 1** shape style to the text box.
14. Use the alignment guides to position the text box vertically aligned with the left margin and horizontally aligned with the first paragraph of text.
15. Set the text wrapping for the picture to **Square**, increase its height to **2.5"** and use alignment guides to align vertically with the right margin and horizontally with the top of the second paragraph.
16. Correct the picture to **Brightness: 0% (Normal) Contrast +20%**, and then apply the **Simple Frame, Black** picture style.
17. Insert a caption for the picture and adjust caption formats as follows:
    a. In the Insert Caption dialog box, click **New Label** to open the New Label dialog box.
    b. Type **Picture** in the Label box and then click **OK**.
    c. Click **Numbering**, click the **Format** down arrow, and click the **A, B, C** format.
    d. Click **OK** to apply the caption.
18. Nudge the caption down slightly so it doesn't obscure the picture shadow.
19. Drag the grouped shapes up to overlap the lower right of the picture. Bring the group forward to layer it on top of the picture.
20. Save the changes to the document.
21. **With your teacher's permission**, print the document. It should look similar to Figure 9-2.
22. Close the document, saving changes, and exit Word.

Figure 9-2

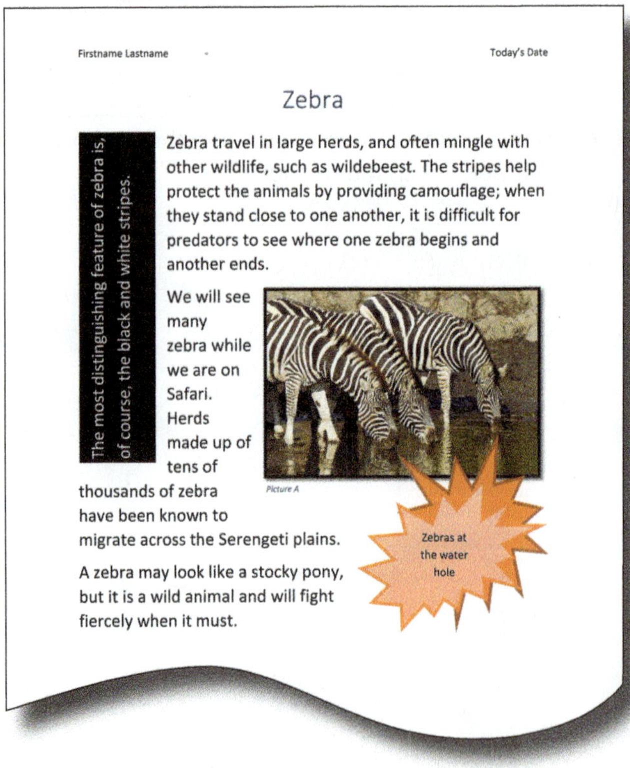
Firstname Lastname Today's Date

Zebra

The most distinguishing feature of zebra is, of course, the black and white stripes.

Zebra travel in large herds, and often mingle with other wildlife, such as wildebeest. The stripes help protect the animals by providing camouflage; when they stand close to one another, it is difficult for predators to see where one zebra begins and another ends.

We will see many zebra while we are on Safari. Herds made up of tens of thousands of zebra have been known to migrate across the Serengeti plains.

Picture A

Zebras at the water hole

A zebra may look like a stocky pony, but it is a wild animal and will fight fiercely when it must.

Lesson 10

Working with SmartArt Graphics, Text Effects, and Page Borders

➤ What You Will Learn

Inserting a SmartArt Graphic
Entering Text in a SmartArt Graphic
Modifying the Design of a SmartArt Graphic
Creating a SmartArt Graphic from a Picture
Applying Text Effects and WordArt Styles
Applying a Page Border

Software Skills Use the SmartArt feature to create diagrams and charts to illustrate data in reports and other documents. In Word 2013, you can create a SmartArt graphic from any picture. You can also apply effects such as shadows or borders to text characters to make the text stand out.

WORDS TO KNOW

Border
A line placed on one or more sides of a paragraph(s), page, or text box.

Diagram
A chart or graph usually used to illustrate a concept or describe the relationship of parts to a whole.

WordArt
A feature of Word used to transform text into a drawing object.

What You Can Do

Inserting a SmartArt Graphic

- Word comes with a set of SmartArt graphics objects that you can insert to create **diagrams**, such as organization charts or Venn diagrams, in a document.
- Use SmartArt graphics to illustrate information, concepts, and ideas such as the relationship between employees in an organization, or the steps in a procedure.
- To insert SmartArt, click the SmartArt button in the Illustrations group on the INSERT tab of the Ribbon to display the Choose a SmartArt Graphic dialog box.
- From that dialog box, you can select a category of diagrams, and then a specific object to insert.
- When you select an object, a description of it and how to use it also displays in the dialog box.

Try It! Inserting a SmartArt Graphic

1. Start Word, and open **W10Try**. Save the document as **W10Try_xx** in the location where your teacher instructs you to store the files for this lesson.
2. Position the insertion point on the last line of the document.
3. Click the INSERT tab, then, in the Illustrations group, click the SmartArt button.

   ✓ *The Choose a SmartArt Graphic dialog box displays.*

4. Click Hierarchy in the left pane.
5. Click Organization Chart in the center pane.
6. Click OK.
7. Save the changes to the document, and leave it open to use in the next Try It.

Choose a SmartArt Graphic dialog box

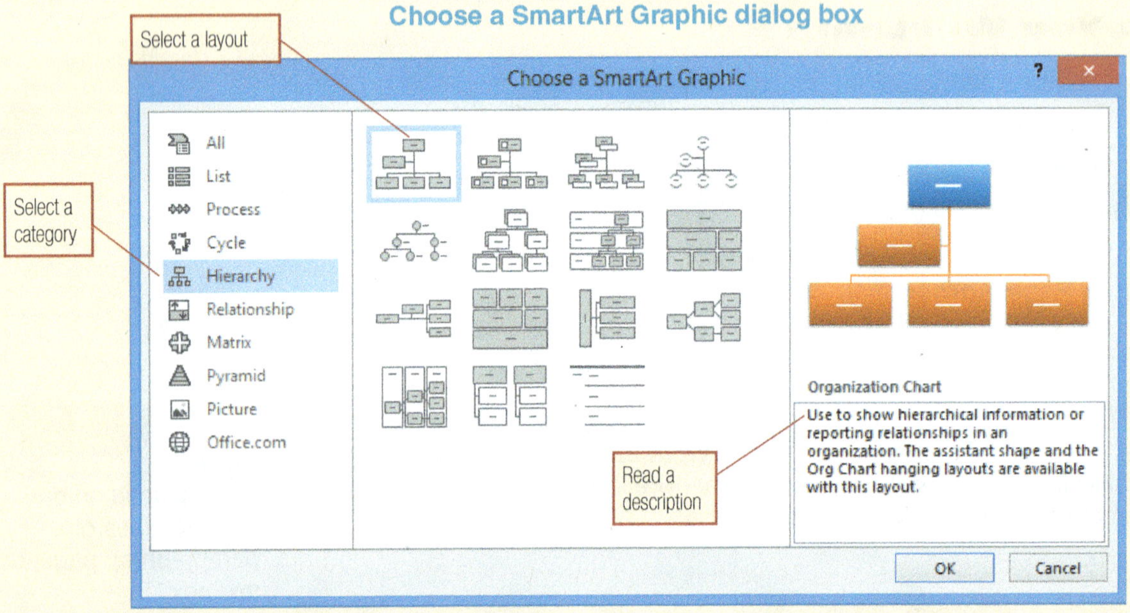

Word 2013, Windows 8, Microsoft Corporation

Entering Text in a SmartArt Graphic

- SmartArt objects are comprised of shapes, to which you can add text labels.
- New SmartArt graphics have placeholders in text boxes grouped with the shapes. Select the placeholder to type the text.
- You can edit and format the text using the same commands used to edit and format text in a text box.
- Most SmartArt graphics also have a Text pane as an alternative location for typing text. Select the placeholder in the Text pane and type the text.
- The Text pane is similar to a task pane; you can drag it to move it around the desktop, open it when you need it, and close it when you don't.

Try It! Entering Text in a SmartArt Graphic

1. In the **W10Try_xx** document with the SmartArt object selected, click the SMARTART TOOLS DESIGN tab.
2. In the Create Graphic group, click the Text Pane button. The button is a toggle; if the Text pane was displayed, clicking the button hides it. If the Text pane was hidden, clicking the button shows it.

   ✓ *You can also click the arrows on the control on the left side of the SmartArt object to display the Text pane.*
3. Click to select the shape at the top of the chart, and then type **President**.
4. Click to select the shape in the middle row and type **Executive Assistant.**
5. In the Text pane, click to select the next placeholder and type **V.P. Sales**.
6. In the Text pane, click to select the next placeholder and type **V.P. Operations**.
7. In the Text pane, click to select the next placeholder and type **V.P. Finance**.
8. Click the Text pane Close button ×.
9. Save the changes to the document, and leave it open to use in the next Try It.

Add text to SmartArt objects

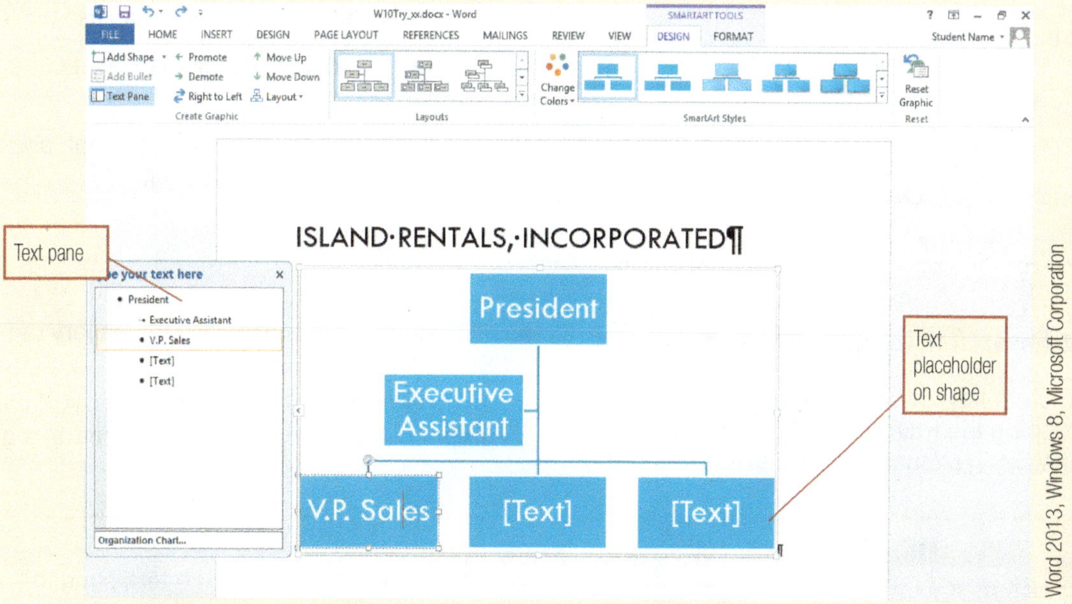

Modifying the Design of a SmartArt Graphic

- SmartArt graphics are inserted using the default design for the selected graphic type.
- You can modify the design of most SmartArt graphics, although the changes depend on the type of graphic you insert. For example, in an organization chart you can promote or demote a shape.
- Use the options on the SMARTART TOOLS DESIGN tab of the Ribbon to modify the design.
- For most SmartArt graphics, you can add shapes, change the order or position of shapes in the graphic, or change the layout.
- You can usually change colors and styles, as well.
- To apply formatting to a SmartArt graphic or the shapes in a SmartArt graphic, use the commands on the SMARTART TOOLS FORMAT tab on the Ribbon.

✓ *For more on formatting objects, refer to Word, Lesson 9.*

Try It! Modifying the Design of a SmartArt Graphic

1. In the **W10Try_xx** document, click the V.P. Sales shape to select it.
2. Click the SMARTART TOOLS DESIGN tab, then, in the Create Graphic group, click the Add Shape button.
3. Type **Regional Manager**, and then click the President shape.
4. Click the Add Shape drop-down arrow Add Shape and click Add Shape Above.
5. Type **CEO**.
6. Click the V.P. Sales shape to select it.
7. Click the Demote button.
8. Click the Regional Manager shape to select it.
9. Click the Move Up button.
10. Click the border around the object to select the entire object.
11. On the SMARTART TOOLS DESIGN tab, in the Layouts group, click the More button.
12. Click the Hierarchy layout (use ScreenTips to identify the layout).
13. If necessary, select the SmartArt object and then click the SMARTART TOOLS DESIGN tab.
14. In the SmartArt Styles group, click the Change Colors button.
15. Under Colorful, click Colorful – Accent Colors.
16. Select the SmartArt object and then click the SMARTART TOOLS DESIGN tab.
17. In the SmartArt Styles group, click the More button.
18. Under 3-D, click Cartoon.
19. If necessary, select the SmartArt object and then click the SMARTART TOOLS DESIGN tab.
20. In the Reset group, click the Reset Graphic button.
21. Save the changes to the document, and leave it open to use in the next Try It.

Creating a SmartArt Graphic from a Picture

- Use the Picture Layout button in the Picture Styles group on the PICTURE TOOLS FORMAT tab to transform a picture into a SmartArt graphic.
- Clicking this button displays the gallery of Picture SmartArt layouts.
- Insert text and modify a picture layout SmartArt graphic as you would any other SmartArt graphic.

Try It! Creating a SmartArt Graphic from a Picture

1. In the **W10Try_xx** file, press CTRL + END to move the insertion point to the end of the document.
2. Press CTRL + ENTER to insert a page break and move to the next page, and then press ENTER to insert a blank paragraph at the top of the page.
3. With the insertion point in the second paragraph on the page, click the INSERT tab, click Pictures in the Illustrations group, navigate to the location where data files for this lesson are stored, click **W10Try_picture.jpg**, and click Insert.
4. With the picture selected, click the PICTURE TOOLS FORMAT tab, and then, in the Picture Styles group, click the Picture Layout button.
5. Click the Snapshot Picture List layout (the second from the right in the first row).
6. On the SMARTART TOOLS DESIGN tab, in the Create Graphic group, click the Text Pane button to display the Text pane.

(continued)

Try It! Creating a SmartArt Graphic from a Picture *(continued)*

7. Type **Family-Friendly Vacation Islands**, and then press ENTER.
8. Click the Demote button ➔, and then type the following entries, pressing ENTER after all but the last entry:

   Martha's Vineyard

   Chincoteague Island

   Sanibel Island

   Hilton Head
9. Close the Text pane.
10. In the SmartArt Styles group, click the More button, and click Intense Effect in the Best Match for Document group.
11. Save the changes to the document, and leave it open to use in the next Try It.

Picture used to create a SmartArt graphic

Applying Text Effects and WordArt Styles

- Text effects such as shadows, fills, and outlines are useful for adding visual interest to text in printed documents, including flyers, brochures, or advertisements, or in documents viewed on a monitor, such as Web pages or presentations.
- Use the Text Effects button in the Font group on the HOME tab of the Ribbon to apply text effects.
- When you click the button, a gallery of text effects displays, or you can use the individual effects options to create your own style.
- Individual effects options include outlines, shadows, reflections, and glows.
- Text effects are not appropriate for use in a business letter or other serious professional document, such as a resume or report.
- Another option for formatting text with special effects is to apply a **WordArt** style.
- WordArt styles look exactly like Text Effects styles, but when you apply a WordArt style to selected text, you transform the text into a WordArt object that can be modified or positioned like any other object.

Try It! Applying Text Effects and WordArt Styles

1. In the **W10Try_xx** document, scroll up and select the text *ISLAND RENTALS, INCORPORATED.*
2. Click the HOME tab, and then, in the Font group, click the Text Effects button.
3. Click the style second from the left in the second row: Gradient Fill – Dark Green, Accent 1, Reflection.
4. Scroll back to page 2 and click in the blank paragraph at the top of the page.
5. Type **Beaches Galore!**.
6. Select the text, click the INSERT tab, and then click Insert WordArt in the Text group.
7. Click the Fill – White, Outline – Accent 2, Hard Shadow – Accent 2 WordArt style. The text becomes a WordArt object.
8. With the WordArt object selected, on the DRAWING TOOLS FORMAT tab, click Position and then click Position in Top Center with Square Text Wrapping.
9. Save the changes to the document, and leave it open to use in the next Try It.

Applying a Page Border

- You can apply a **border** to pages in a document.
- Basic border and shading options include line style, line width (weight), and line color.
- Additional border options include 3-D or Shadow effects.
- Word also has a built-in list of artwork designed for page borders. Art borders are useful for stationery, invitations, and other informal, decorative documents.
- You apply page borders using the options in the Borders and Shading dialog box which you access from the Page Background group on the DESIGN tab of the Ribbon.

Try It! Applying a Page Border

1. In the **W10Try_xx** document, adjust the zoom so you can see the entire page on your monitor.
2. On the DESIGN tab, in the Page Background group, click the Page Borders button.
3. Click the Page Border tab, if necessary.
4. Click the Color drop-down arrow and under Standard Colors, click Blue.
5. Click the Width drop-down arrow and click 1 pt.
6. In the Setting list, click Box.
7. Click OK.
8. Click the DESIGN tab and then click the Page Borders button.
9. Click the Page Border tab, if necessary.
10. Click the Art drop-down arrow to display a gallery of art borders.
11. Scroll down the gallery and click a border of palm trees.
12. Click OK.
13. Close **W10Try_xx**, saving changes, and exit Word.

Lesson 10—Practice

Restoration Architecture has recently reorganized its management structure. In this project, you use SmartArt graphics to draw a company organization chart in a document. You apply text effects and page borders to enhance the appearance of the document.

DIRECTIONS

1. Start Word, if necessary, create a blank document, and save the document as **W10Practice_xx** in the location where your teacher instructs you to store the files for this lesson.
2. Display the rulers and nonprinting characters, if necessary.
3. Double-click in the header area and type your full name. Press ENTER and type today's date.
4. Double-click in the main document area to position the insertion point at the beginning of the document. Type **Restoration Architecture,** press ENTER, and type **Upper Management Organization Chart.**
5. Press ENTER to start a new line.
6. Select the two lines of text. On the **HOME** tab, in the Font group, click the **Font** drop-down arrow and click **Arial** in the list of available fonts.
7. On the **HOME** tab in the Font group, click the **Font Size** drop-down arrow, and click **26** to increase the font size.
8. On the **HOME** tab in the Paragraph group, click the **Center** button to center the text.
9. Move the insertion point to the blank line and click the **INSERT** tab on the Ribbon.
10. Click the **SmartArt** button to display the Choose a SmartArt Graphic dialog box.

11. In the left pane of the dialog box, click **Hierarchy**.
12. In the center pane of the dialog box, click the **Half Circle Organization Chart**, and then click **OK** to insert the graphic.
13. Verify that the shape at the top of the chart is selected, and type **President/CEO**.
14. Click the **SMARTART TOOLS DESIGN** tab, then, in the Create Graphic group, click the **Text Pane** button to display the Text pane.

    ✓ *If the Text pane is already displayed, skip this step.*
15. In the Text pane, click the second text placeholder and type **Vice President of Operations**.
16. Click the third text placeholder and type **Director of Marketing**.
17. Click the fourth text placeholder and type **Director of Architectural Design**.
18. Click the fifth text placeholder and type **Director of Construction Management**.
19. Click the **Text Pane** button to hide the Text pane.
20. On the **SMARTART TOOLS DESIGN** tab, in the SmartArt Styles group, click the **Change Colors** button. Under Accent 2, click the **Colored Outline – Accent 2** style.
21. Click the **SmartArt Styles More** button and, under Best Match for Document, click the **Intense Effect** style.
22. Click the SmartArt graphic to select it, click the **SMARTART TOOLS FORMAT** tab, and click the **Size** button.
23. Use the Shape Height increment arrows to set the Shape Height to **5.0"** and the Shape Width increment arrows to set the Shape Width to **6.5"**.
24. On the **SMARTART TOOLS FORMAT** tab, in the Shape Styles group, click the **Shape Outline** drop-down arrow and under Theme Colors, click **Blue, Accent 5**.
25. Click the **Director of Marketing** shape to select it, then click the **SMARTART TOOLS DESIGN** tab.
26. In the Create Graphic group, click the **Add Shape** drop-down arrow, click **Add Shape Below**, and then type **Communications Manager**.
27. Save the changes to the document.
28. Select the text *Upper Management Organization Chart.*
29. Click the **HOME** tab on the Ribbon and, in the Font group, click the **Text Effects** button.
30. Click the style in the middle of the top—**Fill – Orange, Accent 2, Outline – Accent 2**.
31. Click the **DESIGN** tab and, in the Page Background group, click the **Page Borders** button. Click the **Page Border** tab if necessary.
32. Click the **Color** drop-down arrow and under Theme Colors, click **Orange, Accent 2, Lighter 40%.**
33. Click the **Width** drop-down arrow and click **3 pt**.
34. In the **Setting** area, click **Box**, and then click **OK**.
35. Save the changes to the document.
36. **With your teacher's permission**, print the document. It should look similar to Figure 10-1.
37. Close the document, saving changes, and exit Word.

Figure 10-1

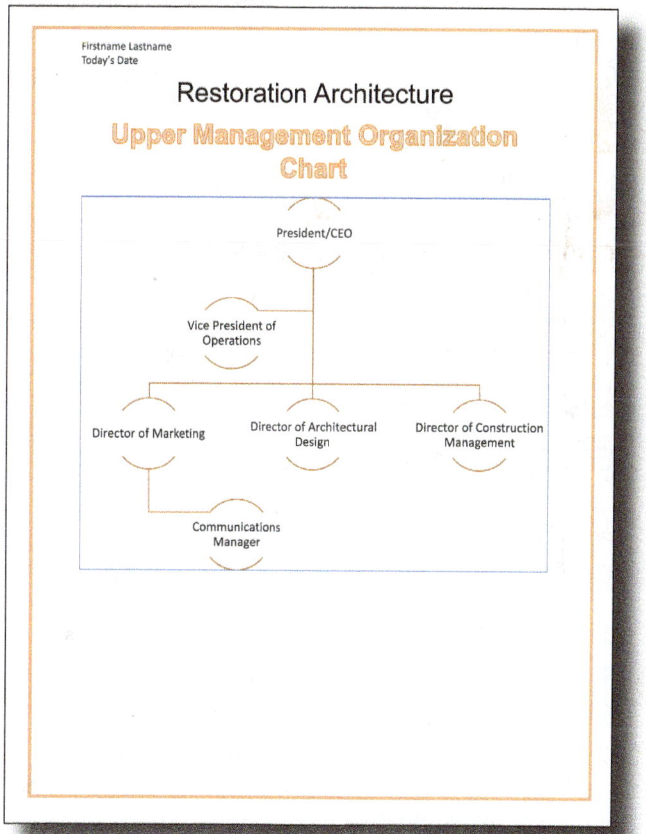

Word 2013, Windows 8, Microsoft Corporation

Lesson 10—Apply

In this project, you use use SmartArt graphics to draw a diagram illustrating Restoration Architecture's new procedures for requesting vacation time off. To improve the appearance of the document, you apply text effects and page borders.

DIRECTIONS

1. Start Word, if necessary, and open **W10Apply** from the data files for this lesson.
2. Save the file as **W10Apply_xx** in the location where your teacher instructs you to store the files for this lesson.
3. Display the rulers and nonprinting characters, if necessary.
4. Type your full name and today's date in the header.
5. Position the insertion point on the last line of the document.
6. Click the **INSERT** tab, and click the **SmartArt** button.
7. Select the **Process** category, and then select the **Basic Process** diagram. Click **OK** to insert the diagram in the document.
8. In the first shape on the left, type the text label **1. Discuss schedule with supervisor.**
9. In the middle shape, type the text label **2. Obtain vacation request form from Human Resources dept.**
10. In the shape on the right, type the text label **3. Complete form and submit to supervisor for signature.**
11. With the third shape selected, select to add a shape after.
12. In the new shape, type the text label **4. Submit signed form to Human Resources dept. for approval.**
13. Change the diagram layout to **Step Down Process**.
14. Change the colors to **Dark 1 Outline**.
15. Apply the **Inset 3-D** SmartArt style.
16. Click the border around the object to select it, then resize the height of the object to **4.5"** inches. Leave the width at 6.0".
17. Position the object in the **Middle Center with Square Text Wrapping**.
18. Left align the object horizontally on the page.
19. Save the changes to the document.
20. Select the text *Restoration Architecture*.
21. Apply the **Fill – Blue, Accent 1, Outline – Background 1, Hard Shadow – Accent 1** WordArt style, and then position the WordArt object in the top center with Square text wrapping.
22. Select the text *Vacation Request Procedure* and apply the **Fill – Blue, Accent 1, Shadow** text effects style.
23. Apply a **Blue-Gray, Text 2, 1½ pt. box** border to the page.
24. **With your teacher's permission**, print the document. It should look similar to Figure 10-2.
25. Close the document, saving changes, and exit Word.

Figure 10-2

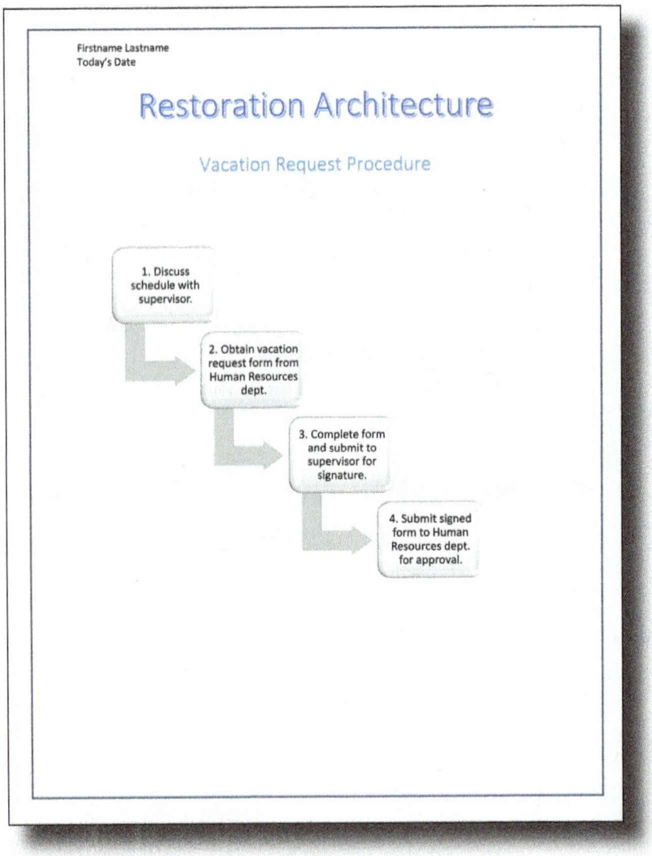
Firstname Lastname
Today's Date

Restoration Architecture

Vacation Request Procedure

1. Discuss schedule with supervisor.

2. Obtain vacation request form from Human Resources dept.

3. Complete form and submit to supervisor for signature.

4. Submit signed form to Human Resources dept. for approval.

End-of-Chapter Activities

➤ Word Chapter 1—Critical Thinking

Write a Letter and Create a Flyer

Becoming involved in a student organization such as Future Business Leaders of America-Phi Beta Lambda, Business Professionals of America, or Family, Career and Community Leaders of America can lead to many opportunities. They sponsor conferences and competitions, encourage leadership, and often offer scholarships for summer programs and college.

In this project, plan an event to publicize student organizations at your school. For example, you might plan a fair at which all organizations have booths or tables where they hand out information, or it might be an assembly at which representatives of the organizations give presentations.

Write a personal business letter to the school principal explaining the event, and asking for permission to hold it. Then design a flyer publicizing the event.

DIRECTIONS

Write the Letter and Create an Envelope

1. Start Word, if necessary. Save a new blank file as **WCT01A_xx** in the location where your teacher instructs you to store the files for this project.
2. Select a theme and a style set and type a letter to the school principal using full-block or modified-block business letter formatting. Be sure to set up the letter correctly, including all the necessary parts, such as a return address, date, and inside address. You may use either open or mixed punctuation.
3. In the letter, explain your project and why it is important. Politely ask for permission to continue planning the event, and to hold the event, if possible. Be specific about the date and time, and where the event would take place.
4. Proofread the letter to find any spelling or grammatical errors, and correct them.
5. Create an envelope for the letter, using the inside address as the delivery address and your own address as the return address.
6. Add the envelope to the document without changing the default return address.
7. **With your teacher's permission**, print both the letter and the envelope. Read your letter out loud to a partner or to the class.
8. Close the document, saving changes.

Create the Flyer

1. Create a new blank document and save it as **WCT01B_xx** in the location where your teacher instructs you to store the files for this lesson.
2. Select a theme and a style set.
3. Enter and format text and graphics to create a flyer publicizing your event.
4. Use text boxes to make it easier to integrate the text with graphics. Use at least two types of graphics—pictures, clip art, scanned images, shapes, text boxes, or SmartArt. Use the Selection Pane to hide objects as necessary while you format other objects.
5. Use font formatting and text effects to enhance the appearance of the document.
6. Use styles and effects to format the graphics objects.
7. Size and position the objects and text to make the document attractive, fun, and easy to read. Use the alignment guides to align objects with each other or with the margins. Apply text wrapping as desired with the Layout Options or Wrap Text gallery.
8. Use line and paragraph spacing to make the text easy to read, and use list formatting where appropriate.

9. As you work, consider the overall organization and appearance of the document. Use colors that work together, and do not overload the page with too much text or formatting.
10. Include your name and the current date somewhere in the header or footer of the document.
11. When you are satisfied with the document, ask a classmate to review it and make comments or suggestions that will help you improve it.
12. Make changes and corrections, as necessary.
13. **With your teacher's permission**, print the document. Present the document to a partner or to the class, explaining why you used specific graphics and formatting.
14. Close the document, saving changes, and exit Word.

➤ Word Chapter 1—Portfolio Builder

Write a Letter and Create an Invitation

Michigan Avenue Athletic Club recently renovated its lobby and locker room. Restoration Architecture was responsible for the design and construction. The club manager has asked you to write a letter to the project manager thanking him for his support during the process and inviting him to the grand reopening celebration.

In this project, you will create and type the letter and an accompanying envelope using modified-block business letter formatting. You will also create an invitation to include with the letter, using graphics, styles, and effects.

DIRECTIONS

Write the Letter and Create an Envelope

1. Start Word, if necessary. Save a new blank file as **WPB01A_xx** in the location where your teacher instructs you to store the files for this project.
2. Apply the **No Spacing** style, change the font to **12-point Times New Roman**, and type the letter shown in Illustration 1A on the next page.
   - Type the business name and address in the header.
   - Set a left tab at **3.25"** and use it to position the date, closing, signature, and job title lines.
   - Replace the sample text **Today's Date** with the actual date and **Student's Name** with your own full name.
   - Apply the Title style to both lines in the header, and then center them horizontally.
   - Insert the **Urgent 1** watermark on the letter.
3. Proofread the letter to find any spelling or grammatical errors, and correct them.
4. Create an envelope for the letter, using the inside address as the delivery address and **235 Michigan Avenue, Chicago, IL 60601** as the return address.
5. Add the envelope to the document without changing the default return address.
6. **With your teacher's permission**, print both the letter and the envelope.
7. Close the document, saving changes.

Create the Invitation

1. Open **WPB01B** from the data files for this lesson. Save it as **WPB01B_xx** in the location where your teacher instructs you to store the files for this lesson.
2. Apply the **Ion Boardroom** theme and the **Centered** style set to the document.
3. Select the first line of text, center it horizontally, and increase the font size to **36 points**. Apply the **Fill – White, Outline – Accent 2, Hard Shadow – Accent 2** text effect.
4. Select the second paragraph and apply the **Title** style, then change the font size to 26 points and justify the text.

Illustration 1A

Michigan Avenue Athletic Club
235 Michigan Avenue, Chicago, IL 60601

Today's Date

Mr. George Hernandez
Project Manager
Restoration Architecture
5566 Elm Street, Suite 25B
Chicago, IL 60601

Dear Mr. Hernandez:

I am writing on behalf of the members and employees of Michigan Avenue Athletic Club to thank you for the excellent job designing and renovating the club's lobby and locker rooms. Everyone is very pleased with the completed results.

All the representatives of Restoration Architecture and all the construction workers were courteous and professional. The work was completed with a minimum of disruption. Best of all, it was done on time and within budget.

We are holding our grand reopening on Sunday, April 14, from 2:00 p.m. to 6:00 p.m. (See the enclosed invitation.) There will be refreshments, tours, and complimentary access to the club's facilities, including the pool, racquetball courts, and fitness rooms. We hope you will be able to join us so we can express our gratitude in person.

Again, thank you very much for an excellent job, well done.

Sincerely,

Student's Name
Assistant Manager

Enclosure
Invitation

URGENT

5. Draw a text box around the selection, and resize the box to **2.7"** high by **5.7"** wide. Format the text box to have no outline, and align it in the center middle of the page. Nudge it down, if necessary so it displays below the first line of text.
6. Select the date and time, increase the font size to **20 points** and draw a text box around the selection. If necessary, increase the size of the text box so all the text displays.
7. Apply the **Subtle Effect – Red, Accent 2** shape style to the text box, and then apply the **Red, 18 pt glow, Accent color 3** Glow shape effect.
8. Position the text box in the **Top Right with Square Text Wrapping**, then change the text wrapping to **Top and Bottom**.
9. Select the five items at the end of the document and increase the font size to **16 points**.
10. Format the items as a bulleted list, using the bullet symbol shown in Illustration 1B on the next page.
11. Change the font color to **Red, Accent 3, Darker 25%.** Change the hanging indent setting to **0.5"**.
12. Draw a text box around the list. Resize the box to **2.0"** high by **4.0"** wide, and apply the **Colored Outline – Red, Accent 2** shape style. Position the text box in the **Bottom Center with Square Text Wrapping**.
13. Insert an **Explosion 1** shape sized to **1.5"** high by **1.7"** wide. Add the text **Food!** to the shape, and format the text as **12-point Bold**. Apply the **Subtle Effect – Plum, Accent 1** shape style and then rotate the shape about **0.5"** to the left.
14. Insert an **Explosion 2** shape sized to **1.5"** high by **2.0"** wide. Add the text **Fun!** to the shape, and format the text as **12-point Bold**. Apply the **Subtle Effect – Purple, Accent 6** shape style and then rotate the shape about **0.5"** to the right.
15. Move the **Explosion 2** shape so it overlaps the **Explosion 1** shape, and layer it behind the Explosion 1 shape (refer to illustration 1-B on the next page).
16. Group the two shapes together, and align them above the list text box, centered horizontally on the page. They may overlap the top of the text box.
17. Use Online Pictures to search for a picture of balloons to insert in the document, or insert the picture file **WPB01_picture**.
18. Recolor the picture to **Plum, Accent color 1 Light**.
19. Resize the picture to **4.0"** high, if necessary, and set the text wrapping to **Behind Text**.
20. Move the picture to the top left of the page.
21. Complete the invitation by adding an art page border of balloons.
22. Save the changes to the document. It should look similar to Illustration 1-B on the next page.
23. Type your name and today's date in the footer of the document. (If the text is hidden by the border, click the HEADER & FOOTER TOOLS DESIGN tab, and change the Footer from Bottom setting to 0.6".)
24. **With your teacher's permission**, print the document.
25. Close the document, saving changes, and exit Word.

Illustration 1B

Sunday, April 14

2:00 p.m. until 6:00 p.m.

Grand Reopening Celebration!

PLEASE JOIN US AT MICHIGAN AVENUE ATHLETIC CLUB TO CELEBRATE OUR NEW AND IMPROVED LOBBY AND LOCKER ROOMS.

- Refreshments!
- Tours!
- Games!
- Raffles!
- Access to the club's facilities!

Firstname Lastname

Today's Date

Chapter 2

(Courtesy East/Shutterstock)

Editing Documents and Working with Tables

Lesson 11 Checking Spelling and Grammar

- Correcting Spelling and Grammar As You Type
- Checking Spelling and Grammar
- Using the Thesaurus
- Controlling Hyphenation
- Analyzing the Use of Hyphens
- Inserting a Non-Breaking Space

Lesson 12 Moving a Selection

- Moving Text
- Using Drag-and-Drop and Cut and Paste
- Using Paste Options
- Using Paste Special

Lesson 13 Copying a Selection

- Using Copy and Paste
- Using Drag-and-Drop Editing to Copy

Lesson 14 Inserting a Table

- Analyzing Tables
- Inserting and Deleting a Table
- Entering Text in a Table
- Selecting in a Table
- Selecting Multiple Components in a Table
- Changing Table Structure
- Formatting a Table
- Viewing Gridlines

Lesson 15 Aligning Tables

- Converting Text to a Table
- Inserting Existing Text into a Table Cell
- Setting Column Width and Row Height
- Setting Alignment in a Table Cell
- Setting Tabs in a Table Cell
- Setting Cell Margins
- Aligning a Table Horizontally on the Page

Lesson 16 Drawing a Table

- Drawing a Table
- Merging and Splitting Cells
- Changing Text Direction in a Table Cell
- Moving and Resizing Tables
- Setting Text Wrapping Around a Table

Lesson 17 Performing Calculations in a Table

- Performing Addition in a Table
- Applying a Number Format
- Sorting Rows in a Table
- Applying Cell Borders and Shading
- Making a Table Accessible
- Converting a Table to Text

Lesson 11

Checking Spelling and Grammar

➤ What You Will Learn

Correcting Spelling and Grammar As You Type
Checking Spelling and Grammar
Using the Thesaurus
Controlling Hyphenation
Analyzing the Use of Hyphens
Inserting a Non-Breaking Space

Software Skills A professional document should be free of spelling and grammatical errors. While it is important to always proofread your work for errors, Word can check the spelling and grammar in a document and recommend corrections. You can also use Word to control hyphenation, and to recommend alternative words to improve your writing.

WORDS TO KNOW

Antonyms
Words with opposite meanings.

Compound modifier
Two words combined to act as an adjective.

Compound word
Two or more words combined to create a new or more specific word.

Hyphen
A horizontal bar character used to indicate a split or incomplete word.

Synonyms
Words with the same meaning.

Thesaurus
A listing of words with synonyms and antonyms.

What You Can Do

Correcting Spelling and Grammar As You Type

- Word checks spelling and grammar as you type and marks suspected errors with a wavy underline. The color of the underline indicates the type of error:
  - Red wavy underlines are spelling errors.
  - Blue wavy underlines are grammatical errors such as incorrect punctuation, mismatched case or tense, sentence fragments, and run-on sentences.
  - Blue underlines are also used for possible word choice errors, which are words that are spelled correctly but may be used in the wrong context. For example, if you type *I red the book*, Word applies a blue wavy underline to the word *red*.
- You can ignore the wavy lines and keep typing, or use a shortcut menu to select a correction. Note that these wavy lines do not appear in the document when printed.
- You can also choose to ignore the error on the shortcut menu, which removes the underline.

- Any word not in the Word dictionary is marked as misspelled, including proper names, words with unique spellings, and many technical terms. You can add words to the Word dictionary so that Word does not mark them as misspelled in the future.
- By default, Word checks for grammar only. You can select to check for grammar and style, and you can even select specific grammar and style rules to check.
- If the wavy underlines distract you from your work, you can turn off the feature.

Try It! Selecting Spelling and Grammar Options

1. Start Word, and open **W11TryA** from the data files for this lesson. Save the file as **W11TryA_xx** in the location where your teacher instructs you to store the files for this lesson.
2. Click FILE > Options.
3. Click Proofing.
4. Verify that the Check spelling as you type check box is selected.
5. Verify that the Mark grammar errors as you type check box is selected.
6. Verify that the Frequently confused words check box is selected.
7. Verify that the Check grammar with spelling check box is selected.

   ✓ *A check mark in a box means the option is already selected. If there is no check mark, click the box to select it.*
8. Click the Settings button to the right of the Writing Style list box.
9. Scroll through the list to see which options are selected.
10. Click the Writing style drop-down arrow and click Grammar & Style.
11. Scroll through the list to see which options are selected.
12. Click the Writing Style drop-down arrow and click Grammar Only.
13. In the Grammar list, click in the Fragments and Run-ons and Subject-verb agreement check boxes.
14. Click OK.
15. Click OK to close the Word Options dialog box.
16. Save the changes to **W11TryA_xx**, and leave it open to use in the next Try It.

Select grammar options

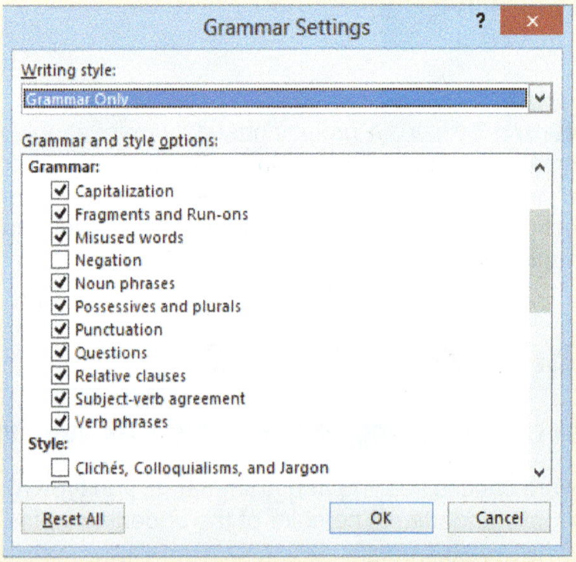

Word 2013, Windows 8, Microsoft Corporation

Try It! Correcting Spelling As You Type

1. In the **W11TryA_xx** file, right-click the first word that has a red, wavy underline: *Advetners*.
2. On the shortcut menu, click Adventures—the correct spelling.
3. Right-click the word *DeShawn*, which also has a red, wavy underline.
4. Click Add to Dictionary.

   ✓ *When you add a word to the dictionary, it is no longer marked as misspelled.*
5. Right-click the word *Weitzel*.
6. Click Ignore All.

   ✓ *When you ignore an error, the underline is removed from that occurrence only. When you Ignore All, it is removed from all occurrences in the document.*
7. Right-click the word that has a blue wavy underline: *companies*.
8. Click company's on the shortcut menu.
9. Save the changes to the **W11TryA_xx** file, and leave it open to use in the next Try It.

Use a shortcut menu to correct errors as you type

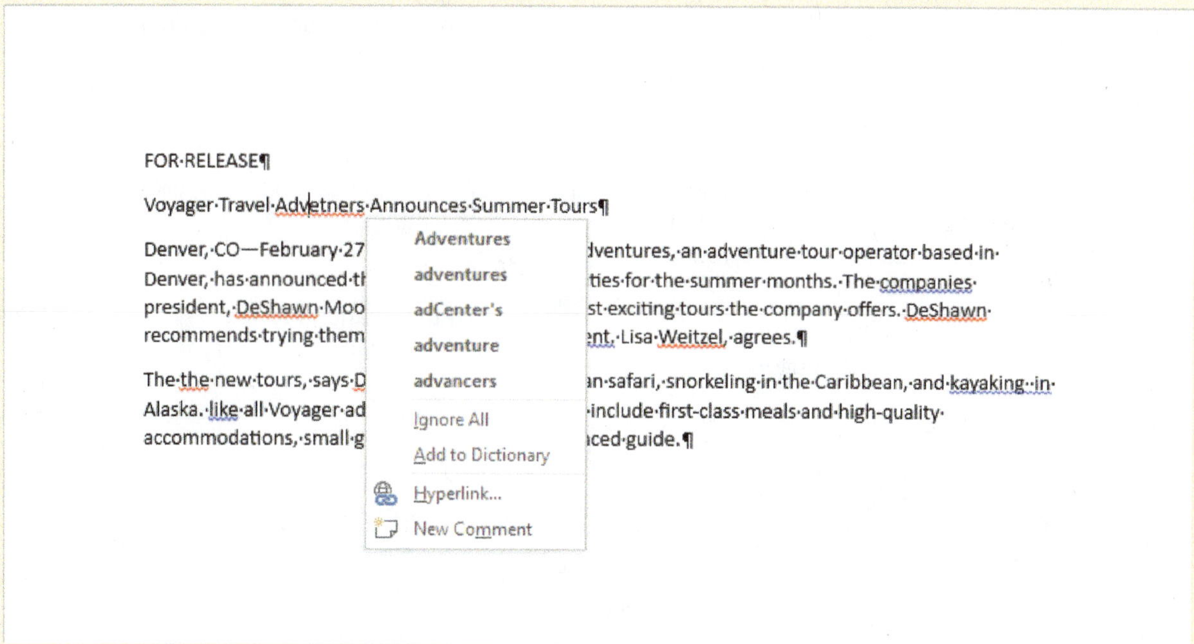

Word 2013, Windows 8, Microsoft Corporation

Try It! Correcting Grammar As You Type

1. In the **W11TryA_xx** file, right-click the first text marked with a blue, wavy underline: *these is.*
2. On the shortcut menu, click these are.
3. Right-click the third text marked with a blue, wavy underline: *like.*
4. On the shortcut menu, click Like.
5. Save the changes to **W11TryA_xx**, and close it. Leave Word open to use in the next Try It.

Checking Spelling and Grammar

- You can check the spelling and grammar in an entire document or in part of a document.
- To check part of a document, you must first select the section you want to check.
- When Word identifies a word that may be misspelled, you can correct the error, ignore it, or add the word to the dictionary.
- When Word identifies a grammatical mistake, you can correct the error or ignore it.
- The task pane that opens when you select the Spelling & Grammar option provides additional information about the spelling and grammar errors identified.
- To check only the spelling, you can clear the Check grammar with spelling check box on the Proofing tab of the Word Options dialog box.

Try It! Checking Spelling and Grammar

1. In Word, open **W11TryB** from the data files for this lesson, and save it as **W11TryB_xx** in the location where your teacher instructs you to store the files for this lesson.
2. Click the REVIEW tab. In the Proofing group, click the Spelling & Grammar button.

   ✓ F7 *is the shortcut key to start the spelling and grammar check.*

3. For the first misspelled word, *Advetners*, click the correct spelling, Adventures, and then click Change.
4. For the first Grammar error, click *company's* and click Change.
5. For the Subject-Verb Agreement, click *these are* and then click Change.
6. For the fragment, remove the period following vice president and replace it with a comma. Then click Resume to continue the check.
7. For the Repeated Word error, click Delete.
8. For the error with extra space between words, click *kayaking in*, and then click Change.
9. For the incorrect *a*, click *an* and click Change.
10. For the Capitalization error, click *Like*, and then click Change.
11. Click OK.
12. Save the changes to **W11TryB_xx**, and leave it open to use in the next Try It.

Use the Spelling and Grammar checker

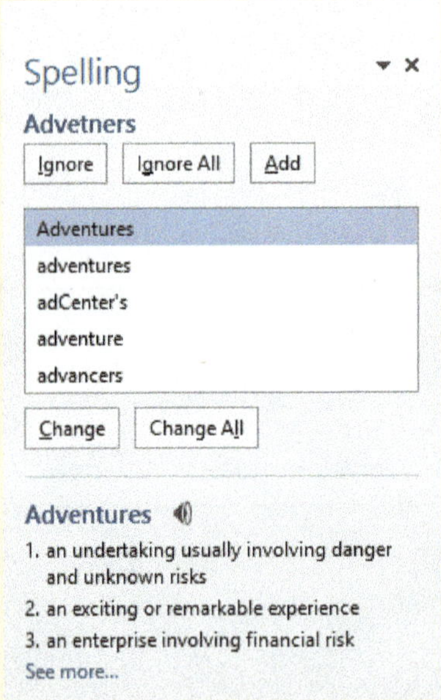

Word 2013, Windows 8, Microsoft Corporation

Try It! Editing the Custom Dictionary

1. Click FILE > Options.
2. Click Proofing.
3. Click Custom Dictionaries.
4. Click the dictionary marked as the default, such as RoamingCustom.dic, and then click Edit Word List.
5. Click DeShawn.
6. Click Delete.
7. Click OK.
8. Click OK.
9. Click OK.
10. Leave the file open to use in the next Try It.

Using the Thesaurus

- A **thesaurus** can improve your writing by helping you to eliminate repetitive use of common words and to choose more descriptive words.
- You can use a shortcut menu to quickly find a **synonym** for any word in a document.
- Use Word's thesaurus to look up synonyms, definitions, and **antonyms** for any word. Word displays a list of results in the Thesaurus task pane. The results are organized under collapsible headings.
  - Click an expand arrow to expand the list to show additional words.
  - Click a collapse arrow to collapse the list to hide some words.
- Use the available drop-down list to insert a word from the results list at the current insertion point location or copy it at a different location, or look it up in the thesaurus.

  ✓ *To see definitions of the selected word, you must sign in to a valid Microsoft account.*
- Use the Back button in the Thesaurus task pane to browse through the content you previously viewed in the Thesaurus pane.
- By default, Word searches an English thesaurus, but you can select to search another reference, such as a French or Spanish thesaurus.

Try It! Using the Thesaurus

1. In the **W11TryB_xx** file, right-click the word *Announces* in the headline.
2. On the shortcut menu, click Synonyms.
3. On the submenu, click Reveals.
4. Click the word *exciting* in the second sentence.
5. On the REVIEW tab, click the Thesaurus button.

   ✓ *A list of synonyms and antonyms for the word* exciting *displays.*
6. In the Thesaurus task pane, click *thrilling* under the first boldfaced heading **thrilling (adj.)**.

   ✓ *A list of synonyms and antonyms for the word* thrilling *displays.*
7. Click the Back button to display the synonyms for exciting again.
8. Rest the mouse pointer on the word *breathtaking*, click the down arrow that displays, and click Insert.
9. Close the Thesaurus task pane.
10. Save the changes to **W11TryB_xx**, and leave it open to use in the next Try It.

Controlling Hyphenation

- Use **hyphens** to break words at the ends of lines instead of wrapping them to the next line.
- Word can automatically insert hyphens in a document or selection. When you edit the document, Word adjusts, or re-hyphenates, the words, as necessary.
- Use optional hyphens to indicate where you want to insert a hyphen if a word falls at the end of a line. Word only uses the optional hyphen if necessary, but you can see it by displaying nonprinting characters.
- Use non-breaking hyphens to prevent a word from breaking at the end of a line. Non-breaking hyphens are useful for hyphenated text that you want to keep together on the same line, such as phone numbers.

Try It! Controlling Hyphenation

1. In the **W11TryB_xx** file, display nonprinting characters, if they are not already displayed.
2. On the PAGE LAYOUT tab, click the Hyphenation button bc.
3. Click Automatic.
4. On the PAGE LAYOUT tab, click Hyphenation bc > None.
5. On the PAGE LAYOUT tab, click Hyphenation bc > Manual.

   ✓ *Word looks for long words that may require hyphenation, and displays the Manual Hyphenation dialog box. It suggests logical positions for hyphens. The cursor flashes on the selected location.*
6. Click Yes to the suggested hyphenation of Denver, recommends, and accommodations.
7. Click OK.
8. Click to position the insertion point to the right of the letter *h* in the word *breathtaking*.
9. Press CTRL + -.
10. Position the insertion point to the right of the hyphen in the word *high-quality*.
11. Press BACKSPACE to delete the hyphen.
12. Press CTRL + SHIFT + -.
13. Save the changes to **W11TryB_xx**, and leave it open to use in the next Try It.

Optional hyphens display as nonprinting characters

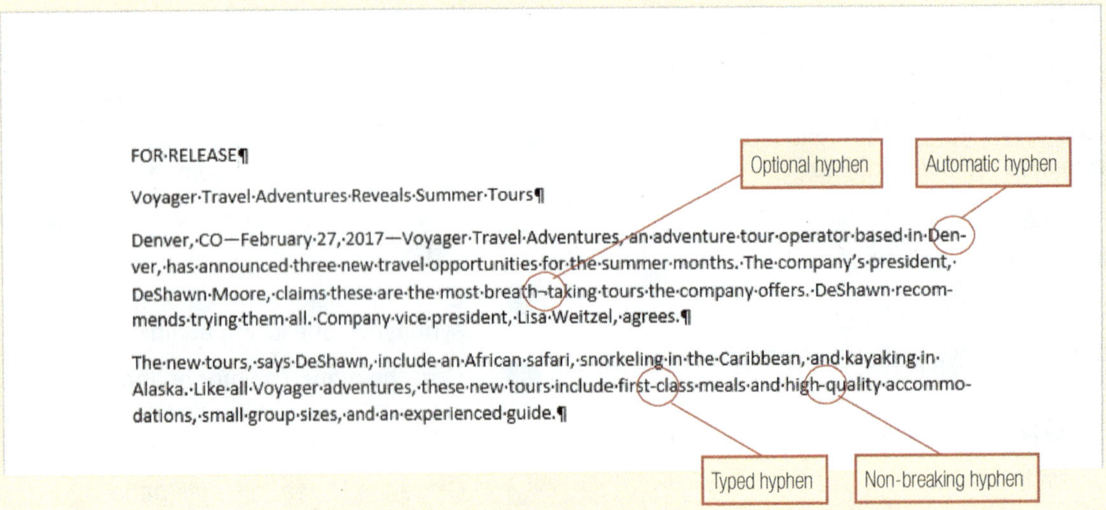

Word 2013, Windows 8, Microsoft Corporation

Analyzing the Use of Hyphens

- Most of the time, it is best not to hyphenate; it makes text harder to read.
- When you do hyphenate, insert the hyphen between syllables at a logical point for pausing. Visually, it looks best if the word is split evenly.
- Hyphens may be used in some **compound words** to make them easier to read. For example, mother-in-law is usually hyphenated.
- Hyphens are usually used in **compound modifiers** that come before the noun they describe. For example, She has a ten-year-old brother includes hyphens; Her brother is ten years old, does not.
- They should also be used if the compound modifier can be misinterpreted. Consider the different meanings of the following two sentences:
  - My first-class teacher assigns a lot of homework.
  - My first class teacher assigns a lot of homework.

Inserting a Non-Breaking Space

- When Word wraps text from one line to the next, it breaks the line at a space or—if hyphenation is on—at a hyphen.
- Insert a non-breaking space to keep two words together on the same line.

Try It! Inserting a Non-Breaking Space

1. In the W11TryB_xx file, delete the space between the words *in* and *Alaska* in the first sentence of the second paragraph.
2. Position the insertion point between the n and the A, and press CTRL + SHIFT + SPACE. Word inserts the non-breaking space—it looks like a small superscript circle—and keeps the two words together on the same line.
3. Close W11TryB_xx, saving changes, and exit Word.

Lesson 11—Practice

The Marketing Director at Michigan Avenue Athletic Club has asked you to create a mission statement for the club. A mission statement is used to define the purpose and goals of a business or organization. In this project, you will create one version of the statement. You will check and correct spelling and grammar, and use the thesaurus to select synonyms. You will also use automatic and manual hyphenation.

DIRECTIONS

1. Start Word, if necessary, create a new document, and save the document as W11Practice_xx in the location where your teacher instructs you to store the files for this lesson.
2. Display the rulers and nonprinting characters, if necessary.
3. Double-click in the header area and type your full name and today's date.
4. Starting on the first line of the document, type the following text exactly as shown:

   The Michigan Avenue Athletic Club is cometted to
5. Right-click the misspelled word **cometted**, and select the correct spelling **committed**.
6. Reposition the insertion point and continue typing:

   excellence. We encourages our employees and our members to strive for the highest goals, meet all challenges with spirit and enthusiasm, and work diligently to achieve personel and professionel harmony.

7. Press ENTER.
8. Right-click the **blue wavy underline** in the second sentence and select the correct word, **encourage**. Do not correct the remaining errors.
9. Reposition the insertion point and type the following second paragraph:

   At MAAC, we respects individuality and value diversity. Under the first-rate guidance of General Manager Raimond Petersun and Exercise Director Chardutta Saroj we hope to provide an enviromnent where people feel comfortable, safe,, and free to pursue there physical fitness goals.
10. Save the changes to the document.
11. Move the insertion point to the beginning of the document.
12. Click the **REVIEW** tab and click the **Spelling & Grammar** button to start the spelling checker.
13. When Word stops on the misspelled word **personel**, click the correct spelling, **personal**, and then click **Change**.
14. When it stops on **professionel**, click **professional** and then click **Change**.
15. When Word stops on the Subject-Verb Agreement for **respects**, click **Change**.
16. Click **Ignore** to skip over the proper name **Raimond**.
17. Click **Add** to add the proper name **Petersun** to the dictionary.
18. Click **Ignore** to skip over the proper names **Chardutta** and **Saroj**.
19. For the Possible Word Choice Error, click **their** and then click **Change**.
20. For the incorrect punctuation, click **Change** to replace the two commas with one.
21. Correct any other errors that Word identifies, and then click **OK** when the spelling and grammar check is complete.
22. Save the changes to the document.
23. Right-click the word **encourage** in the second sentence, click **Synonyms** on the shortcut menu, and click **embolden** in the list of synonyms.
24. Click on the word **guidance** in the second sentence of the second paragraph.
25. Click **REVIEW** > **Thesaurus**.
26. In the Thesaurus task pane, rest the mouse pointer on the word **leadership** below the boldfaced heading **leadership (n.)**, then click the down arrow and click **Insert**.
27. Close the Thesaurus task pane.
28. Click **PAGE LAYOUT** > **Hyphenation** > **Automatic** to automatically hyphenate long words at the end of lines.
29. Click the **Hyphenation** button again, and then click **None**.
30. Click the **Hyphenation** button again, and then click **Manual**.
31. In the first **Manual Hyphenation** dialog box, click **Yes** to accept the hyphen location in the word Manager.
32. Click on the hyphen between the t and the l in the word diligently in the Hyphenate at box to move the hyphen location, and then click **Yes**, and then click **OK**.
33. **With your teacher's permission**, print the document. It should look similar to Figure 11-1 on the next page.
34. Close the document, saving changes, and exit Word.

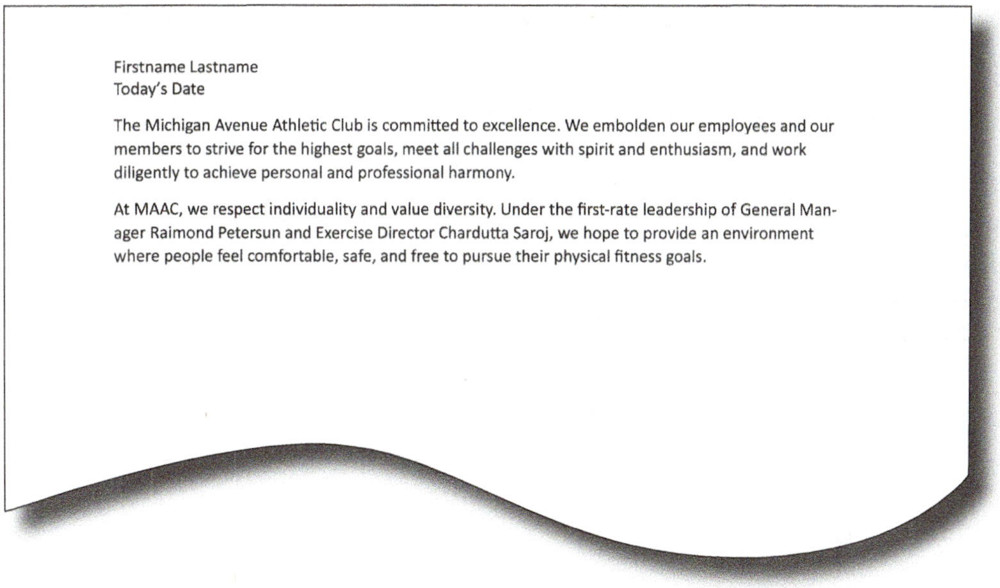
Firstname Lastname
Today's Date

The Michigan Avenue Athletic Club is committed to excellence. We embolden our employees and our members to strive for the highest goals, meet all challenges with spirit and enthusiasm, and work diligently to achieve personal and professional harmony.

At MAAC, we respect individuality and value diversity. Under the first-rate leadership of General Manager Raimond Petersun and Exercise Director Chardutta Saroj, we hope to provide an environment where people feel comfortable, safe, and free to pursue their physical fitness goals.

Figure 11-1

Lesson 11—Apply

In this project, you work on a different version of the Michigan Avenue Athletic Club's mission statement. After correcting spelling and grammar, you fine-tune wording using the Thesaurus and then adjust hyphenation.

DIRECTIONS

1. Start Word, if necessary, and open **W11Apply** from the data files for this lesson.
2. Save the file as **W11Apply_xx** in the location where your teacher instructs you to store the files for this lesson.
3. Display the rulers and nonprinting characters, if necessary.
4. Type your full name and today's date in the header.
5. Right-click the misspelled word *dilligently* in the first paragraph and use the shortcut menu to select the correct spelling.
6. Right-click the grammatical error in the second paragraph. The suggested correction of a single semicolon is incorrect.
7. Press ESC to cancel the shortcut menu and correct the error by selecting the two semicolons and typing a comma.
8. Move the insertion point to the beginning of the document and start the spelling and grammar checker.
9. Correct the misspellings *Ahthletic* and *excllence*.
10. Click **goals** in the list of suggestions and then click **Change All** to correct the misspelling of the word *goles* throughout the document.
11. Ignore all proper names that Word marks as not in the dictionary.
12. Click different in the list and then click **Change All** to correct the misspelling of the word *diferent* throughout the document.
13. Correct the subject-verb agreement in the first sentence of the third paragraph, and correct both word choice errors in the second sentence of the third paragraph. Select **their** in the Suggestions list to replace the word *there*.
14. Click **OK** when the spelling and grammar check is complete, and save the changes to the document.
15. Use a shortcut menu to replace the word *excellent* in the second sentence of the first paragraph with its synonym *outstanding*.
16. Click the word **things** in the first sentence of the third paragraph and use the thesaurus to display a list of synonyms in the Thesaurus task pane.

17. Scroll down the list, and click the word **points** to display its synonyms, then scroll down and click the word **aims** to display its synonyms.
18. Under *goals*, rest the mouse pointer on the word **objectives**, click the down arrow, and click **Insert**, then close the Thesaurus task pane.
19. Start manual hyphenation.
20. Select to insert an optional hyphen between the second and third syllables in the words *responsibility*, *employees*, and *leadership*. Accept the hyphenation suggestion for *provide*. Close the dialog box.
21. Apply the **Title** style to the text *Michigan Avenue Athletic Club*, and the **Heading 1** style to the text *Mission Statement*, and then save the changes to the document.
22. **With your teacher's permission**, print the document. It should look similar to Figure 11-2.
23. Close the document, saving changes, and exit Word.

Figure 11-2

Firstname Lastname
Today's Date

Michigan Avenue Athletic Club

Mission Statement

The Michigan Avenue Athletic Club is committed to excellence. We encourage our outstanding employ-ees and our loyal members to strive for the highest goals, meet all challenges with spirit, and a positive attitude, and to work diligently to achieve personal and professional harmony.

At Michigan Avenue Athletic Club, we respect individuality and value diversity. Under the first-rate leadership of General Manager Raimond Petersun and Exercise Director Chardutta Saroj we hope to pro-vide an environment where people feel comfortable, safe, and free to pursue their physical fitness goals.

At MAAC, we recognize that different people are motivated by different objectives. We take our respon-sibility for making sure every individual can achieve their goals very seriously. Our mission, in a nutshell, is to make the highest quality resources available and to provide a safe and nurturing environment.

Word 2013, Windows 8, Microsoft Corporation

Lesson 12

Moving a Selection

➤ What You Will Learn

Moving Text
Using Drag-and-Drop and Cut and Paste
Using Paste Options
Using Paste Special

Software Skills Move text to rearrange a document quickly without retyping existing information. You can move any amount of text, from a single character to an entire page. You can also move selected graphics and other objects.

What You Can Do

Moving Text

- Word has many features that make it easy to move text from one location to another.
- One of the simplest methods for moving selected text is to use the F2 key on your keyboard.
- You can use the up arrow key in combination with ALT and SHIFT to move a paragraph up into place before the previous paragraph.
- You can use the down arrow key in combination with ALT and SHIFT to move a paragraph down into place after the next paragraph.
- Be sure to consider nonprinting characters when you select text to move:
    - Select the space following a word or sentence to move along with text.
    - Select the paragraph mark following a paragraph or line to move paragraph formatting and blank lines with text.
- Use Undo to reverse a move that you make unintentionally.

WORDS TO KNOW

Cut
To delete a selection from its original location and move it to the Clipboard.

Drag-and-drop editing
The action of using a mouse to drag a selection from its original location and drop it in a new location.

Embed
To insert an object created with one program into a file created with a different program.

Link
To create a connection between two files, or the connection itself.

Office Clipboard
A temporary storage area where a selection may be held until it is pasted into a new location.

Paste
To insert a selection from the Clipboard into a document.

Try It! Moving Text

1. Start Word, and open **W12Try** from the data files for this lesson. Save the file as **W12Try_xx** in the location where your teacher instructs you to store the files for this lesson.
2. Display nonprinting characters.
3. Select the line with the title *Spin with David!* Select the entire line, including the paragraph mark.
4. Press F2.
5. Position the insertion point to the left of the word *David* in the last paragraph.
6. Press ENTER.
7. Click anywhere in the title *Eat Heart Healthy with Sandra!*

   ✓ *Recall that any amount of text that ends with a paragraph mark is a paragraph.*
8. Press ALT + SHIFT + ↑.
9. Press ALT + SHIFT + ↓.
10. Save the changes to **W12Try_xx**, and leave it open to use in the next Try It.

Using Drag-and-Drop and Cut and Paste

- Use **drag-and-drop editing** to move a selection by dragging it with the mouse.
- Drag-and-drop editing is convenient when you can see the selection to move and the new location on the screen at the same time.
- Use the Cut and Paste commands to move a selection in a document.

  ✓ *For more information on using Cut and Paste and the Office Clipboard, refer to Lesson 5 of the Basics section of this book.*
- The **Cut** command deletes selected text from its original location and moves it to the **Office Clipboard**.
- The **Paste** command copies the selection from the Clipboard to the insertion point location.
- The Cut and Paste commands are in the Clipboard group on the HOME tab of the Ribbon or on the shortcut menu when you right-click a selection.
- The shortcut key combination for cutting a selection is CTRL + X.
- The shortcut key combination for pasting a selection is CTRL + V.

Try It! Using Drag-and-Drop and Cut and Paste

1. In the **W12Try_xx** file, adjust the zoom to 90% so you can see all text in the document.
2. Select the line with the title *Eat Heart Healthy with Sandra!* Include the paragraph mark. (It may still be selected from the previous Try It.)
3. Move the mouse pointer anywhere over the selection.
4. Press and hold the left mouse button.
5. Drag the mouse to position the insertion point at the beginning of the first line of text—*Are all sugars bad?*

   ✓ *As you drag, the mouse pointer changes to the move pointer, which is a box with a dotted shadow attached to an arrow.*
6. Release the mouse button.
7. Select the text *Do carbs really boost my endurance?*
8. On the HOME tab, in the Clipboard group, click the Cut button.
9. Position the insertion point at the beginning of the paragraph, to the left of the word *Are*.
10. On the HOME tab, click the Paste button. (If necessary, type a space.)
11. Save the changes to **W12Try_xx**, and leave it open to use in the next Try It.

Using Paste Options

- Use paste options to select formatting for a pasted selection.
- Paste options vary depending on the selection. For text, they usually include the following:
  - *Keep Source Formatting* to maintain formatting from original location.
  - *Merge Formatting* to apply formatting used in the destination location to the pasted selection.
  - *Keep Text Only* to remove formatting.
- For graphics and other objects, paste options may also include:
  - *Use Destination Theme* to apply formatting used in the destination location to the pasted object.
  - *Keep Source Formatting & Link Data* to link the object to the source file and maintain the source formatting.
  - *Use Destination Theme & Link Data* to link the object to the source file, but apply formatting used in the destination location.
  - *Picture* to insert the object as a picture.
- The available paste options display when you click the drop-down arrow on the Paste button in the Clipboard group on the HOME tab.
- Rest the mouse pointer over a paste option before selecting it to preview how completing the paste will affect the document.
- When you paste a selection in a document, Word displays the Paste Options button (Ctrl). Click the button to access a menu of available paste options.

✓ *If the Paste Options button does not display, click FILE > Options > Advanced, and select the Show Paste Options button when content is pasted check box.*

Try It! Using Paste Options

1. In the **W12Try_xx** file, select the line *Eat Heart Healthy with Sandra!* including the paragraph mark.
2. On the HOME tab, click the Cut button.
3. Position the insertion point at the end of the fourth sentence in the paragraph, to the right of the question mark.
4. On the HOME tab, click the Paste drop-down arrow.
5. Under Paste Options, rest the mouse pointer over the Keep Source Formatting button.
6. Look at the document to preview how the text will look if you keep the source formatting.
7. Under Paste Options, click the Merge Formatting button.
8. In the document, click the Paste Options button (Ctrl).
9. Click the Keep Text Only button. Type a space, if necessary.
10. Save the changes to **W12Try_xx**, and leave it open to use in the next Try It.

Using Paste Special

- As an alternative to paste options, you can use the Paste Special dialog box to choose the formatting you want to apply to a pasted selection.
- Paste Special provides additional options, and lets you select specific formatting, such as pasting the selection as a .jpg picture or a .gif picture.
- You also use Paste Special to **link** or **embed** an object created in a different program into a Word document.

Try It! Using Paste Special

1. In the **W12Try_xx** file, select the line *Spin with David!* including the paragraph mark.
2. On the HOME tab, click the Cut button.
3. Position the insertion point at the end of the last paragraph, to the left of the paragraph mark.
4. Click the Paste drop-down arrow.

   ✓ *Notice that there are three paste options available.*

5. Click Paste Special to display the Paste Special dialog box.

   ✓ *Notice there are more than three paste options available in the As list in the Paste Special dialog box. The options in the box vary depending on the type of content on the Clipboard.*

6. In the As list, click Picture (Enhanced Metafile), and then click OK.
7. In the document, click on the pasted selection. Note that it is now a picture object: a bounding box and sizing handles display, and the PICTURE TOOLS FORMAT tab becomes available on the Ribbon.
8. Close **W12Try_xx**, saving changes, and exit Word.

Paste Special dialog box

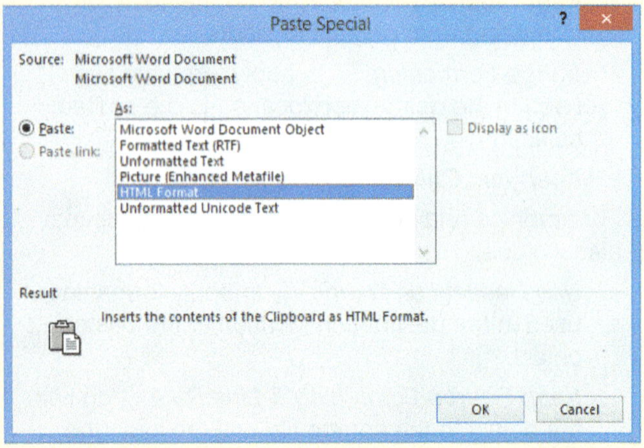

Word 2013, Windows 8, Microsoft Corporation

Lesson 12—Practice

A summer intern at Voyager Travel Adventures tried to combine multiple documents to create pages for a travel brochure, but was not successful. In this project, you will use several methods to rearrange paragraphs in the document.

DIRECTIONS

1. Start Word, if necessary, and open **W12Practice** from the data files for this lesson. Save the file as **W12Practice_xx** in the location where your teacher instructs you to store the files for this lesson.
2. Display the rulers and nonprinting characters, if necessary.
3. Double-click in the header area and type your full name and today's date.
4. Take a moment to look over the document and note how the paragraphs are in the wrong order.
5. Select the first paragraph under the title *Wildebeest!*.
6. Press F2.
7. Scroll down and position the insertion point at the beginning of the second paragraph under the title *Lion!*.
8. Press ENTER.
9. Select the first sentence under the title *Lion!*.
10. Adjust the zoom so you can see the selection and the top of the document on your screen at the same time.
11. Position the mouse pointer over the selection.

12. Press and hold the left mouse button and drag the selection to position the insertion point between the first and second sentences under the title *Wildebeest*.
13. Release the mouse button to drop the selection.
14. Select the text *Zebra!* at the beginning of the last paragraph in the document.
15. Click the **HOME** tab, and then click the **Cut** button.
16. Position the insertion point at the beginning of the document to the left of the title **Wildebeest!**.
17. Click the **Paste** drop-down arrow.
18. Under **Paste Options**, rest the mouse pointer on the **Keep Source Formatting** button.
19. Click the **Merge Formatting** button.
20. Delete the text *Wildebeest!*.
21. Click anywhere in the last sentence in the document.
22. Press ALT + SHIFT + ↑ four times to move the paragraph up into position as the middle paragraph in the description of zebra.
23. Save the changes to the document.
24. **With your teacher's permission**, print the document. It should look similar to Figure 12-1.
25. Close the document, saving changes, and exit Word.

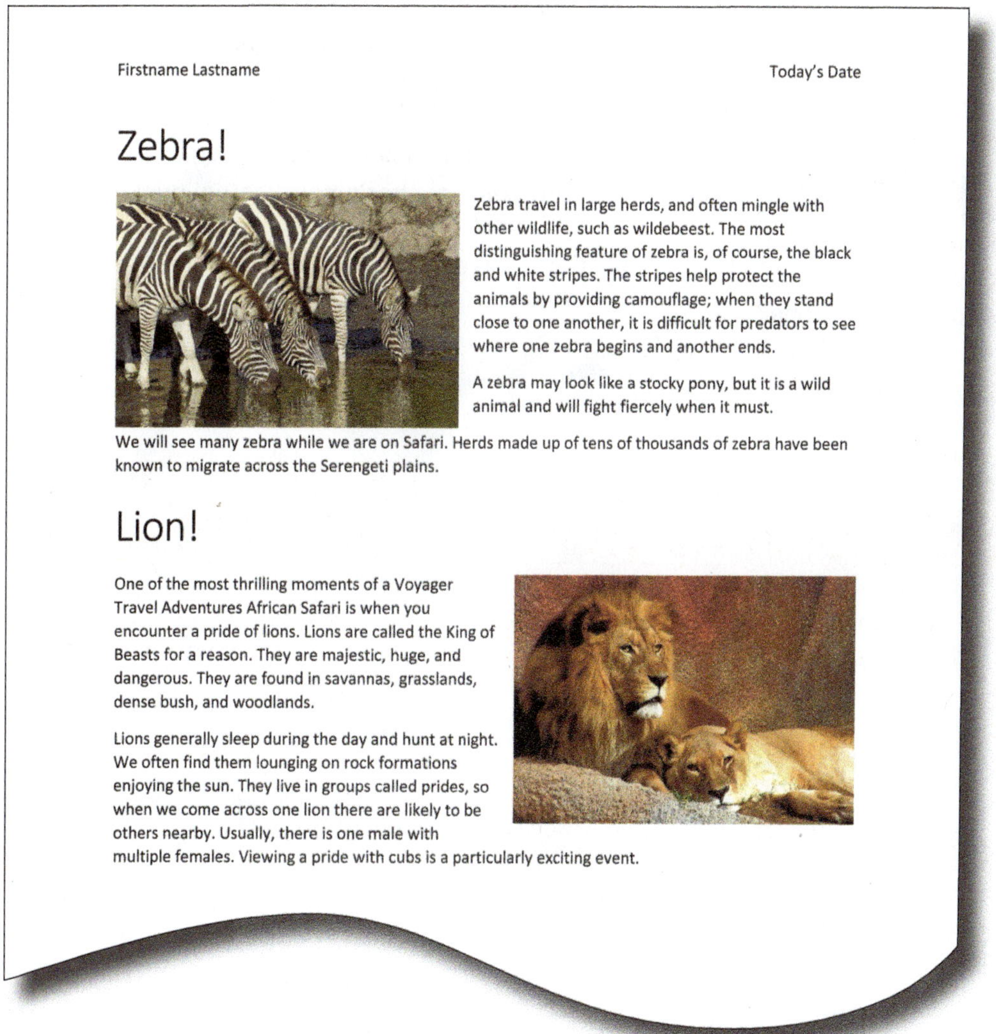

Firstname Lastname Today's Date

Zebra!

Zebra travel in large herds, and often mingle with other wildlife, such as wildebeest. The most distinguishing feature of zebra is, of course, the black and white stripes. The stripes help protect the animals by providing camouflage; when they stand close to one another, it is difficult for predators to see where one zebra begins and another ends.

A zebra may look like a stocky pony, but it is a wild animal and will fight fiercely when it must.

We will see many zebra while we are on Safari. Herds made up of tens of thousands of zebra have been known to migrate across the Serengeti plains.

Lion!

One of the most thrilling moments of a Voyager Travel Adventures African Safari is when you encounter a pride of lions. Lions are called the King of Beasts for a reason. They are majestic, huge, and dangerous. They are found in savannas, grasslands, dense bush, and woodlands.

Lions generally sleep during the day and hunt at night. We often find them lounging on rock formations enjoying the sun. They live in groups called prides, so when we come across one lion there are likely to be others nearby. Usually, there is one male with multiple females. Viewing a pride with cubs is a particularly exciting event.

Figure 12-1

Word 2013, Windows 8, Microsoft Corporation

Lesson 12—Apply

You continue working on the pages for Voyager Travel Adventures' safari brochure. In this project, you use several methods to move paragraphs to their proper locations.

DIRECTIONS

1. Start Word, if necessary, and open **W12Apply** from the data files for this lesson.
2. Save the file as **W12Apply_xx** in the location where your teacher instructs you to store the files for this lesson.
3. Display the rulers and nonprinting characters.
4. Type your full name and today's date in the header.
5. Select the paragraph under the title *Lion* and press F2.
6. Position the insertion point under the title *Hyena* and press ENTER.
7. Click anywhere within the paragraph that describes zebra and press ALT + SHIFT + ↑ as many times as necessary to position it under the title *Zebra*.
8. Select the paragraph that describes elephants and use drag-and-drop editing to move it under the title *Elephant*.
9. Select the paragraph that describes cheetahs and use drag-and-drop editing to move it under the title *Cheetah*.
10. Cut the paragraph that describes giraffes.
11. Position the insertion point under the title *Giraffe*, and preview the available paste options. Paste the selection, keeping the source formatting.
12. Cut the paragraph describing lions and paste it under the title *Lion*.
13. Using any or all of the methods for moving text, arrange the titles and their descriptive paragraphs into alphabetical order.
14. Save the changes to the document.
15. **With your teacher's permission**, print the document.
16. Close the document, saving changes, and exit Word.

Lesson 13

Copying a Selection

➤ What You Will Learn

Using Copy and Paste
Using Drag-and-Drop Editing to Copy

Software Skills Copy a selection from one location to another when you need to reuse content already entered into a document. You can leave the copied selection intact, or edit it. You can copy or move any amount of text, from a single character to an entire document, and you can copy graphics and objects such as pictures as well.

What You Can Do

Using Copy and Paste

- Use the Copy and Paste commands to copy a selection from one location and paste it to another location.

  ✓ *For more information on using Copy and Paste and the Office Clipboard, refer to Lesson 5 of the Basics section of this book.*

- The **Copy** command stores a duplicate of the selection on the Clipboard, leaving the original selection unchanged.
- You can then use the Paste command to paste the selection from the Clipboard to the insertion point location.
- The Copy and Paste commands are in the Clipboard group on the HOME tab of the Ribbon or on the shortcut menu when you right-click a selection.
- The shortcut key combination for copying a selection is CTRL + C.
- The shortcut key combination for pasting a selection is CTRL + V.
- Use Paste Options and Paste Special to control formatting when copying a selection just as you use it when moving text.

  ✓ *For more information about Paste Options and Paste Special, refer to Lesson 12.*

WORDS TO KNOW

Copy
To create a duplicate of a selection.

Try It! Using Copy and Paste

1. Start Word, and open **W13Try** from the data files for this lesson. Save the file as **W13Try_xx** in the location where your teacher instructs you to store the files for this lesson.
2. Select the text *Eat Heart Healthy with Sandra!*, including the paragraph mark.
3. On the HOME tab, in the Clipboard group, click the Copy button.
4. Press CTRL + END to move the insertion point to the end of the document.
5. On the HOME tab, in the Clipboard group, click the Paste button.
6. In the document, click the Paste Options button (Ctrl), and click the Merge Formatting button.
7. Save the changes to **W13Try_xx**, and leave it open to use in the next Try It.

Using Drag-and-Drop Editing to Copy

- Use drag-and-drop editing to copy a selection by dragging it with the mouse.
- Drag-and-drop is convenient when you can see the content to copy and the new location on the screen at the same time.

Try It! Using Drag-and-Drop Editing to Copy Text

1. In the **W13Try_xx** file, select the text *Spin with David!* without the paragraph mark.
2. Move the mouse pointer anywhere over the selection.
3. Press and hold CTRL.
4. Press and hold the left mouse button and drag the mouse to the end of the document.

   ✓ *As you drag, the mouse pointer changes to the copy pointer, which is a box with a dotted shadow attached to an arrow.*
5. Release the mouse button.
6. In the document, click the Paste Options button (Ctrl), and click the Merge Formatting button.
7. Close **W13Try_xx**, saving changes, and exit Word.

Lesson 13—Practice

Whole Grains Bread has asked you to type up a page listing three new franchise locations. The information about each location is similar. Once you type one, you can copy it to use for the other two.

DIRECTIONS

1. Start Word, and save a new blank document as **W13Practice_xx** in the location where your teacher instructs you to store the files for this lesson.
2. Display the rulers and nonprinting characters.
3. Double-click in the header area and type your full name and today's date.
4. On the first line of the document, type **New Franchise Information**, and format it using the **Title** style.
5. Press ENTER at the end of the line to start a new paragraph, and type **Park City, Utah**. Format the text using the **Heading 1** style.
6. Press ENTER at the end of the line to start a new paragraph, increase the font size to 12 points, and type **The Park City store is scheduled to open on April 1. It includes a bakery and a cafe that serves sandwiches, pastries, and other light meals. It uses the standard Whole Grains Bread interior design and color scheme, but the exterior has been customized to complement the unique character of the neighborhood.**
7. Press ENTER to start a new line.
8. Type **Seattle, Washington**. Format the text using the **Heading 1** style, and then press ENTER to start a new line.
9. Select the paragraph of text under the heading *Park City, Utah*.
10. On the **HOME** tab, in the Clipboard group, click the **Copy** button.
11. Position the insertion point on the blank line under the heading *Seattle, Washington*.
12. On the HOME tab, in the Clipboard group, click the **Paste** button.
13. Edit the text in the pasted paragraph to replace the text *Park City* with the text **Seattle**, and the date *April 1* with the date **April 15**.
14. Move the insertion point to the blank line at the end of the document and type **Taos, New Mexico**.
15. Format the text using the **Heading 1** style, and then press ENTER to start a new line.
16. Select the paragraph of text under the heading *Seattle, Washington*.
17. Press and hold CTRL, press and hold the left mouse button, and drag the selection to the blank line under the heading *Taos, New Mexico*.
18. Release the mouse button when the insertion point is in the correct location.
19. Edit the text in the copied paragraph to replace the text *Seattle* with the text **Taos**, and the date *April 15* with the date **May 1**.
20. Save the changes to the document.
21. **With your teacher's permission**, print the document. It should look similar to Figure 13-1 on the next page
22. Close the document, saving changes, and exit Word.

Figure 13-1

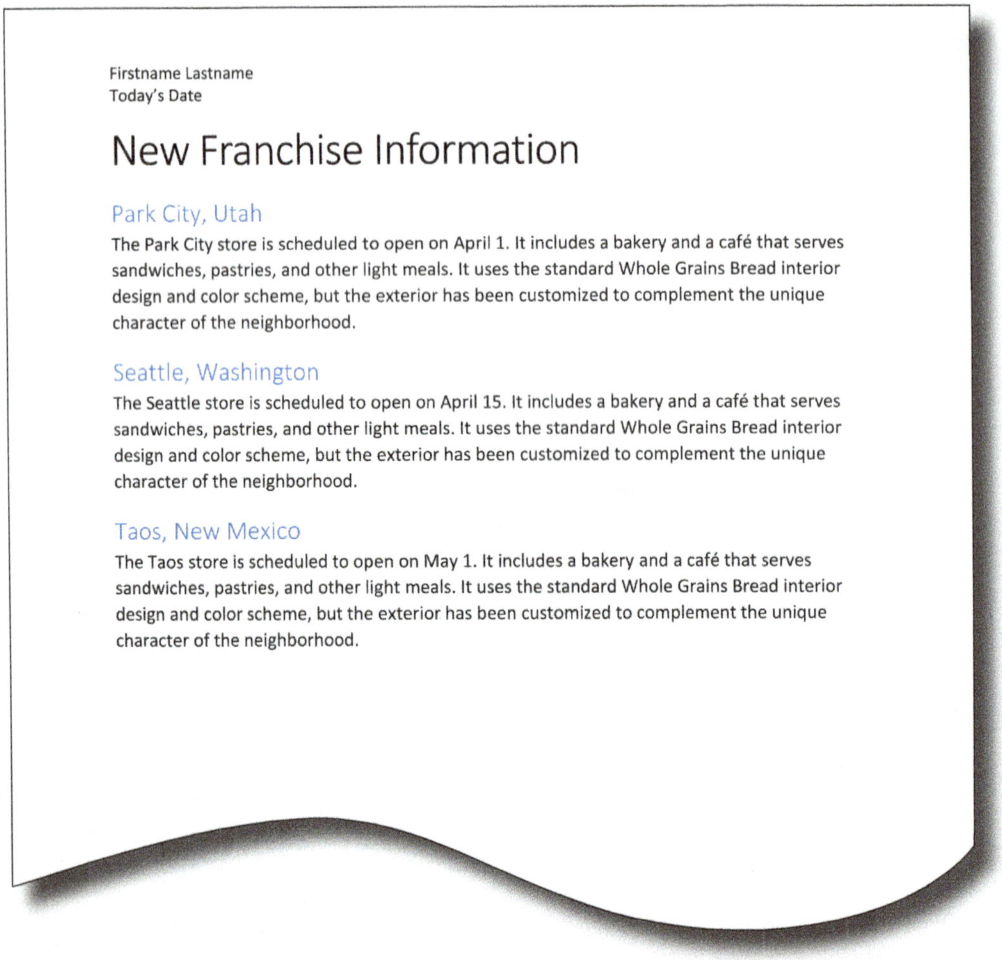

Firstname Lastname
Today's Date

New Franchise Information

Park City, Utah

The Park City store is scheduled to open on April 1. It includes a bakery and a café that serves sandwiches, pastries, and other light meals. It uses the standard Whole Grains Bread interior design and color scheme, but the exterior has been customized to complement the unique character of the neighborhood.

Seattle, Washington

The Seattle store is scheduled to open on April 15. It includes a bakery and a café that serves sandwiches, pastries, and other light meals. It uses the standard Whole Grains Bread interior design and color scheme, but the exterior has been customized to complement the unique character of the neighborhood.

Taos, New Mexico

The Taos store is scheduled to open on May 1. It includes a bakery and a café that serves sandwiches, pastries, and other light meals. It uses the standard Whole Grains Bread interior design and color scheme, but the exterior has been customized to complement the unique character of the neighborhood.

Lesson 13—Apply

In this project, you use copying techniques to complete a press release announcing new developments at the company to accompany the list you created in the Lesson 13—Practice project.

DIRECTIONS

1. Start Word, if necessary, and open **W13Apply** from the data files for this lesson.
2. Save the file as **W13Apply_xx** in the location where your teacher instructs you to store the files for this lesson.
3. Display the rulers and nonprinting characters.
4. Replace the sample text *Today's Date* with the actual date, and *Student's Name* with your own name.
5. Move the insertion point to the end of the last paragraph, above the text *For more information contact*.
6. Press [ENTER] to start a new line and type **New franchise opening dates:**.
7. Press [ENTER] to start a new line. Change the style to **No Spacing**.
8. Set a left indent at **0.5"**, and a left tab stop at **2.5"**.
9. Select the text *Park City, Utah* in the first paragraph, and copy it to the new blank line you inserted in step 7.
10. Press [TAB].
11. Select the text *April 1* in the second paragraph, and copy it to the right of the tab stop. Press [ENTER] to start a new line.

12. Copy the text *Seattle, Washington* and the date *April 15* to the new blank line.
13. Press Enter to start a new blank line, and copy the text *Taos, New Mexico* and the date *May 1* to the new blank line.
14. Press Enter to insert a blank line after the list.
15. Save the changes to the document.
16. **With your teacher's permission**, print the document. It should look similar to Figure 13-2.
17. Close the document, saving changes, and exit Word.

Figure 13-2

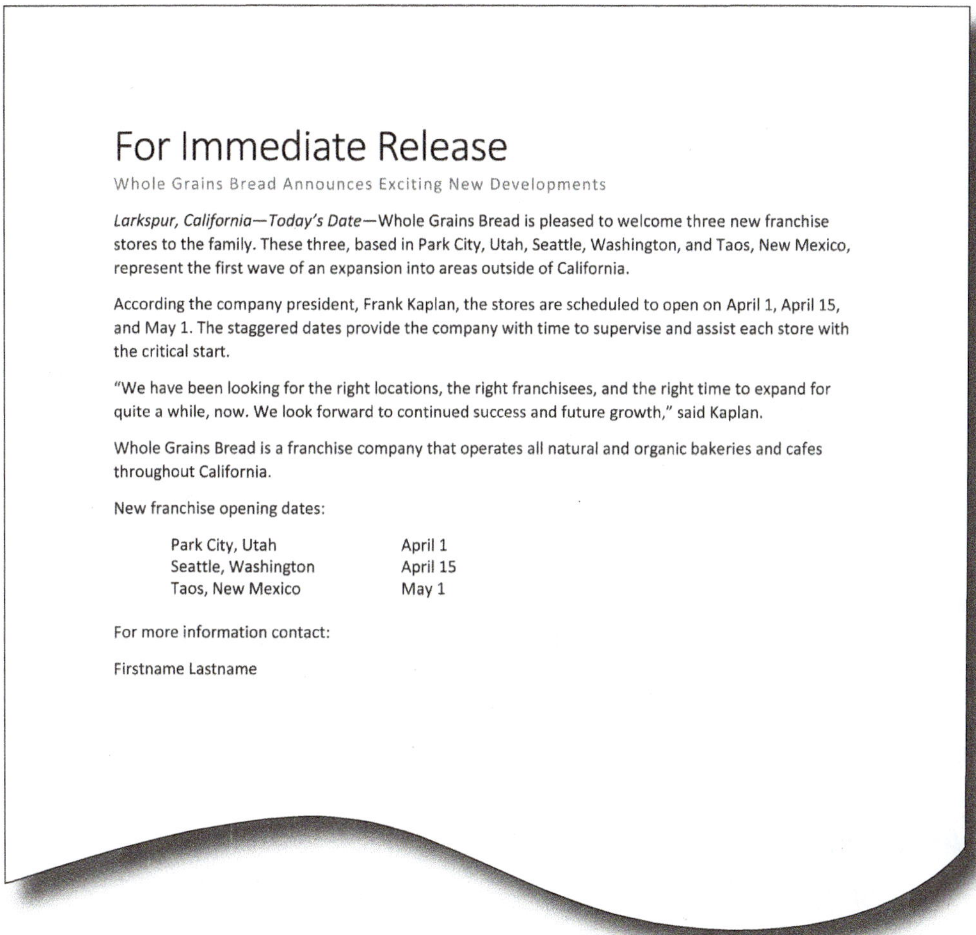

For Immediate Release

Whole Grains Bread Announces Exciting New Developments

Larkspur, California—Today's Date—Whole Grains Bread is pleased to welcome three new franchise stores to the family. These three, based in Park City, Utah, Seattle, Washington, and Taos, New Mexico, represent the first wave of an expansion into areas outside of California.

According the company president, Frank Kaplan, the stores are scheduled to open on April 1, April 15, and May 1. The staggered dates provide the company with time to supervise and assist each store with the critical start.

"We have been looking for the right locations, the right franchisees, and the right time to expand for quite a while, now. We look forward to continued success and future growth," said Kaplan.

Whole Grains Bread is a franchise company that operates all natural and organic bakeries and cafes throughout California.

New franchise opening dates:

Park City, Utah	April 1
Seattle, Washington	April 15
Taos, New Mexico	May 1

For more information contact:

Firstname Lastname

Word 2013, Windows 8, Microsoft Corporation

Lesson 14

Inserting a Table

WORDS TO KNOW

Border
A line drawn around the edges of an element, such as a table or a table cell. Borders can also be drawn around graphics, paragraphs, and pages.

Cell
The rectangular area at the intersection of a column and a row in a table, into which you enter data or graphics.

Column
A vertical series of cells in a table.

Column markers
Markers on the horizontal ruler that indicate column dividers.

Column width
The width of a column in a table, measured in inches.

Contiguous
Adjacent, or next to each other.

Dividers
The lines that indicate the edges of cells in a table. Dividers do not print, although they are indicated onscreen by either gridlines or borders.

End of row/cell markers
Nonprinting characters used to mark the end of a cell or a row in a table.

➤ What You Will Learn

Analyzing Tables
Inserting and Deleting a Table
Entering Text in a Table
Selecting in a Table
Selecting Multiple Components in a Table
Changing Table Structure
Formatting a Table
Viewing Gridlines

Software Skills Create tables to organize data into columns and rows. Any information that needs to be presented in side-by-side columns can be set up in a table. For example, a price list, an invoice, and a resume are all types of documents for which you could use a table. The table format lets you align information side by side and across the page so the information is easy to read.

What You Can Do

Analyzing Tables

- A **table** is an object that you insert in a Word document.
- Tables are easier to use than tabbed columns when setting up and organizing data in **columns** and **rows**.
- You can format an entire document using a table, or integrate a table with text and other objects on a page.
  - You might use a table to provide the layout for a form, because a table allows you to line up and position elements attractively.
  - You might insert a table in a report so you can include statistical data.
- When you select a table, the TABLE TOOLS DESIGN and TABLE TOOLS LAYOUT tabs become available on the Ribbon. You use the commands on these tabs to edit, design, and format the table.

Inserting and Deleting a Table

- Use the Table drop-down menu in the Table group on the INSERT tab to select commands for inserting a table.
  - You can use the Table grid to select the number of columns and rows you want in the table.
  - You can open the Insert Table dialog box to specify the number of columns and rows.
  - You can insert a Quick Table from a gallery of built-in tables that you can then customize as needed.
- Word inserts the table at the insertion point location.
- **Column markers** on the horizontal ruler show the location of the right **divider** of each column.
- By default, Word places a ½-point **border** around all **cells** in a table.
- Tables also have three nonprinting elements:
  - **End of cell markers**, which display at the end of all content entered in a cell.
  - **End of row markers**, which display at the end of each row.
  - **Gridlines**, which you can choose to display along the row and column dividers if there are no printing table borders applied to the table.
- When you delete a table, you delete all the data in the table as well.

Gridlines
Nonprinting lines that can be displayed around cells in a table.

Noncontiguous
Not adjacent, or not next to, each other.

Row
A horizontal series of cells in a table.

Row height
The height of a row in a table, measured in inches.

Table
A grid comprised of horizontal rows and vertical columns into which you can enter data.

Try It! Inserting and Deleting a Table

1. Start Word, and open **W14Try** from the data files for this lesson. Save the file as **W14Try_xx** in the location where your teacher instructs you to store the files for this lesson.
2. Display the rulers and nonprinting characters.
3. Position the insertion point on the blank line following the text *You can insert a Quick Table*.
4. Click INSERT > Table > Quick Tables.
5. Scroll down the gallery of Quick Tables and click the Tabular List table.
6. Position the insertion point on the blank line following the next paragraph of text, *You can drag across the Table grid to insert a table*.
7. Click INSERT > Table.
8. On the grid, position the mouse pointer over the third cell from the left in the third row, so a grid of three rows and three columns is highlighted. The label at the top of the grid displays *3x3 Table,* as shown in the figure at the right.
9. Click to insert a table with three columns and three rows.
10. Move the insertion point to the end of the document.
11. On the INSERT tab, click the Table button.
12. Click Insert Table.
13. Use the Number of columns increment arrows to set the value to 4.

Inserting a table with 3 columns and 3 rows

Word 2013, Windows 8, Microsoft Corporation

(continued)

Try It! Inserting and Deleting a Table *(continued)*

14. Use the Number of rows increment arrows to set the value to 3.
15. Click OK.
16. Click in any cell in the third table.
17. On the TABLE TOOLS LAYOUT tab, click the Delete button, and then click Delete Table.
18. Save the changes to W14Try_xx, and leave it open to use in the next Try It.

Entering Text in a Table

- You enter text in the cells of a table.
- **Row height** increases automatically to accommodate the text.
- **Column width** does not change automatically when you type. Text wraps at the right margin of a cell the same way it wraps at the right margin of a page.
- To move to the next cell, you press TAB, →, or click the cell with the mouse.
- When you press ENTER in a cell, Word starts a new paragraph within the cell.
- The keyboard shortcuts for moving the insertion point within a table are listed in Table 14-1.

Table 14-1 Keyboard Shortcuts for Moving the Insertion Point in a Table

To Select	Press
One cell left	SHIFT + TAB
One cell right	TAB
One cell up	↑
One cell down	↓
First cell in column	ALT + PG UP
Last cell in column	ALT + PG DN
First cell in row	ALT + HOME
Last cell in row	ALT + END

Try It! Entering Text in a Table

1. In the W14Try_xx file, click in the top-left cell in the second table.
2. Type Group A.
3. Press TAB.
4. Type Group B.
5. Press TAB.
6. Type Group C.
7. Press TAB.
8. Type Manufacturing.
9. Press TAB.
10. Type Marketing.
11. Press TAB
12. Type Accounting.
13. Save the changes to W14Try_xx, and leave it open to use in the next Try It.

Selecting in a Table

- As with other Word features, you must select table components before you can affect them with commands.
- You select text within a cell using the standard selection commands. For example, double-click a word to select it, or drag across the text to select.
- You can select one or more columns, one or more rows, one or more cells, or the entire table.
- The commands for selecting table components are in the Table group on the TABLE TOOLS LAYOUT tab of the Ribbon.
- You can also use your mouse to select components in a table.
- Selected table components are highlighted.

Try It! Selecting in a Table

1. In the W14Try_xx file, click in the middle cell of the top row of the second table.
2. On the TABLE TOOLS LAYOUT tab, click the Select button.
3. Click Select Cell.
4. Click in the middle cell of the top row.
5. On the TABLE TOOLS LAYOUT tab, click Select > Select Column.
6. Click in the middle cell of the top row.
7. On the TABLE TOOLS LAYOUT tab, click Select > Select Row.
8. Click in the middle cell of the top row.
9. On the TABLE TOOLS LAYOUT tab, click Select > Select Table.
10. In the cell on the right end of the second row, position the insertion point over the area to the left of the text and the right of the column divider. When the pointer changes to a small black arrow pointing diagonally up and right, click.
11. Position the mouse pointer above the cell on the right end of the first row—outside the table border. When the pointer changes to a small black arrow pointing down, click.
12. Position the mouse pointer to the left of the first cell in the first row—outside the table border. When the pointer changes to a typical selection pointer, click.
13. In the upper-left corner of the table, click on the table move handle.
14. Save the changes to W14Try_xx, and leave it open to use in the next Try It.

Selecting Multiple Components in a Table

- Sometimes you may want commands to affect more than one component at a time.
- For example, you may want to apply the bold font style to all text in the top row, or increase the font size of numbers in multiple cells.
- Press and hold SHIFT to select **contiguous** components.
- Press and hold CTRL to select **noncontiguous** components.
- You can also drag across contiguous components to select them.

Try It! Selecting Multiple Components in a Table

1. In the **W14Try_xx** file, in the cell on the left end of the first row of the second table, position the insertion point to the left of the text and the right of the column divider, and click.

   ✓ *This selects the first cell.*

2. Press and hold SHIFT.
3. In the cell on the left end of the second row, position the insertion point to the left of the text and the right of the column divider, and click.

   ✓ *This selects the second, contiguous, cell.*

4. Press and hold CTRL.
5. In the cell on the right end of the first row, position the insertion point to the left of the text and the right of the column divider, and click.
6. Save the changes to **W14Try_xx**, and leave it open to use in the next Try It.

Changing Table Structure

- Change a table's structure by inserting and deleting columns, rows, or cells.
- To quickly add a row to the bottom of a table, position the insertion point in the last cell and press TAB.
- To quickly insert a row or column anywhere in a table, use the insert bar that displays when you move the mouse pointer near a row or column divider.
- Other commands for inserting and deleting columns and rows are on the TABLE TOOLS LAYOUT tab in the Rows & Columns group.
  - You can insert rows above or below the current row.
  - You can insert columns to the left or right of the current column.
- Use the Insert Cells or Delete Cells dialog box to insert or delete individual cells.
  - When you insert a cell, you choose whether to shift existing cells to the right or down to make room for the new cell.
  - When you delete a cell, you choose whether to shift existing cells left or up to fill in the space left by the deleted cell.
- To insert multiple components, select that number before selecting the insert command. For example, to insert three rows, select three rows.

Try It! Changing Table Structure

1. In the **W14Try_xx** file, move the mouse pointer near the left edge of the second table, at the divider between the second and third rows.
2. When the insert bar displays, click the plus sign ⊕ to insert a new row.
3. Click in the middle cell of the top row.
4. On the TABLE TOOLS LAYOUT tab, click the Insert Below button.
5. Click in the right cell of the top row.
6. On the TABLE TOOLS LAYOUT tab, click the Insert Right button.
7. Click in the right cell of the bottom row.
8. On the TABLE TOOLS LAYOUT tab, click the Rows & Columns dialog box launcher.
9. In the Insert Cells dialog box, click Shift cells right, and then click OK.
10. Click in the right cell of the bottom row—the one you inserted in step 9.

(continued)

Try It! Changing Table Structure *(continued)*

Insert columns, rows, and cells to change table structure

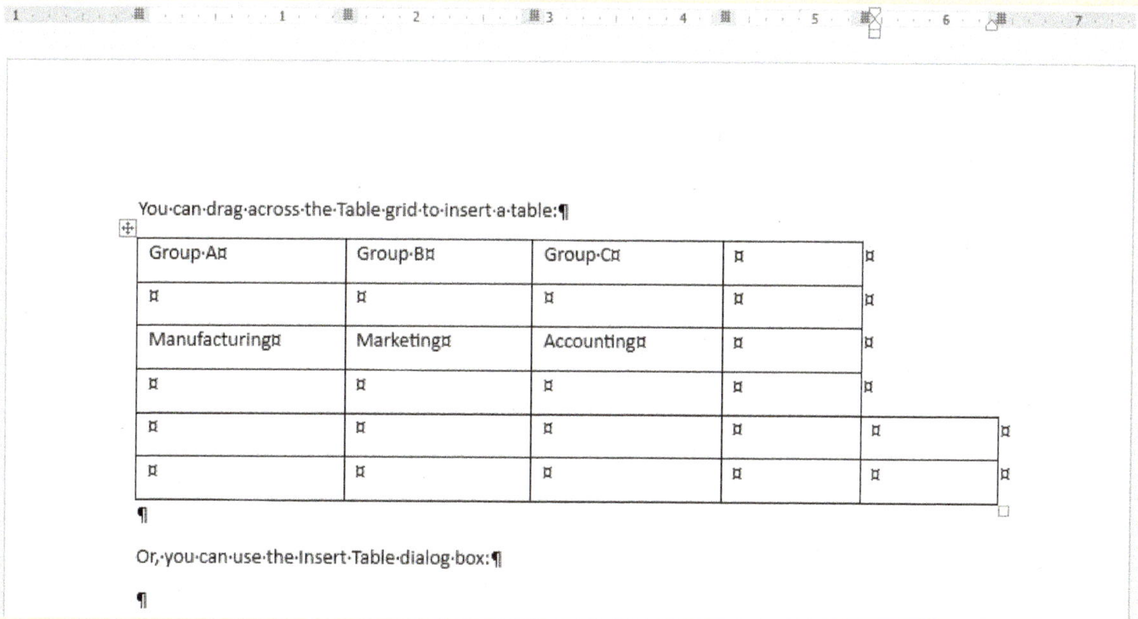
You·can·drag·across·the·Table·grid·to·insert·a·table:¶

Group·A¤	Group·B¤	Group·C¤	¤	
¤	¤	¤	¤	
Manufacturing¤	Marketing¤	Accounting¤	¤	
¤	¤	¤	¤	
¤	¤	¤	¤	¤
¤	¤	¤	¤	¤

¶

Or,·you·can·use·the·Insert·Table·dialog·box:¶

¶

Word 2013, Windows 8, Microsoft Corporation

11 Press TAB.

12 Click in any cell in the bottom row.

13 On the TABLE TOOLS LAYOUT tab, click Delete > Delete Rows.

14 Click in the cell on the right end of the top row.

15 On the TABLE TOOLS LAYOUT tab, click Delete > Delete Columns.

16 Click in the cell on the right end of the bottom row.

17 On the TABLE TOOLS LAYOUT tab, click Delete > Delete Cells.

18 In the Delete Cells dialog box, click Shift cells left, and then click OK.

19 Save the changes to **W14Try_xx**, and leave it open to use in the next Try It.

Formatting a Table

- You can format text within a table using standard Word formatting techniques. For example, use font formatting and alignments to enhance text in a table.
- You can apply formatting to selected text, or to selected cells, columns, or rows.
- To quickly apply a set of formatting effects to an entire table, you can select a table style from the gallery of styles in the Table Styles group on the TABLE TOOLS DESIGN tab of the Ribbon.
- Rest the mouse pointer on a table style in the gallery to preview how it will affect the current table, and to see the style name in a ScreenTip.
- When you select a table style, it overrides existing formatting. Therefore, you should apply a style first, and then modify the formatting as needed.

Try It! Formatting a Table

1. In the **W14Try_xx** file, click in any cell in the table.
2. Click the TABLE TOOLS DESIGN tab, then, in the Table Styles group, click the More button.
3. In the Table Styles gallery, under List Tables, click the style that is second from the left in the second row—List Table 2 – Accent 1.
4. Double-click the text *Manufacturing* in the left cell of the third row.
5. Click HOME > Bold **B** to toggle the Bold style off.
6. Select the top row in the table.
7. On the HOME tab, click the Font Size drop-down arrow and click 14.
8. With the first row still selected, on the HOME tab, click the Center button.
9. Save the changes to **W14Try_xx**, and leave it open to use in the next Try It.

Table Styles gallery

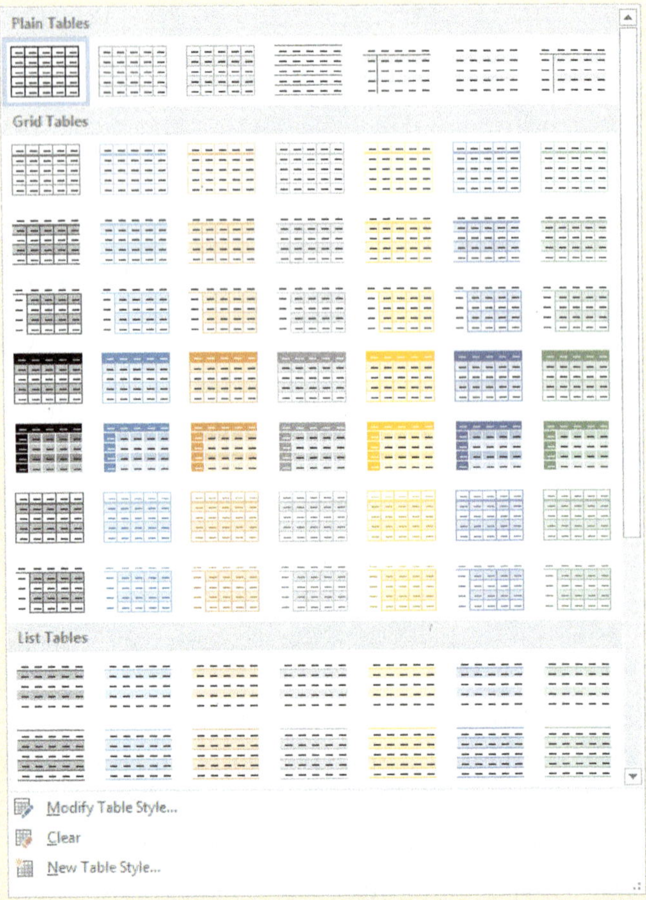

Word 2013, Windows 8, Microsoft Corporation

Viewing Gridlines

- When a table is not formatted with printing borders, you cannot see the cell dividers onscreen.
- Toggle nonprinting gridlines on so you can identify where one cell ends and the next begins.
- Gridlines display as dotted lines.

Try It! Viewing Gridlines

1. In the **W14Try_xx** file, click in any cell in the table.
2. Click the TABLE TOOLS LAYOUT tab, then click the View Gridlines button.

   ✓ *Click the button again to toggle gridlines off.*
3. Close **W14Try_xx**, saving changes, and exit Word.

Lesson 14—Practice

Restoration Architecture is offering in-house computer training courses. In this project, you create a memo that uses a table to list the names of instructors teaching the courses.

DIRECTIONS

1. Start Word, create a new document, and save the document as **W14Practice_xx** in the location where your teacher instructs you to store the files for this lesson.
2. Display the rulers and nonprinting characters.
3. On the **PAGE LAYOUT** tab, set paragraph spacing **Before** to **24** points and paragraph spacing **After** to **36** points.
4. Type **MEMO**, and press ENTER .
5. On the **HOME** tab, in the Styles group, click the **No Spacing** style.
6. On the horizontal ruler, set a left tab stop at **0.75"**.
7. Type **To:**, press TAB, and type **All Employees**. Press ENTER .
8. Type **From:**, press TAB, and type your own name. Press ENTER .
9. Type **Date:**, press TAB, and type or insert today's date. Press ENTER .
10. Type **Subject:**, press TAB, and type **Training Courses**. Press ENTER twice.
11. Apply the **Normal** style and type the following: **In response to many requests, here are the names of the instructors who will be teaching the courses next week.**
12. Press ENTER .
13. Click **INSERT** > **Table** .
14. Move the mouse pointer across the table grid to select two columns and two rows, and then click in the lower right selected cell to insert the table.
15. Click in the top left cell and type **Course Name**. Press TAB and type **Instructor Name**.
16. Press TAB and type **Word for Beginners**. Press TAB and type **Marilyn Pak**.
17. Press TAB and type **Advanced Excel**. Press TAB and type **Ben Thompson**.
18. Click **TABLE TOOLS LAYOUT** > **Insert Above** .
19. In the new row, click in the cell on the left and type **Introduction to the Internet**. Press TAB and type **Suni Patel**.
20. On the **TABLE TOOLS DESIGN** tab, in the Table Styles group, click the **More** button .
21. In the Table Styles gallery, click the style on the left end of the second to last row—**List Table 6 Colorful**.
22. Click the **table move handle** to select the entire table.
23. Click **HOME** > **Font Size** drop-down arrow > **12** to increase the font size.
24. Check and correct the spelling and grammar in the document, and then save the changes.
25. **With your teacher's permission**, print the document. It should look similar to Figure 14-1 on the next page.
26. Close the document, saving changes, and exit Word.

Figure 14-1

MEMO

To: All Employees
From: Firstname Lastname
Date: Today's Date
Subject: Training Courses

In response to many requests, here are the names of the instructors who will be teaching the courses next week.

Course Name	Instructor Name
Word for Beginners	Marilyn Pak
Introduction to the Internet	Suni Patel
Advanced Excel	Ben Thompson

Lesson 14—Apply

In this project, you edit the memo you prepared in the Practice project to add a course schedule.

DIRECTIONS

1. Start Word, if necessary, and open **W14Apply** from the data files for this lesson.
2. Save the file as **W14Apply_xx** in the location where your teacher instructs you to store the files for this lesson.
3. Display the rulers and nonprinting characters.
4. Replace the sample text *Student's Name* with your own name, and *Today's Date* with the actual date.
5. Press CTRL + END to move the insertion point to the end of the document.
6. Press ENTER and type: **Following is the schedule and location of courses:** and press ENTER.
7. Insert a table with three columns and four rows.
8. Enter the following data in the table:

Course Name	**Location**	**Time**
Word for Beginners	**Conference Room A**	**8:30 – 11:45**
Advanced Excel	**Conference Room B**	**8:30 – 11:45**
Introduction to the Internet	**Media Lab**	**1:30 – 3:30**

   To enter an en dash between the times, simply type a space, a hyphen, and a space. By default, AutoFormat automatically replaces the hyphen and spaces with an en dash after the second number is typed.
9. Select the last two rows in the table and insert two rows above them.

10. Enter the following data in the new rows:

Advanced Word	Conference Room A	8:30 – 11:45
Excel for Beginners	Conference Room B	1:30 – 3:30

11. Insert a column to the right of the Time column.
12. Starting in the top cell, enter the following data in the new column:
    Days
    Tuesday, Thursday
    Monday, Wednesday
    Tuesday, Wednesday
    Monday, Thursday
    Friday
13. Delete the row for the Word for Beginners course.
14. Apply the **Grid Table 6 Colorful - Accent 2** table style to the table.
15. Increase the font size of all text in the table to 12 points.
16. Check and correct the spelling and grammar in the document, and then save the changes.
17. **With your teacher's permission**, print the document. It should look similar to Figure 14-2.
18. Close the document, saving changes, and exit Word.

Figure 14-2

MEMO

To: All Employees
From: Firstname Lastname
Date: Today's Date
Subject: Training Courses

In response to many requests, here are the names of the instructors who will be teaching the courses next week.

Course Name	Instructor Name
Word for Beginners	Marilyn Pak
Introduction to the Internet	Suni Patel
Advanced Excel	Ben Thompson

Following is the schedule and location of courses:

Course Name	Location	Time	Days
Advanced Word	Conference Room A	8:30 – 11:45	Monday, Wednesday
Excel for Beginners	Conference Room B	1:30 – 3:30	Tuesday, Wednesday
Advanced Excel	Conference Room B	8:30 – 11:45	Monday, Thursday
Introduction to the Internet	Media Lab	1:30 – 3:30	Friday

Lesson 15

Aligning Tables

➤ What You Will Learn

Converting Text to a Table
Inserting Existing Text into a Table Cell
Setting Column Width and Row Height
Setting Alignment in a Table Cell
Setting Tabs in a Table Cell
Setting Cell Margins
Aligning a Table Horizontally on the Page

Software Skills Use alignment options and tabs to make tables easy to read. Numbers are usually aligned flush right in a cell, while text can be flush left, centered, justified, or rotated to appear vertical. You can vertically align data with the top, center, or bottom of a cell as well. Decimal tabs are especially useful in tables for aligning dollar values. Other ways to improve the appearance of a table include aligning the table horizontally on the page and adjusting column width and row height.

What You Can Do

Converting Text to a Table

- You can convert existing text to a table using commands in the Tables group on the INSERT tab of the Ribbon.
- If the existing text includes paragraph marks, Word will start a new row at every paragraph mark.
- If the existing text includes tabs, Word will start a new column at every tab.
- You can choose to separate text at a different character in the Convert Text to Table dialog box.

Try It! Converting Text to a Table

1. Start Word, and open **W15Try** from the data files for this lesson. Save the file as **W15Try_xx** in the location where your teacher instructs you to store files for this lesson.
2. Select the line beginning with *Paper goods* and the three lines below it.
3. Click the INSERT tab, then click the Table button.
4. Click Convert Text to Table to open the Convert Text to Table dialog box.
5. Click OK.
6. Save the changes to **W15Try_xx**, and leave it open to use in the next Try It.

Inserting Existing Text into a Table Cell

- You can copy or move existing text into a table cell. For example, you can move an existing heading to become the table title.
- Inserting existing text into a table cell saves you the time and effort of retyping information.
- You can change the formatting of text you insert in a cell, using standard text formatting commands. For example, you can apply font formatting, and even bullet or numbered list formats.

Try It! Inserting Existing Text into a Table Cell

1. In the **W15Try_xx** file, position the insertion point in any cell in the top row.
2. Click TABLE TOOLS LAYOUT > Insert Above.
3. Select the text *Party Budget*. (Do not select the paragraph mark.)
4. Right-click the selection and click Cut on the shortcut menu.
5. Click in the blank cell on the left of the new row.
6. Click HOME > Paste.
7. Select the left column.
8. On the HOME tab, click the Bullets button.
9. Click in the top left cell of the column, and click the Bullets button again to remove the formatting from the text in that cell.
10. Save the changes to **W15Try_xx**, and leave it open to use in the next Try It.

Setting Column Width and Row Height

- By default, Word creates table columns of equal column width, sized so the table extends from the left margin to the right margin.
- Rows are sized according to the line spacing on the line where the table is inserted. Row height automatically increases to accommodate lines of text typed in a cell.
- You can automatically adjust the column width and row height to fit the contents of each cell, or to fit the width of the current window.
- You can drag with your mouse to change column width or row height:
  - Drag column dividers to increase or decrease column width.
  - Drag row dividers to increase or decrease row height.

  ✓ *Press and hold* ALT *as you drag the divider to see measurements displayed on the ruler.*
- You can set precise measurements for column width and row height using the options in the Cell Size group on the TABLE TOOLS LAYOUT tab of the Ribbon.
- Alternatively, you can select to automatically distribute the height of the rows equally among the total height of selected rows.
- You can also automatically distribute the width of the columns equally across the total width of selected columns.

Try It! Setting Column Width and Row Height

1. In the **W15Try_xx** file, click in the cell at top left.
2. Click TABLE TOOLS LAYOUT > AutoFit > AutoFit Contents.

   ✓ *To quickly resize a column to automatically fit the contents, double-click the column divider. To resize a row automatically to fit the contents, double-click the row divider.*

3. Click the AutoFit button again, and then click AutoFit Window.
4. Rest the mouse pointer on the column divider between the left and right columns.

   ✓ *The pointer changes to a double vertical line with arrows pointing left and right.*

5. Click and drag the divider about 0.5" to the left.
6. Release the mouse button to resize the columns.
7. Rest the mouse pointer on the divider between the first and second rows.

   ✓ *The pointer changes to a double horizontal line with arrows pointing up and down.*

8. Click and drag down about 0.5".
9. Release the mouse button to resize the row.
10. Click in any cell in the right column.
11. On the TABLE TOOLS LAYOUT tab, use the Table Column Width increment arrows to set the column width to 1.5".
12. Select rows two through five.
13. On the TABLE TOOLS LAYOUT tab, use the Table Row Height increment arrows to set the row height to 0.5".
14. Click the table move handle to select the entire table.
15. On the TABLE TOOLS LAYOUT tab, click the Distribute Rows button.
16. Click the Distribute Columns button.
17. Save the changes to **W15Try_xx**, and leave it open to use in the next Try It.

Drag to resize a column

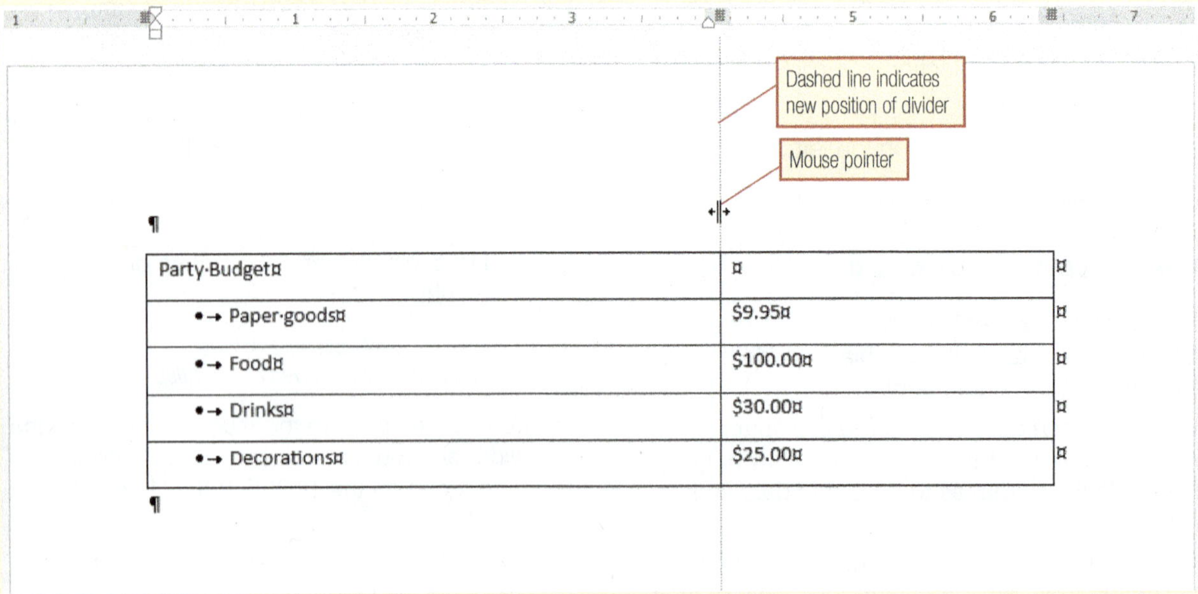

Setting Alignment in a Table Cell

- You can set horizontal and vertical alignment within a cell.
- Set alignment for the cell in which the insertion point is currently located, or for all cells in a selection.
- There are nine possible alignments available on the TABLE TOOLS LAYOUT tab in the Alignment group:
  - Align Top Left
  - Align Top Center
  - Align Top Right
  - Align Center Left
  - Align Center
  - Align Center Right
  - Align Bottom Left
  - Align Bottom Center
  - Align Bottom Right
- You can also use the horizontal alignment buttons in the Paragraph group on the HOME tab to align text horizontally in a cell.

✓ *If you justify text in a cell, be sure you have at least three lines of text.*

Try It! Setting Alignment in a Table Cell

1. In the **W15Try_xx** file, click in the cell where the text *Party Budget* displays.
2. On the TABLE TOOLS LAYOUT tab, click the Align Center button to center the text horizontally and vertically in the cell.
3. Select the four cells containing the bulleted items.
4. Click the Align Bottom Right button.
5. Select the four cells containing the dollar values, and then click the Align Bottom Left button.
6. Save the changes to **W15Try_xx**, and leave it open to use in the next Try It.

Setting Tabs in a Table Cell

- All tab stops can be used within a table cell.
- Decimal tab stops are often used in a table to automatically align numbers such as dollar values within a cell or a column.
- To advance to a tab stop within a table cell, you must press CTRL + TAB.

✓ *For more information on tabs, refer to Lesson 5.*

Try It! Setting Tabs in a Table Cell

1. In the **W15Try_xx** file, select the four cells containing dollar values.
2. Verify that the left tab indicator displays in the Tab selector box. If not, click the Tab selector box until the left tab indicator displays.
3. Click at 4.0" on the horizontal ruler to set a left tab.
4. Click the Tab selector box until the decimal tab indicator displays.
5. Click at 4.5" on the horizontal ruler to set a decimal tab.
6. Position the insertion point to the left of the dollar value in the second row and press CTRL + TAB to advance the data to the left tab stop.
7. Press CTRL + TAB again to advance the data to the decimal tab stop.
8. Repeat steps 6 and 7 to advance the dollar values in rows 3, 4, and 5 so they align on the decimal tab.
9. Save the changes to **W15Try_xx**, and leave it open to use in the next Try It.

Setting Cell Margins

- By default, top and bottom margins in a cell are set to 0" and left and right margins are set to 0.08".
- You can use the Table Options dialog box to set margins within a cell.
- The margins affect all cells in the table.
- By default, Word resizes the cells so the content fits.

Try It! Setting Cell Margins

1. In the **W15Try_xx** file, click in any cell.
2. On the TABLE TOOLS LAYOUT tab, click the Cell Margins button.
3. In the Table Options dialog box, use the Top increment arrows to set the top margin to 0.1".
4. Use the Left increment arrows to set the left margin to 0.1".
5. Use the Bottom increment arrows to set the bottom margin to 0.1".
6. Use the Right increment arrows to set the right margin to 0.1".
7. Click OK.
8. Save the changes to **W15Try_xx**, and leave it open to use in the next Try It.

Aligning a Table Horizontally on the Page

- You can left-align, right-align, or center a table on the page.
- The options for aligning a table on the page are found in the Table Properties dialog box, which you can open from the Table group on the TABLE TOOLS LAYOUT tab of the Ribbon.

Try It! Aligning a Table Horizontally on the Page

1. In the **W15Try_xx** file, position the insertion point anywhere in the table.
2. On the TABLE TOOLS LAYOUT tab, click the Properties button.
3. Click the Table tab if it is not already active.
4. Under Alignment, click the Center button.
5. Click OK.
6. Click the Properties button again.
7. Under Alignment, click the Right button.
8. Click OK.
9. Close **W15Try_xx**, saving changes, and exit Word.

Table Properties dialog box

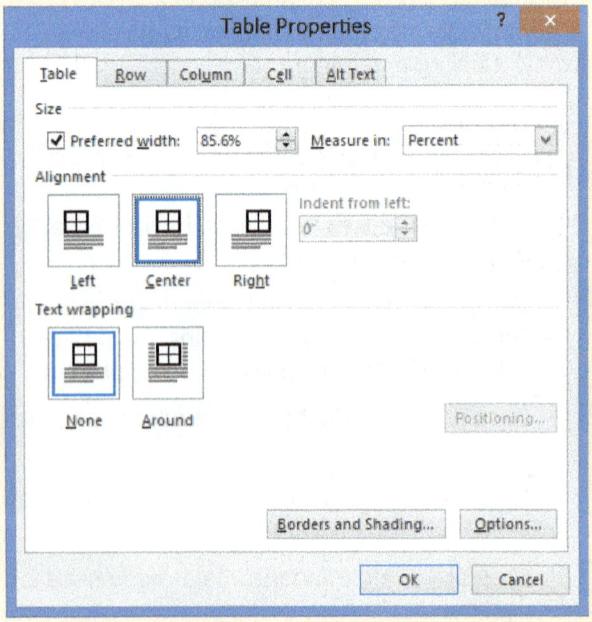

Word 2013, Windows 8, Microsoft Corporation

Lesson 15—Practice

Michigan Avenue Athletic Club is planning a major renovation. In preparation, it has surveyed members to find whether they want more tennis courts, more racquetball courts, more equipment rooms, or a lap pool. In this project, you create a table to display the potential cost of each area or renovation.

DIRECTIONS

1. Start Word, create a new document, and save the document as **W15Practice_xx** in the location where your teacher instructs you to store the files for this lesson.
2. Display the rulers and nonprinting characters.
3. Double-click in the header area and type your full name and today's date.
4. In the main document area, type the following list, separating the area names from the potential cost values using a left tab stop:

Area	Potential Cost
Reception	$8,500.00
Tennis court	$50,000.00
Racquetball court	$50,000.00
Equipment room	$75,000.00
Lap pool	$115,000.00

5. Select the six lines you typed in step 4.
6. Click **INSERT** > **Table** > **Convert Text to Table** to display the Convert Text to Table dialog box.
7. Click **OK** to create the table.
8. Select the cells in rows 2 through 6 in the left column (the area names).
9. Click **HOME** > **Bullets**.
10. Click the **table move handle** to select the entire table.
11. Click **TABLE TOOLS LAYOUT** > **AutoFit** > **AutoFit Contents**.
12. With the entire table still selected, use the Table Row Height increment arrows to set the row height to **0.4"**.
13. Click in any cell in the right column, and use the Table Column Width increment arrows to set the right column width to **1.6"**.
14. Select the top row.
15. On the **TABLE TOOLS LAYOUT** tab, click the **Align Center** button to center the text horizontally and vertically in the cell.
16. Select rows 2 through 6.
17. On the **TABLE TOOLS LAYOUT** tab, click the **Align Center Left** button.
18. Select the cells in rows 2 through 6 in the right column (the dollar values).
19. Click the **Tab selector** box until the decimal tab indicator displays.
20. Click at **3.0"** on the horizontal ruler to set a decimal tab. Word automatically aligns the selected data with the tab stop.
21. Click in the left cell in the top row.
22. On the **TABLE TOOLS LAYOUT** tab, click the **Cell Margins** button to display the Table Options dialog box.
23. Use the **Top** increment arrows to set the top cell margin to **0.05"** and the **Bottom** increment arrows to set the bottom cell margin to **0.05"**.
24. Click **OK**.
25. On the **TABLE TOOLS LAYOUT** tab, click the **Properties** button to display the Table Properties dialog box.
26. On the **Table** tab, under Alignment, click **Center**, and then click **OK**.
27. **With your teacher's permission**, print the document. It should look similar to Figure 15-1 on the next page.
28. Close the document, saving changes, and exit Word.

Figure 15-1

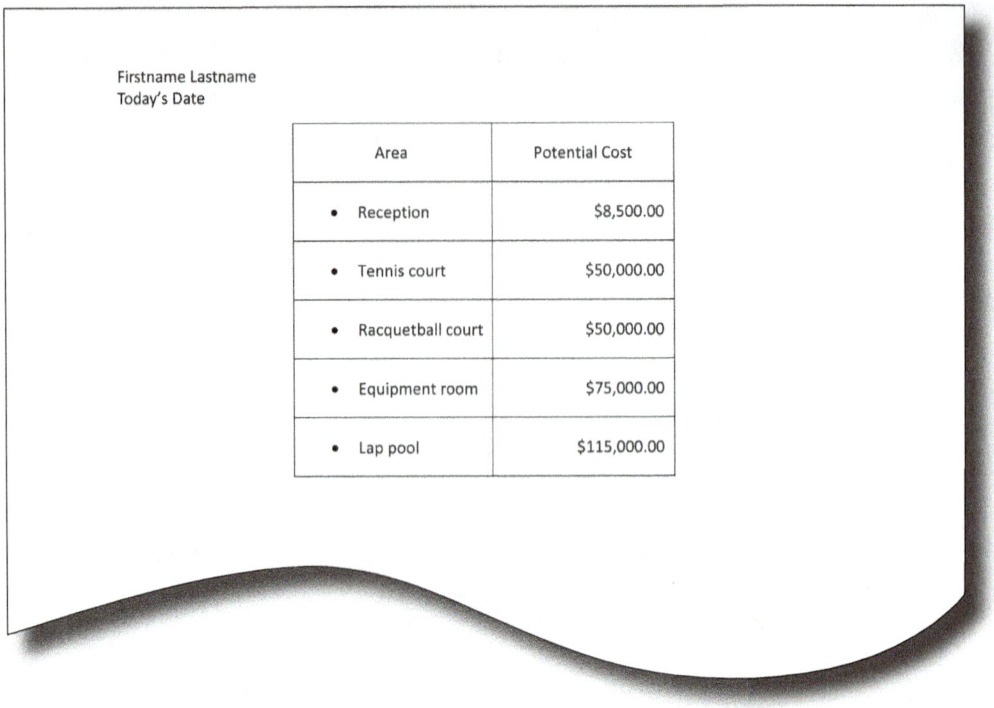
Firstname Lastname
Today's Date

Area	Potential Cost
• Reception	$8,500.00
• Tennis court	$50,000.00
• Racquetball court	$50,000.00
• Equipment room	$75,000.00
• Lap pool	$115,000.00

Lesson 15—Apply

In this project, you create a memo to the Michigan Avenue Athletic Club's general manager that includes the survey results and potential costs.

DIRECTIONS

1. Start Word, if necessary, and open **W15Apply** from the data files for this lesson.
2. Save the file as **W15Apply_xx** in the location where your teacher instructs you to store the files for this lesson.
3. Display the rulers and nonprinting characters.
4. Replace the sample text *Student's Name* with your own name, and *Today's Date* with the actual date.
5. Use the following steps to create the document shown in Figure 15-2 on the next page.
6. Select the six lines where the tabbed survey results are listed.
7. Convert the selection into a table with 5 columns and 6 rows, separating the text at the tabs.
8. In column 1, apply the **Align Bottom Center** alignment.
9. In columns 2, 3, and 4, apply the **Align Bottom Right** alignment.
10. In column 5, apply the **Align Bottom Left** alignment.
11. In row 1, apply the **Align Center** alignment.
12. In the cells that contain dollar values, insert a decimal tab at **6.25"** on the horizontal ruler to align the costs.
13. Change the font formatting of the text in the first column and the first row to 12-point Arial, bold.
14. Set the widths of columns 1 and 5 to **1.5"**.
15. Set the width of columns 2, 3, and 4 to **0.8"**.
16. Set the height of all rows to **0.5"**.

17. Center the entire table horizontally on the page.
18. Apply the **Title** style to the text **Memo**.
19. **With your teacher's permission**, print the document. It should look similar to Figure 15-2.
20. Close the document, saving changes, and exit Word.

Figure 15-2

MEMO

To: General Manager
From: Firstname Lastname
Date: Today's Date
Subject: Renovation Survey Results

Here are the results of the member survey. I have also included information about the potential costs associated with each item. We can use this data to help us decide where we want to focus our resources during the renovation.

Area	Want	Do not Care	Do not Want	Potential Cost
Reception	15	18	2	$8,500.00
Tennis court	19	10	5	$50,000.00
Racquetball court	25	15	7	$50,000.00
Equipment room	45	22	2	$75,000.00
Lap pool	8	5	12	$115,000.00

Lesson 16

Drawing a Table

➤ What You Will Learn

Drawing a Table
Merging and Splitting Cells
Changing Text Direction in a Table Cell
Moving and Resizing Tables
Setting Text Wrapping Around a Table

WORDS TO KNOW

Header row
A row across the top of a table in which heading information is entered.

Merge
Combine multiple adjacent cells together to create one large cell.

Sizing handle
A nonprinting icon that displays outside the lower right corner of a table that you use to resize the table.

Split
Divide one cell into multiple cells, either vertically to create columns or horizontally to create rows.

Software Skills Word's Draw Table tool gives you great flexibility to organize tables. You can lay out the table cells exactly as you want them; not necessarily in rigid columns and rows. You can then move and resize the table, if necessary, merge and split cells, and rotate the text to achieve the exact effect you need.

What You Can Do

Drawing a Table

- Word's Draw Table feature lets you create tables with uneven or irregular columns and rows by dragging the mouse.
- Access Draw Table from the Tables group on the INSERT tab of the Ribbon, or in the Draw group on the TABLE TOOLS LAYOUT tab.
- You can draw a new table, or add columns, rows, or cells to an existing table.
- When you draw a table, the mouse pointer looks and functions like a pencil .
- You drag the pointer to draw one cell, then drag to draw lines vertically or horizontally to create cell dividers.
- Word creates straight lines at 90 degree angles to existing cell dividers, even if you do not drag in a straight line.
- You can draw a diagonal line across a cell as a visual element or border, not to split the cell diagonally.
- New cells can be drawn anywhere. Rows and columns do not have to extend across the entire table.
- The Draw Table tool remains active until you turn it off.
- You must use Print Layout view to draw a table.

Try It!

Drawing a Table

1. Start Word and open **W16Try** from the data files for this lesson, and save it as **W16Try_xx** in the location where your teacher instructs you to store the files for this lesson. Display nonprinting characters and the rulers.
2. Click the INSERT tab, then click the Table button.
3. Click Draw Table on the INSERT table drop-down menu.

   ✓ *The mouse pointer change to resemble a pencil.*
4. Position the mouse pointer just below the paragraph mark at the end of the document, press and hold the left mouse button, and drag diagonally down and to the right.

   ✓ *Notice that lines on the rulers indicate the current position of the mouse.*
5. When the cell is approximately 2" high by 5" wide, release the mouse button.
6. Position the mouse pointer at the mid-point along the top border of the cell.
7. Click and drag straight down. When the dotted divider line reaches the bottom border, release the mouse button.
8. Position the mouse pointer at the mid-point along the cell divider you drew in step 7, and then click and drag to the right. When the divider line reaches the right border, release the mouse button.
9. Press ESC to turn off Draw Table
10. Click TABLE TOOLS LAYOUT > Draw Table.
11. Position the mouse pointer on the lower left corner of the table.
12. Click and drag down about 0.5" and to the right until the new cell is the same width as the current table.
13. Release the mouse button.
14. Click and drag to draw eight vertical cell dividers across the new cell you drew in step 12.
15. Click the Draw Table button again to turn the feature off.
16. Save the changes to **W16Try_xx**, and leave it open to use in the next Try It.

Merging and Splitting Cells

- You can **merge** horizontally or vertically adjacent cells using commands in the Merge group on the TABLE TOOLS LAYOUT tab of the Ribbon.
- You can use the Eraser tool in the Draw group on the TABLE TOOLS LAYOUT tab to erase dividers between cells, thus merging the cells.
- If you erase a divider on the outer edge of the table, you simply erase the border line, not the divider.
- Merging is useful for creating a **header row** across a table.
- **Split** a cell to insert dividers to create additional columns or rows in an existing table.
- You can split a cell using the Split Cells dialog box to select the number of columns or rows you want to create.

  ✓ *Alternatively, use the Draw Table tool to draw divider lines, as you learned in the previous Try It.*

Try It! Merging and Splitting Cells

1. In the W16Try_xx file, select the two cells on the left end of the bottom row.
2. Click TABLE TOOLS LAYOUT > Merge Cells.
3. Click anywhere in the table.
4. Click TABLE TOOLS LAYOUT > Eraser.

   ✓ *The mouse pointer changes to resemble an eraser.*
5. Click on a vertical divider line in the bottom row.
6. Click another vertical divider line in the bottom row.
7. Press ESC to turn off the feature.
8. Click in the cell in the top right corner of the table.
9. Click TABLE TOOLS LAYOUT > Split Cells to open the Split Cells dialog box.
10. Use the Number of columns increment arrows to set the number of columns to 3.
11. Use the Number of rows increment arrows to set the number of rows to 2.
12. Click OK.
13. Save the changes to W16Try_xx, and leave it open to use in the next Try It.

Changing Text Direction in a Table Cell

- By default, when you type text in a table cell it runs from left to right, like text in a document.
- You can change the text direction so it runs from top to bottom or from bottom to top.

Try It! Changing Text Direction in a Table Cell

1. In the W16Try_xx file, click in the top-left cell in the table and type Voyager Travel Adventures.
2. On the TABLE TOOLS LAYOUT tab, click the Text Direction button to rotate the text so it runs top to bottom.

   ✓ *Notice that the Text Direction button changes to show the direction of the text in the current cell.*
3. Click the Text Direction button again to rotate the text so it runs bottom to top.

   ✓ *The Text Direction button changes again.*
4. Click the Text Direction button again to rotate the text so it runs left to right.
5. Save the changes to W16Try_xx, and leave it open to use in the next Try It.

Moving and Resizing Tables

- Drag the table move handle to move a table anywhere on the page.
- Existing text will wrap around the table in its new position.
- Drag the table's **sizing handle** to change the table size.
- The table move handle and sizing handle only display when the mouse pointer is resting on the table or if the table is selected.

Try It! Moving and Resizing Tables

1. In the **W16Try_xx** file, rest the mouse pointer over the table so the table move handle ⊞ displays.
2. Click and drag the table move handle ⊞ straight up.

   ✓ *As you drag, the mouse pointer changes to a four-headed arrow ✥, and a dotted line moves with the pointer to indicate the new location.*

3. Release the mouse button when the pointer is positioned on the space between the two paragraphs to drop the table in the new location.

   ✓ *Notice that the text now wraps around the table.*

4. Rest the mouse pointer over the table so the sizing handle displays.
5. Click and drag the sizing handle diagonally up and to the left.

   ✓ *As you drag, the mouse pointer changes to resemble a cross-hair.*

6. Release the mouse button when the table is about 2" high by 4" wide.
7. Save the changes to **W16Try_xx**, and leave it open to use in the next Try It.

Drag the table sizing handle to resize a table

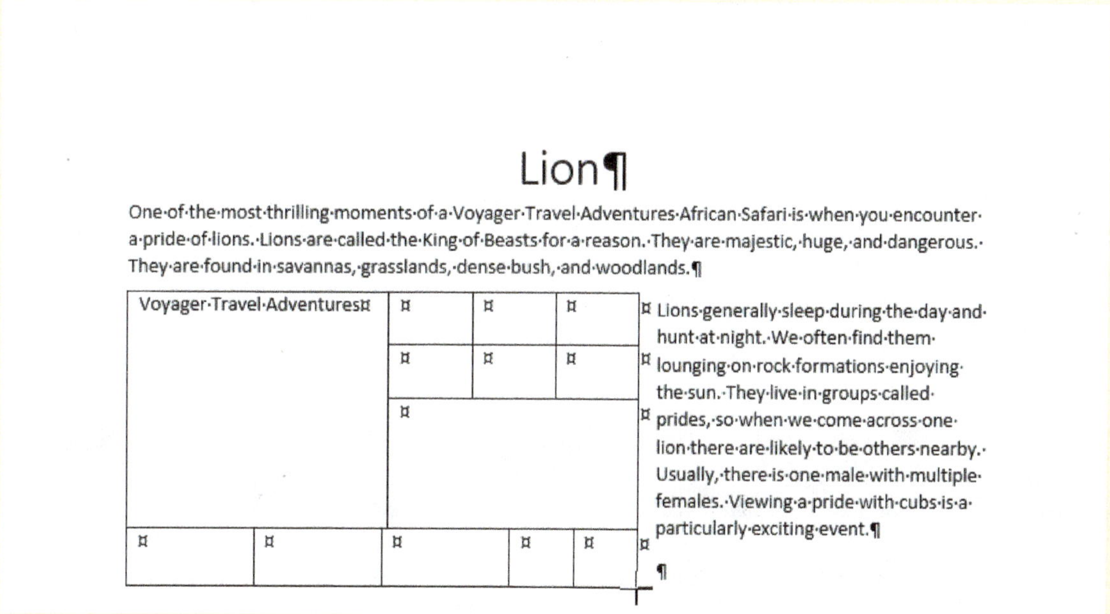

Lion¶

One·of·the·most·thrilling·moments·of·a·Voyager·Travel·Adventures·African·Safari·is·when·you·encounter· a·pride·of·lions.·Lions·are·called·the·King·of·Beasts·for·a·reason.·They·are·majestic,·huge,·and·dangerous.· They·are·found·in·savannas,·grasslands,·dense·bush,·and·woodlands.¶

Voyager·Travel·Adventures

Lions·generally·sleep·during·the·day·and· hunt·at·night.·We·often·find·them· lounging·on·rock·formations·enjoying· the·sun.·They·live·in·groups·called· prides,·so·when·we·come·across·one· lion·there·are·likely·to·be·others·nearby.· Usually,·there·is·one·male·with·multiple· females.·Viewing·a·pride·with·cubs·is·a· particularly·exciting·event.¶

Word 2013, Windows 8, Microsoft Corporation

Setting Text Wrapping Around a Table

- There are two text-wrapping options in the Table Properties dialog box for integrating a table with text on a page.
  - Choose None to display text above and below the table.
  - Choose Around to wrap text around the sides of the table.
- By default, tables are inserted on a blank line above or below existing text.
- When you drag a table to a new location, text automatically wraps around the table.
- Wrapping text around a table integrates the table object into the text so text appears above, below, and on either side of the table.

Try It! Setting Text Wrapping Around a Table

1. In the **W16Try_xx** file, click in any cell in the table.
2. Click TABLE TOOLS LAYOUT > Properties to open the Table Properties dialog box.
3. Under Text Wrapping, click None.
4. Click OK. Word removes text wrapping so text flows above and below the table.

   ✓ *The position of the table in relation to the text depends on the size of your table. It may not look exactly like the figures.*
5. On the TABLE TOOLS LAYOUT tab, click the Properties button again.
6. Under Text Wrapping, click Around, and then click OK. Word wraps the text around the table.

   ✓ *The position of the table in relation to the text depends on the size of your table. It may not look exactly like the figures.*
7. Close **W16Try_xx**, saving changes, and exit Word.

Text wrapping is set to None (left) and Around (right)

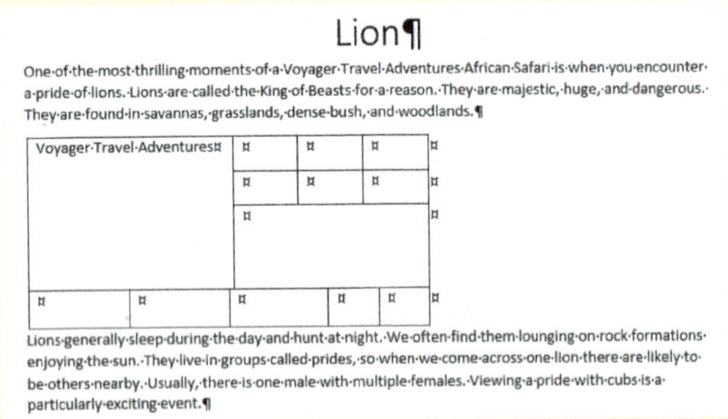
Lion¶

One·of·the·most·thrilling·moments·of·a·Voyager·Travel·Adventures·African·Safari·is·when·you·encounter·a·pride·of·lions.·Lions·are·called·the·King·of·Beasts·for·a·reason.·They·are·majestic,·huge,·and·dangerous.·They·are·found·in·savannas,·grasslands,·dense·bush,·and·woodlands.¶

Voyager·Travel·Adventures¤

Lions·generally·sleep·during·the·day·and·hunt·at·night.·We·often·find·them·lounging·on·rock·formations·enjoying·the·sun.·They·live·in·groups·called·prides,·so·when·we·come·across·one·lion·there·are·likely·to·be·others·nearby.·Usually,·there·is·one·male·with·multiple·females.·Viewing·a·pride·with·cubs·is·a·particularly·exciting·event.¶

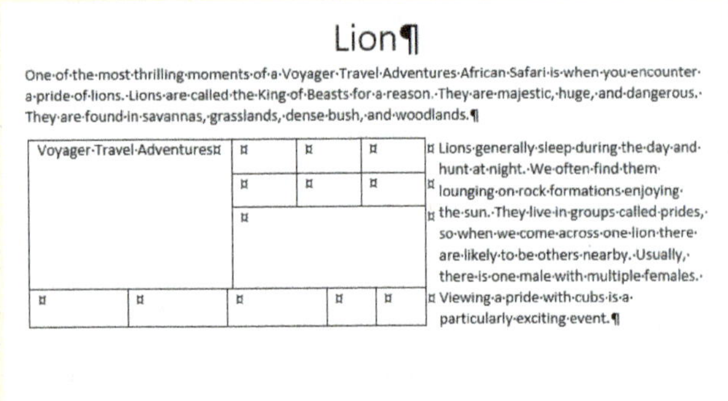
Lion¶

One·of·the·most·thrilling·moments·of·a·Voyager·Travel·Adventures·African·Safari·is·when·you·encounter·a·pride·of·lions.·Lions·are·called·the·King·of·Beasts·for·a·reason.·They·are·majestic,·huge,·and·dangerous.·They·are·found·in·savannas,·grasslands,·dense·bush,·and·woodlands.¶

Voyager·Travel·Adventures¤

Lions·generally·sleep·during·the·day·and·hunt·at·night.·We·often·find·them·lounging·on·rock·formations·enjoying·the·sun.·They·live·in·groups·called·prides,·so·when·we·come·across·one·lion·there·are·likely·to·be·others·nearby.·Usually,·there·is·one·male·with·multiple·females.·Viewing·a·pride·with·cubs·is·a·particularly·exciting·event.¶

Word 2013, Windows 8, Microsoft Corporation

Lesson 16—Practice

The exercise director at Michigan Avenue Athletic Club has asked you to design a flyer announcing a series of new classes. In this project, you will create a draft of the table you will use in the flyer.

DIRECTIONS

1. Start Word, create a new document, and save the document as **W16Practice_xx** in the location where your teacher instructs you to store the files for this lesson.
2. Display the rulers and nonprinting characters.
3. Double-click in the header area and type your full name and today's date.
4. On the first line of the document, increase the font size to 12 points and then type the following paragraph:

   Work Out with David is a series of three classes designed to introduce members to some of the exercise opportunities here at Michigan Avenue Athletic Club. Each hour-long session focuses on two complementary types of exercises.

5. Press ENTER to start a new line.
6. Click **INSERT** > **Table** > **Draw Table**.
7. Starting at the current insertion point location, click and drag down and to the right with the mouse pointer to draw a cell approximately **3"** wide by **3"** high.
8. Click and drag to draw a vertical line dividing the cell into two columns so that the left column is **1"** wide and the right column is **2"** wide.
9. Click and drag to draw two horizontal lines dividing the table into three 1" high rows.
10. On the TABLE TOOLS LAYOUT tab, click the **Draw Table** button to turn the feature off.
11. Select the left column of the table.
12. Click **TABLE TOOLS LAYOUT** > **Merge Cells**.
13. Change the font size to 22 points and then type **Work Out with David**.
14. Click **TABLE TOOLS LAYOUT** > **Text Direction** twice to rotate the text so it runs bottom to top.
15. Click in the top cell in the right column.
16. Click the **Split Cells** button to open the Split Cells dialog box.
17. Use the **Number of columns** increment arrows to set the value to **1**.
18. Use the **Number of rows** increment arrows to set the value to **2**.
19. Click **OK**.
20. Click in what is now the third row in the right column, and then click the **Repeat** button on the Quick Access Toolbar.
21. Click in what is the fifth row in the right column, and then click the **Repeat** button on the Quick Access Toolbar again.
22. Rest the mouse pointer anywhere over the table so the sizing handle displays.
23. Click and drag the **sizing handle** to the right to increase the width of the table to **4"**.
24. Rest the mouse pointer anywhere over the table so the table move handle displays.
25. Click and drag the **table move handle** up and release the mouse button when the mouse pointer is even with the beginning of the first line of text.
26. Check and correct the spelling and grammar in the document, and then save the changes.
27. **With your teacher's permission**, print the document. It should look similar to Figure 16-1.
28. Close the document, saving changes, and exit Word.

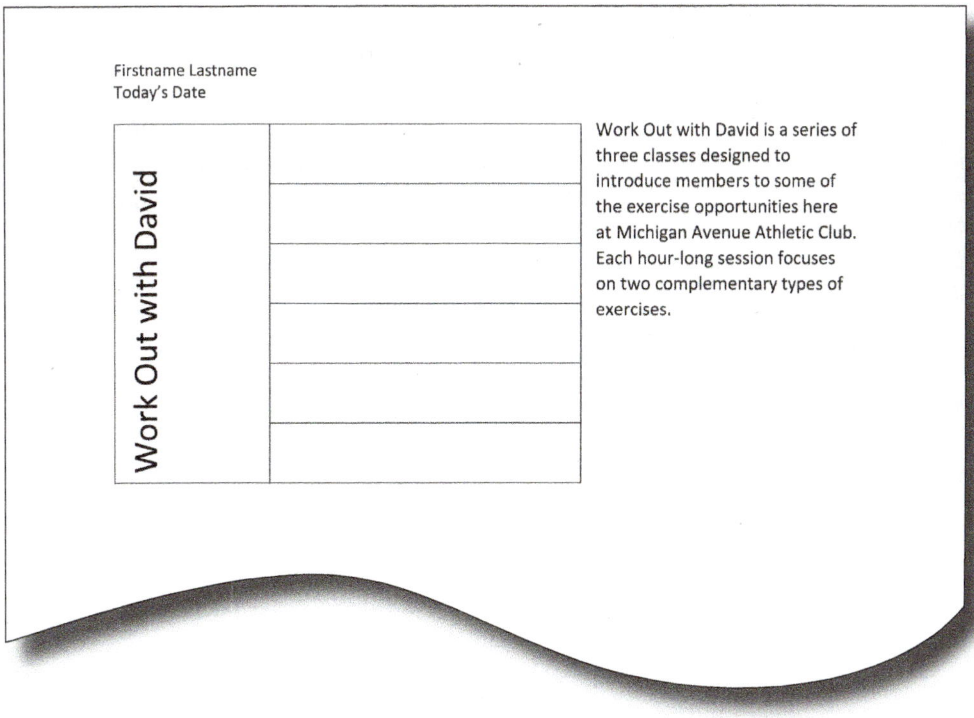

Figure 16-1

Lesson 16—Apply

In this project, you create the flyer for Michigan Avenue Athletic Club that includes a table and other information.

DIRECTIONS

1. Start Word, if necessary, and open **W16Apply** from the data files for this lesson.
2. Save the file as **W16Apply_xx** in the location where your teacher instructs you to store the files for this lesson.
3. Display the rulers and nonprinting characters.
4. Type your full name and today's date in the header area.
5. Use the following steps to complete the table and format the document as shown in Figure 16-2 on the next page.
6. Click anywhere in the table and then use the **Draw Table** tool to draw a vertical line to split the current column into two columns of equal width.
7. Use the **Eraser** tool to merge the top two cells in the left column into one cell.
8. Select what are now the second and third cells in the left column and merge them.
9. Select what are now the bottom two cells in the left column and merge them.
10. Draw a new row across the bottom of the table, sized 0.5" high.
11. Draw a new column along the left side of the table, sized about 0.5" wide.

    ✓ *If you cannot draw the column correctly with the Draw Table tools, use Insert Left to insert a new column along the left side of the table and adjust its width to 0.5". Merge all cells in the new column.*
12. Drag the **table move handle** ⊞ to move the entire table on the page so its top aligns with the top of the second paragraph, and its left edge aligns with the left margin.
13. Draw a new row across the top of the table, sized 0.5" high.
14. Drag the **sizing handle** to resize the table so it is about 4" wide by 4" high.
15. Enter the text as shown in Figure 16-2 on the next page.
    a. Set the font size of the header row and the dates to 20 points, and center align the text horizontally and vertically.
    b. Set the font size of the class names to 18 points and align them with the bottom left of the cells.
    c. Set the font size in the bottom row to 14 points and center align the text horizontally and vertically.
    d. Set the text direction for the left column to run from bottom to top, set the font size to 28 points, and center align the text horizontally and vertically.
16. Change the font of the first three lines of text in the document to 16-point Calibri Light bold, and center them horizontally.
17. Add 18 points of space after the third line.
18. Check and correct the spelling and grammar in the document, and then save the changes.
19. **With your teacher's permission**, print the document. It should look similar to Figure 16-2 on the next page.
20. Close the document, saving changes, and exit Word.

Figure 16-2

Firstname Lastname
Today's Date

Work Out with David
A series of introductory exercise classes with
Personal Trainer David Fairmont

Work Out with David is a series of three classes designed to introduce members to some of the exercise opportunities here at Michigan Avenue Athletic Club. Each hour-long session focuses on two complementary types of exercises.

Schedule		
Work Out with David	January 8	Step Aerobics
		Pilates
	January 15	Spinning
		Yoga
	January 22	Kickboxing
		Free Weights
	Space is limited. Please sign up as soon as possible!	

The first 15 minutes of each class will be spent learning about the exercises, including the equipment that may be involved. The rest of each class includes a warm up, active participation, followed by cool down exercises and stretching.

David Fairmont is out newest personal trainer. He holds a master's degree in health management from the University of Vermont in Burlington, VT, and he is certified in cardiovascular exercise and strength training.

Work Out with David is geared toward those who are new to our exercise class offerings, but all members are welcome to join. There is no fee for participation

but class size is limited. Please see Katie at the front desk to enroll.

Lesson 17

Performing Calculations in a Table

➤ What You Will Learn

Performing Addition in a Table
Applying a Number Format
Sorting Rows in a Table
Applying Cell Borders and Shading
Making a Table Accessible
Converting a Table to Text

WORDS TO KNOW

Formula
A mathematical equation.

Function
A built-in formula for performing calculations, such as addition, in a table.

Line style
The appearance of a line.

Line weight
The thickness of a line.

Shading
A color or pattern used to fill the background of a cell.

Spreadsheet
A document created with an application, such as Microsoft Office Excel 2013, used for setting up mathematical calculations.

Software Skills Perform basic calculations in a table to total values in a column or row. If the values change, you can update the result without redoing the math. At the same time, you can format the calculation results with one of Word's built-in number formats. Sorting rows helps you keep your tables in order, while cell borders and shading let you dress up your tables to make them look good as well as to highlight important information. Use accessibility options to make a table more meaningful for someone using a screen reader. Convert a table to restore it to text format.

What You Can Do

Performing Addition in a Table

- Use Word's **Formula** command to access basic **spreadsheet** functions so you can perform calculations on data entered in a table.
- The Formula command is in the Data group on the TABLE TOOLS LAYOUT tab.
- Word enters the result in a field, so it can be updated if the values in the table change.
- You must update the total each time one of the values used in the formula is changed. The total does not update automatically.
- By default, Word assumes you want to use the SUM **function** to add the values entered in the column above the current cell or in the row beside the current cell.
- You can enter a different formula by typing it into the Formula text box in the Formula dialog box.

- You can also select a function from the Paste function drop-down list in the Formula dialog box.
- For anything other than basic calculations, use an Excel worksheet, not a Word table.

✓ *For information on using Excel functions, and formulas, refer to the Excel section in this book.*

Try It! Performing Addition in a Table

1. Start Word and open **W17Try** from the data files for this lesson. Save the file as **W17Try_xx** in the location where your teacher instructs you to store the files for this lesson.
2. In the first table, click in the bottom cell in the right column.
3. Click TABLE TOOLS LAYOUT > Formula *fx*.
4. Verify that the Formula box displays the formula for adding the values in the cells above the current cell: =SUM(ABOVE).
5. Click OK.
6. Click in the bottom cell of the left column in the first table (Total).
7. On the TABLE TOOLS LAYOUT tab, click the Insert Above button.
8. Click in the left column of the new row and type **Taxi**.
9. Press TAB and type **$53.65**.
10. Right-click on the value in the bottom cell of the right column.
11. On the shortcut menu, click Update Field.

    ✓ *The shortcut key for updating a total is* F9.
12. Save the changes to **W17Try_xx**, and leave it open to use in the next Try It.

Applying a Number Format

- When you set up a calculation in a table, you can select a number format in the Formula dialog box to apply to the calculation result.
- Number formats include dollar signs, commas, percent signs, and decimal points.

Try It! Applying a Number Format

1. In the **W17Try_xx** file, click in the last cell in the right column of the second table.
2. On the TABLE TOOLS LAYOUT tab, click the Formula button *fx*.
3. Verify that the Formula box displays the formula for adding the values in the cells to the left of the current cell: =SUM(LEFT).
4. Click the Number format drop-down arrow.
5. Click the third format from the top of the list: $#,##0.00;($#,##0.00).
6. Click OK. Word inserts the result of the formula and applies the selected format.
7. Save the changes to **W17Try_xx**, and leave it open to use in the next Try It.

Select a Number format in the Formula dialog box

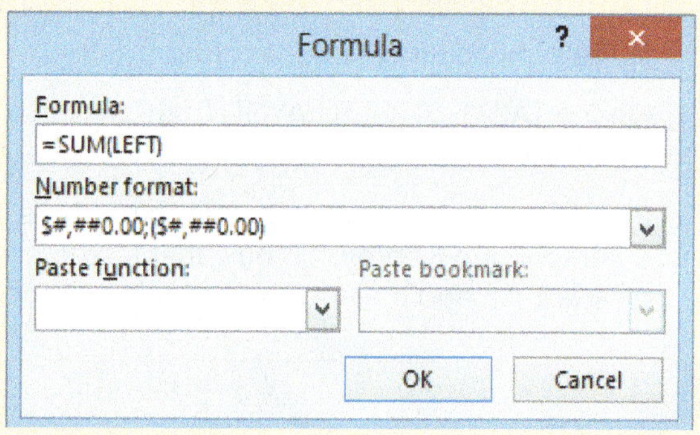

Word 2013, Windows 8, Microsoft Corporation

Sorting Rows in a Table

- Sort rows in a table using the Sort dialog box, the same way you sort lists or paragraphs.

  ✓ *See Word, Lesson 7.*

- For tables, the Sort command is available in the Data group on the TABLE TOOLS LAYOUT tab of the Ribbon.
- Rows can be sorted according to the data in any column.
- Word rearranges the rows in the table but does not rearrange the columns.
- For example, in a table of names and addresses, rows can be sorted alphabetically by name or by city, or numerically by postal code.
- By default, Word identifies the type of data in the selected column as Text, Number, or Date.
- The default sort order is ascending, but you can select descending if you want.
- You can specify whether or not the table includes a header row that you do not want to include in the sort.
- Word identifies the columns by the label in the header row, if there is one. If not, it numbers the columns consecutively from left to right. For example, in a three-column table, Column 1 is on the left, Column 2 is in the middle, and Column 3 is on the right.
- You can even sort by up to three columns. For example, you can sort a single table alphabetically by name and then numerically by postal code.
- You cannot sort rows containing merged cells.

Try It! Sorting Rows in a Table

1. In the **W17Try_xx** file, select the right column in the first table.
2. On the TABLE TOOLS LAYOUT tab, click the Sort button.
3. In the Sort dialog box, verify that Column 2 is entered in the Sort by text box, that the data type is Number, that the Sort order is Ascending, and that the No header row option button is selected.
4. Click OK to sort the rows in ascending order based on the dollar values in the right column.
5. Click in the top row of the first table.
6. Insert a row above the current row so you can set up a header row.
7. In the left column, type **Expense**.
8. In the right column, type **Amount**.
9. On the TABLE TOOLS LAYOUT tab, click the Sort button.
10. In the Sort dialog box, verify that Expense is entered in the Sort by text box, that the data type is Text, and that the sort order is Ascending.
11. Click the first Then by drop-down arrow and click Amount. Verify that the data type is Number, the sort order is Ascending, and that the Header row option button is selected.
12. Click OK.
13. Save the changes to **W17Try_xx**, and leave it open to use in the next Try It.

Sort dialog box

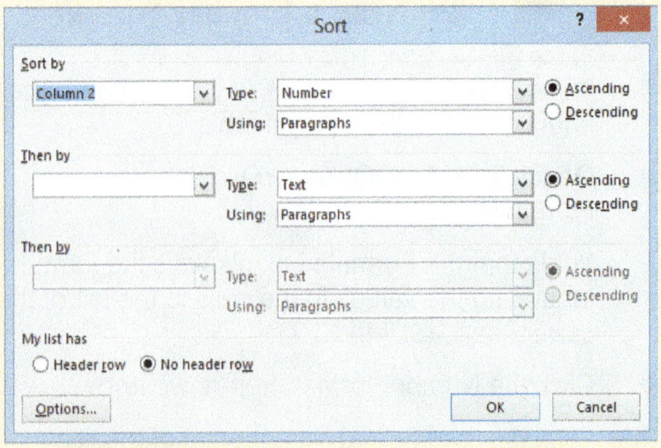

Word 2013, Windows 8, Microsoft Corporation

Applying Cell Borders and Shading

- By default, Word applies a ½-point black solid line border around all table cells.
- You can select to display or hide border lines along one or more sides of a cell.
- To change the appearance of the borders, you select a **line style**, **line weight**, and pen color, and then select the border style you want to apply.
- For example, you might apply a green, dashed border around the outside of selected cells, or a purple triple-line border across the bottom of the selected cells.
- When you select border formatting, the Border Painter tool becomes active so you can use it to apply the selected formatting.
- You can apply background color or **shading** to a cell.
- Selected border and shading formatting remain in effect until new formatting is selected.
- Table style formatting takes precedence over direct border and shading formatting. Apply Table styles first, then modify the styles if necessary using the direct formatting.

✓ *When table borders are removed, you can see table cells onscreen by displaying gridlines. Refer to Word, Lesson 14 for information on showing and hiding gridlines.*

Try It! Applying Cell Borders and Shading

1. In the W17Try_xx file, select the first table.
2. Click TABLE TOOLS DESIGN > Line Style.
3. From the Line Style gallery, click the double-line line style.

   ✓ *Notice that the Border Painter tool becomes active.*
4. Click TABLE TOOLS DESIGN > Line Weight ½ pt.
5. From the Line Weight gallery, click 1½ pt.
6. Click the Pen Color drop-down arrow.
7. Under Standard Colors, click Red.
8. Click the Borders drop-down arrow.
9. From the Borders gallery, click Outside Borders. Word applies an outside border around the selected cells, using the selected border formatting.

   ✓ *Border styles are toggles—click on to display border; click off to hide border.*
10. Select the top row in the second table.
11. On the TABLE TOOLS DESIGN tab, click the Shading drop-down arrow.
12. Under Standard Colors, click Orange.
13. Save changes to W17Try_xx, and leave it open for the next Try It.

Making a Table Accessible

- Many people who have vision challenges use screen readers to read document text and describe objects such as pictures, diagrams, and table.
- To help such a reader understand table content, you can use alternative text to provide a title and description of the table.
- Use the Alt Text tab in the Table Properties dialog box to specify the table title and description.

Try It! Making a Table Accessible

1. In the **W17Try_xx** file, click anywhere in the first table.
2. Click TABLE TOOLS LAYOUT > Properties and then click the Alt Text tab.
3. Click in the Title box and type the following title: **Travel Expenses Table**
4. Click in the Description box and type the following description: **Lists expenses for standard travel categories such as airfare and lodging**
5. Click OK.
6. Save the changes to **W17Try_xx**, and leave it open to use in the next Try It.

Supplying alternative text for a table

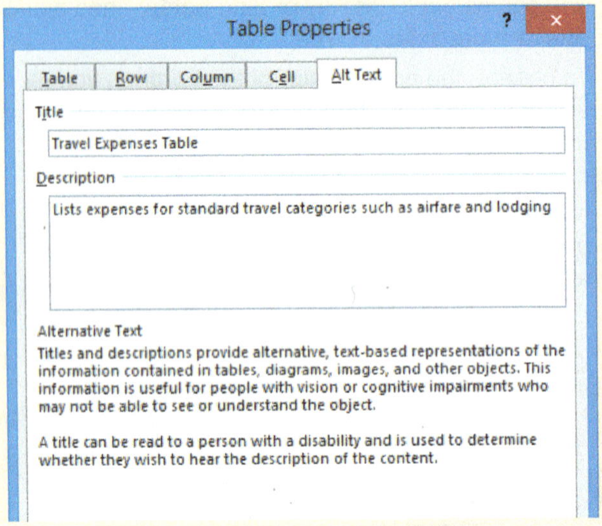

Word 2013, Windows 8, Microsoft Corporation

Converting a Table to Text

- Convert an entire table or selected table rows into regular document text.
- Word inserts the specified separator character into the text at the end of each column.
- Word starts a new paragraph at the end of each row.

Try It! Converting a Table to Text

1. In the **W17Try_xx** file, select the second table, and then click HOME > Copy.
2. Click in the last paragraph in the document, and then click HOME > Paste.
3. Select the pasted table, and then click TABLE TOOLS LAYOUT > Convert to Text.
4. Click OK to separate the text with tabs.
5. Close **W17Try_xx**, saving changes, and exit Word.

Lesson 17—Practice

A Whole Grains Bread franchise is offering a special gift basket for Earth Day. In this project, you will create a document to advertise the gift basket. You will use a table to organize the information and to calculate costs.

DIRECTIONS

1. Start Word, create a new document, and save the document as **W17Practice_xx** in the location where your teacher instructs you to store the files for this lesson.
2. Display the rulers and nonprinting characters.
3. Double-click in the header area and type your full name and today's date. Close the Header area.

4. Set the font to 14-point Calibri and type:
   Celebrate Earth Day by sending someone you love a beautiful gift basket filled with organic treats. The basket includes all of the items listed below, as well as an Earth Day surprise. The basket is beautifully arranged and wrapped using recycled materials. Local delivery is included in the special price.
5. Press ENTER.
6. Click **INSERT** > **Table**. Drag across the INSERT table grid to insert a table with two columns and three rows.
7. Enter the following data in the table cells:

Muffins	15.99
Fruit Preserves	12.99
Granola	10.99

8. Select the left column.
9. Click **TABLE TOOLS LAYOUT** > **Sort**.
10. Verify that Column 1 is entered in the Sort by text box, that the data type is Text, that the sort order is Ascending, and that the No header row option is selected.
11. Click **OK**.
12. Insert a new row at the bottom of the table.
13. In the left column of the new row, type **Total**.
14. Click in the right column of the new row, then click **TABLE TOOLS LAYOUT** > **Formula**.
15. Verify that the formula is =SUM(ABOVE).
16. Click the **Number format** drop-down arrow and click the third format from the top of the list: $#,##0.00;($#,##0.00).
17. Click **OK**.
18. Click in the bottom row.
19. Click **TABLE TOOLS DESIGN** > **Line Style** and click the solid line style.
20. Click the **Line Weight** button ½ pt and click **3 pt**.
21. Click the **Pen Color** drop-down arrow and, under Theme Colors, click **Blue-Gray, Text 2**.
22. Drag the **Border Painter** pointer along the top border of the last row to apply the selected formats.
23. Select the right column of the table and set a decimal tab stop at **4.0"** on the ruler.
24. Check and correct the spelling and grammar in the document, and then save the changes.
25. **With your teacher's permission**, print the document. It should look similar to Figure 17-1.
26. Close the document, saving changes, and exit Word.

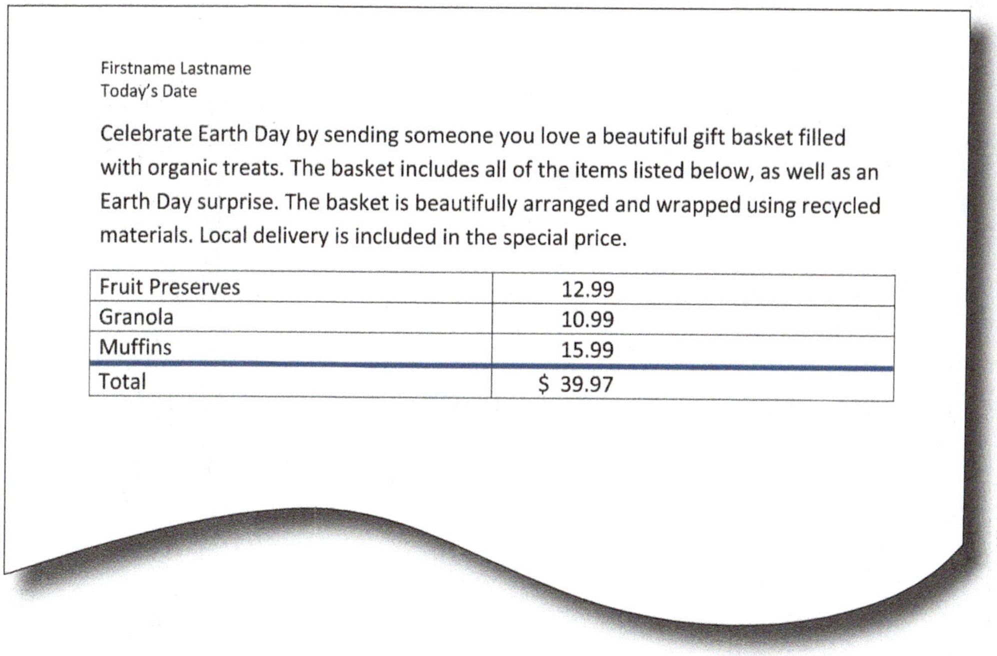
Firstname Lastname
Today's Date

Celebrate Earth Day by sending someone you love a beautiful gift basket filled with organic treats. The basket includes all of the items listed below, as well as an Earth Day surprise. The basket is beautifully arranged and wrapped using recycled materials. Local delivery is included in the special price.

Fruit Preserves	12.99
Granola	10.99
Muffins	15.99
Total	$ 39.97

Word 2013, Windows 8, Microsoft Corporation

Figure 17-1

Lesson 17—Apply

In this project, you continue to work with the gift basket flyer. You add rows and sort them, and then format the table using cell borders and shading.

DIRECTIONS

1. Start Word, if necessary, and open **W17Apply** from the data files for this lesson.
2. Save the file as **W17Apply_xx** in the location where your teacher instructs you to store the files for this lesson.
3. Display the rulers and nonprinting characters.
4. In the header, type your full name and today's date. Use the following steps to complete and format the table, as shown in Figure 17-2.
5. Click in the bottom right cell in the table and insert a formula to add the values in the cells above. Format the result as dollars.
6. Insert a row at the top of the table. In the left cell of the new row, type **Organic Whole Grain Banana Bread**. In the right cell of the new row, type **16.35**.
7. Update the result of the formula in the bottom right cell to include the new value.
8. Sort the table rows into ascending order based first on the data in column 1 and then by the data in column 2.
9. Insert another new row at the top of the table.
10. In the left cell of the new row, type **Basket Includes:**.
11. In the right cell of the new row, type **Regular Price:**.
12. Select the top row of the table and apply the **Green, Accent 6** shading.
13. With the top row still selected, remove all borders from the top row.
14. Select the bottom row of the table and apply a **solid-line, 2¼ pt. Green, Accent 6** outside border.
15. With the bottom row still selected, apply **Green, Accent 6, Lighter 80%** shading.
16. Add a title and description of the table as alternate text.
17. Check and correct the spelling and grammar in the document, and then save the changes.
18. **With your teacher's permission**, print the document. It should look similar to Figure 17-2.
19. Close the document, saving changes, and exit Word.

Figure 17-2

Firstname Lastname
Today's Date

Earth Day Gift Basket
Specially Priced at $49.99

Celebrate Earth Day by sending someone you love a beautiful gift basket filled with organic treats. The basket includes all of the items listed below, as well as an Earth Day surprise. The basket is beautifully arranged and wrapped using recycled materials. Local delivery is included in the special price.

Basket Includes:	Regular Price:
Granola	10.99
Natural Fruit Preserves	12.99
Organic Pears	13.75
Organic White Grape Juice	7.35
Organic Whole Grain Banana Bread	16.35
Organic Whole Grain Muffins	15.99
Total	$ 77.42

Word 2013, Windows 8, Microsoft Corporation

Lesson 18

Improving a Document with Find and Replace and AutoCorrect

➤ What You Will Learn

- Using Find
- Using Advanced Find
- Using Find and Replace
- Inserting a Bookmark
- Using Go To
- Using the Navigation Pane
- Using AutoCorrect
- Editing the AutoCorrect List

Software Skills Word's Navigation pane provides access to tools such as Find, Headings, and Pages that help you quickly move to a specific location in a document. Word's AutoCorrect feature automatically replaces typed characters with something else. You can use it to correct common spelling errors—such as to replace *teh* with *the*—or to insert formatted text and graphics by simply typing two or three characters.

WORDS TO KNOW

AutoCorrect
A feature available in most Microsoft Office 2013 programs that automatically corrects common spelling errors as you type.

Navigation pane
A task pane that opens on the left side of the document window. Features in the Navigation pane help you quickly locate and go to a specific location in a document.

Thumbnails
Small pictures.

What You Can Do

Using Find

- Use Word's Find feature to locate and highlight all occurrences of a word or phrase within a document
- You type the text to find in the **Navigation pane**; Word displays a list of occurrences in the Navigation pane and highlights the text in the document. Click an item in the list to move the insertion point to it.

Try It! Using Find

1. Start Word, and open **W18Try** from the data files for this lesson. Save the file as **W18TryA_xx** in the location where your teacher instructs you to store the files for this lesson.
2. On the HOME tab, click the Find button to display the Navigation pane.

   ✓ *By default, the most recently searched for text displays in the Navigation pane text box.*
3. In the text box at the top of the Navigation pane, delete any text that displays and type **business**. Word displays a list of occurrences in the Navigation pane, and highlights the text throughout the document.
4. Delete the text *business* in the Navigation pane text box and type **entre**. Word finds and highlights the text throughout the document.
5. Click the third occurrence of the text in the list in the Navigation pane. Word moves the insertion point to that occurrence.
6. Click the Navigation pane Close button ×.
7. Save the changes to **W18TryA_xx**, and leave it open to use in the next Try It.

Use Find in the Navigation pane

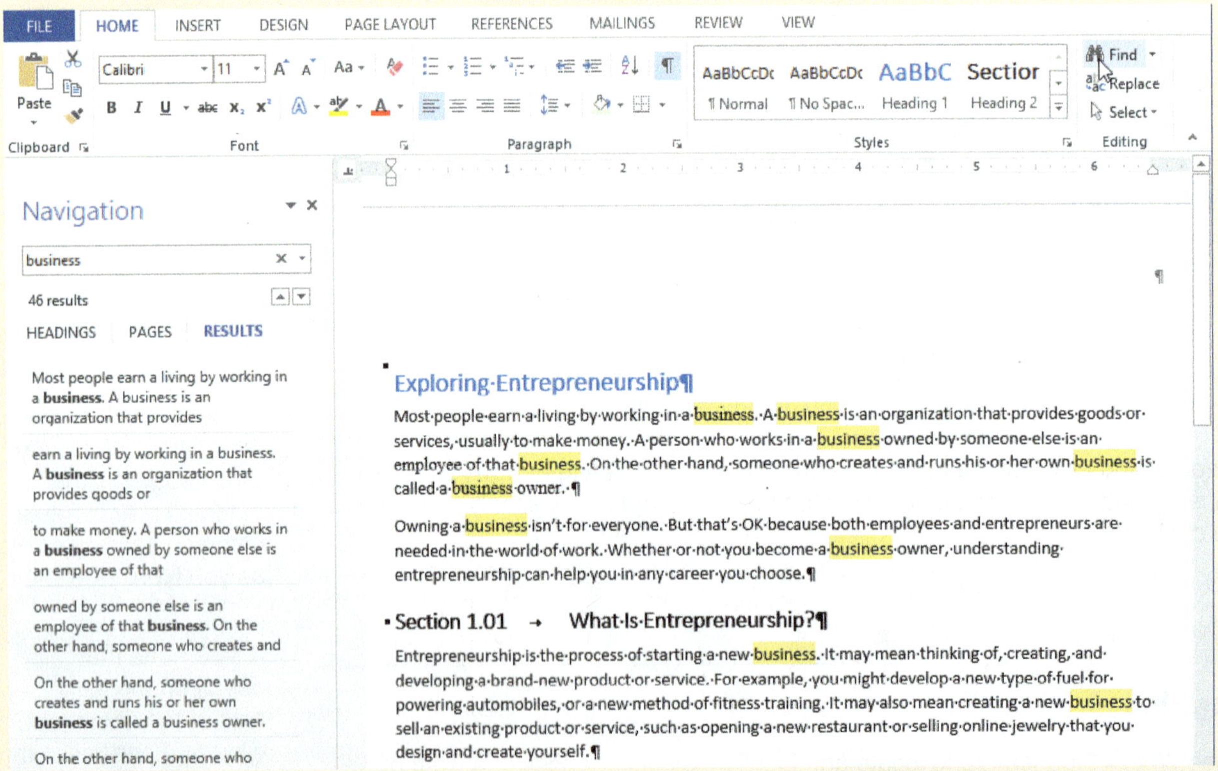

Word 2013, Windows 8, Microsoft Corporation

Using Advanced Find

- Use Advanced Find in the Find and Replace dialog box when you want to find and/or replace text or other content, such as formatting, nonprinting characters such as spaces or paragraph marks, symbols, graphics, objects, or other items.
- You can also use Advanced Find to expand the search options to look through headers and footers as well as the main document, to move one by one through each occurrence of the Find text, and to specify criteria, such as matching upper- or lowercase or finding whole word matches only.

Try It! Using Advanced Find

1. In the **W18TryA_xx** file, press CTRL + HOME to move the insertion point to the beginning of the document.
2. On the HOME tab, click the Find drop-down arrow and then click Advanced Find to open the Find and Replace dialog box.

   ✓ *You can also open the Find and Replace dialog box from the Navigation pane. Click the drop-down arrow in the text box at the top of the pane, and click Advanced Find.*
3. In the Find what text box, replace the existing text by typing **Business Owner**.
4. Click Find Next. Word finds and highlights the first occurrence of the text. Notice that even though you typed *Business Owner* with initial capitalization, Word highlights the text *business owner*. By default, case does not matter.

   ✓ *You can drag the dialog box out of the way, if necessary.*
5. Click the More button to expand the dialog box to show all of the search options.
6. Click to select the Match case check box.

   ✓ *A check mark indicates the option is selected.*
7. Click Find Next. Word highlights the text *Business Owner*, matching the case you typed.
8. In the Find and Replace dialog box, click Cancel.
9. Save the changes to **W18TryA_xx**, and leave it open to use in the next Try It.

Using Find and Replace

- Use options on the Replace tab of the Find and Replace dialog box when you want to replace occurrences of a word or phrase with something else.
- Replace is useful for correcting errors that occur several times in a document, such as a misspelled name.
- You can also use Replace to apply formatting to words that you find. For example, you can apply a highlight or a font style such as bold or italics.
- You can use the expanded search options to refine the procedure just as with Advanced Find.

Try It! Using Find and Replace

1. In the **W18TryA_xx** file, press CTRL + HOME to move the insertion point to the beginning of the document.
2. On the HOME tab, click the Replace button ab→ac to open the Find and Replace dialog box. The Replace tab should be active, with the criteria for the previous search still entered.
3. In the Find what text box, replace any existing text by typing **a business owner**.
4. Click in the Replace with text box and type **an entrepreneur**.
5. Verify that the Match case check box is still selected, and then click Find Next. Word finds and highlights the first occurrence of the text *a business owner*.
6. Click Replace. Word replaces the text *a business owner* with the text *an entrepreneur*, and highlights the next occurrence.
7. Click Replace All. Word replaces all occurrences, and displays a dialog box telling you how many replacements it made.

(continued)

Try It! Using Find and Replace *(continued)*

8 Click OK.

9 Click outside the Find and Replace dialog box and move the insertion point to the top of the document. Then click in the Find and Replace dialog box to make it active.

10 Delete text in the Find what box and type **Entrepreneurship**.

11 Click in the Replace with box and delete existing text, but do not enter any other text. Verify that the Match case check box is still selected.

12 Click the Format button and then click Highlight.

13 Click Find Next to display the first instance of *Entrepreneurship*. Do not replace it.

14 Click Find Next, and then click Find Next again.

15 Replace the next two instances of Entrepreneurship in the body text, and then click OK.

16 In the Find and Replace dialog box, click Close.

17 Save the changes to **W18TryA_xx**, and leave it open to use in the next Try It.

Use Find and Replace

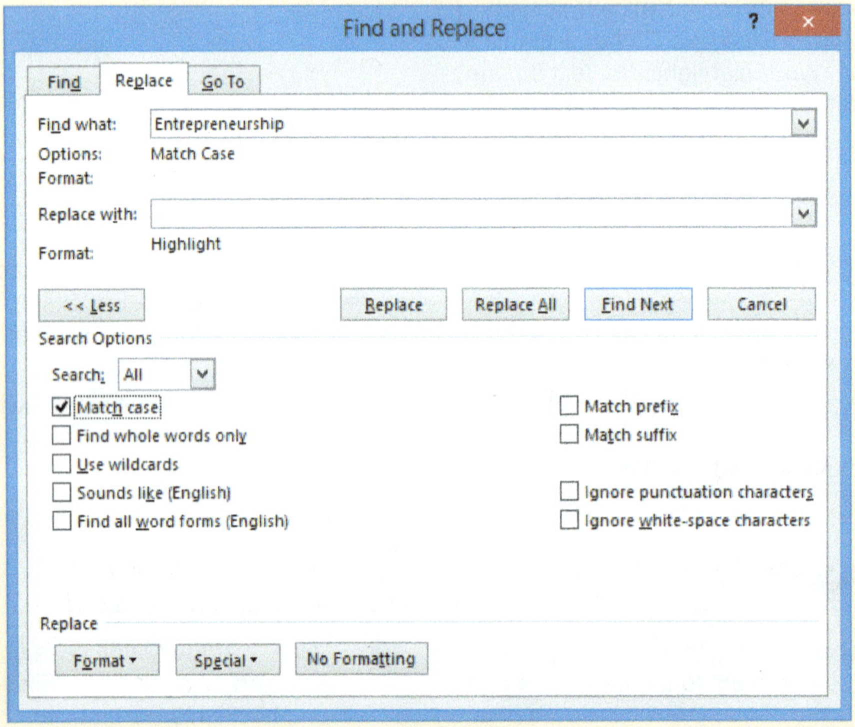

Word 2013, Windows 8, Microsoft Corporation

Inserting a Bookmark

- You can insert a bookmark to make it easy to find a specific location or specific text in a document.
- Use the Bookmark dialog box to name a new bookmark or delete a bookmark.
- Bookmarks are not visible in the text. To move to a bookmarked location or text, you can use Go To in the Bookmark dialog box or the Go To command on the Find menu.

✓ *You work with Go To in the next section.*

Try It! Inserting a Bookmark

1. In the W18TryA_xx document, go to page 2 and locate the word *money* in the first sentence under the Section 1.03 heading.
2. Select the word *money* and then click INSERT > Bookmark to display the Bookmark dialog box.
3. In the Bookmark name box, type **money** and then click Add. The dialog box closes automatically.
4. Save the changes to W18TryA_xx, and leave it open to use in the next Try It.

Using Go To

- Use the Go To tab in the Find and Replace dialog box to move the insertion point to a particular part of the document, such as a page, heading, table, or graphic.

Try It! Using Go To

1. In the W18TryA_xx file, click CTRL + HOME to go to the top of the first page.
2. On the HOME tab, click the Find drop-down arrow and then click Go To to open the Find and Replace dialog box with the Go To tab active.
3. Click Bookmark in the Go to what list box. The bookmark name displays in the Enter bookmark name box.
4. Click Go To. Word moves to the word *money* that you bookmarked in the previous Try It.
5. In the Go to what list box, click Page.
6. In the Enter page number text box, type **2**, and then click Go To. Word moves the insertion point to the top of page 2.
7. In the Go to what list box, scroll down and click Heading, and then click the Next button. Word moves the insertion point to the next heading.
8. Click in the Enter heading number text box and type **-2**.
9. Click Go To. Word moves the insertion point back two headings.
10. In the Find and Replace dialog box, click Close.
11. Save the changes to W18TryA_xx, and leave it open to use in the next Try It.

Use Go To

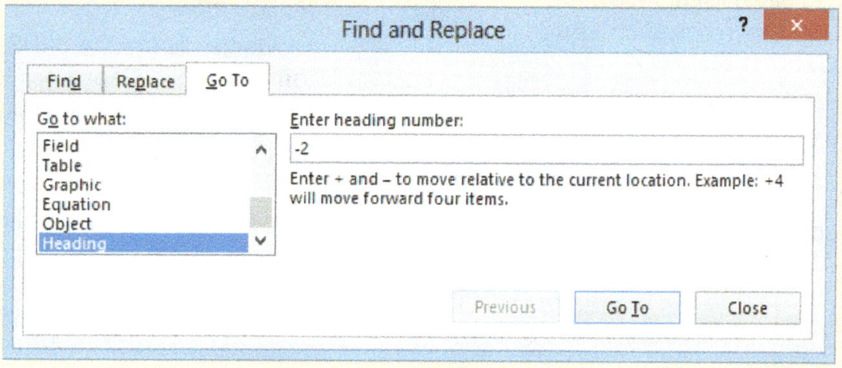

Word 2013, Windows 8, Microsoft Corporation

Using the Navigation Pane

- The Navigation pane provides access to two tools that are useful for navigating through long documents: Headings and Pages.
- When you click Headings, paragraphs formatted as headings display in an outline format.
- Click a heading to move the insertion point to that location in the document.
- You can collapse the heading outline to make it easier to navigate through a long document.
- If there are no headings, the Navigation pane displays information about how to add headings to the document.
- When you click Pages, Word displays **thumbnails** representing each page in the document.
- Click a thumbnail to go to that page.

Try It! Using the Navigation Pane

1. In the W18TryA_xx file, click the VIEW tab, and then click the Navigation Pane check box to select it.
2. Click the Navigation Pane check box again to clear the check mark and close the pane.
3. Display the Navigation pane.
4. In the Navigation pane, under the Search document text box, click Headings.
5. In the Navigation pane, click the heading Section 1.04. Word moves the insertion point to that heading.
6. In the Navigation pane, click the heading Section 1.01. Word moves the insertion point to that heading.
7. In the Navigation pane, click the small black downward-pointing collapse arrow to the left of the *Exploring Entrepreneurship* heading to hide the subheadings below it.
8. In the Navigation pane under the Search document text box, click Pages.
9. Click the page 1 thumbnail. Word moves the insertion point to the beginning of page 1.
10. Click the page 2 thumbnail. Word moves the insertion point to the beginning of page 2.
11. Click the Navigation pane Close button ×.
12. Close the W18TryA_xx file, saving changes, and leave Word open to use in the next Try It.

Using AutoCorrect

- **AutoCorrect** automatically replaces typed characters with something else as soon as you press the spacebar after typing.
- It is particularly useful for correcting common spelling errors.
- Word comes with a built-in list of AutoCorrect entries including common typos such as *adn* for *and* and *teh* for *the*.
- There are also AutoCorrect entries for replacing regular characters with symbols, such as the letters T and M enclosed in parentheses (TM) with the trademark symbol, ™, and for inserting accent marks in words such as café, cliché, crème, and déjà vu.
- By default, AutoCorrect corrects capitalization errors as follows:
  - TWo INitial CApital letters are replaced with one initial capital letter.
  - The first word in a sentence is automatically capitalized.
  - The days of the week are automatically capitalized.
  - Accidental use of the cAPS LOCK feature is corrected if the Caps Lock key is set to ON.
- If AutoCorrect changes text that was not incorrect, you can use Undo or the AutoCorrect Options button to reverse the change.
- If you find AutoCorrect distracting, you can disable it.
- The AutoCorrect list is shared among the Microsoft Office programs.

Try It! Using AutoCorrect

1. In Word, create a new blank file and save it as **W18TryB_xx** in the location where your teacher instructs you to store the files for this lesson.
2. Type **Mike adn Jane**. Notice that as soon as you press the spacebar after the misspelled word *adn*, Word corrects the spelling.
3. Type **recieved a package**. Again, as soon as you press the spacebar after the misspelled word *recieved*, Word corrects the spelling.
4. Move the mouse pointer over the corrected word *received*. A small blue rectangle displays below the word.
5. Rest the mouse pointer on the rectangle to display the AutoCorrect Options button.
6. Click the AutoCorrect Options button to display available options.
7. Click anywhere in the document outside the AutoCorrect Options menu.
8. Save changes to **W18TryB_xx**, and leave it open to use in the next Try It.

Editing the AutoCorrect List

- You can add words to the AutoCorrect list in the AutoCorrect dialog box. For example, if you commonly misspell someone's name, you can add it to the list.
- You can even use AutoCorrect to replace a code with a phrase, paragraph, and even objects, such as pictures. For example, you can set AutoCorrect to replace the text *MyAddress* with your actual address, or the word *letterhead* with a company letterhead.
- You can delete AutoCorrect entries.
- If you want to permanently stop AutoCorrect from replacing certain words, you can add them to the Exceptions list. Access the Exceptions list by clicking the Exceptions button in the AutoCorrect dialog box.

Try It! Editing the AutoCorrect List

1. In Word, click FILE > Options to open the Word Options dialog box.
2. Click Proofing.
3. Click AutoCorrect Options to open the AutoCorrect dialog box.
4. Click in the Replace text box and type **Suzie**.
5. Click in the With text box and type **Suzy**.
6. Click Add.
7. Click OK.
8. Click OK to close the Word Options dialog box.
9. In the **W18TryB_xx** file, press ENTER to start a new line, type **Suzie**, and press SPACE. As soon as you press the spacebar, Word replaces *Suzie* with *Suzy*.
10. Press ENTER, and type your full name and address as you would if you were addressing an envelope.
11. Apply the No Spacing style to the address, increase the font size to 14 points, and apply the Bold font style.
12. Select all lines in the address.
13. Click FILE > Options > Proofing.

(continued)

Try It! Editing the AutoCorrect List *(continued)*

14. Click AutoCorrect Options. Notice that the selected text displays in the With text box.
15. Click in the Replace text box and type **MyAddress**.
16. Click Add.
17. Click OK.
18. Click OK to close the Word Options dialog box.
19. In the **W18TryB_xx** file, double-click in the header area.
20. Type **MyAddress** and press SPACE. As soon as you press the spacebar, Word replaces the text with your formatted address.
21. In Word, click FILE > Options > Proofing > AutoCorrect Options.
22. Click in the Replace text box and type **Suzie**.
23. In the list of AutoCorrect entries, click Suzie|Suzy.
24. Click Delete.
25. Click in the Replace text box and replace the text *Suzie* by typing **MyAddress**.
26. In the list of AutoCorrect entries, click MyAddress.
27. Click Delete.
28. Click OK.
29. Click OK to close the Word Options dialog box.
30. Save the **W18TryB_xx** file, close it, and exit Word.

AutoCorrect dialog box

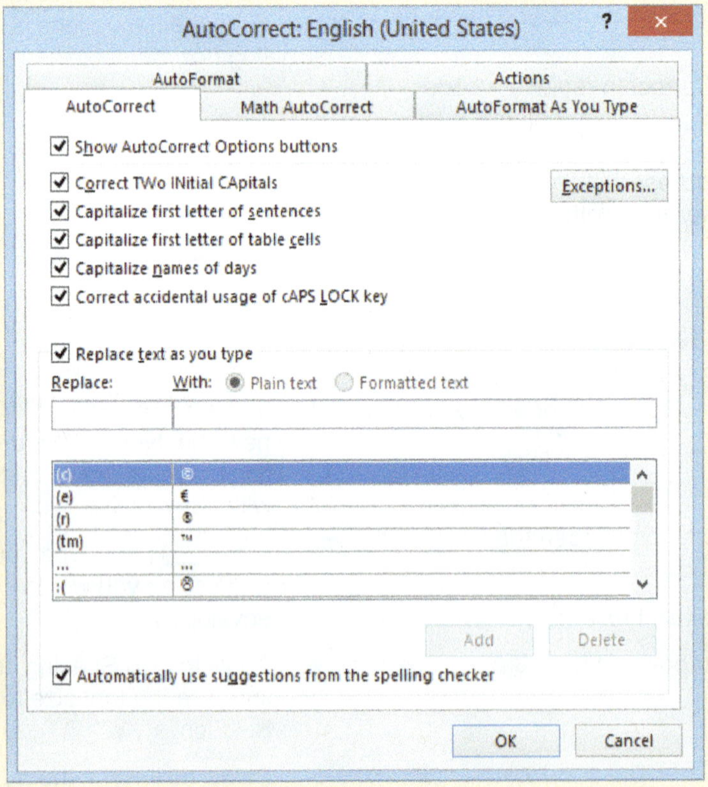

Word 2013, Windows 8, Microsoft Corporation

Lesson 18—Practice

You have been working to complete a report on exercise for Michigan Avenue Athletic Club. In this project, you will edit a version of the document using Find and Replace. You will use the Navigation pane to find headings and paragraphs, and AutoCorrect to correct typing errors and to insert a header.

DIRECTIONS

1. Start Word, and open **W18PracticeA** from the data files for this lesson.
2. Select the line of text in the document, including the paragraph mark.
3. Click **FILE** > **Options** > **Proofing**.
4. Click **AutoCorrect Options**. Notice that the selected text displays in the With text box.
5. Click in the **Replace** text box and type **letterhead**.
6. Click **Add**.
7. Click **OK**.
8. Click **OK** to close the Word Options dialog box.
9. Close **W18PracticeA** without saving any changes.
10. Open **W18PracticeB** from the data files for this lesson. Save it as **W18PracticeB_xx** in the location where your teacher instructs you to store the files for this lesson.
11. Format the first line of the document with the **Title** style.
12. Replace the sample text *Student's Name* with your own name, and replace the sample text *Today's Date* with the actual date.
13. On the HOME tab, click the **Find** button to display the Navigation pane.
14. In the text box at the top of the Navigation pane, delete any text that displays and type **<H1>**.
15. In the document, click in the text *Introduction* next to the highlighted *<H1>*, and apply the **Heading 1** style.
16. Click in the text box at the top of the Navigation pane and press ENTER to repeat the search.
17. Repeat steps 15 and 16 to format the text next to each occurrence of *<H1>* in the Heading 1 style.
18. Select the text *<H1>* in the Navigation pane text box and replace it with the text **<H2>**.
19. In the document, click in the text *Disease Control* next to the first highlighted *<H2>*, and apply **Heading 2** style.
20. Click in the text box at the top of the Navigation pane and press ENTER to repeat the search.
21. Repeat steps 19 and 20 to format the text next to each occurrence of *<H2>* in the Heading 2 style.
22. In the Navigation pane, click **Pages**.
23. Click the page 1 thumbnail to move the insertion point to the beginning of the document.
24. Double-click in the header area and type **letterhead**, then press SPACE to insert the letterhead AutoCorrect entry.
25. Double-click in the document area to close the header and make the document active.
26. Click the Navigation pane **Close** button × to close the pane.
27. On the HOME tab, click the **Replace** button to open the Find and Replace dialog box.
28. Delete the text in the Find what box and type **<H1>**. Delete all text from the Replace with text box. Clear the Match case check box, if necessary.
29. Click **Replace All**. Word replaces all occurrences of <H1> with nothing.
30. Click **OK**.
31. Edit the text in the Find what text box to **<H2>**, and click **Replace All**. Word replaces all occurrences of <H2> with nothing.
32. Click **OK**, and then click **Close** in the Find and Replace dialog box.
33. Check and correct the spelling and grammar in the document, and then save the changes.
34. **With your teacher's permission**, print the document. Page 1 should look similar to Figure 18-1 on the next page.
35. Close the document, saving changes, and exit Word.

Figure 18-1

Michigan Avenue Athletic Club

Exercise for Life

Prepared by
Firstname Lastname
Today's Date

Introduction

The benefits of regular exercise cannot be overstated. Studies have shown that people who exercise regularly live longer, are healthier, and enjoy a better quality of life than those who do not exercise. It is now generally accepted knowledge that even moderate physical activity performed regularly improves the health and well-being of all individuals.

Despite this knowledge, studies show that more than 60% of American adults are not regularly active and that an astonishing 25% of adults are not active at all. Therefore, the government recommends that schools and communities provide education to promote exercise to people of all ages.

This report has been prepared for Michigan Avenue Athletic Club in order to help spread the word on the importance of physical activity for the health of our members. It is meant as an introduction only. For more information about the health benefits of exercise, or about a particular type of exercise program, please contact any member of our staff. He or she will be happy to help you find the information you need.

The Impact on Your Health

It is believed that lack of physical activity and poor diet taken together are the second largest underlying cause of death in the United States. Studies show that even the most inactive people can gain significant health benefits if they accumulate 30 minutes or more of physical activity per day. Some of the known benefits of exercise include disease prevention and control, weight control, and improved mental health.

Exercise can also have an impact on your lifestyle as well. Exercising may improve your social life by giving you an opportunity to meet new people. It may open up opportunities for your career as well. For example, it is commonly believed that a lot of business is conducted on the golf course or tennis court!

Disease Control

Daily physical activity can help prevent heart disease and stroke by strengthening the heart muscle, lowering blood pressure, raising the levels of good cholesterol and lowering bad cholesterol, improving blood flow, and increasing the heart's working capacity.

By reducing body fat, physical activity helps prevent obesity and may help to prevent and control noninsulin-dependent diabetes.

By increasing muscle strength and endurance and improving flexibility and posture, regular exercise helps to prevent back pain. Regular weight-bearing exercise promotes bone formation and may prevent many forms of bone loss associated with aging.

Weight Control

Research shows that regular physical activity, combined with healthy eating habits, is the most efficient and healthful way to control your weight. Regular physical activity uses excess calories that otherwise would be stored as fat. It also builds and preserves muscle mass and improves the body's ability to use calories.

Lesson 18—Apply

In this project, you work with another version of the document you edited in the Practice project. You insert AutoCorrect text, use Find and Replace, and navigate in the document using the Navigation pane.

DIRECTIONS

1. Start Word, if necessary, and open **W18Apply** from the data files for this lesson.
2. Save the file as **W18Apply_xx** in the location where your teacher instructs you to store the files for this lesson.
3. Replace the sample text *Student's Name* with your own name, and *Today's Date* with the actual date.
4. Make the header active and type **letterhead**. Press SPACE to insert the letterhead AutoCorrect entry.

   ✓ *If the letterhead AutoCorrect entry is not available on your system, follow steps 1 through 9 of Lesson 18—Practice to create it.*
5. Close the header area.
6. Open the Find and Replace dialog box.
7. Find all occurrences of the text *Obese people*, and replace it with **Those who are overweight**. Be sure to match the case.
8. Replace all occurrences of the text *obese people*, with **those who are overweight**.
9. Find all occurrences of the text *physical activity* and format them in italics:
   a. Type the search string in the Find what box.
   b. Remove all text from the Replace with box and leave it blank.
   c. Click **Format** in the Find and Replace dialog box, and then click **Font**.
   d. In the Replace Font dialog box, click **Italic** in the Font style list.
   e. Click **OK** and then click **Replace All**.
10. When the procedure is complete, close the Find and Replace dialog box.
11. Display the Navigation pane.
12. In the Navigation pane, click **HEADINGS**.
13. Go to the heading, *Doctor Supervision*. Close the Navigation pane.
14. Click at the end of the paragraph under the heading and type **The doctor will check for signs that your body might not be able to withstand physical activity. If there is a problem, he or she might place limitations on the type of activity you can do.**
15. Insert a bookmark named **stress** that will take a reader to the end of the paragraph under the *Mental Health* heading.
16. Click **FILE** > **Options** > **Proofing** > **AutoCorrect Options**.
17. Click in the **Replace** text box and type **letterhead**.
18. In the list of AutoCorrect entries, click **letterhead**.
19. Click **Delete**.
20. Click **OK**.
21. Close the Word Options dialog box.
22. Check and correct the spelling and grammar in the document, and then save the changes.
23. **With your teacher's permission**, print the document.
24. Close the document, saving changes, and exit Word.

Lesson 19

Working with Templates and Different File Types

WORDS TO KNOW

Content controls
Automated features such as a pop-up calendar or drop-down list that make it easier to enter or format information.

File extension
A dot followed by three or four characters at the end of a file name, used to indicate the file type.

File icon
The icon used to represent a file in a file list.

File type
The format in which a file is stored. Usually, the file type corresponds to the program used to create the file.

OneDrive
Online storage location to which you can save documents to share with others.

Placeholder
Sample text or graphics that marks a location in a document where content should be placed.

Resume
A document summarizing an individual's employment experience, education, and other information a potential employer needs to know.

➤ What You Will Learn

- Recognizing File Types
- Opening and Saving Compatible Files
- Saving a Word Document As a PDF
- Opening a PDF Document in Word
- Analyzing a Resume
- Creating a Document Based on a Template
- Using Content Controls
- Saving a Word Document As a Template
- Exploring Online Templates
- Sharing Documents on OneDrive

Software Skills Templates help you create consistent documents efficiently—and time after time. Templates include page setup and formatting settings to ensure that new documents will be uniform. In many cases they include standard text and graphics as well. You can use Word to open files created with different word processing programs, and to save Word documents in different formats.

What You Can Do

Recognizing File Types

- Files are saved in different **file types**, depending on the application used to create, save, and open the file.
- File types are sometimes referred to as file formats.
- All files have a **file extension** that indicates the file type. For example, a Word 2013 file has a .docx file extension.

- By default, file extensions do not display in Windows. Instead, the name of the program and the **file icon** indicate the file type.
- Table 19-1 lists some common file types and their extensions. Figure 19-1 shows how they may appear in File Explorer.

Table 19-1 Common File Types

File Type	File Extension
Word 2013, 2010, and 2007 documents	.docx
Word 2013, 2010, and 2007 templates	.dotx
Word 97-2003 documents	.doc
Word 97-2003 templates	.dot
Text files	.txt
Web pages	.htm
Excel 2013, 2010, and 2007 workbooks	.xlsx
Excel 97-2003 workbooks	.xls
PowerPoint 2013, 2010, and 2007 files	.pptx
PowerPoint 97-2003 files	.ppt
Portable Document Format	.pdf
Graphics Interchange Format	.gif
Joint Photography Experts Group	.jpg
Windows Media Audio	.wma
Windows Media Video	.wmv
MPEG audio	.mp4

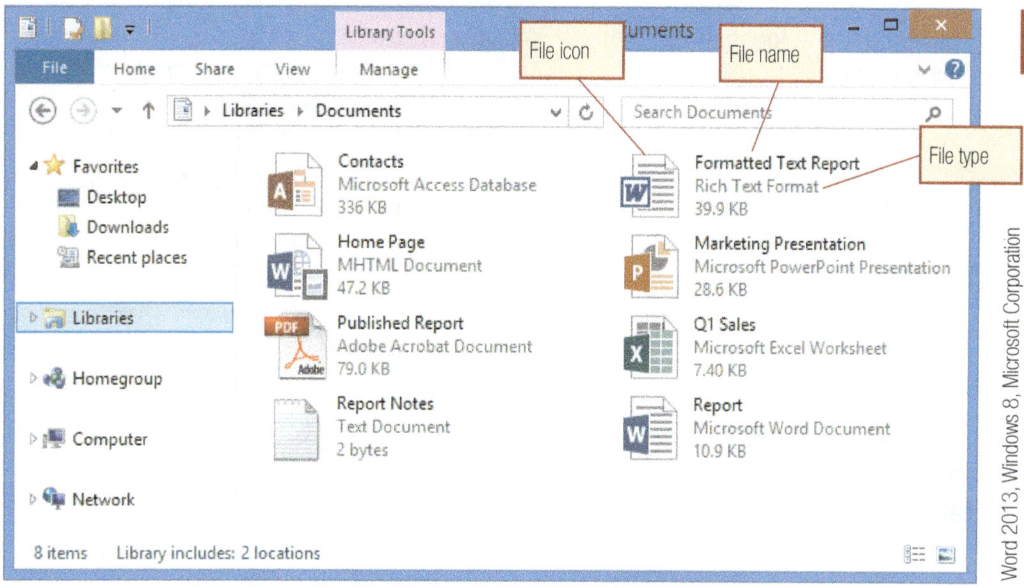

Figure 19-1

Opening and Saving Compatible Files

- You can save a Word document in a variety of file types, including .pdf, .htm, .txt, and .rtf.
- Use the Save As dialog box to save a Word file in a compatible file type, or to save a compatible file in its original file type or as a Word document.
- Word 2013 can open documents saved in compatible file types. For example, Word can open text files, Web page files, XML files, and files created with other versions of Word.
- Use the Open dialog box to open any file type that is compatible with Word 2013.
- By default, only Word documents display in the Open dialog box, but you can select to display a specific file type, or all files.
- Compatible files open in Compatibility Mode in Word; the text [Compatibility Mode] displays in the title bar.
- If some Word 2013 features are not supported by the selected file type when you save or open the file, Word displays a File Conversion or Compatibility Checker dialog box that shows you how the new format will affect the document contents.
- For example, a plain text file cannot display graphics or style formatting.

Try It! Opening and Saving Compatible Files

1. Start Word, and open **W19TryA** from the data files for this lesson.
2. Click FILE > Save As.
3. Type **W19TryA_xx**.
4. Click the Save as type button to display a list of compatible file types.
5. Click Plain Text.
6. Navigate to the location where your teacher instructs you to store the files for this lesson.
7. Click Save.
8. Click OK in the File Conversion dialog box.
9. Close **W19TryA_xx**. Leave Word open.
10. Click FILE > Open and navigate to the location where you are storing files for this lesson.
11. Click the File Type button to display a list of available file types.

    ✓ *The text on the File Type button changes depending on your most recent selection. If you have never changed the file type, it will display All Word Documents.*
12. Click All Files to display all files in the current storage location.
13. Click the text document **W19TryA_xx**.
14. Click Open.
15. If Word displays a File Conversion dialog box, click OK.
16. Double-click the word *Zebra* to select it, and then on the HOME tab, in the Font group, click the Bold button **B** .
17. Click the Save button on the Quick Access Toolbar.
18. In the warning dialog box, click Yes to save the file in the current format—plain text.

    ✓ *Click No to open the Save As dialog box so you can save the file in Word document format. You can select any file format in the Save As dialog box, change the storage location, and enter a new file name, if you want.*
19. Close the **W19TryA_xx** file, but leave Word open to use in the next Try It.

Saving a Word Document As a PDF

- Portable Document Format is a file type that can be opened in many different programs.
- You can use the Save As dialog box to save a Word document in .pdf format.

Try It! Saving a Word Document As a PDF

1. In Word, open W19TryB from the data files for this lesson.
2. Click FILE > Save As.
3. Type W19TryB_xx.
4. Click the Save as type button to display a list of compatible file types.
5. Click PDF.
6. In the Save As dialog box, navigate to the location where your teacher instructs you to store the files for this lesson.
7. Click Save.

   ✓ *The pdf file may display in Adobe Reader. Click the Close button to exit the program.*

8. Close W19TryB without saving any changes, and leave Word open to use in the next Try It.

Opening a PDF Document in Word

- Word 2013 allows you to open PDF files and edit them in Word.
- Word's PDF text reflow feature captures information from the PDF file, including text, graphics, and tables, and converts the content so that you can modify it just as you would any Word content.
- You may find that the PDF content does not look exactly the same in Word as it did on the PDF page, but you can easily adjust text formats and graphic layout.
- When you have finished editing the document, you can save it as a Word document.

Try It! Opening a PDF Document in Word

1. In your PDF reader application, open W19TryC from the data files for this lesson.
2. Scroll through the document to see how the text, table, and graphics are laid out in the PDF document.
3. Close the PDF reader application.
4. In Word, open W19TryC from the data files for this lesson. Click OK in the Optimization dialog box.
5. Scroll through the document to see that the PDF content has been converted for use in Word.
6. Click anywhere in the table and apply the Grid Table 5 Dark – Accent 6 table style.
7. Select the entire table and change the row height to 0.2".
8. Select the first text paragraph, then hold down CTRL and select the remaining text paragraphs.
9. On the HOME tab, click the Paragraph dialog box launcher.
10. In the Paragraph dialog box, set both the Left and Right Indentation value to 0", and change the Special indent setting to (none). Change Spacing After to 8 pt and change Line spacing to 1.5 lines.
11. Click OK.
12. Move the organization chart on page 2 to the top of the page to force text back to page 1. Make any other adjustments to the position of graphics to improve the document.
13. Use the layout guides to align the flowchart graphic with the right margin and the top of the second paragraph below the table.
14. Save W19TryC as a Word file with the name W19TryC_xx in the location where your teacher instructs you to store the files for this lesson, and then close the file. Leave Word open to use in the next Try It.

(continued)

Try It! Opening a PDF Document in Word *(continued)*

Realign the graphic in the document

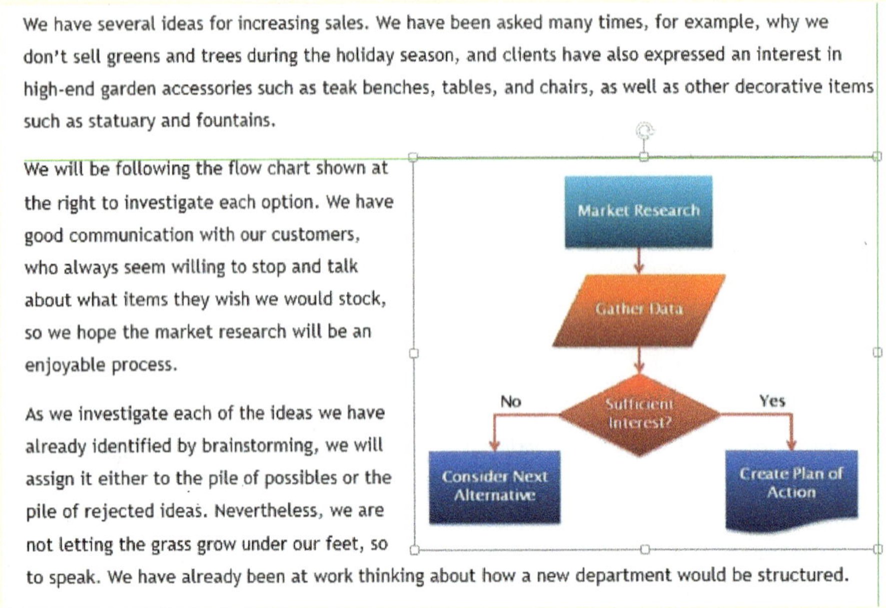
We have several ideas for increasing sales. We have been asked many times, for example, why we don't sell greens and trees during the holiday season, and clients have also expressed an interest in high-end garden accessories such as teak benches, tables, and chairs, as well as other decorative items such as statuary and fountains.

We will be following the flow chart shown at the right to investigate each option. We have good communication with our customers, who always seem willing to stop and talk about what items they wish we would stock, so we hope the market research will be an enjoyable process.

As we investigate each of the ideas we have already identified by brainstorming, we will assign it either to the pile of possibles or the pile of rejected ideas. Nevertheless, we are not letting the grass grow under our feet, so to speak. We have already been at work thinking about how a new department would be structured.

Word 2013, Windows 8, Microsoft Corporation

Analyzing a Resume

- When you apply for a job, you submit a **resume** which summarizes your qualifications, education, and experience. A resume is sometimes called a CV, which stands for Curriculum Vitae, Latin for "course of life."

  ✓ *You usually send a cover letter along with your resume. Refer to Word, Lesson 6 for information on writing a cover letter.*

- A resume is usually the first way a potential employer learns about you, so it is important to make it easy to read and informative.
- To make a positive impression, a resume should be neatly printed on white paper, truthful, and free of any typographical, grammatical, or spelling errors.
- An employer may spend less than a minute looking at your resume; the way it is formatted can help make important information stand out. For example, you should not crowd too much on the page, or use a font that is difficult to read. Using bullets can help the reader identify key points quickly.
- An effective resume has four main parts:
  - Your contact information, including name, address, phone, and e-mail.
  - An objective that describes your career goals.
  - A list of your educational experience, including the names of all schools where you earned a degree, with the most recent school at the top. You can also include special courses or certificates you have earned.
  - A list of your work experience, including all full-time and part-time jobs, internships, and volunteer experience, with the most recent at the top. Include the dates of employment, the job title, company name, and company location. You should briefly list your responsibilities and accomplishments.
- You may also include a section for listing skills, such as an ability to speak multiple languages or to use computer programs, and interests, such as co-curricular activities, awards, honors, and club or organization memberships.

Creating a Document Based on a Template

- All new Word documents are based on a template, which is a file that includes settings for page and text formatting.
- Blank documents are based on the Normal template, which includes settings for creating typical business documents. For example, the Normal template page size is 8.5 inches by 11 inches.
- All new documents based on the same template will have the same default formatting settings and will display the same placeholder text and graphics.
- Word comes with sample templates for creating documents such as flyers, calendars, letters, and resumes. Many additional templates are available online.

✓ *You can also use templates you create yourself, or use an existing Word document as a template for a new document.*

- You select and preview templates in the Backstage view.
- Templates usually come in a variety of themes. Each theme includes different formatting, so you can select a theme that best suits your purpose.
- For a professional, consistent look, you can coordinate your documents by theme. For example, you can select a letter template and a resume template in the same theme.

Try It! Creating a Document Based on a Template

1. In Word, click FILE > New. Available templates display in the backstage.
2. Scroll down the available templates and click one of the Student report templates. Word displays a preview of the selected template in a window; the report's pages are animated so you can see the sample content.
3. Click the preview's Close button ×.
4. If you do not see a resume template among those displayed, click Resume in the Suggested searches list at the top of the tab, and then click Basic resume (Timeless design).
5. Click the Create button.
6. Save the file as W19TryD_xx in the location where your teacher instructs you to store the files for this lesson, and leave it open to use in the next Try It.

Using Content Controls

- Most templates include sample text, formatting, graphics, and **content controls** that prompt you to enter information to complete the document.
- You replace the sample text, change the formatting, or replace or delete the graphics using standard editing and formatting commands. For example, you can select and replace text by typing.
- Content controls display with brackets around them, like this: [Street Address]; sample, or **placeholder**, text does not have brackets.
- To enter text in a content control, click it, and type the text.
- When you click a content control, a handle displays. Some content control handles have a drop-down arrow. Click the arrow to display a list of options you can use to automatically insert information into the document.
- You can remove content controls you do not need.

Try It! Using Content Controls

1. In the **W19TryD_xx** file, click the name text in the blue-gray bar. The content control for the name is called Your Name.

   ✓ *Word picked up the name from the user information you use to log in to the system.*

2. If necessary, edit the name to display your full first name and last name.
3. Click the Street Address content control and type the street address of your school.
4. Click the Category content control and type the city, state, and ZIP code of your school.
5. Click the Telephone content control and type your school phone number.
6. Right-click the Website content control.
7. On the shortcut menu, click Remove Content Control, and then press DEL to remove the blank line.
8. Click the Email content control and type your e-mail address.
9. Save the changes to the **W19TryD_xx** file, and close it. Leave Word open to use in the next Try It.

Use content controls to enter and edit information

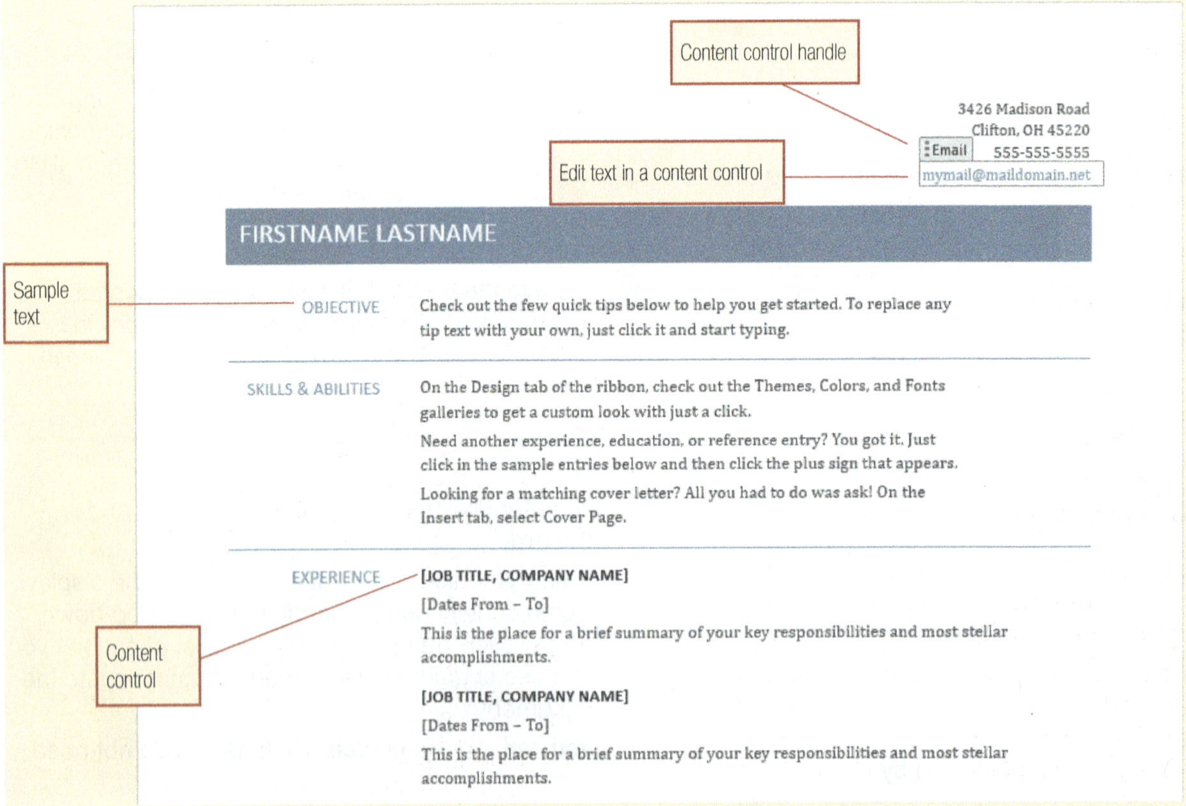

Word 2013, Windows 8, Microsoft Corporation

Saving a Word Document As a Template

- You can create your own template by saving a Word document as a template file.
- Template files in the most recent version of Word have a .dotx file extension.
- Template files from Word versions prior to 2007 have a .dot file extension.
- Template file icons look similar to Word file icons, with a blue bar across the top.
- You can include formatting, themes, style sets, and sample text in your template.

✓ *You can also insert content controls to help others create documents based on the template.*

- New documents you create based on the template will include the elements you save with the template file.

Try It! Saving a Word Document As a Template

1. In Word, create a new, blank document.
2. Click DESIGN > Themes > Retrospect.
3. Click DESIGN > Document Formatting > Centered.
4. On the first line of the document, type your full name, and format it with the Title style.
5. Click FILE > Save As.
6. Type **W19TryE_xx**.
7. Click the Save as type button and click Word Template in the list of file types.
8. Navigate to the location where your teacher instructs you to store the files for this lesson.
9. Click Save.
10. Close the **W19TryE_xx** file, but leave Word open.
11. Click File Explorer on the Windows taskbar.
12. Navigate to the location where you save the files for this lesson.
13. Right-click the **W19TryE_xx** file.
14. Click New. Word creates a new document that has the same formatting and sample text as the template file.
15. Close the new document without saving changes. Leave Word open to use in the next Try It.

Exploring Online Templates

- If you have a connection to the Internet, you can explore the lengthy list of templates that are available online.
- The templates are organized by category. For example, you can browse templates for creating reports, or templates for creating calendars.
- Some of the templates are provided by Microsoft, but many are created by users, like you. The name of the person who created the template is listed next to the preview in the Backstage view, along with a rating.
- You can explore and preview the available templates without actually downloading one; before you download any file, you must have permission from your teacher.

Try It! **Exploring Online Templates**

1. In Word, click FILE > New.
2. Click in the Search online templates text box, type **Letterhead**, and then click the Start searching button.
3. In the Category at the right, click Business.
4. Click any of the letterhead designs to preview it. Click the Close button × to close the preview.
5. To the left of the search box, click Home to return to the backstage.
6. In the list of suggested searches, click Calendar.
7. In the Category list, click Single page.
8. Exit Word.

Sharing Documents on OneDrive

- Office 2013 makes it easier than ever to share documents with others using Microsoft's OneDrive, an online storage location where authorized users can post and access files.
- Documents stored on OneDrive are available to anyone who is given permission to access them. The ability to access online documents from any Internet-connected computer can be very helpful for teams whose members may work in different offices or different geographical locations.
- To use OneDrive, you must have a Microsoft account, such as the one you use to log in to Office 2013 applications.
- Commands to save documents to OneDrive and open documents from OneDrive are conveniently located on Word 2013's FILE menu.
- Once a document has been stored on OneDrive, you can open it in the browser to edit it, using Word Online, or open it in Word on your computer.
- You can use the Share button to send a link to your document to a colleague so that he or she can view or edit the document.
- Multiple users can work on the same document at the same time, and the next time you open it, you can update it to see changes from all reviewers.

Try It! **Save a Document to OneDrive**

1. In Word, open **W19TryF** from the data files for this lesson.
2. Save the document as **W19TryF_xx** in the location where your teacher instructs you to store the files for this lesson.
3. Click FILE > Save As, and click the OneDrive option for your login name in the Save As list.
4. Click the Browse button in the right pane to open the Save As dialog box, double-click Documents to open that folder, and then click Save to store the document with the same name on OneDrive.
5. Close the **W19TryF_xx** file, and leave Word open.

Try It! View and Edit a Document on OneDrive

1. Start Internet Explorer and type **https://onedrive.live.com** in the address bar. Press ENTER.
2. If necessary, click Sign in and supply your Microsoft account information to open OneDrive in your browser.
3. Click the Documents folder to display the document you saved to the OneDrive.
4. Click the document name to open it in Word Online.
5. Click Edit Document, and then click Edit in Word Online.
6. At the location of the insertion point, type **Contents**, and then apply the Heading 1 style.
7. Click OPEN IN WORD.
8. Click Yes when asked if you want to allow the website to open the program on your computer.
9. The document opens in Word. Note that the edit you made on the OneDrive now displays in the document.
10. Save **W19TryF_xx** to the location where you are storing files for this lesson, overwriting the previous version of the document. Close the document and exit Word and your browser.

Document stored in the Documents folder of the OneDrive

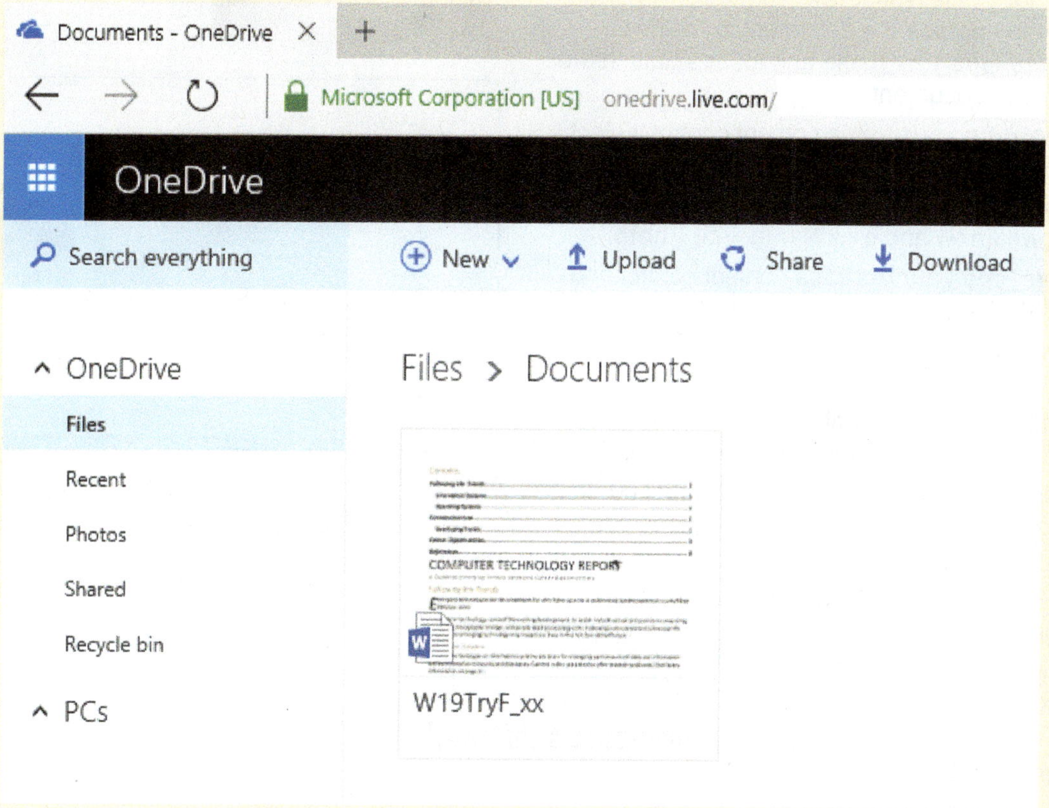

Word 2013, Windows 8, Microsoft Corporation

Lesson 19—Practice

Vocation Opportunities, Inc., a career counseling company, offers a service helping clients develop effective job search materials. In this project, you will use a Word template to create a resume for a client.

DIRECTIONS

1. Start Word.
2. Click **FILE** > **New** and then click **Resume** in the Suggested searches list.
3. Scroll down the list of templates and click **Resume (Origin theme)**.
4. Click **Create** to create a document based on the Origin Resume template.
5. Save the document as **W19PracticeA_xx** in the location where your teacher instructs you to store the files for this lesson. Click FILE > Convert, and then OK to upgrade the document to the newest file format. Type your name and today's date in the footer of the document.
6. Click the **Type your name** content control, select the text, and type **Sandra Tsai**.
7. Click the **Resume Name** content control handle drop-down arrow and click **Name with Photo**.
8. Click the **Type your address** content control and type **2555 North Clark, Chicago, IL 60614**.
9. Click the **Type your phone number** content control and type **555-555-5555**.
10. Click the **Type your e-mail address** content control and type **sandrat@mailservice.net**.
11. Right-click the **Type your website** content control and click **Remove Content Control** on the shortcut menu.
12. Select the text **Website:** and press DEL.
13. Replace the remaining content control and sample text using the information shown in Figure 19-2 on the next page.
14. Check and correct the spelling and grammar in the document, and then save the changes.
15. **With your teacher's permission**, print the document. It should look similar to Figure 19-2.
16. Click **FILE** > **Save As**.
17. Type **W19PracticeB_xx**.
18. Click the **Save as type** button to display a list of compatible file types.
19. Click **Rich Text Format**.
20. Navigate to the location where your teacher instructs you to save the files for this lesson.
21. Click **Save**. If necessary, click **Continue** in the Microsoft Word Compatibility Checker.

    ✓ *The name may be removed from the Resume Name content control. Save the document as is.*

22. Close the document, saving changes, and exit Word.

Figure 19-2

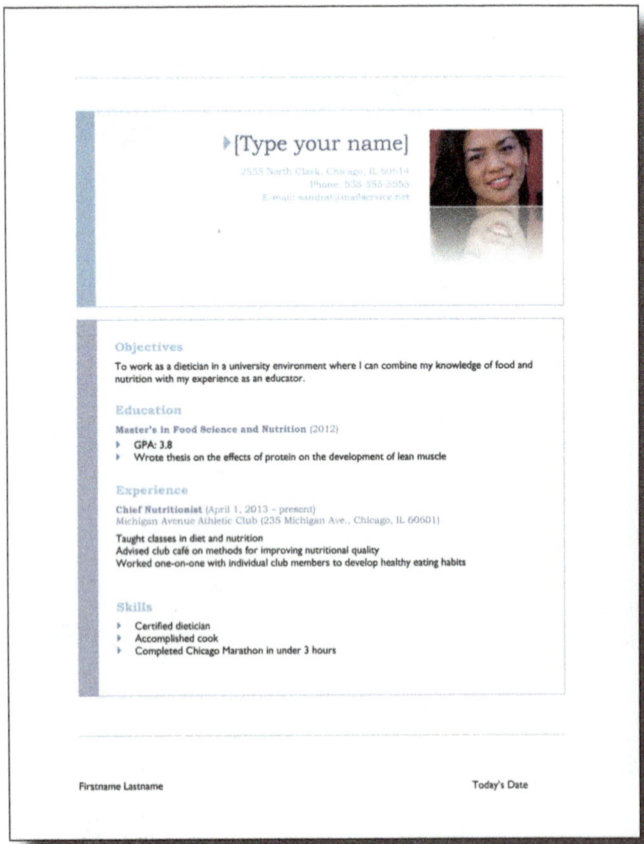

Word 2013, Windows 8, Microsoft Corporation

Lesson 19—Apply

In this project, you continue to work with Sandra Tsai's resume. You will save the file as a PDF, and then open the PDF in Word for further editing.

DIRECTIONS

1. Start Word, if necessary, and open **W19Apply** from the data files for this lesson.
2. Save the file as a Word document with the name **W19ApplyA_xx** in the location where your teacher instructs you to store the files for this lesson. Type your name and today's date in the footer of the file, and save the changes.
3. Save the file again as a **PDF** in the location where your teacher instructs you to store the files for this lesson with the name **W19ApplyB_xx**.
4. View the resume in your PDF reader and then close the document.
5. Close the **W19ApplyA** document in Word.
6. In Word, open the **W19ApplyB_xx** PDF file.
7. Remove the blank table row at the bottom of the first section of the resume.
8. Change alignment of the contact information lines to right.
9. Change the font of all text formatted with Bookman Old Style to Times New Roman.
10. Delete the name and date at the end of the document and insert your name and today's date in the footer.
11. Save the document as a Word document with the name **W19ApplyC_xx**. Your page should look similar to Figure 19-3.
12. **With your teacher's permission**, print the document.
13. Save the document to your OneDrive.
14. Close the document, saving changes, and exit Word.
15. Launch your OneDrive, open the document you saved, and **with your teacher's permission**, share the document with a classmate or your teacher.
16. Close your browser.

Figure 19-3

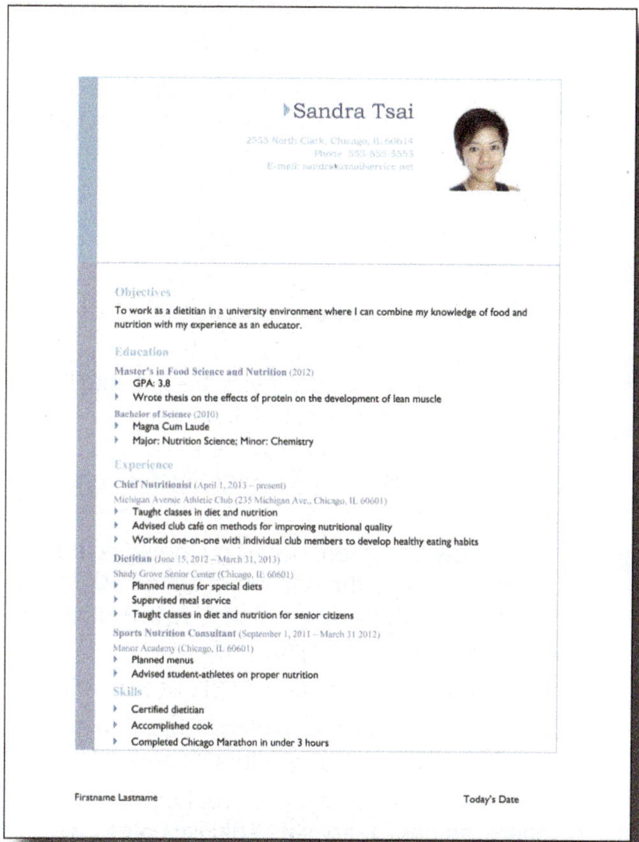

Sandra Tsai

2555 North Clark, Chicago, IL 60614
Phone 555-555-5555

Objectives

To work as a dietitian in a university environment where I can combine my knowledge of food and nutrition with my experience as an educator.

Education

Master's in Food Science and Nutrition (2012)
- GPA: 3.8
- Wrote thesis on the effects of protein on the development of lean muscle

Bachelor of Science (2010)
- Magna Cum Laude
- Major: Nutrition Science; Minor: Chemistry

Experience

Chief Nutritionist (April 1, 2013 – present)
Michigan Avenue Athletic Club (235 Michigan Ave., Chicago, IL 60601)
- Taught classes in diet and nutrition
- Advised club café on methods for improving nutritional quality
- Worked one-on-one with individual club members to develop healthy eating habits

Dietitian (June 15, 2012 – March 31, 2013)
Shady Grove Senior Center (Chicago, IL 60601)
- Planned menus for special diets
- Supervised meal service
- Taught classes in diet and nutrition for senior citizens

Sports Nutrition Consultant (September 1, 2011 – March 31 2012)
Manor Academy (Chicago, IL 60601)
- Planned menus
- Advised student-athletes on proper nutrition

Skills
- Certified dietitian
- Accomplished cook
- Completed Chicago Marathon in under 3 hours

Firstname Lastname Today's Date

Word 2013, Windows 8, Microsoft Corporation

End-of-Chapter Activities

➤ Word Chapter 2—Critical Thinking

Create a Resume

Your resume may be the most important job search document you ever create. As such, it is important to take the time to get it right. Once you have a resume that you feel accurately describes you and your goals, you can keep it up-to-date and ready to send any time you want to apply for a job.

In this project, explore the available resume templates and choose one that best highlights your education, work and volunteer experience, and skills so they stand out to someone who might just glance at it quickly. If you do not like any of the resume templates, create your own using table and document formatting skills you have learned in the first two chapters in this section of the book.

Use the template to create your own resume. Before you begin, you may want to research resume writing tips online or in your school's library or career center.

DIRECTIONS

1. Start Word. Explore the available sample resume templates.
2. **With your teacher's permission**, explore online resume templates.
3. Select a resume template. If you are not satisfied with any of the templates, create a resume template of your own, using a theme, document format, and tables to align content professionally on the page.
4. Create a new document based on the selected template, and save the document as WCT02A_xx in the location where your teacher instructs you to store the files for this project.
5. Enter your own information into the document.
6. Include your contact information, education and work experience, and your interests and skills.
7. Include contact information for your employers or teachers, as necessary, and specific dates.
8. Be truthful and accurate.
9. Check the spelling and grammar in the document and correct any errors. If you make the same spelling errors frequently, add them to the AutoCorrect list.
10. Ask a classmate to review your resume and offer suggestions on how you might improve the information and the design. For example, it is good to use interesting action words to describe your experience. If you have worked at a sandwich shop, instead of writing *I made sandwiches*, you might write *Prepared sandwiches in a busy shop*. You can use the thesaurus to help you make interesting and accurate word choices.
11. Make the improvements to the resume, and check the spelling and grammar again.
12. **With your teacher's permission**, print the resume.
13. Save it as a PDF as WCT02B_xx.
14. Close the document, saving changes, and exit Word.

➤ Word Chapter 2—Portfolio Builder

Customer Demographics Fax

Voyager Travel Adventures has been collecting demographic information about clients who participate in adventure travel vacations. The information is available in a text document. In this project, you will open the text document and save it in Word document format.

You will create tables, apply formatting, and use features such as cut and paste, find and replace, and AutoCorrect to complete the document. You will save the document as a PDF so it can be viewed outside of Word. You will then use a sample template to create a fax cover sheet so you can fax the document to the vice president of marketing, who is at an offsite meeting.

DIRECTIONS

Open a Plain Text File and Save It As a Word Document

1. Start Word.
2. Open the plain text file **WPB02**. Move the insertion point to the end of the file, insert a blank line and then type your full name and today's date.
3. Save the file in plain text format as **WPB02A_xx** in the location where your teacher instructs you to store the files for this project.
4. Apply the **Title** style to the first two lines of text, and center both lines horizontally, apply the **Heading 1** style to the third line—*Respondant Survey Results*—and apply the **Normal** style to the rest of the text in the document.
5. Use the Thesaurus to look up synonyms for the word *Favored*. Insert **Preferred** in its place.
6. Save the document in Word document format as **WPB02B_xx** in the location where your teacher instructs you to store the files for this project.
7. Move your name and today's date into the footer of the document.
8. Add an entry to the AutoCorrect list to replace the word **Motto** with the first two lines of the document formatted in the **Title** style.
9. Add an entry to the AutoCorrect list to replace the word **respondant** with the correctly spelled word **respondent**.
10. Check the spelling and grammar in the document and make all necessary corrections.
11. Find and replace all occurrences of the word **Respondent** with the word **Customer**.
12. Save the changes to the document.

Create and Format Tables

1. Select the six lines of text under the heading *Customer Survey Results* and convert them into a table with 3 columns, separated at tabs.
2. Insert a new row at the top of the table.
3. Merge the three cells in the new row.
4. In the new row, type the text **CUSTOMER DEMOGRAPHICS** in all uppercase letters.
5. Apply the **Grid Table 2** table style to the table.
6. Increase the font size of all text in the table to **12 points**, and then adjust the column width to automatically fit the contents.
7. Change the alignment of the cells displaying percentages to **Align Top Right**.
8. On the second blank line below the table, insert a new table with 3 columns and 3 rows.
9. Change the font size to **12 points**, and then enter the following text to complete the table:

Gender		
	Male	54%
	Female	46%

10. Apply the **List Table 2** table style to the table, and adjust the column width to automatically fit the contents.
11. Apply a **1½ point solid line Blue, Accent 5** border around the outside of the table, and center the table horizontally on the page.
12. Use the Border Painter to apply the same border outline format to the Demographics table.
13. Select the last six lines of text in the document and move them above the *Customer Demographics* table.

14. Convert the six lines of text to a table with 2 columns and 6 rows, separated at the tabs.
15. Delete the top row.
16. Sort the remaining five rows into alphabetical order based on the content in column 1.
17. Insert a new row across the bottom of the table. In the left column type **Total**. In the right column, insert a formula to add the values in the cells above.
18. Right-align the text **Total** and increase the font size for all the text in the table to 12 points.
19. Adjust the column width to automatically fit the contents of the table, and center the table horizontally on the page.
20. Use the Draw Table tool to draw a cell on the left side of the table. Size it to the same height as the current table, and 0.75" wide.
21. In the new cell, change the text direction to **Bottom to Top**. Set the font to **12-point Arial** and type **Preferred Activity (Per Respondant)**. Note that AutoCorrect should correct the misspelled word respondent.
22. Apply **Blue, Accent 1, Lighter 60%** shading to the cell, and a **1½ point solid line Blue, Accent 5** border around the outside of the entire table.
23. Add 24 points of space after the *Customer Survey Results* heading.
24. Check the spelling and grammar in the document and correct any errors. Save the document.
25. **With your instructor's permission**, print the document. It should look similar to Illustration 2A on the next page.
26. Save the document as a PDF with the file name **WPB02C_xx**. View the document in your PDF reader and then close it.
27. Close **WPB02B_xx**, saving changes.

Create a Fax Cover Sheet Based on a Template

1. In Word, create a new document based on the **Fax (Urban theme)** template.
2. Save the file as **WPB02D_xx** in the location where your teacher instructs you to store the files for this project.
3. In the header, type **Motto** and press SPACE to insert the AutoCorrect entry.
4. Replace the content controls in the template using the following information:

   Company name: **Voyager Travel Adventures**

   Company address: **1635 Logan Street, Denver, CO 80205**

   Phone number: **555-555-5550**

   Remove the Web address content control.

   Date: **Today's date**

   To: **Dan Euell, V.P. Marketing**

   Recipient company name: **Voyager Travel Adventures**

   Fax: **555-555-5552**

   Phone: **555-555-0005**

   From: Your Name

   Pages: **2, including cover**

   Fax: **555-555-5551**

   Phone: **555-555-5550**

   Remove the CC: content control and delete the sample text.

   RE: **Survey results**

   Comments: **Dan – I thought you might want a preview of these survey results. Based on the responses, we should consider targeting families with teenagers, and focusing on trips that involve water!**
5. Check the spelling and grammar in the document and correct any errors.
6. **With your instructor's permission**, print the document. It should look similar to Illustration 2B on page 265.
7. Delete the **Motto** AutoCorrect entry.
8. Delete the **Respondant/Respondent** AutoCorrect entry.
9. Close the document, saving changes, and exit Word.

Illustration 2A

Voyager Travel Adventures
"Active Vacations for All Ages"

Customer Survey Results

Preferred Activity (Per Respondent)		
	Backpacking	25
	Biking	43
	Kayaking	95
	River Rafting	77
	Sightseeing	10
	Total	250

CUSTOMER DEMOGRAPHICS		
Age	0 – 18	3%
	19 – 25	17%
	26 – 35	20%
	36 – 45	30%
	46 – 55	20%
	55 +	10%

Gender	
Male	54%
Female	46%

Firstname Lastname

Today's Date

Illustration 2B

Voyager Travel Adventures
"Active Vacations for All Ages"

VOYAGER TRAVEL ADVENTURES
1635 Logan Street, Denver, CO 80205
555-555-5550

Today's Date

Fax

TO: Dan Euell, V.P. Marketing	**FROM: Firstname Lastname**
VOYAGER TRAVEL ADVENTURES	PAGES: 2, including cover
FAX: 555-555-5552	FAX: 555-555-5551
PHONE: 555-555-0005	PHONE: 555-555-5550

RE: Survey results

COMMENTS:
Dan—I thought you might want a preview of these survey results. Based on the responses, we should consider targeting families with teenagers, and focusing on trips that involve water!

☐ Urgent
☐ Please review
☐ Please comment
☐ For your records

Chapter 3

(Courtesy Sergej Khakimullin/Shutterstock)

Creating Reports and Newsletters

Lesson 20
Changing Case and Managing Document Properties

- Using Uppercase Mode
- Changing Case
- Managing Document Properties
- Customizing the Ribbon

Lesson 21
Formatting a One-Page Report

- Analyzing Document Production
- Inserting a File in a Document
- Setting Margins
- Inserting a Section Break
- Setting Page Orientation
- Inserting Page Numbers
- Checking the Word Count
- Formatting a One-Page Report

Lesson 22
Managing Sources and Controlling Text Flow

- Inserting a Hard Page Break
- Controlling Pagination
- Inserting Footnotes and Endnotes
- Inserting Citations
- Analyzing Citations
- Creating a Reference Page
- Viewing a Document in Read Mode

Lesson 23
Working with Newsletter Columns

- Understanding Desktop Publishing
- Creating Newsletter Columns
- Setting Column Width
- Inserting a Column Break
- Balancing Columns
- Analyzing Page Layout and Design

Lesson 24
Enhancing Paragraphs with Dropped Capitals, Borders, and Shading

- Inserting Dropped Capitals
- Enhancing a Paragraph with Borders and Shading
- Analyzing Time Management

Lesson 25
Using Format Painter, Highlights, Symbols, and Quick Parts

- Copying Formatting
- Highlighting Text
- Inserting Symbols
- Inserting Quick Parts
- Working with Building Blocks
- Analyzing Teamwork

Lesson 26
Creating Letters and Labels with Mail Merge

- Understanding Mail Merge and the Mail Merge Process
- Understanding Merge Fields
- Removing Extra Space from the Address Block
- Merging to a New Document
- Creating Mailing Labels by Merging Manually
- Creating an Address List
- Arranging, Previewing, and Printing the Labels

End-of-Chapter Activities

Lesson 20

Changing Case and Managing Document Properties

➤ What You Will Learn

Using Uppercase Mode
Changing Case
Managing Document Properties
Customizing the Ribbon

WORDS TO KNOW

Case
The specific use of upper- or lowercase letters.

Document properties
Categories of information about a document.

Keywords
Important words found in a document. Keywords can be used to classify a document.

Metadata
Data about data, such as the size of a file. Another term for document properties.

Software Skills Document properties are details that help you to identify a file, such as the name of the author and the main topic. The properties remain attached to the file so you can use them for recordkeeping and data management. If you find you often need to use a command that is not already on the Ribbon, you can customize the Ribbon to add the command.

What You Can Do

Using Uppercase Mode

- Use uppercase mode to type all capital letters without pressing SHIFT.
- When uppercase mode is on, press SHIFT to insert a lowercase letter.
- The Caps Lock key on your keyboard is a toggle that turns uppercase mode off and on.
- When uppercase mode is on, the Caps Lock indicator on your keyboard is lit.
- You can add the Caps Lock indicator to the status bar to display whether uppercase mode is off or on.
- Uppercase mode affects only letter characters.

Try It! Using Uppercase Mode

1. Start Word, and save a default blank document as **W20Try_xx** in the location where your teacher instructs you to store the files for this lesson.
2. Right-click the status bar, click to select Caps Lock on the shortcut menu, and then press ESC.
3. On your keyboard, press CAPS LOCK.
4. Type today's date and press ENTER. Press and hold SHIFT and type the first character of your first name. Release SHIFT and type the rest of your first name.
5. Press CAPS LOCK again to turn uppercase mode off.
6. Type your last name.
7. Right-click the status bar, click to clear the check mark from the Caps Lock option, and then press ESC.
8. Save the changes to **W20Try_xx**, and leave it open to use in the next Try It.

Changing Case

- You can easily change the **case** of selected text in a document using the Change Case button in the Font group on the HOME tab of the Ribbon.
- There are five case options:
  - Sentence case: First character in a sentence is uppercase.
  - lowercase: All characters are lowercase.
  - UPPERCASE: All characters are uppercase.
  - Capitalize Each Word: First character in each word is uppercase.
  - tOGGLE cASE: Case is reversed for all selected text.

Try It! Changing Case

1. In the **W20Try_xx** file, press ENTER to start a new line and type: **Microsoft Word 2013 provides many features that make it easier to create professional documents.**
2. Select the sentence you typed in step 1.
3. On the HOME tab, click the Change Case button Aa▾.
4. Click lowercase.
5. Click the Change Case button Aa▾ and click Capitalize Each Word.
6. Click the Change Case button Aa▾ and click tOGGLE cASE.
7. Save the changes to **W20Try_xx**, and leave it open to use in the next Try It.

Managing Document Properties

- **Document properties**, or **metadata**, are bits of unique information that you save as part of a document.
- Document properties display on the Info tab in the Backstage view.
- Some properties are updated automatically when you create or modify a document, such as the file name and type, the author, and the file size.
- You can enter more specific properties to help differentiate the file from other similar documents.
- You can also use the Document Information Panel to view, enter, and edit summary properties, such as Author, Title, Subject, and **Keywords**, or you can use the Properties dialog box to manage advanced document properties.
- You can print a document listing the document properties.

Try It! Managing Document Properties

1. In the **W20Try_xx** file, click FILE to display the Info tab in Backstage view.
2. In the Preview pane, under Properties, click the content control Add a title, and then type **Changing Case**.
3. Click the content control Add a tag and type **uppercase, properties**.
4. Click Add comments and type **Practice document for lesson 20**.
5. Click Show All Properties to expand the list to display all properties.
6. Click Show Fewer Properties to collapse the list.
7. Save the changes to **W20Try_xx**, and leave it open to use in the next Try It.

Try It! Using the Document Information Panel

1. In the **W20Try_xx** file, in the Backstage view, click Properties, and then click Show Document Panel to display the panel below the Ribbon.
2. Click in the Subject box in the Document Information Panel and type **Learning Word 2013**.
3. Click the Close the Document Information Panel button × .
4. Save the changes to **W20Try_xx**, and leave it open to use in the next Try It.

Try It! Viewing a Properties Dialog Box

1. In the **W20Try_xx** file, click FILE to display the Info tab in the Backstage view.
2. In the Preview pane, click Properties, and then click Advanced Properties to display the document's Properties dialog box.
3. Click the Summary tab.
4. Click the Statistics tab.
5. Click OK to close the dialog box.

   ✓ *Alternatively, right-click a document name in File Explorer or an Office dialog box and click Properties to open the Properties dialog box.*
6. Save the changes to **W20Try_xx**, and leave it open to use in the next Try It.

Try It! Printing Document Properties

1. In the **W20Try_xx** file, click FILE > Print.
2. Under Settings, click the top button—it may display Print All Pages—to display a list of items you can choose to print.
3. Click Document Info.

   ✓ *Select other print settings and options as necessary.*
4. Click the Print button.
5. Save the changes to **W20Try_xx**, and leave it open to use in the next Try It.

Customizing the Ribbon

- If you find that you often want to use a command that is not already on the Ribbon, you can customize the Ribbon to add that command for easy reference.
- To add a command to the Ribbon, you must first insert a new group on a tab.
- Commands for customizing the Ribbon are on the Customize Ribbon tab of the Word Options dialog box.

Try It! Customizing the Ribbon

1. In the **W20Try_xx** file, right-click anywhere on the Ribbon and click Customize the Ribbon.
2. On the right side of the Word Options dialog box, under Main Tabs, click the plus sign next to View to see the groups on the View tab.
3. Click View to make the tab active, and then click New Group to add a new group at the bottom of the View list.
4. Click the Rename button, and type **Properties**. Click OK.
5. Click the Choose commands from drop-down arrow and click Commands Not in the Ribbon.
6. In the list of commands, click Advanced Document Properties, and then click the Add button. The command is added to the new Properties group on the View tab.
7. Click OK, and then click the VIEW tab on the Ribbon to view the new group and the new command.
8. Right-click anywhere on the Ribbon and click Customize the Ribbon.
9. In the Word Options dialog box, click the Reset button and then click Reset all customizations.
10. Click Yes in the confirmation dialog box and then click OK.
11. Save the changes to **W20Try_xx**, close it, and exit Word.

Lesson 20—Practice

You work in the personnel department at Voyager Travel Adventures. In this project, you write a job offer letter to offer the position of communications director to Jeremy LeBlanc. You will prepare the letter using Word's features for controlling case and managing document properties.

DIRECTIONS

1. Start Word, if necessary, and create a new document using the Single spaced template. Save the document as **W20Practice_xx** in the location where your teacher instructs you to store the files for this lesson.
2. Type the full-block business letter shown in Figure 20-1 on the next page.
   a. Use uppercase mode as necessary to type text that displays in all uppercase letters.
   b. Replace the sample text *Today's Date* with the actual date.
   c. Replace the sample text *Student's Name* with your own name.
3. Select the company name in the return address.
4. On the **HOME** tab, click the **Change Case** button Aa▾ and click **Capitalize Each Word**.
5. Select the company name in the first sentence of the letter, click the **Change Case** button Aa▾, and click **Capitalize Each Word**.

Figure 20-1

VOYAGER TRAVEL ADVENTURES
1635 Logan Street
Denver, CO 80205

Today's Date

Mr. Jeremy LeBlanc
555 Main Street
Boulder, CO 80309

Dear Mr. LeBlanc:

JOB OFFER

Voyager travel adventures is pleased to offer you a position as Communications Director. We believe that your experience, skills, and abilities will make you a valuable member of our team.

The position comes with the following compensation:

- Salary: annual gross salary of $67,500 paid in monthly installments.
- Performance bonus: up to three percent of your annual gross salary, paid quarterly.
- Benefits: standard benefits for salaried, exempt employees, including the following:
    - 401(k) retirement account
    - Health, dental, life, and disability insurance
    - Educational assistance
    - Personal days for vacation, illness, and family care based on length of employment
    - One voyager travel adventures trip per calendar year

To accept or decline this offer, please sign and date this letter where indicated below and return it to my attention at the address listed above by May 1, 2014.

We hope that you will accept this offer, and we look forward to working with you. Please contact me if you have any questions or concerns.

Sincerely,

Student's Name
Personnel Director

I, Jeremy LeBlanc, ACCEPT THIS OFFER OF THE POSITION OF COMMUNICATIONS DIRECTOR.
Signature:______________________________ Date:________________

I, Jeremy LeBlanc, DECLINE THIS OFFER OF THE POSITION OF COMMUNICATIONS DIRECTOR.
Signature:______________________________ Date:________________

6. Select the company name in the last bullet item, click the **Change Case button** Aa▾, and click **Capitalize Each Word**.
7. Select the text *ACCEPT THIS OFFER OF THE POSITION OF* above the first signature line near the end of the document.
8. Click **HOME** > **Change Case** Aa▾, and click **lowercase**.
9. Select the text *COMMUNICATIONS DIRECTOR* at the end of the sentence above the first signature line.
10. Click **HOME** > **Change Case** Aa▾, and click **Capitalize Each Word**.
11. Select the text *DECLINE THIS OFFER OF THE POSITION OF* above the second signature line at the end of the document.
12. Click **HOME** > **Change Case** Aa▾, and click **lowercase**.
13. Select the text *COMMUNICATIONS DIRECTOR* at the end of the sentence above the second signature line.

14. Click **HOME** > **Change Case** Aa▾, and click **Capitalize Each Word**.
15. Check and correct the spelling and grammar in the document, and then save the changes.
16. **With your teacher's permission,** print the document.
17. Click **FILE** to display the Info tab in the backstage.
18. In the Preview pane under Properties, click **Add a title** and type **Job Offer Letter**.
19. Click **Add a tag** and type **letter, job offer, Jeremy LeBlanc**.
20. Click **Properties** and then click **Show Document Panel**.
21. In the Subject box, type **Communications Director Position**.
22. In the Category box, type **Personnel Department**.
23. In the Status box, type **Open**.
24. Click the **Close the Document Information Panel** button ×.
25. Save the changes to the file.
26. Click **FILE** > **Print**.
27. Under Settings, click the top button to display a list of items you can choose to print, and click **Document Info**.
28. **With your teacher's permission,** click the **Print** button to print the document properties.
29. Close the document, saving changes, and exit Word.

Lesson 20—Apply

In this project, you write a job offer letter to Annabel Martin to offer her the position of tour leader. You will edit the letter you created for Jeremy LeBlanc to complete this letter.

DIRECTIONS

1. Start Word, if necessary, and open **W20Apply** from the data files for this lesson.
2. Save the file as **W20Apply_xx** in the location where your teacher instructs you to store the files for this lesson.
3. Edit the document to create the letter shown in Figure 20-2 on the next page.
   a. Replace the sample text *Student's Name* with your own name, and *Today's Date* with the actual date.
   b. Turn on uppercase mode and type the subject **JOB OFFER** between the salutation and the first sentence of the letter.
   c. Use the Change Case feature to change all text in tOGGLE cASE to Capitalize Each Word.
   d. Edit the recipient's name from *Jeremy LeBlanc* to **Annabel Martin** in all three places it displays, and *Mr. LeBlanc* to **Ms. Martin** where it displays.
   e. Edit the inside address as shown.
   f. Edit the job title from *Communications Director* to **Tour Guide** in all three places it displays.
   g. Edit the salary from *$67,500* to **$28,000**.
4. Check and correct the spelling and grammar in the document, and then save the changes.
5. **With your teacher's permission,** print the document.
6. Display the Info tab in the Backstage view, and then open the Document Information Panel.
7. In the Subject box, change *Communications Director Position* to **Tour Guide Position**.
8. In the Keywords box, change *Jeremy LeBlanc* to **Annabel Martin**.
9. In the Comments box, type **Excellent travel experience; certified teacher**.
10. Close the Document Information Panel.
11. Save the changes to the file.
12. **With your teacher's permission,** print the document properties.
13. Close the document, saving changes, and exit Word.

Figure 20-2

Voyager Travel Adventures
1635 Logan Street
Denver, CO 80205

Today's Date

Annabel Martin
1001 South Street
Taos, NM 87571

Dear Ms. Martin:

JOB OFFER

Voyager Travel Adventures is pleased to offer you a position as Tour Guide. We believe that your experience, skills, and abilities will make you a valuable member of our team.

The position comes with the following compensation:

- Salary: annual gross salary of $28,000 paid in monthly installments.
- Performance bonus: up to three percent of your annual gross salary, paid quarterly.
- Benefits: standard benefits for salaried, exempt employees, including the following:
    - 401(k) retirement account
    - Health, dental, life, and disability insurance
    - Educational assistance
    - Personal days for vacation, illness, and family care based on length of employment
    - One Voyager Travel Adventures trip per calendar year

To accept or decline this offer, please sign and date this letter where indicated below and return it to my attention at the address listed above by May 1, 2014.

We hope that you will accept this offer, and we look forward to working with you. Please contact me if you have any questions or concerns.

Sincerely,

Firstname Lastname
Personnel Director

I, Annabel Martin, accept this offer of the position of Tour Guide.
Signature:______________________________________ Date:______________________

I, Annabel Martin, decline this offer of the position of Tour Guide.
Signature:______________________________________ Date:______________________

Lesson 21

Formatting a One-Page Report

➤ What You Will Learn

Analyzing Document Production
Inserting a File in a Document
Setting Margins
Inserting a Section Break
Setting Page Orientation
Inserting Page Numbers
Checking the Word Count
Formatting a One-Page Report

Software Skills Format a one-page report so that it is attractive and professional. Import existing text to append it to the current document. Set margins to meet expected requirements and to improve the document's appearance and readability. For example, leave a wider margin in a report if you expect a reader to make notes or comments; leave a narrower margin to fit more text on a page.

What You Can Do

Analyzing Document Production

- There are three basic steps to producing any business document: planning, creating, and publishing.
- The planning stage requires you to think about such questions as the type of document you want to create, the purpose of the document, the audience for whom you are creating the document, and whether there are any special publishing requirements.
- For example, you might consider what paper to print on, if color ink should be used, how many copies to print, or whether you will need to print on both sides of a page.

WORDS TO KNOW

Gutter
Space added to the margin to leave room for binding.

Landscape orientation
Positioning document text so it displays and prints horizontally across the longer side of a page.

Margins
The amount of white space between the text and the edge of the page on each side.

Portrait orientation
The default position for displaying and printing text horizontally across the shorter side of a page.

Section
In Word, a segment of a document defined by a section break. A section may have different page formatting from the rest of the document.

Word count
The number of words in a document or selection.

- If the project seems too complex, you may decide to use a desktop publishing package, such as Microsoft Publisher, instead of using a word processing package, such as Microsoft Word.
- During the planning stage you should create a schedule that includes milestones, such as how long it will take to gather the information you need, when the first draft will be complete, how long it will take for a review process, and when the final document will be complete.
- The creation stage involves selecting page and document settings, such as margins and page size, and entering and formatting the text and graphics.
- The document you create should explore the topic clearly, concisely, and accurately. You should thoroughly check grammar, spelling, punctuation, and usage to make sure the document has no errors that will detract from its message.
- The publishing stage involves outputting the document using either your desktop printer or a commercial printer. In some cases, the document may be published electronically on a Web site.

Inserting a File in a Document

- You can insert one file into another file to incorporate the first file's contents into the second file.
- The contents of the inserted file are appended—that is, added—to the second file. No content is removed when the file is inserted.
- The entire contents are saved as part of the second file, and the first file remains unchanged.
- Use the Text from File command to insert a file in another document.

Try It! Inserting a File in a Document

1. Start Word, and open **W21TryA** from the data files for this lesson.
2. Save the file as **W21TryA_xx** in the location where your teacher instructs you to store the files for this lesson.
3. Display nonprinting characters, position the insertion point at the end of the last paragraph, and press ENTER.
4. On the INSERT tab, in the Text group, click the Object button drop-down arrow, and click Text from File.
5. In the Insert File dialog box, navigate to the location of the data files, select **W21TryB**, and click Insert.
6. Delete the two blank paragraphs at the end of the inserted text.
7. Save the changes to **W21TryA_xx**, and leave it open to use in the next Try It.

Setting Margins

- **Margins** are measured in inches.
- The normal default margins in Word 2013 are 1" on the left, right, top, and bottom.
- You can select from a list of preset margins by clicking the Margins button in the Page Setup group on the PAGE LAYOUT tab.
- Alternatively, you can set custom margins.
- If you set custom margins, you can also specify a **gutter** width to leave room for binding multiple pages.
- Margin settings can affect an entire document or the current section.

  ✓ *To set margins for a single paragraph, use indents.*

- On the rulers, areas outside the margins are shaded gray, while areas inside the margins are white.
- Light gray bars mark the margins on the rulers.
- You can set Word to display margins on the page as nonprinting lines called text boundaries.

Try It! Selecting a Preset Margin

1. In the W21TryA_xx file, on the PAGE LAYOUT tab, in the Page Setup group, click the Margins button.
2. Click Narrow.
3. In the Page Setup group, click the Margins button again, and click Wide.
4. Save the changes to W21TryA_xx, and leave it open to use in the next Try It.

Try It! Setting Custom Margins

1. In the W21TryA_xx file, click PAGE LAYOUT > Margins.
2. Click Custom Margins to open the Page Setup dialog box.
3. Under Margins, use the increment arrows to set the Top, Bottom, Left, and Right margins to 1.3".
4. Click OK.
5. Save the changes to W21TryA_xx, and leave it open to use in the next Try It.

✓ *To quickly set a margin, drag a margin marker on the ruler. Press and hold* ALT *while you drag to see the margin width.*

Try It! Showing or Hiding Text Boundaries

1. In the W21TryA_xx file, click FILE > Options > Advanced.
2. Under Show document content, click to select the Show text boundaries check box.
3. Click OK.
4. Repeat the steps to clear the check box to hide the boundaries.
5. Save the changes to W21TryA_xx, and leave it open to use in the next Try It.

Inserting a Section Break

- A default Word document contains one **section**.
- Using commands in the Page Setup group on the PAGE LAYOUT tab, you can divide a document into multiple sections.
- Document sections can be formatted separately to apply different kinds of formats. Using sections, you can create a document within a document.
  - You can set different margins, page layout options, or orientation for each section.
  - You can apply different header and footer options to each section to change numbering or display different chapter titles.
  - You can use a section break to move a title into a new section and then format that title as desired.
- After you have inserted a section break to create a new section, you can insert another section break to revert back to the formats of a previous section.
- There are four types of section breaks:
  - Next page: Inserts a section break and a page break so that the new section will start on the next page.
  - Continuous: Inserts a section break so that the new section will start at the insertion point.
  - Even page: Inserts a section break and page breaks so the new section will start on the next even-numbered page.
  - Odd page: Inserts a section break and page breaks so the new section will start on the next odd-numbered page.
- In Print Layout view, section breaks display only if nonprinting characters display.

Try It! Inserting a Section Break

1. In the **W21TryA_xx** file, position the insertion point at the beginning of the heading *Zebra*.
2. On the PAGE LAYOUT tab, in the Page Setup group, click the Breaks button.
3. From the Breaks gallery, under Section Breaks, click Continuous.
4. Click on the section break in the document and press DEL to remove it.
5. Click the Breaks button again.
6. From the Breaks gallery, under Section Breaks, click Next Page.
7. Save the changes to **W21TryA_xx**, and leave it open to use in the next Try It.

A Continuous section break

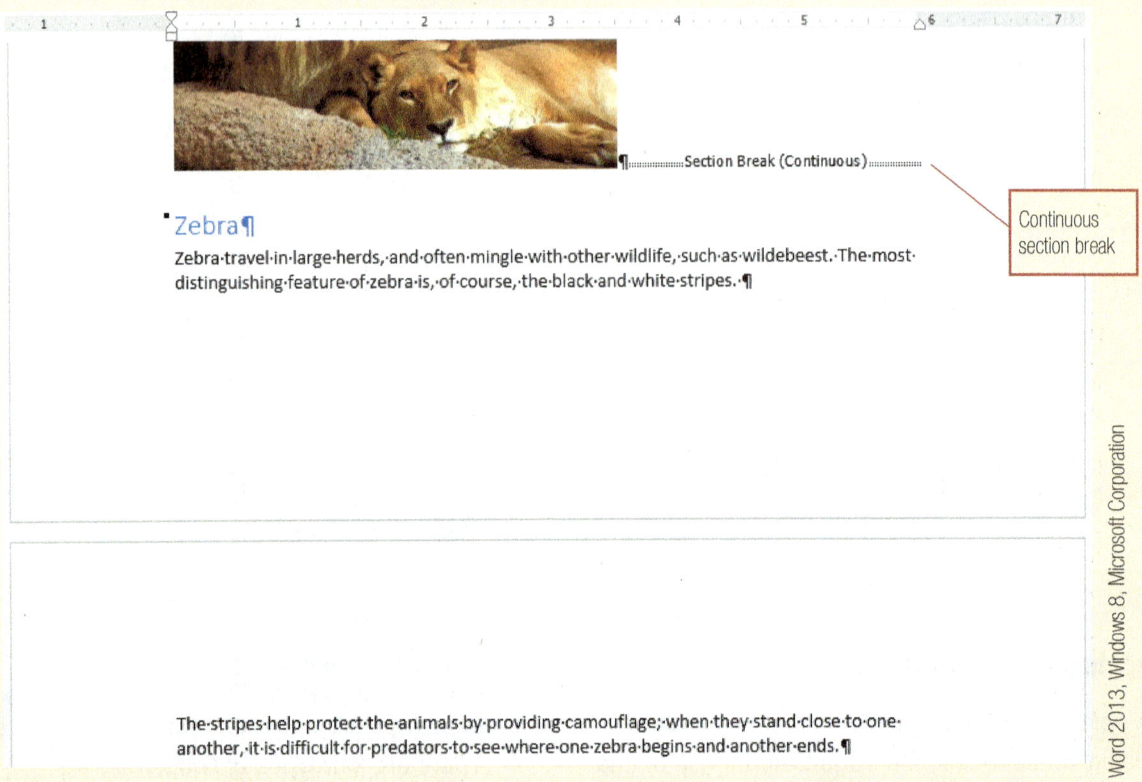

Word 2013, Windows 8, Microsoft Corporation

Setting Page Orientation

- Orientation is either **portrait** or **landscape**.
  - Select Portrait orientation—the default—when you want data displayed across the shorter length of a page.
  - Select Landscape orientation when you want data displayed across the wider length of a page.
- Portrait orientation is used for most documents, including letters, memos, and reports.
- Use landscape orientation to display a document across the wider length of the page. For example, if a document contains a table that is wider than the standard 8.5" page, Word will split it across two pages. When you change to landscape orientation, the table may fit on the 11" page.
- You can set the orientation for the entire document, or for a section.
- The orientation options are in the Page Setup group on the PAGE LAYOUT tab.

Try It! Setting Page Orientation

1. In the W21TryA_xx file, make sure the insertion point is still on the same line as the heading *Zebra*.

   ✓ *The heading should be at the top of page 2, at the beginning of the second section.*

2. On the PAGE LAYOUT tab, click the Orientation button.

3. Click Landscape. The orientation for the second section of the document changes to Landscape; the first section remains in Portrait.

4. Save the changes to W21TryA_xx, and leave it open to use in the next Try It.

Change the orientation

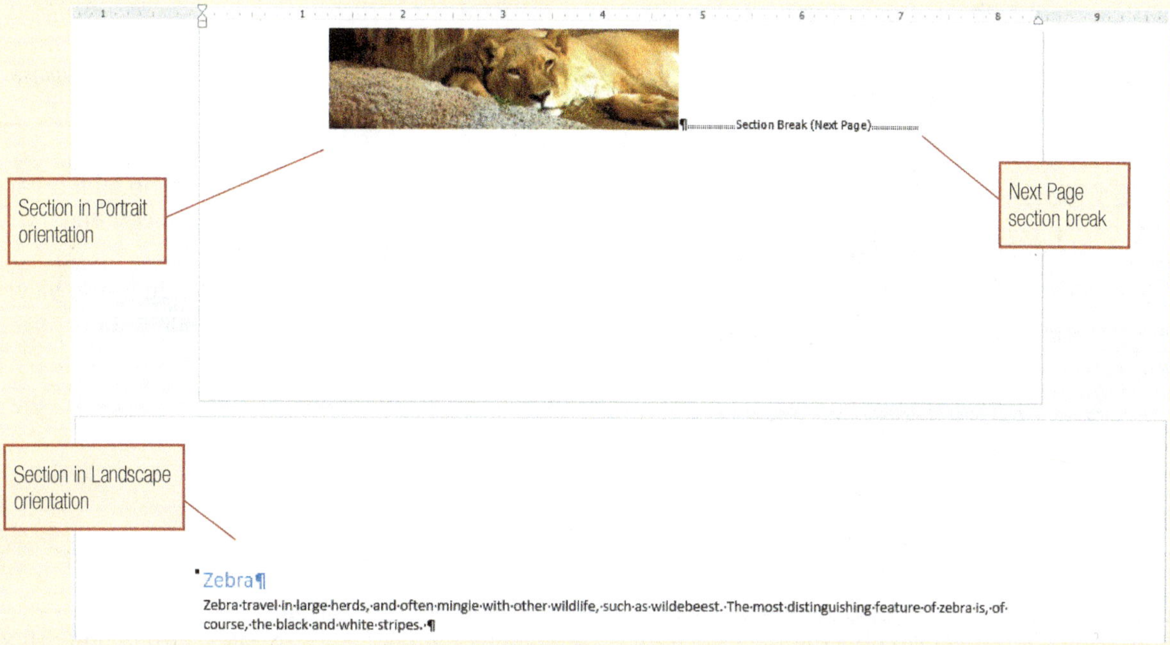

Word 2013, Windows 8, Microsoft Corporation

Inserting Page Numbers

- You can insert a page number into the header or footer of a document. Numbers automatically display on each page, numbered consecutively.
- You can select from a collection of built-in page number styles, or you can apply your own formatting.
- Once you insert a page number, you can select options such as to restart numbering for a new section, or to change the number format.
- Restarting page numbering is useful when your document has a title page that you do not want numbered.

Try It! Inserting Page Numbers

1. In the **W21TryA_xx** file, press CTRL + HOME to move the insertion point to the beginning of the document.
2. Click INSERT > Page Number.
3. Click Top of Page to display a gallery of page number formats to display in the header, and then click Plain Number 3.
4. On the HEADER & FOOTER TOOLS DESIGN tab, click the Next button to move the insertion point to the page number in the header on page 2.
5. Click the Page Number button on the Ribbon and click Format Page Numbers to open the Page Number Format dialog box.
6. Under Page numbering, click the Start at option button. Leave the page number set to 1, and click OK.
7. Click the Close Header and Footer button, then save the changes to **W21TryA_xx**, and leave it open to use in the next Try It.

   ✓ *To remove all page numbers, on either the INSERT tab or the HEADER & FOOTER TOOLS DESIGN tab, click the Page Number button and click Remove Page Numbers.*

Checking the Word Count

- Word keeps track of the **word count** as part of the statistics properties for each document.

  ✓ *For more about document properties refer to Word, Lesson 20.*

- By default the word count displays on the status bar.
- If you select part of the document, the status bar displays the word count of the selection and the total word count.
- You can open the Word Count dialog box to view additional statistics such as the number of lines, paragraphs, and characters.

Try It! Checking the Word Count

1. In the **W21TryA_xx** file, locate the word count on the status bar and take note of the number of words in the document.

   ✓ *If the word count does not display, right-click the status bar, click to select Word Count, and then close the shortcut menu.*

2. Move the insertion point to the end of the title *Safari with Voyager*, press the spacebar, and type **Travel Adventures**.
3. Locate the word count on the status bar again. The value should have increased by 2 to 319.
4. Select the title. Now, the word count on the status bar displays 5 of 319 WORDS, indicating that 5 of the total 319 words are selected.
5. Cancel the selection, and then click the REVIEW tab.
6. In the Proofing group, click the Word Count button to open the Word Count dialog box where you can view the number of words, pages, characters with or without spaces, paragraphs, and lines.
7. Click Close.
8. Save the changes to **W21TryA_xx**, and close it. Leave Word open to use in the next Try It.

Formatting a One-Page Report

- Traditionally, a one-page report is set up as follows:
  - Left and right margins are 1".
  - Orientation is Portrait.
  - The title is positioned 1" to 2" from the top of the page.

    ✓ *The position of the title depends on the amount of text on the page.*
  - The report title is centered and in either all uppercase or title case.
  - Spacing after the title is 54 points (1").
  - Body text is in a 12-point serif font, such as Times New Roman.
  - Text is justified.
  - Lines are double-spaced.
  - First-line indents are between 0.5" and 1".
  - Spacing before and after paragraphs is 0.
  - Author's name and the date are right-aligned in the header.
- There are many variations of one-page report formatting that are acceptable, and your teacher may request that you use alternative formatting. For example, some teachers request a wider margin so there is room for writing comments, and want the teacher's name and class information left-aligned above the title, or in the header.

Try It! Formatting a One-Page Report

1. In Word, open **W21TryC** from the data files for this lesson.
2. Save the file as **W21TryC_xx** in the location where your teacher instructs you to store the files for this lesson.
3. Select the four paragraphs of body text under the heading and change the font to 12-point Times New Roman. Justify the paragraph alignment.
4. Change the line spacing to Double and the spacing before and after paragraphs to 0.

   ✓ *Refer to Word, Lesson 4 for a refresher on changing spacing.*
5. Apply a first-line indent of 0.5".
6. Click PAGE LAYOUT > Margins > Normal.
7. Center the title and apply 54 points of space before and after.
8. Double-click in the header, type your name, press ENTER, and type today's date.
9. Right-align your name and the date in the header.
10. Save the changes to **W21TryC_xx**, close it, and exit Word.

Lesson 21—Practice

Member Services at Michigan Avenue Athletic Club has decided to publish a series of information sheets on various topics. The goal is to keep the reports to fewer than 250 words so they fit on one page, and to make them available to members in print and online. In this project, you create and format a sheet that explains what a personal trainer is and how to select one.

DIRECTIONS

1. Start Word, if necessary, and save a blank document as **W21Practice_xx** in the location where your teacher instructs you to store the files for this lesson.
2. Double-click in the header, type your name, press ENTER, and type today's date.
3. Right-align your name and the date in the header.
4. On the first line of the document, type the title **Is Personal Training Right for You?**
5. Apply the **Title** style to the text, and center it horizontally. Set the spacing before and after the title to 54 points and press ENTER to start a new line.
6. Change the font and font size to 12-point Times New Roman.
7. Set the line spacing to **Double**. Set the alignment to **Justified**. Set the first line indent to **0.5"**. Set the spacing before and after paragraphs to **0**.
8. Type the following paragraphs of text:

   Almost everyone could benefit from the services of a personal trainer. In addition to designing a personalized workout program, a good trainer provides motivation and encouragement. He or she helps you understand how to fit exercise into your life and teaches you how to make the most out of your exercise time. The lessons you learn from a trainer help ensure a safe, effective workout, even when you are exercising on your own.

   Working with a trainer should be a satisfying and rewarding experience. There are many different reasons for hiring a personal trainer. Some people want the motivation of a workout partner, others require specialized services for rehabilitation, and still others are interested in achieving weight loss goals. Before hiring a trainer, make sure he or she has experience helping people with goals similar to your own. Ask for references and then contact at least three of them. You should also interview the trainer to find out if you are compatible. You should feel comfortable talking and working together, and you should trust the trainer to respect your time and efforts.

   Verify that the trainer is certified by a nationally recognized organization such as the American Council on Exercise, the American College of Sports Medicine, or the National Strength and Conditioning Association. Many trainers have degrees in subjects such as sports medicine, physical education, exercise physiology, or anatomy and physiology.

   For more information about personal training at Michigan Avenue Athletic Club, contact Candace at extension 765.

9. Click **REVIEW** > **Word Count**. Check the word count in the document. It should be 253. Note how many words you must delete to meet the 250 word limit.
10. Close the Word Count dialog box.
11. In the last sentence of the document, delete the eight words: *about personal training at Michigan Avenue Athletic Club*. Check the word count again to verify that it is now less than 250.
12. Click **INSERT** > **Page Number**.
13. Click **Bottom of Page** and then click **Plain Number 2**.
14. Click **PAGE LAYOUT** > **Orientation** > **Landscape**. Adjust the zoom so you can see the entire document on your screen.
15. Click **PAGE LAYOUT** > **Orientation** > **Portrait**. Increase the zoom to at least 100%.
16. Check the spelling and grammar in the document and correct errors as necessary.
17. **With your teacher's permission,** print the document. It should look similar to Figure 21-1 on the next page.
18. Close the document, saving changes, and exit Word.

Figure 21-1

Firstname Lastname
Today's Date

Is Personal Training Right for You?

Almost everyone could benefit from the services of a personal trainer. In addition to designing a personalized workout program, a good trainer provides motivation and encouragement. He or she helps you understand how to fit exercise into your life and teaches you how to make the most out of your exercise time. The lessons you learn from a trainer help ensure a safe, effective workout, even when you are exercising on your own.

Working with a trainer should be a satisfying and rewarding experience. There are many different reasons for hiring a personal trainer. Some people want the motivation of a workout partner, others require specialized services for rehabilitation, and still others are interested in achieving weight loss goals. Before hiring a trainer, make sure he or she has experience helping people with goals similar to your own. Ask for references and then contact at least three of them. You should also interview the trainer to find out if you are compatible. You should feel comfortable talking and working together, and you should trust the trainer to respect your time and efforts.

Verify that the trainer is certified by a nationally recognized organization such as the American Council on Exercise, the American College of Sports Medicine, or the National Strength and Conditioning Association. Many trainers have degrees in subjects such as sports medicine, physical education, exercise physiology, or anatomy and physiology.

For more information, contact Candace at extension 765.

1

Lesson 21—Apply

In this project, you work on a second information sheet for Michigan Avenue Athletic Club. This sheet explores the relationship between diet and exercise.

DIRECTIONS

1. Start Word, if necessary, and open **W21Apply** from the data files for this lesson.
2. Save the file as **W21Apply_xx** in the location where your teacher instructs you to store the files for this lesson.
3. Type your name and today's date in the header, and right-align both lines.
4. Display the text boundaries, and then set the margins to **Normal—1"** on each side.
5. Apply the **Title** style to the first line of the document, and center it horizontally. Set the spacing before and after the title to **54 points**.
6. Capitalize every word in the title.
7. Select the rest of the text in the document and apply formatting as follows:
   a. Change the font and font size to 12-point Times New Roman.
   b. Set the line spacing to **Double**.
   c. Set the alignment to **Justified**.
   d. Set the first line indent to **0.5"**.
   e. Set the spacing before and after paragraphs to **0**.
8. Check the word count. Note how many words you must delete to be under the 250 word limit.
9. In the second paragraph of body text, delete the sentence *But that's exactly what it is: the fuel your body needs to operate.*
10. Check the word count again. In the last sentence of the fifth paragraph, delete the text *Although there is no magic diet that will dramatically increase athletic ability or endurance,* and change the *B* in the word *by* to uppercase.
11. Check the word count again.
12. Insert a page number flush left in the footer.
13. Hide the text boundaries.
14. Check the spelling and grammar in the document and correct errors as necessary.
15. **With your teacher's permission,** print the document. It should look similar to Figure 21-2 on the next page.
16. Close the document, saving changes, and exit Word.

Figure 21-2

Firstname Lastname
Today's Date

Food As Fuel: How Diet Affects Exercise

You may know that diet can directly affect the performance of professional athletes. Do you know it can affect the performance of people who exercise for fun and health benefits? Understanding how food fuels your body can help you get the most out of your workout.

Most people think about food as something that curbs hunger and tastes good. We rarely think of it as fuel. Just as a car will stop if it runs out of gasoline, your body will not be able to perform if it runs out of the nutrients provided by food.

Include complex carbohydrates in your diet before exercise to help your muscles stay strong. Avoid simple carbs that are full of sugar, such as candy or soft drinks, because that may actually decrease your ability to perform.

Water is the most important nutrient. It is vital that you drink water during and after a workout to replace the water you lose by sweating. Protein is also important for recovering after a strenuous workout. It supports growth and tissue repair.

Proper diet can help you achieve your exercise and weight goals. It provides energy, helps you build lean muscle mass, and enables you to maintain the heart rate necessary to improve your physical fitness over time. By eating right, you can improve your strength, develop lean muscles, and keep your body healthy.

For more information about nutrition and exercise, contract Sandra at extension 43.

1

Lesson 22

Managing Sources and Controlling Text Flow

➤ What You Will Learn

Inserting a Hard Page Break
Controlling Pagination
Inserting Footnotes and Endnotes
Inserting Citations
Analyzing Citations
Creating a Reference Page
Viewing a Document in Read Mode

WORDS TO KNOW

Bibliography
A list of sources.

Citation
A reference to a source of information. In legal documents, it is a reference to previous court decisions or authoritative writings.

Common knowledge
Facts that can be found in many—at least three—independent sources and are known by a lot of people.

Copyright
The exclusive right to perform, display, copy, or distribute an artistic work or form of expression, such as words, music, images, or objects.

Endnote
An explanation or reference to additional material that prints at the end of a document.

Software Skills Make a long document easier to read and work in by using page breaks and pagination to control where a new page should start. You can also use Read Mode to view a document onscreen. Include footnotes or endnotes in documents to provide information about the source of quoted material, or to supplement the main text. Insert citations to mark references and to create a reference page or bibliography for your report.

What You Can Do

Inserting a Hard Page Break

- A default Word document page is the size of a standard 8.5" by 11" sheet of paper.
- With 1" top and bottom margins, a page has 9" of vertical space for entering text.

✓ *The number of lines depends on the font size and spacing settings.*

- Word inserts a **soft page break** to start a new page when the current page is full.
- Soft page breaks adjust automatically if text is inserted or deleted, so a break always occurs when the current page is full.
- Insert a **hard page break** to start a new page before the current page is full. For example, insert a hard page break before a heading that falls at the bottom of a page; the break forces the heading to the top of the next page.

- You can insert a hard page break using the Breaks button in the Page Setup group on the PAGE LAYOUT tab or the Page Break button in the Pages group on the INSERT tab.

  ✓ *The shortcut key combination for inserting a hard page break is* CTRL + ENTER.

- Breaks move like characters when you insert and delete text. Therefore, you should insert hard page breaks after all editing is complete to avoid having a break occur at an awkward position on the page.
- In Draft view, a soft page break is marked by a dotted line across the page.
- By default, in Print Layout view page breaks are indicated by a space between the bottom of one page and the top of the next page; if you have nonprinting characters displayed, the space where you insert a hard page break is marked by a dotted line with the words *Page Break* centered in it.
- You can double-click the space between pages to hide it in Print Layout view. If you do, page breaks are marked by a solid black line. Double-click the black line to show the space.
- In Draft view, a hard page break is marked by a dotted line with the words *Page Break* centered in it.

Try It! **Inserting a Hard Page Break**

1. Start Word, and open **W22TryA** from the data files for this lesson.
2. Save the file as **W22TryA_xx** in the location where your teacher instructs you to store the files for this lesson.
3. Display nonprinting characters.
4. Position the insertion point at the beginning of the heading *Zebra*.
5. On the INSERT tab, in the Pages group, click the Page Break button.
6. Click Undo on the Quick Access Toolbar.
7. On the PAGE LAYOUT tab, in the Page Setup group, click the Breaks button and click Page.
8. Double-click the space between pages, then double-click the black line to reveal the space again.
9. Select the line on which the nonprinting page break displays and press DEL twice to remove the page break and the extra paragraph.
10. Save the changes to **W22TryA_xx**, and leave it open to use in the next Try It.

Controlling Pagination

- Use **pagination** options to control the way Word breaks paragraphs and lines at the top and bottom of a page. For example, you can control whether or not a heading stays on the same page as the paragraph that follows it.
- The following pagination options are available on the Line and Page Breaks tab of the Paragraph dialog box:
  - **Widow/Orphan** control. Select this option to prevent either the first or last line of a paragraph from printing on a different page from the rest of the paragraph.

Fair use doctrine
Part of copyright law that provides for the limited use of copyrighted work without permission.

Footnote
An explanation or reference to additional material that prints at the bottom of a page.

Hard page break
A nonprinting character inserted to force the start of a new page.

Note reference mark
A number or character inserted in the document to refer to footnote or endnote text.

Note text
The text of the footnote or endnote citation.

Orphan
The first line of a paragraph printed alone at the bottom of a page.

Pagination
The system used for numbering pages in a document. In Word, it also means using features to control the way paragraphs and lines break at the top and bottom of a page.

Plagiarism
The unauthorized use of another person's ideas or creative work without giving credit to that person.

Soft page break
The location where Word automatically starts a new page because the current page is full.

Widow
The last line of a paragraph printed alone at the top of a page.

- Keep with next. Select this option to prevent a page break between the current paragraph and the following paragraph.
- Keep lines together. Select this option to prevent a page break within a paragraph.
- Page break before. Select this option to force a page break before the current paragraph.

- You can also press SHIFT + ENTER to manually insert a hard line break. A hard line break forces Word to wrap text before reaching the right margin.

  ✓ *To see hard line breaks onscreen, display nonprinting characters.*

Try It! Controlling Pagination

1. In the **W22TryA_xx** file, position the insertion point in the heading *Photography Tips*.
2. On the PAGE LAYOUT tab, click the Paragraph group dialog box launcher to display the Paragraph dialog box.

   ✓ *You can also click the Paragraph group dialog box launcher on the HOME tab.*
3. Click the Line and Page Breaks tab.
4. Under Pagination, click to select the Keep with next check box, and then click OK. The heading is now kept with the next paragraph.
5. Save the changes to **W22TryA_xx**, and leave it open to use in the next Try It.

Inserting Footnotes and Endnotes

- **Footnotes** or **endnotes** are required in documents that include quoted material, such as research papers.
- Standard footnotes and endnotes include the following information:
  - The author of the quoted material (first name first) followed by a comma.

    ✓ *This information may not always be available.*
  - The title of the book (in italics) followed by the city of publication followed by a colon, the publisher followed by a comma, and the date.
  - If the source is not a book, the title of the article (in quotation marks), or Web page (in quotation marks) followed by a comma, the name of the publication if it is a magazine or journal (in italics), the publication volume, number, and/or date (date in parentheses) followed by a colon.
  - The page number(s) where the material is located, followed by a period.
  - If the source is a Web page, the citation should also include the URL address, enclosed in angle brackets <> and the date you accessed the information, followed by a period.

  ✓ *There are other styles used for footnotes and endnotes. If you are unsure which style to use, ask your teacher for more information.*
- Footnotes or endnotes can also provide explanations or supplemental text. For example, an asterisk footnote might provide information about where to purchase a product mentioned in the text.
- When you insert a footnote, Word first inserts a **note reference mark** in the text, then a separator line following the last line of text on the page, and finally the note number corresponding to the note mark below the separator line. You then type and format the **note text** in the note area below the separator line.
- Endnotes include the same parts as footnotes but are printed on the last page of a document.
- Word uses Arabic numerals for footnote marks; if endnotes are used in the same document, the endnote marks are roman numerals.
- You can adjust footnote and endnote formats in the Footnote and Endnote dialog box. For instance, you can change the location of footnotes and endnotes from their default position or change the number format for the notes.
- By default, numbering is consecutive from the beginning of the document. You can have Word restart numbering on each page or each section. You can also change the starting number.

- Word automatically updates numbering if you add or delete footnotes or endnotes, or rearrange the document text.
- To delete a footnote or endnote, position the insertion point to the right of the note mark in the text and press BACKSPACE twice.

Try It! Inserting Footnotes

1. In the **W22TryA_xx** file, position the insertion point at the end of the last sentence in the first paragraph under the heading *Lions*. The point should be between the period and the paragraph mark.

   ✓ *Insert footnotes after punctuation marks.*

2. Click REFERENCES > Insert Footnote AB¹ .
3. Type **"African Wildlife Foundation: Wildlife: Lion," <http://www.awf.org/content/wildlife/detail/lion>, Today's date.**

   ✓ *If Word automatically removes the brackets and/or formats the URL as a hyperlink, you can right-click the text, click Remove Hyperlink, and then retype the brackets, if necessary.*

4. Right-click the note text you just typed and then click Note Options to display the Footnote and Endnote dialog box.
5. In the Location section, click the Bottom of page down arrow and select Below text.
6. Click Apply. The footnote moves from the bottom of the page to sit just below the last paragraph of text.
7. Click Undo to reverse the change.
8. Save the changes to **W22TryA_xx**, and leave it open to use in the next Try It.

Insert a footnote

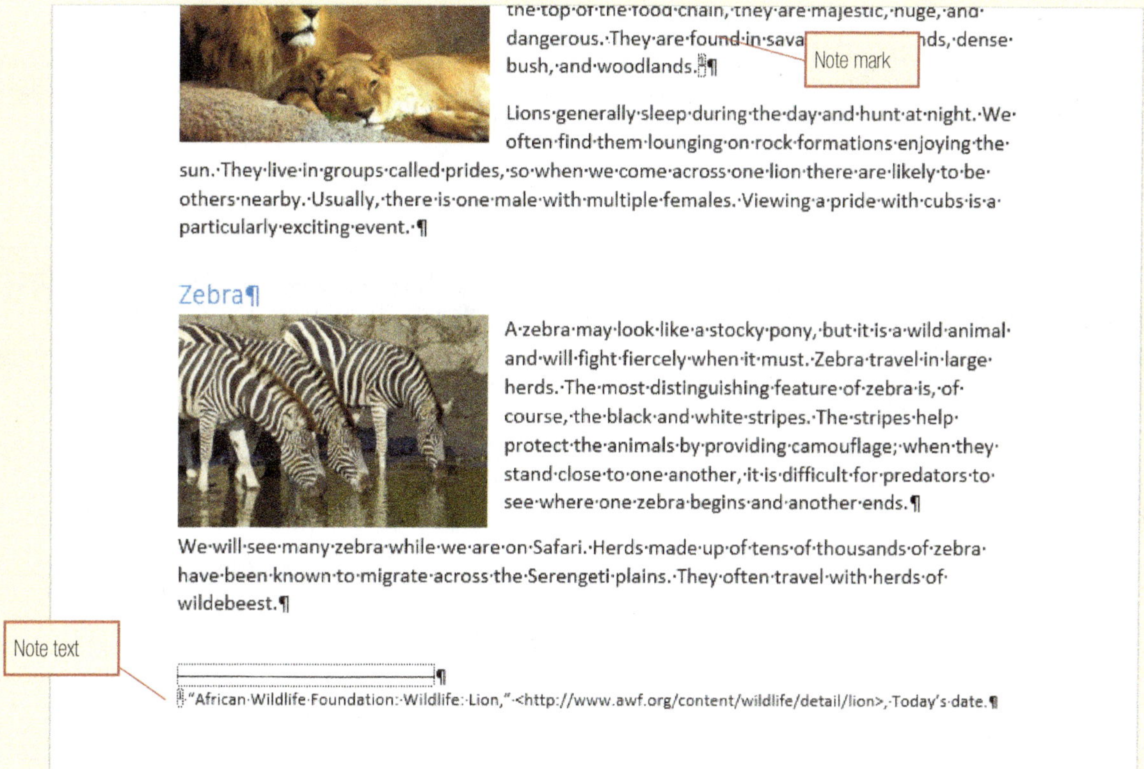
the·top·of·the·food·chain,·they·are·majestic,·huge,·and·dangerous.·They·are·found·in·sava... ...nds,·dense·bush,·and·woodlands.¹¶

Lions·generally·sleep·during·the·day·and·hunt·at·night.·We·often·find·them·lounging·on·rock·formations·enjoying·the·sun.·They·live·in·groups·called·prides,·so·when·we·come·across·one·lion·there·are·likely·to·be·others·nearby.·Usually,·there·is·one·male·with·multiple·females.·Viewing·a·pride·with·cubs·is·a·particularly·exciting·event.·¶

Zebra¶

A·zebra·may·look·like·a·stocky·pony,·but·it·is·a·wild·animal·and·will·fight·fiercely·when·it·must.·Zebra·travel·in·large·herds.·The·most·distinguishing·feature·of·zebra·is,·of·course,·the·black·and·white·stripes.·The·stripes·help·protect·the·animals·by·providing·camouflage;·when·they·stand·close·to·one·another,·it·is·difficult·for·predators·to·see·where·one·zebra·begins·and·another·ends.¶

We·will·see·many·zebra·while·we·are·on·Safari.·Herds·made·up·of·tens·of·thousands·of·zebra·have·been·known·to·migrate·across·the·Serengeti·plains.·They·often·travel·with·herds·of·wildebeest.¶

¹·"African·Wildlife·Foundation:·Wildlife:·Lion,"·<http://www.awf.org/content/wildlife/detail/lion>,·Today's·date.¶

Try It! Inserting Endnotes

1. In the **W22TryA_xx** file, position the insertion point at the end of the last sentence in the second paragraph under the heading *Zebra*.
2. Click REFERENCES > Insert Endnote.
3. Type **The movement of wildebeest, zebra, and other grazing animals across the plains is known as the Great Migration.**
4. Click the Footnotes dialog box launcher.
5. In the Format section of the Footnote and Endnote dialog box, click the Number format down arrow and select the symbol format that begins with an asterisk.
6. Click Apply. Note that the endnote mark changes in text as well as in the note.
7. Save the changes to **W22TryA_xx**, and leave it open to use in the next Try It.

Inserting Citations

- When you use words, pictures, video, sounds, or ideas that come from someone else in a paper or report, you must insert a **citation** to identify the source.
- A proper citation gives credit to the source, and provides the tools a reader needs to locate the source on his or her own.
- To create a citation, you select the citation style, then enter source information such as the type of source, the author, the publisher, and the publication date into a Create Source dialog box.
- The citation displays inline at the insertion point location; the format depends on the selected citation style.
- For example, in MLA (Modern Language Association) style, the author's last name displays in parentheses.
- The citations are stored with the document. They are also added to a master list of sources which is available for use with any Word document you create or edit.
- If you know you need a citation but do not yet have the information for it, you can insert a citation placeholder. You can then edit the placeholder to add the correct information when you have it.

Try It! Inserting Citations

1. In the **W22TryA_xx** file, position the insertion point after the third sentence in the second paragraph under the heading *Lions*.
2. On the REFERENCES tab, click the Style drop-down arrow Style: APA to display a list of available citation styles.
3. Click MLA Seventh Edition.
4. Click the Insert Citation button and click Add New Source to display the Create Source dialog box.
5. Verify that the Type of Source is Book.

   ✓ *If necessary, click the Type of Source down arrow and click Book.*
6. Fill in the information as follows:
   - Author: **George B. Schaller**
   - Title: **The Serengeti Lion: A Study of Predator-Prey Relations**
   - Year: **2009**
   - City: **Chicago**
   - Publisher: **The University of Chicago Press**
7. Click OK. Press the SPACEBAR if necessary to insert a space following the citation.

   ✓ *To insert a citation using the same information you have already inserted in the same document, click the Insert Citation button and click the source to insert.*

(continued)

Try It! Inserting Citations *(continued)*

8. Click at the end of the first paragraph under the *Zebra* heading.
9. Click the Insert Citatation button and click Add New Placeholder.
10. In the Placeholder Name dialog box, type **zebra** and click OK. A citation placeholder displays with that text inserted.
11. Save the changes to **W22TryA_xx**, and close it. Leave Word open to use in the next Try It.

Analyzing Citations

- Citations can help you ensure that the material you are using comes from an accurate and reliable source.
- If you do not cite your sources, you are guilty of **plagiarism**.
- You should insert a citation when you quote someone else, summarize or paraphrase another's work, use an idea that has been expressed by someone else, and when you make reference to someone else's work.
- When you reference information that is considered **common knowledge**, you do not have to include a citation; however, the definition of common knowledge varies. It is better to be safe and cite the source.
- Sometimes, a citation is not enough to ensure that you are in compliance with the law. Artistic creations such as music, text, and artwork—both printed and electronic—are protected by **copyright**.
- You must have permission from the copyright holder in order to use the work.
- Part of copyright law referred to as the **fair use doctrine** allows you to use a limited amount of copyrighted material without permission, as long as the purpose is not to make money from the material. For example, you can quote a few lines of a song or a passage from a book.

Creating a Reference Page

- Use Word's Bibliography feature to automatically create a reference page or **bibliography** by compiling a list of all citations in the document.
- Commands for creating a reference page are on the REFERENCES tab in the Citations & Bibliography group.
- A reference page may also be called a Works Cited page.
- The page is inserted as a content control and formatted in the selected citation style.
- Word comes with built-in designs for bibliography, references, and works cited, or you can simply insert the bibliography as a list.
- If you add or edit sources, you can update the reference page.

Try It! Creating a Reference Page

1. In Word, open **W22TryB** from the data files for this lesson.
2. Save the file as **W22TryB_xx** in the location where your teacher instructs you to store the files for this lesson.
3. Press CTRL + END to move the insertion point to the end of the document.
4. Press CTRL + ENTER to insert a hard page break.
5. On the REFERENCES tab, click the Bibliography button to display a gallery of available designs.
6. Click the Works Cited design. Word inserts the bibliography at the insertion point location.

   ✓ *To update a bibliography if you add or edit citations, click in the list to select the content control, and then click Update Citations and Bibliography on the content control handle.*

7. Save the changes to **W22TryB_xx**, and leave it open for the next Try It.

Viewing a Document in Read Mode

- Read Mode allows you to see a document at expanded size with a clean, uncluttered interface that makes it easy to concentrate on the text. Read Mode has been designed to work well on a variety of devices, such as desktop monitors and tablets.
- By default, a document displays in Read Mode in two columns, each column showing a page.
- You can adjust column width to show three columns across the width of the screen or only a single column.
- You can also change the layout to show a single page at a time as it would appear in Print Layout view.
- You can change the page color from the default white to make reading easy no matter what the light conditions.
- You have access to only a few tools in Read Mode.
- You can display the Navigation pane, for instance, to search the document or navigate by headings or pages.
- You can also use the Find feature, or access the Bing search engine to search the Web.
- Images in the document may not appear at the same size as in Print Layout view, but you can use the object zoom feature to enlarge a graphic in Read Mode.
- Several other new Word 2013 features are useful in Read Mode as well as in Print Layout view.
  - Rest the insertion point on a heading to display the collapse arrow to its left. Clicking this arrow hides text and graphics in the section below the heading so you can keep track of how far you have read.
  - If you close a multipage document before you have finished working on it, and then reopen it, the Resume Reading prompt appears to ask you want to return to your previous position in the document.

Try It! Viewing a Document in Read Mode

1. In the W22TryB_xx file, with the insertion point anywhere in page 3, click the Read Mode button on the status bar to change to Read Mode.
2. Click the previous page button twice to display the first page of the document.
3. On the VIEW tab, point to Column Width and then click Narrow.
4. On the VIEW tab, point to Column width and then click Default.
5. On the VIEW tab, point to Page Color and then click Sepia.
6. On the VIEW tab, point to Page Color and then click None.
7. Double-click the lion picture to display it in the center of the screen, and then click the object zoom button to zoom the image to full-page size.
8. Press ESC to turn off object zoom.
9. Move the insertion point to the *Lions* heading to display the collapse arrow to the left of the heading, and then click on the arrow to hide the text and graphics on lions.
10. Collapse the section under the *Zebra* heading.
11. Click the next page button to move to the last page of the document.
12. Click FILE > Save, and then click FILE > Close to close the document while leaving Word open.
13. Click FILE and then click W22TryB_xx in the Recent Documents list to reopen the document. The document opens in Read Mode, the view you were using when you closed it.
14. Move the mouse pointer, and after a moment, the Resume Reading icon displays just above the status bar toward the right side of the screen. Click the icon to move to the page you were viewing when you closed the document, page 5.

(continued)

Try It! Viewing a Document in Read Mode *(continued)*

15. Click the Print Layout button to return to Print Layout view.

16. Save the changes to **W22TryB_xx**, close it, and exit Word.

The section under the Lions heading has been collapsed

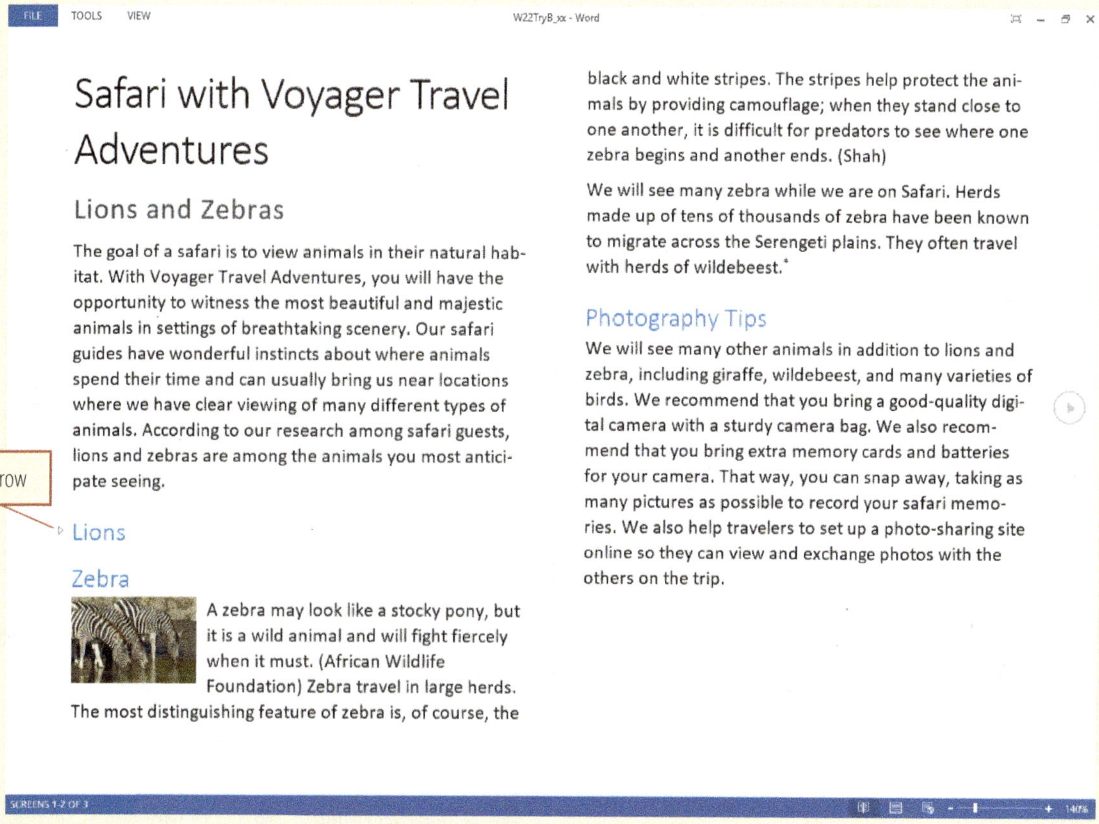

FILE TOOLS VIEW W22TryB_xx - Word

Safari with Voyager Travel Adventures

Lions and Zebras

The goal of a safari is to view animals in their natural habitat. With Voyager Travel Adventures, you will have the opportunity to witness the most beautiful and majestic animals in settings of breathtaking scenery. Our safari guides have wonderful instincts about where animals spend their time and can usually bring us near locations where we have clear viewing of many different types of animals. According to our research among safari guests, lions and zebras are among the animals you most anticipate seeing.

Lions

Zebra

A zebra may look like a stocky pony, but it is a wild animal and will fight fiercely when it must. (African Wildlife Foundation) Zebra travel in large herds. The most distinguishing feature of zebra is, of course, the black and white stripes. The stripes help protect the animals by providing camouflage; when they stand close to one another, it is difficult for predators to see where one zebra begins and another ends. (Shah)

We will see many zebra while we are on Safari. Herds made up of tens of thousands of zebra have been known to migrate across the Serengeti plains. They often travel with herds of wildebeest.

Photography Tips

We will see many other animals in addition to lions and zebra, including giraffe, wildebeest, and many varieties of birds. We recommend that you bring a good-quality digital camera with a sturdy camera bag. We also recommend that you bring extra memory cards and batteries for your camera. That way, you can snap away, taking as many pictures as possible to record your safari memories. We also help travelers to set up a photo-sharing site online so they can view and exchange photos with the others on the trip.

SCREENS 1-2 OF 3 140%

Expand arrow

Word 2013, Windows 8, Microsoft Corporation

Lesson 22—Practice

In this project, you will work to develop a report on exercise for the Michigan Avenue Athletic Club. You will use page breaks and pagination features to control the position of text at the top and bottom of pages. You will also insert footnotes and endnotes, add citations, and view the document in Read Mode.

DIRECTIONS

1. Start Word, if necessary, and open **W22Practice** from the data files for this lesson.
2. Save the file as **W22Practice_xx** in the location where your teacher instructs you to store the files for this lesson.
3. Double-click in the header and type your full name, press ENTER, and type today's date. Align the text flush right.
4. Position the insertion point at the beginning of the heading *The Impact on Your Health*.
5. Click **PAGE LAYOUT** > **Breaks** > **Page**.
6. Select the heading *Mental Health* and the paragraph after it.
7. On the **PAGE LAYOUT** tab, click the **Paragraph** group dialog box launcher to open the Paragraph dialog box.
8. Click the **Line and Page Breaks** tab.
9. Under Pagination, click to select the **Keep with next** check box and then **Keep lines together** check box, and then click **OK**.
10. Position the insertion point at the beginning of the heading *Safety*.
11. Click **PAGE LAYOUT** > **Breaks** > **Page**.
12. Position the insertion point at the end of the first paragraph of the introduction—to the right of the final punctuation.
13. Click **REFERENCES** > **Insert Footnote** AB¹.
14. Type **National Center for Chronic Disease Prevention and Health Promotion, "Physical Activity and Health: A Report of the Surgeon General," Executive Summary (11/17/99): page 12.**
15. Position the insertion point at the end of the second paragraph under the heading *The Impact on Your Health*.
16. Click **REFERENCES** > **Insert Endnote**.
17. Type **For more information, write to the President's Council on Physical Fitness and Sports, Room 738-H Humphrey Building, 200 Independence Avenue, SW, Washington, DC 20201-0004.**
18. Position the insertion point at the end of the second paragraph under the Introduction head.
19. Click **REFERENCES** > **Insert Citation** > **Add New Placeholder**.
20. Type **Aging** and click **OK**.
21. Position the insertion point at the end of the first sentence under the heading *The Impact on Your Health*.
22. Click **REFERENCES** > **Style** drop-down arrow Style: APA > **Chicago Sixteenth Edition**.
23. Click the **Insert Citation** button and click **Add New Source**.
24. Click the **Type of Source** down arrow and click **Document From Web site**.
25. Click to select the **Corporate Author** check box and then fill in the source information as follows:
    - Corporate Author: **National Institute on Aging**
    - Name of Web Page: **Exercise & Physical Activity: Your Everyday Guide from the National Institute on Aging**
    - Name of Web Site: **U.S. National Institutes of Health**
    - Year: **2011**
    - Month: **May**
    - Day: **28**
    - Year Accessed: **2014**
    - Month Accessed: **October**
    - Day Accessed: **11**
    - URL: **http://www.nia.nih.gov/health/publication/exercise-physical-activity-your-everyday-guide-national-institute-aging-0**
26. Click **OK**. Press SPACEBAR to insert a space after the citation.

27. Position the insertion point at the end of the paragraph under the heading *Mental Health*.
28. Click **REFERENCES** > **Insert Citation** > **Add New Source**.
29. Click the **Type of Source** down arrow and click **Book**.
30. Fill in the source information as follows:
    - Author: **G. Faulkner**
    - Title: **Exercise, Health and Mental Health: Emerging Relationships**
    - Year: **2006**
    - City: **Oxford**
    - Publisher: **Routledge**
31. Click **OK**.
32. Press CTRL + END to move the insertion point to the end of the document and then press CTRL + ENTER to insert a hard page break.
33. Click **REFERENCES** > **Bibliography**.
34. Click the **Works Cited** design to insert the bibliography.
35. Click **Read Mode** on the status bar to view the document in Read Mode.
36. Click the previous page button until the first page of the document displays.
37. Click **VIEW** > **Navigation Pane** and then click the *The Impact on Your Health* heading in the Navigation pane.
38. Collapse the *The Impact on Your Health* heading. Notice that the text under this heading and the subheadings under the heading are hidden.
39. Click Page Layout on the status bar.
40. Close the Navigation pane, and expand the *The Impact on Your Health* heading, if necessary.
41. Check and correct the spelling and grammar in the document, and then save the changes.
42. **With your teacher's permission,** print the document. The last page should look similar to Figure 22-1.
43. Close the document, saving changes, and exit Word.

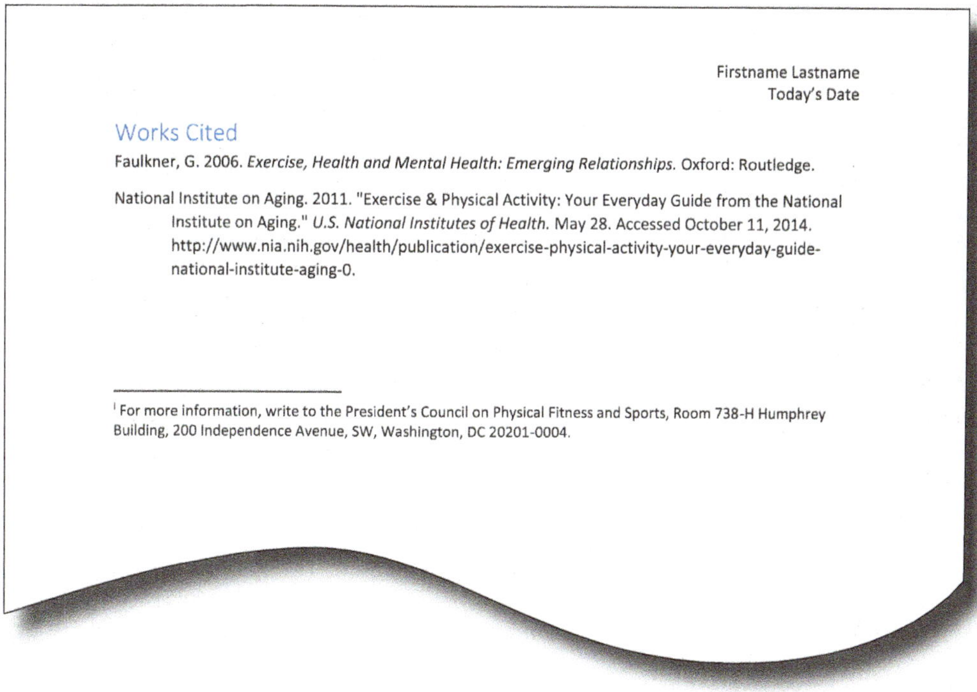
Firstname Lastname
Today's Date

Works Cited

Faulkner, G. 2006. *Exercise, Health and Mental Health: Emerging Relationships.* Oxford: Routledge.

National Institute on Aging. 2011. "Exercise & Physical Activity: Your Everyday Guide from the National Institute on Aging." *U.S. National Institutes of Health.* May 28. Accessed October 11, 2014. http://www.nia.nih.gov/health/publication/exercise-physical-activity-your-everyday-guide-national-institute-aging-0.

[1] For more information, write to the President's Council on Physical Fitness and Sports, Room 738-H Humphrey Building, 200 Independence Avenue, SW, Washington, DC 20201-0004.

Figure 22-1

Lesson 22—Apply

In this project, you continue to work on the exercise report for Michigan Avenue Athletic Club. You make further adjustments to page flow, insert sources, and add a reference page.

DIRECTIONS

1. Start Word, if necessary, and open **W22Apply** from the data files for this lesson.
2. Save the file as **W22Apply_xx** in the location where your teacher instructs you to store the files for this lesson.
3. Double-click in the header and type your full name, press ENTER, and type today's date. Align the text flush right.
4. Insert a page break before the heading *The Impact on Your Health*.
5. Use the Keep with next and Keep lines together pagination options to keep the heading *Mental Health* and the next paragraph together on the same page and to keep the bulleted list items and the preceding line together. (This will keep the items on the same page when viewed in Read Mode.)
6. Save changes and use FILE > Close to close the document while leaving Word open.
7. Reopen the document, and use the Resume Reading prompt at the right side of the screen to return to the page where you adjusted text flow for the bulleted list.
8. Position the insertion point after the paragraph under the heading *Weight Control* and insert the following footnote: **Faithe Wempen, *Food & Nutrition for You* (Upper Saddle River: Pearson Education, Inc., 2013): 94.**
9. Position the insertion point after the second paragraph under the heading *Disease Control*. Select the citation style **MLA Seventh Edition** and insert a citation using the following information:
   - Type of Source: **Book**
   - Author: **Faithe Wempen**
   - Title: **Food & Nutrition for You**
   - Year: **2013**
   - City: **Upper Saddle River**
   - Publisher: **Pearson Education, Inc.**
10. At the end of the second paragraph under the heading *Introduction*, select and delete the Aging placeholder, click the **Insert Citation** button, and click the **National Institute on Aging** source to insert it in the document.
11. Start a new page at the end of the document and create a Works Cited page.
12. Change the numbering format for the endnote to use capital letters.
13. View the document in Read Mode, changing the layout to default columns and Inverse page color.
14. Zoom in on one of the graphics in the document.
15. Change column layout to Narrow and page color to None, and then switch back to Print Layout view.
16. Check and correct the spelling and grammar in the document, and then save the changes.
17. **With your teacher's permission,** print the document. The first page should look similar to Figure 22-2 on the next page.
18. Close the document, saving changes, and exit Word.

Figure 22-2

Firstname Lastname
Today's Date

Exercise for Life

Introduction

The benefits of regular exercise cannot be overstated. Studies have shown that people who exercise regularly live longer, are healthier, and enjoy a better quality of life than those who do not exercise. It is now generally accepted knowledge that even moderate physical activity performed regularly improves the health and well-being of all individuals.[1]

Despite this knowledge, studies show that more than 60% of American adults are not regularly active and that an astonishing 25% of adults are not active at all. Therefore, the government recommends that schools and communities provide education to promote exercise to people of all ages. (National Institute on Aging)

This report has been prepared for Michigan Avenue Athletic Club in order to help spread the word on the importance of physical activity for the health of our members. It is meant as an introduction only. For more information about the health benefits of exercise, or about a particular type of exercise program, please contact any member of our staff. He or she will be happy to help you find the information you need.

[1] National Center for Chronic Disease Prevention and Health Promotion, "Physical Activity and Health: A Report of the Surgeon General," Executive Summary (11/17/99): page 12.

1

Lesson 23

Working with Newsletter Columns

➤ What You Will Learn

Understanding Desktop Publishing
Creating Newsletter Columns
Setting Column Width
Inserting a Column Break
Balancing Columns
Analyzing Page Layout and Design

WORDS TO KNOW

Balance
A basic principle of design that describes the visual weight of objects on a page, and the way the objects are arranged in relation to each other.

Column gutter
The space between column margins.

Commercial printer
A business that provides printing, copying, and publishing services.

Consistency
The use of repetition to create a uniform and predictable design or layout.

Software Skills Word's desktop publishing features let you design and publish eye-catching documents such as newsletters using your computer and printer. Designing a document with columns lets you present more information on a page, as well as create a visually interesting page. Newsletter-style columns are useful for creating documents such as newsletters, pamphlets, articles, or brochures.

What You Can Do

Understanding Desktop Publishing

- **Desktop publishing** refers to designing and producing printed documents using a desktop computer.
- Some common documents you can create with desktop publishing include reports, newsletters, brochures, booklets, manuals, and business cards.
- Most word-processing programs, such as Microsoft Word 2013, include desktop publishing features that are sufficient for producing many types of published documents.
- Some programs, such as Microsoft Publisher 2013, are designed exclusively for desktop publishing applications. These programs offer more sophisticated features for designing documents, including the ability to import text and graphics to create the final publication.
- Many documents can be **published** using the computer, printer, and software that you already have at home, work, or school.

- If you have complex publishing requirements such as color matching or binding, you may be able to design the document on your own equipment, but you may need to use a **commercial printer** to produce the final product.
- A third alternative for publishing a document is to create a file, then deliver it or e-mail it to a copy shop for reproduction.

Creating Newsletter Columns

- Use Word's Columns feature to divide a document into more than one **newsletter-style column**.
- There are five preset column styles available on the PAGE LAYOUT tab, in the Page Setup group, which you can apply to the entire document or the current section:
  - One is the default format. It has one column the width of the page from the left margin to the right margin.
  - Two creates two columns of equal width.
  - Three creates three columns of equal width.
  - Left creates a narrow column on the left and a wider column on the right.
  - Right creates a narrow column on the right and a wider column on the left.
- By dividing a document into sections using section breaks, you can combine different numbers of columns within a single document. For example, you can have a title or headline across the width of the page, and then divide the body text into multiple columns.

Try It! Creating Newsletter Columns

1. Start Word, and open **W23Try** from the data files for this lesson.
2. Save the file as **W23Try_xx** in the location where your teacher instructs you to store the files for this lesson.
3. Adjust the zoom so you can see the entire page on screen at once, and display nonprinting characters and the ruler.

   ✓ *Notice that there is a continuous section break between the title and the first heading.*
4. Move the insertion point anywhere in the second section of the document.
5. On the PAGE LAYOUT tab, click the Columns button.
6. Click Three.
7. Save the changes to **W23Try_xx**, and leave it open to use in the next Try It.

(continued)

Contrast
A basic design principle in which elements with opposite or complementary features are positioned to create visual interest.

Desktop publishing
The process of designing and printing a document using a computer and printer.

Newsletter-style columns
Columns in which text flows from the bottom of one column to the top of the next column.

Page layout
The way text, graphics, and space are organized on a document page.

Publish
Output a document so it can be distributed to readers.

Try It! Creating Newsletter Columns *(continued)*

Newsletter-style columns

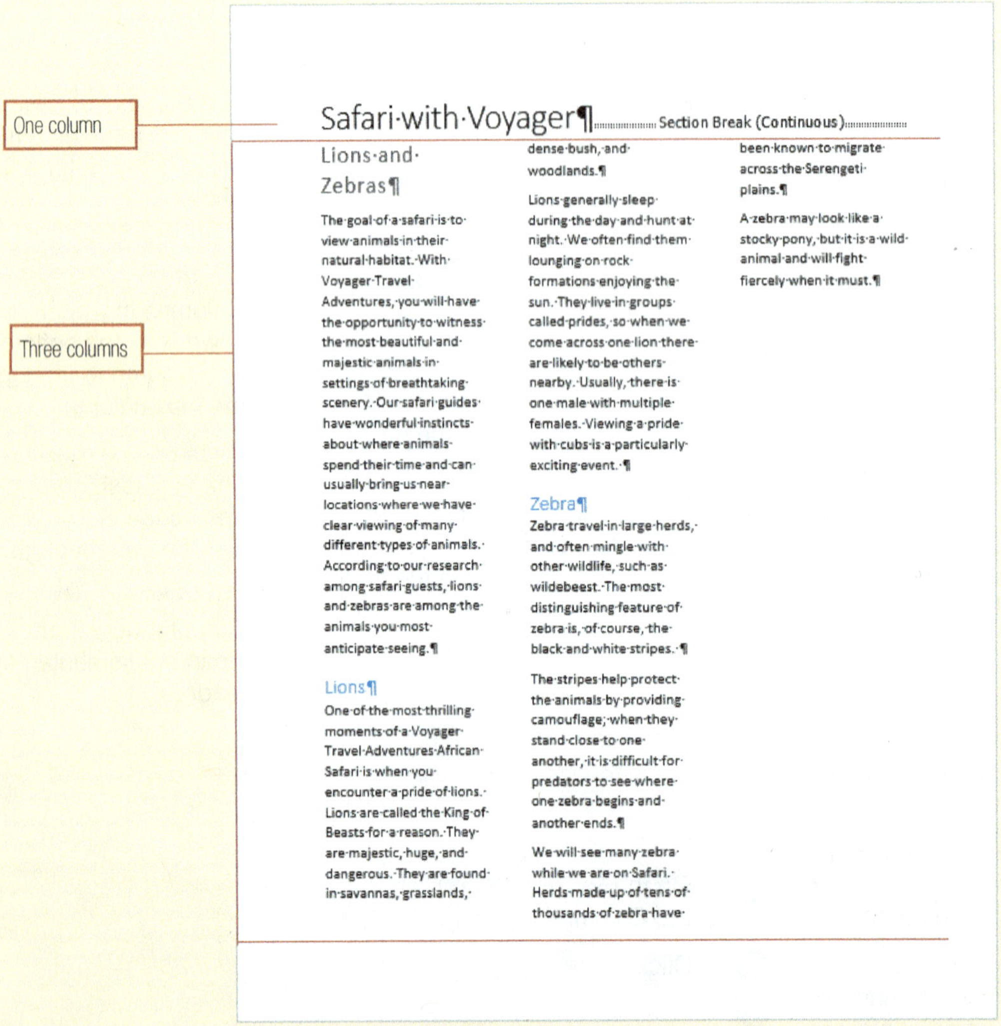

Safari with Voyager¶ Section Break (Continuous)

Lions and Zebras¶

The goal of a safari is to view animals in their natural habitat. With Voyager Travel Adventures, you will have the opportunity to witness the most beautiful and majestic animals in settings of breathtaking scenery. Our safari guides have wonderful instincts about where animals spend their time and can usually bring us near locations where we have clear viewing of many different types of animals. According to our research among safari guests, lions and zebras are among the animals you most anticipate seeing.¶

Lions¶

One of the most thrilling moments of a Voyager Travel Adventures African Safari is when you encounter a pride of lions. Lions are called the King of Beasts for a reason. They are majestic, huge, and dangerous. They are found in savannas, grasslands, dense bush, and woodlands.¶

Lions generally sleep during the day and hunt at night. We often find them lounging on rock formations enjoying the sun. They live in groups called prides, so when we come across one lion there are likely to be others nearby. Usually, there is one male with multiple females. Viewing a pride with cubs is a particularly exciting event. ¶

Zebra¶

Zebra travel in large herds, and often mingle with other wildlife, such as wildebeest. The most distinguishing feature of zebra is, of course, the black and white stripes. ¶

The stripes help protect the animals by providing camouflage; when they stand close to one another, it is difficult for predators to see where one zebra begins and another ends.¶

We will see many zebra while we are on Safari. Herds made up of tens of thousands of zebra have been known to migrate across the Serengeti plains.¶

A zebra may look like a stocky pony, but it is a wild animal and will fight fiercely when it must.¶

Word 2013, Windows 8, Microsoft Corporation

Setting Column Width

- Use the Columns dialog box to customize column formatting.
- You can create more than three columns, set a specific column width, and adjust the **column gutter** spacing.
- You can also select to display a line between columns.
- You can also drag the column margins on the ruler to adjust column widths and gutter spacing. Press and hold ALT as you drag to see the width and/or spacing measurement.

Try It! Setting Column Width

1. In the **W23Try_xx** file, verify that the insertion point is anywhere within the second section.
2. Click PAGE LAYOUT > Columns > More Columns to open the Columns dialog box.
3. Under Presets, click Left.
4. Under Width and spacing, use the increment arrows to change the width of column 1 to 2".
5. Use the increment arrows to change the Spacing between the columns to 1".
6. Click to select the Line between check box.
7. Click OK.
8. Save the changes to **W23Try_xx**, and leave it open to use in the next Try It.

Inserting a Column Break

- By default, text flows to the top of the next column when the current column is filled.
- Use a column break to force text to flow to the top of the next column before the current column is filled.
- Column breaks are useful for moving headings or headlines to the top of a column.

Try It! Inserting a Column Break

1. In the **W23Try_xx** file, click PAGE LAYOUT > Columns > Two to divide section 2 of the document into two columns of equal width.
2. Position the insertion point at the beginning of the heading *Zebra*.
3. Click PAGE LAYOUT > Breaks > Column to insert a column break.
4. Save the changes to **W23Try_xx**, and leave it open to use in the next Try It.

Insert a column break

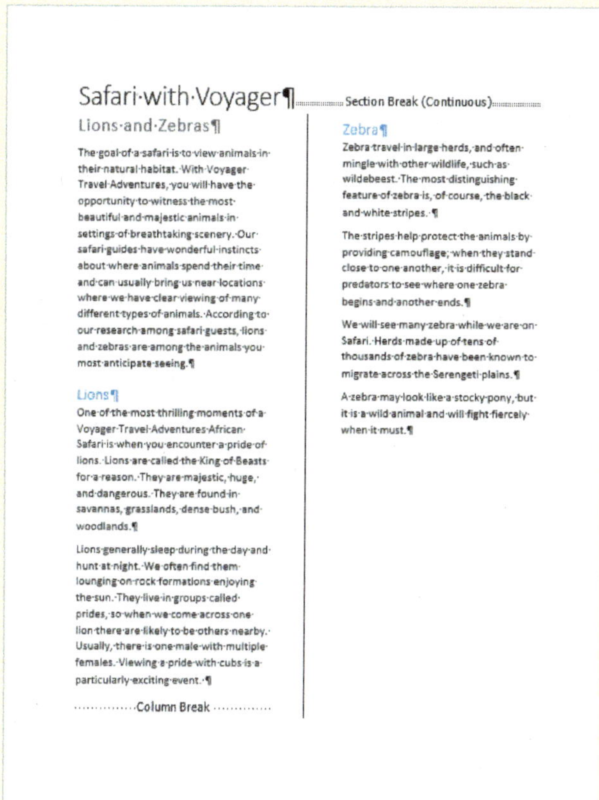
Safari with Voyager¶ ::::::::Section Break (Continuous)::::::::

Lions and Zebras¶

The goal of a safari is to view animals in their natural habitat. With Voyager Travel Adventures, you will have the opportunity to witness the most beautiful and majestic animals in settings of breathtaking scenery. Our safari guides have wonderful instincts about where animals spend their time and can usually bring us near locations where we have clear viewing of many different types of animals. According to our research among safari guests, lions and zebras are among the animals you most anticipate seeing.¶

Lions¶

One of the most thrilling moments of a Voyager Travel Adventures African Safari is when you encounter a pride of lions. Lions are called the King of Beasts for a reason. They are majestic, huge, and dangerous. They are found in savannas, grasslands, dense bush, and woodlands.¶

Lions generally sleep during the day and hunt at night. We often find them lounging on rock formations enjoying the sun. They live in groups called prides, so when we come across one lion there are likely to be others nearby. Usually, there is one male with multiple females. Viewing a pride with cubs is a particularly exciting event. ¶

..............Column Break..............

Zebra¶

Zebra travel in large herds, and often mingle with other wildlife, such as wildebeest. The most distinguishing feature of zebra is, of course, the black and white stripes. ¶

The stripes help protect the animals by providing camouflage; when they stand close to one another, it is difficult for predators to see where one zebra begins and another ends.¶

We will see many zebra while we are on Safari. Herds made up of tens of thousands of zebra have been known to migrate across the Serengeti plains.¶

A zebra may look like a stocky pony, but it is a wild animal and will fight fiercely when it must.¶

Word 2013, Windows 8, Microsoft Corporation

Balancing Columns

- If there is not enough text to fill the last column in a document, the columns will appear uneven.
- You can balance the amount of text in multiple columns on a page by inserting a continuous section break at the end of the last column on the page.
- Column breaks take precedence over balancing; if there is a column break, the columns will not balance as expected.

Try It! Balancing Columns

1. In the **W23Try_xx** file, position the insertion point on the column break at the bottom of the left column and press DEL to delete it.
2. Position the insertion point at the end of text in the right column.
3. Click PAGE LAYOUT > Breaks > Continuous.
4. Save the changes to **W23Try_xx**, close it, and exit Word.

Balanced columns

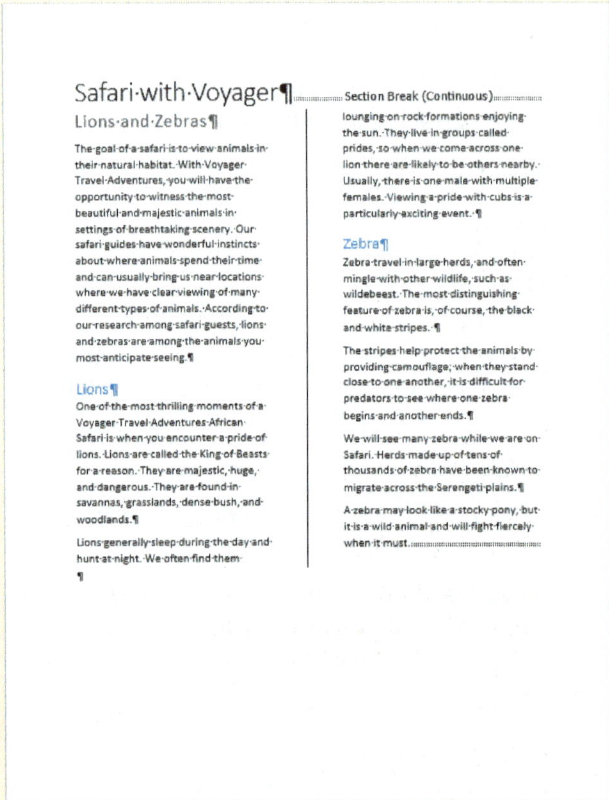

Safari with Voyager

Section Break (Continuous)

Lions and Zebras

The goal of a safari is to view animals in their natural habitat. With Voyager Travel Adventures, you will have the opportunity to witness the most beautiful and majestic animals in settings of breathtaking scenery. Our safari guides have wonderful instincts about where animals spend their time and can usually bring us near locations where we have clear viewing of many different types of animals. According to our research among safari guests, lions and zebras are among the animals you most anticipate seeing.

Lions

One of the most thrilling moments of a Voyager Travel Adventures African Safari is when you encounter a pride of lions. Lions are called the King of Beasts for a reason. They are majestic, huge, and dangerous. They are found in savannas, grasslands, dense bush, and woodlands.

Lions generally sleep during the day and hunt at night. We often find them lounging on rock formations enjoying the sun. They live in groups called prides, so when we come across one lion there are likely to be others nearby. Usually, there is one male with multiple females. Viewing a pride with cubs is a particularly exciting event.

Zebra

Zebra travel in large herds, and often mingle with other wildlife, such as wildebeest. The most distinguishing feature of zebra is, of course, the black and white stripes.

The stripes help protect the animals by providing camouflage; when they stand close to one another, it is difficult for predators to see where one zebra begins and another ends.

We will see many zebra while we are on Safari. Herds made up of tens of thousands of zebra have been known to migrate across the Serengeti plains.

A zebra may look like a stocky pony, but it is a wild animal and will fight fiercely when it must.

Word 2013, Windows 8, Microsoft Corporation

Analyzing Page Layout and Design

- The way you set up a page affects the way the reader sees and interprets the textual information.
- Effective **page layout** uses the basic principles of design, including **contrast**, **balance**, and **consistency** to highlight the text and capture the reader's attention.
- In addition to newsletter columns, you can use features such as themes, style sets, tables, borders, font formatting, lists, alignment, pictures, and spacing to create interesting and informative documents.

Lesson 23—Practice

As a communications assistant at Vocation Opportunities, Inc., a career counseling company, you are responsible for producing publications such as newsletters, articles, and brochures. In this project, you create and format an article about proper business attire.

DIRECTIONS

1. Start Word, if necessary, and open **W23Practice** from the data files for this lesson.
2. Save the file as **W23Practice_xx** in the location where your teacher instructs you to store the files for this lesson.
3. Click **DESIGN** > **Themes** > **Retrospect**.
4. Click **DESIGN**, click the **Document Formatting More** button, and click **Casual**.
5. Position the insertion point at the beginning of the first line of text, type **Dress for Success** and press ENTER.
6. Type the following paragraph:

   "What should I wear?" Whether you are heading out to a job interview, your first day at a new job, or your company has started a "casual Friday" policy, it is important to understand the type of clothing that you should wear. In this article we will discuss the three levels of business attire: traditional, general, and business casual. Selecting appropriate attire shows your supervisor and your co-workers that you are professional, responsible, and worthy of respect.
7. Press ENTER.
8. Apply the **Title** style to the title, *Dress for Success*.
9. Apply the **Strong** style to the headings *Traditional Business Attire*, *General Business Attire*, *Business Casual Attire*, *Specific Circumstances*, and *The Bottom Line*.
10. Position the insertion point at the beginning of the heading *Traditional Business Attire*.
11. Click **PAGE LAYOUT** > **Breaks** > **Continuous**.
12. Click **PAGE LAYOUT** > **Columns** > **Two**.
13. Position the insertion point at the beginning of the heading *Business Casual Attire*.
14. Click **PAGE LAYOUT** > **Breaks** > **Column**.
15. Click **PAGE LAYOUT** > **Columns** > **More Columns** to open the Columns dialog box.
16. Click to select the **Line between** check box, and then click **OK**.
17. Type your full name and today's date in the header.
18. Check and correct the spelling and grammar in the document, and then save the changes.
19. **With your teacher's permission,** print the document. It should look similar to Figure 23-1 on the next page.
20. Close the document, saving changes, and exit Word.

Figure 23-1

Firstname Lastname
Today's Date

Dress for Success

"What should I wear?" Whether you are heading out to a job interview, your first day at a new job, or your company has started a "casual Friday" policy, it is important to understand the type of clothing that you should wear. In this article we will discuss the three levels of business attire: traditional, general, and business casual. Selecting appropriate attire shows your supervisor and your co-workers that you are professional, responsible, and worthy of respect.

Traditional Business Attire

Traditional—or formal—business attire means a suit and dress shirt for both men and women. Suits should be conservative in color—black or blue is most appropriate.

Men should wear a properly tied necktie and dress shoes. Women should wear hosiery—stockings or pantyhose and closed-toe, closed-heeled shoes.

It is important to note the difference between "formal" business attire and formalwear. Formalwear refers to evening dress for a black-tie party, such as a gown for women and a tuxedo for men. No one expects you to wear a tuxedo to the office.

General Business Attire

General business attire is similar to traditional attire, but is not strictly limited to suits. A sport coat or a jacket may be worn with tailored slacks, but a tie is still called for. Women may wear a dress, or a skirt or slacks coordinated with an appropriate top.

Business Casual Attire

In some businesses, casual attire is appropriate, and even encouraged. Of course, business casual does not mean shorts and flip-flops. Rather, it means chinos and khakis, a collared shirt such as a polo, and sweaters. Men may leave off the tie, and casual shoes are appropriate.

Specific Circumstances

Some modern or contemporary offices develop their own dress code. When the environment is more relaxed, so are the expectations for what to wear. Clean jeans with no holes and fresh sneakers may be acceptable. If you wear a uniform be sure it fits properly, and that you keep it clean and neat.

The Bottom Line

You will be judged by your appearance. Keep yourself clean and well-groomed. Never show too much skin. Make sure your clothing fits properly. Tone down hair color, makeup, and piercings. When you are unsure, ask a co-worker or someone in the personnel department what is appropriate.

Lesson 23—Apply

You continue your work for Vocation Opportunities by formatting a publication about how to interview for a job.

DIRECTIONS

1. Start Word, if necessary, and open **W23Apply** from the data files for this lesson.
2. Save the file as **W23Apply_xx** in the location where your teacher instructs you to store the files for this lesson.
3. Apply the **Ion** theme.
4. Apply the **Basic (Simple)** style set.
5. Apply the **Title** style to the title, *Interviewing Skills for the Job-Seeker*.
6. Apply the **Strong** style to the headings *The Interview Process* and *Making the Most of a Job Interview*.
7. Insert a Continuous section break between the introductory paragraph and the heading *The Interview Process*.
8. Format the second section with the **Left** column preset.
9. Apply numbered list formatting to the five paragraphs under the heading *The Interview Process* in the narrow, left column.
10. Apply bulleted list formatting to the 11 items following the full paragraph under the heading *Making the Most of a Job Interview*.
11. Insert a column break to force the heading *Making the Most of a Job Interview* to the top of the right column.
12. Increase the column gutter spacing to **0.6"**.
13. Type your full name and today's date in the footer.
14. Check and correct the spelling and grammar in the document, and then save the changes.
15. **With your teacher's permission,** print the document.
16. Close the document, saving changes, and exit Word.
17. Now that you have completed several desktop publishing projects in Word, with your teacher's permission, research on the Internet to identify other technologies available for desktop publishing. Try to answer the following questions, and then write a report on your findings:
    a. What software applications are specifically designed to handle desktop publishing tasks?
    b. How much do they cost, and how easy are they to use?
    c. What applications are designed to create and edit images you might use in DTP projects?
    d. What options do you have for printing DTP projects besides using your desktop printer?

Lesson 24

Enhancing Paragraphs with Dropped Capitals, Borders, and Shading

➤ What You Will Learn

Inserting Dropped Capitals
Enhancing a Paragraph with Borders and Shading
Analyzing Time Management

WORDS TO KNOW

Dropped capital
An enlarged capital letter that drops below the first line of body text in the paragraph.

Goal-setting
A plan to obtain or achieve something.

Opacity
A measurement of the transparency of a color.

Prioritize
Rank in order of importance.

Responsibilities
Things people expect you to do or that you must accomplish.

Time management
Controlling and organizing a schedule so you can accomplish tasks and meet responsibilities.

Software Skills Dropped capital letters, borders, and shading can call attention to a single word, a line, a paragraph, or an entire page. They make a document visually appealing and interesting to the reader, so the reader will be more likely to take the time to read and remember the text.

What You Can Do

Inserting Dropped Capitals

- A **dropped capital** letter, called a *drop cap*, is used to call attention to an opening paragraph.
- Word 2013 comes with two preset drop cap styles that drop the character three lines.
  - The Dropped style places the drop cap within the paragraph text.
  - The In margin style places the drop cap in the margin to the left of the paragraph.
- You can select options in the Drop Cap dialog box to change the font of the drop cap, the number of lines that the character drops, and the distance the drop character is placed from the paragraph text.
- Selecting a font that is different and more decorative than the paragraph font can enhance the drop cap effect.
- Options for applying and formatting drop caps are in the Text group on the INSERT tab of the Ribbon.

Try It! Inserting Dropped Capitals

1. Start Word, and open **W24Try** from the data files for this lesson.
2. Save the file as **W24Try_xx** in the location where your teacher instructs you to store the files for this lesson.
3. Click in the first paragraph under the heading *Lions*.
4. Click INSERT > Drop Cap.
5. Click In margin.
6. Click in the first paragraph under the heading *Zebra*.
7. Click INSERT > Drop Cap > Dropped.

   ✓ *Click None in the Drop Cap gallery to remove a drop cap style from selected text.*

8. Save the changes to **W24Try_xx**, and leave it open to use in the next Try It.

Try It! Customizing a Dropped Capital

1. In the **W24Try_xx** file, make sure the insertion point is in the first paragraph under the heading *Zebra*.
2. Click INSERT > Drop Cap > Drop Cap Options to open the Drop Cap dialog box.
3. Click the Font down arrow and click Algerian.
4. Use the increment arrows to set the Lines to drop to 5.
5. Click OK.
6. Save the changes **W24Try_xx**, and leave it open to use in the next Try It.

Two styles of drop cap

Word 2013, Windows 8, Microsoft Corporation

Enhancing a Paragraph with Borders and Shading

- You can apply borders and/or shading to paragraphs.
- Paragraph borders and shading can be applied to a single paragraph or selected paragraphs.
- Paragraph border and shading options are similar to those for tables and pages.

✓ *Refer to Word, Lesson 10 for information on applying page borders; refer to Word, Lesson 17 for information on table borders and shading.*

- Border options include line style, line width (weight), and line color. You can also apply 3D or shadow effects.
- Shading options include solid color fills, or you can select a pattern style and color.
- The pattern styles include built-in geometric patterns as well as percentages of **opacity**.
  - The higher the percentage, the more opaque the color, with 100% being solid.
  - The lower the percentage, the more transparent the color, with 0% being no color.

Try It! Enhancing a Paragraph with Borders

1. In the W24Try_xx file, position the insertion point in the title *Safari with Voyager*.
2. Click DESIGN > Page Borders to open the Borders and Shading dialog box.
3. Click the Borders tab.
4. In the Style list box, scroll down and click the border that has a thin line above and below a thick middle line.
5. Click the Color drop-down arrow and under Theme Colors, click Orange, Accent 2.
6. If necessary, click the Width drop-down arrow and click 3 pt.
7. In the Setting list, click None, and then in the Preview area, click the Bottom border button.

   ✓ *The border buttons in the Preview area and in the Setting list are toggles; click once to select and again to clear.*
8. Click OK.
9. Save the changes W24Try_xx, and leave it open to use in the next Try It.

Try It! Enhancing a Paragraph with Shading

1. In the W24Try_xx file, position the insertion point in the title *Safari with Voyager*.
2. Click DESIGN > Page Borders to open the Borders and Shading dialog box.
3. Click the Shading tab.
4. Click the Fill drop-down arrow and under Theme Colors, click Gray-25%, Background 2.
5. Click OK.
6. Click the Page Borders button again, and click the Shading tab.
7. Under Patterns, click the Style drop-down arrow and click 10%.
8. Click the Color drop-down arrow and under Theme Colors, click Orange, Accent 2.
9. Click OK.
10. Save the changes to W24Try_xx, close it, and exit Word.

Analyzing Time Management

- **Time management** is a critical skill for succeeding at school and at work.
- Use time management techniques to organize and **prioritize** the tasks you must accomplish, and to make sure you meet your **responsibilities**.
- Time management techniques include analyzing exactly how you currently spend your time, making a list of tasks you must accomplish, ranking the tasks in order of importance, and creating a realistic schedule to complete each task.
- Combining **goal-setting** with time management is an effective way to make sure you get things done.
- You can practice time management in class and at home to ensure that you complete your work on time.

Lesson 24—Practice

The articles for Vocation Opportunities have been very well received. Your supervisor would like you to combine them to create a two-page newsletter. She is leaving for an off-site meeting in the morning and would like to take a draft of the newsletter with her to show off. You will need to use time management techniques to make sure you complete your assigned tasks on time. In this project, you begin setting up and formatting the newsletter.

DIRECTIONS

Time Management

1. Before beginning this project, make a time journal listing how you spend your time every day. The journal will help you analyze your current use of time.
2. Make a to-do list of tasks you must accomplish today. Include the projects for this lesson on your list.
3. Prioritize the tasks, putting this project at the top.
4. Create a schedule that clearly shows how you will spend the time you have available to complete the tasks on your to-do list.

Create the Newsletter

1. Start Word, if necessary, and save a default blank document as **W24Practice_xx** in the location where your teacher instructs you to store the files for this lesson.
2. Apply the **Banded** theme and the **Basic (Stylish)** style set.
3. Double-click in the header and type your full name and today's date.
4. On the first line of the document, type **Opportunity Knocks**. Format it with the **Title** style.
5. Press ENTER and type **A Publication of Vocation Opportunities, Inc.** Format it with the **Heading 2** style and center it horizontally on the line.
6. Press ENTER. Change the font size to 12 points, set the paragraph spacing before to 12 points, and type the following paragraph: **Welcome to the first edition of Opportunity Knocks, a monthly newsletter published by Vocation Opportunities, Inc. Our goal with this newsletter is to provide information that will help you achieve your career goals. Content will include articles, tips, and interviews with industry insiders. We hope you find it useful and entertaining!**
7. Press ENTER.
8. Click in the paragraph you typed in step 6.
9. Click **INSERT** > **Drop Cap** > **Dropped**. Justify the paragraph text.
10. Select the second line in the document—*A Publication of Vocation Opportunities, Inc.*
11. Click **DESIGN** > **Page Borders**.
12. Click the **Borders** tab.
13. In the Style list, click the single solid line border.
14. Click the **Color** drop-down arrow and, under Theme Colors, click **Gold, Accent 1**.
15. Click the **Width** drop-down arrow and click **2¼ pt**.
16. In the preview area, click to toggle on the **Top border** button and the **Bottom border** button.

17. Click the **Shading** tab in the Borders and Shading dialog box.
18. Click the **Fill** drop-down arrow and under Theme Colors, click **White, Background 2**.
19. Click **OK**.
20. Check and correct the spelling and grammar in the document, and then save the changes.
21. **With your teacher's permission,** print the document. It should look similar to Figure 24-1.
22. Close the document, saving changes, and exit Word.

Figure 24-1

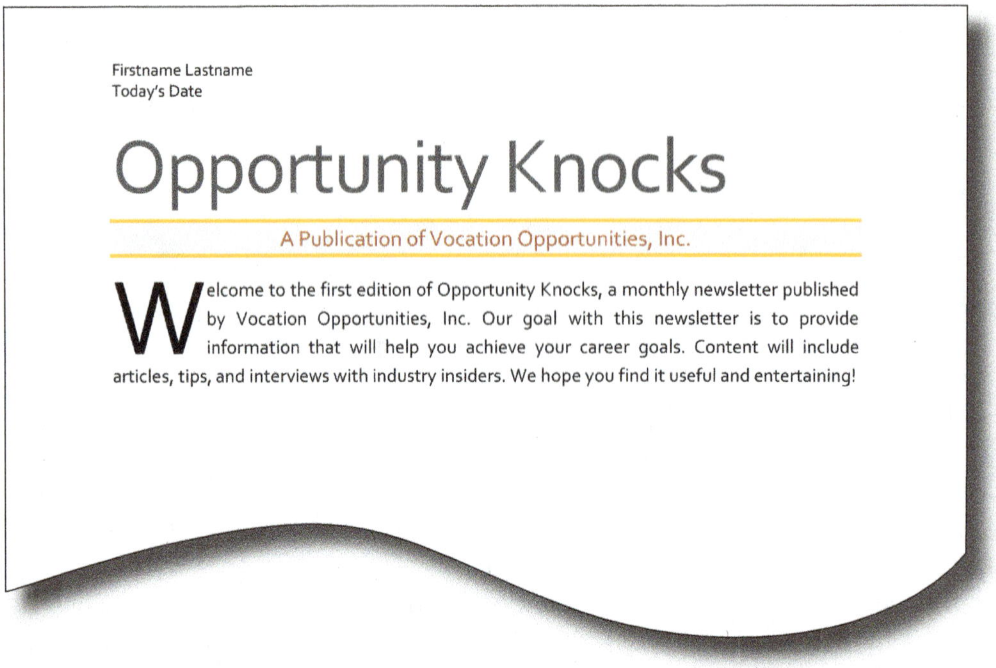
Firstname Lastname
Today's Date

Opportunity Knocks

A Publication of Vocation Opportunities, Inc.

Welcome to the first edition of Opportunity Knocks, a monthly newsletter published by Vocation Opportunities, Inc. Our goal with this newsletter is to provide information that will help you achieve your career goals. Content will include articles, tips, and interviews with industry insiders. We hope you find it useful and entertaining!

Lesson 24—Apply

In this project, you continue to work on the newsletter for Vocation Opportunities, Inc. You format the newsletter with columns and add shading and borders to emphasize various parts of the newsletter.

DIRECTIONS

1. Start Word, if necessary, and open **W24Apply** from the data files for this lesson.
2. Save the file as **W24Apply_xx** in the location where your teacher instructs you to store the files for this lesson.
3. Type your full name and today's date in the header.
4. Insert page numbers flush right in the footer.
5. Insert continuous section breaks before the headings *Dress for Success*, *Interviewing Skills for the Job-Seeker*, *The Interview Process*, and *Time Management Tips*.
6. Apply two-column formatting to section 2 (*Dress for Success*) and apply Left column formatting to section 4 (*The Interview Process*).
7. Insert a column break in section 4 before the heading *Making the Most of a Job Interview*.
8. In the first paragraph under the heading *Dress for Success*, insert a drop cap using the Dropped style customized to drop 5 lines.
9. In the first paragraph under the heading *Interviewing Skills for the Job Seeker*, insert a drop cap using the default Dropped style.

10. Select the heading *The Bottom Line* and the paragraph following it and apply a single line, **1½ pt., Orange, Accent 2 Shadow** border and an **Ice Blue, Background 2** fill.
11. Select the heading *Time Management Tips*, the paragraph, and the four numbered items following it and apply a single line, **Olive Green, Text 2, 2¼ pt. Box** border on all sides, and a **20% Tan, Accent 5** color pattern.
12. Check and correct the spelling and grammar in the document, and then save the changes.
13. **With your teacher's permission,** print the document. (Use two-sided printed if available.) It should look similar to Figure 24-2.
14. Close the document, saving changes, and exit Word.

Figure 24-2

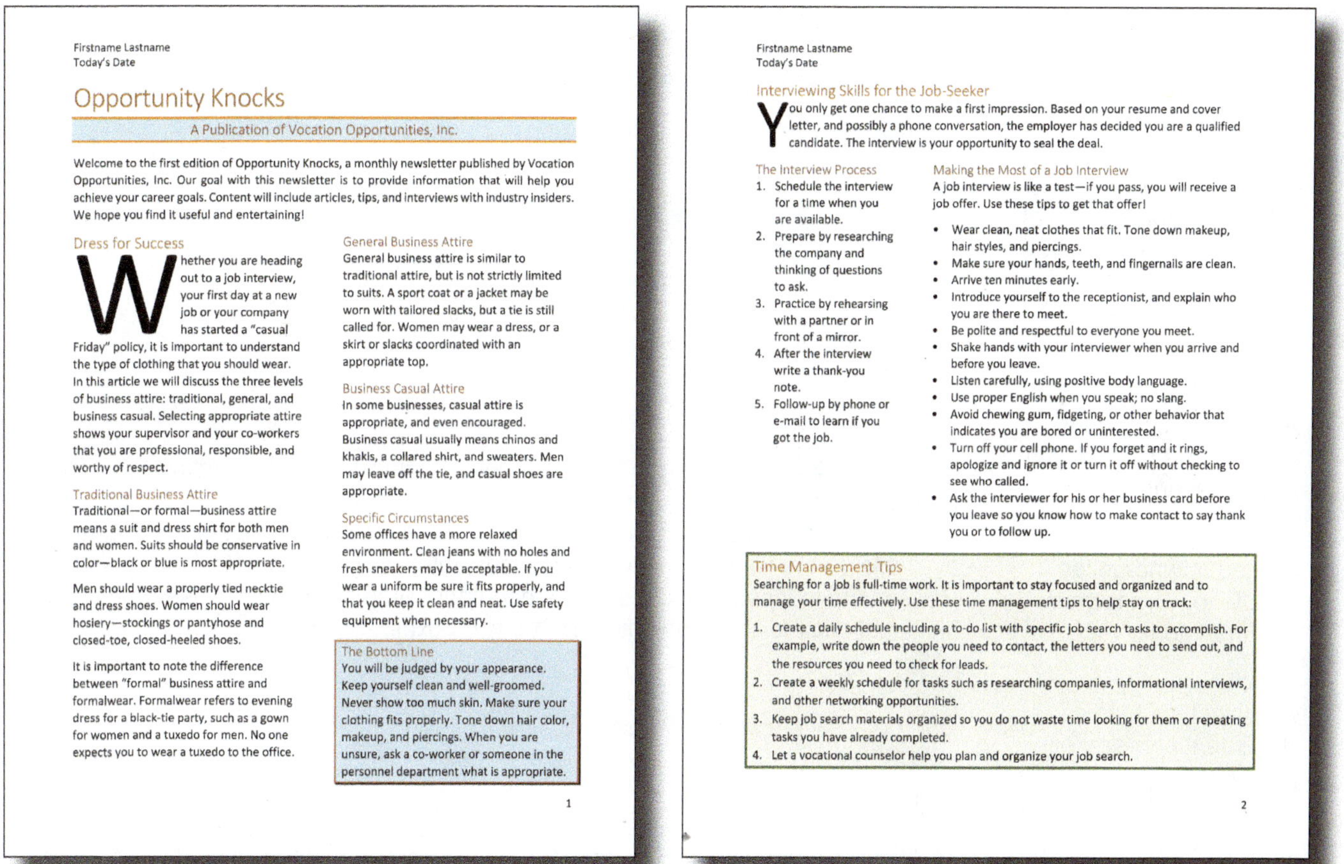
Firstname Lastname
Today's Date

Opportunity Knocks

A Publication of Vocation Opportunities, Inc.

Welcome to the first edition of Opportunity Knocks, a monthly newsletter published by Vocation Opportunities, Inc. Our goal with this newsletter is to provide information that will help you achieve your career goals. Content will include articles, tips, and interviews with industry insiders. We hope you find it useful and entertaining!

Dress for Success

Whether you are heading out to a job interview, your first day at a new job or your company has started a "casual Friday" policy, it is important to understand the type of clothing that you should wear. In this article we will discuss the three levels of business attire: traditional, general, and business casual. Selecting appropriate attire shows your supervisor and your co-workers that you are professional, responsible, and worthy of respect.

Traditional Business Attire

Traditional—or formal—business attire means a suit and dress shirt for both men and women. Suits should be conservative in color—black or blue is most appropriate.

Men should wear a properly tied necktie and dress shoes. Women should wear hosiery—stockings or pantyhose and closed-toe, closed-heeled shoes.

It is important to note the difference between "formal" business attire and formalwear. Formalwear refers to evening dress for a black-tie party, such as a gown for women and a tuxedo for men. No one expects you to wear a tuxedo to the office.

General Business Attire

General business attire is similar to traditional attire, but is not strictly limited to suits. A sport coat or a jacket may be worn with tailored slacks, but a tie is still called for. Women may wear a dress, or a skirt or slacks coordinated with an appropriate top.

Business Casual Attire

In some businesses, casual attire is appropriate, and even encouraged. Business casual usually means chinos and khakis, a collared shirt, and sweaters. Men may leave off the tie, and casual shoes are appropriate.

Specific Circumstances

Some offices have a more relaxed environment. Clean jeans with no holes and fresh sneakers may be acceptable. If you wear a uniform be sure it fits properly, and that you keep it clean and neat. Use safety equipment when necessary.

The Bottom Line

You will be judged by your appearance. Keep yourself clean and well-groomed. Never show too much skin. Make sure your clothing fits properly. Tone down hair color, makeup, and piercings. When you are unsure, ask a co-worker or someone in the personnel department what is appropriate.

1

Firstname Lastname
Today's Date

Interviewing Skills for the Job-Seeker

You only get one chance to make a first impression. Based on your resume and cover letter, and possibly a phone conversation, the employer has decided you are a qualified candidate. The interview is your opportunity to seal the deal.

The Interview Process

1. Schedule the interview for a time when you are available.
2. Prepare by researching the company and thinking of questions to ask.
3. Practice by rehearsing with a partner or in front of a mirror.
4. After the interview write a thank-you note.
5. Follow-up by phone or e-mail to learn if you got the job.

Making the Most of a Job Interview

A job interview is like a test—if you pass, you will receive a job offer. Use these tips to get that offer!

- Wear clean, neat clothes that fit. Tone down makeup, hair styles, and piercings.
- Make sure your hands, teeth, and fingernails are clean.
- Arrive ten minutes early.
- Introduce yourself to the receptionist, and explain who you are there to meet.
- Be polite and respectful to everyone you meet.
- Shake hands with your interviewer when you arrive and before you leave.
- Listen carefully, using positive body language.
- Use proper English when you speak; no slang.
- Avoid chewing gum, fidgeting, or other behavior that indicates you are bored or uninterested.
- Turn off your cell phone. If you forget and it rings, apologize and ignore it or turn it off without checking to see who called.
- Ask the interviewer for his or her business card before you leave so you know how to make contact to say thank you or to follow up.

Time Management Tips

Searching for a job is full-time work. It is important to stay focused and organized and to manage your time effectively. Use these time management tips to help stay on track:

1. Create a daily schedule including a to-do list with specific job search tasks to accomplish. For example, write down the people you need to contact, the letters you need to send out, and the resources you need to check for leads.
2. Create a weekly schedule for tasks such as researching companies, informational interviews, and other networking opportunities.
3. Keep job search materials organized so you do not waste time looking for them or repeating tasks you have already completed.
4. Let a vocational counselor help you plan and organize your job search.

2

Word 2013, Windows 8, Microsoft Corporation

Lesson 25

Using Format Painter, Highlights, Symbols, and Quick Parts

WORDS TO KNOW

Building block
A feature of Microsoft Office 2013 that lets you insert reusable pieces of content such as headers, footers, or tables created from saved text and graphics.

Conflict
A disagreement between two or more people who have different ideas.

Leader
Someone who unites people to work toward common goals.

Quick Part
An object such as a document property or field you can insert from a gallery.

Symbol
Shapes, mathematical and scientific notations, currency signs, and other visual elements you can insert in documents by using the Symbol dialog box.

Team
A group of two or more people who work together to achieve a common goal.

➤ What You Will Learn

Copying Formatting
Highlighting Text
Inserting Symbols
Inserting Quick Parts
Working with Building Blocks
Analyzing Teamwork

Software Skills Use the Format Painter to quickly copy formatting from one location to another. You can highlight text to change the color around the text without changing the font color. Use symbols to supplement the standard characters available on the keyboard and to add visual interest to documents. Use Word's Quick Parts menu to insert objects such as document properties and fields and building block galleries to insert objects such as text boxes.

What You Can Do

Copying Formatting

- Use the Format Painter to copy formatting from existing formatted text to another part of the document.
- You can copy formatting one time, or leave the Format Painter active so you can copy the same formatting to multiple locations.
- The Format Painter button is in the Clipboard group on the HOME tab of the Ribbon.

Try It! Copying Formatting

1. Start Word and open **W25Try** from the data files for this lesson.
2. Save the file as **W25Try_xx** in the location where your teacher instructs you to store the files for this lesson.
3. Click in the heading *Lions*.
4. Click HOME > Format Painter.

   ✓ *The mouse pointer changes to the Painter pointer.*
5. Click the heading *Zebra* at the top of the right column.
6. Click in the paragraph under the heading *Lions*, then double-click the Format Painter button.
7. Drag over the first paragraph under the heading *Zebra*.
8. Select the remaining paragraphs under the heading *Zebra*.
9. Click the Format Painter button to turn the feature off.
10. Save the changes to **W25Try_xx**, and leave it open to use in the next Try It.

Highlighting Text

- Highlighting calls attention to text by applying a color background.
- You can highlight text as a decorative or visual effect, but Word's Highlighter feature is commonly used like a highlighter pen on paper to mark text that requires attention.
- The Text Highlight Color button is in the Font group on the HOME tab of the Ribbon.
- Click the button to apply the current color displayed on the button, or click the drop-down arrow to select a different color from the Text Highlight Color palette.

Try It! Highlighting Text

1. In the **W25Try_xx** file, select the text *sleep at night and hunt during the day* in the first sentence of the second paragraph under the heading *Lions*.
2. Click HOME > Text Highlight Color.
3. In the last sentence of the first paragraph under the heading *Zebra*, select the text *the red and white stripes*.
4. Click HOME > Text Highlight Color drop-down arrow and click Pink on the color palette.
5. Select the text *and white stripes* again.
6. Click the Text Highlight Color drop-down arrow again and click No Color.
7. Click the Text Highlight Color drop-down arrow and click Bright Green on the color palette.

   ✓ *The mouse pointer changes to the Highlight Text pointer.*
8. Drag across the last sentence in the second paragraph under the heading *Lions*: *Viewing a pride with cubs is a particularly exciting event.*
9. Click the Text Highlight Color button to turn the feature off.
10. Save the changes to **W25Try_xx**, and leave it open to use in the next Try It.

Inserting Symbols

- **Symbols** are characters that cannot be typed from the keyboard, such as hearts, stars, and other shapes, as well as foreign alphabet characters.
- Symbols can be selected, edited, and formatted in a document just like regular text characters.
- Several symbol fonts come with Microsoft Office 2013 and others are available online for download.
- Many regular fonts also include some symbol characters.
- You can also insert special characters such as paragraph marks and ellipses.
- You can select from a gallery of common and recently used symbols by clicking the Symbol button on the INSERT tab, or you can select from all available symbols in the Symbol dialog box.
- Some symbols have number codes you can use for identification, and some have shortcut keys you can use to insert the symbol into a document.
- When you insert symbols, the default font formatting is applied to the character. You can change the font size, style, and effects just as you can for regular text characters.

Try It! Inserting Symbols

1. In the **W25Try_xx** file, position the insertion point on the blank line between the first paragraph and the section break.
2. Click INSERT > Symbol Ω > More Symbols to open the Symbol dialog box.

   ✓ *If the symbol you want displays in the Symbols gallery, click it to insert it in the document.*
3. Click the Font drop-down arrow and click Wingdings.
4. Click the flower symbol in the sixth row—Wingdings 123—and then click Insert. The dialog box stays open.
5. Click the flower symbol to the right—Wingdings 124—and click Insert.
6. Click Close to close the dialog box.
7. Save the changes to **W25Try_xx**, and leave it open to use in the next Try It.

Try It! Inserting a Special Character

1. In the **W25Try_xx** file, position the insertion point after the word *Safari* in the first sentence of the first paragraph under the heading *Lions*.
2. Click INSERT > Symbol Ω > More Symbols to open the Symbol dialog box.
3. Click the Special Characters tab.
4. Click the Registered symbol and then click Insert.
5. Click Close to close the dialog box.
6. Save the changes to **W25Try_xx**, and leave it open to use in the next Try It.

Special Characters tab in the Symbol dialog box

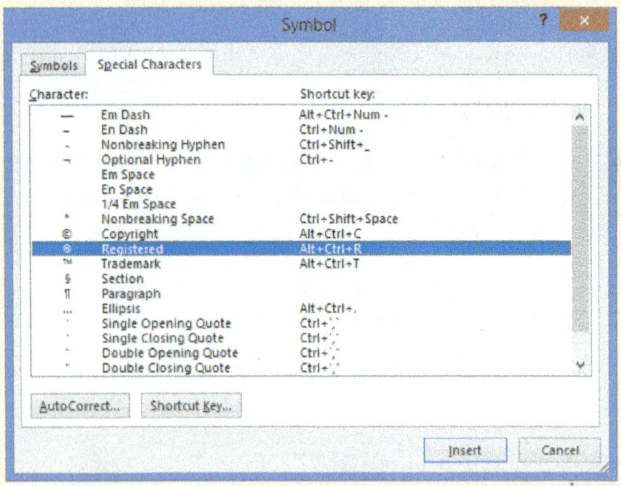

Word 2013, Windows 8, Microsoft Corporation

Inserting Quick Parts

- **Quick Parts** are elements you can select from Word's Quick Parts gallery to insert in a document.
- The Quick Parts gallery allows you to insert three types of Quick Parts:
  - AutoText: AutoText is a word or phrase you save to the AutoText gallery so that you can quickly insert it anywhere in any document. You might save your name, for example, so that you can insert it in the header of any document.
  - Document Property: The list of document properties you can insert are the same as those you find on the Info tab in Backstage view.
  - Field: A field is a placeholder used to insert information that changes, such as the date, the time, a page number, or the results of a calculation. Selecting this option opens the Field dialog box, where you can choose from a wide variety of fields to insert and customize.

Try It! Inserting Quick Parts

1. In the W25Try_xx file, double-click in the footer area to open the footer.
2. Click HOME > Center to apply center alignment.
3. Type **Published on** and press SPACEBAR.
4. On the INSERT tab, in the Text group, click Quick Parts.
5. Click Document Property, and then click Publish Date. The Publish Date content control displays with a down arrow that allows you to select a date.
6. Click the down arrow and select Today.
7. Click outside the content control and press ENTER.
8. Type **By** and press SPACEBAR.
9. On the INSERT tab, in the Text group, click Quick Parts.
10. Click Field to open the Field dialog box, and then click Author in the Field names list. Click OK. The Author field displays your name.
11. Click the Close Header and Footer button to close the footer.
12. Save the changes to W25Try_xx, and leave it open for the next Try It.

Working with Building Blocks

- **Building blocks** make it easy to save content so you can insert it into any document at any time.
- Word 2013 comes with many built-in building blocks that display in galleries available using commands on the Ribbon.
- For example, there are building block galleries for bibliographies, cover pages, headers, footers, equations, page numbers, tables of contents, tables, text boxes, and watermarks.
- Click a building block in a gallery to insert it in a document, and then adjust formatting as necessary.
- You can create your own custom building blocks to reuse in any document.
- Select the text and/or graphics you want to save as a building block and then use the Create New Building Block dialog box to enter properties for the building block, such as a name and a description.
- The gallery property determines in which gallery the building block will display. For example, if you are creating a header building block, it should be stored in the Header gallery.
- When you exit Word after creating or modifying a building block, the program asks if you want to save the changes to the Building Blocks template.
- You use the Building Blocks Organizer dialog box to edit, insert, view, or delete a building block.
- By default, building blocks are listed by gallery. You can change the sort order by clicking a heading at the top of the list.
- Click a building block to view a preview on the right side of the Building Blocks Organizer dialog box, or to select it for editing, deletion, or to insert.

Try It! Working with Building Blocks

1. In the **W25Try_xx** file, click INSERT > Text Box > Banded Quote to insert a built-in text box building block.
2. With the text box selected, adjust the text box width to 3". Click in the color bar at the top of the quote and type **TRAVEL TIP**.
3. Select the color bar and apply the Intense Effect – Green, Accent 6 shape style.
4. Click the outside of the text box to select the entire object, and then click INSERT > Quick Parts > Save Selection to Quick Part Gallery.
5. In the Name box, type **Travel Tip**. Click the Gallery down arrow and select Text Boxes. Click the Category down arrow and select General. Click OK.
6. Delete the text box you customized, and then click INSERT > Text Box. Scroll down on the gallery to the bottom to locate your custom building block, and click to insert it.
7. Click INSERT > Quick Parts > Building Blocks Organizer.
8. Click the Name heading to sort the building blocks by name, and then scroll down to locate the Travel Tip building block.
9. Click the Travel Tip building block, click Delete, and then click Yes to remove it from the Organizer. Click Close.
10. Save the changes to **W25Try_xx**, close it, and exit Word.

Building Blocks Organizer

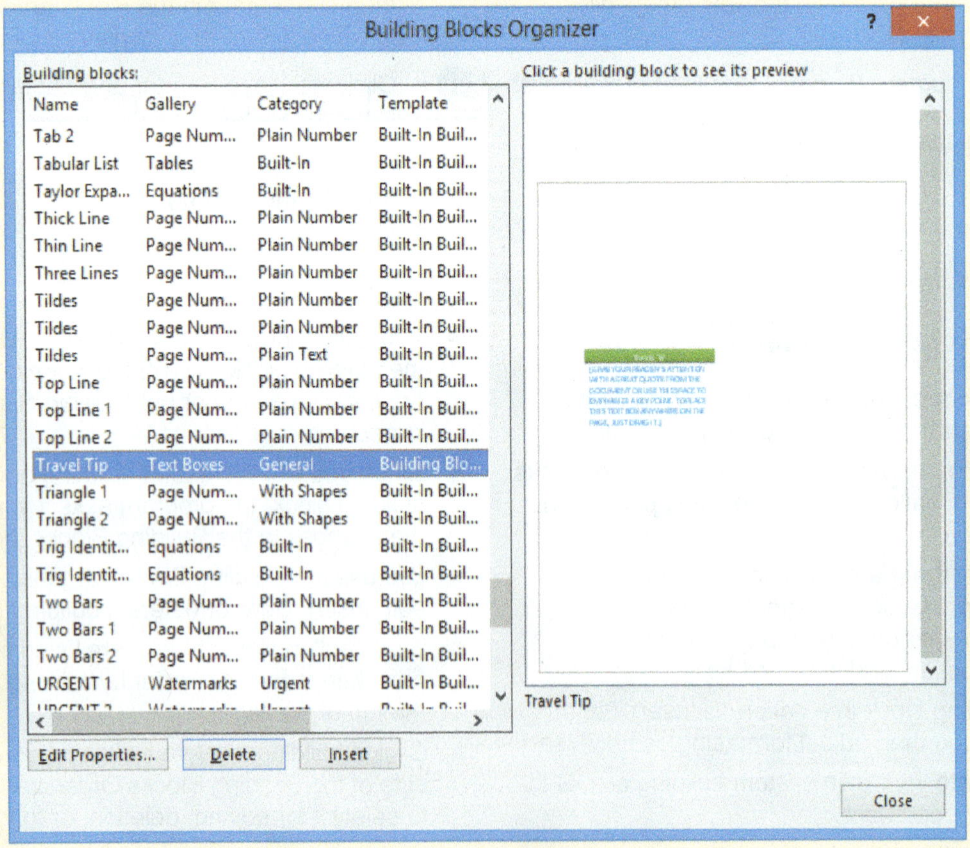

Word 2013, Windows 8, Microsoft Corporation

Analyzing Teamwork

- Being able to work as part of a **team** is an important skill for succeeding at school and at work.
- A successful team is made up of people who trust and respect one another. They work together to make decisions, solve problems, and achieve common goals.
- **Conflict** can interfere with the team's ability to achieve its goals. Effective communication is an important way to avoid or resolve conflict.
- Team members must be committed to the group's success, and willing to work hard to meet their responsibilities.
- Teams are more likely to succeed when the members are open-minded, cooperative, trustworthy, and friendly, and when they feel comfortable speaking out, listening, and compromising when necessary.
- Often, a team **leader** keeps the team on track and focused on achieving its goals. He or she organizes the team's activities, encourages communication, and motivates team members.

Lesson 25—Practice

You have been working as part of a team planning new winter tours at Voyager Travel Adventures. The team member responsible for writing press releases about the tours is having trouble completing his assignments, and the other team members are chipping in to help. In this project, you will use the Format Painter to copy formatting to complete the document. You will highlight text you think might be incorrect so another team member can check the facts. You will also insert a document property Quick Part and add symbols.

DIRECTIONS

1. Start Word, if necessary, and open **W25Practice** from the data files for this lesson.
2. Save the file as **W25Practice_xx** in the location where your teacher instructs you to store the files for this lesson.
3. Replace the sample text *Student's Name* with your own name.
4. Select Today's Date, and then click **INSERT** > **Quick Parts** > **Document Property** > **Publish Date**.
5. Click the down arrow on the Publish Date content control and click Today.
6. Click in the blue, bold text *Voyager Travel Adventures* in the first paragraph.
7. Click **HOME** > **Format Painter**.
8. Drag across the text *Voyager Travel Adventures* at the beginning of the last paragraph to copy the blue, bold formatting.
9. Click in the paragraph that begins with the text *While on board*.
10. On the **HOME** tab, in the **Clipboard** group, double-click **Format Painter**.
11. Drag across the first four indented paragraphs.
12. Drag across the last two lines of the document. Then click the Format Painter to turn it off.
13. Select the text *8-day/7-night*.
14. Click **HOME** > **Text Highlight Color** button to apply the default yellow highlight to the selection.

    ✓ *If yellow is not the color displayed on the button, click the drop-down arrow and click Yellow on the Text Highlight Color palette.*
15. Click the **Text Highlight Color** drop-down arrow and click **Bright Green** on the color palette.
16. Drag across the text *48-foot, fully-equipped catamaran*.
17. Drag across the word *spelunking*.
18. Drag across the year *1998*.
19. Click the **Text Highlight Color** button to turn the feature off.
20. Click to the left of the paragraph that begins *The 8-day/7-night*.
21. Click **INSERT** > **Symbol** > **More Symbols**.
22. In the Wingdings font, select symbol **70**, a hand with a finger pointing to the right. Click **Close**.

23. Insert the same symbol from the Symbol Gallery to the left of the next three paragraphs.
24. Check and correct the spelling and grammar in the document, and then save the changes.
25. **With your teacher's permission,** print the document.
26. Close the document, saving changes, and exit Word.

Lesson 25—Apply

In this project, you continue to work with your teammates to format a second press release. You will use the Format Painter, highlights, symbols, and Quick Parts to complete the document.

DIRECTIONS

1. Start Word, if necessary, and open **W25Apply** from the data files for this lesson.
2. Save the file as **W25Apply_xx** in the location where your teacher instructs you to store the files for this lesson.
3. In the blank paragraph at the top of the document, insert the Title document property from the Quick Parts gallery. Type the text **For Immediate Release**.
4. Replace the sample text *Student's Name* with your own name using the Author field that you access from the Quick Parts gallery. Replace *Today's Date* with the Publish Date document property Quick Part.
5. Display the Building Blocks Organizer, sort the building blocks by Gallery, and select and insert the Ion (Dark) built-in footer.
6. Copy the blue, bold formatting from the text *Voyager Travel Adventures* in the first paragraph to the text *Voyager Travel Adventures* in the last paragraph.
7. Copy the paragraph formatting from the first paragraph to the second, third, fourth, and fifth paragraphs. (Do not drag the Format Painter pointer over the fifth paragraph, or you will remove the formatting you applied in step 4.)
8. Insert two snowflake symbols (Wingding 84) to the left of the subtitle (*Winter in Yellowstone*) and two to the right of the subtitle.
9. Apply Blue font color from the Standard palette to the first snowflake, and then apply Bold font style.
10. Use the Format Painter to apply these formats to the remaining snowflake symbols.
11. Click just to the right of the word *everyone* in the last full paragraph, and insert an em dash from the Special Characters tab in the Symbol dialog box. Press DEL to remove the space before the word *from*.
12. Highlight the word *wasteland* in turquoise.
13. Highlight the text *5-day/6-night* and the year *1998* in pink.
14. Highlight in yellow the sentence, *This rugged adventure is for experienced winter campers only*.
15. Check and correct the spelling and grammar in the document, and then save the changes.
16. **With your teacher's permission,** print the document. It should look similar to Figure 25-1 on the next page.
17. Close the document, saving changes, and exit Word.

Figure 25-1

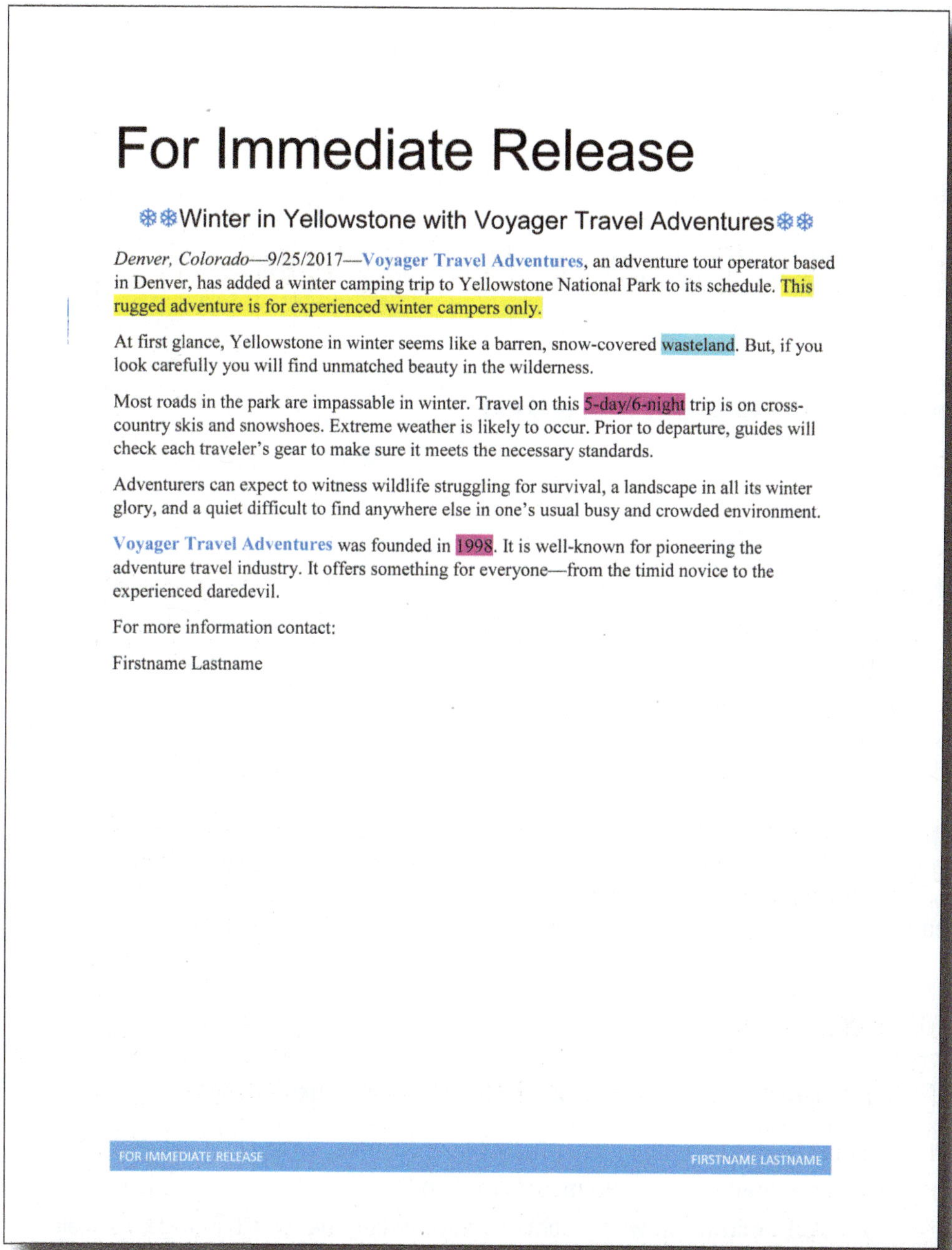

For Immediate Release

❄❄Winter in Yellowstone with Voyager Travel Adventures❄❄

Denver, Colorado—9/25/2017—**Voyager Travel Adventures**, an adventure tour operator based in Denver, has added a winter camping trip to Yellowstone National Park to its schedule. This rugged adventure is for experienced winter campers only.

At first glance, Yellowstone in winter seems like a barren, snow-covered wasteland. But, if you look carefully you will find unmatched beauty in the wilderness.

Most roads in the park are impassable in winter. Travel on this 5-day/6-night trip is on cross-country skis and snowshoes. Extreme weather is likely to occur. Prior to departure, guides will check each traveler's gear to make sure it meets the necessary standards.

Adventurers can expect to witness wildlife struggling for survival, a landscape in all its winter glory, and a quiet difficult to find anywhere else in one's usual busy and crowded environment.

Voyager Travel Adventures was founded in 1998. It is well-known for pioneering the adventure travel industry. It offers something for everyone—from the timid novice to the experienced daredevil.

For more information contact:

Firstname Lastname

FOR IMMEDIATE RELEASE FIRSTNAME LASTNAME

Lesson 26

Creating Letters and Labels with Mail Merge

➤ What You Will Learn

Software Skills Use Mail Merge to customize mass mailings. For example, you can store a document with standard text, such as a form letter, and then insert personalized names and addresses on each copy that you generate or print. You can also use Mail Merge to generate labels for sending the form letters.

WORDS TO KNOW

Address list
A simple data source file stored in Access file format, which includes the information needed for an address list, such as first name, last name, street, city, state, and so on.

Data source
The document containing the variable data that will be inserted during the merge.

Mail merge
A process that inserts variable information into a standardized document to produce a personalized or customized document.

Main document
The document containing the standardized text that will be printed on all documents.

Merge block
A set of merge fields stored as one unit. For example, the Address block contains all the name and address information.

What You Can Do

Understanding Mail Merge and the Mail Merge Process

- Use Mail Merge to create mass mailings, envelopes, e-mail messages, or labels.
- To create a **mail merge**, you must have two files:
  - A **main document**, which contains information that won't change, as well as **merge fields** and **merge blocks**, which act as placeholders for variable information. For example, you might have a form letter that has merge fields where the address and greeting should be.
  - A **data source** file, which contains variable information such as names and addresses. You can use many types of data source files for a merge, including an **address list**, an Outlook contact list, or an Access database.
- During the merge, Word generates a series of **merge documents** in which the variable information from the data source replaces the merge fields entered in the main document.

Figure 26-1

A main document and a merge document

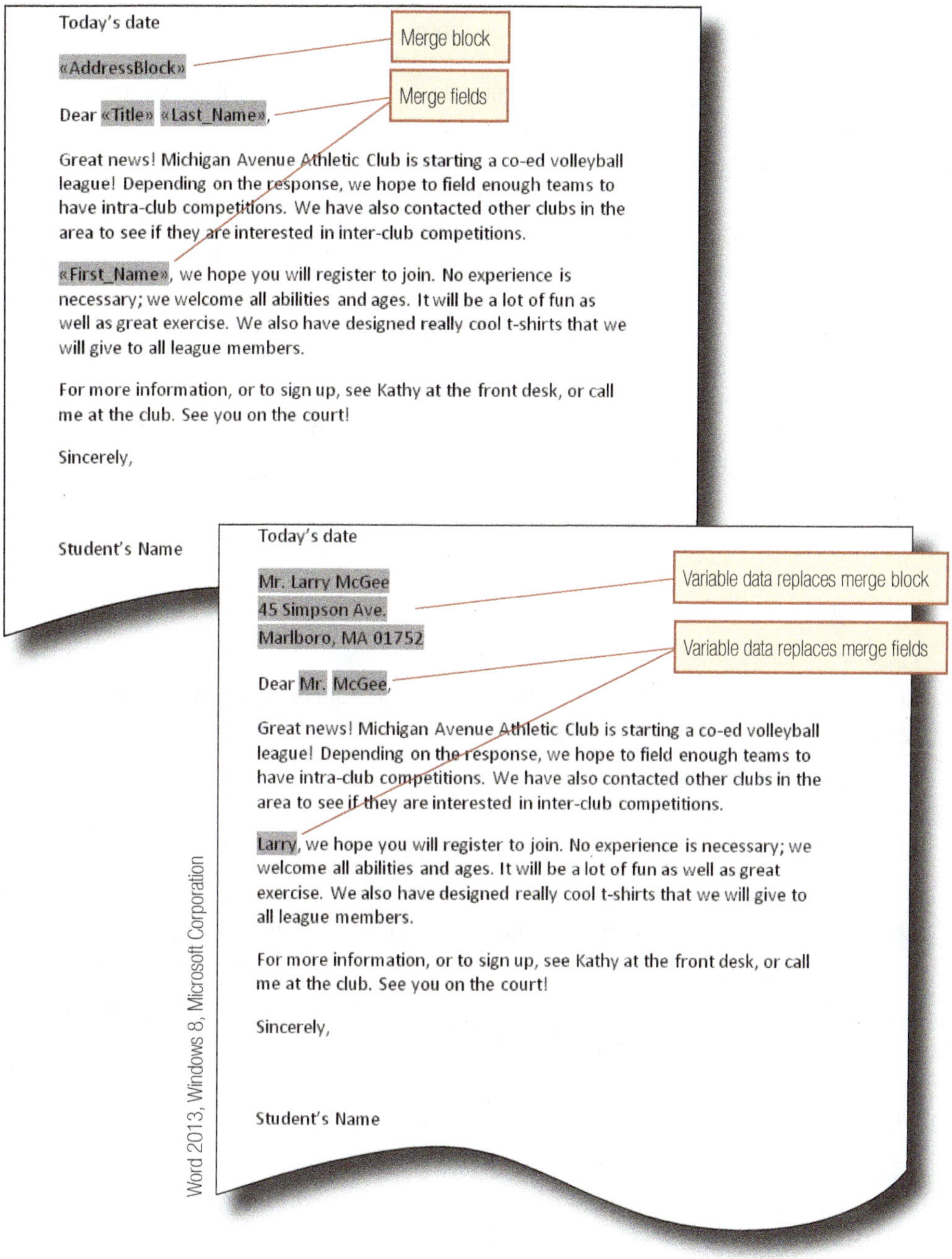

Merge document
The customized document resulting from a merge.

Merge field
A placeholder in the main document that marks where and what will be inserted from the data source document.

Recipient
The entity—a person or organization—who receives a mailing. The recipient's contact information is stored in the data source.

Record
A collection of variable data about one person or thing. In a form letter merge, for example, each record contains variable data for each person receiving the letter: first name, last name, address, city, state, and ZIP code.

- There are six steps involved in completing a merge:
  1. The first step is to select the type of main document you want to create. These types are shown in Table 26-1.
  2. The second step is to select a starting document. You may select to start from the current document, an existing document, or a new document based on a template.
  3. The third step is to select **recipients**. In this step, you locate or create the data source file, and then select the individual recipients to include in the merge.

     If you select to create a new list, Word prompts you through the steps for creating the data source file by entering the variable data for each recipient.
  4. The fourth step is to create the main document. In this step, you type and format the data you want included in each merge document, and you insert the merge fields or merge blocks where Word will insert the variable data.

     If the text is already typed in the document, you simply insert the merge fields and merge blocks in step 4.
  5. The fifth step is to preview the merge documents. In this step, you have the opportunity to see the merge documents before you print them. This lets you check for spelling, punctuation, and grammatical errors and make corrections.
  6. The final step is to complete the merge. You have the option of printing the merge documents, or saving them in a new file for later use.
- You may use the commands on the MAILINGS tab of the Ribbon to conduct a merge.
- Alternatively, the Mail Merge Wizard prompts you through the step-by-step process of conducting a merge.
- You may also use a combination of the two methods.

Table 26-1 Documents to Merge

Document Type	Used For
Letters	Letters or other regular Word documents such as reports, flyers, or memos
E-mail messages	Messages to send via e-mail
Envelopes	Personalized envelopes
Labels	Personalized labels
Directories	Lists such as rosters, catalogs, or telephone lists

Understanding Merge Fields

- You insert the merge fields or blocks in the main document at the location where you want the corresponding variable data to print.
- Word has a preset list of merge fields that correspond to variable information typically used in a mail merge, such as First Name, Last Name, and ZIP Code. These are used to create the address block that is generated when you insert the <<AddressBlock>> field.
- Each of those fields can also be inserted individually.
- There are also other blocks you can use. For example, the <<GreetingLine>> block inserts the word *Dear* followed by a code for the person's name.
- You must type all spaces and punctuation between merge fields. Merge blocks, however, include standard punctuation and spacing, such as a comma between the city and state in an address.
- By default, when you insert a merge field, you see the field name enclosed in merge field characters (<< >>). The field may be shaded, depending on your settings.

  ✓ *To change whether fields are highlighted, click MAILINGS > Highlight Merge Fields.*
- You may insert merge fields more than once in a document. For example, you can insert a name merge field in multiple locations in order to personalize a letter.

Try It! Performing a Mail Merge with the Mail Merge Wizard

1. Start Word, and open **W26TryA** from the data files for this lesson.
2. Save the document as **W26TryA_xx** in the location where your teacher instructs you to store the files for this lesson.
3. Click MAILINGS > Start Mail Merge > Step-by-Step Mail Merge Wizard. The Mail Merge task pane opens.
4. At the bottom of the task pane, click Next: Starting document.
5. Click Next: Select recipients.

   ✓ *In steps 3 and 4, the default selections are appropriate, so no changes are needed.*

6. Under Use an existing list in the task pane, click Browse. Navigate to the location where the data files for this lesson are stored, and click **W26TryB**.
7. Click Open. In the Mail Merge Recipients dialog box, click OK.
8. Click Next: Write your letter at the bottom of the task pane.
9. Click to place the insertion point on the second paragraph below the date.
10. In the task pane, click Address block. The Insert Address Block dialog box appears. Click OK.

The Mail Merge Recipients dialog box

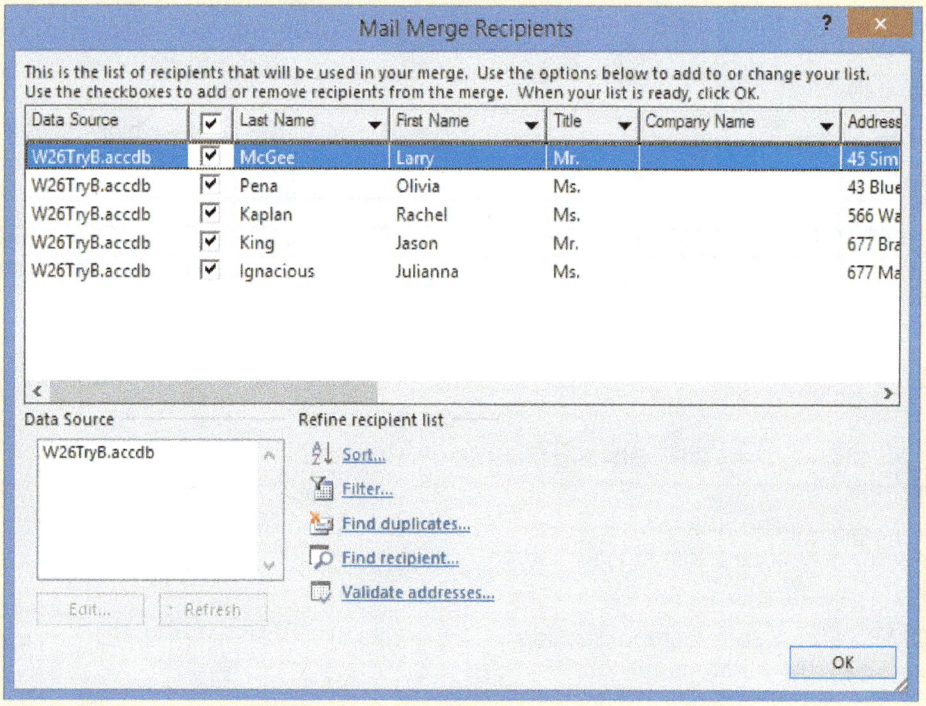

Word 2013, Windows 8, Microsoft Corporation

(continued)

Try It! Performing a Mail Merge with the Mail Merge Wizard *(continued)*

11 Click to place the insertion point immediately before the colon that follows *Dear*.

12 In the task pane, click More items. The Insert Merge Field dialog box opens.

13 Click First Name and click Insert. Then, click Close.

14 Click MAILINGS > Preview Results. A copy of the merged letter appears for the first record.

15 Click Preview Results again. The document goes back to showing the fields.

16 Save the changes to **W26TryA_xx**, and leave it open for the next Try It.

The Insert Merge Field dialog box

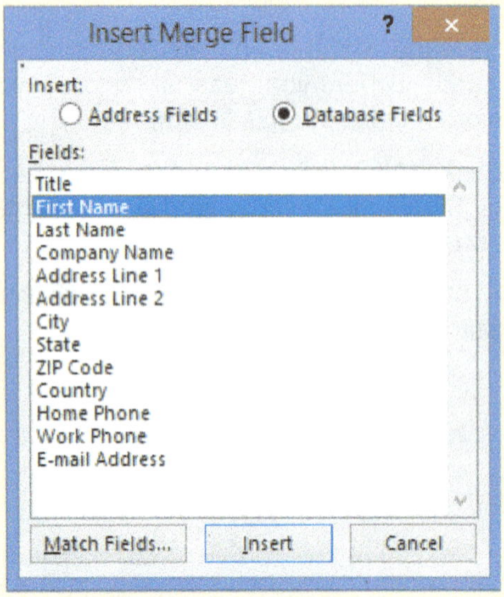

Word 2013, Windows 8, Microsoft Corporation

Removing Extra Space from the Address Block

- As you saw when you previewed the results in the previous steps, the <<AddressBlock>> code places each line of the address in its own paragraph, with the standard amount of vertical spacing between the paragraphs.
- To make the address block text appear more like a real mailing address, you may want to remove that extra spacing.
- To do so, format the <<AddressBlock>> code to remove the spacing after the paragraph.

Try It! Removing Extra Space from the Address Block

1 In the **W26TryA_xx** file, click the <<AddressBlock>> code to move the insertion point into that paragraph.

2 Click HOME > Line and Paragraph Spacing > Remove Space After Paragraph.

3 Click MAILINGS > Preview Results to check that the address block no longer produces extra vertical space.

4 Click Preview Results again to return to viewing the fields.

5 Save the changes to **W26TryA_xx**, and leave it open for the next Try It.

Remove the space following the paragraph that contains the address block

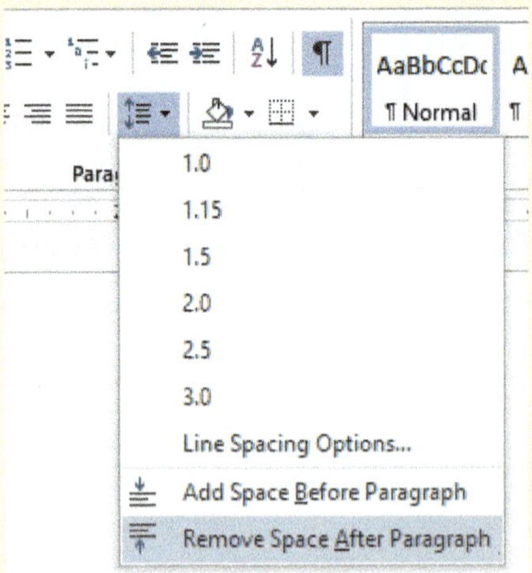

Word 2013, Windows 8, Microsoft Corporation

Merging to a New Document

- You can merge directly to the printer, but this may result in wasted paper if there is an error in the merge operation.
- A more conservative approach is to merge to a new document, examine the merged copies, and then either print them or make changes to them.
- After merging to a new document, you can also save the new document as a regular Word file, to be printed later, rather than printing immediately.

Try It! Merging to a New Document

1. In the W26TryA_xx file, click MAILINGS > Finish & Merge > Edit Individual Documents. The Merge to New Document dialog box opens.
2. Click OK.
3. Scroll through the new document, examining the copies for errors.
4. Close the new document without saving changes. Close W26TryA_xx, saving changes, and leave Word open for the next Try It.

Creating Mailing Labels by Merging Manually

- To create mail merged labels, you follow many of the same steps as when creating form letters.
- Instead of selecting letter as the main document, select labels. Then, select the label type and size that match the actual labels on which you will print.
- To perform a manual mail merge, you use commands on the MAILINGS tab of the Ribbon rather than following the steps in the Mail Merge Wizard task pane.

Try It! Start a Mailing Label Manual Merge

1. In Word, start a new blank document and save it as W26TryC_xx in the location where your teacher instructs you to store the files for this lesson.
2. Click MAILINGS > Start Mail Merge > Labels.
3. In the Label Options dialog box, click the Label vendors drop-down arrow and click Avery US Letter.

   ✓ *Avery is a company that sells mailing labels; you would select the type of label you have on which to print.*

Label Options dialog box

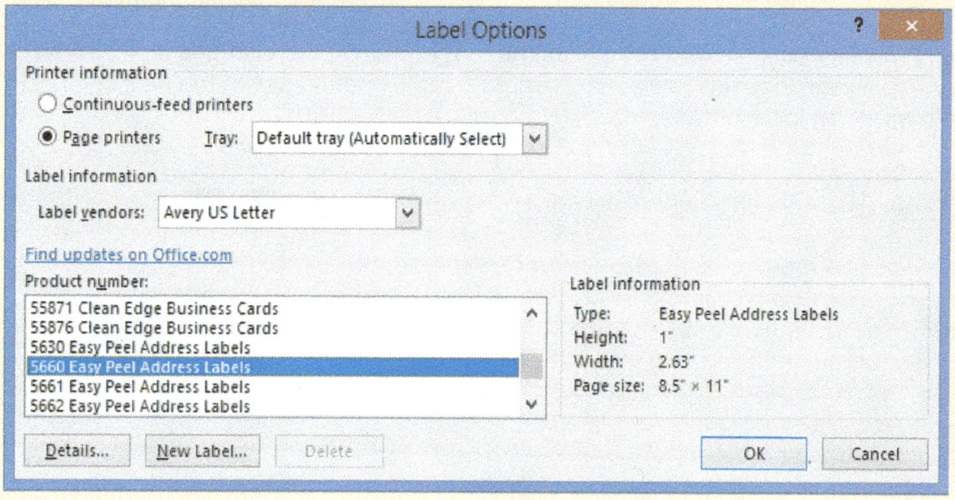

Word 2013, Windows 8, Microsoft Corporation

(continued)

Try It! Start a Mailing Label Manual Merge *(continued)*

4. In the Product number list, click 5660 Easy Peel Address Labels, and then click OK. Word creates a table that has cells the same size and in the same layout as the labels you selected.

✓ *If you cannot see the cells in the document, click the TABLE TOOLS LAYOUT tab and, in the Table group, click View Gridlines.*

5. Save the changes to **W26TryC_xx**, and leave it open to use in the next Try It.

Creating an Address List

- As part of the manual mail merge process, you can choose to create a new address list.
- Word creates a data source that contains fields appropriate for mailings, such as name, address, city, and so on. Word saves the data in Microsoft Access format. You do not have to own a copy of Access in order to use this feature.
- The data is stored in a tabular format, with each column containing one field of information and each row containing the **record** for one recipient.
- If a field in the data source is blank, the information is left out of the merge document for that record.
- As part of the process, you are prompted to specify a name and storage location for the data file.

Try It! Creating an Address List

1. In the **W26TryC_xx** file, click MAILINGS > Select Recipients > Type a New List. The New Address List dialog box opens.
2. Type **Mr.**, press TAB, type **John**, press TAB, and type **Smith**.
3. Press TAB twice to move to the Address Line 1 field.
4. Type **111 Main Street**, and press TAB twice to move to the City field.
5. Type **Macon**, press TAB, type **IL**, press TAB, and type **62544**.
6. Click the New Entry button. Word completes the first entry and moves to a new row so you can type the information for another entry.
7. Repeat steps 2 through 6 to enter the following information for two more recipients.
8. Click OK. The Save Address List dialog box opens.
9. Navigate to the folder where you have been instructed to store the files for this lesson.
10. In the File name box, type **W26TryD_xx**. Click OK.
11. Word positions the insertion point in the first cell of the label document, and inserts the <<Next Record>> field in the other cells.
12. Save the changes to **W26TryC_xx**, and leave it open to use in the next Try It.

Title	First Name	Last Name	Address Line 1	Address Line 2	City	State	ZIP Code
Ms.	**Kendra**	**Johnson**	**902 Chestnut Street**	**Apt. 5**	**Newtown**	**CT**	**02211**
Mr.	**Oliver**	**White**	**61 Frederick Street**		**Omaha**	**NE**	**68101**

Arranging, Previewing, and Printing the Labels

- Insert the merge block or merge fields on the first label.
- Once the first label is complete, you update the remaining labels to match.
- For labels, it is easiest to use the <<AddressBlock>> merge block, which includes all fields for a standard mailing address.
- If you insert individual fields, such as first name, last name, and ZIP Code, you must type the required punctuation, such as the comma between the city and state.
- Preview the labels the same way you learned earlier in this lesson.
- You can then merge the labels to a new document, if desired, or print them from the merge document.

Try It! Arranging the Labels

1. In the **W26TryC_xx** file, click in the first paragraph of the first label.
2. Click MAILINGS > Address Block. The Insert Address Block dialog box displays.
3. Verify that the Insert recipient's name in this format check box is selected and that *Mr. Joshua Randall Jr.* is highlighted in the list.
4. Click to clear the Insert company name check box.
5. Verify that the Insert postal address check box is selected and that the Only include the country/region if different than option button is selected.
6. Verify that the Format address according to the destination country/region check box is selected.
7. Click OK. Word inserts the <<AddressBlock>> merge block in the first cell.
8. Click MAILINGS > Update Labels to copy the layout from the first cell to the remaining cells.
9. Save the changes to **W26TryC_xx**, and leave it open to use in the next Try It.

Insert Address Block dialog box

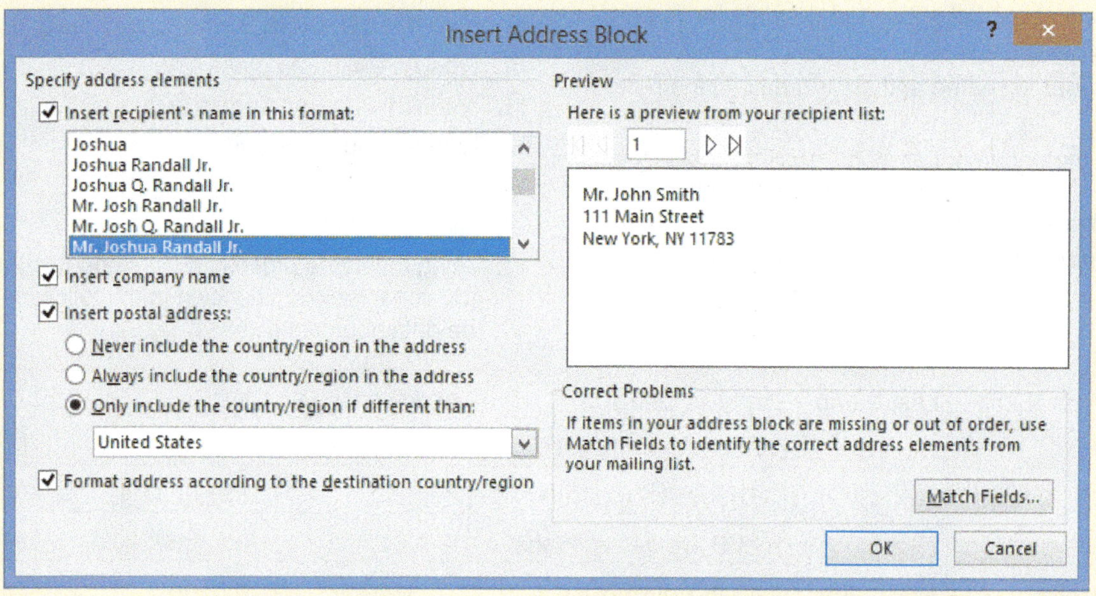

Word 2013, Windows 8, Microsoft Corporation

Try It! Previewing and Printing the Labels

1. In the W26TryC_xx file, on the MAILINGS tab, click Preview Results.
2. Word displays the label document with the actual addresses in place of the merge block fields. Note that the text in the label with four lines does not fit within the cell.
3. Click Preview Results to return to the merge codes.
4. Select the first table cell, click the PAGE LAYOUT tab, and use the Spacing Before increment arrows to set the spacing to 0.
5. On the MAILINGS tab, click Update Labels.
6. Preview the labels to make sure the spacing change worked.
7. Click Finish & Merge.
8. **With your teacher's permission**, click Print Documents. The Merge to Printer box displays.
9. Click OK to print the labels.

   ✓ *You can print the labels on plain paper.*
10. Save the changes to W26TryC_xx, close it, and exit Word.

Lesson 26—Practice

A letter inviting Michigan Avenue Athletic Club members to join a volleyball team becomes a simple task using the Mail Merge feature. The form letter will be personalized with each person's name and address. In this project, you will create the letter document and the data source address list, and you will merge them to generate the letters.

DIRECTIONS

1. Start Word, if necessary, and in a new blank document, type the text shown in Figure 26-2 on the next page. Substitute today's date for *Today's date.*
2. Type your full name and today's date in the header area.
3. Save the document as **W26PracticeA_xx** in the location where your teacher instructs you to store the files for this lesson.
4. Click **MAILINGS** > **Start Mail Merge** > **Letters**.
5. Click **Select Recipients** > **Type a New List**.
6. Type **Mr.**, and press TAB.
7. Type **Jeffrey**, and press TAB.
8. Type **Halloran**, and press TAB twice.
9. Type **3535 N. Clark Street**, and press TAB.
10. Type **Apt. 4B**, and press TAB.
11. Type **Chicago**, and press TAB.
12. Type **IL**, and press TAB.
13. Type **60601**.
14. Click **New Entry**.
15. Using the same process as in steps 6–14, add the additional recipients shown in the following table to the data source file:

Title	First Name	Last Name	Address Line 1	Address Line 2	City	State	ZIP Code
Ms.	**Liz**	**Rupert**	**221 N. Rush Street**	**#351**	**Chicago**	**IL**	**60601**
Ms.	**Kathy**	**Figit**	**562 S. Michigan Avenue**		**Chicago**	**IL**	**60601**
Mr.	**Charles**	**Huang**	**125 E. Delaware Place**	**#26**	**Chicago**	**IL**	**60601**
Mr.	**Keith**	**Newmann**	**882 W. Polk Street**		**Chicago**	**IL**	**60601**

16. Click **OK**.
17. In the Save Address List dialog box, navigate to the folder where you are storing the files for this lesson.
18. In the File name box, type **W26PracticeB_xx** and click **Save**.
19. Click to move the insertion point to the line immediately below today's date.
20. Click **MAILINGS** > **Address Block**.
21. Click **OK** to accept the default address block settings.
22. Move the insertion point to the blank line below <<AddressBlock>>.
23. Type **Dear**, and press SPACEBAR once.
24. Click **MAILINGS** > **Insert Merge Field** > **First_Name**.
25. Type a colon (**:**).
26. Click **MAILINGS** > **Preview Results**. Repeat to return to viewing the merge codes.
27. Close the document, saving changes, and exit Word.

Figure 26-2

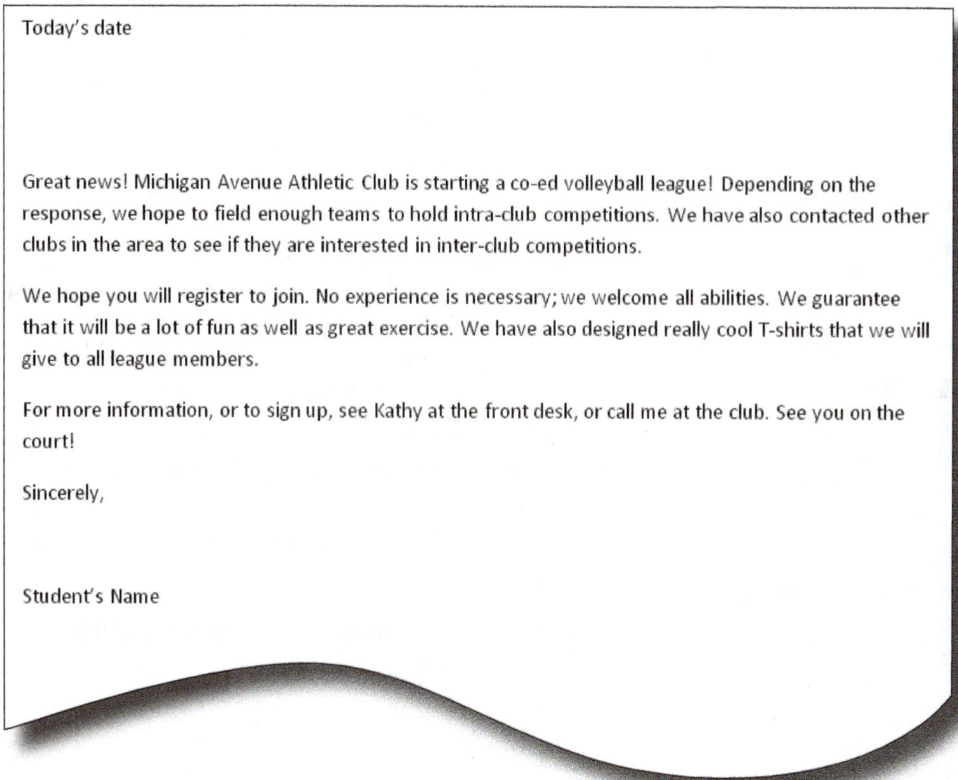

Today's date

Great news! Michigan Avenue Athletic Club is starting a co-ed volleyball league! Depending on the response, we hope to field enough teams to hold intra-club competitions. We have also contacted other clubs in the area to see if they are interested in inter-club competitions.

We hope you will register to join. No experience is necessary; we welcome all abilities. We guarantee that it will be a lot of fun as well as great exercise. We have also designed really cool T-shirts that we will give to all league members.

For more information, or to sign up, see Kathy at the front desk, or call me at the club. See you on the court!

Sincerely,

Student's Name

Word 2013, Windows 8, Microsoft Corporation

Lesson 26—Apply

In this project, you modify the merge letter you created in the Lesson 26—Practice project, and you also create mailing labels for sending the letters to club members.

DIRECTIONS

1. Start Word, if necessary, and open **W26ApplyA** from the data files for this lesson. Click **Yes** when prompted to attach the merge file. If the Select Data Source dialog box opens, select **W26ApplyB** and click **Open**.
2. Save the document as **W26ApplyA_xx** in the location where your teacher instructs you to store the files for this lesson.
3. Type your full name and today's date in the header area.
4. Preview the merge. Then switch back to viewing the field codes.
5. Remove the extra vertical space from the **<<AddressBlock>>**.

   ✓ *Add an extra paragraph break after the <<AddressBlock>> field to maintain the needed spacing between the address and the greeting.*
6. Replace the greeting paragraph with a **<<GreetingLine>>** code. (Click **MAILINGS** > **Greeting Line** to do this.) Use the default settings.
7. Insert the **<<First_Name>>** field at the beginning of the second paragraph, and edit the text as shown in Figure 26-3 on the next page.
8. Save your work.
9. Merge to a new document. Save the new document as **W26ApplyC_xx** in the location where your teacher instructs you to store the files for this lesson.
10. Save and close both documents, and leave Word open.
11. Start a new, blank document and save it as **W26ApplyD_xx** in the location where your teacher instructs you to store the files for this lesson.
12. Start the Mail Merge Wizard.
13. Select to create a Labels main document using Avery US Letter 5263 Shipping Labels.
14. Select to use an existing list. Click the **Browse** button and navigate to the location where the data files for this lesson are stored. Select **W26ApplyB** and click **Open**. Click **OK** to use all of the recipients in the Mail Merge Recipients dialog box.
15. Insert an Address Block on the first label, and remove extra space between lines of the address.
16. Update the labels, preview the labels, and then complete the merge.
17. **With your teacher's permission**, print the labels.

    ✓ *You can print the labels on plain paper.*
18. Close the document, saving changes, and exit Word.

Figure 26-3

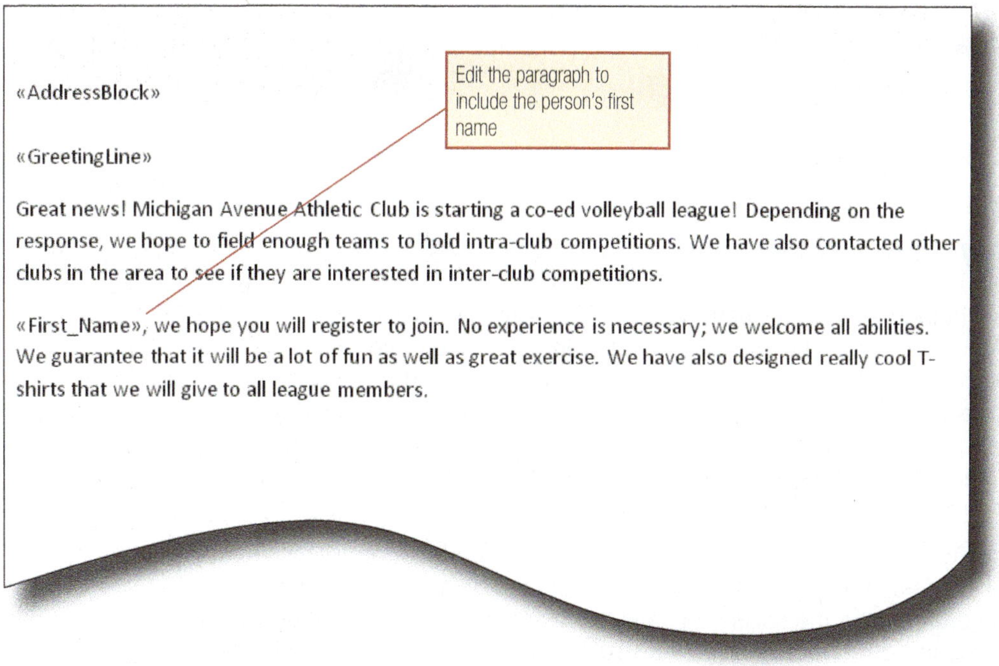

«AddressBlock»

«GreetingLine»

Great news! Michigan Avenue Athletic Club is starting a co-ed volleyball league! Depending on the response, we hope to field enough teams to hold intra-club competitions. We have also contacted other clubs in the area to see if they are interested in inter-club competitions.

«First_Name», we hope you will register to join. No experience is necessary; we welcome all abilities. We guarantee that it will be a lot of fun as well as great exercise. We have also designed really cool T-shirts that we will give to all league members.

End-of-Chapter Activities

➤ Word Chapter 3—Critical Thinking

Technology Trends Newsletter

Trends in technology impact the way we work. For example, thanks to collaborative technologies such as cloud computing and voice-over-Internet protocols, teams can work together even when they are located hundreds of miles apart. Technology trends also impact career opportunities by making some old careers obsolete and making new careers possible. For example, the Internet allows retailers to market world-wide, but robots have replaced many manufacturing jobs.

In this project, work with a team to create a multipage newsletter about emerging trends in computer technology and how they affect employment opportunities. To complete the project, use the skills you have learned in this chapter, set goals, prioritize tasks, and develop a realistic schedule that you will be able to achieve.

DIRECTIONS

1. As a team, work together to plan the project. Develop a schedule, allocate assignments, and set goals. Assign each team member the responsibility of writing at least one article for the newsletter.
2. Use the Internet, magazines, and books to research current trends in technology to gather the information you will need to write your articles. Be sure to use reliable sources. Take notes and record source information so you can enter citations as necessary. When possible, copy images that accompany articles so that they can be added to the newsletter.
3. Work cooperatively to develop and edit the articles. Meet as a team to read and discuss each other's work, offering and accepting constructive criticism.
4. When the articles are complete, start Word and create a new document.
5. Save the document as **WCT03_xx** in the location where your teacher instructs you to store the files for this chapter.

   ✓ *Pick one member of the team and use that student's name in the document file name.*
6. Select a theme and style set for the document. Set the margins and page orientation, and insert page numbers.
7. Import each team member's original document into the newsletter document by inserting their files. Adjust formats after importing to ensure consistency throughout the newsletter.
8. Design the newsletter using section breaks and newsletter-style columns. For example, you probably want the newsletter title in one column, but the articles in two or three columns.
9. Adjust spacing and select options to control pagination and make the text easier to read.
10. Enhance the document using drop caps, borders, and shading. Insert symbols as accents or illustrations.
11. Import any images copied from Internet sources, adding source captions as necessary. Or import images you find using appropriate online searches. Position the images and wrap text attractively.
12. At the end of the document, insert a page break and create a Works Cited page to accompany the newsletter.
13. Enter document properties to help identify the document. Put the names of all team members in the footer.
14. Check the spelling and grammar in the document and correct errors as necessary.
15. Ask a classmate who is not part of your team to review the newsletter and make suggestions for how you might improve it. Incorporate your classmate's suggestions into the document and then do a final review of the document in Read Mode.
16. **With your teacher's permission,** print the newsletter and share it with your class.
17. Close the document, saving changes, and exit Word.

➤ Word Chapter 3—Portfolio Builder

Job Search Strategies Report

Vocation Opportunities, Inc. wants to create a report of no more than 350 words about strategies for getting a job search started. In this project, you will create the one-page report. You will include endnotes and enhance the document with borders, shading, and drop caps. When the document is complete, you will create labels using an existing address list so you can mail the report to clients.

DIRECTIONS

Create a One-Page Report

1. Start Word and open **WPB03A** from the data files for this chapter.
2. Save the file as **WPB03A_xx** in the location where your teacher instructs you to store the files for this chapter.
3. Insert Quick Part document properties for Author and Publish Date in the header and right-align.
4. Apply the **Centered** style set and the **Integral** theme.
5. Apply the **Title** style to the first line of text. Center it, and change the paragraph spacing to **30** points before and after.
6. Format the first paragraph in 12-point Times New Roman, justified. Set the line spacing to double. Apply a first line indent of **0.5"** and set paragraph spacing before and after to **0**.
7. Copy the formatting from the first paragraph to the rest of the paragraphs in the document.
8. Insert an endnote after the first sentence as follows: **Bob Corlett, "How long will your job search take?" <http://www.bizjournals.com/washington/blog/2012/07/how-long-will-your-job-search-take.html> (July 2012).**
9. Insert an endnote after the second paragraph as follows: **Why Learn About Me?, <http://www.careeronestop.org/ExploreCareers/SelfAssessments/WhyLearnAboutMe.aspx> (2012).**
10. Insert page numbers in the center of the footer.
11. Change the page margins to **Moderate**.
12. Apply an In margin drop cap to the first paragraph, customized to drop two lines.
13. Apply a solid line, 2¼ pt. border to the top and bottom of the report title. Apply a Teal, Accent 6, Lighter 60% shading to the title as well.
14. Enter the following document properties:
    - Title: **Getting a Job Search Started**
    - Subject: **Job search strategies**
    - Keywords: **job search, careers, tips, strategies, networking, online resources**
    - Category: **job search**
    - Status: **mailed**
15. Check the word count to see if it is under 350 words.
16. Check the spelling and grammar in the document and correct errors as necessary.
17. **With your teacher's permission,** print the document. It should look similar to Illustration 3A shown on the next page.
18. Close the document, saving changes. Leave Word open to use in the next part of this project.

Illustration 3A

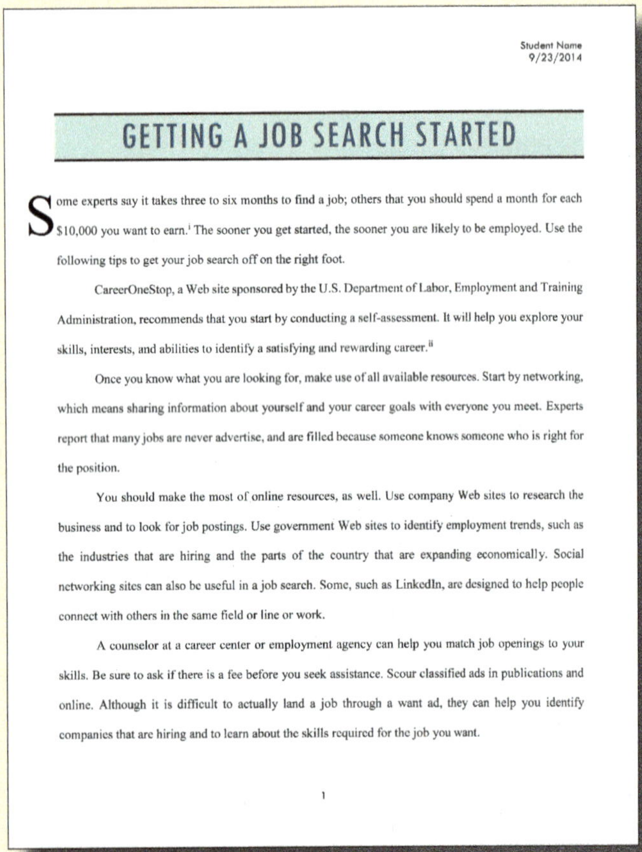

Student Name
9/23/2014

GETTING A JOB SEARCH STARTED

Some experts say it takes three to six months to find a job; others that you should spend a month for each $10,000 you want to earn.[i] The sooner you get started, the sooner you are likely to be employed. Use the following tips to get your job search off on the right foot.

CareerOneStop, a Web site sponsored by the U.S. Department of Labor, Employment and Training Administration, recommends that you start by conducting a self-assessment. It will help you explore your skills, interests, and abilities to identify a satisfying and rewarding career.[ii]

Once you know what you are looking for, make use of all available resources. Start by networking, which means sharing information about yourself and your career goals with everyone you meet. Experts report that many jobs are never advertise, and are filled because someone knows someone who is right for the position.

You should make the most of online resources, as well. Use company Web sites to research the business and to look for job postings. Use government Web sites to identify employment trends, such as the industries that are hiring and the parts of the country that are expanding economically. Social networking sites can also be useful in a job search. Some, such as LinkedIn, are designed to help people connect with others in the same field or line or work.

A counselor at a career center or employment agency can help you match job openings to your skills. Be sure to ask if there is a fee before you seek assistance. Scour classified ads in publications and online. Although it is difficult to actually land a job through a want ad, they can help you identify companies that are hiring and to learn about the skills required for the job you want.

1

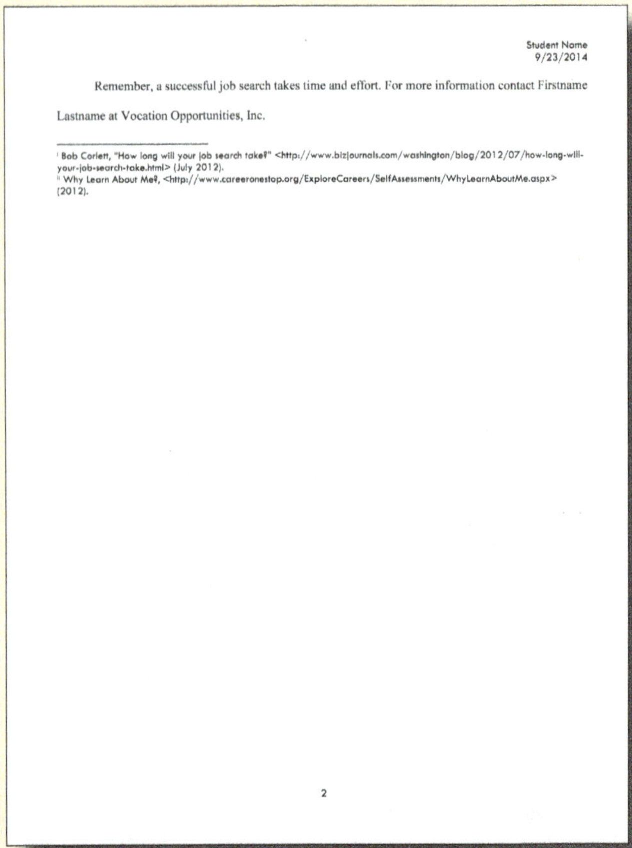

Student Name
9/23/2014

Remember, a successful job search takes time and effort. For more information contact Firstname Lastname at Vocation Opportunities, Inc.

[i] Bob Corlett, "How long will your job search take?" <http://www.bizjournals.com/washington/blog/2012/07/how-long-will-your-job-search-take.html> (July 2012).
[ii] Why Learn About Me?, <http://www.careeronestop.org/ExploreCareers/SelfAssessments/WhyLearnAboutMe.aspx> (2012).

2

Word 2013, Windows 8, Microsoft Corporation

Create Mailing Labels

1. In Word, create a new, blank document and save it as **WPB03B_xx** in the location where your teacher instructs you to store the files for this lesson.
2. Use the Mail Merge Wizard to create mailing labels to print on Microsoft 30 Per Page Address Labels that are 1" high and 2.63" wide.
3. Use all the names in the **WPB03C** data file as the data source.
4. Adjust formatting as necessary so the addresses fit on the labels
5. **With your teacher's permission**, print the labels.

   ✓ *You can print the labels on plain paper.*
6. Close the document, saving changes, and exit Word.

Chapter 1

(Courtesy Yuri Arcurs/Shutterstock)

Getting Started with Microsoft Excel 2013

Lesson 1
Touring Excel

- Starting Excel
- Naming and Saving a Workbook
- Exploring the Excel Window
- Exploring the Excel Interface
- Navigating the Worksheet
- Changing Worksheet Views
- Closing a Workbook and Exiting Excel

Lesson 2
Worksheet and Workbook Basics

- Creating a New (Blank) Workbook
- Entering Text and Labels
- Editing Text
- Using Undo and Redo
- Clearing Cell Contents
- Inserting a Built-In Header or Footer
- Previewing and Printing a Worksheet

Lesson 3
Adding Worksheet Contents

- Opening an Existing Workbook and Saving It with a New Name
- Entering and Editing Numeric Labels and Values
- Using AutoComplete
- Using Pick From List
- Using AutoCorrect
- Checking the Spelling in a Worksheet

Lesson 4
Worksheet Formatting

- Choosing a Theme
- Applying Cell Styles
- Applying Font Formats
- Merging and Centering Across Cells
- Applying Number Formats

Lesson 5
More on Cell Entries and Formatting

- Entering Dates
- Filling a Series
- Aligning Data in a Cell
- Wrapping Text in Cells
- Changing Column Width and Row Height
- Using Keyboard Shortcuts

Lesson 6
Working with Ranges

- Selecting Ranges
- Entering Data by Range
- Making a Range Entry Using a Collapse Button

Lesson 7
Creating Formulas

- Entering a Formula
- Using Arithmetic Operators
- Editing a Formula
- Copying a Formula Using the Fill Handle
- Using the SUM Function

Lesson 8
Copying and Pasting

- Copying and Pasting Data
- Copying Formats
- Copying Formulas Containing a Relative Reference
- Copying Formulas Containing an Absolute Reference

Lesson 9
Techniques for Moving Data

- Inserting and Deleting Cells
- Inserting, Deleting, Hiding, and Unhiding Columns and Rows
- Cutting and Pasting Data
- Using Drag-and-Drop Editing
- Transposing Columns and Rows

Lesson 10
Sheet, Display, and Print Operations

- Displaying, Printing, and Hiding Formulas
- Printing Titles
- Changing Orientation
- Scaling a Printout to Fit
- Previewing and Printing a Worksheet

End-of-Chapter Activities

Lesson 1

Touring Excel

➤ What You Will Learn

Starting Excel
Naming and Saving a Workbook
Exploring the Excel Window
Exploring the Excel Interface
Navigating the Worksheet
Changing Worksheet Views
Closing a Workbook and Exiting Excel

Software Skills When you want to analyze business, personal, or financial data and create reports in a table format consisting of rows and columns, use the Microsoft Excel 2013 spreadsheet application in the Microsoft Office 2013 suite.

What You Can Do

Starting Excel

- Start Excel from the Windows 8 Start screen.
  - Click the Excel 2013 tile to start the program.
  - You can also find the program on the Apps screen. Scroll to the Excel 2013 tile and click to start.
- When you create a new blank worksheet, Excel displays a list of recently used files and a gallery of available **templates**.
- Click the Blank workbook tile to create a new Excel document.
- When Excel starts, it displays an empty **workbook** with one **worksheet**.
- A worksheet contains rows and columns that intersect to form **cells**.
- Gridlines mark the boundaries of each cell.

WORDS TO KNOW

Active cell
The active cell contains the cell pointer. There is a dark outline around the active cell.

The Backstage view
A feature of Microsoft Office 2013 from which you access file and program management commands.

Cell
A cell is the intersection of a column and a row on a worksheet. You enter data into cells to create a worksheet.

Cell address or cell reference
The location of a cell in a worksheet as identified by its column letter and row number.

Formula bar
As you enter data in a cell, it simultaneously appears in the formula bar, which is located above the worksheet.

OneDrive
A file hosting service that allows you to upload and sync files to a virtual, or cloud, storage environment. Files can then be accessed from a Web browser or a local device.

Scroll
A way to view locations on the worksheet without changing the active cell.

Sheet tabs
Tabs that appear at the bottom of the workbook window, which display the name of each worksheet.

Tab scrolling buttons
Buttons that appear to the left of the sheet tabs, which allow you to scroll hidden tabs into view.

Template
A document that contains formatting, styles, and sample text that you can use to create new documents.

Workbook
An Excel file with one or more worksheets.

Worksheet
The work area for entering and calculating data made up of columns and rows separated by gridlines (light gray lines). Also called a spreadsheet.

Try It! Starting Excel

1. From the Windows Start screen, click the Excel 2013 program tile.

   ✓ *If your keyboard has a Windows key (a key with the Windows logo on it), you can press that key at any time to display the Start screen.*

   OR

   a. Right-click a blank area of the Windows Start screen.
   b. Click the All apps button.
   c. Scroll to the Excel 2013 tile.
   d. Click Excel 2013.

   OR

   a. Move the mouse pointer to the lower-left corner of the screen.
   b. When you see the Windows Start screen icon, click to open the start screen.

2. Click Blank workbook.
3. Explore the features of the Excel program window.
4. Leave the file open to use in the next Try It.

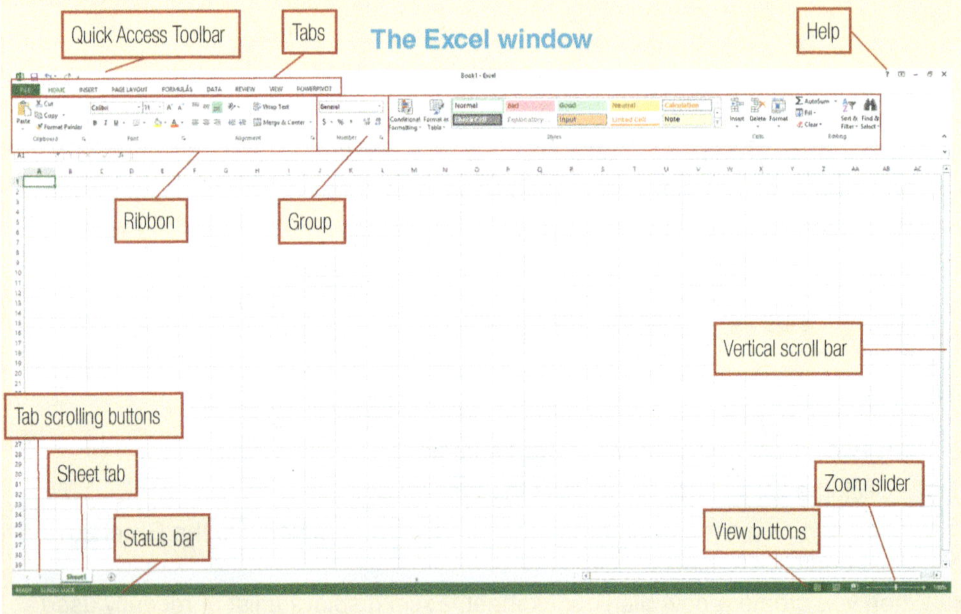

The Excel window

Excel 2013, Windows 8, Microsoft Corporation

Naming and Saving a Workbook

- After entering data in a workbook, you must save it, or that data will be lost when you exit Excel.
- A saved workbook is referred to as a file.
- A file may be saved on a hard disk, a removable disk, a shared group drive, or to the **OneDrive**. Files saved to the OneDrive are stored virtually on Microsoft's OneDrive Web site.
- You must provide a name for the file when you save it. File names should be descriptive, with a limit of 255 characters for the name, disk drive, and path.
- A file name may contain letters, numbers, and spaces, but not \ / : * ? " < > or | .
- Excel automatically adds a period and a file type extension (usually .xlsx) to the end of a file name when you save it.

- You must select a location in which to save your file, for example, the Documents folder. You can also create new folders in which to store your workbooks.
- The default Excel file format is .xlsx, or Strict Open XML Spreadsheet file format. This XML-based file format allows your workbooks to integrate more easily with outside data sources and results in smaller workbook file sizes than in earlier versions of Excel.

  ✓ *You can install updates to some older versions of Excel so they can read the new .xlsx format.*

- Data can also be saved in other formats, such as HTML, Excel Binary (a file format for very large workbooks), or older versions of Excel (.xls).

  ✓ *You might want to save data in a different format in order to share that data with someone who uses a different version of Excel or a Web browser to view your data.*

- **The Backstage view** shows the places in which you can save your file, such as the OneDrive or Computer. The the Backstage view will display the first time you save a file.

  ✓ *You can exit the the Backstage view by clicking the Back button.*

- When you select Computer, the Recent Folders list provides the locations of folders you have recently opened.
- You can select a different storage location by double-clicking Computer or by clicking Browse.
- Once you've saved a workbook, you need only click the Save button as you work to resave any changes made since the last save action. You will not need to reenter the file name.
- You can save a previously saved file with a different name by using the Save As tab in the the Backstage view.
- Click Browse to browse to a location and the Save As dialog box will open.

  ✓ *If the location where you want to store the file displays in the the Backstage view, click it instead of clicking Browse.*

- In the Save As dialog box, you can rename the file, browse to a location, and save the file.

Try It! Naming and Saving a Workbook

1. Click the FILE tab.

   OR

   Click the Save button on the Quick Access Toolbar.
2. Click Save As.
3. Click Computer and then click Browse.

   OR

   Double-click Computer.
4. In the File name text box, type **E01Try_xx**.

   ✓ *Replace xx with your own name or initials, as instructed by your teacher. For example, if your name is Mary Jones, type* **E01Try_MaryJones** *or* **E01Try_MJ**.
5. Use the Navigation pane to navigate to the location where your teacher instructs you to store the files for this lesson.

   ✓ *Use the drop-down lists at the top of the Save As dialog box or the locations in the Navigation pane at the left to select the folder to save to. Clicking the triangle beside any disk or folder in the Navigation pane displays or hides that location's contents. If saving to a USB drive, make sure it is inserted. Scroll down the Navigation pane at left, and click the USB drive under Computer. Refer to Lesson 1 of the Basics section of this book for more information on navigating.*
6. Click the Save button.
7. Leave the file open to use in the next Try It.

Exploring the Excel Window

- In the worksheet, a green border appears around the **active cell.**
- You can change the active cell using the mouse, touch device, or keyboard.
- Data is entered into the active cell.
- The Name box, located on the left side of the **formula bar,** displays the **cell reference** or **cell address** of the active cell (its column letter and row number). For example, A1 is the cell in the first row of the first column. B5 is the address for the cell in the fifth row of the second column.
- To help you identify the cell reference for the active cell, Excel surrounds the cell with a dark border and highlights its column letter (at the top of the worksheet) and row number (to the left of the worksheet). The column letters and row numbers are also known as the column and row headings.
- You can use the arrow keys [↑] [↓] [←] [→] (alone or in combination with other keys), special key combinations, the mouse, a touch device, or Go To [F5] to select a cell on the current worksheet.

Try It! Exploring the Excel Window

1. In the **E01Try_xx** file, press [→] twice.
2. Press [↓] four times.
3. Click in the Name box, type **b3**, and press [ENTER].
4. Press [↓].
5. Click cell F13.
6. Press [CTRL] + [HOME].
7. Save the **E01Try_xx** file, and leave it open to use in the next Try It.

Key worksheet features

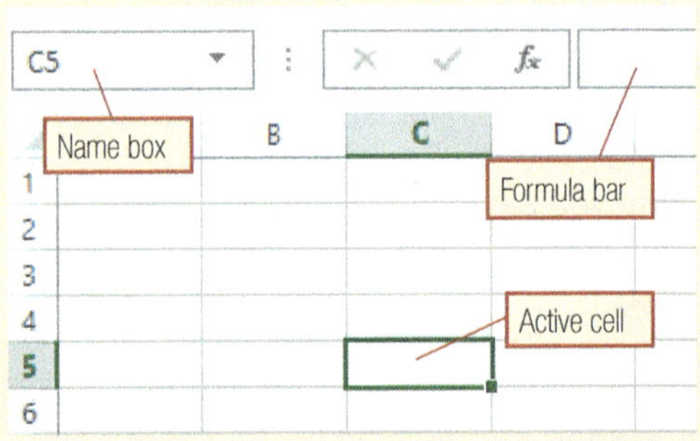

Excel 2013, Windows 8, Microsoft Corporation

Exploring the Excel Interface

- In the Microsoft Office Basics section, you learned that you can access common commands such as Save and Undo through the buttons on the Quick Access Toolbar.
- Through the FILE tab, you can access commands for managing files such as New, Open, Save, and Print. Clicking the FILE tab displays the Backstage view.
- The Ribbon, located at the top of the Excel window, offers buttons for the most common Excel commands.
- The Ribbon offers several tabs, and on each tab, related command buttons are arranged in groups. Click a tab to display its contents, and then click a button to choose a command or display further choices.
- Some tabs, called contextual tabs, appear only when you've selected an item to which the tab's commands apply.
- To access Help, click the Help button ? .

Try It! Exploring the Excel Interface

1. In the **E01Try_xx** file, click the FILE tab.
2. In the list at the left of the Backstage view, click Print.
3. Click the Back button in the upper-left corner of the window to go back to your document.
4. Click the FORMULAS tab.
5. On the FORMULAS tab, in the Function Library group, click the Date & Time button.
6. Press ESC .
7. Click the HOME tab.
8. Save the **E01Try_xx** file, and leave it open to use in the next Try It.

Navigating the Worksheet

- There are 16,384 columns and 1,048,576 rows available in a worksheet, but you don't need to fill the entire worksheet in order to use it—just type data in the cells you need.
- Since the workbook window displays only a part of a worksheet, you **scroll** through the worksheet to view another location.
- With the mouse or a touch device, you can scroll using the horizontal or vertical scroll bars.

  ✓ *Using the mouse or touch device to scroll does not change the active cell.*

- With the keyboard, you can scroll by pressing specific keys or key combinations.

  ✓ *Scrolling with the keyboard does change the active cell.*

- You can move to a specific cell that's not onscreen using Go To or the Name box.

  ✓ *You can also use the Name box to go directly to a named cell or range. This is discussed in Lesson 13.*

- The Go To function allows you to go to a specific cell and make that cell active.
- You can open the Go To dialog box by clicking HOME > Find & Select > Go To.

  ✓ *In this book, the symbol > is used to indicate a series of steps.*

- When you type the cell address into the Reference box and select OK, that cell will become the active cell.

Try It! Navigating the Worksheet

1. In the **E01Try_xx** file, click the down scroll arrow on the vertical scroll bar to scroll one row down.
2. Click the right scroll arrow on the horizontal scroll bar to scroll one column right.
3. Roll the mouse wheel down until row 52 comes into view. (Do not press the wheel, just lightly roll it with your fingertip.)

   ✓ *If you are using a touchpad, click the down arrow on the vertical scroll bar.*

4. Click above the scroll box on the vertical scroll bar once or twice to redisplay row 1.
5. Drag the scroll box on the horizontal scroll bar all the way to the left to redisplay column A.
6. Click HOME > Find & Select > Go To.
7. In the Reference text box, type **ZZ88**.
8. Click OK.
9. Press CTRL + HOME to return to cell A1.
10. Save the **E01Try_xx** file, and leave it open to use in the next Try It.

Changing Worksheet Views

- To view or hide the formula bar, ruler, column and row headings, or gridlines, select or deselect them by checking or clearing the applicable check box in the Show group on the VIEW tab.

  ✓ *Hiding screen elements shows more rows onscreen.*

- To hide and redisplay the Ribbon, double-click any tab.
- Normal view is the default working view.
- Page Layout view is used to view data as it will look when printed and make adjustments.
- Page Break Preview is used before printing, to adjust where pages break.

  ✓ *You'll learn more about Page Layout view and Page Break Preview in later lessons.*

- You can use the view buttons on the status bar to change to the most common views.
- You also can use the buttons in the Workbook Views group on the VIEW tab to change views.
- Use Zoom to magnify cells in a worksheet by any amount up to 400%.
- Change the zoom using the Zoom slider on the status bar.
- You can also change the zoom using the mouse, touch device, or the buttons in the Zoom group on the VIEW tab.

Try It! Changing Worksheet Views

1. In the **E01Try_xx** file, click the VIEW tab on the Ribbon.
2. In the Show group, click one of the following:
   - Ruler
   - Formula Bar
   - Gridlines
   - Headings
3. Click the item you clicked in step 2 again to redisplay it.
4. Double-click the VIEW tab to hide the Ribbon.
5. Double-click the VIEW tab again to redisplay the Ribbon.
6. Click the Page Layout button in either the Workbook Views group or near the zoom slider to change to Page Layout view.
7. In the Zoom group, click the Zoom button. The Zoom dialog box offers the following magnifications:
   - 200%
   - 25%
   - 100%
   - Fit Selection
   - 75%
   - Custom
   - 50%
8. Click 50%, and then click OK.
9. On the status bar, click Zoom In once.
10. On the status bar, use the zoom slider to change the view to more than 100%.
11. On the status bar, drag the Zoom slider to the middle to change the view to 100%.
12. On the VIEW tab, in the Zoom group, click the Zoom to Selection button.
13. In the Zoom group, click the 100% button.
14. In the Workbook Views group, click the Normal button.
15. Save the **E01Try_xx** file, and leave it open to use in the next Try It.

Key worksheet features

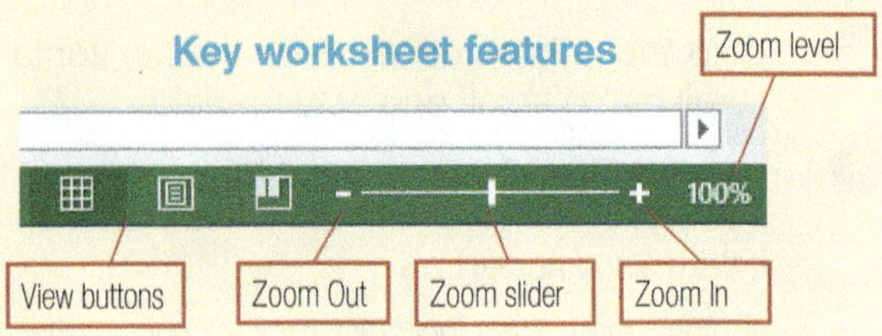

Excel 2013, Windows 8, Microsoft Corporation

Closing a Workbook and Exiting Excel

- When your worksheet is complete and you want to close the Excel workbook, use the Close command after clicking on the FILE tab.
- You can also click the File button on the Quick Access Toolbar, and then click Close.
- Closing a workbook file removes it from the screen without exiting Excel.
- Save a workbook before you close it or you will lose the current data or updated entries that you made.
- If you attempt to close a workbook or close Excel before saving, you will be prompted to save the changes.
- If you have more than one file open, Excel allows you to close and save all of the files before you exit the program.
- Exit the Excel application by clicking the Close button × at the right end of the program's title bar.

Try It! Closing a Workbook and Exiting Excel

1. In the **E01Try_xx** file, click the FILE tab on the Ribbon.
2. Click Close.
3. If necessary, click the Save button to save your changes to the file and close the workbook.
4. Click the **Close** button at the right end of the program's title bar to exit the Excel application.

Lesson 1—Practice

In this project, you will open an Excel worksheet, navigate the worksheet, change views, and close using the skills you learned in this lesson.

DIRECTIONS

1. Click **Excel 2013** and open a **Blank workbook** file.
2. Press → four times to select cell E1.
3. Press ↓ four times to select cell E5.
4. Click cell **H9** to make it the active cell, and then view its cell address in the Name box.
5. Click **HOME** > **Find & Select** > **Go To**.
6. In the Reference text box, type **T98**.
7. Click **OK**. The active cell changes to T98.
8. Click in the Name box to change the active cell to the following, pressing ENTER after typing each new cell address:
   a. **B1492** (row 1492, column B)
   b. **XFD1048576** (bottom right of worksheet)
9. Press CTRL + HOME to move to cell A1.
10. Click cell **D4**.
11. Point to the horizontal scroll bar and click the right scroll arrow. The worksheet moves right by one column but the active cell does not change.
12. Point to the horizontal scroll bar and click to the left of the scroll box. The worksheet moves back left but the active cell does not change.
13. Point to the horizontal scroll bar, and then drag the scroll box all the way to the right. The view of the worksheet has changed again but the active cell does not change.
14. Click the down scroll arrow on the vertical scroll bar three times. The worksheet moves down three rows but the active cell does not change.
15. On the **VIEW** tab, in the Show group, deselect the **Formula Bar** check box to hide the formula bar.
16. Change to the **Page Layout** view by clicking its button on the status bar. Notice that the rulers have appeared just above the column headings and to the left of the row numbers.

17. On the **VIEW** tab, change to Normal view by clicking the **Normal** button.
18. In the Show group, select the **Formula Bar** check box to redisplay the formula bar.
19. In the Zoom group, click the **Zoom** button to display the Zoom dialog box.
20. Click in the Custom box, type **150**, and then click **OK**. The Zoom changes to 150%, so cells appear much larger.
21. Click the **Zoom Out** button on the Status bar twice. The Zoom changes to 130%.
22. Drag the **Zoom slider** to the left until the zoom is set to **70%**. The current zoom percentage shows on the Zoom button as you drag. If you have trouble setting the zoom to an exact percentage using the slider, drag the slider to roughly 70%, then click the Zoom Out or Zoom In button as needed to jump to exactly 70%.
23. Drag the **Zoom slider** to the middle to change the view to 100%.
24. Click the **FILE** tab and then click **Close** to close the workbook. If asked to save the workbook, click **Don't Save**.
25. Click the Close button × at the right end of the program's title bar to exit Excel.

Lesson 1—Apply

You've recently been hired as a marketing specialist for Bike Tours and Adventures, and you've enrolled yourself in a class to learn to use Excel. In this project, you will start Excel, familiarize yourself with the Excel window, change your view of the worksheet, and practice moving around the worksheet using the mouse and the keyboard.

DIRECTIONS

1. Start Excel, if necessary, and open **E01Apply** from the data files for this lesson.
2. Save the file as **E01Apply_xx** in the location where your teacher instructs you to store the files for this lesson.

   ✓ *Replace the text xx with your own first name and last name or initials as directed by your teacher.*

3. Click cell **B1**, type your name, and press ENTER.
4. Increase the zoom to **150%**. Your document should appear as shown in Figure 1-1 on the next page. Scroll to the left and up, if necessary, to see your name.
5. Hide and redisplay these screen elements:
   a. Ribbon.
   b. Formula bar.
   c. Gridlines.
6. Change to **Page Layout** view, and then back to **Normal** view.
7. Click **HOME** > **Find & Select** > **Go To**.
8. In the **Reference** text box, type **AL29**.
9. Click **OK**.
10. Click **HOME** > **Copy** to copy the contents of cell AL29.
11. Click **HOME** > **Find & Select** > **Go To**.
12. In the **Reference** text box, type **F5**.
13. Click **OK**.
14. Click **HOME** > **Paste** to paste the contents of cell AL29 to cell F5.
15. Press CTRL + HOME to return to cell A1.
16. Save and close the file, and exit Excel.

Figure 1-1

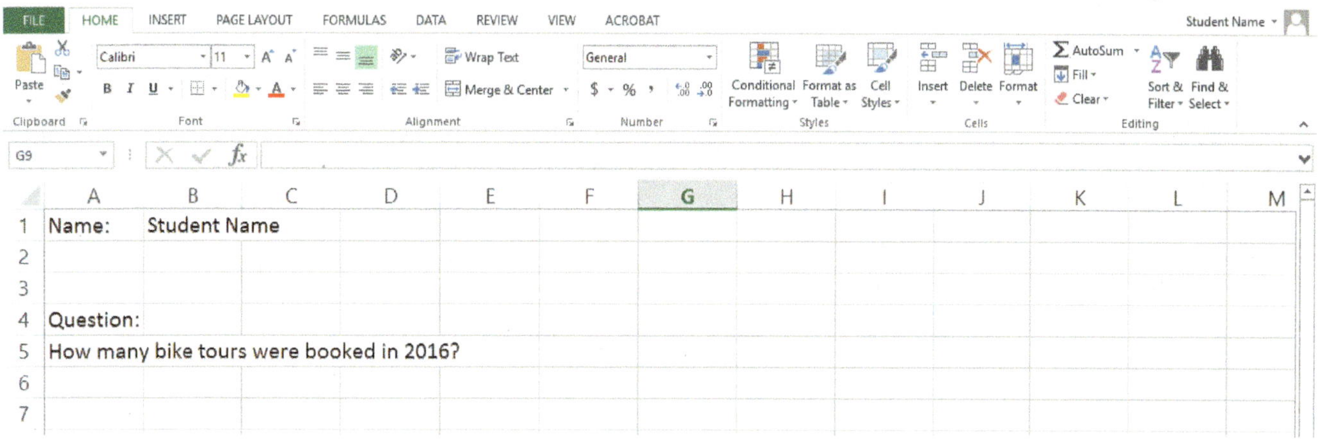

Excel 2013, Windows 8, Microsoft Corporation

Lesson 2

Worksheet and Workbook Basics

➤ What You Will Learn

Creating a New (Blank) Workbook
Entering Text and Labels
Editing Text
Using Undo and Redo
Clearing Cell Contents
Inserting a Built-In Header or Footer
Previewing and Printing a Worksheet

WORDS TO KNOW

Blank workbook
A new, empty workbook contains one worksheet (sheet).

Clear
To remove a cell's contents and/or formatting.

Default
The standard settings Excel uses in its software, such as column width or bottom alignment of text in a cell.

Footer
Descriptive text, such as page numbers, that appears at the bottom of every page of a printout.

Header
Descriptive text, such as page numbers, that appears at the top of every page of a printout.

Label
Text entered to identify the type of data contained in a row or column.

Software Skills Building a workbook involves creating a new file, entering text to identify the data that will be calculated, making changes, and adding an identifying header and footer, among other information. You also can save and print a workbook before closing it. You'll learn these skills in this lesson.

What You Can Do

Creating a New (Blank) Workbook

- You can create a new workbook file any time after you begin working in Excel.
- A **blank workbook** file that you create has one worksheet by **default**, just like the blank workbook that appears when you start Excel.
- Use the Blank workbook choice in the Backstage view to create a blank file. Click the FILE tab > New > Blank workbook.

  ✓ *You can press* CTRL + N *at any time to create a blank file without displaying the Backstage view.*

- You can create a workbook using a template in the the Backstage view. You can choose from sample templates installed with Excel, or templates in a variety of categories on Office.com.
- During the current work session, Excel applies a temporary name to any new workbook you create. The first blank workbook that appears is named Book1 until you save it with a new name. Subsequent blank files you create are named Book2, Book3, and so on.

Try It! Creating a New Workbook in Excel

1. From the Windows Start screen, click the Excel 2013 program tile and then click Blank workbook. Excel starts and opens a blank workbook file.

   ✓ *If your keyboard has a Windows key (a key with the Windows logo on it), you can press that key at any time to display the Start menu.*

2. Click FILE > New > Blank workbook.

   ✓ *Throughout this book, you will see instructions provided in a sequence format; for example, "Click FILE > New" means to click the FILE tab and then click New.*

3. A second new, blank workbook appears, with its sequentially numbered temporary name, *Book2*.

4. Save the file as **E02Try_xx** in the location where your teacher instructs you to store the files for this lesson.

5. Leave the file open for the next Try It.

The new file shown in title bar

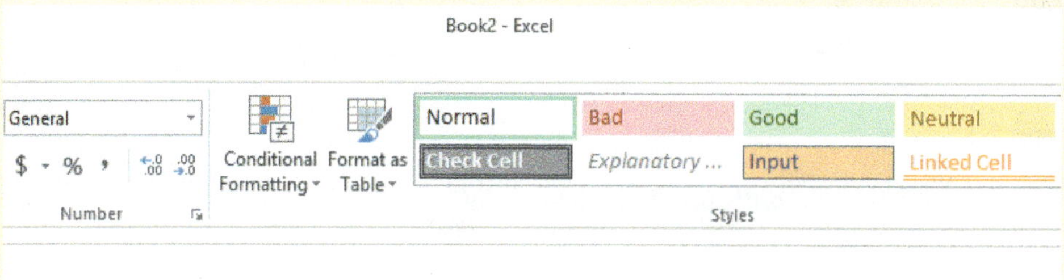

Excel 2013, Windows 8, Microsoft Corporation

Preview
To see how a worksheet will look when printed.

Redo
The command used to redo an action you have undone.

Text
An alphanumeric entry in a worksheet that is not a cell or range address.

Undo
The command used to reverse one or a series of editing actions.

Entering Text and Labels

- The first character entered in a cell determines what type of cell entry it is—a label or **text**, number, or formula.
- If you enter an alphabetical character or a symbol (` ~ ! # % ^ & * ( ) _ \ | { } ; : ' " < > , ?) as the first character in a cell, you are entering a label.
- A **label** may be text data, such as the labels: Blue, Sally Smith, Ohio, or Above Average.
- Or, a label may be used to identify data in the row beside it or the column below it, such as the labels: Sales, Qtr 1, or January.
- As you type a label in a cell, it appears in the cell and in the formula bar.
- To enter the label in the cell, type the text and then do any of the following to finalize the entry: press the [ENTER] key, an arrow key, the [TAB] key, click another cell, or click the Enter button ✔ on the formula bar.

✓ *To enter multiple lines in a cell such as* Overtime above *and* Hours below, *type* Overtime, *press* [ALT] + [ENTER]. *Type* Hours *on the second line in the cell and press* [ENTER] *to finalize the entry.*

- You also can press CTRL + ENTER to finish a cell entry and leave the current cell selected. This is a good technique to use if you later need to copy the cell's contents.
- The default width of each cell is 8.43 characters in the standard font (Calibri, 11 point).
- A label longer than the cell width displays the complete text only if the cell to the right is blank, or if you make the column wide enough to fit the entry.
- If you enter a lot of text in a cell, that text may not fully display in the formula bar. You can expand the formula bar (make it taller) by clicking the Expand Formula Bar button at the right end of the formula bar.
- A label automatically aligns to the left of the cell, making it a left-justified entry.

Try It! Entering Labels (Text)

1. In the **E02Try_xx** file, click cell A1, type **Client Survey**, and press ENTER twice.
2. Type **Client ID**, and press ENTER twice.
3. Type the following entries, pressing ENTER after each one:

   Was the room temperature appropriate?
   Were the staff members cordial?
   Was your appointment administered on time?
   Were your treatments explained in advance?
   Were your treatments explained in advance?
   Were you offered a beverage?

4. Click cell E4. Type **A Rating**, and press TAB.
5. Type **B Rating** and **C Rating** in the next two cells to the right, pressing TAB to complete each entry.
6. Click the Save button on the Quick Access Toolbar to save the file, and leave it open for the next Try It.

The file with label entries

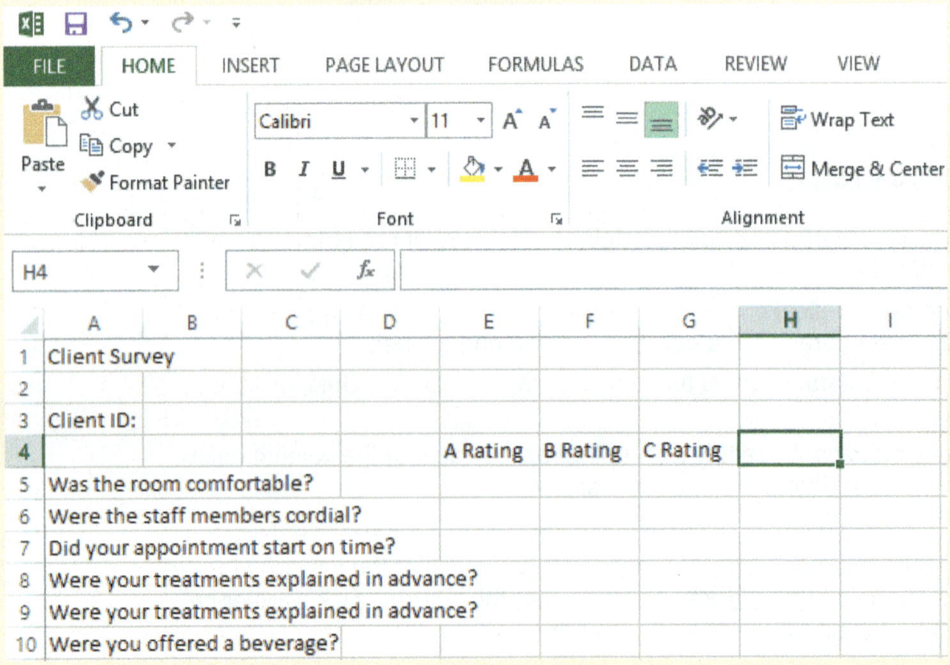

Excel 2013, Windows 8, Microsoft Corporation

Editing Text

- As you type data in a cell, if you notice a mistake before you press ENTER (or any of the other keys that finalize an entry), you can press the BACKSPACE key to erase characters to the left of the insertion point.
- Before you finalize an entry, you can press the ESC key or click the Cancel button ✕ on the formula bar to cancel it.
- After you enter data, you can make the cell active again (by clicking it, pressing an arrow key, etc.) and then type a new entry to replace the old one.
- You can double-click a cell in which the entry has been finalized to enable in-cell editing (also called Edit mode) and then make changes to only part of the entry.
- When in Edit mode, in a cell with data, the word *EDIT* displays at the left end of the status bar.
- Use the BACKSPACE, DEL, and other keys and selection techniques (as in Word) as needed to select and replace data.

Try It! Editing Text

1. In the **E02Try_xx** file, click cell A9. This cell has a repeated entry that you want to replace.
2. Type **Were you relaxed during the process?**, and press CTRL + ENTER to finish the entry.
3. Click cell A5 and press F2. Drag over *temperature appropriate* to select those words, type **comfortable**, and press ENTER.
4. Double-click cell A7, and press HOME to make sure the insertion point is at the beginning of the cell entry. Press and hold SHIFT while pressing → three times to select *Was*. Type **Did**.
5. With the cell still in Edit mode, double-click *administered* to select it.
6. Type **start**, and press ENTER.
7. With cell A8 selected, click in the formula bar to the right of the word *explained*, press SHIFT and click to the right of the word *advance*, press DEL, and then press ENTER. This finishes the current edits.
8. Press CTRL + S to save your changes to the **E02Try_xx** file, and leave it open to use in the next Try It.

Editing a text entry

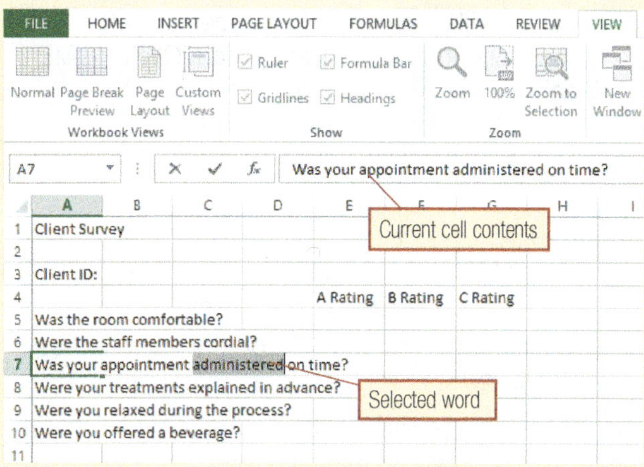

Excel 2013, Windows 8, Microsoft Corporation

The edited text

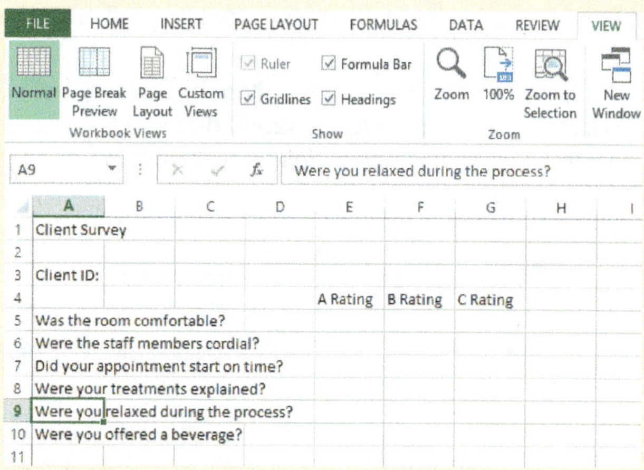

Excel 2013, Windows 8, Microsoft Corporation

Using Undo and Redo

- Use the **Undo** button on the Quick Access Toolbar to reverse any editing action.
- Some actions can't be undone (such as saving a workbook); in such cases, the Undo button will not be available and will be grayed out.
- You can reverse up to 100 previous editing actions with Undo.

✓ *The default number of Undo actions is 25.*

- The Undo button's name changes to reflect the most recent editing action.
- You can also redo (reinstate any action you've undone in error) up to 100 reversed actions using the **Redo** button.
- Both the Undo and Redo buttons include a drop-down list that enables you to undo or redo multiple edits at once.

Try It! Using Undo and Redo

1. In the **E02Try_xx** file, click cell E4.
2. Type **Yes**, and press TAB.
3. In cell F4, type **No** and press CTRL + ENTER to finish the entry.
4. On the HOME tab, in the Font group, click the Bold button **B**.
5. Click the Undo button on the Quick Access Toolbar.
6. Click the Redo button on the Quick Access Toolbar.
7. Click the Undo drop-down arrow on the Quick Access Toolbar, and click the third choice in the menu, which should be **Typing 'Yes' in E4**.
8. Click the **Redo** button on the Quick Access Toolbar twice.
9. Save the **E02Try_xx** file, and leave it open to use in the next Try It.

Clearing Cell Contents

- Press ESC or click the Cancel button ✕ on the formula bar to clear a cell's contents before finalizing any cell entry.
- To erase a finished cell entry, select the cell and then press DEL.
- You also can use the **Clear** button Clear in the Editing group of the HOME tab to delete the cell's contents or to selectively delete its formatting or contents only.
- Right-click a selected cell or range and click Clear Contents on the shortcut menu to remove the contents of the selected cell or range.
- You can clear the formatting of a selected cell or range by clicking HOME > Clear > Clear Formats.
- Clear All will clear the selected cell or range completely (format, contents, etc.). Click HOME > Clear > Clear All.

Try It! Clearing Cell Contents

1. In the **E02Try_xx** file, drag over the range E4:G4 to select it.

   ✓ *The above instruction means to drag the mouse from cell E4 across to cell G4. The shorthand E4:G4 is the address for the range of cells. Lesson 6 provides more detail about selecting and working with ranges.*

2. In the Font group of the HOME tab, click the **Bold** button **B**.
3. Click cell G4, and press DEL.
4. Click the Undo button on the Quick Access Toolbar.
5. With cell G4 still selected, click HOME > Clear Clear > Clear All.
6. Drag over the range E4:F4 to select it.
7. Click HOME > Clear Clear > Clear Formats.
8. Save the **E02Try_xx** file, and leave it open to use in the next Try It.

Inserting a Built-In Header or Footer

- When you want to repeat the same information at the top of each printed page, create a **header**.
- When you want to repeat the same information at the bottom of each printed page, create a **footer.**
- Header and footer information only appears in the Page Layout view or the printed worksheet.
- You can select a predesigned header or footer or create customized ones.
- To create a predesigned header or footer, click the INSERT tab, go to the Text group, and the Header & Footer button to display the HEADER & FOOTER TOOLS DESIGN tab. Then click either the Header or Footer buttons, and choose one of the predefined headers or footers.
- To customize the header/footer from there, type text in the appropriate section of the header or footer area: left, center, or right.

✓ *From here on, you will need to add a header with your name, the current date, and a page number print code to all the project workbooks.*

- You can also click buttons in the Header & Footer Elements group to insert print codes for the page number, total pages, current date, current time, file path, file name, or sheet name.

✓ *A print code is a set of characters that represent an element. For example, &[Page] is the print code for a page number.*

- You can also insert a graphic or picture (such as a company logo) in a header or footer.
- You can change the font, font style, and font size of the header or footer using the tools on the HOME tab.
- Press ESC to finish editing a custom header or footer and close the HEADER & FOOTER TOOLS DESIGN tab.

Try It! Inserting a Built-In Header or Footer

1. In the **E02Try_xx** file, click cell A1.
2. On the INSERT tab, in the Text group, click the Header & Footer button.
3. On the HEADER & FOOTER TOOLS DESIGN tab, in the Header & Footer group, click the Header button, and then click **E02Try_xx, Page 1** on the menu. The header appears in PAGE LAYOUT view.

   ✓ *If you've entered your name as the user name in Excel's options, you can choose a predefined header or footer that includes your name.*

4. Click INSERT > Header & Footer.
5. On the HEADER & FOOTER TOOLS DESIGN tab in the Navigation group, click the Go to Footer button.
6. With the insertion point in the center box of the footer, type your name, and then press TAB to move the insertion point to the right box.
7. On the HEADER & FOOTER TOOLS DESIGN tab in the Header & Footer Elements group, click the Current Date button to insert a code that will display and print the current date.
8. Press TAB to finish the entry in the right box.
9. Press ESC to finish working with the header and footer.
10. Review the footer you created, then scroll up and view the header.
11. Click VIEW > Normal to return to Normal view.
12. Save the **E02Try_xx** file, and leave it open to use in the next Try It.

Previewing and Printing a Worksheet

- You may print the selected worksheet(s), an entire workbook, or a selected data range.
- You can **preview** a worksheet before you print it. Previewing enables you to see a more accurate representation of how the worksheet will look when printed, so you don't waste paper printing a sheet with the wrong settings.

✓ *In Lesson 20, you learn how to print an entire workbook and a selected range.*

- Before you print a worksheet, you have the opportunity to review its appearance in the Backstage view.
- You also can specify print options in the Backstage view.
- If you decide not to print, click the HOME tab to leave the Backstage view.

Try It! Previewing and Printing a Worksheet

1. In the E02Try_xx file, click FILE > Print.
2. Review the document preview at the right side of the Backstage view. The preview shows the placement of headers and footers and all entries on the page.

   ✓ *If the worksheet you were printing consisted of multiple pages, you could use the buttons at the lower left to move between them.*

3. The various print settings appear in the Print pane area of the Backstage view.
4. Make sure that Print Active Sheets is selected under Settings.
5. **With your teacher's permission**, click the Print button. Otherwise, click the HOME tab.
6. Save and close the file, and exit Excel.

Print Preview

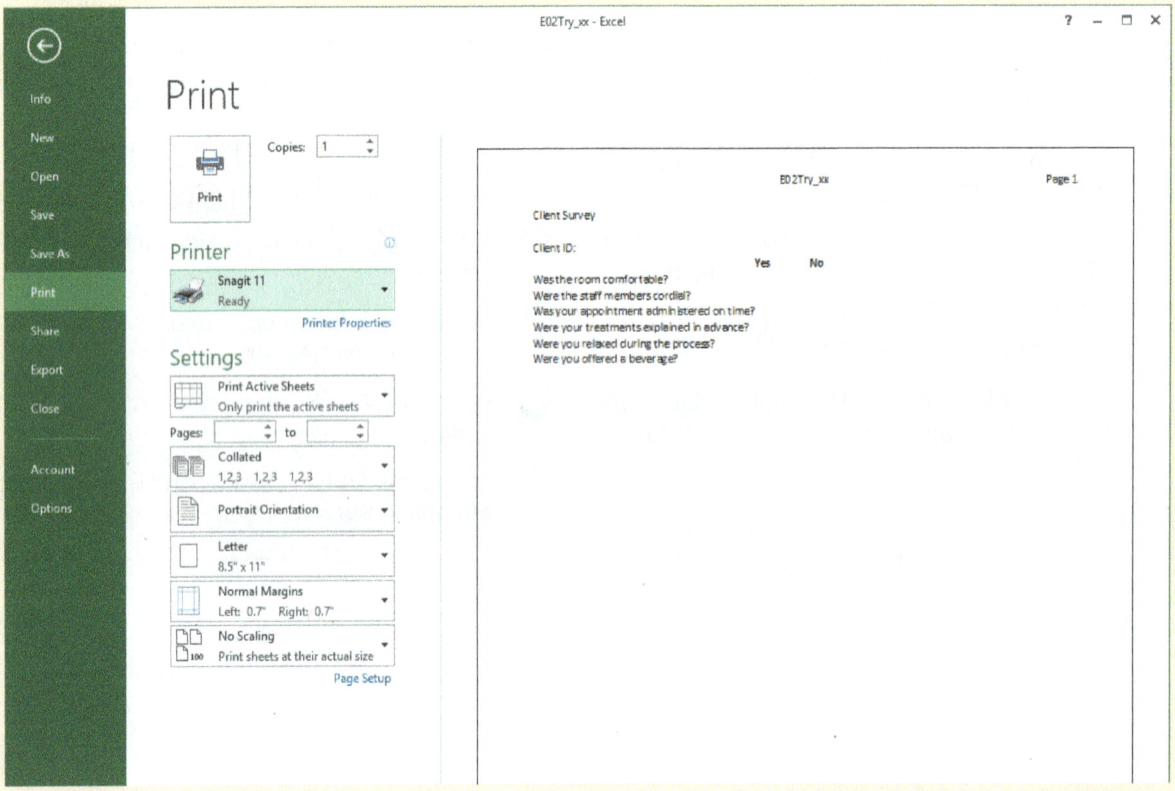

Excel 2013, Windows 8, Microsoft Corporation

Lesson 2—Practice

Excel is an outstanding tool to use when creating business documents such as invoices, where Excel's calculation capability helps you prepare an accurate summary of charges. In this project, you will create a new Excel worksheet containing the text portion of an invoice, insert a built-in header, and undo and redo editing actions using the skills you learned in this lesson.

DIRECTIONS

1. Start Excel, if necessary.
2. Click **Blank workbook**.
3. Save the blank file that appears as **E02Practice_xx** in the location where your teacher instructs you to store the files for this lesson.
4. Click **INSERT** > **Header & Footer**.
5. In the HEADER & FOOTER TOOLS DESIGN tab, click **Header**, and click the **Page 1** choice.
6. Click **INSERT** > **Header & Footer**.
7. Type **your name** in the left header box, and press TAB twice to move to the right header box.
8. In the HEADER & FOOTER TOOLS DESIGN tab, click **Current Date** to insert a date printing code.
9. Press TAB and then ESC to finish creating the header.
10. Click **VIEW** > **Normal** to return to Normal view.
11. Type **Invoice** in cell **A1**, and press ENTER twice.
12. Type **Remit To:** and press TAB.
13. Type **Serenity Health Club**, press ENTER, and press → if needed to select cell B4.
14. Type **200 W. Michigan Ave.** and press ENTER.
15. In cell **B5**, type **Chicago, IL 60614**, and press ENTER.
16. In cell **B6**, type **606-555-1200**, and press ENTER.
17. Click cell **A8**, and type the following three entries, pressing ENTER after each:
    a. **Time:**
    b. **Number:**
    c. **Due Date:**
18. Press ENTER again to select cell **A12**, and make the following two entries, pressing ENTER after each:
    a. **Client ID:**
    b. **Client:**
19. Click the **Undo** button on the Quick Access Toolbar twice to undo the previous two entries.
20. Click the **Redo** button on the Quick Access Toolbar twice to redo your entries.
21. Scroll up and drag over the range **B3:B6** to select it.
22. Click **HOME** > **Clear** Clear > **Clear Contents**.
23. Click the **Undo** button on the Quick Access Toolbar.
24. Click cell **A8**, type **Date:**, and press ENTER to replace that cell's entry.
25. With cell **A9** selected, press F2, press CTRL + ← to move the insertion point to the beginning of the cell, type **Invoice**, press SPACE, and press ENTER.
26. Drag over cell A10's entry in the formula bar, type **Terms:**, and click the **Enter** button ✓ on the formula bar to replace the entry. The finished worksheet appears as shown in Figure 2-1 on the next page.
27. Click **FILE** > **Print**.
28. **With your teacher's permission**, click the **Print** button. Otherwise, click the Back button to exit the Backstage view.
29. Click the **Save** button on the Quick Access Toolbar, and then click the Close button × at the end of the program's menu bar to exit Excel.

Figure 2-1

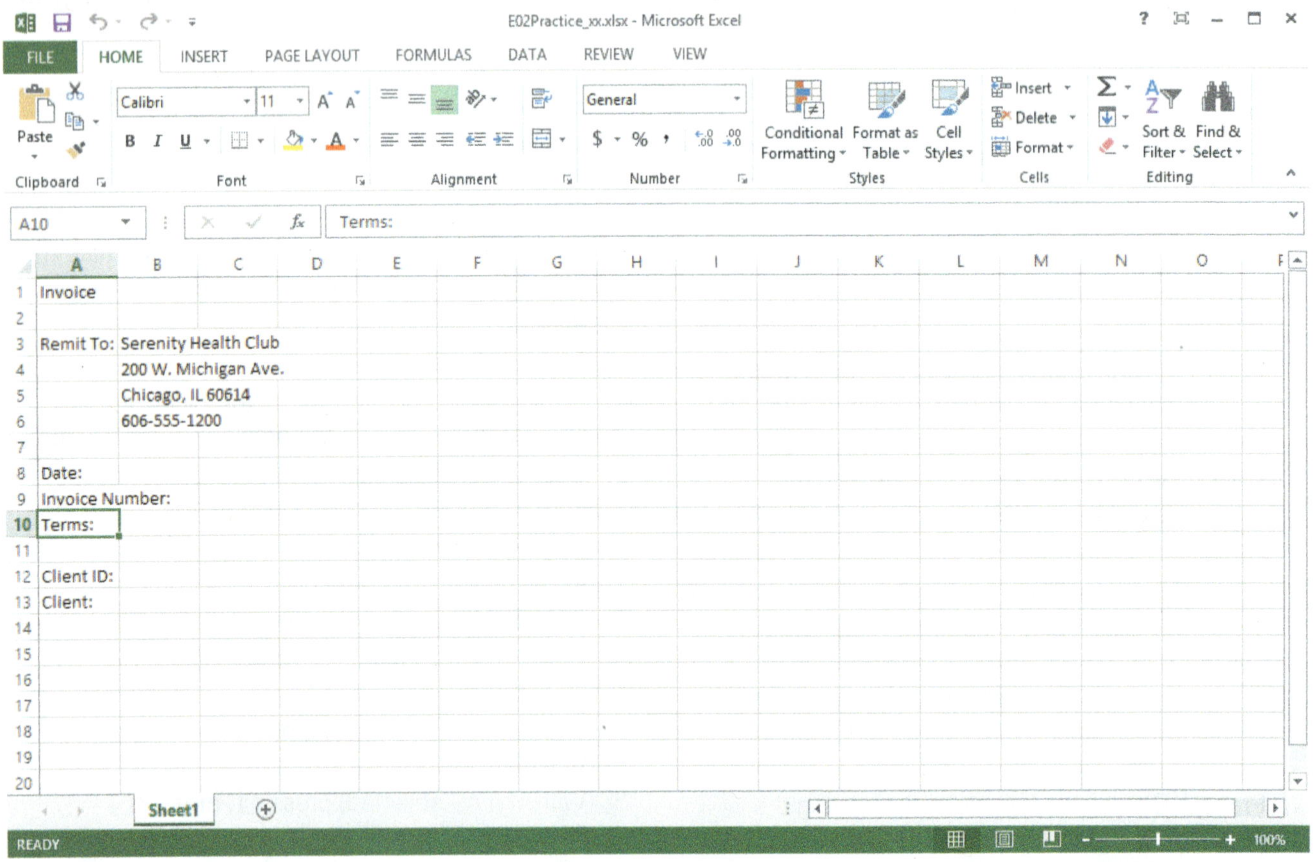

Excel 2013, Windows 8, Microsoft Corporation

Lesson 2—Apply

You are the Accounts Receivable Supervisor at the Serenity Health Club. A member has charged several services but has not yet paid for them. You need to create an invoice detailing the charges.

DIRECTIONS

1. Start Excel, if necessary, and open **E02Apply** from the data files for this lesson.
2. Save the file as **E02Apply_xx** in the location where your teacher instructs you to store the files for this lesson.
3. Add a header that has your name at the left, the date code in the center, and the page number at the right.
4. Change back to **Normal** view.
5. Enter the following data in cells **B8:B10**:
   a. **1/3/14**
   b. **546**
   c. **Due on receipt**
6. Click cell **A9** and replace **Number** with **No.**.
7. Click cell **B10**, and then click **HOME** > **Align Right** in the Alignment group.
8. Clear the formatting you just applied in cell B10.
9. Click the **Undo** button on the Quick Access Toolbar to undo the formatting change.

10. Change the entries in cells **A12:A13** to the following:
    a. **Member ID:**
    b. **Member:**
11. Click cell **B12**, and enter **A1054**.
12. Enter the following data in cells **B13:B15**:
    a. **Joy Wen**
    b. **12 W. 21st St.**
    c. **Chicago, IL 60602**
13. Make entries in the portion of the invoice that calculates the invoice charges, as follows:
    a. cell **A18: 2**
    b. cell **B18: Massage Hours**
    c. cell **C18: 45**
    d. cell **A19: 1**
    e. cell **B19: Facial**
    f. cell **C19: 75**
    g. cell **A20: 3**
    h. cell **B20: Personal Trainer Hours**
    i. cell **C20: 50**
14. Scroll down. Notice that the worksheet already has calculations built in, so it calculates values in the Amount column and Total cell for you.
15. You have been informed that the rate for personal training has changed. Click the **Undo** button on the Quick Access Toolbar, and then enter a rate of **55** in cell C20.
16. Click **FILE** > **Print** to preview the file in the Backstage view.
17. **With your teacher's permission**, click the **Print** button. Otherwise, click the Back button to exit the Backstage view. Submit the printout or the file for grading as required.
18. Save and close the file, and exit Excel.

Lesson 3

Adding Worksheet Contents

➤ What You Will Learn

Opening an Existing Workbook and Saving It with a New Name
Entering and Editing Numeric Labels and Values
Using AutoComplete
Using Pick From List
Using AutoCorrect
Checking the Spelling in a Worksheet

WORDS TO KNOW

AutoComplete
A feature used to complete an entry based on previous entries made in the column containing the active cell.

AutoCorrect
A feature used to automate the correction of common typing errors.

Numeric label
A number entered in the worksheet as a label, not as a value—such as the year 2014 used as a column label.

Pick From List
A shortcut used to insert repeated information.

Spelling checker
A tool used to assist you in finding and correcting typographical or spelling errors.

Value
A cell entry that consists of a number and numeric formatting only.

Software Skills Save a copy of a workbook with a new name to use it as the basis for another workbook. You also need to know how to enter numeric values, which are the basis for calculations. When entering data, take advantage of the many time-saving features Excel offers. Excel's AutoComplete feature, for example, automatically completes certain entries based on previous entries that you've made. AutoCorrect automatically corrects common spelling errors as you type, while the spelling checker checks your worksheet for any additional errors.

What You Can Do

Opening an Existing Workbook and Saving It with a New Name

- When you have saved and closed a workbook file, you can open it from the same disk drive, folder, and file name you used during the save process.
- When Excel starts, you can access a recently used file from the Recent list on the left. Click a file to open it.

  ✓ *You can also click Open Other Workbooks to go to the Backstage view and select a file from a specific location.*

- Click FILE > Open to display the Backstage view and access recently opened workbooks, the OneDrive, and Computer. The Recent Workbooks window is displayed by default. Click a workbook or location to open it.
- Click OneDrive to access files from Microsoft's virtual storage location.
- Click Computer to access files from a specific location on your computer. Click Browse to open the Open dialog box.
- In the Open dialog box, use the arrows in the text box at the top to navigate the disks, libraries, and folders on your computer.

- You also can use the Navigation pane at the left to go to the location of the workbook. Clicking the triangle beside any location displays the location's contents, and clicking again hides its contents.
- The default file location, the Documents library in Windows 8, appears in the Navigation pane by default. You can navigate to other libraries, favorite locations (under Favorites), locations on your computer, locations on the network, and locations on the OneDrive. You can also navigate to Homegroup (local network) locations if that feature is enabled.
- Click the Change your view button in the Open dialog box to preview a file, change the list to display file details, or display the properties of a file.
- You can pin a recently used workbook or location to the Recent lists so it is always easily accessible.
- A newly opened workbook becomes the active workbook and hides any other open workbook.

Try It! Opening an Existing Workbook and Saving It with a New Name

1. Start Excel.
2. In the Excel opening screen, click Open Other Workbooks.
3. Navigate to and select the folder containing the data files for this lesson.
4. Double-click the **E03Try** file. The file appears onscreen.
5. Add a header that has your name at the left, the date code in the center, and the page number code at the right, and change back to Normal view.
6. Click FILE > Save As.
7. Navigate to the folder where your teacher instructs you to store the files for this lesson.
8. Click in the File name text box, and edit the file name to read **E03Try_xx**.
9. Click the Save button to finish saving the file, and leave it open to use in the next Try It.

Renaming the file

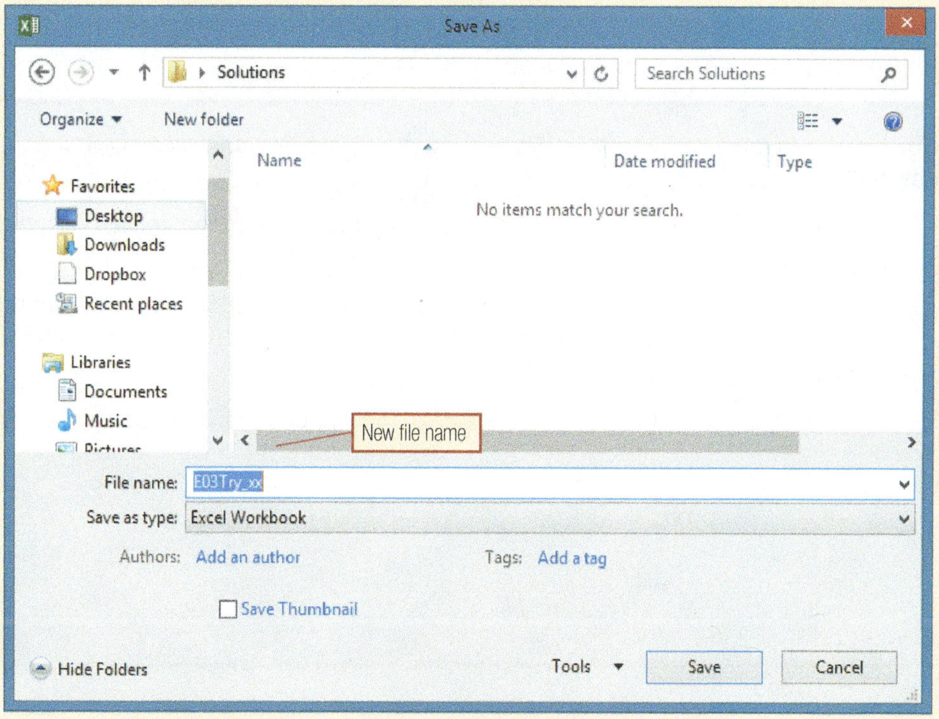

Excel 2013, Windows 8, Microsoft Corporation

Entering and Editing Numeric Labels and Values

- A cell contains a **value** when its first character begins with either a number or one of the following symbols (+, –, =, $).
- Type the value, and then do one of the following to enter it in the cell:
  - Press ENTER.
  - Press an arrow key.
  - Click the Enter button ✓ on the formula bar.
  - Click another cell.
- The default cell format in Excel is General.
- To display any number in a different format, apply the number format you want to use, as explained in Lesson 4.
- If you see pound signs displayed in a cell instead of a number, widen the column to display the value.
- You can enter some numbers with their formatting and Excel will recognize them as numbers, including:
  - Thousands: You can enter numbers with thousands separators, as in 1,543,009.24
  - Currency values: You can enter values with currency formatting, as in $1,299.60.
  - Percentages: You can enter a percent symbol to specify a percentage, as in 54%.
- When you enter numbers that contain hyphen formatting—such as Social Security numbers, phone numbers, and Zip codes—Excel treats the entries as text, and they cannot be used in calculations.
- A **numeric label**, such as a year number above a column of data that identifies the data's timing, is a number that typically will not be used in calculations.
- Begin the entry of a numeric label with an apostrophe (') as a label prefix to indicate that the number should be treated as a label (text) and not as a value. The entry will align at the left of the cell, unlike other value entries, which align right.
- Although the label prefix (') is shown on the formula bar, it is not displayed on the worksheet or printed.
- When you enter a value with an apostrophe, Excel displays a green triangle in the upper left-hand corner of the cell. Select the cell again, and an error button appears. You can:
  - Click the button and click Ignore Error to confirm that the number is really a label.
  - Click the button and click Convert to Number if the apostrophe was entered in error and the entry should be treated as a number.
- Edit a cell with a value or numeric label using the same techniques as editing a cell with a text entry.

Try It! Entering and Editing Numeric Labels and Values

1. In the **E03Try_xx** file, click cell A12, type **Roll**, and press TAB.
2. Type **Spelt** and press TAB.
3. Type **8** and press TAB.
4. Type **.35** and press ENTER.
5. In cell A13 type **Mini Roll**, and press TAB.
6. Type **Oat** and press TAB.
7. Type **'24** and press TAB. Notice that the number left aligns in the cell and a green triangle appears.
8. Click cell C13, click the Error button, and click Convert to Number. The entry right aligns in the cell.

(continued)

Try It! Entering and Editing Numeric Labels and Values *(continued)*

9. Press TAB, type **$.20**, and press CTRL + ENTER.
10. Click cell D8, type **$1.15**, and press ENTER to replace the current entry.
11. Click cell C10, press F2, press BACKSPACE, type **8**, and press ENTER.
12. Save the **E03Try_xx** file, and leave it open to use in the next Try It.

Converting a numeric label to text

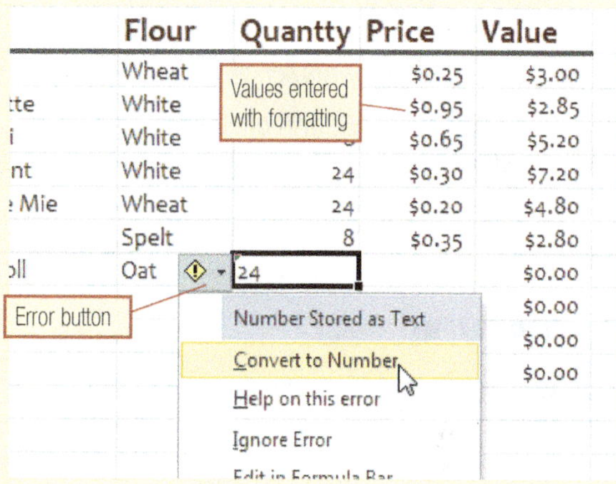

Excel 2013, Windows 8, Microsoft Corporation

Using AutoComplete

- When you need to repeat a label that has already been typed in the same column, the **AutoComplete** feature allows you to enter the label automatically.
- Type part of the label. If an entry with the same characters has already been entered in the column above, a suggestion for completing the entry appears in black.
- To accept the AutoComplete suggestion, press TAB or ENTER. Otherwise, continue typing the rest of the entry.

Try It! Using AutoComplete

1. In the **E03Try_xx** file, click cell A14.
2. Type **Pan**. An AutoComplete suggestion appears in the cell.
3. Press TAB to accept the AutoComplete entry and move to cell B14.
4. Type **Whe**, and press TAB to accept the AutoComplete entry and move to cell C14.
5. Type **8**, and press TAB.
6. Type **$.70**, and press ENTER.
7. Save the **E03Try_xx** file, and leave it open to use in the next Try It.

An AutoComplete suggestion

Excel 2013, Windows 8, Microsoft Corporation

Using Pick From List

- If several labels are entered in a list and the next items to be typed are repeated information, you also can use the **Pick From List** feature to make entries. Right-click a cell and then click the Pick From Drop-down List command on the shortcut menu.

✓ *The cells in the list and the cell to be typed must be next to each other and in the same column. Use the Undo button on the Quick Access Toolbar to reverse any editing action.*

- Click the desired choice in the list of entries that appears to enter it in the cell, and then press TAB or ENTER to move to the next cell, if needed.

Try It! Using Pick From List

1. In the **E03Try_xx** file, right-click cell A15, and click Pick From Drop-down List.
2. In the list that appears, click Roll.
3. Right-click cell B15, and click Pick From Drop-down List.
4. In the list that appears, click White, and then press TAB.
5. Type **36**, and then press TAB.
6. Type **$.23**, and then press TAB.
7. Save the **E03Try_xx** file, and leave it open to use in the next Try It.

Using AutoCorrect

- If you type a word incorrectly and it is in the **AutoCorrect** list, Excel automatically changes the word as you type.
- AutoCorrect automatically capitalizes the names of days of the week; corrects incorrectly capitalized letters in the first two positions in a word; and undoes accidental use of the Caps Lock key.
- When certain changes are made with AutoCorrect, you're given an option to remove the corrections by clicking the arrow on the AutoCorrect Options button that appears, and selecting the action you want.
- You can add words to the AutoCorrect list that you often type incorrectly. Click FILE > Options. In the Excel Options dialog box, click Proofing in the list at the left. Click the AutoCorrect Options button. Type entries in the Replace and With text boxes, and then click the Add button. Repeat as needed, and then click OK to close both dialog boxes.

Try It! Using AutoCorrect

1. In the **E03Try_xx** file, click cell A16.
2. Type **Cafe Biscotti**, and press TAB. Notice that when you press SPACE to finish the first word, Excel adds the accent to correct its spelling.
3. Type **O**, and then press TAB. AutoComplete fills in the word *Oat* for you.
4. Type **92**, and then press TAB.
5. Type **$.28**, and then press TAB.
6. Click FILE > Options.
7. In the Excel Options dialog box, click Proofing in the list at the left.
8. Click the AutoCorrect Options button.
9. Type **quantty** in the Replace text box, and **quantity** in the With text box.
10. Click the Add button.
11. Click the OK button twice.

   ✓ *If your teacher asks you to, reopen the AutoCorrect Options dialog box, select the quantty correction, and click Delete.*

12. Click cell A18 to select it.
13. Type **quantty**, and then press ENTER. Notice that AutoCorrect corrects the text you typed.
14. Click Undo.
15. Save the **E03Try_xx** file, and leave it open to use in the next Try It.

Checking the Spelling in a Worksheet

- To check the spelling of text in a worksheet and obtain replacement word suggestions, use the **spelling checker** feature.
- Start the spelling check from cell A1 to ensure it checks all sheet contents.

✓ *If you don't start the spell check from the beginning of the worksheet, Excel completes the spell check and then displays "Do you want to continue checking at the beginning of the sheet?"*

✓ *Press CTRL + HOME to go to the beginning of the worksheet.*

- To start the spelling checker, click the REVIEW tab and in the Proofing group, click the Spelling button.

✓ *Pressing F7 also starts a spelling check.*

✓ *Checking spelling in Excel works much as it does in Word.*

Try It! Checking the Spelling in a Worksheet

1. In the **E03Try_xx** file, click cell A1.
2. Click REVIEW > Spelling.
3. At the first misspelling, Quantty, make sure the proper spelling is selected in the Suggestions list, and click the Change button.
4. At the next misspelling, Pannini, make sure the proper spelling is selected in the Suggestions list, and click the Change All button.
5. Save and close the file, and exit Excel.

Lesson 3—Practice

In this project, you will enter and edit text, undo and redo editing actions, and check the spelling in a worksheet.

DIRECTIONS

1. Start Excel, if necessary.
2. Click **Blank workbook** to open a new file.
3. Save the file as **E03Practice_xx** in the location where your teacher instructs you to store the files for this lesson.
4. Add a header that has your name at the left, the date code in the center, and the page number code at the right, and change back to **Normal** view.
5. Type **Whole Garins Bread (r)** in cell A1, and press SPACE. (Type the entry exactly as shown; errors will be corrected later.) Notice that the AutoCorrect feature changes the (r) entry to a register mark: ®.
6. Press ENTER three times.
7. Type **Bakery Schedule**, and press ENTER.
8. Type **10/10/14**, and press ENTER twice.
9. Type the following cell entries, pressing TAB after each:
   a. **Customer**
   b. **Item**
   c. **Qty Needed**
   d. **Qty Shipped**
   e. **Qty to Bake**
10. Click cell **A8**, and type the following cell entries exactly as shown, pressing ENTER after each (note AutoCorrect in action again):
    a. **Cafe Latte**
    b. **Java Cafe**
    c. **Villige Green**
11. Click cell **B8**, and type the following cell entries exactly as shown, pressing ENTER after each:
    a. **Bagels**
    b. **Croissants**
    c. **Wheat Bread**
12. Click cell **C8**, and type the following cell entries exactly as shown, pressing ENTER after each:
    a. **325**
    b. **100**
    c. **25**
13. Click cell **D8**, and type the following cell entries exactly as shown, pressing ENTER after each:
    a. **300**
    b. **100**
    c. **25**

14. Click cell **A11**, type **J**, and press TAB to complete the cell entry using AutoComplete.
15. Type the following cell entries, pressing TAB after each:
    a. **Pastries**
    b. **150**
    c. **125**
16. Click cell **A1**.
17. Click **REVIEW** > **Spelling**.
18. At the first misspelling, *Garins*, make sure that **Grains** is selected in the Suggestions list, and then click the **Change** button.
19. At the next misspelling, *Qty*, click the **Ignore All** button.
20. At the next misspelling, *Villige*, make sure that **Village** is selected in the Suggestions list, and then click the **Change** button.
21. In the message box that informs you that the spelling check is complete, click the **OK** button. The finished spreadsheet appears as shown in Figure 3-1.
22. **With your teacher's permission**, print the worksheet. Submit the printout or the file for grading as required.
23. Save and close the file, and exit Excel.

Figure 3-1

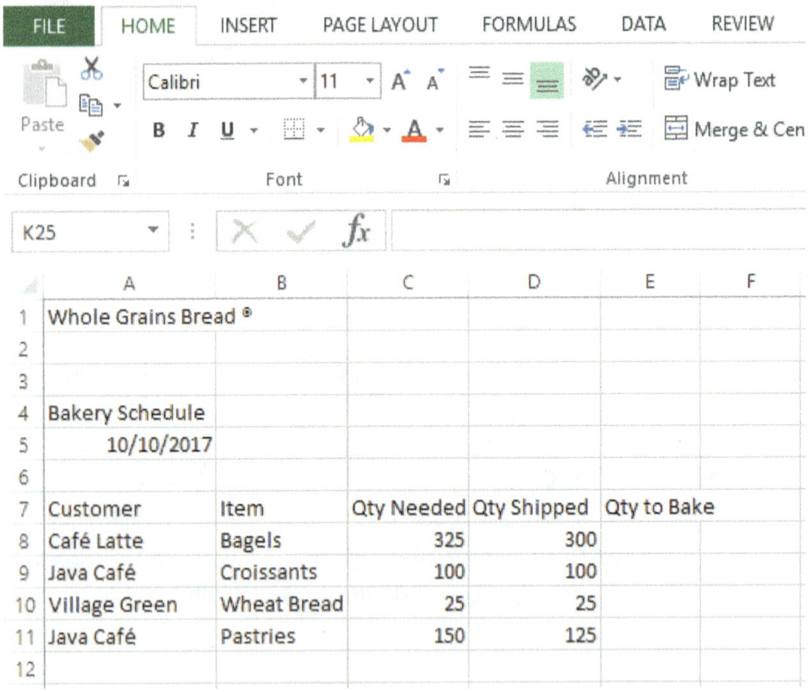

Excel 2013, Windows 8, Microsoft Corporation

Lesson 3—Apply

You're the team leader at Whole Grains Bread, and you need to complete the baking schedule for today so the other chefs will know what needs to be done for delivery tomorrow. You want to compare today's schedule with yesterday's, in order to compile a list of any items that were not completed on time. Those items will be given the highest priority.

DIRECTIONS

1. Start Excel, if necessary, and open the **E03Apply** file from the data files for this lesson.
2. Save the file as **E03Apply_xx** in the location where your teacher instructs you to store the files for this lesson.
3. Add a header that has your name at the left, the date code in the center, and the page number code at the right, and change back to **Normal** view.
4. In cell **A12**, use **Pick From Drop-down List** to enter **Village Green**.
5. Click cell **A13**, and make the following entries, using AutoComplete where applicable and pressing ENTER after each:
   a. **Mike's Steak House**
   b. **Gribaldi's Risorante**
   c. **Java Café**
   d. **Café Latte**
   e. **Village Green**
6. Click cell **B12**, and make the following entries exactly as shown, using AutoComplete where applicable and pressing ENTER after each:
   a. **White Bread**
   b. **Pastry Assortment**
   c. **Garlic Bread**
   d. **Muffin Assotment**
   e. **Muffin Assortment**
   f. **Wheat Rolls**
7. Click cell **C12**, and make the following entries, pressing ENTER after each:
   a. **9**
   b. **200**
   c. **125**
   d. **100**
   e. **225**
   f. **700**
8. Click cell **D12**, and make the following entries, pressing ENTER after each:
   a. **9**
   b. **200**
   c. **125**
   d. **100**
   e. **175**
   f. **650**
9. Click cell **D10**, and change the entry to **0**.
10. Click cell **D13**, and change the entry to **160**.
11. Click cell **D15**, and change the entry to **48**.
12. Click cell **A1**.
13. Check the spelling in the worksheet.
14. At the first misspelling, *Qty*, click the **Ignore All** button.
15. At the next misspelling, *Gribaldi's*, click the **Ignore Once** button.
16. At the next misspelling, *Risorante*, edit the entry to read **Ristorante**, and then click the **Change** button. Click **Yes** to change the word even though it's not in the dictionary.
17. At the next misspelling, *Assotment*, make sure the right correction is selected in the Suggestions list, and click the **Change** button.
18. In the message box that informs you that the spelling check is complete, click **OK**.
19. **With your teacher's permission**, print the worksheet. Submit the printout or the file for grading as required.
20. Save and close the file, and exit Excel.

Figure 3-2

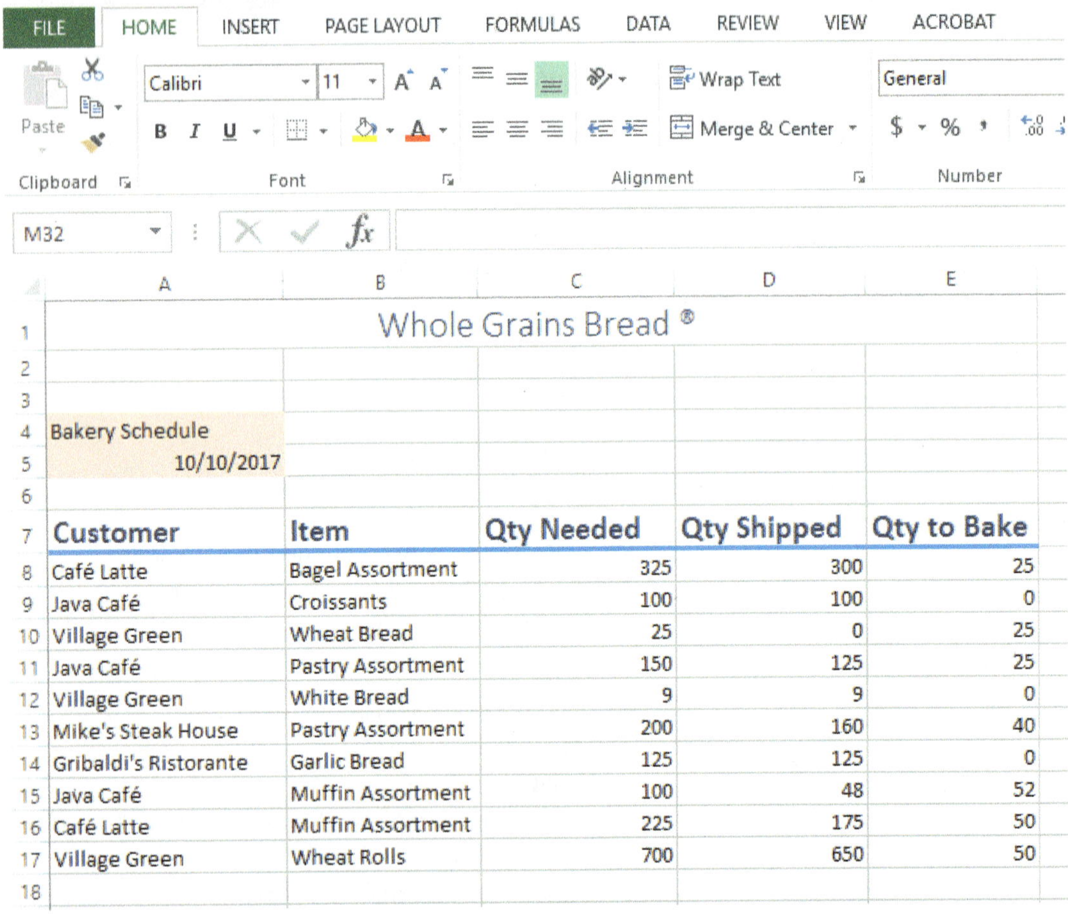
FILE
HOME
INSERT
PAGE LAYOUT
FORMULAS
DATA
REVIEW
VIEW
ACROBAT
Calibri
11
Wrap Text
General
Merge & Center
Paste
Clipboard
Font
Alignment
Number
M32
Whole Grains Bread ®
Bakery Schedule
10/10/2017
Customer Item Qty Needed Qty Shipped Qty to Bake
Café Latte Bagel Assortment 325 300 25
Java Café Croissants 100 100 0
Village Green Wheat Bread 25 0 25
Java Café Pastry Assortment 150 125 25
Village Green White Bread 9 9 0
Mike's Steak House Pastry Assortment 200 160 40
Gribaldi's Ristorante Garlic Bread 125 125 0
Java Café Muffin Assortment 100 48 52
Café Latte Muffin Assortment 225 175 50
Village Green Wheat Rolls 700 650 50

Lesson 4

Worksheet Formatting

➤ What You Will Learn

Choosing a Theme
Applying Cell Styles
Applying Font Formats
Merging and Centering Across Cells
Applying Number Formats

Software Skills When you change the appearance of worksheet data by applying various formats, you also make that data more attractive and readable.

What You Can Do

Choosing a Theme

- To make your worksheet readable and interesting, you can manually apply a set of formats.
- You manually **format** data by selecting cells and then clicking options on the HOME tab, such as the Font Calibri (Body) and Font Color buttons.
- Using too many manual formats can make the worksheet seem disjointed and chaotic.
- To make your worksheet more professional-looking, use a **theme** to apply a coordinated set of formats.
- By default, the Office theme is applied to all new workbooks; if you select a different theme, the **fonts** and colors in your workbook will automatically change.
- If you don't want to change the fonts in your worksheet, you can apply just the theme colors from a theme.
- Likewise, you can change theme fonts and the theme effects applied to graphics without affecting the colors already in your worksheet.
- You select a theme from the Themes gallery in the Themes group on the Page Layout tab.
- As you move the mouse over the themes shown in the gallery, the worksheet automatically shows a **Live Preview** of the data.
- When you type data in a cell, it's automatically formatted using the font in the current theme.

WORDS TO KNOW

Accounting format
A style that vertically aligns dollar signs ($), thousands separators (,), and decimal points.

Cell style
A combination of a font, text color, cell color, and other font attributes applied to a single cell.

Comma format
A style that displays numbers with a thousands separator (,).

Currency format
A style that displays dollar signs ($) immediately preceding the number and includes a thousands separator (,).

Fill
A color that fills a cell, appearing behind the data.

Font
The typeface or design of the text.

Font size
The measurement of the typeface in points (1 point = 1/72 of an inch).

Format
To apply attributes to cell data to change the appearance of the worksheet.

Live Preview
A feature that shows you how a gallery formatting choice will appear in the worksheet when you move the mouse pointer over that choice.

Merge and Center
A feature that enables you to automatically combine cells and center the contents of the original far left cell in the new cell.

Number format
A format that controls how numerical data is displayed, including the use of commas, dollar signs (or other symbols), and the number of decimal places.

Percent format
A style that displays decimal numbers as a percentage.

Theme
A collection of coordinated fonts, colors, and effects for graphic elements, such as charts and images, that can be quickly applied to all sheets in a workbook.

- You can apply a cell color (called a **fill**) or a text color. Click the down arrow on the Fill Color or Font Color buttons in the Font group of the HOME tab, and then click one of the choices under Theme Colors.
- If you apply a theme color to text or as a fill and later switch themes, Excel updates the color according to the new theme.
- If you choose one of the standard colors or use the More Colors option, the selected color will not change if you later change the theme.

Try It! Choosing a Theme

1. Start Excel.
2. Open the **E04Try** file from the data files for this lesson.
3. Save the file as **E04Try_xx** in the location where your teacher instructs you to store the files for this lesson.
4. Add a header that has your name at the left, the date code in the center, and the page number code at the right, and change back to Normal view.
5. On the PAGE LAYOUT tab, click the Themes button.

Previewing a theme

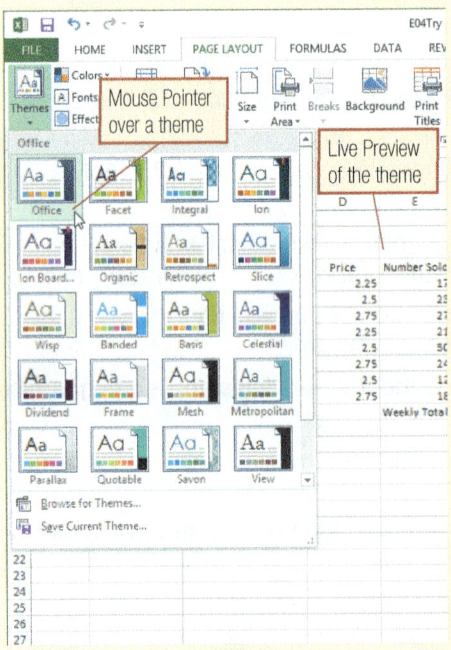

Excel 2013, Windows 8, Microsoft Corporation

6. Move the mouse pointer over the Integral choice in the Themes gallery. Notice how the fonts applied on the worksheet change.
7. Click the Slice theme.
8. Double-click the right column header border for columns C and E to make them wider to accommodate the text due to the theme font change. (Lesson 5 covers this technique in more detail.)

   ✓ *Move the mouse pointer over the right border of the column header you want to resize until you see the resizing pointer, which is a vertical bar with left and right arrows, then double-click to resize the column.*

9. Drag over the range B2:F2 to select it.
10. On the HOME tab in the Font group, click the Fill Color drop-down arrow. Under Theme Colors, click the Red, Accent 6, Lighter 40% fill color in the tenth column. The selected range shows a Live Preview of the color. Click the color to apply it.
11. Click cell F13.
12. Click Fill Color drop-down arrow. Under Standard Colors, click the Green color.
13. Save the **E04Try_xx** file, and leave it open to use in the next Try It.

(continued)

Try It! Choosing a Theme *(continued)*

Applying a theme color

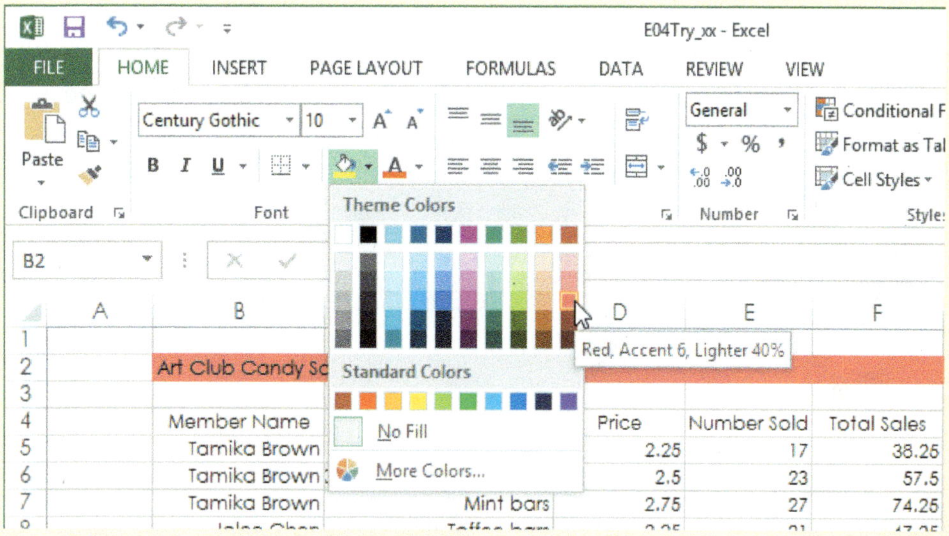

Excel 2013, Windows 8, Microsoft Corporation

Applying Cell Styles

- Themes contain a coordinated set of colors, fonts, and other elements, such as **cell styles**.
- Cell styles in a theme include various styles you can apply to column headings or totals and title and heading styles.
- If you apply any of the title, headings, or themed cell styles, the cells using that style will update automatically if you change themes.
- You also can apply cell styles that aren't changed if you change themes, such as formats you might use to highlight good or bad values, a warning, or a note.
- There are also some number format cell styles available that won't change if you change themes.

✓ *Sometimes applying a cell style to a cell holding a label causes the label to be cut off rather than spilling over into the cell to the right as you might expect. If this happens and you don't want to change the column width, also apply the style to the next cell to the right.*

- If you have a widescreen monitor and display Excel using the full screen, the Cell Styles button will change to the Styles gallery.
- After you select a cell or ranges of cells, you can use the Cell Styles button or the Styles gallery to apply a style. Use the gallery scroll arrows to scroll through the styles. You can also use the More button to view the styles in one window.

Try It! Applying Cell Styles

1. In the **E04Try_xx** file, drag over the range B4:F4 to select it.
2. On the HOME tab in the Styles group, click the Cell Styles button to display the gallery of cell styles.

   OR

   On the HOME tab, click the More button.
3. In the second column under Themed Cell Styles, move your mouse pointer over the 60% - Accent2 choice. The selected range shows a Live Preview of the cell style. Click the cell style to apply it.
4. Drag over the range E13:F13 to select it.
5. On the HOME tab, in the Styles group, click Cell Styles.

(continued)

Try It! Applying Cell Styles *(continued)*

6 Under Titles and Headings, click the Total choice in the far right column.

✓ *Notice that the standard color you applied to cell F13 doesn't change when you apply the cell style.*

7 Double-click the right column header border for columns B, E, and F to adjust the column widths due to the new styles.

8 Save the **E04Try_xx** file, and leave it open to use in the next Try It.

Styles gallery preview

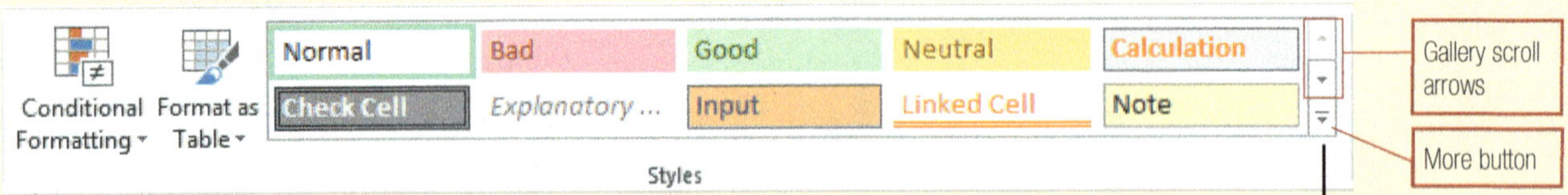

Excel 2013, Windows 8, Microsoft Corporation

Styles gallery

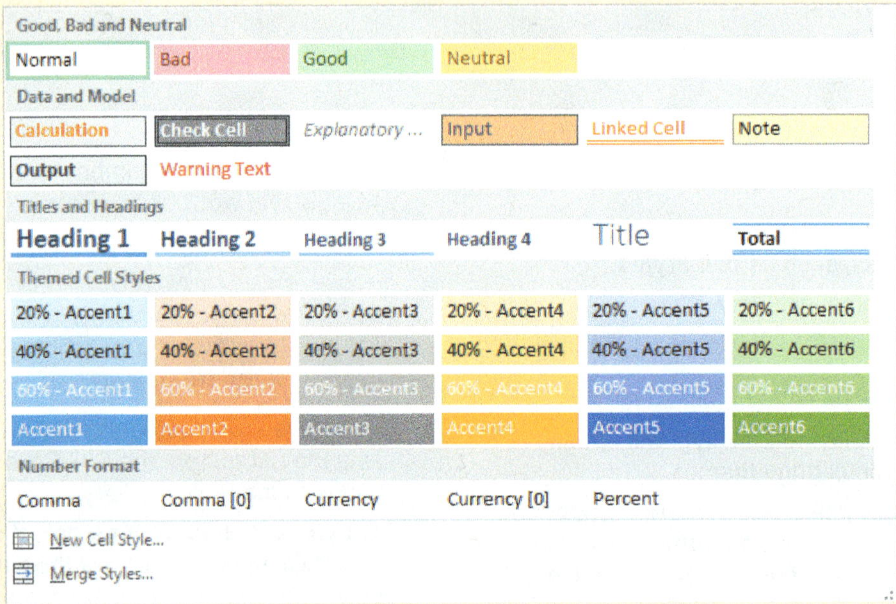

Excel 2013, Windows 8, Microsoft Corporation

Applying Font Formats

- The Font group on the HOME tab of the Ribbon offers choices for formatting text, including font size, color, and attributes such as bold and italics.

  ✓ *This type of formatting is sometimes called direct formatting.*

- The Font group settings you apply override the formatting applied by the current theme.
- If a cell has formatting you applied directly using the Font group tools, such as bold or underlining, that formatting will NOT change if you change themes.
- Theme fonts, font colors, and cell colors appear at the top of the selection list when you click the appropriate button. For example, if you click the Font drop-down arrow, the theme fonts appear at the top of the list.
- Standard fill or text colors will not change if you select a different theme.

- The way in which your data appears after making font and font size changes is dependent on your monitor and printer.
- The available fonts depend on those installed in Windows.
- When you change **font size**, Excel automatically adjusts the row height but does not adjust the column width.

Try It! Applying Font Formats

1. In the E04Try_xx file, click cell B2.
2. Click HOME > Font drop-down arrow.
3. Scroll down the list, and click Arial Black.
4. Click HOME > Font Size drop-down arrow.
5. Move the mouse pointer over the 24 size, view the Live Preview, and then click 24.

   ✓ *When you increase the font size, the row height increases automatically.*

6. Save the E04Try_xx file, and leave it open to use in the next Try It.

Applying a new font size

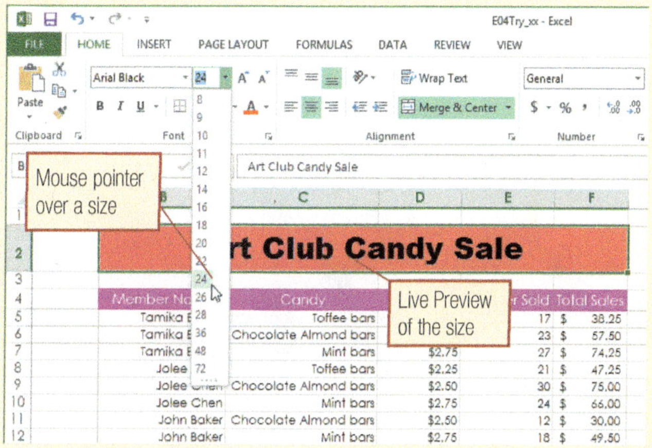

Excel 2013, Windows 8, Microsoft Corporation

Merging and Centering Across Cells

- You can center a worksheet's title across the columns that contain the worksheet data.
- To center a label across several columns, use the **Merge & Center** button Merge & Center in the Alignment group of the HOME tab.

  ✓ *The Merge & Center command actually merges the selected cells into one large cell and then centers the data in the newly merged cell.*

  ✓ *You can align merge cells left or right instead of centering the data. Click the Merge & Center drop-down arrow and click Merge Across to merge the cells with the current alignment (left or right).*

- For Merge & Center to work properly, enter the data in the first cell in a range, and then select adjacent cells to the right.
- Merged cells act as a single cell. Applying formatting to a merged cell formats the entire merged area.
- You can unmerge, or separate, merged cells by selecting the cell and clicking the Merge & Center button Merge & Center again.

Try It! Merging and Centering Across Cells

1. In the **E04Try_xx** file, drag over the range B2:F2 to select it.
2. On the HOME tab, in the Alignment group, click the Merge & Center button Merge & Center.
3. Drag over the range B13:E13 to select it.
4. On the HOME tab, in the Alignment group, click the Merge & Center button Merge & Center.
5. Leave the merged cell selected. On the HOME tab in the Styles group, click Total in the gallery of styles.
6. Save the **E04Try_xx** file, and leave it open to use in the next Try It.

Merge & Center aligns headings over all the data

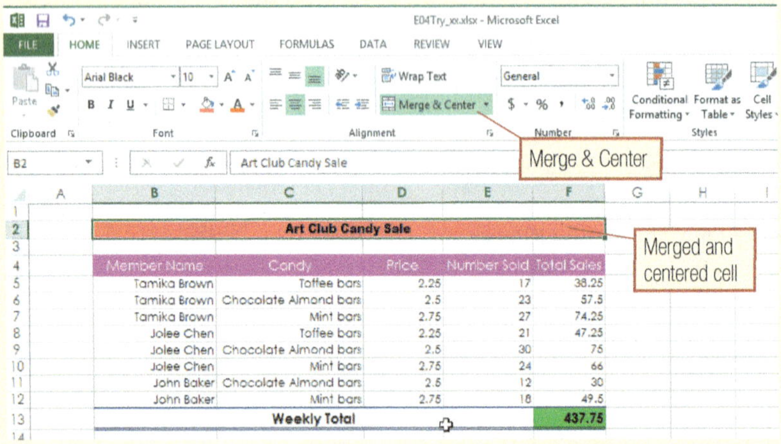

Excel 2013, Windows 8, Microsoft Corporation

Applying Number Formats

- When formatting numerical data, you may want to change more than just the font and font size—you may want to also apply a **number format.**
- Number formats are grouped together in the Number group on the HOME tab.
- The number format determines the number of decimal places and the display of zeros (if any) before/after the decimal point.
- Number formats also include various symbols such as dollar signs, percentage signs, or negative signs.
- Changing the format of a cell does not affect the actual value stored there or used in calculations—it affects only the way in which that value is displayed.
- There are buttons for quickly applying three commonly used number formats:
  - **Accounting format** $ 21,008.00, which includes a decimal point with two decimal places, the thousands separator (comma), and a dollar sign aligned to the far left of the cell.
  - **Percent format** 32%, which includes a percentage sign and no decimal points.

  ✓ *32% is entered as **.32** in the cell. If you type 32 and apply the Percent format, you'll see 3200%.*

  - **Comma format** 178,495.00, which includes two decimal places and the thousands separator (comma).
- Using the Number Format list, you can also apply a variety of other number formats such as Currency, Long Date, and Fraction.
- The **Currency format** is similar to Accounting format, except that the dollar sign is placed just to the left of the data, rather than left-aligned in the cell.
- If you don't see a number format you like, you can create your own by applying a format that's close. For example, you might apply the Accounting format and then change the number of decimal places using the Increase Decimal or Decrease Decimal buttons.
- You can also make selections in the Format Cells dialog box to design a custom number format. Click the Number group dialog box launcher to open the dialog box.

Try It! Applying Number Formats

1. In the **E04Try_xx** file, click cell F5.
2. On the HOME tab, in the Number group, click the Accounting Number Format button $ ▾. Excel formats the cell with the Accounting format.
3. Click cell D5.
4. On the HOME tab, in the Number group, click the Number Format drop-down arrow > Currency. Excel formats the cell with the Currency format. Notice the difference between it and the Accounting format in cell F5.
5. Drag over the cell range D6:D12 to select it.
6. Click the Number Format arrow > Currency.
7. Drag over the range F6:F13 to select it.
8. Click the Accounting Number Format $ ▾.
9. Drag over the range E5:E12 to select it.
10. In the Number group, click the Increase Decimal button twice.
11. In the Number group, click the Decrease Decimal button twice.
12. Save and close the file, and exit Excel.

Applying Currency format

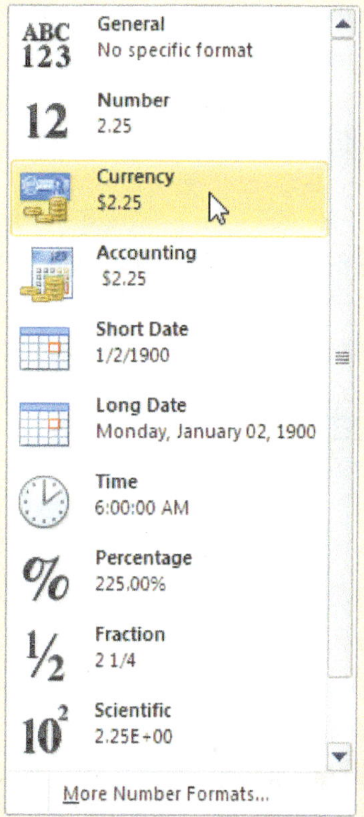

Excel 2013, Windows 8, Microsoft Corporation

Lesson 4—Practice

In this project, you will apply font and number formats to cells, merge and center cells, apply cell styles, and apply a workbook theme using the skills you learned in this lesson.

DIRECTIONS

1. Start Excel, if necessary, and open the **E04Practice** file from the data files for this lesson.
2. Save the file as **E04Practice_xx** in the location where your teacher instructs you to store the files for this lesson.
3. Add a header that has your name at the left, the date code in the center, and the page number code at the right, and change back to **Normal** view.
4. Drag over the row headers for rows **1** through **4** to select them.
5. Click **HOME** > **Clear** > **Clear Formats**.
6. Click cell **A4**, type **11/30/14**, and press CTRL + ENTER.
7. On the **HOME** tab, in the Number group, click the dialog box launcher to open the Format Cells dialog box. Date should already be selected in the Category list.
8. Click **14-Mar** in the Type list, and then click **OK**.
9. Click **PAGE LAYOUT** > **Themes**.
10. Move the mouse pointer over the **Facet** theme to view a Live Preview of its appearance.
11. Click the **Ion** theme to apply it.

12. Drag over the range **A1:I1** to select it.
13. Click **HOME** > **Merge & Center** Merge & Center ▾
14. In the Styles group, click **Cell Styles**, and click **Title**.
15. Drag over the range **A3:I3** to select it.
16. Click **Merge & Center** Merge & Center ▾
17. Click **Cell Styles** and then click **Heading 2**.
18. Drag over the range **A4:I4** to select it.
19. Click **Merge & Center** Merge & Center ▾
20. Click **Bold** **B**.
21. Drag over the range **D5:G5** to select it.
22. Click **Merge & Center** Merge & Center ▾
23. Click **Cell Styles** > **20% - Accent 3**.
24. Click cell **D7**, and type the following cell entries, pressing ENTER after each:
    a. **1**
    b. **3**
    c. **2**
    d. **2**
25. Click cell **E7**, and type the following cell entries, pressing ENTER after each:
    a. **2**
    b. **4**
    c. **2**
    d. **1**
26. Drag over the range **C7:C29** to select it.
27. Click **Accounting Number Format** $ ▾.
28. Press CTRL + HOME. Your worksheet should look like the one shown in Figure 4-1.
29. **With your teacher's permission**, print the worksheet. Submit the printout or the file for grading as required.
30. Save and close the file, and exit Excel.

Figure 4-1

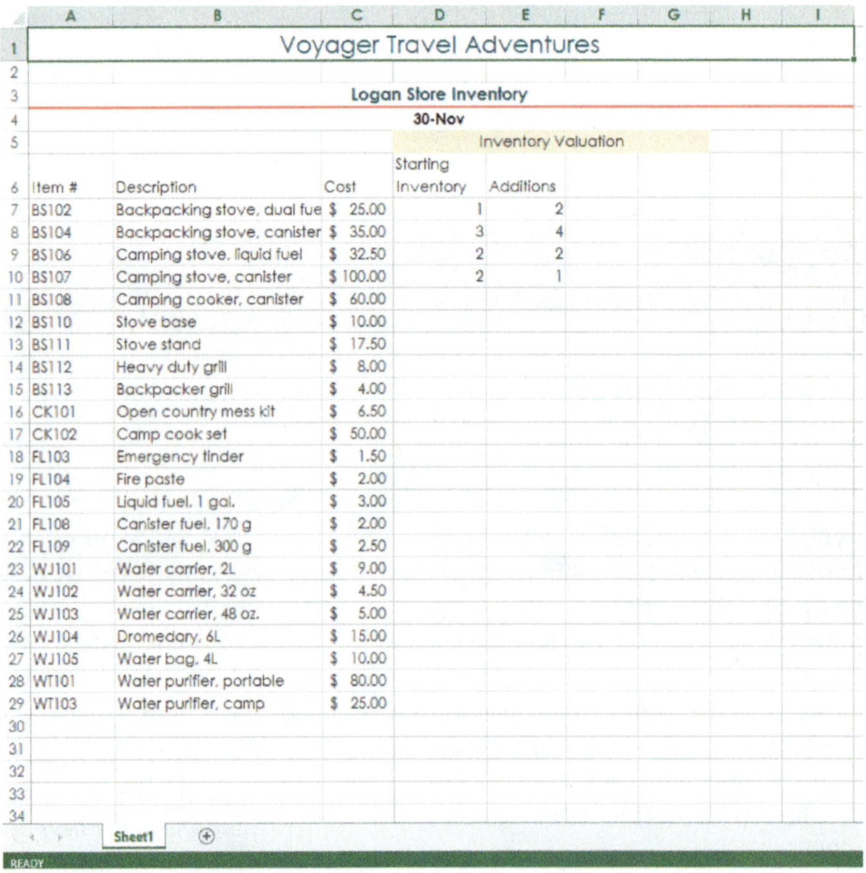

	A	B	C	D	E	F	G	H	I
1	Voyager Travel Adventures								
2									
3	Logan Store Inventory								
4	30-Nov								
5				Inventory Valuation					
6	Item #	Description	Cost	Starting Inventory	Additions				
7	BS102	Backpacking stove, dual fue	$ 25.00	1	2				
8	BS104	Backpacking stove, canister	$ 35.00	3	4				
9	BS106	Camping stove, liquid fuel	$ 32.50	2	2				
10	BS107	Camping stove, canister	$ 100.00	2	1				
11	BS108	Camping cooker, canister	$ 60.00						
12	BS110	Stove base	$ 10.00						
13	BS111	Stove stand	$ 17.50						
14	BS112	Heavy duty grill	$ 8.00						
15	BS113	Backpacker grill	$ 4.00						
16	CK101	Open country mess kit	$ 6.50						
17	CK102	Camp cook set	$ 50.00						
18	FL103	Emergency tinder	$ 1.50						
19	FL104	Fire paste	$ 2.00						
20	FL105	Liquid fuel, 1 gal.	$ 3.00						
21	FL108	Canister fuel, 170 g	$ 2.00						
22	FL109	Canister fuel, 300 g	$ 2.50						
23	WJ101	Water carrier, 2L	$ 9.00						
24	WJ102	Water carrier, 32 oz	$ 4.50						
25	WJ103	Water carrier, 48 oz.	$ 5.00						
26	WJ104	Dromedary, 6L	$ 15.00						
27	WJ105	Water bag, 4L	$ 10.00						
28	WT101	Water purifier, portable	$ 80.00						
29	WT103	Water purifier, camp	$ 25.00						
30									
31									
32									
33									
34									

Lesson 4—Apply

As the Inventory Manager of the Voyager Travel Adventures retail store, you want to enhance the appearance of an inventory worksheet you have created. You have already compiled the inventory data, and you want to spruce up the worksheet prior to printing by adding some formatting.

DIRECTIONS

1. Start Excel, if necessary, and open the **E04Apply** file from the data files for this lesson.
2. Save the file as **E04Apply_xx** in the location where your teacher instructs you to store the files for this lesson.
3. Add a header that has your name at the left, the date code in the center, and the page number code at the right, and change back to **Normal** view.
4. Apply the **Organic** theme to the file. Notice how the fonts and colors in the worksheet change.
5. Select the range **I7:I29** and apply the **Percent** style. Then, format the data for two decimal places.
6. Select the range **G7:G29** and apply the **Accounting** number format.
7. Select the range **A6:I6** and apply the **Accent3** cell style and **Center** alignment.
8. Select the range **A7:A29** and apply the **60% - Accent3** cell style.
9. Click cell **A4** and apply the ***Wednesday, March 14, 2017** date format.
10. Go to cell **A1**. Your worksheet should look like the one shown in Figure 4-2.
11. **With your teacher's permission**, print the worksheet. Submit the printout or the file for grading as required.
12. Save and close the file, and exit Excel.

Figure 4-2

Voyager Travel Adventures

Logan Store Inventory

Thursday, November 30, 2017

Inventory Valuation

	Item #	Description	Cost	Starting Inventory	Additions	Ending Inventory	Value	Full Stock Level	Current Stock Percentage
7	BS102	Backpacking stove, dual fuel	$ 25.00	1	2	3	$ 75.00	4	75.00%
8	BS104	Backpacking stove, canister	$ 35.00	3	4	7	$ 245.00	8	87.50%
9	BS106	Camping stove, liquid fuel	$ 32.50	2	2	4	$ 130.00	5	80.00%
10	BS107	Camping stove, canister	$ 100.00	2	1	3	$ 300.00	5	60.00%
11	BS108	Camping cooker, canister	$ 60.00	2	0	2	$ 120.00	2	100.00%
12	BS110	Stove base	$ 10.00	1	1	2	$ 20.00	3	66.67%
13	BS111	Stove stand	$ 17.50	2	1	3	$ 52.50	3	100.00%
14	BS112	Heavy duty grill	$ 8.00	2	0	2	$ 16.00	3	66.67%
15	BS113	Backpacker grill	$ 4.00	5	4	9	$ 36.00	10	90.00%
16	CK101	Open country mess kit	$ 6.50	4	3	7	$ 45.50	10	70.00%
17	CK102	Camp cook set	$ 50.00	2	1	3	$ 150.00	4	75.00%
18	FL103	Emergency tinder	$ 1.50	9	7	16	$ 24.00	15	106.67%
19	FL104	Fire paste	$ 2.00	12	6	18	$ 36.00	24	75.00%
20	FL105	Liquid fuel, 1 gal.	$ 3.00	18	15	33	$ 99.00	36	91.67%
21	FL108	Canister fuel, 170 g	$ 2.00	20	5	25	$ 50.00	36	69.44%
22	FL109	Canister fuel, 300 g	$ 2.50	21	13	34	$ 85.00	36	94.44%
23	WJ101	Water carrier, 2L	$ 9.00	10	2	12	$ 108.00	15	80.00%
24	WJ102	Water carrier, 32 oz	$ 4.50	12	6	18	$ 81.00	24	75.00%
25	WJ103	Water carrier, 48 oz.	$ 5.00	3	15	18	$ 90.00	24	75.00%
26	WJ104	Dromedary, 6L	$ 15.00	6	6	12	$ 180.00	15	80.00%
27	WJ105	Water bag, 4L	$ 10.00	10	2	12	$ 120.00	15	80.00%
28	WT101	Water purifier, portable	$ 80.00	15	5	20	$ 1,600.00	20	100.00%
29	WT103	Water purifier, camp	$ 25.00	12	0	12	$ 300.00	12	100.00%

Lesson 5

More on Cell Entries and Formatting

➤ What You Will Learn

Entering Dates
Filling a Series
Aligning Data in a Cell
Wrapping Text in Cells
Changing Column Width and Row Height
Using Keyboard Shortcuts

WORDS TO KNOW

Auto Fill
The feature that enables Excel to create a series automatically.

Date
A cell entry that indicates a date or time and is stored as a date code in Excel.

Default column width
The default number of characters that display in a column based on the default font.

Fill handle
A black box on the lower-right corner of the selected cell or range that you can use to fill (copy) a series or formula.

Key Tips
Keyboard shortcuts for choosing Ribbon commands that you display by pressing Alt.

Software Skills Use dates to identify when you created a worksheet or to label a column or row of data by time period. After typing dates, labels, and numbers in a worksheet, you can improve its appearance by changing the alignment of data and the widths of columns. If you need to enter a series of labels (such as Monday, Tuesday, Wednesday) or values (such as 1, 2, 3), using Excel's Auto Fill feature saves data entry time and reduces errors.

What You Can Do

Entering Dates

- Enter a **date** when you need to indicate the timing for data. Excel stores dates as special date codes, but automatically applies a Date number format depending on how you type in the date.
- You can enter a date using one of these date formats:
  - mm/dd/yy, as in 1/14/14 or 01/14/14
  - mm/dd, as in 1/14
  - dd-mmm-yy, as in 14-Jan-14
  - dd-mmm, as in 14-Jan

  ✓ *The current year is assumed for any date entry that doesn't include a year.*

- To enter today's date quickly, press CTRL + ; and then press ENTER.
- To enter the current time, press CTRL + SHIFT + ; and then press ENTER.

- After entering a date, you can change its number format as needed. For example, you can change the date 1/14/14 to display as January 14, 2014.
- To enter a time, follow a number with a or p to indicate AM or PM, like this: 10:43 p.
- You can enter a date and time in the same cell, like this: 10/16/14 2:31 p.

Keyboard shortcuts
Specific keyboard keys that you press together or in sequence to execute commands or apply settings.

Series
A list of sequential numbers, dates, times, or text.

Wrap text
A feature that causes long cell entries to appear on multiple lines.

Try It! Entering Dates

1. Start Excel.
2. Open the **E05Try** file from the data files for this lesson.
3. Save the file as **E05Try_xx** in the location where your teacher instructs you to store the files for this lesson.
4. Add a header that has your name at the left, the date code in the center, and the page number code at the right, and change back to Normal view.
5. Click cell C3 to select it.
6. Press CTRL + ;, and then press ENTER to insert the current date. It appears in the mm/dd/yyyy format.
7. Click cell C3 to select it again.
8. Click HOME > Number Format drop-down arrow > General. The date code for the date appears in the cell. The date code that you see will vary depending on the date you entered.
9. Click HOME > Number Format drop-down arrow > Short Date.
10. Save the **E05Try_xx** file, and leave it open to use in the next Try It.

A date code

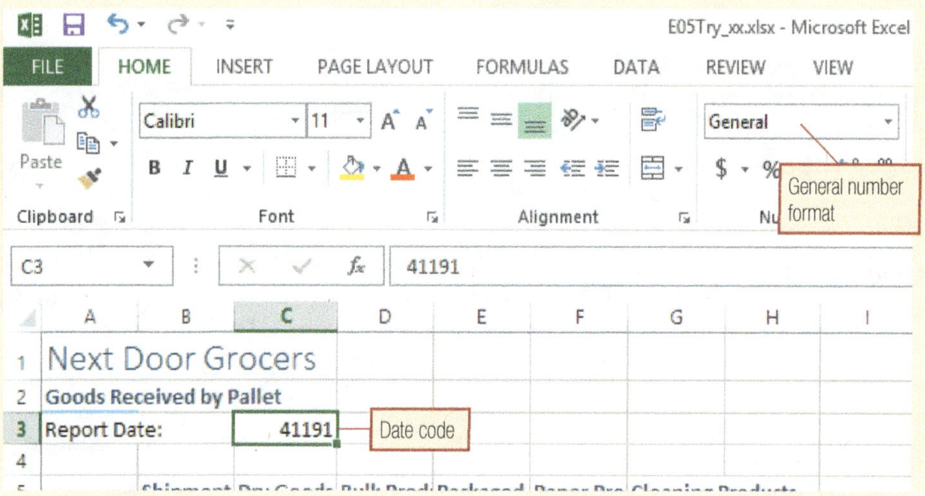

Excel 2013, Windows 8, Microsoft Corporation

Filling a Series

- A **series** is a sequence of numbers (such as 1, 2, 3), dates (such as 10/21/14, 10/22/14, 10/23/14), times (such as 2:30, 2:45, 3:00), or text (such as January, February, March). The feature or process for creating a series in Excel is called **Auto Fill.**
- To enter a series based on the active cell, drag the **fill handle**, a small square in the lower-right corner of the active cell that turns into a plus sign (+), over the range of cells you want to fill with the series.
- Excel can create some series automatically. For example, type January in a cell, and then drag the fill handle down or to the right to create the series January, February, March, and so on.
- A yellow ScreenTip appears under the mouse pointer, displaying the cell values of the series as you drag. The series values appear in the cells after you release the mouse button.
- To create an incremental series (i.e., 1, 3, 5, 7), enter the data for the first and second cells of a series, select the two cells, and then drag the fill handle over the range of cells to fill.
- You can also use the fill handle to copy formatting only (such as bold, italics, and so on) from one cell to adjacent cells, and not its value, or the value only without formatting. To do so, click the Auto Fill Options button that appears when you perform the fill, and then click Fill Formatting Only or Fill Without Formatting.

Try It! Filling in a Series

1. In the **E05Try_xx** file, click cell B6 to select it.
2. Type **4/2** and press [ENTER]. This enters the date with the format 2-Apr.
3. Type **4/9** and press [ENTER]. This is the second date in the sequence that you're entering.
4. Drag over the range B6:B7 to select it.
5. Drag the fill handle down until the ScreenTip reads *30-Apr*, and then release the mouse button.

   ✓ *When you enter dates with the abbreviated format used in steps 2 and 3, Excel applies the year specified by your current system date, so your results may vary from those shown in this chapter.*
6. Click cell C6 to select it.
7. Type **1** and press [CTRL] + [ENTER].
8. Drag the fill handle right through cell G6, and then release the mouse button.

   ✓ *Notice that a single number just repeats and doesn't automatically increment.*
9. Click cell C7 to select it.
10. Type **2** and press [ENTER].
11. Drag over the range C6:C7 to select it.

Filling a series

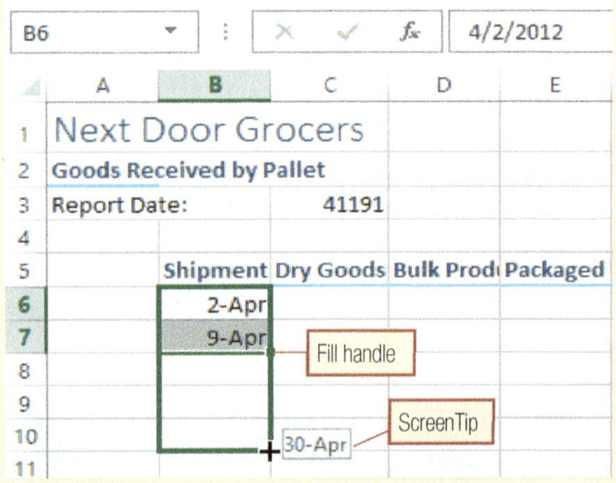

Excel 2013, Windows 8, Microsoft Corporation

12. Drag the fill handle down until the ScreenTip reads 5, and then release the mouse button.
13. With the range still selected, drag the fill handle right through column G. This fills the values across the columns, replacing the 1s already in row 6.
14. Save the **E05Try_xx** file, and leave it open to use in the next Try It.

Using Flash Fill

- When you have a series of labels in one column that you want to format, the Flash Fill feature in Excel can recognize the pattern in the text and change the format of the text for the series.
- Flash Fill can change the case of names that have been typed in lowercase to uppercase or change the format of phone numbers to include parentheses for the area code.
- Flash Fill only works when your text is in a single column.
- In the first cell next to the column you want to change, type the text the way you want it and press ENTER. Flash Fill begins to learn the pattern in the text.
- Next, type text into the second cell.

✓ *If you select another cell or click on the Ribbon before typing in the second cell, the Flash Fill feature will not be available.*

- When you type in the second cell, Flash Fill shows a preview of suggested changes for the rest of the series. Press ENTER to accept the suggestions.

✓ *To continue typing without using Flash Fill suggestions, press the ESC key.*

- You can use the Flash Fill Options button to accept or undo the suggestions.

✓ *If the Quick Analysis Lens displays, press the ESC key. You will learn about the Quick Analysis Lens in Chapter 2.*

- Flash Fill also can separate labels (such as names or addresses) into different columns or combine labels from several columns into one.
- When you want to separate first and last names that are in one column, use Flash Fill to create two new columns with first names in one column and last names in another column.
- When you want to combine first names, middle initials, and last names that are in three columns, use Flash Fill to create a new column with the complete name.
- Flash Fill is case sensitive and works best with consistent labels. For example, all of the last names in a series need to be lowercase for Flash Fill to change the names to be uppercase.

✓ *If the labels are not consistent, Flash Fill may not always separate the data elements correctly.*

Try It! Using Flash Fill

1. In the **E05Try_xx** file, click cell I6 and type the following cell entries, pressing ENTER after each:
   a. **Michael W. Penn**
   b. **Rosie L. Patton**
   c. **Jameson P. Falcon**
   d. **Jon D. Stalwart**
   e. **Mia A. Dawson**
2. Click cell J6 to select it, type **Penn, Michael W.**, and press ENTER.
3. In cell J7, type **Pa**. The Flash Fill preview suggestions appear.
4. Press ENTER to fill cells J7:J10 with the series of last names, a comma, first names, and middle initials.
5. Click the Flash Fill Options button > Undo Flash Fill.
6. Click the Undo button twice.
7. In cell J6, type **Michael**, and press ENTER.
8. In cell J7, type **Ro**, and press ENTER. Flash Fill fills the series of last names in cells J7:J10.
9. In cell K6, type **W.**, and press ENTER.
10. Click cell L6 to select it, type **Penn**, and press ENTER.
11. In cell L7, type **Pa**.
12. Click the Flash Fill Options button > Accept Suggestions.
13. Drag over the range J6:L10 to select it.
14. On the HOME tab, in the Editing group, click Clear Clear > Clear All.
15. Save the **E05Try_xx** file, and leave it open to use in the next Try It.

Aligning Data in a Cell

- When you type a label, Excel automatically aligns it to the left of the cell. Excel aligns values and dates to the right by default.
- In addition, cell entries are aligned along the bottom edge of the cell.
- To improve the appearance of a worksheet, you can change the alignment (both vertically and horizontally) of column labels, row labels, and other data.
- To align data, select the cells to format and use the buttons in the Alignment group on the HOME tab.
- Align data between the top and bottom sides of a cell using the Top Align, Middle Align, or Bottom Align buttons.
- Align data between the left and right sides of a cell using the Align Left, Center, or Align Right buttons.

✓ *Use the Decrease Indent and Increase Indent buttons to add or remove space at the left end of the cell for left-aligned entries.*

Try It! Aligning Data in a Cell

1. In the **E05Try_xx** file, drag over the range B6:B10 to select it.
2. On the HOME tab, click the Align Text Left button.
3. Drag over the range C6:G10 to select it.
4. On the HOME tab, click the Center button.
5. Drag over the range A1:I1 to select it.
6. On the HOME tab, click Merge & Center Merge & Center.
7. On the HOME tab, click Cell Styles > Accent5.

   ✓ *If you are working on a widescreen monitor, the Cell Styles button will change to the Styles gallery.*
8. On the HOME tab, click Increase Font Size five times.
9. On the HOME tab, click Middle Align.

   ✓ *You will only see a subtle vertical alignment change in cell A1 at this point.*
10. Save the **E05Try_xx** file, and leave it open to use in the next Try It.

Center aligned cells

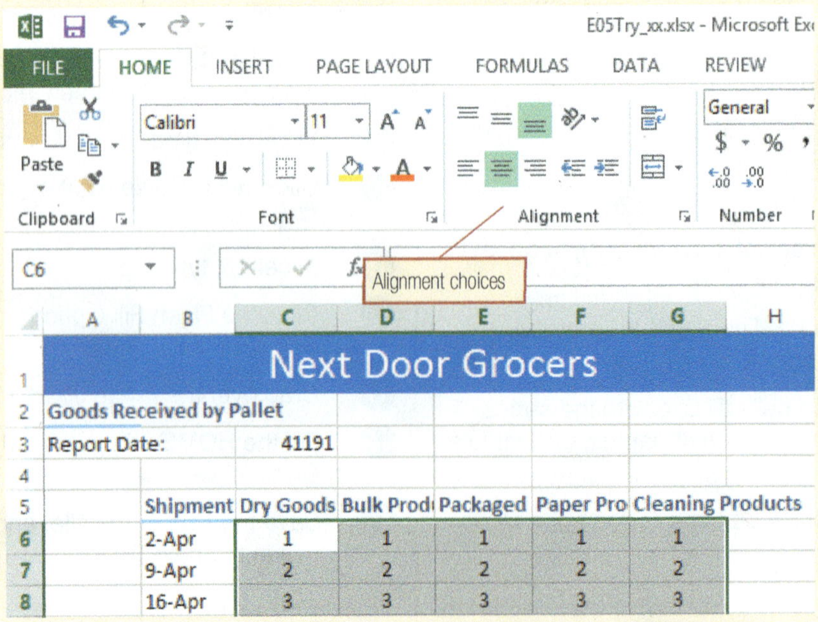

Excel 2013, Windows 8, Microsoft Corporation

Wrapping Text in Cells

- When a cell with a long label entry is too wide to display, you can use the **wrap text** feature to wrap the text to multiple lines.
- The Wrap Text button is in the Alignment group on the HOME tab of the Ribbon. Click it to apply and remove wrapping in the selected cell or range.
- Wrapping sometimes causes a line of text to break within a word, so you may need to adjust the column width for some columns after applying the wrapping.

Try It! Wrapping Text in Cells

1. In the E05Try_xx file, click cell A2 to select it.
2. On the HOME tab, click the Wrap Text button .
   ✓ *You will correct the column widths soon.*
3. Drag over the range B5:I5 to select it.
4. On the HOME tab, click Wrap Text .
5. Save the E05Try_xx file, and leave it open to use in the next Try It.

Changing Column Width and Row Height

- In a workbook file using the default Office theme, the default column width is 8.43 characters in the Calibri, 11 point font. The **default column width** varies in characters depending on the theme applied.
- You can quickly adjust a column to fit the longest entry in that column by double-clicking the right border of the column header, as you've seen in earlier lessons. Drag the right border to resize the width manually.
- The default row height in a workbook using the Office theme is 15 points.
- In some cases, such as when you apply a new number format, the column width increases automatically.
- In some cases, such as when you increase the font size of text or wrap text in a cell, the row height increases automatically.
- Double-click the bottom border of the row header to fit the row size automatically. Drag the border to resize it manually.
- Drag over multiple column or row headers or over cells in multiple columns or rows to resize all the selected rows or columns at once.
- Clicking the Format button in the Cells group on the HOME tab opens a menu with commands for automatically sizing (AutoFit Row Height and AutoFit Column Width) or manually sizing (Row Height and Column Width) rows and columns.

Try It! Changing Column Width and Row Height

1. In the E05Try_xx file, move the mouse pointer over the right border of the column A column header until you see the resizing pointer, which is a vertical bar with left and right arrows.
2. Drag right until the ScreenTip shows a width of 10.00, and then release the mouse button to finish resizing the column.
3. Drag over the range B5:G5 to select it.
4. On the HOME tab, click Format > Column Width.

Changing column width by dragging

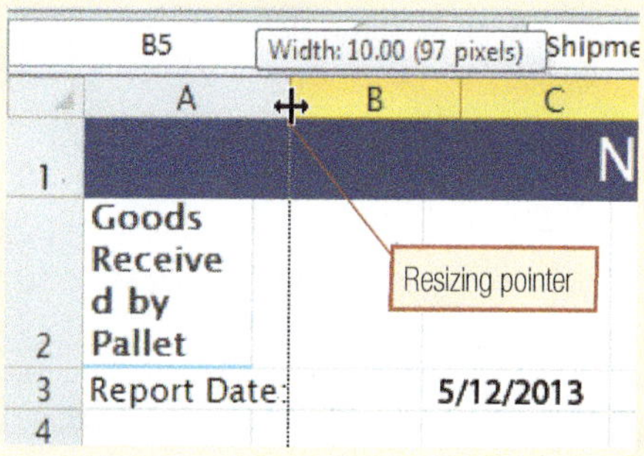

(continued)

Try It! Changing Column Width and Row Height *(continued)*

5 Type 9.57 in the Column width text box of the Column Width dialog box, and then click OK.

6 Move the mouse pointer over the bottom border of the row 1 row header until you see the resizing pointer.

7 Drag down until the ScreenTip shows a height of 42.00, and then release the mouse button to finish resizing the row.

8 Save the E05Try_xx file, and leave it open to use in the next Try It.

Using Keyboard Shortcuts

- You can use **keyboard shortcuts**—combinations of two or more keys pressed together or in sequence—to perform many commands in Excel.

  ✓ *Many keyboard shortcuts are the same as they've been in previous versions of Excel, such as CTRL + O to display the Open pane.*

- Several of the formatting choices have keyboard shortcuts, such as CTRL + B for applying bold. Move the mouse pointer over a Ribbon button, and the ScreenTip lists a keyboard shortcut if one exists.
- Pressing the ALT key displays **Key Tips**, which are keys you can press to select commands on the Ribbon.
- After pressing ALT, press the Key Tip for the desired Ribbon tab, and then the Key Tip for the command.

  ✓ *The Help topic "Keyboard shortcuts in Excel 2013" explains Key Tips in detail and lists all the available keyboard shortcuts.*

- You learned earlier about keyboard techniques for navigating and making selections, such as using the arrow keys to move from cell to cell.

Try It! Using Keyboard Shortcuts

1 In the E05Try_xx file, click cell C3 to select it.

2 Press ALT. The tab Key Tips appear onscreen.

3 Press P. The Page Layout tab appears.

4 Press ALT twice to redisplay the tab Key Tips.

5 Press H. The HOME tab appears.

6 Press J. The Cell Styles gallery opens.

7 Press ↓ four times to select the 20%-Accent1 style, and then press ENTER.

8 Press ↓ three times and ← once to select cell B6.

9 Press and hold SHIFT and press ↓ four times to select the range B6:B10.

10 Press CTRL + B to apply bold to the selection.

11 Press CTRL + I to apply italics to the selection.

12 Press CTRL + S to save the file.

13 Press ALT + F to display the the Backstage view.

14 Press C to exit Excel.

Lesson 5—Practice

In this project, you will align data in cells, wrap text in cells, change column width and height, fill a series of cells with data, and use keyboard shortcuts.

DIRECTIONS

1. Start Excel, if necessary, and open the **E05Practice** file from the data files for this lesson.
2. Save the file as **E05Practice_xx** in the location where your teacher instructs you to store the files for this lesson.
3. Add a header that has your name at the left, the date code in the center, and the page number code at the right, and change back to **Normal** view.
4. Click cell **J3**, type **7/6/14**, and press ENTER .
5. Click cell **D6**, type **Jan**, and press CTRL + ENTER .
6. Drag the **fill handle** right through cell **I6** to automatically fill with the series of month labels.
7. Drag over the range **D7:I7** to select it.
8. Drag the **fill handle** down through cell **I14**. This fills all the selected cells with the values from the selection.
9. Click cell **D14**, type **25**, and press TAB.
10. Type **50**, and press TAB.
11. Drag over the range **D14:E14** to select it.
12. Drag the **fill handle** right through cell **I14**. Excel fills the cells with a series that increments based on the first two entries.
13. Drag over the range **C6:J6** to select it.
14. Press ALT + H to select the HOME tab and display its Key Tips.
15. Press A + R to align the labels to the right.
16. Click cell **C3** to select it.
17. In the HOME tab, click **Wrap Text** .
18. Click cell **C7** to select it.
19. Type **Clark, Joe** and press ENTER .
20. In cell C8, type **Hi** and press ENTER . Flash Fill fills the range C8:C14 with the series.
21. Drag over the range A7:B14 to select it.
22. On the HOME tab, click **Clear** > **Clear Contents**.
23. Drag over the column headers for columns A and B to select them.
24. Move the mouse over the **column B** header right border until you see the resizing pointer, and drag left until the ScreenTip displays a width of **1.00**. Release the mouse button to resize the columns.
25. Click the **column J** header.
26. Double-click the **column J** header right border. This automatically AutoFits the selected column.
27. Drag over the column headers for columns D through I to select them.
28. On the HOME tab, click **Format** > **Column Width**.
29. Type **8.43** in the Column width text box in the Column Width dialog box, and then click **OK**.
30. Double-click the **column C** header right border to AutoFit the column.
31. Double-click the **row 3** and **row 6** header bottom borders to AutoFit the rows.
32. Click cell **C1** to select it.
33. On the HOME tab, click **Format** > **Row Height**.
34. Type **52** in the Row height text box in the Row Height dialog box, and then click **OK**.
35. On the HOME tab, click **Middle Align** . Press CTRL + S to save the file. Your worksheet should look like the one shown in Figure 5-1 on the next page.
36. **With your teacher's permission**, print the worksheet. Submit the printout or the file for grading as required.
37. Press ALT + F and then C to close the file.

Figure 5-1

	A	B	C	D	E	F	G	H	I	J
1	Serenity Health Club									
2										
3			Client Account Tracking							7/6/2017
4										
5				Payments by Month						
6			Client Name	Jan	Feb	Mar	Apr	May	Jun	Total
7			Clark, Joe	$150	$150	$150	$150	$150	$150	$900
8			Higgins, Mary	$150	$150	$150	$150	$150	$150	$900
9			Stevens, Gary	$150	$150	$150	$150	$150	$150	$900
10			Roberts, Paul	$150	$150	$150	$150	$150	$150	$900
11			Moyer, Anne	$150	$150	$150	$150	$150	$150	$900
12			Santos, Antonio	$150	$150	$150	$150	$150	$150	$900
13			Jones, Brett	$150	$150	$150	$150	$150	$150	$900
14			Stewart, Dorothy	$25	$50	$75	$100	$125	$150	$525
15										
16			Totals	$1,075	$1,100	$1,125	$1,150	$1,175	$1,200	$6,825

Excel 2013, Windows 8, Microsoft Corporation

Lesson 5—Apply

You are the Accounts Receivable Supervisor at the Serenity Health Club. You need to compile data on client payments and extra services sold in a worksheet and improve its formatting.

DIRECTIONS

1. Start Excel, if necessary, and open the **05Apply** file from the data files for this lesson.
2. Save the file as **E05Apply_xx** in the location where your teacher instructs you to store the files for this lesson.
3. Add a header that has your name at the left, the date code in the center, and the page number code at the right, and change back to **Normal** view.
4. Click cell **A3**, type **7-6-14**, and press ENTER .
5. Click cell **G3** to select it.
6. Wrap the text and align the text right.
7. Click cell **A1** and top align the data.
8. Adjust the height of row 1 using AutoFit.
9. Click cell **C6** and fill to cell **G6** to fill with a series of label entries.
10. Click cell **A8**. Drag the **fill handle** down to **A11** to fill four week labels.
11. Select the range **C8:C9**.
12. Drag the **fill handle** down to cell **C11** to fill with a series of increasing values.
13. Click cell **B8**, type **Week 1**, and press ENTER .
14. In cell B9, type **Week 2**.
15. Drag the **fill handle** down to cell **B11** to fill the series of capitalized labels.
16. Select the range **A8:A11** and clear the contents of the cells.
17. Select the range **D8:D9**.
18. Drag the **fill handle** down to cell **D11** to fill a series of decreasing values.
19. Select the range **A5:G6**.
20. Wrap the text in the selection.
21. With the range still selected, apply bold to the entries.
22. With the range still selected, change the column width to **13.5**.

23. With the range still selected, apply Center alignment.
24. Resize row 7 to a height of **6.00**. A thin filled row or column like this is another method for creating a border.
25. Select the range **C11:G11** and apply the Underline style.
26. Go to cell **A1**. Your worksheet should look like the one in Figure 5-2.
27. **With your teacher's permission**, print the worksheet. Submit the printout or the file for grading as required.
28. Save and close the file, and exit Excel.

Figure 5-2

A	B	C	D	E	F	G
Serenity Health Club						
7/6/2017						Extra Services Sold
Service Name Service Code		Swedish Massage Serv001	Aromatherapy Massage Serv002	Hot Stone Massage Serv003	Exfoliating Salt Scrub Serv004	Aromatherapy Facial Serv005
	Week 1	$525	$600	$445	$75	$150
	Week 2	$550	$575	$550	$225	$300
	Week 3	$575	$550	$575	$300	$450
	Week 4	$600	$525	$425	$225	$300
		$2,250	$2,250	$1,995	$825	$1,200

Excel 2013, Windows 8, Microsoft Corporation

Lesson 6

Working with Ranges

➤ What You Will Learn

Selecting Ranges
Entering Data by Range
Making a Range Entry Using a Collapse Dialog Box Button

WORDS TO KNOW

Contiguous range
A block of adjacent cells in a worksheet.

Noncontiguous range
Cells in a worksheet that act as a block, but are not necessarily adjacent to each other.

Collapse Dialog box button
A button in a dialog box that you click to downsize a dialog box to make a selection on the sheet, and then click again to restore the dialog box to its regular size.

Range
A block of cells in an Excel worksheet.

Software Skills Select a group of cells (a range) to copy, move, or erase the data in them in one step, or to quickly apply the same formatting throughout the range. You also can fill a range of cells with an entry, or perform calculations on cell ranges—creating sums and averages, for example. Some dialog boxes include a Collapse Dialog box button that enables you to specify a range entry in a text box.

What You Can Do

Selecting Ranges

- A **range** is an area made up of two or more cells.
- When you select cells A1, A2, and A3, for example, the range is indicated as A1:A3.
- The range A1:C5 is defined as a block of cells that includes all the cells in columns A through C in rows 1 through 5.
- A range of cells can be contiguous (all cells are adjacent to each other or in a solid block) or noncontiguous (not all cells are adjacent to each other).
- To select a **contiguous range**, drag over it. You also can click the first cell, press and hold SHIFT, and use the arrow keys to extend the selection or click the cell that's at the lower-right corner of the range to select.
- To select a **noncontiguous range**, select the first portion of the range. Then press and hold the CTRL key while dragging over additional areas or clicking additional cells. Release the CTRL key when finished selecting all the noncontiguous areas.
- When a range is selected, the active cell is displayed normally (with a white background), but the rest of the cells appear highlighted.

✓ *You also can assign a name to a range and use it to select or refer to the range. See "Using Named Ranges" in Lesson 13.*

- Clicking the column or row header selects the entire row or column. You also can press CTRL + SPACE to select the column holding the active cell or SHIFT + SPACE to select the row holding the active cell.

Try It! Selecting Ranges

1. Start Excel.
2. Open the **E06Try** file from the data files for this lesson.
3. Save the file as **E06Try_xx** in the location where your teacher instructs you to store the files for this lesson.
4. Add a header that has your name at the left, the date code in the center, and the page number code at the right, and change back to Normal view.
5. With cell A1 selected, press and hold the SHIFT key while pressing → four times.
6. On the HOME tab, click Merge & Center Merge & Center.
7. Drag over the range A5:A10 to select it.

A noncontiguous range selection

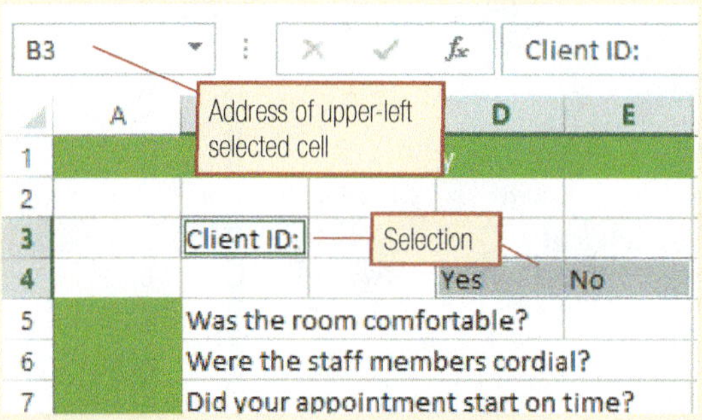

Excel 2013, Windows 8, Microsoft Corporation

8. On the HOME tab, click Cell Styles, and then click Accent6.
9. Drag over the range D4:E4 to select it. Press and hold the CTRL key, and click cell B3.
10. On the HOME tab, click Cell Styles, and then click Accent6.
11. Click the column C column header to select the column.
12. On the HOME tab, click Cell Styles, and then click Accent6.
13. Drag over the range B5:B10 to select it.
14. On the HOME tab, click Wrap Text.
15. Move the mouse pointer over the right border of the column B column header and drag right until the ScreenTip shows a width of 20.00.
16. On the HOME tab, click Format > AutoFit Row Height.
17. Move the mouse pointer over the right border of the column C column header and drag left until the ScreenTip shows a width of 1.00.
18. Save the **E06Try_xx** file, and leave it open to use in the next Try It.

Entering Data by Range

- In the last lesson, you learned how to enter data by using the fill handle. There are a couple of other methods you can use to fill a range.
- To fill all the cells in a selected range with the same entry, first select the range. Then type the desired entry, and press CTRL + ENTER.
- The Fill button in the Editing group on the HOME tab offers choices that enable you to fill cells in the desired direction in a selected range and to create custom series. For example, you can click Down to fill down the column, or Right to fill across the row. Click Series to create a series to fill.

Try It! Entering Data by Range

1. In the **E06Try_xx** file, drag over the range A5:A10 to select it.
2. Type **1** and press ENTER.
3. On the HOME tab, click Fill > Series.
4. In the Series dialog box, make sure the Columns and Linear options are selected and that 1 appears in the Step value text box, and then click OK.
5. Drag over the range D5:D6 to select it.
6. Press and hold CTRL, and click cells E7, D8, D9, and E10.

   ✓ *Be sure to release the CTRL key when you finish.*

7. Type **X**, and press CTRL + ENTER. Excel fills all the selected cells with the entry.
8. Save the changes to **E06Try_xx**, and leave it open to use in the next Try It.

Filling a range

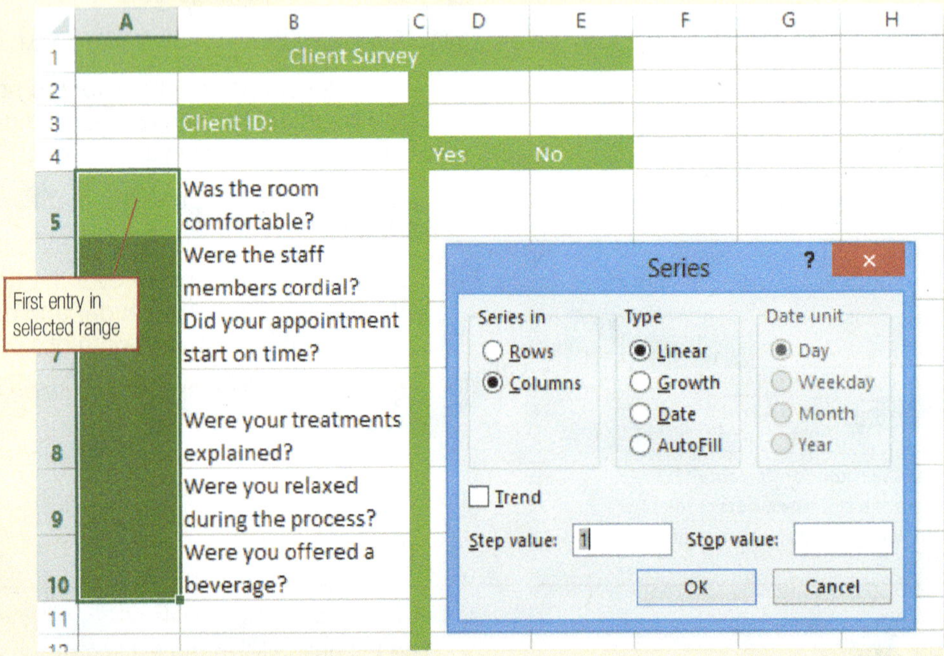

Excel 2013, Windows 8, Microsoft Corporation

Making a Range Entry Using a Collapse Dialog Box Button

- You will most likely set options in Excel using the buttons on the Ribbon, however, occasionally, you may use a dialog box.
- Dialog boxes appear when you click the dialog box launcher within a particular group on the Ribbon.
- To enter cell addresses or ranges in a dialog box, you can click the **Collapse Dialog box button** on the right end of the text box to shrink the dialog box so you can see the worksheet and select the range, rather than type it.
- After selecting the range, click the Collapse Dialog button to restore the dialog box to its normal size, and then finalize your selections.

Try It! Making a Range Entry Using a Collapse Dialog Box Button

1. In the **E06Try_xx** file, on the PAGE LAYOUT tab, in the Page Setup group, click the dialog box launcher.
2. Click the Sheet tab.
3. Click the Collapse Dialog box button at the right end of the Print area text box.
4. Drag over the range A1:E10 to select it and enter it in the text box.
5. Click the Collapse Dialog box button again.
6. Click OK.
7. Save and close the file, and exit Excel.

Using the Collapse button

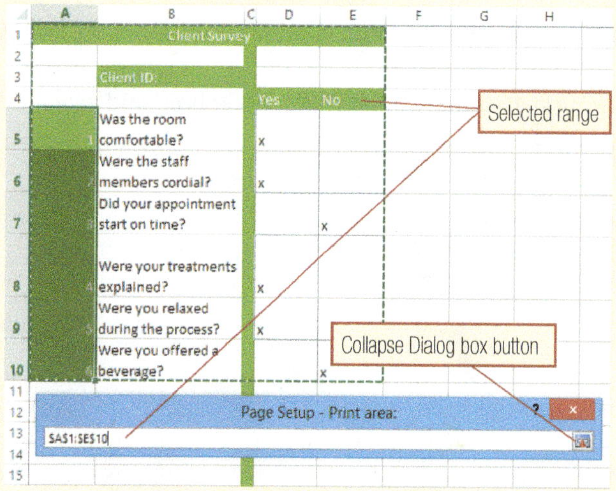

Excel 2013, Windows 8, Microsoft Corporation

Lesson 6—Practice

In this project, you will select a range of cells and fill a series using the skills you learned in this lesson.

DIRECTIONS

1. Start Excel, if necessary, and open the **E06Practice** file from the data files for this lesson.
2. Save the file as **E06Practice_xx** in the location where your teacher instructs you to store the files for this lesson.
3. Add a header that has your name at the left, the date code in the center, and the page number code at the right, and change back to **Normal** view.
4. Click cell **B25**, type **Frieda**, and press TAB.
5. Type **Randall**, and press ENTER.
6. Click cell B26, type **John**, and press TAB.
7. Type **Henson**, and press ENTER.
8. Drag over the range **A1:E1** to select it, and on the HOME tab, click **Merge & Center**.
9. Drag over the range **A2:E2** to select it, and on the HOME tab, click **Merge & Center**.
10. Drag over the range **A4:E5** to select it, and on the HOME tab, click **Cell Styles** > **Accent2**.
11. Drag over the range **A9:E9** to select it, and click **HOME** > **Cell Styles** > **Accent2**.
12. Drag over the range **A5:E5** to select it, and on the HOME tab, click **Wrap Text** > **Center**.
13. Click cell **A6** to select it.
14. Type **1**, and press ENTER.
15. Drag over the range **A6:E6** to select it.
16. On the HOME tab, click **Fill** > **Series**.
17. Make sure that the Rows and Linear options are selected and that **1** is entered as the Step value, and click **OK**.
18. Drag over the range **D11:D12** to select it.
19. Press and hold CTRL, and click cells **D15**, **D18**, **D21**, **D22**, and **D26**. Be sure to release CTRL after clicking the last cell.
20. Type **3**, and press CTRL + ENTER.
21. Click cell **D19** to select it.
22. Type **4**, and press CTRL + ENTER.

23. Select the range **D19:D20** to select it.
24. On the HOME tab, click **Fill** > **Down**.
25. Drag over the column headings for columns A through E.
26. Right-click the selected column headings, and click **Column Width**.
27. Type **13** in the Column width text box, and click **OK**.
28. Press CTRL + HOME. Your worksheet should look like the one in Figure 6-1.
29. **With your teacher's permission**, print the worksheet. Submit the printout or the file for grading as required.
30. Save and close the file, and exit Excel.

Figure 6-1

	A	B	C	D	E
1	Overview Academy				
2	Instructor Performance Ratings				
3					
4	Scale: 1-5				
5	Unacceptable	Needs Improvement	Acceptable	Exceeds Expectations	Outstanding
6	1	2	3	4	5
7					
8					
9	Course	First Name	Last Name	2013 Rating	2014 Rating
10	Band	Angela	Green		
11	Business	Markus	Wright	3	
12	Calculus	Vincent	Gambel	3	
13	Chemistry	Linda	Brown		
14	Computer Basi	Robert	Cardo		
15	Computer Grap	Phyllis	Weaver	3	
16	Computer Prog	Ramon	Ramirez		
17	English	Terry	Kaminsky		
18	Fine Arts	Stella	Andrews	3	
19	French	Francoise	Martine	4	
20	Geometry	Allen	Chang	4	
21	Health/Phys Ed	Axel	Jones	3	
22	History	Fred	Wilson	3	
23	Life Manageme	Stewart	Bing		
24	Science	Carl	Tyrell		
25	Social Studies	Frieda	Randall		
26	Spanish	John	Henson	3	

Excel 2013, Windows 8, Microsoft Corporation

Lesson 6—Apply

You are the Principal of Overview Academy, a small private school. You want to create a worksheet to track instructor performance ratings from two prior years. You need to finish entering some of the worksheet data, including the ratings, apply some formatting, and specify the range to print.

DIRECTIONS

1. Start Excel, if necessary, and open the **E06Apply** file from the data files for this lesson.
2. Save the file as **E06Apply_xx** in the location where your teacher instructs you to store the files for this lesson.
3. Add a header that has your name at the left, the date code in the center, and the page number code at the right, and change back to **Normal** view.
4. Adjust the width of **column A** using AutoFit.
5. Drag over the range **A8:E8** to select it.
6. Open the **Format Cells** dialog box, and click the **Alignment** tab, if necessary.
7. Open the **Horizontal** drop-down list and click **Fill**. Then click **OK**. This fills the selected range with the symbol character in cell A8, another way of creating a border.
8. Select the following non-contiguous cells: **D10**, **E10**, **E17**, **E18**, **E22**, **E23**, and **E25**.
9. Type **4**, and press CTRL + ENTER.
10. Click cell **E11** to select it.
11. Type **5**, and press CTRL + ENTER.
12. Fill the range **E12:E14** with the same value.
13. Enter the following data in the blank cells in column D:
    a. **5**
    b. **5**
    c. **2**
    d. **2**
    e. **5**
    f. **5**
    g. **2**
14. Enter the following data in the blank cells in column E:
    a. **3**
    b. **3**
    c. **5**
    d. **5**
    e. **4**
    f. **3**
    g. **2**
15. Open the **Page Setup** dialog box, and on the **Sheet** tab, set the Print area to **A1:E26**. Your worksheet should look like the one in Figure 6-2 on the next page.
16. **With your teacher's permission**, print the worksheet. Submit the printout or the file for grading as required.
17. Save and close the file, and exit Excel.

Figure 6-2

	A	B	C	D	E
1	Overview Academy				
2	**Instructor Performance Ratings**				
3					
4	Scale: 1-5				
5	Unacceptable	Needs Improvement	Acceptable	Exceeds Expectations	Outstanding
6	1	2	3	4	5
7					
8	●●				
9	Course	First Name	Last Name	2013 Rating	2014 Rating
10	Band	Angela	Green	4	4
11	Business	Markus	Wright	3	5
12	Calculus	Vincent	Gambel	3	5
13	Chemistry	Linda	Brown	5	5
14	Computer Basics	Robert	Cardo	5	5
15	Computer Graphics	Phyllis	Weaver	3	3
16	Computer Programming	Ramon	Ramirez	2	3
17	English	Terry	Kaminsky	2	4
18	Fine Arts	Stella	Andrews	3	4
19	French	Francoise	Martine	4	5
20	Geometry	Allen	Chang	4	5
21	Health/Phys Ed.	Axel	Jones	3	4
22	History	Fred	Wilson	3	4
23	Life Management	Stewart	Bing	5	4
24	Science	Carl	Tyrell	5	3
25	Social Studies	Frieda	Randall	2	4
26	Spanish	John	Henson	3	2

Excel 2013, Windows 8, Microsoft Corporation

Lesson 7

Creating Formulas

➤ What You Will Learn

Entering a Formula
Using Arithmetic Operators
Editing a Formula
Copying a Formula Using the Fill Handle
Using the SUM Function

Software Skills Creating formulas to perform calculations in Excel provides one of its powerful benefits: automatic recalculation. When you make a change to a cell that is referenced in a formula, Excel automatically recalculates the formula to reflect the change and displays the new formula result.

WORDS TO KNOW

Arithmetic (mathematical) operators
Symbols used in mathematical operations: **+** for addition, **-** for subtraction, ***** for multiplication, **/** for division, and **^** for exponentiation.

Formula
An instruction Excel uses to calculate a result.

Order of precedence
The order in which Excel performs the mathematical operations specified in a formula, based on the types of mathematical operators used.

SUM function
A built-in calculation used to add a range of values together.

What You Can Do

Entering a Formula

- A **formula** is a worksheet instruction that performs a calculation.
- Enter a formula in the cell where the result should display.
- As you type a formula, it displays in the cell and in the formula bar.
- If you enter a long formula in a cell, that text may not fully display in the formula bar. You can expand the formula bar (make it taller) by clicking the Expand Formula Bar button ⌄ at the right end of the formula bar.
- When you select a cell that has a formula, the answer displays in the cell while the formula appears in the formula bar when the cell is selected.
- Use cell or range references, values, and mathematical operators in formulas.

  ✓ *A formula can also contain Excel's predefined functions, which are covered in Lesson 11, or use named ranges, which are covered in Lesson 13.*

- You must start each formula by typing the equal sign (=). For example, the formula =B2+B4+B6 adds together the values in those three cell locations.
- When you change the value in a cell that is referenced in a formula, the answer in the formula cell automatically changes.
- When typing a percentage as a value in a formula, you can enter it with the percent symbol or as a decimal.
- You can click a cell or drag a range to enter its address in the formula. This method can be more accurate than typing cell or range addresses.

Try It! Entering a Formula

1. Start Excel.
2. Open the **E07Try** file from the data files for this lesson.
3. Save the file as **E07Try_xx** in the location where your teacher instructs you to store the files for this lesson.
4. Add a header that has your name at the left, the date code in the center, and the page number code at the right, and change back to Normal view.
5. Click cell F4 to select it.
6. Type **=D4+E4**, and press ENTER.
7. Click cell D5 to select it.
8. Type **=**, click cell B5, type *****, and click cell C5.

Entering a formula

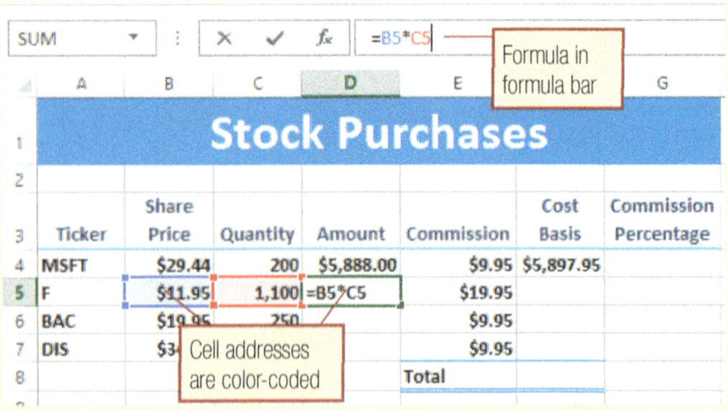

Excel 2013, Windows 8, Microsoft Corporation

9. Press ENTER to finish the formula.
10. Save the **E07Try_xx** file, and leave it open to use in the next Try It.

Using Arithmetic Operators

- Use the following standard **arithmetic (mathematical) operators** in formulas:
  - \+ Addition
  - \- Subtraction
  - * Multiplication
  - / Division
  - ^ Exponentiation
- Excel performs mathematical operations in a particular order, called **order of precedence**. This is the order in which Excel calculates:
  1. Operations enclosed in parentheses.
  2. Exponentiation.
  3. Multiplication and division.
  4. Addition and subtraction.
- When a formula has multiple operators of the same precedence level, such as multiple multiplication operations, Excel performs the calculations from left to right.
- Keeping the order of mathematical operations in mind, the easiest way to control which part of a complex formula is calculated first is to use parentheses. Here are two examples:

  =8+3*5 result: 23

  Excel multiplies first, then adds.

  =(8+3)*5 result: 55

  Excel adds the values in parentheses, then multiplies.

Try It! Using Arithmetic Operators

1. In the **E07Try_xx** file, click cell G4 to select it.
2. Type **=E4/F4** and press ENTER.
3. Press ← to select cell F5.
4. Type **=B5*C5+E5** and press TAB.

   ✓ *The formula you just entered is an alternate way of performing a calculation you created earlier. You could also enter this formula as* ***=D5+E5*** *to calculate the correct result.*

5. In cell G5, type **=E5/(B5*C5+E5)** and press ENTER.

   ✓ *The formula you just entered is an alternate way of performing a calculation you created in cell G4. You could also enter this formula as* ***=E5/F5*** *to calculate the correct result.*

6. Save the **E07Try_xx** file, and leave it open to use in the next Try It.

Editing a Formula

- Excel automatically provides assistance in correcting common mistakes in a formula (for example, omitting a closing parenthesis).
- You can edit a formula as needed to update its calculation or if you see an error message such as #NUM! or #REF! in the cell.
- Editing a formula works just like editing any other data in a cell. Click the cell, and then press F2 or double-click the cell to enter edit mode. Work in the cell or the formula bar to make the changes, and then press ENTER or click the Enter button ✓ on the formula bar to finish the entry.

✓ *Function lock must be enabled to use the function keys.*

Try It! Editing a Formula

1. In the **E07Try_xx** file, click cell F5 to select it, and press F2 to enter edit mode.

   ✓ *If needed, press the F Lock key to turn function lock on.*

2. In cell F5, drag over B5*C5, click cell D5 to replace the selection, and press TAB to finish the change.
3. With cell G5 selected, drag over (B5*C5+E5) in the formula bar to select it.
4. Type **F5** to replace the selected part of the formula, and press ENTER.
5. Save the **E07Try_xx** file, and leave it open to use in the next Try It.

Editing in the formula bar

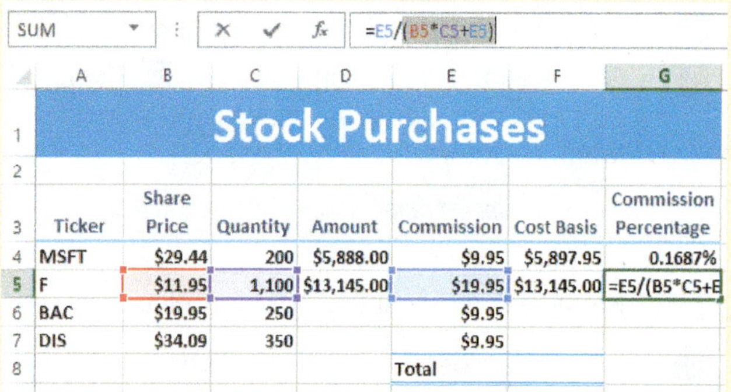

Excel 2013, Windows 8, Microsoft Corporation

Copying a Formula Using the Fill Handle

- You can use the fill feature to copy a formula that you've created to the cells below or to the right of it.
- Excel automatically adjusts cell addresses so the filled formulas apply to the correct data.

  ✓ *Lesson 8 explains more about how and why Excel adjusts cell and range addresses.*

- Drag the fill handle over the range of cells to fill with the formula.
- Also use the Fill button in the Editing group on the HOME tab to fill formulas.

Try It! Copying a Formula Using the Fill Handle

1. In the E07Try_xx file, click cell D5 to select it.
2. Drag the fill handle down through cell D7 to fill the formula.
3. Click cell F5 to select it.
4. Drag the fill handle down through cell F7 to fill the formula.
5. Click cell G5 to select it.
6. Drag the fill handle down through cell G7 to fill the formula.
7. Save the E07Try_xx file, and leave it open to use in the next Try It.

Using the SUM Function

- The most basic and perhaps most often used function is the **SUM function**, which adds the values in the specified cells or range together.
- You can enter the SUM function by typing it into the cell just like any other cell entry. For example, you could enter =SUM(A6,A9,B12) or =SUM(A6:B9).

  ✓ *Formulas and functions are not case sensitive, so an entry like =sum(a6:b9) would calculate correctly. This book shows cell addresses, formulas, and functions in uppercase to make them easier to read in the text.*

- Enclose the cell addresses or range to sum in parentheses, and use commas to separate individual cell references.
- Enter the SUM function more quickly using one of the following three methods:
  - Press ALT + =.
  - Click the Sum button Σ in the Editing group on the HOME tab. Note that this button is also called the AutoSum.
  - Click the AutoSum button Σ AutoSum ▾ in the Function Library group on the FORMULAS tab.

Try It! Using the Sum Function

1. In the E07Try_xx file, click cell F8 to select it.
2. On the HOME tab, click AutoSum Σ. Excel automatically starts the formula and selects the range above it.

   ✓ *If the selected range is incorrect, you can drag to change it.*

3. Press ENTER to finish the SUM formula.
4. Save and close the file, and exit Excel.

Summing a column of data

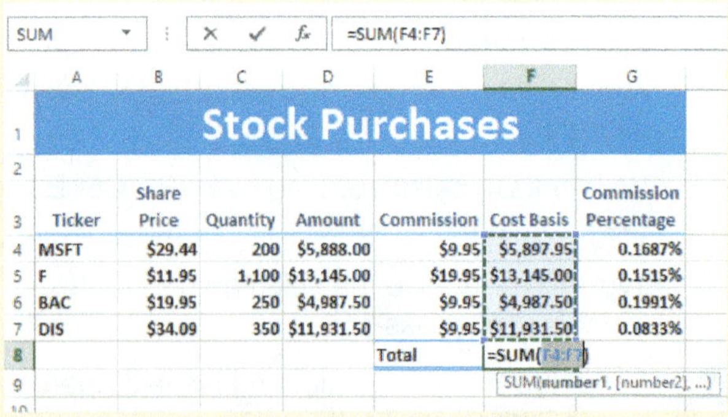

Excel 2013, Windows 8, Microsoft Corporation

Lesson 7—Practice

In this project, you will add basic formulas to a spreadsheet using the skills you learned in this lesson.

DIRECTIONS

1. Start Excel, if necessary, and open the **E07Practice** file from the data files for this lesson.
2. Save the file as **E07Practice_xx** in the location where your teacher instructs you to store the files for this lesson.
3. Add a header that has your name at the left, the date code in the center, and the page number code at the right, and change back to **Normal** view.
4. Click cell **B12**, type **=B8+B9+B10+B11**, and press ENTER twice.
5. Type **=B12/G12**, and press ENTER. Excel should display a #DIV/0! error message because cell G12 is currently empty.
6. Click cell **C12** to select it.
7. Type **=sum(C8:C11)**, and press ENTER.
8. Click cell **G8** to select it.
9. Type **=B8+C8+D8+E8+F8**, and press ENTER. Your worksheet should look like the one shown in Figure 7-1.
10. **With your teacher's permission**, print the worksheet. Submit the printout or the file for grading as required.
11. Save and close the file, and exit Excel.

Figure 7-1

	A	B	C	D	E	F	G
1	Serenity Health Club						
2							
3	9/4/2017						Extra Services Sold
4							
5	Service Name	Swedish Massage	Aromatherapy Massage	Hot Stone Massage	Exfoliating Salt Scrub	Aromatherapy Facial	Weekly Total
6	Service Code	Serv001	Serv002	Serv003	Serv004	Serv005	
7							
8	Week 1	$665	$600	$445	$400	$150	$2,260
9	Week 2	$550	$600	$550	$225	$300	
10	Week 3	$575	$550	$575	$300	$450	
11	Week 4	$600	$550	$625	$225	$300	
12	Total	$2,390	$2,300				
13							
14	Percentage	#DIV/0!					

Excel 2013, Windows 8, Microsoft Corporation

Lesson 7—Apply

You are the Accounts Receivable Supervisor at the Serenity Health Club. You have some new data in a spreadsheet, and need to add basic formulas to calculate the data.

DIRECTIONS

1. Start Excel, if necessary, and open the **E07Apply** file from the data files for this lesson.
2. Save the file as **E07Apply_xx** in the location where your teacher instructs you to store the files for this lesson.
3. Add a header that has your name at the left, the date code in the center, and the page number code at the right, and change back to **Normal** view.
4. Click cell **D12** to select it and sum the values in the cells above.
5. Drag the fill handle right through cell **G12** to fill the formula.
6. Click cell **G8** and double-click the fill handle to fill the entry down the column.
7. Click cell **B14** and drag the fill handle right through cell **F14**. When you release the mouse button, you should see the error message #DIV/0! in each of the filled cells. This is because Excel changed the reference to cell G12 and you don't want it to do that.
8. Edit each of the formulas in the range **C14:F14** to change the divisor (the right cell address) to **G12**.
9. Select the range **B14:F14**. Look in the status bar next to the view buttons. The sum displayed there should be 100.00%, meaning that the corrected formulas each accurately calculate the percentage of the total. Your worksheet should look like the one shown in Figure 7-2.

   ✓ *When you want to see a quick sum of cells without building a formula, drag over the cells and check the status bar.*

10. **With your teacher's permission**, print the worksheet. Submit the printout or the file for grading as required.
11. Save and close the file, and exit Excel.

Figure 7-2

Excel 2013, Windows 8, Microsoft Corporation

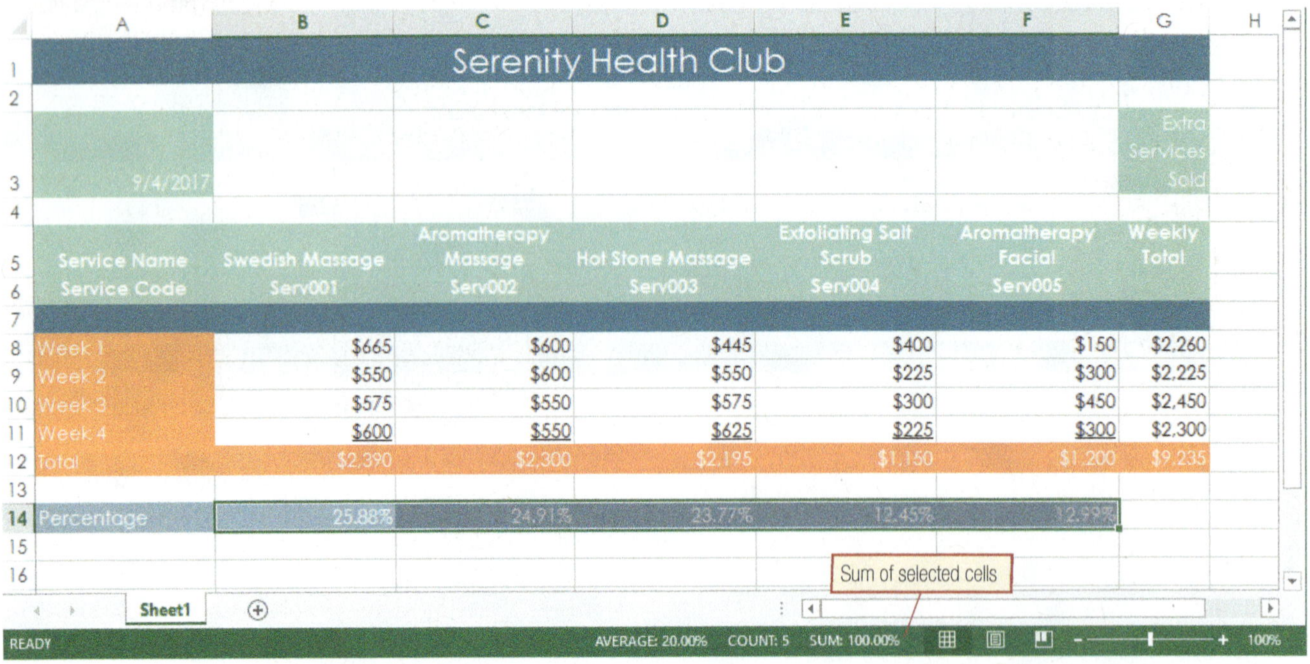

Lesson 8

Copying and Pasting

➤ What You Will Learn

Copying and Pasting Data
Copying Formats
Copying Formulas Containing a Relative Reference
Copying Formulas Containing an Absolute Reference

Software Skills Excel provides many time-saving shortcuts to help you enter data and build formulas in your worksheets. For example, you can use the copy and paste features to reuse data and formulas in the same worksheet, in another worksheet, or in another workbook. You also can copy formats. When copying formulas, you need to understand how to keep a cell reference from changing if needed.

What You Can Do

Copying, Cutting, and Pasting Data

- When you **copy** data, the copy is placed on the **Clipboard.**
- After you copy data, **paste** it to place the copy from the Clipboard to the new location.
- You can copy labels, values, and formulas to another cell, a range of cells, another worksheet, or another workbook. You also can copy Excel data to documents created in other programs, such as Word.
- To copy a selected cell or range of data to a new location, use the Copy and Paste buttons in the Clipboard group on the HOME tab of the Ribbon.

✓ *CTRL + C and CTRL + V are the shortcuts for copying and pasting, respectively.*

- If the cells to which you want to copy data are adjacent to the original cell, you can use the fill handle to copy the data.
- Excel automatically copies the formats applied to data, which overrides any formatting in the destination cell.
- You can copy just the data and formulas without copying formatting.

✓ *Clicking the bottom half of the Paste button, with the arrow on it, displays a menu with additional paste options. For example, you can paste formulas, formulas with number formatting, keep the column widths, and so on.*

WORDS TO KNOW

Absolute reference
A cell address in a formula that will not change when you copy the formula to another location. Dollar signs indicate an absolute cell reference.

Clipboard
A Windows feature that holds data or graphics you cut or copy prior to pasting to another location.

Copy
The command used to place a copy of data from the selected cell or range on the Clipboard.

Format Painter
A tool that enables you to copy formatting from a cell and apply it to another cell or range.

Paste
The command used to place data from the Clipboard to a location on the worksheet.

Relative reference
A cell address that can change in a copied formula, so the new address is expressed in relation to the cell containing the copied ormula. For example, if you copy a relative reference to A5 one row down, it becomes A6.

- Pasting overwrites data in the destination cell or range.
- You can link data as you paste it so the data changes automatically whenever the original data changes. Lesson 36 explains how to link data.

Try It! Copying, Cutting, and Pasting Data

1. Start Excel.
2. Open the **E08Try** file from the data files for this lesson.
3. Save the file as **E08Try_xx** in the location where your teacher instructs you to store the files for this lesson.
4. Add a header that has your name at the left, the date code in the center, and the page number code at the right, and change back to Normal view.
5. Click cell H5 to select it.
6. On the HOME tab, click Cut.
7. Click cell E5 to select it.
8. On the HOME tab, click Paste.
9. Drag over the range A3:E4 to select it.
10. On the HOME tab, click Copy.
11. Click cell A13 to select it.
12. On the HOME tab, click Paste.
13. Drag over the range A5:C11 to select it.
14. On the HOME tab, click Copy.
15. Click cell A15 to select it.
16. On the HOME tab, click the Paste drop-down arrow > Values. Excel pastes the range without pasting the formatting applied in the original range.
17. Press ESC to remove the selection marquee from the copied range.

    ✓ *A selection marquee is a visible dashed line around a selected area.*
18. Click cell B21 to select it. You still need a formula in this cell, so you need to update it.
19. Type **=MEDIAN(B15:B20** and press ENTER. Excel automatically fills in the closing parenthesis for you.
20. Save the **E08Try_xx** file, and leave it open to use in the next Try It.

Copied range

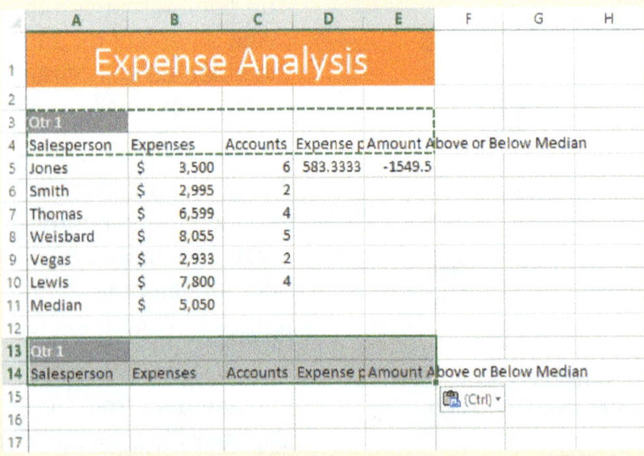

Excel 2013, Windows 8, Microsoft Corporation

Copying Formats

- You can copy formatting from one cell to another, without copying the original cell's value.
- The Format Painter button in the Clipboard group on the HOME tab enables you to copy formatting from one cell to another.
- **Format Painter** copies a cell's font, font size, font color, border, fill color, number formats, column widths (in some cases), cell alignment, and conditional formatting (formatting that depends on the current value in a cell).
- Select the cell with the formatting to copy, and then on the HOME tab, in the Clipboard group, click Format Painter. Click a destination cell or drag over a destination range to apply formatting in that location.
- To paste the formatting to multiple areas, double-click the Format Painter button. It will remain on until you click it again or press ESC to turn it off.

Try It! Copying Formats

1. In the E08Try_xx file, click cell E4 to select it.
2. On the HOME tab, click Wrap Text.
3. On the HOME tab, click Format Painter.
4. Drag over cells A4:D4 to copy the wrapping to them.
5. Click the column header for column C, and drag its right border to the right to resize the column to a width of 9.00.
6. Click cell E4 to select it.
7. On the HOME tab, click Format Painter.
8. Drag over cells D14:E14 to copy the wrapping to them.
9. Click cell B5 to select it.
10. Double-click the Format Painter button.
11. Drag over cells D5:E11 to copy the number formatting.
12. Scroll down and drag over cells B15:B21 to copy the number formatting.
13. Press ESC.
14. Save the E08Try_xx file, and leave it open to use in the next Try It.

Copying Formulas Containing a Relative Reference

- Formulas often have **relative references** to cells. This means that if you copy the formula to another location, the cell reference changes to reflect the position of its copied location relative to the original location.
- For example, the formula =B4+B5 entered in column B becomes =C4+C5 when copied to column C, =D4+D5 when copied to column D, and so on.
- Relative references make it easy to copy formulas across a row to total values above, for example.
- Relative references also work best when you want to fill formulas across a row or down a column.

Try It! Copying Formulas Containing a Relative Reference

1. In the E08Try_xx file, scroll down so row 4 is the first row visible.
2. Click cell D5 to select it.
3. On the HOME tab, click Copy.
4. Drag over the range D6:D10 to select it.
5. Press ENTER. Excel pastes the formula to fill the destination range.

   ✓ *In some cases, you can select a range or click in the upper-left cell of a range and press ENTER to complete a paste rather than using the Paste button.*
6. Drag over the range D5:D10 to select it.

(continued)

Try It! Copying Formulas Containing a Relative Reference *(continued)*

A pasted formula with relative references

D5 | f_x =B5/C5

	A	B	C	D	E
4	Salesperson	Expenses	Accounts	Expense per Account	Amount Above or Below Median
5	Jones	$ 3,500	6	$ 583	$ (1,550)
6	Smith	$ 2,995	2	$ 1,498	
7	Thomas	$ 6,599	4	$ 1,650	
8	Weisbard	$ 8,055	5	$ 1,611	
9	Vegas	$ 2,933	2	$ 1,467	
10	Lewis	$ 7,800	4	$ 1,950	
11	Median	$ 5,050			

Excel 2013, Windows 8, Microsoft Corporation

7. Press CTRL + C.
8. Click cell D15 to select it.
9. Press CTRL + V.
10. Click cell B15 to select it.
11. Type **4240** and press ENTER. The value in cell D15 recalculates as you'd expect.
12. Click cell D15 to select it. The cell references in the formula have been updated to refer correctly to other cells on row 15.
13. Save the **E08Try_xx** file, and leave it open to use in the next Try It.

Copying Formulas Containing an Absolute Reference

- Sometimes, you do not want a cell reference to change when you copy the formula, so you need to create an **absolute reference**.
- To make a cell reference absolute, enter a dollar sign ($) before both the column letter and row number of that cell in the formula.
- For example, the formula =$B$4+$B$5 contained in a cell in column B remains =$B$4+$B$5 when copied to column C. The cell addresses do not adjust based on the new formula location.
- You can also create mixed cell references, where the column letter part of a cell address is absolute, and the row number is relative, or vice-versa.
- For example, the formula =B$4+B$5 contained in a cell in column B changes to =C$4+C$5 when copied to any cell in column C. The cell addresses partially adjust based on the new formula location.
- Press the F4 key as you type a cell reference in a formula to change to an absolute reference. Pressing F4 additional times cycles through the mixed references and then returns to a relative reference.

Try It! Copying a Formula Using an Absolute Reference

1. In the **E08Try_xx** file, click cell E5 to select it.
2. Drag the fill handle down through cell E10 to fill the formula. Cell E8 displays an error message, so you know there must be a problem with the copied formula.
3. Click cell E5 to select it again. Notice that it subtracts the median value calculated in cell B11 from Jones' expenses. You need for each of the formulas in the column to subtract the value in B11 rather than changing, so you need to change to an absolute reference for cell B11.

Copying a formula with an absolute reference

	A	B	C	D	E	F
1	Expense Analysis					
2			Absolute reference			
3	Qtr 1					
4	Salesperson	Expenses	Accounts	Expense per Account	Amount Above or Below Median	
5	Jones	$ 3,500	6	$ 583	$ (1,550)	
6	Smith	$ 2,995	2	$ 1,498	$ (2,055)	
7	Thomas	$ 6,599	4	$ 1,650	$ 1,550	
8	Weisbard	$ 8,055	5	$ 1,611	$ 3,006	
9	Vegas	$ 2,933	2	$ 1,467	$ (2,117)	
10	Lewis	$ 7,800	4	$ 1,950	$ 2,751	
11	Median	$ 5,050				
12						

Excel 2013, Windows 8, Microsoft Corporation

(continued)

Try It! **Copying a Formula Using an Absolute Reference** *(continued)*

4. Press F2 to enter edit mode.
5. Press F4 to add dollar signs for the row letter and column number for cell B11 in the formula, and then press ENTER to finish the change.
6. Click cell E5 to select it.
7. Drag the fill handle down through cell E10 to fill the formula. Now it fills correctly.
8. With the range E5:E10 still selected, on the HOME tab, click Copy.
9. Click cell E15 to select it.
10. On the HOME tab, click Paste. Look at the formula bar. The absolute reference in the formula still refers to cell B11, but for this set of data, you need for it to refer to cell B21.
11. Click cell E15 to select it.
12. Use the method of your choice to change the absolute reference in the formula from $B$11 to **$B$21**.
13. With cell E15 selected, drag the fill handle down through cell E20 to fill the formula.
14. Save and close the file, and exit Excel.

Lesson 8—Practice

In this project, you will copy and paste formatting and formulas using the skills you learned in this lesson.

DIRECTIONS

1. Start Excel, if necessary, and open the **E08Practice** file from the data files for this lesson.
2. Save the file as **E08Practice_xx** in the location where your teacher instructs you to store the files for this lesson.
3. Add a header that has your name at the left, the date code in the center, and the page number code at the right for each sheet, and change back to **Normal** view.
4. Click cell **D9** to select it.
5. Click **HOME** > **Copy**.
6. Drag over the range **D10:D19** to select it.
7. On the HOME tab, click **Paste**.
8. Drag over the range **J9:K19** to select it.
9. On the HOME tab, click **Copy**.
10. Click cell **B9** to select it.
11. On the HOME tab, click **Paste**.
12. Drag over the range J9:K19 to select it and clear the contents. Your worksheet should look like the one shown in Figure 8-1 on the next page.
13. **With your teacher's permission,** print both worksheets. Submit the printouts or the file for grading as required.
14. Save and close the file, and exit Excel.

Figure 8-1

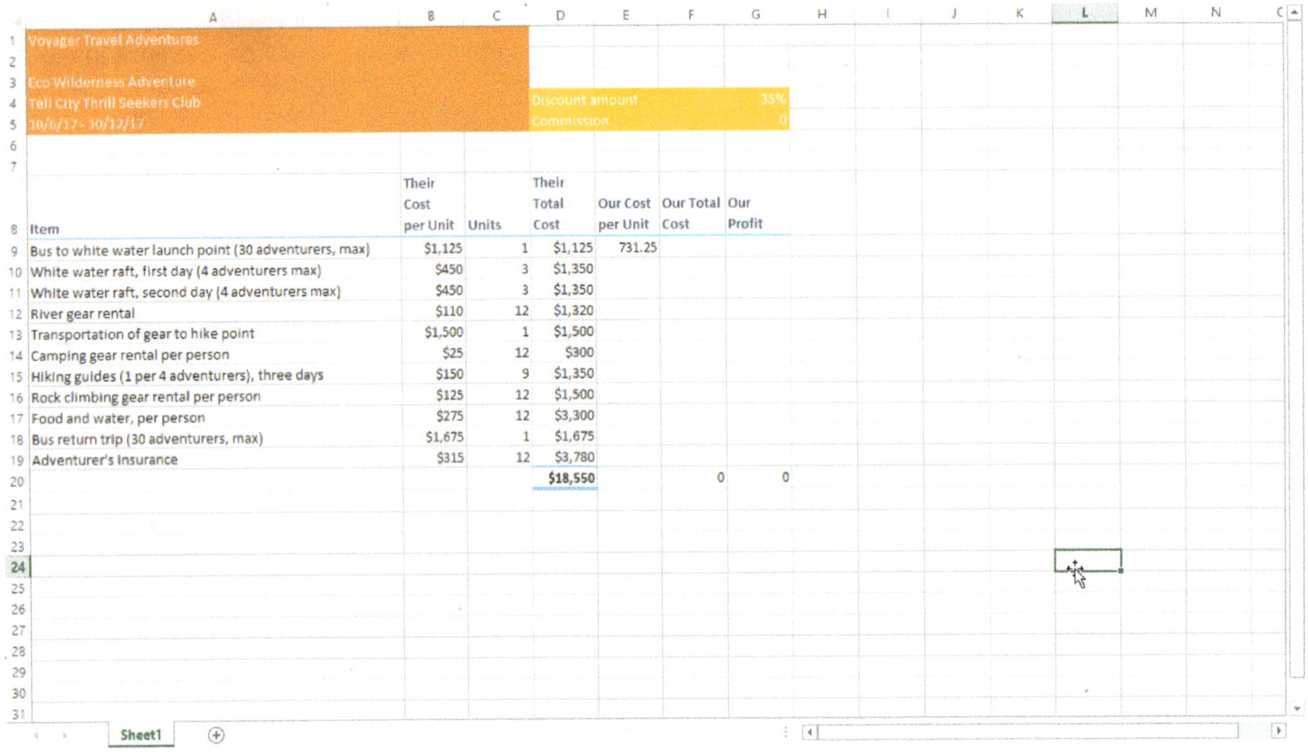

Excel 2013, Windows 8, Microsoft Corporation

Lesson 8—Apply

As an Adventure Coordinator for Voyager Travel Adventures, you make all the arrangements necessary to create a unique and thrilling adventure vacation for your clients. Today, the Tell City Thrill Seekers Club has asked for an estimate of expenses per person for a special trip that combines white water rafting, back country hiking, and rock climbing. You have started both a trip budget for the club and a profit worksheet. To complete the two worksheets, you need to copy formulas, data, and formatting.

DIRECTIONS

1. Start Excel, if necessary, and open the **E08Apply** file from the data files for this lesson.
2. Save the file as **E08Apply_xx** in the location where your teacher instructs you to store the files for this lesson.
3. Add a header that has your name at the left, the date code in the center, and the page number code at the right for each sheet, and change back to **Normal** view.
4. Click cell **I9** to select it, and copy the formula.
5. Click cell **E9** to select it, and paste the formula. An error message appears in cell E9, so you know there's a problem with the formula. Notice that to calculate the discounted price, the formula has to use the discount percentage in cell G4. That cell reference needs to be changed to an absolute reference for the formula to copy correctly.
6. In Edit mode, change the **C4** cell reference, to an absolute reference to cell **G4**.
7. Also in Edit mode, change the **#REF!** cell reference to **B9**.
8. Copy cell **E9** and paste it to the range **E10:E19**.

9. Delete the contents of cell **I9**.
10. Enter the formula **=C9*E9** in cell **F9**. Copy or fill the formula down through cell **F19**.
11. Enter the formula **=D9-F9** in cell **G9**. Copy or fill the formula down through cell **G19**.
12. Select cells **F20:G20**, and apply the **Total** cell style to them.
13. Click cell **G5**, and apply the **Currency** number format to it.
14. Click the cell range **F20:G20**, and apply the **Currency** number format. Apply the Total cell style to the same range. Your worksheet should look like the one shown in Figure 8-2.
15. **With your teacher's permission**, print the worksheet. Submit the printout or the file for grading as required.
16. Save and close the file, and exit Excel.

Figure 8-2

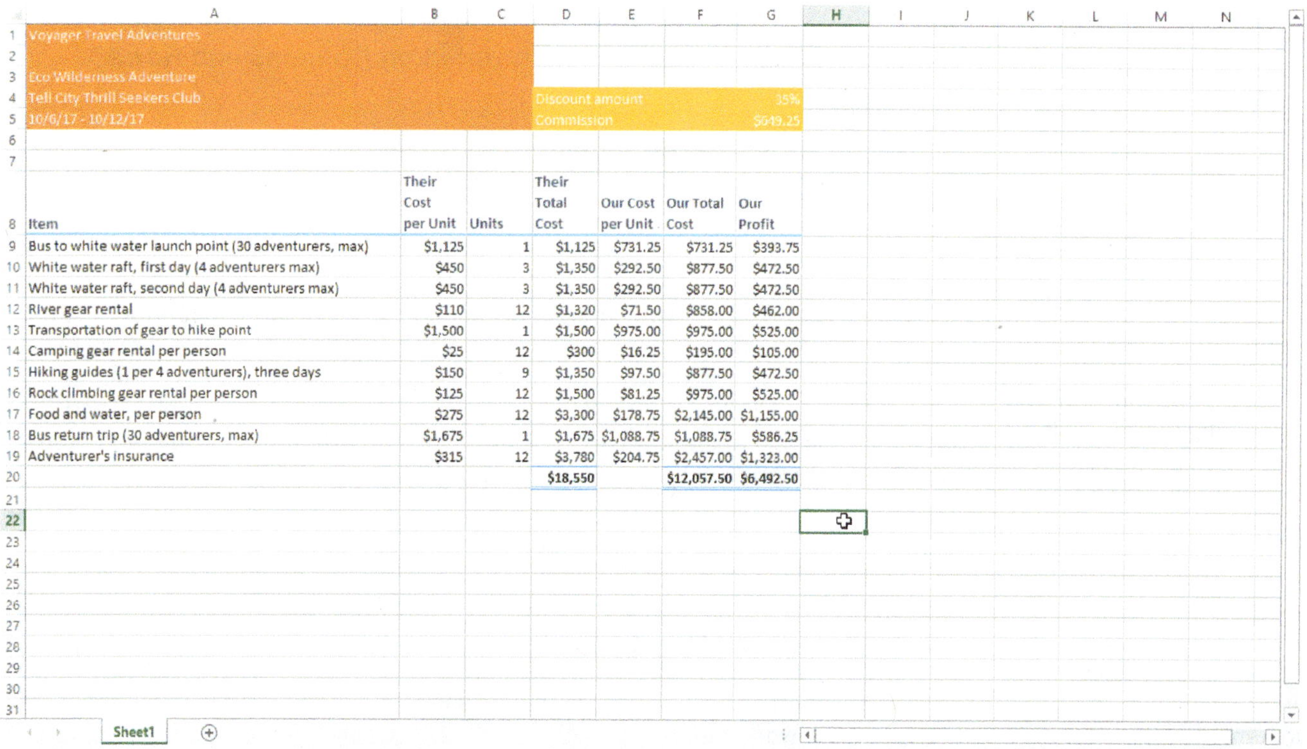

	A	B	C	D	E	F	G
1	Voyager Travel Adventures						
2							
3	Eco Wilderness Adventure						
4	Tell City Thrill Seekers Club			Discount amount			35%
5	10/6/17 - 10/12/17			Commission			$649.25
6							
7							
8	Item	Their Cost per Unit	Units	Their Total Cost	Our Cost per Unit	Our Total Cost	Our Profit
9	Bus to white water launch point (30 adventurers, max)	$1,125	1	$1,125	$731.25	$731.25	$393.75
10	White water raft, first day (4 adventurers max)	$450	3	$1,350	$292.50	$877.50	$472.50
11	White water raft, second day (4 adventurers max)	$450	3	$1,350	$292.50	$877.50	$472.50
12	River gear rental	$110	12	$1,320	$71.50	$858.00	$462.00
13	Transportation of gear to hike point	$1,500	1	$1,500	$975.00	$975.00	$525.00
14	Camping gear rental per person	$25	12	$300	$16.25	$195.00	$105.00
15	Hiking guides (1 per 4 adventurers), three days	$150	9	$1,350	$97.50	$877.50	$472.50
16	Rock climbing gear rental per person	$125	12	$1,500	$81.25	$975.00	$525.00
17	Food and water, per person	$275	12	$3,300	$178.75	$2,145.00	$1,155.00
18	Bus return trip (30 adventurers, max)	$1,675	1	$1,675	$1,088.75	$1,088.75	$586.25
19	Adventurer's insurance	$315	12	$3,780	$204.75	$2,457.00	$1,323.00
20				$18,550		$12,057.50	$6,492.50

Sheet1

Excel 2013, Windows 8, Microsoft Corporation

Lesson 9

Techniques for Moving Data

➤ What You Will Learn

Inserting and Deleting Cells
Inserting, Deleting, Hiding, and Unhiding Columns and Rows
Cutting and Pasting Data
Using Drag-and-Drop Editing
Transposing Columns and Rows

WORDS TO KNOW

Cut
The command used to remove data from a cell or range of cells and place it on the Clipboard.

Drag-and-drop
A method used to move or copy the contents of a range of cells by dragging the border of a selection from one location in a worksheet and dropping it in another location.

Transpose
A method to rearrange data by switching the positions of columns and rows.

Software Skills After you create a worksheet, you may want to rearrange data or add more information. For example, you may need to insert additional rows to a section of your worksheet because new employees have joined a department or been promoted. With Excel's editing features, you can easily add, delete, and rearrange cells and entire rows and columns. You can also move or drag and drop sections of the worksheet with ease.

What You Can Do

Inserting and Deleting Cells

- You can insert or delete cells when necessary to change the arrangement of the data on the worksheet.
- When you select a cell or range of cells, you can use the Insert and Delete buttons in the Cells group on the HOME tab to insert and delete cells. You also can click the drop-down arrows for these buttons for more commands, or right-click a selected cell and use the Insert and Delete commands on the shortcut menu.
- The Insert or Delete button will add or remove the number of cells specified by your selection.
- When you insert a cell in a worksheet, existing cells shift their position down. For example, if you select cell B2 and then insert a cell, the data that was in cell B3 is shifted down and becomes cell B4.
- When you select a range of cells and then click the Insert or Delete buttons, the Insert or Delete dialog box will open.
- You can choose the direction to shift the surrounding cells in the Insert or Delete dialog box, for example, right or down.

- After inserting a cell or group of cells, you can use the Format Options button to choose whether or not formatting should be applied to the new cell(s).
- When you delete a cell, existing cells shift left or up to close the gap. Any data in the rows or columns you select for deletion is erased.

Try It! Inserting and Deleting Cells

1. Start Excel.
2. Open the **E09Try** file from the data files for this lesson.
3. Save the workbook as **E09Try_xx** in the location where your teacher instructs you to store the files for this lesson.
4. Add a header that has your name at the left, the date code in the center, and the page number code at the right, and change back to Normal.
5. Click cell C6 to select it.
6. On the HOME tab, in the Cells group, click the Insert button.

   ✓ *Be sure to click the top part of the Insert button, not the drop-down arrow on the bottom part.*
7. Click the Insert Options button next to the cell, and click Format Same As Below.
8. Type **3091**, and press CTRL + ENTER. Notice that the number is formatted for currency.
9. Right-click on cell C6, select delete, make sure Shift cells up is selected, and click OK.
10. Save the **E09Try_xx** file, and leave it open to use in the next Try It.

The Delete dialog box

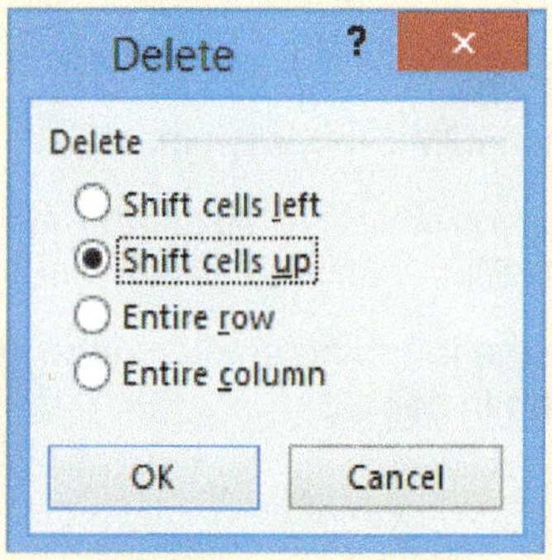

Excel 2013, Windows 8, Microsoft Corporation

Inserting, Deleting, Hiding, and Unhiding Columns and Rows

- You can insert or delete columns or rows when necessary to change the arrangement of the data on the worksheet.
- When you select a row or column, or multiple rows or columns, you can use the Insert and Delete buttons in the Cells group on the HOME tab to insert and delete columns and rows. You also can right-click a selected column or row's heading and use the Insert and Delete commands on the shortcut menu.

  ✓ *Drag over multiple row or column headings to select multiple rows or columns. Then, using the shortcut menu to insert or delete will add or remove the number of rows or columns specified by your selection.*
- When you insert column(s) in a worksheet, existing columns shift their position to the right. For example, if you select column C and then insert two columns, the data that was in column C is shifted to the right and becomes column E.
- If you insert row(s) in a worksheet, existing rows are shifted down to accommodate the newly inserted row(s). For example, if you select row 8 and insert two rows, the data that was in row 8 is shifted down to row 10.
- After inserting a column or row, you can use the Insert Options button to choose whether or not formatting from a nearby row or column should be applied to the new rows or columns.
- When you delete a column or row, existing columns and rows shift left or up to close the gap. Any data in the rows or columns you select for deletion is erased.
- You can also hide columns or rows temporarily and then redisplay them as needed. Right-click the column/row heading and click Hide. Drag over headings surrounding the hidden row/column, right-click, and click Unhide.

Try It! Inserting, Deleting, Hiding, and Unhiding Columns and Rows

1. In the **E09Try_xx** file, right-click the column B column heading and click Hide on the shortcut menu.
2. Drag across column headings A though C and right-click the selected headings. Click Unhide on the shortcut menu.
3. Click the column B column heading to select the column.
4. On the HOME tab, click Delete. Excel removes the column.

   ✓ *Be sure to click the top part of the Delete button, not the drop-down arrow on the bottom part.*
5. Click the column C column heading to select it.
6. On the HOME tab, click Insert.

   ✓ *Be sure to click the top part of the Insert button, not the drop-down arrow on the bottom part.*
7. Make the following entries in the new column, starting in cell C3:

   February
   8282
   9087
   10443
   9731
   8367
8. Fill the formulas from cells B9 and B10 to the right to cells C9 and C10.
9. Right-click the row 8 row heading and click Hide on the shortcut menu.
10. Drag across row headings 7 though 9 and right-click the selected headings. Click Unhide on the shortcut menu.
11. Click the row 8 row heading to select it.
12. On the HOME tab, click Insert.
13. Make the following entries in the new row, starting in cell A8:

    Vegas
    8042
    6639
    8088
14. Save the **E09Try_xx** file, and leave it open to use in the next Try It.

Cutting and Pasting Data

- To move data from one place in the worksheet to another, use the Cut and Paste options in the Clipboard group on the HOME tab. This removes the data from its original location.
- When you **cut** data from a location, it is temporarily stored on the Clipboard. That data is then copied from the Clipboard to the new location when you paste.
- If data already exists in the location you wish to paste to, Excel overwrites it.
- Instead of overwriting data with the Paste command, you can insert the cut cells and have Excel shift cells with existing data down or to the right.
- When you move data, its formatting moves with it. You can override this and move just the data using choices on the Paste button's drop-down list.

Try It! Cutting and Pasting Data

1. In the **E09Try_xx** file, drag over the range **A8:E9** to select it.
2. On the HOME tab, in the Clipboard group, click Cut.
3. Click cell G4 to select it.
4. On the HOME tab, in the Clipboard group, click Paste.

   ✓ *Be sure to click the top part of the Paste button, not the drop-down arrow on the bottom part.*
5. Save the changes to **E09Try_xx** file, and leave it open to use in the next Try It.

Using Drag-and-Drop Editing

- The **drag-and-drop** feature enables you to use the mouse to copy or move a range of cells simply by dragging them.
- To use drag-and-drop, select a range to copy or move, and then you use the border surrounding the range to drag the data to a different location. When you release the mouse button, the data is "dropped" in that location.
- An outline of the selection appears as you drag it to its new location on the worksheet.
- You can use drag-and-drop to move data and to copy it. To copy data using drag-and-drop, simply hold down the CTRL key as you drag.
- Insert, delete, move, and copy operations may affect formulas, so you should check the formulas after you have used drag-and-drop to be sure that they are correct.
- When a drag-and-drop action does not move data correctly, use the Undo feature to undo it.

Try It! Using Drag-and-Drop Editing

1. In the **E09Try_xx** file, drag over the range A7:E7 to select it.
2. Point to the border of the selection. When the mouse pointer changes to a four-headed arrow, drag down one row. When the ScreenTip reads A8:E8, release the mouse button.
3. Drag over the range G4:K4 to select it.
4. Use drag-and-drop to move the selection to row 7 of the sales data.
5. Click the row 9 row heading to select it.
6. On the HOME tab, click Delete.
7. Save the changes to **E09Try_xx** file, and leave it open to use in the next Try It.

Moving a range with drag-and-drop

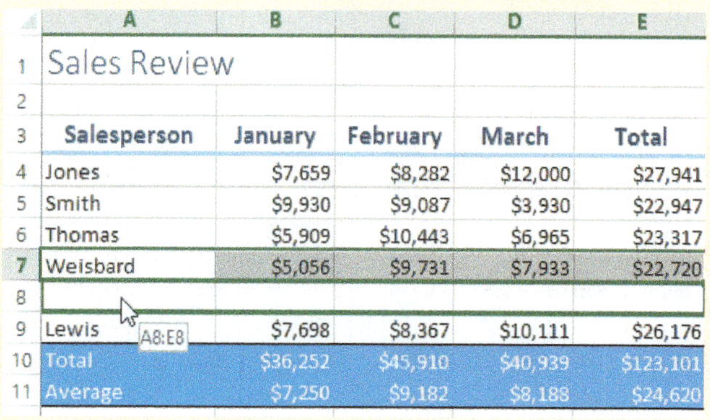

	A	B	C	D	E
1	Sales Review				
2					
3	Salesperson	January	February	March	Total
4	Jones	$7,659	$8,282	$12,000	$27,941
5	Smith	$9,930	$9,087	$3,930	$22,947
6	Thomas	$5,909	$10,443	$6,965	$23,317
7	Weisbard	$5,056	$9,731	$7,933	$22,720
8					
9	Lewis	$7,698	$8,367	$10,111	$26,176
10	Total	$36,252	$45,910	$40,939	$123,101
11	Average	$7,250	$9,182	$8,188	$24,620

Excel 2013, Windows 8, Microsoft Corporation

Transposing Columns and Rows

- You can use the **transpose** feature to rearrange the columns and rows of data in a worksheet.
- To use the transpose feature, select the data you want to transpose, which can include row or column labels, and then copy it.

  ✓ *You must use Copy with the transpose feature; you cannot use Cut.*

- Transposed data must be placed in blank cells.
- To place the transposed data, right-click the first cell where you want the tranposed data to be pasted, and choose Transpose in the Paste Options menu.
- Transposing may affect formulas, so you should check the formulas after you have used the transpose feature to be sure that they are correct.
- When a transpose action does not move data correctly, use the Undo feature to undo it.

Try It! Transposing Columns and Rows

1. In the **E09Try_xx** file, select the cell range A3:D8.
2. On the HOME tab, in the Clipboard group, click Copy.
3. Right-click cell A13.
4. In the Paste Options menu, click Transpose. The column headings have now been transposed to row headings, and vice versa. Notice that the data has been transposed also.
5. Save and close the file, and exit Excel.

The Transpose button in the Paste Options drop-down menu

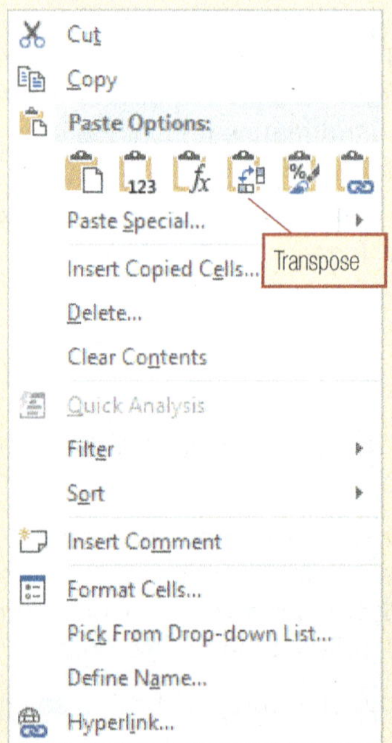

Excel 2013, Windows 8, Microsoft Corporation

Lesson 9—Practice

In this project, you will insert, delete, hide, and unhide columns and rows using the skills you learned in this lesson.

DIRECTIONS

1. Start Excel, if necessary, and open the **E09Practice** file from the data files for this lesson.
2. Save the file as **E09Practice_xx** in the location where your teacher instructs you to store the files for this lesson.
3. Add a header that has your name at the left, the date code in the center, and the page number code at the right, and change back to **Normal** view.
4. Click the **row 14** row heading to select it.
5. On the HOME tab, click **Insert**.
6. Click the **row 4** row heading to select it.
7. Move the mouse pointer over the border of the selection, press and hold CTRL, and drag the selection down to **row 15**. When you release the mouse button, Excel copies the selection.
8. Click cell **A15** to select it, type **Hourly Employees**, and press ENTER.
9. Click the **column D** column heading to select it.
10. On the HOME tab, click **Delete**.
11. Right-click the **row 14** row heading and select **Hide**.
12. Click the row headings for **rows 13-15**, right-click, and select **Unhide**.
13. **With your teacher's permission**, print the worksheet. Submit the printout or the file for grading as required.
14. Save and close the file, and exit Excel.

Lesson 9—Apply

You are the Payroll Manager at Whole Grains Bread. The conversion to an in-house payroll system is next week, and you want to test out a payroll worksheet the staff will use to collect and enter payroll data in the computer system. You need to finish entering data and formulas in the worksheet. This will require adding, deleting, hiding, and unhiding rows and columns, and moving data by cutting and pasting and drag-and-drop techniques. You also will transpose the hourly employee data to show a different way of presenting this information.

DIRECTIONS

1. Start Excel, if necessary, and open the **E09Apply** file from the data files for this lesson.
2. Save the file as **E09Apply_xx** in the location where your teacher instructs you to store the files for this lesson.
3. Add a header that has your name at the left, the date code in the center, and the page number code at the right, and change back to **Normal** view.
4. Select the range **B5:J13** and move it left one column.
5. Select the range **B16:H24** and move it left one column.
6. Adjust column widths as needed.
7. Select the range **G5:I13**, press and hold the CTRL key, and use drag-and-drop to copy the data to the range **H16:J24**.

   ✓ *When using drag-and-drop to copy data, remember to use the CTRL key.*

8. Select **row 12**, and insert a new row.
9. Cut the range **A22:D22**, and paste it in the new **row 12**.

10. In row 12, change the Rate to **765**. For the rest of the columns, fill the formulas down from the row above to row 12.
11. Delete **row 22**.
12. Select **row 15** and hide the row.
13. Select **column B** and hide the column.
14. Select the cell range **A17:J24**.
15. On the HOME tab, in the Clipboard group, click **Copy**.
16. Right-click cell **A27**.
17. In the Paste Options menu, click **Transpose**. Adjust the column widths, if necessary. Your worksheet should look like the one shown in Figure 9-1.
18. **With your teacher's permission**, print the worksheet. Submit the printout or the file for grading as required.
19. Save and close the file, and exit Excel.

Figure 9-1

	A	C	D	E	F	G	H	I	J	K
1	Whole Grains Bread									
2	Home Office Payroll									
3										
4	Salaried Employees									
5	Employee Name	Rate	Regular Hours	Gross Pay	Fed Tax	SS Tax	State Tax	Net Pay		
6	Anthony Splendoria	$ 2,175.00	40.00	$2,175.00	$ 543.75	$ 169.65	$ 65.25	$1,396.35		
7	Eileen Costello	$ 1,895.00	40.00	$1,895.00	$ 473.75	$ 147.81	$ 56.85	$1,216.59		
8	Carol Chen	$ 895.00	40.00	$ 895.00	$ 223.75	$ 69.81	$ 26.85	$ 574.59		
9	Marty Gonzales	$ 684.00	40.00	$ 684.00	$ 171.00	$ 53.35	$ 20.52	$ 439.13		
10	Maria Nachez	$ 1,665.00	40.00	$1,665.00	$ 416.25	$ 129.87	$ 49.95	$1,068.93		
11	Mika Gritada	$ 1,023.00	40.00	$1,023.00	$ 255.75	$ 79.79	$ 30.69	$ 656.77		
12	Vickie Helms	$ 765.00	40.00	$ 765.00	$ 191.25	$ 59.67	$ 22.95	$ 491.13		
13	Randall Lohr	$ 1,545.00	40.00	$1,545.00	$ 386.25	$ 120.51	$ 46.35	$ 991.89		
14	Abe Rittenhouse	$ 1,231.00	40.00	$1,231.00	$ 307.75	$ 96.02	$ 36.93	$ 790.30		
16	Hourly Employees									
17	Employee Name	Rate	Regular Hours	Overtime Hours	Gross Pay	Fed Tax	SS Tax	State Tax	Net Pay	
18	Thomas Cortese	$ 8.25	40.00	2.00	$ 354.75	$ 53.21	$ 27.67	$ 10.64	$ 263.22	
19	Javier Cortez	$ 7.75	40.00	3.00	$ 344.88	$ 51.73	$ 26.90	$ 10.35	$ 255.90	
20	Allen Gaines	$ 7.25	40.00	6.00	$ 355.25	$ 53.29	$ 27.71	$ 10.66	$ 263.60	
21	Freda Gage	$ 8.00	40.00	3.00	$ 356.00	$ 53.40	$ 27.77	$ 10.68	$ 264.15	
22	Isiah Herron	$ 10.95	40.00	5.50	$ 528.34	$ 79.25	$ 41.21	$ 15.85	$ 392.03	
23	Thomas Kaminski	$ 9.75	40.00	4.00	$ 448.50	$ 67.28	$ 34.98	$ 13.46	$ 332.79	
24	Chris Nakao	$ 11.25	40.00	3.00	$ 500.63	$ 75.09	$ 39.05	$ 15.02	$ 371.46	
25										
26										
27	Employee Name	Javier Cortez	Allen Gaines	Freda Gage	Isiah Herron	Thomas Kaminski	Chris Nakao			
28	Employee ID	21154	23455	27855	33252	37881	29958			
29	Rate	$ 7.75	$ 7.25	$ 8.00	$ 10.95	$ 9.75	$ 11.25			
30	Regular Hours	40.00	40.00	40.00	40.00	40.00	40.00			
31	Overtime Hours	3.00	6.00	3.00	5.50	4.00	3.00			
32	Gross Pay	$ 344.88	$ 355.25	$ 356.00	$ 528.34	$ 448.50	$ 500.63			
33	Fed Tax	$ 51.73	$ 53.29	$ 53.40	$ 79.25	$ 67.28	$ 75.09			
34	SS Tax	$ 26.90	$ 27.71	$ 27.77	$ 41.21	$ 34.98	$ 39.05			
35	State Tax	$ 10.35	$ 10.66	$ 10.68	$ 15.85	$ 13.46	$ 15.02			
36	Net Pay	$ 255.90	$ 263.60	$ 264.15	$ 392.03	$ 332.79	$ 371.46			

Lesson 10

Sheet, Display, and Print Operations

➤ What You Will Learn

Displaying, Printing, and Hiding Formulas
Printing Titles
Changing Orientation
Scaling a Printout
Previewing and Printing a Worksheet

Software Skills A few of the options available for adjusting a printout make a great difference in how easy it is to read the worksheet data. Repeating rows or columns with labels on multipage printouts ensures that the data will be identified on every page; choosing the right page orientation ensures enough columns will fit on screen; and scaling a printout to fit to a specified number of pages helps ensure that rows or columns aren't "orphaned" from the rest of the data. You might also want to display and print formulas to review them and preview the worksheet so you can see how it will look when printed.

What You Can Do

Displaying, Printing, and Hiding Formulas

- The **Show Formulas** command displays formulas in cells in which they are entered rather than formula results.
- Showing formulas enables you to review the worksheet to ensure that the formulas refer to the correct cells and ranges and accurately perform the desired calculations.
- Print the worksheet with the formulas displayed to create a printout of the formulas for later reference.
- Use the Show Formulas button in the Formula Auditing group on the FORMULAS tab to turn formula display on and off. You also can press CTRL + `.

✓ *The accent grave character (`) is on the same key as the tilde, typically found to the left of the 1 on the row of numbers at the top of the keyboard or beside the Spacebar in rarer cases.*

WORDS TO KNOW

Orientation
The position for displaying and printing text either horizontally across the shorter side of a page, the default Portrait orientation, or along the wider side of the page, Landscape orientation.

Print titles
Row and column labels that reprint on each page of a printout.

Scale
Adjust the size proportionately.

Show Formulas
A command that enables you to display the formulas in a worksheet so that you can check them.

Try It! Displaying, Printing, and Hiding Formulas

1. Start Excel, if necessary, and open the **E10Try** file from the data files for this lesson.
2. Save the file as **E10Try_xx** in the location where your teacher instructs you to store the files for this lesson.
3. Scroll down so that row 105 is visible.
4. Click FORMULAS > Show Formulas.
5. Click FILE > Print.
6. Under Settings, click No Scaling > Custom Scaling > Fit Sheet on One Page.

   ✓ *It's often necessary to scale the sheet when formulas are displayed because the formula display makes the columns wider.*

7. **With your teacher's permission**, print the worksheet by clicking the Print button. Otherwise, click the Back button.
8. Press CTRL + ` to toggle off the formula display.

   ✓ *The ` is usually above the TAB key.*

9. Save the **E10Try_xx** file, and leave it open to use in the next Try It.

Formulas displayed in worksheet

	A	B	C	D	E	F
94	KLAC	KLA-Tencor	32.25	1:29pm	5.482B	3.356
95	MGM	MGM Resorts International	12.42	1:29pm	5.481B	-37.953
96	CEA	China Eastern Air	48.25	1:12pm	5.441B	0
97	FLS	Flowserve Corp.	96.88	1:29pm	5.431B	25.771
98	LM	Legg Mason Inc.	33.09	1:29pm	5.411B	3.915
99	RDY	Dr. Reddy's Labor	31.6	1:28pm	5.335B	2.587
100	AIG	American International	39.49	1:29pm	5.334B	-9.384
101	ATI	Allegheny Technology	53.28	1:29pm	5.250B	2.216
102						
103						
104						
105	Averages		=AVERAGE(C4:C101)			=AVERAGE(F4:F101)
106						
107						

Excel 2013, Windows 8, Microsoft Corporation

Printing Titles

- Using the Sheet tab of the Page Setup dialog box, you can specify rows or columns with the **print titles** that need to appear on every page of a printout.

  ✓ *Print titles do not affect or replace worksheet headers or footers.*

- You also can use the Print Titles button in the Page Setup group of the PAGE LAYOUT tab on the Ribbon to add print titles.

  ✓ *Click the dialog box launcher for the Page Setup group to open the Page Setup dialog box.*

- The row and column labels make it possible for you to identify the data on every page, which is useful when the sheet has many rows or many columns of information.

Try It! Printing Titles

1. In the **E10Try_xx** file, add a header that has your name at the left, the date code in the center, and the page number code at the right, and change back to Normal view.
2. Click PAGE LAYOUT > Print Titles.
3. On the Sheet tab in the Page Setup dialog box, click in the Rows to repeat at top text box, click the Collapse Dialog box button, and then click the row 3 row header. The row address for row 3, which holds the labels for the columns of data, appears in the box.
4. Click OK.
5. Save the **E10Try_xx** file, and leave it open to use in the next Try It.

Specifying print titles

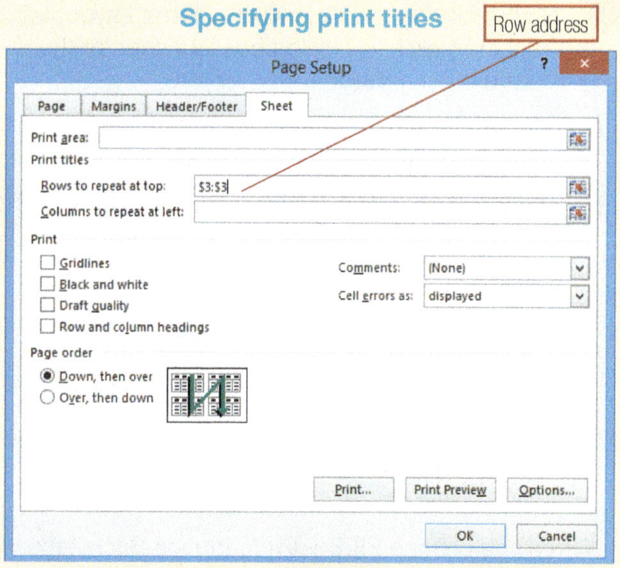

Excel 2013, Windows 8, Microsoft Corporation

Changing Orientation

- You can change the **orientation** to help a worksheet fit better on paper.
- The default orientation is Portrait (tall or vertical).
- Changing to Landscape (wide or horizontal) orientation allows for more columns to fit on each page when a worksheet has many columns.
- Change orientation on the Page tab of the Page Setup dialog box, or use the Orientation button choices in the Page Setup group of the PAGE LAYOUT tab.

Try It! Changing Orientation

1. In the **E10Try_xx** file, click PAGE LAYOUT > Orientation > Landscape.
2. Save the **E10Try_xx** file, and leave it open to use in the next Try It.

Scaling to Fit

- You can **scale** the data to print to a larger or smaller size to help it fill a page or print on fewer pages.
- Specify scaling in the Scaling section of the Page tab of the Page Setup dialog box.
- You can scale the printout to a percentage of normal size, or specify how many pages wide and tall it should be.

✓ *For many worksheets, changing to Landscape orientation and then scaling to 1 page wide prevents orphaned columns on a nearly blank page.*

- You also can use the choices in the Scale to Fit group on the Page Layout tab to specify the printout Width and Height in number of pages or a Scale percentage.

Try It! **Scaling to Fit**

1. In the E10Try_xx file, click the Page Layout tab, and then click the dialog box launcher for the Scale to Fit group.
2. On the Page sheet, click the Fit to button, and then adjust the accompanying text box entries to set up the printout to be 1 page(s) wide by 2 tall.
3. Click the Print Preview button.
4. At the bottom of Backstage view, click the Next Page (right arrow) button to display the second page of the printout.
5. Save the E10Try_xx file, and leave it open to use in the next Try It.

Previewing and Printing a Worksheet

- You may print the selected worksheet(s), an entire workbook, or a selected data range.

  ✓ *You learn how to print an entire workbook and a selected range in Lesson 20.*

- When you choose FILE > Print, the the Backstage view automatically shows you a preview of the printout. Review it carefully and adjust print settings there before printing.
- Settings you can change appear in the middle column of the Backstage view. These include specifying how many copies to print, what printer to use, page orientation, page size, margins, and scaling.

Try It! **Previewing and Printing a Worksheet**

1. In the E10Try_xx file, click FILE > Print.
2. In the Settings area, in the Orientation option, check that Portrait Orientation is selected.
3. Under Settings, click the Page Setup link.
4. In the Page Setup dialog box, click the Margins tab.
5. Click the Horizontally and Vertically check boxes under Center on page to select them, and then click OK.
6. Review the changes in the preview.
7. **With your teacher's permission,** print the worksheet by clicking the Print button. Otherwise, click the Back button to return to your document.
8. Save and close the file, and exit Excel.

   ✓ *Notice that when you save a file from the Backstage view, you exit the Backstage view.*

(continued)

Try It! Previewing and Printing a Worksheet *(continued)*

Preparing and previewing before printing

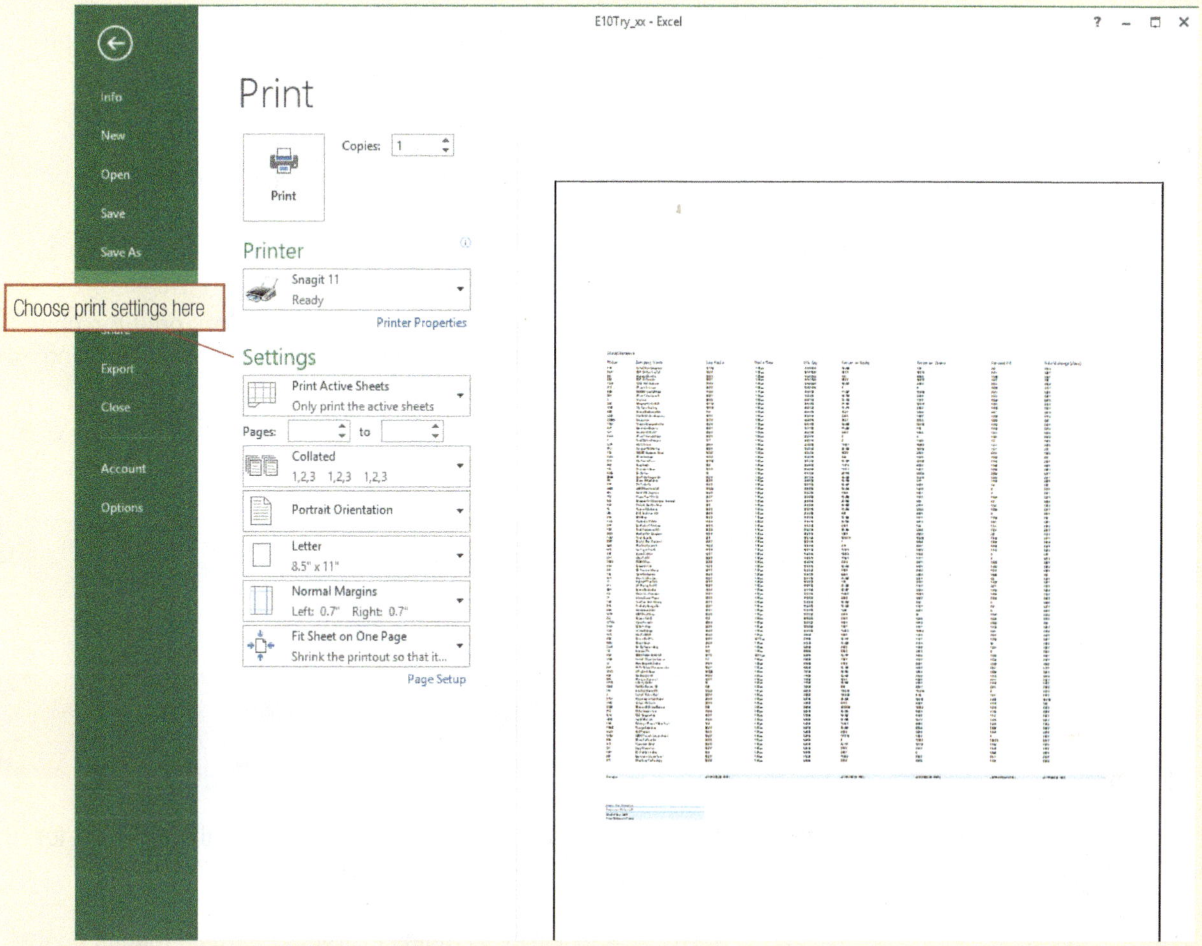

Excel 2013, Windows 8, Microsoft Corporation

Lesson 10—Practice

In this project, you will review and print formulas, change the page orientation and scaling, and preview and print a worksheet using the skills you learned in this lesson.

DIRECTIONS

1. Start Excel, if necessary, and open the **E10Practice** file from the data files for this lesson.
2. Save the file as **E10Practice_xx** in the location where your teacher instructs you to store the files for this lesson.
3. Add a header that has your name at the left, the date code in the center, and the page number code at the right, and change back to **Normal** view.
4. Click **FORMULAS** > **Show Formulas**. The formulas instead of the formula results are now displayed on the worksheet.
5. Click **FILE** > **Print**.
6. Under Settings, click **Portrait Orientation** > **Landscape Orientation**.
7. Under Settings, click **No Scaling** > **Fit Sheet on One Page**.
8. **With your teacher's permission**, print the chart sheet. Submit the printout or the file for grading as required.
9. Save and close the file, and exit Excel.

Lesson 10—Apply

You are the Chief Financial Officer for Hyland Manufacturing. You are finalizing the company's balance sheet for fiscal year 2014. You want to review and print the formulas, and preview and print the finished worksheet.

DIRECTIONS

1. Start Excel, if necessary, and open the **E10Apply** file from the data files for this lesson.
2. Save the file as **E10Apply_xx** in the location where your teacher instructs you to store the files for this lesson.
3. Add a header that has your name at the left, the date code in the center, and the page number code at the right, and change back to **Normal** view.
4. Display formulas instead of formula results on the worksheet.
5. Change the print settings so that the sheet fits on one page.
6. **With your teacher's permission**, print the worksheet. Submit the printout or the file for grading as required.
7. Save and close the file, and exit Excel.

End-of-Chapter Activities

➤ Excel Chapter 1—Critical Thinking

Safety Consulting Services

You have recently started your own business providing safety consulting services to large businesses. You need to create a worksheet to help you track, report, and bill work for each client at two billing rates. You will create and format the sheet, and then enter example data to test how it works.

DIRECTIONS

1. Start Excel, if necessary, and create a new, blank file if necessary.
2. Save the file as **ECT01_xx** in the location where your teacher instructs you to store the files for this chapter.
3. Add a header that has your name at the left, the date code in the center, and the page number code at the right, and change back to **Normal** view.
4. Enter the following data:

A1	**Timesheet**
A3	**Client Name**
A5	**Rate A**
A6	**Rate B**
B5	**50**
B6	**75**
D5	**Weekly Retainer**
F5	**1750**
A8	**Day**
B8	**Date**
C8	**Hours Rate A**
D8	**Hours Rate B**
E8	**Amount Rate A**
F8	**Amount Rate B**
G8	**Total**
D17	**Total**
D18	**Percentage of Retainer**

5. Enter **Monday** in cell **A9**. Fill the days Monday through Sunday down through cell A15.
6. Enter **4/2/17** in cell **B9**. Fill the date entry down the column through 4/8/2017 in cell B15.
7. Insert a column to the left of **column C**.
8. Enter **Monday 4/2/2017** in cell **C9** of the new column C.
9. Enter **Tuesday 4/3/2017** in cell **C10**.
10. Use Flash Fill to fill the series in the range **C9:C15** with the day and date combined.
11. Delete **column C**.
12. Enter the formula **=C9*$B$5** in cell **E9**. Fill the formula down through cell E15.
13. Enter the formula **=D9*$B$6** in cell **F9**. Fill the formula down through cell F15.
14. In cell **G9**, enter a formula that adds the values in cells **E9** and **F9**. Fill the formula down through cell G15.
15. In cell **E17**, enter a formula with the SUM function that totals the values above. Fill the formula right through cell **G17**.
16. In cell **G18**, enter a formula that divides the overall total in cell **G17** by the weekly retainer amount in cell **F5**.
17. Apply the **Ion** theme to the file.
18. Apply the **Title** cell style to cell A1, and merge and center cells **A1:G1**.
19. Apply the **60%-Accent1** style to the label in cell **A3**, then copy the formatting to the other labels in the document (except for the dates).
20. Wrap and center align the range **A8:G8**. Adjust column widths as necessary to display all text.
21. Merge the range **D18:F18**.
22. In cells **B5**, **B6**, and **F5**, apply the **Currency** format with zero decimal places to the entries.
23. Apply the **Currency** format with two decimal places to all the other cells calculating dollar values.

24. Format cell **G18** as a **Percentage** with one decimal place.
25. Enter the following sample data to test the sheet:

    C9 **2.25**
    D9 **4.5**
    C10 **2**
    D10 **1.25**

26. **With your teacher's permission**, print the worksheet. Submit the printout or the file for grading as required. Your worksheet should look like the one in Illustration 1A.
27. Save and close the file, and exit Excel.

Illustration 1A

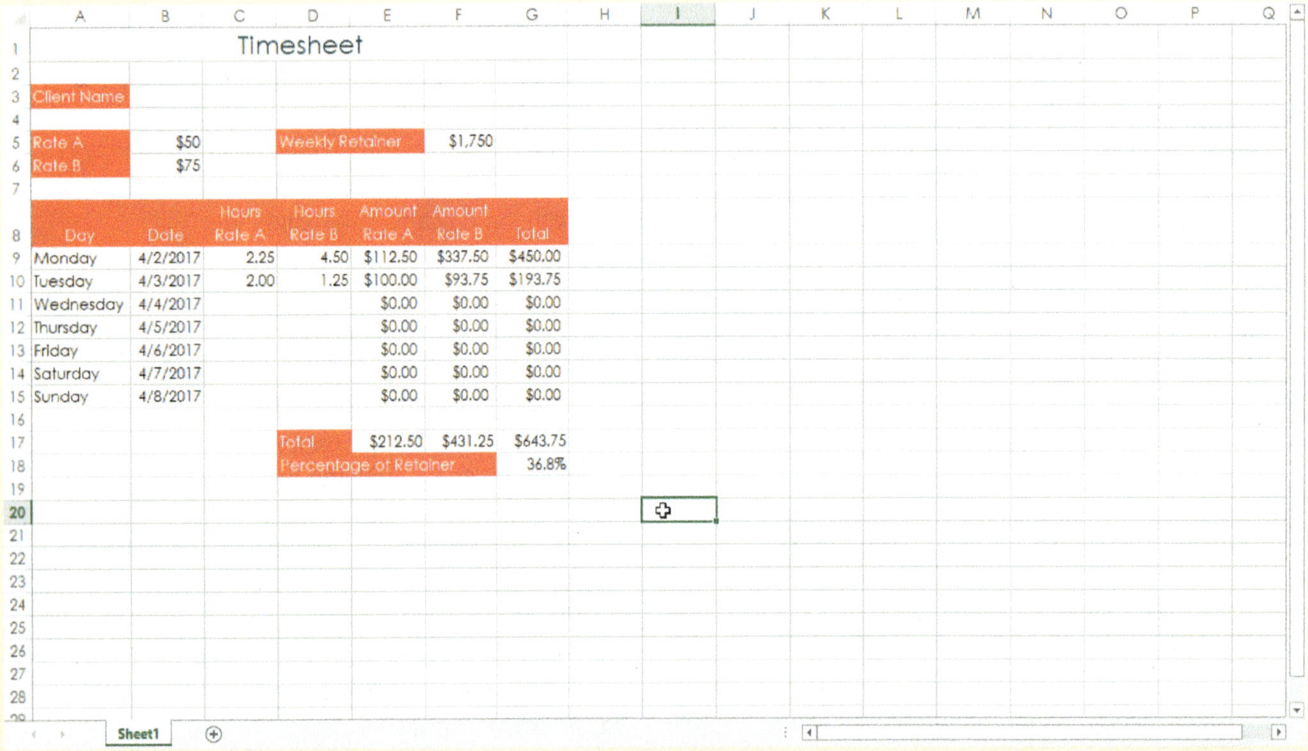

Excel 2013, Windows 8, Microsoft Corporation

➤ Excel Chapter 1—Portfolio Builder

Personal Budget

You want to save for a car and need to get a better handle on your income and expenses in order to do so. In this project, you finish a basic budget worksheet by adding formulas and by making sure items are arranged properly. You'll apply attractive formatting and adjust the print settings.

DIRECTIONS

1. Start Excel, if necessary, and open the **EPB01** file from the data files for this chapter.
2. Save the file as **EPB01_xx** in the location where your teacher instructs you to store the files for this chapter.
3. Add a header that has your name at the left, the date code in the center, and the page number code at the right, and change back to **Normal** view.
4. Insert a column to the left of **column C**.
5. Use Flash Fill to fill the range **C9:C12** with the combined text from columns A and B.
6. Copy the data from the range **C9:C12** and paste it to the range **A9:A12**.
7. Resize **column A**.
8. Delete **columns B** and **C**.
9. Enter the formula **=B5+B6** in cell **B7**. Fill the formula across through cell G7.
10. In cell **B13**, enter a formula that sums **B9:B12**. Fill the formula across through cell G13.
11. Insert a blank row above the *Expenses* row.
12. Review the items in the *Expenses* section. You realize that the Gifts row really belongs in the *Income* area.
13. Insert a new row 6, drag-and-drop row 13 to row 6, and then delete the blank row 13.
14. Click cell **B8**, and review its formula in comparison with the original formula you created in step 4. Because it totals specific cells, it does not include the Gifts data that you have moved to the *Income* section. Edit the formula to correct the calculation, and then copy or fill it across the row.
15. In cell **B15**, enter a formula that subtracts the expense subtotal from the income subtotal. Fill the formula across through cell G15.
16. Add a blank row above the *Surplus* row.
17. Apply a different theme to the workbook.
18. Format the labels as desired and apply the **Accounting** format with zero decimal places to the numeric data.
19. Hide row 2.
20. Display formulas.
21. Preview the sheet, scaling to fit the sheet on one page with the formulas displayed.
22. **With your teacher's permission**, print the worksheet. Submit the printouts or the file for grading as required.
23. Save and close the file, and exit Excel.

Chapter 2

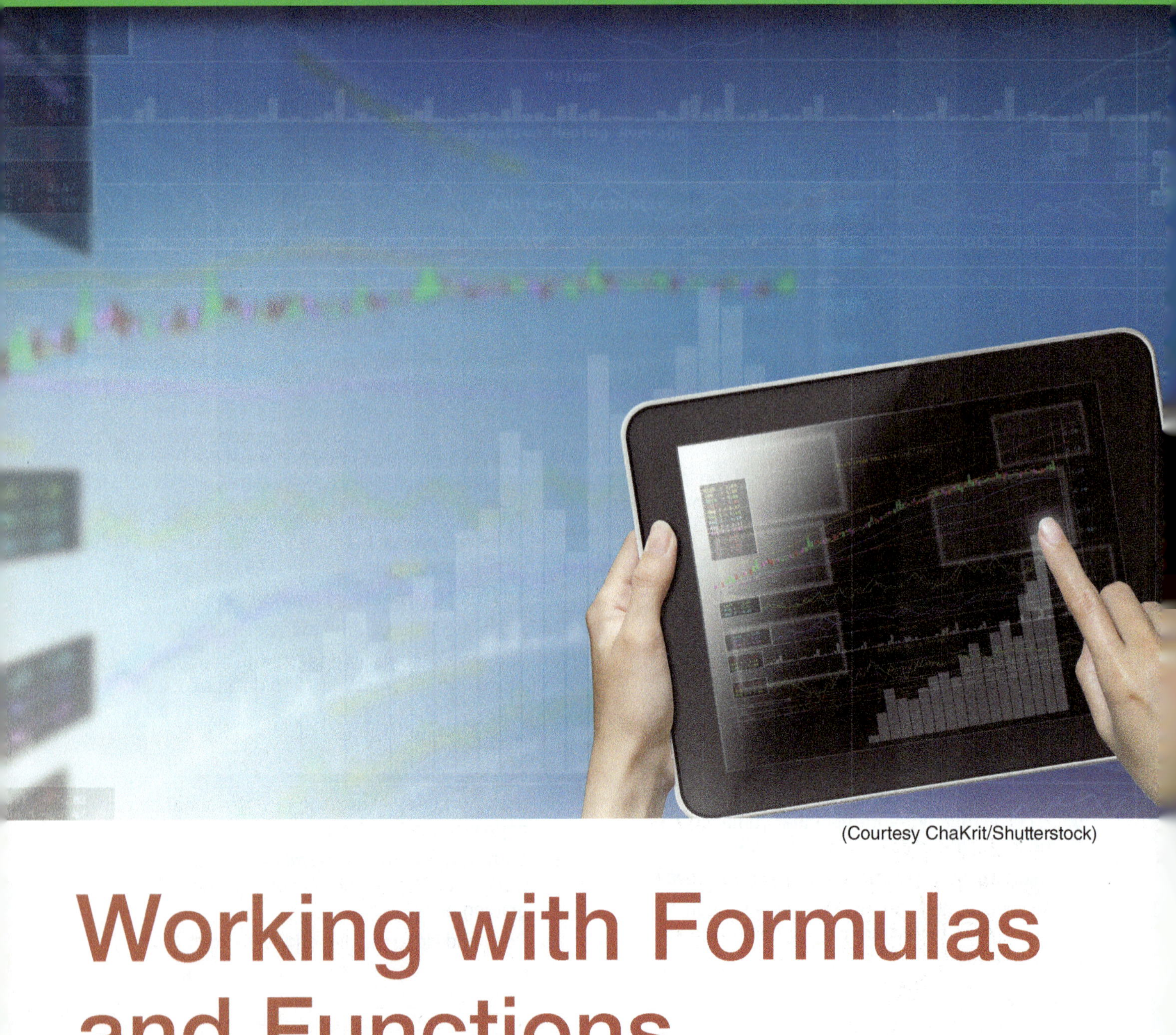

(Courtesy ChaKrit/Shutterstock)

Working with Formulas and Functions

Lesson 11
Getting Started with Functions

- Using Functions (SUM, AVERAGE, MEDIAN, MIN, and MAX)
- Inserting a Function
- Using AutoCalculate
- Inserting Subtotals

Lesson 12
Using Excel Tables

- Creating an Excel Table
- Formatting an Excel Table
- Sorting and Filtering an Excel Table
- Converting a Table to a Range

Lesson 13
Working with the NOW Function and Named Ranges

- Using the NOW Function to Display a System Date
- Using Named Ranges

Lesson 14
Working with IF Functions

- Understanding IF Functions
- Nesting Functions
- Using SUMIF and SUMIFS Functions
- Using COUNTIF and COUNTIFS Functions
- Using the AVERAGEIF Function

Lesson 15
Working with Text Functions

- Using the CONCATENATE Function
- Using the UPPER and LOWER Function
- Using the RIGHT, LEFT, and MID Functions
- Using the TRIM Function

Lesson 16
Using Frozen Labels and Panes

- Freezing Labels While Scrolling
- Splitting a Worksheet into Panes

Lesson 17
Using Conditional Formatting and Find and Replace

- Applying Conditional Formatting
- Using Find and Replace

Lesson 18
Rotating Entries and Resolving #### Errors

- Rotating Cell Entries
- Resolving a #### Error Message

Lesson 19
Managing Worksheets and Performing Multi-Worksheet Operations

- Inserting, Deleting, Copying, Moving, and Renaming Worksheets
- Changing the Color of a Worksheet Tab
- Changing Between Worksheets
- Hiding Sheets
- Grouping Worksheets for Editing
- Creating a Summary Workbook
- Updating a Summary Workbook

Lesson 20
Modifying Print Options

- Printing a Selection
- Printing All the Worksheets in a Workbook
- Inserting Page Breaks
- Using Page Break Preview
- Setting the Print Area
- Repeating Row and Column Labels
- Selecting Other Sheet Tab Options

End-of-Chapter Activities

Lesson 11

Getting Started with Functions

➤ What You Will Learn

Using Functions (SUM, AVERAGE, MEDIAN, MIN, and MAX)
Inserting a Function
Using AutoCalculate
Inserting Subtotals

WORDS TO KNOW

Argument
The values and other inputs that a function uses to calculate the result. You specify the cell or range that holds the value(s) for each argument or input a particular value.

AutoCalculate
A feature that temporarily performs the following calculations on a range of cells without the user having to enter a formula: AVERAGE, COUNT, MIN, MAX, or SUM.

Formula AutoComplete
A feature that speeds up the manual entry of functions.

Function
A predefined formula that performs a specific calculation using the inputs you specify.

Function name
The name given to one of Excel's predefined formulas.

Nest
To use a function as an argument within another function.

Software Skills Use an Excel function to help you write a formula to perform more advanced calculations in your worksheets. Excel's Insert Function feature provides a list of available functions and "fill-in-the-blanks" assistance to complete a formula. Excel's AutoCalculate feature allows you to quickly calculate the AVERAGE, COUNT, COUNTA, MAX, MIN, or SUM for a cell range without entering a formula. The Function Library group also enables you to select functions by category.

What You Can Do

Using Functions (SUM, AVERAGE, MEDIAN, MIN, and MAX)

- Excel provides built-in formulas called **functions** to perform special calculations.
- To create a formula with a function, enter these elements in the following order:
  - The equal sign (=).
  - The **function name**, in upper- or lowercase letters.
  - An open parenthesis to separate the arguments from the function name.
  - The **argument(s)** identifying the data required to perform the function.
  - A close parenthesis to end the argument.
- For example, =SUM(A1:A40) adds the values in the cells specified by the argument, which in this case is a single range of cells A1 through A40.
- Most functions allow multiple arguments, separated by commas. For example, =SUM(A1:A40,C1:C40) adds the values in the ranges A1:A40 and C1:C40.
- A function may be inserted into a formula. For example, =B2/SUM(C3:C5) takes the value in cell B2 and divides it by the sum of the values in the range C3:C5.
- When a function is used as an argument for other functions, it is **nested** within those functions.

- For example, =ROUND(SUM(B12:B23),2)) totals the values in the range, B12:B23, and then rounds that total to two decimal places.
- Following are commonly used functions:
  - =SUM( ) adds the values in a range of cells.
  - =AVERAGE( ) returns the arithmetic mean of the values in a range of cells.
  - =COUNT( ) counts the cells containing numbers in a range of cells (blank cells or text entries are ignored).
  - =COUNTA( ) counts the number of non-blank cells.
  - =MAX( ) finds the highest value in a range of cells.
  - =MIN( ) finds the lowest value in a range of cells.
  - =ROUND( ) adjusts a value to a specific number of digits.

✓ *When a cell is formatted to a specified number of decimal places, only the display of that value is affected. The actual value in the cell is still used in all calculations. For example, if a cell contains the value 13.45687, and you decide to display only the last two decimal places, then the value 13.46 will display in the cell, but the value, 13.45687, will be used in all calculations.*

- If you are familiar with a formula and its required arguments, you can type it into the cell where you want the result to display. The formula name must be typed correctly.
- After you type =, the function name, and the opening parenthesis, a ScreenTip shows you what argument(s) to enter for the function.
- When you type = and then type the beginning of a function name, the **Formula AutoComplete** feature displays a list of possible matching function names. Use the ↓ key to select the desired function, and then press TAB to enter it in the formula.

✓ *You also can use Formula AutoComplete to enter other listed items such as a range name.*

- Use the drop-down arrow on the AutoSum button Σ in the Editing Group on the HOME tab to quickly insert a SUM, AVERAGE, COUNT, MAX, or MIN function. The AutoSum button Σ is also located in the Function Library group on the FORMULAS tab.

Try It! Using Functions (SUM, AVERAGE, MEDIAN, MIN, and MAX)

1. Start Excel.
2. Open the **E11TryA** file from the data files for this lesson.
3. Save the workbook as **E11TryA_xx** in the location where your teacher instructions you to store the files for this lesson
4. Add a header that has your name at the left, the date code in the center, and the page number code at the right, and change back to Normal view.
5. Click cell B10 to select it.
6. Type **=sum(**, and then drag over the range B5:B9 to select it.
7. Press ENTER. Excel adds the closing parenthesis for you and displays the formula result in the cell.
8. Press ↓ once to select cell B12.
9. Type **=av**. Press ↓ once to select AVERAGE.
10. Press TAB, type **B5:B9** to specify that range as the argument, and press ENTER to finish the formula and select cell B13.
11. On the HOME tab, in the Editing group, click the AutoSum drop-down arrow Σ AutoSum ▾, and then click Max. Type or select the range **B5:B9**, and press ENTER to complete the formula and select cell B14.
12. On the FORMULAS tab, in the Function Library group, click the AutoSum drop-down arrow Σ AutoSum ▾, and then click Min. Type or select the range **B5:B9**, and press ENTER to complete the formula and select cell B15.
13. Save the **E11TryA_xx** file, and leave it open to use in the next Try It.

(continued)

Try It! Using Functions (SUM, AVERAGE, MEDIAN, MIN, and MAX) *(continued)*

Typing a Function

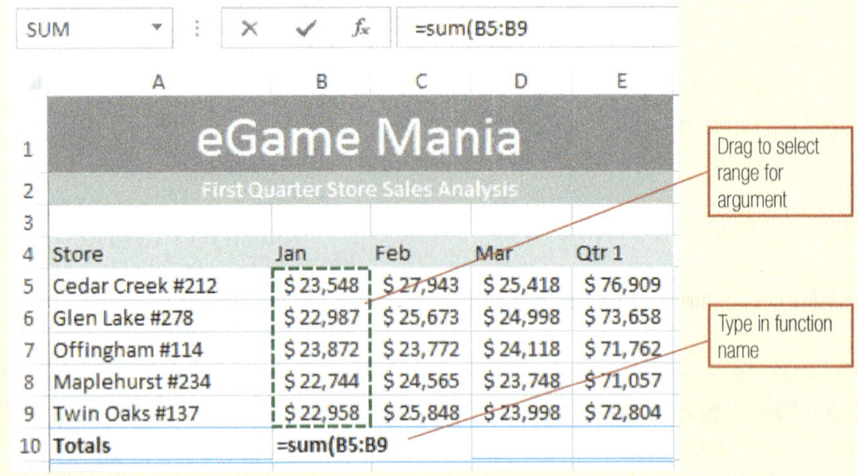

Excel 2013, Windows 8, Microsoft Corporation

Selecting a function with Formula AutoComplete

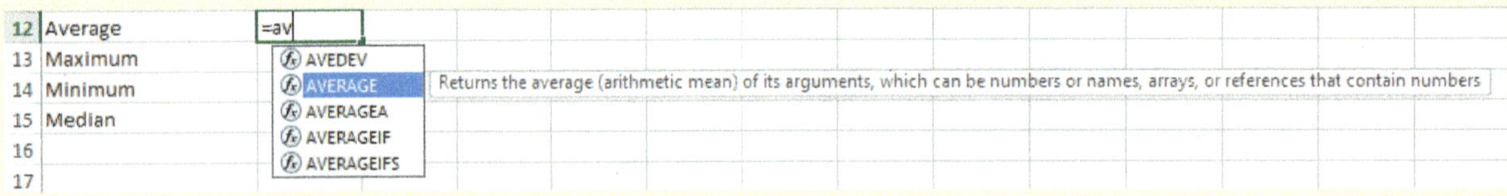

Excel 2013, Windows 8, Microsoft Corporation

Inserting a Function

- If you know what category a function falls in, you can insert it by clicking the FORMULAS tab, clicking the category name in the Function Library group, and then clicking the function.
- Clicking More Functions displays a menu with additional categories. Click the desired category, and then the desired function.
- If you need to search for a function, click the Insert Function button *fx* on the formula bar. You also can click the Insert Function button *fx* in the Function Library group of the FORMULAS tab. Either method opens the Insert Function dialog box.
- In the Insert Function dialog box, you can type a brief description of the function you want to use to display a list of corresponding functions. For example, you could type the description "add numbers" to find a function you could use to add a column of numbers.
- You can also display functions by typing the name of the function (if you know it), or by choosing a category from the Or select a category list.
- When you enter a formula using Insert Function, Excel automatically enters the equal sign (=) in the formula.
- After you select a function and click OK in the Insert Function dialog box, the Function Arguments dialog box appears to prompt you to enter the arguments needed for the function.
- In the Function Arguments dialog box, you can select cells instead of typing them by using the Collapse Dialog button located at the right of each text box.

✓ *You also can type another function as an argument for the current function.*

- Required argument names appear in bold.
- As you enter the arguments, the value of that argument is displayed to the right of the text box.
- Excel calculates the current result and displays it at the bottom of the dialog box.

✓ *If you need help understanding a particular function's arguments, click the Help on this function link, located in the lower left-hand corner of the dialog box.*

Try It! Inserting a Function

1. With cell B15 still selected in the **E11TryA_xx** file, on the FORMULAS tab, click More Functions > Statistical, and then scroll down and click MEDIAN.
2. In the Number1 text box of the Function Arguments dialog box, type **B5:B9** to replace the suggested entry, and click OK.
3. Click cell C10 to select it.
4. Click the Insert Function button *fx* on the formula bar.
5. Click the Or select a category list drop-down arrow, and click Math & Trig.
6. Scroll down the Select a function list, click SUM, and then click OK.
7. In the Function Arguments dialog box, make sure that C5:C9 appears in the Number1 text box, and then click OK.
8. Use the fill handle to copy the formula from cell C10 to D10:E10.
9. Select the range B12:B15, and use the fill handle to copy the formulas from those cells to C12:E15 to the right.
10. Adjust the column widths if needed.
11. Save the **E11TryA_xx** file, and close it.

The Insert Function dialog box

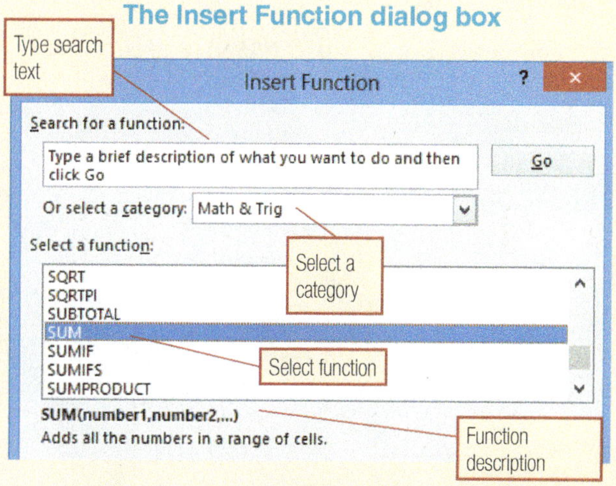

Excel 2013, Windows 8, Microsoft Corporation

Using AutoCalculate

- To quickly calculate the AVERAGE, COUNT, COUNTA, MAX, MIN, or SUM for a cell range without entering a formula, use **AutoCalculate**.
- Select the range, and the Average, Count (COUNTA), and Sum results appear on the Status bar.
- To control which function results appear on the Status bar, right-click the Status bar and click one of the six functions that appear.

Try It! Using AutoCalculate

1. In the **E11TryA_xx** file, drag over the range E5:E9 to select it.
2. Observe the Status bar. The Average calculated by AutoComplete should match the result in cell E12. The Sum calculated by AutoComplete should match the result in cell E10.
3. With the range E5:E9 still selected, right-click the Status bar, click Maximum, and press ESC.
4. Observe the Status bar. It now includes a Max value that should match the result shown in cell E13.
5. Right-click the Status bar, click Maximum, and press ESC.
6. Click cell A1 to select it.
7. Save the **E11TryA_xx** file, and close it.

(continued)

Try It! Using AutoCalculate *(continued)*

Working with AutoCalculate

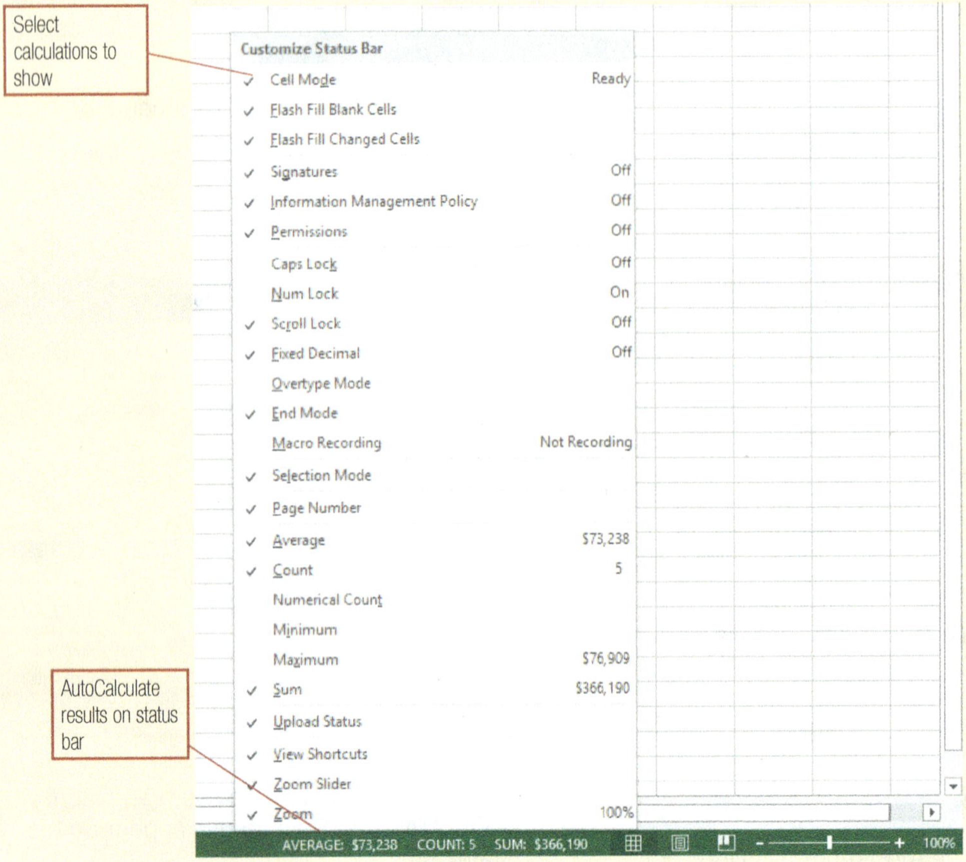

Excel 2013, Windows 8, Microsoft Corporation

Inserting Subtotals

- With the Subtotal feature, you can quickly insert subtotals between similar rows in an Excel list without having to create custom functions.

  ✓ *You cannot use the Subtotal feature with an Excel table. You will learn more about Excel tables in the Lesson 12.*

- Instead of entering formulas or using functions to total a field for particular rows, you can use the Subtotal feature. For example, you can subtotal a sales list to compute the amount sold by each salesperson on a given day.
- The Subtotal feature does the following:
  - Calculates subtotals for all rows that contain the same entry in one column. For example, if you select the field Salesperson, Excel will create subtotals for each salesperson.
  - Inserts the totals in a row just below that group of data.
  - Calculates a grand total.
  - Inserts a label for each group totaled/subtotaled.
  - Displays the outline controls.

    ✓ *The outline controls allow you to control the level of detail displayed.*

- For the Subtotal feature to work, all records containing values that contribute to that subtotal (or other calculation) must be sorted together.

  ✓ *You will learn about sorting data in Lesson 31.*

- Excel inserts a subtotal line whenever it detects a change in the value of the chosen field—for instance, a change from each sales office name.

- Also, if the subtotal line is to show the average pledge amount for all callers to the Sacramento office, then each pledge must contain "Sacramento" in one column—preferably one with a meaningful field name, such as "Office."
- When you click the Subtotal button on the DATA tab, a dialog box displays from which you can make several choices:
  - *At each change in*—Select the field name by which you want to total.
  - *Use function*—Select a function.
  - *Add subtotal to*—Select one or more fields to use with the database function you selected.
  - *Replace current subtotals*—Select this option to create a new subtotal within a database, removing any current subtotals. Deselect this option to retain current subtotals.
  - *Page break between groups*—Places each subtotaled group on its own page.
  - *Summary below data*—Inserts the subtotals/grand total below each group, rather than above it.
  - *Remove All*—Removes all subtotals.
- Subtotals act just like any other formula or function; if you change the data, the total will recalculate automatically.
- The Subtotal feature displays the outline controls around the worksheet frame. With the outline controls, you can hide or display the records within any given group.

✓ *You will learn more about working with outlines in Lesson 34.*

Try It! Creating Subtotals

1. Open the **E11TryB** file from the data files for this lesson.
2. Save the workbook as **E11TryB_xx** in the location where your teacher instructs you to store the files for this lesson.
3. Add a header that has your name at the left, the date code in the center, and the page number code at the right, and change back to Normal.
4. Select the range A5:G29 and click DATA > Subtotal.
5. In the At each change in drop-down list, select Item Type, if necessary.

   ✓ *A new subtotal will be calculated at each change within the column you choose here.*
6. In the Use function box, select Sum.
7. In the Add Subtotal to box, select Items Sold and Value Sold. Unselect PriceperCase, if necessary.
8. Select Replace current subtotals, and Summary below data, if necessary.
9. Click OK. Notice that the item types are now subtotaled.
10. Save the **E11TryB_xx** file, and close it.

The Subtotal dialog box

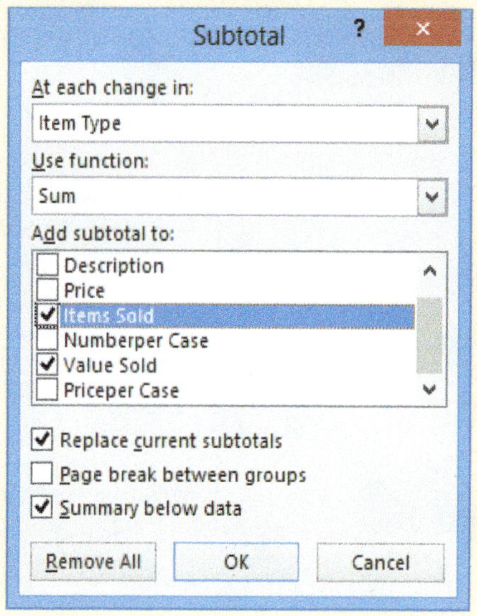

Excel 2013, Windows 8, Microsoft Corporation

Lesson 11—Practice

In this project, you will insert functions into formulas and create subtotals using the skills you learned in this lesson.

DIRECTIONS

1. Start Excel, if necessary, and open the **E11Practice** file from the data files for this lesson.
2. Save the workbook as **E11Practice_xx** in the location where your teacher instructs you to store the files for this lesson.
3. Add a header that has your name at the left, the date code in the center, and the page number code at the right, and change back to **Normal** view.
4. In cell **E4**, enter the formula **=sum(B4,C4)**, and press TAB.
5. In cell **F4**, enter the formula **=sum(B4,D4)**, and press CTRL + ENTER.
6. Drag over the range **E4:F4** to select it, and then double-click the fill handle to copy the formulas down through row 14.
7. Click cell **B16** to select it.
8. Type **=B11**, and press CTRL + ENTER.
9. Drag the fill handle right through cell **F16** to fill the formula across.
10. Select the range **A3:G14** and click **DATA** > **Subtotal**.
11. In the **At each change in** drop-down list, select **Lot**.
12. In the **Use function** box, select **Count**.
13. Select **Replace current subtotals** and **Summary below**, if necessary.
14. Click **OK**.
15. Press CTRL + HOME. Your worksheet should look like the one shown in Figure 11-1.
16. **With your teacher's permission**, print the worksheet. Submit the printout or the file for grading as required.
17. Save and close the file, and exit Excel.

Figure 11-1

	A	B	C	D	E	F	G
1	Bid Results - Canal Street Home Restoration Project						
2							
3		Unit Bid	Option Pkg. #1	Option Pkg. #2	Base Bid + #1	Base Bid + #2	Lot
4	BJW, Ltd.	$ 97,854	$ 6,981	$ 9,726	$ 104,835	$ 107,580	Lot A
5	Craftsman, Inc.	$ 89,475	$ 7,051	$ 8,974	$ 96,526	$ 98,449	Lot A
6	Meguro Construction	$ 92,441	$ 6,200	$ 9,795	$ 98,641	$ 102,236	Lot A
7	Mendoza Inc.	$ 88,459	$ 7,500	$ 8,945	$ 95,959	$ 97,404	Lot A
8						Lot A Count	4
9	New Mark Designs	$ 99,487	$ 5,985	$ 9,760	$ 105,472	$ 109,247	Lot B
10	Ravuru Renovations	$ 92,335	$ 6,193	$ 8,554	$ 98,528	$ 100,889	Lot B
11	Renovation Ventures	$ 91,415	$ 6,300	$ 10,000	$ 97,715	$ 101,415	Lot B
12	Restoration Architecture	$ 89,445	$ 6,115	$ 9,784	$ 95,560	$ 99,229	Lot B
13						Lot B Count	4
14	TOH Construction	$ 91,225	$ 6,451	$ 10,800	$ 97,676	$ 102,025	Lot C
15	Williams Brothers Renovators, Ltd.	$ 96,485	$ 5,531	$ 9,875	$ 102,016	$ 106,360	Lot C
16	Woo Home Designs	$ 93,415	$ 6,751	$ 10,633	$ 100,166	$ 104,048	Lot C
17						Lot C Count	3
18						Grand Count	11
19	Analysis						
20	Restoration Architecture	$ 89,445	$ 6,115	$ 9,784	$ 95,560	$ 99,229	
21	Average of All Bids						
22	Difference (+/-)						
23	Lowest Bid						
24	Difference (+/-)						
25	Highest Bid						
26	Difference (+/-)						
27							
28	Median						

Excel 2013, Windows 8, Microsoft Corporation

Lesson 11—Apply

You're the owner of Restoration Architecture, a large design and construction firm specializing in the remodeling, redesign, and restoration of existing properties. You submitted a bid to restore several homes purchased by a neighborhood revitalization organization. The group solicited bids from a number of firms. You want to analyze the bidding results to evaluate how competitive your bid was.

DIRECTIONS

1. Start Excel, if necessary, and open the **E11Apply** file from the data files for this lesson.
2. Save the workbook as **E11Apply_xx** in the location where your teacher instructs you to store the files for this lesson.
3. Add a header that has your name at the left, the date code in the center, and the page number code at the right, and change back to **Normal** view.
4. Click cell **B20**, type **=av**, click **AVERAGE** in the Formula AutoComplete list, and press TAB. Drag over the range **B6:B16** to enter it in the formula, and finish the formula.
5. Use the fill handle to fill the formula across the row.
6. In cell **B21**, enter a formula that subtracts the value in cell **B20** from the value in cell **B19**. Fill the formula across the row.
7. Use the **AutoSum** button Σ to enter a formula in cell **B22** that finds the lowest (MIN) value in the range **B6:B16**. Fill the formula across the row.
8. In cell **B23**, enter a formula that subtracts the value in cell **B22** from the value in cell **B19**. Fill the formula across the row.
9. Use the **More Functions** button **Statistical** submenu to enter a formula in cell **B24** that finds the highest (MAX) value in the range **B6:B16**. Fill the formula across the row.
10. In cell **B25**, enter a formula that subtracts the value in cell **B24** from the value in cell **B19**. Fill the formula across the row.
11. Use the **Insert Function** button *fx* on the formula bar to enter a formula in cell **B27** that finds the median value in the range **B6:B16**. Fill the formula across the row.
12. Select the range **F6:F16**. Observe the AutoCalculate results in the status bar.
13. Select the range **A5:G16** and click **DATA** > **Subtotal**.
14. In the **At each change in** drop-down list, select **Lot**.
15. In the **Use function** box, select **Count**.
16. Select **Replace current subtotals** and **Summary below**, if necessary.
17. Click **OK**. Adjust column widths as necessary to display all data. Your worksheet should look like the one shown in Figure 11-2 on the next page.
18. **With your teacher's permission**, print the worksheet. Submit the printout or the file for grading as required.
19. Save and close the file, and exit Excel.

Figure 11-2

	A	B	C	D	E	F	G
1	Bid Results - Canal Street Home Restoration Project						
2							
3	**No. of homes to be restored:**	**11**					
4							
5		**Unit Bid**	**Option Pkg. #1**	**Option Pkg. #2**	**Base Bid + #1**	**Base Bid + #2**	**Lot**
6	BJW, Ltd.	$ 97,854	$ 6,981	$ 9,726	$ 104,835	$ 107,580	Lot A
7	Craftsman, Inc.	$ 89,475	$ 7,051	$ 8,974	$ 96,526	$ 98,449	Lot A
8	Meguro Construction	$ 92,441	$ 6,200	$ 9,795	$ 98,641	$ 102,236	Lot A
9	Mendoza Inc.	$ 88,459	$ 7,500	$ 8,945	$ 95,959	$ 97,404	Lot A
10						**Lot A Count**	4
11	New Mark Designs	$ 99,487	$ 5,985	$ 9,760	$ 105,472	$ 109,247	Lot B
12	Ravuru Renovations	$ 92,335	$ 6,193	$ 8,554	$ 98,528	$ 100,889	Lot B
13	Renovation Ventures	$ 91,415	$ 6,300	$ 10,000	$ 97,715	$ 101,415	Lot B
14	Restoration Architecture	$ 89,445	$ 6,115	$ 9,784	$ 95,560	$ 99,229	Lot B
15						**Lot B Count**	4
16	TOH Construction	$ 91,225	$ 6,451	$ 10,800	$ 97,676	$ 102,025	Lot C
17	Williams Brothers Renovators, Ltd.	$ 96,485	$ 5,531	$ 9,875	$ 102,016	$ 106,360	Lot C
18	Woo Home Designs	$ 93,415	$ 6,751	$ 10,633	$ 100,166	$ 104,048	Lot C
19						**Lot C Count**	3
20						**Grand Count**	11
21							
22	**Analysis**						
23	Restoration Architecture	$ 89,445	$ 6,115	$ 9,784	$ 95,560	$ 99,229	
24	Average of All Bids	$ 92,912	$ 6,460	$ 9,713	$ 99,372	$ 102,626	
25	Difference (+/-)	$ (3,467)	$ (345)	$ 71	$ (3,812)	$ (3,397)	
26	Lowest Bid	$ 88,459	$ 5,531	$ 8,554	$ 95,560	$ 97,404	
27	Difference (+/-)	$ 986	$ 584	$ 1,230	$ -	$ 1,825	
28	Highest Bid	$ 99,487	$ 7,500	$ 10,800	$ 105,472	$ 109,247	
29	Difference (+/-)	$(10,042)	$ (1,385)	$ (1,016)	$ (9,912)	$ (10,018)	
30							
31	Median	$ 92,335	$ 6,300	$ 9,784	$ 98,528	$ 102,025	
32							

Lesson 12

Using Excel Tables

➤ What You Will Learn

Creating an Excel Table
Formatting an Excel Table
Sorting and Filtering an Excel Table
Converting a Table to a Range

Software Skills Formatting a range as an Excel table enables you to apply formatting and create calculations more easily. You also can sort and filter the data in the table to organize it for analysis. You'll learn how to create and format a table, perform calculations, and sort and filter in this lesson, as well as how to convert a table back to a regular range of cells.

What You Can Do

Creating an Excel Table

- An **Excel table** is a range of data with special features that enable you to reference a column of data in a formula more naturally and build formulas more easily.
- You can perform other functions with the special column headers in an Excel table such as sorting and filtering data.
- Excel tables are best for data that's organized primarily by columns, because some automatic totals and other functions can be inserted by column, and not by row.
- You create a table by clicking in a range of data that includes headings for every column, and then using the Table button in the Tables group of the INSERT tab.
- You select an overall table format and other formatting settings on the TABLE TOOLS DESIGN tab.
- Excel automatically names the table, although you can change the table name.
- You can reference the table name and table column headers in formulas. References to the table and columns are called **structured references**.
- Adding a formula in a cell in the column to the right of the table automatically creates a calculated column that becomes part of the table.
- Structured references make the formulas easy to understand and also adjust automatically when you add data to the table.

WORDS TO KNOW

Banded rows or columns
The shading of alternating rows or columns to make a table easier to read.

Column specifier
The structured reference to a table column, which consists of the table column header name in square brackets.

Criterion
A value, some text, or an expression that defines the type of content you want to see.

Excel table
Data arranged in columns and specially formatted with column headers that contain commands that allow you to sort, filter, and perform other functions on the table.

Filter
Hide nonmatching rows in a table or list of data according to the criterion or criteria you specify.

Sort
Arrange the rows in a table or list of data in a new order according to the entries in one or more columns.

Structured references
Using the table name or a table column header in a formula to refer to data in the entire table or specified column.

Table style
A combination of cell color, border, shading, and other formatting attributes applied to a table.

Total row
A row you can display below a table to calculate data in the columns above using a function you choose.

- For example, =SUM(SalesDept[Jan]) totals the range of cells in the Jan column in the SalesDept table.
- The structured reference to a table column header is called a **column specifier**.
- To enter formulas that reference table data, use Formula AutoComplete so it can supply you with valid table names, column specifiers, and other structured references.
- In a formula, you enclose column specifiers and structured references in square brackets, and precede them with the table name, as in =AVERAGE(Sales[June])
- Excel provides several structured references you can use to refer to specific areas in a table.
  - [#ALL]—refers to the entire table range, including column headers, table data, and the totals row (if any).
  - [#DATA]—refers to the table data range.
  - [#HEADERS]—refers to the cells in the header row.
  - [#TOTALS]—refers to the cells in the total row.
  - [#THISROW]—refers to table cells located in the same row as the formula. This might include non-data cells.
- For example, =SUM(SalesDept[[#TOTALS], [April]:[June]]) totals the values in the Totals cells in columns April through June.
- You can display the **total row** below the table data range and set it up to perform calculations using the functions you specify.

Try It! Creating an Excel Table

1. Start Excel.
2. Open the **E12Try** file from the data files for this lesson.
3. Save the workbook as **E12Try_xx** in the location where your teacher instructs you to store the files for this lesson.

Creating an Excel table

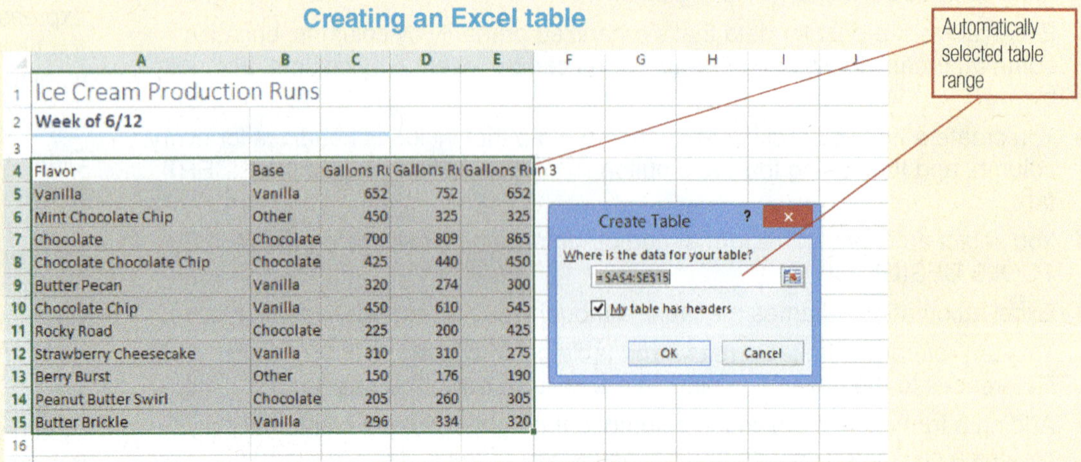

Excel 2013, Windows 8, Microsoft Corporation

(continued)

Try It! Creating an Excel Table *(continued)*

4. Add a header that has your name at the left, the date code in the center, and the page number code at the right, and change back to Normal view.

5. Click cell B7 to select it.

6. Click the INSERT tab > Table . The Create Table dialog box appears, suggesting the correct range as the data range for the table.

   ✓ *Because the selected cell is in a range of data that has column header labels, Excel can identify the proper range for the table. Otherwise, you can drag to select the desired range.*

7. Click OK. Excel automatically creates the table, applies a table style, and displays the TABLE TOOLS DESIGN tab.

8. On the TABLE TOOLS DESIGN tab, in the Table Styles group, click the More button and then click Table Style Medium 7 under Medium in the gallery.

9. Click cell F5 to select it.

10. Type **=[Gallons Run 1]+[Gallons Run 2]+[Gallons Run 3]** and press ENTER. Excel automatically adds a new column to the table and copies the formula with structured references in the whole column.

    ✓ *This formula's structured references are the column headers, or column labels for the table. Notice that you didn't need to type in the table name in this instance.*

11. Press CTRL + Z three times to undo the new column.

12. With cell F5 still selected, on the HOME tab, click AutoSum Σ, and press ENTER. This method also creates a formula with structured references and adds a new column to the table.

13. Change the entry in cell F4 to Gallons Total.

14. Click TABLE TOOLS DESIGN > Total Row. The total row appears below the table data. Note that by default, Total is entered in cell A16, and a sum formula in cell F16.

    ✓ *Note that the function used to create the sum is actually a SUBTOTAL function.*

15. Change the entry in cell A16 to **Averages**.

Calculating with structured references

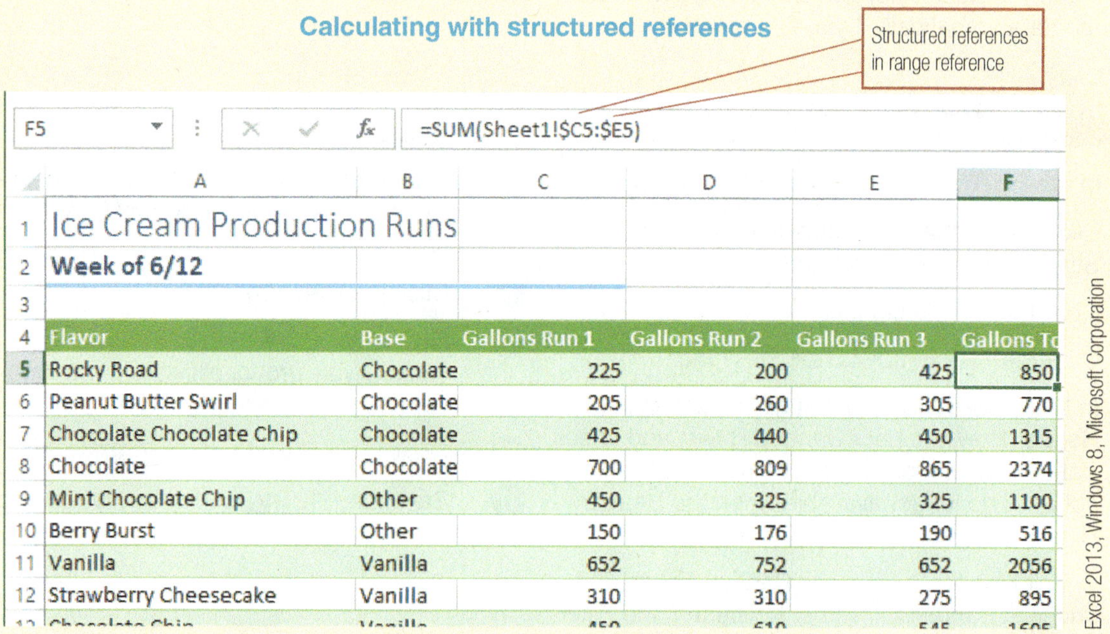

(continued)

Try It! Creating an Excel Table *(continued)*

16 Click cell F16, click the down arrow button, and then click None to remove the sum.

17 Click cell C16, click the down arrow button, and click Average.

18 Add Average calculations for cells D16 and E16.

19 Drag over the range C16:E16 to select it.

20 On the HOME tab, click the dialog box launcher for the Number group.

21 In the Format Cells dialog box, on the Number tab, in the Category list, click Number. Reduce the Decimal places entry to 0, and then click OK.

22 Save the E12Try_xx file, and leave it open to use in the next Try It.

Formatting an Excel Table

- **Table styles** include various formatting elements you can apply to column headings or totals and title and heading styles.
- To select a table style, click the More drop-down button in the Table Styles group on the TABLE TOOLS DESIGN tab.
- You also can select a table style from the Format as Table drop-down gallery in the Styles group on the HOME tab.
- As you move the mouse over the table styles shown in the gallery, the worksheet automatically shows a Live Preview of the new style.
- If you apply a table style, the table using that style will update automatically if you change themes.
- You can control the appearance of rows and columns by using the Table Style Options on the TABLE TOOLS DESIGN tab.
- Table Style Options include bolding the first and last column, including a header and total row, **band rows and columns**, or including a filter button to sort and display data.
- Checking a selection in the Table Style Options will include the table formatting element and unchecking a selection will remove it.
- You can remove the entire table style by clicking the Clear button from the More styles gallery in the Table Styles group on the TABLE TOOLS DESIGN tab.

Try It! Formatting an Excel Table

1 In the E12Try_xx file, click cell A5 to select it.

2 Click the Format as Table button in the Styles group on the HOME tab.

3 Click Table Style Light 7.

4 Click the TABLE TOOLS DESIGN tab.

5 In the Table Styles Options group, uncheck Header Row, uncheck Banded Rows, and check Banded Columns. Notice that the Filter Button option is no longer available when the Header Row is unselected.

6 Check Header Row, check Banded Rows, and uncheck Banded Columns. Notice that the Filter Button becomes available when the Header Row is selected.

7 On the TABLE TOOLS DESIGN tab, in the Table Styles group, click the More drop-down button.

8 Click the Clear button.

9 On the TABLE TOOLS DESIGN tab, in the Table Styles group, click the More drop-down button

10 Click Table Style Medium 7.

11 Save the E12Try_xx file, and leave it open to use in the next Try It.

Sorting and Filtering an Excel Table

- Each column header in an Excel table has a down arrow button. Clicking the button displays a menu with choices for changing the display of the table rows.
- Using a column header menu, you can **sort** the table, or change the order of the rows according to the entries in the column header by which you're sorting.
- You can sort in ascending order: A to Z, lowest to highest, or least recent to most recent.
- You also can sort in descending order: Z to A, highest to lowest, or most recent to least recent.
- Clearing a sort does not undo the sort. So, either use Undo to remove a sort immediately or add a column that numbers the rows so that you can return the rows to their original order.
- To sort by multiple columns, use the Sort button in the Sort & Filter group on the DATA tab. In the Sort dialog box, specify the top level sort in the first Sort by row, then to sort within those results, use the Add Level button to sort by another field within those results.
- To limit the list to display only rows that have a particular entry (**criterion**) in one of the columns, **filter** the list.
- For example, you can filter a list of sales transactions to show transactions for only one client or salesperson.
- Choose (Select All) or Clear Filter from *"Column"* in the column header menu to remove the filter.

Try It! Sorting and Filtering an Excel Table

1. In the **E12Try_xx** file, click the down arrow button for the Base column header.
2. In the menu, click Sort A to Z. Notice that the rows change order and are listed according to the entry in the Base column.

   ✓ *Look at the entries in the Flavor column. They are not sorted. For example, the rows with the Vanilla base appear in this order according to Flavor: Vanilla, Butter Pecan, Chocolate Chip, Strawberry Cheesecake, and Butter Brickle.*
3. Select the range B5:B15.
4. Click DATA > Sort .
5. In the Sort dialog box, click the Add Level button. In the Then by drop-down list that appears, choose Flavor. Open the Order drop-down list for that row, and click Z to A.
6. Click OK.

   ✓ *The rows reorder so that the Flavor column entries now appear in descending order within each Base grouping. The rows with the Vanilla base now appear in this order according to Flavor: Vanilla, Strawberry Cheesecake, Chocolate Chip, Butter Pecan, and Butter Brickle.*
7. Click the down arrow button for the Base column header.
8. In the menu, click the check box beside (Select All) to uncheck it. Then, click the check box beside Chocolate to check it and click OK.

   ✓ *The table changes to show results based on the filtered data only.*
9. Click the down arrow button for the Base column header.
10. In the menu, click Clear Filter From "Base".
11. On the DATA tab, click Sort .
12. Click the Delete Level button twice, and then click OK.
13. Save the **E12Try_xx** file, and leave it open to use in the next Try It.

(continued)

Try It! Sorting and Filtering an Excel Table *(continued)*

Use a column header menu to sort or filter the table

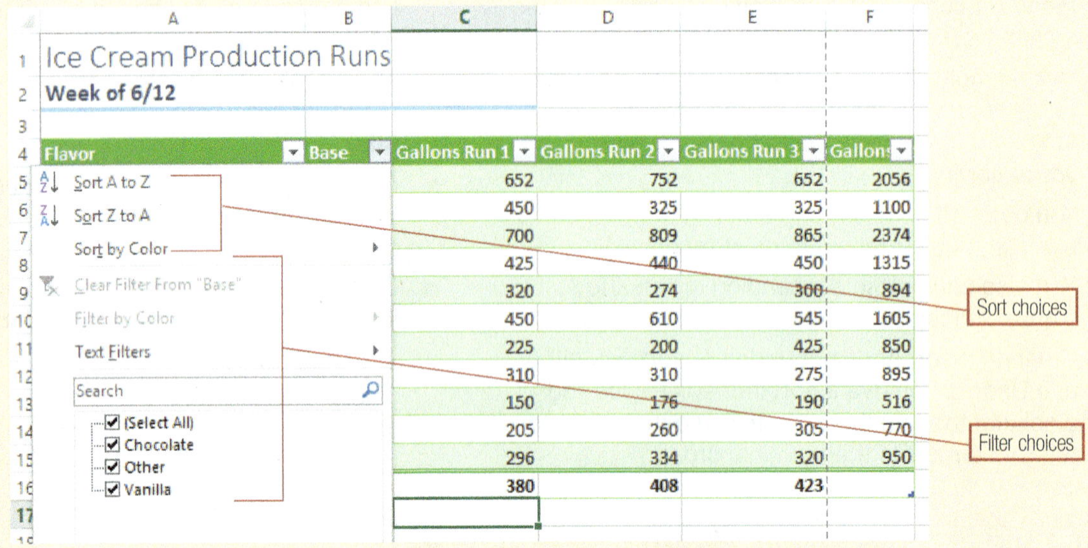

Excel 2013, Windows 8, Microsoft Corporation

Converting a Table to a Range

- Converting a table to a range removes the special table functionality.
- The converted range retains any formatting you applied.
- Use the Convert to Range button in the Tools group of the TABLE TOOLS DESIGN tab to convert the table, or right-click the table, point to Table, and click Convert to Range in the submenu.

Try It! Converting a Table to a Range

1. In the **E12Try_xx** file, click any cell in the table.
2. Click TABLE TOOLS DESIGN > Convert to Range.
3. In the dialog box that appears to ask you to confirm the conversion, click Yes.
4. Click cell F6 to select it. Notice that the structured references have been converted to regular references.
5. Click cell C16 to select it. Notice that the formula is a subtotal formula.
6. Save the **E12Try_xx** file, and close it.

Lesson 12—Practice

In this project, you will create a table, perform calculations, sort and filter the table, and convert the table to a range using the skills you learned in this lesson.

DIRECTIONS

1. Start Excel, if necessary, and open the **E12Practice** file from the data files for this lesson.
2. Save the workbook as **E12Practice_xx** in the location where your teacher instructs you to store the files for this lesson.
3. Add a header that has your name at the left, the date code in the center, and the page number code at the right, and change back to **Normal** view.
4. In cell **G5**, enter the formula **=sum(D5:F5)**, and press CTRL + ENTER.
5. Double-click the fill handle to fill the formula down the column.
6. Click cell **C8** to select it.
7. Click the **INSERT** > **Table**.
8. In the Create Table dialog box, click **OK**.
9. On the **TABLE TOOLS DESIGN** tab, in the Table Styles group, click the **More** button, and click **Table Style Medium 23** under Medium.
10. Click the down arrow button for the Type column header.
11. In the menu, click **Sort A to Z**.
12. Right-click anywhere in the table > **Table** > **Convert to Range** > **Yes** to confirm that you want to convert the table to a normal range.
13. Use **Undo** to undo the conversion of the table to a normal range.
14. Change the label in cell **A4** to **Project**. Your worksheet should look like the one in Figure 12-1.
15. **With your teacher's permission,** print page one of the worksheet. Submit the printout or the file for grading as required.
16. Save and close the file, and exit Excel.

Figure 12-1

	A	B	C	D	E	F	G	H
1	Restoration Architecture							
2	3rd Qtr Revenues by Project							
3								
4	Project	Type	Project Manager	July	August	September	Qtr 3 Totals	
5	18 South Pendleton Ave.	Commercial	Jansen	$ 7,855	$ 27,958	$ 31,225	$ 67,038	
6	Old Barn Quilts	Commercial	Nolo	$ 4,522	$ 12,889	$ 18,645	$ 36,056	
7	Faster Library	Public	Nolo	$ 41,325	$ 78,945	$ 85,664	$ 205,934	
8	Cramer Theater	Public	Timson	$ 125,995	$ 285,941	$ 275,884	$ 687,820	
9	Freemont Park Amphitheater	Public	Jansen	$ 72,145	$ 63,145	$ 21,778	$ 157,068	
10	Rossen House	Residential	Jansen	$ 328,118	$ 456,221	$ 298,485	$ 1,082,824	
11	512 N. Oak Street	Residential	Nolo	$ 32,995	$ 28,445	$ 18,445	$ 79,885	
12								

Excel 2013, Windows 8, Microsoft Corporation

Lesson 12—Apply

You are the Chief Financial Officer (CFO) of Restoration Architecture, and it's time for the quarterly revenue recap. You want to organize the information in a table so that you can add formulas and sort and filter to make the information easier to follow.

DIRECTIONS

1. Start Excel, if necessary, and open the **E12Apply** file from the data files for this lesson.
2. Save the workbook as **E12Apply_xx** in the location where your teacher instructs you to store the files for this lesson.
3. Add a header that has your name at the left, the date code in the center, and the page number code at the right, and change back to **Normal** view.
4. In cell **H5**, enter a function to calculate the average revenues for July, August, and September.
5. Change the column header for the new calculated column to **Qtr 3 Averages** and adjust the column width.
6. Add a total row to the table using the **TABLE TOOLS DESIGN** tab.
7. Change the entry in cell **A12** to **Averages**.
8. Remove the calculation from cell **H12**, and add average calculations to cells **D12:G12**.
9. Sort the table in ascending order by **Type**.
10. Filter the table to show only projects by **Jansen**.
11. Adjust column widths if needed. Your worksheet should look like the one in Figure 12-2.
12. **With your teacher's permission,** print page one of the worksheet. Submit the printout or the file for grading as required.
13. Save and close the file, and exit Excel.

Figure 12-2

	A	B	C	D	E	F	G	H
1	Restoration Architecture							
2	3rd Qtr Revenues by Project							
3								
4	Project	Type	Project Manager	July	August	September	Qtr 3 Totals	Qtr 3 Averages
5	18 South Pendleton Ave.	Commercial	Jansen	$ 7,855	$ 27,958	$ 31,225	$ 67,038	$ 22,346
9	Freemont Park Amphitheater	Public	Jansen	$ 72,145	$ 63,145	$ 21,778	$ 157,068	$ 52,356
10	Rossen House	Residential	Jansen	$ 328,118	$ 456,221	$ 298,485	$ 1,082,824	$ 360,941
12	Averages			$ 136,039	$ 182,441	$ 117,163	$ 435,643	
13								

Excel 2013, Windows 8, Microsoft Corporation

Lesson 13

Working with the NOW Function and Named Ranges

➤ What You Will Learn

Using the NOW Function to Display a System Date
Using Named Ranges

Software Skills If you don't add a header or footer including the date print code to a worksheet, you can instead insert the NOW function to add the system date and time to any cell on the sheet. Many users find it easier to reference a cell or range of cells using a descriptive name rather than cell addresses. Using range names makes worksheet formulas easier to understand, as well as helping with other operations such as formatting and printing.

WORDS TO KNOW

Name Box
The box at the far-left end of the formula bar that you can use to create and navigate to named ranges.

Range name
An identifying label assigned to a group of cells. Also known as defined name.

Volatile
A function that updates and displays a new result each time you open the workbook.

What You Can Do

Using the NOW Function to Display a System Date

- When you need to include a date and time that automatically updates on the worksheet, insert the NOW function. Rather than performing a calculation, this function displays the current system date and time.
- The NOW function doesn't require any arguments, so you enter it as =NOW().
- The results of the now function are **volatile**, meaning that they change based on the current system date and time when you open the workbook file rather than reflecting values on a worksheet.
- When you enter the NOW function in a cell, Excel automatically applies a date format that includes the time to the cell. You can change to another format if desired.
- You can enter the NOW function by typing it in, using Formula AutoComplete, or inserting it as you've learned earlier in the chapter.

Try It! Using the NOW Function to Display a System Date

1. Start Excel.
2. Open the **E13Try** file from the data files for this lesson.
3. Save the file as **E13Try_xx** in the location where your teacher instructs you to store the files for this lesson.
4. Add a header that has your name at the left, the date code in the center, and the page number code at the right, and change back to Normal view.
5. Click cell A2 to select it.
6. Type **=NOW()** and press CTRL + ENTER. The date and time appear in the cell.

The result of the NOW function

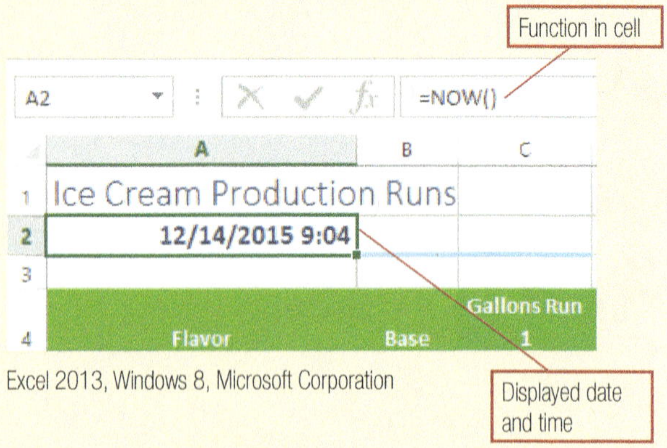

Excel 2013, Windows 8, Microsoft Corporation

7. Save the **E13Try_xx** file, and leave it open to use in the next Try It.

Using Named Ranges

- You create a descriptive **range name** for a range of cells (or a single cell) in order to reference it by name rather than by cell addresses.
- After naming a range, you can use the range name any place the range address might otherwise be entered—within a formula, defining the print range, selecting a range to format, and so on.
- As you learned in Lesson 13, you don't have to name ranges to use column labels in formulas. Instead, you can format your data as an Excel table.
- If you use the range name in a formula, you can use Formula AutoComplete to enter it quickly.
- You can also insert range names in a formula using the Use in Formula button list in the Defined Names group of the FORMULAS tab.
- If a range name is defined within a worksheet, it can only be used within that sheet, unless you precede it with the sheet name and an exclamation point, as in *Sheet1!RangeName*.
- If defined within a workbook, the range name can be used on any sheet in that workbook.
- A range name may use up to 255 characters, although short descriptive names are easier to read and remember.
- Range naming rules include:
  - No spaces allowed. Use the underscore character in place of a space.
  - Do not use range names that could be interpreted as a cell address or a number, such as Q2 or Y2012.
  - A range name may include letters, numbers, underscores (_), backslashes (\), periods (.), and question marks (?).
  - Do not begin a range name with a number.
  - Range names are not case sensitive, so you can use uppercase or lowercase letters.
  - Avoid using your column labels as range names, because they could create errors if you should format the range as a table and attempt to use range names as table names or vice versa.
- You can define a range name using the **Name Box** at the left end of the formula bar. Type a name and press ENTER.
- You also can use the Define Name button in the Defined Names group of the FORMULAS tab to define a range name. This method enables you to select the scope where the name applies (a particular worksheet or the entire workbook), and to enter a comment which might help in identifying the purpose of the range name.

- Right-click a selected range, and click Define Range to begin the naming process.
- If you have a lot of named ranges in a workbook, you can insert a list of named ranges with their corresponding cell references in the worksheet.
- If you are working with a list or table of data, you may need to sort the data prior to assigning range names.
- Use the Name Manager dialog box, opened from the Defined Names group on the FORMULAS tab, to edit or delete named ranges.

Try It! Using Named Ranges

1. In the **E13Try_xx** file, select the range C5:C8.
2. Click in the Name Box, type **ChocRun1**, and press ENTER.
3. Use the technique in step 2 to assign the following names to the specified ranges:
   D5:D8................**ChocRun2**
   E5:E8................**ChocRun3**
   F5:F8................**ChocTotal**
4. Select the range C9:C10, right-click it, and click Define Name. Type **OthRun1** in the Name text box of the New Name dialog box, and then click OK.
5. Use the technique in step 4 to assign the following names to the specified ranges:
   D9:D10................**OthRun2**
   E9:E10................**OthRun3**
   F9:F10................**OthTotal**
6. Select the range C11:C15. Click FORMULAS > Define Name. Type **VanRun1** in the Name text box of the New Name dialog box, and then click OK.
7. Use the technique in Step 6 to assign the following names to the specified ranges:
   D11:D15..............**VanRun2**
   E11:E15..............**VanRun3**
   F11:F15..............**VanTotal**
8. Click in the Name Box, type **ChocRun1**, and press ENTER. Excel selects the range that you named ChocRun1 earlier.
9. Click cell C16. Type **=sum(ChocRun1,OthRun1,VanRun1)**, and press TAB.
10. Type **=sum(cho**, press ↓ to select ChocRun2, and press TAB. Type **,OthRun2,VanRun2** and press TAB.

    ✓ *Step 10 is an example of using Formula AutoComplete to enter a range name.*
11. Use the techniques of your choice to enter formulas that total the Gallons Run 3 and Gallons Total columns.

    ✓ *Named ranges are absolute references, so you can't fill them.*
12. Select cell C18, and enter the formula **=sum(ChocRun1)**. Continue by entering the following formulas:
    C19..........**=sum(OthRun1)**
    C20.........**=sum(VanRun1)**
    D18.......**=sum(ChocRun2)**
    D19..........**=sum(OthRun2)**
    D20.........**=sum(VanRun2)**
    E18.......**=sum(ChocRun3)**
    E19..........**=sum(OthRun3)**
    E20.........**=sum(VanRun3)**
    F18........**=sum(ChocTotal)**
    F19...........**=sum(OthTotal)**
    F20...........**=sum(VanTotal)**
13. Save the **E13Try_xx** file, and close it.

(continued)

Try It! Using Named Ranges *(continued)*

Using range names in formulas

F16 =SUM(ChocTotal,OthTotal,VanTotal)

Formula with range names

	A	B	C	D	E	F
1	Ice Cream Production Runs					
2	12/19/2015 12:28					
3						
4	Flavor	Base	Gallons Run 1	Gallons Run 2	Gallons Run 3	Gallons Total
5	Rocky Road	Chocolate	225	200	425	850
6	Peanut Butter Swirl	Chocolate	205	260	305	770
7	Chocolate Chocolate Chip	Chocolate	425	440	450	1315
8	Chocolate	Chocolate	700	809	865	2374
9	Mint Chocolate Chip	Other	450	325	325	1100
10	Berry Burst	Other	150	176	190	516
11	Vanilla	Vanilla	652	752	652	2056
12	Strawberry Cheesecake	Vanilla	310	310	275	895
13	Chocolate Chip	Vanilla	450	610	545	1605
14	Butter Pecan	Vanilla	320	274	300	894
15	Butter Brickle	Vanilla	296	334	320	950
16	Totals		4,183	4,490	4,652	13,325
17						
18	Chocolate Subtotal		1,555	1,709	2,045	5,309
19	Other Subtotal		600	501	515	1,616
20	Vanilla Subtotal		2,028	2,280	2,092	6,400
21						

Formula result

Excel 2013, Windows 8, Microsoft Corporation

Lesson 13—Practice

In this project, you will insert the NOW function to add the system date and time to a cell using the skills you learned in this lesson.

DIRECTIONS

1. Start Excel, if necessary, and open the **E13Practice** file from the data files for this lesson.
2. Save the workbook as **E13Practice_xx** in the location where your teacher instructs you to store the files for this lesson.
3. Add a header that has your name at the left, the date code in the center, and the page number code at the right, and change back to **Normal** view.
4. In cell **C2**, enter the formula **=NOW()**, and press CTRL + ENTER.
5. Drag over the range **A4:H11** to select it.
6. Click **DATA** > **Sort**.
7. In the Sort dialog box, click the **Sort by** down arrow, and click **Project Manager**.
8. Click **OK**.
9. Drag over the range **A5:H11** to select it.
10. Click the **HOME** tab, in the Styles group click **Cell Styles**, and then click **40% - Accent1**. Your worksheet should look like the one shown in Figure 13-1 on the next page.
11. **With your teacher's permission,** print the worksheet. Submit the printout or the file for grading as required.
12. Save and close the file, and exit Excel.

Figure 13-1

	A	B	C	D	E	F	G	H
1	Restoration Architecture							
2	3rd Qtr Revenues by Project		12/14/2015 9:12					
3								
4	**Project**	**Type**	**Project Manager**	**July**	**August**	**September**	**Qtr 3 Totals**	**Qtr 3 Averages**
5	18 South Pendleton Ave.	Commercial	Jansen	$ 7,855	$ 27,958	$ 31,225	$ 67,038	$ 22,346
6	Freemont Park Amphitheater	Public	Jansen	$ 72,145	$ 63,145	$ 21,778	$ 157,068	$ 52,356
7	Rossen House	Residential	Jansen	$ 328,118	$ 456,221	$ 298,485	$ 1,082,824	$ 360,941
8	Old Barn Quilts	Commercial	Nolo	$ 4,522	$ 12,889	$ 18,645	$ 36,056	$ 12,019
9	Faster Library	Public	Nolo	$ 41,325	$ 78,945	$ 85,664	$ 205,934	$ 68,645
10	512 N. Oak Street	Residential	Nolo	$ 32,995	$ 28,445	$ 18,445	$ 79,885	$ 26,628
11	Cramer Theater	Public	Timson	$ 125,995	$ 285,941	$ 275,884	$ 687,820	$ 229,273
12	**Averages**			**$ 87,565**	**$ 136,221**	**$ 107,161**	**$ 330,946**	**$ 110,315**
13								
14	Jansen Totals							
15	Nolo Totals							
16	Timson Totals							
17								
18	Overall Total							

Excel 2013, Windows 8, Microsoft Corporation

Lesson 13—Apply

As the CFO of Restoration Architecture, you review a great deal of financial and other data. So you want to add features that make your worksheets faster to use, such as a date that updates automatically and named ranges to make it easier to build and review formulas. In this exercise, you'll modify a recent revenue analysis worksheet so it updates with the current date and time and includes range names for use in calculations.

DIRECTIONS

1. Start Excel, if necessary, and open the **E13Apply** file from the data files for this lesson.
2. Save the workbook as **E13Apply_xx** in the location where your teacher instructs you to store the files for this lesson.
3. Add a header that has your name at the left, the date code in the center, and the page number code at the right, and change back to **Normal** view.
4. Select the range **D5:D7**. Use the Name Box to assign the name **JansenJuly** to the range.
5. Also use the Name Box to assign the following range names:
   a. **E5:E7** **JansenAugust**
   b. **F5:F7** **JansenSeptember**
   c. **G5:G7** **JansenTotal**
6. Select the range **D8:D10**. Right-click the range and click **Define Name**. Type **NoloJuly** in the **Name** text box of the New Name dialog box, change the **Scope** to **Sheet1**, and click **OK**.
7. Use the same technique used in step 6 to assign the following range names and limit their scope to Sheet1:
   a. **E8:E10** **NoloAugust**
   b. **F8:F10** **NoloSeptember**
   c. **G8:G10** **NoloTotal**
8. Use the method of your choice to assign the following range names:
   a. **D11** **TimsonJuly**
   b. **E11** **TimsonAugust**
   c. **F11** **TimsonSeptember**
   d. **G11** **TimsonTotal**
9. Click **D14**, and enter a formula that sums the **JansenJuly** range.

10. Enter formulas that total the other three Jansen ranges in cells **E14:G14**.
11. Enter formulas that sum the ranges for the other two project managers in the applicable cells in the range **D15:G16**.
12. Click cell **D18** and enter a formula that sums the July ranges for all three project managers. (Hint: The first formula is =SUM(JansenJuly,NoloJuly, TimsonJuly).)
13. Enter formulas that sum the August, September, and Total data for the three project managers in cells **E18:G18**. Your worksheet should look like the one shown in Figure 13-2.
14. **With your teacher's permission,** print the worksheet. Submit the printout or the file for grading as required.
15. Save and close the file, and exit Excel.

Figure 13-2

	A	B	C	D	E	F	G	H
1	Restoration Architecture							
2	3rd Qtr Revenues by Project		12/14/2015 9:17					
3								
4	**Project**	**Type**	**Project Manager**	**July**	**August**	**September**	**Qtr 3 Totals**	**Qtr 3 Averages**
5	18 South Pendleton Ave.	Commercial	Jansen	$ 7,855	$ 27,958	$ 31,225	$ 67,038	$ 22,346
6	Freemont Park Amphitheater	Public	Jansen	$ 72,145	$ 63,145	$ 21,778	$ 157,068	$ 52,356
7	Rossen House	Residential	Jansen	$ 328,118	$ 456,221	$ 298,485	$ 1,082,824	$ 360,941
8	Old Barn Quilts	Commercial	Nolo	$ 4,522	$ 12,889	$ 18,645	$ 36,056	$ 12,019
9	Faster Library	Public	Nolo	$ 41,325	$ 78,945	$ 85,664	$ 205,934	$ 68,645
10	512 N. Oak Street	Residential	Nolo	$ 32,995	$ 28,445	$ 18,445	$ 79,885	$ 26,628
11	Cramer Theater	Public	Timson	$ 125,995	$ 285,941	$ 275,884	$ 687,820	$ 229,273
12	**Averages**			**$ 87,565**	**$ 136,221**	**$ 107,161**	**$ 330,946**	**$ 110,315**
13								
14	Jansen Totals			$ 408,118	$ 547,324	$ 351,488	$ 1,306,930	
15	Nolo Totals			$ 78,842	$ 120,279	$ 122,754	$ 321,875	
16	Timson Totals			$ 125,995	$ 285,941	$ 275,884	$ 687,820	
17								
18	Overall Total			$ 612,955	$ 953,544	$ 750,126	$ 2,316,625	

Excel 2013, Windows 8, Microsoft Corporation

Lesson 14

Working with IF Functions

➤ What You Will Learn

Understanding IF Functions
Nesting Functions
Using SUMIF and SUMIFS Functions
Using COUNTIF and COUNTIFS Functions
Using the AVERAGEIF Function

Software Skills IF functions enable you to test for particular conditions and then perform specific actions based on whether those conditions exist or not. For example, with an IF function, you could calculate the bonuses for a group of salespeople on the premise that bonuses are only paid if a sale is over $1,000. With the SUMIF function, you could total up the sales in your Atlanta office, even if those sales figures are scattered through a long list of sales figures. With the COUNTIF function, you could count the number of sales that resulted in a bonus being paid. With the AVERAGEIF function, you could find the average bonus amount paid out.

WORDS TO KNOW

Expression
A type of equation (such as B6>25) that returns a value, such as TRUE or FALSE. Excel uses expressions to identify cells to include in certain formulas such as IF and SUMIF.

Nesting
Using a function as an argument within another function.

What You Can Do

Understanding IF Functions

- IF() is a Logical function.
- With an IF function, you can tell Excel to perform one of two different calculations based on whether your data matches a logical test.
- For example, you can use an IF function to have Excel calculate a 10% bonus if total sales are over $500,000 and just a 3% bonus if they are not.
- The format for an IF function is: =IF(logical_test,value_if_true,value_if_false)
    - The *logical test* is a condition or **expression** whose result is either true or false.
    - If the condition is true, the formula displays the *value_if_true* argument in the cell.
    - If the condition is false, the formula displays the *value_if_false* argument in the cell.
- For example, to calculate the bonus described above, you would type **=IF(B2>500000,B2*.10,B2*.03)**
- The above function says, "If total sales (cell B2) are greater than $500,000, then take total sales times 10% to calculate the bonus. Otherwise, take total sales times 3%."

- Notice that in the IF function, the value, $500,000, is entered without the dollar sign or the comma.
- You can have text appear in a cell instead of a calculated value. For example, you might type **=IF(B2>500000,"We made it!","Good try.")** to display the words *We made it!* if total sales are over $500,000, or the words *Good try.* if they are not.
- Surround the text you want to appear with quotation marks ("") in the formula.

  ✓ *The ampersand (&) may be used inside the function to join text.*

- IF functions may use the comparison operators below to state the condition:

  = Equals
  <> Not equal to
  > Greater than
  >= Greater than or equal to
  < Less than
  <= Less than or equal to

- Like any other function, you can enter an IF function manually, use Formula AutoComplete, or use the Insert Function dialog box or Function Library group drop-down lists to help.

Try It! Understanding IF Functions

1. Start Excel.
2. Open the **E14Try** file from the data files for this lesson.
3. Save the workbook as **E14Try_xx** in the location where your teacher instructs you to store the files for this lesson.
4. Add a header that has your name at the left, the date code in the center, and the page number code at the right, and change back to Normal view.
5. Click cell F4 to select it.
6. Click FORMULAS > Logical > IF. The Function Arguments dialog box appears.
7. Type **d4>=20** in the Logical_test text box, and press TAB.
8. Type **Yes** in the Value_if_true text box, and press TAB.

   ✓ *The Function Arguments dialog box adds the quotation marks around text entries for you.*

9. Type **No** in the Value_if_false text box, and press TAB.
10. Click OK. Because the entry in cell D4 is 17 (less than 20), a result of No displays in cell F4.
11. Drag the fill handle down to fill the formula through cell F21.
12. Click the Auto Fill Options button > Fill Without Formatting.
13. Save the **E14Try_xx** file, and leave it open to use in the next Try It.

Building an IF function

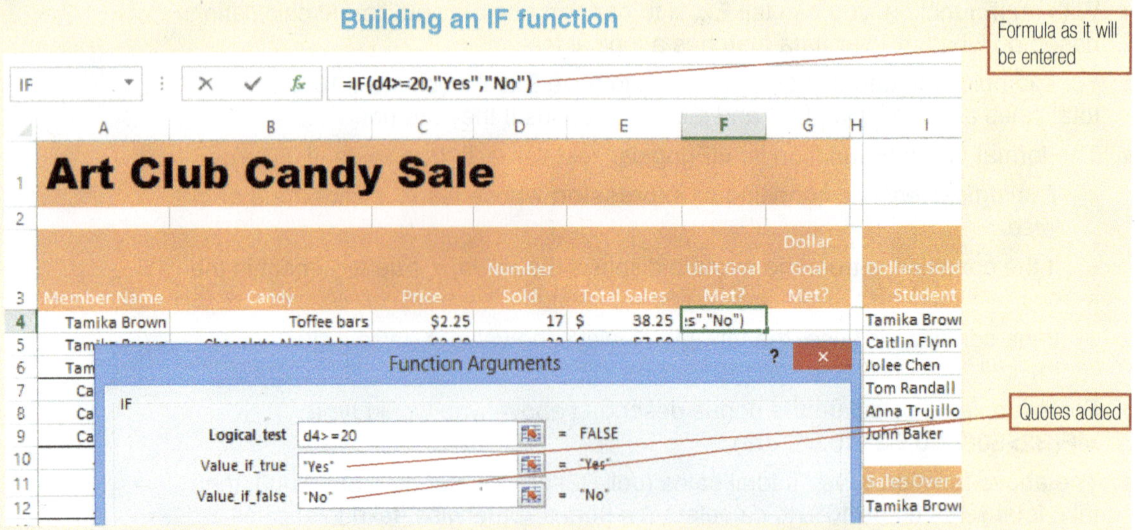

Excel 2013, Windows 8, Microsoft Corporation

Nesting Functions

- You can **nest** any function as one of the arguments for another function in a formula.
- The arguments in IF functions often use nested functions, either in the logical test or of the possible outcome values, or both.
- For example, consider the formula: =IF(C3>92,"A",IF(C3>83,"B",IF(C3>73,"C", IF(C3>65,"D","F"))))
- The above formula says that if the average score in cell C3 is greater than 92, then the student gets an A; if the score is less than or equal to 92 but greater than 83, the student gets a B; if the score is less than or equal to 83 but greater than 73, the student gets a C; and so on.

Try It! Nesting Functions

1. In the **E14Try_xx** file, click cell G4 to select it.
2. Click the Insert Function button *fx* on the formula bar.
3. Open the Or select a category list, and click Logical. In the Select a function list, click IF. Click OK. The Function Arguments dialog box appears.
4. Type **E4>=60** in the Logical_test text box, and press TAB.
5. Type **Yes** in the Value_if_true text box, and press TAB.
6. Type **No** in the Value_if_false text box, and press TAB.
7. Click OK. Because the entry in cell E4 is less than $60, a result of No displays in cell G4.
8. Drag the fill handle down to fill the formula through cell G21.
9. Click the Auto Fill Options button > Fill Without Formatting.
10. Save the **E14Try_xx** file, and leave it open to use in the next Try It.

Using SUMIF and SUMIFS Functions

- SUMIF() is a Math & Trig function that uses a condition to add certain data.
- If the condition is true, then data in a corresponding cell is added to the total; if it is false, then the corresponding data is skipped.
- Here is how you enter a SUMIF function: =SUMIF(range,criteria,sum_range).
  - The *range* is the range of cells you want to review.
  - The *criteria* is an expression that is either true or false, and defines which cells should be added to the total.
  - If you specify an optional *sum_range*, values from the sum_range on the rows where the range data results in a true result for the *criteria* are added to the total.
  - If you do not specify a sum_range, the formula adds the values from the *range* rows that evaluate as true.
- Use the same comparison operators (such as >,<>, etc.) as for an IF function in the criteria. However, here, you must enclose the condition in quotation marks ("") if it is not a cell reference.
- For example, if you had a worksheet listing sales for several different products, you could total only sales for chocolate by using this formula: =SUMIF(D2:D55,"Chocolate",G2:G55).
  - Assume in this example that column D contains the name of the product being sold and column G contains the total amount for that sale. If column D contains the word *Chocolate*, then the amount for that sale (located in column G) is added to the running total.
- You can leave the last argument off if you want to sum the same range that you're testing; for example: =SUMIF(G2:G10,"<=500"). This formula calculates the total of all values in the range G2 to G10 that are less than or equal to 500.
- SUMIFS is a function similar to SUMIF except that it allows you to enter multiple qualifying conditions.

- The format for a SUMIFS statement is: =SUMIFS(sum_range,criteria_range1,criteria1,criteria_range2,criteria2,etc.).
  - The *criteria_range1* is the first range of cells you want to test.
  - The *criteria1* is an expression that is either true or false, and defines which cells should be added to the total.
  - If the criteria1 result is true, the corresponding cell in sum_range is added to the total.
  - If the criteria1 result is false, the corresponding cell in sum_range is not added to the total.
  - You can add conditions and additional ranges to test as needed. You can specify the same range to test or use a different one.
  - All ranges, the sum_range and the criteria ranges, must be the same size and shape.
- Using the earlier example, if you wanted to total all the sales of chocolate bars and toffee bars, you could use a formula such as: =SUMIFS(G2:G55, D2:D55,"Chocolate Bars",D2:D55,"Toffee Bars").
- Again, column D contains the name of the product being sold, and column G contains the total amount for that sale.

Try It! Using SUMIF and SUMIFS Functions

1. In the **E14Try_xx** file, click cell K4 to select it.
2. Click the Insert Function button fx on the formula bar.
3. Open the Or select a category list, and click Math & Trig. In the Select a function list, click SUMIF. Click OK. The Function Arguments dialog box appears.
4. Drag over the range A4:A21 to specify it in the Range text box, press F4 to make the range address absolute, and press TAB.

   ✓ *Because you will be copying the formula, you need to make the range references absolute.*
5. Click cell I4 to specify it in the Criteria text box, and press TAB.

   ✓ *Using a cell reference rather than typing in the student name in this case will enable you to fill the formula down and get an accurate result for each student.*
6. Drag over the range E4:E21 to specify it in the Sum_range text box, press F4 to make the range address absolute, and press TAB.
7. Click OK. Excel calculates a total of $170.00 in sales for the specified student.
8. Drag the fill handle down to fill the formula through cell K9.
9. Click cell K12 to select it.
10. Click the Insert Function button fx on the formula bar.
11. Open the Or select a category list, and click Math & Trig. In the Select a function list, click SUMIFS. Click OK. The Function Arguments dialog box appears.
12. Drag over the range E4:E21 to specify it in the Sum_range text box, press F4 to make the range address absolute, and press TAB.

Using the SUMIF function

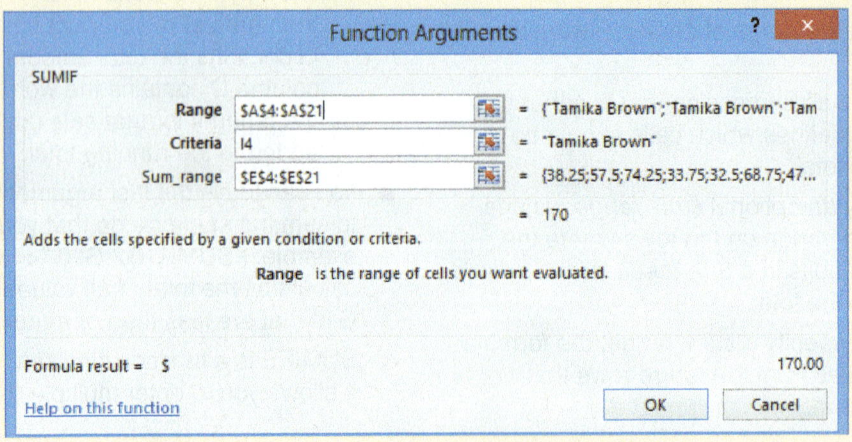

Excel 2013, Windows 8, Microsoft Corporation

(continued)

Try It! Using SUMIF and SUMIFS Functions *(continued)*

13 Drag over the range A4:A21 to specify it in the Criteria_range1 text box, press F4 to make the range address absolute, and press TAB.

14 Click cell I12 to specify it in the Criteria1 text box, and press TAB.

15 Drag over the range D4:D21 to specify it in the Criteria_range2 text box, press F4 to make the range address absolute, and press TAB.

16 Type >20 in the Criteria2 text box.

17 Click OK. Excel calculates a total of $131.75 for sales where the specified student sold more than 20 units of a product.

18 Drag the fill handle down to fill the formula through cell K17.

19 Save the E14Try_xx file, and leave it open to use in the next Try It.

Specify as many criteria as needed with the SUMIFS function

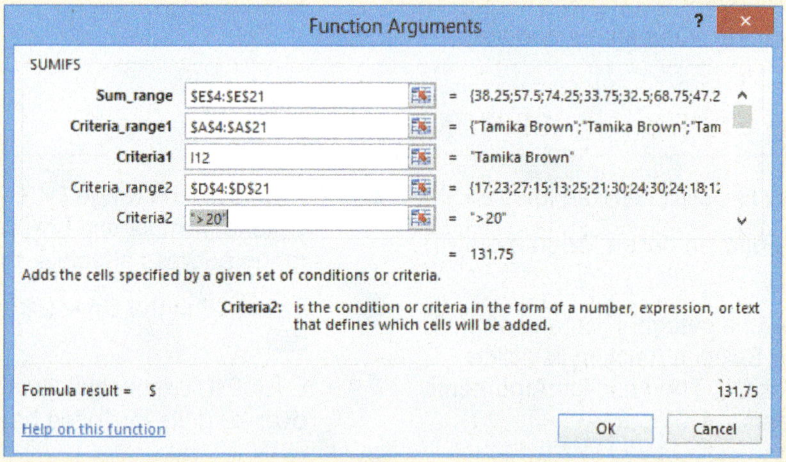

Excel 2013, Windows 8, Microsoft Corporation

Using COUNTIF and COUNTIFS Functions

- COUNTIF is a Statistical function that uses a criteria to count the number of items in a range.
  - ✓ *You learned about two similar functions, COUNT and COUNTA, in Lesson 11.*
- If the result of the criteria is true, then the item is added to a running count; if it is false, then the item is skipped.
- The format for a COUNTIF function is: =COUNTIF(range, criteria).
  - The *range* is the range of cells holding the values to test (and count).
  - The *criteria* is an expression that is either true or false, defining which cells should be counted.
- Use the same comparison operators as for the IF function when writing the criteria. As for SUMIF, you must enclose the condition in quotation marks ("") if it is not a cell reference.
- For example, if you want to count the number of individual Chocolate Bars sales in the earlier example, you could use this formula: =COUNTIF(D2:D55,"Chocolate Bars"). Assume here that column D contains the name of the product being sold; for each cell in column D that contains the words *Chocolate Bars*, 1 is added to the running total of the number of chocolate bar sales.
- Because Chocolate Bars is a text label, you must enclose it in quotation marks ("").
- To compute the number of chocolate bars sold or the value of those sales, use SUMIF.
- You can combine functions to create complex calculations: =SUMIF(D3:D13,"PASS",C3:C13)/ COUNTIF(D3:D13,"PASS"). This formula computes the average score of all the students who passed the course. Assume that column D contains the words *Pass* or *Fail* based on the student's final score. The final score is located in column C. The formula sums the scores of all the students who passed and divides that by the number of students who passed, calculating an average score for passing students.

- COUNTIFS is a function similar to COUNTIF except that it allows you to enter multiple qualifying conditions.
- The format for a COUNTIFS statement is: =COUNTIFS(criteria_range1,criteria1,criteria_range2,criteria2,etc.).
  - The *criteria_range1* is the range of cells you want to test.
  - The *criteria1* is an expression that is either true or false, and defines which cells should be counted.
  - You can add additional conditions and ranges to test as needed. You can specify the same range to test or use a different one.
  - All ranges must be the same shape and size.
- Using the earlier example, if you wanted to count all Chocolate Bars sales with a value over $100, you could use a formula such as: =COUNTIFS(D2:D55,"Chocolate Bars",G2:G55, ">100").
- Again, column D contains the name of the product being sold, and column G contains the total amount for that sale.
- Since there are 54 rows in the two ranges, the highest answer you might get is 54. A row is counted only if it contains both the words Chocolate Bars in column D, and a value greater than 100 in column G.

Try It! Using COUNTIF and COUNTIFS Functions

1. In the **E14Try_xx** file, click cell K20 to select it.
2. Click the Insert Function button *fx* on the formula bar.
3. Open the Or select a category list, and click Statistical. In the Select a function list, click COUNTIFS. Click OK. The Function Arguments dialog box appears.
4. Drag over the range B4:B21 to specify it in the Criteria_range1 text box, press F4 to make the range address absolute, and press TAB.
5. Type **I20** to specify it in the Criteria1 text box, and press TAB.
6. Drag over the range D4:D21 to specify it in the Criteria_range2 text box, press F4 to make the range address absolute, and press TAB.
7. Type **>20** in the Criteria2 text box, and press TAB.
8. Click OK. Excel calculates a total of 3 sales of over 20 units for Toffee bars.
9. Drag the fill handle down to fill the formula through cell K22.
10. Save the **E14Try_xx** file, and close it.

Using multiple criteria to count with the COUNTIFS function

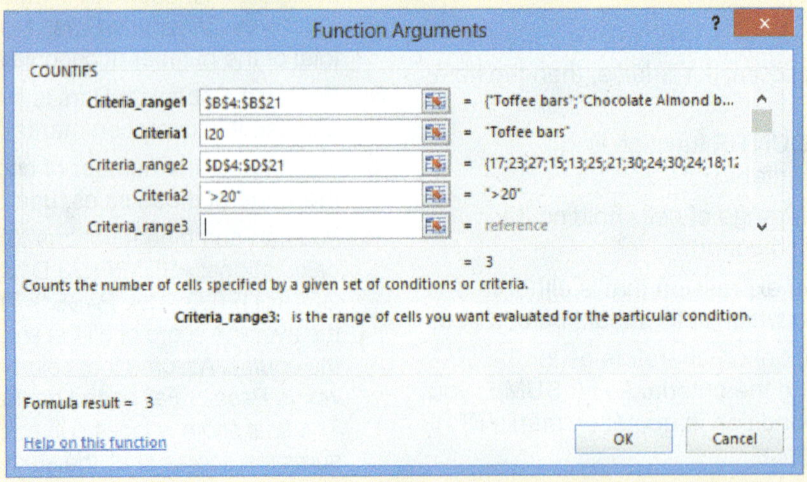

Excel 2013, Windows 8, Microsoft Corporation

Using the AVERAGEIF Function

- AVERAGEIF is a Statistical function that uses a condition to return the average of all cells in a range that meet specific criteria.
- The IF portion of the function indicates what data meets the specific criteria and the AVERAGE portion calculates the mean or average.
- If the result of the criteria is true, then AVERAGEIF will calculate the average. If the result is false, then the item is skipped.
- The format for an AVERAGEIF statement is: =AVERAGEIF(range,criteria,average_range).
  - The *range* is the range of cells holding the values to test (and average).
  - The *criteria* is an expression that is either true or false, defining which cells should be averaged.
  - If you specify an optional *average_range*, values from the average_range on the rows where the range data results in a true result for the criteria are calculated.
  - If you do not specify a average_range, the formula averages the values from the range rows that evaluate as true.
- Use the same comparison operators as for the IF function when writing the criteria. You must enclose the condition in quotation marks ("") if it is a text label and not a cell reference.
- For example, if you had a worksheet listing sales of different types of chocolate bars and you wanted to know the average sale for each chocolate bar, you could use this formula: =AVERAGEIF(D2:D55,"Chocolate Bar",G2:G55).
  - Assume in this example that column D contains the name of the product being sold and column G contains the total amount for that sale. If column D contains the words *Chocolate Bar*, then the amount for that sale (located in column G) is added to the averaged total.

Try It! Using the AVERAGEIF Function

1. In the **E14Try_xx** file, click cell K25 to select it.
2. Click the Insert Function button *fx* on the formula bar.
3. Open the Or select a category list, and click Statistical. In the Select a function list, click AVERAGEIF. Click OK. The Function Arguments dialog box appears.
4. Drag over the range B4:B21 to specify it in the Range text box, press F4 to make the range address absolute, and press TAB.

   ✓ *Because you will be copying the formula, you need to make the range references absolute.*
5. Click cell I25 to specify it in the Criteria text box, and press TAB.

Using the AVERAGEIF function to find the average for a specific criterion

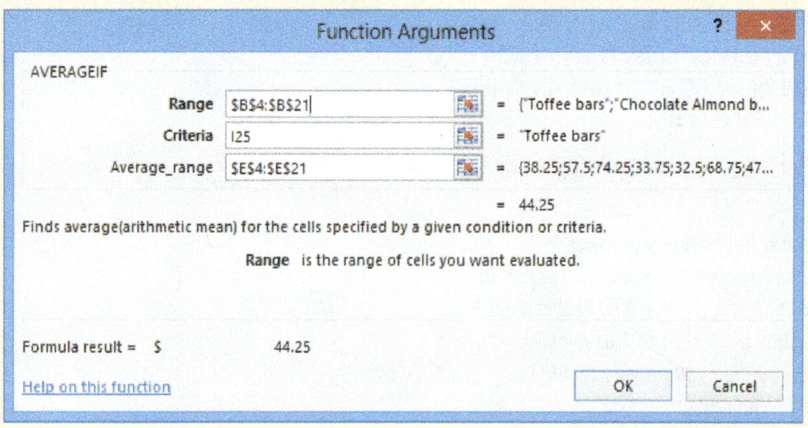

Excel 2013, Windows 8, Microsoft Corporation

(continued)

Try It! **Using the AVERAGEIF Function** *(continued)*

6. Drag over the range E4:E21 to specify it in the Average_range text box, press F4 to make the range address absolute, and press OK. Excel calculates an average of $44.25 in sales for the specified candy bar.

7. Drag the fill handle down to fill the formula through cell K27.

8. Save the **E14Try_xx** file, and close it.

Lesson 14—Practice

In this project, you will use IF functions to perform calculations using the skills you learned in this lesson.

DIRECTIONS

1. Start Excel, if necessary, and open the **E14Practice** file from the data files for this lesson.
2. Save the workbook as **E14Practice_xx** in the location where your teacher instructs you to store the files for this lesson.
3. Add a header that has your name at the left, the date code in the center, and the page number code at the right, and change back to **Normal** view.
4. Enter the date **12/3/14** in cell **B4**, and increase the column width as needed to display the date.
5. Click cell **U8**. Notice that the Name Box displays the name already assigned to this cell. All the cells holding prices have names assigned.
6. Because your company gives a discount for white bread on Mondays, you need to enter a formula in cell U8 to calculate the discounted amount for that day of the week. Use the **IF** function with a nested **WEEKDAY** function in the formula. The formula should return a value of $2.00 if the date in cell B4 is a Monday, and $2.55 if it is not.

   ✓ *Hint: Use =IF(WEEKDAY(argument)=something,then do this, else do this).*

   ✓ *The WEEKDAY function requires one argument, in parentheses. The required argument is the address of the cell that contains the date to look at, which in this case is cell B4. WEEKDAY returns a value from 1 to 7, telling you what day of the week the date you provide as the first argument is. By default, Sunday is counted as day 1, so if the date in cell B4 is a Monday, WEEKDAY() will return a value of 2.*

7. Enter a similar formula in cell **U9**, charging $2.00 for wheat bread if it's Monday and $2.60 if it's not. Notice the values calculated in the Order Total column.
8. Change the date in cell **B4** to **12/8/14**. Notice how the Order Total values recalculate to reflect that the date is now a Monday.
9. Undo the change to return the date in cell B4 to 12/3/14.
10. Display the formulas, and increase the width of column U so that the two new formulas display completely. Your worksheet should look like the one in Figure 14-1 on the next page.
11. **With your teacher's permission,** print the Price List print area. Submit the printout or the file for grading as required.
12. Save and close the file, and exit Excel.

Figure 14-1

T	U
Price List	
White Bread	=IF(WEEKDAY(B4)=2,2,2.55)
Wheat Bread	=IF(WEEKDAY(B4)=2,2,2.6)
Honey Wheat Bagel	1.1
Blueberry Bagel	1.25
Cinnamon Bagel	1.25
Wheat Rolls	0.32
White Rolls	0.3
Garlic Bread	2.25
Blueberry Muffin	1.95
Bran Muffin	1.85
Croissant	1.32
Baguette	1.95

Lesson 14—Apply

You're the manager of a Whole Grains Bread store in Olympia, Washington, and you've been developing a new worksheet for tracking retail bread sales. You've just learned about various IF functions, and, along with some other new functions you've discovered, you know you can refine the worksheet so that it's simple for your employees to use. With the sales analysis the worksheet will provide, you can refine the retail end of your business to maximize your profits.

DIRECTIONS

1. Start Excel, if necessary, and open the **E14Apply** file from the data files for this lesson.
2. Save the workbook as **E14Apply_xx** in the location where your teacher instructs you to store the files for this lesson.
3. Add a header that has your name at the left, the date code in the center, and the page number code at the right, and change back to **Normal** view.
4. In cell **C36**, use the **COUNT** function to create a formula that counts the number of coupon sales. (Refer to Figure 14-2 throughout this exercise to double-check that you are getting the correct results.) Remember that the COUNT function counts how many cells in the range contain numbers (values or formula results).

Figure 14-2

34				
35	Daily Summary			
36	Coupon Sales		11	$146.46
37	Sales w/o Coupon		13	$289.84
38	Credit Sales		14	$271.98
39	Cash Sales		10	$164.32
40	Total Sales		24	$436.30
41	Credit Sales < $10		2	$ 15.48
42	Average Credit Sale			$ 19.43
43				

5. In cell **C37**, use the **COUNTBLANK** function to create a formula that counts the number of non-coupon sales.
6. In cell **C38**, use the **COUNTIF** function to create a formula that counts the number of credit card sales, using x as the criteria.
7. In cell **C39**, use the **COUNTIF** function to create a formula that counts the number of cash sales, using x as the criteria.
8. In cell **C40**, use the **COUNT** function to count the number of sales for the day, based on the Total Sale column.
9. In cell **C41**, use the **COUNTIFS** function to create a formula that counts the number of credit card sales for less than $10.

   ✓ *Calculations like this could help you determine whether your business should continue to accept credit card payments for small purchases.*

10. In cell **D36**, use the **SUMIF** function to create a formula that calculates the revenue from coupon sales.
11. In cell **D37**, use the **SUMIF** function to create a formula that calculates the revenue from non-coupon sales.

    ✓ *Hint: You want to find blank values ("") in the Coupon column and add the values from the corresponding rows in the Total Sale column.*

12. In cell **D38**, use the **SUMIF** function to create a formula that calculates the revenue from credit card sales.
13. In cell **D39**, use the **SUMIF** function to create a formula that calculates the revenue from cash sales.
14. In cell **D40**, use the method of your choice to make a cell reference to the cell with the sum of Total Sales.
15. In cell **D41**, use the **SUMIFS** function to total the value of credit card sales less than $10.
16. In cell **D42**, use the AVERAGEIFS function to find the average credit sale.
17. Apply the **Accounting** cell style to **D36:D42**, and adjust column widths as needed. Your worksheet should look like Figure 14-2 on the previous page.
18. **With your teacher's permission,** print the worksheet. Submit the printout or the file for grading as required.
19. Save and close the file, and exit Excel.

Lesson 15

Working with Text Functions

➤ What You Will Learn

Using the CONCATENATE Function
Using the UPPER and LOWER Functions
Using the LEFT, RIGHT, and MID Functions
Using the TRIM Function

Software Skills Excel's text functions help you manage the text data in your worksheets. For example, the CONCATENATE function would allow you to join together first and last names. Then you could use the UPPER and LOWER functions to correct any capitalization of the names. With the RIGHT, LEFT, and MID functions, you could separate the parts of a phone number into area code, prefix, and line number. Finally, you could use the TRIM function to remove unwanted spaces in the text.

WORDS TO KNOW

Case
The use of capital (uppercase) and small letters (lowercase) in text.

Concatenation
The linking of elements together in a series.

What You Will Learn

Using the CONCATENATE Function

- You can use **concatenation** to join together cell data.
- CONCATENATE is a Text function that joins together words, cell references, blank spaces, or numbers.

✓ *You learned in Lesson 5 that FlashFill also can be used to concatenate data.*

- Access Text functions from the Text button in the Function Library on the FORMULAS tab.
- You also can access Text functions from the Insert Function button *fx* on the formula bar. In the Function Arguments dialog box, click Text in the Or select a category list and then click a text function name in the Select a function list.
- The CONCATENATE function requires a text argument.
- You can add up to 255 text entries to the CONCATENATE function. Each entry must be separated by a comma.

- The format for a CONCATENATE function is: =CONCATENATE(text1,text2).
  - In this example, *text1* is the first text item to be concatenated and *text2* is the second text item to be concatenated.
  - If *text1* is the word *voice* and *text2* is the word *mail*, then the returned result is *voicemail*.
- The CONCATENATE function does not automatically leave a blank space between words or other data.
- You must specify any spaces or punctuation that you want to appear in the results as an argument enclosed in quotation marks; for example, =CONCATENATE(A1," ",B1). The second argument in this example is a space character (" ").
  - In this example, the returned result is the contents of cell A1, a space, and the contents of cell B1.

Try It! Using the CONCATENATE Function

1. Start Excel.
2. Open the **E15Try** file from the data files for this lesson.
3. Save the workbook as **E15Try_xx** in the location where your teacher instructs you to store the files for this lesson.
4. Add a header that has your name at the left, the date code in the center, and the page number code at the right, and change back to Normal.
5. Click cell D4 to select it.
6. Click the Insert Function button *fx* on the formula bar. The Insert Functions dialog box appears.
7. Open the Or select a category list, and click Text. In the Select a function list, click CONCATENATE. Click OK. The Function Arguments dialog box appears.
8. In the Text1 arguments box, type **A4**, and press TAB.
9. In the Text2 arguments box, type " " (a quotation mark, space, and another quotation mark), and press TAB.
10. In the Text3 arguments box, type **B4**, and click OK.
11. Drag the fill handle down to fill the formula through cell D9.
12. Save the **E15Try_xx** file, and leave it open to use in the next Try It.

Using the CONCATENATE function

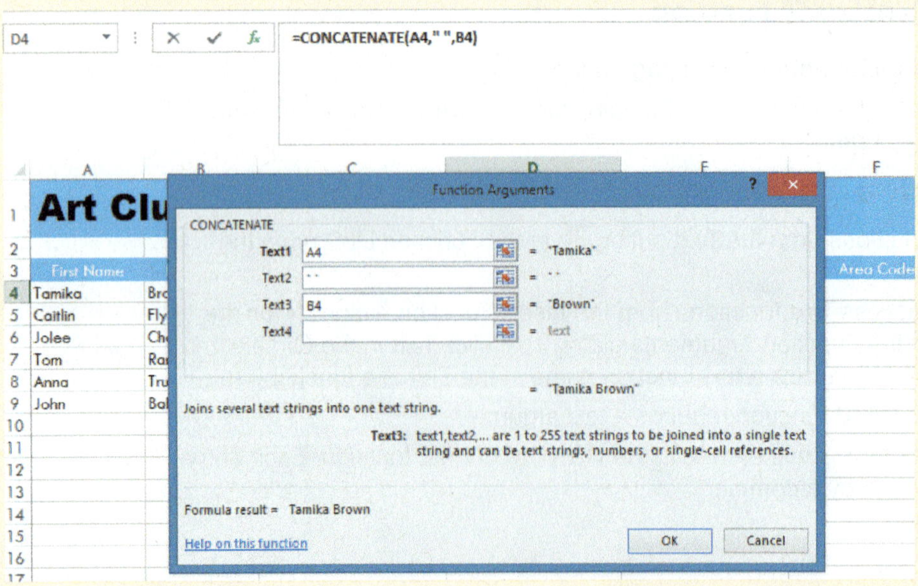

Using the UPPER and LOWER Functions

- When text data is imported or copied into an Excel spreadsheet, you may have to correct the capitalization.
- UPPER and LOWER Text functions can change the **case** of text. The UPPER function capitalizes text, and the LOWER function lowercases text.
- Both UPPER and LOWER functions require a text argument. The argument can be a cell reference or text.

  ✓ *When using text in an argument, you must enclose the text in quotation marks.*

- The format for an UPPER function is: =UPPER(text).
  - For example, the argument *text* can be a reference to a cell, and will return a result of all uppercase text in that cell.
- The format for a LOWER function is: =LOWER(text).
  - For example, the argument *text* can be typed text such as *INCOME STATEMENT,* which will return a result of all lowercase text (i.e., *income statement*).
- The LOWER function only affects letters; it does not change numbers or characters such as ampersands (&), percentage signs (%), or parentheses (()).

Try It! Using the UPPER and LOWER Functions

1. In the E15Try_xx file, click cell D12 to select it.
2. Type =UPPER(D4) and press ENTER. The text is now all uppercase.
3. Drag the fill handle down to fill the formula through cell D17.
4. Clear the contents of the cell range D12:D17.
5. Click cell C12 to select it.
6. Click the Insert Function button *fx* on the formula bar.

Using the LOWER function to change the case of text

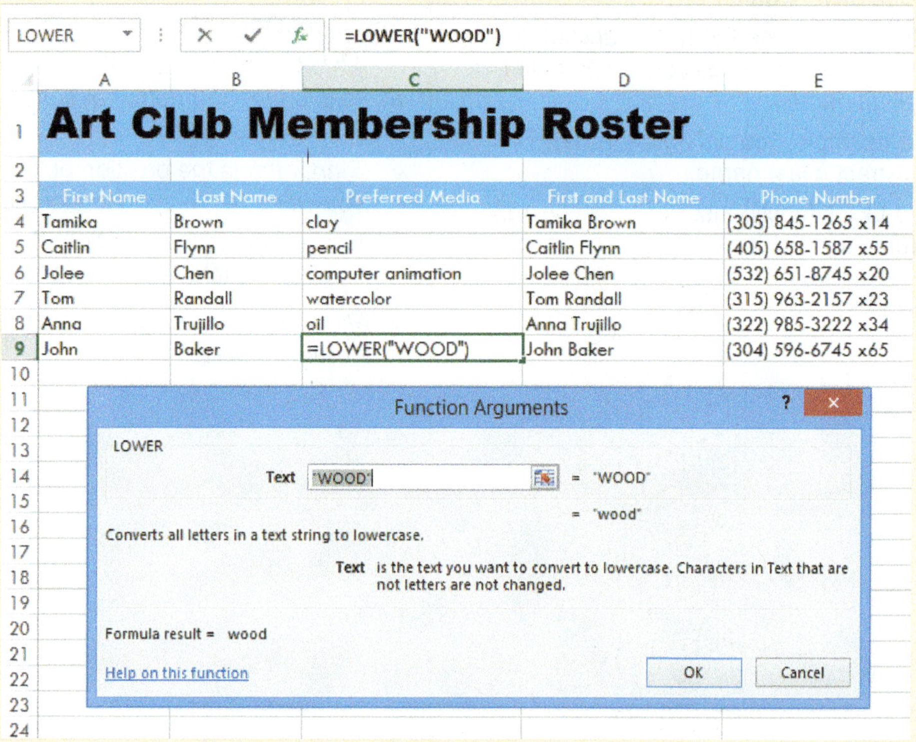

Excel 2013, Windows 8, Microsoft Corporation

(continued)

Try It! **Using the UPPER and LOWER Functions** *(continued)*

7. In the Function Arguments dialog box, click Text in the Or select a category list, click LOWER in the Select a function list, and click OK. The Function Arguments dialog box appears.
8. In the Text box, type **"PENCIL"** and click OK.
9. Drag and drop the cell C12 to replace cell C5.
10. Click OK to replace the current data.
11. Click cell C12 to select it.
12. Click FORMULAS > Text > LOWER. The Function Arguments dialog box appears.
13. In the Text box, type **"WOOD"** and click OK.
14. Drag and drop the cell C12 to replace cell C9.
15. Click OK to replace the current data.
16. Save the **E15Try_xx** file, and leave it open to use in the next Try It.

Using the LEFT, RIGHT, and MID Functions

- You can use Excel's LEFT, RIGHT, and MID functions to remove unwanted characters from your data.
- You also can use these functions to extract specific characters from your data.

✓ *All of your data must be consistent in the cells where you choose to use the LEFT, RIGHT, and MID functions.*

- The LEFT function targets characters from the left side, and the RIGHT function targets characters from the right side of your data.
  - For example, you can use the LEFT function to extract a first name from a cell containing a first, middle, and last name.
  - In the above example, you can use the RIGHT function to extract a last name.
- The format for a LEFT function is: =LEFT(Text, Num_chars).
- The format for a RIGHT function is: =RIGHT(Text, Num_chars).
  - *Text* is the argument that contains the character you want to extract. This also can be a cell reference.
  - *Num_chars* is the number of characters you want the function to extract.
- The MID function targets characters in the middle of your data.
  - For example, you can use the MID function to extract a middle name from a cell containing a first, middle, and last name.
- The format for a MID function is: =MID(Text, Start_num, Num_chars).
  - *Text* is the argument that contains the character you want to extract.
  - *Start_num* is the position of the first characters you want the function to extract.
  - *Num_chars* is the number of characters you want the function to remove or extract.

✓ *When using text in an argument, you must enclose the text in quotation marks.*

Try It! Using the LEFT, RIGHT, and MID Functions

1. In the **E15Try_xx** file, click cell F4 to select it.
2. Click the Insert Function button *fx* on the formula bar.
3. In the Insert Function dialog box, click Text in the Or select a category list, click LEFT in the Select a function list, and click OK. The Function Arguments dialog box appears.
4. In the Text box, type **E4** and press TAB.
5. In the Num_chars box, type **5** and click OK. The area code is extracted from the phone number.
6. Drag the fill handle down to fill the formula through cell F9.
7. Click cell G4 to select it.
8. Click the Insert Function button *fx* on the formula bar.
9. In the Insert Function dialog box, click Text in the Or select a category list, click MID in the Select a function list, and click OK. The Function Arguments dialog box appears.
10. In the Text box, type **E4** and press TAB.
11. In the Start_num box, type **7** and press TAB.
12. In the Num_chars box, type **3** and click OK. The prefix is extracted from the phone number.
13. Drag the fill handle down to fill the formula through cell G9.
14. Click cell H4 to select it.
15. Type **=RIGHT(E4,3)** and press ENTER. The extension is extracted from the phone number.
16. Drag the fill handle down to fill the formula through cell H9.
17. Save the **E15Try_xx** file, and leave it open to use in the next Try It.

Using the MID function

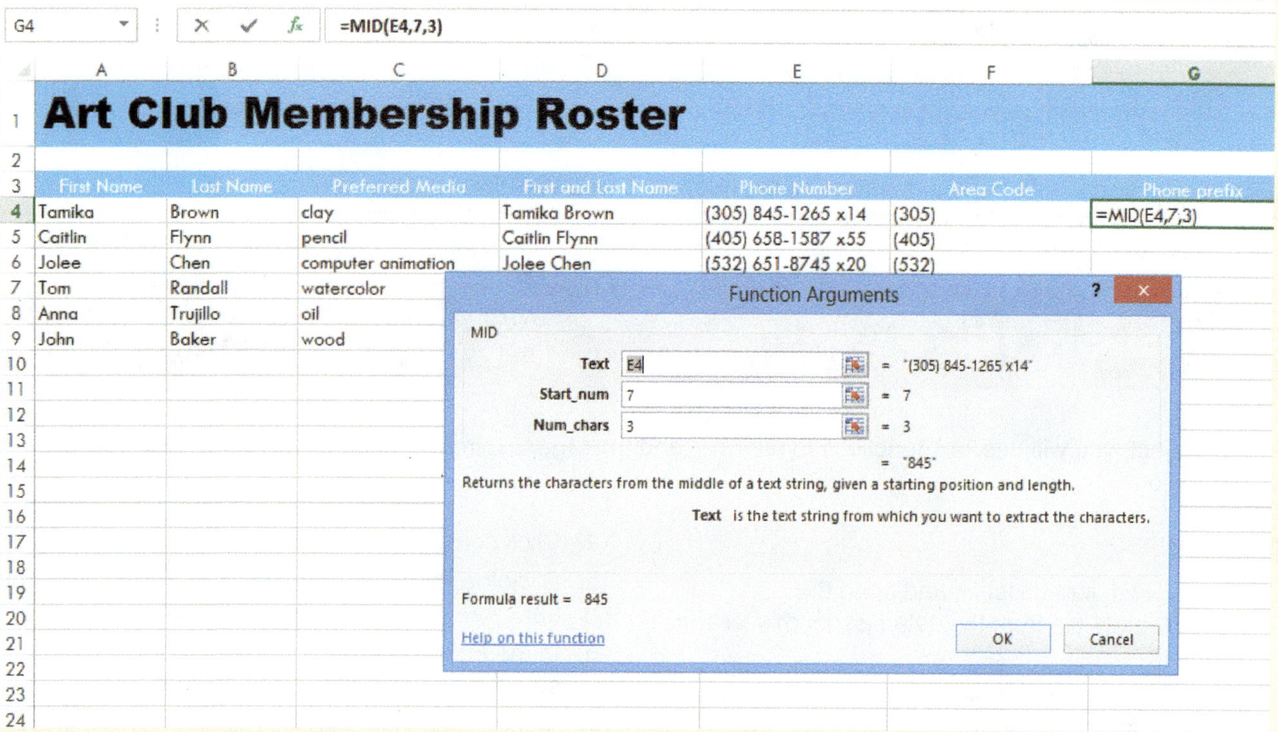

Excel 2013, Windows 8, Microsoft Corporation

Using the TRIM Function

- You can use Excel's TRIM function to remove unwanted spaces from your data.
- The format for a TRIM function is: =TRIM(Text).
  - *Text* is the argument that contains the character you want to extract. This also can be a cell reference.

Try It! Using the TRIM Function

1. In the **E15Try_xx** file, click cell C12 to select it.
2. Click FORMULAS > Text > TRIM. The Function Arguments dialog box appears.
3. In the Text box, type **C6** and click OK. The ten spaces are trimmed from the text in cell C6. Notice that the space between words is not removed.
4. Clear the contents of cell C12.
5. Save the **E15Try_xx** file, and close it.

Using the TRIM function to remove unwanted spaces

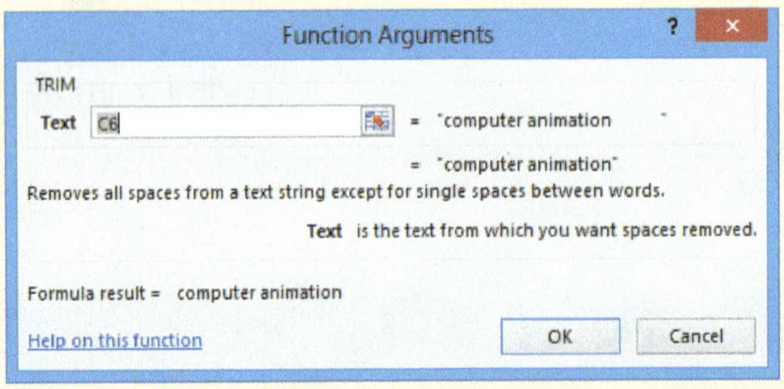

Excel 2013, Windows 8, Microsoft Corporation

Lesson 15—Practice

In this project, you will use Text functions to reformat and manage text in a worksheet using the skills you learned in this lesson.

DIRECTIONS

1. Start Excel, if necessary, and open the **E15Practice** file from the data files for this lesson.
2. Save the workbook as **E15Practice_xx** in the location where your teacher instructs you to store the files for this lesson.
3. Add a header that has your name at the left, the date code in the center, and the page number code at the right, and change back to **Normal** view.
4. Click cell **D6** to select it.
5. Click the **Insert Function** button *fx* on the formula bar.
6. In the Function Arguments dialog box, in the Or select a category list, click **Text**.
7. In the Select a function list, click **LOWER**, and click **OK**.
8. In the Function Arguments dialog box, in the Text box, type **C6** and click **OK**.

9. Drag the fill handle down to fill the formula through cell **D13**.
10. Click cell **A18** to select it.
11. Click the **Insert Function** button *fx* on the formula bar.
12. In the Insert Functions dialog box, open the Or select a category list, and click **Text**.
13. In the Select a function list, click **CONCATENATE**, and click **OK**.
14. In the Function Arguments dialog box, in the Text1 arguments box, type **A6**, and press TAB.
15. In the **Text2** arguments box, type **": "**, and press TAB.
16. In the **Text3** arguments box, type **D6**, and click **OK**.
17. Drag the fill handle down to fill the formula through cell **A25**. Adjust the column width.
18. Select cell **C18** to select it.
19. Click the **Insert Function** button *fx* on the formula bar.
20. In the Insert Function dialog box, open the Or select a category list, and click **Text**.
21. In the Select a function list, click **RIGHT**, and click **OK**.
22. In the **Function Arguments** dialog box, in the **Text** box, type **B6**, and press TAB.
23. In the **Num_chars** box, type **5**, and click **OK**.
24. Drag the fill handle down to fill the formula through cell **C25**.
25. Select cell **E18** to select it.
26. Type **=TRIM(E6)**, and click **OK**. Adjust the column width, if necessary.
27. Drag the fill handle to fill the series through cell **E25**. Your worksheet should look like Figure 15-1.
28. **With your teacher's permission**, print the worksheet. Submit the printout or the file for grading as required.
29. Save and close the file, and exit Excel.

Figure 15-1

	A	B	C	D	E
1	Whole Grains Bread				
2	Affiliate Retail Stores				
3					
4					
5	Store Name	Store Address	Store Code		Manager
6	ABC Bakery	234 SE 183RD Street, Portland, oR 97321	1B-2c	1b-2c	Jay Ray Burns
7	Baked Goods, Inc.	19 houston Ave., austin, tx 73301	10k-104D	10k-104d	Margie Ann Jackson
8	Better Breads, Corp.	923 1sT St., Seattle, WA 98101	3B-84d	3b-84d	Jose Angelo Marquez
9	Great Harvester	10 Market StrEET, San Diego, ca 92101	18e-99X	18e-99x	Mark Dean Smith
10	More Better Bread	2-b NorTH Wygandt Rd., DES moines, io 50301	4p-14w	4p-14w	Rob Beau Washington
11	My Best Bread, Inc.	209 9th AVE., BalTIMOre, Md 21201	8t-8O	8t-8o	Richard Benjamin Tiller
12	Very Best Bread	100 Charleston AveNUE, Boise, ID 83702	33d-1y	33d-1y	Diane Lea Ross
13	Your Whole Bread Store	88 wickersham lane, Lexington, KY 40505	8r-9P	8r-9p	Paris Renee Mills
14					
15					
16					
17	Store Name & Code		Store ZIP Code		Manager
18	ABC Bakery: 1b-2c		97321		Jay Ray Burns
19	Baked Goods, Inc.: 10k-104d		73301		Margie Ann Jackson
20	Better Breads, Corp.: 3b-84d		98101		Jose Angelo Marquez
21	Great Harvester: 18e-99x		92101		Mark Dean Smith
22	More Better Bread: 4p-14w		50301		Rob Beau Washington
23	My Best Bread, Inc.: 8t-8o		21201		Richard Benjamin Tiller
24	Very Best Bread: 33d-1y		83702		Diane Lea Ross
25	Your Whole Bread Store: 8r-9p		40505		Paris Renee Mills

Excel 2013, Windows 8, Microsoft Corporation

Lesson 15—Apply

You're the manager of a Whole Grains Bread store in Olympia, Washington, and you've been sent a worksheet with information about other affiliate retail bread stores. The names in the worksheet have not been consistently typed and there are extra spaces within the cells. You've just learned about various Text functions, and you want to reformat the text in the worksheet so that it looks more professional.

DIRECTIONS

1. Start Excel, if necessary, and open the **E15Apply** file from the data files for this lesson.
2. Save the workbook as **E15Apply_xx** in the location where your teacher instructs you to store the files for this lesson.
3. Add a header that has your name at the left, the date code in the center, and the page number code at the right, and change back to **Normal** view.
4. In cell **A18**, use the **TRIM** function to create a formula that removes the extra spaces in the text.
5. Fill the formula down through cell **A25**.
6. In cell **B18**, use the **UPPER** function to create a formula that changes the text in cell **B6** to uppercase.
7. Fill the formula down through cell **B25**.
8. In cell **C18**, use the **LEFT** function to create a formula that extracts the area code. Remember to include the parentheses.
9. Fill the formula down through cell **C25**.
10. In cell **D18**, use the **MID** function to create a formula that extracts the phone prefix. Remember to count the space as a character for the start_num value.
11. Fill the formula down through cell **D25**.
12. In cell **E18**, use the **RIGHT** function to create a formula that extracts the phone line number (the last four digits of the phone number).
13. Fill the formula down through cell **E25**.
14. In cell **F18**, use the **CONCATENATE** function to create a formula that combines the first, middle, and last name of the manager. Remember to insert a space between each name.
15. Fill the formula down through cell **F25**. Adjust the column width, if necessary. Your worksheet should look like Figure 15-2.
16. **With your teacher's permission**, print the worksheet. Submit the printout or the file for grading as required.
17. Save and close the file, and exit Excel.

Figure 15-2

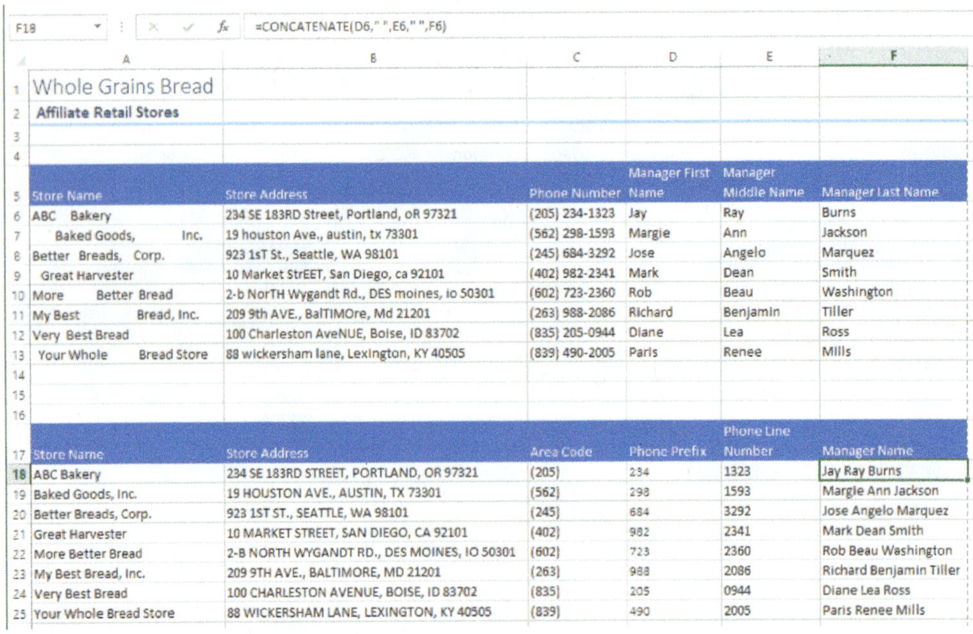

F18 =CONCATENATE(D6," ",E6," ",F6)

	A	B	C	D	E	F
1	Whole Grains Bread					
2	Affiliate Retail Stores					
3						
4						
5	Store Name	Store Address	Phone Number	Manager First Name	Manager Middle Name	Manager Last Name
6	ABC Bakery	234 SE 183RD Street, Portland, oR 97321	(205) 234-1323	Jay	Ray	Burns
7	Baked Goods, Inc.	19 houston Ave., austin, tx 73301	(562) 298-1593	Margie	Ann	Jackson
8	Better Breads, Corp.	923 1sT St., Seattle, WA 98101	(245) 684-3292	Jose	Angelo	Marquez
9	Great Harvester	10 Market StrEET, San Diego, ca 92101	(402) 982-2341	Mark	Dean	Smith
10	More Better Bread	2-b NorTH Wygandt Rd., DES moines, io 50301	(602) 723-2360	Rob	Beau	Washington
11	My Best Bread, Inc.	209 9th AVE., BalTIMOre, Md 21201	(263) 988-2086	Richard	Benjamin	Tiller
12	Very Best Bread	100 Charleston AveNUE, Boise, ID 83702	(835) 205-0944	Diane	Lea	Ross
13	Your Whole Bread Store	88 wickersham lane, Lexington, KY 40505	(839) 490-2005	Paris	Renee	Mills
14						
15						
16						
17	Store Name	Store Address	Area Code	Phone Prefix	Phone Line Number	Manager Name
18	ABC Bakery	234 SE 183RD STREET, PORTLAND, OR 97321	(205)	234	1323	Jay Ray Burns
19	Baked Goods, Inc.	19 HOUSTON AVE., AUSTIN, TX 73301	(562)	298	1593	Margie Ann Jackson
20	Better Breads, Corp.	923 1ST ST., SEATTLE, WA 98101	(245)	684	3292	Jose Angelo Marquez
21	Great Harvester	10 MARKET STREET, SAN DIEGO, CA 92101	(402)	982	2341	Mark Dean Smith
22	More Better Bread	2-B NORTH WYGANDT RD., DES MOINES, IO 50301	(602)	723	2360	Rob Beau Washington
23	My Best Bread, Inc.	209 9TH AVE., BALTIMORE, MD 21201	(263)	988	2086	Richard Benjamin Tiller
24	Very Best Bread	100 CHARLESTON AVENUE, BOISE, ID 83702	(835)	205	0944	Diane Lea Ross
25	Your Whole Bread Store	88 WICKERSHAM LANE, LEXINGTON, KY 40505	(839)	490	2005	Paris Renee Mills

Lesson 16

Using Frozen Labels and Panes

➤ What You Will Learn

Freezing Labels While Scrolling
Splitting a Worksheet into Panes

Software Skills When working with a large worksheet, you can freeze row and/or column labels to keep them in view, so that you can always identify your data no matter how far you've scrolled. You also can split the worksheet window into two or four panes, enabling you to view multiple parts of a worksheet at the same time—in order to compare or copy data, for example.

WORDS TO KNOW

Freeze
A method to keep specified rows and columns—usually ones containing labels for data—in view when scrolling through a worksheet.

Panes
Sections or areas in a window that enable you to see different parts of the worksheet at the same time.

What You Can Do

Freezing Labels While Scrolling

- When you need to keep labels or titles in view at the top or left edge of the worksheet as you scroll through it, you can **freeze** them in place.

  ✓ *Note that freezing rows and columns onscreen does not freeze them in a printout.*

- Position the insertion point in the column to the right or the row below the data to be frozen, and then use the Freeze Panes button in the Window group on the VIEW tab of the Ribbon.
- You can freeze just the column labels, the row labels, or both.
- Click a cell to specify which rows and columns to freeze. Rows above and columns to the left of the selected cell will be frozen. To freeze only rows, make sure you click a cell in column A. To freeze only columns, click a cell in row 1.
- You also can instantly freeze either the top row or the first column of the worksheet.
- Thin lines indicate the borders of the frozen area. You can scroll the area outside of these borders, and the frozen row/column labels will remain in view.
- To remove the freeze, use the Unfreeze Panes command found on the Freeze Panes drop-down list.

Try It! Freezing Labels While Scrolling

1. Start Excel.
2. Open the **E16Try** file from the data files for this lesson.
3. Save the workbook as **E16Try_xx** in the location where your teacher instructs you to store the files for this lesson.
4. Add a header that has your name at the left, the date code in the center, and the page number code at the right, and change back to Normal view.
5. Click cell C4 to select it.
6. Click View > Freeze Panes > Freeze Panes.

   ✓ *Use the Freeze Top Row or Freeze First Column choices to freeze row 1 or column A.*
7. Scroll down and to the right until cell I70 is visible. Notice how rows 1 through 3 and columns A and B remain visible onscreen.
8. On the VIEW tab, click Freeze Panes > Unfreeze Panes. The scrolling panes are removed and the worksheet scrolls back up.
9. Save the **E16Try_xx** file, and leave it open to use in the next Try It.

Frozen panes

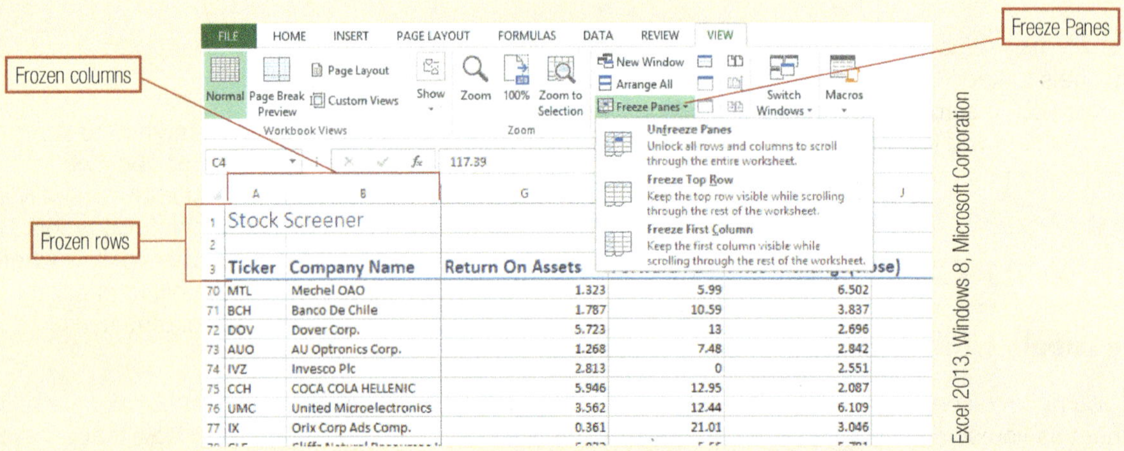

Excel 2013, Windows 8, Microsoft Corporation

Splitting a Worksheet into Panes

- When you need to view different parts of a large worksheet at the same time, possibly at different zoom levels, split the worksheet horizontally or vertically into **panes**.

  ✓ *Panes also do not affect the appearance of a printout.*
- To split a worksheet, use the Split button in the Window group of the VIEW tab.
- Click a cell to specify where the panes appear. The pane divider bars appear to the left of and above the selected cell.
- When you position the insertion point in a cell in row 1 and use the Split command, the vertical panes scroll together when scrolling up and down, and independently when scrolling left to right.
- When you position the insertion point in a cell in column A and use the Split command, the horizontal panes scroll together when scrolling left to right, and independently when scrolling up and down.
- When you need to cancel the split, click the Split button again.

Try It! Splitting a Worksheet into Panes

1. In the **E16Try_xx** file, click cell C15 to select it.
2. On the VIEW tab, click Split.
3. Drag the vertical divider bar so that column C displays completely in the left pane.
4. In the right pane, scroll right so that columns A through D scroll out of view.
5. In the bottom pane, scroll down until row 60 is visible.
6. Scroll left so that column A is once again visible.
7. Scroll the bottom pane down until you see the Screener Criteria Conditions in the range A112:B115.
8. Save the **E16Try_xx** file, and close it.

Scrolling panes

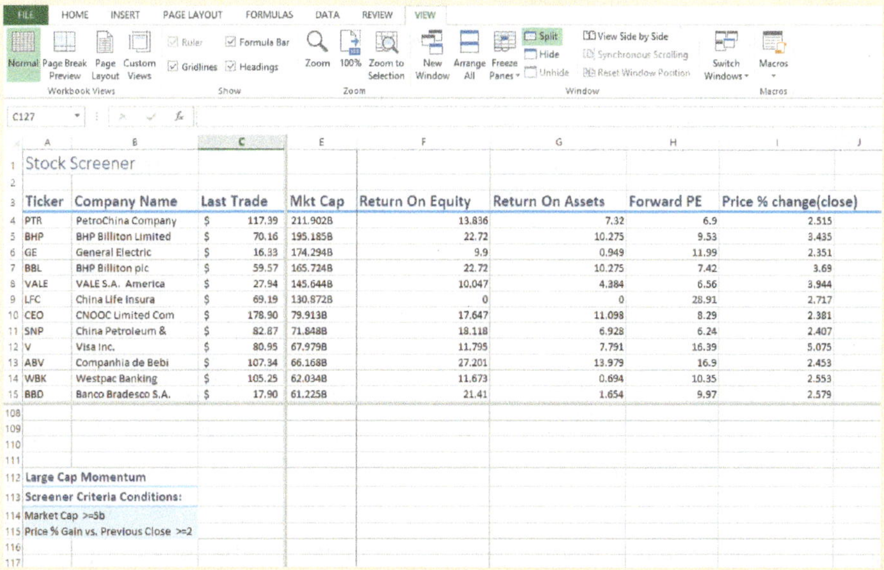

Excel 2013, Windows 8, Microsoft Corporation

Lesson 16—Practice

In this project, you will freeze a row label using the skills you learned in this lesson.

DIRECTIONS

1. Start Excel, if necessary, and open the **E16Practice** file from the data files for this lesson.
2. Save the workbook as **E16Practice_xx** in the location where your teacher instructs you to store the files for this lesson.
3. Add a header that has your name at the left, the date code in the center, and the page number code at the right, and change back to **Normal** view.
4. Scroll down to row 33, and make the following cell entries:
   a. **A33** **ZG020**
   b. **B33** **Sleeping bag, 20 degrees**
   c. **C33** **75**
   d. **D33** **3**
   e. **E33** **1**
   f. **H33** **3**

5. Press CTRL + HOME.
6. Click cell **A7** to select it.
7. Click **VIEW** > **Freeze Panes** > **Freeze Panes**.
8. Scroll down again so that row 34 is visible, and make the following cell entries.
   a. **A34** **ZG030**
   b. **B34** **Sleeping bag, 30 degrees**
   c. **C34** **70**
   d. **D34** **5**
   e. **E34** **2**
   f. **H34** **8**
9. **With your teacher's permission,** print the worksheet. Submit the printout or the file for grading as required.
10. Save and close the file, and exit Excel.

Lesson 16—Apply

You manage the Logan retail store for Voyager Travel Adventures. You've made some updates to your inventory worksheet, and need to use the features that enable you to divide the worksheet into panes so that you can complete your evaluation of current inventory levels for summer outdoor gear.

DIRECTIONS

1. Start Excel, if necessary, and open the **E16Apply** file from the data files for this lesson.
2. Save the workbook as **E16Apply_xx** in the location where your teacher instructs you to store the files for this lesson.
3. Add a header that has your name at the left, the date code in the center, and the page number code at the right. After completing the header, change back to Normal view.
4. Click cell **D20**, and split the window into panes.
5. Scroll down the bottom pane to display the range title *Inventory Evaluation*.
6. In cell **C49**, enter a formula that sums the values in the range **F7:F34**, entering that range in the formula by dragging over it in the upper-right pane.
7. In cell **C50**, enter a formula that sums the Value column entries in the upper-right pane. Adjust the position of the vertical split divider once you enter the formula and widen the column if necessary.
8. In cell **C51**, enter a formula that calculates a carrying cost of 2.5% of the Item Value you just calculated in cell C50.

   ✓ *Hint: Multiply the Item Value by 2.5%.*
9. In cell **C52**, enter a formula that calculates the average of the Current Stock Percentage entries. Your worksheet should resemble Figure 16-1 on the next page.
10. **With your teacher's permission,** print the worksheet. Submit the printout or the file for grading as required.
11. Save and close the file, and exit Excel.

Figure 16-1

	A	B	C	D	E	F	G	H	I	J
15	BS113	Backpacker grill	$ 4.00	5	4	9	$ 36.00	10	90.00%	
16	CK101	Open country mess kit	$ 6.50	4	3	7	$ 45.50	10	70.00%	
17	CK102	Camp cook set	$ 50.00	2	1	3	$ 150.00	4	75.00%	
18	FL103	Emergency tinder	$ 1.50	9	7	16	$ 24.00	15	106.67%	
19	FL104	Fire paste	$ 2.00	12	6	18	$ 36.00	24	75.00%	
20	FL105	Liquid fuel, 1 gal.	$ 3.00	18	15	33	$ 99.00	36	91.67%	
21	FL108	Canister fuel, 170 g	$ 2.00	20	5	25	$ 50.00	36	69.44%	
22	FL109	Canister fuel, 300 g	$ 2.50	21	13	34	$ 85.00	36	94.44%	
23	WJ101	Water carrier, 2L	$ 9.00	10	2	12	$ 108.00	15	80.00%	
24	WJ102	Water carrier, 32 oz	$ 4.50	12	6	18	$ 81.00	24	75.00%	
25	WJ103	Water carrier, 48 oz.	$ 5.00	3	15	18	$ 90.00	24	75.00%	
26	WJ104	Dromedary, 6L	$ 15.00	6	6	12	$ 180.00	15	80.00%	
27	WJ105	Water bag, 4L	$ 10.00	10	2	12	$ 120.00	15	80.00%	
28	WT101	Water purifier, portable	$ 80.00	15	5	20	$ 1,600.00	20	100.00%	
29	WT103	Water purifier, camp	$ 25.00	12	0	12	$ 300.00	12	100.00%	
30	ZG005	Day pack, light	$ 35.00	3	1	4	$ 140.00	5	80.00%	
31	ZG009	Rugged pack, frameless	$ 55.00	2	2	4	$ 220.00	3	133.33%	
32	ZG010	Rugged pack, light frame	$ 65.00	2	1	3	$ 195.00	3	100.00%	
33	ZG020	Sleeping bag, 20 degrees	$ 75.00	3	1	4	$ 300.00	3	133.33%	
34	ZG030	Sleeping bag, 30 degrees	$ 70.00	5	2	7	$ 490.00	8	87.50%	
35										
36										
41										
42										
43										
44										
45										
46										
47										
48		Inventory Evaluation								
49		Items in Stock	297							
50		Item Value	$5,308.00							
51		Carrying Cost	$ 132.70							
52		Average Inventory Level	86.87%							
53										
54										

Excel 2013, Windows 8, Microsoft Corporation

Lesson 17

Using Conditional Formatting and Find and Replace

➤ What You Will Learn

Applying Conditional Formatting
Using Find and Replace

WORDS TO KNOW

Color scales
A type of conditional formatting that applies a background fill color that varies depending on the relative value stored in each of the formatted cells.

Conditional formatting
Variable formatting that changes the formatting applied based on the contents of the cells in the formatting range.

Data bars
A type of conditional formatting that creates filled background bars reflecting the relative value stored in each of the formatted cells.

Highlight cells rules
A method of applying conditional formatting based on how cell contents compare with a specified criterion, such as a Less Than comparison.

Software Skills Conditional formatting is a volatile type of formatting that changes depending on what the values or calculated results in the cells are. This type of formatting enables you to identify key data, and it updates automatically if you update worksheet values and formulas. The Find and Replace function in Excel works just like it does in Word, enabling you to update text information by changing spellings and words globally. You learn to use both of these features in this lesson.

What You Can Do

Applying Conditional Formatting

- When you want cells to have different formatting depending on their contents, you can apply **conditional formatting**.
- Excel 2013 offers more forms of conditional formatting than its predecessors. You can now apply these types of conditional formatting to a cell or range:
  - Use **highlight cells rules** to apply specified formatting to cells only when the contents meet a certain rule or criterion, such as being greater than 100 or text that contains a particular phrase.
  - To format the cells holding the highest or lowest values in a range, use **top/ bottom rules** conditional formatting. You can find the top or bottom 10 items or top or bottom 10%, or format values that are above or below average.
  - The **data bars** conditional formatting method creates a colored horizontal bar in every cell. The length of the colored bars varies according to the values in the cells, basically creating a chart of the data right within the range holding the values.

- Use the **color scales** type of conditional formatting when you want to apply different cell fill colors depending on the values in the cells.
- If you prefer graphical indicators of the relative values in cells, use **icon sets** conditional formatting. You can choose variations from four different types of icons, including ones that indicate ratings.

■ To apply conditional formatting to a selected range, click the Conditional Formatting button in the Styles group of the HOME tab. Click an overall conditional formatting type from the menu that appears, and then choose the specific type of conditional formatting to apply.

■ You can create a custom conditional format using the New Rule command, clear conditional formatting using the Clear Rules command, or edit a conditional format with the Manage Rules choice.

■ You also can apply conditional formatting using the Quick Analysis Lens. When you select a range of cells, the **Quick Analysis Lens** button appears to the bottom right of your data.

■ The formatting options available in the Quick Analysis Lens will change based on the type of data you select.

■ You also can use the Quick Analysis Lens to clear the format of cells.

✓ *You will learn more about the Quick Analysis Lens in Chapter 4.*

Icon sets
A type of conditional formatting that includes one of a set of icons reflecting the relative value stored in each of the formatted cells.

Quick Analysis Lens
A tool that provides formatting for data analysis.

Top/Bottom rules
Conditional formatting rules that format the highest or lowest values in the formatted range, or those that are above or below average.

Try It! Applying Conditional Formatting

1. Start Excel.
2. Open the E17Try file from the data files for this lesson.
3. Save the workbook as E17Try_xx in the location where your teacher instructs you to store the files for this lesson.
4. Add a header that has your name at the left, the date code in the center, and the page number code at the right, and change back to Normal view.
5. Select the range with Q1 sales data, excluding the column titles.

   ✓ *The worksheet has predefined names for each of the ranges with quarterly sales (SalesQ1 through SalesQ4) and the average data (Average).*
6. On the HOME tab, click Conditional Formatting > Highlight Cell Rules > Greater Than.
7. In the Greater Than dialog box, change the suggested value to 3000. Open the with drop-down list and click Green Fill with Dark Green Text. Click OK.
8. Select the range with Q2 sales data.
9. Click the Quick Analysis Lens button > Data Bars.
10. Click the Quick Analysis Lens button > Clear Format.
11. Click Conditional Formatting > Top/Bottom Rules > Bottom 10 Items.
12. In the Bottom 10 Items dialog box, change the suggested value to 5. Click OK.
13. Select the range with Q3 sales data.
14. Click Conditional Formatting > Data Bars > Gradient Fill > Orange Data Bar.

(continued)

Try It! Applying Conditional Formatting *(continued)*

15 Select the range with Q4 sales data.

16 Click Conditional Formatting > Color Scales > Green-Yellow-Red Color Scale. (It's the first choice in the first row.)

17 Select the range with Average sales data.

18 Click Conditional Formatting > Icon Sets > Ratings > 3 Stars.

19 Reselect the range with the Q2 sales data.

20 Click Conditional Formatting > Manage Rules.

21 In the Conditional Formatting Rules Manager dialog box, click the Edit Rule button.

22 Under Edit the Rule Description, change the entry in the center text box to **15** and click the % of the selected range check box to check it, then click OK.

23 Click OK in the Conditional Formatting Rules Manager dialog box.

24 Save the **E17Try_xx** file, and leave it open to use in the next Try It.

Applying conditional formatting

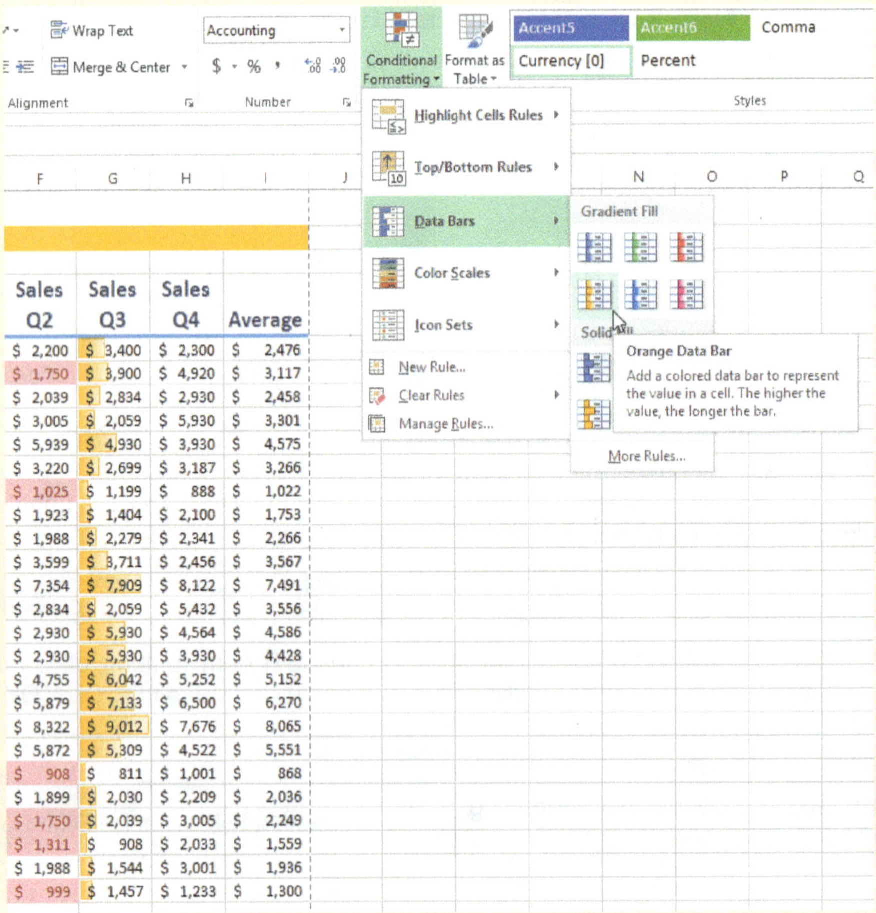

Excel 2013, Windows 8, Microsoft Corporation

Using Find and Replace

- Similar to the Find and Replace feature used in Word 2013, Excel also offers Find and Replace, and you can use it to replace all or part of a cell entry.
- To open the Find and Replace dialog box, click HOME > Find & Select > Replace.
- Enter the Find what and Replace with entries. Then, either use the Find Next and Replace buttons to replace selected entries, or Replace All to replace all entries.
- Click the Options button in the Find and Replace dialog box to display additional choices, such as the ability to find and replace formatting or search the entire workbook rather than just the current sheet.

Try It! Using Find and Replace

1. In the **E17Try_xx** file, select cell A1.

   ✓ *As for a spell check, it's a good practice to start a find and replace from the top of the sheet.*
2. On the HOME tab, click Find & Select > Replace.
3. Type **Mens** in the Find what text box, press TAB, and type **M**.
4. Click the Options button to display all the options, and click the Match entire cell contents check box to check it.
5. Click the Replace All button, then click OK in the dialog box informing you that Excel made 12 replacements. Note that a number of entries in column B are replaced.
6. Change the Find what and Replace with entries to **Womens** and **W**, respectively, click the Replace All button, and click OK.
7. Change the Find What to **White** and Replace with to **Ivory**.
8. Click the Find Next button seven times to skip the first six instances of White in column D, rows 5 through 10.
9. Click the Replace button six times to replace the second six instances of White in rows 11 through 16.
10. Click the Match entire cell contents check box to clear it, and then click the Close button to close the Find and Replace dialog box.
11. Save the **E17Try_xx** file, and close it.

Lesson 17—Practice

In this project, you will find and replace terms in the worksheet using the skills you learned in this lesson.

DIRECTIONS

1. Start Excel, if necessary, and open the **E17Practice** file from the data files for this lesson.
2. Save the workbook as **E17Practice_xx** in the location where your teacher instructs you to store the files for this lesson.
3. Add a header that has your name at the left, the date code in the center, and the page number code at the right, and change back to **Normal** view.
4. On the HOME tab, click **Find & Select** > **Replace**.
5. Type **Operations** in the **Find what** text box, and press TAB.
6. Type **Operating** in the **Replace with** box, and click the **Find Next** button.
7. Click **Replace** to replace the first match in cell A15.
8. Click in the worksheet, and press CTRL + HOME to return to cell A1.

9. Select the existing entry in the **Find what** text box in the Find and Replace dialog box, type **Expensives**, and press TAB.
10. Type **Expenses** in the **Replace with** box.
11. Click the **Replace All** button, and then click **OK** in the message box.
12. Click **OK** to confirm that Excel made two replacements.
13. Click the **Close** button to close the Find and Replace dialog box.
14. **With your teacher's permission,** print the worksheet. Submit the printout or the file for grading as required.
15. Save and close the file, and exit Excel.

Lesson 17—Apply

You are the CFO for Telson Tech, a small manufacturer of custom circuit boards. You are finalizing a Profit & Loss statement that compares this year's sales, expenses, and profit information with data from last year. Businesses like Telson Tech use Profit & Loss statements to summarize their revenues, costs, and expenses so they can plan how to increase revenue and reduce expenses. You will use Find and Replace to fix some text errors, and then use conditional formatting to help evaluate the financial performance of your company.

DIRECTIONS

1. Start Excel, if necessary, and open the **E17Apply** file from the data files for this lesson.
2. Save the workbook as **E17Apply_xx** in the location where your teacher instructs you to store the files for this lesson.
3. Add a header that has your name at the left, the date code in the center, and the page number code at the right, and change back to **Normal** view.
4. Select the following noncontiguous cells and ranges (using the CTRL key):
   a. **D11**
   b. **D13:E13**
   c. **D21:E21**
   d. **D23:E23**
   e. **D27:E27**
5. Apply the **Green-White Color Scale** conditional format to the selection.

   ✓ *This formatting will apply deeper green shades to the revenue and profit items that have improved the most.*
6. Select the following noncontiguous cells and ranges:
   a. **D12 :E12**
   b. **D16:E19**
   c. **D25:E25**
7. Apply the **Red-White Color Scale** conditional format to the selection.

   ✓ *This formatting will apply deeper red shades to the expense items that have worsened (increased) the most.*
8. Select cell **B5**. Apply a highlight cell rules conditional format that changes the cell formatting to a Light Red Fill if the margin fell below 50%.
9. Select cell **B6**. Apply a highlight cell rules conditional format that changes the cell formatting to a Green Fill with Dark Green Text if the return exceeds 10%.
10. **With your teacher's permission,** print the worksheet. Submit the printout or the file for grading as required.
11. Save and close the file, and exit Excel.

Lesson 18

Rotating Entries and Resolving Errors

➤ What You Will Learn

Rotating Cell Entries
Resolving a #### Error Message

Software Skills Rotating cell entries provides another choice you can use to better organize worksheet data and make it more attractive. One formatting problem—having columns that are two narrow—produces an #### error message. In this lesson, you learn how to apply rotation and how to fix column width errors.

WORDS TO KNOW

Rotate
To change the angle of the contents of a cell.

What You Can Do

Rotating Cell Entries

- You can **rotate** the entry in a cell to change the angle of the entry.
- The Orientation button in the Alignment group of the HOME tab offers five preset rotation choices.
  - Angle Counterclockwise: 45 degrees, right end angled up.
  - Angle Clockwise: -45 degrees, left end angled up.
  - Vertical Text: Does not rotate the letters, but stacks them top to bottom.
  - Rotate Text Up: 90 degrees, right end up.
  - Rotate Text Down: -90 degrees, left end up.
- You also can specify a custom rotation in the Orientation area on the Alignment tab in the Format Cells dialog box. The Format Cell Alignment command at the bottom of the Orientation menu is another way to display that dialog box.
- You can use rotation in conjunction with other formatting methods, such as cell merging.

Try It! Rotating Cell Entries

1. Start Excel.
2. Open the **E18Try** file from the data files for this lesson.
3. Save the workbook as **E18Try_xx** in the location where your teacher instructs you to store the files for this lesson.
4. Add a header that has your name at the left, the date code in the center, and the page number code at the right, and change back to Normal view.
5. Drag over the range A5:A10 to select it.
6. On the HOME tab, click the Merge & Center drop-down arrow Merge & Center > Merge Cells.
7. On the HOME tab, click the Orientation > Angle Counterclockwise.
8. Repeat the techniques in steps 6 and 7 to merge and rotate the following ranges:
   A11:A16
   A17:A22
   A23:A28
9. Double-click the right border of the column A column header to AutoFit the column width to the rotated values.
10. On the HOME tab, click the Border drop-down arrow > Bottom Border to apply bottom borders to these ranges:
    A10:I10
    A16:I16
    A22:I22
    A28:I28
11. Save the **E18Try_xx** file, and leave it open to use in the next Try It.

Rotating a cell entry

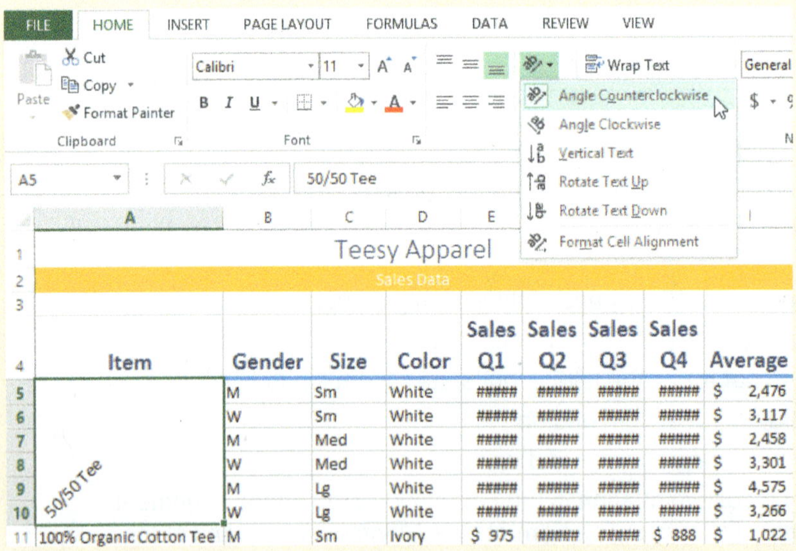

Excel 2013, Windows 8, Microsoft Corporation

Resolving a #### Error Message

- If a column is too narrow to display a value, formula result, or date entry in a cell, the cell will fill with pound signs (#).
- You can correct this error by using any technique to increase the column width until all #### errors disappear from the column.

Try It! Resolving a #### Error Message

1. In the **E18Try_xx** file, double-click the right border of the column E column header to resize the column. All #### errors should disappear from the column.
2. Drag over the column headers for columns F through H to select those columns.
3. On the HOME tab, click Format > AutoFit Column Width. All #### errors should disappear from the selected columns.
4. Save the **E18Try_xx** file, and close it.

Lesson 18—Practice

In this project, you will fix column widths using the skills you learned in this lesson.

DIRECTIONS

1. Start Excel, if necessary, and open the **E18Practice** file from the data files for this lesson.
2. Save the workbook as **E18Practice_xx** in the location where your teacher instructs you to store the files for this lesson.
3. Add a header that has your name at the left, the date code in the center, and the page number code at the right, and change back to **Normal** view.
4. Click the column **E** column header.
5. On the **HOME** tab, click **Format** > **AutoFit Column Width**.
6. Drag over the column headers for columns **I** and **J** to select them.
7. Double-click the right border of the column **I** column header. Your worksheet should look like Figure 18-1.
8. **With your teacher's permission,** print the worksheet. Submit the printout or the file for grading as required.
9. Save and close the file, and exit Excel.

Figure 18-1

Whole Grains Bread

Home Office Payroll

Salaried Employees

Employee Name	Employee ID	Rate	Regular Hours	Gross Pay	Fed Tax	SS Tax	State Tax	Net Pay
Anthony Splendoria	38748	$ 2,175.00	40.00	$2,175.00	$ 543.75	$ 169.65	$ 65.25	$1,396.35
Eileen Costello	21544	$ 1,895.00	40.00	$1,895.00	$ 473.75	$ 147.81	$ 56.85	$1,216.59
Carol Chen	38448	$ 895.00	40.00	$ 895.00	$ 223.75	$ 69.81	$ 26.85	$ 574.59
Marty Gonzales	61522	$ 684.00	40.00	$ 684.00	$ 171.00	$ 53.35	$ 20.52	$ 439.13
Maria Nachez	34789	$ 1,665.00	40.00	$1,665.00	$ 416.25	$ 129.87	$ 49.95	$1,068.93
Mika Gritada	22785	$ 1,023.00	40.00	$1,023.00	$ 255.75	$ 79.79	$ 30.69	$ 656.77
Vickie Helms	31851	$ 765.00	40.00	$ 765.00	$ 191.25	$ 59.67	$ 22.95	$ 491.13
Randall Lohr	38514	$ 1,545.00	40.00	$1,545.00	$ 386.25	$ 120.51	$ 46.35	$ 991.89
Abe Rittenhouse	22854	$ 1,231.00	40.00	$1,231.00	$ 307.75	$ 96.02	$ 36.93	$ 790.30

Hourly Employees

Employee Name	Employee ID	Rate	Regular Hours	Overtime Hours	Gross Pay	Fed Tax	SS Tax	State Tax	Net Pay
Thomas Cortese	21875	$ 8.25	40.00	2.00	$ 354.75	$ 53.21	$ 27.67	$ 10.64	$263.22
Javier Cortez	21154	$ 7.75	40.00	3.00	$ 344.88	$ 51.73	$ 26.90	$ 10.35	$255.90
Allen Gaines	23455	$ 7.25	40.00	6.00	$ 355.25	$ 53.29	$ 27.71	$ 10.66	$263.60
Freda Gage	27855	$ 8.00	40.00	3.00	$ 356.00	$ 53.40	$ 27.77	$ 10.68	$264.15
Isiah Herron	33252	$ 10.95	40.00	5.50	$ 528.34	$ 79.25	$ 41.21	$ 15.85	$392.03
Thomas Kaminski	37881	$ 9.75	40.00	4.00	$ 448.50	$ 67.28	$ 34.98	$ 13.46	$332.79
Chris Nakao	29958	$ 11.25	40.00	3.00	$ 500.63	$ 75.09	$ 39.05	$ 15.02	$371.46

Lesson 18—Apply

You are the Payroll Manager at Whole Grains Bread. Your assistant worked on a version of the payroll worksheet and introduced errors in the column formatting, so you need to make corrections. You also want to use rotated cell entries to improve worksheet formatting.

DIRECTIONS

1. Start Excel, if necessary, and open the **E18Apply** file from the data files for this lesson.
2. Save the workbook as **E18Apply_xx** in the location where your teacher instructs you to store the files for this lesson.
3. Add a header that has your name at the left, the date code in the center, and the page number code at the right, and change back to **Normal** view.
4. Select rows 4 and 16 (at the same time), and delete them from the sheet.
5. Insert a new column A, and move the entries in cells **B1:B2** left to **A1:A2**.
6. Select the range **A5:A13**, and merge it into one cell.
7. Enter **Salaried** in the merged cell A5, apply the **Accent1** cell style, and increase the text size to **24**.
8. Change the Orientation for the merged cell A5 to **Rotate Text Up**. Apply Middle and Center alignment.
9. Repeat the techniques used in steps 6 through 8 to merge **A16:A22** and create a rotated label that says **Hourly** to match the salaried label formatting.
10. Select column **F** and double-click its right column border to AutoFit the column width. Your worksheet should look like Figure 18-2.
11. **With your teacher's permission**, print the worksheet. Submit the printout or the file for grading as required.
12. Save and close the file, and exit Excel.

Figure 18-2

Excel 2013, Windows 8, Microsoft Corporation

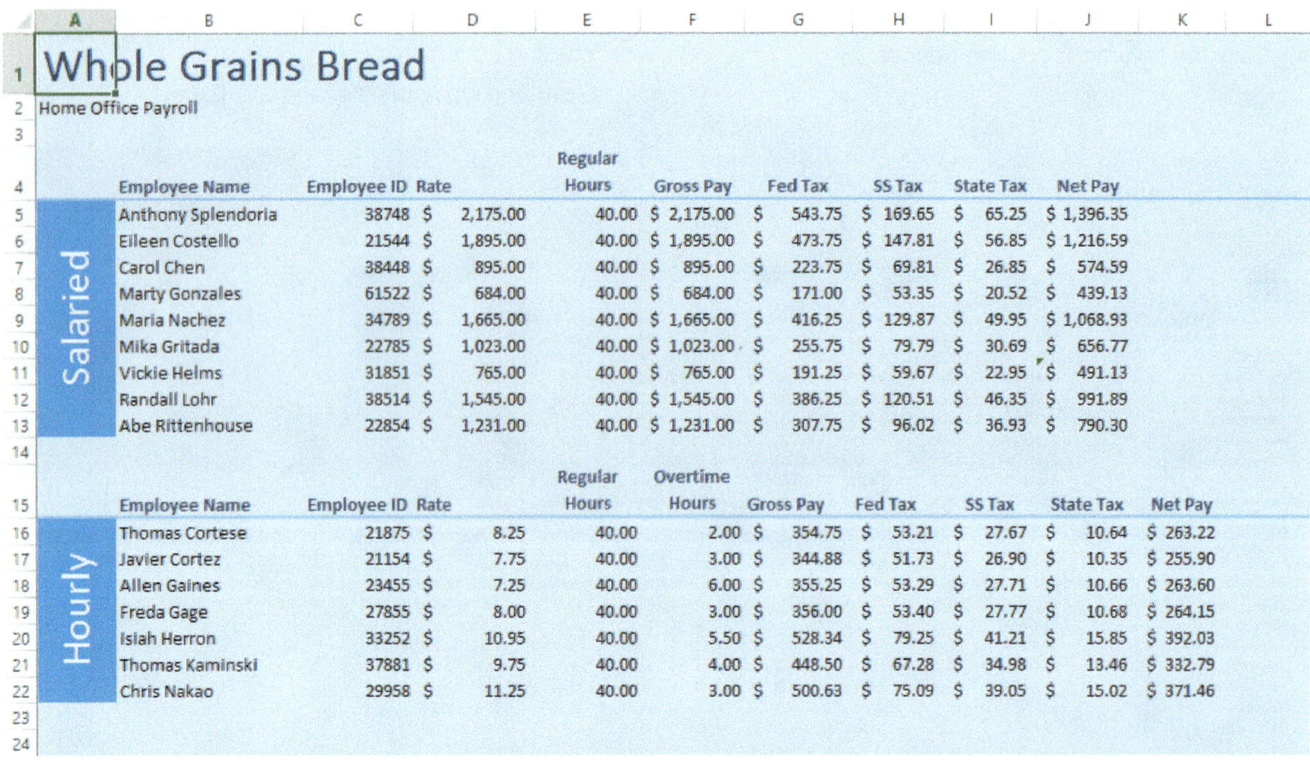

Whole Grains Bread

Home Office Payroll

	Employee Name	Employee ID	Rate	Regular Hours	Gross Pay	Fed Tax	SS Tax	State Tax	Net Pay
Salaried	Anthony Splendoria	38748	$ 2,175.00	40.00	$ 2,175.00	$ 543.75	$ 169.65	$ 65.25	$ 1,396.35
	Eileen Costello	21544	$ 1,895.00	40.00	$ 1,895.00	$ 473.75	$ 147.81	$ 56.85	$ 1,216.59
	Carol Chen	38448	$ 895.00	40.00	$ 895.00	$ 223.75	$ 69.81	$ 26.85	$ 574.59
	Marty Gonzales	61522	$ 684.00	40.00	$ 684.00	$ 171.00	$ 53.35	$ 20.52	$ 439.13
	Maria Nachez	34789	$ 1,665.00	40.00	$ 1,665.00	$ 416.25	$ 129.87	$ 49.95	$ 1,068.93
	Mika Gritada	22785	$ 1,023.00	40.00	$ 1,023.00	$ 255.75	$ 79.79	$ 30.69	$ 656.77
	Vickie Helms	31851	$ 765.00	40.00	$ 765.00	$ 191.25	$ 59.67	$ 22.95	$ 491.13
	Randall Lohr	38514	$ 1,545.00	40.00	$ 1,545.00	$ 386.25	$ 120.51	$ 46.35	$ 991.89
	Abe Rittenhouse	22854	$ 1,231.00	40.00	$ 1,231.00	$ 307.75	$ 96.02	$ 36.93	$ 790.30

	Employee Name	Employee ID	Rate	Regular Hours	Overtime Hours	Gross Pay	Fed Tax	SS Tax	State Tax	Net Pay
Hourly	Thomas Cortese	21875	$ 8.25	40.00	2.00	$ 354.75	$ 53.21	$ 27.67	$ 10.64	$ 263.22
	Javier Cortez	21154	$ 7.75	40.00	3.00	$ 344.88	$ 51.73	$ 26.90	$ 10.35	$ 255.90
	Allen Gaines	23455	$ 7.25	40.00	6.00	$ 355.25	$ 53.29	$ 27.71	$ 10.66	$ 263.60
	Freda Gage	27855	$ 8.00	40.00	3.00	$ 356.00	$ 53.40	$ 27.77	$ 10.68	$ 264.15
	Isiah Herron	33252	$ 10.95	40.00	5.50	$ 528.34	$ 79.25	$ 41.21	$ 15.85	$ 392.03
	Thomas Kaminski	37881	$ 9.75	40.00	4.00	$ 448.50	$ 67.28	$ 34.98	$ 13.46	$ 332.79
	Chris Nakao	29958	$ 11.25	40.00	3.00	$ 500.63	$ 75.09	$ 39.05	$ 15.02	$ 371.46

Lesson 19

Managing Worksheets and Performing Multi-Worksheet Operations

➤ What You Will Learn

- Inserting, Deleting, Copying, Moving, and Renaming Worksheets
- Changing the Color of a Worksheet Tab
- Hiding Sheets
- Grouping Worksheets for Editing and Formatting
- Creating a Summary Worksheet
- Updating a Summary Worksheet

Software Skills Use workbook sheets to divide and present data in logical chunks. For example, rather than placing an entire year's sales on one sheet, create a sales sheet for each month. You can add, delete, move, and rename sheets as needed. You can group sheets to work on them simultaneously, such as applying the same formatting to all the selected sheets. You also can combine data from different worksheets to perform summary calculations. When you do this, you can still change data on the individual worksheets. Excel recalculates the summary formula results to reflect the changes.

WORDS TO KNOW

Active sheet tab
The selected worksheet; the tab name of an active sheet is bold.

Grouping
Worksheets that are selected as a unit; any action performed on this unit will affect all the worksheets in the group.

What You Can Do

Inserting, Deleting, Copying, Moving, and Renaming Worksheets

- The sheet tab displays the name of the sheet. The **active sheet tab** name appears in bold.
- You can add or delete worksheets as needed, using the Insert and Delete drop-down lists in the Cells group of the HOME tab. You also can use the Insert Worksheet tab ⊕ that appears to the right of the right-most sheet in the workbook.
- You also can right-click a sheet tab to display a shortcut menu that allows you to insert, delete, rename, move, and copy worksheets.

- You do not need to delete unused sheets from a workbook, since they do not take up much room in the file; however, if you plan on sharing the file, you may want to remove unused sheets to create a more professional look.
- When you copy a worksheet, you copy all of its data and formatting. However, changes you later make to the copied sheet do not affect the original sheet.
- Moving sheets enables you to place them in a logical order within the workbook.
- Renaming sheets make it easier to keep track of the data on individual sheets.

Try It! Inserting, Deleting, Copying, Moving, and Renaming Worksheets

1. Start Excel.
2. Open the **E19TryA** file from the data files for this lesson.
3. Save the workbook as **E19TryA_xx** in the location where your teacher instructs you to store the files for this lesson.
4. Add a header that has your name at the left, the date code in the center, and the page number code at the right, and change back to Normal view.
5. Click the Insert Worksheet tab ⊕ to insert a new, blank sheet named Sheet2.
6. Click Sheet1, and then click Sheet2.
7. On the HOME tab, click Delete drop-down arrow > Delete Sheet. Excel removes the new sheet from the workbook.
8. Right-click the Sheet1 tab and click Rename.
9. Type **2015**, and press ENTER.
10. Right-click the 2012 sheet tab, and click Move or Copy.
11. In the Move or Copy dialog box, click (move to end) in the Before sheet list, click the Create a copy check box to check it, and click OK. The new sheet appears, with the name 2012 (2).
12. Double-click the name on the new sheet tab, type **2016**, and press ENTER.

Shortcut menu with commands for working with sheets

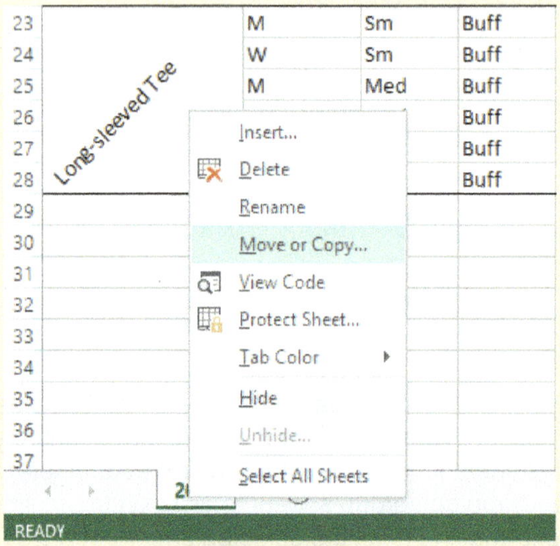

Excel 2013, Windows 8, Microsoft Corporation

13. Select the 2012 sheet. Drag it to the right of the 2013 sheet tab. As you drag, the mouse pointer includes a page and a black triangle shows you the move location. When you release the mouse button, the sheet moves into that new position.
14. Create a copy of the 2012 sheet, name the copy **2017**, and move it to the far left to make it the first sheet.
15. Save the **E19TryA_xx** file, and leave it open to use in the next Try It.

Changing the Color of a Worksheet Tab

- Change the color of a worksheet's tab to further distinguish sheets with different types of data.
- Choosing a tab color from the current theme colors enables you to maintain a color-coordinated look. If you change themes, the colors in the worksheet and the colors of your tabs will change to those in the new theme.
- If you change the color of a sheet tab, that color appears when the tab is not selected.
- When a colored sheet tab is clicked, its color changes to white, with a small line of its original color at the bottom of the tab. For example, an orange sheet tab changes to white with a thin orange line at the bottom.

Try It! Changing the Color of a Worksheet Tab

1. In the E19TryA_xx file, right-click the 2014 sheet tab, point to Tab Color, and click the Green, Accent 6 color in the top row.
2. Right-click the 2013 sheet tab, point to Tab Color, and click the Blue, Accent 1 color in the top row.
3. Right-click the 2012 sheet tab, point to Tab Color, and click the Orange, Accent 2 color in the top row.
4. Save the E19TryA_xx file, and leave it open to use in the next Try It.

Hiding Sheets

- Hide a worksheet temporarily when you need to put sensitive data out of sight.
- Hiding a sheet simply hides its sheet tab from view.
- Access the Hide & Unhide feature by clicking Format in the Cells group on the HOME tab. The Hide & Unhide submenu is in the Visibility group.
- The Hide & Unhide submenu includes the Hide Sheet and Unhide Sheet commands. You also can right-click the sheet tab and use the Hide and Unhide commands.
- Hiding provides a simple layer of protection, but does not provide any real security for confidential data because the Unhide commands become active whenever a sheet is hidden.
- If you rename your worksheets and hide the ones you don't want seen, it's difficult for a user to detect that a sheet is hidden because the sheet names are no longer sequential.

Try It! Hiding Sheets

1. In the E19TryA_xx file, click the 2013 sheet tab to select it.
2. On the HOME tab, in the Cells group, click Format > Hide & Unhide > Hide Sheet.
3. Right-click the 2012 sheet tab, and click Hide.
4. On the HOME tab, click Format > Hide & Unhide > Unhide Sheet.
5. Select 2013 in the Unhide sheet list of the Unhide dialog box, and click OK.
6. Save the E19TryA_xx file, and leave it open to use in the next Try It.

Grouping Worksheets for Editing and Formatting

- If you want to work on several worksheets simultaneously, select multiple worksheets and create a **grouping**.
- Grouped sheet tabs appear white when selected, the name of the active sheet tab appears in bold, and [Group] appears in the title bar.
- To group adjacent sheets, click the first sheet tab and SHIFT + click on the last one. Or, CTRL + click to select nonadjacent sheets.
- When you select a grouping, any editing, formatting, or new entries you make to the active sheet are simultaneously made to all the sheets in the group.
- For example, you can select a group of sheets and format, move, copy, or delete them in one step. You can also add, delete, change, or format the same entries into the same cells on every selected worksheet.
- Remember to deselect the grouping when you no longer want to make changes to all the sheets in the group. Right-click one of the selected sheet tabs, and click Ungroup Sheets.

Try It! Grouping Worksheets for Editing and Formatting

1. In the **E19TryA_xx** file, click the 2014 sheet tab, and then SHIFT + click the 2013 sheet tab.
2. Select the range E5:H28.
3. On the HOME tab, click Clear (Clear ▾) > Clear Contents.
4. Select cell A2.
5. On the HOME tab, in the Styles group, click Accent2.
6. Right-click the 2014 sheet tab, and click Ungroup Sheets.
7. Click the 2013 sheet tab. The changes you made appear on this tab as well as the 2014 tab.
8. Save the **E19TryA_xx** file, and close it.

Creating a Summary Worksheet

- A formula on one worksheet can refer to cells in another worksheet in the same workbook file.

  ✓ *Formulas also can refer to cells in other workbook files.*

- As when using a named range for another sheet, a reference to a cell on another sheet includes the sheet name and an exclamation point, as in Income!E9.

  ✓ *Lesson 13 covered using named ranges.*

- You can type in references to cells on another sheet, or to save time, enter the reference by pointing (clicking the sheet tab and then clicking the cell to enter in the formula).

Try It! Creating a Summary Worksheet Using Reference Formulas

1. Start Excel, if necessary.
2. Open the **E19TryB** file from the data files for this lesson.
3. Save the workbook as **E19TryB_xx** in the location where your teacher instructs you to store the files for this lesson.
4. Click the Qtr 1 sheet tab, and then SHIFT +click the Summary sheet tab to group the sheets. (You are grouping the sheets to apply the header to all three sheets.)
5. Add a header that has your name at the left, the date code in the center, and the sheet name code at the right, and change back to Normal view.

(continued)

Try It! Creating a Summary Worksheet Using Reference Formulas *(continued)*

6. Right-click the Summary sheet tab, and click Ungroup Sheets.
7. Click cell B5 on the Summary sheet.
8. Type **=sum(**, click the Qtr 1 sheet tab, click cell B5 on that sheet, and type a **,** (comma).
9. Click the Qtr 2 sheet tab, click cell B5 on that sheet, press CTRL + ENTER.
10. Fill the formula down through cell B10.
11. Click cell C5 in the Summary sheet.
12. Type **=sum(**, click the Qtr 1 sheet tab, click cell D5 on that sheet, and type a **,** (comma).

    ✓ *If a Formula AutoComplete tip appears in the way, you can drag it to another location before clicking cell D5.*

13. Click the Qtr 2 sheet tab, click cell D5 on that sheet, and press CTRL + ENTER.

Formula referencing other sheets

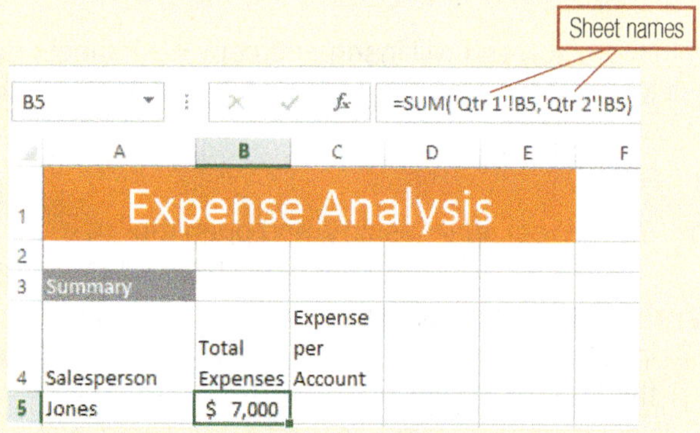

Excel 2013, Windows 8, Microsoft Corporation

14. Fill the formula down through cell C10, and apply the Currency with zero decimal place cell style to the selected range.
15. Save the **E19TryB_xx** file, and leave it open to use in the next Try It.

Updating a Summary Worksheet

- Formulas that summarize or perform calculations using data from other sheets work just like regular formulas.
- Just change entries on the referenced sheets as desired, and formulas on the summary sheet will recalculate results accordingly.

Try It! Updating a Summary Worksheet

1. In the **E19TryB_xx** file, review the data calculated on the Summary sheet. For example, the totals for Thomas are $13,198 and $3,300, respectively.
2. Click the Qtr 2 sheet tab.
3. Change the entries in the range B5:B10 to these values:

   4250
   3300
   4599
   6654
   4952
   7300

4. Click the Summary sheet tab, and review its data again. Now the totals for Thomas are $11,198 and $2,800.
5. Save the **E19TryB_xx** file, and close it.

Lesson 19—Practice

In this project, you will insert and copy worksheets, and color and rename tabs, using the skills you learned in this lesson.

DIRECTIONS

1. Start Excel, if necessary, and open the **E19Practice** file from the data files for this lesson.
2. Save the workbook as **E19Practice_xx** in the location where your teacher instructs you to store the files for this lesson.
3. Add a header that has your name at the left, the date code in the center, and the sheet name code at the right, and change back to **Normal** view.
4. Click the **Insert Worksheet** button to the right of the Monday sheet tab. A blank Sheet1 appears.
5. Right-click the tab for the new sheet, and click **Rename**. Type **Notes**, and press ENTER.
6. Right-click the **Monday** sheet tab, and click **Move or Copy**.
7. In the Move or Copy dialog box, click **(move to end)**, click the **Create a copy** check box to check it, and click **OK**.
8. Double-click the new sheet tab, type **Tuesday**, and press ENTER.
9. Right-click the new sheet tab, point to **Tab Color**, and click **Orange, Accent 2, Lighter 40%**.
10. Repeat steps 6 to 9 to create another copy of the Monday sheet, naming the copy **Wednesday** and assigning the **Green, Accent 6, Lighter 40%** color to the sheet tab.
11. Drag the **Notes** sheet tab to the far right of the other tabs, and reselect the **Monday** sheet. The tabs should now appear as shown in Figure 19-1.
12. **With your teacher's permission,** print the **Monday** worksheet. Submit the printout or the file for grading as required.
13. Save and close the file, and exit Excel.

Figure 19-1

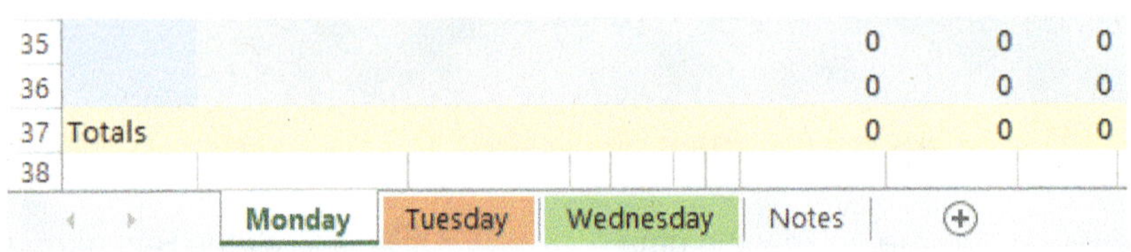

Excel 2013, Windows 8, Microsoft Corporation

Lesson 19—Apply

As the Manager of Spa Services at Serenity Health Club, you are reviewing the popularity of four services provided by a particular group of associates. You've developed a worksheet to total the invoiced amounts for these services on a daily basis. You've created the first day's sheet, and need to copy and update it for additional days of the week. You also want to create a summary worksheet.

DIRECTIONS

1. Start Excel, if necessary, and open the **E19Apply** file from the data files for this lesson.
2. Save the workbook as **E19Apply_xx** in the location where your teacher instructs you to store the files for this lesson.
3. On each sheet, add a header that has your name at the left, the date code in the center, and the sheet name code at the right, and change back to **Normal** view.
4. Group the **Monday**, **Tuesday**, **Wednesday**, and **Summary** sheets.

5. Increase the font size in cell **A3** to **14**.
6. Select **row 11**, wrap the text, apply bold, and align the text to the center.
7. Adjust column widths as needed.
8. Change the entry in cell **C7** to **65**.
9. Ungroup the sheets. Make sure that your changes have been applied to all four sheets.
10. In cell **C6** on the **Summary** sheet, enter a formula that averages cell C6 on the **Monday**, **Tuesday**, and **Wednesday** tabs, and press CTRL + ENTER. Your workbook should look like Figure 19-2.
11. **With your teacher's permission,** print one of the worksheets. Submit the printout or the file for grading as required.
12. Save and close the file, and exit Excel.

Figure 19-2

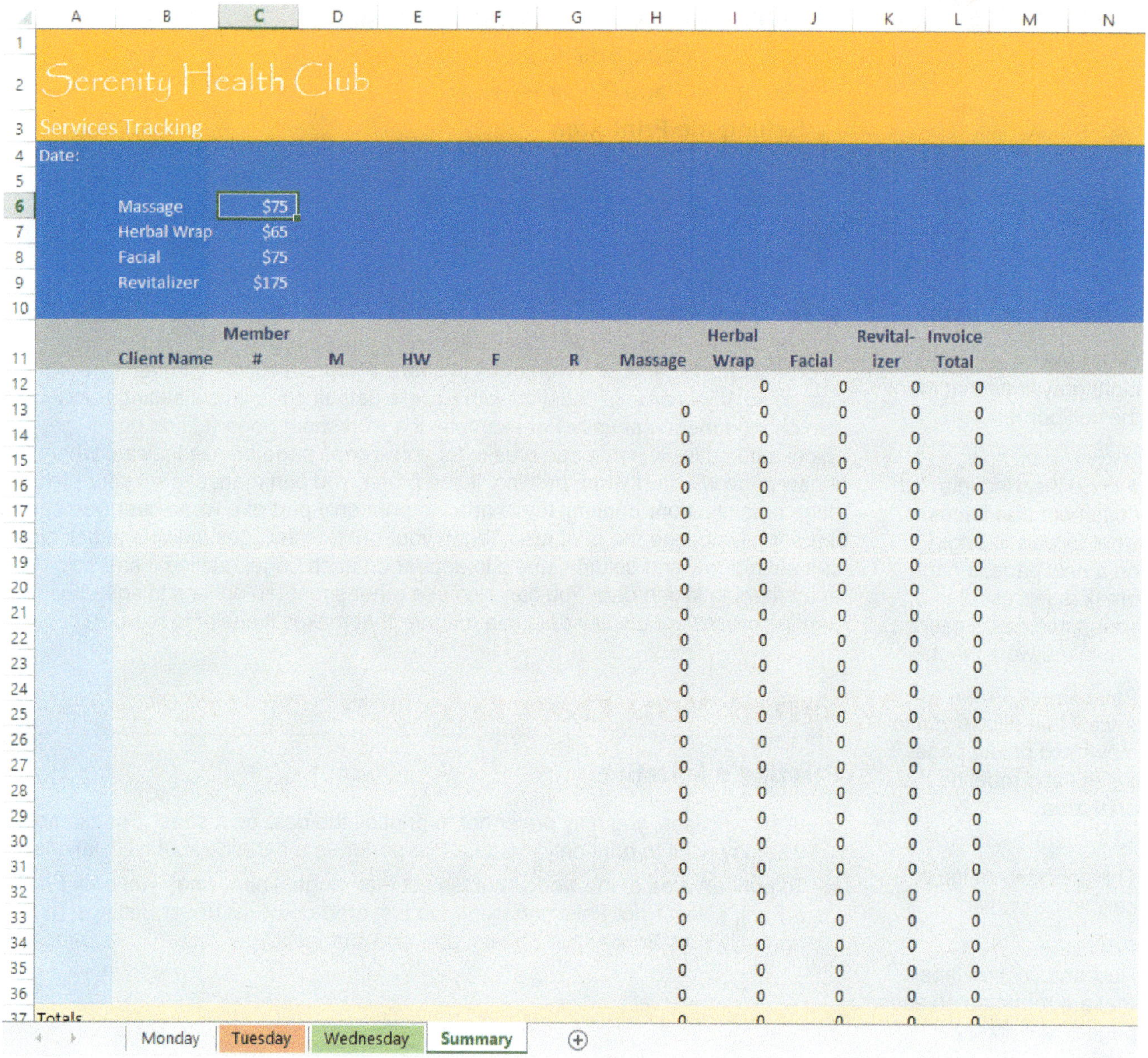

Excel 2013, Windows 8, Microsoft Corporation

Lesson 20

Modifying Print Options

➤ What You Will Learn

Printing a Selection
Printing All the Worksheets in a Workbook
Inserting Page Breaks
Using the Page Break Preview
Setting the Print Area
Repeating Row and Column Labels
Selecting Other Sheet Tab Options

WORDS TO KNOW

Gridlines
Light gray lines that mark the cell borders.

Page break
A code inserted in a document that forces what follows to begin on a new page; a page break is represented on your screen as a dashed line in the worksheet.

Page Break Preview
A view that allows you to move and delete page breaks and redefine the print area.

Print area
The specified range of cells to be printed.

Print titles
Row and column labels that are reprinted on each page of a worksheet printout.

Software Skills Excel gives you great flexibility in printing. If you need to print only part of a worksheet, you can select and print a specific area. Or, if you need to print all worksheets in a workbook to share comprehensive information, you can do so. If you are not satisfied with Excel's default page layout settings, you can change them manually. For example, if a worksheet doesn't fit on one page, Excel automatically sets page breaks for you. These page breaks indicate where a new page will start when printing. If you prefer, you can manually set your own page breaks before printing. If you need to print only part of a worksheet, you can temporarily change the print area. When your printout includes multiple pages, you can set the row and column labels to appear on each page, making it easier for you and others to locate data. You can also use other sheet tab options to speed up the printing process or display data in a manner that makes it easier to read.

What You Can Do

Printing a Selection

- In some cases, you may prefer not to print all the data on a sheet. For example, you may want to print only the data that performs a certain set of calculations.
- To print an area of the worksheet, select that range. Then, when you click FILE > Print, select Print Selection using the first drop-down list under Settings. (It normally says Print Active Sheets, until you change it.)

Try It! Printing a Selection

1. Start Excel.
2. Open the **E20Try** file from the data files for this lesson.
3. Save the workbook as **ETry20_xx** in the location where your teacher instructs you to store the files for this lesson.
4. Add a header that has your name at the left, the date code in the center, and the sheet name code at the right, and change back to Normal view.
5. Select the range A8:C9.
6. Click FILE > Print.
7. Click the top option under Settings, which initially reads Print Active Sheets, and click Print Selection on the menu. The Preview immediately shows you that only the selection will print. You could then click the Print button to send it to the printer.
8. Click Save to save your changes to the file, and return to the HOME tab.
9. Leave the **ETry20_xx** file open to use in the next Try It.

Printing a worksheet selection.

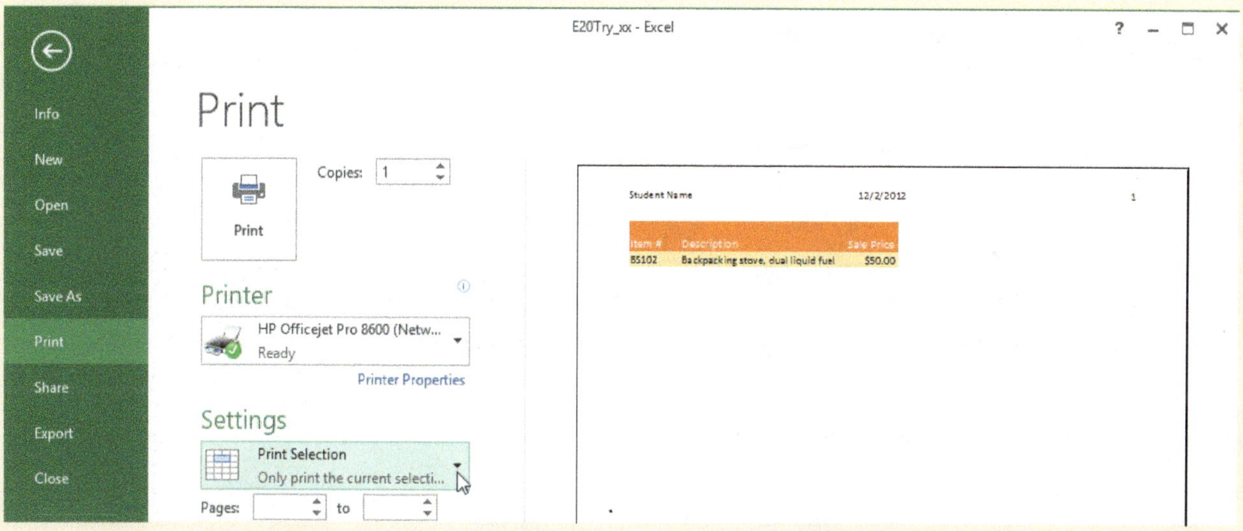

Excel 2013, Windows 8, Microsoft Corporation

Printing All the Worksheets in a Workbook

- Workbooks with multiple sheets of data often contain information that needs to be shared with others for making business decisions.
- Excel enables you to print all the sheets in a workbook file in a single print operation, to save you the trouble of printing each sheet individually.
- Click FILE > Print, select Print Entire Workbook using the first drop-down list under Settings. (It normally says Print Active Sheets, until you change it.)

Try It! Printing All the Worksheets in a Workbook

1. In the ETry20_xx file, click FILE > Print.
2. Click the top option under Settings, which by default reads Print Active Sheets but in this instance will read Print Selection due to the last Try It, and click Print Entire Workbook on the menu.
3. Use the Next button below the preview to view the print preview of all four sheets. Notice that the page breaks need to be adjusted.
4. Save the ETry20_xx file, and leave it open to use in the next Try It.

Inserting Page Breaks

- When worksheet data will not fit on one page, Excel inserts automatic **page breaks** based on the paper size, margins, and scaling options.
- Automatic page breaks appear as dashed lines on the worksheet.

  ✓ *Page breaks appear on the worksheet after you adjust Page Setup options, preview the worksheet, or print it.*

- If you prefer, you can override automatic page breaks and set manual page breaks before printing.
- While automatic page breaks (those created by Excel, based on your page setup options) appear as dashed lines, manual page breaks (those you create by either moving the automatic page breaks, or inserting new ones) display on the worksheet as solid lines.

Try It! Setting Manual Page Breaks

1. In the ETry20_xx file, click cell A30.

   ✓ *Unless you click in row 1, a horizontal page break will be inserted above the cell you click.*

   ✓ *Unless you click in column A, a vertical page break will be inserted to the left of the cell you click.*

2. On the PAGE LAYOUT tab, click the Breaks button.
3. Click Insert Page Break.

   ✓ *Automatic page breaks that follow a manual page break will adjust automatically.*

4. Save the changes to the ETry20_xx file, and leave it open to use in the next Try It.

Viewing page breaks in Normal view

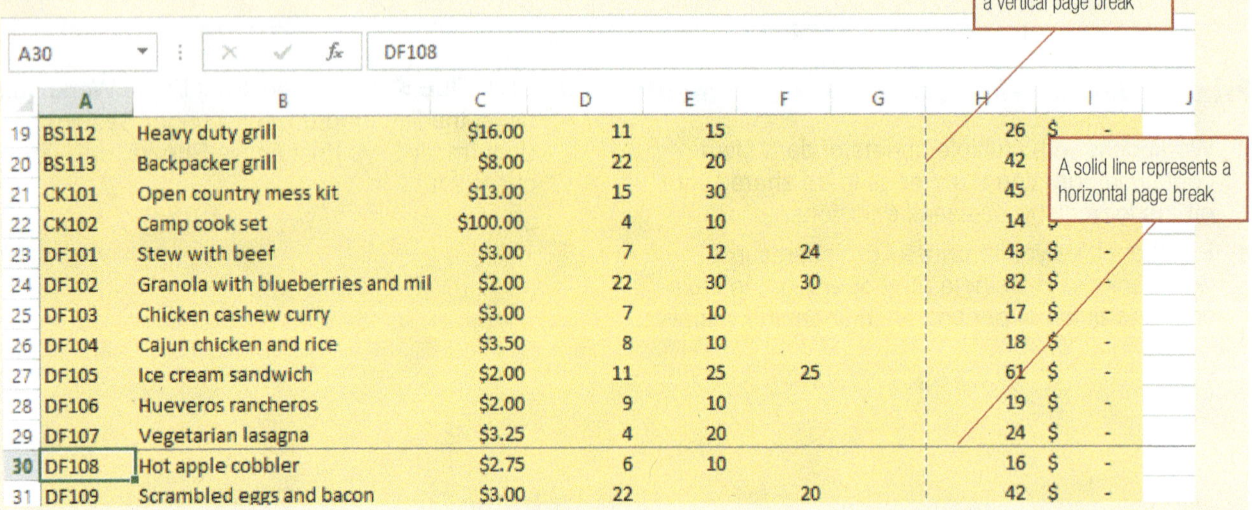

Excel 2013, Windows 8, Microsoft Corporation

Using Page Break Preview

- **Page Break Preview** is a special view that displays both automatic and manual page breaks, and allows you to adjust them.
- You can change to Page Break Preview using the Page Break Preview button on the VIEW tab of the Ribbon or the Page Break Preview button on the Status bar.

✓ *You can also see where page breaks occur in Normal and Page Layout views.*

- When you display a worksheet in Page Break Preview, lines appear, subdividing the worksheet into sections.
  - Each section represents a different print page.
  - Each section is marked in the center with a large page number displayed in light gray.
  - You can change the page breaks by dragging these lines.
- In Page Break Preview, when you drag a dashed line (automatic page break) to move it, it changes to a solid line (manual page break).
- In Page Break Preview, drag a dashed line off the worksheet to remove the page break and reset the page breaks.
  - Page breaks can be inserted and removed in any view, by clicking the cell located below or to the right of the page break and using the Breaks button in the Page Setup group on the PAGE LAYOUT tab on the Ribbon
- You can also edit worksheet data and resize the print area from Page Break Preview.
  - The Print Area button in the Page Setup group on the PAGE LAYOUT tab also lets you adjust the print area.
- If you adjust a page break to include a few more columns or rows on a page, Excel automatically adjusts the scale (font size) to make that data fit on the page.
- You can also use Page Break Preview to adjust how embedded charts print.

✓ *Embedded charts and other objects cover page breaks, so sometimes it can be difficult to see that a chart spans two pages.*

Try It! Changing Page Breaks Using Page Break Preview

1. In the ETry20_xx file, click the VIEW tab, then click the Page Break Preview button.

   OR

   Click the Page Break Preview button on the Status bar.

Page breaks viewed in Page Break Preview

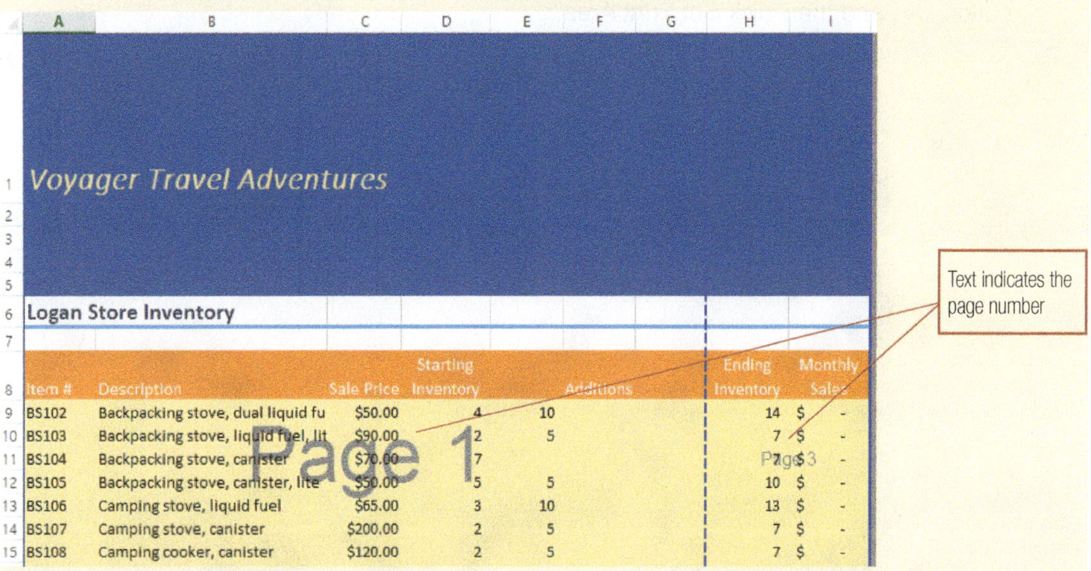

Excel 2013, Windows 8, Microsoft Corporation

(continued)

Try It! Changing Page Breaks Using Page Break Preview *(continued)*

2. Drag the dashed line between column G and H to the right margin of column I.
   - ✓ *The automatic page break dashed line changes to a solid line.*
   - ✓ *When a manual page break is moved outside of the print area, the automatic page break is restored.*
3. Drag the solid blue line between column I and J to the right margin off the worksheet.
4. Save the changes to the ETry20_xx file, and leave it open to use in the next Try It.

Setting the Print Area

- To print only a selected area of data on a worksheet, adjust the **print area**.
- You can set the print area using Page Break Preview, the Print Area button on the PAGE LAYOUT tab of the Ribbon, or the Page Setup dialog box.
- In Normal view, the print area appears on the worksheet with a dashed border.
- In Page Break Preview, the print area appears in full color, while data outside the area to be printed appears on a gray background.
- You can define a unique print area for each worksheet in your workbook.
- You can set multiple print areas by first setting one print area, selecting the second print area, clicking the Print Area button on the PAGE LAYOUT tab, and select Add to Print Area.
- To print the entire worksheet again, you must either clear the print area setting or reset the print area to include all the data.

Try It! Setting the Print Area

1. In the ETry20_xx file, switch to Page Break Preview, if necessary.
2. Select A1:I20 as the range to print.
3. On the PAGE LAYOUT tab, click the Print Area button, and then click Set Print Area.
4. On the PAGE LAYOUT tab, click the Print Area button > Clear Print Area.
5. Save the changes to the ETry20_xx file, and leave it open to use in the next Try It.

Setting the print area

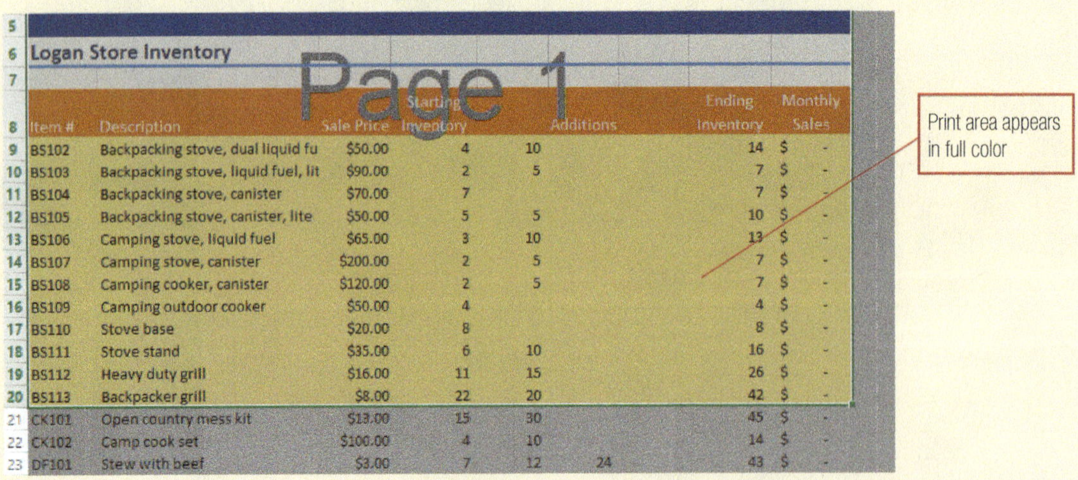

Repeating Row and Column Labels

- Using the Sheet tab of the Page Setup dialog box, you can select to reprint the **print titles** on each page of a worksheet printout.
- You can also use the Print Titles button in the Page Setup group on the PAGE LAYOUT tab to add print titles.
- Without the row and column labels printed on each page, it might be difficult to decipher your data.

Try It! Repeating Row and Column Labels

1. In the ETry20_xx file, click the PAGE LAYOUT tab, then click the Print Titles button .
2. On the Sheet tab, click the Collapse Dialog box button on the Rows to repeat at top box.
3. Select rows 1 through 8.
4. Click the Expand Dialog box button .
5. In the Columns to repeat at left, type **$A:$C**.
6. Click OK.
7. Save the changes to the ETry20_xx file, and leave it open to use in the next Try It.

The Sheet tab in the Page Setup dialog box

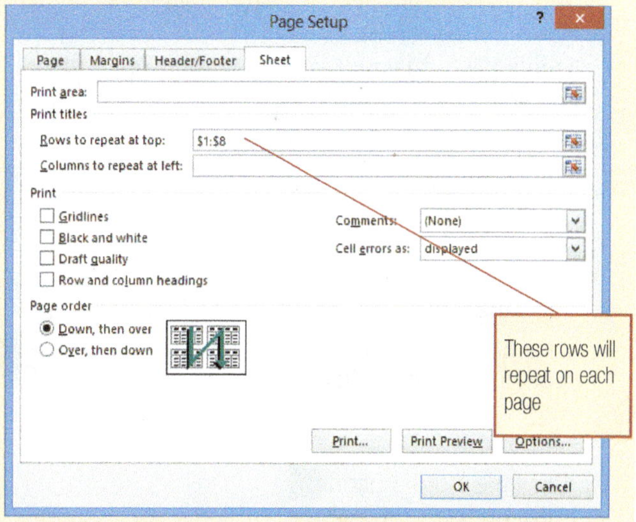

Excel 2013, Windows 8, Microsoft Corporation

Selecting Other Sheet Tab Options

- The Sheet tab of the Page Setup dialog box provides an option for printing **gridlines** with your data.
  - You can also choose to print gridlines using the Gridlines Print option on the PAGE LAYOUT tab of the Ribbon.
- You can print your worksheet in black and white (even if it includes color fills or graphics), in draft mode (faster printing, lower quality), with your comments, and with errors displayed.
- For large worksheets, you can specify the page order (the order in which data is selected to be printed on subsequent pages).
- You can add gridlines to your printouts to make your data more readable.

Try It! Selecting Sheet Tab Options

1. In the ETry20_xx file, click the PAGE LAYOUT tab, if necessary.
2. Click the Page Setup dialog box launcher .
3. In the Page Setup dialog box, click the Sheet tab.
4. In the Print section, click Draft quality.
5. In the Print section, click Gridlines.
6. Click OK.
7. Save the changes to the ETry20_xx file, and close it.

Lesson 20—Practice

In this project, you will set page breaks before printing, change the print area, use other sheet tab options, and print a worksheet using the skills you learned in this lesson.

DIRECTIONS

1. Start Excel, if necessary, and open the **E20Practice** file from the data files for this lesson.
2. Save the workbook as **E20Practice_xx** in the location where your teacher instructs you to store the files for this lesson.
3. Add a header that has your name at the left, the date code in the center, and the sheet name code at the right, and change back to **Normal** view.
4. Click **FILE** > **Print**. A preview of the worksheet appears in the preview pane.
5. Click the **Next Page** button at the bottom of the preview pane to move through the entire printout. Notice that the worksheet is set to print on four pages, but the chart is split up and impossible to interpret.
6. Click the **Back** button.
7. Click the **PAGE LAYOUT** tab. Notice the page breaks indicated by the dashed lines.
8. On the PAGE LAYOUT tab, click the **Orientation** button and select **Landscape**.
9. Click **FILE** > **Print**. Notice the changes to the preview.
10. Click the **Back** button.
11. On the **VIEW** tab, click the **Page Break Preview** button. The worksheet appears in Page Break Preview.
12. Drag the automatic page break located between columns G and H to the right of column K of the worksheet data on page 1.
13. Drag the automatic page break located below row 54 up to the bottom of row 37. Your worksheet should look like Figure 20-1 on the next page.
14. On the PAGE LAYOUT tab, click the Page Setup dialog box launcher.
15. In the Page Setup dialog box, click the **Sheet** tab and select **Draft Quality** in the Print area. Click **Print** to view the preview.
16. **With your teacher's permission**, print the worksheet in draft quality. Submit the printout or the file for grading as required.
17. Save and close the file, and exit Excel.

Figure 20-1

Student Name 12/14/2015 1

HelpNow
Medical Center 2017

Current ratio:	0.950
Quick ratio:	0.922

Current Assets					
Cash and cash equivalents	$	8,755			
Accounts receivable	$	28,957			
Accounts receivable (past due)	$	1,897			
Short-term investments	$	32,750			
Long-term investments	$	256,987			
Inventory	$	11,265			
Income taxes collected (not due)	$	41,859			
Total Current Assets			$	382,470	
Fixed Assets					
Land	$	32,185			
Land improvements	$	11,250			
Buildings (at cost)	$	285,975			
Building improvements	$	112,958			
Equipment (at cost)	$	1,452,375			
Total property, building, and equipment			$	1,894,743	
Less depreciation			$	29,785	
Property, buildings, and equipment (net)			$	1,864,958	
Prepaid expenses	$	25,789			
Other assets	$	118,956			
Total Fixed Assets			$	2,009,703	
Total Assets					$ 2,392,173

Current Liabilities					
Notes payable	$	9,785			
Accounts payable (current)	$	3,128			
Accounts payable (past due)	$	-			
Current portion long-term debt	$	21,875			
Accrued retirement contributions	$	297,551			
Other current liabilities	$	16,145			
Interest payable	$	54,019			
Total Current Liabilities			$	402,503	
Income Taxes					
Federal tax (current)	$	88,175.00			
State tax (current)	$	31,064.00			
Total Income Taxes			$	119,239	
Long-Term Liabilities					
Mortgage debt due after 1 year	$	402,875			
Equipment debt due after 1 year	$	1,287,556			
Long-term Liabilities			$	1,690,431	
Net Worth					
Orlinda Marquez, M.D.	$	45,000			
Michael Lombardi, Ph.D.	$	45,000			
Gwendolyn Green, M.D.	$	30,000			
Jane Medura, M.D.	$	30,000			
Azade Yedding, M.D.	$	30,000			
Total Net Worth			$	180,000	
Total Liabilities and Net Worth					$ 2,392,173

Excel 2013, Windows 8, Microsoft Corporation

Lesson 20—Apply

As the new franchise director at HelpNow Medical Center, you've spent a lot of time creating reports that describe your company's fiscal strength. The balance sheet is ready for printing, but you want to add a repeating row and column label and modify the print settings so it will print exactly as you want.

DIRECTIONS

1. Start Excel, if necessary, and open the **E20Apply** file from the data files for this lesson.
2. Save the workbook as **E20Apply_xx** in the location where your teacher instructs you to store the files for this lesson.
3. Add a header that has your name at the left, the date code in the center, and the sheet name code at the right, and change back to **Normal** view.
4. Click **PAGE LAYOUT** > **Print Titles**.
5. Set the cell range **A1:B9** as the repeating row (print title) for this worksheet.
6. Change the sheet print setting to **Draft quality**.
7. Create two print areas (**A1:K37** and **A39:K71**). Refer to Figures 20-2 and 20-3.

   ✓ *Hint: Set one print area and then select the second print area. When you click the Print Area button on the Page Layout tab, select Add to Print Area.*

8. Display the worksheet in Print Preview.

   ✓ *Because you selected two different ranges for the print area, they print on separate pages.*

9. **With your teacher's permission**, print the worksheet. Submit the printout or the file for grading as required.
10. Save and close the file, and exit Excel.

Figure 20-2

Excel 2013, Windows 8, Microsoft Corporation

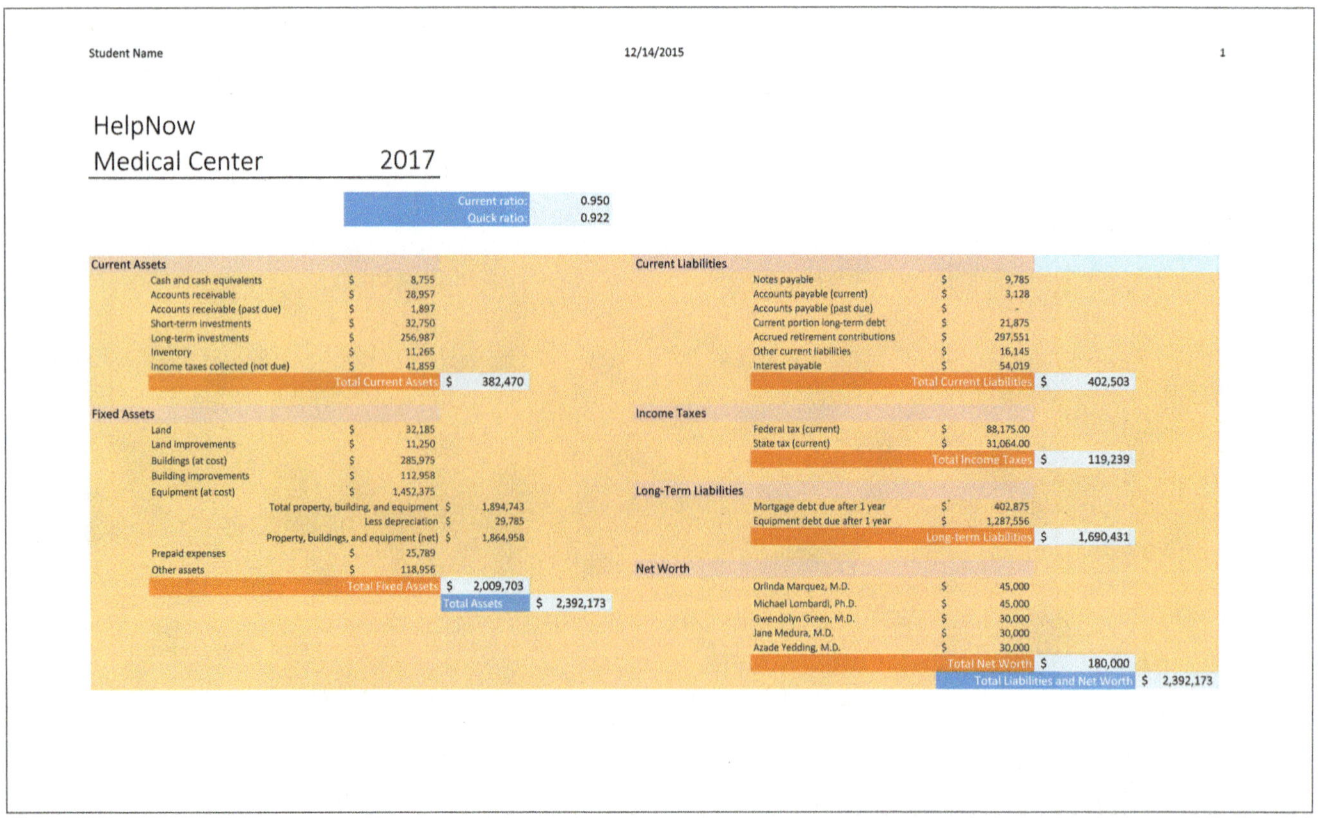

Figure 20-3

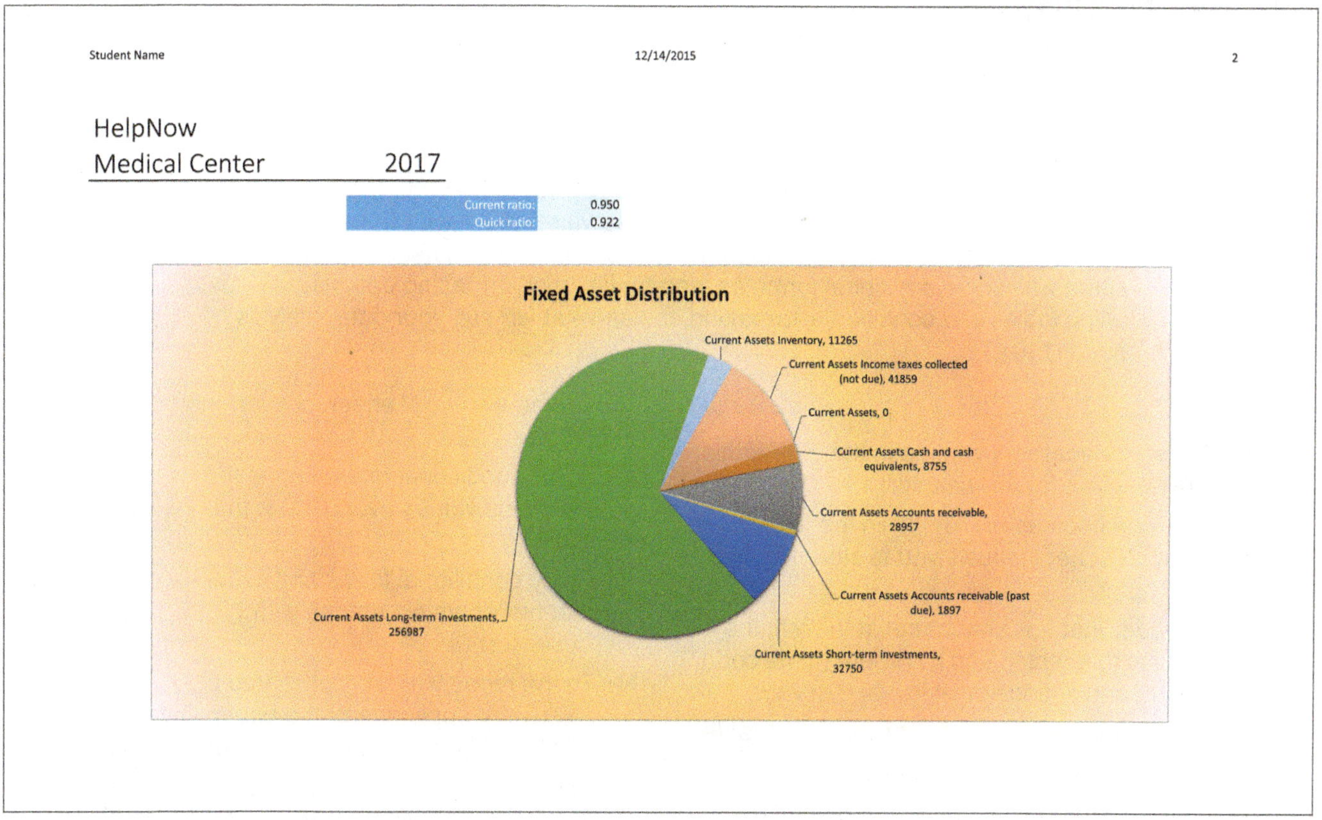

Excel 2013, Windows 8, Microsoft Corporation

End-of-Chapter Activities

➤ Excel Chapter 2—Critical Thinking

Client Activity Worksheet

You have a business called Fry Landscape Services. You have created a worksheet to record and evaluate monthly client activity. You need to complete the sheet with some additional formulas, and try different formatting options, such as using tables and conditional formatting, to see what will suit your data analysis needs best.

DIRECTIONS

1. Start Excel, if necessary, and open the **ECT02** file from the data files for this chapter.
2. Save the workbook as **ECT02_xx** in the location where your teacher instructs you to store the files for this chapter.
3. Add a header that has your name at the left, the date code in the center, and the sheet name code at the right, and change back to **Normal** view.
4. Select the range **A4:D32**, and convert it to a table.
5. Apply the **Table Style Light 20** table style.
6. Add a total row, and adjust it so a *Sum total* displays for the **Fee** column only.
7. In cell **G5**, enter a formula that sums only the fees that have been paid.
8. In the range **G7:G10**, enter formulas that sum only the fees paid for each type of service.
9. Rename **Sheet1** to **Version1**.
10. Copy the **Version1** sheet, naming the copy **Version2** and placing it after the copied sheet.
11. On the **Version2** sheet, convert the table back to a range.
12. Apply conditional formatting to the **Fee** column that highlights values over $100 with a **Yellow Fill with Dark Yellow Text**.
13. Apply conditional formatting to the Paid column that highlights *No* entries with **Light Red Fill with Dark Red Text**.
14. To the range with the calculated paid values **(G7:G10)**, apply one of the Green Data Bar conditional formats (either gradient or solid).
15. In both sheets, replace the Customer name *Tayson* with **Tyler**. Your sheet should resemble Illustration 2A on the next page.
16. Set **row 4** as the print titles on both sheets.
17. **With your teacher's permission,** print the workbook. Submit the printouts or the file for grading as required.
18. Save and close the file, and exit Excel.

Illustration 2A

	A	B	C	D	E	F	G	H
1	Fry Landscape Services							
2	**Client Activity**							
3								
4	**Customer**	**Service**	**Fee**	**Paid**				
5	Hoover	Mowing	$ 75	Yes		Amount Collected	$ 1,995	
6	Jackson	Trimming	$ 60	Yes				
7	Tyler	Mowing	$ 75	Yes		Aeration Paid	$ 500	
8	Renfro	Mowing	$ 100	No		Mowing Paid	$ 800	
9	Allen	Aeration	$ 100	Yes		Other Paid	$ 575	
10	Friend	Other	$ 65	Yes		Trimming Paid	$ 120	
11	Keeger	Mowing	$ 50	Yes				
12	Tyler	Other	$ 85	Yes				
13	Hoover	Other	$ 150	No				
14	Poland	Mowing	$ 75	Yes				
15	Manders	Other	$ 125	Yes				
16	Nodine	Mowing	$ 100	No				
17	Welty	Aeration	$ 100	Yes				
18	Tyler	Mowing	$ 50	Yes				
19	Guertler	Aeration	$ 100	Yes				
20	Fanson	Mowing	$ 100	No				
21	Molton	Mowing	$ 200	Yes				
22	Davis	Other	$ 100	Yes				
23	Fiver	Trimming	$ 50	No				
24	Olson	Mowing	$ 75	Yes				
25	Erland	Mowing	$ 100	No				
26	Walton	Aeration	$ 100	Yes				
27	Stilson	Trimming	$ 60	Yes				
28	Reece	Mowing	$ 125	Yes				
29	Anders	Other	$ 200	Yes				
30	Tyler	Aeration	$ 100	Yes				
31	Branson	Mowing	$ 75	Yes				
32	Carson	Other	$ 275	No				
33	**Total**		**$ 2,870**					
34								

➤ Excel Chapter 2—Portfolio Builder

Fundraising Worksheet

You are the Executive Director of Crossmont Services, a nonprofit organization that provides food assistance to needy families in Crossmont County. Your organization is holding a ball as a fundraiser. You created a budget for the ball and just entered actual information after the event. Now you need to evaluate the actual information to see if the event was a financial success. You will work with a summary worksheet and use formatting to help identify trouble spots so you can plan the event more effectively next year.

DIRECTIONS

1. Start Excel, if necessary, and open the **EPB02** file from the data files for this chapter.
2. Save the workbook as **EPB02_xx** in the location where your teacher instructs you to store the files for this chapter.
3. Group **Sheet1** through **Sheet3**.
4. Add a header that has your name at the left, the sheet name code in the center, and the page number code at the right, and change back to **Normal** view.
5. Format cell **A1** with the **Title** cell style.
6. Format range **A2:E2** with the **Heading 3** cell style.
7. Format the range **A4:E4** with the **Heading 3** cell style, and rotate it using the **Angle Counterclockwise** setting.
8. In cell **D2**, enter the date and time using the **NOW** function.
9. Adjust column widths as needed, and then ungroup the worksheets.
10. Rename the sheets as follows:
    Sheet1 **Expenses**
    Sheet2 **Income**
    Sheet3 **Summary**
11. On the **Expenses** sheet, select the range **C5:C13**. Review the AutoCalculate results on the status bar.
12. In cells **B14** and **C14** of the **Expenses** sheet, enter formulas using the SUM function to calculate the values above. Adjust column widths, as necessary.
13. In cells **B9** and **C9** of the **Income** sheet, enter formulas using the SUM function to calculate the values above. Adjust column widths, as necessary.
14. In cells **B5:C5** of the **Summary** sheet, enter formulas that summarize the applicable data from the other two sheets.

    ✓ *Hint: Subtract the Expenses from the Income.*
15. On the **Income** sheet, change the actual ticket sales value to **53500**.
16. Return to the **Summary** sheet to review the recalculated results. Review the revised results, which appear in Illustration 2B.
17. **With your teacher's permission,** print all worksheets in the workbook in one print operation. Submit the printouts or the file for grading as required.
18. Save and close the file, and exit Excel.

Illustration 2B

	A	B	C	D	E	F
1	Crossmont Services					
2	Fundraising Ball Budget			12/14/2015 9:35		
3						
4		Estimated	Actual	Difference $	Difference %	
5	Event Profit	$ 52,200	$53,275	$ 1,075	2.06%	
6						

Excel 2013, Windows 8, Microsoft Corporation

Chapter 3

(Courtesy Chad McDermott/Shutterstock)

Charting Data

Lesson 21
Building Basic Charts

- Understanding Chart Basics
- Selecting Chart Data
- Reviewing Chart Elements
- Creating a Chart
- Using Recommended Charts
- Changing Chart Types
- Selecting a Chart
- Resizing, Copying, Moving, or Deleting a Chart

Lesson 22
Showing Percentages with a Pie Chart

- Calculating Percentages
- Creating a Pie Chart on a Chart Sheet

Lesson 23
Enhancing a Pie Chart

- Applying 3-D to a Pie Chart
- Rotating Slices in a Pie Chart
- Exploding and Coloring a Pie Chart
- Formatting the Chart Area of a Pie Chart

Lesson 24
Adding Special Elements to a Chart or Sheet and Updating a Chart

- Inserting a Text Box in a Chart
- Using WordArt in a Worksheet
- Updating a Chart

Lesson 25
Completing Chart Formatting

- Changing Data Series Orientation
- Formatting a Chart
- Formatting a Chart Element
- Changing Chart Text
- Enhancing the Chart Plot Area
- Formatting Category and Value Axes

Lesson 26
Comparing and Analyzing Data

- Using Parentheses in a Formula
- Calculating a Value After an Increase
- Performing What-If Analysis
- Creating a Line Chart to Compare Data

Lesson 27
Chart Printing and Publishing

- Printing a Chart
- Preparing and Printing a Chart Sheet
- Publishing a Chart to the Internet/Intranet

Lesson 28
Using Charts in Other Files

- Pasting a Picture of a Chart
- Embedding a Chart in a Word Document
- Linking a Chart
- Editing a Linked or Embedded Chart

Lesson 29
Making Special Purpose Charts

- Creating Organization Charts
- Creating Other SmartArt Diagrams

End-of-Chapter Activities

Lesson 21

Building Basic Charts

➤ What You Will Learn

Understanding Chart Basics
Selecting Chart Data
Reviewing Chart Elements
Creating a Chart
Using Recommended Charts
Changing Chart Types
Selecting a Chart
Resizing, Copying, Moving, or Deleting a Chart

Software Skills A chart presents Excel data in a graphical format—making the relationship between data items easier to understand. To present your data in the best format, you must select the proper chart type. For example, if you wanted to highlight your department's recent reduction in overtime, you might use a column or bar chart. Or, to compare your division's sales to those of other divisions, you might use a pie chart.

WORDS TO KNOW

Categories
In most cases, each column of charted worksheet data contains a category. Selecting multiple rows of chart data creates multiple categories. The chart displays categories along the horizontal axis.

Chart
A graphic that compares and contrasts worksheet data in a visual format. A chart is also known as a graph.

Chart sheet
A chart that occupies its own worksheet.

Column chart
The default chart type that displays each data point as a vertical column.

Data marker
The shape—bar, column, line, pie slice, and so on—representing each data point of a chart.

What You Can Do

Understanding Chart Basics

- **Charts** provide a way of presenting and comparing data in a graphical format.
- You can create **embedded charts** or **chart sheets**.
- When you create an embedded chart, the chart exists as an object in the worksheet alongside the data.
- When you create a chart sheet, the chart exists on a separate sheet in the workbook.
- All charts are linked to the charted data, which appears in the **plot area**. (The plot area is contained within the overall chart area.) When you change worksheet data linked to the charted **data points**, the **data markers** in the chart plot area change automatically.

Selecting Chart Data

- To create a chart, you first select the data to plot.
- The selection should not contain blank columns or rows.
- If the data is not in a single range, press CTRL and select each range separately, making sure not to select blank rows or columns that may separate the ranges.
- You can select multiple ranges to plot on a single chart.
- You can hide columns or rows you do not wish to chart.

✓ *The selection should include the labels for the data when possible.*

- A blank cell in the upper-left corner of a selection tells Excel that the data below and to the right of the blank cell contains labels for the values to plot.
- Excel assumes each row includes a series. However, you may change the orientation as desired.

Reviewing Chart Elements

- As you move the mouse pointer over a chart, the name of the chart element appears in a ScreenTip.
- A chart or **infographic** may include some or all of the parts shown in Figure 21-1.
- In this example, each community is a **data series** listed on its own row in the worksheet. On the chart, each data series is represented on the chart by a different data marker—columns in the example.
- The **legend** at the right is a key that identifies the series by name.
- Each kind of data for each item is a data point. For each series in the example there are three data points—Planned, Started, and Completed—as noted on the **horizontal axis** (X axis). These are the **categories** of data.

Excel 2013, Windows 8, Microsoft Corporation

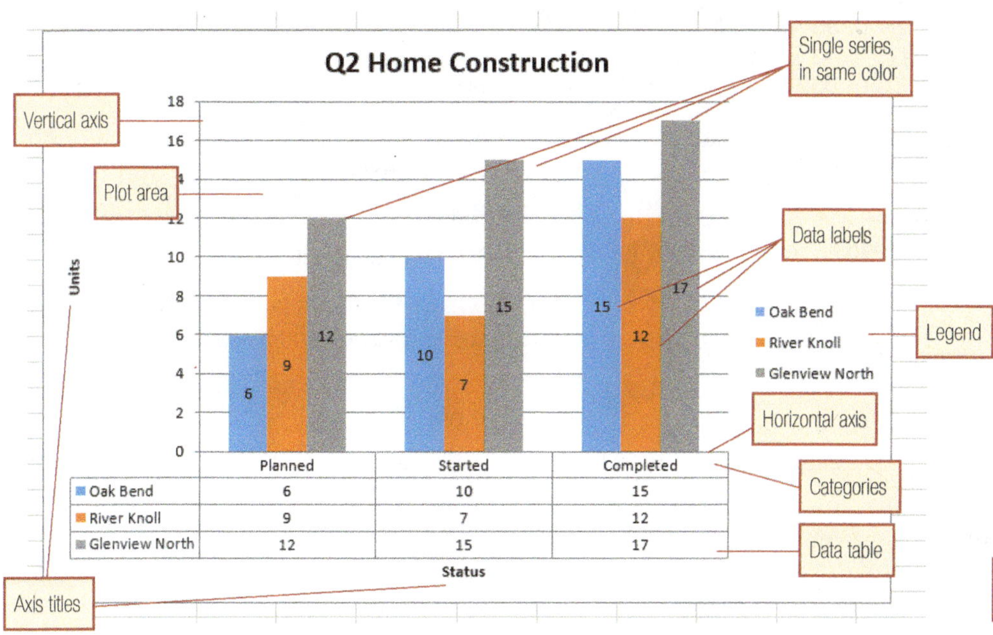

Figure 21-1

Data points
The specific values plotted on a chart.

Data series
A set of related data points to be charted. In most cases, each row of charted worksheet data holds a data series. Selecting multiple columns of data for a chart creates multiple data series. The chart presents each data series in its own color bar, line, or column.

Embedded chart
A chart placed as an object within a worksheet.

Horizontal axis
The horizontal scale of a chart on which categories are plotted, sometimes called the X axis.

Infographic
An information graphic that visually depicts basic or complex data.

Legend
A key that identifies each of the data series in a chart.

Plot area
The area that holds the data points on a chart.

Vertical axis
The vertical scale of a chart on which the values from each category is plotted, sometimes called the Y axis.

- If desired, you can identify each specific data point by displaying data labels. These labels appear on or near the data markers.
- For charts that use axes (generally all charts except pie charts and some 3-D charts), the **vertical axis** or Y axis provides the scale for the values being charted.

  ✓ *For bar charts the axes are reversed. The vertical axis charts categories and the horizontal axis charts values.*

  ✓ *3-D charts typically have a third axis representing the amount of 3-D rotation.*

- The horizontal axis title describes the categories data. (Status in the example.)
- The vertical axis title describes the types of values being plotted. (Units in the example.)
- The chart title identifies the chart overall and axis titles describe the axes. You have to add these titles when you want them to appear.
- So a user can easily view the data that's plotted on the chart, you can add a data table below the chart.
- The data table looks like a small worksheet, and it lists the data used to create the chart.
- You can view chart options using the three buttons that appear in the upper right corner next to the selected chart: Chart Elements, Chart Styles, and Chart Filters.

  ✓ *The Chart Elements, Chart Styles, and Chart Filters buttons provide a limited selection of the most commonly used formatting choices.*

- You can use the Chart Elements button to select the chart elements you want to display. The chart elements available will vary depending on the type of chart you select.

  ✓ *You will learn about Chart Styles and Chart Filters in Lesson 25.*

Try It! Reviewing Chart Elements

1. Start Excel.
2. Open the **E21Try** file from the data files for this lesson.
3. Save the file as **E21Try_xx** in the location where your teacher instructs you to store the files for this lesson.
4. Add a header that has your name at the left, the date code in the center, and the page number code at the right, and change back to Normal view.
5. On the Example sheet, scroll down until you can see the entire chart.
6. Move the mouse pointer over the title at the top of the chart. A ScreenTip that reads *Chart Title* appears.
7. Using Figure 21-1 as a guide, move the mouse pointer over these areas of the chart to view the ScreenTips, verifying that you've identified the correct parts of the chart:
   - Legend
   - Any data marker for the Oak Bend series
   - Any data marker for the River Knoll series
   - Any data marker for the Glenview North series
   - Plot area
   - Vertical axis
   - Title for each axis
   - Data table
8. Click the chart to select it.
9. Click the Chart Elements button + to the right of the chart and review the available elements.
10. Save the **E21Try_xx** file, and leave it open to use in the next Try It.

Creating a Chart

- The first step to creating a chart is selecting the data to chart on the worksheet, as discussed earlier in the lesson.
- Create charts using the buttons in the Charts group on the INSERT tab.
- The buttons in the group enable you to create each type of chart: Column; Bar; Stock, Surface or Radar; Line; Area; Combo; Pie or Doughnut; and Scatter or Bubble charts.
- Each chart type contains chart subtypes, which are variations on the selected chart type.
- After selecting data to chart—including labels for the data—press ALT + F1 to insert an embedded default column chart on the worksheet.

✓ *After selecting the data to chart, pressing the F11 key will create a column chart on its own **chart sheet**.*

✓ *Lesson 25 explains how to use the Chart Tools contextual tabs to work with elements, such as adding chart text.*

- You can also insert an embedded default **column chart** by selecting the data and using the CHARTS feature in the Quick Analysis tool that appears in the lower right of your selection.
- The theme applied to the workbook file determines the chart's color scheme.

Try It! Creating a Chart

1. In the **E21Try_xx** file, select the Practice sheet.
2. Add a header that has your name at the left, the date code in the center, and the page number code at the right, and then change back to Normal view.
3. Drag over the range A5:D8 to select it.
4. On the INSERT tab, click the Insert Bar Chart button, and click 3-D Clustered Bar in the 3-D Bar group.
5. Drag the new chart so that its upper-left corner is over cell F2. Notice how the charted data is selected in the worksheet.
6. Leave the data selected, and press ALT + F1. A default column chart appears.

   OR

   With the data selected, click the Quick Analysis tool that appears in the lower right of your selection, click CHARTS, and click the first Clustered Column.
7. Drag the new chart so that its upper-left corner is over cell F18. Compare how the different chart types present the same data.
8. Save the **E21Try_xx** file, and leave it open to use in the next Try It.

A new bar chart

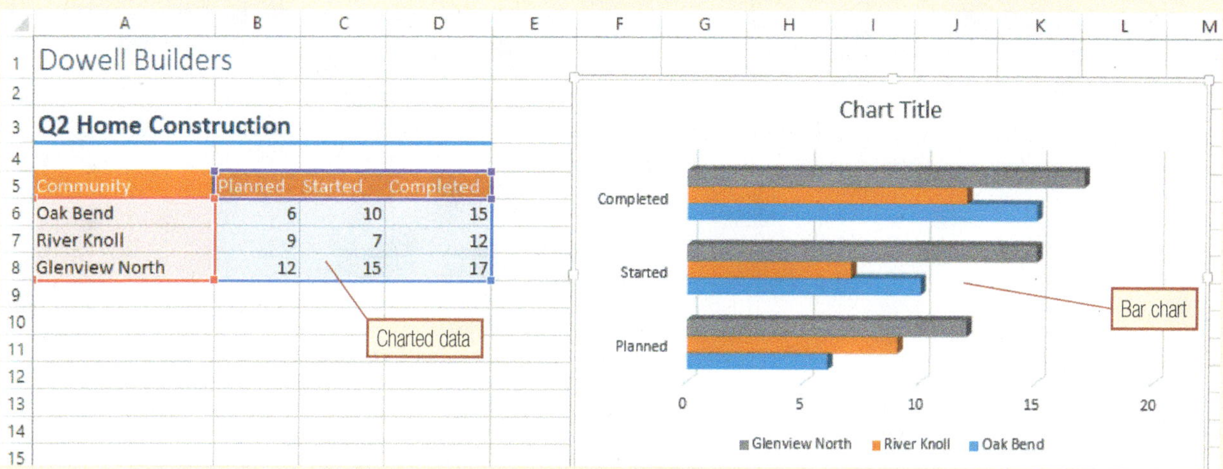

Excel 2013, Windows 8, Microsoft Corporation

Using Recommended Charts

- Excel's Recommended Charts feature examines your data and provides recommended chart types based on the type of your data.
- When you select your data, the Quick Analysis tool appears in the lower-right corner next to the chart.
- You can click the Quick Analysis tool, and then select CHARTS to view and preview the recommended charts.
- You can also access Recommended Charts by clicking on the INSERT tab, and clicking the Recommended Charts button.
- Use the More Charts button if you want to view additional recommended charts. The Insert Charts dialog box will open.

✓ *You can also access More Charts in the Charts group on the INSERT tab.*

Try It! Using Recommended Charts

1. In the **E21Try_xx** file, drag over the range A5:D8 to select it again.
2. At the bottom right of the data, click the Quick Analysis tool.
3. Click CHARTS, and click the first Stacked Column chart. Notice that the Community names are the horizontal axis labels.
4. Drag the new chart so that its upper-left corner is over cell P2.
5. Save the **E21Try_xx** file, and leave it open to use in the next Try It.

Viewing Recommended Charts in the Quick Analysis tool

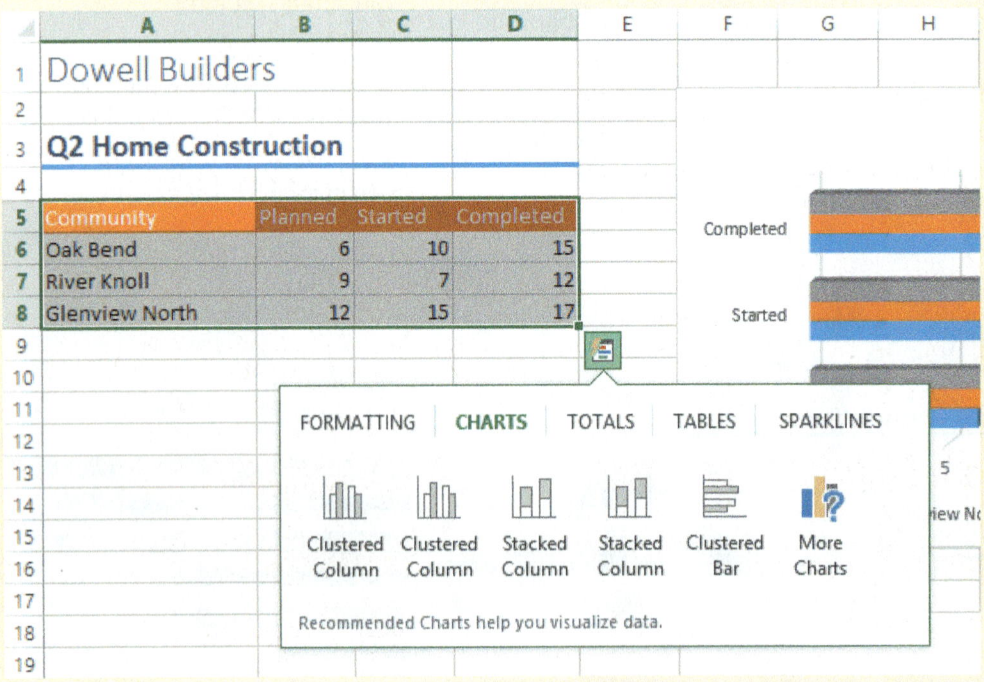

Changing Chart Types

- After creating a chart, you can easily change its chart type.
- Select the chart and click Change Chart Type in the Type group of the CHART TOOLS DESIGN tab to open the Change Chart Type dialog box.
- Column charts, the default chart type, compare individual or sets of values. The height of each bar corresponds to its value in the worksheet, relative to other values in the chart.

  ✓ *Most chart types also have 3-D subtypes.*

- Line charts connect points of data, making them effective for showing changes over time, such as trends.
- Circular pie charts show the relationship of each value in a single series to the total for the series. The size of a pie wedge represents the percentage that value contributes to the total, and adding data labels clarifies the proportions even more.

  ✓ *Charting one more series of data in a pie chart results in an inaccurate chart because Excel will combine all selected series into a single chart.*

- A bar chart is basically a column chart turned on its side. Like column charts, bar charts compare the values of various items.
- Area charts are like "filled in" line charts; you can use area charts to track changes over time.
- Scatter charts, also called XY charts, represent data points as dots. The dots for each series appear in a different color. Any overall direction to the position of the dots reveals a trend.
- Excel also offers many specialty chart types such as Stock, Surface, Doughnut, Bubble, and Radar.

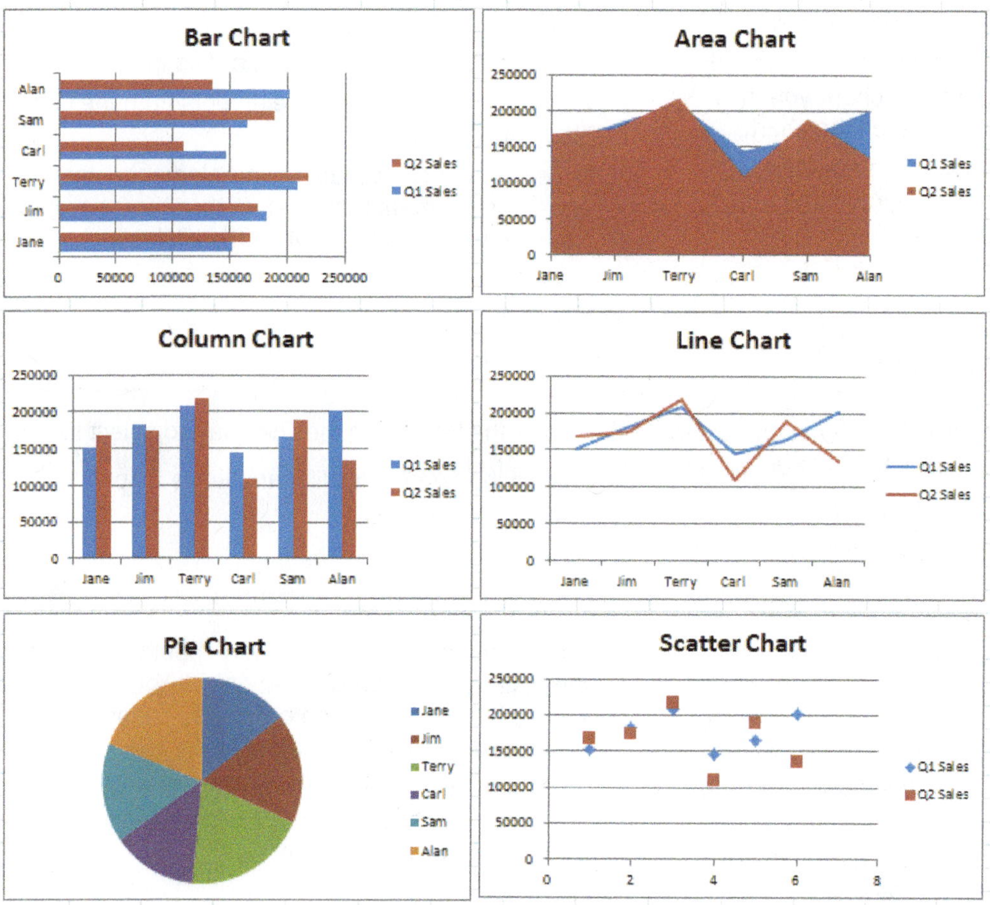

Figure 21-2

Excel 2013, Windows 8, Microsoft Corporation

Try It! Changing Chart Types

1. In the **E21Try_xx** file, click the bar chart that you created first (positioned starting in cell F2) to select it.
2. On the CHART TOOLS DESIGN tab, click Change Chart Type. The Change Chart Type dialog box appears.
3. In the list at the left, click the Area chart type. Notice that the chart choices have different horizontal axis labels.
4. Click the 3-D Area choice above Area.
5. Click OK. Observe the changes. You determine that the 3-D Area chart is too imprecise for the data, so you will change the chart again.
6. On the CHART TOOLS DESIGN tab, click Change Chart Type. The Change Chart Type dialog box appears.
7. In the list at the left, click the Line chart type.
8. Click the Line with Markers choice above Line.
9. Click OK.
10. Save the **E21Try_xx** file, and leave it open to use in the next Try It.

Selecting a Chart

- You can copy a chart and then edit it to produce a different chart that uses the same worksheet data.
- To resize, copy, move, or format a chart, you must first select it by clicking anywhere on the chart.
- A selected chart is surrounded by a border with evenly spaced square handles at the corners and middle of each side.
- Use the square handles on the border of a selected chart to resize the chart.
- Once the chart itself is selected, click an individual chart element such as an axis or title to select it.
- You can select some chart elements from the Chart Elements button +.
- To select from all available chart elements, use the Add Chart Element button in the Chart Layouts group on the CHART TOOLS DESIGN tab.

Try It! Selecting a Chart

1. In the **E21Try_xx** file, click the column chart with the upper-left corner in cell F18. The border with the square handles appears.
2. Click the line chart above it to select it, instead.
3. Click the legend on the line chart to select it.
4. Save the **E21Try_xx** file, and leave it open to use in the next Try It.

Resizing, Copying, Moving, or Deleting a Chart

- You can resize, copy, or move an embedded chart as needed using the same methods as for moving and resizing other objects.
- You can't resize a chart on a chart sheet; however, you can copy or move the chart around on the sheet.
- You can move a chart on a chart sheet to another sheet, creating an embedded object. You can reverse the process when needed to change an embedded chart into a chart sheet.
- If you copy a chart, you can change the copied chart type to present data in a different way, such as using another chart type.

Try It! Resizing, Copying, Moving, or Deleting a Chart

1. In the E21Try_xx file, click the border of the line chart itself to reselect the whole chart.
2. Press DEL.
3. Click the stacked bar chart with the upper-left corner starting at cell P2, and drag it so that its upper-left corner starts at cell F2.
4. With the chart still selected, click HOME > Copy .
5. Click the New sheet button ⊕.
6. On the HOME tab, click Paste .
7. With the chart still selected, drag it down so its upper-left corner is on cell B3.
8. Drag the lower-right handle down to cell K21 to increase the chart size.
9. Reset the page break to fit the chart on one page.
10. Save the E21Try_xx file, and close it.

Lesson 21—Practice

In this project, you will create a chart, change its chart type, and resize the chart using the skills you learned in this lesson.

DIRECTIONS

1. Start Excel, if necessary, and open the **E21Practice** file from the data files for this lesson.
2. Save the file as **E21Practice_xx** in the location where your teacher instructs you to store the files for this lesson.
3. Group the sheets. Add a header that has your name at the left, the date code in the center, and the page number code at the right, and change back to **Normal** view. Ungroup the sheets.
4. Select the product names in the range **A6:L6**.
5. Scroll down, press and hold CTRL, and drag over the daily sales figures in the range **A31:L31**.
6. Click **INSERT** > **Insert Line Chart** > **Line with Markers** in the 2-D Line group.
7. With the new chart still selected, click **HOME** > **Cut** .
8. Click the **Charts** sheet tab.
9. On the **HOME** tab, click **Paste** .
10. Drag the chart so its upper-left corner is in cell **B2**.
11. Drag the lower-right corner of the chart up and to the left, through cell **G12**. Your chart should resemble Figure 21-3 on the next page.
12. **With your teacher's permission**, print the **Charts** worksheet. Submit the printout or the file for grading as required.
13. Save and close the file, and exit Excel.

Figure 21-3

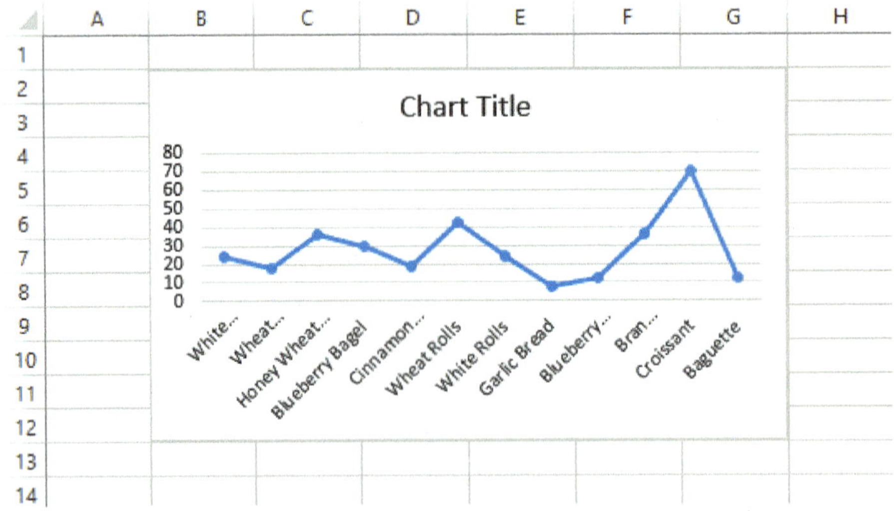

Excel 2013, Windows 8, Microsoft Corporation

Lesson 21—Apply

The modifications you made to your daily bread sales worksheet is working out very well. Now, as manager of a Whole Grains Bread store, you're ready to analyze the data further with charts. Being able to visually compare the sales of the various items in your retail store will help you to produce the right products you need to maximize profits. In this project, you will add two charts.

DIRECTIONS

1. Start Excel, if necessary, and open the **E21Apply** file from the data files for this lesson.
2. Save the file as **E21Apply_xx** in the location where your teacher instructs you to store the files for this lesson.
3. Group the sheets. Add a header that has your name at the left, the date code in the center, and the page number code at the right, and change back to **Normal** view. Ungroup the sheets.
4. Go to the **Daily Sales** sheet and scroll down to the Daily Summary area.
5. Select the nonadjacent ranges **A38:A39** and **D38:D39**.
6. Insert a pie chart using the **3-D Pie** subtype.
7. Cut the new pie chart from the **Daily Sales** sheet, and paste it on the **Charts** sheet.
8. Drag the chart down so its upper-left corner is over cell **B16**.
9. Resize the chart so that its lower-right cell is over cell **G27**.
10. Change the chart type to a column chart, **3-D Clustered Column** subtype.
11. Deselect the chart.
12. **With your teacher's permission**, print the **Charts** worksheet. Submit the printout or the file for grading as required.
13. Save and close the file, and exit Excel.

Lesson 22

Showing Percentages with a Pie Chart

➤ What You Will Learn

Calculating Percentages
Creating a Pie Chart on a Chart Sheet

Software Skills Finding relative percentages of values provides a way to measure performance or compare parts to a whole. You can build formulas from scratch to calculate percentages, or you can create a pie chart, which automatically calculates percentages. You can also place a pie chart on a separate chart sheet so you can print it separately and manage it more easily.

What You Can Do

Calculating Percentages

- A percentage is a calculation of proportion. It tells you how much one value represents when compared with a total.
- Calculate a percentage of a total by dividing the individual value by the total value.

  ✓ *For example, if you want to find the chocolate ice cream sales percentage of total ice cream sales, substitute the division operator for "percentage of" to see how to structure your formula: =chocolate sales/total sales.*

- If you know the percentage you need to calculate of a value, use multiplication and specify the percentage as a decimal.
- For example, if you want to calculate 25% of total sales, change the percentage to a decimal and substitute the multiplication operator for "of" to see how to structure your formula: =.25*total sales.

Try It! Calculating Percentages

1. Start Excel.
2. Open the **E22Try** file from the data files for this lesson.
3. Save the file as **E22Try_xx** in the location where your teacher instructs you to store the files for this lesson.
4. Add a header that has your name at the left, the date code in the center, and the page number code at the right, and change back to Normal view.
5. Click cell J4 to select it.
6. Use the method of your choice to enter the formula that calculates the first student's sales as a percentage of the Weekly Total sales: **=I4/E22**.
7. Press F4 to make the reference to cell E22 an absolute reference, which changes the formula to =I4/$E$22, and press CTRL + ENTER.

   ✓ *You can also manually type the dollar signs.*
8. Use the fill handle to fill the formula down through cell J9.
9. Use the same process to create formulas in cells J12:J14 to calculate each type of candy's percentage of Weekly Total sales.
10. In cell G17, enter a formula that calculates 33% of the Weekly Total sales in cell E22, or **=.33*E22**.
11. Save the **E22Try_xx** file, and leave it open to use in the next Try It.

Finding a percentage

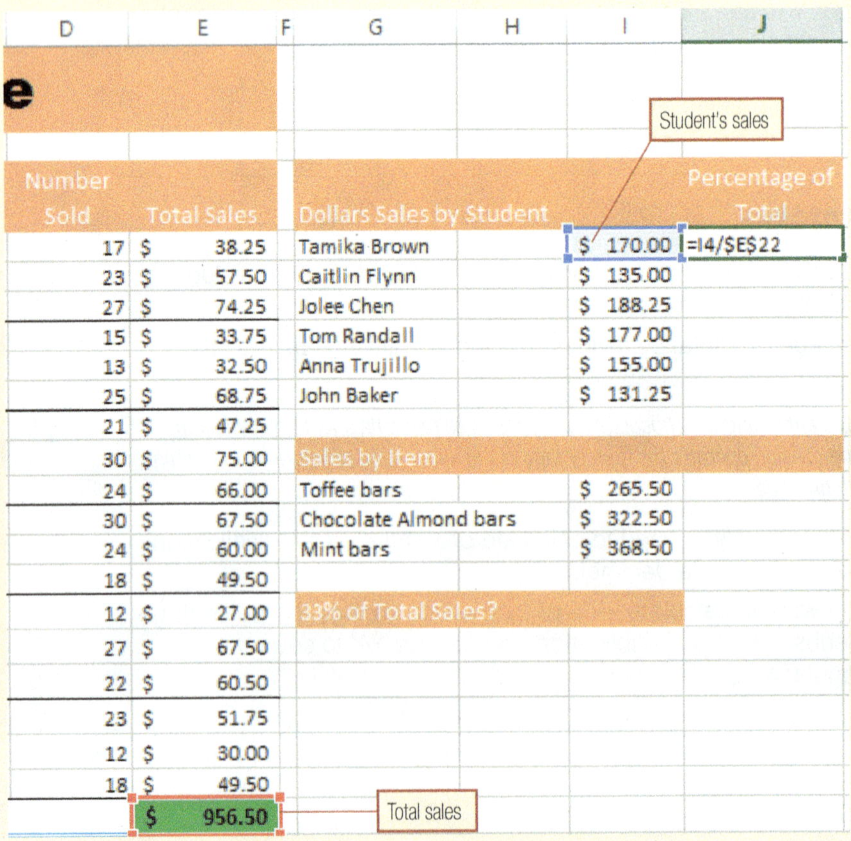

D	E	F	G	H	I	J
e						
Number Sold	Total Sales		Dollars Sales by Student			Percentage of Total
17	$ 38.25		Tamika Brown		$ 170.00	=I4/$E$22
23	$ 57.50		Caitlin Flynn		$ 135.00	
27	$ 74.25		Jolee Chen		$ 188.25	
15	$ 33.75		Tom Randall		$ 177.00	
13	$ 32.50		Anna Trujillo		$ 155.00	
25	$ 68.75		John Baker		$ 131.25	
21	$ 47.25					
30	$ 75.00		Sales by Item			
24	$ 66.00		Toffee bars		$ 265.50	
30	$ 67.50		Chocolate Almond bars		$ 322.50	
24	$ 60.00		Mint bars		$ 368.50	
18	$ 49.50					
12	$ 27.00		33% of Total Sales?			
27	$ 67.50					
22	$ 60.50					
23	$ 51.75					
12	$ 30.00					
18	$ 49.50					
	$ 956.50					

Excel 2013, Windows 8, Microsoft Corporation

Creating a Pie Chart on a Chart Sheet

- A pie chart automatically calculates the total of the values in the selected range, and represents each individual value as a percentage of that total.

✓ *Lesson 25 will explain how to make changes such as adding percentage data labels to pie slices, and Lesson 23 will explain other changes specific to working with slices.*

- After you create a pie chart, you can move it to its own chart sheet using the Move Chart button in the Location group on the CHART TOOLS DESIGN tab.
- This opens the Move Chart dialog box, where you can click New sheet, enter a chart sheet name, and then click the OK button.
- Or, you can select data to chart and press F11 to create a column chart on a new chart sheet, and then change the chart to a pie chart.
- When you insert a header or footer on a chart sheet, the Page Setup dialog box appears, with the Header/Footer tab selected. Click the Custom Header or Custom Footer button, and then use the dialog box that appears to specify what information appears in each section of the header or footer.

Try It! Creating a Pie Chart on a Chart Sheet

1. In the **E22Try_xx** file, use CTRL to select the nonadjacent ranges G4:G9 and I4:I9.
2. Click INSERT > Insert Pie or Doughnut Chart > Pie in the 2-D Pie group
3. On the CHART TOOLS DESIGN tab, in the Location group, click Move Chart.
4. Click the New sheet option button, and type **Student Pie Chart** as the name for the new sheet.
5. Click OK. Review the chart.
6. Click INSERT > Header & Footer.
7. On the Header/Footer tab, click Custom Header.
8. In the Left section edit box, type your name, and press TAB.
9. In the Center section edit box, click the Insert Date button, and press TAB.
10. In the Right section edit box, click the Insert Page Number button, and press OK twice.
11. Click FILE > Print, and preview the chart sheet with the custom header.
12. Save the **E22Try_xx** file, and close it.

Lesson 22—Practice

In this project, you will add percentage calculations using the skills you learned in this lesson.

DIRECTIONS

1. Start Excel, if necessary, and open the **E22Practice** file from the data files for this lesson.
2. Save the file as **E22Practice_xx** in the location where your teacher instructs you to store the files for this lesson.
3. Add a header that has your name at the left, the date code in the center, and the page number code at the right, and change back to **Normal** view.
4. In cell **F5**, enter the formula **=E5/$E$9**, and press CTRL + ENTER.
5. Drag the fill handle to fill the formula down through cell **F8**.
6. In cell **G5**, enter the formula **=.05*E5**, and press CTRL + ENTER.
7. Drag the fill handle to fill the formula down through cell **G8**, as shown in Figure 22-1.
8. **With your teacher's permission**, print the worksheet. Submit the printout or the file for grading as required.
9. Save and close the file, and exit Excel.

Figure 22-1

	A	B	C	D	E	F	G	H
1	Telson Tech							
2	Q3 Sales							
3								
4	Rep	July	August	September	Total	Percentage	5% Bonus	
5	Parker	$ 65,000	$ 45,982	$ 68,256	$ 179,238	27.96%	$ 8,962	
6	Jones	$ 35,990	$ 62,834	$ 51,045	$ 149,869	23.38%	$ 7,493	
7	Anderson	$ 51,030	$ 22,930	$ 73,454	$ 147,414	22.99%	$ 7,371	
8	Chen	$ 46,113	$ 29,288	$ 89,224	$ 164,625	25.68%	$ 8,231	
9	**Total**	**$ 198,133**	**$ 161,034**	**$ 281,979**	**$ 641,146**			
10								

Excel 2013, Windows 8, Microsoft Corporation

Lesson 22—Apply

You are the vice president of sales for Telson Tech. You are performing a review of quarterly sales, and you want to review how the sales made by individual sales reps contribute to overall revenue. You also want to calculate 5% bonus values. You will develop formulas to find percentages, and create reviewing percentages via a pie chart.

DIRECTIONS

1. Start Excel, if necessary, and open the **E22Apply** file from the data files for this lesson.
2. Save the file as **E22Apply_xx** in the location where your teacher instructs you to store the files for this lesson.
3. Select the nonadjacent ranges **A5:A8** and **E5:E8**.
4. Insert a pie chart using the **3-D Pie** subtype.
5. Move the chart to its own sheet named **Sales Percentage Pie**. The finished chart should resemble Figure 22-2.
6. Add a header to the chart sheet that has your name at the left, the date code in the center, and the page number code at the right, and change back to **Normal** view.
7. **With your teacher's permission**, print the chart sheet. Submit the printout or the file for grading as required.
8. Save and close the file, and exit Excel.

Figure 22-2

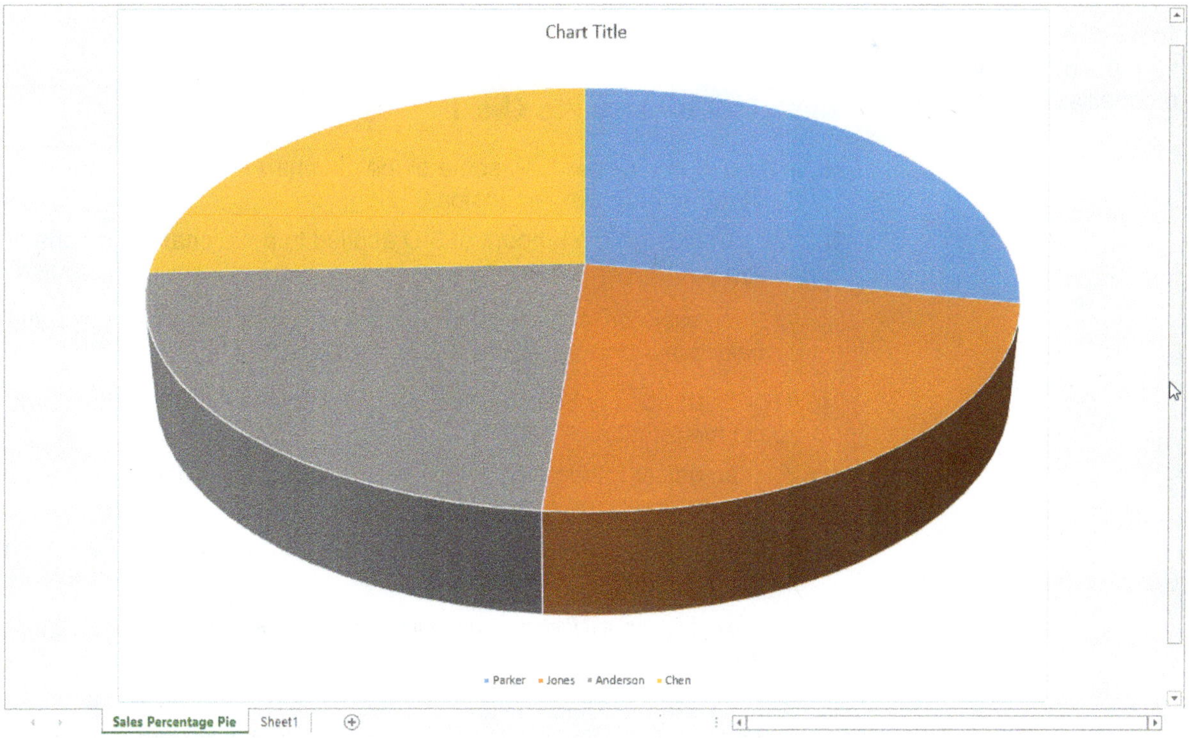

Lesson 23

Enhancing a Pie Chart

➤ What You Will Learn

Applying 3-D to a Pie Chart
Rotating Slices in a Pie Chart
Exploding and Coloring a Pie Chart
Formatting the Chart Area of a Pie Chart

WORDS TO KNOW

Chart area
The overall background for the chart and all its elements, such as titles.

Explode
To move a pie slice away from the pie chart, for emphasis.

Software Skills With the themes available in Excel, even a basic pie chart looks attractive. However, you can present the data even more effectively by working with several pie chart formatting settings. You can work with the amount of 3-D applied to the pie chart, rotate the slices to a new position, explode a slice or change slice color, and add formatting to the area behind the chart.

What You Can Do

Applying 3-D to a Pie Chart

- As you saw in Lesson 22, some of the pie chart subtypes are three-dimensional (3-D) rather than two dimensional (2-D).
- You can change the amount of 3-D applied to a pie chart using one of the 3-D subtypes.

✓ *Some users believe that excessive 3-D distorts the appearance of the chart, making interpreting the data more difficult.*

- If the chart does not use a 3-D subtype, change to a 3-D subtype and then adjust the rotation.
- You can adjust rotation for either an embedded chart or chart on a chart sheet. Be sure to select the embedded chart to change it.
- You can apply formatting and effects, such as rotation, to a chart or chart element using the Format task pane.

✓ *When you select a different chart element, the task pane displays available options for the new chart element.*

- You can use the Effects button ⬠ in the CHART OPTIONS tab of the Format Chart Area task pane to view the effects you can add to a chart or chart element. Click a heading to view specific effect options.

- You can also right-click to view the shortcut menu, and select Format Chart Area.
- When you right-click a chart and click 3-D Rotation, the 3-D Rotation options will display.
- With 3-D ROTATION selected the Format Chart Area dialog box, change the entries in the X Rotation and Y Rotation boxes to adjust the amount of horizontal and vertical rotation, respectively.

Try It! Applying 3-D to a Pie Chart

1. Start Excel.
2. Open the **E23Try** file from the data files for this lesson.
3. Save the file as **E23Try_xx** in the location where your teacher instructs you to store the files for this lesson.
4. Display the Student Pie Chart sheet, if necessary, and add a header that has your name at the left, the date code in the center, and the page number code at the right.
5. Select the chart, and click CHART TOOLS DESIGN > Change Chart type > 3-D Pie > OK.
6. Right-click the chart > 3-D Rotation.
7. Change the Y Rotation value to 50°.
8. Close the Format Chart Area pane.
9. Save the **E23Try_xx** file, and leave it open to use in the next Try It.

Rotating the pie chart

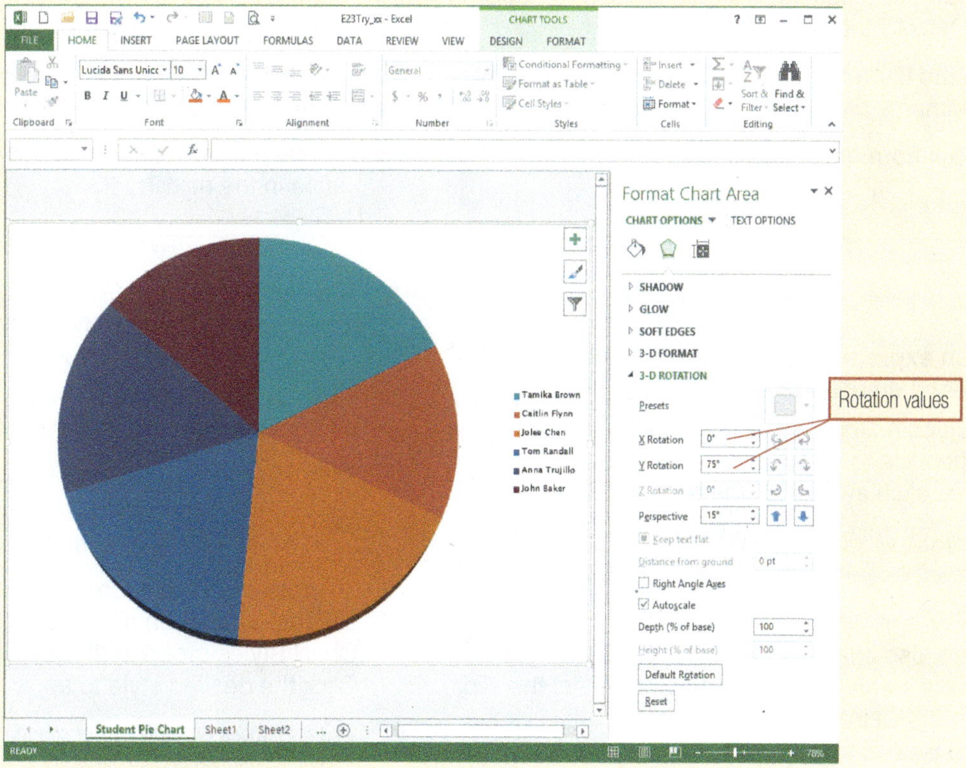

Rotating Slices in a Pie Chart

- You can rotate a pie chart's slices to help enhance a chart's appearance. For example, a pie chart might look best visually with the thinnest slices at the bottom.
- You can select the pie chart itself or a slice to apply the rotation.
- The Chart Elements drop-down list in the Current Selection group will display your selection.

✓ *If you select the pie chart itself, the Chart Elements drop-down box displays Series "xx," where "xx" is the name of the data series.*

✓ *If you select a slice, the Chart Elements drop-down box displays Series "xx" Point, where "xx" is the name of the data point.*

- After selecting the pie chart or slice you want to rotate, click the Format Selection button in the Current Selection group on the CHART TOOLS FORMAT tab to display the SERIES OPTIONS.
- Use the slider below Angle of first slice to rotate the pie chart.

Try It! Rotating Slices in a Pie Chart

1. In the E23Try_xx file, with the chart sheet and chart still selected, click the CHART TOOLS FORMAT tab.
2. In the Current Selection group, click the Chart Elements drop-down arrow > Series 1.
3. Click Format Selection .
4. In the Format Data Series task pane, in the SERIES OPTIONS, under Angle of first slice, drag the slider right to a setting of 280.
5. Click the Close button × on the Format Data Series task pane.
6. Save the E23Try_xx file, and leave it open to use in the next Try It.

Exploding and Coloring a Pie Chart

- You can **explode** a pie slice to separate it from the others and emphasize it.
- To explode a single slice, first click the pie, then click the slice to select it individually. Drag the selected slice away from the rest of the slices.

✓ *To explode all slices, select the entire pie chart, click the Format Selection button, and drag the slider under Pie Explosion.*

- You can also change the coloring for the entire chart or a single slice or data point. Select the slice, and on the CHART TOOLS FORMAT tab click the Format Selection button . The Format Data Point task pane appears. Click the Fill&Line button , and click FILL.
- You can select Solid fill, and then use the Color button to select a color. Note that you can also fill a slice with a gradient, picture, or pattern.
- You can also change the coloring by right-clicking on the entire chart or element, and using the Fill button .

✓ *Use the techniques described here to change the coloring for elements in any chart type.*

- To recolor the entire chart, click CHART TOOLS DESIGN, and then click the More button in the Chart Styles group to display a gallery of styles. Click the desired style to apply it.

✓ *Chart styles typically do not change any separate formatting you've applied previously, such as changing rotation.*

Try It! Exploding and Coloring a Pie Chart

1. In the E23Try_xx file, with the chart sheet and chart still selected, click CHART TOOLS DESIGN, and click the More button in the Chart Styles group, if necessary.
2. Click Style 3 from the gallery, which is third from the left in the first row.
3. Click the chart, and then click the slice for Jolee Chen, who was the top seller. It is the orange slice beside the legend. Right-click the selected slice, and then click Format Data Point on the shortcut menu.
4. In the Format Data Point task pane, click the Fill & Line button > FILL.
5. Under FILL, click the Solid fill option button.
6. Click the Color button, and then click Green under Standard Colors.
7. Click the Close button × on the task pane.
8. With the green slice still selected, drag it away from the pie to explode it.
9. Save the E23Try_xx file, and leave it open to use in the next Try It.

Formatting the Chart Area of a Pie Chart

- The **chart area** is the background that holds all of the elements of the chart, including the plot area.
- You can fill the chart area with a solid color, gradient, picture or texture, or pattern, just as for individual data points and series.

✓ *Use the techniques described here to change the formatting of the chart area for any type of chart.*

- Select the chart area, and then use the Format Selection button in the Chart Layouts group to open the Format Chart Area task pane, where you can apply the formatting.
- Be careful when applying a picture or texture fill. If the fill is too busy looking, it can make other elements of the chart, such as axis labels, difficult to read.

Try It! Formatting the Chart Area of a Pie Chart

1. In the E23Try_xx file, with the chart sheet and chart still selected, click CHART TOOLS FORMAT > Chart Elements drop-down arrow > Chart Area.
2. Click Format Selection.
3. Make sure FILL is selected, and click the Gradient fill option button.
4. Click the Preset gradients button, and then click Light Gradient - Accent 5, which is the fifth from the left on the top row.
5. Click the Close button × on the task pane.
6. Save the E23Try_xx file, and close it.

Lesson 23—Practice

In this project, you will change worksheet data and update an existing pie chart using the skills you learned in this lesson.

DIRECTIONS

1. Start Excel, if necessary, and open the **E23Practice** file from the data files for this lesson.
2. Save the file as **E23Practice_xx** in the location where your teacher instructs you to store the files for this lesson.
3. On the **Sales Percentage Pie** chart sheet, add a header that has your name at the left, the date code in the center, and the page number code at the right, and change back to **Normal** view.
4. Click the **Sheet1** sheet tab.
5. Right-click the row **7** row header, and click **Insert**.
6. Enter the following data across the new row to cell E7:
   Bronsky
   8504
   9250
   11904
   15172
7. Select cells **F6:G6**, and use the fill handle to fill the formulas down to row 7.
8. Change the entry in cell **B8** to **31030**.
9. Click the **Sales Percentage Pie** sheet tab to return to that sheet. As shown in Figure 23-1, the chart has automatically updated to reflect the data changes.
10. **With your teacher's permission**, print the chart sheet. Submit the printout or the file for grading as required.
11. Save and close the file, and exit Excel.

Figure 23-1

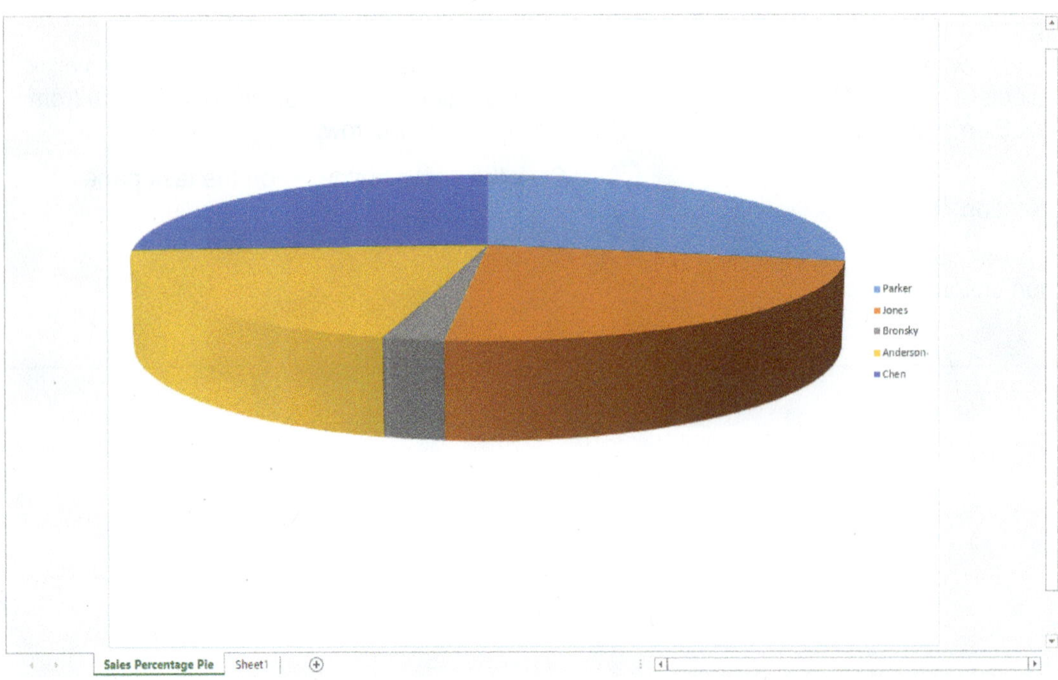

Excel 2013, Windows 8, Microsoft Corporation

Lesson 23—Apply

As vice president of sales for Telson Tech, you are continuing the review of quarterly sales. You've received updates to the sales data, so you want to make those changes. You also want to enhance the pie chart by working with 3-D settings, exploding the slice for the leading salesperson, and applying coloring.

DIRECTIONS

1. Start Excel, if necessary, and open the **E23Apply** file from the data files for this lesson.
2. Save the file as **E23Apply_xx** in the location where your teacher instructs you to store the files for this lesson.
3. On the **Sales Percentage Pie** chart sheet, add a header that has your name at the left, the date code in the center, and the page number code at the right, and change back to **Normal** view.
4. Right-click the **chart area** > **3-D Rotation**.
5. In the Format Chart Area task pane, change the **Y Rotation** to **20°**.
6. Select the pie chart series. The Format Data Series task pane will appear.

   ✓ *Make sure the Chart Elements drop-down displays Series 1.*
7. Click the **Series Options** button, drag the slider under **Angle of first slice** right to a setting of **150**, and then click the Close button on the task pane.
8. Explode the blue slice for **Parker** at the bottom of the chart.
9. Format the exploded slide to fill it with the **Granite** texture.
10. Apply a **Gold, Accent 4, Lighter 60%** solid fill to the chart area.
11. **With your teacher's permission**, print the chart sheet. Submit the printout or the file for grading as required.
12. Save and close the file, and exit Excel.

Lesson 24

Adding Special Elements to a Chart or Sheet and Updating a Chart

➤ What You Will Learn

Inserting a Text Box in a Chart
Using WordArt in a Worksheet
Updating a Chart

WORDS TO KNOW

Text box
A free-floating box added to a sheet or chart that contains any text you specify and that can be formatted separately.

WordArt
A free-floating text object added to a sheet or chart, to which you can apply special formatting effects.

Software Skills Even though a chart is graphical in itself, you can still enhance it with other elements. For example, you can add a text box with information to elaborate on a particular data point, or use WordArt to create a jazzy title. You can also change the actual data charted.

What You Can Do

Inserting a Text Box in a Chart

- When you need to be able to position text freely on a chart, chart sheet, or worksheet, you can insert a **text box**.
- A text box can hold any text you specify, and it can be sized, positioned, and formatted.
- To insert a text box on a chart, make sure the chart is selected first.
- Use the Text Box in the Text group of the INSERT tab, and click on the location where you want to insert the text box.
- You can also click and hold, and then drag the mouse pointer to insert a text box with the dimensions you outline.
- You can reposition a text box by selecting it and dragging it to the desired position.
- Use the HOME tab and DRAWING TOOLS FORMAT tab choices to apply desired formatting.

Try It! Inserting a Text Box in a Chart

1. Start Excel.
2. Open the **E24Try** file from the data files for this lesson.
3. Save the file as **E24Try_xx** in the location where your teacher instructs you to store the files for this lesson.
4. On the Student Pie Chart Sheet, add a header that has your name at the left, the date code in the center, and the page number code at the right, and change back to Normal view.
5. Click INSERT > Text Box.
6. Click on the exploded pie slice to create a text box.
7. Type **Great job!** in the text box.
8. Drag over the text in the text box.
9. Using the tools in the Font group of the HOME tab, increase the font size to 20 and change the font color to White, Background 1.
10. Resize the text box so the text is on one line, and reposition the text to fit on the pie slice, if needed.
11. Save the **E24Try_xx** file, and leave it open to use in the next Try It.

Using WordArt in a Worksheet

- You can create a **WordArt** object to add decorative text on a worksheet or chart sheet.
- You can also apply WordArt styles to existing text, such as a chart title.

  ✓ *You will learn more about adding and working with chart text formatting in Lesson 25.*

- Use the WordArt button in the Text group on the INSERT tab to create a WordArt object.
- When you create WordArt, you choose from a gallery of styles that are compatible with the theme applied to the workbook file.
- You can format the WordArt object using the choices on the DRAWING TOOLS FORMAT tab.
- Use the HOME tab and DRAWING TOOLS FORMAT tab choices to change the font size and apply desired formatting.

Try It! Using WordArt in a Worksheet

1. In the **E24Try_xx** file, with the chart sheet and chart selected, click INSERT > WordArt.
2. In the gallery, click the Fill - Red, Accent 2, Outline 2 - Accent 2 style, which is on the top row, third from left. The WordArt object appears with placeholder text.
3. Type **Top**, press ENTER, and type **Sellers**.
4. Drag the WordArt object to the upper-right corner of the chart area. The WordArt object can overlap the pie slice.
5. Click below the legend to deselect the WordArt.
6. Select the *Great job!* text box, and click DRAWING TOOLS FORMAT.
7. In the WordArt Styles group, click the More button.
8. Click the Fill - Blue, Accent 4, Soft Bevel style, which is on the top row, fifth from the left.
9. Save the **E24Try_xx** file, and leave it open to use in the next Try It.

Updating a Chart

- In Lesson 23, you saw how adding data within the range of charted data was automatically added to the pie chart and changes made to the chart data also resulted in automatic chart updates. In other cases, you may need to make your own changes to the charted data to update the chart.
- For example, you may want to sort the charted range to present the data in a different order, or remove part of the charted range from the chart.

✓ *Sorting data does change the order of the pie slices, so be sure to fix that.*

- Make any changes you want to the chart data first.
- Then, with the chart selected, click CHART TOOLS DESIGN > Select Data. Change the entry in the Chart data range text box as needed, either by typing a new range or using the Collapse Dialog button.

✓ *If the chart is on the chart sheet, Excel automatically displays the sheet holding the charted data.*

- When you change the data of a chart, Excel's chart engine animates the change within the chart. The chart animation feature can show you how the changed data will affect the chart overall.

Try It! Updating a Chart

1. In the **E24Try_xx** file, click the Sheet1 sheet to select it.
2. Select the range G3:J9.
3. Click DATA > Sort.
4. In the Sort dialog box, click the My data has headers box.
5. In the Sort by drop-down list, select Percentage of Total.
6. Review the Sort On drop-down list, and make sure it reads Values.
7. In the Order drop-down list, select Largest to Smallest, and click OK.
8. Click the Student Pie Chart sheet tab.
9. Select the chart, and click CHART TOOLS DESIGN > Select Data.
10. In the Select Data Source dialog box, change the range to:

    =Sheet1!$G$4:$G$6,Sheet1!$I$4:$I$6

    This will eliminate the bottom three contributors from the chart.
11. Click OK.
12. Drag the green slice back to the rest of the pie, right-click it, and click Reset to Match Style.
13. Select the *Great job!* text box and drag it over the top slice for Jolee Chen, the top seller.
14. Click below the legend to deselect the text box.
15. Save the **E24Try_xx** file, and close it.

Lesson 24—Practice

In this project, you will insert a WordArt object and reposition it using the skills you learned in this lesson.

DIRECTIONS

1. Start Excel, if necessary, and open the **E24Practice** file from the data files for this lesson.
2. Save the file as **E24Practice_xx** in the location where your teacher instructs you to store the files for this lesson.
3. On the **Sales Percentage Pie** chart sheet, add a header that has your name at the left, the date code in the center, and the page number code at the right, and change back to **Normal** view.
4. With the chart sheet displayed, click **INSERT** > **WordArt** .
5. In the gallery, click the **Fill - Orange, Accent 2, Outline - Accent 2** style, which is on the top row, third from the left.
6. Type **Q3 Sales by Rep**.
7. Drag the WordArt object above the chart, and click outside it to deselect it.
8. **With your teacher's permission**, print the chart sheet. Submit the printout or the file for grading as required.
9. Save and close the file, and exit Excel.

Lesson 24—Apply

As vice president of sales for Telson Tech, you continue to work with the quarterly sales worksheet and chart. You also will add a text box to explain the exploded pie slice, and update chart information.

DIRECTIONS

1. Start Excel, if necessary, and open the **E24Apply** file from the data files for this lesson.
2. Save the file as **E24Apply_xx** in the location where your teacher instructs you to store the files for this lesson.
3. On the **Sales Percentage Pie** sheet, add a header that has your name at the left, the date code in the center, and the page number code at the right, and change back to **Normal** view.
4. On **Sheet1**, select the range **A4:G9**, and sort the data by the **Total** column, from smallest to largest, making sure that the **My data has headers** check box is checked.
5. Click the Sales Percentage Pie sheet, and click **CHART TOOLS DESIGN** > **Select Data** .
6. Use the method of your choice to change the selected ranges to **A6:A9** and **E6:E9**, to eliminate the Bronsky data.
7. Drag the exploded slice back to the pie, right-click it, and click **Reset to Match Style**.
8. Rotate the pie so that the gold slice for Parker is at the lower right, and then explode that slice.

   ✓ *You can use an X Rotation of more than 200°.*
9. Add a text box at the center-bottom with the following text:
   Bronsky data eliminated because she was in training.
   Parker was top seller.
10. Format the text box text with the **Gradient Fill - Blue, Accent 1, Reflection** WordArt style.
11. Deselect the text box.
12. **With your teacher's permission**, print the chart sheet. Submit the printout or the file for grading as required.
13. Save and close the file, and exit Excel.

Lesson 25

Completing Chart Formatting

➤ What You Will Learn

Changing Data Series Orientation
Formatting a Chart
Formatting a Chart Element
Changing Chart Text
Enhancing the Chart Plot Area
Formatting Category and Value Axes

WORDS TO KNOW

Chart layout
A formatting arrangement that specifies the location and sizes of chart elements, such as the chart title and legend.

Object
Any element on a worksheet or chart that can be manipulated independently. Some chart elements are also objects.

Tick marks
Lines of measurement along the category and value axis.

Walls
The areas of a 3-D chart that frame the data series. These can include side walls and a back wall.

Software Skills There are many ways in which you can enhance your chart: you can add and format chart text, add color or a pattern to the chart plot area, format the value and category axes so that the numbers are easier to read, and add a legend.

What You Can Do

Changing Data Series Orientation

- When you create a chart, Excel assumes the data series are arranged in rows.
- For example, if you had a worksheet with several stores listed in different rows, and sales for each month listed in columns, then each store would be a different data series and be represented with a unique color.
- If you switched the orientation of the data series from columns to rows, then the sales in the columns would become the series rather than the categories.
- Use the Switch Row/Column button in the Data group on the CHART TOOLS DESIGN tab to change the data orientation for the selected chart.

Try It! Changing Data Series Orientation

1. Start Excel.
2. Open the **E25Try** file from the data files for this lesson.
3. Save the file as **E25Try_xx** in the location where your teacher instructs you to store the files for this lesson.
4. Group the sheets. Add a header that has your name at the left, the date code in the center, and the page number code at the right, and change back to Normal view. Ungroup the sheets.

✓ *You may need to adjust the page breaks after adding the headers.*

5. Click the Practice sheet tab, and click the chart.
6. Click CHART TOOLS DESIGN > Switch Row/Column. The statuses become the series and the communities become the categories.
7. Save the **E25Try_xx** file, and leave it open to use in the next Try It.

Formatting a Chart

- When a chart is created, it contains a legend and labels along each axis.
- Apply a different **chart layout** to add common features such as a chart title, axis titles, and data table.
- You can also select individual chart elements such as a legend or a chart title, and add or remove them from your chart layout to personalize it.
- You can use the shortcut buttons that appear at the upper right corner outside of the chart to format chart elements and chart styles. Use the Filter shortcut button to display selected data elements of a chart.
- In addition to its default chart layout, every new chart is formatted with a default style.
- The Chart Layouts and Chart Styles galleries are found on the CHART TOOLS DESIGN tab.
- As you learned in Lesson 23, you can quickly recolor and format the selected chart by simply changing chart styles. The technique presented in that lesson works for any chart type.
- Regardless of the style you select, you can still apply manual formatting to any selected chart element using special Format dialog boxes.
- You can use the Quick Layout button in the Chart Layouts group to change the layout of the chart to one of Excel's preset layouts.
- You can also quickly change the coloring of a chart using the Change Colors button in the Chart Styles group.

Try It! Formatting a Chart

1. In the **E25Try_xx** file, click the Large Chart sheet tab to select it.
2. Click the chart to select it.
3. Click CHART TOOLS DESIGN > Quick Layout button > Layout 9, which is third from the left in the third row of the gallery. The layout adds a placeholder chart title and axis titles.
4. Click CHART TOOLS DESIGN > Chart Styles More button > Style 8. This applies a dark background and lighter formatting to the chart.
5. Click the Chart Title placeholder to select it.
6. Click HOME > Font Color drop-down arrow, and apply the Orange, Accent 2, Lighter 40% color.
7. Save the **E25Try_xx** file and leave it open to use in the next Try It.

(continued)

Try It! Formatting a Chart *(continued)*

Chart formatting tools

Excel 2013, Windows 8, Microsoft Corporation

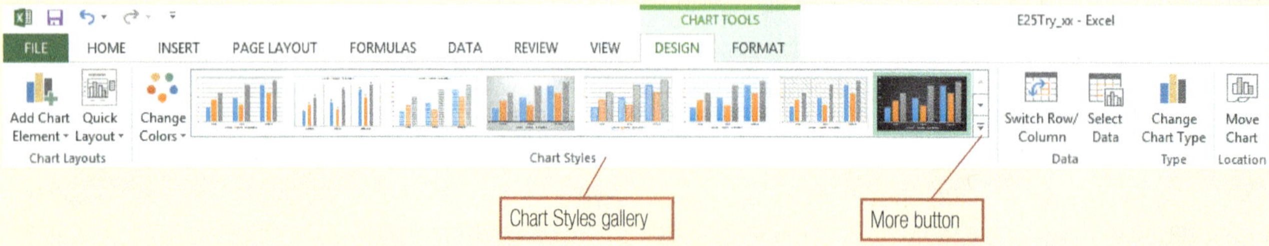

Formatting a Chart Element

- Before you can resize, move, or delete a chart element, also called an **object**, you must first select it.
- By adding, resizing, moving, or deleting the parts of your chart, you may make it more attractive and easier to read.
- If you resize an object that contains text, the font size of the text changes correspondingly.
- When you delete an object from a chart, the remaining parts of the chart are enlarged to fill the gap.
- You can also use the CHART ELEMENTS shortcut button + to select the chart elements you want to display.
- You can change the value represented by a column or bar by resizing it.
- You can format chart elements, such as the legend, the axis labels, and data labels.
- You can format some of the chart elements as a group, for example, in a 3-D chart you can format the side and back **walls** at the same time by selecting Walls in the Chart Elements drop-down list of the CHART TOOLS FORMAT tab.

Try It! Formatting a Chart Element

1. In the **E25Try_xx** file, on the Large Chart sheet with the chart selected, click the legend to select it.
2. Drag the legend to the lower-right corner of the chart area.
3. Click the horizontal Axis Title placeholder to select it.
4. Press DEL to delete the placeholder.
5. Click the CHART ELEMENTS shortcut button +, and click the Legend checkbox to deselect it.
6. Move the mouse pointer to the right of the Legend element, and click the More arrow ▸ that appears.

   ✓ *If using a touch device, touch to the right of the Legend element to display the More arrow.*
7. Click Right. Notice that the Legend chart element checkbox is selected, and the legend is now placed to the right of the chart.
8. Save the **E25Try_xx** file, and leave it open to use in the next Try It.

Changing Chart Text

- You can edit chart text or change its formatting. For example, you can change the size, font, and attributes of a chart's title.
- Usually, you can select a new text object or placeholder, type the new text, and press ENTER to update the text. The text you type appears in the formula bar.

✓ *Double-clicking the text with the text object will insert the cursor within the placeholder text, which you can delete and replace with your own text.*

- You can also click within a text box and edit the text, and then click outside the text box to finish the change.
- The Data Labels options in the Chart Elements shortcut menu provides options for displaying individual chart labels and varying their position.
- Click the More Options button at the bottom of the menu to display the Format Data Labels task pane.
- For charts with multiple series, you have to format the data labels for each series independently.

✓ *Click the drop-down arrow next to LABEL OPTIONS in the Format Data Labels task pane to change labels or chart elements.*

Try It! Changing Chart Text

1. In the **E25Try_xx** file, on the Large Chart sheet click the chart to select it, and click the Chart Title placeholder to select it.
2. Type **Buildout Status**, and press ENTER.
3. Click the vertical Axis Title placeholder to select it.
4. Type **Units**, and press ENTER.
5. Click HOME > Increase Font Size four times to make the axis title larger.
6. Click the Chart Elements shortcut menu, click the More arrow next to the Data Labels option, and click Inside End. Data labels are added to the column chart bars.
7. Click one of the data labels for the River Knoll series. Notice that the entire River Knoll series data labels are now selected.
8. On the CHART TOOLS FORMAT tab, click the Text Fill drop-down arrow, and then click Automatic. The text becomes black.
9. Click above the legend to deselect all objects.
10. Save the **E25Try_xx** file, and leave it open to use in the next Try It.

Enhancing the Chart Plot Area

- In Lesson 23, you learned how to apply a background to the chart area. You can use that same method to apply a fill to the chart area for any chart type.
- You can also apply a separate fill to the smaller plot area.
- You can:
  - Add a border around the background area.
  - Apply a color to the background.
  - Apply a fill effect, such as a gradient (a blend of two colors), texture (such as marble), pattern (such as diagonal stripes), or picture (a graphic file).
  - Add a shadow effect behind the border.
  - Shape the corners to create a 3-D look.
- To select the plot area, click it or choose Chart Area in the Chart Elements drop-down list in the Current Selection group on the CHART TOOLS DESIGN tab. Click the Format Selection button to display the Format Chart Area task pane and its formatting options.
- You can also use the choices in the CHART TOOLS FORMAT Shape Styles group to change the plot area formatting.
- You can remove a plot area fill by right-clicking on the plot area, and clicking Fill > No fill.

Try It! Enhancing the Chart Plot Area

1. In the **E25Try_xx** file, in the Large Chart sheet, click CHART TOOLS FORMAT > Chart Elements drop-down list arrow > Plot Area.
2. Click Format Selection.
3. In the Format Plot Area task pane, click FILL > No fill.
4. On the CHART TOOLS FORMAT tab, click Shape Fill drop-down arrow Shape Fill > Gray-50%, Accent 3, Lighter 80% (seventh choice in the second row of Theme Colors).
5. Click above the legend to deselect the plot area.
6. Save the **E25Try_xx** file, and leave it open to use in the next Try It.

Formatting the plot area

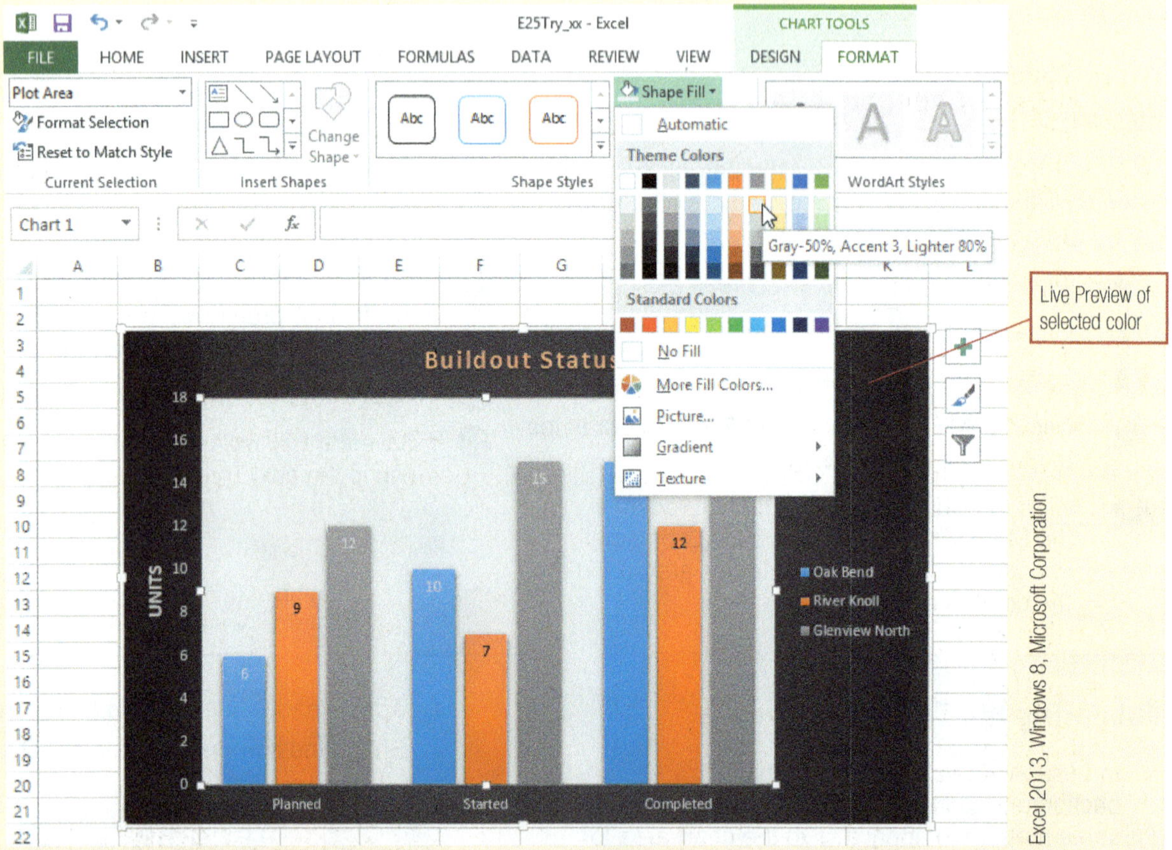

Formatting Category and Value Axes

- Categories and data series are plotted along the category or horizontal axis.
- The vertical or value axis provides a scale for the values of the data for most chart types. (For example, for bar charts, the axes are reversed.)
- You can change the font, size, color, attributes, alignment, and placement of text or numbers along both the category and value axes.
- You can add a color fill, border, line, shadow, or 3-D effect to the labels along either axis.
- You can also change the appearance of the **tick marks**, or add or remove gridlines.
- In addition, you can adjust the scale used along the value axis.
- You can use the Axes option in the Chart Elements shortcut menu to control whether either axis displays overall.

- You can also select an axis in the Chart Elements drop-down list on the CHART TOOLS FORMAT tab, and make changes in the Format Axis task pane.
- You can control whether the axis includes major gridlines, minor gridlines, or both, by clicking More Options in the Gridlines option of the Chart Elements shortcut menu. Use the task pane to make changes to the gridlines.
- After selecting an axis, use CHART TOOLS DESIGN > Format Selection to see more detailed settings.

Try It! Formatting Category and Value Axes

1. In the **E25Try_xx** file, with the Large Chart sheet and chart selected, click the Chart Elements shortcut button + > Axes arrow > More Options. The Format Axis task pane opens.
2. Below Format Axis, click the AXIS OPTIONS drop-down arrow > Vertical (Value) Axis.
3. Click the Axis Options button, and expand the AXIS OPTIONS submenu.
4. Under Units, in the Minor box, change the entry to 1.
5. Scroll down if necessary, expand the TICK MARKS submenu, and select Inside in the Major type drop-down list.
6. Click the Close button × on the task pane.
7. Save the **E25Try_xx** file, and close it.

Lesson 25—Practice

In this project, you will change the data orientation and layout of a chart using the skills you learned in this lesson.

DIRECTIONS

1. Start Excel, if necessary, and open the **E25Practice** file from the data files for this lesson.
2. Save the file as **E25Practice_xx** in the location where your teacher instructs you to store the files for this lesson.
3. Group the sheets. Add a header that has your name at the left, the date code in the center, and the page number code at the right, and change back to **Normal** view. Ungroup the sheets.
4. Click the **Charts** sheet tab to select it.
5. Click the bottom pie chart and press the DEL key to remove it.
6. Click the top chart to select it, and click **HOME** > **Copy**.
7. Click cell **B25** > **HOME** > **Paste**.
8. Click **CHART TOOLS DESIGN** > **Switch Row/ Column**.
9. Scroll up and compare the appearance of the top chart with that of the bottom chart. As shown in Figure 25-1 on the next page, changing the data orientation reduced the categories but increased the number of series.
10. **With your teacher's permission**, print the **Charts** sheet. Submit the printout or the file for grading as required.
11. Save and close the file, and exit Excel.

Figure 25-1

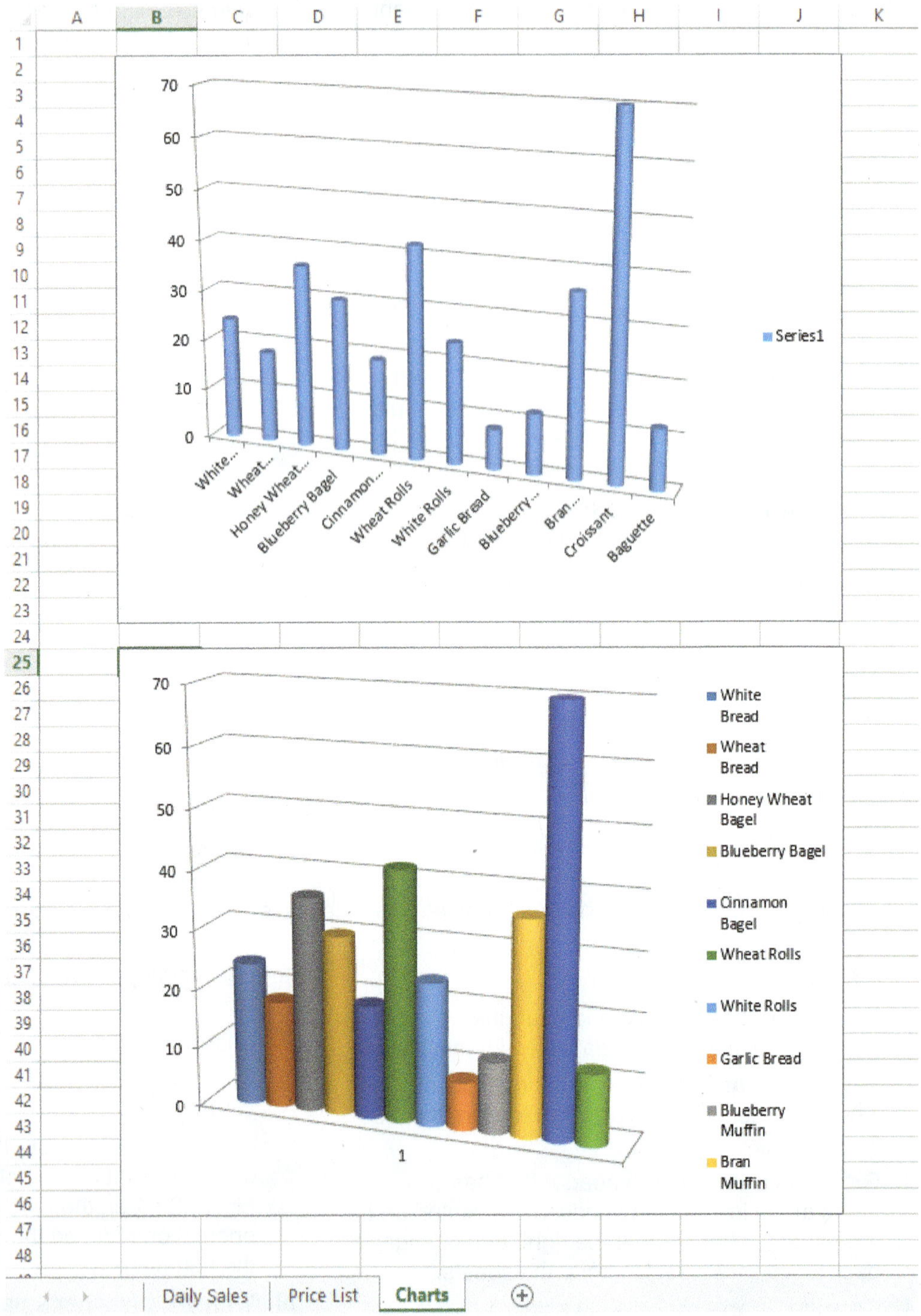

Excel 2013, Windows 8, Microsoft Corporation

Lesson 25—Apply

The charts you created to analyze daily bread sales at your Whole Grains Bread retail store are almost completed. Before printing, you want to format them to make them more professional looking and easier to understand.

DIRECTIONS

1. Start Excel, if necessary, and open the **E25Apply** file from the data files for this lesson.
2. Save the file as **E25Apply_xx** in the location where your teacher instructs you to store the files for this lesson.
3. Group the sheets. Add a header that has your name at the left, the date code in the center, and the page number code at the right, and change back to **Normal** view. Ungroup the sheets.
4. Click the **Charts** sheet tab.
5. Select the horizontal axis for the top chart, and format it so it displays without axis labels.
6. On the same chart display data labels that are the category names.
7. Use the Format Data Labels task pane to show the category name only.
8. Use the TEXT OPTIONS in the Format Data Labels task pane to change the text direction to Rotate all text 270°.
9. Select the **Croissant** data label, and move it just to the left of the top of its data point cylinder, within the plot area.
10. Delete the legend.
11. Add a chart title above the chart that reads **Daily Sales**.
12. Add an **Orange, Accent 2, Lighter 40%** fill to the walls.
13. Select the data marker (cylinder) for the Croissant data point, and change its fill color to **Green, Accent 6, Darker 50%**.
14. Scroll down, if necessary, and select the bottom chart.
15. Apply the **Style 10** chart style.
16. Change the position of the legend to **Right**.
17. Add a rotated vertical axis title that reads **Unit Sales**, and increase its font size to **16** pts.
18. Select the Chart Area, and use the Format Chart Area task pane to add a **Pink tissue paper** texture fill set to **25%** transparency to the chart area.
19. Scroll to compare the charts. They should resemble Figure 25-2 on the next page.
20. **With your teacher's permission**, print the **Charts** sheet. Submit the printout or the file for grading as required.
21. Save and close the file, and exit Excel.

Figure 25-2

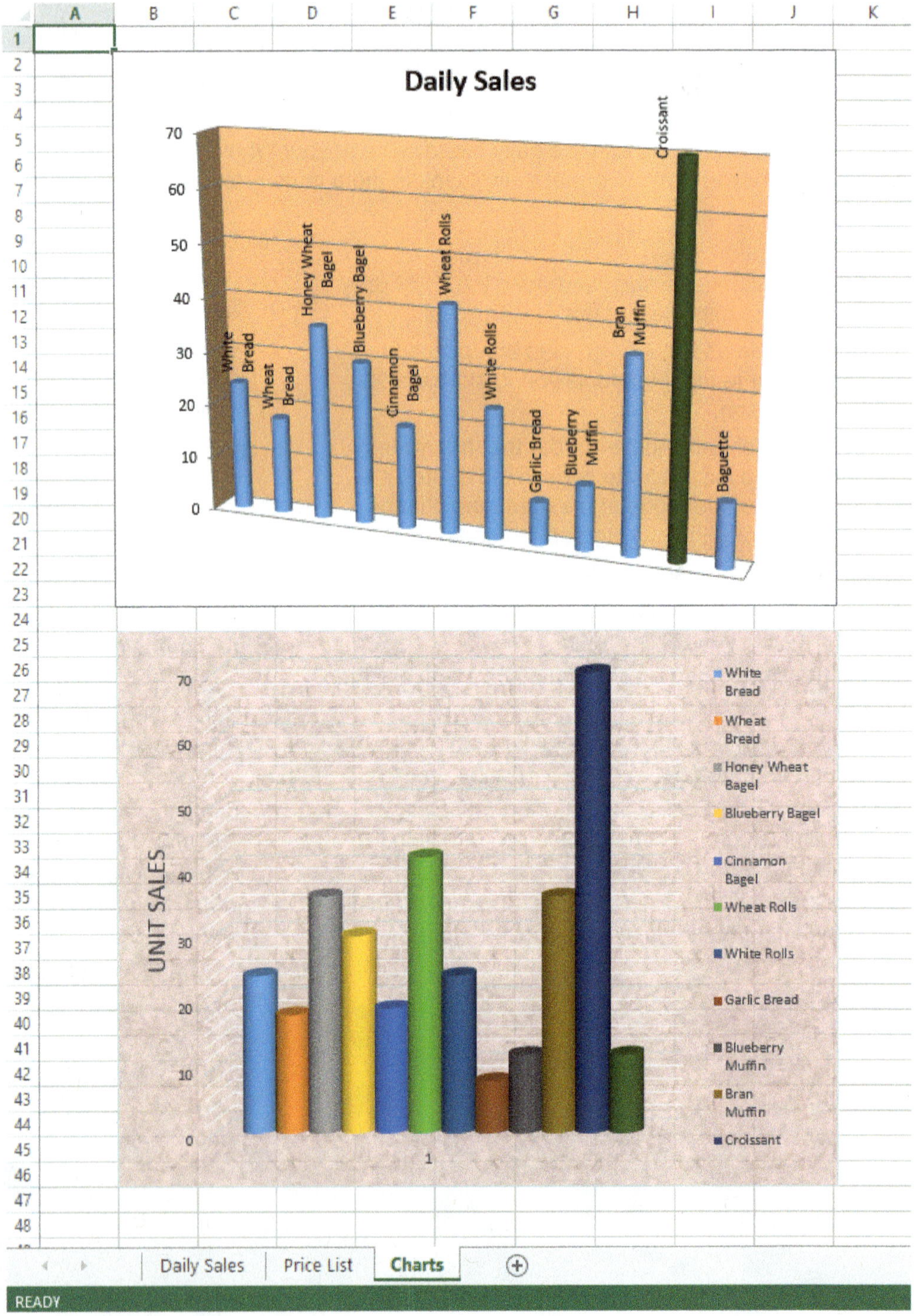

Excel 2013, Windows 8, Microsoft Corporation

Lesson 26

Comparing and Analyzing Data

➤ What You Will Learn

- Using Parentheses in a Formula
- Calculating a Value After an Increase
- Performing What-If Analysis
- Creating a Line Chart to Compare Data

Software Skills Forecasting is an important business function. You can't plan for the future unless you can anticipate how various scenarios will develop and play out numerically. Excel offers a number of techniques that you can use to evaluate data based on your answer to the question, "What if?" In this lesson, you will explore the use of parentheses in formulas, calculating a value based on a percentage increase, creating a formula that performs a basic what-if analysis, and using a line chart to visualize the what-if scenario.

WORDS TO KNOW

What-if analysis
Using formulas and other tools in Excel to examine the results of changing particular data, for planning purposes.

What You Can Do

Using Parentheses in a Formula

- Parentheses, along with operator precedence, control the order of calculations in formulas.

  ✓ *Excel Lesson 7 first introduced the concept of how to use parentheses in formulas. This lesson provides more examples.*

- A business that calculates payroll can use parentheses in a formula to sum the federal, state, and other payroll tax rates and then multiply that sum by wages to determine the amount of withholding.
- When there are multiple nested pairs of parentheses, Excel calculates from the innermost pair, working outward.
- Improperly placed parentheses can cause logic flaws in a formula Excel might not necessarily flag with an error message or indicator. Look at the use of parentheses if your formula results are not what you expected.

Try It! Using Parentheses in a Formula

1. Start Excel.
2. Open the **E26Try** file from the data files for this lesson.
3. Save the file as **E26Try_xx** in the location where your teacher instructs you to store the files for this lesson.
4. Add a header that has your name at the left, the date code in the center, and the page number code at the right, and change back to Normal view.
5. Select cell F6 and enter **=((B6/C6)+(D6/E6))/2**.

   ✓ *The parentheses cause the formula to calculate the individual quarterly averages, and then average the two values.*
6. Use the fill handle to copy the formula from cell F6 through F11.
7. Save the **E26Try_xx** file, and leave it open to use in the next Try It.

Calculating a Value After an Increase

- In Lesson 22, you learned how to calculate the percentage of a total value represented by a single value. In that case, you create a formula that divides the individual value by the total value to yield the percentage.
- You also learned in that lesson that to find a particular percentage of a value, you convert the percentage to a decimal, and then multiply.
- Calculating the result of an increase works the same as calculating a percentage of a value, in most cases. That's because increases are often stated in terms of percentage increases.
- So while you still convert to a decimal and multiply, you first add 1 (to represent 100% of the original value) to the decimal, so the result reflects the original value with the percentage increase added.
  - For example, suppose you pay a $215 membership fee this year and that value is in cell B2. The fee will go up 15% next year, and that value (.15) is in cell B3. To find the new fee, use the formula =(1+B3)*B2, or simply =1.15*B2.

Try It! Calculating a Value After an Increase

1. In the **E26Try_xx** file, select cell G6.
2. Assume that Q3 travel expenses will be 2% more than the average for the first two quarters. Enter the formula **=F6*1.02** in the cell.
3. Use the fill handle to copy the formula from cell G6 through G11.
4. Save the **E26Try_xx** file, and leave it open to use in the next Try It.

A formula that calculates an increase

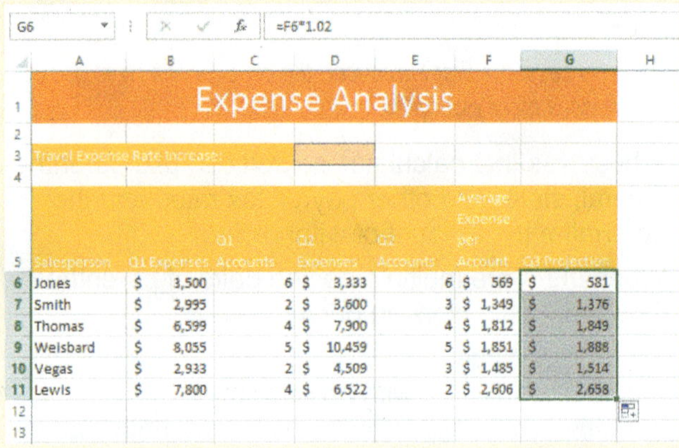

Excel 2013, Windows 8, Microsoft Corporation

Performing What-If Analysis

- A **what-if analysis** entails looking at how future results might change based on varying inputs or data.
- For example, businesses often want to plan for sales increases or decreases, tax increases or decreases, or other expense increases or decreases.
- You can perform some what-if analyses in Excel simply by creating formulas that refer to an input cell whose entry you can change to see differing results.

✓ *Excel Lesson 34 covers built-in tools that help automate what-if analysis. These tools include what-if data tables, Goal Seek, and Solver.*

Try It! Performing What-If Analysis

1. In the E26Try_xx file, select cell G6.
2. Change the formula to calculate the increased projected quarterly expense amount using an absolute reference to D3. The formula should read =F6*(1+$D$3).
3. Use the fill handle to copy the formula from cell G6 through G11.
4. Enter 2.5 in cell D3. Note how the column G values update.
5. Enter 3.5 in cell D3. Review the new values in column G again.
6. Save the E26Try_xx file, and leave it open to use in the next Try It.

Creating a Line Chart to Compare Data

- Line charts provide a great data analysis tool.
- Not only do line charts identify data points, but they also show how data changed between data points. You can draw the lines further to anticipate how data might change beyond the charted timeframes.
- When performing what-if analysis, charting the most recent actual data and the projected data as separate series provides an idea of how the projected data varies based on changes in projected inputs.

Try It! Creating a Line Chart to Compare Data

1. In the E26Try_xx file, select the nonadjacent ranges A5:A11 and F5:G11.
2. Click INSERT > Insert Line Chart > Line with Markers.
3. Drag the chart down below the sheet data.
4. Change the entry in cell D3 to 7.5. View the results in the chart.
5. Save the E26Try_xx file, and close it.

(continued)

Try It! Creating a Line Chart to Compare Data *(continued)*

A line chart that shows a what-if analysis result

D3 | *fx* 7.5%

Expense Analysis

Travel Expense Rate Increase: 7.50%

Changing input value

Salesperson	Q1 Expenses	Q1 Accounts	Q2 Expenses	Q2 Accounts	Average Expense per Account	Q3 Projection
Jones	$ 3,500	6	$ 3,333	6	$ 569	$ 612
Smith	$ 2,995	2	$ 3,600	3	$ 1,349	$ 1,450
Thomas	$ 6,599	4	$ 7,900	4	$ 1,812	$ 1,948
Weisbard	$ 8,055	5	$ 10,459	5	$ 1,851	$ 1,990
Vegas	$ 2,933	2	$ 4,509	3	$ 1,485	$ 1,596
Lewis	$ 7,800	4	$ 6,522	2	$ 2,606	$ 2,801

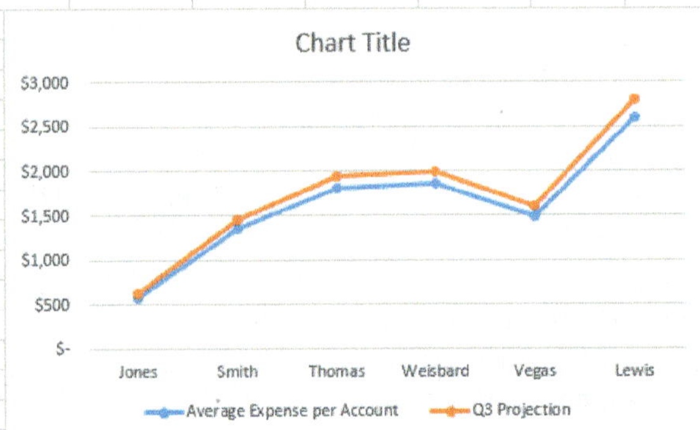

Excel 2013, Windows 8, Microsoft Corporation

Lesson 26—Practice

In this project, you will use parentheses in formulas to calculate a value based on a percentage increase using the skills you learned in this lesson.

DIRECTIONS

1. Start Excel, if necessary, and open the **E26Practice** file from the data files for this lesson.
2. Save the file as **E26Practice_xx** in the location where your teacher instructs you to store the files for this lesson.
3. Add a header that has your name at the left, the date code in the center, and the page number code at the right, and change back to **Normal** view.
4. Click cell **B14**.
5. Enter a formula that adds the 2013 tax rates and multiplies by the Q1 2013 wages. It should be **=($B$7+$B$8+$B$9)*B13**.
6. Use the fill handle to copy the formula from cell B14 through F14. Increase column widths, as necessary.
7. Copy the formula from cell **B14** to cell **B16**.
8. Edit the absolute references in the copied formula in cell B16 to refer to column C. Edit the relative cell reference to refer to cell B15.
9. Use the fill handle to copy the formula from cell B16 to F16. Your worksheet should look like the one shown in Figure 26-1.
10. **With your teacher's permission**, print the worksheet. Submit the printout or the file for grading as required.
11. Save and close the file, and exit Excel.

Figure 26-1

	A	B	C	D	E	F
1	Cantrell Resources					
2	2017 Projections					
3						
4	Proposed State Tax Increase					
5						
6		2016	2017			
7	Av. Federal Tax Rate	25.00%	25.00%			
8	State Tax Rate	6.00%	6.00%			
9	Other Payroll Taxes	15.30%	15.30%			
10						
11						
12		Q1	Q2	Q3	Q4	Total
13	2016 Wages	$ 626,254.00	$ 832,999.00	$ 709,241.00	$ 906,888.00	$ 3,075,382.00
14	2016 Withholding	$ 289,955.60	$ 385,678.54	$ 328,378.58	$ 419,889.14	$ 1,423,901.87
15	2017 Wages (+1.9%)					
16	2017 Withholding	$ -	$ -	$ -	$ -	$ -
17						
18						

Lesson 26—Apply

You are the CEO for Cantrell Resources, a firm that provides temporary labor, placement, and payroll services. The state legislature in your state is debating a possible increase in the state income tax for next year. You are already anticipating that gross wages will increase by 1.9% for the coming year, so you want to examine how different increased state tax levels will affect quarterly withholding taxes for your firm by adding the formulas and charts needed to make these projections.

DIRECTIONS

1. Start Excel, if necessary, and open the **E26Apply** file from the data files for this lesson.
2. Save the file as **E26Apply_xx** in the location where your teacher instructs you to store the files for this lesson.
3. Add a header that has your name at the left, the date code in the center, and the page number code at the right, and change back to **Normal** view.
4. Select cell **C8**, and enter a formula that multiples 1 plus the input rate in cell **C4** times the previous tax rate in cell **B8**.
5. In cell **B15**, create a formula that increases the wages in cell **B13** by **1.9%**. Fill the formula through cell **F15**, and adjust column widths, as necessary.
6. Enter **1** as the base rate in cell **C4**.
7. Select the noncontiguous ranges **A12:E12**, **A14:E14**, and **A16:E16**.
8. Insert a line chart using the **Line with Markers** subtype.
9. Adjust the minimum bound of the vertical axis to a minimum value of **250000**, and a maximum value of **450000**.

   ✓ *Use the Minimum and Maximum text boxes in the Bounds group in the AXIS OPTIONS of the Format Axis task pane.*
10. If necessary, adjust the Major units to a value of **20000**, and adjust the Minor units to a value of **4000**.
11. Remove the decimal places from the axis display.

    ✓ *See the NUMBER choices in the Format Axis task pane.*
12. Increase the size of the chart as desired and position it below the data.
13. Change the entry in cell **C4** to **4**. Observe the calculations in the data and the chart. Your chart should resemble Figure 26-2 on the next page.
14. **With your teacher's permission**, print the worksheet. Submit the printout or the file for grading as required.
15. Save and close the file, and exit Excel.

Figure 26-2

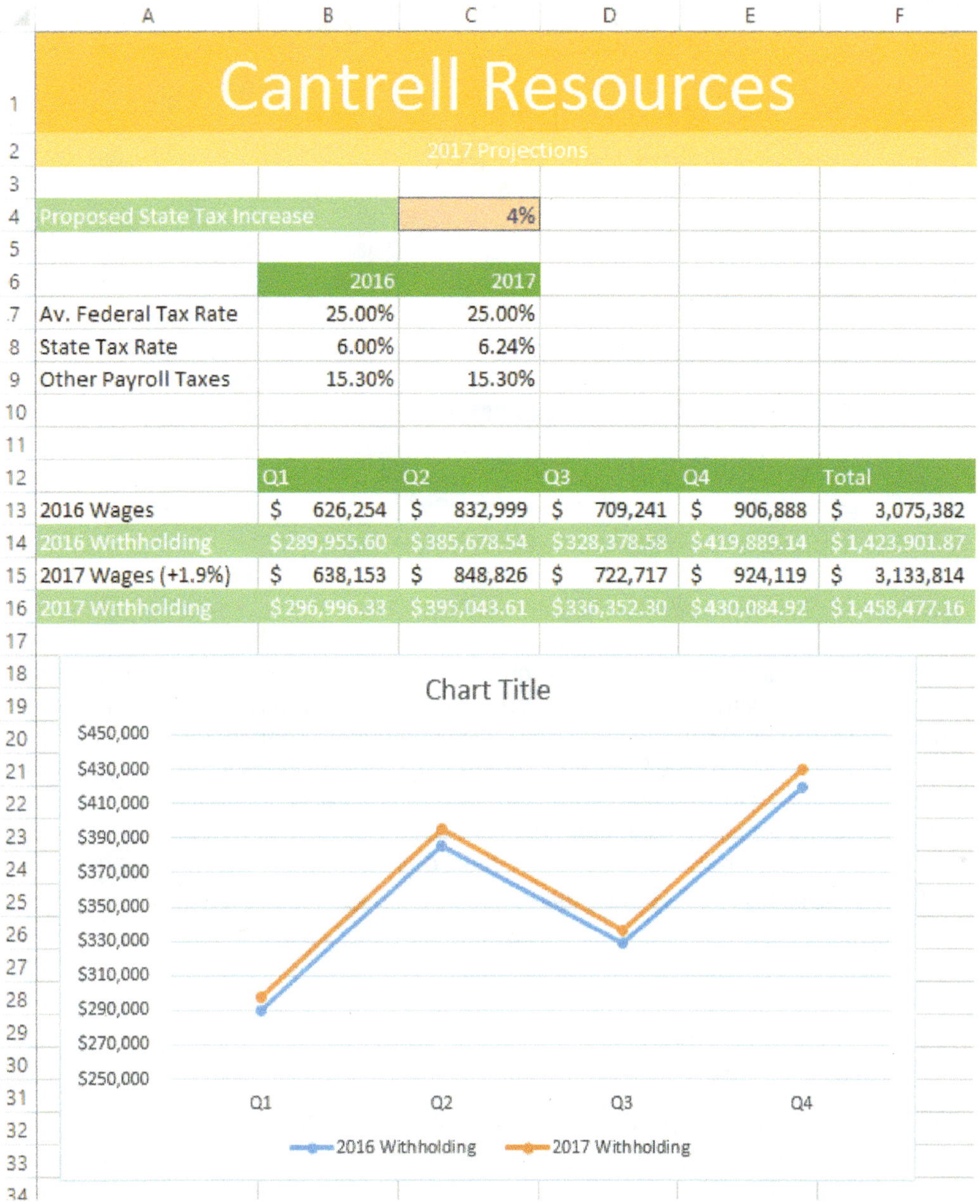

	A	B	C	D	E	F
1	Cantrell Resources					
2	2017 Projections					
3						
4	Proposed State Tax Increase		4%			
5						
6		2016	2017			
7	Av. Federal Tax Rate	25.00%	25.00%			
8	State Tax Rate	6.00%	6.24%			
9	Other Payroll Taxes	15.30%	15.30%			
10						
11						
12		Q1	Q2	Q3	Q4	Total
13	2016 Wages	$ 626,254	$ 832,999	$ 709,241	$ 906,888	$ 3,075,382
14	2016 Withholding	$289,955.60	$385,678.54	$328,378.58	$419,889.14	$1,423,901.87
15	2017 Wages (+1.9%)	$ 638,153	$ 848,826	$ 722,717	$ 924,119	$ 3,133,814
16	2017 Withholding	$296,996.33	$395,043.61	$336,352.30	$430,084.92	$1,458,477.16

Excel 2013, Windows 8, Microsoft Corporation

Lesson 27

Chart Printing and Publishing

➤ What You Will Learn

Printing a Chart
Preparing and Printing a Chart Sheet
Publishing a Chart to the Internet/Intranet

WORDS TO KNOW

Intranet
A private network of computers within a business or organization.

Publish
The process of saving data to an intranet or Internet.

Software Skills After creating a chart, you may want to print it out so you can share your data with others. You can print the chart with the rest of the worksheet data, or simply print just the chart, which is even easier when the chart is on a separate chart sheet. Another way to share your information is to publish your chart to the Internet, or to your company's intranet. You can even make your online chart *interactive*, so that users can change the data in the chart as well as view it. This is especially useful when the data for the chart comes from several sources, such as different departments in your company.

What You Can Do

Printing a Chart

- Embedded charts typically print with the worksheet on which they are located.
- If you select an embedded chart before choosing the Print command, you will only be able to print the chart.
- Typical print settings, such as changing the orientation and scaling, are available when printing a chart.

Try It! Printing a Chart

1. Start Excel.
2. Open the E27Try file from the data files for this lesson.
3. Save the file as E27Try_xx in the location where your teacher instructs you to store the files for this lesson.
4. On the Example sheet, add a header that has your name at the left, the date code in the center, and the page number code at the right, and change back to Normal view.
5. Make sure the Example sheet is selected.
6. Click FILE > Print. Examine the preview of the printout. Under Settings, notice that the Print Active Sheets option is set to only print the active sheets.
7. **With your teacher's permission**, click the Print button to print the sheet and chart.
8. Save the E27Try_xx file, and leave it open to use in the next Try It.

Preparing and Printing a Chart Sheet

- When printing a chart sheet, the Print Active Sheet option is selected by default so that only the chart sheet prints. You would have to change that setting to print the whole workbook.
- When you insert a header or footer on a chart sheet using INSERT > Header & Footer, the Page Setup dialog box appears with the Header/Footer tab selected. Use the Custom Header or Custom Footer button to build a header or footer.

  ✓ *You also have to use this method to add a header or footer to an embedded chart if you want to print it by itself.*

- The FILE > Print command also enables you to print the chart sheet.

Try It! Preparing and Printing a Chart Sheet

1. In the E27Try_xx file, click the Large Chart sheet.
2. Click the Buildout Status chart to select it, and then click INSERT > Header & Footer.
3. Click the Custom Header button. The Header dialog box appears.
4. Using the sections in the dialog box, add a header that has your name at the left, the date code in the center, and the page number code at the right, and then click OK twice.
5. Click FILE > Print. Examine the preview of the printout. Notice that the Large Chart sheet is using a different orientation than the Example sheet.
6. **With your teacher's permission**, click the Print button to print the chart.
7. Save the E27Try_xx file, and leave it open to use in the next Try It.

Publishing a Chart to the Internet/Intranet

- The process of saving worksheet data to the Internet or your company's **intranet** is called **publishing**.
- To publish a chart on the Internet or an intranet, Excel converts the chart to HTML format.
- There are actually two different HTML formats: Web Page (HTM) and Single File Web Page (MHT).
- HTM or HTML format is the standard Web page format in which the text and page format is stored in one file, and the graphics and other elements are stored in separate files linked to the main file.
- MHT or MHTML format is a single file Web page format in which the text, page format, and supporting graphics for a Web page are stored in one file.
- Both formats work perfectly well in most Web browsers; the MHT format does make it easier to relocate a Web page file if needed.
- If the chart is an embedded chart, the chart and its supporting data is published.
- You can publish a chart sheet or the entire workbook.
- Choose the Web format to save to from the Save as type drop-down list in the Save As dialog box. After choosing one of the Web formats, click the Publish button to open the Publish as Web Page dialog box, where you can navigate to a Web destination.
- In the Publish as Web Page dialog box, you must also open the Choose drop-down list under Item to publish, and then click Entire workbook. Otherwise, only the current sheet will be published, even if you chose Entire workbook in the Save As dialog box.
- Once your data is published, you can republish it when needed to update the data.
- You can have Excel automatically republish the data whenever you change the workbook, using the AutoRepublish option in the Publish as Web Page dialog box.
- You can also save Web page data on your hard disk, and transfer it to a Web location using another method.

  ✓ *When transferring Web page data to a Web location, be sure to transfer all the subfolders and contents created when the Web page was published; otherwise, the Web page will not display correctly.*

- Using an HTML editor, you can make changes to the Web page after it's saved to improve its appearance.

Try It! Publishing a Chart to the Internet/Intranet

1. In the **E27Try_xx** file, make sure the Large Chart sheet is selected.
2. Click FILE > Save As.
3. Browse to the location where your teacher instructs you to store the files for this lesson.
4. In the File name box enter **E27Try_HTM_xx**. Open the Save as type drop-down list, and click Single File Web Page.
5. Click the Change Title button Change Title..., type **Progress in Construction** as the title, and click OK.
6. Click the Selection: Chart button.
7. Click the Publish button Publish....
8. If necessary, use the Browse button to specify the location where your teacher instructs you to store the files for this lesson.
9. Click the Open published web page in browser check box, and then click the Publish button Publish.
10. View the published chart in the system's Web browser, and then close the browser.
11. Save and close the **E27Try_xx** file, and exit Excel.

Publishing settings

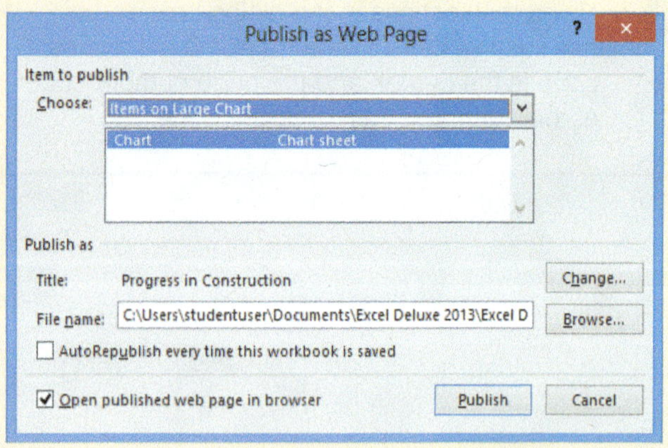

Excel 2013, Windows 8, Microsoft Corporation

Lesson 27—Practice

In this project, you will print a worksheet and a chart using the skills you learned in this lesson.

DIRECTIONS

1. Start Excel, if necessary, and open the **E27Practice** file from the data files for this lesson.
2. Save the file as **E27Practice_xx** in the location where your teacher instructs you to store the files for this lesson.
3. For the **Data** sheet, add a header that has your name at the left, the date code in the center, and the page number code at the right, and change back to **Normal** view.
4. Click **FILE** > **Print**. Notice that the right side of the data and chart are cut off, and that 1 of 2 appears at the bottom of the preview to indicate the number of pages in the file.
5. Under Settings, change the orientation to **Landscape**.
6. **With your teacher's permission**, print the worksheet.
7. On the **Data** sheet, click the chart to select it.
8. Click **INSERT** > **Header & Footer** > **Custom Header**.
9. In the text edit boxes, type your name at the left, the date code in the center, and the page number code at the right.
10. Click **OK** twice.
11. **With your teacher's permission**, print the chart. Submit the printout or the file for grading as required.
12. Save and close the file, and exit Excel.

Lesson 27—Apply

You are the CFO of Restoration Architecture and you've been preparing an important report for the CEO on fourth quarter revenues. The most important part is the chart you've prepared. You're going to print it out for inclusion in the final report, and publish the chart to the Web.

DIRECTIONS

1. Start Excel, if necessary, and open the **E27Apply** file from the data files for this lesson.
2. Save the file as **E27Apply_xx** in the location where your teacher instructs you to store the files for this lesson.
3. For both the **Revenue Chart** and **Data** sheets, add a header that has your name at the left, the date code in the center, and the page number code at the right, and change back to **Normal** view.
4. Preview the Revenue Chart sheet.
5. **With your teacher's permission**, print the sheet.
6. Save the chart sheet as a Single File Web Page in the location where your teacher instructs you to store the files for this lesson.
7. Click **Selection: Chart**.
8. Add a title of **Q4 Revenue Chart**.
9. Click **Save**.
10. In the Publish as Web Page dialog box, click the **Open published web page in browser** check box to select it if it isn't already selected.
11. Click **Publish**, and view the published chart in the Web browser program.
12. Close the browser.
13. **With your teacher's permission**, print the chart sheet. Submit the printout or the file for grading as required.
14. Save and close the file, and exit Excel.

Lesson 28

Using Charts in Other Files

➤ What You Will Learn

Pasting a Picture of a Chart
Embedding a Chart in a Word Document
Linking a Chart
Editing a Linked or Embedded Chart

WORDS TO KNOW

Embed
To insert an object in a destination document so that it can still be edited by the source application. When you double-click an embedded object, the source application (or its tools) appear, so you can edit the object. The original object remains unchanged because no link exists.

Link
A reference in a destination document to an object (such as a chart) in a source document. Changes to the linked object in the source document are automatically made to the object in the destination document.

Software Skills You can link or embed an Excel chart into another document, such as a Word document. If the source data is likely to change, you should link the data to its source, so that your chart will automatically update. This is especially useful when the source data is updated by several different people in your organization. You can also embed the chart in your Word document to ensure that your changes will not affect the original data.

What You Can Do

Pasting a Picture of a Chart

- The simplest way to include an Excel chart within another document, such as a Word document, is to paste its picture.
- The advantage of using a picture of a chart is that it will not significantly affect the size of your Word file.
- The disadvantage of using a chart picture is that the data is static—meaning if the data changes in the original Excel workbook, the picture of the chart is not updated.
- To update the picture, you would need to change the data in Excel and paste a new picture.
- After pasting the chart, click the Paste Options button that appears to the lower-right of the chart and then click Picture to paste the chart as a picture.

Try It! Pasting a Picture of a Chart

1. Start Excel.
2. Open the **E28TryA** file from the data files for this lesson.
3. Save the file as **E28TryA_xx** in the location where your teacher instructs you to store the files for this lesson.
4. Add a header that has your name at the left, the date code in the center, and the page number code at the right, and change back to Normal view.
5. Start Word.
6. Open the **E28TryB** file from the data files for this lesson.
7. Save the document as **E28TryB_xx** in the location where your teacher instructs you to store the files for this lesson.
8. Press CTRL + END and type your name.
9. Press ↑ three times to position the insertion point where you'd like the chart to appear.
10. In the **E28TryA_xx** workbook, on the Expenses tab, click the chart.
11. On the HOME tab, click Copy.
12. In the **E28TryB_xx** Word document, on the HOME tab, click Paste.
13. Click the Paste Options button, and click the Picture button.
14. Drag the sizing handle in the upper-left corner of the chart to make the chart smaller, so it will fit within the margins of the page.
15. Save the **E28TryB_xx** file, and leave it open to use in the next Try It.

Embedding a Chart in a Word Document

- When you **embed** a chart in a Word document, the chart data is also copied to the Word file and stored there.
- Making data or formatting changes to an embedded chart does not affect the original data or chart, since there is no link to the original chart.

✓ *Although this lesson discusses pasting charts into another document, you can use these same procedures to embed worksheet data rather than chart data. You can also use these procedures to share data in PowerPoint. See Excel Lesson 45 to learn more about using Paste Special.*

- An embedded chart in the destination file may also be displayed as an icon.
- After pasting the chart, you can use the Paste Options button that appears to the lower right of the chart to select either Use Destination Theme & Embed Workbook or Keep Source Formatting & Embed Workbook to insert the chart.

✓ *Rather than pasting and then choosing a paste method, you can use the HOME > Paste > Paste Options to choose the paste method when performing the initial paste. This is true of all the procedures covered in this lesson.*

Try It! Embedding a Chart in a Word Document

1. In the **E28TryB_xx** Word file, double-click the pasted chart picture. Notice that Excel does not open.

   ✓ *If the Format Chart Area task pane opens, click Close to close it.*

2. With the picture selected, press DEL to remove the picture from the file.
3. On the HOME tab, click the Paste button drop-down arrow ▾.

   ✓ *Because the chart is already on the Clipboard, there is no need to copy it again. However, if you copy any other data or information in a situation like this, you would need to return to Excel and select and copy the chart again.*

(continued)

Try It! Embedding a Chart in a Word Document *(continued)*

4. In the Paste Options drop-down options, click the Keep Source Formatting & Embed Workbook button.
5. Double-click the chart. Notice that the Chart Tools contextual tabs appear on Word's Ribbon.
6. Save the **E28TryB_xx** file, and leave it open to use in the next Try It.

Linking a Chart

- If you want to be able to edit your chart after pasting it into another document, you can **link** the chart.
- When you paste a chart into a destination file (Word document) as a linked chart, it remains connected to its source data (in Excel).
- When you change the data or chart formatting in a linked chart and open the destination file again, the link causes the destination chart to update as well.
- The link also enables you to start Excel from within the destination file (from within Word, for example), display the chart, and make your changes.
- To maintain the link, the files must remain in their original locations.
- Linked data in the destination file may also be displayed as an icon.
- After pasting the chart, click the Paste Options button that appears to the lower right of the chart and then click either Use Destination Theme & Link Data or Keep Source Formatting & Link Data to establish the link.

Try It! Linking a Chart

1. In the **E28TryB_xx** Word file, double-click the pasted chart picture. Notice that the Format Chart Area task pane opens, but that Excel does not open.
2. With the embedded chart selected, press DEL to remove the chart from the file.
3. On the HOME tab, click the Paste button drop-down arrow.
4. In the Paste Options drop-down options, click the Use Destination Theme & Link Data button.
5. Double-click the chart. Notice that the Chart Tools contextual tabs appear on Word's Ribbon.
6. Save the **E28TryB_xx** file and leave it open to use in the next Try It.

Editing a Linked or Embedded Chart

- Because linked data is stored in the source document, you can open that document in Excel to edit a linked chart. Save the source document to preserve the changes.
- When you change the worksheet data in Excel, the corresponding chart is updated.
- Open the destination document and the chart is either updated automatically or when you manually update the link.
- You can open Excel from within the destination document if you like, rather than starting Excel separately.
- Click a linked or embedded chart to display Excel's CHART TOOLS tabs in the destination application.

✓ *When you make formatting changes to a chart either in the source or destination workbook for a linked chart, those changes do not flow between the two chart locations.*

- Right-click a linked or embedded chart and click Edit Data to open the Excel window for editing data.

- If the data is linked, the source document opens in Excel. If the data is embedded, the Excel window shows the Chart name in the title bar, indicating the data is stored in the destination file, with the embedded chart.
- Make the changes you need. For a linked chart, save the source worksheet and close the Excel window. For an embedded chart, simply close the Excel window.
- If you've updated a source linked chart and the updates don't appear in the destination document, click the chart in the destination document and use the Refresh Data button on the CHART TOOLS DESIGN tab.

Try It! **Editing a Linked or Embedded Chart**

1. In Word, save the **E28TryB_xx** file and close it.
2. In the **E28TryA_xx** Excel file, select the chart title.
3. Edit the title to read **Projected 2014 Expenses**.
4. Click cell A6 and change its entry to **Computers & Software**.
5. Change the entries for book expenses in cells B4 and C4 to **375** and **450**, respectively.
6. Save the **E28TryA_xx** file, and exit Excel.
7. In Word, open the **E28TryB_xx** file.
8. Click the chart to select it > CHART TOOLS DESIGN tab > Refresh Data. Notice that the changes to the book expenses and the new series name appear in the chart. The title does not change, because that is a formatting change.
9. Save the **E28TryB_xx** file, and exit Word.

Lesson 28—Practice

In this project, you will paste a chart in a Word document as a picture using the skills you learned in this lesson.

DIRECTIONS

1. Start Excel, if necessary, and open **E28PracticeA** from the data files for this lesson.
2. Save the file as **E28PracticeA_xx** in the location where your teacher instructs you to store the files for this lesson.
3. Group the sheets. Add a header that has your name at the left, the date code in the center, and the page number code at the right, and change back to Normal view. Ungroup the sheets.
4. Open **E28PracticeB** from the data files for this lesson.
5. Save the document as **E28PracticeB_xx** in the location where your teacher instructs you to store the files for this lesson.
6. Type the date and your name in the *Date Prepared* and *Prepared By* headings, respectively.
7. In Word, add a footer that has your name at the left, the date code in the center, and the page number code at the right.

   ✓ *The Blank (Three-Columns) Footer will provide a footer similar to the heading you have been using in the Excel exercises.*

   ✓ *To insert a page number in a Word footer, click the Type Here placeholder > Page Number > Current Position > Plain Number.*

   ✓ *Click Close Header and Footer on the HEADER & FOOTER TOOLS DESIGN tab to close the header or footer and return to your document.*

8. In the **E28PracticeA_xx** Excel file, click the **2017 Charts** tab.
9. Click the top chart to select it.
10. On the **HOME** tab, click **Copy**.
11. In the **E28PracticeB_xx** Word file, click below the Asset Summary heading, and click **HOME** > **Paste** drop-down arrow > **Picture**. The picture appears in the document.
12. **With your teacher's permission**, print the Word document. Submit the printout or the file for grading as required.
13. Save and close both files, and exit Word and Excel.

Lesson 28—Apply

As CFO of Hyland Manufacturing, you need to prepare an executive summary of balance sheet data for the board of directors. You've prepared the charts, and you need to incorporate the charts in the executive summary Word document.

DIRECTIONS

1. Start Excel, if necessary, and open **E28ApplyA** from the data files for this lesson.
2. Save the file as **E28ApplyA_xx** in the location where your teacher instructs you to store the files for this lesson.
3. Group the sheets. Add a header that has your name at the left, the date code in the center, and the page number code at the right, and change back to Normal view. Ungroup the sheets.
4. Open **E28ApplyB** from the data files for this lesson.
5. Save the document as **E28ApplyB_xx** in the location where your teacher instructs you to store the files for this lesson.
6. In the **E28ApplyB_xx** document, type the date and your name in the *Date Prepared* and *Prepared By* headings, respectively.
7. Add a footer that has your name at the left, the date code in the center, and the page number code at the right.
8. In the Excel file, click the **2014 Charts** tab.
9. Select and copy the top chart.
10. In the Word document, paste the chart using the destination theme and link the data under the Asset Summary heading.
11. Repeat steps 8 through 10 to paste and link the bottom chart under the Liability Summary heading. Review the appearance of both charts.
12. In the Excel file, click the **2017 Balance Sheet** sheet tab.
13. Change the entry in cell **B15** to **4095**.
14. Change the entry in cell **E19** to **1813**.
15. Save the **E28ApplyA_xx** Excel file, and exit Excel.
16. In the Word document, review the changes to the charts, particularly the Liabilities chart.
17. **With your teacher's permission**, print the Word document. Submit the printout or the file for grading as required.
18. Save the **E28ApplyB_xx** Word file, and exit Word.

Lesson 29

Making Special Purpose Charts

➤ What You Will Learn

Creating Organization Charts
Creating Other SmartArt Diagrams

Software Skills With an organization chart, you can easily show the relationship between objects or people. For example, you could show how your department is organized. With other conceptual charts, you could show the progress of a project—from conception to completion, areas of overlapping responsibility within a department or on a group project, or the cycle of events with a school or calendar year.

WORDS TO KNOW

Organization chart
Displays the relationships within an organization, such as the managers in an office, the people they manage, and who they report to.

SmartArt graphic
A pre-drawn graphic used to illustrate a specific data relationship, such as a list, process, cycle, hierarchy, matrix, pyramid, or other relationship.

What You Can Do

Creating Organization Charts

- To show relationships within a group such as an office, the government, or a school, create an **organization chart**.
- An organization chart is just one of many **SmartArt graphics** you can insert on a worksheet.
- On the INSERT tab, use the SmartArt button to open the Choose a SmartArt Graphic dialog box. The Hierarchy group in the Choose a SmartArt Graphic dialog box provides a selection of organization and layout charts.
- When you start an organization chart, Excel provides a sample chart showing several basic relationships.
- Enter data for the organization chart using the Text Pane, which displays a bulleted list that shows the relationship between people.

  ✓ *Use the Text Pane button on the SMARTART TOOLS DESIGN tab to open and close the Text Pane.*

- You can paste this list from another source or enter it manually.
- Use the Add Shape button on the SmartArt Tools Design tab to add the desired relationships.

- You can add shapes before, after, above, or below the currently selected shape. You can also add an assistant shape.
- If you add a shape before or after, that shape is placed on the same level in the hierarchy as the current shape.
- If you add a shape above or below, the shape is placed above or below the current shape in the organizational hierarchy.

✓ *After typing text in the Text Pane, press ENTER to create another shape at the same level. Use SHIFT + TAB to decrease the level, or TAB to increase the level.*

- An assistant shape is placed out to one side, indicating a different relationship than an employee-manager or employee-employee relationship.
- Remove shapes (relationships) you don't need for your chart by selecting the shape, and pressing DEL.
- For other graphics such as charts, you can select from predefined layouts and styles, and apply them with a single click. The SMARTART TOOLS DESIGN tab offers Layouts and SmartArt Styles galleries.
- You can also apply your own formatting (outlines, fills, shadows, glows, and other effects) to individual shapes and the background. These choices are on the SMARTART TOOLS FORMAT tab.
- You can format the text of individual shapes or the whole chart.
- Using the Layout button in the Create Graphic group on the SMARTART TOOLS DESIGN tab, you can change the way in which relationships are displayed within the chart.

✓ *If you've already created an organization chart or other SmartArt graphic in Word or PowerPoint, you can save time by simply copying and pasting it into Excel.*

Try It! Creating Organization Charts

1. Start Excel, and create a new blank workbook file.
2. Save the file as **E29Try_xx** in the location where your teacher instructs you to store the files for this lesson.
3. Add a header that has your name at the left, the date code in the center, and the page number code at the right, and change back to Normal view.
4. Click PAGE LAYOUT > Orientation > Landscape.
5. Click INSERT > SmartArt.
6. In the list at the left, click Hierarchy.
7. In the list in the middle, click the third layout in the top row, Name and Title Organization Chart, and click OK.
8. In the Text Pane that appears to the left of the chart, type the following names in order, clicking the next placeholder after finishing each one:
   Aliyah Brown
   Linda Williams
   Bill Whittaker
   Marlow Aronstein
   Katie Martin
9. Click the smaller text box at the lower right of each shape, and type the following titles:
   President
   Assistant
   HR Director
   Product Director
   Sales Director
10. Click the Katie Martin shape > SMARTART TOOLS DESIGN > Add Shape drop-down arrow > Add Shape Below.
11. In the new shape, add **Ron Crane** and **Deputy Sales Director** as the name and title.
12. On the SMARTART TOOLS DESIGN tab, click the SmartArt Styles More button, and click Polished, the first style under 3-D.
13. Click the Linda Williams shape to select it.
14. Click SMARTART TOOLS FORMAT > Shape Fill (Shape Fill) > Green, Accent 6, Darker 25%.
15. With the Linda Williams shape still selected, click SMARTART TOOLS FORMAT > Shape Outline > Green, Accent, Lighter 80%.

(continued)

Try It! Creating Organization Charts *(continued)*

16. Click the Close button on the Text Pane.
17. Drag the chart up so its upper-left corner is over cell B2.
18. Save the **E29Try_xx** file and leave it open to use in the next Try It.

Organization chart with names and titles added

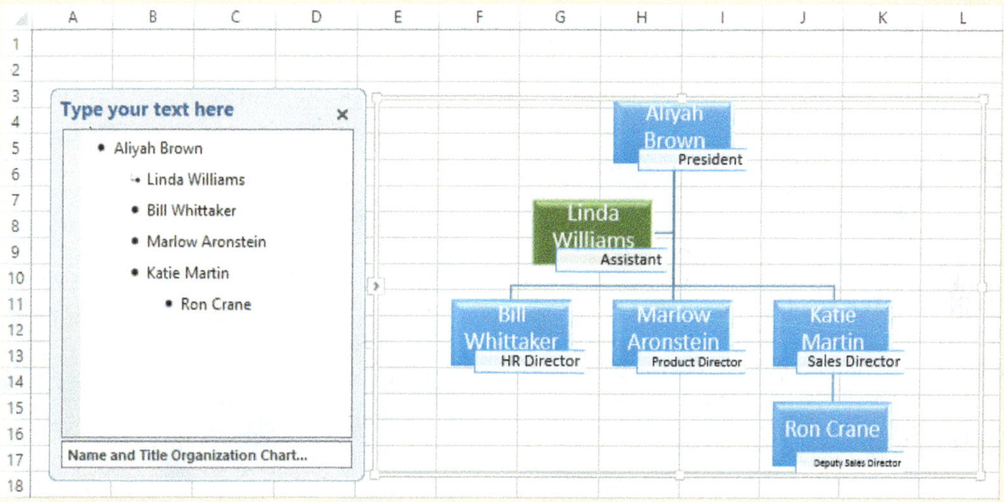

Excel 2013, Windows 8, Microsoft Corporation

Creating Other SmartArt Diagrams

- In addition to organization charts, Excel enables you to create several other types of conceptual charts using the Choose a SmartArt Graphic dialog box.
- You can choose these overall diagram types from the list at the left side of the dialog box.

  ✓ *You can use the Office.com choice to see the latest added diagrams available for download.*

- There are numerous layouts available for each of the SmartArt diagram types.
- After you create the diagram, you can easily change from one layout to another until you find the one that properly conveys the relationship between your data items. You can use the More button in the Layouts group on the SMARTART TOOLS DESIGN tab to view the layouts. You can use the More Layouts button at the bottom of the menu to change to another type of diagram. The More Layouts choice at the bottom of the menu even enables you to change to another type of diagram.

Try It! Creating Other SmartArt Diagrams

1. In the **E29Try_xx** file, click INSERT > SmartArt. The SmartArt Graphic Dialog box opens.
2. In the list at the left, click Cycle.
3. In the list in the middle, click the first layout in the second row, Continuous Cycle, and click OK.
4. Drag the new chart down below the organization chart. Scroll down, if necessary.
5. On the SMARTART TOOLS DESIGN tab, in the Create Graphic group, click Text Pane.

(continued)

Try It! Creating Other SmartArt Diagrams *(continued)*

6. In the Text Pane, type the following text for the boxes, clicking the next placeholder after finishing each one:

   Startup

   Initial Diagnostics

   Operational Cycle

   Cleaning Cycle

   Auto Power Cycle

7. Click Text Pane to close the Text Pane.
8. With the mouse pointer still in the Auto Power Cycle box, click Add Bullet.
9. Type **Manual power cycle every 14 days**.
10. On the SMART TOOLS DESIGN tab, in the SmartArt Styles group, click Change Colors > Colorful > Colorful Range - Accent Colors 2 to 3 (the second choice in the Colorful group).
11. Click SMARTART TOOLS FORMAT > Shape Fill Shape Fill > Gradient > Dark Variations > From Center (second on the second row).
12. Click SMARTART TOOLS DESIGN > Layouts More button > More Layouts.
13. In the list at the left, click List.
14. In the list in the middle, click the second layout in the second row, Vertical Box List, and click OK.
15. Click the Close button on the Text Pane to close the Text Pane.
16. Save and close the file, and exit Excel.

Cycle diagram with fill gradient

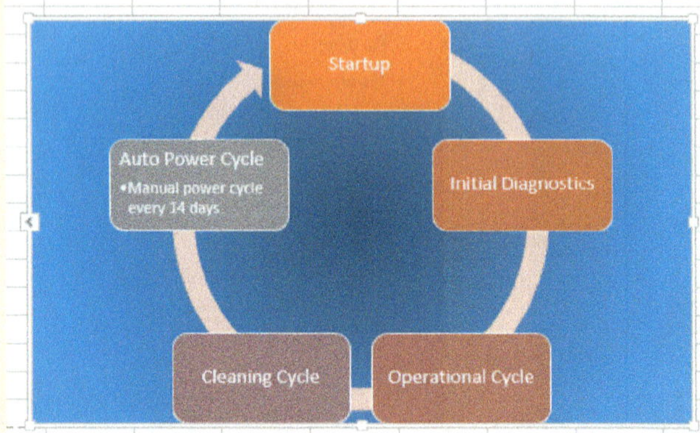

Excel 2013, Windows 8, Microsoft Corporation

Lesson 29—Practice

In this project, you will use SmartArt to create a process diagram using the skills you learned in this lesson.

DIRECTIONS

1. Start Excel, if necessary, and open **E29Practice** from the data files for this lesson.
2. Save the file as **E29Practice_xx** in the location where your teacher instructs you to store the files for this lesson.
3. Add a header that has your name at the left, the date code in the center, and the page number code at the right, and change back to **Normal** view.
4. Click **INSERT** > **SmartArt**.
5. In the list at the left, click **Process**.
6. In the middle list, click **Vertical Chevron List**, and click **OK**.
7. In the Text Pane, add the following text:

   Rapid Prototyping

       Reduced Time

       Reduced Waste

   Production Pilot

       Build Process

       Document Process

   Testing

       Safety Testing

       Performance Testing

8. After the last entry, press ENTER and then SHIFT + TAB. This creates another shape at the top level.
9. Type **Production Release**, press ENTER and then TAB. This indents to the bullet-level shape.
10. Type **Continuous Quality Improvement**, press ENTER, and then type **RFID Tracking**.
11. On the SMARTART TOOLS DESIGN tab, click **Text Pane** to hide the Text Pane.
12. Drag the diagram up so its upper-left corner is on cell **B4**. Your chart should resemble Figure 29-1.
13. **With your teacher's permission**, print the worksheet. Submit the printout or the file for grading as required.
14. Save and close the file, and exit Excel.

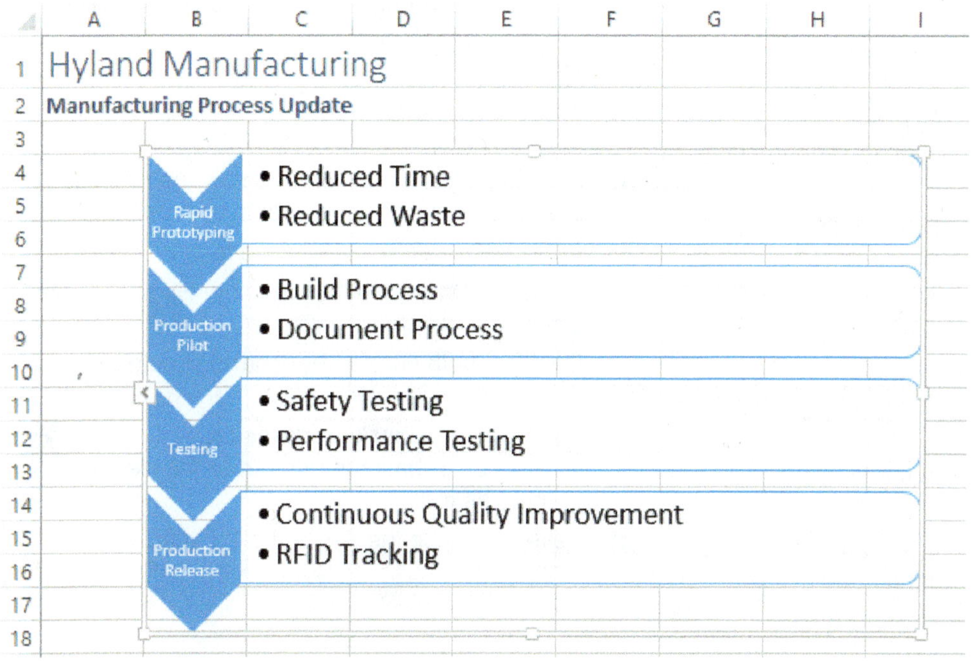

Excel 2013, Windows 8, Microsoft Corporation

Figure 29-1

Lesson 29—Apply

You are the Chief Operating Officer (COO) of Hyland Manufacturing. The company has developed a new manufacturing process, and you need to provide information about it to key customers to reassure them that their future orders will be handled seamlessly under the new process. You will send two SmartArt diagrams—one that illustrates the process itself, and another that is an organization chart of the team managing the process.

DIRECTIONS

1. Start Excel, if necessary, and open **E29Apply** from the data files for this lesson.
2. Save the file as **E29Apply_xx** in the location where your teacher instructs you to store the files for this lesson.
3. Add a header that has your name at the left, the date code in the center, and the page number code at the right, and change back to **Normal** view.
4. Create an organization chart using the **Horizontal Organization Chart** layout.
5. Delete the Assistant shape (the text box above the relationship line).
6. Enter **Production Director** in the top level box on the left.
7. Enter **Engineering Manager**, **Quality Manager**, and **Production Manager** in the three stacked text boxes.
8. Right-click the Engineering Manager box, click **Change Shape**, and click the **Pentagon** block arrow.
9. Apply the **Pentagon** block arrow shape to the other two lower-level boxes.
10. Drag the organization chart below the process chart, so its upper-left corner is over cell **B20**.
11. Apply the **Inset** SmartArt style to both charts.
12. Apply the **Dark 2 Fill** colors under Primary Theme Colors to both charts.
13. Deselect both charts. Your charts should resemble Figure 29-2.
14. **With your teacher's permission**, print the worksheet. Submit the printout or the file for grading as required.
15. Save and close the file, and exit Excel.

Figure 29-2

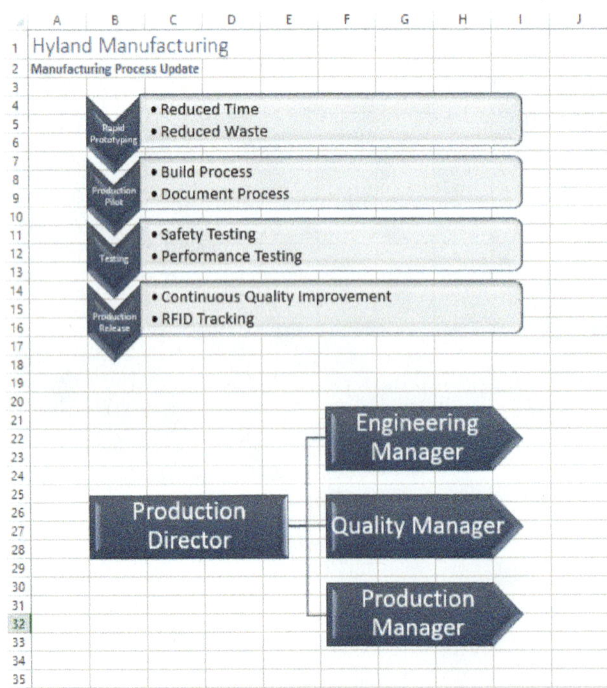

Excel 2013, Windows 8, Microsoft Corporation

End-of-Chapter Activities

➤ Excel Chapter 3—Critical Thinking

Investment Portfolio

You are a certified financial planner with Solid Investments, LLC. You are putting some sample data together to help illustrate stock performance and investment potential and risk for new clients who are also new to investing overall. You will chart historical stock price data, create formulas that show how a sample portfolio of investments will change if the market goes up or down, and chart that sample portfolio data.

DIRECTIONS

1. Start Excel, if necessary, and open **ECT03** from the data files for this chapter.
2. Save the file as **ECT03_xx** in the location where your teacher instructs you to store the files for this chapter.
3. Group the named sheets. Add a header that has your name at the left, the date code in the center, and the page number code at the right, and change back to **Normal** view. Ungroup the sheets.
4. On the **Ford Historical Prices** sheet, select the range **A5:E27**, and insert a **Stock** chart using the **Open-High-Low-Close** subtype.
5. Apply the **Layout 1** layout to the chart, and the **Style 3** chart style.
6. Change the scale of the primary vertical axis so that its minimum value is **9**. This scales the data bars so that they are easier to interpret.
7. Change the chart title to **Ford June 2010**.
8. Drag the chart so its upper-left corner is over cell **I3**.
9. Go to the **Portfolio Analysis** tab.
10. In cell **E8**, enter a formula that will recalculate the value from the Total column based on an increase percentage entered in cell **D4**. Use an absolute reference to cell D4.
11. Copy the formula in cell **E8** down through cell **E12**.
12. In cell **F8**, enter a formula that will recalculate the value from the Total column based on a decrease percentage entered in cell **D5**. Use an absolute reference to cell D5.

    ✓ *You can use a similar formula to the one you created in step 10, but subtract, instead.*
13. Copy the formula in cell **F8** down through cell **F12**. Adjust column widths, if necessary.
14. To test your formulas, enter **7** in cell **D4** and **5** in cell **D5**. Verify that the values in column E increased by 7% and that the values in column F decreased by 5%. If not, correct your formulas.
15. Select the ranges **D7:F7** and **D13:F13** and insert a **Clustered Column** chart.
16. Add a title above the chart that reads **Sample Portfolio Results**.
17. Move the chart so its upper-left corner is over cell **I4**.
18. Adjust the page breaks in Page Break Preview for both worksheets to print on a single page.

    ✓ *Adjust the Print Settings to Print Entire Workbook and Fit Sheet on One Page, as needed.*
19. **With your teacher's permission**, print the workbook. Submit the printouts or the file for grading as required.
20. Save and close the file, and exit Excel.

➤ Excel Chapter 3—Portfolio Builder

Sales Data Chart and Web Page

You are the CFO for Teesy Apparel, a T-shirt manufacturer. You have developed a worksheet with quarterly sales data that also tracks sales by product line and size. You need to chart all this information for future production planning, and create a SmartArt diagram that ranks potential new product ideas. After you chart the data, you will publish the data as a Single File Web Page to the company intranet to give the planning team easier access.

DIRECTIONS

1. Start Excel, if necessary, and open **EPB03** from the data files for this chapter.
2. Save the file as **EPB03_xx** in the location where your teacher instructs you to store the files for this chapter.
3. Create a **Clustered Column** chart of the quarterly sales totals on its own chart sheet. Name the sheet **Q Sales**.
4. Use the Select Data Source dialog box to assign the range **='Sales Data'!$E$4:$H$4** as the horizontal axis label range. (Hint: Select an existing axis label entry, and click **Edit**.)
5. Add a title above the chart that reads **Strong Quarterly Product Sales**.
6. Apply chart **Style 16** to the chart.
7. On the **Sales Data** sheet, create **3-D Pie** charts for the Sales by Product Line and Sales by Size data, placing each chart on its own sheet and giving the sheets appropriate names.
8. Apply the **Layout 1** layout to each pie chart, and make the chart title the same as the sheet name.
9. Apply a solid fill of **Gold, Accent 4, Lighter 80%** to each of the pie chart areas.
10. Explode the smallest slice for each pie chart.
11. Add a sheet titled **Potential Products**.
12. Insert a **Matrix** SmartArt diagram that uses the **Grid Matrix** layout.
13. Open the Text Pane, and use it to add these entries to the diagram:

    Organic Cotton Socks

    Organic Cotton Sweatshirts

    Natural Dyes Line

    Children's Tees
14. Hide the Text Pane, apply **Colorful - Accent Colors** to the diagram, and drag it to the upper-left corner of the worksheet.
15. On the **Sales Data** sheet, select cell **A1**. Publish the entire workbook as a **Single File Web Page**, adding **Teesy Apparel** as a title. (Hint: In the Publish as Web Page dialog box, remember to also open the Choose drop-down list under Item to publish, and then click Entire workbook.) Save the Web page as **EPB03_HTM_xx**.
16. The workbook opens in your Web browser. If necessary, allow blocked content to be viewed in the browser. The file has a tab for every tab in the worksheet, as shown in Illustration 3A on the next page. Click the various tabs to review the charts that you have created. Close the Web browser when you finish.
17. For all chart sheets and worksheets, add a header that has your name at the left, the date code in the center, and the page number code at the right, and change back to **Normal** view.
18. **With your teacher's permission**, print all worksheets in the workbook, scaling each to fit a single page. Submit the printouts or the file for grading as required.
19. Save and close the file, and exit Excel.

Illustration 3A

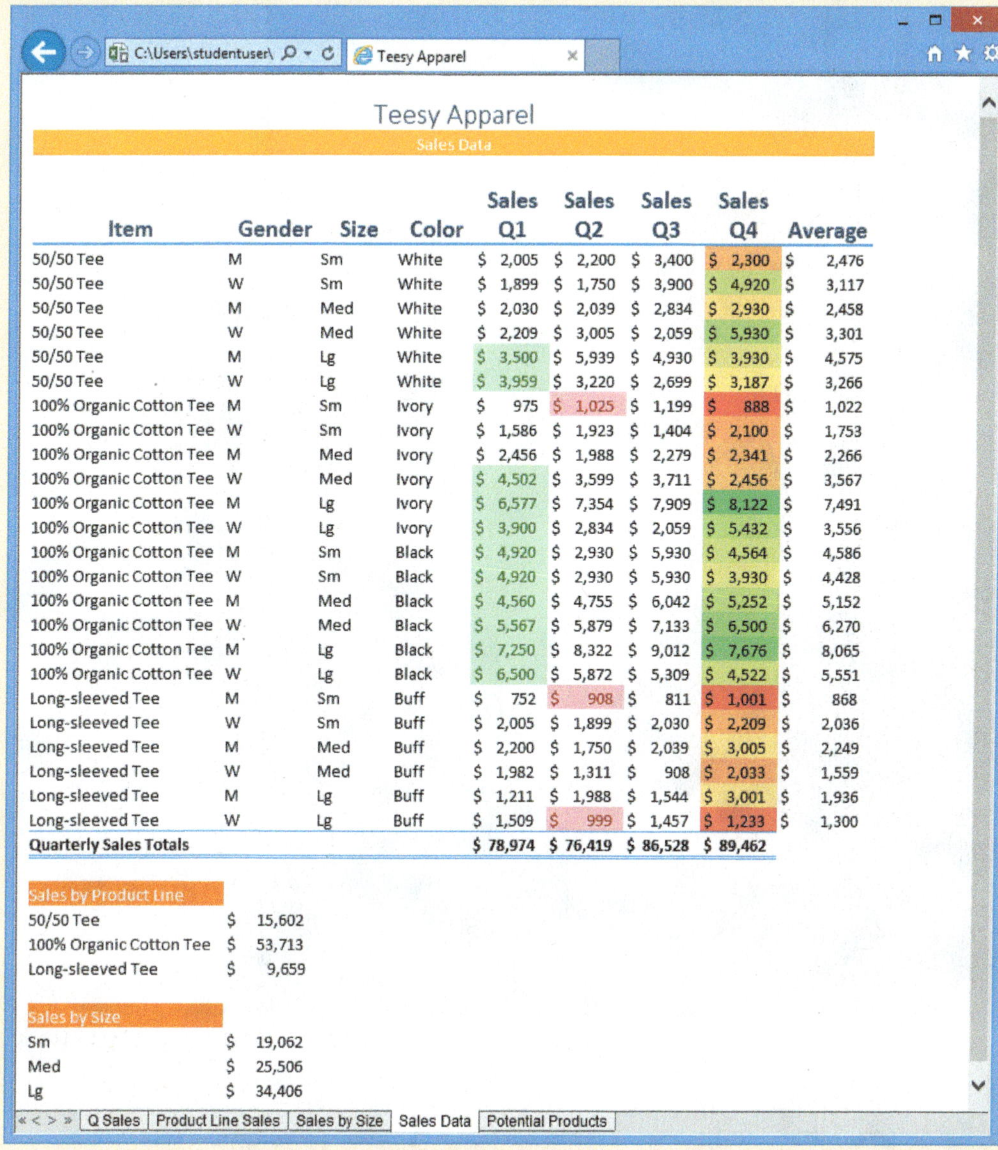

C:\Users\studentuser\ Teesy Apparel

Teesy Apparel

Sales Data

Item	Gender	Size	Color	Sales Q1	Sales Q2	Sales Q3	Sales Q4	Average
50/50 Tee	M	Sm	White	$ 2,005	$ 2,200	$ 3,400	$ 2,300	$ 2,476
50/50 Tee	W	Sm	White	$ 1,899	$ 1,750	$ 3,900	$ 4,920	$ 3,117
50/50 Tee	M	Med	White	$ 2,030	$ 2,039	$ 2,834	$ 2,930	$ 2,458
50/50 Tee	W	Med	White	$ 2,209	$ 3,005	$ 2,059	$ 5,930	$ 3,301
50/50 Tee	M	Lg	White	$ 3,500	$ 5,939	$ 4,930	$ 3,930	$ 4,575
50/50 Tee	W	Lg	White	$ 3,959	$ 3,220	$ 2,699	$ 3,187	$ 3,266
100% Organic Cotton Tee	M	Sm	Ivory	$ 975	$ 1,025	$ 1,199	$ 888	$ 1,022
100% Organic Cotton Tee	W	Sm	Ivory	$ 1,586	$ 1,923	$ 1,404	$ 2,100	$ 1,753
100% Organic Cotton Tee	M	Med	Ivory	$ 2,456	$ 1,988	$ 2,279	$ 2,341	$ 2,266
100% Organic Cotton Tee	W	Med	Ivory	$ 4,502	$ 3,599	$ 3,711	$ 2,456	$ 3,567
100% Organic Cotton Tee	M	Lg	Ivory	$ 6,577	$ 7,354	$ 7,909	$ 8,122	$ 7,491
100% Organic Cotton Tee	W	Lg	Ivory	$ 3,900	$ 2,834	$ 2,059	$ 5,432	$ 3,556
100% Organic Cotton Tee	M	Sm	Black	$ 4,920	$ 2,930	$ 5,930	$ 4,564	$ 4,586
100% Organic Cotton Tee	W	Sm	Black	$ 4,920	$ 2,930	$ 5,930	$ 3,930	$ 4,428
100% Organic Cotton Tee	M	Med	Black	$ 4,560	$ 4,755	$ 6,042	$ 5,252	$ 5,152
100% Organic Cotton Tee	W	Med	Black	$ 5,567	$ 5,879	$ 7,133	$ 6,500	$ 6,270
100% Organic Cotton Tee	M	Lg	Black	$ 7,250	$ 8,322	$ 9,012	$ 7,676	$ 8,065
100% Organic Cotton Tee	W	Lg	Black	$ 6,500	$ 5,872	$ 5,309	$ 4,522	$ 5,551
Long-sleeved Tee	M	Sm	Buff	$ 752	$ 908	$ 811	$ 1,001	$ 868
Long-sleeved Tee	W	Sm	Buff	$ 2,005	$ 1,899	$ 2,030	$ 2,209	$ 2,036
Long-sleeved Tee	M	Med	Buff	$ 2,200	$ 1,750	$ 2,039	$ 3,005	$ 2,249
Long-sleeved Tee	W	Med	Buff	$ 1,982	$ 1,311	$ 908	$ 2,033	$ 1,559
Long-sleeved Tee	M	Lg	Buff	$ 1,211	$ 1,988	$ 1,544	$ 3,001	$ 1,936
Long-sleeved Tee	W	Lg	Buff	$ 1,509	$ 999	$ 1,457	$ 1,233	$ 1,300
Quarterly Sales Totals				**$ 78,974**	**$ 76,419**	**$ 86,528**	**$ 89,462**	

Sales by Product Line	
50/50 Tee	$ 15,602
100% Organic Cotton Tee	$ 53,713
Long-sleeved Tee	$ 9,659

Sales by Size	
Sm	$ 19,062
Med	$ 25,506
Lg	$ 34,406

Q Sales | Product Line Sales | Sales by Size | Sales Data | Potential Products

Excel 2013, Windows 8, Microsoft Corporation

Chapter 4

(Courtesy Stephen Coburn/Shutterstock)

Advanced Functions, PivotCharts, and PivotTables

Lesson 30
Working with Hyperlinks

- Using a Hyperlink in Excel
- Creating a Hyperlink in a Cell
- Modifying Hyperlinks
- Modifying Hyperlinked Cell Attributes
- Removing a Hyperlink

Lesson 31
Using Advanced Sort

- Sorting Excel Items
- Understanding the Rules for Advanced Sorting
- Sorting on Multiple Columns
- Removing a Sort

Lesson 32
Using Advanced Filtering

- Using AutoFilter to Filter Tables
- Using AutoFilter to Filter by Custom Criteria
- Filtering Items without Creating a Table
- Filtering by Using Advanced Criteria
- Removing an In-Place Advanced Filter
- Extracting Filtered Rows
- Using Sum, Average, and Count in a Filtered Table
- Using Slicers

Lesson 33
Using Advanced Functions to Predict Trends

- Creating Predictions and Estimations
- Using FORECAST
- Using TREND
- Using GROWTH

Lesson 34
Using Advanced Functions for Data Analysis

- Using the PMT Function
- Creating What-If Data Tables
- Solving a Problem with Goal Seek
- Using Solver to Resolve Problems
- Working with Outlines

Lesson 35
Using Lookup Functions

- Creating Lookup Functions

Lesson 36
Working with PivotTables and PivotCharts

- Creating PivotTables
- Using the PivotTable Fields Task Pane
- Applying PivotTable Styles
- Creating PivotCharts

Lesson 37
Working with Data Models

- Understanding the Excel Data Model
- Drilling into PivotTable Data
- Using a PivotTable Timeline
- Using a Trendline

Lesson 38
Working with Excel Online

- Creating a Web Query
- Sharing Workbook Data on OneDrive

End-of-Chapter Activities

Lesson 30

Working with Hyperlinks

➤ What You Will Learn

Using a Hyperlink in Excel
Creating a Hyperlink in a Cell
Modifying Hyperlinks
Modifying Hyperlinked Cell Attributes
Removing a Hyperlink

WORDS TO KNOW

Hyperlink
Text or graphics linked to related information in the same workbook, another workbook, or another file.

URL
Short for Uniform Resource Locator. The address or location of a page or file on the Internet.

Web pages
Documents (frequently including multimedia elements) that can be accessed with a Web browser.

Software Skills A hyperlink can connect a worksheet to specific locations within any worksheet in any workbook, or to information on the Internet or a company intranet. Using a hyperlink is a convenient way to provide quick access to related information. For example, in a sales worksheet, you could provide a hyperlink to an area in the workbook (or in another workbook) that provides product costs or other revenues.

What You Can Do

Using a Hyperlink in Excel

- A **hyperlink** is text or a graphic that, when clicked, displays related information elsewhere in the worksheet or in another file.
  - You can link to information in the same worksheet, another worksheet in the same workbook, another workbook, or anywhere on the Internet.
  - You can also link to any other file, such as a Word document, sound file, graphic image or movie, as shown in Figure 30-1 on the next page.
  - These files may be located on your hard disk, the company network, the Internet or an intranet.

    ✓ *If you link to other files, make sure that the location of the file you are linking to will not change.*

  - You can link to your e-mail address, to help the user send you an e-mail message.
  - You can also create a new workbook to link to.
- When you move the mouse pointer over a hyperlink, it changes to a pointing hand.
  - This change helps you distinguish hyperlinks from regular text, and hyperlink graphics from regular pictures.
  - Because the mouse pointer changes to a hand when over a hyperlink, you must use special techniques to select the link for editing.

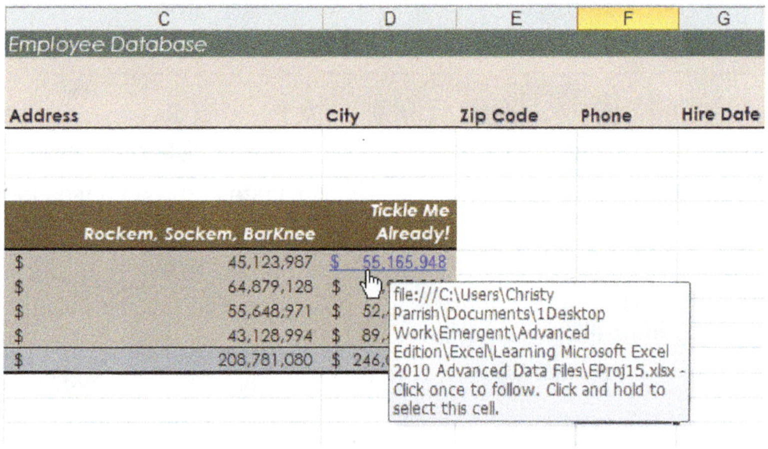

Figure 30-1

Excel 2013, Windows 8, Microsoft Corporation

- When a mouse pointer moves over a hyperlink, a ScreenTip appears, displaying the **URL** of the linked file or e-mail address.
  - You can override this default ScreenTip with a short description of the linked file or e-mail address.
- Text hyperlinks are typically formatted in a different color and underlined.
  - When you click a text hyperlink and then later return to it, you'll probably notice that it has changed to purple underlined text.
  - This change helps you quickly identify the links you've used (and those you haven't).
- Clicking a hyperlink moves you to the associated location.
  - If the hyperlink involves another file, that file is opened automatically.
  - If you want the user to move to a particular place within a worksheet, you might want to create a range name so that you can use that name in the link.

    ✓ *If you don't want to create a range name, you can still link to a specific place within a worksheet by typing its cell address.*
- You can create hyperlinks that connect a user to data in the current workbook or workbooks located on a company intranet.
- You can also connect to data on the Internet.
  - You can connect to Excel files or to HTML/MHTML files, since Excel can display either.
  - This capability allows you to include links to related **Web pages** (since they're coded in HTML or MHTML) within your worksheets.
- You can include hyperlinks in ordinary Excel worksheets or in workbooks that you have converted to HTML format.

Creating a Hyperlink in a Cell

- If you want to create a hyperlink, enter the text or graphic image before you follow the steps to create the hyperlink.
- Normally, you insert a hyperlink using the Insert Hyperlink dialog box.
- If you want to create a hyperlink to a Web page or an intranet document, you can bypass the Insert Hyperlink dialog box and type the Web page address (URL) or intranet location into a cell.
  - Excel will instantly recognize the address as a URL, and create a hyperlink from it automatically.
  - A Web address might look like this: http://www.fakeco.com/augsales.html
- You can also type an e-mail address directly in a cell, and Excel will convert it to a hyperlink. When a user clicks this type of hyperlink, an e-mail message is automatically created, with the recipient's address included.

Try It! Creating a Hyperlink to Another File

1. Start Excel, and open **E30TryA** from the data files for this lesson.
2. Save the file as **E30TryA_xx** in the location where your teacher instructs you to store the files for this lesson.
3. For all worksheets, add a header that has your name at the left, the date code in the center, and the page number code at the right, and change back to Normal view.
4. On the Sept Sales worksheet, click cell B8 > INSERT > Hyperlink.
5. Navigate to the data files for this lesson and click **E30TryB**.
6. In the Link to menu on the left, check that Existing File or Web Page is selected, and click OK.
7. Save the **E30TryA_xx** file, and leave it open to use in the next Try It.

The Insert Hyperlink dialog box

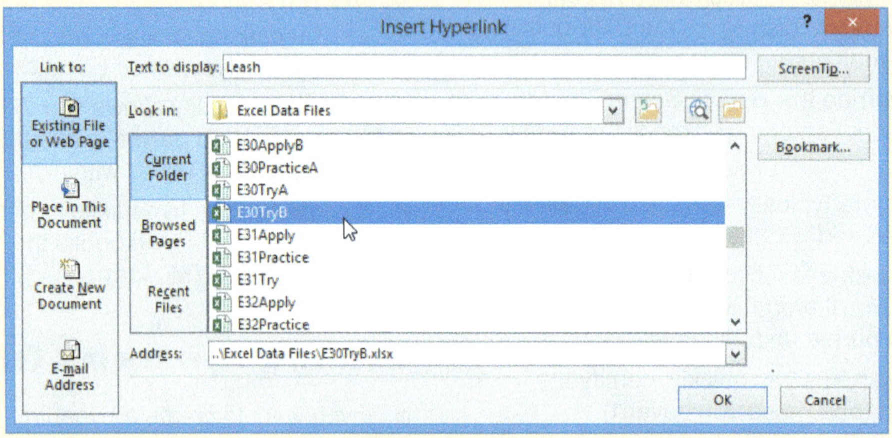

Excel 2013, Windows 8, Microsoft Corporation

Try It! Creating a Hyperlink to a Web Page

1. In the **E30TryA_xx** file, click cell B6.
2. Click INSERT > Hyperlink.
3. Check that Existing File or Web Page is selected, and type **http://www.akc.org/** in the Address box.
4. Click OK.
5. Save the **E30TryA_xx** file, and leave it open to use in the next Try It.

Try It! Inserting a Hyperlink to a Location in the Current Workbook

1. In the **E30TryA_xx** file, click cell D7.
2. Click INSERT > Hyperlink.
3. Click Place in This Document.
4. In the Or select a place in this document section, select Customers.
5. Click OK.
6. Save the **E30TryA_xx** file, and leave it open to use in the next Try It.

(continued)

Try It! Inserting a Hyperlink to a Location in the Current Workbook *(continued)*

Creating a hyperlink to a location in the current workbook

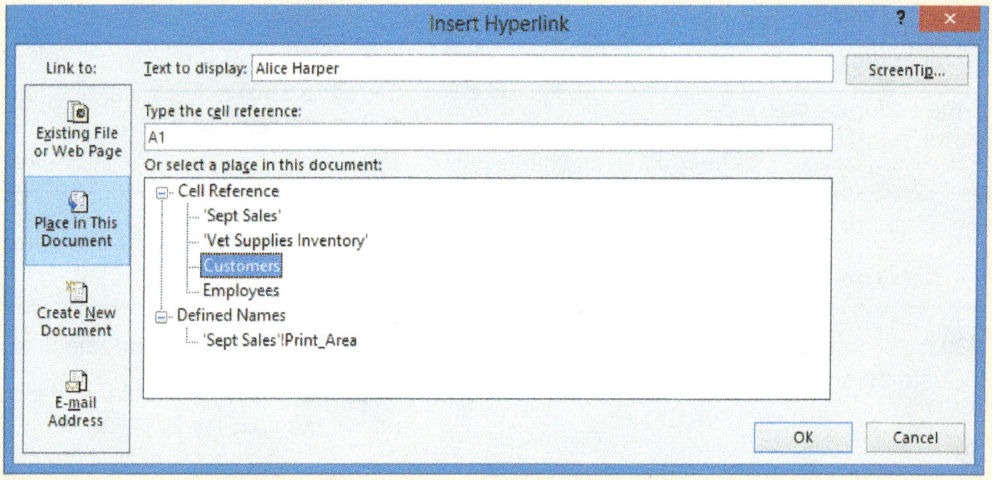

Excel 2013, Windows 8, Microsoft Corporation

Try It! Inserting a Hyperlink to a New Workbook

1. In the **E30TryA_xx** file, click cell B10.
2. Click INSERT > Hyperlink.
3. Click Create New Document.
4. In the Name of the new document box, type **E30TryC_xx.xlsx**.
5. Click Change, if necessary, and select the location your teacher instructs you to store files for this lesson.

✓ *When linking files, the file locations must stay the same for the links to remain intact.*

6. Under When to edit, click Edit the new document later option button, and click OK.
7. Save the **E30TryA_xx** file, and leave it open to use in the next Try It.

Creating a hyperlink to a new workbook

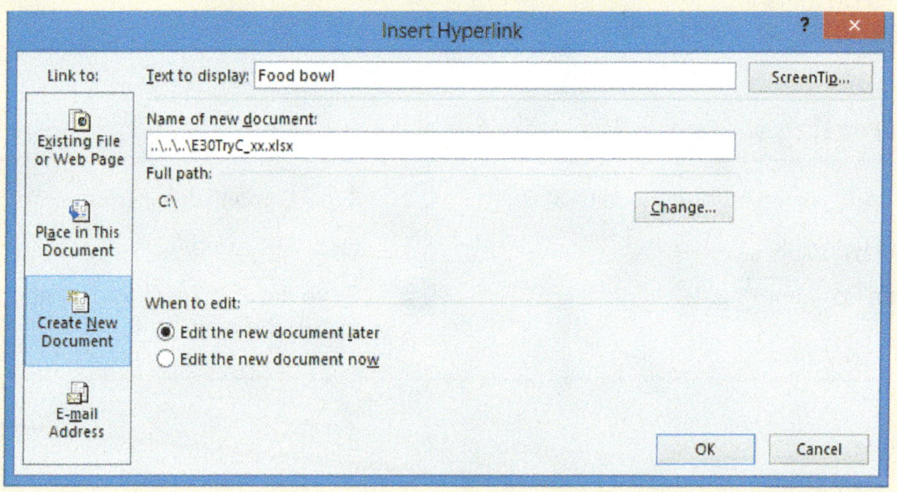

Excel 2013, Windows 8, Microsoft Corporation

Try It! Inserting a Hyperlink to an E-mail Address

1. In the **E30TryA_xx** file, click cell A3.
2. Click INSERT > Hyperlink.
3. Click E-mail Address.
4. In the E-mail address box, type **accounting@petes_pets.com**.
5. In the Subject box, type **Request for additional sales information**.
6. Click OK.
7. Save the **E30TryA_xx** file, and leave it open to use in the next Try It.

Try It! Activating a Hyperlink

1. In the **E30TryA_xx** file, click the hyperlink in cell D7. The Customers worksheet is displayed.
2. Click the Sept Sales worksheet tab.
3. Save the **E30TryA_xx** file, and leave it open to use in the next Try It.

Modifying Hyperlinks

- You can modify a hyperlink by providing a custom ScreenTip, by changing the destination for the link, or by editing the screen text.

Try It! Modifying a Hyperlink

1. In the **E30TryA_xx** file, select cell C8, and press the left arrow key one time.
2. Type **Collar**.
3. Right-click cell D7 > Edit Hyperlink.
4. Change the destination of the link by clicking Place in This Document.
5. Click Employees in the destination list, type **A6** in the Type the cell reference box, and click OK.
6. Save the **E30TryA_xx** file, and leave it open to use in the next Try It.

Try It! Creating a Custom ScreenTip for a Hyperlink

1. In the **E30TryA_xx** file, right-click cell A3.
2. Select Edit Hyperlink.
3. Click ScreenTip ScreenTip... .
4. Type **E-mail us for more information**.
5. Click OK twice.
6. Save the **E30TryA_xx** file, and leave it open to use in the next Try It.

(continued)

Try It! Creating a Custom ScreenTip for a Hyperlink *(continued)*

Creating a custom ScreenTip for a hyperlink

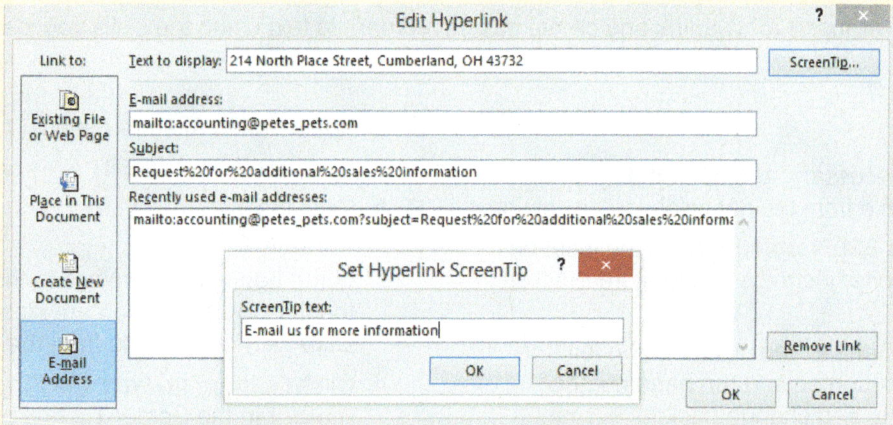

Excel 2013, Windows 8, Microsoft Corporation

Modifying Hyperlinked Cell Attributes

- When you add a hyperlink to a cell, you might find that the resulting link colors do not look good with the existing formatting of the worksheet.
- You can modify the appearance of hyperlinked cells using the Cell Styles button on the HOME tab. You can also manually change your worksheet's formatting, including theme and font colors and other text attributes.

Try It! Modifying Hyperlinked-Cell Attributes

1. In the **E30TryA_xx** file, select cells A3:F3.
2. Click HOME > Cell Styles.
3. In the Cell Styles gallery, select Accent1 in the Themed Cell Styles.
4. Save the **E30TryA_xx** file, and leave it open to use in the next Try It.

Removing a Hyperlink

- There are many ways to remove a hyperlink from a worksheet depending on whether you want to eliminate the hyperlink itself or remove the cell contents as well.

Try It! Removing a Hyperlink

1. In the **E30TryA_xx** file, right-click cell B6.
2. Select Remove Hyperlink.
3. Save the **E30TryA_xx** file, and close it.

Lesson 30—Practice

In this project, you will insert a hyperlink and create custom screen tip text using the skills you learned in this lesson.

DIRECTIONS

1. Start Excel, if necessary, and open the **E30PracticeA** file from the data files for this lesson.
2. Save the file as **E30PracticeA_xx** in the location where your teacher instructs you to store the files for this lesson.
3. Add a header that has your name at the left, the date code in the center, and the page number code at the right, and change back to **Normal** view.
4. Open the **E30PracticeB** file from the data files for this lesson.
5. Save the file as **E30PracticeB_xx** in the location where your teacher instructs you to store the files for this lesson.
6. Add a header that has your name at the left, the date code in the center, and the page number code at the right, and change back to Normal.
7. Save and close the **E30PracticeB_xx** file.
8. Create a link to Akemi's medical history:
   a. Click cell **A6** > **INSERT** > **Hyperlink** .
   b. Click the **Existing File or Web Page** button on the Link to bar.
   c. In the Look in list, browse to the folder where the files for this lesson are stored, and click the **E30PracticeB_xx** file from the list.
   d. Click **ScreenTip**, type **Akemi's medical history** in the ScreenTip text box, and click **OK**.
   e. Click **OK** to create the hyperlink.
9. Click cell **A6** to test the hyperlink. Accept the conditions of the security warning, if needed. The **E30PracticeB_xx** file should appear onscreen.

   ✓ *Remember that when you click a link, only the linked workbook appears on the screen, unless you arrange the view so you can see both.*
10. Close the **E30PracticeB_xx** file.
11. Save and close the **E30PracticeA_xx** file, and exit Excel.

Lesson 30—Apply

You've been put in charge of tracking patient services at Wood Hills Animal Clinic. You've put together a patient worksheet listing the various pets that have recently visited the clinic and a separate worksheet listing owner information. Before you get too far on your project, you want to test out its usability by adding hyperlinks that connect each pet with its owner's personal data.

DIRECTIONS

1. Start Excel, if necessary, and open **E30ApplyA** from the data files for this lesson.
2. Save the file as **E30ApplyA_xx** in the location where your teacher instructs you to store the files for this lesson.
3. Add a header that has your name at the left, the date code in the center, and the page number code at the right, and change back to **Normal** view.
4. Open the **E30ApplyB** file from the data files for this lesson.
5. Save the file as **E30ApplyB_xx** in the location where your teacher instructs you to store the filesfor this lesson.
6. Add a header that has your name at the left, the date code in the center, and the page number code at the right, and change back to Normal.
7. Save and close the **E30ApplyB_xx** file.

8. Create a hyperlink to information about Akemi's owner:
   a. Click cell **E6** > **INSERT** > **Hyperlink**.
   b. Click the **Existing File or Web Page** button on the Link to bar, if necessary.
   c. In the Look in list, browse to the folder where the files for this lesson are stored, and select the **E30ApplyB_xx** file from the list.
   d. Create a ScreenTip that says **View owner information**.
   e. Click the **Bookmark** button.
   f. Select the range name **woo_daniel**, and click **OK**.
   g. Click **OK** to create the hyperlink.
9. Test the hyperlink on the worksheet. See Figure 30-2.

   ✓ *The linked workbooks have been arranged onscreen so you can see how they are linked. To do the same click VIEW > Arrange All > Cascade, and resize the windows.*
10. Close the **E30ApplyB_xx** file.
11. Save and close the file, and exit Excel.

Figure 30-2

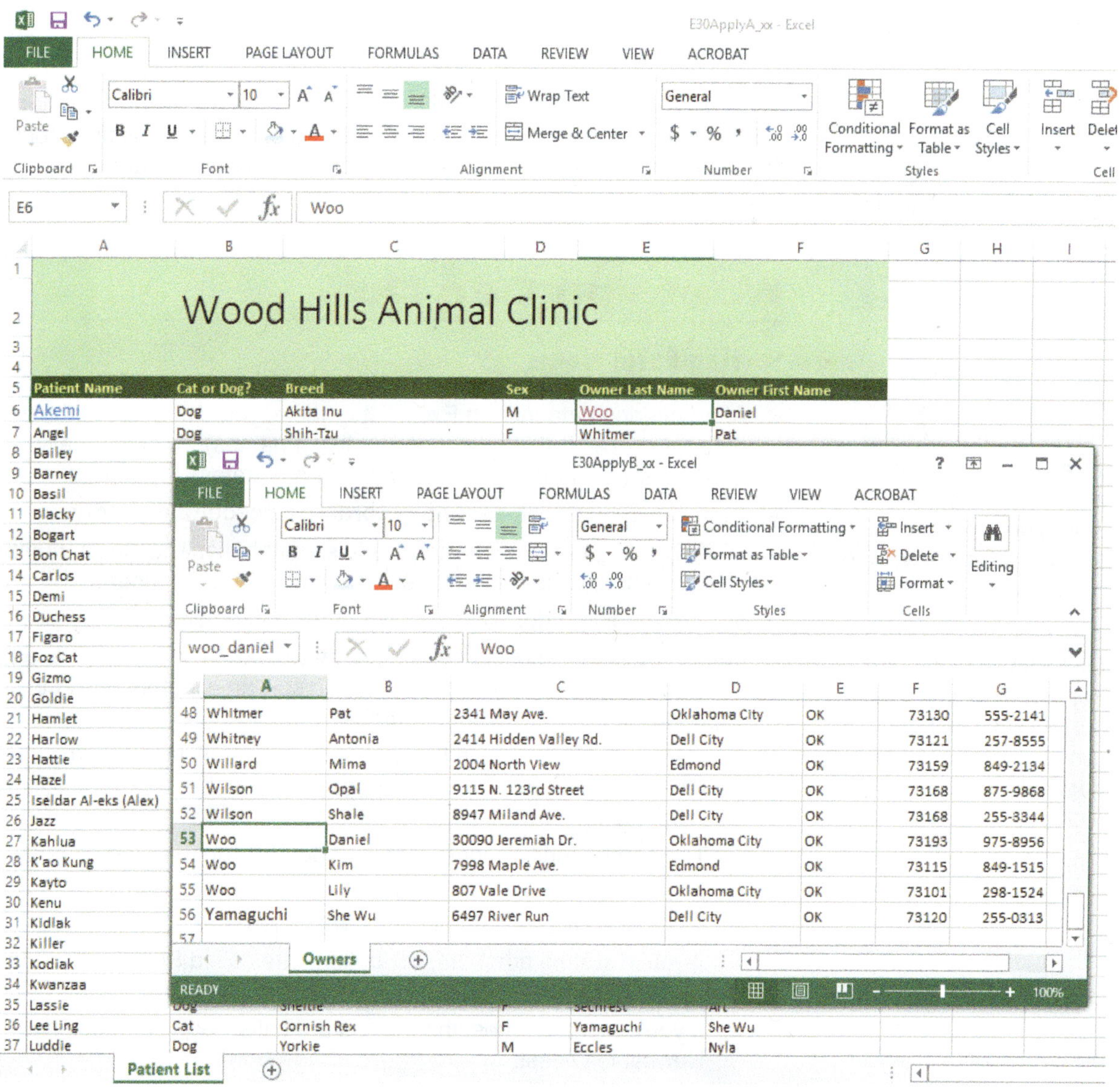

Excel 2013, Windows 8, Microsoft Corporation

Lesson 31

Using Advanced Sort

➤ What You Will Learn

Sorting Excel Items
Understanding the Rules for Advanced Sorting
Sorting on Multiple Columns
Removing a Sort

WORDS TO KNOW

Ascending order
An arrangement of items in alphabetical order (A to Z) or numerical order (1, 2, 3, and so on). Dates are arranged from oldest to most recent.

Descending order
An arrangement of items in reverse alphabetical order (Z to A) or reverse numerical order (10, 9, 8, and so on). Dates are arranged from newest to oldest.

Key
One level within a sort. For example, you might sort a list by last name (one key) and then sort duplicate last names by first name (another key).

Software Skills Entering data in random order might make the job a bit easier, but trying to find information in a disorganized spreadsheet is time consuming. So the first order of business after entering data into a list is ordering (or sorting) the data.

What You Can Do

Sorting Excel Items

- After entering data into an Excel list or table, you can arrange the items in any order: alphabetically (for example, a list of names), or numerically (a price list), or date order (a list of employees and their hire dates).
- Lists can be sorted in **ascending order** or **descending order.**
  - Ascending order will arrange labels alphabetically (A to Z), numbers from smallest to largest, and dates from oldest to most recent.
  - Descending order is the reverse of ascending order.
- You can sort any contiguous data in the worksheet; it doesn't have to be a list or table. For example, you might want to sort an expense report to list all the expenses in order by account number.
- You can sort data by using the sort buttons on the DATA tab, the HOME tab or with the down-arrow button that appears beside the field names in the top row of an Excel table.
  - The sort buttons change names depending on the type of data you're trying to sort.
  - If you're sorting text, the buttons are called Sort A to Z and Sort Z to A.
  - If you're sorting numbers, the buttons are called Sort Smallest to Largest and Sort Largest to Smallest.
  - If you're sorting dates, the buttons are called Sort Oldest to Newest and Sort Newest to Oldest.

Understanding the Rules for Advanced Sorting

- Excel sorts data based on the actual cell content, not the displayed results.
- If you choose to sort in ascending order, items are arranged as follows:
  - Numeric sort—Numbers are sorted from the largest negative number to the largest positive number. For example, -3, -2, -1, 0, 1, 2, and so on.
  - Alphanumeric sort—Labels (text or text/number combinations) are sorted first by symbols, then by letters.
  - Hyphens (-) and apostrophes (') are ignored in alphanumeric sorts if the cell's contents are identical apart from a hyphen or apostrophe, in which case the cell containing the symbol is placed last.
  - If names in the list contain spaces (for example, de Lancie), the sort results may differ from what you expect. Because spaces sort to the top of the list, de Lancie lands above Dean and Debrazzi.
  - When number/text combinations are sorted alphanumerically, combinations like 1Q through 11Q, for example, sort like this 10Q, 11Q, 1Q, 2Q, 3Q, and so on.
  - Dates are sorted chronologically. For example, 1/10/14 would come before 2/12/14.
  - If a cell in the sort column is blank, that record is placed at the end of the list.
- As an example of sorted records, consider this list:
  - Jay's Grill 1256 Adams Ave.
  - CompuTrain 12 Brown Street
  - Central Perk
  - Carriage Club Carriage Center
  - Giving Tree Mark Building
- If the list is sorted by address (ascending order), you'll end up with:
  - Compu Train 12 Brown Street
  - Jay's Grill 1256 Adams Ave.
  - Giving Tree Mark Building
  - Carriage Club Carriage Center
  - Central Perk
- Notice that the record that doesn't contain an address is placed last when you sort by address.
- Using the Sort Options dialog box, you can sort left to right (across a row) rather than top to bottom (down a column). This option is useful if your list is organized with a horizontal rather than a vertical orientation.
- You also can sort with case sensitivity. In a case-sensitive sort, capital letters are sorted after lowercase letters, so kit appears above Kit.

Try It! Sorting a List in Ascending or Descending Order

1. Start Excel, and open **E31Try** from the data files for this lesson.
2. Save the file as **E31Try_xx** in the location where your teacher instructs you to store the files for this lesson.
3. For all worksheets, add a header that has your name at the left, the date code in the center, and the page number code at the right, and change back to Normal view.
4. Click cell B8 on the Employees worksheet.
5. Click DATA > Sort A to Z.
6. On the DATA tab, click Sort Z to A. Notice that the names are sorted from highest to lowest.
7. Save the **E31Try_xx** file, and leave it open to use in the next Try It.

The Sort & Filter Group

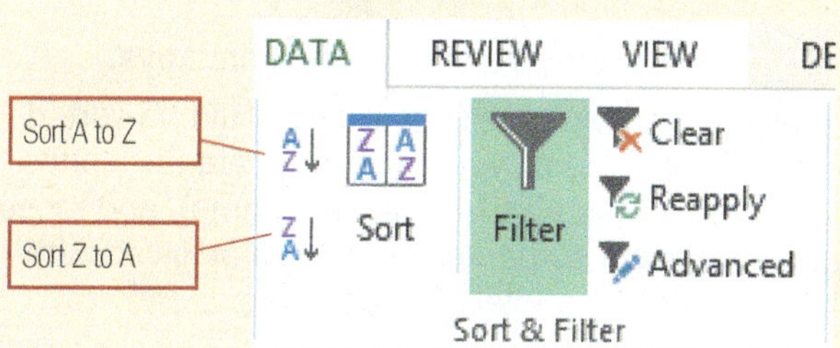

Excel 2013, Windows 8, Microsoft Corporation

Try It! Sorting in a Table in Ascending or Descending Order

1. In the **E31Try_xx** file, click the arrow next to the First Name column heading.
2. Click Sort A to Z.
3. Click the arrow next to the Hire Date column heading.
4. Click Sort Newest to Oldest.
5. Save the **E31Try_xx** file, and leave it open to use in the next Try It.

Try It! Sorting in a Table by Formatting

1. In the **E31Try_xx** file, click the arrow next to the Last Name column heading.
2. Select Sort by Color.
3. Select the Green fill color.
4. Save the **E31Try_xx** file, and leave it open to use in the next Try It.

Table sort options

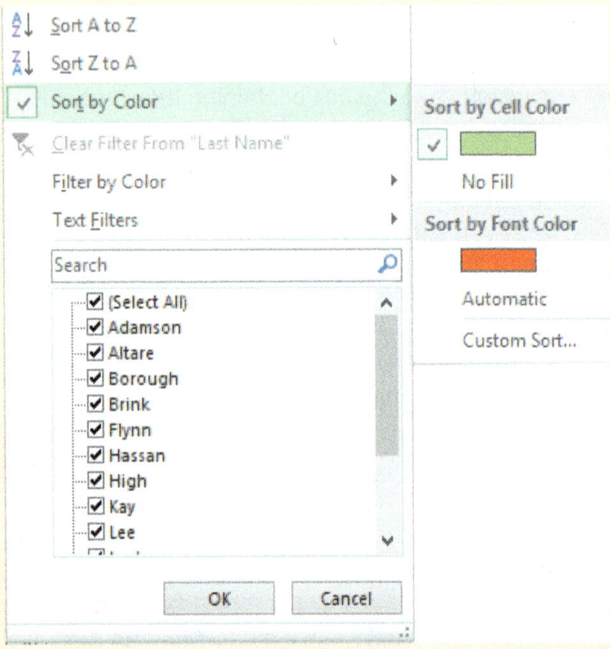

Excel 2013, Windows 8, Microsoft Corporation

Sorting on Multiple Columns

- Data can be sorted using one or more **keys**.
- For example, an employee listing could be sorted by ZIP code. Employees with duplicate ZIP codes are then sorted by surname (last name), and those with duplicate surnames are sorted by given name (first name) for a total of three keys.
- You can use the Sort dialog box to create a custom sort that contains multiple sort levels.

Try It! Creating a Custom Sort

1. In the E31Try_xx file, click cell B8, if needed.
2. Click DATA > Sort.

   ✓ *Notice that the last sort appears as the first sort level.*
3. Click the Add Level button, click the Column Then by down arrow, and select Last Name.
4. In the level you added, click the Sort On down arrow, and select Font Color.
5. Click the Automatic down arrow and select the Red font color.
6. Click the Add Level button, click the new Column Then by down arrow, and select Start Time.
7. Click OK.
8. Save the E31Try_xx file, and leave it open to use in the next Try It.

The Sort dialog box

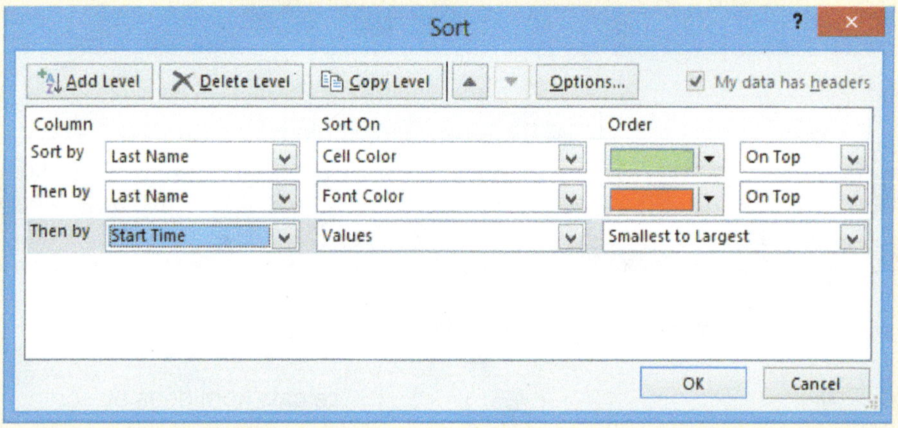

Excel 2013, Windows 8, Microsoft Corporation

Removing a Sort

- You can undo a sort if you click the Undo button immediately after completing the sort.
- If you don't undo a sort immediately, the original sort order is lost.
- To protect your data, always save the workbook prior to sorting.

  ✓ *If something goes wrong, close the workbook without saving changes, and open the previously saved version.*
- If you want to keep your original sort order as well as the new, sorted list, copy the original list to another sheet in the workbook and then sort.
- Another way to restore the original record order of data that has been sorted is to include a unique field in every record.
  - For example, you could include a field called Record Number, and fill in unique numbers for each record. (Make sure all numbers are the same length.)
  - To restore the original order, sort by the Record Number column.

Try It! **Removing a Sort**

1. In the **E31Try_xx** file, right-click the column F heading and select Insert. A table column is inserted to the left and becomes the new column F.
2. In cell F5, type **Record Number**.
3. In cell F6, type **1**, and in cell F7 type **2**.
4. Select cells F6 and F7, and drag the fill handle down to cell F20 so that AutoFill completes the record number list.
5. Click cell A11 > DATA > Sort A to Z.
6. Click the arrow next to the Hire Date column heading.
7. Click Sort Oldest to Newest.
8. Click Undo.
9. Click the arrow next to the Record Number heading.
10. Click Smallest to Largest.
11. Save the **E31Try_xx** file, and close it.

Lesson 31—Practice

In this project, you will sort a table of data using the skills you learned in this lesson.

DIRECTIONS

1. Start Excel, if necessary, and open **E31Practice** from the data files for this lesson.
2. Save the file as **E31Practice_xx** in the location where your teacher instructs you to store the files for this lesson.
3. Add a header that has your name at the left, the date code in the center, and the page number code at the right, and change back to **Normal** view.
4. Click the arrow next to the Breed field name and click **Sort A to Z**.
5. Divide cats from dogs by sorting:
   a. Click cell **B8**.
   b. Click **DATA** > **Sort A to Z**.

   ✓ *Notice that the cat breeds and the dog breeds are still sorted alphabetically as well because of the sort you performed earlier.*
6. **With your teacher's permission**, print the worksheet. It should look similar to Figure 31-1 on the next page.
7. Save and close the file, and exit Excel.

Figure 31-1

Wood Hills Animal Clinic

	Patient Name	Cat or Dog?	Breed	Sex	Owner Last Name	Owner First Name
6	Figaro	Cat	Abyssian	M	Damir	Rafiquil
7	Foz Cat	Cat	American Bobtail - Longhair	M	Echols	Jyoti
8	Mayhem	Cat	American Bobtail - Longhair	F	Thompson	Doug
9	K'ao Kung	Cat	Balinese	N	Whitaker	Verna
10	Bogart	Cat	British SH	M	Scott	Kate
11	Hamlet	Cat	British SH	M	Turner	Teresa
12	Lee Ling	Cat	Cornish Rex	F	Yamaguchi	She Wu
13	Basil	Cat	Devon Rex	M	Lee	Wu
14	Harlow	Cat	DSH	F	Wasserman	Jay
15	Hazel	Cat	DSH	F	Whitney	Antonia
16	Kwanzaa	Cat	DSH	M	Whitaker	Shamir
17	Maddie	Cat	DSH	F	Askren	Mollica
18	Nikki	Cat	DSH	F	Arzate	Lisa
19	Pyewackett	Cat	DSH	M	Woo	Kum
20	Bon Chat	Cat	Himalayan	F	Russell	Melissa
21	Mai Tai	Cat	Himalayan	M	Thorton	Vanessa
22	Maiimoto	Cat	Korat	M	Ryan	Meghan
23	Marshall	Cat	Maine Coon	M	Sweeney	Dyan
24	Jazz	Cat	Ocicat	F	Ryan	Shakur
25	Rahjah	Cat	Persian	M	Willard	Mima
26	Kahlua	Cat	Russian Blue	F	Sventeck	Robert
27	Kayto	Cat	Siamese	F	Waters	Alyce
28	Sagwa	Cat	Siamese	F	Wilson	Shale
29	Spice Cat	Cat	Siamese	F	Flynn	Katerina
30	Akemi	Dog	Akita Inu	M	Woo	Daniel
31	Tamami	Dog	Akita Inu	F	Peyton	Tony
32	Barney	Dog	Beagle	M	Nuniez	Juan
33	Snowball	Dog	Bichon Frise	M	Rwizi	Jorita
34	Carlos	Dog	Chihuahua	M	Leaminson	Carl
35	Maggie	Dog	Cocker Spaniel	F	Waters	Kim
36	Sherlock	Dog	German Shepherd	M	Alvarez	Rita
37	Goldie	Dog	Golden Retriever	F	Russell	Jacob
38	Rayna	Dog	Great Dane	F	Broussard	Steve
39	Blacky	Dog	Labrador Retriever	M	Hassan	Eram
40	Duchess	Dog	Labrador Retriever	F	Vidito	Jewel
41	Shamrock	Dog	Labrador Retriever	M	Nguyen	Chu Gi
42	Wheatley	Dog	Lhasa Apso	M	Teasley	Carlos
43	Demi	Dog	Newfoundland	F	Pferrer	Jacob
44	Killer	Dog	Pit Bull Terrier	M	Washington	Tyrell
45	Sandy	Dog	Poodle German Shepherd Mix	F	Walters	Corrine
46	Pearl	Dog	Pug	F	Jones	Mikalia
47	Hattie	Dog	Scottish Terrier	F	Edwards	Betty
48	Bailey	Dog	Shar-Pei	M	Woo	Lily
49	Lassie	Dog	Sheltie	F	Sechrest	Art
50	McGreggor	Dog	Sheltie	M	Hanslow	Molly
51	Angel	Dog	Shih-Tzu	F	Whitmer	Pat

Lesson 31—Apply

You are responsible for adding new patients to the list of cats and dogs at the Wood Hills Animal Clinic. However, the records system adds new patients at the end of the patients list. You need to use Excel to sort the entries alphabetically.

DIRECTIONS

1. Start Excel, if necessary, and open **E31Apply** from the data files for this lesson.
2. Save the file as **E31Apply_xx** in the location where your teacher instructs you to store the files for this lesson.
3. Add a header that has your name at the left, the date code in the center, and the page number code at the right, and change back to **Normal** view.
4. Sort the table by cat or dog, then sex (males first), then breed (see Figure 31-2 on the next page):
   a. Click anywhere inside the table.
   b. Click **DATA** > **Sort**.
   c. Select **Cat or Dog?** from the **Sort by** list.
   d. Select **Values** from the **Sort On** list.
   e. Select **A to Z** from the **Order** list.
   f. Click **Add Level**.
   g. Select **Sex** from the **Column Then by** list.
   h. Select **Values** from the **Sort On** list.
   i. Select **Z to A** from the **Order** list.
   j. Click **Add Level**.
   k. Select **Breed** from the **Then by** list.
   l. Select **Values** from the **Sort On** list
   m. Select **A to Z** from the **Order** list.
   n. Click **OK**.
5. **With your teacher's permission**, print the worksheet.
6. Save and close the file, and exit Excel.

Figure 31-2

	A	B	C	D	E	F
1						
2	Wood Hills Animal Clinic					
3						
4						
5	Patient Name	Cat or Dog?	Breed	Sex	Owner Last Name	Owner First Name
6	Figaro	Cat	Abyssian	M	Damir	Rafiquil
7	Foz Cat	Cat	American Bobtail - Longhair	M	Echols	Jyoti
8	K'ao Kung	Cat	Balinese	M	Whitaker	Verna
9	Hamlet	Cat	British SH	M	Turner	Teresa
10	Bogart	Cat	British SH	M	Scott	Kate
11	Basil	Cat	Devon Rex	M	Lee	Wu
12	Kwanzaa	Cat	DSH	M	Whitaker	Shamir
13	Pyewackett	Cat	DSH	M	Woo	Kum
14	Mai Tai	Cat	Himalayan	M	Thorton	Vanessa
15	Maiimoto	Cat	Korat	M	Ryan	Meghan
16	Marshall	Cat	Maine Coon	M	Sweeney	Dyan
17	Rahjah	Cat	Persian	M	Willard	Mima
18	Mayhem	Cat	American Bobtail - Longhair	F	Thompson	Doug
19	Lee Ling	Cat	Cornish Rex	F	Yamaguchi	She Wu
20	Maddie	Cat	DSH	F	Askren	Mollica
21	Nikki	Cat	DSH	F	Arzate	Lisa
22	Harlow	Cat	DSH	F	Wasserman	Jay
23	Hazel	Cat	DSH	F	Whitney	Antonia
24	Bon Chat	Cat	Himalayan	F	Russell	Melissa
25	Jazz	Cat	Ocicat	F	Ryan	Shakur
26	Kahlua	Cat	Russian Blue	F	Sventeck	Robert
27	Sagwa	Cat	Siamese	F	Wilson	Shale
28	Spice Cat	Cat	Siamese	F	Flynn	Katerina
29	Kayto	Cat	Siamese	F	Waters	Alyce
30	Akemi	Dog	Akita Inu	M	Woo	Daniel
31	Barney	Dog	Beagle	M	Nuniez	Juan
32	Snowball	Dog	Bichon Frise	M	Rwizi	Jorita
33	Carlos	Dog	Chihuahua	M	Leaminson	Carl
34	Sherlock	Dog	German Shepherd	M	Alvarez	Rita
35	Blacky	Dog	Labrador Retriever	M	Hassan	Eram
36	Shamrock	Dog	Labrador Retriever	M	Nguyen	Chu Gi
37	Wheatley	Dog	Lhasa Apso	M	Teasley	Carlos
38	Killer	Dog	Pit Bull Terrier	M	Washington	Tyrell
39	Bailey	Dog	Shar-Pei	M	Woo	Lily
40	McGreggor	Dog	Sheltie	M	Hanslow	Molly
41	Iseldar Al-eks (Alex	Dog	Shih-Tzu	M	Navarro	Maria
42	Kodiak	Dog	Siberian Husky	M	Wilson	Opal
43	Kidlak	Dog	Siberian Husky	M	Sweares	Lucy
44	Luddie	Dog	Yorkie	M	Eccles	Nyla
45	Gizmo	Dog	Yorkshire Terrier	M	Hu	Joi
46	Tamami	Dog	Akita Inu	F	Peyton	Tony
47	Maggie	Dog	Cocker Spaniel	F	Waters	Kim
48	Goldie	Dog	Golden Retriever	F	Russell	Jacob
49	Rayna	Dog	Great Dane	F	Broussard	Steve
50	Duchess	Dog	Labrador Retriever	F	Vidito	Jewel
51	Demi	Dog	Newfoundland	F	Pfeffer	Jacob

Lesson 32

Using Advanced Filtering

➤ What You Will Learn

Using AutoFilter to Filter Tables
Using AutoFilter to Filter by Custom Criteria
Filtering Items without Creating a Table
Filtering by Using Advanced Criteria
Removing an In-Place Advanced Filter
Extracting Filtered Rows
Using Sum, Average, and Count in a Filtered Table
Using Slicers

WORDS TO KNOW

Calculated column
A special column that can be added to a table, in which a single formula is automatically applied to each row.

Criteria range
Area of the worksheet in which you specify the criteria for selecting records from the list or table.

Excel table
Data arranged in columns and specially formatted with column headers that contain commands that allow you to sort, filter, and perform other functions on the table.

Extract
Copy records that match specified criteria to another place in the worksheet where they can be changed, sorted, formatted, printed, and so on.

Software Skills When you're looking for particular records in a long list, you can use a filter to reduce the number of records to the ones you want to view right now. You can use an advanced filter to extract the matching records and then format, sort, and make other changes to them without affecting the records in the list. This is handy when you want to print or format a subset of the list. In addition, advanced filters let you create complex criteria using formulas, multiple conditions applied to a single field, and so on, to filter the list.

What You Can Do

Using AutoFilter to Filter Tables

- You can use the AutoFilter feature to find pertinent information in a worksheet quickly.
- Use AutoFilter to filter the data in multiple columns.
- When you use AutoFilters, the AutoFilter drop-downs take the place of the column headers when scrolling through long **lists** so that you can easily see your categories.
- You can access the AutoFilter search settings by clicking the AutoFilter drop-downs.

Try It! Using AutoFilter to Filter Tables

1. Start Excel, and open **E32Try** from the data files for this lesson.
2. Save the file as **E32Try_xx** in the location where your teacher instructs you to store the files for this lesson.
3. For both worksheets, add a header that has your name at the left, the date code in the center, and the page number code at the right, and change back to Normal view.
4. On the Sept Sales worksheet, click the arrow next to the Salesperson heading.
5. Deselect the (Select All) option, select Alice Harper, and click OK.
6. Hover on the Filter indicator for the Salesperson column to see the ScreenTip.
7. Save the **E32Try_xx** file, and leave it open to use in the next Try It.

Use the Filter Indicator to see your filter criteria

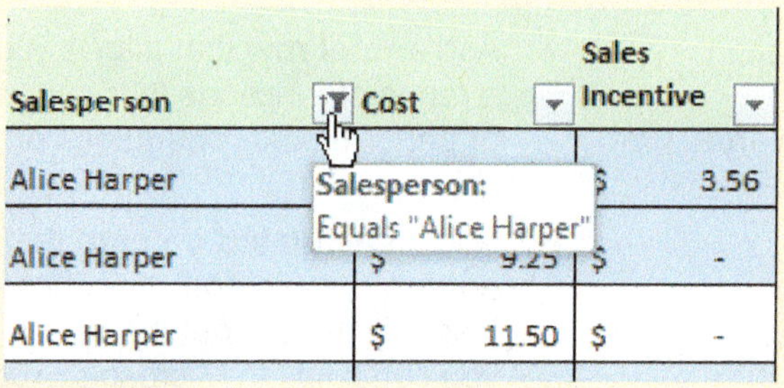

Excel 2013, Windows 8, Microsoft Corporation

Filter
Hide nonmatching rows in a table or list of data according to the criterion or criteria you specify.

List
A range of Excel data organized primarily in columns.

Slicer
An easy-to-use filtering component that contains a set of buttons to enable you to quickly filter data.

Total row
A row you can display below a table to calculate data in the columns above using a function you choose.

Using AutoFilter to Filter by Custom Criteria

- In Excel 2013, you can search for specific criteria within an AutoFilter. This allows you to quickly jump to the information you want without having to scroll through a long list of values.
- You can set up an AutoFilter based on specific numeric or text values, formatting, or based on specific custom criteria.

Try It! Using AutoFilter to Filter by Custom Criteria

1. In the **E32Try_xx** file, on the Sept Sales worksheet, click the arrow next to the Cost heading.
2. Point to Number Filters, and select Greater Than from the list.
3. In the box to the right of the is greater than box, type **15**, and click OK.
4. Click the arrow next to the Description heading.
5. Point to Text Filters, and select Custom Filter from the list.
6. In the first box, scroll down and click does not contain, and in the second box, type **puppy**.

(continued)

Try It! Using AutoFilter to Filter by Custom Criteria *(continued)*

7. Check that the And option button is selected, and in the first box of the second row, select *does not end with*.
8. In the second box, type **n**. Click OK.
9. Click the arrow next to the *Product Type* heading.
10. Point to Filter by Color, and select the blue fill color.
11. Save the **E32Try_xx** file, and leave it open to use in the next Try It.

The Custom AutoFilter dialog box

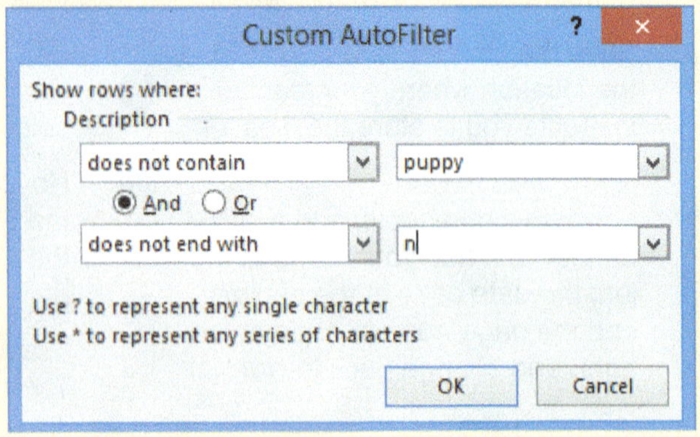

Excel 2013, Windows 8, Microsoft Corporation

Filtering Items Without Creating a Table

- As mentioned earlier, you do not need to convert a list into an **Excel table** in order to **filter** its data.
- A table, however, does give you several advantages. With a table, you can:
  - Create formulas that reference the columns in the table by their name.
  - Format the table with a single click.
  - Add a **total row** that allows you to select from a range of functions that sum, average, count, or perform other operations on the data in a column.
  - Add a **calculated column** that allows you to enter a formula and have that formula copied instantly throughout the column. For example, you could link to Microsoft Excel data during a presentation.

Try It! Filtering Items Without Creating a Table

1. In the **E32Try_xx** file, click the Pet Supplies Inventory worksheet tab.
2. Click anywhere in the range A5:H32 > DATA > Filter .

   ✓ *Arrow buttons appear next to each column name.*
3. Click the arrow next to the Current Inventory heading.
4. Point to Number Filters, and select Less Than Or Equal To from the list.
5. In the second box of the first row, type **10**, and click OK.
6. Click the arrow next to the *Description* heading.
7. Deselect the (Select All) option.
8. Type **Collar** in the Search box. Click OK.
9. Save the **E32Try_xx** file, and leave it open to use in the next Try It.

(continued)

Try It! Filtering Items without Creating a Table *(continued)*

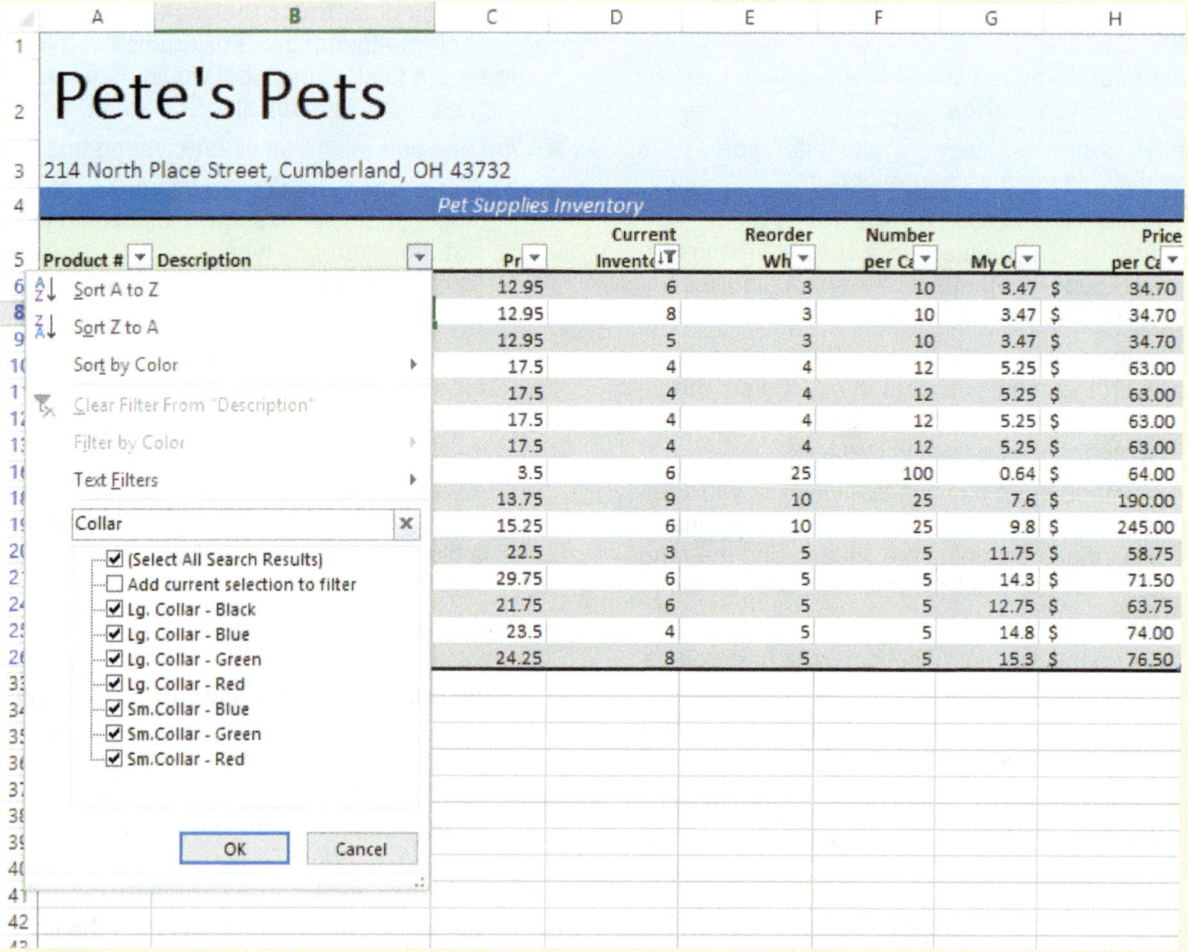

A list offers most of the same filter features as a table

Excel 2013, Windows 8, Microsoft Corporation

Try It! Removing a Filter from a List

1. In the **E32Try_xx** file, in the Pet Supplies Inventory worksheet, click any cell in the list.
2. Click DATA > Filter.

✓ *This process will redisplay all records and remove the filter arrows from a list, but not a table.*

3. Save the **E32Try_xx** file, and leave it open to use in the next Try It.

Filtering by Using Advanced Criteria

- With an advanced filter, you can filter records to hide records that do not match the criteria you specify—in much the same way as with a regular filter.
- Prior to using an advanced filter, you must first set up your **criteria range**.
- An advanced filter allows you to enter more complex criteria than a regular filter:
  - Instead of selecting criteria from a drop-down list, you enter it in a special area in the workbook—perhaps a worksheet unto itself—set aside for that purpose.
  - In the marked cells of this criteria range, you enter the items you want to match from the list, or expressions that describe the type of comparison you wish to make.
  - You then open a dialog box in which you specify the range where the list or table is contained, the range containing the criteria, and the range to which you want records copied/extracted (if applicable).
- To set up the criteria range, copy the field names from the top of the list to another area of the worksheet, or to a separate worksheet in the same workbook.

  ✓ *The labels in the criteria range must exactly match the labels used in the list, which is why you should copy them rather than typing them.*

Guidelines for Entering Criteria

- After the criteria range is established, you enter criteria in the criteria range, below the field names you copied.
  - For example, to display only records belonging to Smith, you might type Smith under the Last Name field name in the criteria range you've established.
- If you want to establish an AND condition, where two or more criteria must be true for a record to match, then type the criteria under their proper field names in the same row.
  - For example, to display records where the quantity on hand is over 25 AND the cost is less than $10, type both criteria in the same row, each in their respective column.
- If you want to establish an OR condition, where any of two or more criteria will qualify a record as a match, then type the criteria under their proper field names, but in separate rows.
- When you enter text, Excel looks for any match beginning with that text. For example, typing Sam under the First Name label would match records such as Sam, Samuel, and Samantha.
- You can use wildcards when entering text criteria.
  - A question mark (?) can be used to replace a single character in a specific position within the text. For example, type Sm?th under the Last Name label to get Smith and Smyth.
  - An asterisk (*) can be used to replace one or several characters within the text. For example, type Sm*th under the Last Name label to get Smith, Smyth, Smouth, and Smaningfith.
  - Because ? and * are assumed to be wildcards, if you want to find records that actually contain those characters, you must precede them with a tilde (~). For example, type RJ4~?S2 to get RJ4?S2.
- You can use operators to compare text, numbers, or dates.
  - Operators include < (less than), > (greater than), <= (less than or equal to), >= (greater than or equal to), <> (not equal to), and = (equal to). For example, type >256000 under the Annual Salary label to get all records that contain an annual salary over $256,000.
  - You can use operators with dates as well. For example, type >=01/01/08 under the Hire Date label to get all records with a hire date on or after January 1, 2008.
  - You can also use operators with text, as in <M, which will display all records beginning with the letters A through L.
- You can use formulas to specify criteria.
  - For example, to display only records where the total sale (stored in column G) is greater than the average of column G, you could enter something like this for cell G5: =G5>AVERAGE($G$5:$G$21).

    ✓ *G5 in this example is the first cell in the list or table in column G.*

- You could also use the label cell (G4) or the label itself, as in this formula: ="Total Sales">AVERAGE($G$5:$G$21).
- The comparison cell address uses relative cell addressing, while the rest of the formula must use absolute cell addresses (preceded by $).

■ To use a formula to specify criteria, type it in a cell that doesn't have a label above it.

✓ *For this reason, it's usually best to type a formula in the first column to the right of the criteria range you originally established.*

- Be sure to redefine the criteria range to include the cell that contains the formula and the blank cell above it.
- You can use more than one formula by typing the second formula in the next column, and adjusting the criteria range again.

✓ *If you need to use two formulas, and either one may be true in order to get a match, then type them in the same column in different rows.*

✓ *See examples in the next section for placement of formulas in the criteria range.*

Examples of Advanced Criteria

■ To display records for Smith and Jones from the sample shown here, type these criteria, in two rows, under the Name field:

Name	Computer	Sale Amt.
Smith		>1300
Jones		

✓ *As on the preceding pages, the following examples show typical list or table field names. Be sure to copy the actual field names from your own list/table to the criteria range.*

■ To display records for Jones where the total sale amount is over $1,300, type these criteria in one row under the appropriate field names:

Name	Computer	Sale Amt.
Jones		>1300

✓ *You could also display these records with the proper selections from two columns in filtered list or table.*

Figure 32-1

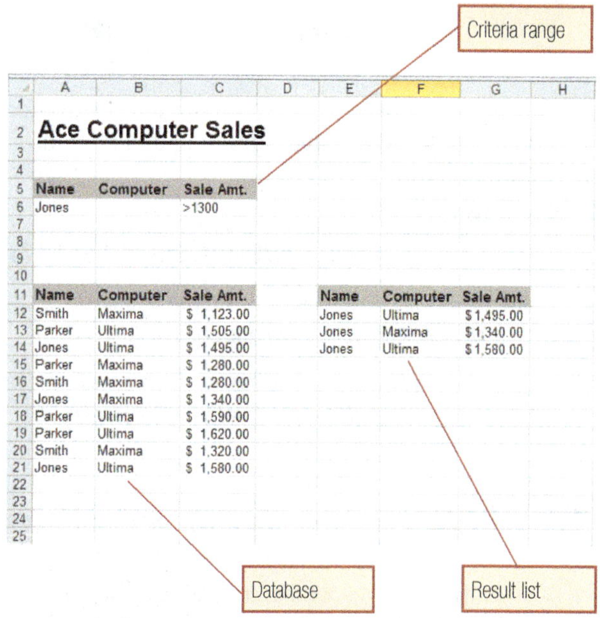

Excel 2013, Windows 8, Microsoft Corporation

■ To display Smith's sales records of Maxima computers with a total sales amount more than $1,250, type this in one row:

Name	Computer	Sale Amt.
Smith	Maxima	>1250

✓ *Again, you could display these records using a regular filter.*

■ To display records for both Smith and Jones that have a sale amount over $1,250, type this in two rows:

Name	Computer	Sale Amt.
Smith		>1250
Jones		>1250

■ To display records that have a sale amount over $1,250 or that involve Maxima computers (no matter what amount), type this in two rows:

Name	Computer	Sale Amt.
	Maxima	
		>1250

■ To display records of sales of Maxima computers over $1,250, type this in one row:

Name	Computer	Sale Amt.
	Maxima	>1250

- To display records of sales of Maxima or Ultima computers over $1,250, type this in two rows:

Name	Computer	Sale Amt.
	Maxima	>1250
	Ultima	>1250

- To display records whose sale amount is greater than or equal to the average, type this in a cell without a label:

Sale Amt.	
	=C2>AVERAGE($C$2:$C$17)

✓ *Be sure to include the cell in which you type the formula and the blank cell above it, within the criteria range.*

✓ *The formula includes an expression of comparison, featuring the > operator, and which evaluates to TRUE or FALSE.*

- To display records whose sale amounts are between $1,250 and $2,000, type this in two cells without a label in the same row, but in different columns:

Computer	Sale Amt.		
	=C2>1250		=C2<2000

✓ *Place formulas in cells without a label above them.*

- To display records whose total sale is greater than the average OR over $2,000, type this in two rows, but in the same column:

Sale Amt.	
	=C2>AVERAGE($C$2:$C$17)
	=C2>2000

Try It! Setting Up a Criteria Range and an Advanced Filter

1. In the **E32Try_xx** file, in the Pet Supplies Inventory worksheet, select the range A5:H5.
2. Click HOME > Copy.

   ✓ *Typically, you create a criteria range above or to the right of the list or table, separated from it by a few rows or columns, although you can create a separate Criteria worksheet if you like.*

3. Click cell J5 and press CTRL + V. Adjust the column widths as necessary.

   ✓ *Remember that formulas, if you use them, must be entered in cells that don't have a label above them.*

4. Type the following criteria.

Cell	Type
K7	**Cat***
M6	**<10**
N6	**<10**
P7	**>1.00**

5. Click any cell within the range A6:H32 > DATA > Advanced.
6. If necessary, select Filter the list, in-place.
7. In the List range text box, type **$A$6:$H$32** or select the range containing the list or table.
8. In the Criteria range text box, select the range J5:Q7.

   ✓ *Include the criteria label(s) with the criteria.*

   ✓ *If the criteria includes a formula, include the blank cell(s) above the cell(s) containing the formula.*

9. Click OK.
10. Save the **E32Try_xx** file, and leave it open to use in the next Try It.

(continued)

Try It! Setting Up a Criteria Range and an Advanced Filter *(continued)*

Setting up an advanced filter

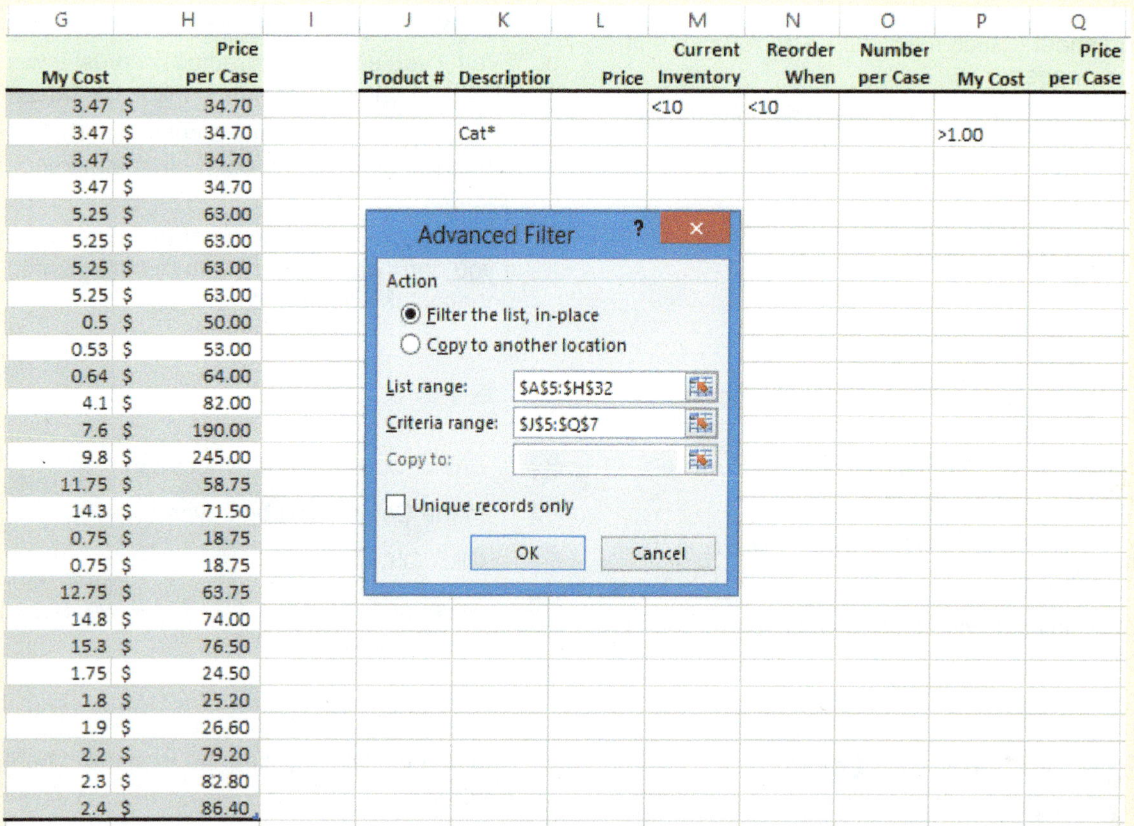

Removing an In-Place Advanced Filter

- Unlike a regular filter, an advanced filter applied in-place to a list or table (rather than copied to another area of the worksheet) isn't easily detectable.
- If the row numbers in the list or table are blue and the filter down-arrow buttons aren't visible, an advanced filter is in place.
- To remove an in-place advanced filter, click in the list/table and click the Clear button on the DATA tab.

Try It! Removing an In-Place Advanced Filter

1. In the **E32Try_xx** file, in the Pet Supplies Inventory worksheet, click any cell in the table or list within the cell range A4:H6.
2. Click DATA > Clear.
3. Click the Sept Sales worksheet tab, and click any cell in the table or list with the cell range A5:F45.
4. Click DATA > Clear.
5. Save the **E32Try_xx** file, and leave it open to use in the next Try It.

Extracting Filtered Rows

- With an advanced filter, you can **extract** (copy) records to another place in the worksheet.
- The extracted records are copied to another area of the worksheet (called the results list). You can edit them as needed.
- The results list must appear in the same worksheet as the source list from which its records were copied.

✓ *The destination range must be located in the same worksheet as the list or table.*

✓ *If you indicate a single cell as the Copy to range, Excel copies the filtered results to cells below and to the right of the cell, overwriting existing data without warning.*

- You can change, format, print, sort, delete, and otherwise manipulate the extracted records.
- Even if you alter the extracted records, it won't affect the original records in the list or table.
- This allows you to create a customized, professional-looking report with the extracted records.
- You can even delete some of the extracted records if you don't want to work with them; again, this does not affect the original data.

Try It! Extracting Filtered Rows

1. In the **E32Try_xx** file, click the Pet Supplies Inventory worksheet tab.

   ✓ *For this exercise, you'll use the same criteria and range as before.*

2. Click any cell within the table or list within the cell range A5:H32 > DATA > Advanced.
3. Select Copy to another location.
4. In the Copy to text box, type **$A$40**.
5. Click OK.
6. Save the **E32Try_xx** file, and leave it open to use in the next Try It.

Using Sum, Average, and Count in a Filtered Table

- Using tables provides a lot of flexibility when it comes to managing columnar data.
  - For example, it's easy to add totals and perform other calculations on the columns in a table by simply adding a total row.
  - Once a total row is added, click in the total row at the bottom of a column you want to calculate, and choose an available function such as SUM, AVERAGE, or MIN.
  - You can select a different function for each column, or none at all.
  - You can also enter text in the total row if needed.
- You can temporarily hide the total row when needed.
- Another easy way to add calculations to a table is to use calculated columns.
  - A calculated column can be located in a blank column inserted between existing table columns, or in the first blank column to the right of a table.
  - To create a calculated column, type a formula in the blank column you've inserted in the table, or in a blank column to the right of the table.
  - The formula is instantly copied down the column.
  - If new rows are added to the table, the formula is copied to that new row automatically.

Try It! Using Sum, Average, and Count in a Filtered Table

1. In the E32Try_xx file, click the Sept Sales worksheet tab.
2. Click in the list with the cell range A5:F45 > TABLE TOOLS DESIGN > Total Row.
3. Click cell F46, and click the down arrow that appears to the right of the cell. Select Sum, if necessary.
4. Click cell E46, and click the down arrow. Select Average.
5. Click cell D46, and click the down arrow. Select Count.
6. Save the E32Try_xx file, and leave it open to use in the next Try It.

Working with a Total Row in a filtered table

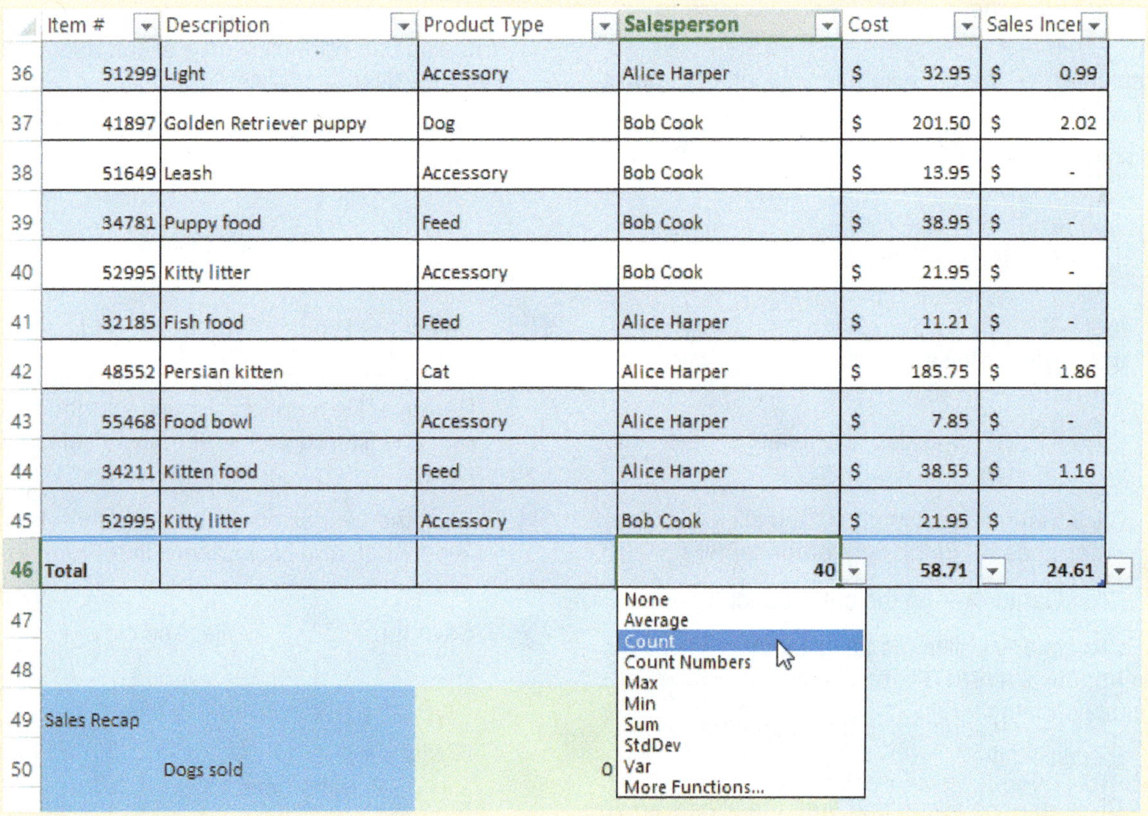

Excel 2013, Windows 8, Microsoft Corporation

Using Slicers

- When you filter on multiple criteria, it is not always easy to see which filters are being used.
- **Slicers** provide buttons that you can click to filter data in a table.
- You can use slicers to quickly see the current filtering state when you filter on multiple items.
- If you have multiple tables, you can create a slicer for each table.
- You can insert a slicer using the Slicer button in the Filter group on the INSERT tab.
- You can select the data you want your table to display from the Insert Slicers dialog box.
- To select more than one item in a slicer, hold down CTRL, and click the items on which you want to filter.
- A slicer is displayed for every field that you select.
- After you create a slicer, it appears on the worksheet alongside the table. If needed, you can move a slicer to another location on the worksheet.
- If you have more than one slicer, the slicers are displayed in layers.
- Select the item or items on which you want to filter from the Insert Slicers dialog box.
- To remove a filter, click the Clear Filter button on the slicer.
- You can change the slicer settings or apply slicer styles from the SLICER TOOLS OPTIONS tab.
- You can resize a slicer.
- Click on a slicer, and press DEL to delete a slicer. You also can right-click on a slicer, and click Remove "Name of slicer."

✓ *When you delete a slicer, the filter(s) applied to your data are not removed.*

Try It! Using Slicers

1. In the **E32Try_xx** file, on the Sept Sales worksheet, click any cell in the table with the cell range A5:F46.
2. Click INSERT > Slicer. The Insert Slicers dialog box appears.
3. Click the Product Type box, and click OK. The slicer appears to the right of the table.
4. Click Cat to filter on the cat product type.
5. Click in any cell in the table with the cell range A5:F46 > INSERT > Slicer.
6. Click the Description and Salesperson boxes, and click OK.
7. Click on each slicer, and drag the slicers so you can see all three of them.
8. On the Product Type slicer, click Dog.
9. On the Description slicer, scroll down, and click Scottie puppy. Notice that the Salesperson slicer automatically filters on Bob Cook because he is the only salesperson to sell a Dog that was a Scottie puppy.
10. On the Description slicer, click the Clear Filter button. Notice that all dogs are now showing.
11. Select the Product Type slicer, and press DEL.
12. Right-click the Description slicer, and click Remove "Description." Notice that the table remains filtered on the items you selected in the slicers.
13. Click the filter arrow at the end of the Product Type label, and click Clear Filter From "Product Type."
14. Save the **E32Try_xx** file, and close it.

An example of a slicer

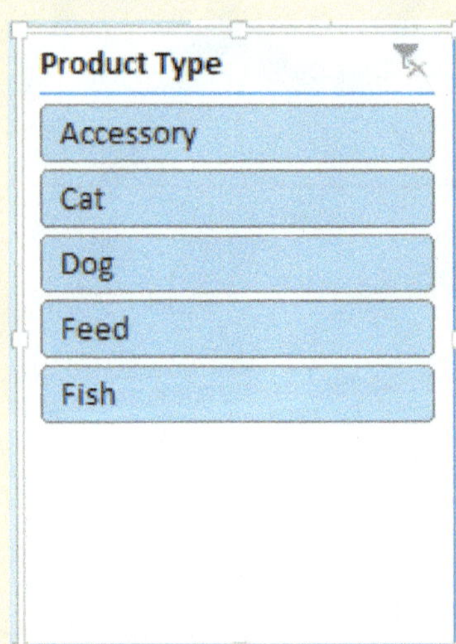

Lesson 32—Practice

In this project, you will filter a large data table using the skills you learned in this lesson.

DIRECTIONS

1. Start Excel, if necessary, and open **E32Practice** from the data files for this lesson.
2. Save the file as **E32Practice_xx** in the location where your teacher instructs you to store the files for this lesson.
3. Add a header that has your name at the left, the date code in the center, and the page number code at the right, and change back to **Normal** view.
4. Display only the heart medications:
   a. Click on any cell in the table > **INSERT** > **Slicer**.
   b. In the **Insert Slicers** dialog box, click the **For use on** box > **OK**.
   c. Move the slicer so the entire table is visible, if necessary.
   d. In the **For use on slicer**, click **Heart**.
   e. Sort the records by price by clicking the arrow next to **Item Cost**, and choosing **Sort Smallest to Largest**.
5. **With your teacher's permission**, adjust the print settings, and print the worksheet.
6. Right-click the For use on slicer, and click "Remove For use on."

   ✓ *Remember that removing a slicer does not clear its filter.*
7. Display only items with 100 or more units remaining in inventory:
   a. Clear the filter by clicking **DATA** > **Clear**.
   b. Click the arrow next to **Total Items2**, and point to **Number Filters**.
   c. Select **Greater Than Or Equal To** from the list.
   d. In the box to the right of is greater than or equal to, enter **100**, and click **OK**.
8. Add a total row:
   a. Click anywhere in the table, then click **TABLE TOOLS DESIGN** > **Total Row**.
   b. Click the cell at the bottom of the **Total Items2** column, click the arrow, and click **Average**.
   c. Click the cell at the bottom of the **Total Items** column, click the arrow, and click **Sum**.
9. Display the top **15** selling items:
   a. Clear the filter by clicking **DATA** > **Clear**.
   b. Click the arrow next to **Total Sales** heading, point to **Number Filters**, and click **Top 10**.
   c. In the center box of the Top 10 AutoFilter dialog box, choose **15**, then click **OK**.
10. Select **A1:K95** and click **Page Layout** > **Print Area** > **Set Print Area**.
11. **With your teacher's permission**, print the worksheet. It should look similar to Figure 32-2 on the next page.

    ✓ *To print the selected print area, you may need to change the print settings to Print Selection, Landscape Orientation, and No Scaling.*
12. Save and close the file, and exit Excel.

Figure 32-2

Wood Hills Animal Clinic

August Drug Sales

			Starting Inventory				Ending Inventory			
Drug	For use on	To treat	No. of Cases	Items per Case	Loose Items	Total Items	Total Items2	No. Sold	Item Cost	Total Sales
Droncit Tapewormer	De-wormer	Dog or Cat	6	100	88	688	432	256	$ 28.95	$ 7,411.20
Enacard	Heart	Dog or Cat	12	22	20	284	61	223	$ 25.00	$ 5,575.00
Enacard	Heart	Dog or Cat	14	30	3	423	222	201	$ 31.95	$ 6,421.95
Anipryl	Endocrine	Dog	12	20	19	259	152	107	$ 53.00	$ 5,671.00
Enacard	Heart	Dog or Cat	10	30	14	314	158	156	$ 32.95	$ 5,140.20
Bomazeal Senior	Arthritis	Dog	14	50	42	742	382	360	$ 24.95	$ 8,982.00
Proin	Incontinence	Dog	15	35	33	558	390	168	$ 30.00	$ 5,040.00
Tapazole	Hyperthyroidism	Cat	15	30	29	479	358	121	$ 49.00	$ 5,929.00
Heartgard Plus Blue	Heartworm	Dog	18	75	42	1,392	968	424	$ 14.95	$ 6,338.80
Soloxine	Hyperthyroidism	Dog or Cat	18	20	17	377	51	326	$ 36.95	$ 12,045.70
Revolution	Heartworm	Dog	21	32	6	678	325	353	$ 26.95	$ 9,513.35
Soloxine	Hyperthyroidism	Dog or Cat	21	20	4	424	186	238	$ 40.00	$ 9,520.00
Advantage Green	Flea	Dog	22	25	14	564	268	296	$ 19.95	$ 5,905.20
Heartgard Plus Green	Heartworm	Dog	22	75	36	1,686	1,296	390	$ 19.95	$ 7,780.50
Heartgard Plus Brown	Heartworm	Dog	30	75	19	2,269	918	1,351	$ 24.95	$ 33,707.45
Total						11,137	411			$ 134,981.35

Excel 2013, Windows 8, Microsoft Corporation

Lesson 32—Apply

You're continuing to put together the inventory tracking sheet for Wood Hills Animal Clinic, and it's looking pretty good. It's your job now to make some sense of all this data. You plan to use filtering to organize the information, and make printouts based on particular data the boss has requested.

DIRECTIONS

1. Start Excel, if necessary, and open **E32Apply** from the data files for this lesson.
2. Save the file as **E32Apply_xx** in the location where your teacher instructs you to store the files for this lesson.
3. On all three sheets, add a header that has your name at the left, the date code in the center, and the page number code at the right, and change back to **Normal** view.
4. Set up a criteria range for an advanced filter:
   a. Click the **New sheet** button, and create a new worksheet.
   b. Name the new worksheet **Criteria**, and move it after the Drug Sales for Cats worksheet.
   c. In the Drug Sales for Dogs worksheet, copy cells **A7:K7**, and paste them in the Criteria worksheet in the same position.
   d. Adjust columns widths as necessary to be readable.
5. Use the Criteria worksheet to select the records from the Drug Sales for Dogs worksheet, featuring only those medications for dogs with sales over $2000 and where less than 150 items are left in inventory:
   a. In the Criteria worksheet, in the cell under **To treat**, type **Dog**.
   b. In the cell under **Total Items2**, type **<150**.
   c. In the cell under **Total Sales**, type **>2000**.
   d. Switch to the **Drug Sales for Dogs** worksheet, and click any cell in the list range.
   e. Click **DATA** > **Advanced**.

      ✓ *Under List range, the range $A$7:$K$94 should already appear.*

   f. Next to Criteria range, click the **Collapse Dialog Box** button.
   g. Switch to the Criteria worksheet, select the range **A7:K8**.

      ✓ *The criteria range should always include the entire field names row, plus as many rows beneath it that include criteria values or expressions, in their entirety.*

h. Click the **Restore Dialog Box** button, then choose **Copy to another location**.

i. Next to **Copy to**, click the **Collapse Dialog Box** button.

j. Select cell **O7** in the Drug Sales for Dogs worksheet.

k. Click the **Restore Dialog Box** button to return to the dialog box, click **OK**.

✓ *Excel will copy all records that match the given criteria, including field names, and will format these records exactly as they appear in their original cells, except for their column width.*

l. Adjust column widths as necessary.

6. Select the range **O1:Y17** > **Page Layout** > **Print Area** > **Set Print Area**.

7. **With your teacher's permission**, print the worksheet. It should look similar to Figure 32-3.

✓ *To print the selected print area, you may need to change the print settings to Print Selection, Landscape Orientation, and No Scaling.*

8. Save and close the file, and exit Excel.

Figure 32-3

Student Name 11/22/2015 1

Wood Hills Animal Clinic

August Drug Sales for Dogs

Results

Drug	For use on	To treat	No. of Cases	Items per Case	Loose Items	Total Items	Total Items2	No. Sold	Item Cost	Total Sales
Enacard	Heart	Dog or Cat	6	30	8	188	126	62	$ 41.00	$ 2,542.00
Soloxine	Hyperthyroidism	Dog or Cat	6	20	6	126	74	52	$ 38.50	$ 2,002.00
Revolution	Heartworm	Dog	7	32	21	245	146	99	$ 25.95	$ 2,569.05
Anipryl	Endocrine	Dog	8	20	11	171	110	61	$ 49.00	$ 2,989.00
Anipryl	Endocrine	Dog	9	20	4	184	135	49	$ 60.00	$ 2,940.00
Revolution	Heartworm	Dog	9	32	27	315	145	170	$ 27.95	$ 4,751.50
Deramaxx	Anti-inflamatory	Dog	10	12	8	128	67	61	$ 62.50	$ 3,812.50
Lotagen	Skin Wounds	Dog or Cat	10	15	9	159	104	55	$ 72.15	$ 3,968.25
Enacard	Heart	Dog or Cat	12	22	20	284	61	223	$ 25.00	$ 5,575.00
Soloxine	Hyperthyroidism	Dog or Cat	18	20	17	377	51	326	$ 36.95	$ 12,045.70

Excel 2013, Windows 8, Microsoft Corporation

Lesson 33

Using Advanced Functions to Predict Trends

➤ What You Will Learn

Creating Predictions and Estimations
Using FORECAST
Using TREND
Using GROWTH

WORDS TO KNOW

Sparklines
A tiny chart that can be used to show trend patterns.

Step
Used to calculate a future value. The step is the difference between two existing values.

Trend
A mathematical prediction of future values based on the relationship between existing values.

Software Skills When it comes to business accounting, a crystal ball that predicts the future would come in handy pretty often. Imagine being able to predict sales so accurately you never order too many parts, carry too much inventory, or schedule too many staff members. Excel doesn't come with a crystal ball, but it does provide some nifty equivalents, such as sparklines, and the FORECAST, TREND, and GROWTH functions.

What You Can Do

Creating Predictions and Estimations

- In Excel, you can use the AutoFill feature to create a series of data, such as April, May, June.
- You also can use AutoFill to predict many kinds of future values.
- AutoFill calculates future values by examining the **trend** of existing values.
- With AutoFill, you can choose from two different trend formulas: linear or growth.
  - Linear trend—the **step** is calculated by determining the average difference between the existing values. The step is then added to the second value.

    ✓ *For example, in the series 21, 37, the next value would be 53 (37-21=16; 16+37=53).*

  - Growth trend—the step is calculated by dividing the second selected value by the first selected value. The step is then multiplied by the second value.

    ✓ *For example, in the series 21, 37, the next value would be 65.19048 (37/21=1.761905; 37*1.761905=65.19048).*

- To determine which tool to use, follow this pattern:
  - If existing values seem to follow a straight curve, use the linear trend method.
  - If existing values seem to go up and down a lot, use the growth trend method.

- You can also create a linear trend or growth trend estimate using the Fill button in the Editing group on the HOME tab.

  ✓ *If you want to create an estimate based on more than one set of numbers instead, select Trend from the Insert Series dialog box. You also can enter a specific Step or Stop value.*

- You can use **Sparklines**, as shown in Figure 33-1, to quickly show a trend graphically inside a single cell. This example helps forecast inventory needs for ingredients used at a bread store.
- You also can insert a Column or Win/Loss sparkline to show a trend in these formats.

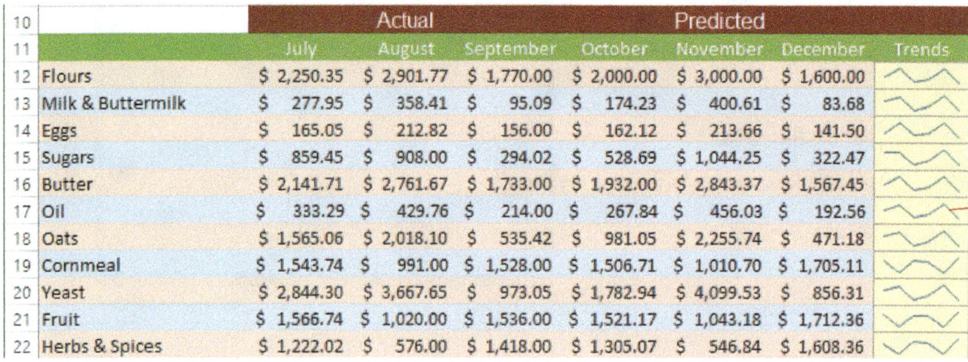

10		Actual			Predicted			
11		July	August	September	October	November	December	Trends
12	Flours	$ 2,250.35	$ 2,901.77	$ 1,770.00	$ 2,000.00	$ 3,000.00	$ 1,600.00	
13	Milk & Buttermilk	$ 277.95	$ 358.41	$ 95.09	$ 174.23	$ 400.61	$ 83.68	
14	Eggs	$ 165.05	$ 212.82	$ 156.00	$ 162.12	$ 213.66	$ 141.50	
15	Sugars	$ 859.45	$ 908.00	$ 294.02	$ 528.69	$ 1,044.25	$ 322.47	
16	Butter	$ 2,141.71	$ 2,761.67	$ 1,733.00	$ 1,932.00	$ 2,843.37	$ 1,567.45	
17	Oil	$ 333.29	$ 429.76	$ 214.00	$ 267.84	$ 456.03	$ 192.56	
18	Oats	$ 1,565.06	$ 2,018.10	$ 535.42	$ 981.05	$ 2,255.74	$ 471.18	
19	Cornmeal	$ 1,543.74	$ 991.00	$ 1,528.00	$ 1,506.71	$ 1,010.70	$ 1,705.11	
20	Yeast	$ 2,844.30	$ 3,667.65	$ 973.05	$ 1,782.94	$ 4,099.53	$ 856.31	
21	Fruit	$ 1,566.74	$ 1,020.00	$ 1,536.00	$ 1,521.17	$ 1,043.18	$ 1,712.36	
22	Herbs & Spices	$ 1,222.02	$ 576.00	$ 1,418.00	$ 1,305.07	$ 546.84	$ 1,608.36	

Sparklines

Figure 33-1

Excel 2013, Windows 8, Microsoft Corporation

Try It! Using AutoFill to Complete a Series and Create Trends

1. Start Excel, and open **E33Try** from the data files for this lesson.
2. Save the file as **E33Try_xx** in the location where your teacher instructs you to store the files for this lesson.
3. Add a header that has your name at the left, the date code in the center, and the page number code at the right, and change back to Normal view.
4. Select cells B2:G2.
5. Click the AutoFill handle and drag to the right to cell J2.
6. Select cells B3:G3.
7. Right-click the AutoFill handle, and drag to the right to cell J3.
8. Release the mouse button at cell J3.
9. In the shortcut menu, select Linear Trend.
10. Select cells B4:G4.
11. Right-click the AutoFill handle, and drag to the right to cell J4.
12. Release the mouse button at cell J4.
13. In the shortcut menu select Growth Trend.
14. Save the changes to the **E33Try_xx** file, and leave it open to use in the next Try It.

AutoFill shortcut menu

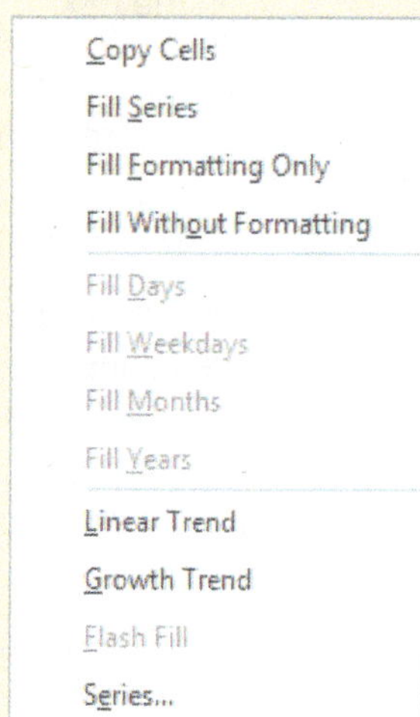

Excel 2013, Windows 8, Microsoft Corporation

Try It! Using the Fill Button to Create a Linear Trend

1. In the **E33Try_xx** file, select cells B5:J5.
2. On the HOME tab, click the Fill button > Series.
3. In the Series in group, click Rows, if necessary.
4. Select Linear as the Type.
5. Click OK.
6. Save the changes to the **E33Try_xx** file, and leave it open to use in the next Try It.

The Series dialog box

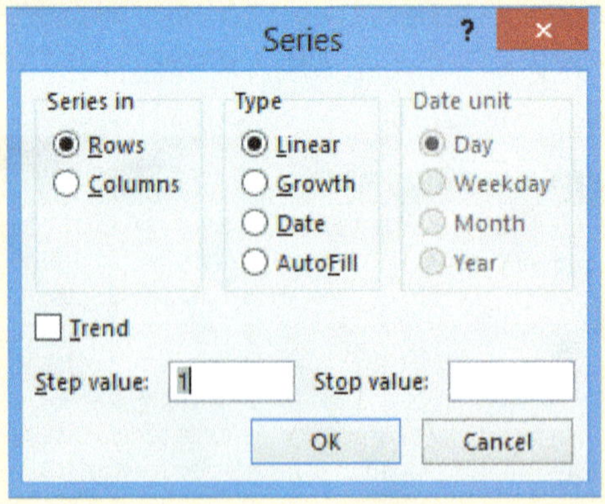

Excel 2013, Windows 8, Microsoft Corporation

Try It! Using Sparklines to Instantly Chart Trends

1. In the **E33Try_xx** file, select cells B5:J5, if needed.
2. On the INSERT tab, click the Line button to show the trend in a line chart.
3. In the Create Sparklines dialog box, enter **$L$5** in the Location Range box.
4. Click OK.
5. Save the changes to the **E33Try_xx** file, and leave it open to use in the next Try It.

The Create Sparklines dialog box

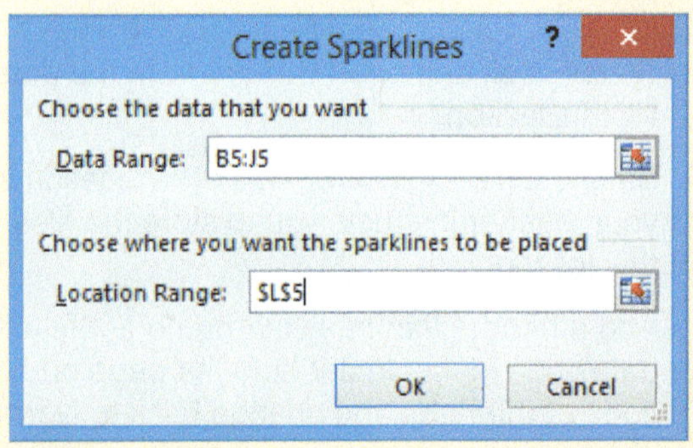

Excel 2013, Windows 8, Microsoft Corporation

Using FORECAST

- The FORECAST function uses a "linear trend" formula to calculate future values.
- FORECAST examines the x-values and their relationship to the y-values, and then, given a new x-value, it calculates the matching y-value.
- Use FORECAST when existing values follow more or less a straight line, with little or no variance (ups or downs).
- FORECAST plots new values along a straight line formed by existing values.
- The FORECAST function requires two sets of related variables—x values and y values.

Try It! Using the FORECAST Function

1. In the E33Try_xx file, click D14.
2. Type =.
3. Type FORECAST.

   ✓ *Notice that when you begin typing the name of the function, Excel provides a list of functions. You can double-click the function of your choice instead of typing the entire name.*
4. Type (.
5. Select D13.
6. Type ,.
7. Select B3:J3.
8. Type ,.
9. Select B2:J2.
10. Type), and press ENTER.
11. Save the changes to the E33Try_xx file, and leave it open to use in the next Try It.

Using TREND

- TREND, like FORECAST, plots new values along the straight line formed by the plotted positions of existing values.
- Use the TREND function when existing values follow more or less a straight line when plotted on a chart.
- The TREND function uses a "linear trend" method of calculating future values.
- You only need known y-values to make a prediction using TREND.
- You can input known x-values in the TREND equation to improve the accuracy of the prediction.
- If you also input a new x-value as an argument, it will produce the same result as FORECAST.
- TREND uses the formula, y=mx+b to plot new values along a straight line.
- If you tell TREND to set the value of b to zero, the x value will be adjusted to begin plotting its trend line at zero.

Try It! Using the TREND Function

1. In the E33Try_xx file, click D15.
2. Type =.
3. Type TREND.
4. Type (.
5. Select cells B4:J4 and skip to Step 6.

   OR

   If desired, add known x-value(s):
   - Type ,.
   - Select B2:J2.

   If desired, add new x-value(s):
   - Type ,.
   - Select D13.

   If desired, set the intercept to zero:
   - Type ,.
   - Type FALSE.
6. Type).
7. Press ENTER.
8. Save the changes to the E33Try_xx file, and leave it open to use in the next Try It.

Using GROWTH

- The GROWTH function predicts future values using an exponential growth formula, y=b*m^x.
- The trend line created by the GROWTH function is curved, not straight.
- Like TREND, the GROWTH function requires only known y-values.
- You can improve the accuracy by supplying known x-values and new x-values if they're available.

Try It! Using the GROWTH Function

1. In the **E33Try_xx** file, click D16.
2. Type **=**.
3. Type **GROWTH**.
4. Type **(**.
5. Select B5:J5.
6. Type **,**.
7. Select B2:J2.
8. Type **,**.
9. Select D13 and skip to Step 10.

   OR

   If desired, set the intercept to zero:
   - Type **,**.
   - Type **FALSE**.
10. Type **)**.
11. Press ENTER.
12. Save the **E33Try_xx** file, and close it.

Lesson 33—Practice

In this project, you will create a FORECAST function using the skills you learned in this lesson.

DIRECTIONS

1. Start Excel, if necessary, and open the **E33Practice** file from the data files for this lesson.
2. Save the workbook as **E33Practice_xx** in the location where your teacher instructs you to store the files for this lesson.
3. For all the worksheets, add a header that has your name at the left, the date code in the center, and the page number code at the right, and change back to **Normal** view.
4. Switch to the **FORECAST** sheet, if necessary, and click cell **E13**.
5. Type **=FORECAST(**.
6. Click cell **E12** and press F4 twice. This will make the row part of the address absolute.

   ✓ *You want to use the value entered in row 12 of each column as the new x-value for the y-value you wish to calculate.*
7. Type **,** (comma), and select the range **B13:D13**.
8. Press F4 three times to make the column part of the range address absolute.

   ✓ *As you copy the formula, you want it to always refer to the known y-values in columns B, C, and D.*
9. Type **,** (comma), and select the range **B12:D12**.
10. Press F4 to make the range address absolute.

    ✓ *As you copy the formula, you want it to always refer to the known x-values in cells B12:D12, which correspond to the new x value entered in row 12 of columns E through G.*
11. Type **)**, and press ENTER to complete the formula.
12. Select cell **E13**, and on the HOME tab, click **Copy** to place the formula on the Office Clipboard.
13. Press SHIFT + click cell **G22** to select the cells where you want to enter the projected fourth quarter data.

14. On the HOME tab, click the **Paste** down arrow Paste and select **Formulas** to fill the range **E13:G22** while maintaining the worksheet formatting. Your worksheet should look like Figure 33-2.

15. **With your teacher's permission,** print the **FORECAST** worksheet. Submit the printout or the file for grading as required.

16. Save and close the file, and exit Excel.

Figure 33-2

	A	B	C	D	E	F	G
1							
2							
3							
4	***Whole Grains Bread***						
5	*Salem, Oregon Office*						
6	Forecasted Inventory Needs						
7							
8							
9							
10		Actual			Predicted		
11		July	August	September	October	November	December
12	Flours	$ 2,250	$ 2,902	$ 1,770	$ 2,000	$ 3,000	$ 1,600
13	Milk & Buttermilk	$ 278	$ 358	$ 95	$ 174	$ 401	$ 84
14	Eggs	$ 165	$ 213	$ 156	$ 162	$ 214	$ 141
15	Sugars	$ 859	$ 908	$ 294	$ 529	$ 1,044	$ 322
16	Butter	$ 2,142	$ 2,762	$ 1,733	$ 1,932	$ 2,843	$ 1,567
17	Oil	$ 333	$ 430	$ 214	$ 268	$ 456	$ 193
18	Oats	$ 1,565	$ 2,018	$ 535	$ 981	$ 2,256	$ 471
19	Cornmeal	$ 1,544	$ 991	$ 1,528	$ 1,507	$ 1,011	$ 1,705
20	Yeast	$ 2,844	$ 3,668	$ 973	$ 1,783	$ 4,100	$ 856
21	Fruit	$ 1,567	$ 1,020	$ 1,536	$ 1,521	$ 1,043	$ 1,712
22	Herbs & Spices	$ 1,222	$ 576	$ 1,418	$ 1,305	$ 547	$ 1,608

Excel 2013, Windows 8, Microsoft Corporation

Lesson 33—Apply

You are the owner of a Whole Grains Bread store in Salem, Washington, and you've been looking for a way to manage inventory more effectively. After learning about Excel's forecasting functions, you've decided to give them a try and see how good they are at predicting your future inventory needs.

DIRECTIONS

1. Start Excel, if necessary, and open the **E33Apply** file from the data files for this lesson.
2. Save the workbook as **E33Apply_xx** in the location where your teacher instructs you to store the files for this lesson.
3. For all worksheets, add a header that has your name at the left, the date code in the center, and the page number code at the right, and change back to **Normal** view.
4. On the **TREND** worksheet, use a simple **TREND** formula to calculate the Flours projection for October.
5. Copy the formula for the rest of the year.
6. In cell **E13**, create a **TREND** formula that projects inventory expenses for Milk & Buttermilk based on its relationship to the flours usage.

   ✓ *Hint: Use the Flours expense for July-Sept as the known x-values and the Flours expense for October as the new x-value.*

7. Use this TREND formula to project the rest of the expenses for the fourth quarter of October, November, and December. (Keep the existing formatting.)
8. On the **GROWTH** worksheet, use a simple **GROWTH** formula to calculate the Flours projection for October.
9. Copy the formula for the rest of the year.
10. In cell **E13**, create a **GROWTH** formula that projects inventory expenses for Milk & Buttermilk based on its relationship to the flours usage.

    ✓ *Hint: Use the Flours expense for July-Sept as the known x-values and the Flours expense for October as the new x-value.*

11. Use this **GROWTH** formula to project the rest of the expenses for the fourth quarter. (Keep the existing formatting.)
12. Apply the Accounting formatting to all expenses in the workbook, and widen the columns, as necessary. Your **GROWTH** worksheet should look like Figure 33-3.
13. Check the spelling in the workbook.
14. **With your teacher's permission,** print the **TREND** and **GROWTH** worksheets. Submit the printouts or the file for grading as required.
15. Save and close the file, and exit Excel.

Figure 33-3

	A	B	C	D	E	F	G
1							
2							
3							
4	***Whole Grains Bread***						
5	*Salem, Oregon Office*						
6	Forecasted Inventory Needs						
7							
8							
9							
10		Actual			Predicted		
11		July	August	September	October	November	December
12	Flours	$ 2,250.35	$ 2,901.77	$ 1,770.00	$ 2,549.38	$ 2,514.61	$ 1,885.29
13	Milk & Buttermilk	$ 277.95	$ 358.41	$ 95.09	$ 277.96	$ 267.27	$ 131.47
14	Eggs	$ 165.05	$ 212.82	$ 156.00	$ 188.71	$ 186.88	$ 156.57
15	Sugars	$ 859.45	$ 908.00	$ 294.02	$ 769.29	$ 744.46	$ 411.04
16	Butter	$ 2,141.71	$ 2,761.67	$ 1,733.00	$ 2,399.13	$ 2,365.14	$ 1,826.68
17	Oil	$ 333.29	$ 429.76	$ 214.00	$ 362.14	$ 354.62	$ 242.63
18	Oats	$ 1,565.06	$ 2,018.10	$ 535.42	$ 1,565.10	$ 1,504.95	$ 740.28
19	Cornmeal	$ 1,543.74	$ 991.00	$ 1,528.00	$ 1,204.79	$ 1,221.65	$ 1,571.08
20	Yeast	$ 2,844.30	$ 3,667.65	$ 973.05	$ 2,844.37	$ 2,735.05	$ 1,345.37
21	Fruit	$ 1,566.74	$ 1,020.00	$ 1,536.00	$ 1,230.78	$ 1,247.10	$ 1,582.84
22	Herbs & Spices	$ 1,222.02	$ 576.00	$ 1,418.00	$ 820.15	$ 843.77	$ 1,410.67
23							

Lesson 34

Using Advanced Functions for Data Analysis

➤ What You Will Learn

- Using the PMT Function
- Creating What-If Data Tables
- Solving a Problem with Goal Seek
- Using Solver to Resolve Problems
- Working with Outlines

Software Skills What-if analysis allows you to determine the optimal values for a given situation. For example, if you know that you can only spend a maximum of $32,000 this year on new computers, you could adjust the monthly budget amount so you could spend the total amount by the end of the year and yet still remain within your department's monthly budgetary constraints. You can use Excel's data features—Goal Seek, Solver, and Auto Outline—to improve and manage list or table data.

What You Can Do

Using the PMT Function

- You can use the PMT (payment) function to calculate a loan payment amount given the principal, interest rate, and number of payment periods.

  ✓ *The PMT result is equal to your principal and interest for the loan, but does not include any other payment parts such as taxes, escrow, points, closing fees, and so on.*

- The arguments for the PMT function are: =PMT(rate,nper,pv).
  - rate: Interest rate per period (for example, annual interest rate/12).
  - nper: Number of payment periods (for example, years*12).
  - pv (present value): The total amount that a series of future payments is worth now (for example, the principal).

    ✓ *The principal is the amount of the loan after any down payment that might have been paid.*

WORDS TO KNOW

Data table
A method of performing what-if analysis, involving a column (and possibly a row) of variables and a formula that Excel solves over and over, using each of the variables. The result is a table of answers.

Goal Seek
A method of performing what-if analysis in which the result (the goal) is known, but the value of a single dependent variable is unknown.

Input cell
A cell in a data table to which your formula refers. Excel copies a variable into this cell, solves the formula, and then goes on to the next variable to create a series of answers.

Outline
A feature that allows groups of data to be displayed or hidden.

Solver
A method of performing what-if analysis in which the result is known, but more than a single variable is unknown. Also, there may be additional constraints upon the final result.

Substitution values
A special name given to the variables used in a data table.

Variable
An input value that changes depending on the desired outcome.

What-if analysis
Excel's term for a series of tools that perform calculations involving one or more variables.

- For example, if you wish to calculate a monthly payment for a $175,000 loan at a 9% annual rate of interest for 25 years, you must enter **.09/12** as the monthly rate and enter **25*12** to get the total number of payments (nper): **=PMT(.09/12,25*12,175000)**
- Both the rate and the number of payment periods (nper) must be in the same timeframe or format, such as monthly or annually.
- You must enter the present value as a negative to get a positive number for the result, as in: **=PMT(.09/12,25*12,-175000)**

Try It! Using the PMT Function

1. Start Excel, and open the **E34Try** file from the data files for this lesson.
2. Save the file as **E34Try_xx** in the location where your teacher instructs you to store the files for this lesson.
3. For all worksheets, add a header that has your name at the left, the date code in the center, and the page number code at the right, and change back to Normal view.
4. Click the PMT worksheet tab to make that sheet active, and click D7.
5. Type **=**.
6. Type **PMT**.
7. Type **(**.
8. Click cell D6, and type **/12**.

   ✓ *This breaks the interest rate into a monthly amount. The rate is a percentage, or .09.*
9. Type **,**.
10. Click cell D5, and type ***12**.

    ✓ *For example, 3*12. The term is the number of years.*
11. Type **,**.
12. Type **–** (minus), and click cell D4.

    ✓ *When you type a minus sign before the principal, the payment amount will appear as a positive amount.*
13. Type **)**.
14. Press ENTER.
15. Save the **E34Try_xx** file, and leave it open to use in the next Try It.

Loan payment calculation using PMT

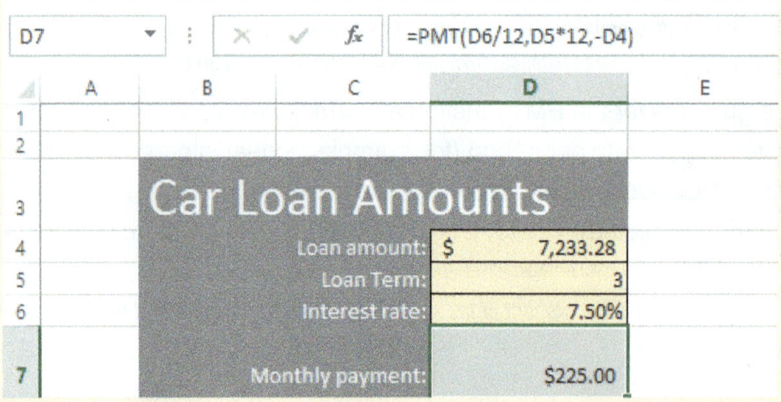

Excel 2013, Windows 8, Microsoft Corporation

Creating What-If Data Tables

- Use **what-if analysis** to evaluate different situations and find the best solution.
- For example when reviewing your personal budget, a what-if table can help you figure out the maximum mortgage you can afford if you want to keep your payments at $1,000 per month given various interest rates.
- The **variables** used in a data table are called **substitution values**, because Excel substitutes each value in the given formula when evaluating the what-if situation.
- Excel uses the **input cell** as a working area during the analysis—it can be blank, or it can contain one of the variables (typically, the first one in the variables list).

  ✓ *The what-if formula must refer to this input cell.*

- Excel places each variable into the input cell as it solves each equation.
- **Data tables** can be either one-input or two-input.
- In a one-input data table, you enter one series of variables, which are then substituted in a formula to come up with a series of answers.
  - You can enter the variables, such as the varying interest rates in this example, in a single column or a single row.
  - You then enter a formula in a cell either one row up and one column to the right, or one row down and one column to the left (for variables entered in a row).
  - The formula points to the input cell, which typically contains a value equal to the first variable in your list.
- In a two-input data table, you enter two series of variables, thus increasing the number of possible solutions.

  ✓ *For example, you can enter both the loan rates and several different loan terms (15-, 20-, 25-, or 30-year) to determine what amounts you can afford under varying plans.*

- In a two-input data table, you enter one set of variables in a row, and the other set in a column to the left of the first row variable.
  - You enter the formula in the cell intersected by the variable row and variable column.
  - The formula refers to two input cells, which again can be blank, or may be filled with the first variable.
- After entering the variables, formula, and input cell precisely, you use a command on the DATA tab to generate the values in the input table.

Try It! Creating a One-Input Data Table

1. In the **E34Try_xx** file, select the One Input Table worksheet.
2. In cell C12, type **=D8**, and press ENTER .
   - ✓ *To enter additional formulas, type them in the cells to the right of the formula cell (if you entered variables in a column), or in the cells below the formula cell (if you entered variables in a row).*
3. Select the range B12:C19.
   - ✓ *Select cells containing the formula and substitution values.*
   - ✓ *Do not select the input cell.*
4. Click DATA > What-If Analysis > Data Table.
5. In the Column input cell box, type **D8**.
6. Click OK.
7. Save the **E34Try_xx** file, and leave it open to use in the next Try It.

A one-variable what-if analysis

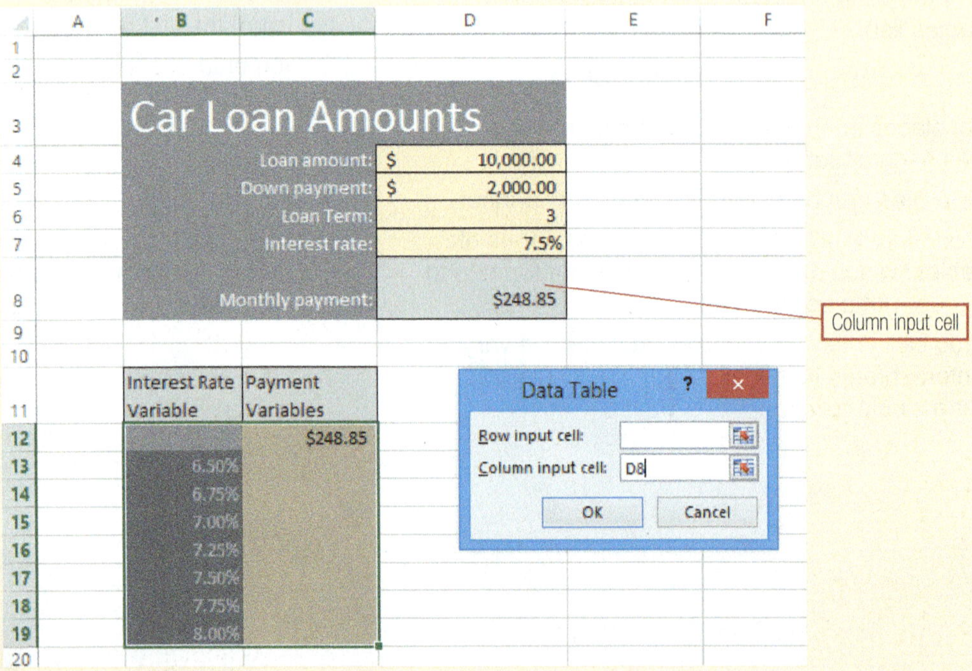

Excel 2013, Windows 8, Microsoft Corporation

Try It! Creating a Two-Input Data Table

1. In the **E34Try_xx** file, select the Two Input Table worksheet.
2. In cell B6, type **=C21**, and press ENTER.
3. Select B6:I13, or all the cells in the data table range.

   ✓ *Select cells containing the formula and the substitution values.*
4. On the DATA tab, click What-If Analysis > Data Table.
5. In the Row input cell, type **C20**.
6. In the Column input cell box, type **C18**.

   ✓ *Excel will automatically create absolute references by adding dollar signs to cell addresses entered in the Data Table dialog box.*
7. Click OK.
8. Save the **E34Try_xx** file, and leave it open to use in the next Try It.

A two-variable what-if analysis

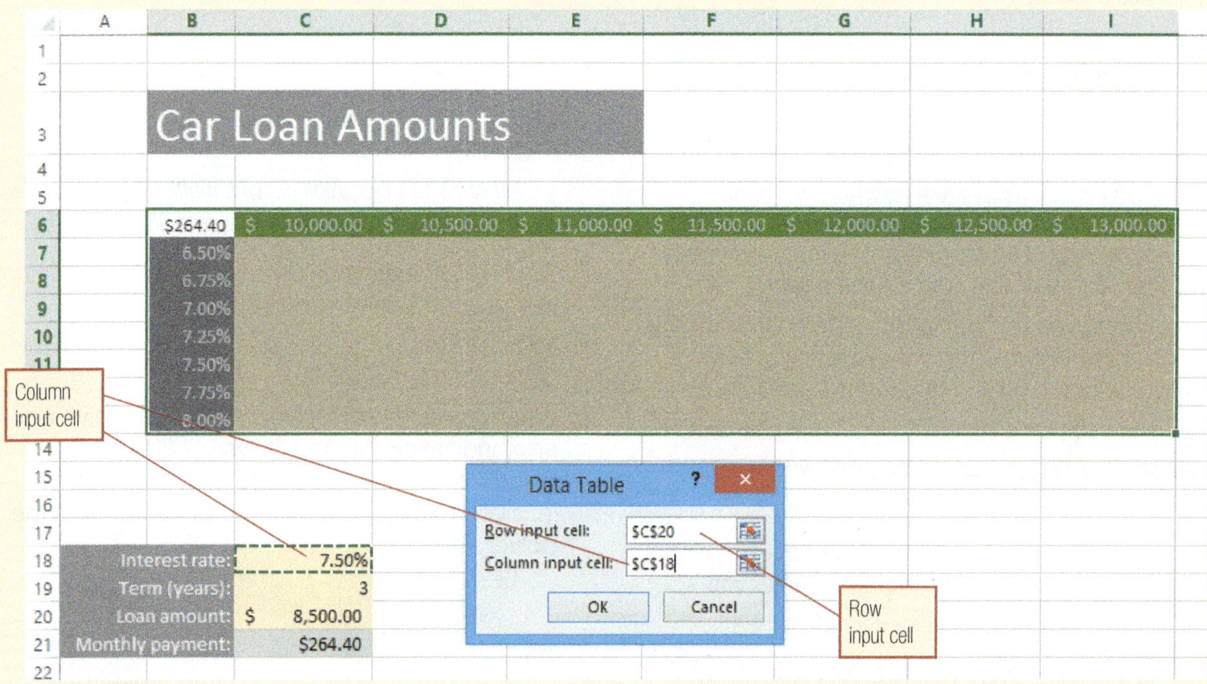

Excel 2013, Windows 8, Microsoft Corporation

Solving a Problem with Goal Seek

- Use **Goal Seek** when you know the result (the goal), but you do not know the value of one of the input variables.
- Goal Seek tests possible variables until it finds the input value that produces the desired result.
- For example, you could use Goal Seek to determine the exact amount you could borrow at 9.25% and keep the payment at $1,000 a month.
- When you input your known variables into Goal Seek, the Goal Seek Status dialog box will show whether it found a solution and, if so, the solution. The values on the worksheet are also changed.

Try It! Using Goal Seek

1. In the **E34Try_xx** file, select the Goal Seek worksheet.
2. On the DATA tab, click What-If Analysis > Goal Seek.
3. In the Set cell box, type **D9**.
4. In the To value box, type **350**.
5. In the By changing cell box, type **D6**.
6. Click OK.

   ✓ *Goal Seek finds a solution and displays it in the Goal Seek Status dialog box. The values on the worksheet are also changed.*
7. In the Goal Seek Status dialog box, click OK to keep the changed cell values.
8. Save the **E34Try_xx** file, and leave it open to use in the next Try It.

The Goal Seek Status dialog box

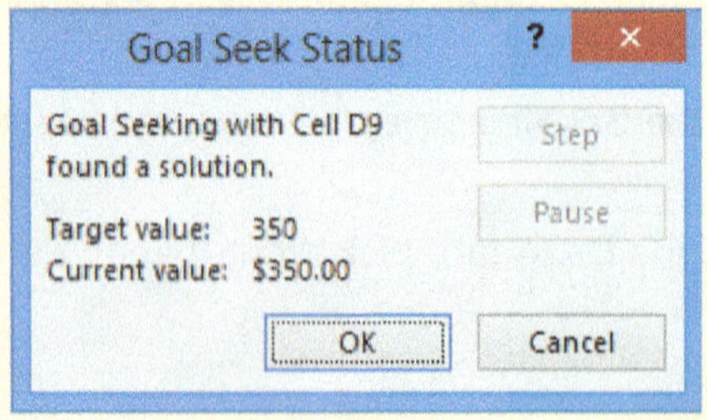

Excel 2013, Windows 8, Microsoft Corporation

Using Solver to Resolve Problems

- With **Solver**, you can resolve problems involving more than one variable with a known result.
- For example, you could use Solver to determine the exact amount you could borrow, spending $1,000 a month, using various interest rates and various down payments.

  ✓ *Use the Value Of option if you plan to solve for a specific result.*
- You can use Solver to determine the best solution to a problem that fits within the constraints you set.

✓ *You can also solve problems with multiple variables using a PivotTable, which is covered in Lesson 36.*

- You must first activate the Solver Add-in before you can use the Solver feature.
- You can enable the Solver Add-in from the Excel Options on the FILE tab.
- When working with Solver, you may receive an error indicating that the Solver.dll file cannot be found. To fix the error, deactivate the Solver add-in, close Excel, reopen Excel, and reactivate the Solver add-in.

Try It! Activating the Solver

1. In the **E34Try_xx** file, click FILE > Options.
2. In the Excel Options dialog box, click Add-Ins.
3. In the Manage drop-down box, select Excel Add-ins > Go.
4. In the Add-Ins dialog box, click Solver Add-in > OK.
5. Save the **E34Try_xx** file, and leave it open to use in the next Try It.

Try It! Using Solver

1. In the E34Try_xx file, select the Solver worksheet.
2. On the DATA tab, in the Analysis group, click Solver .
3. In the Solver Parameters dialog box, click Max.
4. In the Set Objective box, type I4.
5. In the By Changing Variable Cells box, type F5.
6. Click the Add button to add a constraint.
7. In the Cell Reference box, type F5.
8. Select <= from the descriptor drop-down list.
9. In the Constraint box, type I7.
10. Click OK.

    ✓ *Note that the cell reference in the Solver Parameters dialog box makes your cell references absolute.*
11. Click Solve.

    ✓ *Solver finds a solution and displays it in a dialog box. The values on the worksheet are also changed.*
12. Click OK to keep the changed cell values. Adjust the column widths, as needed.

    ✓ *You can save the scenario, restore your previous values, or print reports from the dialog box that appears.*
13. Save the E34Try_xx file, and leave it open to use in the next Try It.

The Solver Parameters dialog box

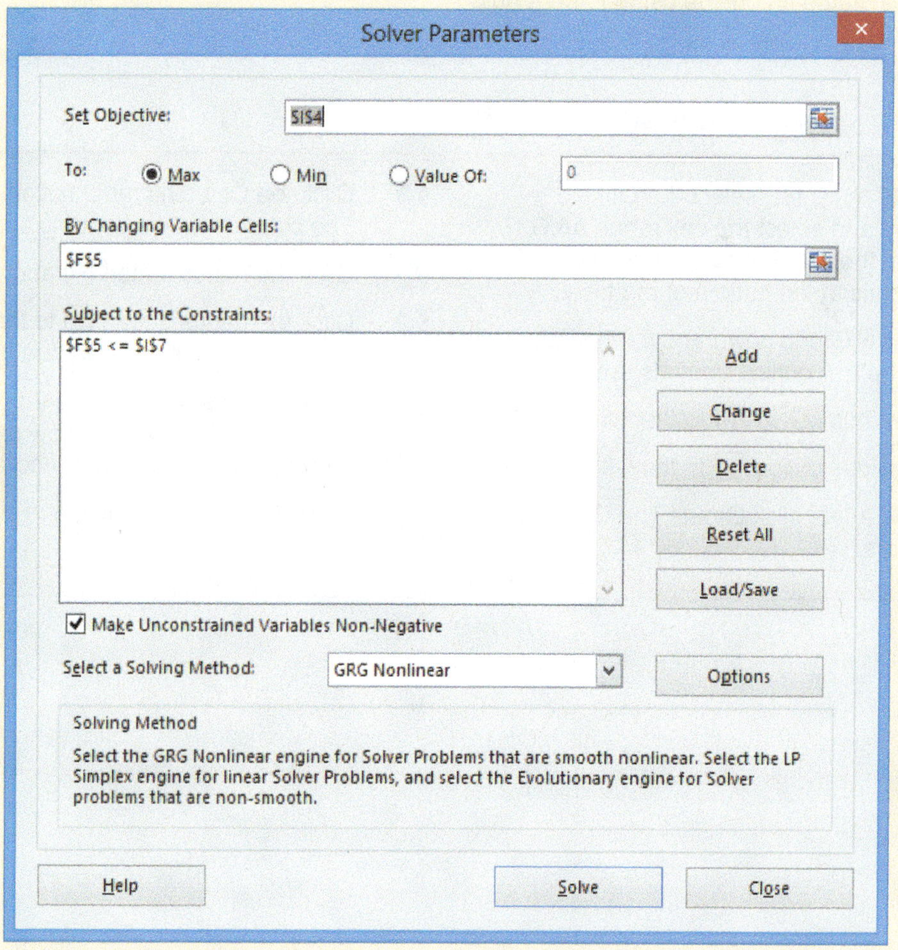

Working with Outlines

- If you have a list of data that you want to group and summarize, you can create an **outline** of up to eight levels, one for each group.
- You can use an outline to quickly display summary rows or columns, or to reveal the detail data for each group.
- You can create an outline of rows, an outline of columns, or an outline of both rows and columns.
- Each column of the data that you want to outline needs to have a label in the first row, similar facts in each column, and no blank rows or columns within the range.
- Outline features are located in the Outline group on the DATA tab.
- To create an outline, select a cell in the range of cells you want to outline, and click the Group button.
- You can quickly create an outline using Excel's Auto Outline feature.

✓ *For the Auto Outline feature to function, the rows of your data need be located below or above a summary row, or a subtotal.*

✓ *You learned about the SUBTOTAL function and creating a subtotal in Lesson 11.*

- You can access Auto Outline from the Group button's drop-down arrow.
- Once you create an outline, the outline controls appear. Row outline controls appear to the left of the list or table. Column outline controls appear above the list or table.
- You can expand or collapse the data in your outline by clicking the plus ⊞ and minus ⊟ outline control buttons.
- You can remove an outline by using the Clear Outline button from the Ungroup button's drop-down arrow.

Try It! Working with Outlines

1. In the **E34Try_xx** file, select the Outline worksheet, and select the cell range A6:G37. Notice that the list already contains two cells with subtotals at the bottom of the table.
2. Click DATA > Group down arrow > Auto Outline. The row outline controls appear.
3. Click the minus button ⊟ to the left of row 20.
4. Click the minus button ⊟ to the left of row 29.
5. On the DATA tab, click Group. The Group dialog box appears.
6. Click the Columns radio button, and click OK. The column outline controls appear.
7. Click the minus button ⊟ above column F.
8. Click the minus button ⊟ to the left of row 37. Notice that all of the rows are now collapsed.
9. Click the plus button ⊞ to the left of row 37. Notice that the rows are now expanded, except for the rows you previously collapsed.
10. Save the **E34Try_xx** file, and close it.

Lesson 34—Practice

In this project, you will use Solver to create a bid projection using the skills you learned in this lesson.

DIRECTIONS

1. Start Excel, if necessary, and open the **E34Practice** file from the data files for this lesson.
2. Save the workbook as **E34Practice_xx** in the location where your teacher instructs you to store the files for this lesson.
3. For all worksheets, add a header that has your name at the left, the date code in the center, and the page number code at the right, and change back to **Normal** view.
4. Select the **Bid Sheet** worksheet, if necessary.
5. On the **DATA** tab, click the **Solver** button. The Solver Parameters dialog box opens.
6. In the **Set Objective** box, click the **Collapse Dialog box** button.
7. Click cell **E14**, and click the **Expand Dialog box** button.
8. Click **Value Of**, and type **300000** in the text box.
9. In the **By Changing Variable Cells** box, click the **Collapse Dialog box** button.
10. Hold down CTRL, and click cells **B20** and **D7**.
11. Click the **Expand Dialog** box button.
12. Click **Add** to open the Add Constraint dialog box.
13. In the **Cell Reference** box, type **B20**.
14. Click **less than or equal** from the descriptor list.
15. Type **22** in the **Constraint** box.
16. Click **Add** to add a second constraint.
17. In the **Cell Reference** box, type **D7**.
18. Click **less than or equal** from the descriptor list.
19. Type **10** in the **Constraint** box, and click **OK** to return to the Solver Parameters dialog box.
20. Click **Solve**.
21. In the **Solver Results** dialog box, select **Keep Solver Solution** and click **OK**. Your document should look like the one shown in Figure 34-1.
22. **With your teacher's permission,** print the **Bid Sheet** worksheet. Submit the printout or the file for grading as required.

    ✓ *If printing, adjust the page breaks, and change the print settings, as necessary.*

23. Save and close the file, and exit Excel.

Figure 34-1

	A	B	C	D	E	F
1						
2						
3						
4	Restoration Architecture					
5	Bid Sheet - Old Highland Library Renovation					
6						
7			Profit	9%		
8						
9		Base Bid	Alt #1	Alt #2	Base Bid + Alt	
10	Materials	$ 173,081.00	$ 33,673.00	$ 7,619.00	$ 214,373.00	
11	Labor	$ 45,749.00	$ 10,023.75	$ 4,977.75	$ 60,750.50	
12	Profit	$ 19,786.48	$ 3,951.03	$ 1,138.99	$ 41,268.53	
13						
14	Total Bid	$ 238,616.48	$ 47,647.78	$ 13,735.74	$ 300,000.00	
15						
16						
17						
18	My estimate on the bid maximum	$ 300,000.00				
19	Minimum profit I need	10%				
20	Maximum I can pay plumbers	$ 22.00				
21						

Excel 2013, Windows 8, Microsoft Corporation

Lesson 34—Apply

As the owner of Restoration Architecture, you're always watching the bottom line. You're preparing a bid for the renovation of your town's library, and you want to run the numbers through Excel before submitting it. You'll create data tables to compute the cost of the small construction loan you'll need if you get the job, and the estimated amount of any increased costs you might encounter if the job runs over deadline.

DIRECTIONS

1. Start Excel, if necessary.
2. Open the **E34Apply** file from the data files for this lesson.
3. Save the workbook as **E34Apply_xx** in the location where your teacher instructs you to store the files for this lesson.
4. For all worksheets, add a header that has your name at the left, the date code in the center, and the page number code at the right, and change back to **Normal** view.
5. Create a two-input what-if analysis on the **Labor** worksheet. Set up the table as shown in Figure 34-2 on the next page:
   a. Type the following formula in cell C19: **=H19*H20**.
      ✓ *This calculates the changes in cost when construction finishes early or late.*
   b. Select the data range **C19:F25**.
   c. Use **H20** for the **Row input cell**.
   d. Use **H19** for the **Column input cell**.
6. Create another two-input table on the **Loan** worksheet. Set up the table as shown in Figure 34-3 on the next page:
   a. In cell **A9**, create a PMT formula using the values in cells **C6**, **C7**, and **F6**.
      ✓ *Be sure to enter the principle value as a negative.*
   b. Select the data range **A9:F15**.
   c. Use **C7** for the **Row input cell**.
   d. Use **C6** for the **Column input cell**.
7. **With your teacher's permission,** print the **Labor** and **Loan** worksheets. Submit the printout or the file for grading as required.
8. Save and close the file, and exit Excel.

Figure 34-2

Restoration Architecture

Estimated Labor Costs - Old Highland Library Renovation

	Hours Estimated to Complete Work					Labor Cost		
	Base Bid	Alt #1	Alt #2	Totals Hours	Hourly Rate Current Quotes	Base Bid	Alt #1	Alt #2
Masonary	215.00			215.00	$ 29.75	$ 6,396.25	$ -	$ -
Carpentry	1,245.00	325.00	114.00	1,684.00	$ 18.75	$ 23,343.75	$ 6,093.75	$ 2,137.50
Electrical	322.00	95.00	85.75	502.75	$ 27.00	$ 8,694.00	$ 2,565.00	$ 2,315.25
Roofers	96.00	21.00		117.00	$ 15.00	$ 1,440.00	$ 315.00	$ -
Plumbing	235.00	42.00	21.00	298.00	$ 22.00	$ 5,170.00	$ 924.00	$ 462.00
Total Bid	2,113.00	483.00	220.75	2,816.75		$ 45,044.00	$ 9,897.75	$ 4,914.75

			Alt #2	Alt #1	Base
		$ 4,423.28	$ 4,914.75	$ 9,897.75	$ 45,044.00
Estimated Cost Reductions/Increases for Schedule Changes	1-Week Early	90%	4,423.28	8,907.98	40,539.60
	On Time	100%	4,914.75	9,897.75	45,044.00
	1 Week Late	112%	5,504.52	11,085.48	50,449.28
	2 Weeks Late	126%	6,192.59	12,471.17	56,755.44
	3 Weeks Late	132%	6,487.47	13,065.03	59,458.08
	4 Weeks Late	141%	6,929.80	13,955.83	63,512.04

$ 4,914.75
90%

Excel 2013, Windows 8, Microsoft Corporation

Figure 34-3

Restoration Architecture

Construction Loan - Old Highland Library Renovation

Loan amount	$ 55,000.00	Term in months	6
Loan rate	5.25%		

$9,307.54	5.25%	5.50%	5.75%	6.00%	6.25%
$55,000.00	$ 9,308	$ 9,314	$ 9,321	$ 9,328	$ 9,334
$60,000.00	$ 10,154	$ 10,161	$ 10,168	$ 10,176	$ 10,183
$65,000.00	$ 11,000	$ 11,008	$ 11,016	$ 11,024	$ 11,032
$70,000.00	$ 11,846	$ 11,855	$ 11,863	$ 11,872	$ 11,880
$75,000.00	$ 12,692	$ 12,701	$ 12,710	$ 12,720	$ 12,729
$80,000.00	$ 13,538	$ 13,548	$ 13,558	$ 13,568	$ 13,577

Excel 2013, Windows 8, Microsoft Corporation

Lesson 35

Using LOOKUP Functions

➤ What You Will Learn

Creating Lookup Functions

WORDS TO KNOW

Range name
The name given to a set of adjacent cells. You might name a range in order to make it more convenient to reference that range in a formula or a function, such as VLOOKUP.

Table
A series of columns and rows used to organize data. Each column typically represents a different field, and each row represents an entire record.

Software Skills With the lookup functions, you can look up information in a table based on a known value. For example, you can look up the salesperson assigned to a particular client. At the same time, you can look up that client's address and phone number. You can also look up the sales discount for a particular customer or calculate the bonuses for a group of salespeople based on a bonus structure. If needed, you can nest a function, such as SUM, within a lookup function in order to look up a sum total within a table. For example, you might want to look up the total cost of the items in an invoice to calculate the cost of delivering them.

What You Can Do

Creating Lookup Functions

- The lookup functions, VLOOKUP and HLOOKUP, locate a value in a **table**.
- Use the VLOOKUP (vertical lookup) function to look up data in a particular column in the table.
- The VLOOKUP function uses this format: =VLOOKUP(item,table-range,column-position)
    - *Item* is the text or value for which you are looking.
        - The item to look up must be located in the first column of the VLOOKUP table.
        - Uppercase and lowercase are treated the same.
        - Depending on the true/false argument used, if an exact match is not found, the next smallest value may be used.

      ✓ *You can use a function here to calculate the item's value. For example, you can use the SUM function to calculate the total cost of items on an invoice and look up the delivery costs in another table to determine the total cost of the invoice.*

- *Table-range* is the range reference or **range name** of the lookup table.
  - Do not include the row containing the column labels.
  - If you are going to copy the lookup function, you should express the range as an absolute reference or as a range name.
- *Column-position* is the column number in the table from which the matching value should be returned.

  ✓ *The far-left column of the table is one; the second column is two, etc.*

- Use the HLOOKUP (horizontal lookup) function to look up data in a particular row in the table.
- You may use a similar formula in a horizontal lookup table: =HLOOKUP(item,table-range,row-position).
  - *Item* is the text or value for which you are looking.
  - *Table-range* is the range reference or range name of the lookup table.

    ✓ *Do not include the column that contains the row labels in this range.*

  - *Row-position* is the row number in the table from which the matching value should be returned.

Try It! Inserting the VLOOKUP Function

1. Start Excel, and open **E35Try** file from the data files for this lesson.
2. Save the file as **E35Try_xx** in the location where your teacher instructs you to store the files for this lesson.
3. Add a header that has your name at the left, the date code in the center, and the page number code at the right, and change back to Normal view.
4. Click cell I18.
5. Type **=**.
6. Type **VLOOKUP(**.

   ✓ *This function's syntax appears in a ScreenTip underneath the selected cell formula. You can click the function's name in the ScreenTip in order to display the related Help screen.*

7. Type **.0725** in the lookup_value position.

   ✓ *This can be an actual value or item or a reference to the cell containing the value or item.*

   ✓ *You can click a cell in the worksheet to insert a cell reference.*

8. Type **,**.
9. Type **B6:I13** for the table_array.

   ✓ *You can also select cells in the worksheet for the cell range.*

10. Type **,**.
11. Type **4** for the col_index_num (column number).
12. Type **)**, and press ENTER.
13. Save the **E35Try_xx** file, and leave it open to use in the next Try It.

Try It! Inserting an HLOOKUP Function Using the Function Wizard

1. In the **E35Try_xx** file, select cell I19.
2. Type **=**.
3. Type **HLOOKUP(**.
4. Click the Insert Function button *fx* on the formula bar.
   - ✓ *This opens the Function Wizard that can help you format the function's arguments.*
5. In the Lookup_value box, type **10500**.
6. Click in the Table_array box, and select cells B6:I13.
   - ✓ *You can use the Collapse Dialog box and Expand Dialog box buttons to hide or expand the dialog box for the selection, if necessary.*
7. In the Row_index_num box, type **MATCH(0.0675,B7:B13)+1**.
   - ✓ *By using the MATCH function, you can have the HLOOKUP function locate the appropriate row index item for you.*
8. Click OK.
9. Save the **E35Try_xx** file, and close it.

The Function Arguments dialog box

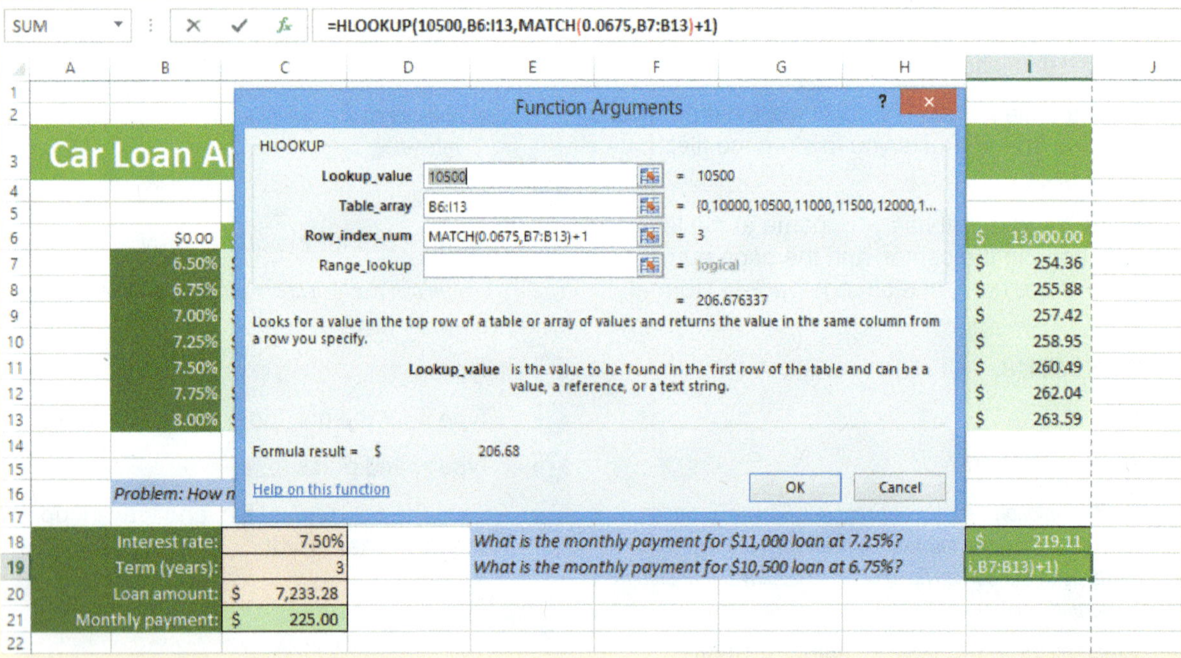

Excel 2013, Windows 8, Microsoft Corporation

Lesson 35—Practice

In this project, you will create VLOOKUP functions to perform income tax calculations using the skills you learned in this lesson.

DIRECTIONS

1. Start Excel, if necessary, and open the **E35Practice** file from the data files for this lesson.
2. Save the workbook as **E35Practice_xx** in the location where your teacher instructs you to store the files for this lesson.
3. For all worksheets, add a header that has your name at the left, the date code in the center, and the page number code at the right, and change back to **Normal** view.
4. Select the **1040** worksheet, if necessary.
5. Click cell **F50**. You'll use this cell to enter a formula to look up your tax based on the provided taxable amount.
6. Type **=VLOOKUP(**, and click the Insert Function button *fx* on the formula bar to open the Function Arguments dialog box.
7. Click in the **Lookup_value** box, and click cell **F49**.

   ✓ *You also can use the Collapse and Expand Dialog box buttons.*
8. Click in the **Table_array** box, click the **Tax Table** worksheet, and select the cell range **A4:C304**.
9. In the **Column_index_num** box, type **2** (the married filing joint column).
10. Click **OK**. Your worksheet should look like Figure 35-1 on the next page.
11. **With your teacher's permission,** print the **1040** worksheet. Submit the printout or the file for grading as required.

    ✓ *If printing, adjust the page breaks, and change the print settings, as necessary.*
12. Save and close the file, and exit Excel.

Figure 35-1

	A	B	C	D	E	F
45	37b	Married filing separately and spouse itemizes				
46	38	Deduction (married jointly)				$ 7,850.00
47	39	Subtract line 38 from line 36				$ 78,530.23
48	40	Multiply $3,000 by tot. exemptions...				$ 12,000.00
49	41	Taxable income				$ 66,530.23
50	42	**Tax**				$ 11,758.00
51	43	Alternative minimum tax				
52	44	**Add lines 42 and 43**				$ 11,758.00
53	45	Foreign tax credit				
54	46	Credit for child and dependent care expenses			$ 682.00	
55	47	Credit for elderly or disabled				
56	48	Education credits				
57	49	Retirement savings credit				
58	50	Child tax credit			$ 1,200.00	
59	51	Adoption credit				
60	52	Credits from form 8396 or 8859				
61	53	Other credits from form 3800 or 8801				
62	54	Total credits				$ 1,882.00
63	55	Subtract line 54 from line 44				$ 9,876.00
64	56	Self-employment tax				
65	57	Social security tax and Medicare tax on tip income				
66	58	Tax on IRAs				
67	59	Advanced EIC payments				
68	60	Household employment taxes				
69	61	**Total tax**				$ 9,876.00
70	62	Federal income tax withheld			$ 9,761.40	
71	63	2010 estimated tax payments				
72	64	Earned income credit				
73	65	Excess social security tax and tier 1 RRTA tax withheld				
74	66	Additional child tax credit				
75	67	Amount paid with extension to file				
76	68	Other payments				
77	69	**Total payments**				$ 9,761.40
78	70	This is the amount you OVERPAID				$ -
79	71a	Amount to be refunded to you				$ -
80	72	Amount to be applied to 2011 tax				
81	73	The amount you OWE				$ 114.60
82	74	Estimated tax penalty				

Amount you owe

Lesson 35—Apply

After learning about the power of Excel's lookup functions, you've decided to use them to make tax time a bit easier. You want to add several lookup functions to your income tax worksheets.

DIRECTIONS

1. Start Excel, if necessary, and open **E35Apply** from the data files for this lesson.
2. Save the workbook as **E35Apply_xx** in the location where your teacher instructs you to store the files for this lesson.
3. Select the **Student Loan** worksheet, if necessary.
4. Add a header that has your name at the left, the date code in the center, and the page number code at the right, and change back to **Normal** view.
5. In cell **F7**, enter a formula to look up the deduction limit, which is based on your filing status. Make sure the formula takes the following into consideration:
   a. Use the **IF** function to determine your filing status.
   b. If the text entered in cell **B7** is equal to "married, filing jointly," then use an **HLOOKUP** function that looks up the value **2** in the table, and displays the dollar amount shown below it.
   c. If the text in cell **B7** is anything else, use **HLOOKUP** to look up the value **1** and display the dollar amount below it.
   d. The **Row Index** for both **HLOOKUP** functions is 2, because the dollar amounts are located in row 2 of the table.
6. Your worksheet should look like Figure 35-2. **With your teacher's permission,** print the **Student Loan** worksheet. Submit the printout or the file for grading as required.

   ✓ *If printing, adjust the page breaks, and change the print settings, as necessary.*
7. Save and close the file, and exit Excel.

	A	B	C	D	E	F
1	Student Loan Interest Deduction Worksheet - 1040 Line 25					
2	**Line**	**Description**				**Amount**
3	1	Interest paid				$ 778.56
4	2	1040, line 22				$ 92,808.79
5	3	1040, lines 23,24,27-33a				$ 1,200.00
6	4	Subtract line 3 from line 2				$ 91,608.79
7	5	Married, filing jointly				$ 100,000.00
8	6	Is line 4 > 5?				No
9	7	Divide line 6 by $30,000				$ -
10	8	Multiply line 1 by 7				$ -
11	9	Student loan interest deduction				$ 778.56
12						
13						
14			1	2		
15		Limit	$50,000.00	$100,000.00		
16						

Figure 35-2

Lesson 36

Working with PivotTables and PivotCharts

➤ What You Will Learn

Software Skills PivotTables make it easier to analyze complex data. For example, if you had a database containing lots of information, such as sales data by product, store, region, and salesperson, you can summarize it in a PivotTable. With the table, you can display totals by region for each product, or you can rearrange the table to display sales totals by office and individual salesperson. You also can combine the tables to display totals by region, office, salesperson, and product. PivotTable can become very hard to navigate depending on their complexity. You can use a PivotChart to visually present your data, and quickly analyze a subset of your data using the filtering controls.

WORDS TO KNOW

Database
An organized collection of records. For example, in an employee database, one record might include:

- Employee name
- Date of hire
- Address
- Phone number
- Salary rate

Field
A single element of a record, such as "Phone number." Multiple related fields, such as one employee's name, address, phone number, etc., make up one record.

PivotChart
A chart based on PivotTable data.

What You Can Do

Creating PivotTables

- A **PivotTable** allows you to summarize complex data, such as a company's sales or accounting records. (See Figure 36-1 on the next page.)
- The advantage of the PivotTable over a regular table of information is that it lets you quickly change how data is summarized.
- For example, you can change from a report that summarizes sales data by region and office to one that summarizes the same data by salesperson and product.
- The source data for your PivotTable can be an external **database**, text file, or query file, or a range or table within an Excel workbook.

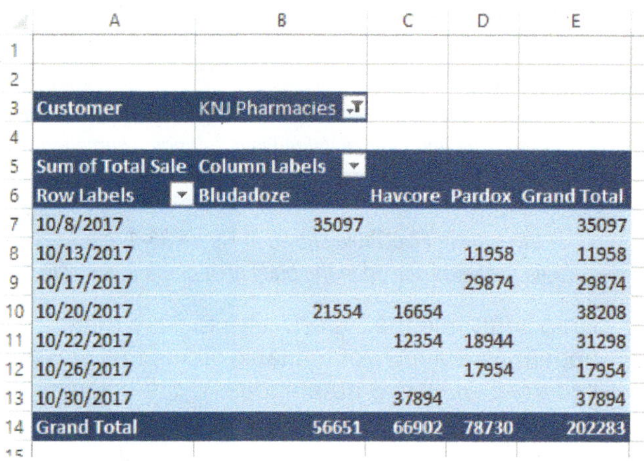

Customer	KNJ Pharmacies			
Sum of Total Sale	Column Labels			
Row Labels	Bludadoze	Havcore	Pardox	Grand Total
10/8/2017	35097			35097
10/13/2017			11958	11958
10/17/2017			29874	29874
10/20/2017	21554	16654		38208
10/22/2017		12354	18944	31298
10/26/2017			17954	17954
10/30/2017		37894		37894
Grand Total	56651	66902	78730	202283

Excel 2013, Windows 8, Microsoft Corporation

Figure 36-1

PivotTable
A rearrangeable table that allows you to analyze complex data in a variety of ways.

Report filter
A field from the database that you can use to filter or limit the data displayed within the PivotTable.

Try It! Creating PivotTables with Excel Data

1. Start Excel, and open **E36Try** from the data files for this lesson.
2. Save the file as **E36Try_xx** in the location where your teacher instructs you to store the files for this lesson.
3. For all worksheets, add a header that has your name at the left, the date code in the center, and the page number code at the right, and change back to Normal view.
4. On the DATA worksheet, click cell A5.
5. Click INSERT > PivotTable.

   ✓ *The range or table containing the cell you selected earlier should appear in the Select a table or range box. If the selection is wrong, you can select the correct range yourself.*
6. Select Existing Worksheet.
7. In the Location box, type **PivotTable!$A$5**.
8. Click OK.
9. Save the **E36Try_xx** file, and leave it open to use in the next Try It.

Create PivotTable dialog box

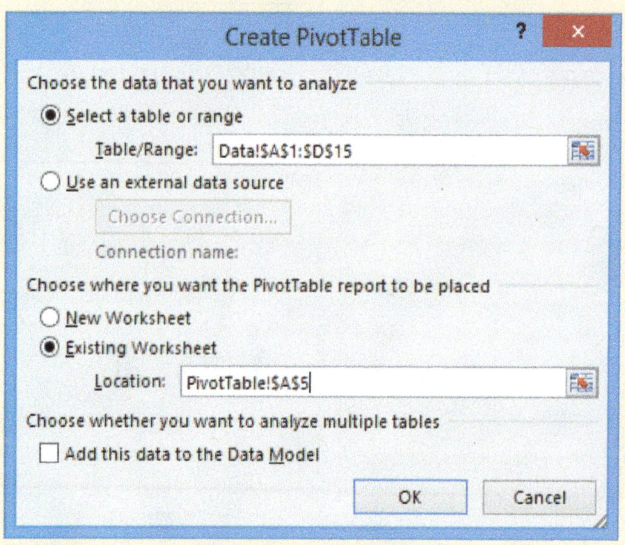

Excel 2013, Windows 8, Microsoft Corporation

Using the PivotTable Fields Task Pane

- The PivotTable Field List allows you to control each of the **fields** (columns) in your original data.
- When you insert a PivotTable in a worksheet, Excel creates the framework for your PivotTable. You then use the items on the PivotTable Fields task pane to arrange (and rearrange) the data to create the table you want.
- To change the way your data is summarized, drag the field name into the report area boxes at the bottom of the PivotTable Fields task pane.
- The PivotTable has four areas into which you can drag your fields: FILTERS, COLUMNS, ROWS, and VALUES.
- Drag numerical items into the VALUES area to summarize them.
  - ✓ *The default format for values on the PivotTable is a sum of the items.*
  - ✓ *To modify the format of the data, click the field item in the Values area and choose Value Field Settings. Then choose the type of value you want, such as Sum, and click OK.*
  - ✓ *In the sample PivotTable shown in Figure 36-1, the Total Sale item was placed in the body area of the PivotTable.*
- Drag items into the ROWS area to have them appear as the rows of the table. Items that you drag into the COLUMNS area appear in the columns of the table.
  - ✓ *In the sample PivotTable shown in Figure 36-1, the Sales Date item was added to the row area, and the Drug Purchased item was added to the column area of the table (see Figure 36-2 to see where to add the items).*

Figure 36-2

Excel 2013, Windows 8, Microsoft Corporation

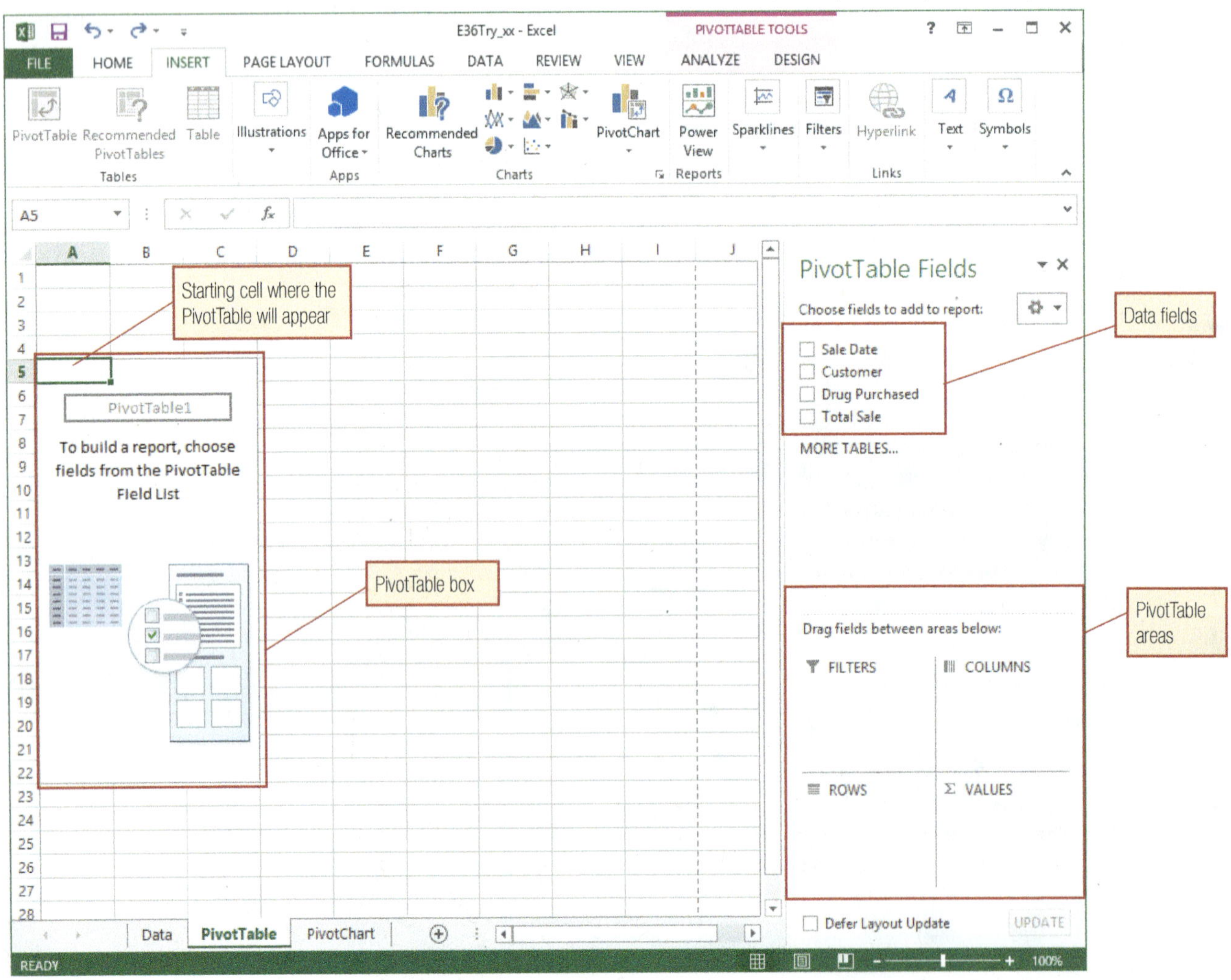

- You can also filter the entire table by dragging a field to the FILTERS area.
- When you use **Report filters**, only the items relating to a particular category are displayed.

  ✓ *In the sample PivotTable shown in Figure 36-1, the Customer item was added to the FILTERS area.*

- When you add an item to a PivotTable, that item becomes a button with a down arrow.
- You can limit what's displayed in the PivotTable by clicking the down arrow on the appropriate item and selecting the item(s) you want to display.

  ✓ *For example, you could click the down arrow on a Sale Date field, and choose a specific date. The PivotTable data would then be limited to activity on that date.*

  ✓ *In the sample PivotTable shown in Figure 36-1 the down arrow on the Customer button was clicked, and "KNJ Pharmacies" was selected. A user could further limit the report to display only the drug sales for Bludadoze and Pardox, or only the sales for 10/22.*

- To rearrange a table, drag fields from area to area at the bottom of the PivotTable Fields List.
- If you don't want to see the changes to the PivotTable as you go, click the Defer Layout Update option. Then, when you're ready, click the Update button.
- To remove an item from a PivotTable, deselect it in the PivotTable Fields List.

Try It! Using the PivotTable Fields Task Pane

1. In the **E36Try_xx** file, click in the PivotTable box on the worksheet.
2. In the PivotTable Fields task pane, drag the Drug Purchased field into the COLUMNS area.
3. Drag the Sale Date field from the PivotTable Fields task pane into the ROWS area.
4. Drag the Total Sale field to the VALUES area.

   ✓ *This item is typically a numerical item, such as total sales.*

5. Drag the Customer field to the FILTERS area.

   ✓ *To rearrange a table, drag fields from area to area at the bottom of the PivotTable Fields List.*

6. Save the **E36Try_xx** file, and leave it open to use in the next Try It.

The PivotTable Fields task pane and Field List

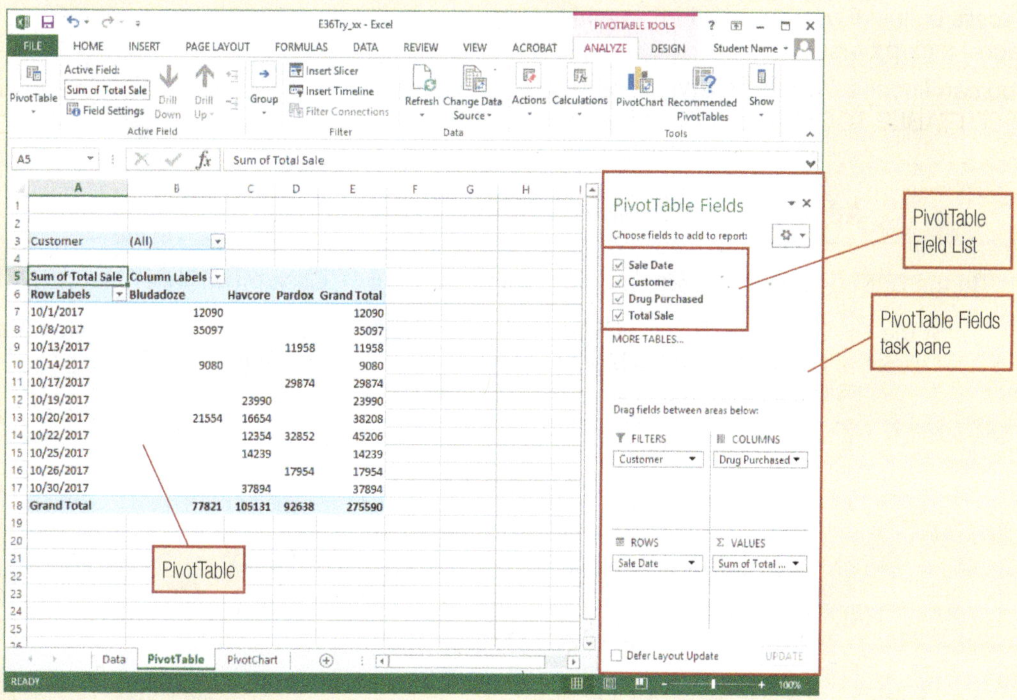

Excel 2013, Windows 8, Microsoft Corporation

Try It! Filtering Report Data

1. In the **E36Try_xx** file, click anywhere within the PivotTable on the PivotTable worksheet.
2. Click the Customer (All) down arrow.
3. Select KNJ Pharmacies.
4. Click OK.
5. Save the **E36Try_xx** file, and leave it open to use in the next Try It.

The Filtered PivotTable

	A	B	C	D	E
1					
2					
3	Customer	KNJ Pharmacies			
4					
5	Sum of Total Sale	Column Labels			
6	Row Labels	Bludadoze	Havcore	Pardox	Grand Total
7	10/8/2017	35097			35097
8	10/13/2017			11958	11958
9	10/17/2017			29874	29874
10	10/20/2017	21554	16654		38208
11	10/22/2017		12354	18944	31298
12	10/26/2017			17954	17954
13	10/30/2017		37894		37894
14	Grand Total	56651	66902	78730	202283

PivotTable drop-down arrows allow you to filter data

Excel 2013, Windows 8, Microsoft Corporation

Applying PivotTable Styles

- After creating a PivotTable report, you can use Excel's built in PivotTable designs to make your report look professional.
- You can find the PivotTable Styles on the PIVOTTABLE TOOLS DESIGN tab.

Try It! Applying a PivotTable Style

1. In the **E36Try_xx** file, click inside the PivotTable.
2. Click the PIVOTTABLE TOOLS DESIGN tab, and click the PivotTable Styles More button.
3. Click Pivot Style Dark 2.
4. Save the **E36Try_xx** file, and leave it open to use in the next Try It.

Creating Pivot Charts

- After creating a PivotTable report, you can create a **PivotChart** that illustrates the data summarized in the report.
- You can publish your PivotTable/PivotChart to the Internet or your company's intranet.
- You also can create a PivotChart without first creating a PivotTable. This is called a decoupled PivotChart.
- You can create a standalone PivotChart using an external data connection to an external data source.
- You can filter the data on a PivotChart as you might filter the data on a PivotTable; select the items you want to show from the appropriate drop-down buttons on the chart.
- You can format and move a PivotChart as you would a regular chart.

Try It! Creating a PivotChart from a PivotTable

1. In the E36Try_xx file, click inside the PivotTable.
2. Click INSERT > PivotChart.
3. Click the Area type, and click 3-D Area as the chart subtype.
4. Click OK.
5. Save the E36Try_xx file, and leave it open to use in the next Try It.

A PivotChart

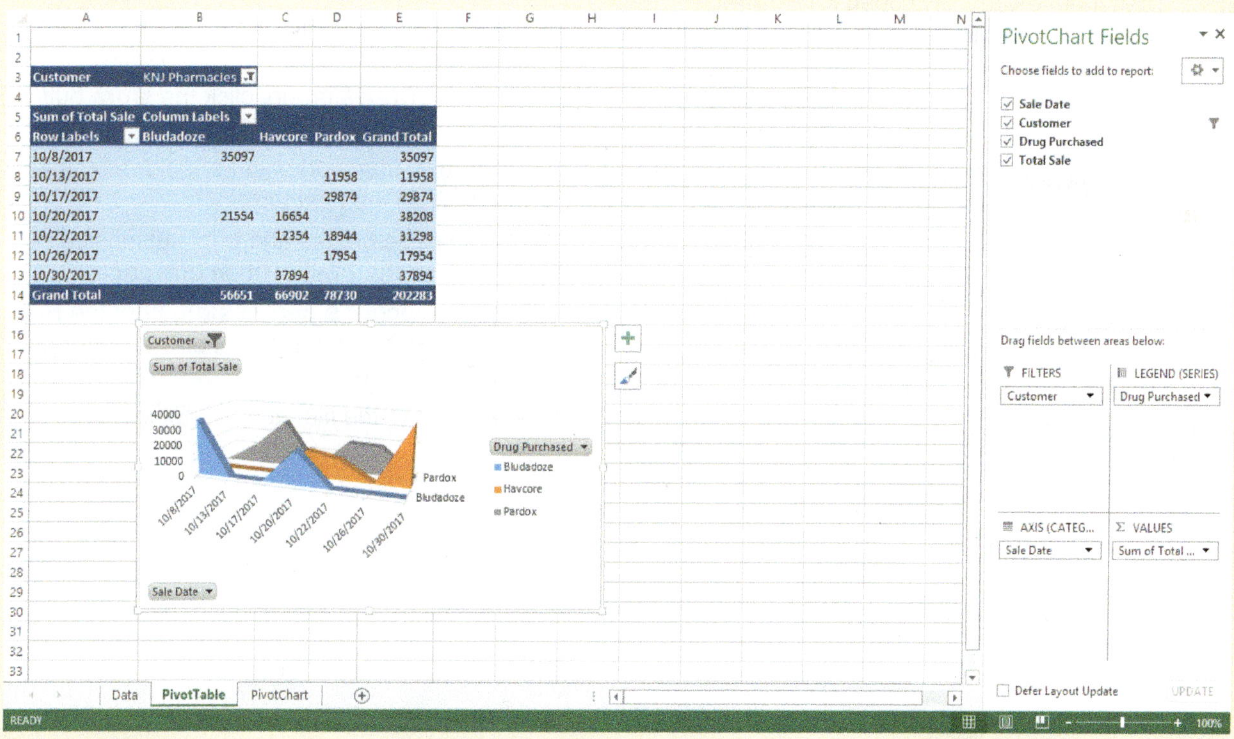

Excel 2013, Windows 8, Microsoft Corporation

Try It! **Moving a PivotChart**

1. In the E36Try_xx file, click the PivotChart to select it.
2. Click PIVOTCHART TOOLS ANALYZE > Move Chart.
3. Select Object in, and click the down arrow.
4. Select PivotChart, and click OK.
5. In the PivotChart worksheet, click on the PivotChart to select it, and drag it so that its upper right corner is over B3.
6. Save the E36Try_xx file, and close it.

Lesson 36—Practice

In this project, you will create and format a PivotChart using the skills you learned in this lesson.

DIRECTIONS

1. Start Excel, if necessary, and open **E36Practice** from the data files for this lesson.
2. Save the file as **E36Practice_xx** in the location where your teacher instructs you to store the files for this lesson.
3. For all the worksheets, add a header that has your name at the left, the date code in the center, and the page number code at the right, and change back to **Normal** view.
4. Click the **Report** tab.
5. Click anywhere within the table.
6. Click **INSERT** > **PivotChart**.
7. Click **Column** > **3-D Clustered Column**.
8. Drag the PivotChart so the upper-left corner is covering G5.
9. With the PivotChart selected, click **PIVOTCHART TOOLS DESIGN**.
10. In the **Chart Styles** group, click the **More** button of the Chart Styles Gallery.
11. Click **Style 3**. Your worksheet should resemble Figure 36-3 on the next page.
12. Adjust the page breaks and print settings so that the table and chart will print on one page.
13. **With your teacher's permission**, print the Report worksheet. Submit the printout or the file for grading as required.
14. Save and close the file, and exit Excel.

Figure 36-3

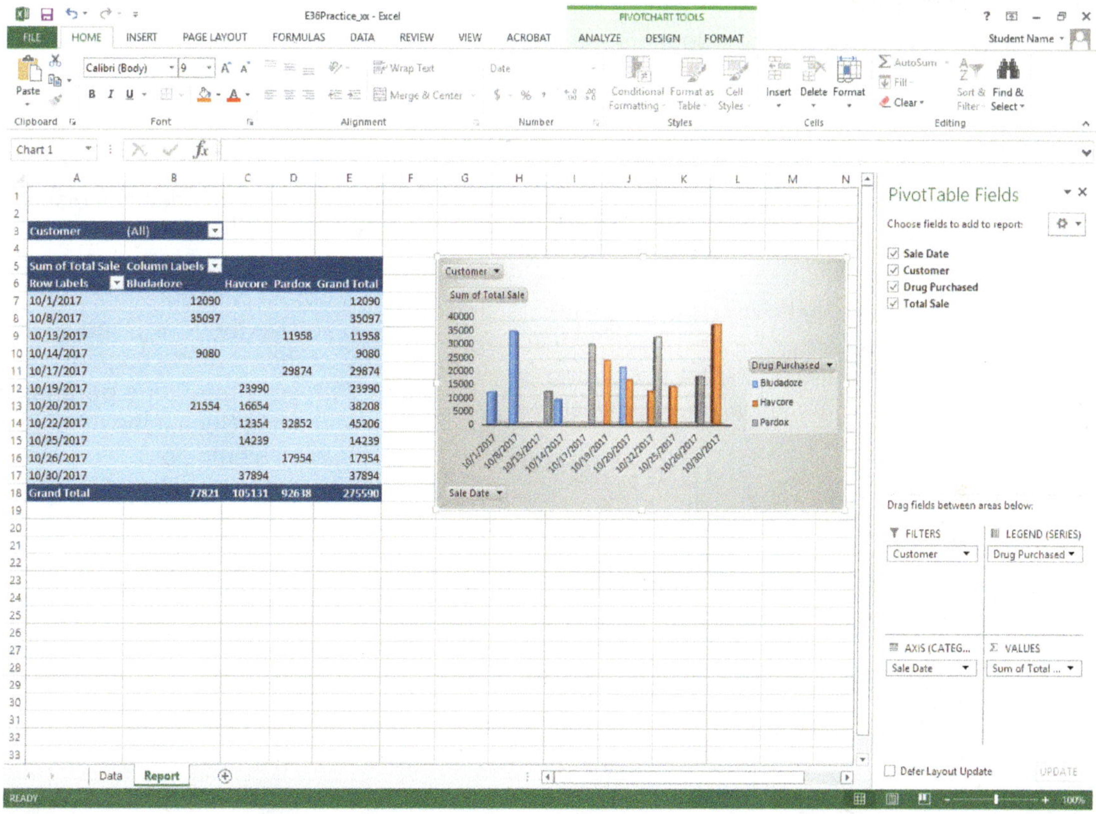

Excel 2013, Windows 8, Microsoft Corporation

Lesson 36—Apply

As the Inventory Manager at Voyager Travel Adventures, you are well aware of the inventory problems at the Logan store. Sometimes the store carries too much of an item, and other times it carries so little there is nothing on the floor to sell. Carrying too many items that don't sell wastes space that costs a lot to rent and makes it difficult to restock the items you do carry. Carrying low inventory on popular items causes customers to get frustrated when they are told they have to come back. You want to use the inventory figures from the previous month to create a PivotTable and PivotChart that will help you quickly see where the problems are.

DIRECTIONS

1. Start Excel, if necessary, and open the **E36Apply** file from the data files for this lesson.
2. Save the workbook as **E36Apply_xx** in the location where your teacher instructs you to store the files for this lesson.
3. For all worksheets, add a header that has your name at the left, the date code in the center, and the page number code at the right, and change back to **Normal** view.
4. On the **Total Inventory** worksheet, click cell **A9** to indicate the data range for the PivotTable.
5. On the INSERT tab, click **PivotTable** . The Create PivotTable dialog box opens.
6. In the Table/Range box, make sure the data range is **'Total Inventory'!$A$8:$L$134**, indicating that the range consists of cells A8:L134 on the Total Inventory worksheet.
7. Click **Existing Worksheet**.

8. Click in the **Location** box, click the **Collapse Dialog box** button, click the **PivotTable** worksheet tab, and click cell **A11**.
9. Click **OK**. A blank PivotTable appears with the PivotTable Fields task pane on the right.
10. Check that cell **A11** on the **PivotTable** worksheet is selected, and set up the PivotTable as follows, as shown in Figure 36-4:
    a. Drag the **Category** field to the **ROWS** area.
    b. Drag the **Subcategory** field to the **COLUMNS** area.
    c. Drag the **Monthly Revenue** field to the **VALUES** area.
    d. Drag the **Type** field to the **FILTERS** area.
    e. Click the **Type** drop-down arrow, select **Men**, and click **OK**.
11. Apply the **Pivot Style Dark 5** style to the PivotTable.
12. Apply the **Accounting** number format to the cell range **B13:D17**. Adjust column widths, if necessary.
13. Create a PivotChart from your table as shown in Figure 36-5 on the next page:
    a. Click **Bar** > **Clustered Bar Chart**.
    b. Use **Cut** and **Paste** to place the PivotChart on the PivotChart worksheet.
    c. Right-click the **X-axis label**, and click **Format Axis**.
    d. Click the **NUMBER** arrow, and format so that there are no decimal places.
    e. Close the Format Axis task pane.
    f. Reposition the PivotChart so that the upper-left corner is at edge of cell B3.
    g. Resize the PivotChart so that the lower-right corner is at the edge of cell K22.
14. **With your teacher's permission,** print the workbook. Submit the printout or the file for grading as required.
15. Save and close the file, and exit Excel.

Figure 36-4

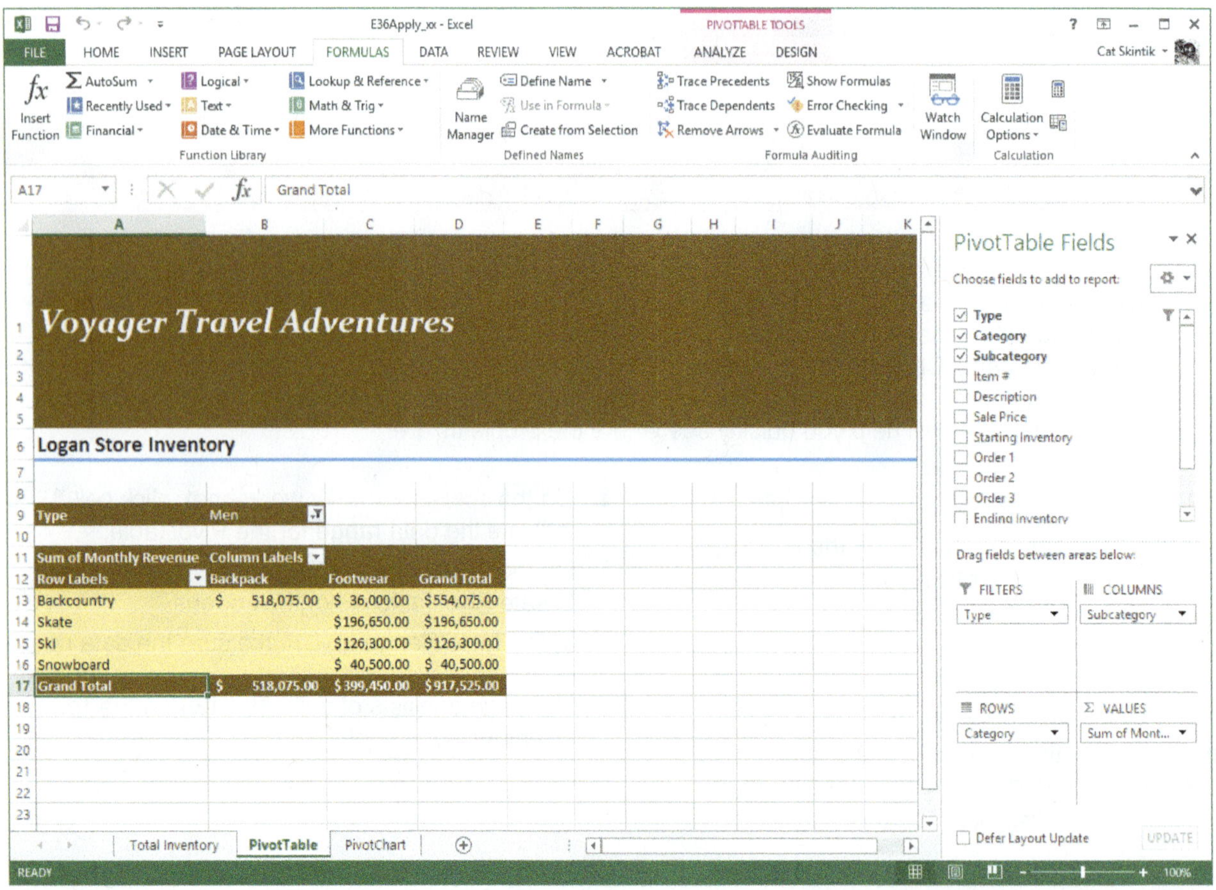

Excel 2013, Windows 8, Microsoft Corporation

Figure 36-5

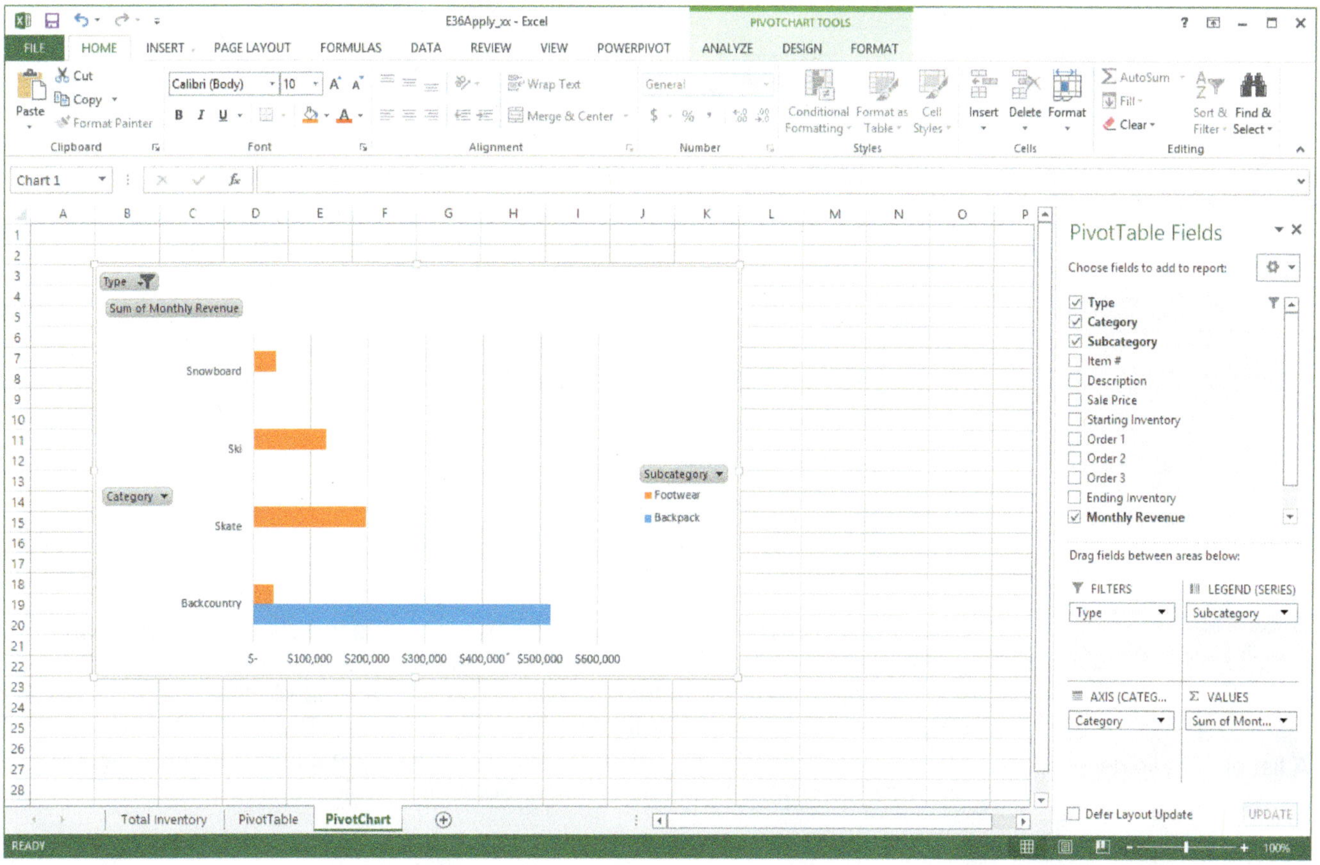

Excel 2013, Windows 8, Microsoft Corporation

Lesson 37

Working with the Excel Data Model

➤ What You Will Learn

Understanding the Excel Data Model
Drilling into PivotTable Data
Using a PivotTable Timeline
Using a Trendline

WORDS TO KNOW

Data Model
The linking of elements together in a series.

Field List
A list of data fields within a PivotTable.

Hierarchy
A type of organization in which items (e.g., data) are ranked one above the other.

Linear
A pattern of data points that looks like a line.

Quick Explore
A feature in Excel that allows you to navigate data tables and drill into specific data.

Timeline
A feature in Excel that filters dates and time, and can zoom in on a specific time period.

Trendline
A feature in Excel that shows trends in the data series of a chart.

Software Skills Excel has powerful data analysis features to help you visualize and present your data. You can use the Excel Data Model to build a relational data source. The Quick Explore feature lets you drill into a Data Model–based PivotTable so you can analyze the details of your data. You can create a timeline to show a specific time period of a PivotTable. You also can create a trendline on a chart to show trends in your data, and to help predict future values.

What You Can Do

Understanding the Excel Data Model

- A **Data Model** is a feature in Excel 2013 that allows you to integrate data from multiple tables.
- The Excel Data Model is displayed as a collection of tables in a **Field List** as shown in the Fields task pane.
- You can use the Excel Data Model to build a relational data source inside a workbook.
- An Excel Data Model is automatically created when you use data in PivotTables, PivotCharts, and Power View reports.

✓ *You will learn about Power View in Lesson 38.*

- The Excel Data Model can contain a single table or multiple tables.
- You can add data from other tables to modify and enhance the same Excel Data Model used in PowerPivot.

✓ *You can only add a table once to a Data Model.*

Drilling into PivotTable Data

- Drilling into large amounts of data in a PivotTable **hierarchy** can be a time-consuming task with lots of expanding, collapsing, and filtering.
- The **Quick Explore** feature in Excel 2013 lets you drill into a Data Model-based PivotTable hierarchy so you can analyze the details of your data.
- The Quick Explore feature acts like a filter to help you navigate to the data you want to see.

  ✓ *You must have at least two PivotTables in your data model to use the Quick Explore feature.*

- The Quick Explore button appears whenever you select an item in a PivotTable field.

  ✓ *You can only drill down one item at a time.*

- You also can right-click an item, and select Quick Explore from the menu.
- When working with multiple tables, it is recommended to name the tables so you can keep track of them.
- You can name a PivotTable from the PivotTable Name box in the PivotTable group on the PIVOTTABLE TOOLS ANALYZE tab.

  ✓ *Remember that you cannot use spaces or special characters in a table name.*

Try It! Drilling into PivotTable Data

1. Start Excel, if necessary, and open the **E37TryA** file from the data files for this lesson.
2. Save the file as **E37TryA_xx** in the location where your teacher instructs you to store the files for this lesson.
3. For all worksheets, add a header that has your name at the left, the date code in the center, and the page number code at the right, and change back to Normal view.
4. Click the Inventory Description tab, and click any cell in the table.
5. Click INSERT > PivotTable.
6. In the Create PivotTable dialog box, check that the table in the Table/Range box is Inv Description.
7. Under Choose where you want the PivotTable report to be placed, click Existing Worksheet.
8. Click the Collapse dialog box, select the cell E3 on the PivotTables worksheet, and click the Expand dialog box to return to the Create PivotTable dialog box.
9. Under Choose whether you want to analyze multiple tables, click the Add this data to the Data Model option.
10. Click OK. Notice that the OrderInfo PivotTable has already been created for you.
11. On the PIVOTTABLE TOOLS ANALYZE tab, in the PivotTable group, in the PivotTable Name box, type **InventoryTable**, and press ENTER.
12. Set up the InventoryTable with the following fields:
    a. Drag the Type field into the FILTERS area.
    b. Drag the Category field into the ROWS area.
    c. Scroll down, and click the Starting Inventory and the Ending Inventory check boxes. Notice that Excel automatically adds these sum fields to the VALUES area, and places the Values in the COLUMNS area.
13. Click cell E4. Notice that the Quick Explore feature appears outside the lower-right corner of the cell.
14. Click Quick Explore.
15. Click Description. Notice that the Drill To box includes Description.
16. Click Drill To Description.
17. Save the **E37TryA_xx** file, and close it.

Using a PivotTable Timeline

- You can use a PivotTable **timeline** to show dates, filter by time, and zoom in on a specific time period.
- You can insert a timeline from the Filter group on the PIVOTTABLE TOOLS ANALYZE tab.
- Once you insert a timeline, you can make changes to the time period on the fly.
- To move a timeline, select the timeline, and drag it to the desired location on the worksheet.
- To resize a timeline, select the timeline, and use the sizing handles to change its size.
- You can apply a Timeline Style to customize the look of a timeline.
- You can clear a timeline by using the Clear Filter button in the Filter group on the PIVOTTABLE TOOLS ANALYZE tab.

✓ *To remove a timeline, you also can right-click the timeline, and click Remove Timeline.*

Try It! Using a PivotTable Timeline

1. Open the E37TryB file from the data files for this lesson.
2. Save the file as E37TryB_xx in the location where your teacher instructs you to store the files for this lesson.
3. For all worksheets, add a header that has your name at the left, the date code in the center, and the page number code at the right, and change back to Normal view.
4. Click the PivotTable tab.
5. Click in any cell in the PivotTable.
6. In the PIVOTTABLE TOOLS ANALYZE tab, in the Filter group, click the Insert Timeline button. The Insert Timelines dialog box appears.
7. Click the Sale Date box, and click OK.
8. Drag the timeline so that the upper-left corner is at the edge of cell B18.
9. Click the MONTHS down arrow, and click DAYS.
10. Scroll to the right, and under OCT 2017, click 1.
11. Save the E37TryB_xx file, and leave it open to use in the next Try It.

A PivotTable timeline

Excel 2013, Windows 8, Microsoft Corporation

Using a Trendline

- You can show trends in your data using a **trendline** in a chart you have created.
- For example, you can extend a trendline beyond your data to help predict future values.
- A **linear** trendline creates a best-fit straight line for simple data.
- Use a linear trendline to show data that is increasing or decreasing at a steady rate.
- You also can show moving averages with a trendline in a chart you have created.
- You can add a trendline to a 2-D chart that is not stacked (such as an area, bar, column line, stock, scatter, or bubble chart).

✓ *You cannot use trendlines with stacked, 3-D, radar, pie, surface, or doughnut charts.*

- Access the trendline feature using the Chart Elements button + next to the upper-right corner of your chart.
- The trendline will begin on the first data point of your data series.
- To choose a different type of trendline, hover the mouse pointer over Trendline, and click the arrow.

- You also can choose More Options, and the Format Trendline task pane will display.
- You can create multiple trendlines on the same chart.
- To delete a trendline, click on the trendline to select it, and press the DEL key.
- To remove all trendlines, uncheck the Trendline box in the CHART ELEMENTS menu.

Try It! Using a Trendline

1. In the E37TryB_xx file, click the PivotChart tab.
2. Click the chart to select it, and click the Chart Elements button +.
3. Click the Trendline box. The Add Trendline dialog box appears.
4. Click Pardox, and click OK.
5. Click the Trendline box to deselect it. The trendline is deleted.
6. In the CHART ELEMENTS menu, hover the mouse pointer over Trendline, and click the arrow.
7. Click Linear Forecast.
8. In the Add Trendline dialog box, click Havcore, and click OK.
9. Save and close the file.

A linear forecast trendline

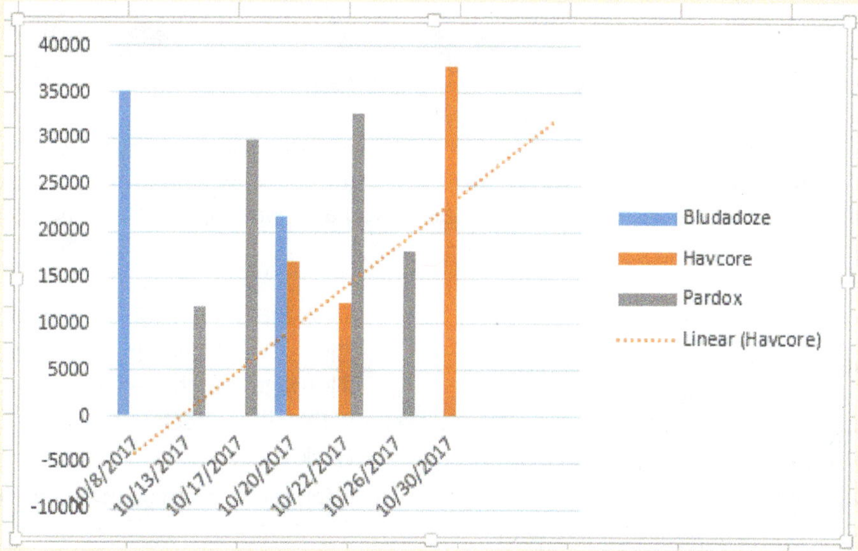

Excel 2013, Windows 8, Microsoft Corporation

Lesson 37—Practice

In this project, you will drill into a PivotTable to view detailed data using the skills you learned in this lesson.

DIRECTIONS

1. Start Excel, if necessary, and open the **E37Practice** file from the data files for this lesson.
2. Save the file as **E37Practice_xx** in the location where your teacher instructs you to store the files for this lesson.
3. For all worksheets, add a header that has your name at the left, the date code in the center, and the page number code at the right, and change back to **Normal** view.
4. Click the **PivotTable** tab, and click cell **C24**.
5. Click the **Quick Explore** button that appears outside the lower-right corner of the cell.
6. Click **Item #**, and click **Drill To Item #**.
7. **With your teacher's permission**, print the worksheet. Submit the printout or the file for grading as required.
8. Save and close the file, and exit Excel.

Lesson 37—Apply

You're the chief financial officer of A-1 Pharmacy based in Portland, Oregon, and you've been sent a worksheet with information about the company's annual drug sales. You want to review data from previous years to see whether the company's profits have increased or decreased. You also want to forecast a trend for next year's profits.

DIRECTIONS

1. Start Excel, if necessary, and open the **E37Apply** file from the data files for this lesson.
2. Save the workbook as **E37Apply_xx** in the location where your teacher instructs you to store the files for this lesson.
3. For all worksheets, add a header that has your name at the left, the date code in the center, and the page number code at the right, and change back to **Normal** view.
4. Click the Report tab.
5. Click any cell in the PivotTable.
6. Click **PIVOTTABLE TOOLS ANALYZE** > **Insert Timeline**.
7. In the Insert Timelines dialog box, click the **Year** box, and click **OK**.
8. Drag the timeline so that the upper-left corner is at the edge of cell A18.
9. Drag the resizing handle in the lower-right corner to the edge of cell E26.
10. Click the **MONTHS** down arrow, and click **YEARS**.
11. Click **2015**. Notice that the PivotTable data is now filtered to the chosen year, and the PivotChart only shows that year's data.
12. Click **Clear Filter**.
13. Click the chart to select it, and click **Chart Elements** +.
14. In the CHART ELEMENTS menu, hover the mouse pointer over Trendline, and click the arrow.
15. Click **Linear Forecast**.
16. In the Add Trendline dialog box, click **Bludadoze** > **OK**.
17. Repeat steps 13–15 to add trendlines for Havcore and Pardox. Your worksheet should look like Figure 37-1 on the next page.
18. **With your teacher's permission**, print the worksheet. Submit the printout or the file for grading as required.
19. Save and close the file, and exit Excel.

Figure 37-1

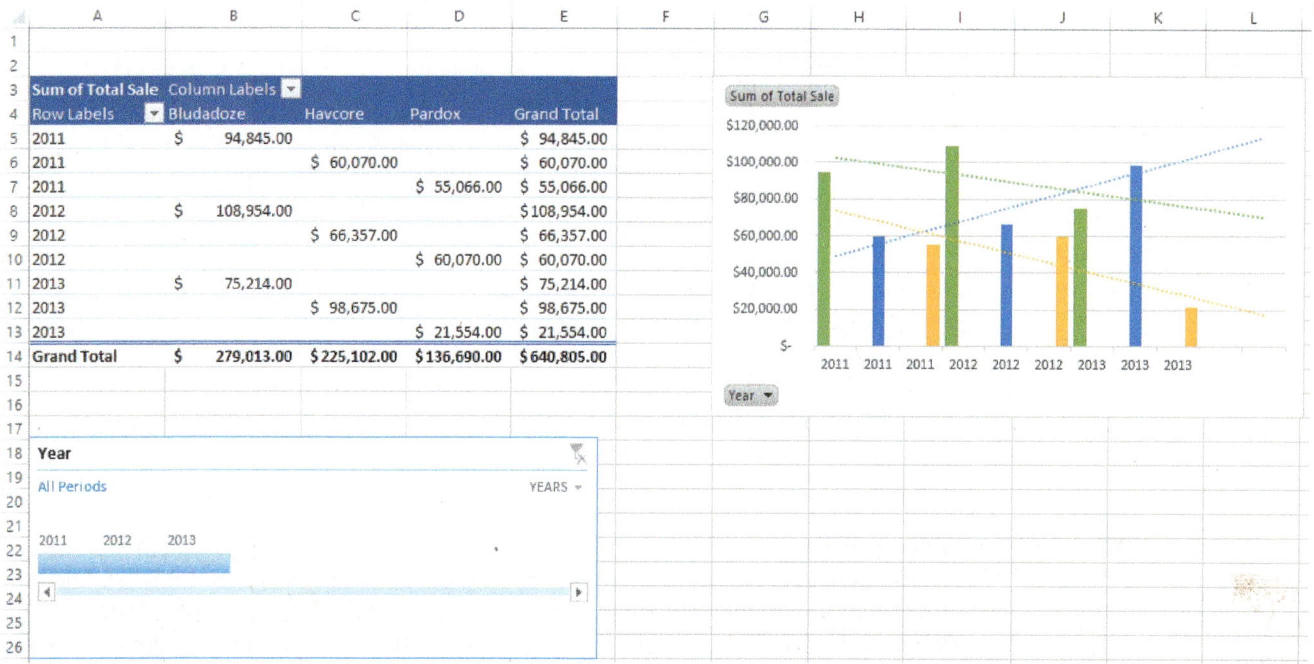

Sum of Total Sale	Column Labels			
Row Labels	Bludadoze	Havcore	Pardox	Grand Total
2011	$ 94,845.00			$ 94,845.00
2011		$ 60,070.00		$ 60,070.00
2011			$ 55,066.00	$ 55,066.00
2012	$ 108,954.00			$108,954.00
2012		$ 66,357.00		$ 66,357.00
2012			$ 60,070.00	$ 60,070.00
2013	$ 75,214.00			$ 75,214.00
2013		$ 98,675.00		$ 98,675.00
2013			$ 21,554.00	$ 21,554.00
Grand Total	**$ 279,013.00**	**$225,102.00**	**$136,690.00**	**$640,805.00**

Excel 2013, Windows 8, Microsoft Corporation

Lesson 38

Working with Excel Online

➤ What You Will Learn

Creating a Web Query
Sharing Workbook Data on OneDrive

WORDS TO KNOW

Web query
The process of pulling data from a Web page into an Excel worksheet.

Refresh
The process of updating the data copied to a worksheet through a query.

Software Skills The Internet contains a vast amount of data that you can use to solve business problems, such as viewing current currency rates for international commerce. A refreshable Web query allows you to make sure your Web data is always up to date. You can use the OneDrive to share data with team members and then edit that data in Excel Online.

Creating a Web Query

- You can create a **Web query** in Excel using a command from the Get External Data group on the DATA tab.
- After a query is created, data from the associated Web page is copied to the worksheet.
- If the data on the Web page changes, you can refresh the query with the **Refresh** command on the Refresh All button drop-down menu in the Connections group on the DATA tab.
- To refresh all the queries in a workbook, you can use the Refresh All button.

✓ *You can set the query to update periodically by clicking the Properties button in the Connections group and setting the Refresh every XX minutes option.*

- You can also use the options in the Refresh All button to learn the status of a refresh operation or to stop a refresh operation.
- When a query is refreshed, current data from the associated Web page is copied to the worksheet, replacing the existing data.
- With the Connections button on the DATA tab, you can change the Web page and specific Web data associated with the query.
- With the Properties button on the DATA tab, you can update the query automatically, after a period of time you specify.

Try It! Creating a Web Query

1. Start Excel and open the **E38Try** file from the data files for this lesson.
2. Save the file as **E38Try_xx** in the location where your teacher instructs you to store the files for this lesson.
3. Add a header that has your name at the left, the date code in the center, and the page number code at the right, and change back to Normal view.
4. Using File Explorer, copy **E38Try_Table** from the data files for this lesson to the location where your teacher instructs you to store the files for this lesson.
5. Using File Explorer, open **E38Try_Table**.
6. With **E38Try_Table** displayed in your Web browser, select the URL in the address bar.
7. Press CTRL + C.
8. In the **E38Try_xx** file, click cell A5.
9. Click DATA > From Web.
10. In the New Web Query dialog box, select the URL in the Address box and press CTRL + V.
11. Click Go.
12. Click the yellow arrow next to the table, as shown in the figure.

    ✓ *Selected arrows will change to green check marks.*

    ✓ *If you click Import without selecting any tables, the entire page will be imported.*
13. Click Import.
14. In the Import Data dialog box, check that the Existing worksheet box has =$A$5.
15. Click OK.
16. Close Internet Explorer.
17. Save the **E38Try_xx** file, and leave it open to use in the next Try It.

A linear forecast trendline

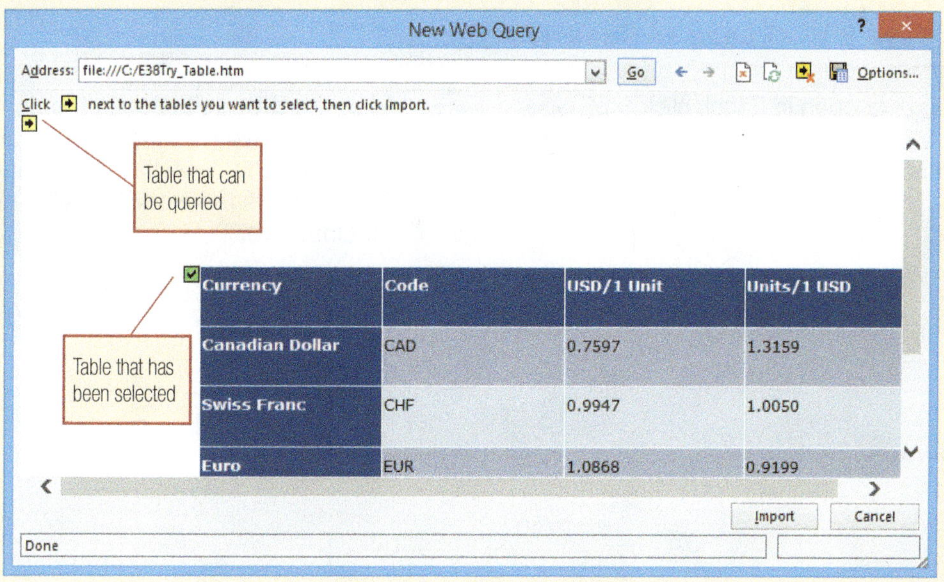

Excel 2013, Windows 8, Microsoft Corporation

Try It! Refreshing a Web Query

1. In the E38Try_xx file, click a cell within the query area (A5:D10).
2. On the DATA tab, in the Connections group, choose a refresh option.
   a. To refresh all external data, click Refresh All.
   b. To refresh the currently selected query only, click the Refresh All drop-down arrow > Refresh.

   ✓ *To learn the status of a refreshing operation, choose Refresh Status.*

   ✓ *To stop a refresh operation, choose Cancel Refresh.*
3. Save the E38Try_xx file, and leave it open to use in the next Try It.

Sharing Workbook Data on OneDrive

- You can use OneDrive to share Excel data with others.
- After you save a workbook to the OneDrive, you can invite others to work on the workbook.
- You (and anyone else sharing the file) can view and edit the workbook in Excel Online, or you can choose to open the workbook in Excel on your computer.
- The next time you open the workbook on the OneDrive, you can update it to see edits from everyone who is sharing the file.
- To invite other people to work on the workbook, click the Share button in Excel Online and then supply the e-mail address of the person you want to share the workbook. That person will receive a message with a link that takes them directly to the workbook so they can view and edit the content.

Try It! Save a Workbook to OneDrive

1. With E38Try_xx open in Excel, click FILE > Save As, and click the OneDrive option for your login name in the Save As list.
2. Click the Browse button in the right pane to open the Save As dialog box, double-click Documents to open that folder, and then click Save to store the workbook with the same name on OneDrive.
3. Close the E38Try_xx file, and leave Excel open.

Try It! View and Edit a Workbook on OneDrive

1. Start Internet Explorer and type **https://onedrive.live.com** in the address bar. Press ENTER.
2. If necessary, click Sign in and supply your Microsoft account information to open OneDrive in your browser.
3. Click the Documents folder to display the workbook you saved to the OneDrive.
4. Click the workbook name to open it in Excel Online.
5. Click Edit in the browser in the message that indicates the Web query will be removed.
6. Insert a row above row 5, and type **Use the following conversions when preparing marketing materials for our international guests.**.
7. Select the range A5:D5 and apply a fill color of your choice.
8. Click OPEN IN EXCEL.
9. Click Yes when asked if you want to allow the website to open the program on your computer.
10. The workbook opens in Excel. Note that the edit you made on the OneDrive now displays in the workbook.
11. Save **E38Try_xx** to the location where you are storing files for this lesson, overwriting the previous version of the workbook. Close the workbook and exit Excel and your browser.

Workbook stored in the Documents folder of the OneDrive

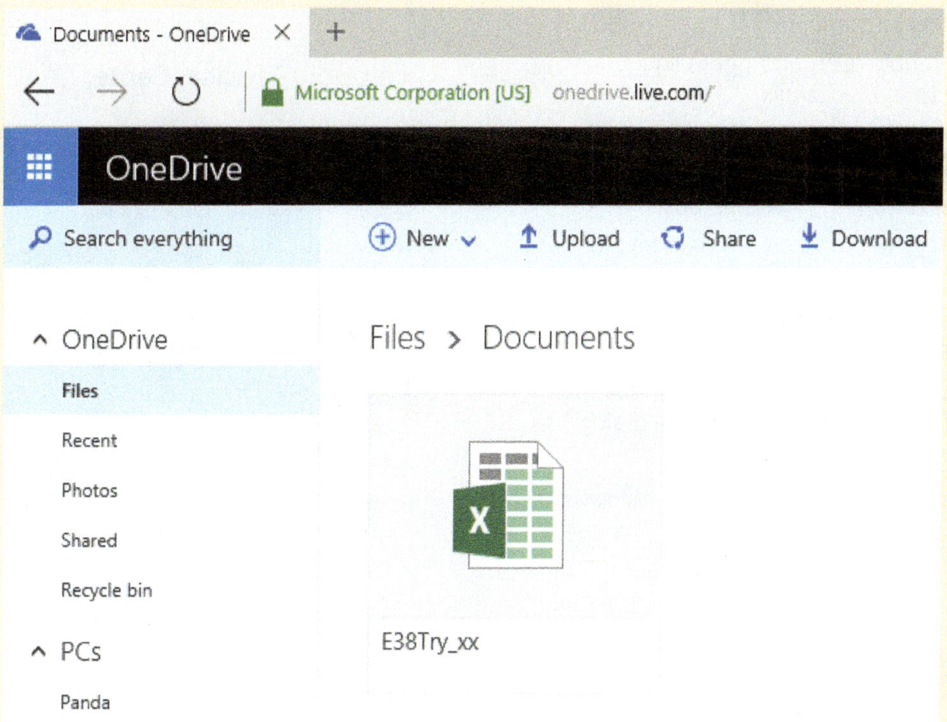

Lesson 38—Practice

In this project, you will be using the skills you learned in this lesson.

DIRECTIONS

1. Start Excel, if necessary, and open the **E38Practice** file from the data files for this lesson.
2. Save the workbook as **E38Practice_xx** in the location where your teacher instructs you to store the files for this lesson.
3. Add a header that has your name at the left, the date code in the center, and the page number code at the right, and change back to **Normal** view.
4. Click cell A5 on the **Infusion Rates** worksheet.
5. Click **DATA** > **From Web**. The New Web Query dialog box opens.
6. Copy the file path for **E38Practice_Medication**.
   a. Open File Explorer, and navigate to the data files for this lesson.
   b. Press and hold SHIFT, and right-click **E38Practice_Medication**.
   c. Click Copy as path.
7. Return to the New Web Query dialog box, and delete the text from the Address box.
8. Press CTRL + V to paste the file path text in the Address box.
9. In the Address box, delete the quotation marks (") from the beginning and end of the file path.
10. Click Go. (Click Yes if a Script Error message appears.) The preview window in the dialog box fills with the requested Web page.

    ✓ *Yellow tabs indicate all of the refreshable information that can be queried.*

11. Click the yellow arrow next to the table containing medication information. The arrow will turn into a green check mark.
12. Click **Import**. The Import Data dialog box opens.
13. Click **OK**. The data is pasted to the worksheet in a refreshable format. Refer to Figure 38-1.
14. **With your teacher's permission**, adjust the page breaks, and print the **Infusion Rates** worksheet. Submit the printout or the file for grading as required.
15. Save and close the file, and exit Excel.

Figure 38-1

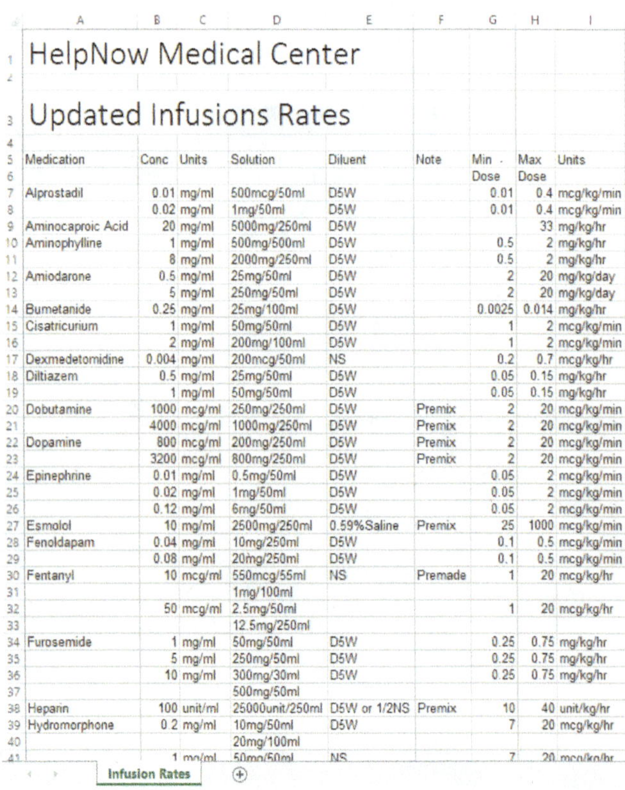

	A	B	C	D	E	F	G	H	I
1	HelpNow Medical Center								
2									
3	Updated Infusions Rates								
4									
5	Medication	Conc	Units	Solution	Diluent	Note	Min	Max	Units
6							Dose	Dose	
7	Alprostadil	0.01	mg/ml	500mcg/50ml	D5W		0.01	0.4	mcg/kg/min
8		0.02	mg/ml	1mg/50ml	D5W		0.01	0.4	mcg/kg/min
9	Aminocaproic Acid	20	mg/ml	5000mg/250ml	D5W			33	mg/kg/hr
10	Aminophylline	1	mg/ml	500mg/500ml	D5W		0.5	2	mg/kg/hr
11		8	mg/ml	2000mg/250ml	D5W		0.5	2	mg/kg/hr
12	Amiodarone	0.5	mg/ml	25mg/50ml	D5W		2	20	mg/kg/day
13		5	mg/ml	250mg/50ml	D5W		2	20	mg/kg/day
14	Bumetanide	0.25	mg/ml	25mg/100ml	D5W		0.0025	0.014	mg/kg/hr
15	Cisatricurium	1	mg/ml	50mg/50ml	D5W		1	2	mcg/kg/min
16		2	mg/ml	200mg/100ml	D5W		1	2	mcg/kg/min
17	Dexmedetomidine	0.004	mg/ml	200mcg/50ml	NS		0.2	0.7	mcg/kg/hr
18	Diltiazem	0.5	mg/ml	25mg/50ml	D5W		0.05	0.15	mg/kg/hr
19		1	mg/ml	50mg/50ml	D5W		0.05	0.15	mg/kg/hr
20	Dobutamine	1000	mcg/ml	250mg/250ml	D5W	Premix	2	20	mcg/kg/min
21		4000	mcg/ml	1000mg/250ml	D5W	Premix	2	20	mcg/kg/min
22	Dopamine	800	mcg/ml	200mg/250ml	D5W	Premix	2	20	mcg/kg/min
23		3200	mcg/ml	800mg/250ml	D5W	Premix	2	20	mcg/kg/min
24	Epinephrine	0.01	mg/ml	0.5mg/50ml	D5W		0.05	2	mcg/kg/min
25		0.02	mg/ml	1mg/50ml	D5W		0.05	2	mcg/kg/min
26		0.12	mg/ml	6mg/50ml	D5W		0.05	2	mcg/kg/min
27	Esmolol	10	mg/ml	2500mg/250ml	0.59%Saline	Premix	25	1000	mcg/kg/min
28	Fenoldapam	0.04	mg/ml	10mg/250ml	D5W		0.1	0.5	mcg/kg/min
29		0.08	mg/ml	20mg/250ml	D5W		0.1	0.5	mcg/kg/min
30	Fentanyl	10	mcg/ml	550mcg/55ml	NS	Premade	1	20	mcg/kg/hr
31				1mg/100ml					
32		50	mcg/ml	2.5mg/50ml			1	20	mcg/kg/hr
33				12.5mg/250ml					
34	Furosemide	1	mg/ml	50mg/50ml	D5W		0.25	0.75	mg/kg/hr
35		5	mg/ml	250mg/50ml	D5W		0.25	0.75	mg/kg/hr
36		10	mg/ml	300mg/30ml	D5W		0.25	0.75	mg/kg/hr
37				500mg/50ml					
38	Heparin	100	unit/ml	25000unit/250ml	D5W or 1/2NS	Premix	10	40	unit/kg/hr
39	Hydromorphone	0.2	mg/ml	10mg/50ml	D5W		7	20	mcg/kg/hr
40				20mg/100ml					
41		1	mg/ml	50mg/50ml	NS		7	20	mcg/kg/hr

Excel 2013, Windows 8, Microsoft Corporation

Lesson 38—Apply

The workbook with financial information for your company, HelpNow Medical Center, needs to be updated by a member of the staff who is currently on assignment in a different office. You can use the OneDrive to share the workbook so your colleague can make the necessary edits. You will view the changes in your OneDrive and then open the workbook in Excel to make a few final edits.

DIRECTIONS

1. Start Excel, if necessary, and open the **E38Apply** file from the data files for this lesson.
2. Save the workbook as **E38Apply_xx** in the location where your teacher instructs you to store the files for this lesson.
3. For all worksheets, add a header that has your name at the left, the date code in the center, and the page number code at the right, and change back to **Normal** view. Select the **2016** sheet.
4. Save the file with the same name in the Documents folder on your OneDrive, and then close it in Excel. Leave Excel open.
5. In your browser, start your OneDrive and open the Documents folder.
6. Click the **E38Apply_xx** file to open it in Excel Online.

   ✓ *The cells needing to be updated have been left unfilled. Assume you are the colleague responsible for providing the Income Taxes information.*

7. In cell I21, type **88175**.
8. In cell I22, type **31064**.
9. Apply **Accounting** format with 0 decimal places to cells I21 and I22.
10. Click **OPEN IN EXCEL** to open the workbook in Excel. Click **Yes** when asked if you want to open the file.
11. Format the range G20:I20 with the same fill color used for other section headings.
12. Format the range H21:I22 with the same fill color used for the background of the balance sheet. Your completed worksheet should look like Figure 38-2.
13. Save the workbook, overwriting the previous version.
14. **With your teacher's permission**, print the **2017** worksheet. Submit the printout or the file for grading as required.
15. Save and close the file, and exit Excel and your browser.

Figure 38-2

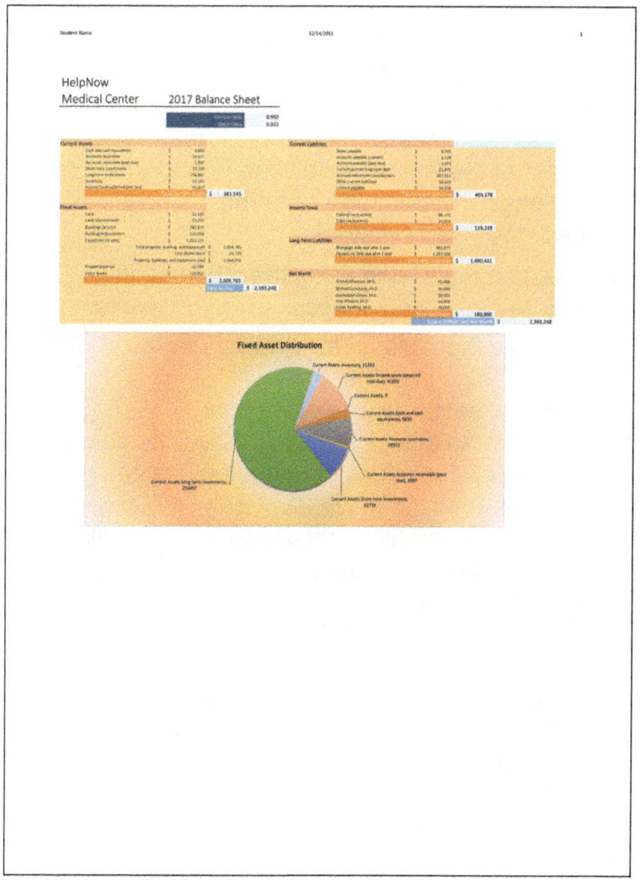

Excel 2013, Windows 8, Microsoft Corporation

End-of-Chapter Activities

➤ Excel Chapter 4—Critical Thinking

Revenue PivotTable

You're the owner of Whole Grains Bread company, and you want to analyze the past year's sales for each of your stores. You've compiled a database of revenues, and with it you'll create a PivotTable you can rearrange as you like, creating as many different revenue reports as you wish. After creating a PivotTable that lists quarterly revenues by city, you'll use its data to predict possible earnings amounts for next year. Finally, you'll use Solver to help you decide on the best price for a new product you'll introduce in your Oregon stores—tomato basil focaccia.

DIRECTIONS

1. Start Excel, if necessary.
2. Open the **ECT04** file from the data files for this chapter.
3. Save the workbook as **ECT04_xx** in the location where your teacher instructs you to store the files for this lesson.
4. For all worksheets, add a header that has your name at the left, the date code in the center, and the page number code at the right, and change back to **Normal** view.
5. Create a PivotTable using the information on the **Revenue** worksheet:
   a. Place the table on the Analysis worksheet, beginning in cell **A10**.
   b. Show each city on its own row.
   c. Show the quarterly totals in separate columns.
   d. Display the values or grand totals of the gross sales.
   e. Add a report filter that allows you to display each state separately.
   f. Apply a currency format with no decimal places to all numerical data.
   g. Display only the Oregon stores.
   h. Apply **Pivot Style Medium 5** style.
   i. Spell check the worksheet.
   j. **With your teacher's permission**, print the PivotTable **Analysis** worksheet (see Illustration 4A).
6. Copy the table data:
   a. Make sure that all cities and states are displayed by removing the **State** field from the **FILTERS** area.
   b. Select the range **B12:E27**, and copy it.
   c. Use Paste Special to paste only the values starting in cell **B9** of the **Forecast** worksheet.
7. Use the GROWTH function to predict future sales (see Illustration 4B):
   a. In cell **F9** of the **Forecast** worksheet, enter a formula that calculates the predicted sales for Bend, OR.
   b. Use the actual sales in cells **B9:E9** as the basis for the prediction.
   c. Copy the formula to the range **B10:B24** to fill Quarter 1.
   d. Copy the formula to the range **G9:I24** to fill Quarters 2–4.
8. Adjust column widths as needed.
9. Spell check the **Forecast** worksheet, and adjust the page breaks, if necessary.
10. **With your teacher's permission,** print the **Forecast** worksheet.
11. Use Solver to change the proposed price of tomato basil focaccia (cell **C15** of the **New Product** sheet) so that the projected weekly profit (cell **C19**) equals **$1,200** (see Illustration 4C):
    a. Allow the coupon discount in cell **D18** to also be changed as needed.
    b. Set constraints that limit the price point to a value between **$3.75** and **$4.25**.
    c. Set constraints that limit the coupon discount (cell **D18**) to a value between **0.50** and **0.75**.
12. Spell check the entire workbook, and adjust the page breaks, if necessary.

13. **With your teacher's permission,** print the **New Product** worksheet. Submit the printout or the file for grading as required.

14. Save and close the file, and exit Excel.

Illustration 4A

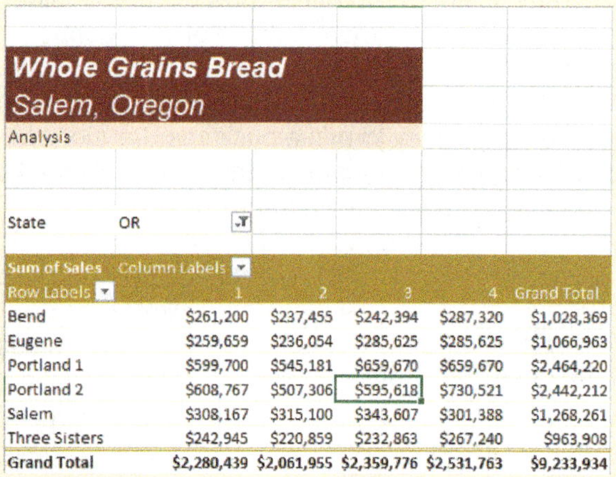

Whole Grains Bread
Salem, Oregon
Analysis

State	OR				
Sum of Sales	**Column Labels**				
Row Labels	**1**	**2**	**3**	**4**	**Grand Total**
Bend	$261,200	$237,455	$242,394	$287,320	$1,028,369
Eugene	$259,659	$236,054	$285,625	$285,625	$1,066,963
Portland 1	$599,700	$545,181	$659,670	$659,670	$2,464,220
Portland 2	$608,767	$507,306	$595,618	$730,521	$2,442,212
Salem	$308,167	$315,100	$343,607	$301,388	$1,268,261
Three Sisters	$242,945	$220,859	$232,863	$267,240	$963,908
Grand Total	**$2,280,439**	**$2,061,955**	**$2,359,776**	**$2,531,763**	**$9,233,934**

Illustration 4B

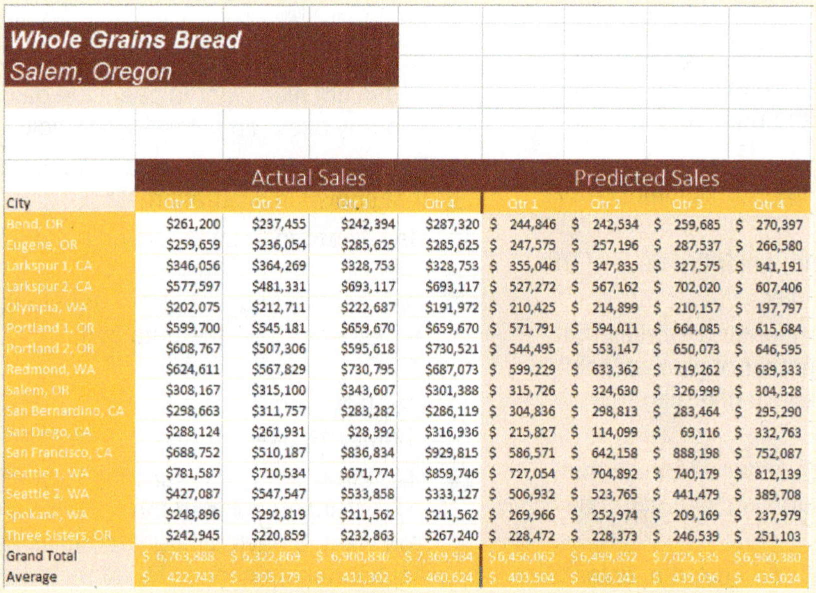

Whole Grains Bread
Salem, Oregon

	Actual Sales				Predicted Sales			
City	Qtr 1	Qtr 2	Qtr 3	Qtr 4	Qtr 1	Qtr 2	Qtr 3	Qtr 4
Bend, OR	$261,200	$237,455	$242,394	$287,320	$ 244,846	$ 242,534	$ 259,685	$ 270,397
Eugene, OR	$259,659	$236,054	$285,625	$285,625	$ 247,575	$ 257,196	$ 287,537	$ 266,580
Larkspur 1, CA	$346,056	$364,269	$328,753	$328,753	$ 355,046	$ 347,835	$ 327,575	$ 341,191
Larkspur 2, CA	$577,597	$481,331	$693,117	$693,117	$ 527,272	$ 567,162	$ 702,020	$ 607,406
Olympia, WA	$202,075	$212,711	$222,687	$191,972	$ 210,425	$ 214,899	$ 210,157	$ 197,797
Portland 1, OR	$599,700	$545,181	$659,670	$659,670	$ 571,791	$ 594,011	$ 664,085	$ 615,684
Portland 2, OR	$608,767	$507,306	$595,618	$730,521	$ 544,495	$ 553,147	$ 650,073	$ 646,595
Redmond, WA	$624,611	$567,829	$730,795	$687,073	$ 599,229	$ 633,362	$ 719,262	$ 639,333
Salem, OR	$308,167	$315,100	$343,607	$301,388	$ 315,726	$ 324,630	$ 326,999	$ 304,328
San Bernardino, CA	$298,663	$311,757	$283,282	$286,119	$ 304,836	$ 298,813	$ 283,464	$ 295,290
San Diego, CA	$288,124	$261,931	$28,392	$316,936	$ 215,827	$ 114,099	$ 69,116	$ 332,763
San Francisco, CA	$688,752	$510,187	$836,834	$929,815	$ 586,571	$ 642,158	$ 888,198	$ 752,087
Seattle 1, WA	$781,587	$710,534	$671,774	$859,746	$ 727,054	$ 704,892	$ 740,179	$ 812,139
Seattle 2, WA	$427,087	$547,547	$533,858	$333,127	$ 506,932	$ 523,765	$ 441,479	$ 389,708
Spokane, WA	$248,896	$292,819	$211,562	$211,562	$ 269,966	$ 252,974	$ 209,169	$ 237,979
Three Sisters, OR	$242,945	$220,859	$232,863	$267,240	$ 228,472	$ 228,373	$ 246,539	$ 251,103
Grand Total	$ 6,763,888	$ 6,322,869	$ 6,900,830	$ 7,369,984	$6,456,062	$6,499,852	$7,025,535	$6,960,380
Average	$ 422,743	$ 395,179	$ 431,302	$ 460,624	$ 403,504	$ 406,241	$ 439,096	$ 435,024

Illustration 4C

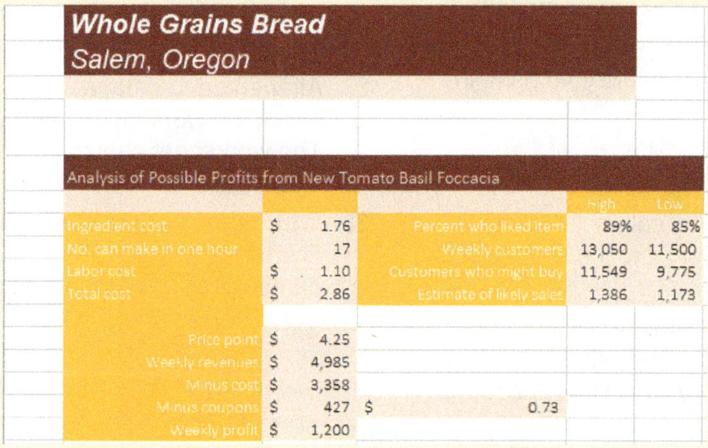

Whole Grains Bread
Salem, Oregon

Analysis of Possible Profits from New Tomato Basil Foccacia

			High	Low
Ingredient cost	$ 1.76	Percent who liked item	89%	85%
No. can make in one hour	17	Weekly customers	13,050	11,500
Labor cost	$ 1.10	Customers who might buy	11,549	9,775
Total cost	$ 2.86	Estimate of likely sales	1,386	1,173
Price point	$ 4.25			
Weekly revenues	$ 4,985			
Minus cost	$ 3,358			
Minus coupons	$ 427	$ 0.73		
Weekly profit	$ 1,200			

➤ Excel Chapter 4—Portfolio Builder

Lemonade Stand Projections

It's difficult to run any business, no matter how simple. Customer purchases are based on many things, some of them outside of your control, such as the weather and social trends. You might think that running a lemonade stand is easy, but it's not, as you'll find in this project. First, you'll gather data for 30 days of lemonade sales. You'll get the opportunity to make business decisions based on the weather and the cost of making your lemonade. In the end, you'll analyze your data using a PivotTable, and make predictions on future sales.

DIRECTIONS

1. Start Excel, if necessary.
2. Open the **EPB04** file from the data files for this chapter.
3. Save the file as **EPB04_xx** in the location where your teacher instructs you to store the files for this lesson.
4. For all worksheets, add a header that has your name at the left, the date code in the center, and the page number code at the right, and change back to **Normal** view.
5. On the Sales Data tab, in the **Day** column, enter the values **1** to **30**.
6. In the **Day of Week** column, enter the days of the week, beginning with Monday.
7. In the **Gross Profit** column, enter a formula that calculates revenue (the number of glasses sold multiplied by the amount you're charging per glass).
8. In the **Advertising** column, enter a formula that calculates the cost of advertising your stand (**0.25** per sign).
9. In the **Cost to Make Lemonade** column, enter a formula that calculates your cost—the cost per glass times the number of glasses you made that day.
10. Finally, enter a formula to calculate your profit in the **Net Profit** column.
11. In the first cell under **Money at Start of Day**, enter **$3**.
12. In the **Money at End of Day** column, enter a formula that adds the net profit to the Money at Start of Day.
13. In the second cell under **Money at Start of Day**, enter a formula that displays the value in the first cell under **Money at End of Day**. Copy the formula down to cell N33.
14. Copy cells **N5** and **O5**. Highlight cells **N6:O33** and click **HOME** > **Paste** to record 30 days' worth of lemonade sales. Format the worksheet to create a professional appearance.
15. Use the data to create a PivotTable so you can analyze your results. Place the PivotTable on the **PivotTable** worksheet.
16. Modify the PivotTable to show the effects of weather and price on the number of glasses sold. You might also want to see if the day of the week had any effect on sales—your choice.
17. Format the PivotTable and worksheet, similar to that shown in Illustration 4D.
18. Use **Paste** to copy the values and formats in the **Gross Profit, Advertising, Cost to Make Lemonade**, and **Net Profit** data to the **Forecast** worksheet. Copy the data in the **Day** and **Day of Week** columns as well.
19. Use this data and the **TREND** function to predict another 15 days' worth of gross sales.
20. Use the **FORECAST** function to predict the advertising costs, and the cost to make lemonade. You want to have different formulas adjacent to each other, so choose to ignore the error indicated by the Error Checker.
21. Use a regular formula to calculate the predicted net profits.
22. After entering data, adjust column widths, spell check the worksheets, and adjust the page breaks. The worksheet should look similar to that shown in Illustration 4E.
23. **With your teacher's permission,** print the **Forecast** and **PivotTable** worksheets. Submit the printout or the file for grading as required.
24. Save and close the file, and exit Excel.

Illustration 4D

Lemonade Sales Analysis

Day of Week: (All)

Count of GlassesSold	Column Labels						
Row Labels	**$ -**	**$0.10**	**$0.12**	**$0.20**	**$0.25**	**$0.30**	**Grand Total**
⊟ Cloudy				2	5	2	9
Cool				1	2	1	4
Storms					2	1	3
Sunny				1	1		2
⊟ Hot						5	5
Hot						4	4
Sunny						1	1
⊟ Rainy	1	1	1	3			6
Cool							
Storms	1	1	1	3			6
⊟ Sunny					2	7	9
Cool						1	1
Hot						3	3
Sunny					2	3	5
Grand Total	**1**	**1**	**1**	**5**	**7**	**14**	**29**

Illustration 4E

Forecasted Sales

Day	Day of Week	Gross Profit	Advertising	Cost to Make Lemonade	Net Profit
1	Monday	$ 7.50	$ 0.50	$ 2.10	$ 4.90
2	Tuesday	$ 3.60	$ 0.50	$ 2.40	$ 0.70
3	Wednesday	$ 0.12	$ 0.25	$ 0.72	$ (0.85)
4	Thursday	$ -	$ -	$ 0.12	$ (0.12)
5	Friday	$ 0.60	$ 0.75	$ 4.80	$ (4.95)
6	Saturday	$ 6.00	$ 0.50	$ 1.40	$ 4.10
7	Sunday	$ 1.00	$ 0.50	$ 1.50	$ (1.00)
8	Monday	$ 9.00	$ 0.75	$ 3.00	$ 5.25
9	Tuesday	$ 7.50	$ 0.50	$ 2.00	$ 5.00
10	Wednesday	$ 5.00	$ 0.50	$ 2.00	$ 2.50
11	Thursday	$ 15.00	$ 0.75	$ 3.50	$ 10.75
12	Friday	$ -	$ 0.50	$ 3.50	$ (4.00)
13	Saturday	$ 0.30	$ 0.50	$ 1.20	$ (1.40)
14	Sunday	$ -	$ -	$ 0.50	$ (0.50)
15	Monday	$ 0.30	$ 0.75	$ 1.60	$ (2.05)
16	Tuesday	$ 13.80	$ 0.75	$ 5.40	$ 7.65
17	Wednesday	$ 7.50	$ 0.50	$ 4.25	$ 2.75
18	Thursday	$ 9.00	$ 0.75	$ 2.40	$ 5.85
19	Friday	$ 12.00	$ 0.75	$ 3.60	$ 7.65
20	Saturday	$ 2.00	$ 0.50	$ 1.80	$ (0.30)
21	Sunday	$ 12.00	$ 0.75	$ 2.40	$ 8.85
22	Monday	$ 2.60	$ 0.50	$ 1.40	$ 0.70
23	Tuesday	$ 12.00	$ 0.75	$ 4.40	$ 6.85
24	Wednesday	$ -	$ -	$ -	$ -
25	Thursday	$ -	$ 0.50	$ 1.50	$ (2.00)
26	Friday	$ -	$ -	$ 0.15	$ (0.15)
27	Saturday	$ 8.70	$ 0.75	$ 3.20	$ 4.75
28	Sunday	$ 7.50	$ 0.50	$ 4.00	$ 3.00
29	Monday	$ -	$ -	$ 0.48	$ (0.48)
30	Tuesday	$ -	$ -	$ -	$ -
31	Wednesday	$ 4.67	$ 0.47	$ 2.16	$ 2.04
32	Thursday	$ 4.68	$ 0.47	$ 2.18	$ 2.02
33	Friday	$ 4.69	$ 0.47	$ 2.17	$ 2.05
34	Saturday	$ 4.70	$ 0.47	$ 2.19	$ 2.04
35	Sunday	$ 4.70	$ 0.49	$ 2.23	$ 1.99
36	Monday	$ 4.71	$ 0.47	$ 2.10	$ 2.14
37	Tuesday	$ 4.71	$ 0.47	$ 2.14	$ 2.11
38	Wednesday	$ 4.72	$ 0.47	$ 2.13	$ 2.12
39	Thursday	$ 4.72	$ 0.46	$ 2.13	$ 2.13
40	Friday	$ 4.73	$ 0.46	$ 2.16	$ 2.10
41	Saturday	$ 4.73	$ 0.46	$ 2.17	$ 2.10
42	Sunday	$ 4.73	$ 0.47	$ 2.20	$ 2.06
43	Monday	$ 4.73	$ 0.46	$ 2.12	$ 2.15
44	Tuesday	$ 4.73	$ 0.45	$ 2.11	$ 2.17
45	Wednesday	$ 4.73	$ 0.46	$ 2.12	$ 2.15

Chapter 1

(Courtesy Hasloo Group Production Studio/Shutterstock)

Getting Started with Microsoft Access 2013

Lesson 1
Planning a Database

- Exploring Database Concepts
- Analyzing a Database Management System
- Analyzing Access Objects and Database Organization
- Understanding How Access Tables Are Related
- Planning Database Tables and Relationships
- Creating an Access Web App
- Planning the Data Types

Lesson 2
Creating a Database with Access

- Starting Access and Creating a New Blank Desktop Database
- Exploring the Access Window
- Setting Access Options
- Creating Table Fields in Datasheet View
- Saving, Closing, and Reopening a Table
- Creating Additional Tables
- Closing, Opening, and Working with a Database
- Saving a Copy of a Database
- Splitting a Database

Lesson 3
Modifying and Adding Data to a Table

- Adding Records
- Entering Data in a Special Field
- Editing Records
- Editing a Hyperlink
- Selecting Records
- Deleting Records
- Adding a Totals Row

Lesson 4
Modifying Fields in a Table

- Setting Field Properties
- Adding a Field
- Renaming a Field
- Moving a Field
- Deleting a Field
- Hiding and Unhiding Fields
- Changing Table Field Widths
- Freezing Fields

Lesson 5
Importing and Protecting Data

- Understanding Data Import and Export Options
- Importing Data from Excel into an Existing Table
- Importing Data from Excel into a New Table
- Importing a Table from an Existing Database
- Previewing and Printing a Table
- Opening a Database Exclusively
- Setting a Database Password
- Changing Database Properties
- Compact & Repair a Database

Lesson 6
Using Table Templates and Design View

- Creating a New Database Using a Template
- Changing the View of the Navigation Pane
- Creating Objects with Application Parts
- Opening a Table in Design View
- Creating a Table in Design View
- Setting a Primary Key in Design View
- Managing the Field List in Design View
- Changing a Field's Data Type in Design View
- Modifying Table and Field Properties

Lesson 7
Creating Other Objects

- Using the Simple Query Wizard to Create a Query
- Creating a Quick Form
- Entering Records Using a Form
- Creating and Modifying a Quick Report
- Previewing and Printing a Report

End-of-Chapter Activities

Lesson 1

Planning a Database

➤ What You Will Learn

Software Skills Before diving into the Access software, you should familiarize yourself with basic database concepts. This includes how Access stores data, how tables are related, and how support objects such as forms, queries, and reports interact with table data.

What You Can Do

Exploring Database Concepts

- A **database** is an organized collection of information about a subject.
- Examples of databases include an address book, a list of tracks on your portable music player, or a filing cabinet full of documents relating to clients.
- A name, address, and phone listing in an address book is an example of a **record** in a common paper database. To update an address of a friend in Denver, you would search for the name, erase or cross out the existing address, and write in the new address.
- While updating one or two addresses in a paper database may not take a lot of effort, searching for all friends in one city or sorting all clients who have done business with you in the last month would take considerable effort.
- Many people prefer to store their databases on computers to make them easier to find and update.

WORDS TO KNOW

Database
An organized collection of information about a subject.

Database management system
A computer program that includes both the stored database and the tools required to use the database.

Datasheet view
A spreadsheet-like view of a table in which each record is a row and each field is a column.

Field
A piece of data stored about each record in a table. For example, ZIP Code is a field in an address book.

Form
A view of a table or query's data, designed for lookup or input of records.

Figure 1-1 Some examples of database records

Name: Jim Ferrara Address: 84 Winthrop Road City: Denver State: CO ZIP: 80209 Telephone: 303-555-5576 Note: Note new address and phone number

Part Number: 001759 Part Description: Socket wrench Cost: $3.50 List price: $14.99 Date received: 2/23/17

Access 2013, Windows 8, Microsoft Corporation

Analyzing a Database Management System

- A **database management system** includes both the database information and the tools to use the database. These tools enable you to input, edit, and verify your data.
- Microsoft Office Access is a popular personal computer database management system. Access makes it easy to organize and update information electronically.
- An Access database file can contain several types of **objects**, including **tables**, **forms**, **queries**, and **reports**. Each Access database file is stored with an .accdb extension for Access 2007–2013 format files or an .mdb extension for Access 2003 and earlier versions.
- With Access, you can sort, find, analyze, and report on information in your database. For example, in a sales management database you can find all clients who bought a mountain bike in the last year and create mailing labels in order to send them an announcement of a new bike trails book.
- You can share data created in Access with other Microsoft Office applications, especially Word and Excel.

Analyzing Access Objects and Database Organization

- The four main types of objects are tables, queries, forms, and reports. Two additional types, macros and modules, are not covered in this book.
- All Access database information is stored in tables. Each table contains information about a particular topic. For example, a sales inventory database may have separate tables for clients, products, and sales.
- Each row of an Access table is a record. A record is a set of details about a specific item. For example, a record for a client may contain the client's name, address, and phone number. A record about a product could include the part number, serial number, and price.
- Each column of an Access table is a **field**. Fields categorize the details of each record. In the client example above, there would be separate fields for name, address, and phone number. Each column is headed by a field name.
- The most common way to look at a table in Access is in **Datasheet view**. In Datasheet view, the table appears in a spreadsheet-like row and column format, with each row representing a record and each column representing a field.
- You can click the View button on the toolbar to change the view of the object you're working with—form, report, query, or table. To change to the view indicated by the graphic, click the button itself. To see a list of other views to choose from, click the arrow next to the button. You will be working with different views throughout the lessons in this text.

Object
An item in an Access database, such as a table, query, form, or report.

Primary key
The field that uniquely identifies each record in a table.

Query
A specification that describes how a set of records should be sorted, filtered, calculated, or presented.

Record
The stored information about one particular instance, such as one person's data in an address book.

Relational database
A database that contains (or can contain) multiple tables with relationships between them.

Report
A printable layout of the data from a table or query.

Table
A collection of records that share the same fields.

Figure 1-2 Tables store information in rows and fields

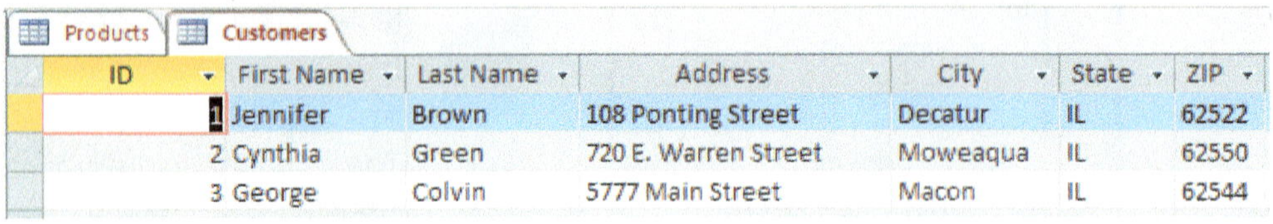

Access 2013, Windows 8, Microsoft Corporation

Figure 1-3 Forms provide a friendly interface for data entry and lookup

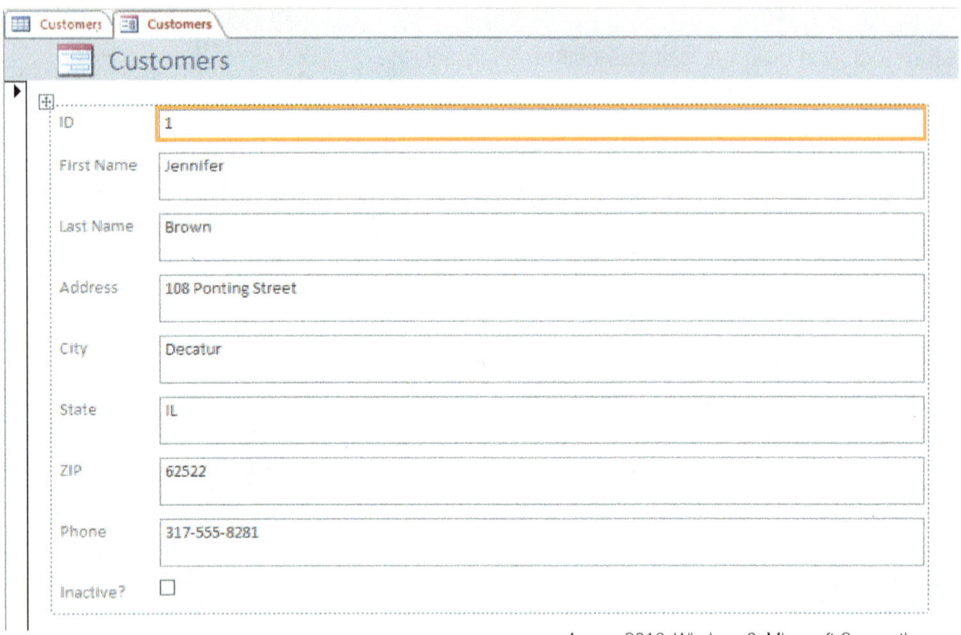

Access 2013, Windows 8, Microsoft Corporation

Figure 1-4 Queries sort, filter, and summarize data

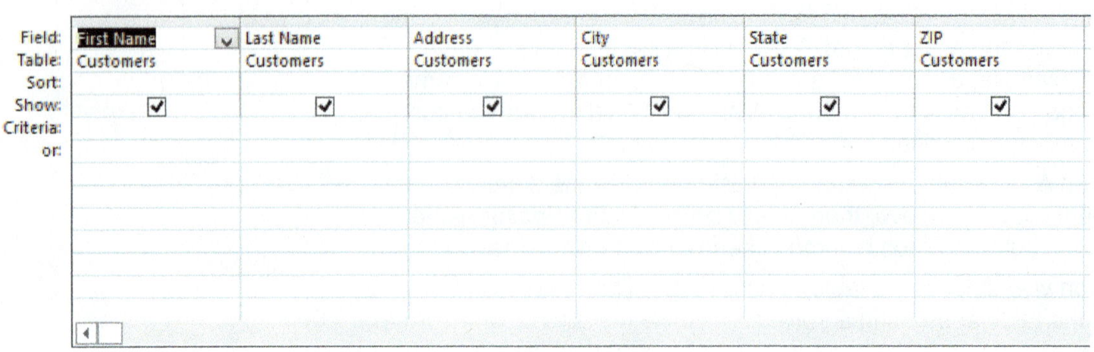

Access 2013, Windows 8, Microsoft Corporation

Figure 1-5 Reports provide attractive printable views of table or query data

Customers

ID	First Name	Last Name	Address
1	Jennifer	Brown	108 Ponting Street
2	Cynthia	Green	720 E. Warren Street
3	George	Colvin	5777 Main Street
4	Jasper	Garrett	992 West Avenue
5	Carrie	Strong	211 West Eckhardt Street
6	Felicia	Adamson	775 North Main Street
7	Norman	Eichmann	55110 Old Church Lane
8	Allison	Norville	522 German Drive
9	Peter	Washington	852 Ronald Parkway

Access 2013, Windows 8, Microsoft Corporation

- A form is a window for viewing the data in one or more tables. Forms make it easy to view, input, and edit data because forms typically show all the information for one record on a single page.
- A query enables you to see or work with a portion of a table by limiting the number of fields and by selecting specific records. For example, you might want to see only the name, city, state, and ZIP of customers who live in Illinois.
- A report is formatted information from a table or query that you can send to a printer. Reports can include a detailed list of records, calculated data from the records, mailing labels, or a chart summarizing the data.

Understanding How Access Tables Are Related

- Database tables that share common fields are related. Most Access databases have multiple tables that are related to each other, which means you can use Access to create a **relational database**.
- A relational database breaks the "big picture" into smaller, more manageable pieces. For example, if you were gathering information about a new product line, each type of information—products, suppliers, customers—would be stored in its own related table rather than in one large, all-inclusive table.
- You relate one table to another through a common field. For example, for a retail business's database, the Order Details table will have a Product field that also appears in the Products table.
- This capability to store data in smaller, related tables gives a relational database great efficiency, speed, and flexibility in locating and reporting information.

Planning Database Tables and Relationships

- Before you create a database, you must decide which fields you want to include and if you need a single table or more than one. Consider what information the database will store and how the information will be used.
- For example, to create a database for a company, you would first analyze the company's data requirements. You can then design the database to meet the specific needs of that company.
- To begin, make a list of the fields you want to store in your database, such as last name, first name, address, phone, and so on.
- Think about the ways you will want to search or sort the data, and plan the fields to support them. For example, if you want to sort by last name, make sure you have separate fields for first name and last name. The same goes for city, state, and ZIP code.

- As you are listing the fields to include, group them according to their purpose. For example, you might have fields for information about your products, fields for information about your customers, and so on. Each of those groups will form a separate table in your database.
- Having multiple tables helps avoid needless repetition, which is not only tedious for data entry people but also potentially introduces errors. For example, you might want to store customer and order information separately so that you do not have to repeat a customer's mailing address every time he or she places an order.
- Each table should have a field in which each record will be unique, such as an ID number field. This field will be the table's **primary key**.
- Plan the relationships between your tables. Make sure that tables to be related have a common field. For example, the ID field in a Customers table might link to the Customer ID field in the Orders table.

  ✓ *Relationships between tables are covered more thoroughly in Chapter 2, Lesson 8.*

- When you've finished identifying fields and tables, you are ready to create your new database file and create the tables within it.

Creating an Access Web App

- You can add an Access database to an online sharing site such as SharePoint by creating an Access Web app.
- Use one of the templates on the New tab (any template with a globe symbol can be used as a Web app), or click Custom web app to start a new custom database.
- You must have an account with an online sharing service such as SharePoint before you can create the new app. SharePoint, for example, provides a default team site to which you can publish your Access app.

  ✓ *You can publish a Web app through Office 365 if your 365 account supports Office 2013. If you publish to SharePoint, SharePoint must be configured as a development environment.*

- Provide a name for the app, if necessary, and then select a location from the list, such as your default SharePoint team site, and then click Create.
- You can work with your Access Web app in your browser in much the same way you would in the desktop version of Access. You can add tables (either blank or predefined tables similar to templates), enter data or import data from other files, and change views.
- You can open the Web app in Access to fine-tune the design or work on the database locally. The Web-based app is synchronized with the version you open on the desktop so that any changes you make on the desktop also display in the Web version.

Try It! Planning a Pets and Owners Database

1. On a blank sheet of paper, write **Pets** and draw a line under it.
2. Under the line, write all the fields that you might need for a table that stores information about pets. The first field should be a **Pet ID** field. Make sure you include an **Owner** field somewhere in the list.
3. Write **Owners** next to **Pets** and draw a line under it.
4. Under the line, write all the fields that you might need for a table that stores information about pet owners. The first field should be an **Owner ID** field.
5. Draw a line to connect the Owner ID field from the Owners table to the Owner field in the Pets table.

Planning the Data Types

- Each field will have a data type in Access, which determines what types of values will be stored in it. Some common data types are Number, Short Text, and Date/Time.
- In general, any fields that will hold alphabetic text should have one of the text types (Short Text, Long Text, etc.). This includes fields that may contain a mixture of letters, numbers, and symbols. Hyperlink fields are considered text, too.
- Phone numbers and ZIP codes are usually set up as text fields, because the numbers they contain will never be used for calculations.
- A Yes/No field is a logical field that has only two possible values. You would use it in situations where every record is one or the other, such as Male/Female, Married/Unmarried, or Active/Not Active.

✓ *When there is a relationship between fields, the fields must have the same type. For example, in the preceding Try It, the Owner ID field will be a Number type, so the Owner field in the Pets table must be a Number type also. The pet owner will be referred to in the Pets table by his or her ID number, rather than by name. This ensures that there is no confusion if several people have the same name.*

Lesson 1—Practice

You have been asked to help plan a database for a friend's new jewelry business. In this project, you will use paper and pencil to sketch out a database design for her, including the tables and fields she should include.

DIRECTIONS

1. Start with a blank sheet of paper. Turn it sideways, so you are writing across the wide edge, and write your name in the upper-right corner.
2. In the upper-left corner, write **Products** and draw a line under it.
3. Under the line, write this list of fields to include in a **Products** table:

   Product ID

   Type

   Name

   Materials Cost

   Labor Cost

   Retail Price

   Build Hours
4. Circle the **Product ID** field; this is the table's primary key.
5. To the right of the Products list, write **Order Details** and draw a line under it.
6. Under the line, write this list of fields to include in an **Order Details** table:

   Order Detail ID

   Order

   Product

   Quantity
7. Circle the **Order Detail ID** field; this is the table's primary key.
8. To the right of the Order Details list, write **Orders** and draw a line under it.
9. Under the line, write this list of fields to include in an **Orders** table:

   Order ID

   Order Date

   Customer

   Salesperson

   Shipper
10. Circle the **Order ID** field; this is the table's primary key.
11. Draw a straight line between the **Order ID** field in the **Orders** table and the **Order** field in the **Order Details** table. This represents a relationship.

    ✓ *Notice that this relationship involves the primary key in one table and a field that is not the primary key in another table. This is typical of most relationships in Access.*
12. Draw a straight line between the **Product ID** field in the **Products** table and the **Product** field in the **Order Details** table. This represents another relationship.
13. If your teacher requests it, turn in the database planning sheet you have created.

Lesson 1—Apply

Using a piece of paper and a pencil, sketch out a database design for your friend's jewelry business database, including the tables and fields she should include.

DIRECTIONS

1. Use the document that you created in Lesson 1—Practice, or open and print the file **A01Practice.pdf** from the data files for this lesson, and write your name at the top of the page. (You will be working on paper for this project.)
2. Discuss with a partner how to choose appropriate software for this activity. You have learned to create tables in Word and Excel. What advantage does creating a database in Access give you?
3. On the paper, fill in a list of fields you want to include in the **Shippers** table about each shipping company.

   ✓ *At a minimum you should include Shipper Name, Account Number, and any other information you might want to record in your database.*
4. On the paper, fill in a list of fields you want to include in the **Employees** table:

   Think about what information about an employee would be needed in the process of fulfilling a customer's order.

   Besides the person's first name and last name, you may want to include his or her position in the company.

   This is not a Human Resources database, so you do not need to include contact information for each employee (such as mailing address or phone number). However, you might want to include a field that contains some way to contact that employee, in case there are questions.
5. On the paper, fill in a list of fields you want to include in the **Customers** table.

   Think about what information you would need to gather about a customer to complete an order. For example, you need a name, mailing address, and at least one way to contact the customer if there is a problem with the order. You may also want to include an e-mail address for sending an order confirmation. If you plan to address the customer with a prefix, such as Mr. or Ms., make sure you include a field for that, too.
6. Circle the primary key fields in the **Customers**, **Employees**, and **Shippers** tables.
7. Draw lines between the primary key fields in the **Customers**, **Employees**, and **Shippers** tables and the corresponding fields in the **Orders** table.
8. Write **Auto** to the right of each primary key field.
9. Write **Number** to the right of each field that is connected via a line to one of the primary key fields.
10. Write the appropriate data type next to each of the remaining fields in each table. Choose from this list:
    - Short Text
    - Number
    - Date/Time
    - Currency
    - Yes/No
    - Hyperlink

    ✓ *The Account Number field for a shipper should be set to Short Text because some account numbers may contain letters.*

    ✓ *Use the Hyperlink type for e-mail addresses and Web sites.*
11. If your teacher requests it, turn in the database planning sheet you have created.
12. Review what you have learned in this lesson about Access database objects, and write a short explanation of how each of these tools could be used to access information from the database you have designed.

Lesson 2

Creating a Database with Access

➤ What You Will Learn

- Starting Access and Creating a New Blank Desktop Database
- Exploring the Access Window
- Setting Access Options
- Creating Table Fields in Datasheet View
- Saving, Closing, and Reopening a Table
- Creating Additional Tables
- Closing, Opening, and Working with a Database
- Saving a Copy of a Database
- Splitting a Database

Software Skills You can create a new database in Access and then add tables to it containing any fields you like. When you finish, you can close the table and save the design changes you have made to it. A database file contains multiple objects such as tables, all stored under a single file name. That file can be opened or closed as well.

WORDS TO KNOW

Extension
A suffix at the end of a file name that indicates its type, such as .accdb.

Object
An item, such as a table, query, form, or report, in an Access database file that is used to store, display, or manage data.

What You Can Do

Starting Access and Creating a New Blank Desktop Database

- The database file contains all Access **objects**, including tables, forms, queries, and reports. Each database file is stored with an .accdb **extension** for Access 2007, 2010, and 2013 format files or an .mdb extension for Access 2003 and earlier versions.
- You must create a database file, or open an existing one, before you can enter any data or create any objects (such as tables or queries).
- If creating a new database, you can start from scratch with a blank one, or you can start with a template that contains one or more database objects already.

✓ *You will learn how to create a database from a template in Chapter 1, Lesson 6.*

Try It! Starting Access and Creating a New Blank Desktop Database

1. On the Windows Start screen, click the Access 2013 tile. Access opens.

   ✓ *If you are running Windows 7, then open Access from All Programs.*

2. On the Access Welcome screen, click Blank desktop database.

3. In the File Name box, type **A02Try_xx**. Replace *xx* with your name or initials, as instructed by your teacher.

4. If necessary, click the Browse button to browse to the location where your teacher instructs you to store the files for this lesson, and click OK.

5. Click Create.

6. Leave the **A02Try_xx** database open to use in the next Try It.

Create a new database

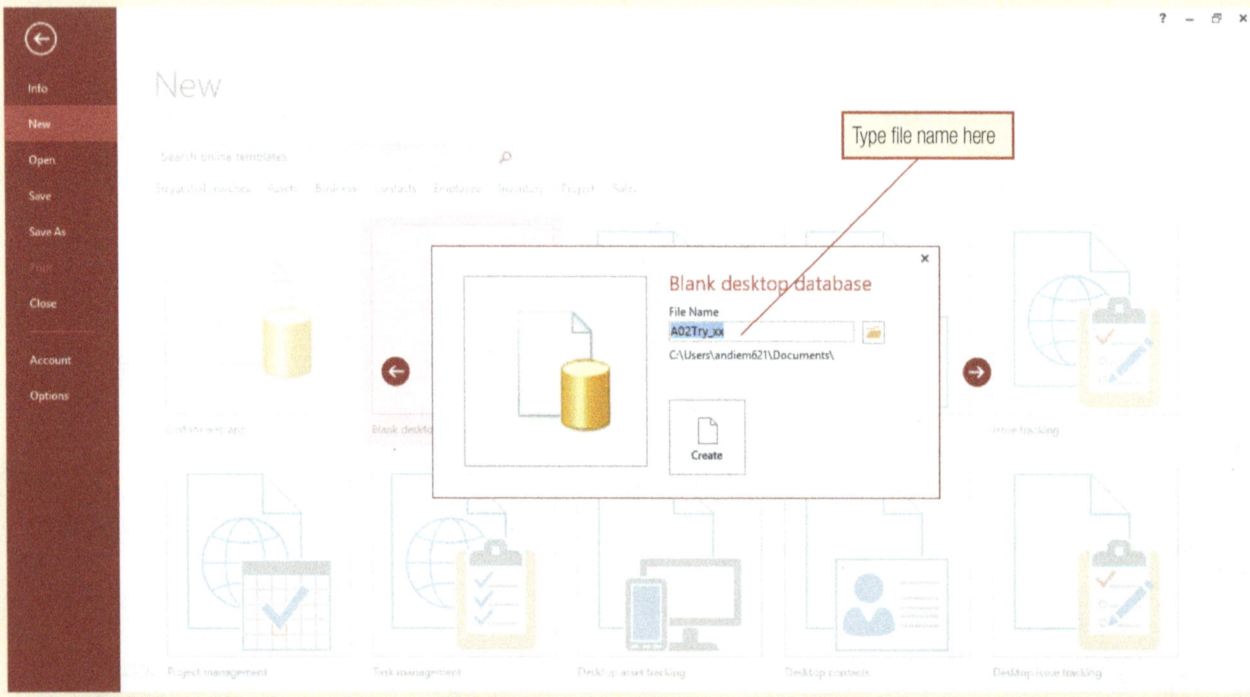

Access 2013, Windows 8, Microsoft Corporation

Exploring the Access Window

- After you create a new blank database, the main Access window appears and a new blank table opens.
- Across the top is the Ribbon, and the status bar is at the bottom, just like in other Office applications.
- At the left is the Navigation pane. By default, it shows all Access objects grouped by type. An object is a table, query, report, form, or other item used to store, display, or manage Access data. You can collapse the Navigation pane to save space onscreen and then expand it when you need it again.
- In the center is the open object—in this case a blank table in Datasheet view. Each open object has a tab that shows its name. The name is Table1 for now because you have not yet saved it and given it a more descriptive name.
- At the right a field list may appear, but it is empty at this point. You can close the field list (if it appears) to make more room to work with the table.

Figure 2-1 Access opens a new table when you create a new blank database

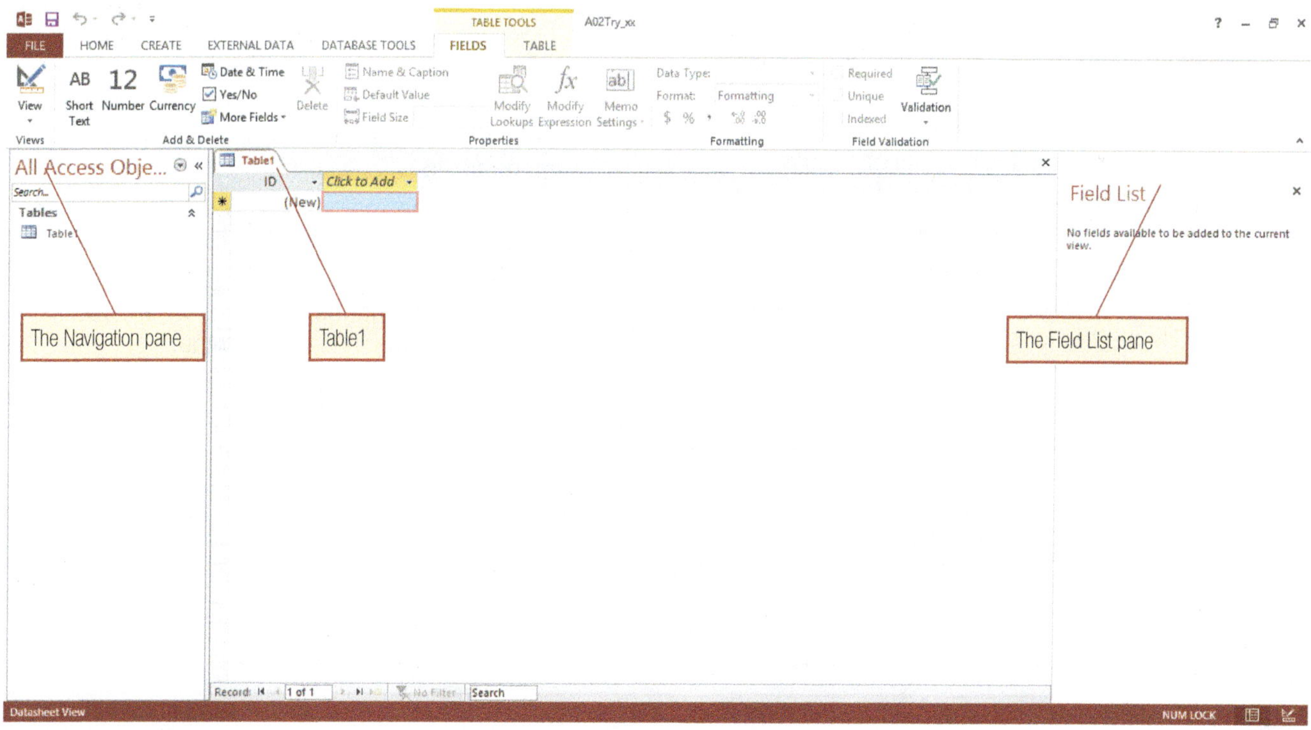

Access 2013, Windows 8, Microsoft Corporation

Try It! Collapsing and Expanding the Navigation Pane

1. In the **A02Try_xx** database, click « in the Navigation pane. The Navigation pane collapses.
2. In the Navigation pane, click ». The Navigation pane expands again.
3. Leave the **A02Try_xx** database open to use in the next Try It.

Try It! Opening and Closing the Field List

1. In the **A02Try_xx** database, press ALT + F8 to display the Field List.

   ✓ *If the Field List is already displayed, pressing ALT + F8 closes it. Press ALT + F8 again to open it.*

2. Click the Close button × in the Field List pane. The pane closes.
3. Leave the **A02Try_xx** database open to use in the next Try It.

Setting Access Options

- The Access Options dialog box enables you to personalize Access 2013 as well as individual databases. Access Options are divided into the following sections:
  - General. The General section is where options can be set for working with all of Access.
  - Current Database. The Current Database section is where options can be set for the current database.
  - Datasheet. The Datasheet section is where options are set for customizing datasheets in Access.
  - Object Designers. The Object Designers section is where options are set to customize the design of database objects in Access.
  - Proofing. The Proofing section is where options are set to change automatic corrections and to customize the dictionary.
  - Language. The Language section is where Office Language Preferences options are set.
  - Client Settings. The Client Settings section is where options are set for editing, display, printing, and other general settings.
  - Customize Ribbon. The Customize Ribbon section is where the task ribbon options are customized.
  - Quick Access Toolbar. The Quick Access Toolbar section is where the Quick Access Toolbar options can be customized.
  - Add-ins. The Add-ins section is where you manage Microsoft Office Add-ins.
  - Trust Center. The trust center is where options can be customized to help prevent issues with your documents and computer.

Try It! Setting Access Options

1. In the **A02Try_xx** database, click FILE > Options. The Access Options dialog box appears.
2. Click Proofing in the list on the left side of the Access options dialog box to display the Proofing options.
3. Click Current Database to display the options for the current database.
4. Click Cancel to close the dialog box without making any changes.
5. Leave the **A02Try_xx** database open to use in the next Try it.

Creating Table Fields in Datasheet View

- Access enables you to create table fields in either Datasheet or Design view. This lesson shows you how to do it in Datasheet view (the easiest method).

  ✓ *You will learn how to create table fields in Design view in Chapter 1, Lesson 6.*
- When creating field names, try to use concise, descriptive names.
- An ID field is created automatically by default for each table created in Datasheet view. This field is set to be unique and automatically numbered for each record.

Try It! Creating Table Fields in Datasheet View

1. In the **A02Try_xx** database, in the open table, click *Click to Add*.
2. Click Short Text on the menu of data types.
3. Type **First Name**.
4. Press ENTER.
5. Leave the **A02Try_xx** database open to use in the next Try It.

Add a field

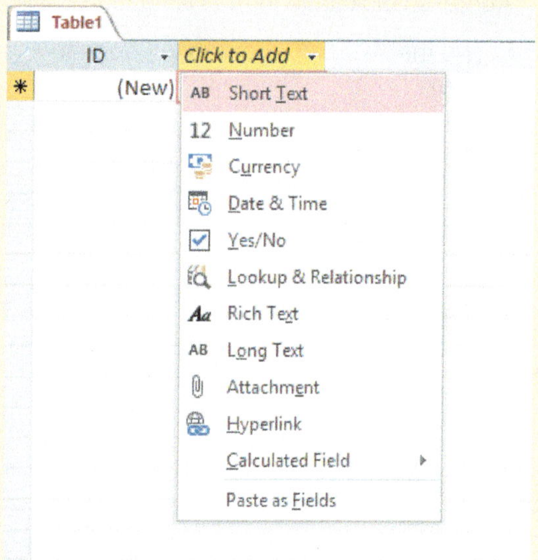

Access 2013, Windows 8, Microsoft Corporation

Saving, Closing, and Reopening a Table

- When you are finished creating the fields in the table, you should save your work.
- When you close a table, you are prompted to save if you have made any structural modifications to it. This includes adding and removing fields as well as changing field properties.
- Saving is necessary only when making changes to the table's structure; any records you enter in the table (covered in Lesson 3) are saved automatically.

Try It! Saving and Closing a Table

1. In the **A02Try_xx** database, right-click the Table1 tab and click Close, or click the Close button × in the upper-right corner of the Table1 table.
2. Click Yes.
3. Type **Address Book**.
4. Click OK.
5. Leave the **A02Try_xx** database open to use in the next Try It.

Try It! Opening a Table

1. In the **A02Try_xx** database, double-click the Address Book table in the Navigation pane.
2. Leave the **A02Try_xx** database open to use in the next Try It.

Double-click to open a table from the Navigation pane

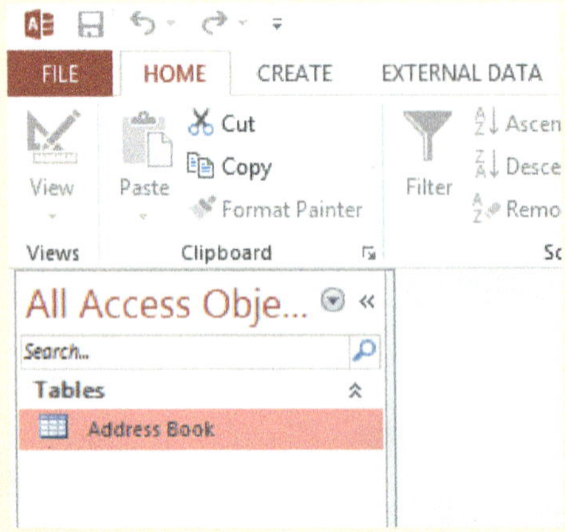

Access 2013, Windows 8, Microsoft Corporation

Creating Additional Tables

- Most databases have more than one table. Having multiple tables and connecting them using relationships helps reduce or eliminate redundancy in a database and reduces the likelihood of data entry errors.

Try It! Creating Additional Tables

1. In the **A02Try_xx** database, click the CREATE tab and then click Table to create a new table.
2. On the FIELDS tab, click Short Text **AB** to assign that type to Field1.
3. Type **Event** and press ENTER to rename Field1 and display the data type list for the next field.
4. On the data type list, click Number **12**.
5. Type **Attendees** and press ENTER.
6. Click the Save button on the Quick Access Toolbar, which is another method of saving a table.
7. Type **Events**.
8. Click OK. The database now includes two tables.
9. Leave the **A02Try_xx** database open to use in the next Try It.

Closing, Opening, and Working with a Database

- When you exit Access, you automatically close the open database and save your changes to it. You can also choose to close a database without exiting Access.
- Opening a different database closes the open one; you can have only one database open at once.
- Opening a database file is much like opening any other file in an Office application. You can click FILE > Open and then choose a recently used database from the Recent list, or select a database stored on your SkyDrive or computer.

Try It! Closing a Database

- In the A02Try_xx database, click FILE > Close.

Try It! Opening a Database from the Recent List

1. Click FILE > Open, and under Recent click A02Try_xx.

   OR

   a. From the Access Welcome screen click Open Other Files. The Open menu appears.

   b. Click Recent, if necessary.

   c. From the Recent list, click A02Try_xx.

   ✓ *If Access displays a Security Warning, click Enable Content.*

2. Close the A02Try_xx database file.

Try It! Opening a Database with the Open Dialog Box

1. Click FILE > Open.
2. Click Computer > Browse.
3. Navigate to the location where the files for this lesson are stored.
4. In the Open dialog box, click A02Try_xx.
5. Click Open.
6. Leave the A02Try_xx database open to use in the next Try It.

Saving a Copy of a Database

- You can save a database with a new name, to a different location, or in a different format.
- A database can be created in an older format by saving the database in an older format using the Save As Type option. Saving a database in an older format will also maintain the backward compatibility of the database.
- Saving a database as a template allows you to re-use the database structure to create a new database.
- To save a database as a template, click FILE > Save As, and then select Template in the Save As pane in the Backstage view.
- Access enables you to save the file in one of the following ways:
  - Access Database: saves the database copy in the default 2007-2013 format.
  - Access 2002-2003 Database: saves the database copy in a format that is compatible with Microsoft Access 2002-2003.
  - Access 2000 Database: saves the database copy in a format that is compatible with Microsoft Office Access 2000.
  - Template: saves the database copy as a database template.
  - Package and Sign: saves the database copy in an Access Deployment (.accdc) file and applies a digital signature. Users can extract the database from the package to use it.
  - Make ACCDE: compiles the database copy into an executable only file (.exe).
  - Back Up Database: saves the database copy as a backup for archiving purposes. Data can be recovered from the back up if the original database becomes corrupt or if errors are introduced.
  - SharePoint: saves the database copy to a SharePoint document management server.

- After saving a copy of a database, the copy opens and the original closes.
  - ✓ *Depending on the location to which you save the copy, certain features may be disabled. If you see an information bar with an Enable Content button, click the Enable Content button. (See Figure 2-2.)*
- You can also save your database to your SkyDrive account so that the file is available from any computer.

Figure 2-2

Access 2013, Windows 8, Microsoft Corporation

Try It! Saving a Copy of a Database

1. In the **A02Try_xx** database, click FILE > Save As > Save Database As.
2. Verify that the Access Database file type is selected and then click Save As. The Save As dialog box opens.
3. If necessary, navigate to the location where your teacher instructs you to store the files for this lesson.
4. In the File name box, type **A02TryA_xx**.
5. Click Save.
6. If the information bar appears, click Enable Content.
7. Leave the **A02TryA_xx** database open to use in the next Try It.

Try It! Backing Up a Database

1. In the **A02TryA_xx** database file, click FILE > Save As > Back Up Database.
2. If necessary, navigate to the location where your teacher instructs you to store the files for this lesson.
3. In the File name box, type **A02TryA_Backup_xx**.
4. Click FILE > Save.

Try It! Saving a Copy of a Database As an Access 2000 Database File

1. Open the **A02TryA_xx** database, click FILE > Save As > Save Database As.
2. Under Database File Types, click Access 2000 Database and then click Save As to open the Save As dialog box.
3. If necessary, navigate to the location where your teacher instructs you to store the files for this lesson.
4. In the File name box, type **A02TryB_xx**.
5. Click Save.
6. If the information bar appears, click Enable Content.
7. Leave the **A02TryB_xx** database open to use in the next Try It.

Splitting a Database

- A database can be split so that several people sharing the database can work on it at the same time. This improves the performance of the database.

Try It! Splitting a Database

1. In the **A02TryB_xx** database file, click DATABASE TOOLS tab and select Access Database.
2. Click Split Database Split Database.
3. If necessary, navigate to the location where your teacher instructs you to store the files for this lesson.
4. In the File Name box, type **A02TryC_xx**, and click Split Split.
5. Click OK in the Database Splitter confirmation box.
6. Close the **A02TryC_xx** file, saving changes, and exit Access.

Lesson 2—Practice

You have been asked to start a database for a friend's new jewelry business. In this project, you will start a new blank database file and populate it with two tables: one for customers and one for products.

DIRECTIONS

1. On the Windows Start screen, click the **Access 2013** tile. Access opens.
2. On the Access Welcome screen, click **Blank desktop database**. In the File name box, type **A02Practice_xx**. Replace *xx* with your name or initials, as instructed by your teacher.
3. Click the **Browse** icon to the right of the box, browse to the location where your teacher instructs you to store the files for this lesson, and click **OK**.
4. Click **Create**. A new blank table opens.
5. Click **Click to Add**. A list of data types appears, as shown in Figure 2-3 on the next page.
6. Click **Short Text**.
7. Type **First Name** and press ENTER.
8. Right-click the **Table1** tab and click **Close**.
9. When asked if you want to save, click **Yes**.
10. Type **Customers**, as shown in Figure 2-4, and press ENTER.
11. Click the **CREATE** tab. In the Tables section, click **Table**. A new table opens.
12. On the **FIELDS** tab, click **Short Text** AB. A new text field appears.
13. Type **Type**, and press ENTER. A list of data types appears for the next new field.
14. Click the **Close** button × in the upper-right corner of the table.
15. When asked if you want to save, click **Yes**.
16. Type **Products**, and press ENTER.
17. Click **FILE** > **Close** to close the database. If instructed, submit this database to your teacher for grading.

Figure 2-3

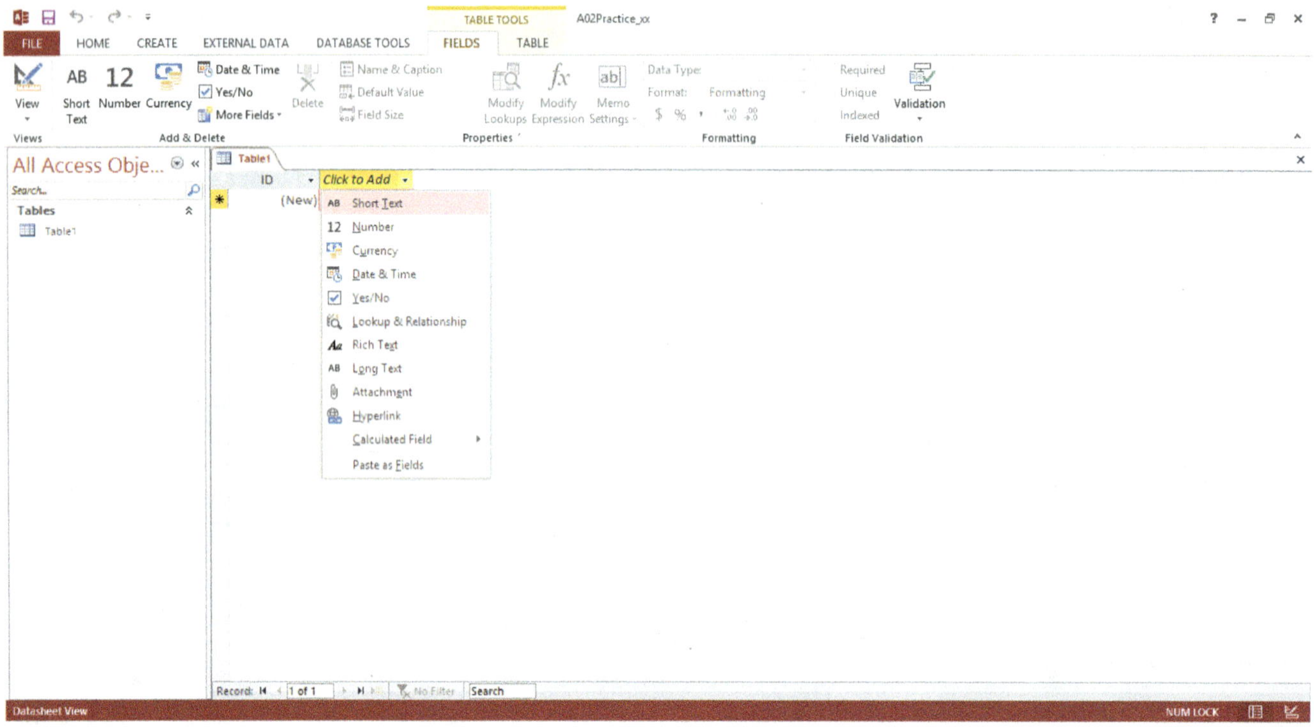

Access 2013, Windows 8, Microsoft Corporation

Figure 2-4

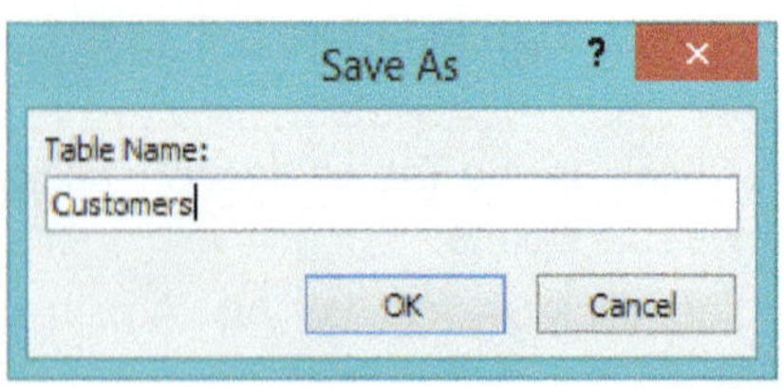

Access 2013, Windows 8, Microsoft Corporation

Lesson 2—Apply

You have been asked to work on a database for a friend's new jewelry business. In this project, you will open an existing database and add fields to two existing tables.

DIRECTIONS

1. Start Access, if necessary.
2. Open **A02Apply** from the data files for this lesson.
3. Save the database as **A02Apply_xx**. Replace *xx* with your name or initials, as instructed by your teacher.
4. Open the Navigation pane if it is hidden, and enable active content if it is blocked.
5. Open the **Customers** table in Datasheet view and enter the following additional fields, in the order listed:

Field	Type
Date Added	Date & Time
Inactive?	Yes/No

6. Close the **Customers** table.
7. Open the **Products** table in Datasheet view and enter the following additional fields, in the order listed:

Field	Type
Product	Short Text
Materials Cost	Currency
Labor Cost	Currency
Retail Price	Currency
Build Hours	Number

8. Close the **Products** table.
9. Click **FILE** > **Close** to close the database. If instructed, submit this database to your teacher for grading.

Lesson 3

Modifying and Adding Data to a Table

➤ What You Will Learn

Adding Records
Entering Data in a Special Field
Editing Records
Editing a Hyperlink
Selecting Records
Deleting Records
Adding a Totals Row

WORDS TO KNOW

Multi-valued field
A field that can contain more than one separate entry per record.

Software Skills After creating a table, the next step is to enter records into it. This data entry forms the basis of your database.

What You Can Do

Adding Records

- When you enter records, they are stored in a table. A table is the only object type that can hold records. Most of the other types of objects are simply ways of looking at the data from one or more tables.
- To enter records in a table, type the information you want in a field and press TAB or ENTER to go to the next field. To skip a field, Tab past it or click to move the insertion point to a different field.
- Access automatically saves a record when you go to another record.

Try It! Adding Records to a Table

1. Open the **A03Try** database from the data files for this lesson. Save the file as **A03Try_xx**. Replace *xx* with your name or initials, as instructed by your teacher. Click Enable Content if necessary any time you see a security warning.
2. Double-click the Events table. It opens in Datasheet view.
3. Press TAB to move past the ID field.
4. In the Event field for the first record, type **Paws for a Cause** and press TAB.
5. In the Sponsor field, type **Hamilton County Humane Society** and press TAB.
6. In the Location field, type **Hamilton County Humane Society** and press TAB.
7. In the Attendees field, type **200** and press TAB.
8. Press TAB to move past the Contact field without entering data. Because this is the last field in the record, the first field in the next record becomes active.
9. Right-click the Events tab and click Close.
10. Leave the **A03Try_xx** database open to use in the next Try It.

Entering Data in a Special Field

- Some data types display drop-down lists or check boxes that you use to enter data.
- A check box appears in a logical (yes/no) field. Mark the check box by clicking it to choose Yes, or leave it cleared to choose No.
- When you select a field that contains a drop-down list, a down arrow appears on the right side of the field. Click that arrow to open a menu and then click your selection from the menu.
- Some drop-down list fields are **multi-valued fields**; you can mark or clear any or all of the check boxes on the list.
- A Hyperlink field formats the entry as either a Web address (http://) or an e-mail address.

Try It! Entering Data in a Special Field

1. In the **A03Try_xx** database, double-click Address Book to open that table.
2. In the first record, click in the State field and then click the down arrow.
3. Click IN on the drop-down list.
4. Click in the E-mail field.
5. Type **tom@sycamoreknoll.com**, and press TAB to move to the next field.
6. Click the down arrow in the Special Needs field.
7. Mark the Handicap Parking and Wheelchair Access check boxes and click OK. Press TAB or ENTER to move to the Inactive field.

   ✓ *It is important to click OK after making selections; otherwise, the changes will not be saved.*
8. In the Inactive field, mark the check box.
9. Right-click the Address Book tab and click Close.
10. Leave the **A03Try_xx** database open to use in the next Try It.

Select values for a multi-valued field

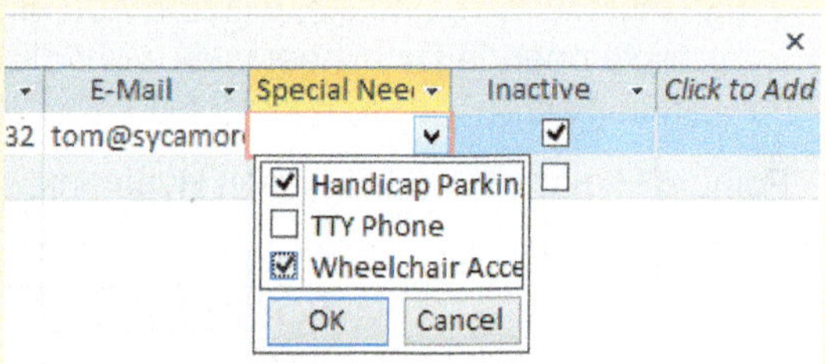

Access 2013, Windows 8, Microsoft Corporation

Editing Records

- You may want to modify field information after you enter it. You can change text in the same way you would in Word or Excel. Click to position the insertion point.
- While you are making changes to a record, a pencil icon appears on the record selector button (to the left of the record). The pencil indicates that any changes are not currently saved.
- Press BACKSPACE to remove text before the insertion point or press DEL to remove text after the insertion point. You can also drag the mouse pointer to select text and then press DEL to remove the text.
- Select text and type new text to replace the selected text. You can double-click on a word to select a word, then type to replace it.
- If you move the mouse pointer to the beginning of a field, the pointer changes to a white plus sign. Click to select the entire content of that field.
- If you want to undo your changes, press ESC once to undo the change to the current field and press ESC again to undo all changes to the current record.
- Changes are automatically saved to the record when you go to another record or close the table or form.

Try It! Editing Field Data

1. In the **A03Try_xx** database, double-click Address Book to open that table.
2. In the First Name field, double-click Tom, and type **Thomas** to replace it.
3. In the Address field, click to move the insertion point after the "a" in Wander. Press BACKSPACE once and type **o**.
4. In the Last Name field, position the mouse pointer on the upper-left part of the field so you see a large white plus sign, and then click to select the entire field.
5. Type **Jones**. Press ESC to cancel the change before it is finalized.
6. Leave the **A03Try_xx** database open to use in the next Try It.

Editing a Hyperlink

- To change data entered in a hyperlink field, edit the hyperlink or delete the data and replace it.
- To delete the data, select it and press DEL.
- To edit the hyperlink, right-click the field, point to Hyperlink, then click Edit Hyperlink to open the Edit Hyperlink box.
- Edit the hyperlink in the Text to display box, and enter the hyperlink destination in the E-mail address box.

  ✓ *Changing the data in the Text to display box is not required.*

Try It! Editing a Hyperlink

1. In the **A03Try_xx** database, with the Address Book table open in Datasheet view, right-click in the E-mail field.
2. Point to Hyperlink, and click Edit Hyperlink.
3. In the Text to display box, change the e-mail address to **thomas@sycamoreknoll.com**.
4. In the E-mail address box, change the e-mail address to **mailto:thomas@sycamoreknoll.com**.

   ✓ *Do not remove the mailto: portion of the entry.*
5. Click OK.

(continued)

Try It! Editing a Hyperlink *(continued)*

6. Right-click the Address Book tab, and click Close.

7. Leave the **A03Try_xx** database open to use in the next Try It.

Edit an e-mail hyperlink

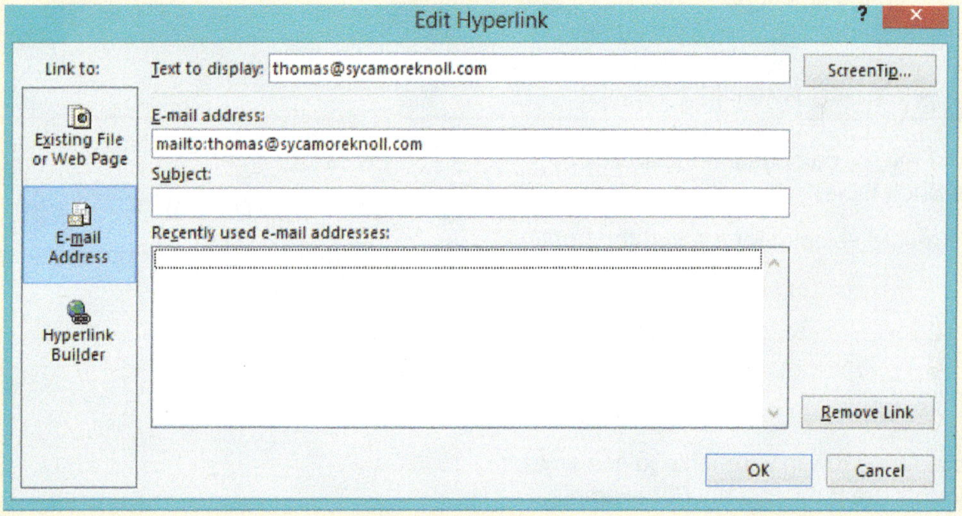

Access 2013, Windows 8, Microsoft Corporation

Selecting Records

- To select a single record, click the record selector button to its left.
- To select multiple contiguous (adjacent) records, select the first one and then hold down SHIFT as you click the record selector of the last one.
- Press CTRL + A to select all records in the table.

Try It! Selecting Records

1. In the **A03Try_xx** database, double-click the States table.
2. Click the record selector for the AR record.

Select a record by clicking its record selector

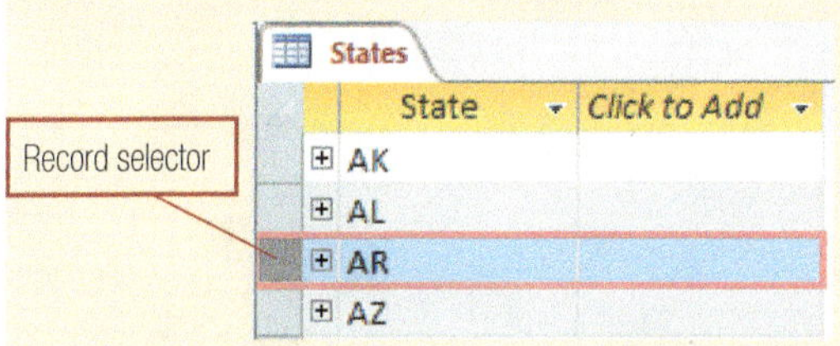

Access 2013, Windows 8, Microsoft Corporation

3. Hold down SHIFT and click the record selector for the MA record.
4. Release SHIFT.
5. Click any record to cancel the selection.
6. Press CTRL + A to select all records.
7. Click any record to cancel the selection.
8. Right-click the States tab, and click Close to close the table.
9. Leave the **A03Try_xx** database open to use in the next Try It.

Deleting Records

- You can delete selected records. To delete, press DEL or click the HOME tab and in the Records group, click Delete.
- When you delete one or more records, Access will ask you to confirm the deletion. After you click Yes, you cannot reverse the deletion.
- Access shows the total number of records at the bottom of the window.
- If you have an AutoNumber field in the table, Access will not reuse the numbers of the deleted records.

Try It! Deleting Records

1. In the **A03Try_xx** database, double-click the Address Book table.
2. Click the record selector for the first (and only) record.
3. Press DEL.
4. Click Yes to confirm.
5. Leave the **A03Try_xx** database open to use in the next Try It.

Adding Total Rows

- You can add a Totals row in your table to see what the total amounts are for a column. For example, you can see the sum of amounts spent or the total number of entries in a column.

Try It! Adding a Total Row

1. In the **A03Try_xx** database, double-click the Events table.
2. Add a new event:

   Event: Dog Walkers

   Sponsors: Pet Inc.

   Location: 100 Main Street

   Attendees: 50
3. On the HOME tab, in the Records group, click the Totals button Σ Totals .
4. Double-click in the Totals row field for Events, select the drop-down arrow and select Count. Save your changes.

   ✓ *The totals row can be toggled on and off.*
5. Click FILE > Close.

Create a totals row

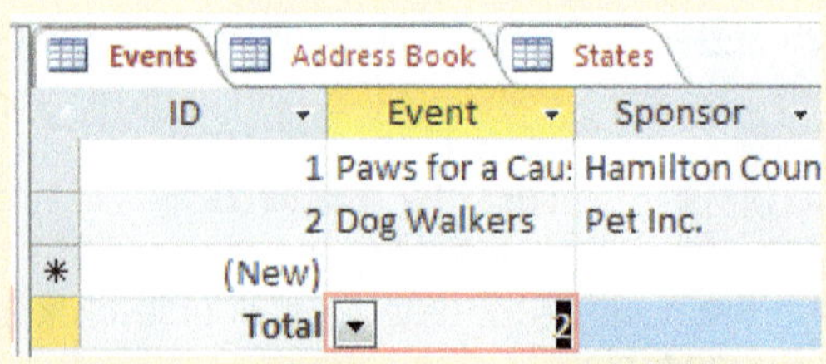

Access 2013, Windows 8, Microsoft Corporation

Lesson 3—Practice

In this project, you will enter a record in the Customers table of your friend's jewelry business database.

DIRECTIONS

1. Start Access, if necessary.
2. Open **A03Practice** from the data files for this lesson.
3. Save the database as **A03Practice_xx** in the location where your teacher instructs you to store the files for this lesson.

   ✓ *If a security warning bar appears, click Enable Content.*
4. Double-click the **Customers** table in the Navigation pane to open it in Datasheet view.
5. Press TAB to move past the **ID** field.
6. In the **First Name** field, type **Ann** and press TAB.
7. In the **Last Name** field, type **Brown** and press TAB.
8. In the **Address** field, type **108 Ponting Street** and press TAB.
9. In the **City** field, type **Macon** and press TAB.
10. In the **State** field, type **IL** and press TAB.
11. In the **ZIP** field, type **62544** and press TAB.
12. In the **Phone** field, type **317-555-8281** and press TAB.
13. In the **Date Added** field, type today's date in this format: **mm/dd/yyyy**. Press TAB. Your entry should look like Figure 3-1.
14. Press TAB to skip the Inactive check box without marking it.
15. Double-click the name in the **First Name** field (*Ann*) and type **Jennifer**.
16. Double-click the name in the **City** field (*Macon*) and type **Decatur**.
17. Click to position the insertion point at the end of the current entry in the **ZIP** field.
18. Press BACKSPACE twice.
19. Type **22**, changing the entry to read **62522**. Refer to Figure 3-2.
20. Right-click the **Customers** tab and click **Close**.
21. Click **FILE** > **Close** to close the database. If instructed, submit this database to your teacher for grading.

Figure 3-1

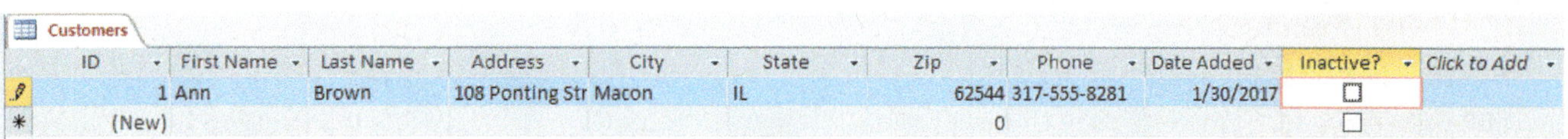

Access 2013, Windows 8, Microsoft Corporation

Figure 3-2

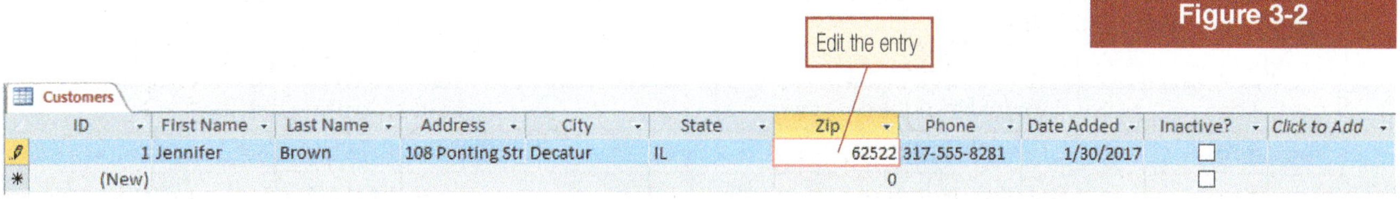

Access 2013, Windows 8, Microsoft Corporation

Lesson 3—Apply

In this project, you will enter records for products and customers in your friend's jewelry business database and make edits to existing records.

DIRECTIONS

1. Start Access, if necessary.
2. Open **A03Apply** from the data files for this lesson.
3. Save the database as **A03Apply_xx** to the location where your teacher instructs you to store the files for this lesson.

   ✓ *If a security warning bar appears, click Enable Content.*
4. Open the **Customers** table in Datasheet view, and enter the following records. Skip the fields (that is, leave them blank) that are not specified. Use today's date as the Date Added:

   Carrie Fulton
   211 West Eckhardt Street
   Pana, IL 61722
   217-555-2273

   Felicia Adamson
   775 North Main Street
   Noblesville, IN 46060
   317-555-1125

   Norman Eichmann
   55110 Old Church Lane
   Boston, MA 02201
   502-555-7755
5. Set Norman Eichmann's record to be Inactive by marking the check box in the **Inactive** field.
6. Change Carrie Fulton's last name to **Strong**.
7. Close the **Customers** table.
8. Open the **Products** table in Datasheet view.
9. Enter the records from the table (shown at the bottom of this page) in the **Products** table. Skip the fields (that is, leave them blank) that are not specified in the table.
10. Enter the materials cost for each necklace:
    - Silver: **$10.00**.
    - Yellow gold: **$20.00**.
    - White gold: **$30.00**.
11. For the labor cost for each product, enter **$20.00**.
12. For the build hours for each product, enter **1**.
13. Delete all the silver necklaces.
14. Close the **Products** table, and close the database. If instructed, submit the database file to your teacher for grading.

Type	Product	Size	Material
Necklace	Clover Necklace	22"	Sterling Silver
Necklace	Clover Necklace	22"	Gold, Yellow, 14K
Necklace	Clover Necklace	22"	Gold, White, 18K
Necklace	Starfish Necklace	22"	Sterling Silver
Necklace	Starfish Necklace	22"	Gold, Yellow, 14K
Necklace	Starfish Necklace	22"	Gold, White, 18K
Necklace	Heart Necklace	22"	Sterling Silver
Necklace	Heart Necklace	22"	Gold, Yellow, 14K
Necklace	Heart Necklace	22"	Gold, White, 18K

Lesson 4

Modifying Fields in a Table

➤ What You Will Learn

Setting Field Properties
Adding a Field
Renaming a Field
Moving a Field
Deleting a Field
Hiding and Unhiding Fields
Changing Table Field Widths
Freezing Fields

Software Skills It is best to edit a table's structure before putting data into it, but occasionally you may need to make changes after data has been entered. In this lesson, you will learn how to modify a table's structure and layout in Datasheet view.

WORDS TO KNOW

Field header
The top block in a vertical field in a table, containing the field name.

Freeze
To set a field so that it always remains onscreen, in the left-most position, as you scroll left to right.

Required field
A field for which each record must contain an entry.

Unique field
A field for which each record must contain a unique entry.

What You Can Do

Setting Field Properties

- On the TABLE TOOLS FIELDS tab, you can set the data type for the active field, from the Data Type drop-down list.
- Changing the data type changes the way the data is stored in the field and may also change the type of data that is allowed in the field.

✓ *Data types are described in more detail in Chapter 1, Lesson 6.*

- If the current data in that field violates the rules for the new data type, an error message appears, and any data that violates the rules is deleted. For example, if you change a field that contains text to a Number field, any character-based entries are removed.
- In a **required field**, each record must include an entry in that field. An error message appears and the record is not saved if that field is empty.
- In a **unique field**, each record must contain a unique entry, which means no duplicates. For example, Social Security Number might be a unique field in a personnel database.
- There are many other properties you can set for a field; some of these can be changed only in Design view.

✓ *Chapter 1, Lesson 6 explains how to modify field properties in Design view.*

Try It! Changing the Data Type

1. Open the **A04Try** database from the data files for this lesson, and save it as **A04Try_xx**. Replace *xx* with your name or initials, as instructed by your teacher. Enable content if necessary.
2. Open the Address Book table in Datasheet view.
3. Click in the E-Mail field in the first (and only) record.
4. Click the TABLE TOOLS FIELDS tab, click the Data Type drop-down arrow in the Formatting group, and click Hyperlink.
5. Leave the **A04Try_xx** database open to use in the next Try It.

Choose Hyperlink as the data type

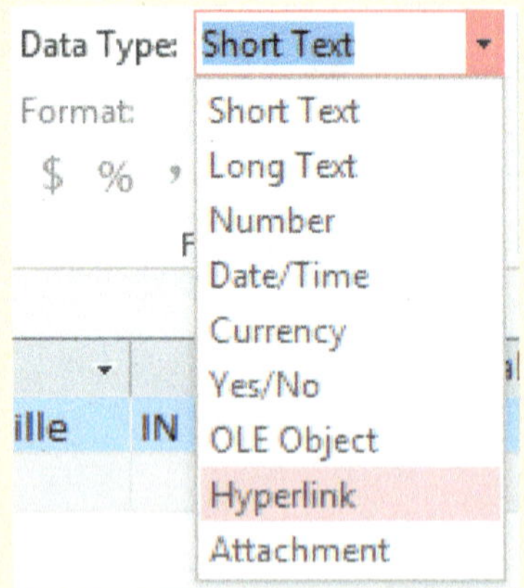

Access 2013, Windows 8, Microsoft Corporation

Try It! Making a Field Required

1. In the **A04Try_xx** database, click the Last Name field.
2. On the TABLE TOOLS FIELDS tab, in the Field Validation group, click the Required check box.
3. Leave the **A04Try_xx** database open to use in the next Try It.

Require an entry for each record

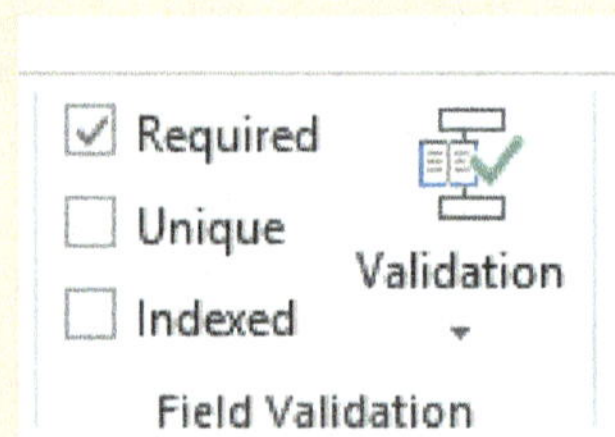

Access 2013, Windows 8, Microsoft Corporation

Try It! Making a Field Unique

1. In the **A04Try_xx** database, click the E-Mail field.
2. On the TABLE TOOLS FIELDS tab, click the Unique check box.
3. Leave the **A04Try_xx** database open to use in the next Try It.

Adding a Field

- There are three ways to create a new field in a table:
  - Use the *Click to Add* empty field to the right of the existing fields in the table, as you did when creating fields in Lesson 2.
  - Right-click the **field header** of an existing field and click Insert Field. A new field with default settings appears to the left of the existing field. The field's name will be a placeholder (Field1, for example). You can rename it.
  - Use one of the buttons on the TABLE TOOLS FIELDS tab in the Add & Delete group to insert a field of a specific type, such as Short Text, Number, and so on.

- If you have already entered data in the table, you will need to go back and fill in the value for the new field for each record.

Try It! Adding a Field by Right-Clicking

1. In the A04Try_xx database, right-click the field header of the First Name field.
2. Click Insert Field. A new text field appears with a generic name.
3. Leave the A04Try_xx database open to use in the next Try It.

Insert a new field by right-clicking

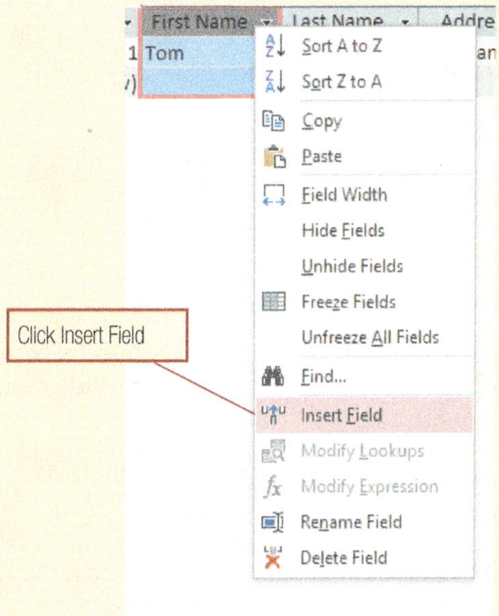

Access 2013, Windows 8, Microsoft Corporation

Try It! Adding a Field from the Ribbon

1. In the A04Try_xx database, click in the Last Name field.
2. On the TABLE TOOLS FIELDS tab, click the Short Text button **AB**.
3. Leave the A04Try_xx database open to use in the next Try It.

Insert a new field from the Ribbon

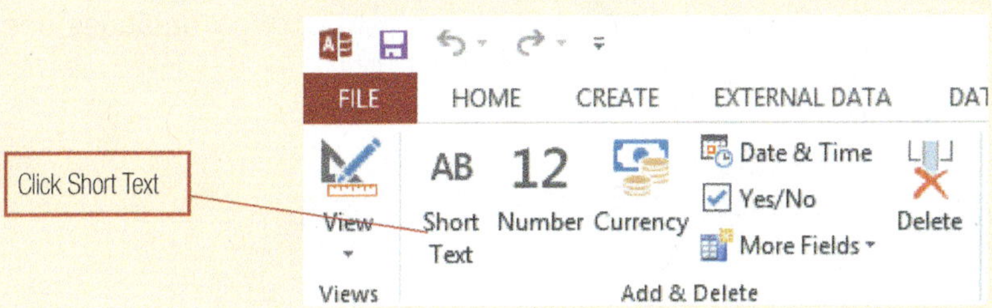

Access 2013, Windows 8, Microsoft Corporation

Renaming a Field

- When you insert new fields, they have generic names; you will want to change these to more descriptive names.
- You might also sometimes need to rename existing fields. For example, you might decide to omit spaces from field names for easier data sharing with other database applications.

Try It! Renaming a Field

1. In the **A04Try_xx** database, double-click the Field1 field header.

   OR

   Right-click the Field1 field header and click Rename Field.
2. Type **Prefix** and press ENTER .
3. Click anywhere in the Field2 field.
4. On the TABLE TOOLS FIELDS tab, click Name & Caption . The Enter Field Properties dialog box opens.
5. In the Name text box, change the name to **Suffix**.
6. Click OK.
7. Leave the **A04Try_xx** database open to use in the next Try It.

Change the name to Suffix

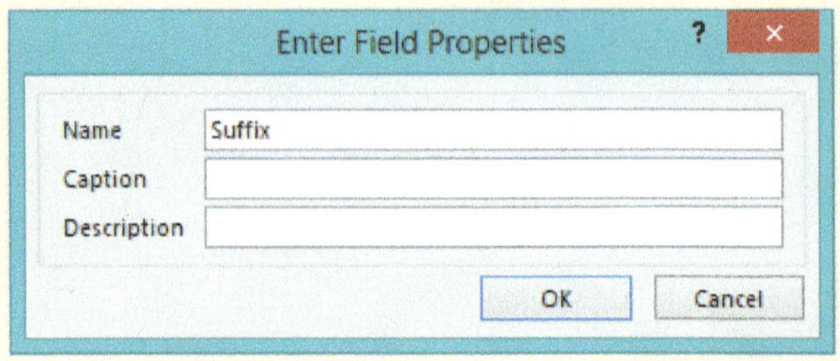

Access 2013, Windows 8, Microsoft Corporation

Moving a Field

- The easiest way to move a field is by dragging it. Click a field header to select it, hold the mouse button down, and then drag. A black vertical line shows where the field will be placed. When you release the mouse button, the field drops into the new location.
- The changes you make to the field order, by moving fields, are made permanent when you save the table. If you do not want the changes to be permanent, do not save the changes to the table when prompted (when closing it).

Try It! Moving a Field

1. In the **A04Try_xx** database, click the E-Mail field header.
2. Click and hold the mouse button down over the E-Mail field header, and drag the field to the left of the Phone field. Then release the mouse button.
3. Leave the **A04Try_xx** database open to use in the next Try It.

Deleting a Field

- Deleting a field from the table removes it from the table's structure and deletes all data in it. Do not delete a field from the table unless you want it permanently gone.

  ✓ *If you just want the field temporarily hidden, use the Hide Fields command, described later in this chapter.*

- There are several ways to delete a field. You can right-click the field header and click Delete Field; select the field and click Delete on the TABLE TOOLS FIELDS tab; or select the field and press DEL .
- Deleting a field is permanent, even if you do not save your changes to the table.

Try It! Deleting a Field

1. In the **A04Try_xx** database, click the E-Mail field and click Delete .
2. Click Yes to confirm.
3. If you see a message about deleting one or more indexes, click Yes to confirm.
4. Leave the **A04Try_xx** database open to use in the next Try It.

Hiding and Unhiding Fields

- If you do not want to view or print certain fields in Datasheet view, you can hide them.
- Hiding a field does not remove it from the table structure, and it does not delete any data.

Try It! Hiding and Unhiding Fields

1. In the **A04Try_xx** database, right-click the field header of the Inactive field and click Hide Fields.
2. Right-click the field header of the Phone field (or any other visible field) and click Unhide Fields.
3. In the Unhide Columns dialog box, click to mark the check box next to Inactive.
4. Click Close.
5. Leave the **A04Try_xx** database open to use in the next Try It.

Mark the check box to unhide a field

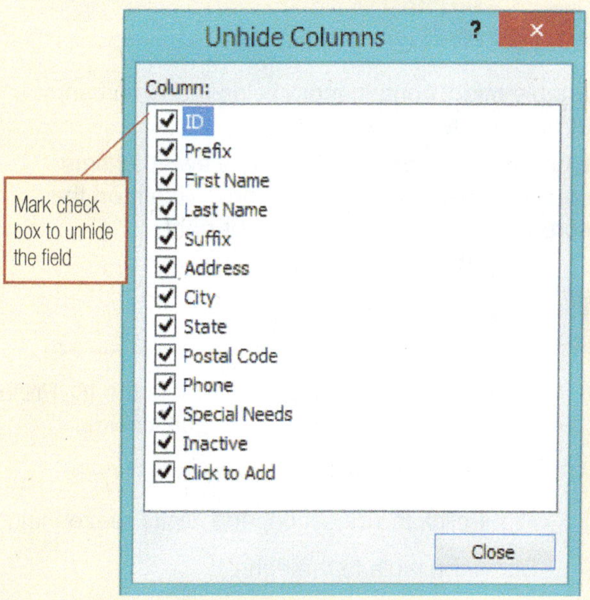

Access 2013, Windows 8, Microsoft Corporation

Changing Table Field Widths

- Data appears truncated, or cut off, when it is wider than the width of the field. To see all of the data, you can widen the field.
- If data in a field is short, you can narrow the field to remove the extra space.
- Column width does not affect the field size (that is, the maximum number of characters the field can contain); column width is only for your convenience when viewing the table.
- To set the field to fit the widest entry, drag the edge of the field to adjust the width manually, or specify an exact width (in number of characters).

Try It! Changing Table Field Widths

1. In the **A04Try_xx** database, position the mouse pointer between the field headers for the Address and the City fields. When the pointer is in the right place, it changes to a bar with horizontal arrows.

Double-click to autosize a field

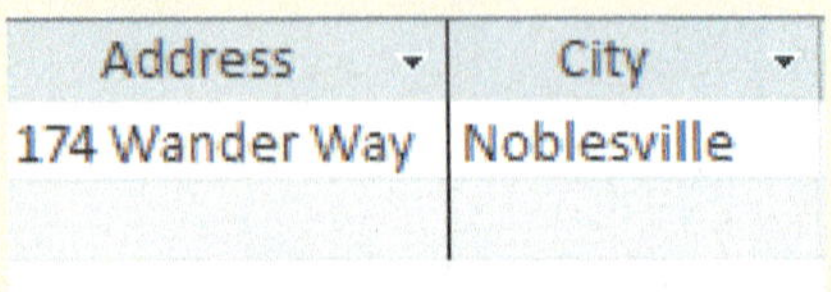

Access 2013, Windows 8, Microsoft Corporation

2. Double-click. The Address field widens to accommodate the widest (and only) entry.
3. Position the mouse pointer between the field headers for Special Needs and Inactive.
4. Hold down the left mouse button and drag to the right approximately one inch, then release the mouse button.
5. If the Special Needs field label still appears truncated, repeat step 4 to widen the field further.
6. Right-click the Prefix field header and click Field Width.
7. In the Column Width dialog box, enter **7**.

   ✓ *Column width is measured in characters.*
8. Click OK.
9. Leave the **A04Try_xx** database open to use in the next Try It.

Freezing Fields

- A table might contain more fields than you can see at once in Datasheet view.
- If certain fields are important to view at all times, you can **freeze** them so that they remain on the screen as you scroll to the left or right.
- If you freeze multiple contiguous fields starting with the left-most field, they will simply appear fixed as you scroll from side to side.
- If you freeze individual fields that are not already at the left-most edge of the table, they will move to the left edge when you freeze them. After unfreezing them, you will need to move them back to their original locations manually.

Try It! Freezing Fields

1. In the **A04Try_xx** database, select the ID, Prefix, First Name, Last Name, and Suffix fields.

   ✓ *Hold down the SHIFT key to select multiple fields.*
2. Right-click the selection, and click Freeze Fields.
3. Scroll the table to the right.

   ✓ *Notice that the frozen fields remain in view.*
4. Right-click any field.
5. Click Unfreeze All Fields.
6. Right-click the Address Book tab and click Close.
7. Click Yes when prompted to save changes.
8. Click FILE > Close to exit the database.

Lesson 4—Practice

You have been asked to make the datasheet in your friend's jewelry business database easier to read. You will rename and move some fields, hide some fields, and widen other fields so their entries are not truncated.

DIRECTIONS

1. Start Access, if necessary.
2. Open **A04Practice** from the data files for this lesson.
3. Save the database as **A04Practice_xx** to the location where your teacher instructs you to store the files for this lesson.

   ✓ *If a security warning bar appears, click Enable Content.*
4. In the Navigation pane, double-click the **Products** table to open it in Datasheet view.
5. Double-click between the **Product** and **Size** field headers to widen the **Product** field to accommodate the longest entry in it.
6. Drag the divider between the **Material** and **Materials Cost** fields to the right to widen the Material field enough that the entries are not truncated.
7. Right-click the **Size** field header, and click **Field Width**.
8. In the Column Width box, type **6** and click **OK**.
9. Select the **Build Hours** field, and press DEL to delete it; click **Yes** to confirm.
10. Select the **Retail Price** field, and drag it (by the header) to the left of the **Materials Cost** field.
11. Select the **Retail Price**, **Materials Cost**, and **Labor Cost** fields.
12. Right-click the selection, and click **Hide Fields**.
13. Double-click the **Field1** field header and type **Category**, renaming it.
14. Select the **Product** field.
15. Click the **TABLE TOOLS FIELDS** tab and click **Short Text**. A new text field appears.
16. Type **Description** and press ENTER, replacing the generic field name with the new field name.
17. Click **FILE** > **Close**. If instructed, submit it to your teacher for grading.

Lesson 4—Apply

In your friend's jewelry business database, you will edit fields to make the datasheet easier to read.

DIRECTIONS

1. Start Access, if necessary.
2. Open **A04Apply** from the data files for this lesson.
3. Save the database as **A04Apply_xx** to the location where your teacher instructs you to store the files for this lesson.

   ✓ *If a security warning bar appears, click Enable Content.*
4. Open the **Customers** table in Datasheet view.
5. Change the widths of all fields so that they are no wider than needed, and yet no entries are truncated.
6. Hide the **Inactive?** field.
7. Delete the **Date Added** field.
8. Unhide the **Inactive?** field, and hide the **Click to Add** field. Redisplay the **Click to Add** field.
9. Close the **Customers** table, saving your changes.
10. Open the **Products** table in Datasheet view.
11. Change the width of the **Description** field to **30**.
12. Change the **ID**, **Category**, and **Material** field widths to fit their contents.
13. Move the **Description** field to the right-most position.
14. Freeze the **Product** field.
15. Close the **Products** table, saving your changes.
16. Click **FILE** > **Close**. If instructed, submit your database to your teacher for grading.

Lesson 5

Importing and Protecting Data

➤ What You Will Learn

Understanding Data Import and Export Options
Importing Data from Excel into an Existing Table
Importing Data from Excel into a New Table
Importing a Table from an Existing Database
Previewing and Printing a Table
Opening a Database Exclusively
Setting a Database Password
Changing Database Properties
Compact & Repair a Database

WORDS TO KNOW

Append
To add to the end of.

Collate
To order copies of a multipage document so that complete sets are together.

Encrypt
To add protection to a file so others cannot read it.

Exclusive mode
A mode in which only one user at a time can work with a file.

Print Preview
A view that shows you exactly how a report will look when printed.

Wizard
A series of dialog boxes that guide you step-by-step through a process.

Software Skills Sometimes it is easier to import data from other sources than to type it into a table from scratch. In this lesson, you will learn how to import Excel data into an existing table and into a new table. You will also learn how to print a table, how to set a database password to protect it, change database properties, and compact and repair a database.

What You Can Do

Understanding Data Import and Export Options

- Data may be imported from a variety of sources, including text files, other Access databases, Excel files, SharePoint lists, XML files, and more. The procedure for doing so is roughly the same for all types: a **wizard** walks you through the process.
- You can import data from the EXTERNAL DATA tab's Import & Link group. Buttons are available there for several types of data sources. The More button opens a menu of additional less-common formats from which you can import.
- Importing from Excel is simple since the data is already pre-delimited into fields. Use the Excel button in the Import & Link group of the EXTERNAL DATA tab to get started.

- You can import data into an existing table, create a new table, or create a link to the original data source.

  ✓ *You cannot directly import data from a Word table, but you can import the Word data into Excel, save it as an Excel file, and then import it into Access.*

- To export an Access database to an alternate format, go to the EXTERNAL DATA tab. In the Exports group, select the appropriate formatting option. You can export to Excel, a text file, PDFs, and other formats.

Figure 5-1

The Import & Link group on the EXTERNAL DATA tab contains options for importing many types of data

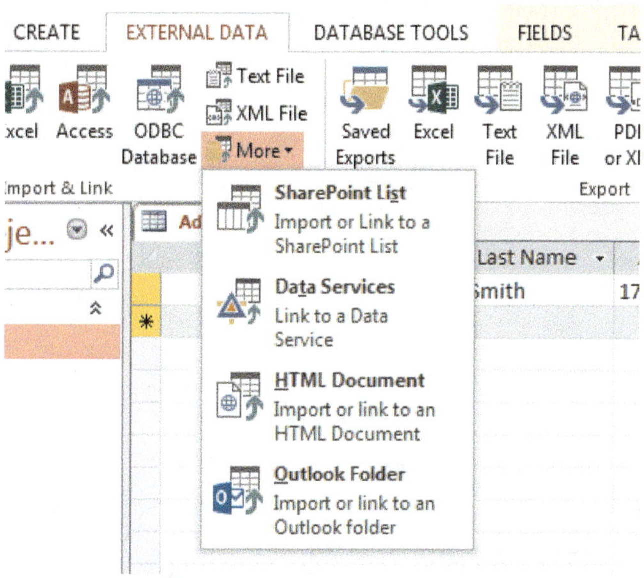

Access 2013, Windows 8, Microsoft Corporation

Importing Data from Excel into an Existing Table

- When you import data into an existing table, the records are **appended** to the end of the table. In Datasheet view, they appear at the bottom of the table.

- Importing data into an existing table works only if the fields have the same names and if the data fits into the fields as they are defined in Access. For example, data in a State field where the state names are spelled out would not import into a State field in Access that had a length limit of two characters. You might have to edit the data in Excel before importing to correct such problems.

Try It! Importing Data into an Existing Table and Exporting Data

1. Open the **A05Try** database from the data files for this lesson and save it as **A05Try_xx**. Click Enable Content.
2. Click the EXTERNAL DATA tab, in the Import & Link group, click Excel.
3. Click Browse and navigate to the folder containing the data files for this lesson.
4. Select **A05Trydata**, and click Open.

   ✓ *The file's path and name appear in the File name box.*
5. Click Append a copy of the records to the table.
6. Make sure that Address Book is selected on the drop-down list.
7. Click OK.

(continued)

Try It! Importing Data into an Existing Table and Exporting Data *(continued)*

8 Click Next.

9 Click Next.

10 Click Finish.

11 Click Close and open the Address Book table to view the imported data.

12 With the Address table still open, on the EXTERNAL DATA tab, Export Group, click PDF or XPS.

13 Save the file as **A05TryPDF_xx**.

14 Click Publish.

15 Close the PDF file, and close the Save Export Steps dialog box.

16 Leave the **A05Try_xx** database open to use in the next Try It.

Choose which table to append the records to

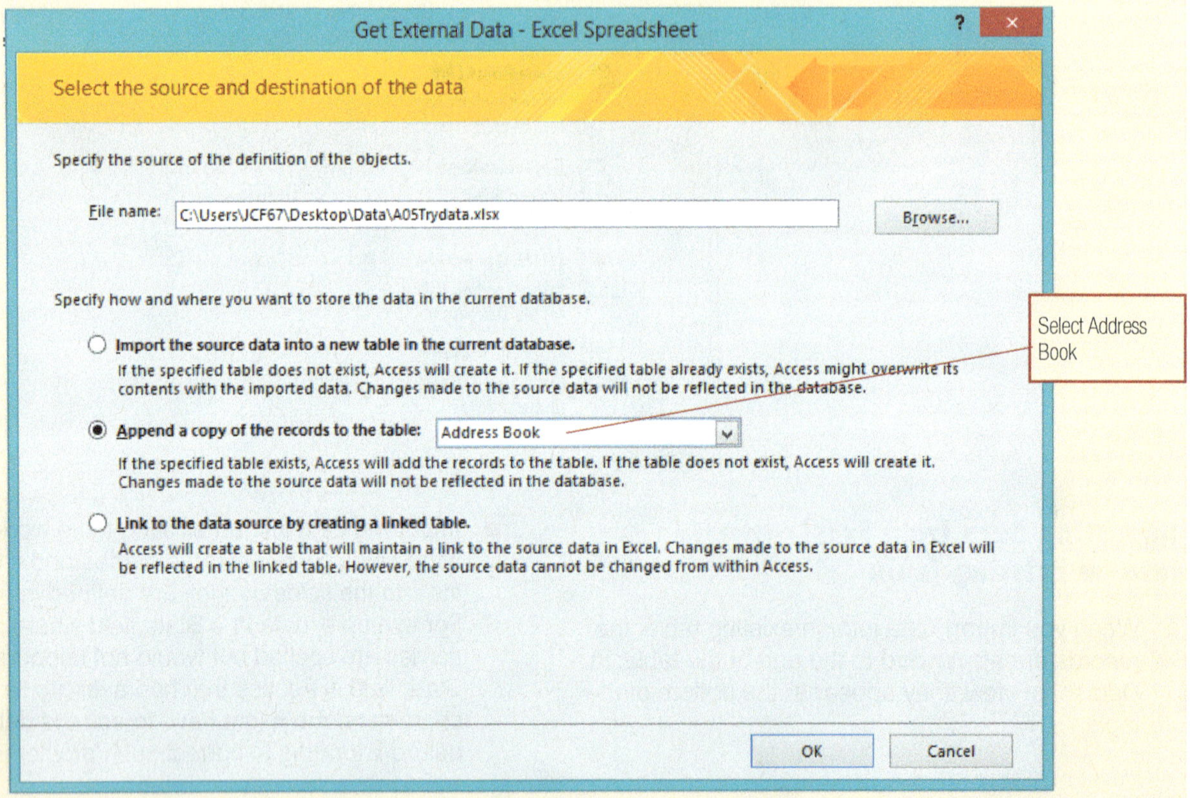

Access 2013, Windows 8, Microsoft Corporation

Importing Data from Excel into a New Table

- When importing data that does not fit in any of the existing tables, you can import it into a new table created on-the-spot. You do not have to create the new table beforehand.
- As part of the import process, you have the opportunity to set the fields' data types.
- You can also exclude certain fields from the import if desired.
- The imported table can be linked to the original source data table, by importing a linked table.
- Changes made to the source data table will appear in the linked Access table, but changes cannot be made to the table from Access.
- If you are importing more than one table, each table must be imported separately.

Try It! Importing Data into a New Table

1. In the **A05Try_xx** database, on the EXTERNAL DATA tab, in the Import & Link group, click Excel.
2. Click Browse and navigate to the folder containing the data files for this lesson.
3. Select the Excel file **A05Trydata_1** and click Open.

   ✓ *The file's path and name appear in the File name box.*
4. Make sure that the Import the source data into a new table in the current database option is selected. Click OK.
5. Click Sheet2.
6. Click Next.
7. Be sure that the First Row Contains Column Headings check box is selected. Click Next.
8. Click the Customer field to select it.
9. Open the Data Type list and click Integer.
10. Click the Salesperson field to select it.
11. Mark the Do not import field (Skip) check box.
12. Click Next.
13. Click Choose my own primary key.

    ✓ *The Order ID field is selected by default in the drop-down list box.*
14. Click Next. In the Import to Table text box, type **Orders**, replacing the default name (Sheet2).
15. Click Finish.
16. Click Close.
17. In the Navigation pane, double-click the Orders table to view it. Right-click the Orders tab and click Close.
18. Leave the **A05Try_xx** database open to use in the next Try It.

Select the worksheet to import

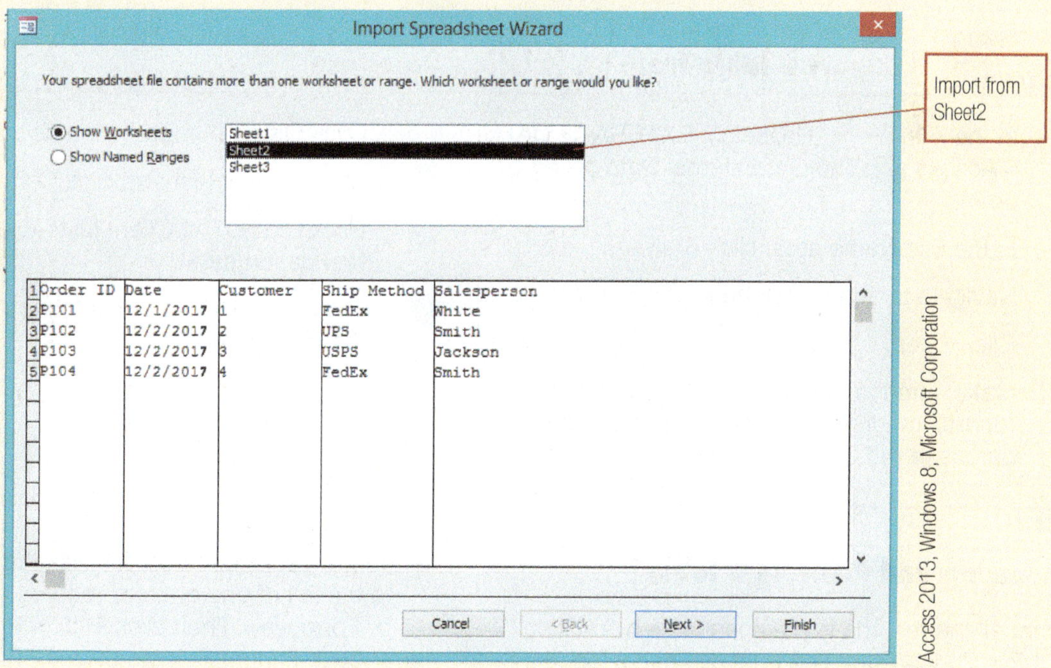

Access 2013, Windows 8, Microsoft Corporation

Try It! Importing a Linked Table

1. In the **A05Try_xx** database, click the EXTERNAL DATA tab.
2. In the Import & Link group, click Excel.
3. Click Browse and navigate to the folder containing the data files for this lesson.
4. Select **ATry05data_1**, and click Open.

   ✓ *The file's path and name appear in the File name box.*
5. Click Link to the data source by creating a linked table.

   ✓ *A table with a link to the source data in the Excel document will be created.*
6. Click OK.
7. Click Next.
8. Click Next.
9. In the Linked Table Name field, type **Excel Address Book**.
10. Click Finish.
11. Click OK. Open the Excel Address Book to view it.

    ✓ *Changes made to the source Excel document will appear in the linked Access table, but changes cannot be made from within Access.*
12. Leave the **A05Try_xx** database open to use in the next Try It.

Importing a Table from an Existing Database

- Tables can be imported from one existing database into another.

Try It! Import a Table from an Existing Database

1. In the **A05Try_xx** file, select EXTERNAL DATA > Access. The Get External Data dialog box opens.
2. In the File Name area, click Browse.
3. Navigate to and select the **A05Trydata_2** file.
4. Click Open.
5. Make sure the Import tables, queries, forms, reports, macros, and modules into the current database radio button is selected.
6. Click OK. The Import Objects dialog box opens.
7. Select Client List and click OK.
8. Click Close. The Client List table is added to the Navigation pane.
9. Leave the **A05Try_xx** database open to use in the next Try It.

Previewing and Printing a Table

- Print all the records in the open table by clicking FILE > Print > Print. The Print dialog box appears. From here you can set the printer, the print range, the number of copies, and more.

  ✓ *To print only certain records, select them before printing.*
- The Name drop-down arrow in the Print dialog box enables you to choose a different printer.
- To print selected records, click the record selector to the left of one or more records in Datasheet or Form view. Then click FILE > Print > Print and choose to print Selected Record(s) in the Print dialog box.
- If desired, type more than 1 in the Number of Copies box, and then check **Collate** if you want to print the document in a complete set; or leave Collate unchecked if you want to print multiple copies of page 1, then page 2, and so on.

- Click FILE > Print > **Print Preview** to see a screen preview of what your printing will look like.
- The page orientation can be changed from Portrait to Landscape, in the Page Layout group.
- Multiple pages can be viewed in Print Preview. To view two pages at once, in the Zoom group, click Two Pages. To view more pages, click the More Pages drop-down list and select the appropriate number of pages to view.
- While in Print Preview, click the Zoom button to toggle between zooming in and zooming out. You can also click the arrow below the Zoom button for a menu with more zoom options.
- The Navigation buttons at the bottom of the screen in Print Preview enable you to see the first, previous, specific, next, or last page.
- To print without changing the print settings, click FILE > Print > Quick Print. The database is sent directly to the default printer.
- To perform a print without changing the print settings, click the FILE tab > Print > Quick Print. The database is sent directly to the default printer.

Try It! Previewing a Table

1. In the **A05Try_xx** database, open the Address Book table in Datasheet view.
2. Click FILE > Print, and then click Print Preview.
3. Click the preview of the page to zoom in.

   ✓ *You may need to scroll to view the data on the page after zooming.*
4. Click the preview of the page again to zoom out.
5. Click the Next Page arrow at the bottom of the screen to view the second page.
6. On the PRINT PREVIEW tab, in the Page Layout group, click Landscape to preview the page in Landscape orientation.
7. Click Portrait to return to Portrait orientation.
8. In the Zoom group, click Two Pages to see two pages at a time.
9. Click One Page to return to single-page view.
10. Click Close Print Preview.
11. Leave the **A05Try_xx** database open to use in the next Try It.

Try It! Printing a Table

1. In the **A05Try_xx** database, open the Address Book table in Datasheet view if it is not already open.
2. Click FILE > Print, and then click Print.
3. In the Print dialog box, click the Pages option button.
4. In the From box, type **1**.
5. In the To box, type **1**.
6. **With your teacher's permission**, click OK to print the table; otherwise, click Cancel.
7. Click FILE > Close to exit the database.

Opening a Database Exclusively

- To set a database password, you have to open the database in **exclusive mode** (no one else can be working in the database). Open Exclusive is most often used to ensure that only one user at a time is trying to change the design of database objects.
- In the Open dialog box, click the down arrow on the Open button and select Open Exclusive.

Try It! Opening a Database Exclusively

1. Click FILE > Open. Navigate to the location where you have been storing the files for this lesson.
2. Click **A05Try_xx**.
3. Click the down arrow on the Open button.
4. Click Open Exclusive.
5. Leave the **A05Try_xx** database open to use in the next Try It.

Open the file exclusively

Access 2013, Windows 8, Microsoft Corporation

Setting a Database Password

- Password-protecting a database prevents others who do not know the password from using the database. Password-protecting in Office applications is also called **encrypting**.
- When you set a password, you must type the password again to verify accuracy. The password does not show when you type; asterisks are displayed instead. Note that passwords are case-sensitive.
- You have to type the password again when you want to remove the password. If you forget your password, you will not be able to open the database.

Try It! Setting a Database Password

1. Click FILE > Info, and then click Encrypt with Password. The Set Database Password dialog box opens.
2. Type **secure** in the Password box. Then, retype the password in the Verify box.
3. Click OK.
4. If a warning appears about row-level locking, click OK.
5. Click FILE > Close.

Set a database password

Access 2013, Windows 8, Microsoft Corporation

Try It! Opening a Password-Protected Database

1. Open **A05Try_xx** exclusively.
2. In the Enter database password dialog box, type **secure**.
3. Click OK.
4. Leave the **A05Try_xx** database open to use in the next Try It.

Try It! Removing the Password from a Database

1. Click FILE > Info, and then click Decrypt Database. Type **secure** in the Unset Database Password dialog box.
2. Click OK.
3. Leave the **A05Try_xx** database open to use in the next Try It.

Changing Database Properties

- Database properties can help others identify a file when it is stored on a file server, and they can help you remember why you created a database and what data it holds.
- Database properties include Title, Subject, Author, Manager, Company, Category, Keywords, Comments, and so on. You can also create custom properties to store information specific to your situation.

Try It! Changing Database Properties

1. In **A05Try_xx**, click FILE > Info > View and edit database properties. A Properties dialog box appears.
2. On the Summary tab, in the Title box, change the text to **Try It Lesson 5**.
3. In the Author box, replace the name with your name.
4. In the Keywords box, type **Lessons**.
5. Click the Custom tab.
6. On the Name list, click Editor.
7. In the Value box, type **Joe Smith**.
8. Click Add.
9. Click OK.
10. Leave the **A05Try_xx** database open to use in the next Try It.

Compact & Repair a Database

- Compacting and repairing a database gets rid of unused space, makes the file easier to share, and improves the performance of the database.

  ✓ *The Compact & Repair Database process is not available for Access apps.*

- Before running the Compact & Repair Database process, make sure the database is backed up.
- The Compact & Repair Database process can be set to run automatically when a database closes.

  ✓ *Setting a Compact & Repair Database process to run automatically is not recommended for multi-user databases, as it can disrupt database availability.*

Try It! Compact & Repair a Database

1. In **A05Try_xx**, click FILE > Info > Compact & Repair Database.
2. Click the Close button × to exit Access.

Lesson 5—Practice

You have received additional data for your friend's jewelry business database and now you need to incorporate it into the database file in Access and print it.

DIRECTIONS

1. Start Access, if necessary.
2. Open **A05Practice** from the data files for this lesson.
3. Save the database as **A05Practice_xx** to the location where your teacher instructs you to store the files for this lesson.

   ✓ *If a security warning bar appears, click Enable Content.*
4. Click **FILE** > **Info** and then click **View and edit database properties**.
5. In the Title box, change the entry to **Jewelry Database**, as shown in Figure 5-2.
6. In the Author box, change the entry to your full name.
7. Click **OK**.

Figure 5-2

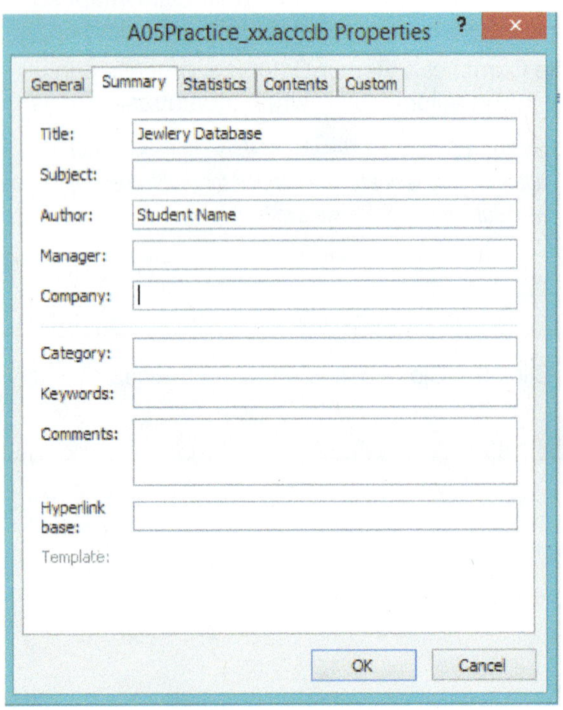

Access 2013, Windows 8, Microsoft Corporation

8. On the Ribbon, click the **EXTERNAL DATA** tab; in the Import & Link group, click **Excel**.
9. Click **Browse**.
10. Navigate to the folder containing the data files for this lesson, and select **A05Practicedata.xlsx**. Then, click **Open**.
11. Click **Append a copy of the records to the table**.
12. Open the drop-down list and select **Products**.
13. Click **OK**. The Import Spreadsheet Wizard opens.
14. Click **Next**.
15. Click **Finish**.
16. Click **Close**.
17. Open the **Products** table in Datasheet view.
18. **If your teacher has instructed you to submit a printout as part of this assignment**, do the following:
    a. Click **FILE** > **Print**, and then click **Print**.
    b. Click **OK**.
19. Click **FILE** > **Close**. If instructed, submit this database to your teacher for grading.

Lesson 5—Apply

You have received additional data for your friend's jewelry business database and now you need to incorporate it into the database file in Access. You also need to print a copy of the Shippers table and password-protect the database file.

DIRECTIONS

1. Start Access, if necessary.
2. Open **A05Apply** from the data files for this lesson.
3. Save the database as **A05Apply_xx** to the location where your teacher instructs you to store the files for this lesson.

   ✓ *If a security warning bar appears, click Enable Content.*
4. Import data without linking from **A05Applydata.xlsx** into two new tables: **Shippers** and **Salespeople**. Pull data from the sheets with the same names in the data file. Include first row column headings. Do not create primary key fields for either table.

   ✓ *Remember that if you are importing more than one table, each table must be imported separately*
5. Close the database, and then reopen it exlusively.
6. Set a password for the database: **admin**.
7. Open the **Shippers** table in Datasheet view and, **with your teacher's permission**, print one copy of it. Write your name on the printout if your teacher wants you to submit it for grading.
8. In the database's Properties box, add a Manager: **Molly Kashon**.
9. Click **FILE** > **Info** > **Compact & Repair Database**.
10. Click **FILE** > **Close**. If instructed, submit this database to your teacher for grading.

Lesson 6

Using Table Templates and Design View

➤ What You Will Learn

Creating a New Database Using a Template
Changing the View of the Navigation Pane
Creating Objects with Application Parts
Opening a Table in Design View
Creating a Table in Design View
Setting a Primary Key in Design View
Managing the Field List in Design View
Changing a Field's Data Type in Design View
Modifying Table and Field Properties

WORDS TO KNOW

Application Parts
Access templates that can be used to create database objects such as tables, forms, or reports.

Caption
Alternate text that appears instead of a field's actual name in tables, forms, and reports.

Composite key
Two or more fields that collectively define the primary key by unique combinations of their values.

Field description
An optional brief comment or explanation of a field. The field description appears in the status bar at the bottom of the window when the field is selected.

Field properties
Characteristics of a field.

Field selector
In Table Design view, the gray rectangle to the left of the field name. Click it to select that field; drag it up or down to move the field in the field list.

Software Skills Access provides a number of database templates that you can use to jumpstart project design. These templates include multiple tables with relationships already established between them in some cases. You can also create tables on your own in Design view, where you have access to a full range of property settings, not just the abbreviated set that is available in Datasheet view.

What You Can Do

Creating a New Database Using a Template

- If the database you plan to create is for some common purpose, such as to store information about events or projects, you may find it easier to use a **template** than to build the database from scratch. The fields in these templates are predefined and formatted appropriately for the data they hold.
- Some templates come preinstalled with Access, and many others are available via Office Online.
- A template creates a ready-to-use database that contains tables, forms, reports, and other Access objects that you might need for that type of database.

Try It! Creating a New Database Using a Template

1. Start Access. The Welcome screen appears with new document options.
   - ✓ *If Access is already open, click FILE > New.*
2. In the Search for online templates search box, type **Events** and click the Start searching icon.
   - ✓ *You will need Internet access to complete this activity. If you do not have Internet access, then use the **A06Try_Template** file for the next Try It. Save the template as **A06Try_xx**.*
3. Click Desktop event management.
4. In the File Name box, type **A06Try_xx**.
5. Click the Browse icon to the right of the box. Navigate to the location where your teacher instructs you to save this file. Click OK.
6. Click Create.
   - ✓ *Click Enable Content, if necessary.*
7. Leave the **A06Try_xx** database open to use in the next Try It.

Create a database with a template

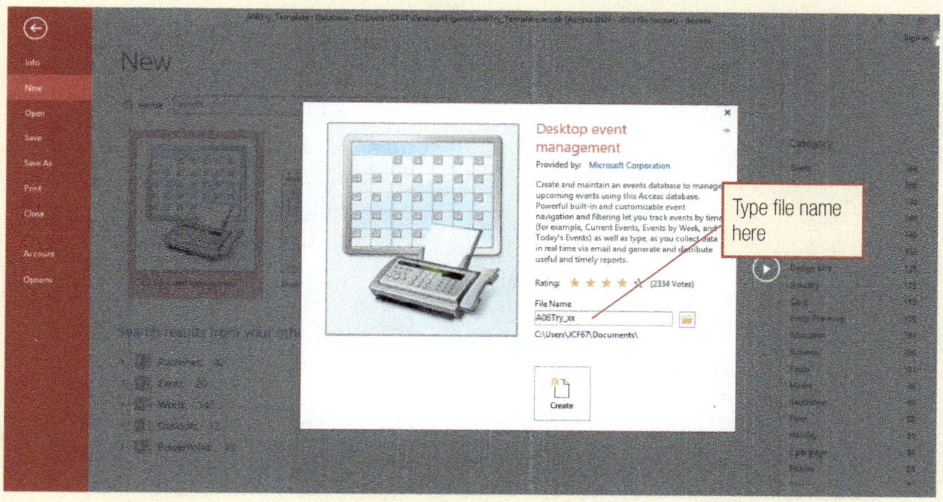

Access 2013, Windows 8, Microsoft Corporation

Primary key
The field that uniquely identifies each record in a table.

Table Design view
A view in which you can add, edit, and delete fields from a table; change data types and descriptions; set a primary key; and more.

Template
A database that contains formatting, styles, and sample text that you can use to create new databases.

Changing the View of the Navigation Pane

- Some templates default to a different arrangement of objects in the Navigation pane than you may be used to; you can change the view from the drop-down menu on the Navigation pane header bar.

Try It! Changing the View of the Navigation Pane

1. In the **A06Try_xx** database, if necessary, click the Navigation pane bar to display it.
2. Click the Supporting Objects heading to expand the list of objects.

Select a view of the Navigation pane

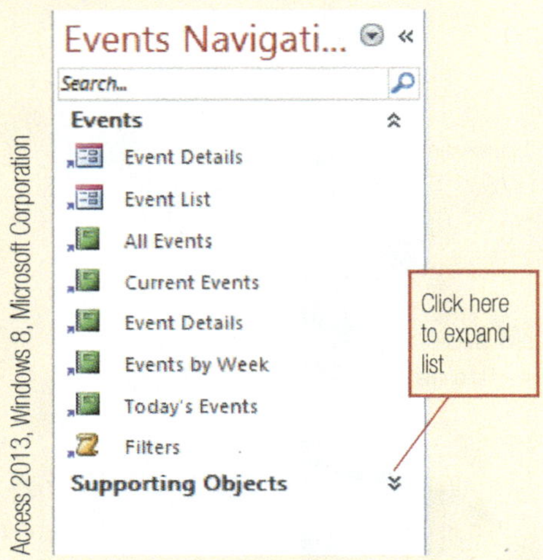

3. Click the down arrow button at the top of the pane.
4. Click Object Type. The Navigation pane changes to show objects grouped by type.
5. Leave the **A06Try_xx** database open to use in the next Try It.

The objects are now grouped by type

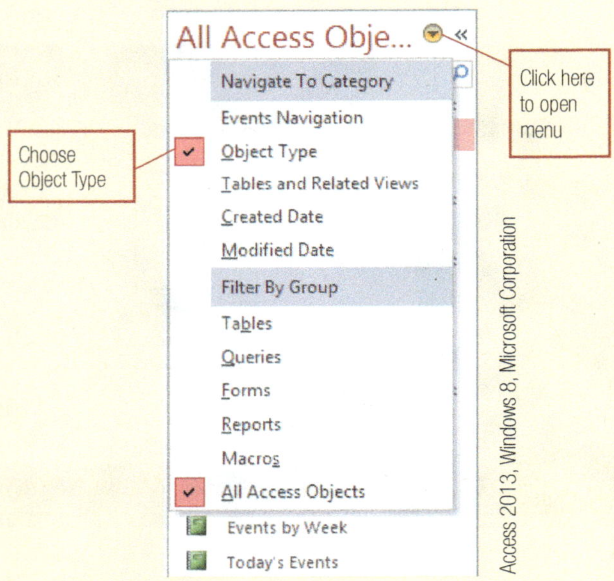

Creating Objects with Application Parts

- **Application Parts** are Access templates that can be used to create database objects such as tables, forms, or reports. Using Applications Parts simplifies adding common components across databases. You can also save your database as Application Parts.
- When you create a table based on a template, you also have the option of creating relationships between the new table and the existing ones in the database.

✓ *You will learn about relationships in Chapter 2, Lesson 8.*

Try It! Creating Objects with Application Parts

1. In the **A06Try_xx** database, click the CREATE tab. Click Application Parts and then click Tasks.
2. If prompted to close all open objects, click Yes.
3. In the Create Relationship dialog box, click There is no relationship.
4. Click Create. The new table appears on the Tables list in the Navigation pane.
5. Double-click the Tasks table to open it. Examine its fields.
6. Leave the **A06Try_xx** database open to use in the next Try It.

Create a table based on the Tasks table template

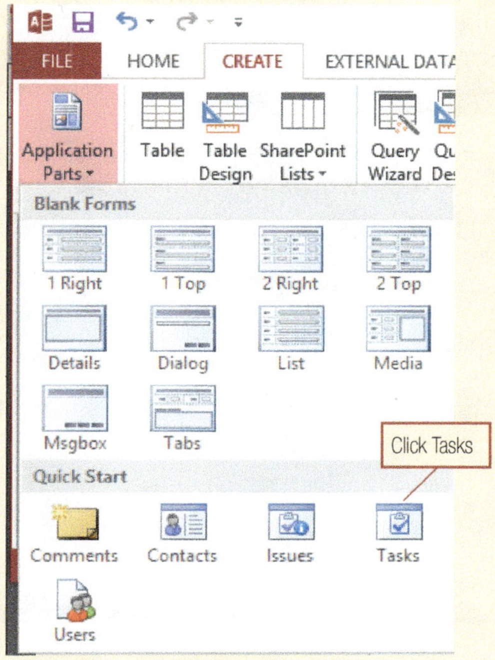

Access 2013, Windows 8, Microsoft Corporation

Opening a Table in Design View

- You can make changes to a table's structure in **Table Design view**.
- The table fields and their data types are listed in the top part of the Design view window.
- The properties for the selected field are shown in the bottom part of the Design view window.

Try It! Opening a Table in Design View

1. In the **A06Try_xx** database, right-click the Tasks table tab.
2. Click Design View.
3. Click the TaskTitle field, as illustrated in the figure on the next page, and examine the properties for that field.
4. Click the StartDate field, and examine the field properties for it.
5. Right-click the Tasks table tab, and click Close to close the table.
6. Leave the **A06Try_xx** database open to use in the next Try It.

(continued)

Try It! Opening a Table in Design View *(continued)*

Click the TaskTitle field

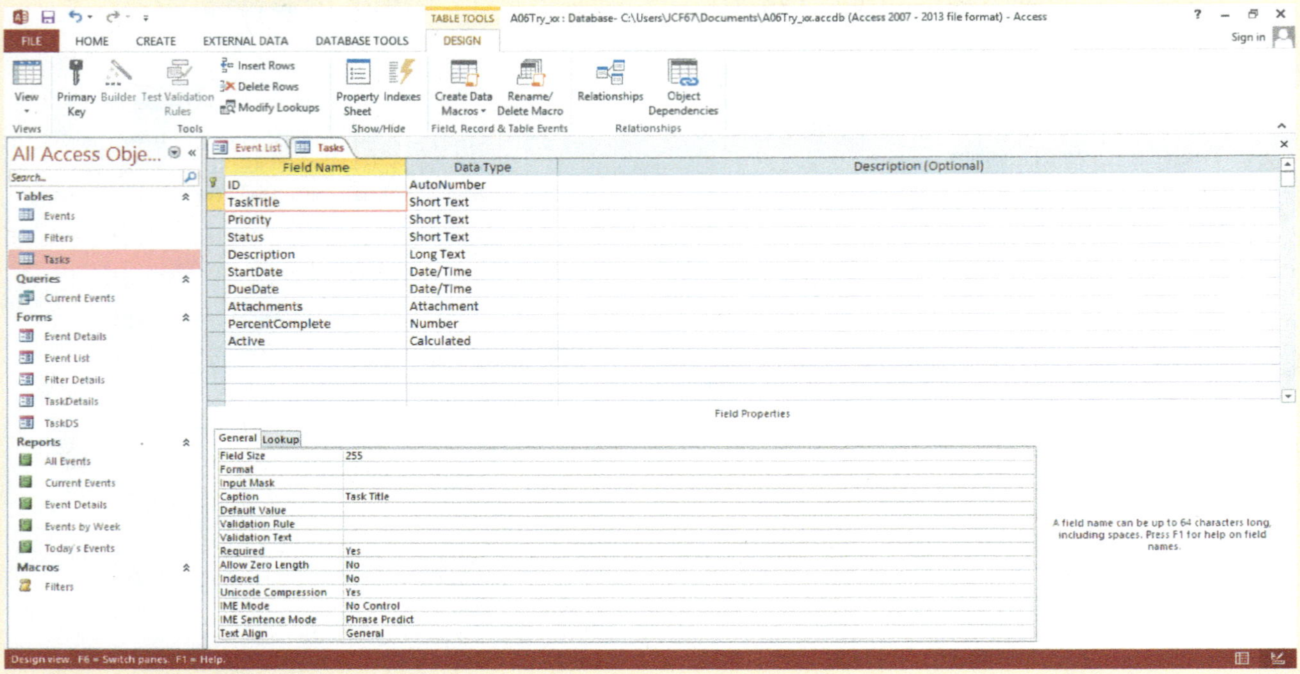

Access 2013, Windows 8, Microsoft Corporation

Creating a Table in Design View

- To start a new table using Design view, click the CREATE tab. In the Tables group, click Table Design.
- Enter the field names in the Field Name field. Although you may use up to 64 characters, you should keep the name short.
- In the Data Type field, you identify what kind of information the field will store. Click the drop-down arrow to choose from the list of data types. You can also type the first letter of the data type to select it.
- The **field description** is optional. In the Description (Optional) cell, you can enter comments or hints about the intended use or limitations of the field. The text you type for the field description will appear on the status bar when the user is in this field on a form.

Try It! Creating a Table in Design View

1. In the **A06Try_xx** database, on the CREATE tab in the Tables group, click Table Design.
2. In the Field Name field, type **LocID** and press TAB.
3. Open the Data Type drop-down list, choose AutoNumber, and then press TAB.

✓ *Instead of choosing from the list, you can type the first letter of the data type option to select it.*

4. In the Description (Optional) field, type **Automatically assigned** and press TAB.
5. In the next row, type **Location** in the Field Name field and press TAB.

(continued)

Try It! Creating a Table in Design View *(continued)*

6. Press TAB to accept the default data type (Short Text).
7. Press TAB to skip the Description (Optional) field.
8. In the next row, type **Capacity** in the Field Name field and press TAB.
9. Open the Data Type drop-down list, choose Number, and then press TAB.
10. Type **Number of people** in the Description (Optional) field.
11. Click the Save button on the Quick Access Toolbar.
12. In the Save As dialog box, type **Locations**.
13. Click OK.

    ✓ *A warning appears that there is no primary key.*
14. Click No.
15. In the Navigation pane, double-click the **Locations** table to view the new information.
16. Right-click the **Locations** tab and click close to close the database.
17. Leave the **A06Try_xx** database open to use in the next Try It.

Enter the fields for the table

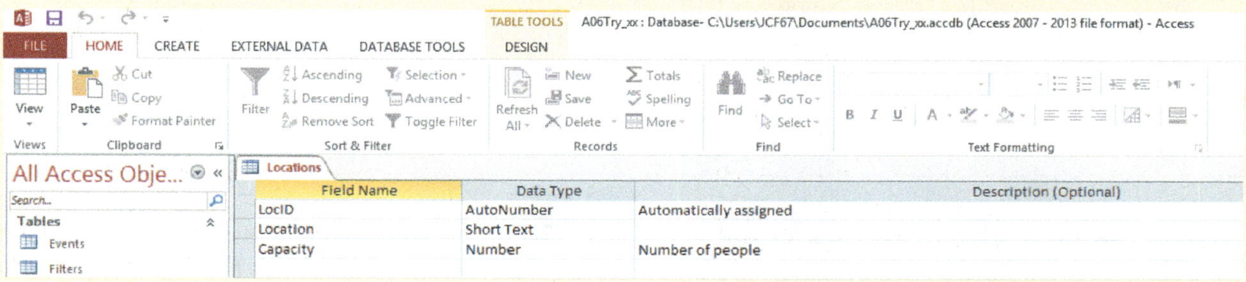

Access 2013, Windows 8, Microsoft Corporation

Setting a Primary Key in Design View

- As explained in Lesson 1, a table can have a **primary key** field that contains unique data for each record. The primary key field helps avoid duplicate records in a table.
- For the primary key field, choose a field that will be unique for each record. FirstName and LastName are not good choices for the primary key because different records could have the same value. For an employee database, the primary key could be the employee's Social Security number, for example. You could also create an ID field to be the primary key field, as in the previous Try It (the LocID field).
- In Design view, you can choose an existing field to be your primary key by selecting it and then clicking the Primary Key button. A key symbol appears to the left of the primary key field.
- When you attempt to save a new table without choosing a primary key field, Access asks whether you want a primary key field to be created automatically. If you do so, the new field receives the name "ID".
- A **composite key** exists when two or more fields together form the primary key. For example, if you designate both FirstName and LastName as keys, no records can have the same combination of those two fields, but duplicates can occur in either of those fields individually. To create a composite key, select two or more fields and click Primary Key.

Try It! Setting a Primary Key

1. In the **A06Try_xx** database, with the Locations table open in Design view, click the LocID field.
2. On the TABLE TOOLS DESIGN tab, in the Tools group, click Primary Key 🔑. A key symbol appears to the left of that field.
3. Leave the **A06Try_xx** database open to use in the next Try It.

Select the primary key field

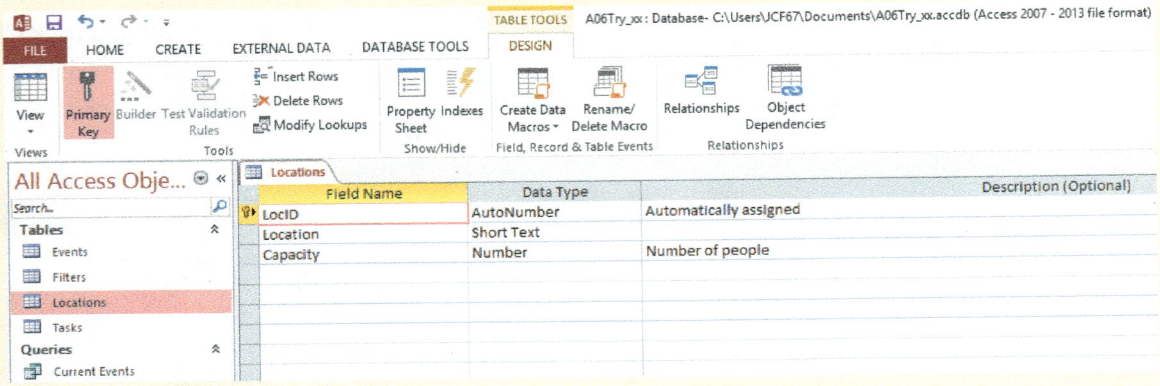

Access 2013, Windows 8, Microsoft Corporation

Managing the Field List in Design View

- You can add fields, delete fields, and reorder fields in Design view.
- To add a field at the bottom of the field list, type the field name into the next blank row.
- To add a field at some other position in the list, you can either insert a blank row using the Insert Rows command, or you can add the field to the bottom of the list and then reorder the list.
- Drag fields up or down on the list to reorder them. Drag a field by its **field selector** (the gray box to the left of the field name).

Try It! Managing the Field List in Design View

1. In the **A06Try_xx** database, with the Locations table open in Design view, click the Capacity field.
2. On the TABLE TOOLS DESIGN tab, in the Tools group, click Insert Rows.
3. In the new row, type **City** in the Field Name field, and press TAB.
4. Click in the first blank row in the Field Name field (after the Capacity field), type **State**, and press TAB.
5. Click the field selector to the left of the State field.
6. Holding the mouse button down, drag the field selector up until the black horizontal line appears below the City field; then release the mouse button.
7. Click the field selector for the City field.
8. On the TABLE TOOLS DESIGN tab, in the Tools group, click Delete Rows.
9. Leave the **A06Try_xx** database open to use in the next Try It.

Changing a Field's Data Type in Design View

- As you learned, a field's data type determines what can be stored in it.
- You can change any field's data format in Design view. Just select a different type from the drop-down list.
- The data types are described in the following table:
- You cannot change a field's type to AutoNumber; the AutoNumber type can be assigned only when the field is created. To configure a field's type to auto-increment in Design view, make sure the data type is AutoNumber. From the General tab, select the New Values drop-down and click Increment.

Data Type	Description
Short Text	Includes any characters up to a maximum of 255 characters (determined by field size). If the data includes a mix of numbers and any amount of letters, choose Short Text. Examples include name and address fields. The default data type is Short Text.
Long Text	Use this data type when Short Text is not large enough. Like Short Text, this data type can also have letters and numbers but can be much larger—up to 65,536 characters. Do not use Long Text unless you need that extra length, however, because you cannot perform certain actions (indexing, for example) on a Long Text field.
Number	Includes various forms of numerical data that can be used in calculations.
Date/Time	Date and time entries in formats showing date, time, or both.
Currency	Use for currency values with up to fifteen digits after the decimal place. This data type is more accurate for large numbers than the Number data type, but generally takes up more space.
AutoNumber	This is typically used to create an identification number for each record. The value for each record increases by one.
Yes/No	Only two possible values can be in this field. Options include Yes/No, True/False, or On/Off. The default style shows a check box with a ☑ for Yes or blank ☐ for No.
OLE Object	This data type enables you to place another file type into your record. Within the field, you can insert a picture (a company logo, for example), a Word document (employee resume), or an Excel spreadsheet (client summary chart).
Hyperlink	This allows you to insert a Web address that will launch when you click it in Datasheet view or on a form. You can also type a path and file name to a file on your hard drive or a network drive.
Attachment	Allows you to attach files from word processing programs, spreadsheets, graphics editing programs, and so on.
Calculated	A new data type available only in Access 2013. You can specify one or more other fields plus a math operation to derive the value of a calculated field.
Lookup Wizard	Creates a lookup field, which displays a list of values from which to choose when entering data.

Try It! Changing a Field's Data Type in Design View

1. In the **A06Try_xx** database, in the Field Name field, type **Rental** in the first empty row and press TAB.
2. In the Data Type field, open the drop-down list and choose Number.
3. Reopen the drop-down list and choose Currency.
4. Leave the **A06Try_xx** database open to use in the next Try It.

Modifying Table and Field Properties

- When a field is selected, its **field properties** appear in the lower half of the Design view window. Field properties specify settings for the field, such as maximum entry length and default value.
- Available properties vary by data type. For example, numeric data types have a Decimal Places property that text fields do not.
- In some cases, multiple data types have a property with the same name, but with different options available. For example, a numeric field has a Format property for which you can choose Currency, General Number, Fixed, and so on; a Yes/No field also has a Format property, with choices such as True/False and Yes/No.
- All data types have the **Caption** property. This property enables you to specify the text that appears in the field header in Datasheet view and also in forms and reports in which the field is inserted.
- Captions are useful when you want to use an abbreviated or cryptic name for the field but still make it look friendly in the forms, reports, and tables that the end-user interacts with. For example, you might have a field named UserFirstName, but on the tables and forms you want it to appear as First Name (with a space between the two words).
- The Field Size property for a text-based field defines the maximum number of characters it can contain.
- For a numeric field, choose a Field Size option on the drop-down list. The main reason to set a field size is to keep the database file as small as possible; choose the field size that uses the fewest bytes per entry and still stores what you want to store.
- The table below shows the most commonly used field sizes for numeric fields.

  ✓ *Use Long Integer for a numeric field that will have a relationship to an AutoNumber field in another table, because you probably do not know at the outset how big a database is going to get and how many records a table will end up containing.*

- Another commonly used field property is Default Value. This property enables you to set a default value, that appears automatically in each new record. This can save you data entry time. For example, if nearly all of your customers live in a certain state, you could set the Default Value of the State field to that state, eliminating the need to type the state name for each record.
- You add the default value by opening the table in Design view, and then entering a value in the Default Value property for the field.
- To add a table description, right-click the table name in the Navigation pane and click Table Properties. Enter a description.

Field Size	Decimal Places	Valid Range	Bytes Used per Record
Byte	No	0 to 255	1
Integer	No	–32,768 to 32,767	2
Long Integer	No	–2,147,483,648 to 2,147,483,647	4
Single	Yes	-3.4×10^{38} to 3.4×10^{38}	4
Double	Yes	-1.797×10^{308} to 1.797×10^{308}	8

Try It! Modifying a Field's Properties

1. In the **A06Try_xx** database, in the Locations table in Design view, select the LocID field.
2. In the Caption property, type **ID**.
3. Select the Capacity field.
4. Click in the Format property box, then click the down arrow to open the drop-down list and select General Number.
5. Select the Rental field.
6. In the Default Value property box, replace the existing value with **500**.
7. Click the Save button on the Quick Access Toolbar.
8. On the HOME tab, in the Views group, click View . The table appears in Datasheet view.
   - ✓ *Notice that the LocID field header appears as ID.*
   - ✓ *Notice that the Rental field contains $500.00 for the empty record.*
9. Click FILE > Close to exit the database.

Lesson 6—Practice

In this project, you will explore one of the templates that comes with Access and customize the field properties in Design view.

DIRECTIONS

1. Start Access. If Access is already running, click **FILE** > **New**.
2. In the Search for online templates field, type **Desktop sales pipeline**.
   - ✓ *You will need Internet access in order to complete this project. If you do not have Internet access, use the **A06Practice_Template** data file and save the file as **A06Practice_xx**.*
3. Click **Desktop Sales Pipeline**.
4. Click the **Browse** icon to the right of the File Name box.
5. Navigate to the location where your teacher instructs you to store the files for this lesson.
6. In the File name box, type **A06Practice_xx**.
7. Click **OK**.
8. Click **Create**.
9. Click **Enable Content**.
10. Display the Navigation pane. Click the **down arrow** button at the top of the Navigation pane.
11. Click **Object Type**.
12. On the CREATE tab, in the Templates group, click **Application Parts** and then click **Comments**.
13. Click **Yes** to close all open objects.
14. Click **There is no relationship**.
15. Click **Create**.
16. In the Navigation pane, right-click the **Comments** table and click **Design View**.
17. Click the **CommentDate** field.
18. On the TABLE TOOLS DESIGN tab, in the Tools group, click **Insert Rows** .
19. In the new row, type **EnteredBy** in the Field Name field, as shown in Figure 6-1 on the next page, and press TAB.
20. Click in the **Caption** box in the Field Properties area at the bottom of the window and type **By**, as shown in Figure 6-2 on the next page.
21. Click the **Save** button on the Quick Access Toolbar to save the changes to the table.
22. Click **FILE** > **Close** to close the database. If instructed, submit this database to your teacher for grading.

Figure 6-1

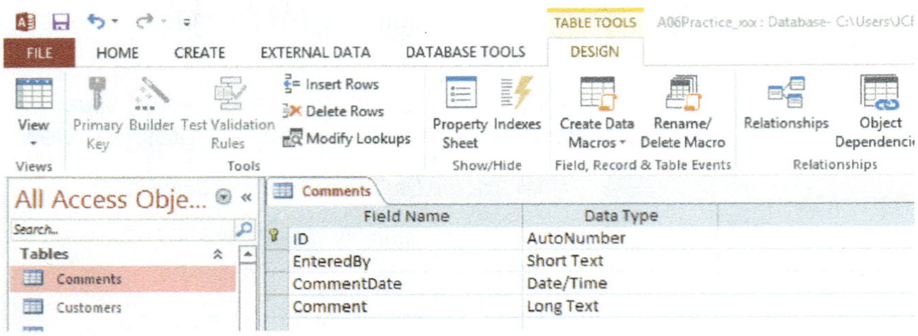

Access 2013, Windows 8, Microsoft Corporation

Figure 6-2

General | Lookup

Field Size	255
Format	
Input Mask	
Caption	By
Default Value	
Validation Rule	
Validation Text	
Required	No
Allow Zero Length	Yes
Indexed	No
Unicode Compression	Yes
IME Mode	No Control
IME Sentence Mode	None
Text Align	General

Access 2013, Windows 8, Microsoft Corporation

Lesson 6—Apply

In this project, you will return to the jewelry business database you have been working with to add more tables to it in Design view. You will set a primary key and customize field properties.

DIRECTIONS

1. Start Access, if necessary.
2. Open **A06Apply** from the data files for this lesson.
3. Save the database as **A06Apply_xx** in the location where your teacher instructs you to store the files for this lesson.

   ✓ *If a security warning bar appears, click Enable Content.*
4. Open the **Customers** table in Design view.
5. Change the **Field Size** property to **50** for the **First Name** and **Last Name** fields.
6. Save and close the **Customers** table. If you see a warning about data possibly being lost, click **Yes**.

   ✓ *The warning in step 6 is not important because there are currently no entries in either of those fields that exceed 50 characters.*
7. Open the **Shippers** table in Datasheet view, and edit the values in the **ID** field to remove the letters. For example, **S1** becomes **1**.
8. In the Navigation pane, right-click the **Shippers** table and click **Design View**. Change the data type for the **ID** field to **Number**.
9. Change the field size for the **ID** field to **Integer**.
10. Open the **Salespeople** table in Design view, and make **Employee ID** the primary key field.
11. Close all open tables, saving all changes to them.
12. Start a new table in Design view. Add the fields and properties shown in the following table. Save the table as **Orders**.
13. If necessary, set the **Order ID** field to be the primary key.
14. Save and close the table.
15. Click **FILE** > **Close** to close the database. If instructed, submit this database to your teacher for grading.

Field Name	Data Type	Description	Properties
Order ID	AutoNumber		
Order Date	Date/Time		Format = Short Date
Customer	Number	Numeric because it is related to the Customer ID field.	
Shipper	Number	Numeric because it is related to the Shipper ID field.	

Lesson 7

Creating Other Objects

➤ What You Will Learn

Using the Simple Query Wizard to Create a Query
Creating a Quick Form
Entering Records Using a Form
Creating and Modifying a Quick Report
Previewing and Printing a Report

Software Skills In addition to tables, you can create a variety of other objects in Access. These objects support and organize table data in a different way. This lesson shows you how to create a query, a form, and a report.

What You Can Do

Using the Simple Query Wizard to Create a Query

- A query is a set of rules that defines how a certain table (or group of tables) should be displayed onscreen (usually in a table).
- Queries are versatile. Here are some of the things a query can do:
  - Show only certain fields
  - Show only certain records
  - Combine the data from multiple tables
  - Create new calculated fields based on the data from other fields
  - Sort the records alphabetically or numerically based on one or more fields
  - Show summary statistics
- The Simple Query Wizard creates a basic query that shows only the fields you specify from the table or tables choice you select.

Try It! Creating a Simple Query

1. Start Access and open the file **A07Try** from the data files for this lesson. Save the file as **A07Try_xx**.

   ✓ *If a warning appears, click Enable Content.*

2. Click the CREATE tab, then click Query Wizard . The New Query dialog box opens.
3. Select Simple Query Wizard, and click OK.
4. Click the Tables/Queries drop-down arrow, and choose Table: Members.
5. Click the First field and click > .
6. Click the Last field and click > .
7. Click the Phone field and click > .
8. Click Next.
9. Type **Phone Listing** as the title for the query.
10. Click Finish. Access displays the query results.
11. Leave the **A07Try_xx** database open to use in the next Try It.

Select the fields to include in the query

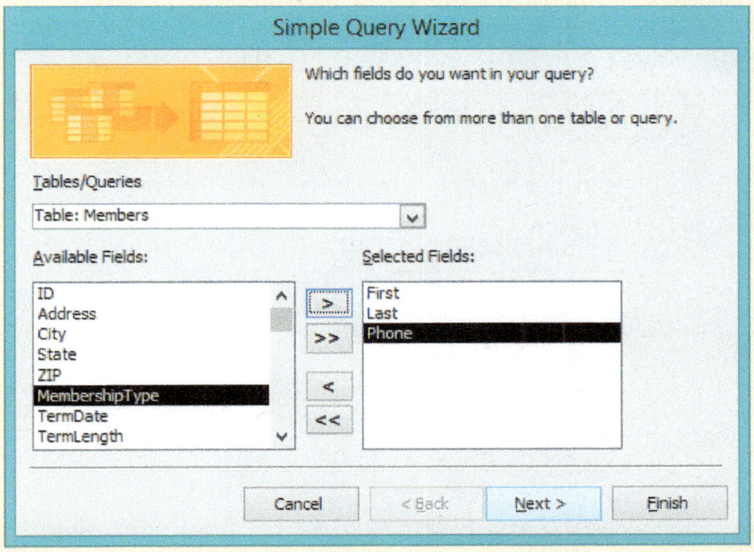

Access 2013, Windows 8, Microsoft Corporation

Creating a Quick Form

- A form provides an attractive interface to use for data entry and lookup. There are a number of ways to create forms, which you will learn more about in Chapter 3.
- The simplest type of form is a Quick Form. It is a basic form that uses all fields in the selected table and arranges them in a list.
- You can also create a multiple-items form to display multiple records in a table format.

Try It! Creating a Quick Form

1. In the **A07Try_xx** database, select the Classes table in the Navigation pane. (Don't open it, just click it once.)
2. On the CREATE tab, in the Forms group, click Form. The form appears.
3. Click the Save button on the Quick Access Toolbar. The Save As dialog box opens.
4. Type **Classes Form** in the Save As dialog box, and click OK to save it.

   ✓ *Including "Form" in the name differentiates the form from the table named Classes.*
5. Right-click the form's tab and click Close.
6. Leave the **A07Try_xx** database open to use in the next Try It.

A new form appears based on the Classes table

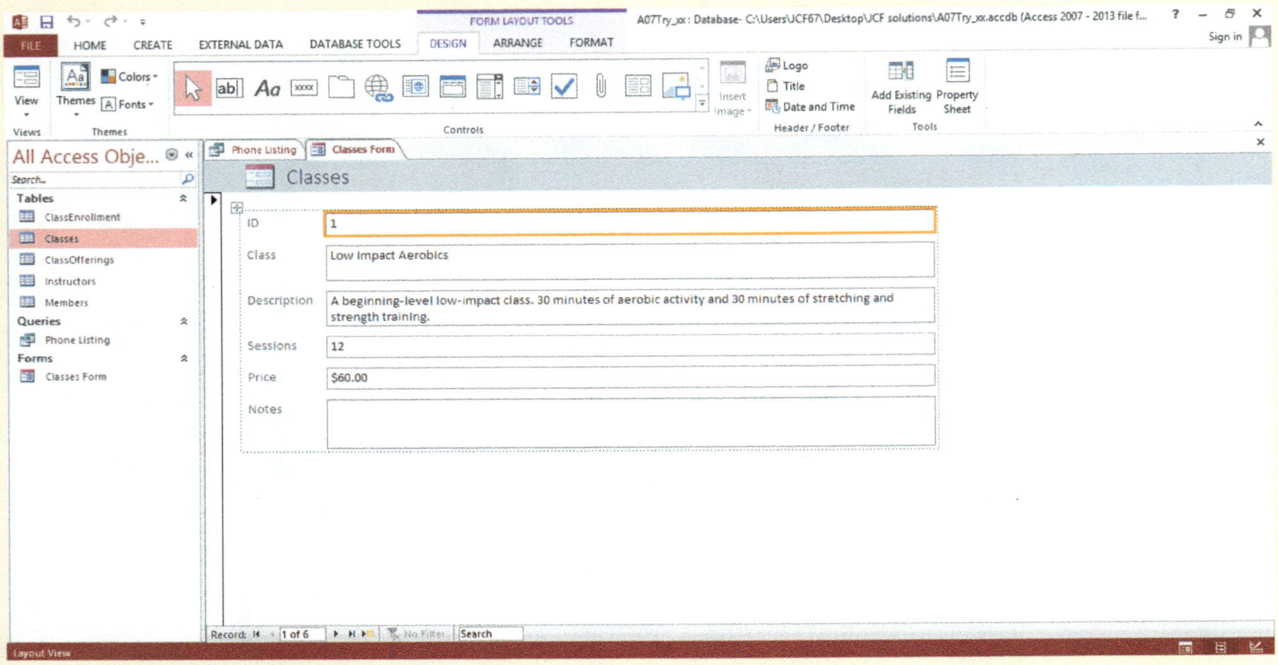

Access 2013, Windows 8, Microsoft Corporation

Try It! Creating a Multiple-Items Form

1. In **A07Try_xx**, select the Members table in the Navigation pane. (Don't open it, just click it once.)
2. On the CREATE tab, in the Forms group, click More Forms and then click Multiple Items. The form appears.
3. Click the Save button on the Quick Access Toolbar. The Save As dialog box opens.
4. Type **Members Form** in the Save As dialog box, and click OK to save it.
5. Right-click the form's tab and click Close.
6. Leave the **A07Try_xx** database open to use in the next Try It.

Entering Records Using a Form

- An advantage of a form over a table is that records are easier to review. For example, the Quick Form you created in the previous section shows one record at a time.
- When working with a form, navigation controls appear at the bottom. You can use them to move between records, and to clear the form so you can add a new record.
- Entering data in a multiple-items form works the same way as in a single-item form; move to the next field by pressing TAB.
- When you create a form, it opens in Layout view. Layout view enables you to see the form, complete with data, and make changes to the form's structure.
- You cannot enter records in Layout view; you must switch to Form view. Closing and reopening the form opens it in Form view. You can also click the View button to switch views.

Figure 7-1 This form shows one record at a time

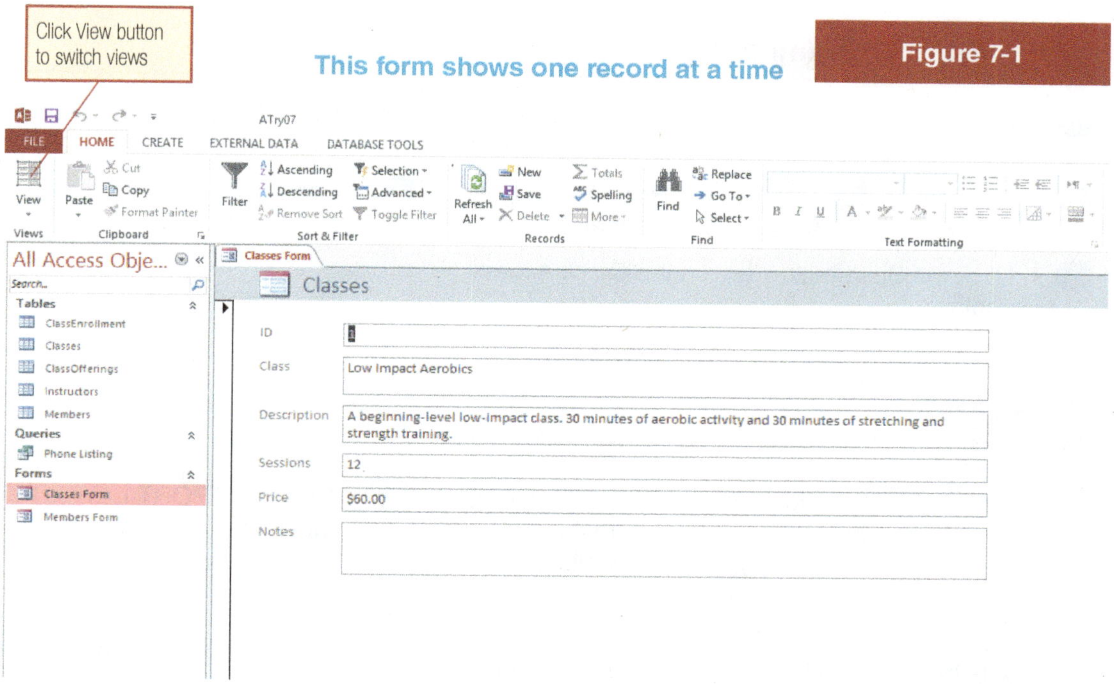

Access 2013, Windows 8, Microsoft Corporation

Try It! Entering Records in a Form

1. In the **A07Try_xx** database, double-click Classes Form in the Navigation pane to open the form in Form view.
2. On the HOME tab, in the Records group, click the New button.
3. Press TAB to move past the ID field.
4. In the Class field, type **Intro to Pilates**, and then press TAB.
5. In the Description field, type **Beginning-level Pilates workout. No previous experience required**. Then, press TAB.
6. In the Sessions field, type **8**, and then press TAB.
7. In the Price field, type **120.00**, and then press TAB.
8. In the navigation controls, click the First record button.
9. Close all open objects.
10. Leave the **A07Try_xx** database open to use in the next Try It.

Creating and Modifying a Quick Report

- A report is a view of a table or query that is designed to be printed. A report contains the same data as the table but is much more attractive and readable.
- After a report is created, it appears in Layout view by default. Layout view enables you to see the report, complete with data, and make changes to the report's structure.
- In Layout view, you can remove fields if they are not necessary. Select the field you want to remove and press DEL.

  ✓ *Editing a form or report does not affect the underlying source data.*
- You can also change the orientation from portrait to landscape, providing more room for fields.
- You can change the widths of the report fields. Drag the right edge of a field to the right or left.

Try It! Creating a Report

1. In the **A07Try_xx** database, select the Members table in the Navigation pane. (Do not open it.)
2. Click the CREATE tab. In the Reports group, click Report. A new report appears.
3. Click the Save button on the Quick Access Toolbar.
4. Click OK to save the report with the name **Members**.
5. Leave the **A07Try_xx** database open to use in the next Try It.

Try It! Deleting Fields from a Report Layout

1. In the **A07Try_xx** database, with the Members report open in Layout view, scroll to the right until the MembershipType field is visible, and click it.
2. On the REPORT LAYOUT TOOLS ARRANGE tab, in the Rows & Columns group, click Select Column.
3. Press DEL.
4. Click the Notes field.
5. On the REPORT LAYOUT TOOLS ARRANGE tab, in the Rows & Columns group, click Select Column.
6. Press DEL.
7. On the REPORT LAYOUT TOOLS PAGE SETUP tab, in the Page Layout group, click Landscape.
8. Leave the **A07Try_xx** database open to use in the next Try It.

Select and delete a field

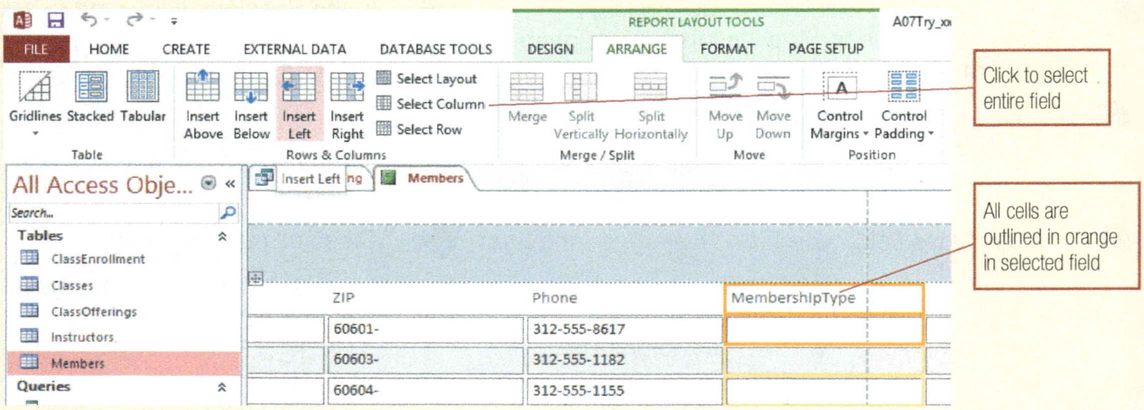

Access 2013, Windows 8, Microsoft Corporation

Try It! Changing Field Widths in a Report

1. In the A07Try_xx database, with the Members report open in Layout view, click any cell in the ID column and then position the mouse pointer over the right edge of the cell until it resembles a two-headed horizontal arrow.
2. Drag to the left until the ID field is as narrow as possible while not wrapping text to additional lines.

   ✓ *If the row height becomes taller, that means the field is too narrow, and the text in at least one row is wrapping. Increase the field width until the row height returns to normal.*
3. Select the First field, then position the mouse pointer over the right edge of any cell in the First field.
4. Drag to the left until the First column is as narrow as possible while not truncating any entries or the field header.
5. Repeat this process for each field in the report until all fields are as narrow as possible without truncating any entries.
6. Leave the A07Try_xx database open to use in the next Try It.

Previewing and Printing a Report

- After a report is created, it appears in Layout view. Layout view is useful for modifying the report's layout, but it does not show the report exactly as it will be printed. For example, it does not show the margins.
- Print Preview lets you see exactly how the report will look when printed. You also can adjust page setup options such as margins and page orientation in Print Preview.
- The navigation buttons at the bottom of the Print Preview window enable you to move from page to page within a report.
- In Print Preview, the mouse pointer appears as a magnifying glass. Click anywhere in the report display to toggle between a view of the whole page and the most recent zoom value. You can set the zoom value from the Zoom button's menu on the PRINT PREVIEW tab.

  ✓ *Report view is similar to Print Preview but designed for onscreen viewing. In Report view, you do not have the capability of zooming in and out on the content as you do in Print Preview. Report view is a more no-frills display method.*
- You can print a report from Print Preview (using the Print button).
- You can also print a report without entering Print Preview by using the FILE > Print > Print command. This opens the Print dialog box, which you learned about in Lesson 5.

Try It! Previewing and Printing a Report

1. In the A07Try_xx database, with the Members report still open, right-click its tab and click Print Preview.
2. On the PRINT PREVIEW tab, in the Page Size group, click Margins and click Normal. This changes the document margins.
3. Click the mouse anywhere on the report. It zooms in. Click again to zoom out.
4. On the PRINT PREVIEW tab, in the Print group, click Print. The Print dialog box opens.
5. **With your teacher's permission**, click OK to print your work; otherwise, click Cancel.
6. On the PRINT PREVIEW tab, click Close Print Preview.
7. With the Members report open, click FILE > Print > Print.
8. **With your teacher's permission**, click OK to print your work; otherwise, click Cancel.

(continued)

Try It! **Previewing and Printing a Report** *(continued)*

9. With the Members report open, click FILE > Print, and then, **with your teacher's permission**, click Quick Print.
10. Right-click the Members tab and click Close.
11. When prompted to save changes, click Yes.
12. Close the database file and exit Access.

Lesson 7—Practice

Now that the structure of the jewelry business database is complete, you will create a form and a report to show your friend examples of what Access can do.

DIRECTIONS

1. Start Access, if necessary.
2. Open **A07Practice** from the data files for this lesson.
3. Save the database as **A07Practice_xx** in the location where your teacher instructs you to store the files for this lesson.

   ✓ *If a security warning bar appears, click Enable Content.*
4. On the Navigation pane, click the **Products** table (do not open it).
5. On the **CREATE** tab, in the Reports group, click **Report**.
6. Click the **Save** button on the Quick Access Toolbar.
7. Type **Product Report** and click **OK**.
8. Right-click the report's tab and click **Close**.
9. On the Navigation pane, click the **Shippers** table (do not open it).
10. On the **CREATE** tab, click **Form**. A new form appears.
11. Click the **Save** button on the Quick Access Toolbar.
12. Type **Shippers Form** and click **OK**.
13. Right-click the form's tab and click **Form View**.
14. On the **HOME** tab, in the Records group, click **New**.
15. In the **Name** field, type **DHL** and press TAB.
16. In the **Account** field, type **D3857**.
17. Right-click the form's tab and click **Close**.
18. Click **FILE** > **Close** to close the database. If instructed, submit this database to your teacher for grading.

Lesson 7—Apply

To give your friend examples of how Access can help with her jewelry business database, you will create a query, a form, and a report.

DIRECTIONS

1. Start Access, if necessary.
2. Open **A07Apply** from the data files for this lesson.
3. Save the database as **A07Apply_xx** in the location where your teacher instructs you to store the files for this lesson.

   ✓ *If a security warning bar appears, click Enable Content.*
4. Use the Simple Query Wizard to create a query that uses the following fields from the **Customers** table:

   First Name

   Last Name

   Address

   City

   State

   ZIP

   Name the query **Customer Mailing Query**.
5. Create a report based on the **Customer Mailing Query**. Save the report as **Customer Mailing Report**.
6. Resize the fields in the report layout so that the entire report fits on one page. (Use Print Preview to check.)

   ✓ *The Page 1 of 1 box at the bottom of the page might be too wide, preventing the entire report from appearing on a single page. You can drag the box's right border to the left to narrow the box and make it fit on the page.*
7. **With your teacher's permission**, print the report and write your name on the printout.
8. Close the report, saving your changes to it.
9. Create a new form for the **Salespeople** table. Name it **Salespeople Form**.
10. Use the new form to enter the following salespeople into the database:

    Employee ID: **557-22-333**

    First: **Rosa**

    Last: **Gonzalez**

    Position: **Manager**

    Commission Rate: **7%**

    Employee ID: **441-22-571**

    First: **Pete**

    Last: **Sanchez**

    Position: **Assistant**

    Commission Rate: **4%**
11. Click **FILE** > **Close** to close the database. If instructed, submit this database to your teacher for grading.

End-of-Chapter Activities

➤ Access Chapter 1—Critical Thinking

Create a New Database

You are responsible for creating a new database for The BFF Travel Club, a group of friends who take vacations together. They will need to store data about members, destinations, and trips. In this exercise, you will design the structure of the database and start creating the tables for it.

DIRECTIONS

1. Write your name at the top of a blank sheet of paper.
2. Make two headings at the top of the paper: **Members** and **Trips**. Beneath each heading, list the fields to include in the table. Make sure that you:
   - Include a field in each table that will be unique for each record.
   - Include enough information about each member to be able to contact him or her in multiple ways in the **Members** table.
   - Think about what you would want to know about a trip if you were planning to go on it, and include fields that contain that information in the **Trips** table.
3. Start Access, and create a new blank database, saving it in the location where your teacher instructs you to store the files for this chapter. Name the file **ACT01_xx**.
4. Using any method you have learned so far, create the two tables, including the fields you have decided to include. Make sure each table has a primary key and uses the appropriate data types for each field.
5. Open the **Trips** table in Datasheet view.
6. Using the Internet, locate information about a guided tour of China that lasts at least seven days, and enter it into the **Trips** table. (If you don't have Internet access, then use other resources or fictional data.) If you find that you need different fields, make changes in Design view.
7. Open the **Members** table in Datasheet view, and enter your own name and contact information in it. If you find that you need different fields, make changes in Design view.
8. Create a form for the **Members** table, and name it **Members Form**.
9. Using the form, enter one other person (real or fictional) into the **Members** table.
10. Close the database, and reopen it exclusively.
11. Set a password of **trip** for the database.
12. Create a report from the **Members** table and name it **Members Report**. Set it in Landscape orientation, and tighten up the field widths as much as possible. **With your teacher's permission**, print one copy of the report, and write your name on the printout. Save and close the report.
13. Click **FILE** > **Close** to close the database. If instructed, submit this database for grading along with your handwritten worksheet from steps 1–2 and the printout from step 12 if you printed one.

➤ Access Chapter 1—Portfolio Builder

Create a New Database with a Template

Student organizations are an important part of any career and technology education course. You are responsible for creating a new Student Organization Database for Planting Senior High School. In this database, you will include the goals and objectives, opportunities, and benefits of each student organization.

DIRECTIONS

1. Start Access. Search for the **Desktop student database** template and select it. (If you do not have Internet access, use **APB_Template** from the data files.) Name the file **APB01_xx** and save it in the location where your teacher instructs you to store the files for this chapter. If necessary, click **Enable Content**.
2. This database includes a Getting Started pop-up window. Close this window and close the **Student List** form (which opens by default when you open the database).
3. Import the data from **APB01data.xlsx** into the **Students** table and append the records.
4. Open the **Students** table in Datasheet view, and widen the columns as needed so that all entries and field names are visible.
5. Freeze the **ID**, **Last Name**, and **First Name** fields.
6. Hide the **Insurance Carrier** and **Insurance Number** fields. Then, close the **Students** table.
7. Create a new table named **Student Organizations** and open it in Datasheet view. Enter the following records.

Organization	Goals and Objectives	Opportunities	Benefits
Finance Club	Learn to participate in the financial world.	Learn about the financial world first hand by working at local non-profit businesses.	Community service
The Government Association	Learn the different roles of the government.	Create a mock government and hold an election.	Student organization conferences/ competitions
Hospitality and Tourism Meetings	Understand the different aspects of working in the hospitality industry.	Learn the business from a local hospitality legend.	Lectures
Marketing Club	Learn the basic concepts and techniques of marketing.	Learn marketing from a philanthropic perspective, by working with a non-profit business.	Philanthropy
FFA (Future Farmers of America)	To unite members ranging from the individual farmer to larger corporations.	Provides programs, institutes, and community service.	Support and education on the opportunities found in agriculture

8. Adjust the field widths so you can read all of the information. **With your teacher's permission**, print the table, and write your name on the printout.
9. In the database's **Properties** box, set the title to **Student Organization Database** and change the author name to your full name.
10. Create a form based on the **Guardians** table, and name the form **Guardian Form**.
11. Create a report based on the **Student Organizations** table, and name it **Student Organizations Report**. Adjust the columns until they all fit on one page. **With your teacher's permission**, print one copy of the report and write your name on the printout. Compare this printout to the one from step 8 to see the difference between a report and a datasheet.
12. Close the database, and reopen it exclusively.
13. Assign a password of **attend** to the database.
14. Click **FILE** > **Close** to close the database. If instructed, submit this database to your teacher for grading along with your printouts if you were instructed to print.

Chapter 2

(Courtesy Konstantin Chagin/Shutterstock)

Working with Queries

Lesson 8
Managing Relationships Between Tables

- Renaming a Table
- Relating Tables
- Showing Additional Tables
- Enforcing Referential Integrity
- Deleting Relationships
- Showing Related Records
- Printing a Relationship Report

Lesson 9
Finding, Replacing, and Sorting Data

- Finding Data
- Replacing Data
- Searching with Wildcards
- Sorting Records in a Table
- Sorting Using Multiple Fields

Lesson 10
Filtering Data

- Filtering by Selection
- Filtering for Multiple Values
- Filtering by Form
- Saving Filter Results As a Query

Lesson 11
Creating a Query in Design View

- Understanding Data Analysis
- Exploring Data Mining Tools, Techniques, and Ethics
- Understanding Database Trends
- Understanding Queries
- Creating a New Select Query in Design View
- Running a Query
- Saving and Printing a Query

Lesson 12
Creating a Multi-Table Query

- Creating a Query Based on More Than One Table
- Sorting Query Results
- Reordering Fields in a Query
- Using All Fields of a Table
- Changing a Column Name
- Saving a Query with a Different Name

Lesson 13
Using Criteria in a Query

- Specifying Text Criteria in a Query
- Specifying Numeric Criteria in a Query
- Specifying Criteria Using a Field Not Displayed in the Query Results
- Using Null Criteria to Find Blank Fields
- Using Make Table and Append Query Types

Lesson 14
Using Comparison Operators

- Using Comparison Operators
- Using Wildcards and the Like Operator
- Using the Between...And Operator
- Using the In Operator
- Combining Criteria with AND or OR Operators

Lesson 15
Using Calculated Fields

- Understanding Calculated Fields
- Creating a Calculated Field in a Table
- Using Calculated Fields in a Query

Lesson 16
Summarizing Data in Queries

- Summarizing with the Simple Query Wizard
- Summarizing Data in Query Design View
- Using the Crosstab Query Type

End-of-Chapter Activities

Lesson 8

Managing Relationships Between Tables

➤ What You Will Learn

Renaming a Table
Relating Tables
Showing Additional Tables
Enforcing Referential Integrity
Deleting Relationships
Showing Related Records
Printing a Relationship Report

WORDS TO KNOW

Cascade delete
When a record in a parent table is deleted, Access deletes all the related records from the child table. Related records are those for which the value in the foreign key matches the value in the primary key.

Cascade update
When the primary key field is updated in a parent table, all corresponding foreign key values in the child table automatically update.

Child field
The related field from the child table of the relationship.

Child table
The second table of a relationship. This is generally the "many" side of the relationship. One record from the parent table (such as clients) can be related to one or more records of the child table (such as sales).

Software Skills In a multi-table database, relationships tie the tables together to form a cohesive database system. When you create relationships between tables, you associate a field in one table with an equivalent field in another. Then the two tables can be used in queries, forms, and reports together. In this lesson, you will learn how to create and manage the relationships between tables.

What You Can Do

Renaming a Table

- You can rename a table at any time. When you rename a table, all references to it in the database automatically change, too. For example, if you have a form and report based on the table, they automatically change to refer to the table by its new name.

Try It! Renaming a Table

1. Start Access, open **A08Try** from the data files for this lesson, and save it as **A08Try_xx**. Enable content if necessary any time you are prompted to do so.
2. In the Navigation pane, right-click the Members table and click Rename.
3. Type **Students** and press ENTER.
4. Leave the **A08Try_xx** database open to use in the next Try It.

Rename the table from the Navigation pane

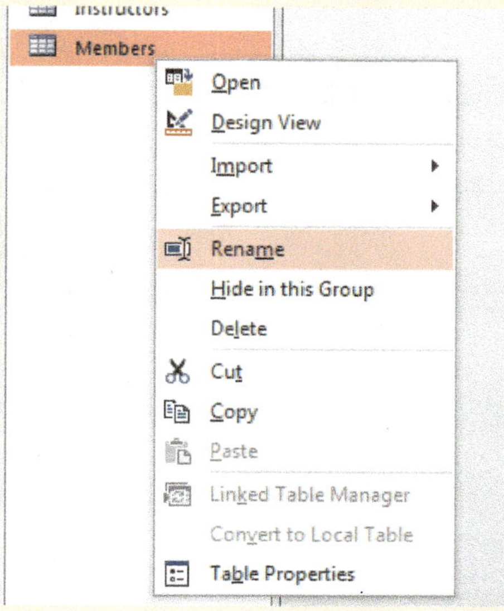

Access 2013, Windows 8, Microsoft Corporation

Relating Tables

- You can create a relationship between two tables that have the same field (or equivalents). It is not required that the field names be identical, but the fields must contain the same data.
- In most cases, the field is unique in one table (usually the primary key) but not unique in the other. This results in a **one-to-many relationship**.
- The related field in the second table is called the **foreign key**. To set a foreign key it must have the same data type as the related primary key, unless the primary key is an AutoNumber type. In that case, the foreign key field must be a Number type. In Figure 8-1, the foreign key is the Class field in the ClassOfferings table.
- The table containing the primary key field is the **parent table**. The primary key field is the "one" side of the relationship, indicated by a "1" in the Relationships grid. In Figure 8-1, the parent table is Classes.
- The table containing the foreign key field is the **child table**. The foreign key field is the "many" side of the relationship, indicated by an infinity sign (∞) in the Relationships grid. In Figure 8-1, the child table is ClassOfferings.

Access 2013, Windows 8, Microsoft Corporation

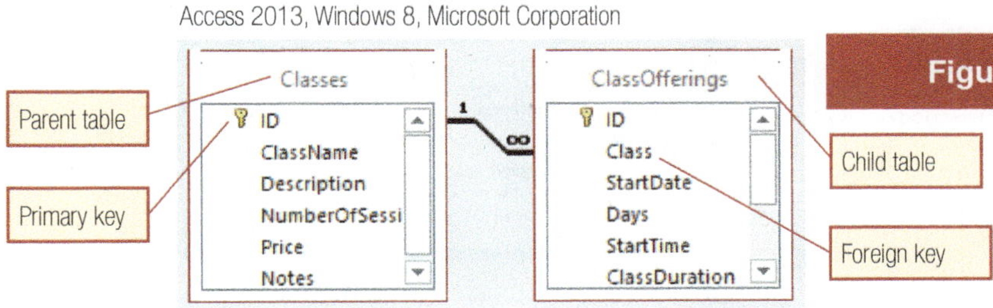

Figure 8-1

Foreign key
A field in the child table that is related to the primary key in the parent table.

Master field
The related field from the main (parent) table of the relationship.

One-to-many relationship
A relationship in which the value of the linked field in the parent table is different for each record, but the value of the linked field in the child table can be the same in multiple records.

Orphan
A value in the foreign key that does not have a corresponding primary key in the parent table.

Parent table
The main table of a relationship. This is the "one" side of the relationship and contains the primary key.

Referential integrity
A property of a relationship between two tables. When Referential Integrity is on, each foreign key value in the child table must have a corresponding primary key value in the parent table.

Subdatasheet
A child table related to the main (parent) table.

Try It! Relating Tables

1. In **A08Try_xx**, click the DATABASE TOOLS tab. In the Relationships group, click Relationships.
2. Drag the Classes table from the Navigation pane into the Relationships grid (the large blank space in the center).
3. Drag the ClassOfferings table into the Relationships grid.
4. Drag the ClassID field from the Classes table and drop it on the Class field in the ClassOfferings table. The Edit Relationships dialog box opens.
5. Click Create. A connector line appears between the two fields.

   ✓ *There is no 1 or infinity symbol (∞) on the line, as shown in Figure 8-1, because referential integrity was not enforced. You will learn about that in the next section.*

6. Leave the **A08Try_xx** database open to use in the next Try It.

Add ClassOfferings to the Relationships grid (step 3)

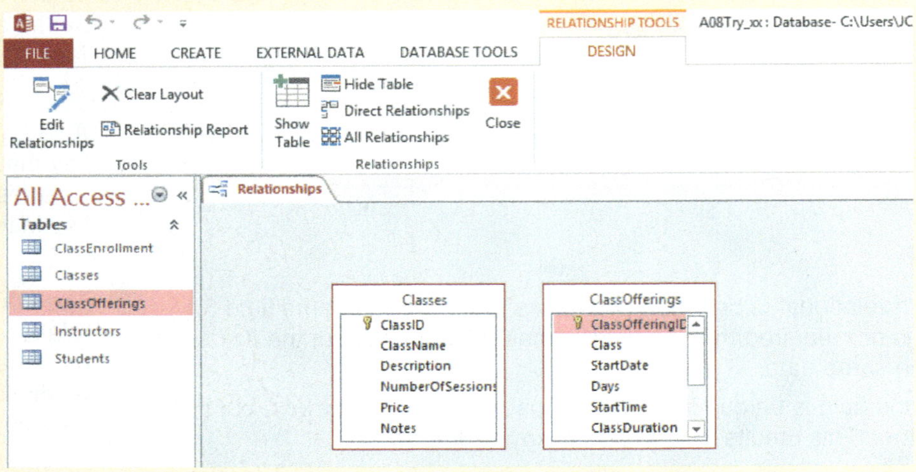

Access 2013, Windows 8, Microsoft Corporation

Create a relationship (step 4)

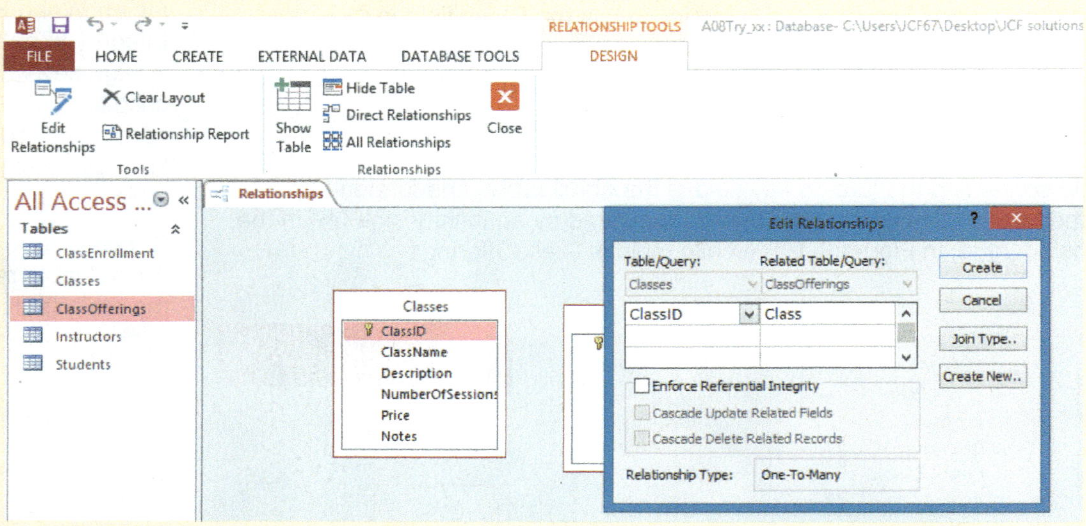

Access 2013, Windows 8, Microsoft Corporation

Showing Additional Tables

- There are two ways to add more tables to the Relationships grid. You can drag them from the Navigation pane, as you did in the preceding steps, or you can use the Show Table dialog box.

✓ *The Show Table dialog box may appear automatically the first time you open the Relationships tab. It did not in the preceding steps because the Relationships tab had already been previously displayed in that database before you opened it.*

Try It! Showing Additional Tables

1. In **A08Try_xx**, on the RELATIONSHIP TOOLS DESIGN tab, click Show Table. The Show Table dialog box opens.
2. Click Students.
3. Hold down the CTRL key and click ClassEnrollment.
4. Click Add. Those two tables appear on the Relationships grid.
5. Click Close.

   ✓ *In this database, relationships between the two tables you just added were already created. The relationships still existed even when the tables involved were not shown on the Relationships grid.*
6. Leave the **A08Try_xx** database open to use in the next Try It.

Enforcing Referential Integrity

- You can choose to Enforce **Referential Integrity** to prevent the creation of **orphan** records in the child table. For example, in a retail business's database, you could select this setting to prevent employees from entering an order for a customer that does not exist.
- If you select Enforce Referential Integrity, you can choose two additional options: Cascade Update Related Fields and Cascade Delete Related Records.
- **Cascade Update** Related Fields means that when you change a value in the primary key of the parent table, the corresponding foreign key values in the child table automatically change as well. If you do not check this box, Access displays an error message when you try to change the primary key.
- **Cascade Delete** Related Records means that when you delete a record in the parent table, all related records in the child table are deleted as well. If you do not check this box, Access displays an error message when you try to delete the record in the parent table.
- When referential integrity is enabled, the parent table shows a "1" next to the primary key, and the child table most often shows an infinity symbol next to the foreign key.
- If the two related fields are primary keys, a "1" appears on both fields.

Try It! Creating a New Relationship with Referential Integrity

1. In **A08Try_xx**, with the Relationships grid displayed, drag the Instructors table onto the grid.
2. Drag the InstructorID field from the Instructors table onto the Instructor field in the ClassOfferings table. The Edit Relationships dialog box opens.
3. Click to mark the Enforce Referential Integrity check box.
4. Click to mark the Cascade Update Related Fields check box.

   ✓ *Cascade Update is used because if an instructor's ID changes, you want the ID updated in all related tables, too.*
5. Click to mark the Cascade Delete Related Records check box.
6. Click Create.
7. Leave the **A08Try_xx** database open to use in the next Try It.

Enforce referential integrity for a relationship

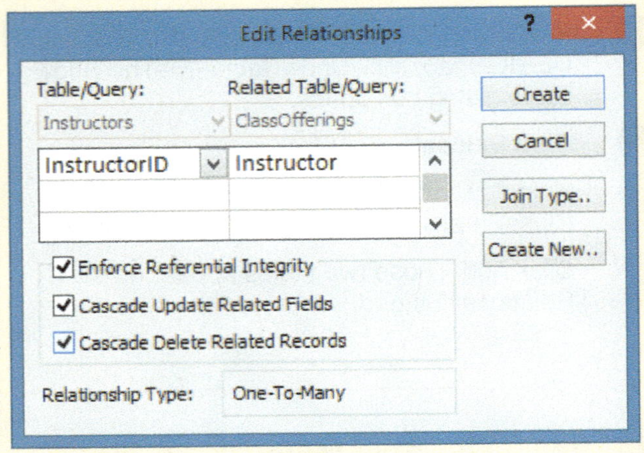

Try It! Modifying an Existing Relationship to Enforce Referential Integrity

1. In **A08Try_xx**, with the Relationships grid displayed, double-click the connector line between the ClassID field in the Classes table and the Class field in the ClassOfferings table. The Edit Relationships dialog box opens.

   ✓ *The ClassID and Class field names should appear in the dialog box. If the dialog box appears blank, you did not double-click in the right spot; cancel and try again.*
2. Click to mark the Enforce Referential Integrity check box.
3. Click to mark the Cascade Update Related Fields check box.
4. Click to mark the Cascade Delete Related Records check box.
5. Click OK.
6. Leave the **A08Try_xx** database open to use in the next Try It.

Deleting Relationships

- Deleting a relationship is sometimes necessary, either because it was erroneously created or because the structure of the database has changed or needs to change. For example, to create a lookup (covered in Chapter 3), you may need to delete an existing relationship between tables.

Try It! Deleting and Re-creating a Relationship

1. In **A08Try_xx**, with the Relationships grid displayed, click the connector line between the Classes and ClassOfferings tables. The line appears bold.

   ✓ *If the line does not appear bold, you did not click in the right spot.*

2. Press DEL.
3. Click Yes.
4. Drag the ClassID field from the Classes table to the Class field in the ClassOfferings table to re-create the relationship.
5. Click Create.
6. Right-click the Relationships tab and click Close.
7. Click Yes.
8. Leave the **A08Try_xx** database open to use in the next Try It.

Showing Related Records

- You can view the parent table and the child table in Datasheet view. After you create a relationship between tables, return to the Datasheet view of the parent table and click the plus sign (+) on the left edge of a record to see the related rows from the child table.
- If you have more than one child table, you can change the **subdatasheet** attached to the datasheet.

Try It! Showing Related Records

1. In **A08Try_xx**, in the Navigation pane, double-click Classes. The Classes table opens in Datasheet view.
2. Click the plus sign to the left of the first class's record. The related records from the ClassOfferings table appear as a subdatasheet.
3. Click the plus sign next to the first record in the ClassOfferings subdatasheet. The related records in the ClassEnrollment table appear in a sub-subdatasheet.
4. Click the minus signs to collapse the subdatasheets.
5. Right-click the Classes tab and click Close to close the datasheet.
6. Leave the **A08Try_xx** database open to use in the next Try It.

View the subdatasheet

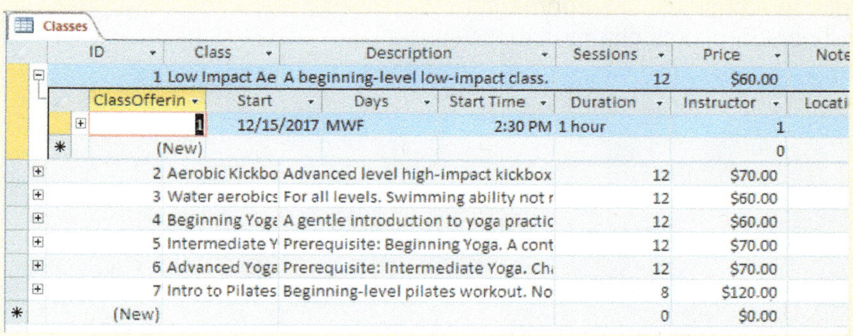

Access 2013, Windows 8, Microsoft Corporation

Try It! Changing the Subdatasheet

1. In **A08Try_xx**, open the ClassOfferings table in Datasheet view.
2. Expand the subdatasheet for the first record.

   ✓ *Notice that the subdatasheet shows the ClassEnrollment table. There are no records in that table right now so it shows a blank row.*
3. Collapse the subdatasheet.
4. On the HOME tab, in the Records group, click More, click Subdatasheet, and then click Subdatasheet again. The Insert Subdatasheet dialog box opens.
5. Click Instructors.

   ✓ *Recommended* ***master fields*** *and* ***child fields*** *in each table appear in the bottom of the dialog box. You can change those if needed, but they are usually right. If those boxes are empty, it means there is no usable relationship between the open datasheet's table and the selected table.*
6. Click OK.
7. Expand the subdatasheet.

   ✓ *Notice that the subdatasheet now shows the Instructors table.*

Choose a different subdatasheet

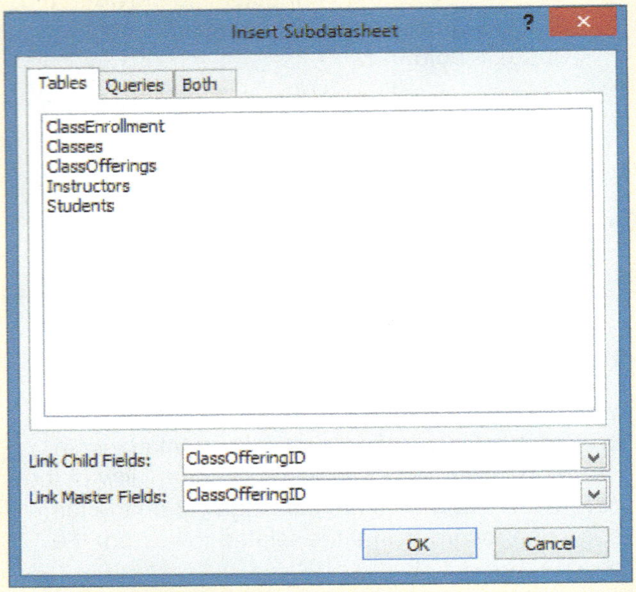

Access 2013, Windows 8, Microsoft Corporation

8. Right-click the ClassOfferings tab, and click Close to close the datasheet.
9. Click Yes to save the changes.
10. Leave the **A08Try_xx** database open to use in the next Try It.

Printing a Relationship Report

- A relationship report is a hard-copy printout of the relationships between the tables in the database. Having one can be useful in documenting the database (for example, in a business environment where more than one person makes changes to the database's structure).

Try It! Printing a Relationship Report

1. In **A08Try_xx**, click DATABASE TOOLS > Relationships.
2. Drag the tables around in the Relationships grid to make an attractive arrangement where all tables are visible and the lines between them are clear.

   ✓ *You can drag a table by its title bar at the top.*
3. On the RELATIONSHIP TOOLS DESIGN tab, in the Tools group, click Relationship Report. A report appears in Print Preview.
4. On the PRINT PREVIEW tab, click Print. The Print dialog box opens.
5. **With your teacher's permission**, click OK to print. Otherwise, click Cancel.
6. Click Close Print Preview to exit Print Preview. The report appears in Design view.
7. Right-click the Report1 tab and click Close.
8. Click No to discard changes. The report is not saved.
9. Click FILE > Close to close the database.

Lesson 8—Practice

Still working in the jewelry business database that you created in Chapter 1, you will now create relationships between the tables that will enable the business owner to enter, edit, and manage the data in multiple tables more easily.

DIRECTIONS

1. Start Access, if necessary, and open **A08Practice** from the data files for this lesson.
2. Save the database as **A08Practice_xx** in the location where your teacher instructs you to store the files for this lesson.

   ✓ *If a security warning bar appears, click Enable Content.*
3. Click **DATABASE TOOLS** > **Relationships**. The Show Table dialog box opens.
4. Click **Customers**, hold down the SHIFT key, and click **Shippers**. All tables become selected, as shown in Figure 8-2.
5. Click **Add**. All tables are added to the Relationships grid.
6. Click **Close** to close the Show Table dialog box.
7. Drag the **ID** field from the **Shippers** table to the Shipper field in the Orders table.
8. Mark the **Enforce Referential Integrity** check box.
9. Mark the **Cascade Update Related Fields** check box.
10. Click **Create**. An error appears, because the fields do not have the same field size.

Figure 8-2

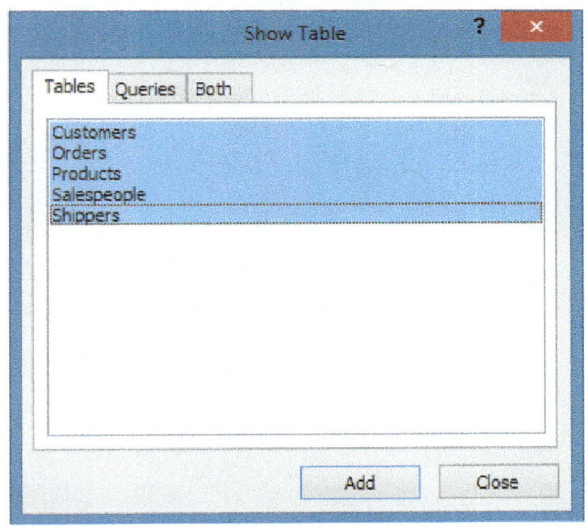

Access 2013, Windows 8, Microsoft Corporation

11. Click **OK** to clear the error message.
12. Click **Cancel** to close the Edit Relationships dialog box.
13. In the Relationships grid, right-click the **Orders** table and click **Table Design**.

    ✓ *Note the Field Size setting for the Shipper field. It is Long Integer.*

14. Close the **Orders** table without saving changes.
15. In the Relationships grid, right-click the **Shippers** table and click **Table Design**.
16. Select the **ID** field.
17. In the Field Size property for the ID field, set the size to **Long Integer**, as shown in Figure 8-3.
18. Click the **Save** button on the Quick Access Toolbar.
19. Right-click the **Shippers** tab, and click **Close** to close the table.
20. On the Relationships grid, drag the **ID** field from the **Shippers** table to the **Shipper** field in the **Orders** table.
21. Click **Enforce Referential Integrity**.
22. Click **Cascade Update Related Fields**.
23. Click **Create**. The relationship is created.
24. Right-click the **Relationships** tab and click **Close**.
25. Click **Yes** to save your work.
26. Click **FILE** > **Close** to close the database. If instructed, submit this database to your teacher for grading.

Figure 8-3

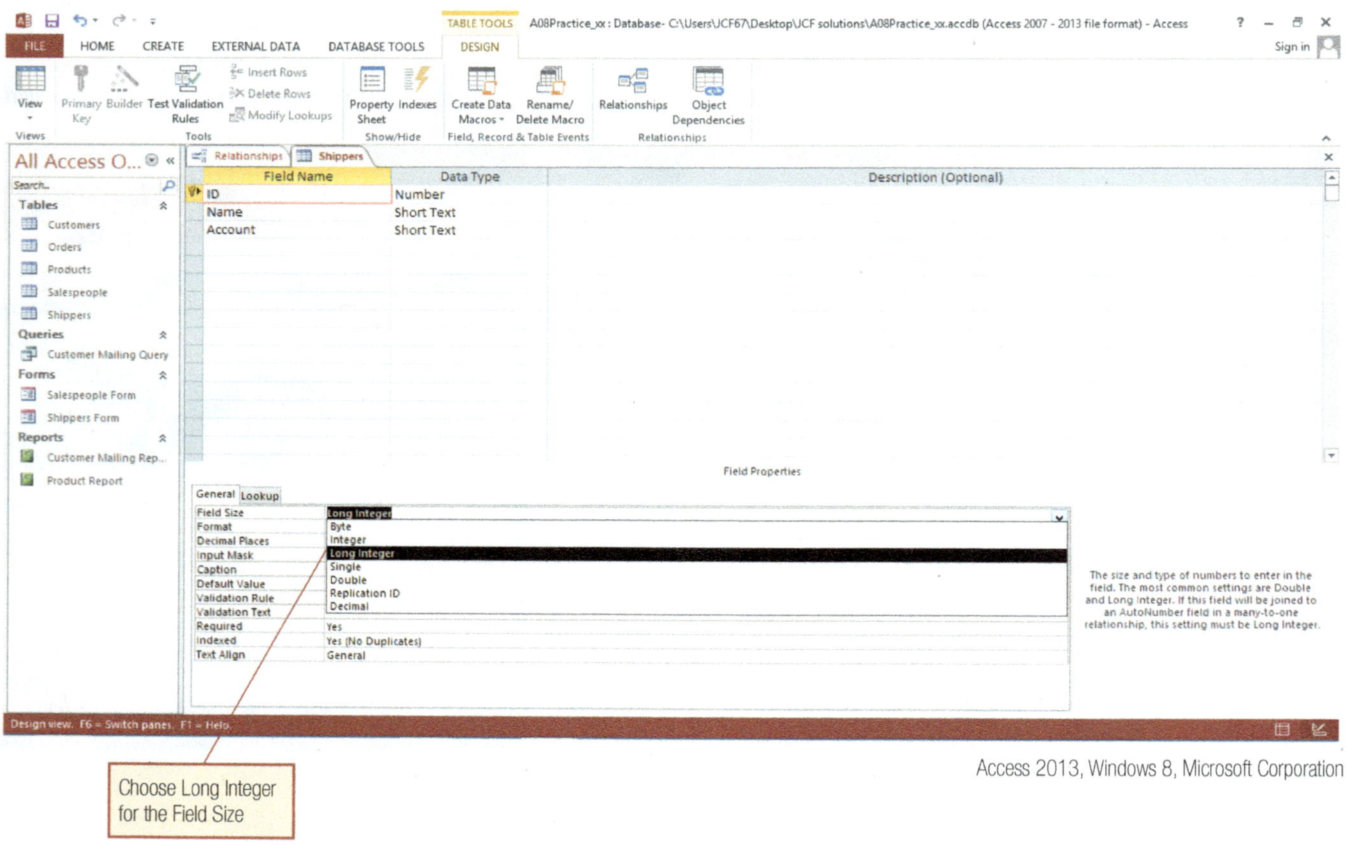

Access 2013, Windows 8, Microsoft Corporation

Lesson 8—Apply

You will now create relationships between the tables that will enable the business owner to enter, edit, and manage the data in multiple tables more easily.

DIRECTIONS

1. Start Access, if necessary, and open **A08Apply** from the data files for this lesson.
2. Save the database as **A08Apply_xx** in the location where your teacher instructs you to store the files for this lesson.

   ✓ *If a security warning bar appears, click Enable Content.*

3. Open the **Relationships** grid.
4. Add the **OrderDetails** table to the grid.
5. Create the relationships shown in the table at the bottom of the page.
6. Arrange the tables on the Relationships grid so that no connector lines cross. Figure 8-4 shows one possible arrangement.
7. Edit the last relationship you created (between the **Products** and **OrderDetails** tables) to turn off **Cascade Delete Related Records**.
8. **If instructed to by your teacher**, print one copy of a Relationships report to your default printer.
9. Close the **Relationships** grid, saving your changes.
10. Open the **Orders** table in Datasheet view, and enter the following record:

    Order ID: (**AutoNumber**)

    Order Date: **12/1/2017**

    Customer: **1**

    Shipper: **1**

    Salesperson: **081-48-281**

    ✓ *You must have at least one record in a table in order for the subdatasheet to be visible. The plus sign that opens the subdatasheet does not appear until you enter a record.*

11. Open the subdatasheet for the first record. Notice that it shows data from the **OrderDetails** table.
12. Using the subdatasheet, enter the following records in the **OrderDetails** table:

    OrderDetailID: (**AutoNumber**)

    Product: **2**

    Quantity: **2**

    OrderDetailID: (**AutoNumber**)

    Product: **3**

    Quantity: **1**

13. Close the datasheet, saving your changes to it when prompted.
14. Click **FILE** > **Close** to close the database. If instructed, submit this database to your teacher for grading.

Figure 8-4

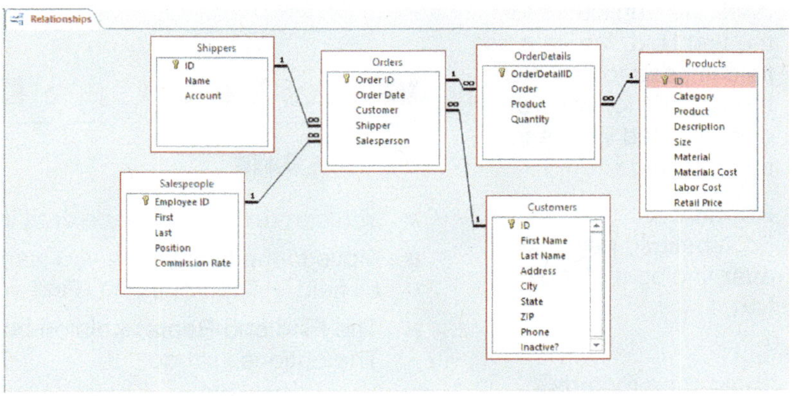

Access 2013, Windows 8, Microsoft Corporation

In Table	From Field	To Field	In Table	Enforce Referential Integrity?	Cascade Update?	Cascade Delete?
Customers	ID	Customer	Orders	Yes	Yes	Yes
Salespeople	Employee ID	Salesperson	Orders	Yes	Yes	No
Orders	Order ID	Order	OrderDetails	Yes	Yes	Yes
Products	ID	Product	OrderDetails	Yes	Yes	Yes

Lesson 9

Finding, Replacing, and Sorting Data

WORDS TO KNOW

Ascending
From A to Z or 1 to 9.

Descending
From Z to A or 9 to 1.

Find
To locate text within a record that matches characters you type.

Multiple sort
To use more than one field to sort records. If there are duplicates for the first field, the second field is used to organize the records for each set of duplicated values in the first field.

Replace
To substitute new text after finding a string of text.

Sort
To arrange records alphabetically or numerically according to a specific field.

Wildcard
A character (? or *) that signifies one or more unspecified characters when finding text.

➤ What You Will Learn

Finding Data
Replacing Data
Searching with Wildcards
Sorting Records in a Table
Sorting Using Multiple Fields

Software Skills One of the primary purposes of a database is to store data so you can look it up later. You use Find procedures to locate data and Find and Replace procedures to locate data and change it to something else. You can search on an exact match or use wildcards that help you find information if you do not know the exact spelling. You can also sort records according to one or multiple fields to find data more easily.

What You Can Do

Finding Data

- You can **find** and replace data in Datasheet view and in Form view.
- Move to the field where you want to search for data (unless you want to search all fields). Then open the Find and Replace dialog box to begin your search.
- The Find and Replace dialog box contains options for how to search for data. The options include:
  - *Find What*
    Type the word or phrase you want to look for. You can include **wildcards**. You can also pick from your last seven searches.
  - *Look In*
    This defaults to the current field.
  - *Match*
    Using the text in the Find What text box, find an exact match using the entire field, any part of the field, or the start of the field.

- *Search*
  You can choose to search the entire list or in a particular direction through the records.
- *Match Case*
  Check this box if you want the capitalization of the Find What entry to match the case of the value in the field exactly. For example, "Broadway" will not match "broadway."
- *Search Fields As Formatted*
  Find exact matches for date and number formats.

■ Click Find Next to find the next record that matches (in the direction indicated in the Search box).

Try It! Finding Data

1. Start Access and open **A09Try** from the data files for this lesson. Save it as **A09Try_xx**.
2. Open the Students table in Datasheet view.
3. Click anywhere in the TermDate field.
4. On the HOME tab, in the Find group, click Find.
5. In the Find and Replace dialog box, type **2017** in the Find What box.
6. Open the Match drop-down list and click Any Part of Field.
7. Click Find Next. The selection highlight jumps to the first record with 2017 as part of the date.
8. Click Find Next again. A message appears that it was not found.

Find records that contain 2015 anywhere in the TermDate field

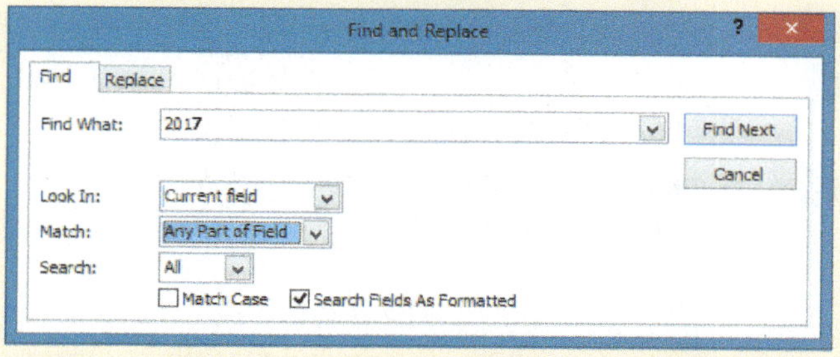

Access 2013, Windows 8, Microsoft Corporation

9. Click OK.
10. Click Cancel.
11. Leave the **A09Try_xx** database open to use in the next Try It.

Replacing Data

■ When you have text that needs to be replaced with other text, you can manually edit it after finding it (as in the previous section).

■ Alternately, you can use the Replace tab of the Find and Replace dialog box. For example, if area code 303 changes to 720, you can replace each occurrence of 303 with 720.

■ If the text is found, you can click Replace to **replace** the text in the current record or Replace All to replace all occurrences in all records. Unless you are sure you will not create errors in your database, you should choose Replace rather than Replace All.

Try It! Replacing Data

1. In **A09Try_xx**, in the Students table in Datasheet view, click in the first record in the Notes field.
2. Click HOME > Replace. The Find and Replace dialog box opens with the Replace tab displayed.
3. In the Find What box, type **Lifetime**.
4. In the Replace With box, type **Unlimited**.
5. If necessary, open the Match drop-down list and click Any Part of Field if it is not already selected.
6. Click Find Next. The first occurrence appears.
7. Click Replace. That occurrence is replaced, and the next occurrence appears.
8. Click Replace All to replace all additional occurrences at once.
9. In the confirmation box, click Yes.
10. Click Cancel to close the Find and Replace dialog box.
11. Leave the **A09Try_xx** database open to use in the next Try It.

Replace all instances of Lifetime with Unlimited

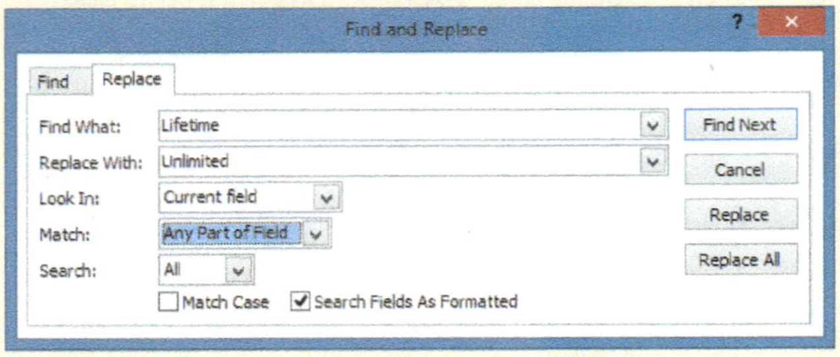

Access 2013, Windows 8, Microsoft Corporation

Searching with Wildcards

- You can use wildcards in the Find What text box if you do not know the exact spelling, but do know some of the characters.
- The most common wildcard is the asterisk (*). The asterisk can replace any number of characters. For example, Sm*th will find Smyth, Smith, and Smooth.
- You can use more than one asterisk. Sm*th* will find Smith, Smooth, Smothers, and Smythe.

✓ *To speed up filling in the Find and Replace dialog box, you do not need to change the Match choice from the default Whole Field option. Type *Broadway* to find a record when Broadway is anywhere within the field.*

- The question mark (?) wildcard is a substitute for an unknown single character. For example, ?oss will find Boss and Hoss, but not Floss.

Try It! Searching with Wildcards

1. In **A09Try_xx**, in the Students table in Datasheet view, click anywhere in the Last field.
2. Click HOME > Find.
3. In the Find What box, type **H???**.
4. Open the Match drop-down list and click Whole Field.
5. Click Find Next.
6. In the Find What box, delete the current entry and type ***g**.
7. Click Find Next.
8. Click Cancel to close the Find and Replace dialog box.
9. Leave the **A09Try_xx** database open to use in the next Try It.

Sorting Records in a Table

- Sorting rearranges records in order by one or more fields. Most types of fields can be sorted.
- You can **sort** records in **ascending** order (A to Z or 1 to 9) or **descending** order (Z to A or 9 to 1).
- Some reasons to sort records might be to:
  - See groups of data (for example, all clients who live in New York or all of yesterday's sales).
  - See information organized from smallest or largest values.
  - Group all records that have blanks in a field.
  - Look for duplicate records.

  ✓ *You can also use filters and queries to sort records (discussed later in this chapter).*

- Before sorting, you must first move the insertion point to the field by which you want to sort the records. For example, if you want to sort a table of clients by last name in ascending order, move to the Last Name field.
- You can sort records by fields that have Short Text, Number, Currency, Date/Time, and Yes/No data types. You cannot sort records by fields that have Long Text, Hyperlink, or OLE Object data types.
- If you save a table or form after sorting, the sort order becomes a property of the table or form. You can change this property by sorting on a different field.
- To remove a sort, you can either sort by a different field or remove all sorts with the Remove Sort command on the HOME tab.
- If there is no primary key, records within a table (and its corresponding forms) are placed in input order when you remove the sort.
- If there is a primary key, records are ordered by the primary key when you remove the sort.

Try It! Sorting Records in a Table

1. In **A09Try_xx**, in the Students table in Datasheet view, click anywhere in the Last field.
2. On the HOME tab, in the Sort & Filter group, click Ascending . The records are sorted in A-to-Z order by last name. An up-pointing arrow appears on the field header to show that the records are sorted by that field.
3. Click HOME > Descending . The records are sorted in Z-to-A order by last name. A down-pointing arrow appears on the field header to show that the records are sorted by that field.
4. Click HOME > Remove Sort . The records return to their default order.
5. Leave the **A09Try_xx** database open to use in the next Try It.

Sort records by last name

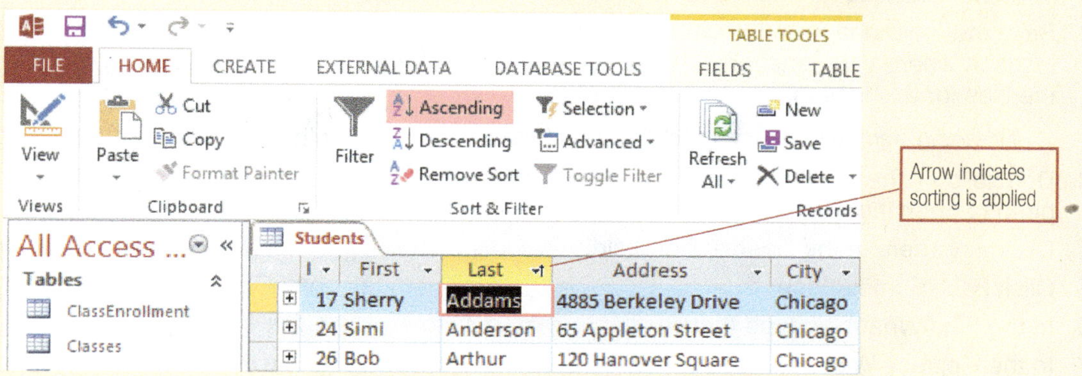

Access 2013, Windows 8, Microsoft Corporation

Sorting Using Multiple Fields

- With a **multiple sort**, you can sort records by more than one field. For example, you could sort by State and then by City. All the records containing CA as the state, for example, would be grouped together, and then all the records with San Diego as the city would be grouped within the CA grouping.
- The two (or more) fields that you sort by must be adjacent on the datasheet. You might need to rearrange the fields to prepare to do the sort.

✓ *To rearrange the fields in a datasheet, select the field and then drag the field header to the right or left. If you do not want the rearrangement to be permanent, drag the fields back to their original positions after sorting, or do not save your changes when you close the datasheet.*

- When sorting records by multiple fields, Access sorts first by the left-most selected field, then by the next-to-leftmost, and so on.

Try It! Sorting Using Multiple Fields

1. In A09Try_xx, in the Students table in Datasheet view, drag the TermLength field to the left of the TermDate field.
2. Select the TermLength field. Hold down SHIFT and click the TermDate field to also select it.
3. Click HOME > Descending. The records are sorted first by term length and then by term date.
4. Click Remove Sort.
5. Click FILE > Close.
6. When prompted to save changes, click No.

Lesson 9—Practice

In this project, you will use the Find and Replace features to make the needed changes. You will also sort records and create printouts of the records in the new sort order.

DIRECTIONS

1. Start Access, if necessary, and open **A09Practice** from the data files for this lesson.
2. Save the database as **A09Practice_xx** in the location where your teacher instructs you to store the files for this lesson.

   ✓ *If a security warning bar appears, click Enable Content.*
3. Double-click the **Products** table in the Navigation pane to open it in Datasheet view.
4. Click anywhere in the **Description** field.
5. Click **HOME** > **Replace**.
6. In the Find What box, type **filagree**.
7. In the Replace With box, type **filigree**.
8. Open the Match drop-down list and click **Any Part of Field**.
9. Click **Replace All**.
10. Click **Yes**.
11. Click **Cancel**.
12. Click anywhere in the **Material** field.
13. Click **HOME** > **Descending**.
14. Click the **Save** button on the Quick Access Toolbar to save the changes to the datasheet.
15. **With your teacher's permission**, do the following:
    a. Click **FILE** > **Print** > **Print**.
    b. If necessary, choose the printer on which you have been instructed to print.
    c. Click **OK**.
    d. Write your name on the printout.
16. Click **FILE** > **Close**. If instructed, submit this database to your teacher for grading.

Lesson 9—Apply

You have received updated information that needs to be input into the jewelry database. In this project, you will use the Find and Replace features to make the needed changes. You will also sort records and create printouts of the records in the new sort order.

DIRECTIONS

1. Start Access, if necessary, and open **A09Apply** from the data files for this lesson.
2. Save the database as **A09Apply_xx** in the location where your teacher instructs you to store the files for this lesson.

   ✓ *If a security warning bar appears, click Enable Content.*

3. Open the **Customers** table in Datasheet view. Use Find to locate the record where the phone number is 502-555-7755. Edit the number to **502-555-7756**.
4. Sort the **Customers** table in ascending order by **State** and **City** (first by state, then by city).

   ✓ *You need to move the State field to the left of the City field temporarily; then move it back to its original position after performing the sort, before the next step. You may need to change the settings of the Look In and Match drop-down lists.*

5. **With your teacher's permission**, print one copy of the datasheet. Write your name on the printout.
6. Save the changes to the table and close it.
7. Open the **Products** table in Datasheet view.
8. In the **Material** field, replace all instances of **Gold, Yellow** with **Yellow Gold**.
9. In the **Material** field, replace all instances of **Gold, White** with **White Gold**.
10. Sort the table in descending order by the **Material** field.
11. **With your teacher's permission**, print one copy of the datasheet. Write your name on the printout.
12. Save the changes to the table and close it.
13. Click **FILE** > **Close** to close the database. If instructed, submit this database to your teacher for grading.

Lesson 10

Filtering Data

➤ What You Will Learn

Filtering by Selection
Filtering for Multiple Values
Filtering by Form
Saving Filter Results As a Query

WORDS TO KNOW

Filter
To display only certain records.

Filter by Form
To use a form that enables you to enter criteria for the filter.

Filter by Selection
To filter based on the data in the selected record and field.

Software Skills Sometimes you will want to look at all records that match certain criteria. Although you could sort a list, it may be easier to isolate (filter) only the records you want to see. Then, when you use the navigation buttons or keys to move through records, you see only relevant records.

What You Can Do

Filtering by Selection

- When you **filter** records, you see a subset of the records in the datasheet or form. The number of records that match the filter appears between the navigation buttons at the bottom of the datasheet or form.
- **Filter by Selection** is the easiest way to filter your records. You can choose to filter for only records that equal or do not equal—or contain or do not contain—the current selection.

Try It! **Filtering by Selection**

1. Start Access, and open **A10Try** from the data files for this lesson. Save it as **A10Try_xx**.
2. Open the Students table in Datasheet view.
3. In record 6, double-click *Unlimited* in the Notes field to select the word.
4. Click HOME, click Selection, and then click Contains "Unlimited." Only the records that contain that value are shown.
5. On the HOME tab, in the Sort & Filter group, click Toggle Filter to remove the filter.
6. In record 6, right-click Unlimited and, on the shortcut menu, click Contains "Unlimited."

(continued)

Try It! Filtering by Selection *(continued)*

7. Right-click Unlimited again and, on the shortcut menu, click Clear filter from Notes.
8. Leave the **A10Try_xx** database open to use in the next Try It.

Filter by a specific value using the Ribbon

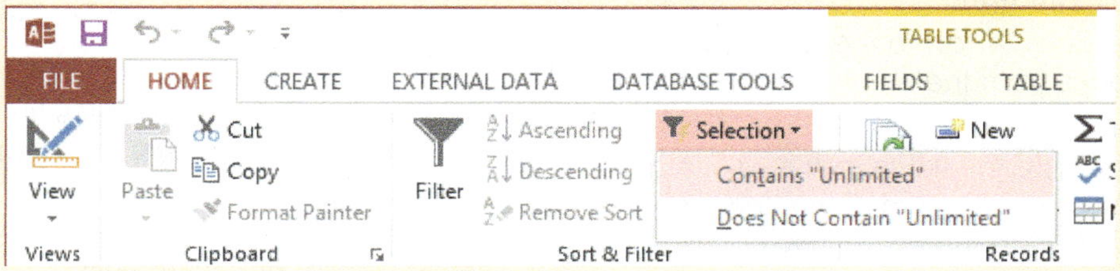

Access 2013, Windows 8, Microsoft Corporation

Filtering for Multiple Values

- You can also filter for multiple values at once. (That is, you can specify multiple values for that field that will all be included in the filter.) For example, you might want a filter on the ZIP field to include several different ZIP codes.

Try It! Filtering for Multiple Values

1. In **A10Try_xx**, in the Students table in Datasheet view, right-click any value in the TermDate column. A shortcut menu opens.
2. Point to Date Filters and then click Last Year. The records are filtered to show only the ones for the previous year.
3. Click Toggle Filter to remove the filter.
4. Right-click any value in the First column.
5. Point to Text Filters, and click Begins With.
6. In the Custom Filter dialog box, type **L** and click OK. The list is filtered to show only people with a first name beginning with L.
7. Click Toggle Filter to remove the filter.
8. Right-click the Students tab, and click Close to close the datasheet. If prompted to save changes, click Yes.
9. Leave the **A10Try_xx** database open to use in the next Try It.

Filter using a data filter on the shortcut menu

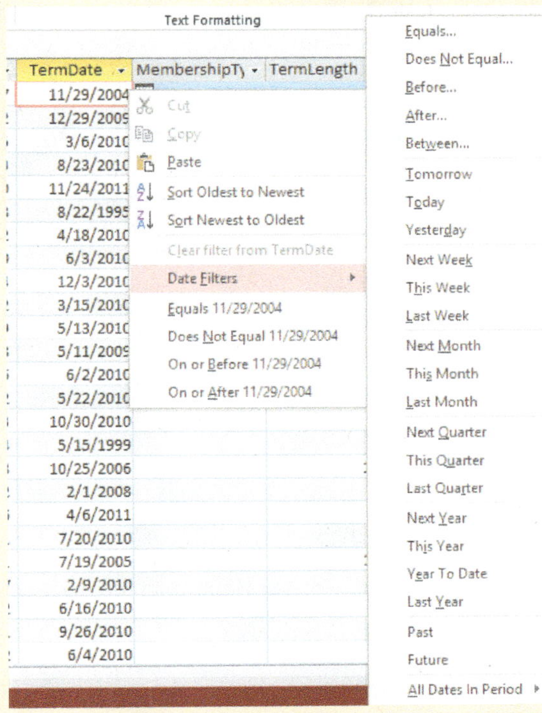

Access 2013, Windows 8, Microsoft Corporation

Filtering by Form

- **Filter by Form** gives you options to filter on multiple fields and to use wildcards in the filter criteria. (Wildcards were covered in Lesson 9.)
- The Filter by Form interface enables you to do any of the following in each field:
  - Type the value you want.
  - Click the drop-down arrow to the right of the field, and choose from the existing entries in the field.
  - Use wildcards: Type the value with a wildcard asterisk (*) for any number of characters or question mark (?) for one character.
  - Use criteria: Type > (greater than), < (less than), >= (greater than or equal to), or <= (less than or equal to) and then a number or text string.

    ✓ *When using greater than or less than, put quotation marks around criteria that should be interpreted alphabetically (such as A being before B in the alphabet).*
  - Type *Between firstvalue and secondvalue*. For example, Between 1/1/2014 and 3/31/2014.
  - Type *Is Null* to find empty fields, or *Is Not Null* to find non-empty ones.
- If you have entries in multiple fields on the Look for tab, Access finds all records that match for all entries. For example, if *Smith* is in Last Name and *Denver* is in City, records that have both Smith and Denver show.

  ✓ *When you use Filter by Form on a Long Text type field, the only choices are Is Null or Is Not Null. If you want more filter options, you must change the field type to Short Text.*
- If you have an entry on the Look for tab and an entry on the Or tab(s), Access finds all records that match any of the entries. For example, if Smith is on the Look for tab and Denver is on the Or tab, Access will find all the Smiths whether or not they live in Denver and all people who live in Denver whether or not their name is Smith.
- Click Toggle Filter to filter the data or to remove the filter.
- From the Filter by Form view, you can click HOME > Advanced > Close to return to the form or datasheet without filtering data, or you can click Toggle Filter twice (once to apply the filter and again to remove it).

Figure 10-1 Filter by Form enables more complex filter criteria

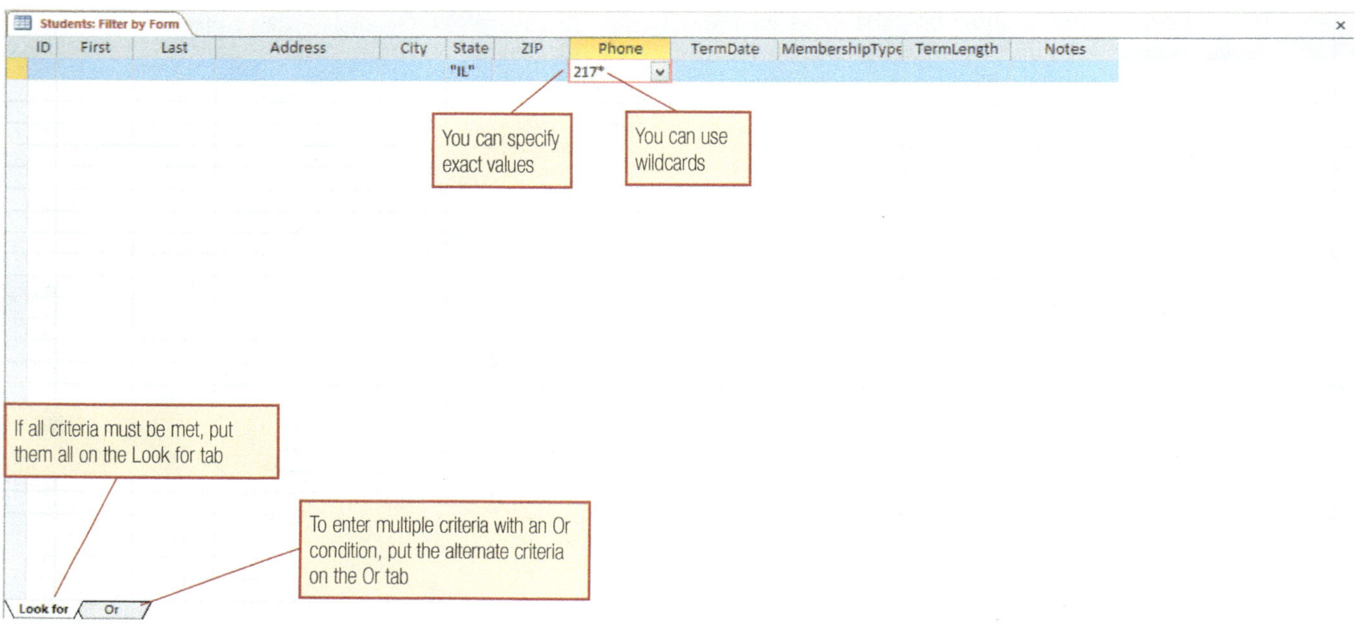

Try It! Filtering by Form

1. In **A10Try_xx**, open the Students table in Datasheet view. On the HOME tab, click Advanced, and then click Filter by Form.
2. If there are any criteria already entered in the form, press DEL to remove them.
3. Click in the TermLength field, click the drop-down arrow, and click 10.
4. Click in the Last field, and type **C*** and press ENTER.

   ✓ *Access automatically changes the entry to* Like "C*".
5. Click the Or tab at the bottom of the window.
6. Click the drop-down arrow in the TermLength field and click 10.
7. In the Last field, type **A*** and press ENTER.
8. Click Toggle Filter. Two records appear in the filter.
9. Click HOME > Advanced > Clear All Filters.
10. Leave the **A10Try_xx** database open to use in the next Try It.

Saving Filter Results As a Query

- When you save a filter to use later, you save it as a query. Queries are covered in more detail in the remaining lessons in this chapter.
- The resulting query is available from the Navigation pane just like any other query.

Try It! Saving a Filter As a Query

1. In **A10Try_xx**, in the Students table in Datasheet view, click HOME > Advanced > Filter by Form.
2. Click the TermLength drop-down arrow and click 10.
3. Click HOME > Advanced > Save As Query. The Save As Query dialog box opens.
4. Type **Term Length 10** and click OK.

   ✓ *Access creates the new query.*
5. Click HOME > Advanced > Close to close the filter form without running the filter.
6. Click FILE > Close.
7. Click Yes.

Save the filter as a query

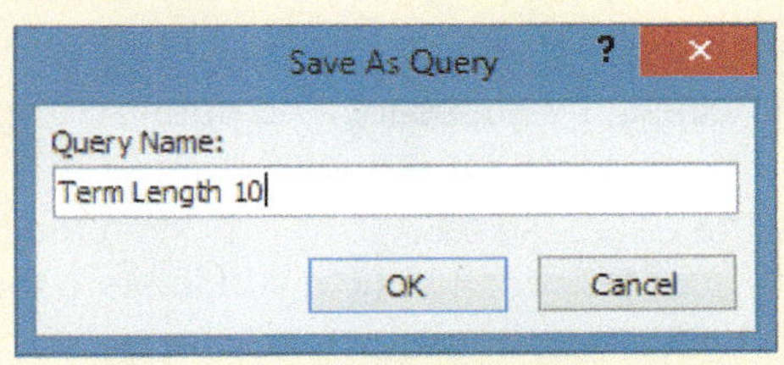

Access 2013, Windows 8, Microsoft Corporation

Lesson 10—Practice

Your friend for whom you have created the jewelry database would like to filter the data in various ways and be able to recall the filters quickly later. You will create a filter and save it as a reusable query.

DIRECTIONS

1. Start Access, if necessary, and open **A10Practice** from the data files for this lesson.
2. Save the database as **A10Practice_xx** in the location where your teacher instructs you to store the files for this lesson.

   ✓ *If a security warning bar appears, click Enable Content.*
3. Double-click the **Products** table to open it.
4. Click the down arrow on the **Category** field header, opening the menu.
5. Click **Select All** to clear all check boxes.
6. Click the **Bracelet** and **Necklace** check boxes.
7. Click **OK**.
8. **With your teacher's permission**, do the following to print the datasheet:
   a. Click **FILE** > **Print** > **Print**.
   b. Click **OK**.
9. Click **HOME** > **Advanced** > **Filter by Form**.
10. Click **HOME** > **Advanced** > **Save As Query**.
11. Type **Necklaces and Bracelets**.
12. Click **OK**.
13. Click **HOME** > **Advanced** > **Close**.
14. Click **FILE** > **Close** to close the database. If instructed, submit this database to your teacher for grading.

Lesson 10—Apply

Your friend for whom you have created the jewelry database liked the filters that you created and would like you to add some additional filters. She also wants the filters to be saved as a reusable query.

DIRECTIONS

1. Start Access, if necessary, and open **A10Apply** from the data files for this lesson.
2. Save the database as **A10Apply_xx** in the location where your teacher instructs you to store the files for this lesson.

   ✓ *If a security warning bar appears, click Enable Content.*
3. Filter the **Customers** table to show only the customers who live in Illinois.
4. Save the filter results as a query named **Illinois Customers**.

   ✓ *First, you will need to Filter by Form and then save the filter as a query. Be sure to remove the filter from the Customers table.*
5. Filter the **Products** table to show only necklaces that are made of any type of yellow gold. The results should contain 4 records.

   ✓ *Here's one way to do step 5: First set up a filter for multiple values (all the values that contain Yellow in the Material field), and then use Filter by Form to add the additional criterion of Necklace in the Category field.*
6. Save the filter results as a query named **Yellow Gold Necklaces**.
7. Filter the **Salespeople** table to show only people whose position is **Manager**.
8. Save the filter results as a query named **Managers**.
9. Click **FILE** > **Close** to close the database. If instructed, submit this database to your teacher for grading.

Lesson 11

Creating a Query in Design View

➤ What You Will Learn

Understanding Data Analysis
Exploring Data Mining Tools, Techniques, and Ethics
Understanding Database Trends
Understanding Queries
Creating a New Select Query in Design View
Running a Query
Saving and Printing a Query

Software Skills It can be challenging to make sense of a large amount of data. Performing data analysis can extract the information you need. This can be done in Access with sorting, filtering, queries, and reports. In this lesson, you will learn about the tools and techniques of data analysis and create queries.

WORDS TO KNOW

Action query
Used to change the data in existing tables or make new tables based on the query's results.

Cloud computing
A model where data and programs are stored on the Internet; users do not own the infrastructure and pay only for the level of services used.

Data analysis
Using software tools to evaluate digital data so you can use the information in meaningful ways.

Data mining
Using data analysis to find patterns in data.

Data warehouse
A database structured for query and analysis rather than for transactional processing.

Parameter query
A query that asks for input every time that you run it.

What You Can Do

Understanding Data Analysis

- **Data analysis** is the process of evaluating information so you can use it in meaningful ways.
- You can use database tools in programs such as Excel or Access to perform data analysis. For example, you can use query and report calculation features in Access to analyze the data, or export the data to Excel and calculate or chart it there to find trends.
- You can also do quick data analysis by sorting or filtering records, whether or not you save as a query. You did basic data analysis in the previous two lessons.
- Data analysis can also include charting. Charting data lets you see a visual representation of the information, which can make it easier to spot trends and make comparisons.

Query
A defined set of operations to be performed on a table (or on the results from another query).

Query design grid
The lower half of the Query Design view that shows the field name, table name, sort order, show box, and criteria rows for selecting records.

Query Design view
A view that enables you to choose the fields in a query, to select the sort order, and to set criteria.

Select query
A query that sorts and filters the records in a table or other query to extract certain fields and records based on criteria you specify. This is by far the most common type of query.

Update query
A query used to change existing data.

Virtualization
A variety of technologies that enable more efficient use of hardware and other resources.

Try It! Analyzing Data

1. Start Access, and open **A11Try** from the data files for this lesson. Save it as **A11Try_xx**.
2. Open the Students table in Datasheet view.
3. Click in the TermDate field, and click HOME > Filter > Date Filters > Before.
4. In the Custom Filter dialog box, type **01/01/2010** and click OK.
5. Click HOME > Advanced > Filter by Form.
6. Open the TermLength drop-down list and click 10.
7. Click the Or tab at the bottom of the window.
8. Open the Notes field's drop-down list and click Is Not Null.
9. Click Toggle Filter. Eight records appear.
10. Right-click the Students tab and click Close. When prompted to save your changes, click No.
11. Leave the **A11Try_xx** database open to use in the next Try It.

Exploring Data Mining Tools, Techniques, and Ethics

- **Data mining** involves using a variety of tools to identify patterns in data and to use that data to make strategic business decisions.
- For example, a supermarket may track your purchases and use data mining to identify the brands you buy most often. It can then send you coupons or special offers to encourage you to try a different brand.
- Data mining is most often performed on samples of data, rather than the full dataset. A representative sample is easier to work with, and if it is a truly random sample, it will likely produce the same results as working with the complete dataset.
- Querying, filtering, and charting tools in database and spreadsheet programs provide basic data mining capabilities, but more sophisticated data mining software is also available.
- Organizations should establish data mining guidelines to ensure that the process is not used for unethical or illegal purposes. For example, an insurance company may not use data mining to identify and discriminate against customers who require expensive medications.
- All employees should be aware of the guidelines, and procedures should be in place for handling ethical breaches of those policies.

Understanding Database Trends

- Data collection and analysis occurs everywhere in society. Retail stores track buying patterns, hospitals track medical care, social networking sites track friend requests, and mobile phones track calling patterns.
- Businesses, organizations, and the government use the information collected in databases to help guide strategic planning, customize products for individuals, and develop new products and services.
- A database structured for analysis rather than transactional processing is referred to as a **data warehouse**. Properly designed, a data warehouse facilitates data mining and business intelligence.
- Trends in both hardware and software are leading to more powerful and customizable databases.
- Two trends to watch include **virtualization** and **cloud computing**:
    - Virtualization is when a variety of technologies are combined to enable more efficient use of hardware and other resources, such as a server hosting multiple operating system environments for multiple customers with each customer accessing his or her applications and data remotely.
    - Cloud computing is when programs and data are stored on Internet servers, relieving customers of the responsibility of owning and maintaining the infrastructure, yet providing access to the information and tools they need at any time, from any location.

Understanding Queries

- A **query** is like an advanced sort or filter, except you can save a query and store it in the database window. In Lesson 10, you learned how to save a custom filter as a query.
- Like sorting and filtering, queries let you specify a sort order and define criteria to select the records you want to see.
- To rename a query, right-click the query in the Navigation pane and click Rename. Enter the appropriate name and press ENTER.
- Unlike sorting and filtering, a query enables you to choose a subset of fields to display. You need not hide the columns you don't want; they simply don't appear in the query results. However, if you've added a field to a query which you later wish to hide, right-click the field header and select Hide Fields.
- You can also use certain fields in the query as filters without including those fields in the query output.
- Queries also make possible some specialized operations such as performing calculations on field values and placing the result in a new column in a datasheet.
- Queries, like tables, can be used as a starting point for reports or forms.
- There are several kinds of queries, but the most common type is a **select query**. The main purpose of a select query is to extract fields and records from a larger table and present the results in a specific sort order.
- **Action queries** modify records based on criteria you add.
- To create an action query, begin with a regular query, and view the datasheet to make sure the selection is what you want to change. Then, modify the query in Design view to apply the action functionality.
- An **Update query** is a type of query that can be used to update records in a database.
- Creating a **parameter query** allows you to use the same query to extract data that meets different criteria.
- You can run a parameter query as a select query or you can change the query type to an action query.
- When you run a parameter query, Access presents you with a dialog box prompting you for the parameter value, which it enters into the appropriate criteria cell. You can have as many parameters as you like in a single query.
- You can format fields within a query by changing its field properties in Query Design view in the Property Sheet pane.
- To export a query, go to the EXTERNAL DATA tab. In the Export group, select the appropriate data type and save the query.
- To delete a query, right-click the appropriate query in the Navigation pane. Click Delete > Yes.

Creating a New Select Query in Design View

- **Query Design view** is a view in which you can define the structure of the query, including choosing the fields to include, the order in which those fields appear, which field to sort the results by (if any), and what criteria to use for filtering records.
- Query Design view consists of two sections. At the top are field lists with which the tables or queries work. At the bottom is the **query design grid**, where you place the individual fields (one per column) and define how they should be acted upon.

Figure 11-1

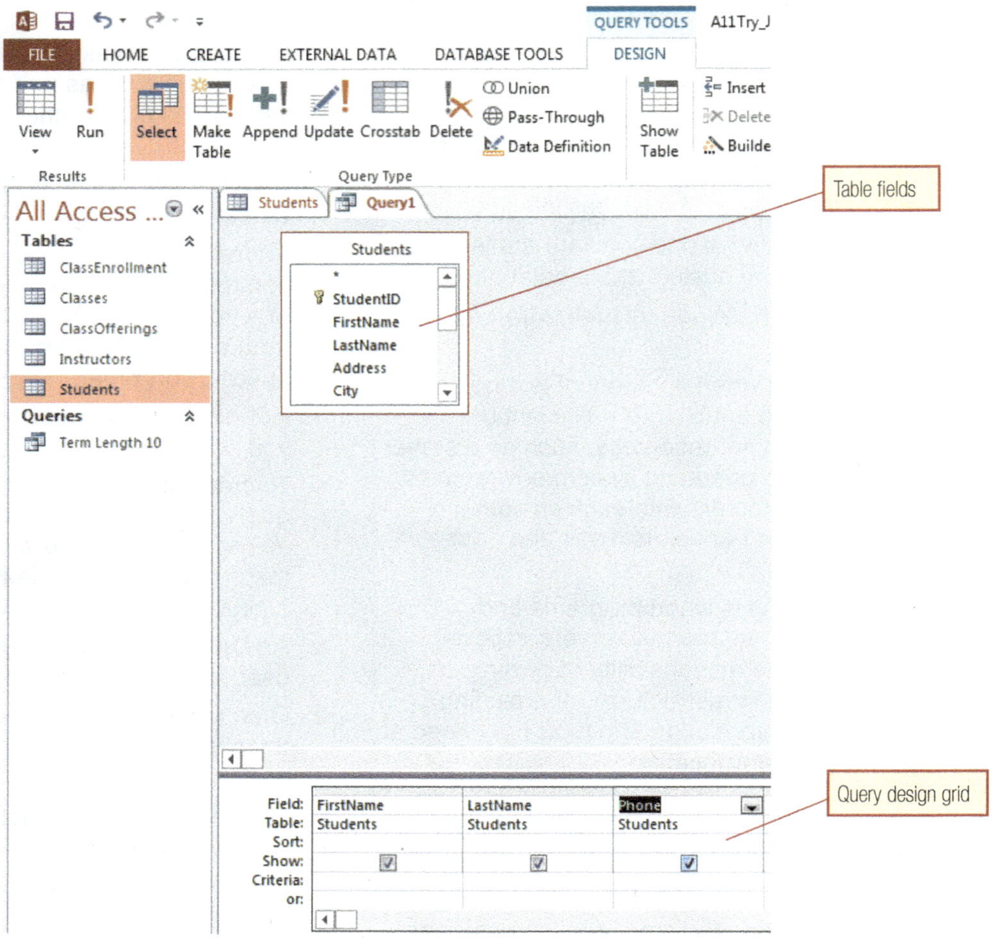

Access 2013, Windows 8, Microsoft Corporation

- After adding the table(s), you select individual fields and place them in the query grid at the bottom of the window.
- The order in which you place the fields in the query design (from left to right in the query grid) determines the column order for the resulting datasheet.
- You can choose a field in any of the following ways:
  - Double-click the field in the table's field list to place the field to the right of the previous field.
  - Drag the field from the field list to a field in the query design grid to insert this field where you want it in the grid. To place a field between two existing fields in the grid, drop the new field on top of the one that it should be to the right of.
  - In the grid, click the drop-down arrow or type in the Field cell to choose a field from the list.
- If you make a mistake in adding a certain field to the query grid, you can remove the field by selecting the entire column and pressing DEL; or, on the QUERY TOOLS DESIGN tab, in the Query Setup group, click Delete Columns.

Try It! Creating a New Select Query in Design View

1. In **A11Try_xx**, click the CREATE tab. In the Queries group, click Query Design. The Show Table dialog box opens.
2. Click Students, and then click Add. Click Close to close the dialog box.
3. Drag down the bottom border of the Students window, expanding the box so that all fields are visible.
4. Leave the **A11Try_xx** database open to use in the next Try It.

Add the Students table to the query design

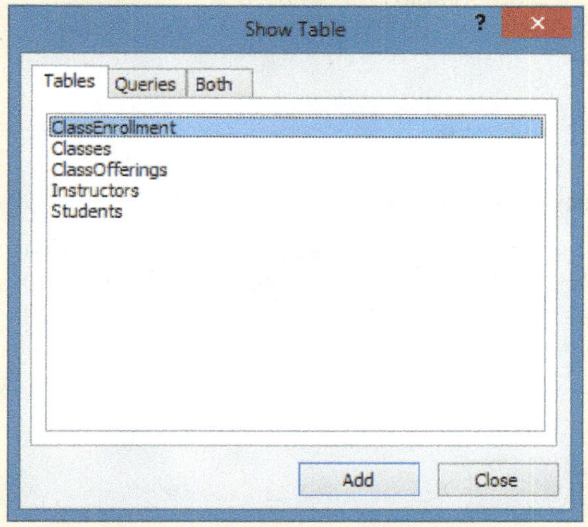

Access 2013, Windows 8, Microsoft Corporation

Try It! Adding Fields to a Query

1. In **A11Try_xx**, in Query Design view, double-click LastName on the Students table field list. LastName is added to the grid.
2. Drag FirstName from the Students table field list and drop it onto the LastName field in the grid, placing FirstName to the left of LastName.
3. Click in the Field cell of the first empty column in the grid.
4. Click the drop-down arrow in the cell, and click Phone on the menu that appears.
5. Double-click the MembershipType field to place it in the next empty column of the grid.
6. Leave the **A11Try_xx** database open to use in the next Try It.

Add fields to a query

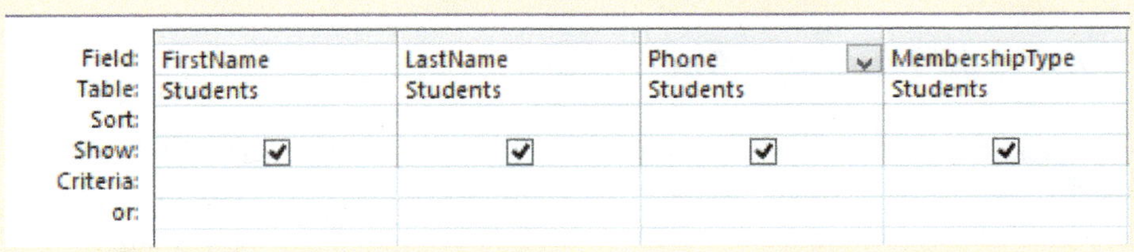

Access 2013, Windows 8, Microsoft Corporation

Try It! Removing Fields from the Query

1. In A11Try_xx, click anywhere in the MembershipType field's column.
2. Click QUERY TOOLS DESIGN > Delete Columns.
3. Leave the A11Try_xx database open to use in the next Try It.

Running a Query

- There are two ways to see the results of a query. One is to switch to Datasheet view to preview the results. The other is to run the query with the Run button !.
- For a select query, there is no real difference between these two methods. However, when you get into action queries that actually perform operations on the data rather than just displaying it, the difference becomes important.
- Query results appear in Datasheet view, just like a table.

Try It! Running a Query

1. In A11Try_xx, on the QUERY TOOLS DESIGN tab, in the Results group, click Run !. The query results appear.
2. Click HOME > View > Design View. Query Design view reappears.
3. Click QUERY TOOLS DESIGN > View > Datasheet View. Datasheet view reappears.
4. Leave the A11Try_xx database open to use in the next Try It.

Saving and Printing a Query

- When you close a query, if you have made design changes to it, you are prompted to save your work. You can also save a query from Design view before you are ready to close it.
- The first time you save a query, you are prompted for a name. Although the name can be a maximum of 64 characters including spaces, you should keep the name short and use no spaces.
- Query results appear in Datasheet view, so you can print them just as you would print any other datasheet.

Try It! Saving and Printing a Query

1. In A11Try_xx, click the Save button on the Quick Access Toolbar.
2. Type Phone List.
3. Click OK.
4. If the query does not already appear in Datasheet view, right-click its tab and click Datasheet View.
5. Click FILE > Print > Print.
6. **With your teacher's permission**, click OK; otherwise, click Cancel.
7. Close the database, and exit Access.

Lesson 11—Practice

In the jewelry database, you will create a query that extracts information (data analysis) from the raw data.

DIRECTIONS

1. Start Access, if necessary, and open **A11Practice** from the data files for this lesson.
2. Save the database as **A11Practice_xx** in the location where your teacher instructs you to store the files for this lesson.

   ✓ *If a security warning bar appears, click Enable Content.*
3. Click **CREATE** > **Query Design**.
4. In the Show Table dialog box, click **Customers**, and click **Add**.
5. Click **Close**.
6. Drag down the bottom of the Customers window until all fields are visible.
7. Double-click the **First Name** field.
8. Double-click the **Last Name** field.
9. Double-click the **City** field.
10. Double-click the **State** field.
11. Double-click the **ZIP** field.
12. Drag the **Address** field into the grid and drop it on the City field, placing it between Last Name and City.
13. Click the **Save** button on the Quick Access Toolbar.
14. Type **Mailing List** and click **OK**.
15. Click **QUERY TOOLS DESIGN** > **Run** **!** to run the query. Your screen should look similar to Figure 11-2.
16. Right-click the query's tab, and click **Close**.
17. Click **FILE** > **Close** to close the database. If instructed, submit this database to your teacher for grading.
18. Working with a partner, research the importance of the design for a data warehouse. How will the structure of the data warehouse limit or facilitate data mining?

Figure 11-2

Mailing List

First Name	Last Name	Address	City	State	ZIP
Jennifer	Brown	108 Ponting Street	Decatur	IL	62522
Cynthia	Green	720 E. Warren Street	Moweaqua	IL	62550
George	Colvin	5777 Main Street	Macon	IL	62544
Jasper	Garrett	992 West Avenue	Indianapolis	IN	46202
Carrie	Strong	211 West Eckhardt Street	Pana	IL	61722
Felicia	Adamson	775 North Main Street	Noblesvile	IN	46060
Norman	Eichmann	55110 Old Church Lane	Boston	MA	02134
Allison	Norville	522 German Drive	Indianapolis	IN	46211
Peter	Washington	852 Ronald Parkway	Fishers	IN	46292
Norman	Greenburg	7755 Peninsula Drive	Moweaqua	IL	62550
*					

Access 2013, Windows 8, Microsoft Corporation

Lesson 11—Apply

In the jewelry database, you will create several additional queries. You will also create a query that displays hidden fields in a table and enter data in those fields.

DIRECTIONS

1. Start Access, if necessary, and open **A11Apply** from the data files for this lesson.
2. Save the database as **A11Apply_xx** to the location where your teacher instructs you to store the files for this lesson.

   ✓ *If a security warning bar appears, click Enable Content.*
3. Discuss with a partner the nature of data mining. Describe the data mining tools that Access provides. Are you aware of other software used for data mining?
4. Open the **Mailing List** query in Design view.

   ✓ *One way to open the Mailing List in Design view is to right-click the query in the Navigation pane and click Design View.*
5. Add the **ID** field to the query grid in the left-most position.
6. Close the query, saving your changes.
7. Create a new query using Query Design view, based on the **Products** table.

   ✓ *Note that the field list contains fields that do not appear in the Datasheet view for this table. That is because these fields are hidden. When you create a query, you have access to all the fields in the table, even the hidden ones.*
8. Add the **Product**, **Material**, **Materials Cost**, and **Labor Cost** fields to the query grid, in that order.
9. Run the query to display its datasheet.
10. In the **Materials Cost** and **Labor Cost** fields in the datasheet, enter the values shown in the following table.
11. Save the query as **Production Costs** and close it.
12. Create a new query based on the **Salespeople** table. Include these fields: **Employee ID**, **First**, **Last**, and **Position**.
13. Save the query as **Sales List** and close it.
14. Rename the query **Salesperson List**.
15. Click **FILE** > **Close** to close the database. If instructed, submit this database to your teacher for grading.

Product	Material	Materials Cost	Labor Cost
Curb Chain	Yellow Gold, 10K	$100.00	$10.00
Curb Chain	White Gold, 14K	$120.00	$10.00
Curb Chain	Sterling Silver	$60.00	$10.00
Frog Bracelet	Sterling Silver	$50.00	$25.00
Snake Bracelet	Sterling Silver	$50.00	$30.00
Hoop Earrings	Yellow Gold, 14K	$40.00	$20.00
Hoop Earrings	White Gold, 14K	$50.00	$20.00
Hoop Earrings	Yellow Gold, 14K	$40.00	$20.00
Hoop Earrings	White Gold, 14K	$50.00	$20.00
Knot Earrings	White Gold, 14K	$40.00	$30.00
Knot Earrings	Yellow Gold, 10K	$30.00	$30.00
Knot Earrings	Sterling Silver	$10.00	$30.00
Three-Diamond Pendant on chain	White Gold, 14K	$350.00	$50.00

Lesson 12

Creating a Multi-Table Query

➤ What You Will Learn

Creating a Query Based on More Than One Table
Sorting Query Results
Reordering Fields in a Query
Using All Fields of a Table
Changing a Column Name
Saving a Query with a Different Name

Software Skills One of the main uses for queries is to join the data from two or more tables into a single datasheet of results. This involves adding multiple tables that have relationships among them to the query design. In this lesson, you will learn how to open a query in Design view and make changes to it, including adding more tables and fields and sorting the results.

WORDS TO KNOW

Alias
An alternative name for a field.

What You Can Do

Creating a Query Based on More Than One Table

- You can use fields from as many tables as you like in a query. The only requirement is that all tables be related to one another in some way.
- There are many benefits to creating queries based on multiple tables. For example, if you have a table that represents related records from another table as numeric entries, it is not always obvious what the numeric entries represent. In Figure 12-1, for example, the ClassEnrollment table shows the classes and students as ID numbers, rather than names.
- In contrast, a datasheet based on a query that combines values from the ClassEnrollment, ClassOfferings, Classes, and Students tables can show all that data in text form, making it easier to understand and interpret. See Figure 12-2.

Figure 12-1

ClassEnrollment

Enrollment I	Class ID	Student ID	Click to Add
1	1	1	
2	1	11	
3	1	24	
4	1	4	
5	1	7	
6	2	15	
7	2	36	
8	2	2	
9	2	9	
10	2	31	
11	2	14	
(New)	0	0	

Figure 12-2

Query 1 | Class Offerin...

Class	Start	Days	First	Last
Low Impact Aerobics	12/15/2017	MWF	Leroy	Critchfield
Low Impact Aerobics	12/15/2017	MWF	Robert	Kroeker
Low Impact Aerobics	12/15/2017	MWF	Simi	Anderson
Low Impact Aerobics	12/15/2017	MWF	Abdul	Norcutt
Low Impact Aerobics	12/15/2017	MWF	Margaret	Faderman
Aerobic Kickboxing	12/19/2017	TTh	Jacob	Hill
Aerobic Kickboxing	12/19/2017	TTh	Marjorie	Pratt
Aerobic Kickboxing	12/19/2017	TTh	Juliana	Smith
Aerobic Kickboxing	12/19/2017	TTh	Anna	Roecher
Aerobic Kickboxing	12/19/2017	TTh	Abby	McNally
Aerobic Kickboxing	12/19/2017	TTh	Melissa	Wilson

Try It! Creating a Multi-Table Query

1. Start Access, open **A12Try** from the data files for this lesson, and save it as **A12Try_xx**.
2. Click CREATE > Query Design.
3. In the Show Table dialog box, click Classes and hold down SHIFT, and click Instructors.
4. Click Add and then click Close. Three tables are added.
5. Drag down the bottom of the tables so that all fields are visible.
6. Drag the FirstName field in the Instructors table to the grid. The field is now added to the grid.
7. Double-click the LastName field in the Instructors table.
8. Double-click the ClassName field in the Classes table.
9. Double-click the Days, StartTime, and Location fields in the ClassOfferings table, in that order.
10. Click QUERY TOOLS DESIGN > Run ! to see the query results. Two records are displayed.
11. Click HOME > View > Design View to return to Design view.
12. Press CTRL + S to open the Save As dialog box.
13. In the Save As dialog box, type **Class Offerings Query** and click OK.
14. Leave the **A12Try_xx** database open to use in the next Try It.

Sorting Query Results

- In the query's design, you can specify that the resulting datasheet be sorted in a certain way. You can sort by one field, or by more than one.
- As with other sorts, the second-level sort applies only in the event of a duplicate value in the first-level sort field.
- If you to sort the records by multiple fields, the sort order is left to right in the query grid.

✓ *If you want to sort in a different order than left to right, there is a workaround. Add a second copy of a field to the query grid and set it to be sorted. Then clear the check box in the Show row for that field so that the copy of the field does not appear in the results.*

Try It! Sorting Query Results

1. In **A12Try_xx**, click in the Sort row for the LastName field.
2. Click the drop-down arrow and click Ascending.
3. Click in the Sort row for the ClassName field.
4. Click the drop-down arrow and click Ascending.
5. Leave the **A12Try_xx** database open to use in the next Try It.

Sort by LastName

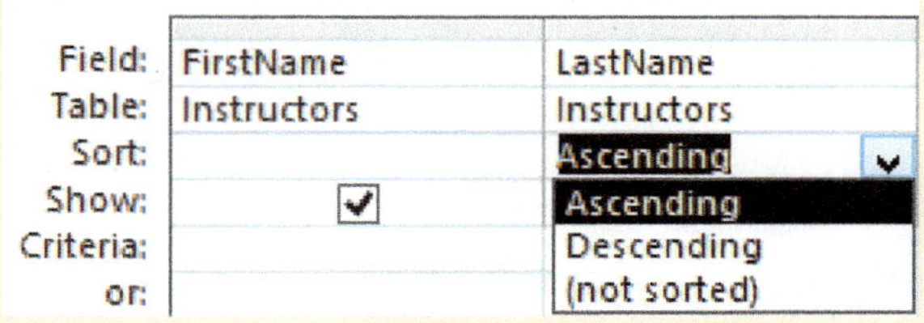

Access 2013, Windows 8, Microsoft Corporation

Reordering Fields in a Query

- To reorder the fields in the query grid, select a field, and then drag it to the right or left.
- To select a field, click the thin gray bar immediately above the field name.

Try It! Reordering Fields in a Query

1. In **A12Try_xx**, in Query Design view, click the thin gray bar above the FirstName field. The column becomes selected.
2. Drag the bar to the right to place the field to the right of the Location field.
3. Click the thin gray bar above the LastName field.
4. Drag the bar to the right to place the field to the right of the FirstName field.
5. Click Run ! to see the query results and then close the query. Click Yes to save the query.
6. Leave the **A12Try_xx** database open to use in the next Try It.

Select the field by clicking the gray bar above it

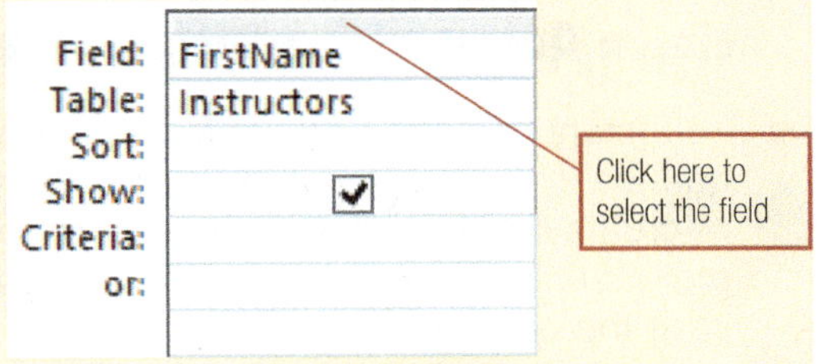

Access 2013, Windows 8, Microsoft Corporation

Using All Fields of a Table

- If you want to include all the fields from a table in the query, drag or double-click the asterisk (*) at the top of the table's field list into the query grid.

Try It! Using All Fields of a Table

1. In A12Try_xx, click CREATE > Query Design to start a new query.
2. Double-click the Classes table to add it to the query, and then close the Show Table dialog box.
3. Double-click the asterisk at the top of the Classes table field list.
4. Click Run ! to see the query results. All fields appear.
5. Click HOME > View > Design View to return to Design view.
6. Right-click the query tab and click Close. Click No when prompted to save your changes.
7. Leave the A12Try_xx database open to use in the next Try It.

Changing a Column Name

- Sometimes when you include a field from a different table, that field's name doesn't make sense in the new context. You can rename the column headings in the query results to show different names. This new name is called an **alias**.
- To assign an alias, in the Field row of the query grid, add the new name in front of the official name, separated by a colon. For example, if the field's actual name is Last and you want the column name to be Salesperson, you would type Salesperson: in front of Last.

Try It! Changing a Column Name

1. In A12Try_xx, right-click the Phone List query in the Navigation pane and click Design View.
2. In the query grid, click to place the insertion point to the left of Phone in the Field row.
3. Type **Telephone:**. The entry in the Field row should now appear as *Telephone:Phone*.
4. Click Run ! to run the query.
5. Right-click the query's tab and click Close. Do not save changes.
6. Leave the A12Try_xx database open to use in the next Try It.

Saving a Query with a Different Name

- You might sometimes want to have several similar queries in the same database. You do not have to re-create the query for each version; you can open the query in Design view, make changes, and then save the query with a different name.

Try It! Saving a Query with a Different Name

1. In **A12Try_xx**, in the Navigation pane, right-click the Phone List query and click Design View.
2. Double-click the Notes field to add it to the query grid.
3. Click FILE > Save As > Save Object As. Click Save As. The Save As dialog box opens.
4. In the Save 'Phone List' to box, type **Phone List with Notes**.
5. Click OK. The Phone List with Notes query appears in the Navigation pane.
6. Close all open objects, close the database, and exit Access.

Lesson 12—Practice

In this project, you will build a multi-table query for your friend to use to analyze her business data.

DIRECTIONS

1. Start Access, if necessary, and open **A12Practice** from the data files for this lesson.
2. Save the database as **A12Practice_xx** to the location where your teacher instructs you to store the files for this lesson.

   ✓ *If a security warning bar appears, click Enable Content.*
3. Click **CREATE** > **Query Design**.
4. In the Show Table dialog box, click **Customers**. Then hold down the CTRL key and click **Orders**.
5. Click **Add** to add both tables to the query, and then click **Close**.
6. On the Customers field list, click **First Name**. Then hold down the CTRL key and click **Last Name**.
7. Drag the selected fields to the grid.
8. Double-click the **Order Date** field in the Orders table to place it into the grid.
9. In the **QUERY TOOLS DESIGN** tab, click **Run** ! to run the query.
10. Click the **Save** button on the Quick Access Toolbar.
11. In the Save As dialog box, type **Customers and Orders** and click **OK**.
12. Click **FILE** > **Close** to close the database. If instructed, submit this database to your teacher for grading.

Lesson 12—Apply

You will continue to build complex and useful multi-table queries in your friend's jewelry database that will help her see the relationships between the tables more clearly.

DIRECTIONS

1. Start Access, if necessary, and open **A12Apply** from the data files for this lesson.
2. Save the database as **A12Apply_xx** to the location where your teacher instructs you to store the files for this lesson.

   ✓ *If a security warning bar appears, click Enable Content.*
3. Save a copy of the **Illinois Customers** query. Name the copy **Indiana Customers**.
4. Modify the **Indiana Customers** query design so that it shows Indiana customers, rather than Illinois customers.

   ✓ *To do so, change the state in the Criteria row of the grid from IL to IN.*
5. Run the **Indiana Customers** query to make sure it shows Indiana customers and then save and close the query.
6. Open the **Customers and Orders** query in Design view, and add the **Shippers** and **Salespeople** tables.
7. Place the **Name** field from the **Shippers** table in the grid to the left of all other fields.
8. Select the **Name** column and drag it to the right of all other fields.
9. Place the **Last** field from the **Salespeople** table in the grid to the right of all other fields.
10. Assign an alias of **Shipper** to the **Name** field.
11. Assign an alias of **Salesperson** to the **Last** field.
12. Run the query to confirm that it works and that the aliases appear correctly. Then, save and close the query.
13. Create a new query in Design view that uses the **Orders**, **Products**, and **OrderDetails** tables.
14. Place the following fields in the grid: **Order Date** from the Orders table, **Product** from the **Products** table, and **Quantity** from the **OrderDetails** table.
15. Set the query to be sorted in **Ascending** order, first by **Order Date** and then by **Product**.
16. Save the query as **Product Ordering**, run it to check the results, and close it.
17. Click **FILE** > **Close** to close the database. If instructed, submit this database to your teacher for grading.

Lesson 13

Using Criteria in a Query

➤ What You Will Learn

Specifying Text Criteria in a Query
Specifying Numeric Criteria in a Query
Specifying Criteria Using a Field Not Displayed in the Query Results
Using Null Criteria to Find Blank Fields
Using Make Table and Append Query Types

Software Skills Criteria (which is the plural of criterion) enable you to apply filters to query results so that only certain records are displayed. In this lesson, you will learn how to apply basic text and numeric criteria and how to use criteria based on a field that does not appear in the query results.

WORDS TO KNOW

Append query
An Append query adds records from one or more table to the end of an existing table.

Criteria
Filtering specifications that determine what records will be included in a query.

Make Table query
This type of query pulls information from one or more tables, and then creates a new table with this information.

Null
A lack of an entry in a field.

What You Can Do

Specifying Text Criteria in a Query

- **Criteria** are filtering specifications that you apply to individual fields. Criteria are very similar to the filters you learned how to create in Lesson 10.
- Criteria can be text-based, numeric, or logical. You can specify an exact value, use one or more wildcards, or enter a formula with a comparison operator such as < (less than) or = (equal to).
- When you specify text-based criteria, the text must be enclosed in quotation marks. If you forget the quotation marks, Access adds them for you automatically.
- If you want to specify more than one possible value, you can enter the second one in the Or row in the query grid. This works for both text and numeric criteria.
- There is no limit to the number of Or lines you can use. However, for practical purposes, you may want to use a wildcard or a comparison operator, as described in Lesson 14, if you have more than two or three possible values to accept.

Try It! Specifying Text Criteria in a Query

1. Start Access, and open **A13Try** from the data files for this lesson. Save it as **A13Try_xx**.
2. Right-click the Classes Being Offered query, and click Design View.
3. In the Criteria row for the Days field, type **MWF** and press TAB. Access automatically encloses the text with quotation marks.
4. Click QUERY TOOLS DESIGN > Run !. The query results show only classes that have MWF in the Days field.
5. Click HOME > View to return to Design view.
6. In the or row below where you typed MWF, type **TTh**.
7. Click Run ! to run the query again. This time records that match either entry appear.
8. Right-click the Classes Being Offered tab, and click Close. Click No when prompted to save changes.
9. Leave the **A13Try_xx** database open to use in the next Try It.

Enter MWF for the Days criteria

Field:	ClassName	StartDate	Days	StartTime	ClassDuration	
Table:	Classes	ClassOfferings	ClassOfferings	ClassOfferings	ClassOfferings	
Sort:						
Show:	☑	☑	☑	☑	☑	☐
Criteria:			"MWF"			
or:						

Access 2013, Windows 8, Microsoft Corporation

Specifying Numeric Criteria in a Query

- Numeric criteria are not enclosed in quotation marks; Access displays numeric criteria as regular numbers in the Criteria row.

Try It! Specifying Numeric Criteria in a Query

1. In **A13Try_xx**, click CREATE > Query Design. In the Show Table dialog box, double-click the Students table and then click Close.
2. In the field list, double-click the FirstName, LastName, and TermLength fields to add them to the grid.
3. In the Criteria row for the TermLength field, type **5**.
4. Click Run !. The query results show only people with a term length of 5.
5. Click View to return to Design view. Leave the query open for later use in this lesson.
6. Leave the **A13Try_xx** database open to use in the next Try It.

Specifying Criteria Using a Field Not Displayed in the Query Results

- You can filter query results based on a criterion that does not appear in the query results themselves. To do this, you add the criteria to the query grid, but then clear the Show check box for the unwanted field(s).

Try It! Filtering by an Undisplayed Field

1. In **A13Try_xx**, the query you created in the previous steps should be open in Design view. In the query grid, click to clear the Show check box for the TermLength field.
2. Click Run **!**. The query results show only the people with a term length of 5, but the TermLength field does not appear.
3. Click View to return to Design view.
4. Mark the Show check box again for the TermLength field.
5. Clear the 5 from the Criteria row. Leave the query open for later use in this lesson.
6. Leave the **A13Try_xx** database open to use in the next Try It.

Clear the Show check box

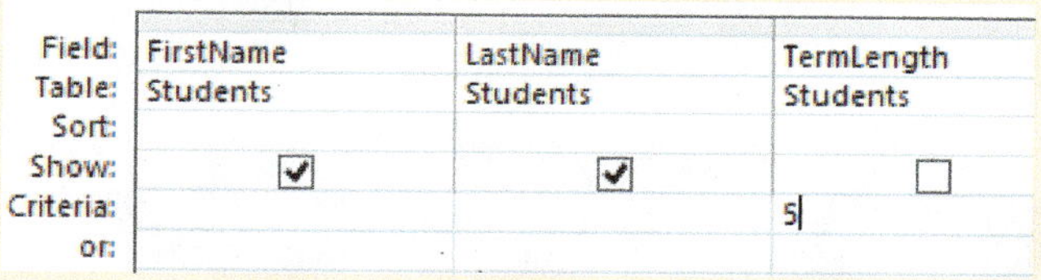

Access 2013, Windows 8, Microsoft Corporation

Using Null Criteria to Find Blank Fields

- **Null** is the word that Access uses to describe a field that is empty. This is different from a zero value, or a text field in which you have clicked and pressed the spacebar. (A space, technically, is a character. A null field contains no characters.)
- You can create a filter criterion based on whether or not a field is null. The words you use for this are *Is Null* and *Is Not Null*, respectively. Enter those words in the Criteria row, without quotation marks.

Try It! Filtering for Null Values

1. In **A13Try_xx**, in the Criteria row for the TermLength field, type **Is Null**.
2. Click Run **!**. The query results show only the records where that field is empty.
3. Click View to return to Design view.
4. In the Criteria row for the TermLength field, replace Is Null with **Is Not Null**.
5. Click Run **!**. The query results show only records where that field is not empty.
6. Close the query without saving changes.
7. Leave the **A13Try_xx** database open to use in the next Try It.

Using Make Table and Append Query Types

- Use the **Make Table query** feature to create a table from a query. This option enables you to sort items into a query and then turn that query into a table.
- To change the query type to the Make Table query type, the query needs to be in Design view.
- An **Append query** enables you to select records from one table and add them to another without removing the records from the original table.
- Make sure the table you are going to append records to has the necessary fields; otherwise, the records will not append.

Try It! Changing a Query to a Make Table Query

1. In **A13Try_xx**, right-click the Phone List query and open it in Design view.
2. In the QUERY TOOLS DESIGN tab, in the Query Type group, click Make Table. The Make Table dialog box opens.
3. In the Table Name field, type **Phone List Query**. Click OK.
4. In the Results group, click Run !. In the dialog box, click Yes.
5. In the Navigation pane, double-click Phone List Query. The table appears.
6. Close the database, and exit Access.

Lesson 13—Practice

In this project, you will create a query that filters data based on numeric criteria.

DIRECTIONS

1. Start Access, if necessary, and open **A13Practice** from the data files for this lesson.
2. Save the database as **A13Practice_xx** to the location where your teacher instructs you to store the files for this lesson.

   ✓ *If a security warning bar appears, click Enable Content.*
3. Right-click the **Product Ordering** query, and click **Design View**.
4. In the Criteria row for the Quantity field, type **1**. Refer to Figure 13-1.
5. Click **Run** ! to run the query, and confirm that the results show only the records where the quantity is 1. Then click **View** to return to Query Design view.
6. In the or row under the Quantity field, type **2**.
7. Click **Run** ! to run the query. This time the results show only the records where the quantity is either 1 or 2.
8. Click **View** to return to Query Design view.
9. Click **FILE** > **Save As** > **Save Object As**. Click **Save As** and save the query as **Orders with 1 or 2 Quantity** and click **OK**.
10. Click **FILE** > **Close** to close the database. If instructed, submit this database to your teacher for grading.

Figure 13-1

Field:	Order Date	Product	Quantity
Table:	Orders	Products	OrderDetails
Sort:	Ascending	Ascending	
Show:	✓	✓	✓
Criteria:			1
or:			

Lesson 13—Apply

You will create two queries that filter data based on multiple criteria in your friend's jewelry database. These queries will provide your friend with useful information about her business.

DIRECTIONS

1. Start Access, if necessary, and open **A13Apply** from the data files for this lesson.
2. Save the database as **A13Apply_xx** in the location where your teacher instructs you to store the files for this lesson.

   ✓ *If a security warning bar appears, click Enable Content.*
3. Create a new query in Design view, and add the **Product Ordering** query to it as a data source.
4. Add all fields to the query grid by adding the asterisk (*) from the field list to the grid.
5. Add the **Product** field to the query grid, and set up a criterion so that the query includes only records where the Product field equals **Curb Chain**.
6. Clear the **Show** check box for the Product field.
7. Run the query and make sure that only one copy of the Product field appears and only curb chain records are displayed.
8. Save the query as **Curb Chain Sales**.
9. Create a new query in Design view, and add the **Products** table to it as a data source.
10. Add all fields to the query grid by adding the asterisk (*) from the field list to the grid.
11. Add the **Size** field to the query grid, and set up a criterion so that the query includes only records where the Size field is null (empty).
12. Clear the **Show** check box for the Size field. Refer to Figure 13-2.
13. Run the query and make sure that only records where the Size field is empty are displayed. You may want to turn on the display of the Size field in the query results temporarily to check.
14. Save the query as **One Size Items Query**.
15. Click **FILE** > **Close** to close the database. If instructed, submit this database to your teacher for grading.

Figure 13-2

Field:	Products.*	Size
Table:	Products	Products
Sort:		
Show:	☑	☐
Criteria:		Is Null
or:		

Access 2013, Windows 8, Microsoft Corporation

Lesson 14

Using Comparison Operators

➤ What You Will Learn

Using Comparison Operators
Using Wildcards and the Like Operator
Using the Between...And Operator
Using the In Operator
Combining Criteria with AND or OR Operators

WORDS TO KNOW

Comparison operator
A symbol or word that represents a comparison to be performed between values.

Software Skills Although you can use multiple Or lines in the query grid to allow for multiple criteria, it is often easier to write an expression that defines the characteristics of the values you want to include. You can do this with wildcards and comparison operators.

What You Can Do

Using Comparison Operators

- **Comparison operators** represent comparisons between two values. For example, in the formula x=y, the equals sign (=) is a comparison operator.
- When using comparison operators with text, enclose the text in quotation marks. When using them with dates, enclose the dates in # (hash marks). If you forget to add those signs, Access will in most cases add them for you.
- Here are the symbols you can use for comparison operators:

Symbol	Meaning	Example
<	Less Than	<30
<=	Less Than or Equal To	<=#1/1/2014#
>	Greater Than	>100
>=	Greater Than or Equal To	>=500
<>	Not Equal To	<>"Denver"

Try It! Using a Comparison Operator in a Query

1. Start Access, and open **A14Try** from the data files for this lesson. Save the file as **A14Try_xx**.
2. Right-click the Classes Under $70 query and click Design View.
3. Double-click the Price field to place it in the grid.
4. In the Criteria row for the Price field, type **<70**.
5. Click to clear the Show check box for the Price field.
6. Click QUERY TOOLS DESIGN > Run to run the query.
7. Click the Save button on the Quick Access Toolbar to save the query.

Enter <70 for the Price criteria

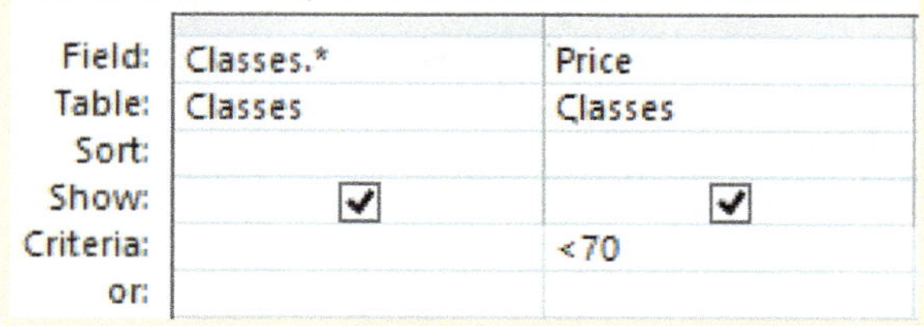

Access 2013, Windows 8, Microsoft Corporation

8. Right-click the query's tab, and click Close.
9. Leave the **A14Try_xx** database open to use in the next Try It.

Using Wildcards and the Like Operator

- Wildcards work in queries the same as in filters (see Lesson 10).
- The asterisk (*) substitutes for any number of characters; the question mark (?) substitutes for any single character.
- If you want to find records where the field includes the text you specify, but not necessarily as the entire entry, precede the criterion with the word *Like*. Then include text and a wildcard character.
- When greater-than or less-than comparison operators are used with text, alphabetical order is used. For example, <="F*" includes entries that begin with letters that come before F alphabetically.

Symbol	Example	Meaning
Like	Like "den*"	Find entries that begin with *den* and include additional characters after *den*.
	Like "den??"	Find entries that begin with *den* and include exactly two other characters after *den*.
	Like "*den"	Find entries that end with *den* and include additional characters before *den*.
	Like "??den"	Find entries that contain exactly two characters followed by *den*.
	Like "*den*"	Find entries that contain *den* and optionally other characters before and/or after *den*.

Try It! Using Wildcards and the Like Operator in a Query

1. In the **A14Try_xx**, right-click the Beginning Classes query and click Design View.
2. Double-click the Description field to add it to the grid.
3. In the Criteria row for the Description field, type **Like "*Beginning*"**.

✓ *Make sure you type the asterisks on both sides of the word, inside of the quotation marks.*

4. Click to clear the Show check box for the Description field.
5. Click Run to run the query. Three records should appear.

(continued)

Try It! Using Wildcards and the Like Operator in a Query *(continued)*

6. Click the Save button on the Quick Access Toolbar.
7. Right-click the query's tab, and click Close.
8. Leave the **A14Try_xx** database open to use in the next Try It.

Place an asterisk (*) at the start and end of the word

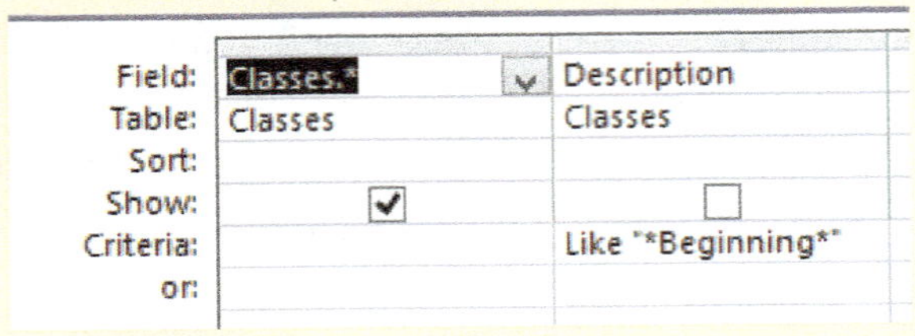

Access 2013, Windows 8, Microsoft Corporation

Using the Between...And Operator

- The word *Between* is used as a comparison operator to specify a range of values.
- For example, *Between #1/1/2014# and #1/15/2014#* finds values that fall between those two dates, inclusive.

Try It! Using the Between...And Operator in a Query

1. In **A14Try_xx**, right-click the Classes Between $60 and $80 query and click Design View.
2. Double-click the Price field to add it to the grid.
3. In the Criteria row for the Price field, type **Between 60 and 80**.
4. Click to clear the Show check box for the Price field.
5. Click Run ! to run the query. Six records should appear.
6. Click the Save button on the Quick Access Toolbar to save the query.

Set up Between criteria for the Price field

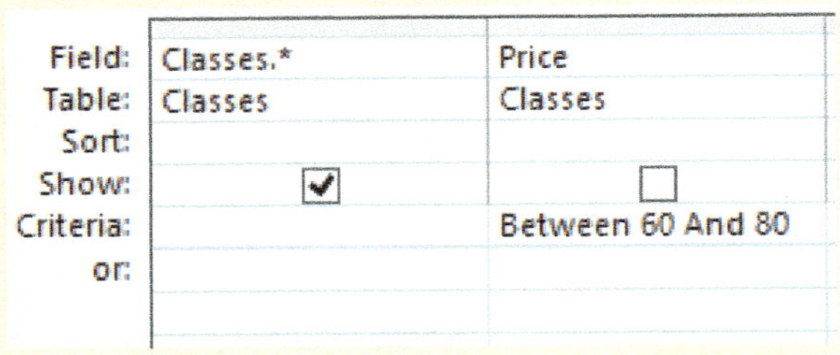

Access 2013, Windows 8, Microsoft Corporation

7. Right-click the query's tab, and click Close.
8. Leave the **A14Try_xx** database open to use in the next Try It.

Using the In Operator

- The word *In* is used as a function to specify a list of values. For example, *In ("NM", "NY", "CA")* would include any fields that contain any of those values.

Try It! Using the In Operator in a Query

1. In **A14Try_xx**, right-click the Term Length 1, 5, or 10 query and click Design View.
2. Double-click the TermLength field to add it to the grid.
3. In the Criteria row for the TermLength field, type **In (1, 5, 10)**.
4. Click to clear the Show check box for the TermLength field.
5. Click Run ! to run the query. Fifteen records should appear.
6. Click the Save button on the Quick Access Toolbar to save the query.

Set up In criteria for the TermLength field

Field:	Students.*	TermLength
Table:	Students	Students
Sort:		
Show:	☑	☐
Criteria:		In (1,5,10)
or:		

Access 2013, Windows 8, Microsoft Corporation

7. Right-click the query's tab, and click Close.
8. Leave the **A14Try_xx** database open to use in the next Try It.

Combining Criteria with AND or OR Operators

- As you saw in the previous lesson, you can use the additional rows under the Criteria row to add conditional logic.
- As an alternative, you can use an OR operator to combine criteria. For example, "GA" OR "CA" would find either value, just the same as if you had entered "GA" in the Criteria row and "CA" in the Or row.
- To use multiple criteria and restrict the results to records where all criteria are matched, use the AND operator. For example, >5 AND <10 finds values between 5 and 10 (but not including 5 and 10 themselves).

Try It! Using the OR Operator in a Query

1. In **A14Try_xx**, right-click the Term Date Not 2006 query and click Design View.
2. Double-click the TermDate field to add it to the grid.
3. In the Criteria row for the TermDate field, type **<#1/1/2017# OR >#12/31/2017#**.

   ✓ *You can widen the TermDate column by dragging so that the criteria are not truncated. It makes no difference in how the query functions, however.*

4. Click to clear the Show check box for the TermDate field.
5. Click Run ! to run the query.

Use an Or operator for the TermDate field

Field:	Students.*	TermDate
Table:	Students	Students
Sort:		
Show:	☑	☐
Criteria:		<#1/1/2017# Or >#12/31/2017#
or:		

Access 2013, Windows 8, Microsoft Corporation

6. Click the Save button on the Quick Access Toolbar to save the query.
7. Right-click the query's tab, and click Close.
8. Close the database, and exit Access.

Lesson 14—Practice

In this project, you will write a Between...And operator query for your friend's jewelry business database.

DIRECTIONS

1. Start Access, if necessary, and open **A14Practice** from the data files for this lesson.
2. Save the database as **A14Practice_xx** to the location where your teacher instructs you to store the files for this lesson.

   ✓ *If a security warning bar appears, click Enable Content.*
3. In the Navigation pane, right-click the **Product Ordering** query and click **Design View**.
4. In the Criteria row for the Quantity field, type **Between 2 and 10**. Refer to Figure 14-1.
5. Click **Run** !. Notice that the records all have quantities from 2 to 10, inclusive.
6. Click **View** to return to Design view.
7. Click **FILE** > **Save As** > **Save Object As**. Click **Save As**, type **Order Quantities 2 to 10** and click **OK**.
8. Right-click the **Order Quantities 2 to 10** tab and click **Close** to close the query.
9. Click **FILE** > **Close** to close the database. If instructed, submit this database to your teacher for grading.

Figure 14-1

Field:	Order Date	Product	Quantity
Table:	Orders	Products	OrderDetails
Sort:	Ascending	Ascending	
Show:	☑	☑	☑
Criteria:			Between 2 and 10
or:			

Access 2013, Windows 8, Microsoft Corporation

Lesson 14—Apply

You will write several queries for your friend's jewelry business database using wildcards and comparison operators to construct more complex filters.

DIRECTIONS

1. Start Access, if necessary, and open **A14Apply** from the data files for this lesson.
2. Save the database as **A14Apply_xx** in the location where your teacher instructs you to store the files for this lesson.

   ✓ *If a security warning bar appears, click Enable Content.*
3. Open the **Products Basic** query in Design view.
4. Use the **Like** operator to create a criterion that includes records with the word "**starfish**" anywhere in the Product field. Run the query to check it (it should return 2 records) and then return to Design view.
5. Save the query as **Starfish Products**.
6. Save the query again as **Animal Products**, and then modify the criteria to show any animal names (Starfish, Frog, or Snake). Run the query (it should return 4 records), and then save and close it.

   ✓ *Use multiple Or criteria.*
7. In Query Design view, create a new query that uses all the fields from the Product Ordering query, but shows only odd-numbered quantities less than 10. (In other words, 1, 3, 5, 7, or 9.) Name the query **Odd-Numbered Quantities**.

   ✓ *Use the In operator.*
8. In Query Design view, create a new query that uses all the fields from the **Product Ordering** query, but shows only orders placed on 12/14/2012. Name the query **Orders 12/14/2012**.
9. Click **FILE** > **Close** to close the database. If instructed, submit this database to your teacher for grading.

Lesson 15

Using Calculated Fields

➤ What You Will Learn

Understanding Calculated Fields
Creating a Calculated Field in a Table
Using Calculated Fields in a Query

Software Skills You can insert calculations in database objects. You can create calculated fields directly within the table's design, or you can create calculated fields in a query's design grid.

What You Can Do

Understanding Calculated Fields

- A **calculated field** contains the result of a computation performed on one or more other fields.
- A calculated field can perform a math operation on a single field. For example, you might have a Markup field that multiplies the Wholesale cost of an item by 1.5.
- A calculated field can perform a math operation on multiple fields. For example, you might have a Cost field that calculates the sum of the LaborCost field and the MaterialCost field.

WORDS TO KNOW

Calculated field
A field that contains the result of a computation performed on one or more other fields.

Creating a Calculated Field in a Table

- You can add calculated fields to a table in table Design view; create a new field and set its data type to Calculated.
- When constructing a calculated field, you use the Expression Builder. This is a dialog box that provides help for building math and logical functions.
- First you choose from the Expression Elements list. This list contains the following elements:
  - Table: The name of the table you are working with. Selecting it allows you to select individual fields from the table to use in the calculation.
  - Functions: Type of operation to be performed in the calculation; same types of functions as provided in Excel.
  - Constants: These are values such as True, False, and Null.
  - Operators: Symbols that represent math operations such as + (addition) or * (multiplication).

- Depending on your choice of expression element, the content in the other two columns changes to help you narrow down further what you want. For example, Operators is the category chosen, <All> is the Expression Category, and * is the Expression Value.
- Once you locate the expression value you want, double-click it to add it to the expression at the top of the dialog box.
- Using the Expression Builder's lists is optional; if you remember the syntax of the formula you want, you can type it at the top of the Expression Builder dialog box rather than build it by selecting from the lists.

Try It! Creating a Calculated Field in a Table

1. Start Access, and open **A15Try** from the data files for this lesson. Save the file as **A15Try_xx**.
2. Right-click the Classes table, and click Design View.
3. Select the Notes field, and click TABLE TOOLS DESIGN > Insert Rows. A new row appears.
4. In the Field Name column, type **Discount Price**.
5. In the Data Type column, open the drop-down list and click Calculated. The Expression Builder opens.
6. Click Classes in the Expression Elements list.
7. In the Expression Categories list, double-click the Price field.
8. Click Operators in the Expression Elements list.
9. In the Expression Values list, double-click the asterisk (*).
10. Click at the end of the formula in the top of the dialog box, and type **.85**.
11. Click OK.

    ✓ *Notice that in the field's properties, the Expression row contains the formula you just created.*
12. Click TABLE TOOLS DESIGN > View. A message prompts you to save.
13. Click Yes to save and to display the datasheet with the new field.
14. Notice that the calculated field does not show the discount price in Currency format. In the TABLE TOOLS DESIGN tab, click View.
15. On the GENERAL tab, select the Format drop-down. Click Currency. In the TABLE TOOLS DESIGN tab, click View. The field should now show the discounted price in currency.
16. Leave the **A15Try_xx** database open to use in the next Try It.

Using Calculated Fields in a Query

- If you do not want a calculated field to appear as a regular part of the table, you can instead create a query based on that table and put the calculated field in the query.
- Adding a calculated field to a query involves constructing a field in the query grid. In the Field row, you type a new field name (that doesn't currently exist). Then you type a colon and then the expression that performs the desired calculation. For example, see Figure 15-1, where a new field named Sale Price is created.
- To set the new field's format, right-click the field in the query grid and choose Properties. On the Property Sheet, select a format from the Format property drop-down list.

Figure 15-1

Access 2013, Windows 8, Microsoft Corporation

Try It! Using Calculated Fields in a Query

1. In **A15Try_xx**, right-click the Expiration Check query and click Design View.
2. In the first blank column in the query grid, in the Field row, type **ExpirationDate:**.

   ✓ *Make sure you type the colon after the text.*
3. Click QUERY TOOLS DESIGN > Builder. The Expression Builder opens.
4. In the Expression Elements list, click Expiration Check. Then, in the Expression Categories list, double-click TermLength.
5. In the Expression Elements list, click Operators. Then in the Expression Values list, double-click *.
6. If <<Expr>> appears at the beginning of the formula at the top of the Expression Builder dialog box, delete it. Then, click at the end of the formula and type **365+**.
7. Click Expiration Check again. In the Expression Categories list, double-click TermDate.
8. Click OK. The formula appears in the Field row.

   ✓ *You can drag to widen the column to see the entire formula if desired.*
9. Click Run ! to see the results of the query, including the new calculated field.
10. Click the Save button on the Quick Access Toolbar.
11. Right-click the query tab, and click Close All.
12. Close the database file, and exit Access.

Set up criteria with the Expression Builder

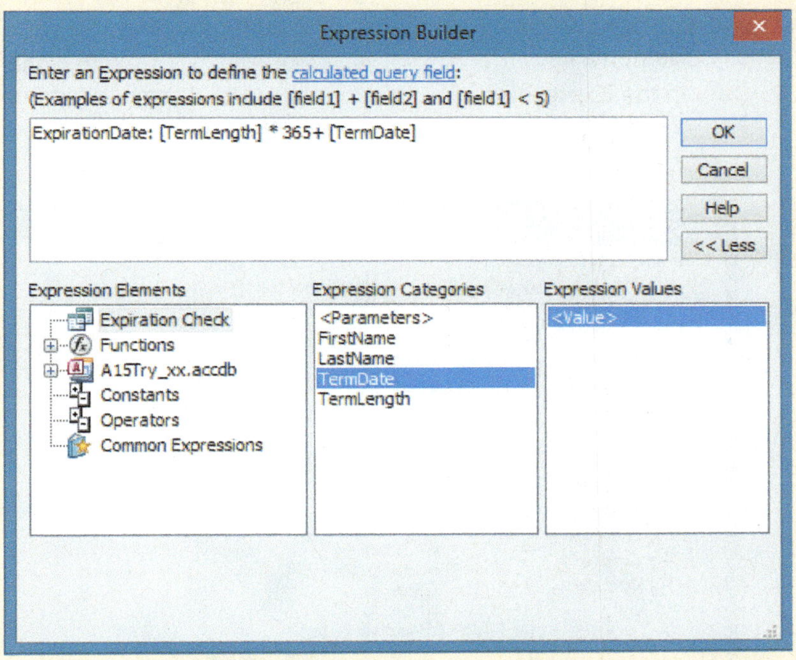

Access 2013, Windows 8, Microsoft Corporation

Lesson 15—Practice

In the jewelry business database you have been working on, you will add several new calculated fields and a new query that will make the business's data easier to understand.

DIRECTIONS

1. Start Access, if necessary, and open **A15Practice** from the data files for this lesson.
2. Save the database as **A15Practice_xx** to the location where your teacher instructs you to store the files for this lesson.

   ✓ *If a security warning bar appears, click Enable Content.*
3. Right-click the **Products** table, and click **Design View**.
4. Click **Retail Price** and click **TABLE TOOLS DESIGN** > **Insert Rows**.
5. In the Field Name column for the new field, type **Cost to Make**.
6. In the Data Type column, open the drop-down list and click **Calculated**.
7. In the Expression Builder dialog box, click **Products** in the Expression Elements list.
8. Double-click **Materials Cost** in the Expression Categories list.
9. At the top of the Expression Builder dialog box, type **+** after [Materials Cost].
10. Double-click **Labor Cost**. Refer to Figure 15-2.
11. Click **OK**.
12. Click **View**.
13. When prompted to save, click **Yes**.
14. Scroll the datasheet to the right to see the new field.
15. Right-click the table's tab, and click **Close**.
16. Right-click the **Gross Sales by Product** query and click **Design View**.
17. In the first empty column, in the Field row, type **Gross Sale: [Quantity]*[Retail Price]**.
18. Click **Save** on the Quick Access Toolbar.
19. Click **QUERY TOOLS DESIGN** > **Run** **!** to view the query results.
20. Click **FILE** > **Close** to close the database. If instructed, submit this database to your teacher for grading.

Figure 15-2

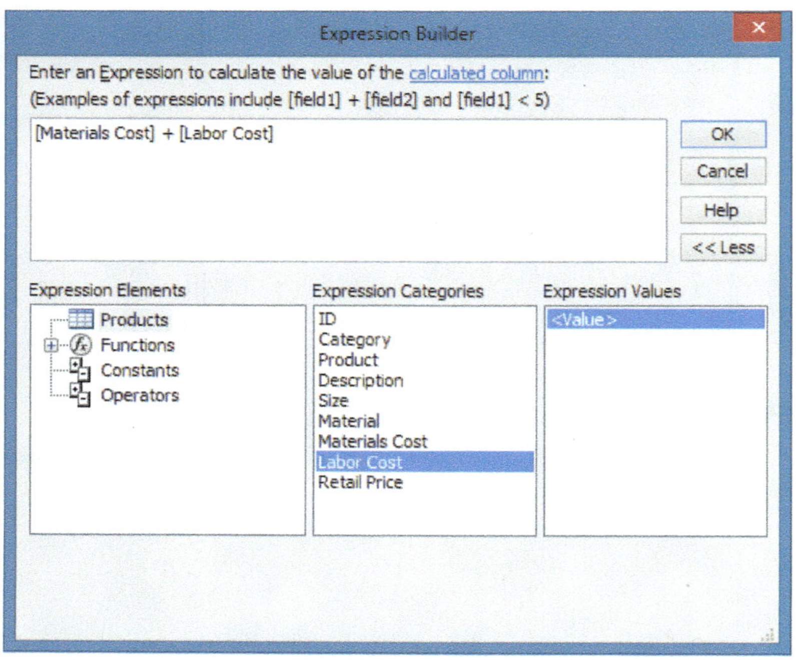

Access 2013, Windows 8, Microsoft Corporation

Lesson 15—Apply

To help your friend with her jewelry business database, you will construct a new query that calculates prices at various discount levels.

DIRECTIONS

1. Start Access, if necessary, and open **A15Apply** from the data files for this lesson.
2. Save the database as **A15Apply_xx** in the location where your teacher instructs you to store the files for this lesson.

   ✓ *If a security warning bar appears, click Enable Content.*
3. Open the **Products** table in Design view.
4. Delete the **Retail Price** field from the table, and replace it with a calculated field named **Retail Price** that multiplies the Cost to Make field's value by 2.2. Set the format to **Currency**.
5. Save your work and view the table in Datasheet view to check it.
6. Create a new query in Design view using the **Products** table.
7. Add the **ID** and **Retail Price** fields to the query grid.
8. Create a new calculated field named **10% Off** that shows the Retail Price multiplied by 0.9.

   ✓ *You multiply by 0.9 because you want to calculate 90% of the original price.*
9. Create a new calculated field named **20% Off** that shows the Retail Price multiplied by 0.8.
10. Create additional calculated fields named **30% Off**, **40% Off**, and **50% Off** that multiply the Retail Price by 0.7, 0.6, and 0.5 respectively.
11. Set the format of each new field to **Currency**.
12. Save the new query as **Discount Prices**, and run the query to check your results.
13. Click **FILE** > **Close** to close the database, and exit Access. If instructed, submit this database to your teacher for grading.

Lesson 16

Summarizing Data in Queries

➤ What You Will Learn

Summarizing with the Simple Query Wizard
Summarizing Data in Query Design View
Using the Crosstab Query Type

WORDS TO KNOW

Aggregate function
Functions that summarize grouped data. These functions include sum, count, average, minimum, and maximum.

Software Skills Sometimes it can be difficult to see the meaning in data if there is too much of it shown in too much detail. It is often helpful to create summary queries that help you pull statistics out of a large pool of data.

What You Can Do

Summarizing with the Simple Query Wizard

- When you create a query that includes numeric data fields, the Simple Query Wizard gives you the option of either a detail or a summary query.
- When you choose Summary, the Summary Options button becomes available. Click it and then choose one or more **aggregate functions** for the query, such as Avg, Min, or Max. The functions available depend on the data type. For text fields, the only option available is to count the records.
- Using the Simple Query Wizard to create a summary query has many advantages, including the ability to group data (such as for a whole month of dates together rather than each date separately) without having to manually write the complex code required to show the data in groups.
- Therefore, the best way to create a summary query is to use the wizard and then edit the query as needed in Query Design view.

Try It! Summarizing with the Simple Query Wizard

1. Start Access, and open **A16Try** from the data files for this lesson. Save the file as **A16Try_xx** in the location where your teacher instructs you to store the files for this lesson.
2. Click CREATE > Query Wizard.
3. In the New Query dialog box, verify that Simple Query Wizard is selected, and click OK.

   ✓ *If a Microsoft Access Security Notice dialog box opens, click Open.*
4. Open the Tables/Queries list, and click Table:Students.
5. In the Available Fields list, scroll down and click TermLength. Click the > button.
6. Click Next.
7. Click Summary, and then click Summary Options [Summary Options ...].
8. In the Summary Options dialog box, click the Avg check box.
9. Click OK.
10. Click Next.
11. In the What title do you want for your query box, type **Average Term Length**.
12. Click Finish. The query results appear in a datasheet.

    ✓ *The results consist of a single field, containing a single value: the average of all records.*
13. Close the query, and leave the **A16Try_xx** database open to use in the next Try It.

Summarizing Data in Query Design View

- You can also create a summary query manually in Query Design view.
- To create a summary query in Design view, click the Totals button Σ in the Show/Hide group on the QUERY TOOLS DESIGN tab. This adds a new row, Total, to the query design grid.
- The default value for each field in the Total row is Group By. The summary will be grouped by each of the fields with this setting.

  ✓ *Include only the essential fields in a summary query. A field should not be present in the query unless it is being used as a criterion, calculated, or grouped by.*
- You can open the drop-down list for the Total row and choose an aggregate function for the field on which you want to calculate.

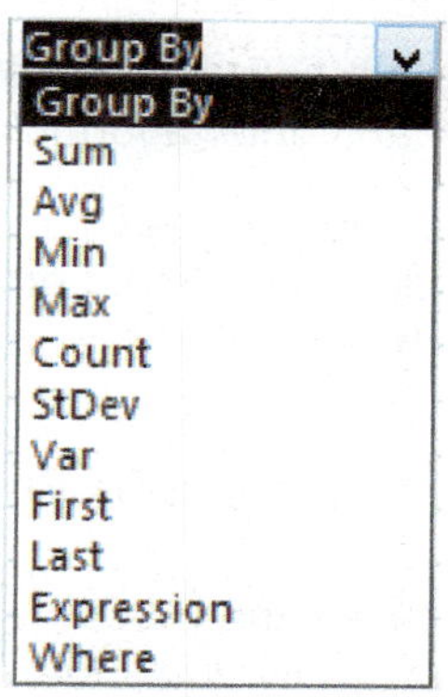

Access 2013, Windows 8, Microsoft Corporation

Figure 16-1

✓ *Some of the aggregate functions, such as Sum, require the data to be numeric; others, such as Count, work on any data type.*

- If you want to show just the calculation(s) for the entire table, do not use any Group By fields.

Here are the aggregate functions you can choose from:

Use	To
Sum	Total the numeric values by each Group By field.
Avg	Total the numeric values and divide by the number of records in each Group By field.
Min	Find the lowest value in each Group By field. If the Min field is text, the function finds the first alphabetical value. If the field is a number, the function finds the lowest number. If the field is a date, the function finds the earliest date.
Max	Find the highest value in each Group By field. If the Max field is text, the function finds the last alphabetical value. If the field is a number, the function finds the largest number. If the field is a date, the function finds the latest date.
Count	Find the number of records in each Group By field.
StDev	Calculate the standard deviation of the numbers by each Group By field. This is used to see how close all the values are to the average.
Var	Calculate the variance of the numbers by each Group By field. This is another measure of how close the values are to the average.
First	Find the field's first record input for each Group By field.
Last	Find the field's last record input for each Group By field.
Expression	If you have a calculated field (for example, Quantity*Price), you can choose Expression in the Total row and enter a formula such as Sum([Quantity]*[Price]) in the Field row.
Where	Refer the query to the Criteria row. This enables you to include fields in the query purely for criteria purposes without grouping or calculating by that field.

Try It! Summarizing Data in Query Design View

1. In **A16Try_xx**, double-click the Class Enrollments query to view its datasheet.
2. Right-click the query's tab, and click Design View.
3. Click QUERY TOOLS DESIGN > Totals Σ. The Total row appears in the query grid.
4. Open the drop-down list for the Total row in the EnrollmentID column and click Count.
5. Click Run ! to display the query results.
   ✓ *Note how the results differ from the results you saw in step 1.*
6. Save and close the Class Enrollments query, and leave the **A16Try_xx** database open to use in the next Try It.

Using the Crosstab Query Type

- The Crosstab query calculates a sum, average, or other aggregate function, and then groups the resulting data into two sets of values. One value is displayed on the top of the datasheet and one is displayed down the left side.
- At least one Row Heading option, Column Heading option, and Value option must be selected.

Try It! Using the Crosstab Query Type

1. In **A16Try_xx**, right-click the Beginning Classes query and open it in Design View.
2. Select the Classes column in the grid. Right-click and click Cut.
3. In the Classes box, double-click ClassName, Price, and Discount Price.
4. In the QUERY TOOLS DESIGN tab, in the Query Type group, click Crosstab. The Crosstab row appears in the grid.
5. In the Description column, open the Crosstab drop-down list and click Row Heading.
6. In the ClassName column, open the Crosstab drop-down list and click Column Heading.
7. In the Price column, open the Total drop-down list and click Sum. In the Crosstab drop-down list, click Row Heading.
8. In the Discount Price column, open the Total drop-down list and click Avg. In the Crosstab drop-down list, click Value.
9. On the QUERY TOOLS DESIGN tab, click Run **!**.
10. Save and close the database, and exit Access.

Lesson 16—Practice

In this project, you will make a query for your friend's jewelry business database that will show her statistics on the orders for each type of product, for example, the total number of orders, the size of the smallest order, and the size of the largest order.

DIRECTIONS

1. Start Access, if necessary, and open **A16Practice** from the data files for this lesson.
2. Save the database as **A16Practice_xx** in the location where your teacher instructs you to store the files for this lesson.

   ✓ *If a security warning bar appears, click Enable Content.*
3. Click **CREATE** > **Query Wizard**.
4. Click **Simple Query Wizard** and click **OK**.

   ✓ *If a Microsoft Access Security Notice dialog box opens, click Open.*
5. Open the drop-down list and click **Query: Product Ordering**.
6. Double-click the **Product** and **Quantity** fields to add them to the Selected Fields list, as shown in Figure 16-2 on the next page. Then click **Next**.
7. Click **Summary**, and then click **Summary Options** [Summary Options ...].
8. In the Summary Options dialog box, mark the **Sum**, **Min**, and **Max** check boxes.
9. Mark the **Count records in OrderDetails** check box.

10. Click **OK**.
11. Click **Next**.
12. In the What title do you want for your query? box, type **Product Order Statistics**.
13. Click **Finish**. The query results appear in a datasheet.
14. Right-click the query's tab and click **Close**. Click **Yes** if prompted to save your changes.
15. Click **FILE** > **Close** to close the database. If instructed, submit this database to your teacher for grading.

Figure 16-2

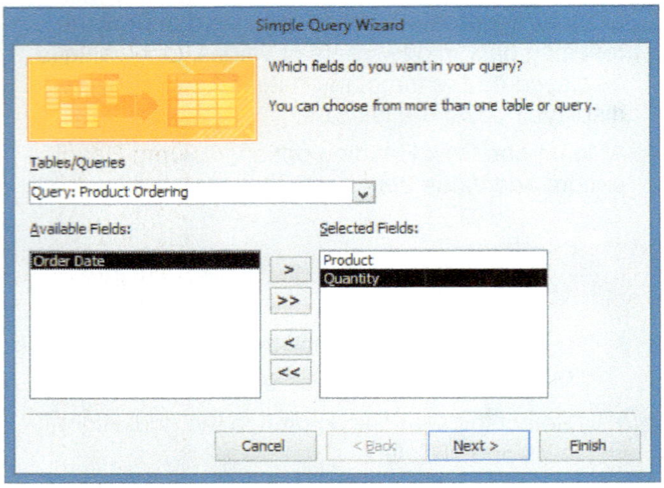

Access 2013, Windows 8, Microsoft Corporation

Lesson 16—Apply

The jewelry business owner would like to know which of her products is selling the best and how much profit she is making. You will help her with data mining techniques by creating new queries to display this information.

DIRECTIONS

1. Start Access, if necessary, and open **A16Apply** from the data files for this lesson.
2. Save the database as **A16Apply_xx** in the location where your teacher instructs you to store the files for this lesson.

   ✓ *If a security warning bar appears, click Enable Content.*

3. In Design view, create a new query based on the Customers table that counts the number of customers from each state. Name it **Customers by State**.

   ✓ *This query should consist of two copies of the State field. In the Total row, one should be set to Group By and one set to Count.*

4. In Design view, create a new query that averages the sales commission for the Salespeople table. Name it **Average Sales Commission**.

   ✓ *This query should consist of one copy of the Commission Rate field, with its Total row set to Avg.*

5. Apply the Percent format to the average. To do this, select the field and open its Property Sheet. Set the Format value to **Percent**.
6. Use the Simple Query Wizard to create a query based on the **Products** table that includes the **Category** and **Retail Price** fields. Set the query to show the Average of the retail prices by Category. Name it **Average Retail Price**.
7. Set the retail price column header to display **Avg of Retail Price** and apply the **Currency** format.
8. Click **FILE** > **Close** to close the database. If instructed, submit this database to your teacher for grading.

End-of-Chapter Activities

➤ Access Chapter 2—Critical Thinking

Little League Database

You are the assistant coach of a little league team and have been given the responsibility of maintaining the database for the team. You have inherited a database that contains several tables, but no queries. You will create relationships between the tables and create several queries that can help extract data from the tables.

DIRECTIONS

1. Open **ACT02** from the data files for this chapter, and save it as **ACT02_xx** in the location where your teacher instructs you to store the files for this chapter.
2. Open the **Relationships** grid, and add all the tables except Venues to the layout.
3. Create the following relationships (with no referential integrity enforced) as shown in the table at the bottom of the page.
4. Edit the last two relationships to enforce referential integrity. Choose both **Cascade Update** and **Cascade Delete** for each.

   ✓ *You cannot enforce referential integrity on the first relationship because neither field involved in the relationship is the primary key field in its table.*
5. Arrange the tables in the **Relationships** grid so that none of the relationship lines cross. Then close the **Relationships** grid, saving your changes.
6. Create a new query using the Simple Query Wizard that shows people's names from the **Roster** table (first and last names) and also shows the name and description of the equipment each person owns (from the **Equipment** table). Name the query **Equipment Ownership**.

   ✓ *To include fields from multiple tables in the query, make your selections from the first table, and then choose a different table from the Tables/Queries drop-down list in the Wizard.*

   ✓ *When the query results appear in the datasheet, you may want to widen the columns so that all the text fits without being truncated. This is optional.*
7. Using Query Design view, create a query that uses the **Categories** and **Roster** tables. Show all fields from the **Roster** table except Category. Include the **MembershipCategory** field from the **Categories** table, and set its criteria to **Active**, but hide it from the query results. Name the query **Active Players**.
8. Display the **Equipment** table in Datasheet view. Filter it to show only items where the Item Type is **Bat**. Save the results of the filter as a new query named **Equipment:Bats**.
9. Click **FILE** > **Close** to close the database. If instructed, submit this database to your teacher for grading.

From	To
ItemType in the **ItemType** table	**ItemType** in the **Equipment** table
CategoryID in the **Categories** table	**Category** in the **Roster** table
ID in the **Roster** table	**Owner** in the **Equipment** table

➤ Access Chapter 2—Portfolio Builder

Book Collection Database

A friend who collects antique books has asked for your help in developing a database for his collection. He has three tables created already, and now would like some queries. You will create several queries for him, to give him some examples of how Access can help him understand his data.

DIRECTIONS

1. Open **APB02** from the data files for this chapter, and save it as **APB02_xx** in the location where your teacher instructs you to store the files for this chapter.
2. Open the **Relationships** grid and enforce referential integrity between the **Books** and **Authors** tables. Use **Cascade Update** and **Cascade Delete**. Then, close the **Relationships** grid.
3. Create a query that shows all the fields for only the books (in the **Books** table) where the **Notes** field is not null. Name the query **Book Notes**.
4. Open the **Books** table in Datasheet view and sort the list in Ascending order by **Author** and then by **Date Published**.

   ✓ *You will need to temporarily rearrange the columns to perform the sort; then put them back the way they were after sorting.*
5. Save the sort as a query named **Books Sorted by Author and Date**. Do not save the changes to the table itself.
6. Create a query that shows all the fields for only authors who were born after 1850. Name the query **Authors Born After 1850**.
7. Create a calculated field in the **Authors** table named **Age at Death** that calculates how old the author was when he or she died. Place the new field immediately before Nationality.
8. Create a query in Design view that displays the first name, last name, and the earliest publication date for each author. Name it **First Published**.

   ✓ *For this query you will need to gather information from both the Author table and the Book table. Be sure to use the Min function in the Total row.*
9. Click **FILE** > **Close** to close the database. If instructed, submit this database to your teacher for grading.

Chapter 3

(Courtesy Jenkedco/Shutterstock)

Working with Forms and Reports

Lesson 17
Creating and Using a Form

- Understanding Forms
- Creating a Form with a Wizard
- Applying a Theme to a Form
- Adding Records to a Table by Using a Form
- Navigating Records in a Form
- Deleting Records from a Table by Using a Form
- Printing a Form

Lesson 18
Working with a Form in Layout View

- Understanding Layout View
- Creating a Form in Layout View
- Sizing a Control
- Moving Controls in the Layout
- Deleting a Control
- Adjusting the Control Margins and Control Padding
- Changing Control Formatting

Lesson 19
Working with a Form in Design View

- Exploring Design View and Resizing Fields
- Moving Controls
- Resetting the Tab Order
- Changing the Form Size
- Inserting an Unbound Label
- Creating a New Form in Design View

Lesson 20
Working with Form Sections

- Understanding Sections
- Displaying and Resizing Sections and Inserting a Form Title
- Adding Date/Time Codes
- Moving Controls Between Sections

Lesson 21
Creating a Report

- Understanding Access Reports
- Creating and Formatting a Report in Layout View
- Creating a Report Using the Report Wizard
- Modifying an Existing Report in Design View
- Working with Print Preview and Report View
- Printing a Report
- Grouping, Sorting, and Filtering Report Data

Lesson 22
Modifying a Report in Design View

- Working with Report Sections
- Moving a Control Between Sections
- Adding Page Number Codes
- Changing Grouping Options
- Adding a Calculated Field to a Report

Lesson 23
Creating Labels

- Understanding Labels
- Using the Label Wizard

Lesson 24
Creating a Lookup List

- Creating a Lookup
- Creating a Value List
- Looking Up Field Values from Another Table
- Creating a Multi-valued Field

Lesson 25
Creating an Input Mask

- Using a Field Validation Rule
- Understanding Input Masks
- Creating an Input Mask Using the Input Mask Wizard
- Creating an Input Mask Using the Input Mask Properties Box

End-of-Chapter Activities

Lesson 17

Creating and Using a Form

➤ What You Will Learn

Understanding Forms
Creating a Form with a Wizard
Applying a Theme to a Form
Adding Records to a Table by Using a Form
Navigating Records in a Form
Deleting Records from a Table by Using a Form
Printing a Form

WORDS TO KNOW

Form
An alternative view of a table or query, displaying the fields in an easy-to-enter arrangement, usually one record at a time.

Split form
A form that shows the related table in a separate pane below the main form.

Software Skills If your table contains many fields, entering records in Datasheet view can become cumbersome. Many people find it easier to create a data entry form that displays all the fields onscreen at once, one record at a time.

What You Can Do

Understanding Forms

- A **form** is an alternative view of a table or query, displaying the fields in an easy-to-enter arrangement, usually one record at a time.
- A form is connected to one or more tables or queries. When you add data to a form, all corresponding objects automatically update.
- To quickly create a form, display a table datasheet and then click the Form button in the Forms group on the CREATE tab. This type of form is very basic and might not be formatted exactly the way you want. You can edit it later if needed.
- A form appears in Layout view after you create it. This view shows the form approximately as it will appear in use, but its layout can also be edited.
- A **split form** is one that shows the related table in a separate pane below the main form, as shown in Figure 17-1 on the next page. To create a split form, display a table datasheet. On the CREATE tab, in the Forms group, click the More Forms button, and click Split Form.
- If you use the Form button to create a quick form from a datasheet that has a related datasheet, Access creates a subform on the form, as shown in Figure 17-2 on the next page. This is different from a split form in that the subform is embedded in the main form; there are not two separate panes.
- You can save a form by right-clicking on the form's tab and clicking Save. If the Save As dialog box opens, enter the appropriate information.

- To delete a form, right-click the form in the Navigation pane and click Delete. In the dialog box, click Yes.

  ✓ *The form must be closed before it can be deleted.*

- An application part is a template that allows you to quickly add an object to a database.
- To create a form from application parts, click the CREATE tab. Click the Application Parts drop-down arrow and select the appropriate option.

  ✓ *All objects must be closed before you can make a form from application parts.*

- A form can be set as a startup option, which means it will automatically display when the database is opened.
- To set a form as the startup option in a database, go to FILE > Options > Current Database. From the Display Form drop-down list, select the appropriate form and click OK.

  ✓ *You must close and reopen the database for the action to take effect.*

- An image can be inserted into the background of a form. From the FORM DESIGN TOOLS FORMAT tab, click the Background Image drop-down arrow Background Image, navigate to the appropriate image, and insert it into the form.
- To sort records in a form, go to HOME > Advanced > Advanced Filter/Sort. To sort a field, add the field to the design grid.
- Records can also be sorted based on calculated values by typing an expression into the field cell.
- A form is based on the data source you used to generate it, usually a table.
- You might decide you want to modify the form's data source. For example, you might want to create a similar table with some of the same fields but also with new fields that are not represented on your form.
- You can change the form's data source to use the fields in the new table.
- You can then add the new fields to your form using the Field List task pane.
- To change the data source, open the form in Design view, and display its Properties sheet. Use the Data tab to change the data source.
- To add new fields to the form, use the Add Existing Fields button to display the Field List. You can then drag the desired fields from the task pane to the form.

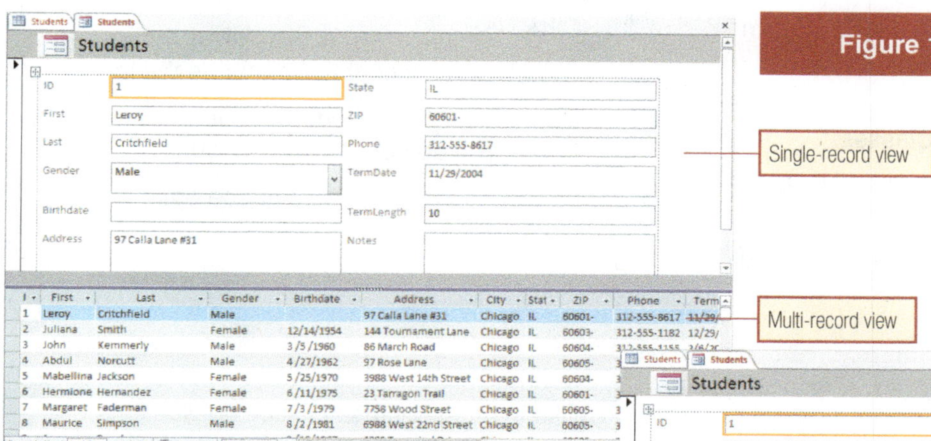

Figure 17-1

Access 2013, Windows 8, Microsoft Corporation

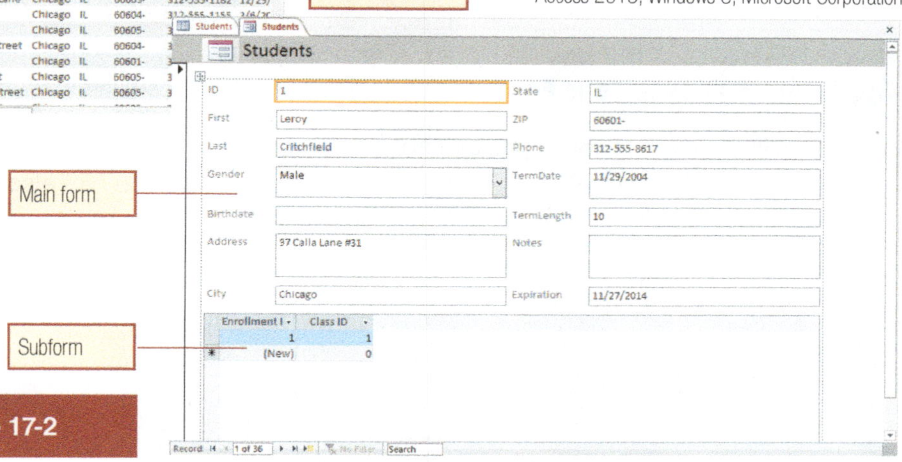

Figure 17-2

Access 2013, Windows 8, Microsoft Corporation

Try It! Creating a Quick Form

1. Start Access, and open the database **A17Try** from the data files for this lesson. Click Enable Content if a security message appears.
2. Save the database as **A17Try_xx** in the location where your teacher instructs you to store the files for this lesson.
3. In the Navigation pane, double-click the Students table.
4. Click CREATE > Form. A new form appears, with the Class Enrollment table in the subform.
5. Right-click the form's tab and click Close. Do not save changes.
6. In the Students table datasheet, click CREATE > More Forms > Split Form. A new split form appears.
7. Right-click the form's tab and click Close. Do not save changes.
8. Right-click the Students table tab and click Close.
9. Leave the **A17Try_xx** database open to use in the next Try It.

Creating a Form with a Wizard

- The Form Wizard asks questions in a series of dialog boxes, walking you step-by-step through the process of selecting tables/queries, fields, and formatting.

Try It! Creating a Form with a Wizard

1. In the **A17Try_xx** file, click CREATE > Form Wizard.
2. In the Form Wizard dialog box, open the Tables/Queries list and click Table:Classes.

   ✓ *If the Microsoft Access Security Notice dialog box opens, click Open.*
3. Click >> to move all the fields to the Selected Fields list.
4. Click Next.
5. Click Next to accept Columnar as the layout.
6. Click Finish. The new form appears. It is already saved; you do not need to resave it.
7. Leave the **A17Try_xx** database open to use in the next Try It.

Applying a Theme to a Form

- To modify an existing form, you can apply a theme, as you do in other Office applications. The theme controls the form's colors and fonts.
- Unlike in other Microsoft Office applications, however, there is no visual effect formatting applied by a theme—only colors and fonts.
- You can also apply a color or font theme separately.

Try It! Applying a Theme to a Form

1. In the **A17Try_xx** file, with the Classes form open from the previous steps, on the HOME tab, in the Views group, click the down arrow on the View button, and click Layout View.

   ✓ *You must switch to Layout or Design view before applying a theme.*

2. Click FORM LAYOUT TOOLS DESIGN > Themes.
3. Click the Ion theme.

   ✓ *The Ion theme is the last theme in the first row of the Office section.*

4. In the FORM LAYOUT TOOLS DESIGN tab, click Colors.
5. Click the Grayscale color theme.
6. In the Themes group, click Fonts A.
7. Click the Calibri font theme.
8. Leave the **A17Try_xx** database open to use in the next Try It.

Adding Records to a Table by Using a Form

- To use a form, you must display it in Form view. Layout view closely resembles Form view in appearance, but records cannot be added or edited in Layout view.
- To start a new record, click the New (blank) record button at the bottom of the form. This clears the form, so a new record can be inserted. Then enter data in the fields, pressing TAB to move to the next field or SHIFT + TAB to move to the previous field.

  ✓ *You can also click in a field to move the insertion point into it.*

- When you press TAB in the last field of the record, Access saves that record and clears the form for you to start another new record.

Try It! Adding a Record to a Table by Using a Form

1. In the **A17Try_xx** file, with the Classes form open, on the HOME tab, click the down arrow on the View button, and click Form View.
2. Click the New (blank) record button at the bottom of the form.
3. Press TAB to move past the ID field.

   ✓ *The ID field is an AutoNumber field.*

4. Type **Beginning Gymnastics** and press TAB.
5. Type **An introduction to gymnastics for adults with no previous gymnastics experience** and press TAB.
6. Type **8** and press TAB.
7. Type **120** and press TAB.
8. Press TAB to move past the Discount Price field.

   ✓ *The Discount Price field is a calculated field.*

9. Type **Ages 18 and older only** in the Notes field.
10. Press TAB. The record is saved and a new blank record opens.
11. Leave the **A17Try_xx** database open to use in the next Try It.

Navigating Records in a Form

- It is important to know how to move between records, especially in a form where only one record appears at a time.
- The navigation buttons at the bottom of the form control which record is displayed. You can use the buttons to move to the first, previous, next, or last record, or you can enter a specific record number in the Current Record text box.

Figure 17-3

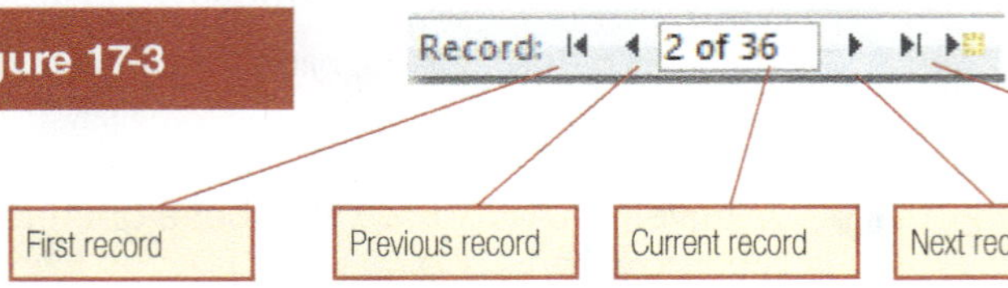

Access 2013, Windows 8, Microsoft Corporation

Try It! Navigating Records in a Form

1. In the **A17Try_xx** file, with the Classes form open, click the First record button ⏮. The Low Impact Aerobics record appears.
2. Click the Next record button ▶. The Aerobic Kickboxing record appears.
3. Click the Last record button ⏭. The Beginning Gymnastics record appears.
4. Leave the **A17Try_xx** database open to use in the next Try It.

Deleting Records from a Table by Using a Form

- You can also delete records from the form. To do so, display the record you want to delete (or select it, if the form displays more than one record at a time), and then delete the record using either of the following methods from Form view:
  - On the HOME tab, in the Records group, click the Delete drop-down arrow, and then click Delete Record.
  - Click the selection bar to the left of the form to select the record and then press DEL.

Figure 17-4

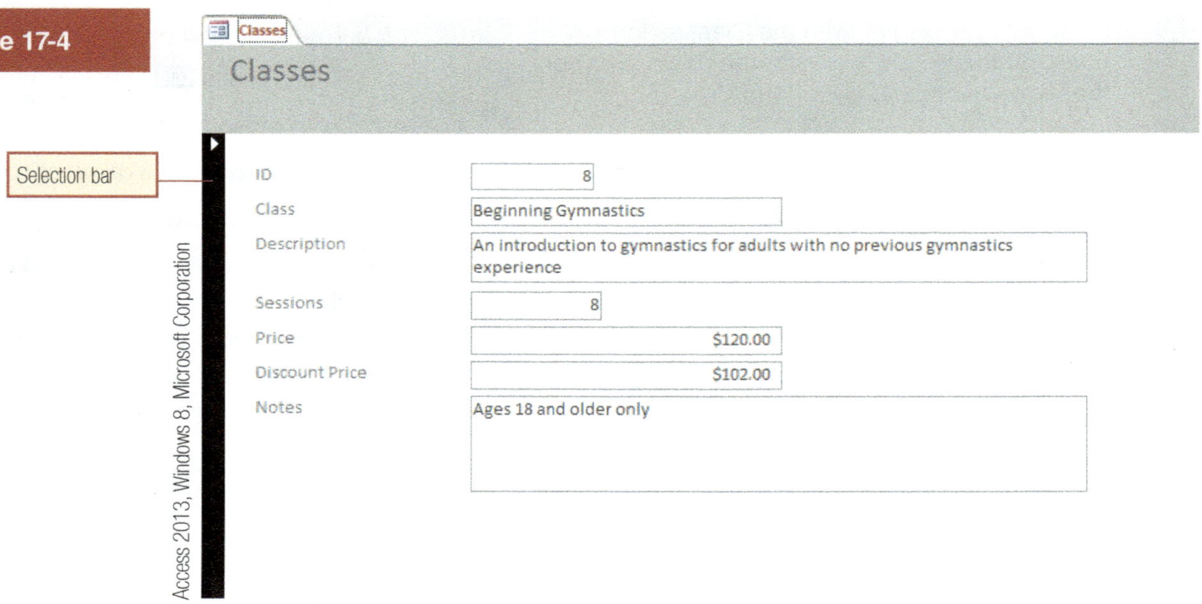

Try It! Deleting a Record from a Form

1. In the A17Try_xx file, with the Classes form open, click the Last record button to make sure the Beginning Gymnastics record is displayed.
2. Click HOME > Delete drop-down arrow > Delete Record.
3. Click Yes to confirm.
4. Leave the A17Try_xx database open to use in the next Try It.

Printing a Form

- Printing a form may be useful if you want people to fill out paper copies of it for later entry in the database.
- You can adjust the print settings in the Page Setup dialog box. There are options for changing the margins, setting columns, or printing the form data without formatting.

Try It! Printing a Form

1. In the A17Try_xx file, with the Classes form open, click FILE > Print > Print. The Print dialog box opens.
2. Click the Setup button Setup... and set the top and bottom margins to 1 inch. Click OK.
3. **With your teacher's permission**, click OK to print. Otherwise, click Cancel.
4. Close the database, saving all changes, and exit Access.

Set margins in the Page Setup dialog box

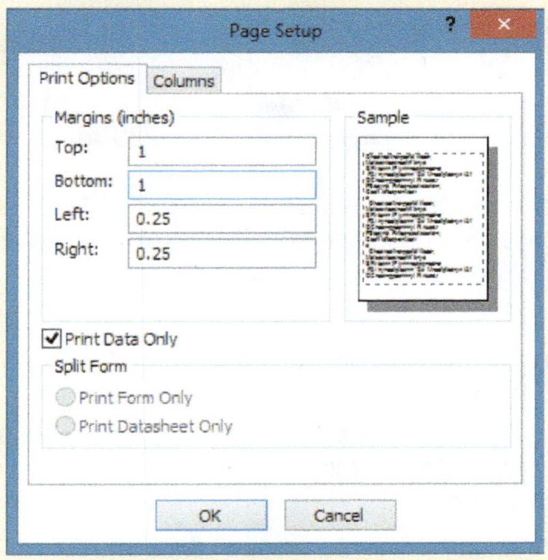

Lesson 17—Practice

In this project, you will create a form for the Orders table and a split form for the Products table.

DIRECTIONS

1. Start Access, if necessary, and open **A17Practice** from the data files for this lesson.
2. Save the database as **A17Practice_xx** in the location where your teacher instructs you to store the files for this lesson.

   ✓ *If a security warning bar appears, click Enable Content.*
3. Double-click the **Orders** table to open it in Datasheet view.
4. Click **CREATE** > **Form**.
5. Click the **Save** button on the Quick Access Toolbar.
6. In the Save As dialog box, type **Orders and Details Form** and click **OK**.
7. Right-click the form's tab and click **Close All**.
8. Double-click the **Products** table to open it in Datasheet view.
9. Click **CREATE** > **More Forms** > **Split Form**.
10. Click the **Save** button on the Quick Access Toolbar.
11. In the Save As dialog box, type **Products Split Form** and click **OK**.
12. Click **FILE** > **Close**. If instructed, submit this database to your teacher for grading.

Lesson 17—Apply

As you add more information to the jewelry database, you're finding that you're spending too much time scrolling through the records in Datasheet view. You've decided to create forms to help navigate through the information.

DIRECTIONS

1. Start Access, if necessary, and open **A17Apply** from the data files for this lesson.
2. Save the database as **A17Apply_xx** in the location where your teacher instructs you to store the files for this lesson.

   ✓ *If a security warning bar appears, click Enable Content.*
3. Use the Form Wizard to create a form for the Salespeople table. Use all the fields, and use the Justified layout. Name the form **Salespeople Form**.
4. Apply the **Whisp** theme to the form.
5. Apply the **Grayscale** color theme to the form.
6. Enter a new salesperson using the form:

   Employee ID: **GC**

   First Name: **Garry**

   Last Name: **Cutler**

   Position: **Manager**

   Commission Rate: **7%**
7. **With your teacher's permission**, print one copy of the form and write your name on the printout.
8. Use the Form Wizard to create a form for the Shippers table. Use all the fields and the **Tabular** layout. Name the form **Shippers Form**.
9. Click **FILE** > **Close**. If instructed, submit this database to your teacher for grading.

Lesson 18

Working with a Form in Layout View

➤ What You Will Learn

Understanding Layout View
Creating a Form in Layout View
Sizing a Control
Moving Controls in the Layout
Deleting a Control
Adjusting the Control Margins and Control Padding
Changing Control Formatting

Software Skills Layout view provides an easy interface for arranging, moving, sizing, and formatting the controls on a form. It is easier to manage these operations in Layout view than in Design view, covered in the next lesson.

WORDS TO KNOW

Control
A generic term for any object on a form or report.

Control margin
The spacing on the inside of the control.

Control padding
The spacing on the outside of the control.

Label
A control that contains descriptive text, such as the name of a field or the form's title.

Text box
A control that pulls information from a table or query and displays it on a form or report.

What You Can Do

Understanding Layout View

- Layout view enables you to create forms by dragging fields onto a grid in which the fields and labels automatically align neatly.
- Each object on the form is generically referred to as a control. A **control** can be a **label**, a **text box** (the field itself), or some other type of object, such as a drop-down list or a picture.
- When you place a field on a form, the field itself appears as a text box, and its name appears in a label adjacent to the text box. Depending on the form's layout, that label may be either to the left of the field or above it.
- The default layout is a stacked layout, which shows each field and its label on a separate row. See Figure 18-1 on the next page.
- The alternative is a tabular layout, in which the labels appear across the top and the fields themselves appear beneath the labels. See Figure 18-2 on the next page.
- To select a field or label in Layout view, click it. An orange border appears around it.
- To select more than one (for example, to apply formatting to more than one control at a time), hold down CTRL as you click each one.

Figure 18-1

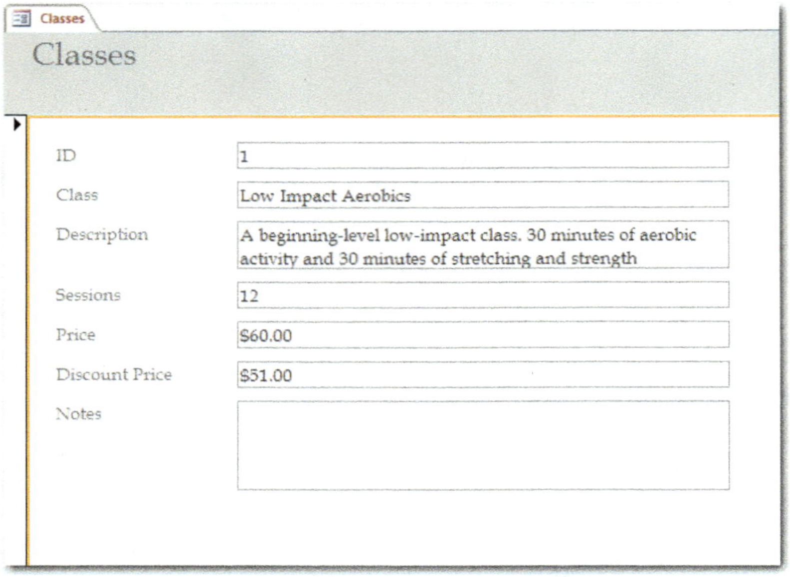

Access 2013, Windows 8, Microsoft Corporation

Figure 18-2

Access 2013, Windows 8, Microsoft Corporation

Try It! Selecting Fields in Layout View

1. Start Access, and open **A18Try** from the data files for this lesson.
2. Save the database as **A18Try_xx** in the location where your teacher instructs you to store the files for this lesson.
3. Right-click the Classes form, and click Layout View.

   ✓ *Make sure you right-click the Classes form, not the Classes table. The Classes form is in the Forms section of the Navigation pane.*
4. Click the ID field's label. The label appears with an orange box around it.
5. Click the ID field's text box (where the ID number appears). The text box appears with an orange box around it.
6. Hold down CTRL and click the ID field's label. Both the label and the text box appear with orange boxes around them.
7. Continue holding down CTRL and click on each of the other labels and text boxes on the form, until they all have orange boxes around them.
8. Click FORMAT LAYOUT TOOLS ARRANGE > Tabular. The layout changes to a tabular one.
9. Press CTRL + Z to undo the last action. The form returns to the default stacked layout.
10. Click outside the fields to deselect them.
11. Right-click the form's tab and click Close. When prompted to save changes, click No.
12. Leave the **A18Try_xx** database open to use in the next Try It.

Select the label and the text box

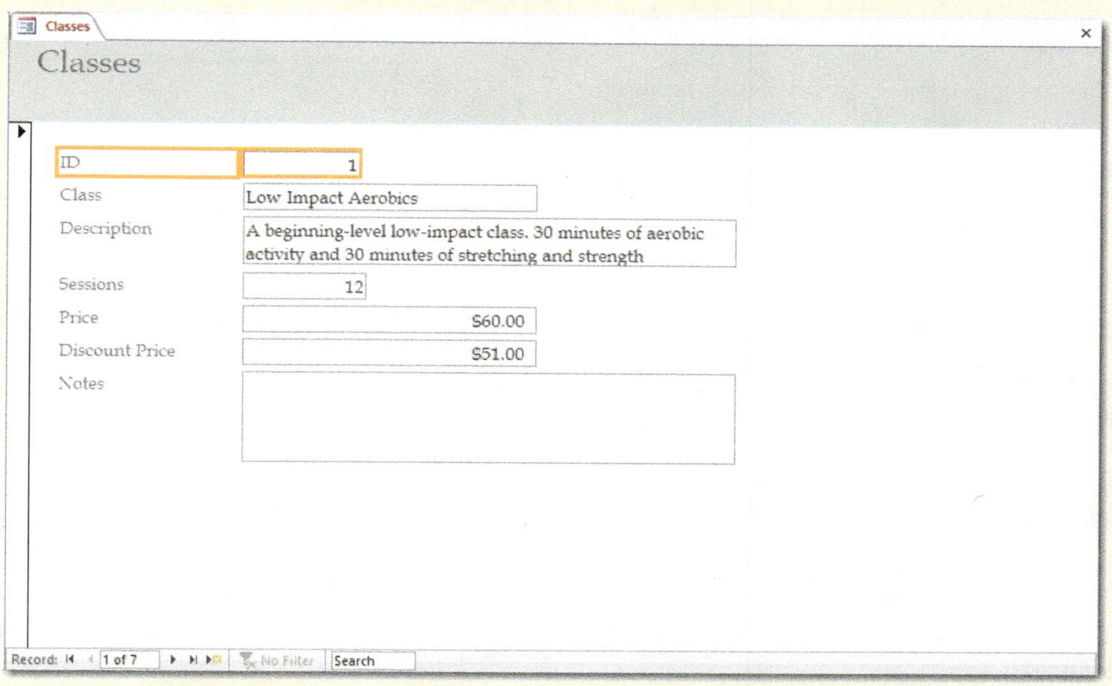

Access 2013, Windows 8, Microsoft Corporation

Creating a Form in Layout View

- Layout view enables you to drag-and-drop fields onto the form without worrying about precise placement. As you add or remove a field in Layout view, placement of the other fields automatically adjusts.
- You can later switch to Design view to fine-tune their placement if desired, as described in Lesson 19.

Try It! Creating a Form in Layout View

1. In the **A18Try_xx** file, click CREATE > Blank Form. A blank form opens, with the Field List pane on the right.
2. In the Field List pane, click Show all tables, then click the plus sign next to the Classes table to open its field list.
3. Drag the ClassID field from the field list to the top of the blank form.
4. Drag the ClassName field onto the form.
5. Drag each of the remaining fields from the Classes table onto the form, in the order they appear in the field list.

   ✓ *The label column appears truncated; this is normal at this point.*
6. Click the Save button on the Quick Access Toolbar. In the Save As dialog box, type **Alternate Class Form** and click OK.
7. Leave the **A18Try_xx** database open to use in the next Try It.

Place the remaining fields on the form

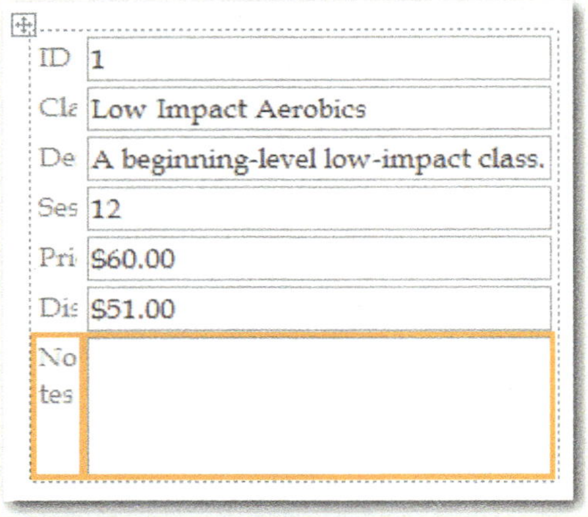

Access 2013, Windows 8, Microsoft Corporation

Creating a Navigation Form

- A Navigation form allows you to navigate to different forms and reports more efficiently.
- Navigation forms are especially helpful if you plan to publish your database to the Web.

Try It! Creating a Navigation Form

1. In the **A18Try_xx** file, click CREATE. In the Forms group, select the Navigation drop-down. Click Horizontal Tabs. The new form opens in Layout view.
2. In the Navigation pane, click and drag the Alternate Class Form to the [Add New] text.
3. In the Navigation pane, click and drag the Classes Form to the [Add New] text. The forms are now added into the navigational form.
4. On the Quick Access Toolbar, click the Save button. In the Save As dialog box, ensure Navigation Form is entered into the Form Name field, and click OK.
5. Right-click the Navigation Form tab, and click Close.
6. Leave the **A18Try_xx** database open to use in the next Try It.

Sizing a Control

- You can resize a control by dragging its border. Select the desired control, and then position the mouse pointer over the border and drag.
- Resizing one control in a column also automatically resizes all other controls in that column so the columns stay even.
- You can double-click the right edge of a selected control label to auto-size it to fit. However, all other controls in that column are resized to that new size as well, even if they need to be wider to avoid being truncated. Therefore, double-clicking to resize works best when performed on the control in that column that requires the greatest width.
- You can set a controls properties in Design view. To set form control properties, select the appropriate control. In FORM DESIGN TOOLS DESIGN click Property Sheet. Edit the appropriate properties.

Try It! Sizing a Control

1. In the **A18Try_xx** file, open the Alternate Class Form in Layout view, and click the ID label.
2. Position the mouse pointer over the right edge of the orange selection box, so the pointer becomes a double-headed arrow.
3. Drag to the right until the column is wide enough to accommodate all labels.
4. Click the Discount Price label to select it.
5. Position the mouse pointer over the right edge of the Discount Price label, so the pointer becomes a double-headed arrow.
6. Double-click to auto-size the label to fit, and all the other labels change size to match.
7. Leave the **A18Try_xx** database open to use in the next Try It.

Auto-size the Discount Price label

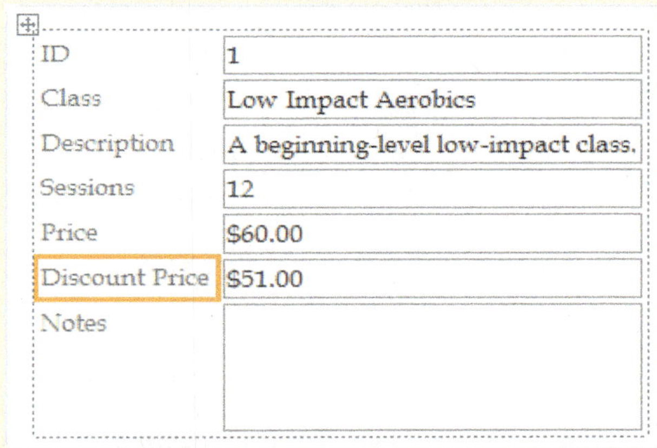

Access 2013, Windows 8, Microsoft Corporation

Moving Controls in the Layout

- Fields within a layout can only be rearranged, not moved around freely on the form. If you need to place a control outside of the layout grid, use Design view, covered in the next lesson.
- To move both the field and its associated label, you must select them both. Otherwise, they move separately.
- To move a control, select it, position the mouse pointer over it so a four-headed arrow appears, and drag it to the new location.
- To rearrange controls in a stacked layout, drag them up or down. To rearrange controls in a tabular layout, drag them to the left or right.

✓ *After reordering the fields, you might need to reset the tab order for the form so that pressing* TAB *moves the insertion point from one field to another in the right order. Resetting the tab order is explained in the next lesson.*

Try It! Moving Controls in a Layout

1. In the **A18Try_xx** file, open the Alternate Class Form in Layout view, and click the Description label.
2. Hold down CTRL and click the Description field (text box).
3. Position the mouse pointer over the Description label and text box so the pointer becomes a four-headed arrow.
4. Drag the field down to the bottom position in the form. A pink horizontal line shows where it is moving.
5. Position the mouse pointer over the bottom border of the Description field. The mouse pointer becomes a vertical double-headed arrow.
6. Drag down to enlarge the Description field to two lines of text.
7. Click the text box, so it is the only box selected, and position the mouse pointer over the right edge of the field and drag to the right to display all text.
8. Leave the **A18Try_xx** database open to use in the next Try It.

Move the Description field to the bottom of the form

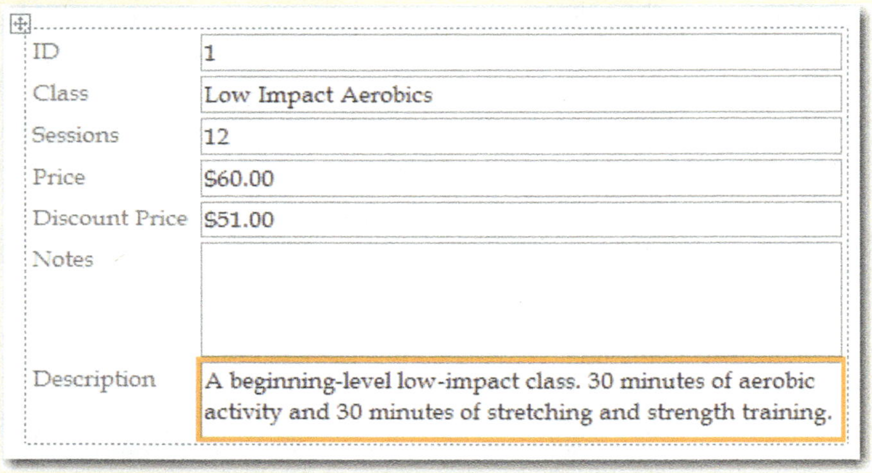

Access 2013, Windows 8, Microsoft Corporation

Deleting a Control

- To delete a field or other control, select the field's text box (not its label) and press DEL. The field and its associated label are both deleted.
- If you select the label (rather than the field itself) before pressing DEL, only the label is deleted; the field remains.

Try It! Deleting a Control

1. In the **A18Try_xx** file, with the Alternate Class form open in Layout view, click the ID field.
2. Press DEL. Both the field and the label are removed.
3. Press CTRL + Z to undo the last action.
4. Click the ID label and press DEL. Only the label is deleted.
5. Click the ID field and press DEL. The field is deleted.
6. Leave the **A18Try_xx** database open to use in the next Try It.

Adjusting the Control Margins and Control Padding

- Each control has its own padding and margins. **Control padding** is the space on the outside of the control (that is, between it and another control). **Control margin** is the space on the inside of the control (that is, between the text inside the control and the control's border).
- To adjust the padding and margins, use the buttons in the Position group on the FORM LAYOUT TOOLS ARRANGE tab. Padding and margins have four possible settings: None, Narrow, Medium, and Wide. The settings apply only to the selected fields and labels.

Try It! Adjusting the Control Margins and Control Padding

1. In the A18Try_xx file, with the Alternate Class Form open in Layout view, press CTRL + A to select all controls on the form.
2. Click FORM LAYOUT TOOLS ARRANGE > Control Margins.
3. Click Narrow.
4. Click FORM LAYOUT TOOLS ARRANGE > Control Padding.
5. Click Medium.
6. Click outside the fields to deselect them.
7. Leave the A18Try_xx database open to use in the next Try It.

Select narrow control margins

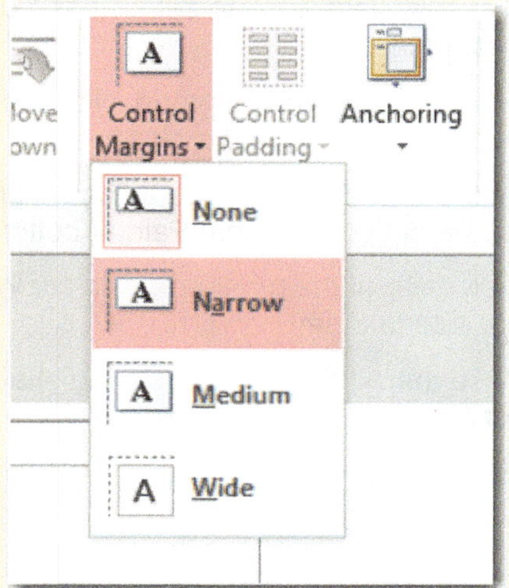

Access 2013, Windows 8, Microsoft Corporation

Changing Control Formatting

- While a control on a form is selected, you can use the controls in the Font group on the FORM LAYOUT TOOLS FORMAT tab or the Text Formatting group on the HOME tab to do any of the following:
  - Change the item's font or font size.
  - Apply bold, italic, or underlined font styles.
  - Choose left-aligned, centered, or right-aligned.
  - Choose background and text color.
- If you make an error while formatting, choose the Undo command immediately after making the error.
- To copy formatting from one control to another, select a control with the formatting you want to copy, click the Format Painter button, and then click the control you want to change.
- If you want to change multiple controls with Format Painter, double-click the Format Painter button and click on each control you want to change. Click the Format Painter button again to turn it off.

Try It! Changing Control Formatting

1. In the **A18Try_xx** file, with the Alternate Class Form open in Layout view, click the Class label.
2. Hold down CTRL and click each of the other labels, so all labels are selected.

   ✓ *Do not select the fields themselves.*

3. Click HOME > Bold **B**, or press CTRL + B.
4. Click HOME > Font Color arrow A and click the bright-red square from the Standard Colors section of the color palette.
5. Click the Class label to select it and deselect all other labels.
6. In the Text Formatting group, click the Font Size drop-down arrow, and click 14.
7. On the HOME tab, in the Clipboard group, double-click the Format Painter button.
8. Click each of the other labels to copy the new font size to them.
9. Close the **A18Try_xx** file, saving changes, and exit Access.

Choose Red as the color for the labels

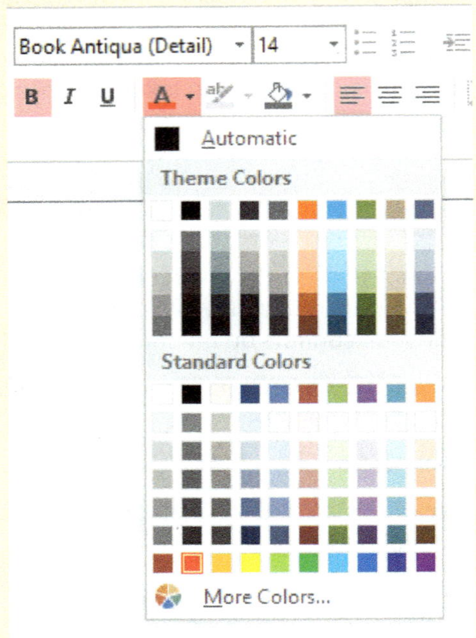

Lesson 18—Practice

In this project, you will create a new form for the Customers table using the tabular layout.

DIRECTIONS

1. Start Access, if necessary, and open **A18Practice** from the data files for this lesson.
2. Save the database as **A18Practice_xx** in the location where your teacher instructs you to store the files for this lesson.

   ✓ *If a security warning bar appears, click Enable Content.*
3. Click **CREATE** > **Blank Form**.
4. In the Field List pane, click **Show all tables** if the list of tables does not already appear.
5. In the Field List pane, click the plus sign next to **Customers** to display the fields for that table. Refer to Figure 18-3.
6. Drag the **First Name** field from the field list to the form.
7. Drag the **Last Name** field from the field list to the form.
8. Select all labels and fields.
9. Click **FORM LAYOUT TOOLS ARRANGE** > **Tabular** to change the form to a tabular layout.
10. Drag the **ID** field onto the form, to the left of the First Name field.

    ✓ *When dragging, position the mouse pointer so a vertical pink line appears to the left of the First Name field, and then release the mouse button.*
11. Position the mouse pointer at the right edge of the **ID** field (selected) and drag to the left, resizing the column to fit the current content.
12. Click the ID field's label to select it.
13. Hold down CTRL and click the **First Name** label, and then the **Last Name** label.
14. Click **HOME** > **Italic** *I*, or press CTRL + I.
15. Click the **Save** button on the Quick Access Toolbar.
16. In the Save As dialog box, type **Customer Basics** and click **OK**.
17. Click **FILE** > **Close**. If instructed, submit this database to your teacher for grading.

Figure 18-3

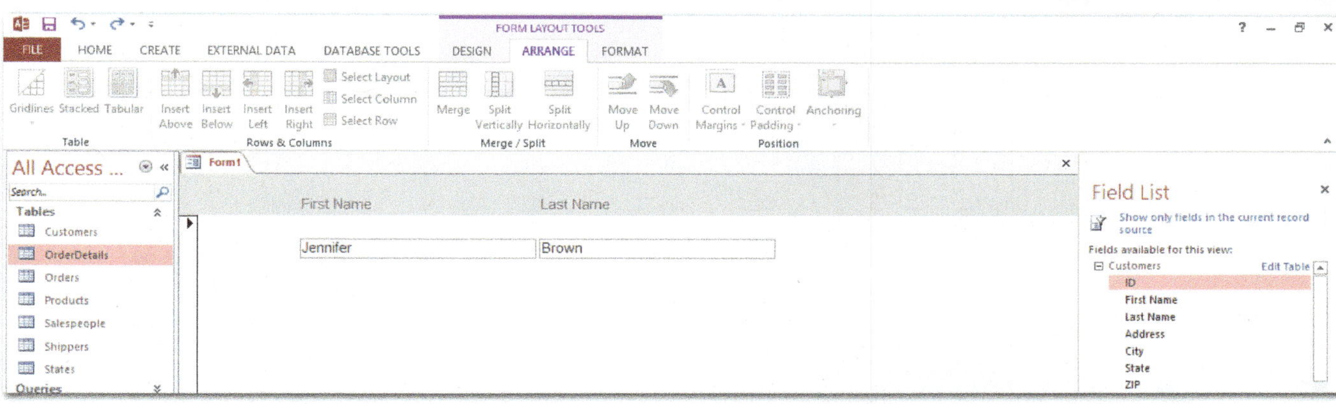

Access 2013, Windows 8, Microsoft Corporation

Lesson 18—Apply

In the jewelry database you have created, you have decided that some of the forms need visual enhancement. You will improve the forms' appearances using Layout view.

DIRECTIONS

1. Start Access, if necessary, and open **A18Apply** from the data files for this lesson.
2. Save the database as **A18Apply_xx** in the location where your teacher instructs you to store the files for this lesson.

   ✓ *If a security warning bar appears, click Enable Content.*
3. Create a new form in Layout view, with Stacked layout, that uses the **Category**, **Product**, **Size**, and **Material** fields from the **Products** table, in that order.
4. Move the **Material** field to immediately follow the Category field.
5. Right-align all the labels.
6. Apply a green text color to the labels.
7. Change the label text size to 12 point.
8. Widen the column containing the fields to approximately twice its original width.
9. Widen the column containing the labels to approximately twice its original width.
10. Save the form as **Product Basics**, and close it.
11. Open the **Shippers** form in Layout view.
12. In the **Name** column, drag the bottom border of one of the fields upward to shrink the height to match the height of the ID field. Do the same thing for the **Account** field.
13. Set the **Control Margins** for all fields on the form to **Narrow**. (Do not include the labels.)
14. Save and close the form.
15. Open the **Orders and Details Form** in Layout view.
16. In the subform, widen the **Product** column so none of the names are truncated.
17. On the main part of the form, widen the column containing the labels so that the **Salesperson** field does not overflow onto an additional line. Your screen should look like Figure 18-4.
18. Save and close the form.
19. Click **FILE** > **Close**. If instructed, submit this database to your teacher for grading.

Figure 18-4

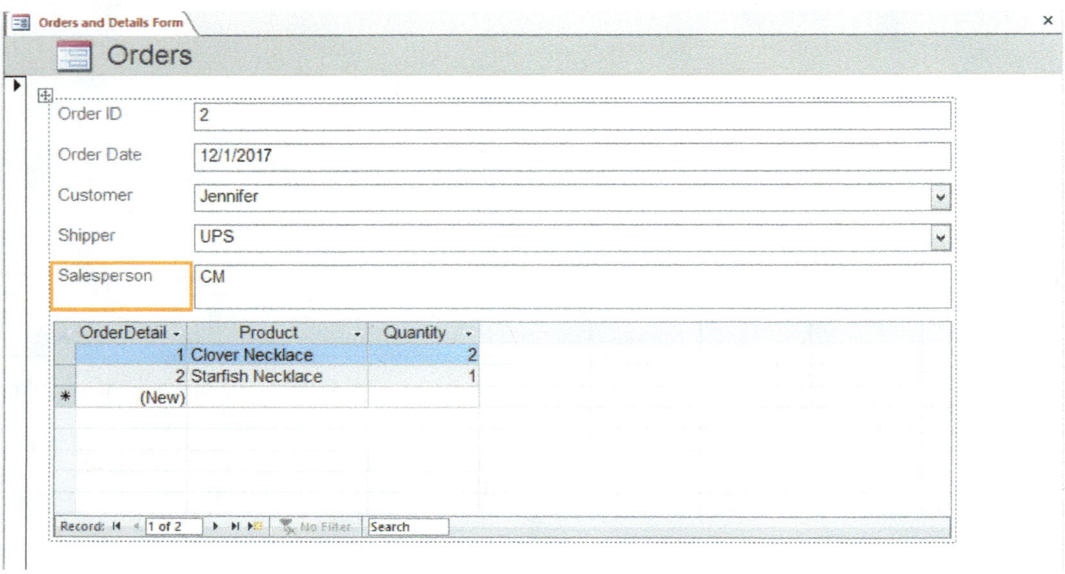

Access 2013, Windows 8, Microsoft Corporation

Lesson 19

Working with a Form in Design View

➤ What You Will Learn

Exploring Design View and Resizing Fields
Moving Controls
Resetting the Tab Order
Changing the Form Size
Inserting an Unbound Label
Creating a New Form in Design View

Software Skills In a form's Design view, you can fine-tune the form's layout, including moving controls around individually. You can also apply formatting and adjust form controls as you do in Layout view.

What You Can Do

Exploring Design View and Resizing Fields

- **Form Design view** consists of a layout grid on which you place fields, labels, and other controls. You can drag them around freely on that grid.
- You can do almost everything in Design view that you can do in Layout view, plus you can add other controls such as drop-down lists, check boxes, and even charts and graphics.
- In Design view, you can place codes on the form that display the date and time, record or page numbers, and other information by using functions similar to those in Excel. These are typically placed in the header or footer, which are covered in Lesson 20.
- You can also fine-tune the placement of items more precisely in Design view and move fields separately from their labels and vice versa.
- Fields behave differently depending on whether they are in a layout. A layout is a structure that automatically arranges and organizes fields, as you saw in Lesson 18. To determine whether a layout is in use, click any label or field. If a **layout selector** ⊞ appears above and to the left of the fields, a layout is present.
- If you created the form in Layout view or with the Form Wizard, the fields are already in a stacked or tabular layout.

WORDS TO KNOW

Form Design view
A view in which you can edit the controls on a form.

Layout selector
The four-headed arrow button ⊞ in the upper-left corner of a layout, visible in Design view when a field or label in the layout is selected.

Selection handles
Squares around the border of a control that can be dragged to resize the control.

Tab order
The sequence in which the insertion point moves from field to field when you press TAB.

Unbound
Not connected to a particular field.

- If you manually create a form in Design view, the fields are free-floating and there is no layout grid. Fields are also free-floating on forms that were upgraded from Access 2010 and earlier versions.
  - ✓ *The layout grid in Access is very much like a table in Word. That same symbol is present when working in a table in Word, but it is called the table selector.*
- To add a control, go to the Controls group under FORM LAYOUT TOOLS DESIGN tab. Select the appropriate control and place it in the form.
- You can drag a control's right border to resize it. This does not change the number of characters that can be stored in a field; that's controlled in the table properties. It only changes the width of the onscreen control that displays the field value.
- When you resize a control that is part of a layout, all the controls in that column are resized. When you resize a free-floating control, only that control is resized.
- You can delete a control by selecting it and pressing DEL.
- You can also insert a background image into a form in Design view. From FORM LAYOUT TOOLS DESIGN, click the Background Image drop-down arrow Background Image. Navigate to and add the appropriate image to the form.

Try It! Exploring Design View and Resizing Fields

1. Start Access, and open **A19Try** from the data files for this lesson.
2. Save it as **A19Try_xx** in the location where your teacher instructs you to store the files for this lesson.
3. In the Navigation pane, right-click Classes With Layout and click Design View.
4. Click the ID label.
   - ✓ *Notice the four-headed arrow in the upper-left corner of the layout and the dashed border that surrounds the controls.*
   - ✓ *All fields are the exact same width and all labels are the exact same width in this form.*
5. Position the mouse pointer at the right edge of the selected ID label and drag to the left.
   - ✓ *All the fields are resized the same amount.*
6. In the Navigation pane, right-click Classes Without Layout and click Design View.
7. Click the text box (the field itself) for the ClassID field.
   - ✓ *Notice that there is no layout selector.*
   - ✓ *Some fields have different widths than others. This is permitted only when a layout is not being used.*
8. Position the mouse pointer at the right edge of the selected ClassID field and drag to the left.
   - ✓ *Only the ClassID field is resized.*
9. Leave the **A19Try_xx** database open to use in the next Try It.

Resize the ClassID field

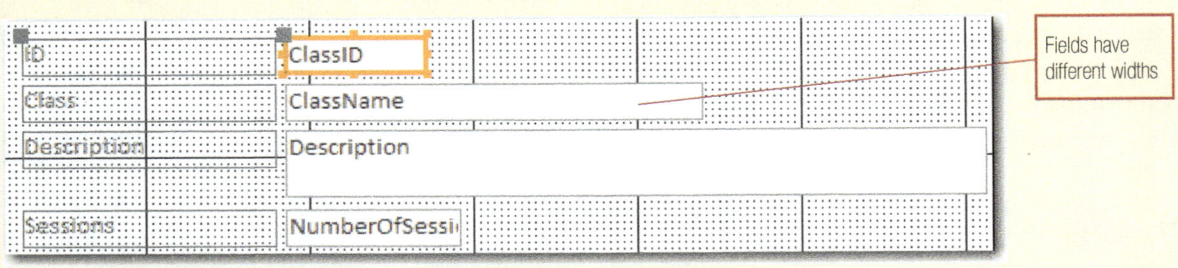

Access 2013, Windows 8, Microsoft Corporation

Moving Controls

- You can drag a control to move it.
- When you drag a control that is part of a layout, you can drag it only to different positions within the layout; you cannot drag it outside of the layout. The label and field move together, regardless of which one you drag.
- When you drag a free-floating control (that is, a control that is not part of a layout), you can place it anywhere you like.

✓ *You cannot drag a control from one section to another. However, you can cut a control (CTRL + X) and then select a different section and paste it (CTRL + V). Sections are covered in Lesson 20.*

- A free-floating control has a large square **selection handle** in its upper-left corner. You can drag the control by that square to move it independently of any associated controls.
- To select multiple controls, click on the first control, hold down the CTRL or SHIFT key, and click on additional controls. You can also "lasso" controls by dragging a box around them.
- The layout that has been applied to the controls can be removed by going to FORM DESIGN TOOLS ARRANGE and clicking Remove Layout in the Table group.

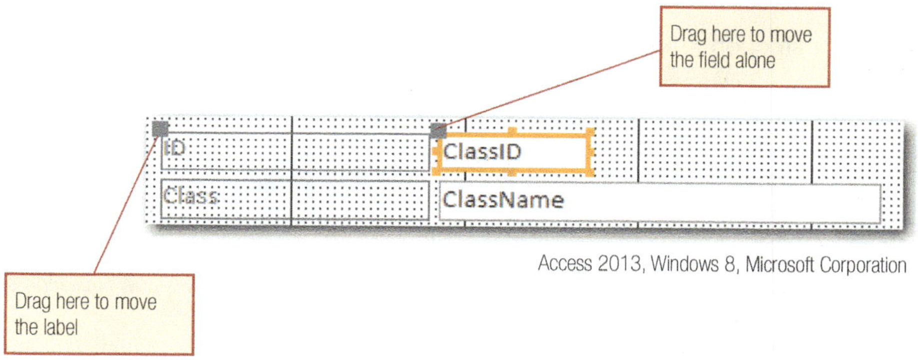

Figure 19-1

Access 2013, Windows 8, Microsoft Corporation

Try It! Moving Fields on a Form

1. In the **A19Try_xx** file, open Classes With Layout in Design view.
2. On the Classes With Layout form, click the Description field.
3. Drag the Description field between the Discount Price and Notes fields.
4. Leave the **A19Try_xx** database open to use in the next Try It.

Resetting the Tab Order

- **Tab order** is the sequence in which pressing the TAB key moves the insertion point from one field to another. The default tab order is from top to bottom on a stacked form, or from left to right on a tabular form.
- If you add or move controls on a form based on a layout, Access automatically adjusts the tab order. For example, earlier in this lesson when you moved the Description field on the Classes With Layout form, Access reset the tab order to reflect the Description field's new position.
- However, if you add or move controls on a form without a layout, you have to change the tab order manually.
- You might also want to set an alternate tab order so that users don't have to tab past a seldom-used field, such as Suffix or Middle Initial during data entry, or past an automatically entered field, such as a calculated or AutoNumber field.
- Tab order can be set to top-to-bottom or left-to-right by selecting Auto Order.
- Auto-ordering forms can be done by going to the Tab Order dialog box and clicking Auto Order.

Try It! Resetting the Tab Order

1. In the **A19Try_xx** file, with the Classes With Layout form open in Design view, click FORM DESIGN TOOLS DESIGN > Tab Order.
2. In the Tab Order dialog box, drag the ClassID field to the bottom of the list. (Click the gray box to the left of the field name to select the field, then drag the gray box to the new position.)
3. Click OK.
4. Click FORM DESIGN TOOLS DESIGN > Tab Order to reopen the dialog box.
5. Click Auto Order Auto Order.
6. Click OK.
7. Leave the **A19Try_xx** database open to use in the next Try It.

Drag a field up or down in the Tab Order dialog box

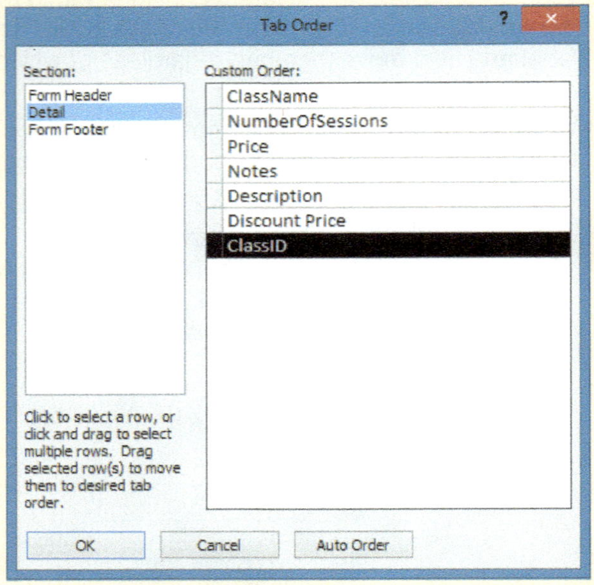

Access 2013, Windows 8, Microsoft Corporation

Changing the Form Size

- By default, forms appear on tabs, so form size is not an issue; the form is as large as the tabbed page on which it is displayed, which is in turn determined by the size of the Access window.
- However, it is also possible to set a form to appear in its own window, in which case the form size is important because it specifies the size of the window.

✓ *Setting a form to appear in a window is beyond the scope of this book.*

- Form size is also (and more commonly) an issue if you want to add additional controls to a form in Design view. The form may need to be enlarged to accommodate the additional controls.

Try It! Changing the Form Size

1. In the **A19Try_xx** file, with the Classes With Layout form open in Design view, position the mouse pointer at the right edge of the form.
2. Drag to the right to expand the form horizontally approximately 2 inches.

   ✓ *Use the ruler above the work area to gauge the distance.*
3. Leave the **A19Try_xx** database open to use in the next Try It.

Drag to enlarge the form horizontally

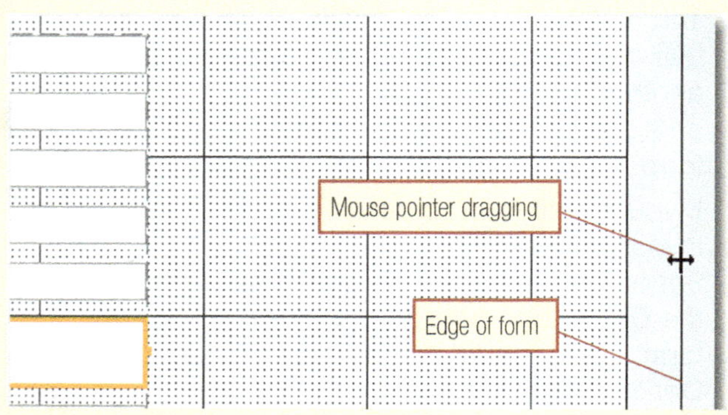

Access 2013, Windows 8, Microsoft Corporation

Inserting an Unbound Label

- An **unbound label** is one that is not associated with any particular field.
- The simplest type of unbound control is a label. Most of the labels on a form are connected to fields, but a form can also contain other labels, too.

Try It! Inserting an Unbound Label

1. In the **A19Try_xx** file, in the Classes With Layout form in Design view, click FORM DESIGN TOOLS DESIGN > Label *Aa*.
2. On the form, in the blank space to the right of the fields, drag to draw a box, approximately 2" by 2" square.
3. In the new box, type **Note: Not all classes are offered every quarter.**
4. Click the outside of the box to select its border. The border appears orange.
5. Position the mouse pointer on the selection handle at the bottom of the box, and drag upward to size the box to fit the text.
6. Right-click the form's tab and click Close. Click Yes when prompted to save changes. If the Classes Without Layout form is still open, close it and save its changes.
7. Leave the **A19Try_xx** database open to use in the next Try It.

Draw a text box in the newly created space

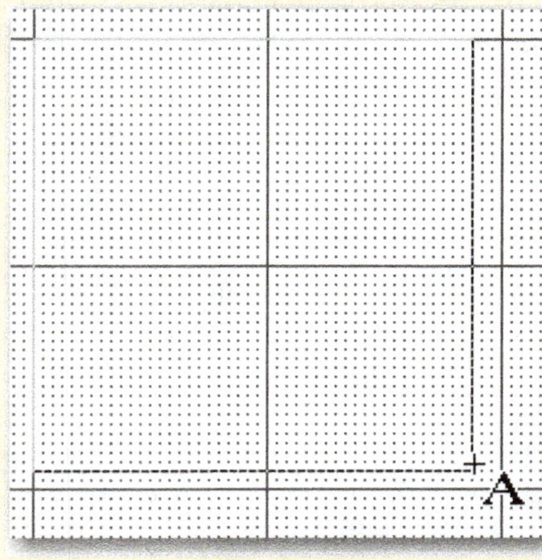

Access 2013, Windows 8, Microsoft Corporation

Resize the text box to fit the text

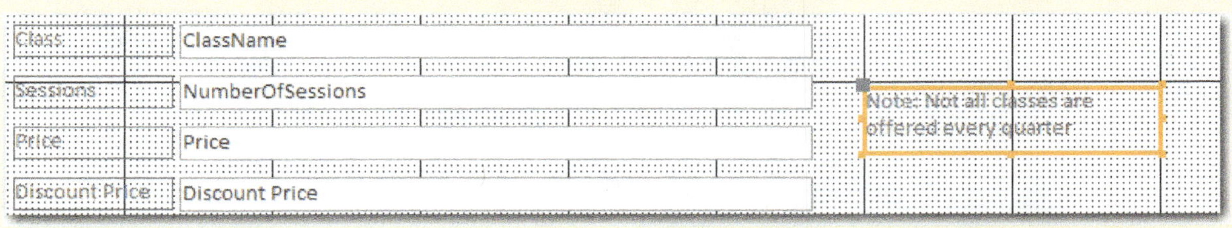

Access 2013, Windows 8, Microsoft Corporation

Creating a New Form in Design View

- Use Design view in order to have more control over the layout of your form. Design view gives you a more detailed view of your form structure.

Try It! Creating a New Form in Design View

1. In the **A19Try_xx** file, in the Classes With Layout form in Design view, click CREATE > Form Design.
2. If necessary, click FORM DESIGN TOOLS DESIGN > Add Existing Fields. The Field List pane opens.
3. If necessary, click Show all tables.
4. Click the plus sign ⊞ to the left of ClassEnrollment.
5. Double-click the EnrollmentID field. It appears on the form.
6. Double-click the ClassOfferingID field.
7. Double-click the StudentID field.
8. Press CTRL + A to select all the fields on the form.
9. Click FORM DESIGN TOOLS ARRANGE > Stacked. The fields are placed in a stacked layout.
10. Close the **A19Try_xx** database without saving the changes to the new form, and exit Access.

Select the layout of the form

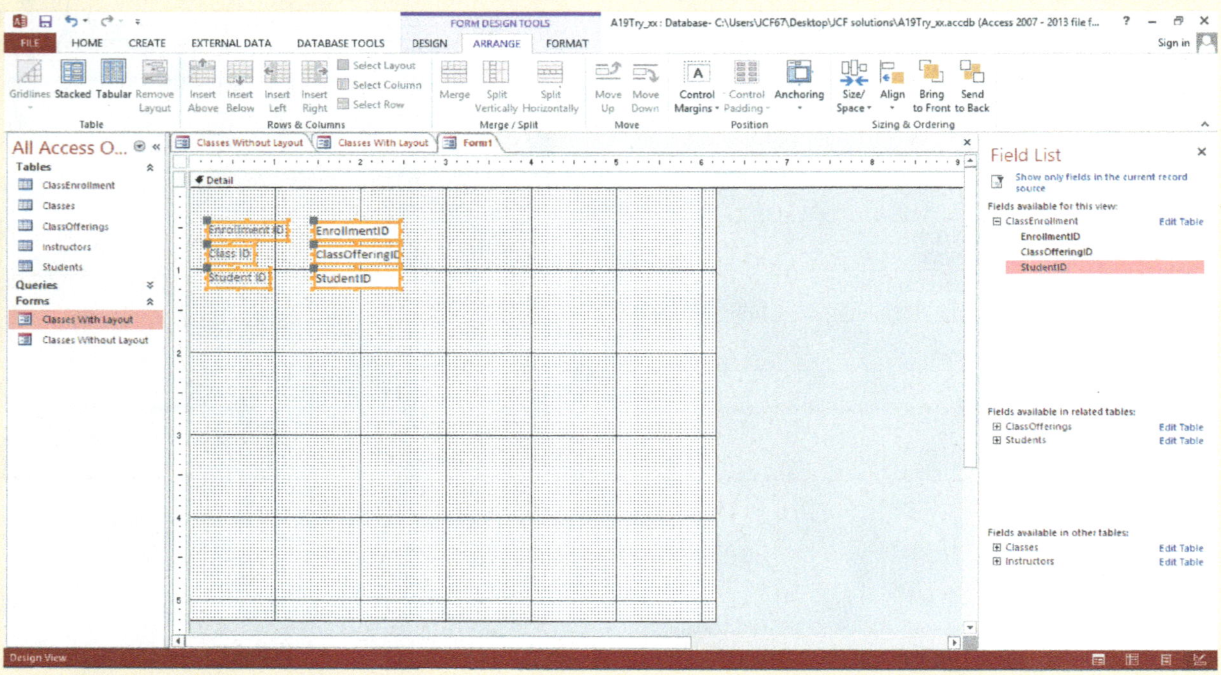

Access 2013, Windows 8, Microsoft Corporation

Lesson 19—Practice

In this project, you will create a new Order Detail Form in Design view.

DIRECTIONS

1. Start Access, if necessary, and open **A19Practice** from the data files for this lesson.
2. Save the database as **A19Practice_xx** in the location where your teacher instructs you to store the files for this lesson.

   ✓ *If a security warning bar appears, click Enable Content.*
3. Click **CREATE** > **Form Design**.
4. If the Field List pane does not appear, click **FORM DESIGN TOOLS DESIGN** > **Add Existing Fields** to display it.
5. Click **Show all tables**.
6. Click the **plus sign** ⊞ next to OrderDetails.
7. Double-click the **OrderDetailID** field to add it to the form.
8. Double-click the **Order** field.
9. Double-click the **Quantity** field.
10. Double-click the **Product** field.
11. Click the **Close** button × on the Field List pane to close it.
12. Press CTRL + A to select all the controls on the form.
13. Drag the selected controls down 1" on the form.
14. Click **FORM DESIGN TOOLS DESIGN** > **Label** *Aa*.
15. Drag to create a label box above the fields.
16. In the label box, type **Order Details**.
17. Click outside the label box to move the insertion point out of it.
18. Click the border of the label box to select it, as shown in Figure 19-2.
19. Click **HOME** > **Font Size** arrow > **20**.
20. Click the **Save** button on the Quick Access Toolbar.
21. In the Save As dialog box, type **Order Detail Form** and click **OK**.
22. Click **FILE** > **Close**. If instructed, submit this database to your teacher for grading.

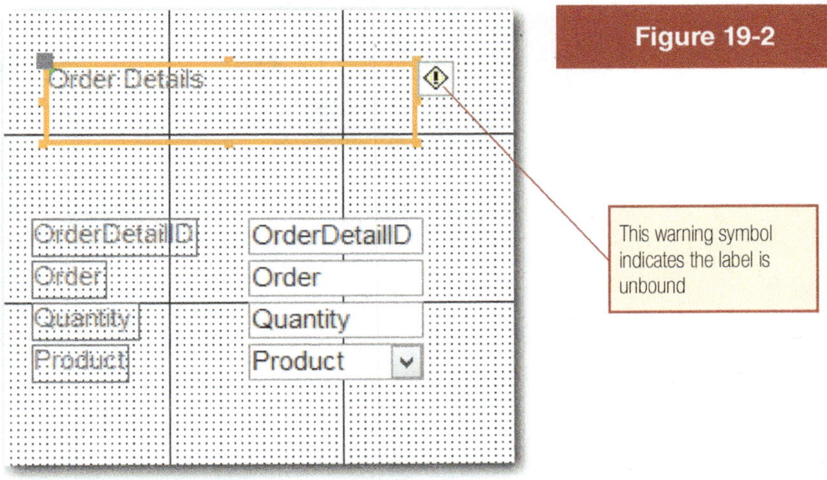

Access 2013, Windows 8, Microsoft Corporation

Figure 19-2

Lesson 19—Apply

In your friend's jewelry business database, you will make changes to forms that cannot be made in Layout view, such as changing the form's size and adding explanatory labels. You will use Design view to make these changes.

DIRECTIONS

1. Start Access, if necessary, and open **A19Apply** from the data files for this lesson.
2. Save the database as **A19Apply_xx** in the location where your teacher instructs you to store the files for this lesson.

   ✓ *If a security warning bar appears, click Enable Content.*
3. Open the **Order Detail Form** in Design view.
4. Change the order of the last three fields to **Order**, **Product**, and **Quantity**.
5. Change the tab order to reflect the new field order.
6. Select all the fields, and place them in a stacked layout.
7. Widen the field column by approximately 1".
8. Close the form, saving your changes.
9. Open the **Customer Basics** form in Design view.
10. Select all fields, and remove them from the layout using the **Remove Layout** command on the FORM DESIGN TOOLS ARRANGE tab.
11. Resize the field widths so they are about the same size as shown in Figure 19-3.
12. Save and close the form.
13. Click **FILE** > **Close**. If instructed, submit this database to your teacher for grading.

Figure 19-3

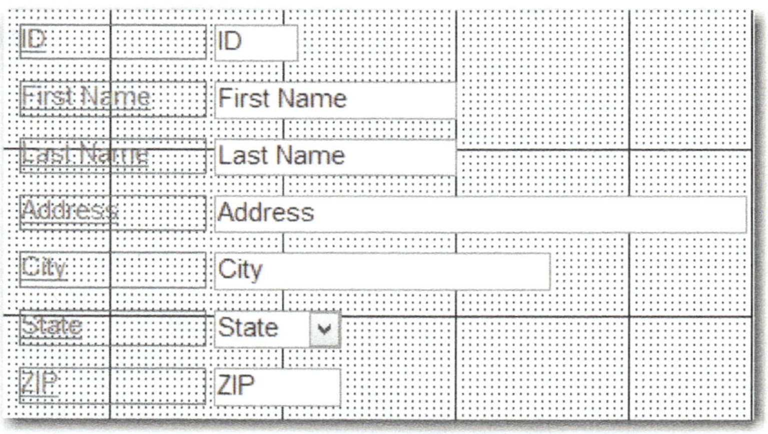

Lesson 20

Working with Form Sections

➤ What You Will Learn

Understanding Sections
Displaying and Resizing Sections and Inserting a Form Title
Adding Date/Time Codes
Moving Controls Between Sections

Software Skills One major benefit of working with a form in Design view is the ability to add and customize additional sections, such as the form header and footer. The header is typically used for a form title; the footer may contain codes such as page numbering or date/time codes.

What You Can Do

Understanding Sections

- A form can have multiple **sections**. The Detail section is the main one, where the fields are placed.
- A form can also have four other sections: Form Header, Page Header, Form Footer, and Page Footer. These header and footer sections provide a place to enter information and objects that relate to the entire form or entire page, rather than to an individual record. They are managed from Design view.
- Forms that you create via the Form Wizard or via the Form button (or Split Form button) automatically have a form header set up. Forms that you create via Design view or via the Blank Form button (Layout view) do not.
- In Form view, the form header appears at the top of the form. The form footer appears at the bottom of the form. See Figure 20-1 on the next page.
- In Design view, there are separate areas for each section, each with its own divider bar at the top. See Figure 20-2 on the next page.
- Whatever you enter on the **form header** appears only once, at the top of the form in Form view or at the beginning of a printout, regardless of the number of pages in the printout.
- Whatever you enter in the **page header** appears at the top of each page of a multipage form or printout. You might place a page numbering code here, for example, to print a page number at the top of each page.

WORDS TO KNOW

Form footer
An area at the bottom of the form, below the Detail area, in which you can enter explanatory text, graphics, or other information that applies to the form as a whole.

Form header
An area at the top of the form, above the Detail area, in which you can enter titles, explanatory text, graphics, or anything else that applies to the form as a whole.

Page footer
Same as form footer except it applies to individual printed pages.

Page header
Same as form header except it applies to individual printed pages instead of the form as a whole.

Section
An area of a form or report layout designed for a specific purpose. For example, the Detail section contains the fields and the Form Header section contains the form title.

- The page header does not appear in Form view.
- Page headers are not typically used, because a typical form is only one page long when printed, so it would be redundant to have both a form header and a page header.
- The **form footer** appears in Form view and on the last page of a printout. The form's footer is a good place for controls that you always want to see if the Detail section requires scrolling.
- The **page footer** appears at the bottom of each page of a multipage form or printout, but does not appear in Form view.
- To select a section, click its bar in Design view. To select the entire form (all sections), click the Select All button in the upper-left corner of the form. See Figure 20-3 on the next page.

Figure 20-1

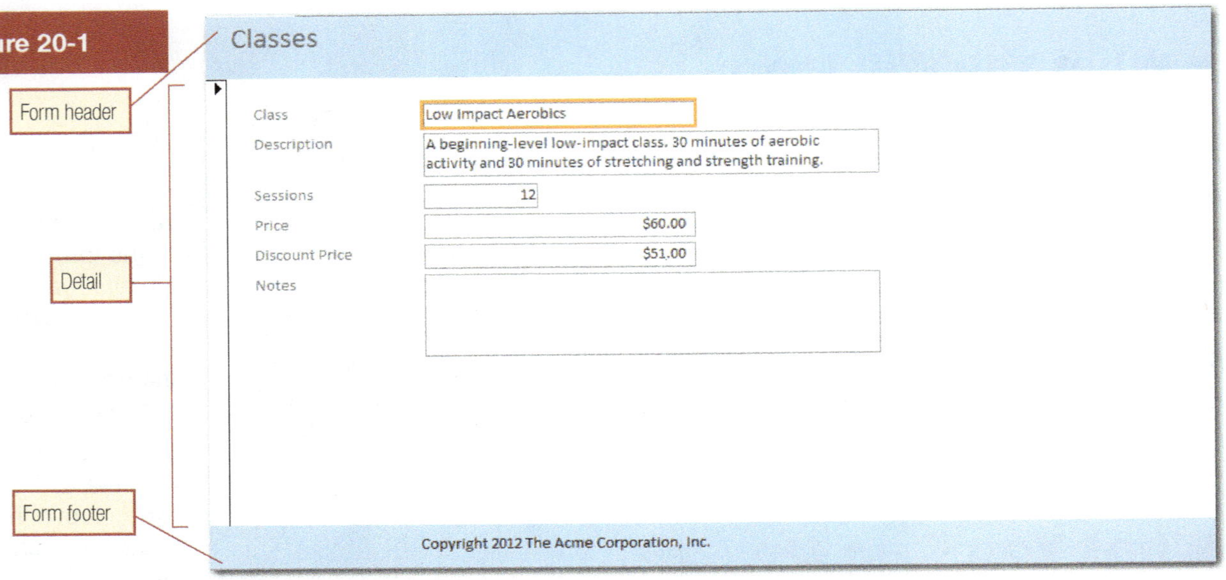

Figure 20-2

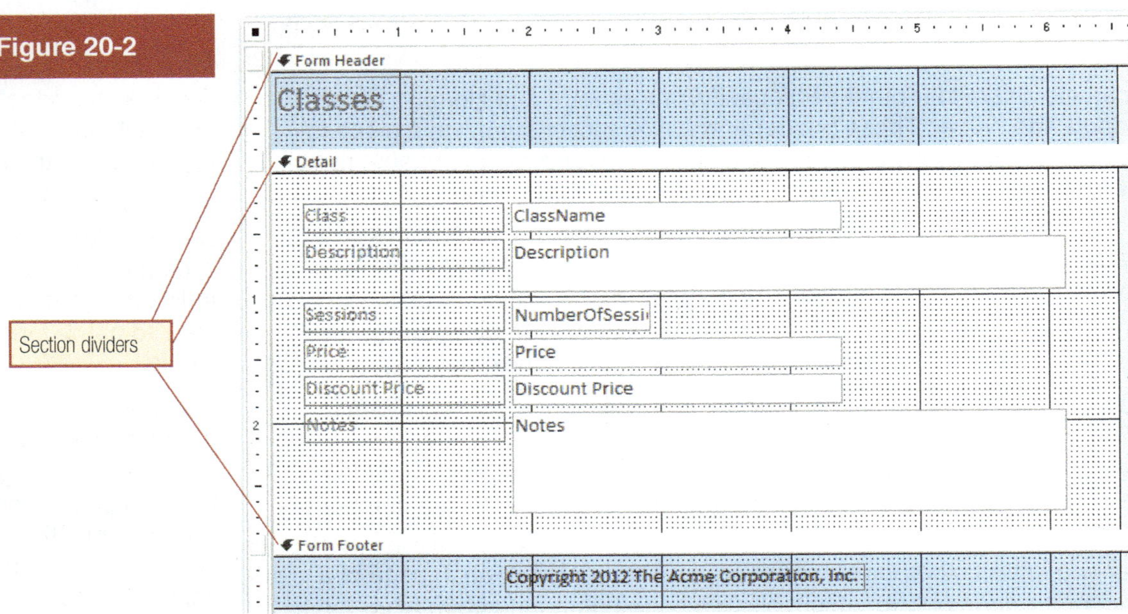

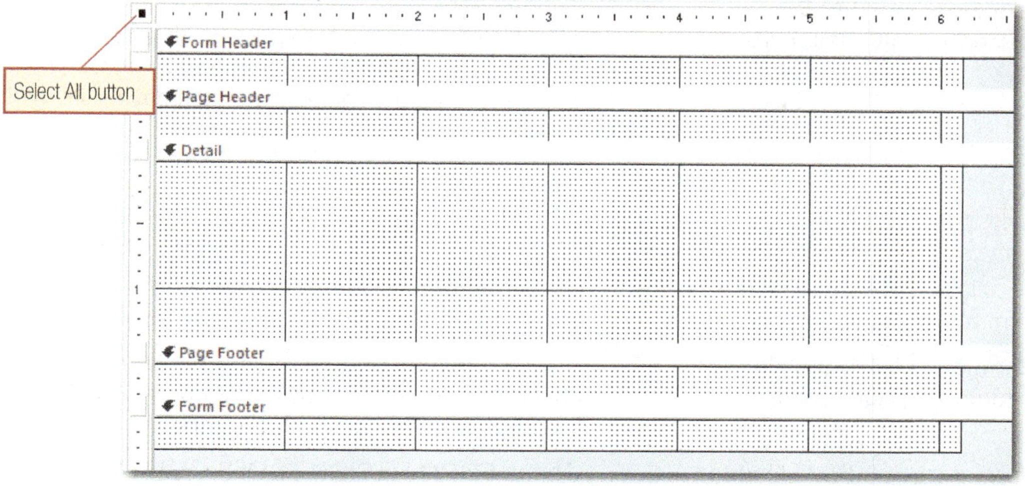

Figure 20-3

Access 2013, Windows 8, Microsoft Corporation

Try It! Selecting Sections of a Form

1. Start Access, and open **A20Try** from the data files for this lesson.
2. Save the database as **A20Try_xx** in the location where your teacher instructs you to store the files for this lesson.
3. Right-click the Sections form, and click Design View.
4. Click the Detail bar. It turns black, indicating it is selected.
5. Click the Select All button. The button appears with a black square in it, and the previously selected bar becomes unselected.
6. Right-click the form's tab, and click Close.
7. Leave the **A20Try_xx** database open to use in the next Try It.

The selected section's divider bar is black

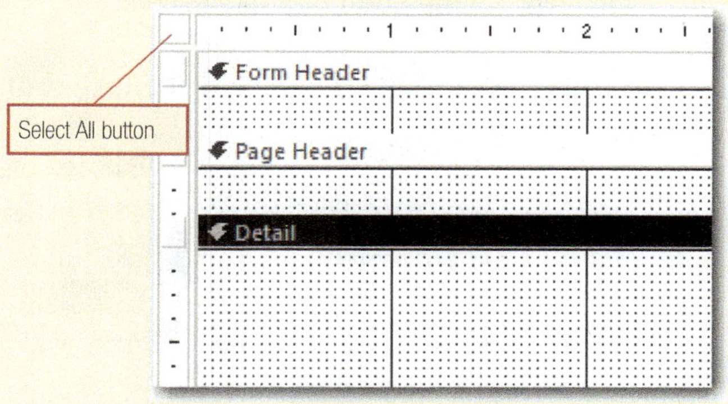

Access 2013, Windows 8, Microsoft Corporation

Displaying and Resizing Sections and Inserting a Form Title

- Depending on how the form was created, certain sections besides Detail may already be displayed and may already contain controls.
- You can drag the bar for each section up or down to decrease or increase the above section's size. For example, to change the size of the Form Header section, drag the Detail bar up or down.

  ✓ *If the Page Header bar is displayed, it should be dragged up and down instead of the Detail bar.*

- The headers and footers are paired, so you cannot display one and hide the other. However, you can resize a section to its smallest size (0" in height), effectively hiding it. In this way, you can have a form with a header but no footer or vice versa.
- Refer to the vertical and horizontal rulers onscreen to help gauge the size of the header or footer when printed. However, the actual size that appears onscreen depends on the monitor size and resolution.
- Hiding a header/footer pair does not just make them invisible; it also deletes any content that was in those sections.

- You can insert a title by manually inserting an unbound label box, as you learned in Lesson 19, in the Form Header section.
- You can also use the Title command to insert a title. The Title command not only inserts an unbound label, but also formats it and, if the Form Header section is not already displayed, it displays it all in one step.

Try It! Displaying and Resizing Sections and Inserting a Form Title

1. In the **A20Try_xx** file, click CREATE > Form Design. A new form appears.
2. Right-click the new form and click Page Header/Footer. The page header and page footer appear.
3. Right-click the new form and click Page Header/Footer again. The page header and page footer are removed.
4. Right-click the new form and click Form Header/Footer. The form header and footer appear.
5. Click the Detail bar to select that section.
6. Position the mouse pointer over the edge of the Detail bar and drag downward ½", increasing the height of the Form Header section.
7. Drag the Form Footer bar upward 1", decreasing the height of the Detail section.
8. Drag the bottom edge of the form footer upward until it touches the Form Footer bar, collapsing the form footer so it no longer appears.
9. On the FORM DESIGN TOOLS DESIGN tab, click Title. A Form1 title placeholder appears in the Form Header.
10. Type **Commerce**. The new text replaces the placeholder.
11. Click outside the label to accept the new text entry.
12. Leave the **A20Try_xx** database open to use in the next Try It.

Increase the height of the Form Header section

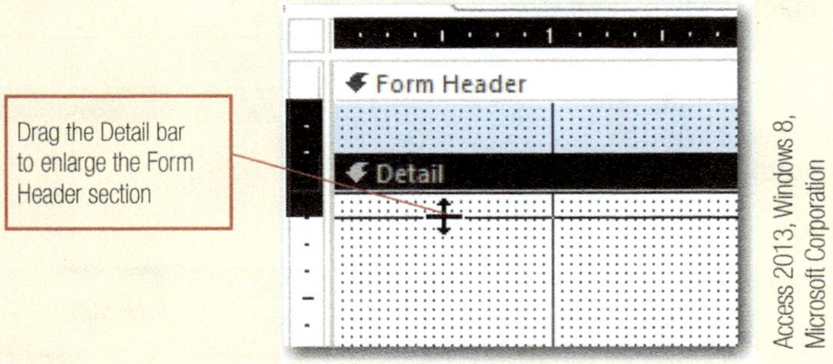

Collapse the Form Footer section

Adding Date/Time Codes

- You can add a date/time code to the form. This code enables the form to display the current date and time in Form view and printouts. Date and time are automatically updated from the computer's internal clock.
- When you choose to insert a date/time code, the Date and Time dialog box appears. You can choose to include the date, time, or both. You can also choose among three formats for each.
- A date/time code is always placed in the form header; you cannot choose where to insert it. You can, however, move it to another section after its insertion. (See the next section.)

Try It! Adding a Date Code

1. In the **A20Try_xx** file, click FORM DESIGN TOOLS DESIGN > Date and Time. The Date and Time dialog box opens.
2. Clear the Include Time check box.
3. Click OK. An =Date( ) code appears in the top right corner of the Form Header.
4. Click HOME > View > Form View to see how the date looks on the form.
5. Click HOME > View > Design View to return to Design view.
6. Leave the **A20Try_xx** database open to use in the next Try It.

Select a format for the date code

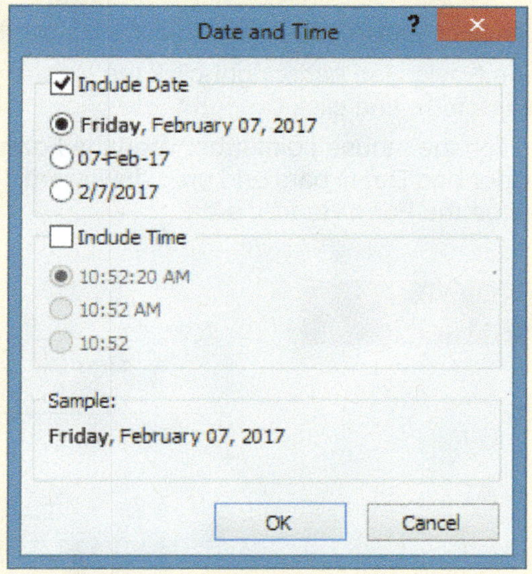

Access 2013, Windows 8, Microsoft Corporation

Moving Controls Between Sections

- You cannot drag-and-drop controls between sections. However, you can use the Cut and Paste commands to move controls from one section to another.

Try It! Moving a Control Between Sections

1. In the **A20Try_xx** file, in Design view, click the Date code that you just inserted. The frame's border appears orange.
2. Press CTRL + X to cut the code to the Clipboard.
3. Click the Form Footer bar to select that section.
4. Press CTRL + V to paste the code from the Clipboard.
5. Close the form without saving changes to it.
6. Close the **A20Try_xx** file, and exit Access.

Lesson 20—Practice

In this project, you will add a title to the Customer Basics form in Design view.

DIRECTIONS

1. Start Access, if necessary, and open **A20Practice** from the data files for this lesson.
2. Save the database as **A20Practice_xx** in the location where your teacher instructs you to store the files for this lesson.

   ✓ *If a security warning bar appears, click Enable Content.*
3. In the Navigation pane, right-click the **Customer Basics** form and click **Design View**.
4. Position the mouse pointer between the Form Header and Detail bars and drag downward 1" to enlarge the Form Header area.
5. Click **FORM DESIGN TOOLS DESIGN** > **Title** to place a title placeholder in the header.
6. Type **Basic Customer Information**, replacing the placeholder.
7. Drag the Detail bar upward until it almost touches the bottom of the title box, tightening up the unused space in the Form Header section, as shown in Figure 20-4.
8. Save and close the form.
9. Click **FILE** > **Close**. If instructed, submit this database to your teacher for grading.

Figure 20-4

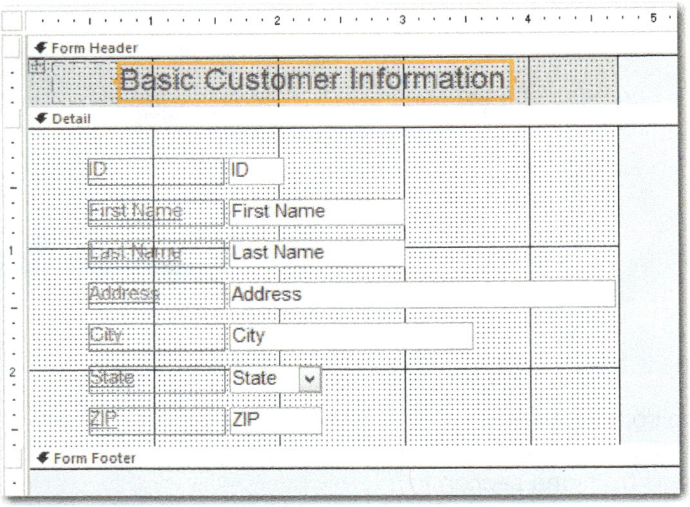

Access 2013, Windows 8, Microsoft Corporation

Lesson 20—Apply

In the jewelry business database, you will enhance the forms by adding and formatting their header and footer sections.

DIRECTIONS

1. Start Access, if necessary, and open **A20Apply** from the data files for this lesson.
2. Save the database as **A20Apply_xx** to the location where your teacher instructs you to store the files for this lesson.

   ✓ *If a security warning bar appears, click Enable Content.*
3. Open the **Customer Basics** form in Design view.
4. Enlarge the Form Footer section by 1" vertically.
5. Insert a code for the current time. It appears in the Form Header.
6. Move the time code into the Form Footer and place it at the right edge of the form.
7. Drag the bottom of the form upward until it almost touches the bottom of the time code, tightening up the unused space in the Form Footer section.
8. Save and close the form.
9. Open the **Product Basics** form in Design view.
10. Click the **Title** button to display the page header and footer.
11. In the Page Header, place the label **Product Information**. Change the font size of the label to 22. See Figure 20-5.
12. Save and close the form.
13. Click **FILE** > **Close**. If instructed, submit this database to your teacher for grading.

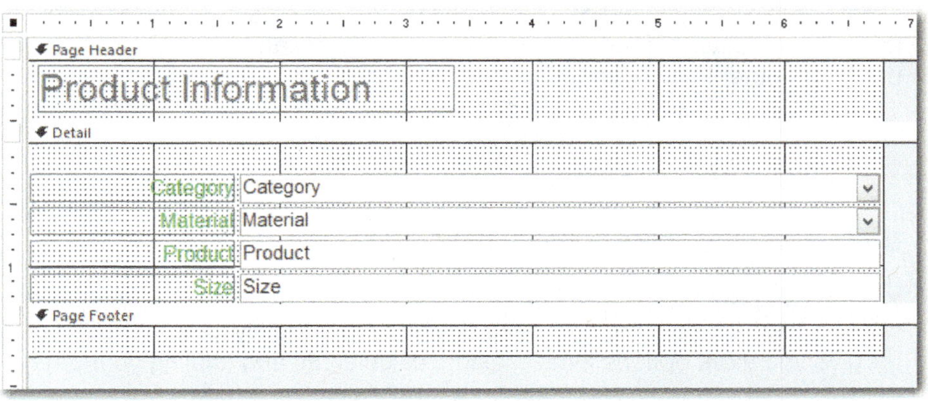

Access 2013, Windows 8, Microsoft Corporation

Figure 20-5

Lesson 21

Creating a Report

➤ What You Will Learn

Understanding Access Reports
Creating and Formatting a Report in Layout View
Creating a Report Using the Report Wizard
Modifying an Existing Report in Design View
Working with Print Preview and Report View
Printing a Report
Grouping, Sorting, and Filtering Report Data

WORDS TO KNOW

Print Preview
A view of the report as it will appear when printed.

Report
A way to present your data for printing with formatting enhancements.

Report Design view
A view of the report that lets you change the report's appearance and content.

Report view
A view of a report similar to Print Preview, but designed for onscreen viewing.

Software Skills Reports give you much more flexibility in producing output than simply printing tables and queries. You can print records in a tabular format that looks like a datasheet but with more attractive fonts, and you can print records one below the other in a columnar format.

What You Can Do

Understanding Access Reports

- You can print tables, queries, and forms, but the printouts may not be attractive. **Reports**, on the other hand, are designed specifically for printed output. Reports give you more options for formatting, calculating, and totaling your data.
- There are four main types of report layouts:
  - In a columnar report (see Figure 21-1 on the next page), all the fields for each record appear together, followed by those for the next record, and so on.
  - In a tabular report (see Figure 21-2 on the next page), each row is a record and each column is a field. It's similar to the printout you get when printing a datasheet.
  - In a justified report (see Figure 21-3 on the next page), the field names appear above the fields for each record, arranged in blocks.
  - In a mailing label report, records are arranged in blocks across and down the page, ready to print on a sheet of self-stick labels. Label reports are covered in Lesson 23.
- Setting margins in a report must be done in either Layout or Design View. Go to REPORT LAYOUT TOOLS PAGE SETUP > Margins. Select the appropriate option.

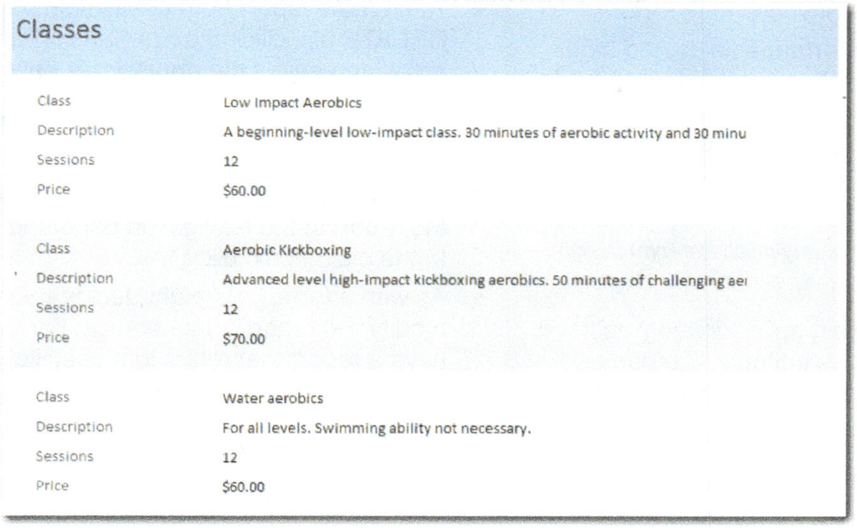

Access 2013, Windows 8, Microsoft Corporation

Figure 21-1

Columnar report

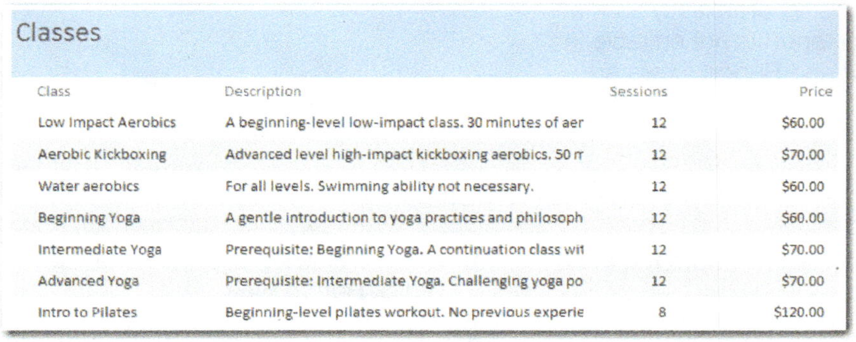

Access 2013, Windows 8, Microsoft Corporation

Figure 21-2

Tabular report

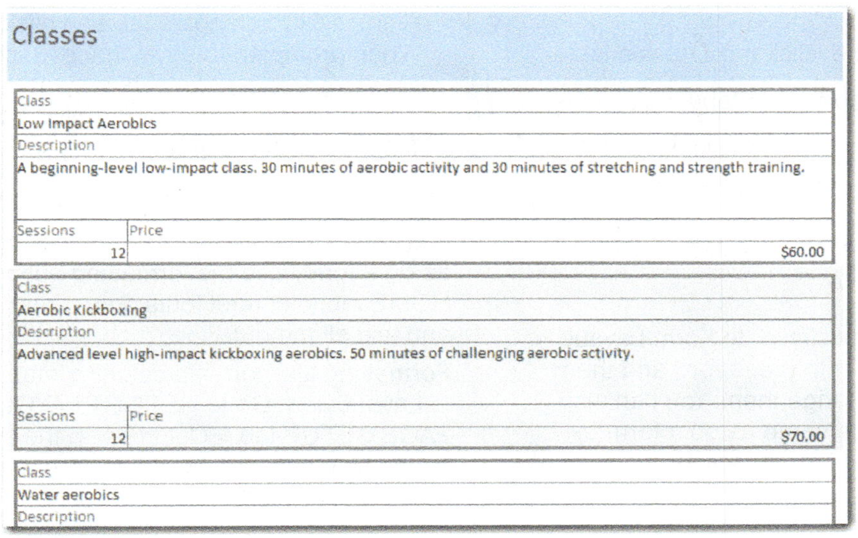

Access 2013, Windows 8, Microsoft Corporation

Figure 21-3

Justified report

- There are four views for working with reports:
  - Design: Uses a grid to arrange fields and other controls precisely; enables you to add non-field controls such as formulas and labels. The layout does not look exactly as it will when printed, so you must switch between this view and others to check your work.

    ✓ *Report Design view works very much like Form Design view, which you learned about earlier in this chapter.*
  - Layout: Shows the report approximately as it will look when printed and is editable. You can add and remove fields, resize controls, and so on.

    ✓ *Report Layout view is very much like Form Layout view.*
  - Report: Shows the report optimized for onscreen viewing. The report is not editable in this view.
  - Print Preview: Shows the report exactly as it will look when printed. The report is not editable in this view. Print Preview and Report views are very similar.
- To create a report from application parts, click the CREATE tab. Click the Application Parts drop-down arrow and select the appropriate option.

  ✓ *All objects must be closed before you can make a report from application parts.*
- To delete a report, it must first be closed. Right-click the report in the Navigation pane and click Delete. In the dialog box, click Yes.
- As with a form, you might decide you want to modify the report's data source. For example, if you have a report that refers to a specific table, but want to create a new report with the same variables, you can change the record source to a different table. When you change the record source, the contents of the field list will also change.

Try It! Creating and Viewing a Tabular Report

1. Start Access, and open **A21Try** from the data files for this lesson.
2. Save the database as **A21Try_xx** in the location where your teacher instructs you to store the files for this lesson.
3. In the Navigation pane, click the Classes table.
4. Click CREATE > Report. A tabular report is created.
5. In the Views group, click the View arrow and click Report View.
6. Right-click the report's tab, and click Design View to switch to Design view.
7. Right-click the report's tab and click Close. When prompted to save changes, click No.
8. Leave the **A21Try_xx** database open to use in the next Try It.

Creating and Formatting a Report in Layout View

- Report Layout view is very similar to Form Layout view. You can drag fields onto the report, and then drag them around to rearrange them. You can also resize fields and labels the same as on a form by dragging the right border of the desired control.
- You can format the controls on a report the same as on a form. Use the formatting buttons on the HOME tab to control fonts, font sizes and colors, and text alignment.
- Formatting a report into columns must be done in Layout view. Go to REPORT LAYOUT TOOLS PAGE SETUP tab > Columns. In the Page Setup dialog box, select the Columns tab and enter the appropriate information.

Try It! Creating and Formatting a Report in Layout View

1. In the **A21Try_xx** file, click CREATE > Blank Report. A blank report opens in Layout view.

   ✓ *If the Field List pane does not appear, click REPORT LAYOUT TOOLS DESIGN > Add Existing Fields.*

2. If necessary, in the Field List pane, click Show all tables. Click the plus sign to the left of Classes.
3. Double-click the ClassName field. The field is added to the report.
4. In the Fields List pane, click the plus sign to the left of ClassOfferings, and then double-click the StartDate field.
5. Click the plus sign to the left of Instructors, and then double-click the LastName field.
6. Click outside the fields to deselect them; then click once on any row in the Class column.
7. Position the mouse pointer at the right edge of the Class field and drag to the right, widening the column so that the longest entry fits on a single row.
8. Click REPORT LAYOUT TOOLS PAGE SETUP tab > Columns.
9. In the Page Setup dialog box, enter **2** in Number of Columns. Click OK.
10. Click any field in the Start column, and click HOME > Align Left.
11. Right-click the report's tab and click Close. Click No when asked if you want to save your work.
12. Leave the **A21Try_xx** database open to use in the next Try It.

Format and align the fields

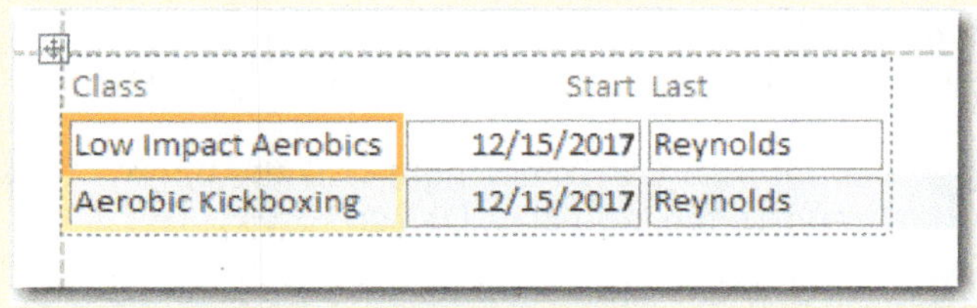

Access 2013, Windows 8, Microsoft Corporation

Creating a Report Using the Report Wizard

- The Report Wizard works like other wizards you have already used in Access.
- You choose the table/query and fields, the layout, and other options for the report, and then Access creates it according to your specifications.
- You can group the records in a report by one or more fields, and then sum, count, or perform some other calculation for each group. For example, you could count the number of clients from each ZIP code.
- You can also specify a sort order. Grouping takes precedence over sorting, so for example, if you group by ZIP and then sort by LastName, the records within each ZIP code will be sorted by LastName.

Try It! Creating a Report Using the Report Wizard

1. In the **A21Try_xx** file, click CREATE > Report Wizard.

   ✓ *If the Microsoft Access Security Notice dialog box opens, click Open.*

2. Open the Tables/Queries list and click Table:ClassOfferings.
3. Click >> to select all the fields, then click Next.
4. The Instructor field is already selected for grouping. Click Next to accept it.
5. Open the 1 drop-down list and click Class. Then, click Next.
6. Under Layout, click Block.
7. Under Orientation, click Portrait. Then, click Next.
8. For the title of the report, type **Class Offerings Report**.
9. Click Finish. The report opens in Print Preview.
10. Leave the **A21Try_xx** database open to use in the next Try It.

Modifying an Existing Report in Design View

- **Report Design view** is similar to Form Design view. To add a control, go to the Controls group under REPORT DESIGN TOOLS DESIGN. Select the appropriate control to add and place it in the report.
- You can move individual controls around by dragging them, cut and paste controls between sections, add titles and dates, and so on.
- You can insert a background image into a report in Design view. From REPORT DESIGN TOOLS DESIGN, click the Background Image drop-down arrow Background Image. Navigate to and add the appropriate image to the report.
- You can also apply a theme to a report to control the reports's colors and fonts. To apply a theme, click REPORT DESIGN TOOLS DESIGN and then select a theme from the Themes drop-down arrow.
- Tabular reports contain the field labels in the Page Header section and the fields themselves in the Detail section. It can be tricky to move fields and their labels when they exist in different sections; it is often better to rearrange fields in Layout view for this reason.

Try It! Modifying an Existing Report in Design View

1. In the **A21Try_xx** file, right-click the open report's tab, and click Design View.
2. Click the Instructor label in the Page Header section.
3. Hold down CTRL, and click the Instructor field in the Detail section.
4. Position the mouse pointer over the border of either selected control and drag to the left, moving the label and field to the left edge of the report.
5. Click the Class label in the Page Header section.
6. Hold down CTRL, and click the Class field in the Detail section.
7. Position the mouse pointer over the left selection handle on either selected control and drag to the left until almost touching the right edge of the Instructor field and label.
8. Click the ClassOfferingID label in the Page Header section and press DEL.
9. Click the ClassOfferingID field in the Detail section and press DEL.
10. Click the Start label in the Page Header section, and click HOME > Align Left.
11. Click the StartDate field in the Detail section and click HOME > Align Left.
12. Click REPORT DESIGN TOOLS DESIGN tab, and then click the Themes drop-down arrow.
13. Select the Ion Boardroom theme (first theme in the 2nd row of Office themes).
14. Leave the **A21Try_xx** database open to use in the next Try It.

Working with Print Preview and Report View

- **Print Preview** lets you see exactly how the report will look when printed. It also contains page setup options such as margins and page orientation.
- In Print Preview, the mouse pointer appears as a magnifying glass. Click anywhere in the report display to toggle between a view of the whole page and the most recent zoom value. You can set the zoom value from the Zoom button's menu on the PRINT PREVIEW tab.

- The navigation buttons at the bottom of the Print Preview window are similar to those for tables, queries, and forms, except they are for moving from page to page within a report.
- **Report view** is similar to Print Preview but designed for onscreen viewing.
- In Report view, you do not have the capability of zooming in and out on the content like in Print Preview. Report view is more of a "no-frills" display method.

Try It! Working with Print Preview and Report View

1. In the A21Try_xx file, click HOME > View > Report View to switch to Report view.
2. Click the View arrow again and click Print Preview to switch to Print Preview.
3. Click anywhere on the report. The view zooms out.
4. Click again on the report. The view zooms in.
5. Drag the View slider to the right. The view zooms in even more.
6. Click anywhere on the report. The view zooms out again.

Drag the slider to zoom in

Access 2013, Windows 8, Microsoft Corporation

7. On the PRINT PREVIEW tab, click the Landscape button.
8. In the Page Size group, click the Margins button, and then click Wide.
9. Click Close Print Preview.
10. Leave the A21Try_xx database open to use in the next Try It.

Printing a Report

- Reports are designed to print and display in a clear and well-organized manner.
- You can change print settings by clicking the Setup button Setup... in the Print dialog box. Here you can modify margins, column widths, and you can print the data without formatting.

Try It! Printing a Report

1. In the A21Try_xx file, with the report displayed in Report view, click FILE > Print > Print.

   ✓ *If you are in Print Preview, you can click the Print button on the PRINT PREVIEW tab.*
2. **With your teacher's permission**, click OK in the Print dialog box. Otherwise, click Cancel.
3. Save and close the report.
4. Leave the A21Try_xx database open to use in the next Try It.

Grouping, Sorting, and Filtering Report Data

Grouping Report Data

- When records are grouped, one field serves as a sub-heading in the report, and records are placed under the appropriate sub-heading depending on their value for that field. See Figure 21-4 on the next page.
- A grouping has a default sort order, which you can change from the group bar in the Group, Sort, and Total pane.
- For more options to define the group operation, click the word More on the bar. The options will vary depending on the field type.
- One of the options you can select there is whether or not to keep a group together on one page.

Figure 21-4

Records are grouped by Class

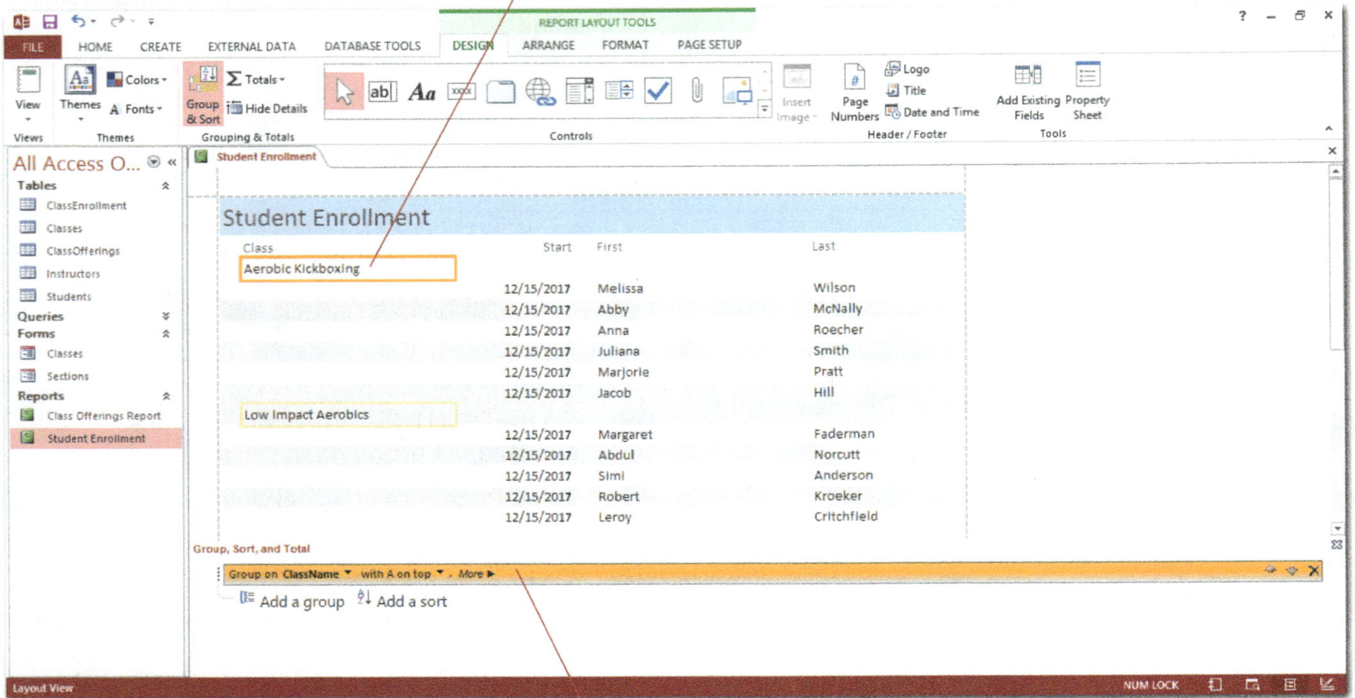

The group bar appears here

Access 2013, Windows 8, Microsoft Corporation

Try It! Grouping Report Data

1. In **A21Try_xx**, right-click Student Enrollment in the Navigation pane and click Layout View.
2. If the Group, Sort, and Total pane does not appear at the bottom of the report, click REPORT LAYOUT TOOLS DESIGN > Group & Sort. The Group, Sort, and Total pane appears at the bottom of the report.
3. In the Group, Sort, and Total pane, click *Add a group*.
4. On the field list that pops up, click StartDate. The report changes so that records are grouped by the start date, and a group bar for the StartDate field appears in the Group, Sort, and Total pane.
5. Leave the report open to use in the next Try It.

A group bar appears for the StartDate field

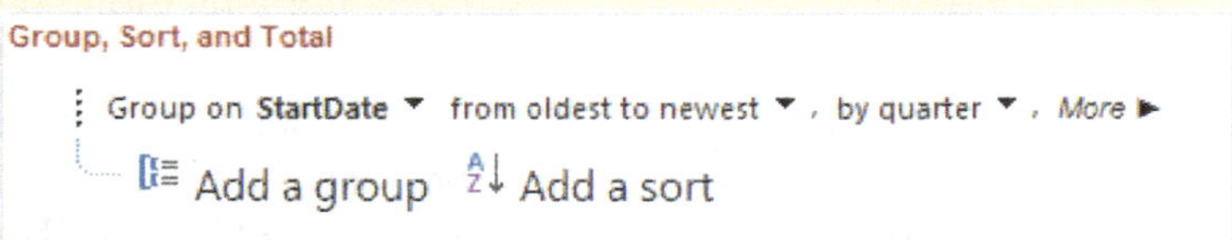

Access 2013, Windows 8, Microsoft Corporation

Try It! Changing Group Options

1. In the Student Enrollment report in the **A21Try_xx** file, click *from oldest to newest* in the Group, Sort, and Total pane. On the pop-up menu that appears, click *from newest to oldest*.
2. Click More. Additional options appear.
3. Click the drop-down arrow to the right of *do not keep group together on one page menu*.
4. Click keep whole group together on one page.
5. Leave the report open to use in the next Try It.

You can keep a group together on a page when the report is printed

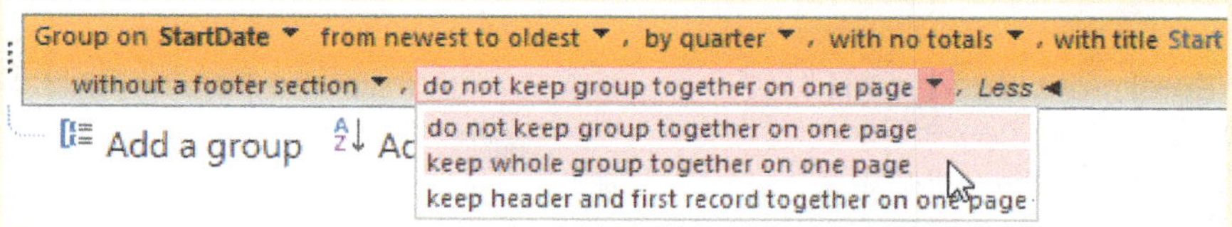

Access 2013, Windows 8, Microsoft Corporation

Sorting Report Data

- Use sorting only if you just want to sort, not group. Grouping includes sorting.
- To sort the records in a report, click Add a sort. A sort bar appears, with a drop-down list from which to select the field by which to sort. Click the desired field.
- The bar shows a default sort order that Access defines for you. The exact wording depends on the type of field. For example, for a date field, it might be "from oldest to newest." You can click this to select an alternate order if you prefer.
- In the event of a duplicate value in the sort field for two or more records, you might want to specify a second-level sort field. To do this, click the Add a sort button beneath the first sort. You can do this beneath a group too if you want additional sorting levels besides the default one that comes with the grouping.

Try It! Sorting Report Data

1. In the Student Enrollment report in the **A21Try_xx** file, click Add a sort under the Group on StartDate bar in the Group, Sort, and Total pane.
2. On the pop-up menu that appears, click ClassName.
3. Click the drop-down arrow to the right of the *with A on top* menu.
4. Click *with Z on top*.
5. Click the Save button on the Quick Access toolbar.
6. Leave the report open to use in the next Try It.

Filtering Report Data

- You can set up filtering for a report from Layout view.
- To filter by example, right-click a field and then choose one of the filter commands on the shortcut menu. This submenu provides Boolean options such as equals, does not equal, and so on.

✓ *It is often just as easy to create a query that filters the data, and then base the report on that query, as it is to set up record filtering on the report layout itself.*

- You can also set up custom filters that enable you to use wildcard characters such as * for any number of characters or ? for single characters.

Try It! Filtering Report Data by Example

1. In the Student Enrollment report in the A21Try_xx file, right-click the Aerobic Kickboxing field in the Class column. A shortcut menu opens.
2. Click Equals "Aerobic Kickboxing." The report changes to show only the records where the class is Aerobic Kickboxing.
3. Right-click the Aerobic Kickboxing field in the Class column again.
4. Click Clear filter from ClassName.
5. Leave the report open to use in the next Try It.

Try It! Filtering Report Data with a Custom Filter

1. In the Student Enrollment report in the A21Try_xx file, right-click anywhere in the Class field's column. A shortcut menu opens.
2. Point to Text Filters. A submenu opens.
3. Click Begins With. A Custom Filter dialog box opens.
4. Type **Aerobic** and click OK. The report shows only class names that begin with Aerobic.
5. Right-click the Class column again.
6. Click Clear filter from ClassName.
7. Right-click the report's tab and click Close. Click No, if prompted to save changes.
8. Close the database, and exit Access.

Lesson 21—Practice

In this project, you will create a report using the Report Wizard for your friend's jewelry business database.

DIRECTIONS

1. Start Access, if necessary, and open **A21Practice** from the data files for this lesson.
2. Save the database as **A21Practice_xx** to the location where your teacher instructs you to store the files for this lesson.

   ✓ *If a security warning bar appears, click Enable Content.*
3. Click **CREATE** > **Report Wizard**.
4. Open the **Tables/Queries** list and click **Query: Customers and Orders**.
5. Click >> to include all fields, then click **Next**.
6. Click **by Salespeople** and click **Next**.
7. For Grouping Levels, click **Order Date** and click > to set it as a grouping field. See Figure 21-5. Then, click **Next**.
8. Click **Next** to skip the sorting criteria selection.
9. Under Layout, click **Block**. Then, click **Next**.
10. For the report's title, type **Orders by Salesperson**. Then, click **Finish**.
11. In the Navigation pane, right-click **Orders by Salesperson** and open in Layout view.
12. In REPORT LAYOUT TOOLS DESIGN, click **Group & Sort**.
13. In the Group, Sort, and Total pane, click **Add a group**. In the pop-up menu, click **Last Name**.
14. Right-click any field in the **Salesperson** column, and click **Text Filters** in the pop-up menu.
15. In the submenu, click **Begins With**.
16. Type **Gonzalez**, and click **OK**.
17. Using any desired method, adjust all of the columns so that all of the text is visible and the report fits on one page.
18. Save and close the report.
19. Click **FILE** > **Close**. If instructed, submit this database to your teacher for grading.

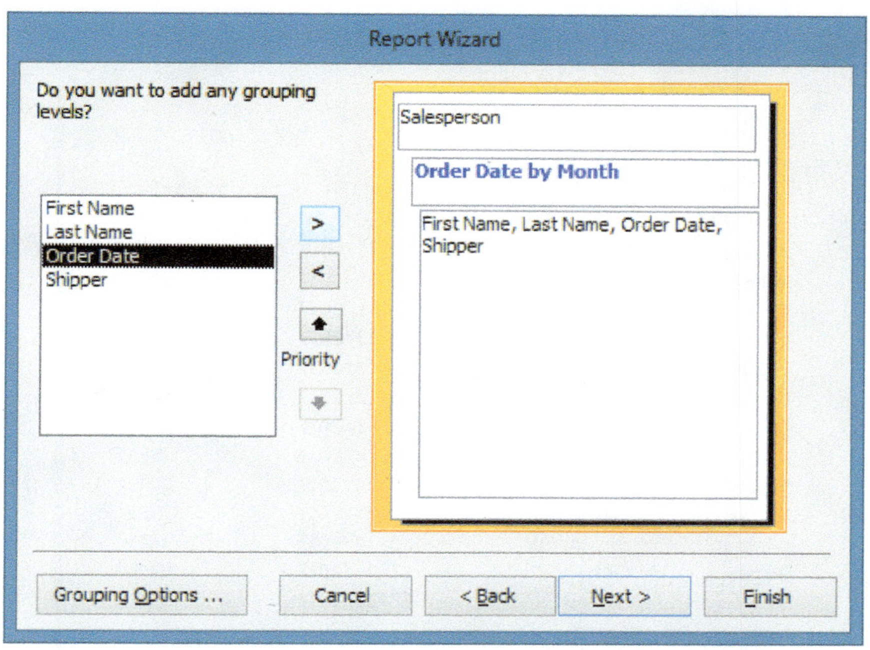

Figure 21-5

Lesson 21—Apply

To help your friend make more readable printouts, you will edit and create reports in the jewelry business database.

DIRECTIONS

1. Start Access, if necessary, and open **A21Apply** from the data files for this lesson.
2. Save the database as **A21Apply_xx** to the location where your teacher instructs you to store the files for this lesson.

   ✓ *If a security warning bar appears, click Enable Content.*
3. Open the **Orders by Salesperson** report in Layout view.
4. Adjust the column widths so no fields or labels are truncated or overlapping, as in Figure 21-6.
5. Set the horizontal alignment for the **Order Date** field to **Left**.
6. Save and close the report.
7. Open the **Products** table in Datasheet view, and create a tabular report from it using the **Report** command.
8. Change the report's orientation to **Landscape**.
9. From either Layout or Design view, adjust the column widths as needed to tighten up the design as much as possible without truncating any fields or labels.
10. Save the report as **Products Report** and close it.
11. Create a new report in Layout view that uses the **Name** and **Account** fields from the **Shippers** table. Save the report as **Shipper List**.
12. Sort the report by Account.
13. View the **Shipper List** report in Print Preview.
14. **With your teacher's permission**, print one copy of the report and write your name on the printout.
15. Save and close the report.
16. Click **FILE** > **Close**. If instructed, submit this database to your teacher for grading. If you printed in step 14, also submit your printout.

Figure 21-6

Orders by Salesperson

Salesperson	Order Date by Month	First Name	Last Name	Order Date	Shipper
Gonzalez	December 2017	Allison	Norville	12/14/2017	USPS
		Peter	Washington	12/15/2017	DHL
Leffler	December 2017	Cynthia	Green	12/2/2017	UPS
		Cynthia	Green	12/13/2017	UPS
		Felicia	Adamson	12/15/2017	USPS
		Norman	Greenburg	12/15/2017	USPS
Mueller	December 2017	Jennifer	Brown	12/1/2017	UPS
		Carrie	Strong	12/3/2017	USPS
		Felicia	Adamson	12/14/2017	UPS
Rodriguez	December 2017	Jasper	Garrett	12/2/2017	USPS
		Norman	Eichmann	12/14/2017	FedEx
		Jasper	Garrett	12/15/2017	UPS
		Jennifer	Brown	12/16/2017	UPS
Sanchez	December 2017	George	Colvin	12/15/2017	USPS

Lesson 22

Modifying a Report in Design View

➤ What You Will Learn

Working with Report Sections
Moving a Control Between Sections
Adding Page Number Codes
Changing Grouping Options
Adding a Calculated Field to a Report

Software Skills Report Design view enables you to make more extensive changes to a report than are possible in Layout view. You can add calculated fields to a report, for example, and move controls between sections. Access also enables you to sort and group data in a report, from either Design or Layout view.

WORDS TO KNOW

Calculated field
A formula on the report that performs a math operation on the records and presents a result, such as counting the number of records, summing the values in a particular field, or multiplying the amount in one field by the amount in another field.

What You Can Do

Working with Report Sections

- Inserting a header or footer section in the report Design view works just as it does in a form's Design view. You can right-click the report and click the applicable header/footer name to turn it on or off.
- Reports can also contain additional headers and footers for the groupings you set up. For example, if you group by salesperson, there will be a Salesperson header and Salesperson footer.

Try It! Working with Report Sections

1. Start Access, and open the database **A22Try** from the data files for this lesson.
2. Save the database as **A22Try_xx** in the location where your teacher instructs you to store the files for this lesson.
3. In the Navigation pane, right-click the Class Offerings Report and click Design View.
4. Position the mouse pointer between the Instructor Header and Detail sections and drag downward, creating a ½" height for the Instructor Header section.
5. Leave the **A22Try_xx** database open to use in the next Try It.

Moving a Control Between Sections

- Most fields should stay in the Detail section; however, all other controls can be moved to any section you wish.
- For example, suppose you have a code that prints today's date in the Page Footer. If you want that date to appear only once in the report, at the very end, you could move that control to the Report Footer section.
- In a report that contains grouping, you might also want to move certain fields or labels into the header section for that field.
- You must use cut-and-paste to move a control between sections; drag-and-drop does not work.

Try It! Moving a Control Between Sections

1. In the A22Try_xx file, with the Class Offerings Report open in Design view, click the Instructor field in the Detail section.
2. Press CTRL + X to cut the control to the Clipboard.
3. Click the bar for the Instructor Header section.
4. Press CTRL + V to paste the control.
5. Drag the Detail bar up slightly, closing up the extra space between the Detail bar and the Instructor field.
6. Click REPORT DESIGN TOOLS DESIGN > View > Report View to preview the report in Report view.
7. Click HOME > View > Design View to return to Design view.
8. Leave the A22Try_xx database open to use in the next Try It.

Decrease the height of the Instructor Header section

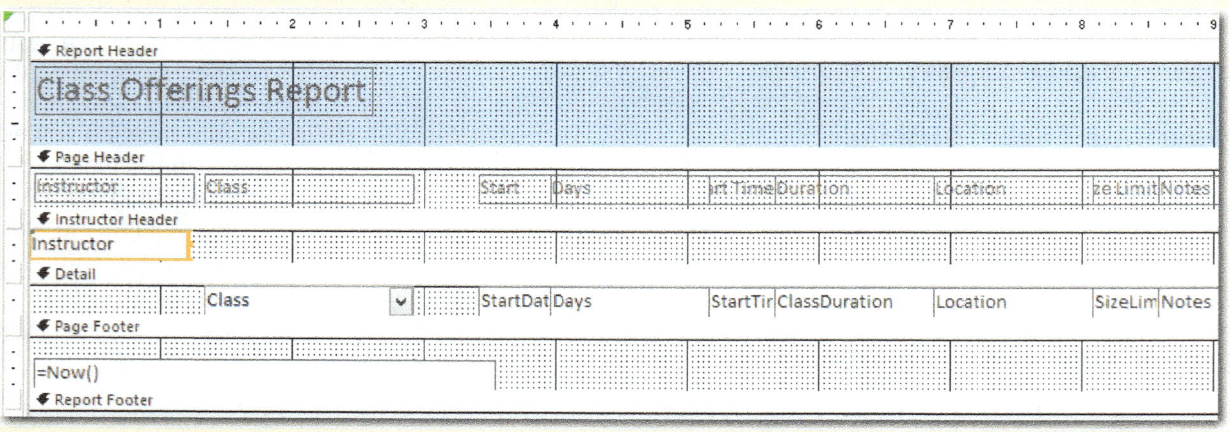

Access 2013, Windows 8, Microsoft Corporation

Adding Page Number Codes

- Page numbering codes are added to a report automatically when you create it with the Report Wizard. You can also manually insert page numbering codes.
  - A page numbering code is a function that consists of a combination of placeholders and literal text. The literal text portions are enclosed in quotation marks. For example: ="Page " & [Page]
  - = signals that it is a function.
  - "Page " is literal text.
  - & is a concatenation operator that joins the literal text to what follows it.
  - [Page] is a code that inserts the correct page number.
- You can manually type a page numbering code into an unbound text box, but there is seldom any need to do so because you can use the Page Numbers command in the Header/Footer group on the REPORT DESIGN TOOLS DESIGN tab instead.

Try It! Adding Page Number Codes

1. In the **A22Try_xx** file, with the Class Offerings Report open in Design view, click REPORT DESIGN TOOLS DESIGN > Page Numbers. The Page Numbers dialog box opens.
2. Click the Page N of M option.
3. Click the Bottom of Page [Footer] option.
4. Open the Alignment drop-down list and click Right.
5. Click OK. The code is placed in the report.
6. Click HOME > View > Report View to see the page number.
7. Right-click the report tab and click Close. Click Yes to save changes.
8. Leave the **A22Try_xx** database open to use in the next Try It.

Add page numbers in the Page Numbers dialog box

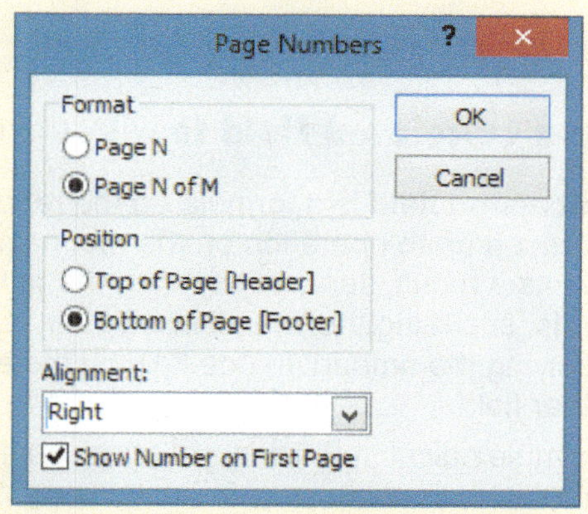

Access 2013, Windows 8, Microsoft Corporation

Changing Grouping Options

- To change the properties of a group, click one of the down-pointing arrows on its bar.
- For example, to change the field on which the report is grouped, click the down arrow following the Group on statement.
- For more options, click the More arrow. More settings appear, each with its own down-pointing arrow you can click to select from a list.

Try It! Changing Grouping Options

1. In the A22Try_xx file, click the Classes table in the Navigation pane.
2. Click CREATE > Report. A report opens in Layout view.
3. If necessary, click REPORT DESIGN TOOLS DESIGN > Group & Sort.

   ✓ *The Group, Sort, and Total pane appears at the bottom of the Access window.*
4. Click Add a group, and then click Price. The report changes so that the classes with the same price are grouped together.
5. In Price group, click the down arrow to the right of *from smallest to largest*, and click *from largest to smallest*.

   ✓ *The order in which the groups are presented in the report is reversed.*
6. Click More. Additional grouping options appear.
7. Click the down arrow to the right of *without a footer section*, and click *with a footer section*.
8. Beneath the Price group, click Add a sort and, on the menu that appears, click NumberOfSessions.
9. Click View > Report View to see the grouped and sorted report.
10. Close the report without saving changes.
11. Leave the A22Try_xx database open to use in the next Try It.

Adding a Calculated Field to a Report

- A **calculated field** is a formula on the report that performs a math operation on the records and presents a result, such as counting the number of records, summing the values in a particular field, or multiplying the amount in one field by the amount in another field.
- For simple calculated fields, you can use the Totals command in the Grouping & Totals group on the REPORT LAYOUT TOOLS DESIGN tab (in Layout view) or on the REPORT DESIGN TOOLS DESIGN tab (in Design view), and select a function from the menu that appears.
- You can also insert an unbound text box and type a function directly in it. Insert a Text Box control to draw a text box, and then in that box type the function.
- Here are some tips for creating your own calculations:
  - Each formula begins with an equals sign.
  - To reference a field name, use square brackets. For example, =[Price]*[Quantity]
  - A function requires parentheses after it. If there are any arguments, they are placed in the parentheses; otherwise, the parentheses are empty. For example, =Now() or =Sum([quantity]).
  - To refer to all records, use an asterisk *. For example, =Count(*) counts all records.

Try It! Adding a Calculated Field to a Report

1. In the **A22Try_xx** file, in the Navigation pane, right-click the Enrollment By Class report and click Design View.

   ✓ *If necessary, click the Group & Sort button to close the Group, Sort, and Total pane.*

2. Position the mouse pointer between the ClassName Footer bar and the Page Footer bar and drag downward ½", creating some space in the ClassName Footer section.
3. Click the ClassName Footer bar to select that section.
4. Click REPORT DESIGN TOOLS DESIGN > Text Box ab|.
5. Click in the ClassName Footer section. An unbound text box appears.

An unbound text box appears

Access 2013, Windows 8, Microsoft Corporation

6. Click outside the control to deselect it. Then, click the label box to the left of the text box (it may overlap the text box, as shown in the illustration).

Select the label box

Access 2013, Windows 8, Microsoft Corporation

7. Press DEL. The label is deleted but the text box remains.
8. Click to select the text box, and then click in the text box so the insertion point appears.
9. Type **=Count([ClassName])** in the text box.
10. Click HOME > View > Report View to view the report in Report view and check your work. Close the report, saving changes.
11. Close the **A22Try_xx** file, and exit Access.

Lesson 22—Practice

In this project, you will edit the layout of a report.

DIRECTIONS

1. Start Access, if necessary, and open **A22Practice** from the data files for this lesson.
2. Save the database as **A22Practice_xx** to the location where your teacher instructs you to store the files for this lesson.

   ✓ *If a security warning bar appears, click Enable Content.*

3. In the Navigation pane, right-click the **Orders by Salesperson** report and click **Layout View**.
4. Click **REPORT LAYOUT TOOLS DESIGN** > **Page Numbers**.
5. Click **Bottom of Page (Footer)** if it is not already selected.
6. Open the **Alignment** drop-down list and click **Outside**.
7. Click **OK**.
8. Click **REPORT LAYOUT TOOLS DESIGN** > **Group & Sort**, if it isn't already selected.
9. In the Group on Salesperson row, click **More**.
10. Click the down arrow to the right of **with no totals**.
11. Click the **Show subtotal in group footer** check box. The count of records in the salesperson grouping appears beneath each salesperson.
12. View the report in Report view. Click the **Save** button on the Quick Access Toolbar.
13. Click **FILE** > **Close**. If instructed, submit this database to your teacher for grading.

Lesson 22—Apply

To improve the reports you've created for your friend's jewelry business database, you will add sorting and grouping to them, as well as a calculated field.

DIRECTIONS

1. Start Access, if necessary, and open **A22Apply** from the data files for this lesson.
2. Save the database as **A22Apply_xx** to the location where your teacher instructs you to store the files for this lesson.

   ✓ *If a security warning bar appears, click Enable Content.*
3. Open the **Orders by Date** report in Design view.
4. Group the report by **Order Date**.
5. Cut and paste the **Order Date** field from the Detail section into the **Order Date Header** section and position it below the **Order Date** label.
6. In the Report Footer section, insert an unbound text box.
7. In the text box's label, change the text to **Total Quantity Ordered**. Adjust the box so it is fully visible and so that the text is not truncated.

   ✓ *Click and drag the text box label from the dark box in the upper-left corner of the box to move it separately from the unbound text box.*
8. In the unbound text box, type **=SUM([Quantity])**.
9. Position both the label and the text box at the right margin, so that when you preview the report in Report view, it appears as shown in Figure 22-1.
10. Save your work, and close the report.
11. Open the **Products Report** in Layout view, and sort it by **Product**.
12. Save and close the report.
13. Click **FILE** > **Close**. If instructed, submit this database to your teacher for grading.

Figure 22-1

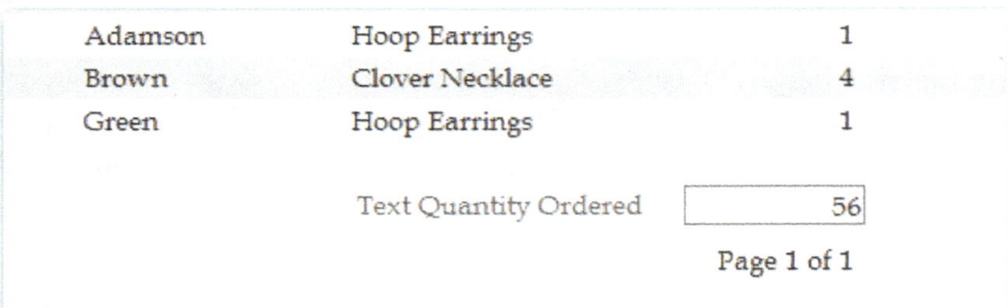

Access 2013, Windows 8, Microsoft Corporation

Lesson 23

Creating Labels

➤ What You Will Learn

Understanding Labels
Using the Label Wizard

Software Skills You can create mailing labels using Microsoft Office applications. You can create them in Word by merging them with a data source. In Access, you can create labels using a table or query as the data source.

What You Can Do

Understanding Labels

- In label format, records are arranged in blocks across and down the page. This format is used to make mailing labels and includes field values, not field names.
- Labels usually are printed on special self-adhesive labels. A variety of manufacturers make such labels, and Access provides automatic formatting for many of the self-adhesive label styles available.
- Although mailing labels are the most common type of label, you can also find labels for manila folders and DVD cases. If you create a database that contains information about your video collection, you can create labels from the database to identify the videos.
- In Access, labels are a type of report.

Using the Label Wizard

- The **Label Wizard** helps you set up a label report quickly and easily.
- Before running the Label Wizard, determine the brand and model number of the labels. If you do not have this information, measure one of the labels with a ruler so you can choose an equivalent that is the same size.

WORDS TO KNOW

Label Wizard
A series of dialog boxes that guides you through the creation of labels.

Try It! Using the Label Wizard

1. Start Access, and open **A23Try** from the data files for this lesson.
2. Save the database as **A23Try_xx** in the location where your teacher instructs you to store the files for this lesson.
3. In the Navigation pane, click the Students table.
4. Click CREATE > Labels.

   ✓ *If the Microsoft Access Security Notice dialog box opens, click Open.*

5. Open the Filter by manufacturer drop-down list and click Avery if it is not already selected.
6. From the Product number list, click 5160. Then, click Next.
7. Open the Font size drop-down list and click 9. Then, click Next.
8. Click the FirstName field, and then click >.
9. Press the spacebar once, click the LastName field, and then click >.
10. Press ENTER to move to the next line. Click the Address field, and click >.
11. Press ENTER, click the City field, and then click >.
12. Type a comma, and then press the spacebar once.
13. Click the State field, and click >.
14. Press the spacebar twice, click the ZIP field, and then click >.
15. Click Next.
16. Click LastName and click > to specify that the labels will be sorted by last name. Then, click Next.
17. Click Finish. A warning appears about some data not being displayed.
18. Click OK. The labels appear in a report in Print Preview.
19. Close the **A23Try_xx** file, and exit Access.

Lesson 23—Practice

In this project, you will create labels for the Products table in your friend's jewelry business database.

DIRECTIONS

1. Start Access, if necessary, and open **A23Practice** from the data files for this lesson.
2. Save the database as **A23Practice_xx** to the location where your teacher instructs you to store the files for this lesson.

   ✓ *If a security warning bar appears, click Enable Content.*

3. In the Navigation pane, click the **Products** table.
4. Click **CREATE** > **Labels**.
5. Click **5963** as the product number, and click **Next**.

   ✓ *Avery should already be selected as the label manufacturer; if not, select it before step 5.*

6. Open the **Font size** drop-down list, click **16**, and then click **Next**.
7. Click **Product**, click >, and then press ENTER.
8. Click **Size**, click >, and then press ENTER.
9. Click **Material**, click >, and then press ENTER.
10. Click **Finish** to accept all remaining default settings.
11. Click **OK** to accept the warning that some data may not be displayed.
12. Click **FILE** > **Close**. If instructed, submit this database to your teacher for grading.

Lesson 23—Apply

Your friend has prepared a catalog of her jewelry items and wants to mail it to customers. You will create mailing labels to affix to the catalogs.

DIRECTIONS

1. Start Access, if necessary, and open **A23Apply** from the data files for this lesson.
2. Save the database as **A23Apply_xx** to the location where your teacher instructs you to store the files for this lesson.

   ✓ *If a security warning bar appears, click Enable Content.*
3. Start the Label Wizard based on the **Customers** table.
4. You do not have the label manufacturer and model number, so browse through the available products and find a label that has the following qualities:
   - 2 labels per row
   - 2" tall
   - 4" wide
   - Sheet fed
5. Format the label text with a dark blue color, 9-point font size, Normal font weight, and Times New Roman font.
6. Include all the fields needed for a postal mailing, in the correct order and format.
7. Sort the labels by ZIP.
8. Accept the default name for the report.
9. **With your teacher's permission**, print one copy of the first page of the label report, and write your name on the printout.
10. Click **FILE** > **Close**. If instructed, submit this database to your teacher for grading.

Lesson 24

Creating a Lookup List

➤ What You Will Learn

Creating a Lookup
Creating a Value List
Looking Up Field Values from Another Table
Creating a Multi-valued Field

WORDS TO KNOW

Lookup field
A list of values from which to choose when entering information in a field.

Software Skills Some fields store data that can contain only a limited range of valid values, such as Marital Status (single, married, etc.) or Gender (male, female). To simplify data entry and prevent entry errors, you can create a lookup for a field that presents the user who is entering records with a drop-down list of options from which to choose. You can also set up fields that hold more than one value and that allow users to select from multiple check boxes during data entry.

What You Can Do

Creating a Lookup

- If the appropriate values for a certain field are limited, such as gender or marital status, consider using a **lookup field**.
- A lookup field appears as a drop-down list during data entry, and you can choose from the list rather than typing an entry. This minimizes data entry errors and ensures consistent formatting (such as capitalization).
- When you enter data for a record, an arrow appears within the lookup field indicating that you can choose from a list of options.
- You can use the Lookup Wizard to create a lookup field with values you enter. This is most appropriate for short lists that do not change frequently.
- You can also use the Lookup Wizard to create a lookup field that looks up values from another table. This is most appropriate for long lists or lists that frequently need updating.
- To create a lookup for a field, go to table Design view and change the field's type to Lookup Wizard. The Lookup Wizard will run automatically.

Creating a Value List

- The Lookup Wizard provides a list in which you can type the values you want to appear on the list.
- This method works well when the values on the list will seldom or never change. If the values change frequently, use the table lookup method instead.

✓ *When creating your list, try to enter the values in a useful order. An alphabetical list of states, for example, is easier to use than one that doesn't have a recognizable order.*

Try It! Creating a Lookup with a Typed Value List

1. Open **A24Try** from the data files for this lesson.
2. Save the database as **A24Try_xx** in the location where your teacher instructs you to store the files for this lesson.
3. In the Navigation pane, right-click the Students table and click Design View.

   ✓ *If a Microsoft Access Security Notice dialog box opens, click Open.*
4. Open the Data Type list for the Gender field and click Lookup Wizard.
5. Click I will type in the values that I want.
6. Click Next.
7. In the Col1 column, in the first blank row, type **Male**.
8. Click in the next blank row, and type **Female**.
9. Click Next.
10. Click the Limit To List check box.
11. Click Finish.
12. Click the Save button on the Quick Access Toolbar.
13. Leave the **A24Try_xx** database open to use in the next Try It.

Type the list items

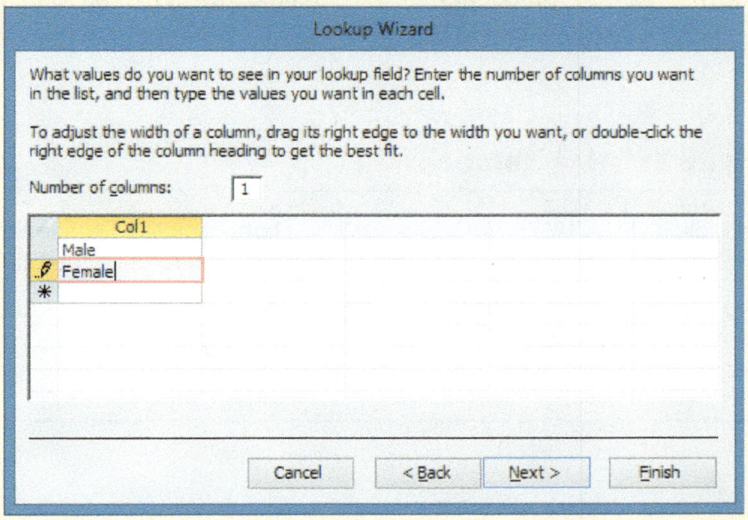

Access 2013, Windows 8, Microsoft Corporation

Try It! Using a Lookup List

1. In the A24Try_xx file, click HOME > View to view the datasheet.
2. For the first record (Leroy Critchfield), click the Gender field.
3. Click the down arrow to open the drop-down list.
4. Click Male.
5. Right-click the table's tab and click Close to close it.
6. Leave the A24Try_xx database open to use in the next Try It.

The lookup list displays the values you entered in the Lookup Wizard

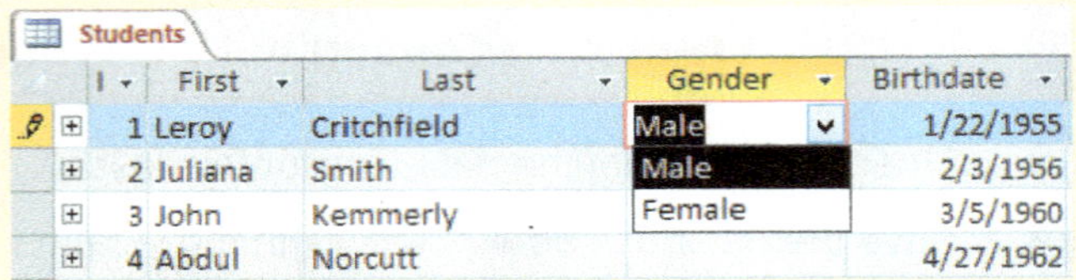

Access 2013, Windows 8, Microsoft Corporation

Looking Up Field Values from Another Table

- If your list often changes, or is long, you might find it easier to create a separate table for the list instead, and then create a lookup field that looks into that table.
- Before creating the lookup, you must first create the additional table. Then run the Lookup Wizard and select the table to be used.
- Creating a lookup also produces a relationship between the tables, which is reflected in the Relationships grid. The new relationship does not enforce referential integrity, but you can edit it to do so later.
- The Lookup Wizard first helps you choose the lookup table or query.
- If there is already a relationship between the two tables, you can't create the lookup until you delete the relationship from the Relationships grid. The Lookup Wizard will re-create the relationship.
- When setting up a lookup based on another table, you are prompted to sort by a particular field if desired, in Ascending or Descending order. This enables the lookup list to display values in a different order than they appear in the table being referenced. If you do not choose a sort order, the values will appear in the same order as in the table.

Try It! Deleting an Existing Relationship

1. In the A24Try_xx file, click DATABASE TOOLS > Relationships.
2. Click the relationship line between the Classes and ClassOfferings tables and press DEL. Click Yes to confirm the deletion.
3. Right-click the Relationships tab and click Close. Click Yes to save the changes, if prompted.
4. Leave the A24Try_xx database open to use in the next Try It.

Try It! Creating a Lookup with Values from Another Table

1. In the **A24Try_xx** file, in the Navigation pane, right-click the ClassOfferings table and click Design View.
2. Open the Data Type list for the Class field and click Lookup Wizard.
3. Click Next.
4. Click Table: Classes and click Next.

Select the table for use for the lookup

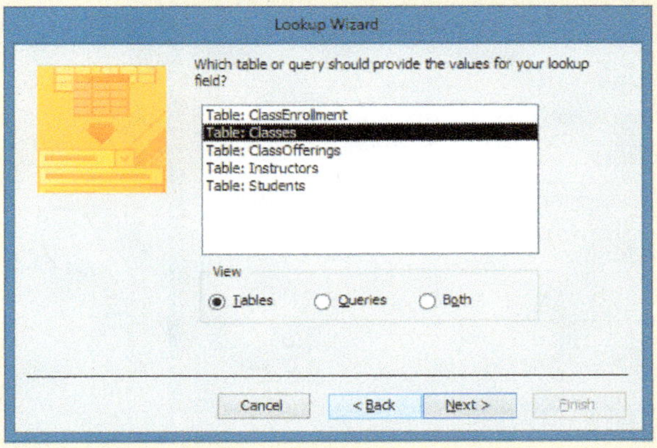

Access 2013, Windows 8, Microsoft Corporation

5. Click the ClassName field and click > to move it to the Selected Fields list.

   ✓ *If the table you choose for the lookup has a primary key field, Access will automatically include it even if you don't select it. The wizard calls it a Key Column. You can choose whether or not to display it in step 8.*

6. Click Next.
7. Open the 1 drop-down list and click ClassName, then click Next.

Select the field by which to sort

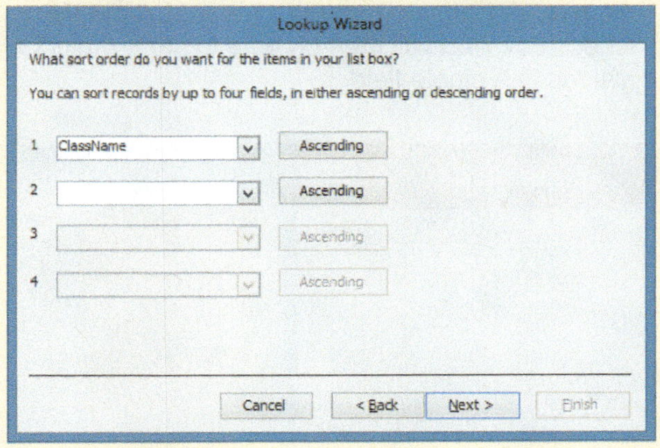

Access 2013, Windows 8, Microsoft Corporation

8. Slightly widen the column by dragging its column heading to the right.

   ✓ *You can clear the Hide key column check box to display the primary key field on which the relationship is based. In this exercise, you will leave the check box checked.*

9. Click Next to accept the list, and then click Finish.
10. When prompted to save the table, click Yes.
11. Click HOME > View to switch to Datasheet view.
12. In the first row, open the drop-down list for the Class field to view the new list.
13. Right-click the table's tab and click Close. If prompted to save changes, click Yes.
14. Leave the **A24Try_xx** database open to use in the next Try It.

Creating a Multi-valued Field

- On the last step of the Lookup Wizard, you also have the opportunity to allow multiple values (see Figure 24-1). If you mark the Allow Multiple Values check box, you will then be able to store multiple values in a single field.
- Rather than selecting from a simple drop-down list, with a multi-valued field you select individual check boxes from the list, and you can mark as many as you like. You learned about using this type of field in Lesson 3.

Figure 24-1

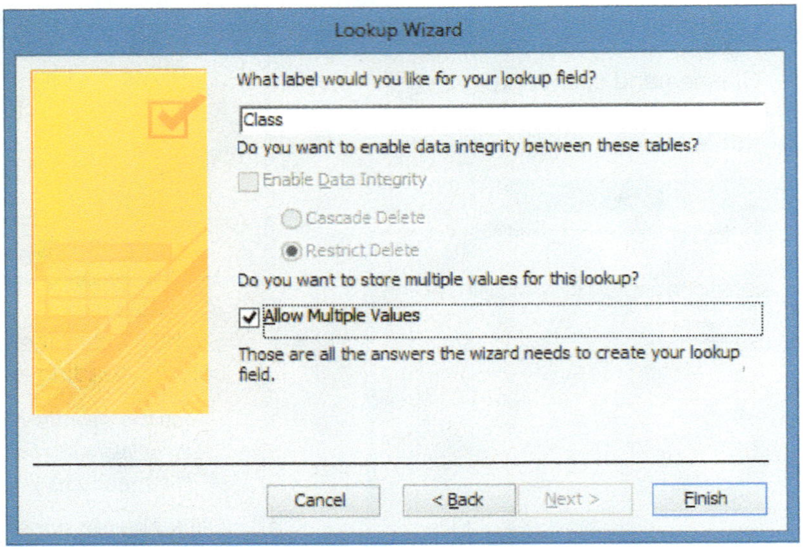

Access 2013, Windows 8, Microsoft Corporation

Try It! Creating a Multi-valued Field

1. In the **A24Try_xx** file, right-click the Instructors table in the Navigation pane and click Design View.
2. Open the Data Type list for the Locations field and click Lookup Wizard.
3. Click I will type in the values that I want, and click Next.
4. In the Col1 column, in the first row, type **Downtown**. In the second row, type **Millbrook**. In the third row, type **Glendale**. In the fourth row, type **Castleton**. Then, click Next.
5. Click the Allow Multiple Values check box.
6. Click Finish.
7. Click Yes to confirm.
8. Click the Save button on the Quick Access Toolbar.
9. Leave the **A24Try_xx** database open to use in the next Try It.

Try It! Using a Multi-valued Field

1. In the **A24Try_xx** file, click HOME > View to view the datasheet.
2. In the first record, open the drop-down list in the Locations field.
3. Click to mark the Downtown and Millbrook check boxes.
4. Click OK.
5. Close the **A24Try_xx** file, and exit Access.

Select multiple values using check boxes

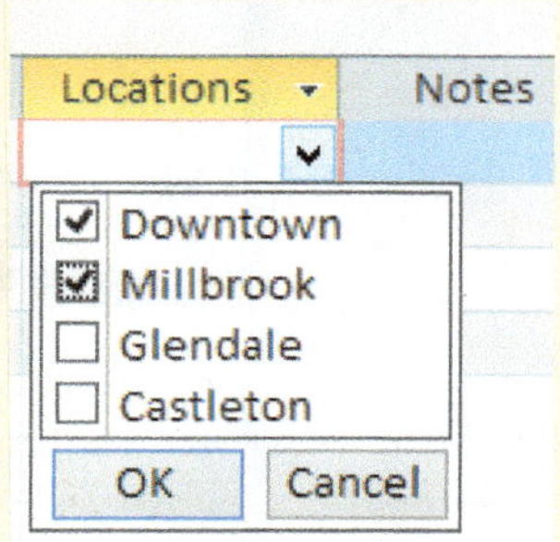

Access 2013, Windows 8, Microsoft Corporation

Lesson 24—Practice

In this project, you will create a lookup for one of the fields in your friend's database.

DIRECTIONS

1. Start Access, if necessary, and open **A24Practice** from the data files for this lesson.
2. Save the database as **A24Practice_xx** in the location where your teacher instructs you to store the files for this lesson.

   ✓ *If a security warning bar appears, click Enable Content.*
3. Click **DATABASE TOOLS** > **Relationships** to open the Relationships grid.
4. Click the relationship between **Shippers** and **Orders**, and press DEL. Click **Yes** to confirm the deletion.
5. Click **RELATIONSHIP TOOLS DESIGN** > **Close**.
6. In the Navigation pane, right-click the **Orders** table and click **Design View**.
7. Open the **Data Type** drop-down list for the Shipper field and click **Lookup Wizard**.

   ✓ *If a Microsoft Access Security Notice dialog box opens, click Open.*
8. Click **Next**.
9. Click **Table: Shippers** and click **Next**.
10. Click the **Name** field and click > to select it. See Figure 24-2 on the next page. Then, click **Next**.
11. Click **Next** to bypass setting a sort order.
12. Click **Next** to accept the default columns.
13. Click **Finish** to accept the default name.
14. Click **Yes** to save the table.
15. Right-click the **Orders** tab and click **Close**.
16. Click **DATABASE TOOLS** > **Relationships**.
17. Select the relationship line between **Shippers** and **Orders**. It turns bold.
18. Click **RELATIONSHIP TOOLS DESIGN** > **Edit Relationships**.
19. Click to mark the **Enforce Referential Integrity** check box.
20. Click to mark the **Cascade Update Related Fields** check box. See Figure 24-3 on the next page.
21. Click **OK**.
22. Click **FILE** > **Close**. If instructed, submit this database to your teacher for grading.

Figure 24-2

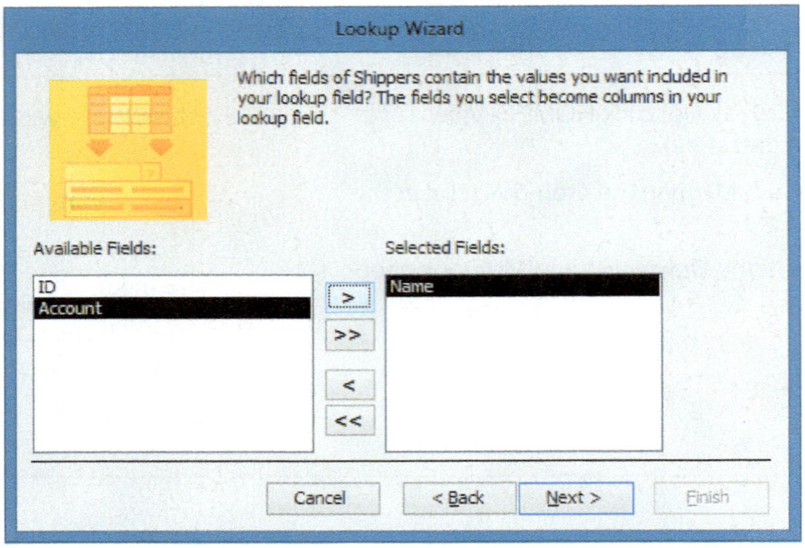

Access 2013, Windows 8, Microsoft Corporation

Figure 24-3

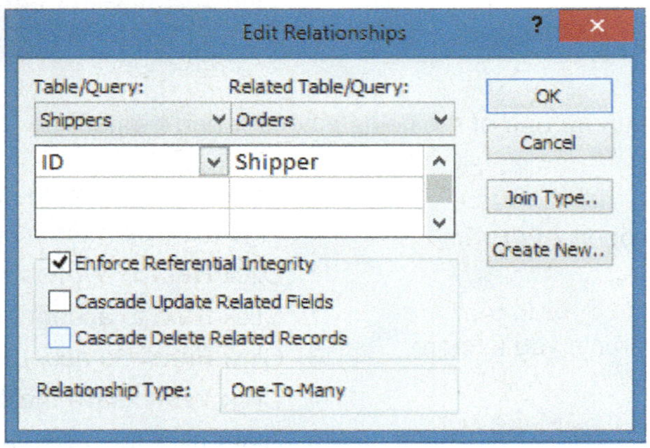

Access 2013, Windows 8, Microsoft Corporation

Lesson 24—Apply

To help your friend enter data into her jewelry business database more efficiently, you will create lookups for several of the database fields.

DIRECTIONS

1. Start Access, if necessary, and open **A24Apply** from the data files for this lesson.
2. Save the database as **A24Apply_xx** in the location where your teacher instructs you to store the files for this lesson.

   ✓ *If a security warning bar appears, click Enable Content.*
3. In the Relationships grid, delete the relationship between **Customers** and **Orders**. Then, close the Relationships grid.
4. Open the **Orders** table in Design view, and change the data type for the **Customer** field to **Lookup Wizard**.
5. Using the Lookup Wizard, create a lookup to **Table: Customers** using the **First Name** and **Last Name** fields. Sort in **Ascending** order by **Last Name**.

   ✓ *The Lookup Wizard re-creates the relationship between the Customers and Orders tables.*
6. Reopen the Relationships grid, and edit the relationship between the **Orders** and **Customers** tables to turn on **Enforce Referential Integrity** and **Cascade Update Related Fields**. Then, close the Relationships grid.
7. Open the **Orders** table in Datasheet view. Make sure that the **Customer** field appears as a drop-down list for each record, and then close the table.

   ✓ *Notice that the first name of the person appears in the Customer field. That's because you selected the First Name field first when creating the lookup; if you had selected the Last Name field first, it would appear here instead.*
8. Open the **Customers** table in Design view.
9. Change the **State** field's data type to **Lookup Wizard**, and create a lookup to the States table, sorted in Ascending order.

   ✓ *This table has only one field, and it's already set up as the primary key.*
10. Save the changes to the table, and check your work in Datasheet view.
11. Open the **Salespeople** table in Design view.
12. Using the Lookup Wizard, create a lookup for the **Commission Rate** field that allows users to select from the following values that you enter yourself: **4%**, **5%**, **6%**, and **7%**. Save the changes to the table, and check your work in Datasheet view.
13. Open the **Products** table in Design view.
14. Create a new field, at the bottom of the field list, named **Special**. Set its Data Type to **Lookup Wizard**, and create a lookup that allows users to select from the following values: **Craftsman Collection**, **Modified Schedule**, and **Special Materials**. On the last screen of the wizard, mark the **Allow Multiple Values** check box.
15. View the **Products** table in Datasheet view and set the **Special** field to **Craftsman Collection** for the first two records.
16. Save the changes to the table, and check your work in Datasheet view.
17. Click **FILE** > **Close**. If instructed, submit this database to your teacher for grading.

Lesson 25

Creating an Input Mask

➤ What You Will Learn

Using a Field Validation Rule
Understanding Input Masks
Creating an Input Mask Using the Input Mask Wizard
Creating an Input Mask Using the Input Mask Properties Box

WORDS TO KNOW

Input mask
A pattern to follow for entering data in a field.

Software Skills When multiple people use a database, inconsistencies can occur that can cause data analysis problems. For example, some people might enter phone numbers with parentheses around the area code and others might not, or someone might enter the wrong number of digits for a ZIP code. An input mask can help users enter data correctly.

What You Can Do

Using a Field Validation Rule

- A Validation Rule enables you to control what can be entered into a database and its objects.
- Field validation rules use data types, field sizes, and table properties to control how data is entered.
- To add a field validation rule in Design view, select the field to change. On the General tab, enter the validation rule into the Validation Rule field.

Understanding Input Masks

- An **input mask** is like a frame that the data is poured into. You use it to ensure that data is entered correctly in specified fields.
- The Input Mask Wizard works only with fields of the Short Text or Date/Time data types. You can manually create an input mask for a Number or Currency data field.
- An input mask streamlines data entry by displaying "helper" characters, such as parentheses around the area code in a phone number or a dash between the fifth and sixth digits of a 9-digit ZIP code.

✓ *When you add an input mask to a table field, any future forms you create based on that table will also use that input mask. However, any existing forms are not affected (unless you delete the affected field from the form and then reinsert it). Forms are covered in Lessons 17, 18, and 19.*

- If you click in a field with an input mask, you will be entering data at a specific position in the input mask, which is not necessarily at the beginning. This can cause errors if there are required characters. Pressing HOME moves the insertion point to the beginning of the field. You can avoid the problem altogether by pressing TAB from the previous field, rather than clicking.
- An input mask does not affect data already entered in the table.

Try It! Using an Input Mask

1. Start Access, and open **A25Try** from the data files for this lesson.
2. Save the database as **A25Try_xx** in the location where your teacher instructs you to store the files for this lesson.
3. Open the Students table in Datasheet view.
4. Click in the Birthdate field for Leroy Critchfield.
5. Press HOME to move the insertion point to the beginning of the field.
6. Type **04121959**.

   ✓ *You do not have to type the slashes; they are already in the field because of the existing input mask.*
7. Click HOME > View to switch to Design view.
8. Click the Birthdate field.
9. In the Properties section, examine the text in the Input Mask box.

   ✓ *Notice the code there: 99/99/0000;0;_. This code creates the mask. Later in this lesson, you will learn what this code means.*
10. Leave the **A25Try_xx** database open to use in the next Try It.

Creating an Input Mask Using the Input Mask Wizard

- The easiest way to create an input mask is to use the Input Mask Wizard. The wizard walks you through the steps for creating any of several common mask types, such as date, ZIP code, Social Security number, or phone number.
- You can fine-tune the input mask by manually editing its codes within the wizard if you like. You will learn about manually editing mask codes in the next section.
- Be careful that your input mask doesn't conflict with the Format property for the field. For example, if your date format is set to Short Date, don't specify an input mask of Medium Date. The input mask and the format will both work, but users may be confused as to which format is correct.
- The wizard lets you specify which placeholder character to use. This is the character that appears in the field before you enter the number. By default, it is an underscore for most mask types, but you can change it to some other character, such as * or #.
- For some mask types, the wizard lets you specify whether or not helper characters should be stored in the field. For example, for a ZIP code, you might have a number like 09123-2842. The dash appears onscreen as part of the mask, to help users input the data. You can choose to not have the dash be stored though, in which case Access stores the data as 091232842.
- Storing helper characters (or not) is an issue for two reasons. One is that each extra character takes up space, making the database file larger. Another is that if you export data to some other program, it may be beneficial or detrimental to have the helper characters included, depending on the program and the usage.

Try It! Creating an Input Mask Using the Input Mask Wizard

1. In the **A25Try_xx** file, with the Students table open in Design view, click the ZIP field.
2. In the grid below, click in the Input Mask property field. A Build button [...] appears.
3. Click the Build button [...]. The Input Mask Wizard runs.

   ✓ *If the Microsoft Access Security Notice dialog box appears, click Open.*
4. Click Zip Code.
5. Click Next. The code for the mask appears.
6. Open the Placeholder character drop-down list and click #.
7. Click Next.
8. Click Next to accept the default data storage (without the symbols in the mask).
9. Click Finish. The mask is created, and the code for it appears in the Input Mask property.
10. Leave the **A25Try_xx** database open to use in the next Try It.

The Input Mask Wizard

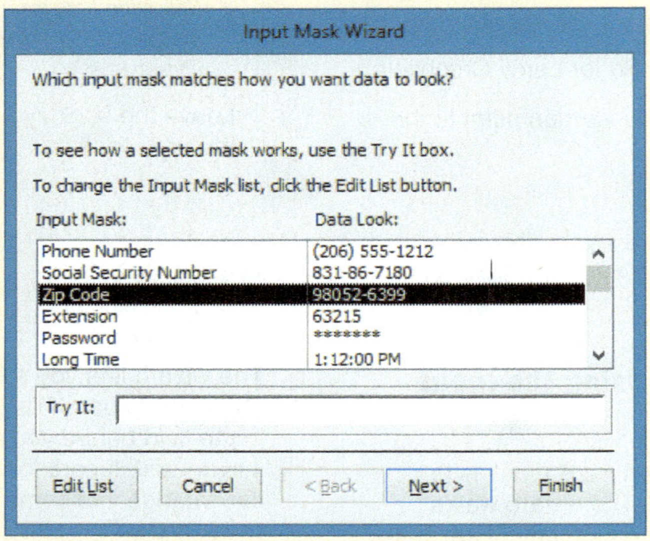

Access 2013, Windows 8, Microsoft Corporation

Creating an Input Mask Using the Input Mask Properties Box

- You can also enter your own input mask by typing characters in a specified format directly in the Input Mask dialog box.
- Alternatively, you can use the wizard to create the mask and then edit it manually to fine-tune it.

  ✓ *You do not have to go all the way through the wizard if you want to accept the default settings.*
- There are up to three sections in the input mask. Each section is separated by a semicolon:

Section	Description	What to type
First	Input mask characters	Type codes shown in the following table.
Second	Store extra characters such as parentheses with the number	Type 0 for yes, or 1 (or leave blank) for no.
Third	Placeholder character to be used	Type any character, such as an underscore. If you want a blank space, type a space in quotation marks.

- The following table shows the characters to use in the first section of the input mask. Different symbols are used depending on whether the user is required to enter that character.

- For example, 00000-9999 requires a five-digit ZIP code (00000), but also allows for an optional extra four characters (9999).

Data	Description	Entry Required	Entry Optional
Number	0 or 9. Plus and minus signs (+ and -) are prohibited.	0	9
Number or space	Leading and trailing spaces are blanks but removed when the field is saved. Plus and minus signs (+ and -) are permitted.	1	#
Letter	Any alphabet character	L	?
Letter or number	Any numeral or any alphabet characters	A	a
Any character or space	Any	&	C

- The second section of the mask is for additional characters or special instructions, as shown in the following table:

. , : ; - /	Decimal, thousand, date, and time separators. Depends on Windows settings.
\	Any character following this symbol is displayed literally.
" "	Any characters within quotes are displayed literally.
>	Converts the following characters to uppercase.
<	Converts the following characters to lowercase.

- For example, an input mask for a 9-digit ZIP code might look like this: 00000-9999;;_. The 00000 specifies five required digits. The 9999 specifies four optional digits. The first semicolon marks the end of the first section. The second section is empty, so another semicolon immediately follows. The _ character is the placeholder.
- The input mask "("999") "999"-"9999;;_ uses quotation marks to include literal characters for the parentheses and the dash. It could also be written as \(999\)999\-9999;;_ instead, but you lose the additional space following the closing parenthesis.
- Adding an exclamation point at the beginning of the code string like this !\(999") "000\-0000;;_ enables you to put numbers anywhere in the field. If you enter only 7 numbers even at the beginning of the field, the numbers will appear to the right of the parentheses. For example, as you type the number 5554567, it will appear as (555) 456-7, but after the number is entered, it will appear as ( ) 555-4567.

Try It! Modifying an Input Mask

1. In the **A25Try_xx** file, in the Students table in Design view, select the ZIP field.
2. In the Input Mask property, delete the # at the end of the code and type an _ (underscore) to replace it.
3. Leave the **A25Try_xx** database open to use in the next Try It.

Try It! **Manually Creating an Input Mask**

1. In the **A25Try_xx** file, in the Students table in Design view, select the Phone field.
2. In the Input Mask property, type the following: **!\(999") "000\-0000;;_**.
3. Click the Save button on the Quick Access Toolbar.
4. Close the **A25Try_xx** file, and exit Access.

Lesson 25—Practice

In this project, you will create two input masks for your friend's database.

DIRECTIONS

1. Start Access, if necessary, and open **A25Practice** from the data files for this lesson.
2. Save the database as **A25Practice_xx** in the location where your teacher instructs you to store the files for this lesson.

   ✓ *If a security warning bar appears, click Enable Content.*
3. Right-click the **Orders** table, and click **Design View**.
4. Click the **Order Date** field, and then click in the **Input Mask** property for that field.
5. Click the **Build** button.
6. Click **Short Date**, and click **Finish**.
7. Click the **Save** button on the Quick Access Toolbar.
8. Click **HOME** > **View** to switch to Datasheet view.
9. Enter a new record in the table:

   Order Date: **12/16/2012**

   Customer: **Jennifer Brown**

   Shipper: **UPS**

   Salesperson: **TR**
10. Right-click the table's tab and click **Close**.
11. Right-click the **Customers** table, and click **Design View**.
12. Click the **ZIP** field, and click in the **Input Mask** property.
13. Type **00000;;_** in the Input Mask property.
14. Click the **Save** button on the Quick Access Toolbar.
15. Click **FILE** > **Close**. If instructed, submit this database to your teacher for grading.

Lesson 25—Apply

Your friend with the jewelry business is getting ready to hire an assistant. To make the database as foolproof as possible you will create input masks to help her.

DIRECTIONS

1. Start Access, if necessary, and open **A25Apply** from the data files for this lesson.
2. Save the database as **A25Apply_xx** in the location where your teacher instructs you to store the files for this lesson.

   ✓ *If a security warning bar appears, click Enable Content.*
3. Open the **Customers** table in Design view.
4. Set up an input mask for the **Phone** field that requires all 10 digits and stores the parentheses as part of the field entry.
5. Save and close the table.
6. Open the **Orders** table in Design view.
7. In the **Salesperson** field, manually enter **LL** into the Input Mask property.
8. Switch to Datasheet view, and enter the following new record. As you do so, try to enter an extra character in the Salesperson field. Access will not let you because of the input mask.

   Order Date: **12/16/2017**

   Customer: **Norman Eichmann**

   Shipper: **UPS**

   Salesperson: **PS**
9. Click **FILE** > **Close**. If instructed, submit this database to your teacher for grading.

End-of-Chapter Activities

➤ Access Chapter 3—Critical Thinking

Medical Office Time Cards

You are a consultant for a medical office where employee data and time cards are stored in an Access database. So far there are only tables and queries in the database. You will create forms and reports that make the data easier to store and retrieve.

DIRECTIONS

1. Start Access, if necessary, and open **ACT03** from the data files for this chapter.
2. Save the database as **ACT03_xx** in the location where your teacher instructs you to store the files for this chapter.

   ✓ *If a security warning bar appears, click Enable Content.*
3. Open the **Employees** table in Design view.
4. Set up the **Positions** table as a lookup for the Position field in the **Employees** table, with the positions sorted in Ascending order.

   ✓ *You may see a warning that some data may be lost; this is okay.*
5. Create an input mask for the **ZIP** field using any standard format you like.

   ✓ *The format you use must be valid for mailings in the United States.*
6. Create an input mask for the **HomePhone** field in which all 10 digits are required. Use any other settings you like.
7. Copy the input mask code you just created into the **CellPhone** and **Pager** fields' Input Mask property.
8. Close the **Employees** table, saving your changes.
9. Using the **CREATE** > **Form** command, create a form for entering data in the **Timecards** table. Save it as **Time Card Entry**.
10. Using the Form Wizard, create a columnar form for entering new employees in the **Employees** table. Use all the fields. Save it as **Employees Form**.
11. Using the Report Wizard, create a report that shows a list of all employees (first and last names), grouped by position. Use the **Positions** field from the Positions table, and the **FirstName** and **LastName** fields from the Employees table. Use the Block layout. Name the report **Employees by Position**.
12. In Layout view, fix the columns so the longest entry in the **Positions** field is not truncated.
13. Create a quick report (**CREATE** > **Report**) based on the **Hours Worked** query. Save it as **Hours Worked Report**.
14. Click **FILE** > **Close**. If instructed, submit this database to your teacher for grading.

➤ Access Chapter 3—Portfolio Builder

Book Collection Database

A friend who collects antique books has asked for your help in continuing to develop a database for his collection. His database currently consists of several tables and queries you created for him earlier. Now you will build forms and reports for him as well.

DIRECTIONS

1. Start Access, if necessary, and open **APB03** from the data files for this chapter.
2. Save the database as **APB03_xx** in the location where your teacher instructs you to store the files for this chapter.

   ✓ *If a security warning bar appears, click Enable Content.*
3. Open the **Authors** table in Design view.
4. For the **Born** field, manually construct an input mask that requires exactly 4 digits.
5. Copy the input mask to the **Died** field.
6. Use the Lookup Wizard to create a lookup for the **Nationality** field that looks up values from the **Countries** table.
7. Create a new form in Layout view that includes all the fields from the **Books** table, in the order they appear in the table.
8. Switch to Design View, and display the **Form Header** and **Form Footer** sections.
9. If necessary, in the Form Header, insert a title of **Books**.
10. In the Form Footer, insert a code that shows the current date (but not the time).

    ✓ *The Date and Time command inserts the code in the Form Header; cut-and-paste it to the Form Footer.*
11. Save the form as **Book Information** and close it.
12. In Layout view, create a new tabular report that lists the books from the **Books** table. Include the **Title**, **Author**, and **Date Published** fields in that order.
13. Adjust the column widths as needed so that no entries wrap to more than one row and nothing is truncated.
14. Group the report by **Author**.
15. Save the report as **Books by Author**. **With your teacher's permission**, print one copy of the first page of the report, and write your name on the printout.
16. Click **FILE** > **Close**. If instructed, submit this database to your teacher for grading.

Chapter 1

(Courtesy Konstantin Chagin/Shutterstock)

Getting Started with Microsoft PowerPoint 2013

Lesson 1
Getting Started with PowerPoint

- About PowerPoint
- Starting PowerPoint
- Using a Storyboard to Plan a Presentation
- Saving and Closing a Presentation
- Opening an Existing Presentation
- Exploring the PowerPoint Window
- Entering Text Using Placeholders
- Applying a Theme
- Checking Spelling in a Presentation
- Previewing a Presentation

Lesson 2
Working with Slides

- Customizing the Quick Access Toolbar
- Viewing PowerPoint Options
- Inserting New Slides
- Selecting Slide Layout
- Moving from Slide to Slide
- Changing List Levels
- Printing a Presentation

Lesson 3
Working with Headers, Footers, and Notes

- Reusing Slides from Other Presentations
- Adding Notes
- Changing Slide Size and Orientation
- Inserting Headers and Footers
- Working with Presentation Properties

Lesson 4
Inserting and Formatting Pictures

- Inserting a Picture from a File
- Formatting Pictures Using the PICTURE TOOLS FORMAT Tab
- Formatting Pictures Using the Format Task Pane

Lesson 5
Formatting Text

- Finding and Replacing Text and Fonts in a Presentation
- Selecting Text and Placeholders
- Changing the Appearance of Text Using Fonts, Font Sizes, Styles, and Colors
- Copying Text Formatting
- Using Undo and Redo
- Clearing Formatting

Lesson 6
Aligning Text

- Aligning Text
- Adjusting Line Spacing
- Adjusting Paragraph Spacing and Indents
- Moving and Copying Text
- Using AutoFit Options
- Adjusting and Formatting Placeholders

Lesson 7
Displaying the Presentation Outline

- Displaying the Presentation Outline
- Viewing a Presentation in Reading View
- Viewing a Presentation in Grayscale or Black and White

Lesson 8
Arranging Slides

- Copying, Duplicating, and Deleting Slides
- Arranging Multiple PowerPoint Windows
- Copying Slides from One Presentation to Another
- Rearranging Slides

Lesson 9
Adding Slide Transitions

- Identifying Guidelines for Using Graphics, Fonts, and Special Effects in Presentations
- Evaluating and Selecting Appropriate Sources of Information
- Adding Slide Transitions
- Controlling Slide Advance

End-of-Chapter Activities

Lesson 1

Getting Started with PowerPoint

➤ What You Will Learn

- About PowerPoint
- Starting PowerPoint
- Using a Storyboard to Plan a Presentation
- Saving and Closing a Presentation
- Opening an Existing Presentation
- Exploring the PowerPoint Window
- Entering Text Using Placeholders
- Applying a Theme
- Checking Spelling in a Presentation
- Previewing a Presentation

WORDS TO KNOW

Normal view
PowerPoint's default view that displays the Slide pane and the Thumbnail pane.

Placeholders
Designated areas in PowerPoint layouts that can be used to easily insert text, graphics, or multimedia objects.

Presentation
A set of slides or handouts that contains information you want to convey to an audience.

Storyboard
A series of drawings used to illustrate the sequence of action or outline of a presentation.

Theme
Formatting feature that applies a background, colors, fonts, and effects to all slides in a presentation.

Software Skills PowerPoint's many features make it easy to create both simple and sophisticated presentations. One way to create a new slide show is to start with a Blank Presentation from the template choices that display when PowerPoint opens. Once a presentation is open, you can enter text and apply a theme to give it a consistent design.

What You Can Do

About PowerPoint

- PowerPoint is a presentation graphics program that lets you create slide shows you can present using a computer projection system or publish online as a slideshow.
- A **presentation** can include handouts, outlines, and speaker notes as well as slides.
- PowerPoint slides may contain text and various other types of content, such as clip art, pictures, videos, tables, or charts.
- You can create all the slide content in PowerPoint or import data from other Microsoft Office programs such as Word and Excel to create slide content.

Starting PowerPoint

- To use PowerPoint 2013 you must first start it so it is running on your computer.
- You use Microsoft Windows to start PowerPoint.
- When PowerPoint starts, it displays a selection of templates for you to choose from. You can start with a blank presentation or one of the other presentation designs.

Try It! Starting PowerPoint

1. Start Windows 8.

   ✓ *If you are using Windows 7, ask your instructor for directions.*

2. In the application tiles at the right side of the Windows 8 Start screen, click PowerPoint 2013.

   ✓ *If PowerPoint 2013 does not appear among the apps displayed on the Start screen, right-click, click All apps near the lower-right corner of the screen, scroll to the right to see the Microsoft Office 2013 applications, and click PowerPoint 2013.*

OR

1. If Windows 8 is already running, point to the lower-left corner of the screen and click to display the Start screen.
2. Locate PowerPoint 2013 as directed previously.

OR

1. From the Windows 8 Start screen, click Desktop.
2. You may then have an option to click a PowerPoint shortcut icon on the desktop or the taskbar.
3. With PowerPoint open, click Blank Presentation to start a new presentation.
4. Leave the blank presentation open to use in the next Try It.

Using a Storyboard to Plan a Presentation

- Before starting PowerPoint and beginning a new presentation, you may find it helpful to create a storyboard to plan what you want to say and show in the presentation.
- A **storyboard** is a series of images that represent the slides you intend to create.
- The slide images might include slide titles, rough notes about the text you want to appear on each slide, and suggestions for supporting graphics, video, or audio files.
- The simplest way to create a storyboard is to sketch the slide images on paper. If you are using a tablet computer with an input stylus, you can draw your storyboard right on the screen to store it digitally.
- You may also want to storyboard using a two-column table in a word processing program such as Microsoft Word 2013. You can quickly type the text you plan to use for your slides in the left column, and after printing, sketch in the right column next to each slide's text the graphics you need for that slide.

  ✓ *An advantage to storyboarding with Word is that you can then copy the text to PowerPoint so you don't have to retype it.*

- You can also use this planning process to decide what kinds of slides you will need, such as a title slide, blank slides on which you intend to draw shapes, slides in which you will have content in two columns, and so on.

Saving and Closing a Presentation

- PowerPoint supplies the default title *Presentation* and a number (for example, *Presentation1*) in the title bar of each new presentation. You should change this default title to a more descriptive title when you save a new presentation so that you can work on it again later.
- By default, a new presentation is saved in XML format, the standard for Office 2010 and Office 2013 applications, giving the file an extension of .pptx.
- If you wish to use a presentation with earlier versions of PowerPoint, you can save the file in PowerPoint 97-2003 Presentation format. You can also save the presentation in several other formats, such as PDF or XPS, or as a template or show.

✓ *You will save presentations as templates and shows in later lessons.*

- Close a PowerPoint presentation the same way you close other Microsoft Office documents and spreadsheets.
- Use the Close button in the upper-right corner of the window to close a presentation. If only one presentation is open, clicking this button closes both the presentation and PowerPoint.
- To close a presentation and leave PowerPoint open, use the Close command on the FILE menu.

Try It! Saving and Closing a Presentation

1. Click Save on the Quick Access Toolbar.

   OR

   a. Click FILE.
   b. Click Save.
2. Click Computer and then click Browse. Navigate to the location where your teacher instructs you to store the files for this lesson.
3. In the File name box, type **P01Try_xx**.

   ✓ *Replace xx with your initials or full name, as instructed by your teacher.*
4. Click Save or press ENTER.
5. Click FILE and then click Close.
6. Leave PowerPoint open to use in the next Try It.

Opening an Existing Presentation

- Open an existing presentation to modify, add, or delete material.
- PowerPoint makes it easy to open presentations on which you have recently worked by listing them in the Recent Presentations list that displays when you click Open on the FILE tab.
- If you do not see the presentation on this list, you can click the place where you stored the file (your OneDrive or Computer) and access a recent folder.
- Or click Browse to display the Open dialog box to navigate to the presentation you want to open.

Try It! Opening an Existing Presentation

1. Click FILE > Open.
2. Click **P01Try_xx** in the Recent Presentations list.
3. Leave **P01Try_xx** open to use in the next Try It.

Exploring the PowerPoint Window

- PowerPoint, like other Microsoft Office 2013 applications, displays the Ribbon interface that groups commands on tabs across the top of the window below the title bar.
- The status bar displays information about the presentation, such as the slide number and view options.
- A presentation opens by default in **Normal view**, which displays the Slide pane and the Thumbnail pane. You can also toggle on the Notes pane by clicking the Notes button on the status bar.
  - Use the Slide pane to insert and modify slide content.
  - Use the Notes pane to add text for personal reference, such as material you want to remember to cover during the presentation.
  - The Thumbnail pane shows a small version of all slides in the presentation and can be used to quickly select slides or reorganize them.

Try It! Exploring the PowerPoint Window

1. In the **P01Try_xx** file, move your mouse pointer over each window element shown in the figure.
2. Leave the **P01Try_xx** file open to use in the next Try It.

The PowerPoint window

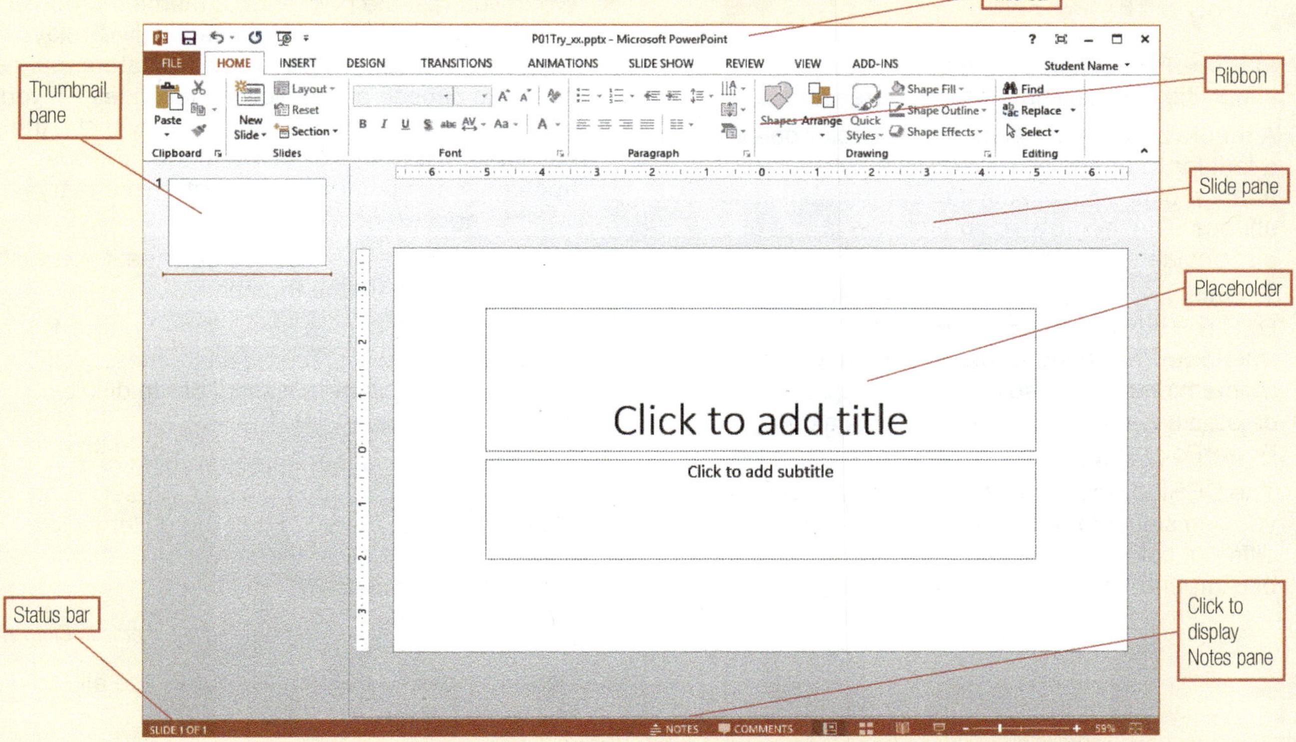

PowerPoint 2013, Windows 8, Microsoft Corporation

Entering Text Using Placeholders

- PowerPoint displays **placeholders** to define the arrangement and location of text and other objects you can add to slides.
- The title slide you see when creating a new presentation has two placeholders: one for the title and one for the subtitle.
- Different types of slides in a presentation have different types of placeholders in which you can insert lists, pictures, tables, charts, or videos.
- To insert text in a placeholder, click inside the placeholder. PowerPoint selects the box and displays a blinking insertion point that shows where text will appear when typed. Begin typing to insert the desired text.

Try It! Entering Text Using Placeholders

1. In the **P01Try_xx** file, click once in the title placeholder to select it and position the insertion point.
2. Type **Premier Soccer Club** in the title placeholder.
3. Click the Click to add subtitle placeholder. Type **Top Travel Soccer Competition for Boys and Girls**.
4. Click outside the placeholder to deselect it.
5. Save the **P01Try_xx** file and leave it open to use in the next Try It.

Applying a Theme

- In PowerPoint, **themes** are used as a means of supplying graphical interest for a presentation.
- A theme provides a background, a color palette, a font for titles and text, distinctive bullets, and a range of special effects that can be applied to shapes. The theme also controls the layout of placeholders on slides.
- Themes are located in the Themes group on the DESIGN tab, as shown in Figure 1-1. The size of the PowerPoint window determines how many theme thumbnails display in the group. If you have created custom themes, they display along with PowerPoint's built-in themes.
- The DESIGN tab also offers a gallery of variants you can select for each theme. Variants supply different color schemes and sometimes different background designs for the chosen theme.
- When you rest the pointer on a theme thumbnail, the slide in the Slide pane immediately displays the theme elements. This Live Preview feature makes it easy to choose a graphic look for slides—if you don't like the look of the theme, simply move the pointer off the theme to return to the previous appearance or point at a different theme to try another appearance.
- Themes have names that you can see if you rest the pointer on a theme thumbnail.
- By default, the Themes group shows only a few of the available themes. To see all themes, click the More button in the theme scroll bar to display a gallery of themes.
- The gallery shows the theme (or themes) currently used in a presentation in the This Presentation area. Options at the bottom of the gallery allow you to search for other themes or save the current theme for future use.

✓ *You will learn how to change and save a theme in Chapter 3.*

- Clicking a theme thumbnail applies it to all slides in the presentation.

Figure 1-1

PowerPoint 2013, Windows 8, Microsoft Corporation

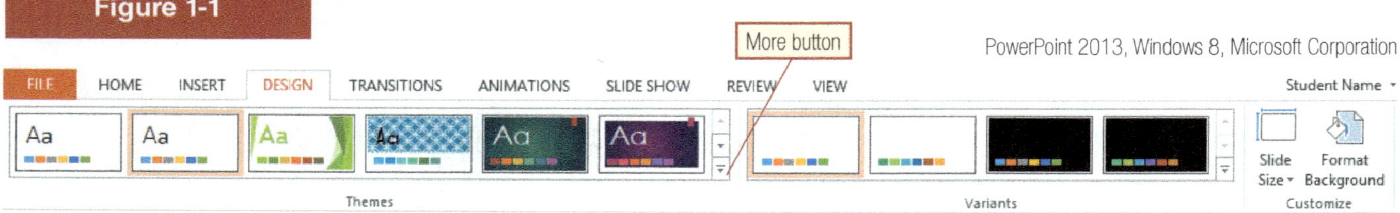

Try It! Applying a Theme

1. In the P01Try_xx file, click the DESIGN tab.
2. Click the More button to display all themes.
3. Point to several themes in the gallery to see them previewed in the presentation.
4. Click the Facet theme to apply it to the presentation.
5. Choose the variant at the far right of the Variants gallery, with the dark background.
6. Save the P01Try_xx file, and leave it open to use in the next Try It.

Checking Spelling in a Presentation

- PowerPoint provides two methods of spell checking in your presentation: automatic and manual.
- Automatic spell checking works while you're typing, displaying a wavy red line under words PowerPoint doesn't recognize. Right-click a wavy underline to see a list of possible correctly spelled replacements.
- To check spelling manually, use the Spelling button on the REVIEW tab. The process of checking spelling in a presentation using the Spelling dialog box is similar to that in other Microsoft Office applications.

Try It! Checking Spelling in a Presentation

1. In the P01Try_xx file, click the subtitle text and select the entire subtitle.
2. Type **The Top Travil Soccer Clubb for Boys and Girls**.

   ✓ *Note: "Travil" and "Clubb" should be typed incorrectly for purposes of the Try It.*
3. Right-click on *Travil* to see a list of suggested spellings. Click Travel to replace with the correct spelling.
4. Click the REVIEW tab, and then click Spelling.
5. Click Change in the Spelling task pane to replace the misspelled word *Clubb* with Club.
6. Click OK.
7. Save the P01Try_xx file, and leave it open to use in the next Try It.

Previewing a Presentation

- Use Slide Show view to see how your presentation will look to your audience.
- Previewing a presentation allows you to check wording, graphics, and other attributes such as transitions and animations.

✓ *You apply transitions later in this chapter and animations in Chapter 3.*

- You can start a slide show from the first slide using the Start From Beginning button on the Quick Access Toolbar or the From Beginning button on the SLIDE SHOW tab, or by pressing F5. To start from the slide currently displayed in the Slide pane, click the Slide Show button in the status bar or the From Current Slide button on the SLIDE SHOW tab.
- Click the left mouse button in Slide Show view to move from slide to slide. If your computer has a touch screen, you can tap the screen to advance slides.
- Click ESC to end a slide show on any slide.

Try It! **Previewing a Presentation**

1. In the **P01Try_xx** file, click the Slide Show button near the right side of the status bar. The presentation's title slide displays in Slide Show view.
2. Click the left mouse button to display the End of slide show screen, and then click again to exit Slide Show view and return to Normal view.
3. Close the **P01Try_xx** file, saving changes, and exit PowerPoint.

Lesson 1—Practice

Wynnedale Medical Center has contacted you to create a presentation to announce the opening of their new laser eye surgery unit. In this project, you create a new presentation, add text to placeholders, apply a theme, and check your spelling.

DIRECTIONS

1. Start PowerPoint, and create a new blank presentation.
2. Click **FILE** > **Save As**. Navigate to the location where your teacher instructs you to store the files for this lesson. Type **P01Practice_xx** in the File name text box, then click **Save**.
3. Click on the title placeholder and type the text **Wynnedale Medical Center**.
4. Click on the subtitle placeholder and type the text **Laser Eye Surgery Unit**.
5. Click the **DESIGN** tab, then click the **More** button to see the gallery of themes.
6. Click the **Slice** theme to apply it, and then select the light orange variant. Your slide should look like Figure 1-2 on the next page.
7. Click **REVIEW** > **Spelling** to check spelling in the presentation.
8. Click Ignore All to skip changing the spelling of Wynnedale, then click OK.
9. Click the Slide Show button on the status bar to preview the presentation.
10. Click the left mouse button twice to end the show and return to Normal view.
11. Close the file, saving changes, and exit PowerPoint.

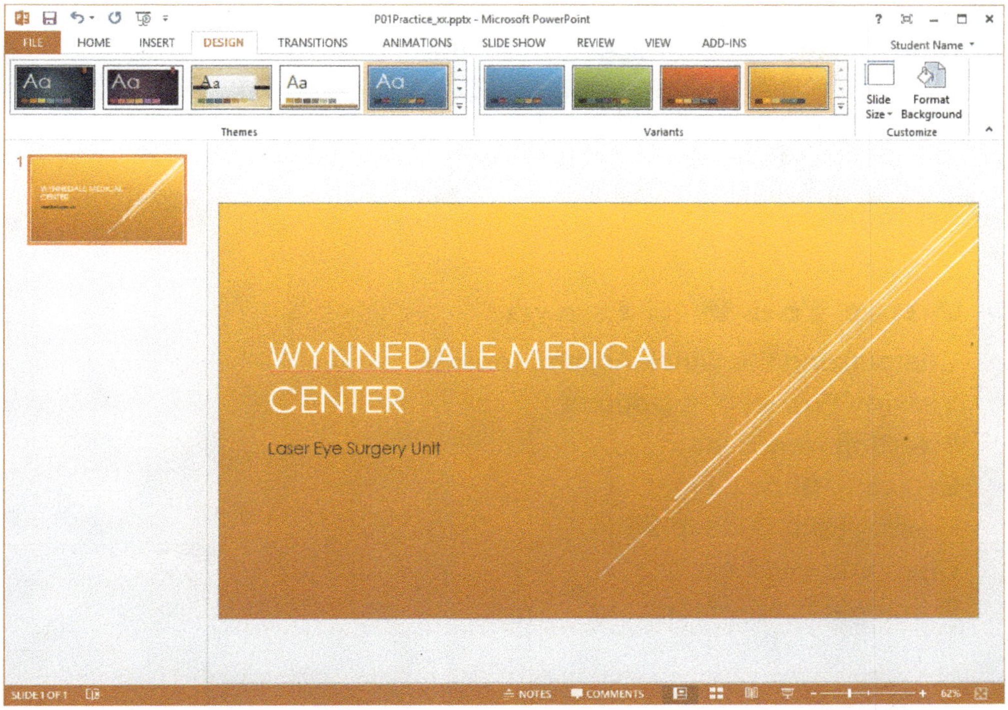

Figure 1-2

PowerPoint 2013, Windows 8, Microsoft Corporation

Lesson 1—Apply

In this project, you create another version of the Wynnedale Medical Center presentation. You add text to placeholders, apply a theme and variant, and check spelling.

DIRECTIONS

1. Start PowerPoint, if necessary.
2. Open **P01Apply** from the data files for this lesson.
3. Save the presentation as **P01Apply_xx** in the location where your teacher instructs you to store the files for this lesson.
4. Click in the subtitle placeholder, click following the word *Unit*, press ENTER, and type the following text: **Find out if Laser Surgery is right for you**
5. Apply the **Ion** theme to the presentation. Apply the blue variant.
6. Check and correct the spelling, and then preview the presentation in Slide Show view.
7. Close the presentation, saving changes, and exit PowerPoint.

Lesson 2

Working with Slides

➤ What You Will Learn

Customizing the Quick Access Toolbar
Viewing PowerPoint Options
Inserting New Slides
Selecting Slide Layout
Moving from Slide to Slide
Changing List Levels
Printing a Presentation

WORDS TO KNOW

Active slide
The slide currently selected or displayed.

Handouts
Printed copies of the presentation for the audience to refer to during and after the slide show.

Slide layout
Prearranged sets of placeholders for various types of slide content.

Software Skills In PowerPoint, you can customize the working interface by adjusting the appearance of the Quick Access Toolbar and by selecting from among a number of PowerPoint options. You can quickly and easily add new slides to a presentation. After adding new slides, you can change the slide layout and change the level of an item in a bulleted list. It's easy to move from one slide to the other, and you can also preview your slide show before printing it or presenting it.

What You Can Do

Customizing the Quick Access Toolbar

- The Quick Access Toolbar in the upper-left corner of the program window displays four commands by default: Save, Undo, Redo (which becomes Repeat after you perform an action), and Start From Beginning.
- Use the Customize Quick Access Toolbar button to add or remove buttons for common commands. You can also choose to add commands from Ribbon tabs.
- You can change the position of the Quick Access Toolbar to move it below the Ribbon.

Try It! Customizing the Quick Access Toolbar

1. Start PowerPoint, and open **P02Try** from the data files for this lesson.
2. Save the presentation as **P02Try_xx** in the location where your teacher instructs you to store the files for this lesson.
3. Click the Customize Quick Access Toolbar button to display a menu of common commands.

   ✓ *A check mark next to a command indicates it is already on the Quick Access Toolbar.*
4. Click Print Preview and Print on the menu. The button for Print Preview and Print is added to the Quick Access Toolbar.
5. Right-click the Copy button on the HOME tab of the Ribbon.
6. Click Add to Quick Access Toolbar.
7. Click the Customize Quick Access Toolbar button and click Show Below the Ribbon.
8. Right-click the Copy button on the Quick Access Toolbar.
9. Click Remove from Quick Access Toolbar.
10. Click the Customize Quick Access Toolbar button and click Show Above the Ribbon.
11. Save the **P02Try_xx** file, and leave it open to use in the next Try It.

Viewing PowerPoint Options

- PowerPoint's PowerPoint Options dialog box offers a number of options for controlling program settings.
- In this dialog box, you will find general options for adjusting the user interface and personalizing PowerPoint, as well as options for making corrections, saving, choosing a default language, and controlling editing tools.
- The PowerPoint Options dialog box also allows you to customize the Ribbon or the Quick Access Toolbar.

Try It! Viewing PowerPoint Options

1. In the **P02Try_xx** file, click FILE and then click Options to open the PowerPoint Options dialog box. The General options display. Note the options under Personalize your copy of Microsoft Office.
2. Click Save in the list on the left side of the dialog box to display the Save options. Locate the default local file location, which is where Office files are saved by default.
3. Click Proofing to display the Proofing options.
4. Click Cancel to close the dialog box without making any changes.
5. Leave the **P02Try_xx** file open to use in the next Try It.

Inserting New Slides

- Most presentations consist of a number of slides. Use the New Slide button on the HOME tab to add a slide to a presentation.
- If you simply click the New Slide button, PowerPoint adds the kind of slide you are most likely to need. With the default title slide displayed, for example, PowerPoint will assume the next slide should be a Title and Content slide.
- If the **active slide**—the currently displayed slide—uses a layout other than Title Slide, PowerPoint inserts a new slide with the same layout as the one currently displayed.
- A new slide is inserted immediately after the active slide.

Try It! Inserting New Slides

1. In the P02Try_xx file, click HOME > New Slide.
2. Press CTRL + M to add another slide.
3. Save the P02Try_xx file, and leave it open to use in the next Try It.

Selecting Slide Layout

- To specify a particular layout for a slide, click the down arrow on the New Slide button to display a gallery of slide layout choices.
- A **slide layout** arranges the standard objects of a presentation—titles, charts, text, pictures—on the slide to make it attractive. Each layout provides placeholders for specific types of content.
- Slide layout choices depend on the slide design. Some slide designs offer more layouts than others, but all offer standard layouts such as Title Slide, Title and Content, Two Content, Comparison, and Blank, among others.
- The New Slide gallery also provides options to Duplicate Selected Slides, add new Slides from Outline, and Reuse Slides.
- You can change the layout of any slide using the Layout command. This command displays the same gallery of choices as the New Slide gallery.
- When you specify a new layout, slide content you have already added to the slide adjusts as necessary to fit the new layout.

Try It! Selecting Slide Layout

1. In the P02Try_xx file, on the HOME tab, in the Slides group, click the New Slide button down arrow. A gallery of available slide types appears.
2. Click the Two Content slide.
3. Click New Slide > Duplicate Selected Slides.
4. Click HOME > Layout Content with Caption to change the layout.
5. Save the P02Try_xx file, and leave it open to use in the next Try It.

The New Slide gallery

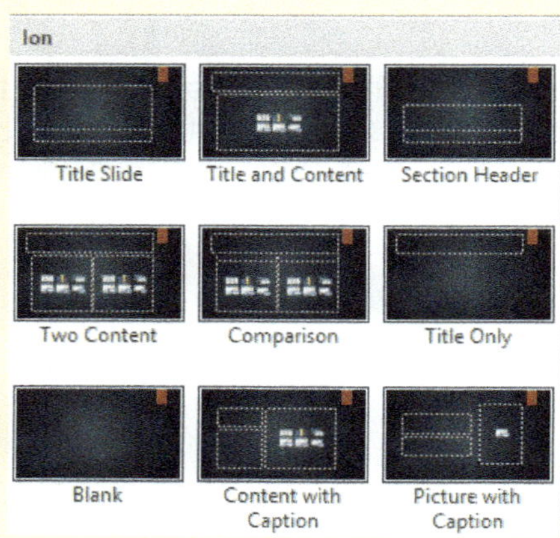

PowerPoint 2013, Windows 8, Microsoft Corporation

Moving from Slide to Slide

- Most presentations include multiple slides. You will need to move from slide to slide in Normal view to enter text and modify the presentation.
- PowerPoint offers a variety of ways to select and display slides. Click in the scroll bar or drag the scroll box to display slides, or use the Previous Slide and Next Slide buttons at the bottom of the scroll bar to move through the slides.
- You can also select slides by clicking them in the Thumbnail pane.
- If you are working in a tablet, you can use standard touch screen gestures to move from slide to slide. To go to the next slide, flick upward on the current slide in the Slide pane. To move to the previous slide, flick downward. To select a specific slide, tap it in the Thumbnail pane.

Try It! Moving from Slide to Slide

1. In the **P02Try_xx** file, click slide 3 in the Thumbnail pane.
2. Click the Next Slide button.
3. Press PG UP twice.
4. Click in the lower part of the scroll bar three times. You should now be on slide 5, as shown by the highlighted slide in the Thumbnail pane.
5. Save the **P02Try_xx** file, and leave it open to use in the next Try It.

Changing List Levels

- Slide text content consists mostly of list items that may or may not be formatted with bullets, depending on the theme. First-level list items are supplied on content placeholders. PowerPoint supplies formatting for five list levels. Each subordinate level uses a smaller font size than the previous level.

✓ *If the list is bulleted, the same bullet symbol is used for all levels.*

- Create subordinate list levels as you type by pressing TAB at the beginning of a line. You can also use the Increase List Level button in the Paragraph group on the HOME tab to apply subordinate level formatting.
- To return to a higher list level, press SHIFT + TAB or use the Decrease List Level button.

Try It! Changing List Levels

1. In the **P02Try_xx** file, click slide 2 in the Thumbnail pane.
2. Click in the title placeholder and type **Tryouts Begin Next Week**.
3. Click in the content placeholder and type **Club tryouts start Wednesday, June 8** and press ENTER.
4. Press TAB. Type **4 p.m. for under-11** and press ENTER.
5. Type **5 p.m. for all others** and press ENTER.
6. Click HOME > Decrease List Level and type **Please be prompt!**
7. Save the **P02Try_xx** file, and leave it open to use in the next Try It.

(continued)

Try It! **Changing List Levels** *(continued)*

Two list levels on a slide

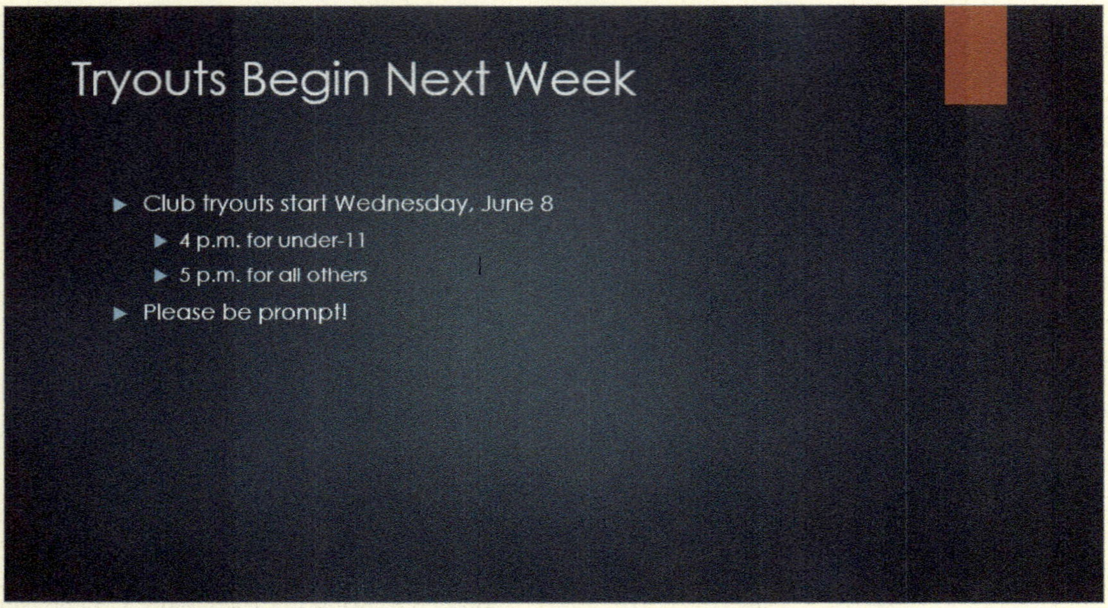

PowerPoint 2013, Windows 8, Microsoft Corporation

Printing a Presentation

- Printing PowerPoint materials is similar to printing pages in other Microsoft Office programs, with a few exceptions.
- A presentation can be printed in various formats: as slides, notes pages, **handouts**, or as an outline. You choose the settings for these formats by clicking the FILE tab and then clicking the Print tab, shown in the illustration in the following Try It.
- Among the options you can choose are:
    - Which slides to print, number of copies to print, and whether hidden slides should be printed.
    - What material (slides, notes pages, handouts, or outline) to print. If you choose to print notes pages, any notes you have typed in the Notes pane will print on the page with the slide.
    - If handouts are to be printed, how many slides per page and the order in which the slides display on the page.
    - Whether the material should be scaled (sized) to fit the page or framed by a box.
    - Whether comments and markup annotations should be printed.
    - Whether to print in grayscale, color, or black and white. You might choose to print in black and white or grayscale to preserve your printer's color ink or toner, or to allow you to concentrate on the text rather than the slide design.
- Printing a presentation can help you prepare to deliver the presentation. You may find it easier to judge the flow of information when you can see the entire presentation on one or two pages.

Try It! Printing a Presentation

1. In the **P02Try_xx** file, click Print Preview and Print on the Quick Access Toolbar. You should see a screen that looks like the following figure.
2. At the bottom of the preview area, click the Previous Page arrow ◀ to preview slide 1.
3. Click Color, then select Grayscale.
4. Click Full Page Slides, then select 2 Slides in the Handouts area of the gallery.
5. Click Grayscale, then select Color.
6. Click Print All Slides, then select Print Current Slide.
7. **With your teacher's permission**, click Print.
8. On the Quick Access Toolbar, right-click Print Preview and Print and click Remove from Quick Access Toolbar.
9. Close the **P02Try_xx** file, saving changes, and exit PowerPoint.

The Print tab

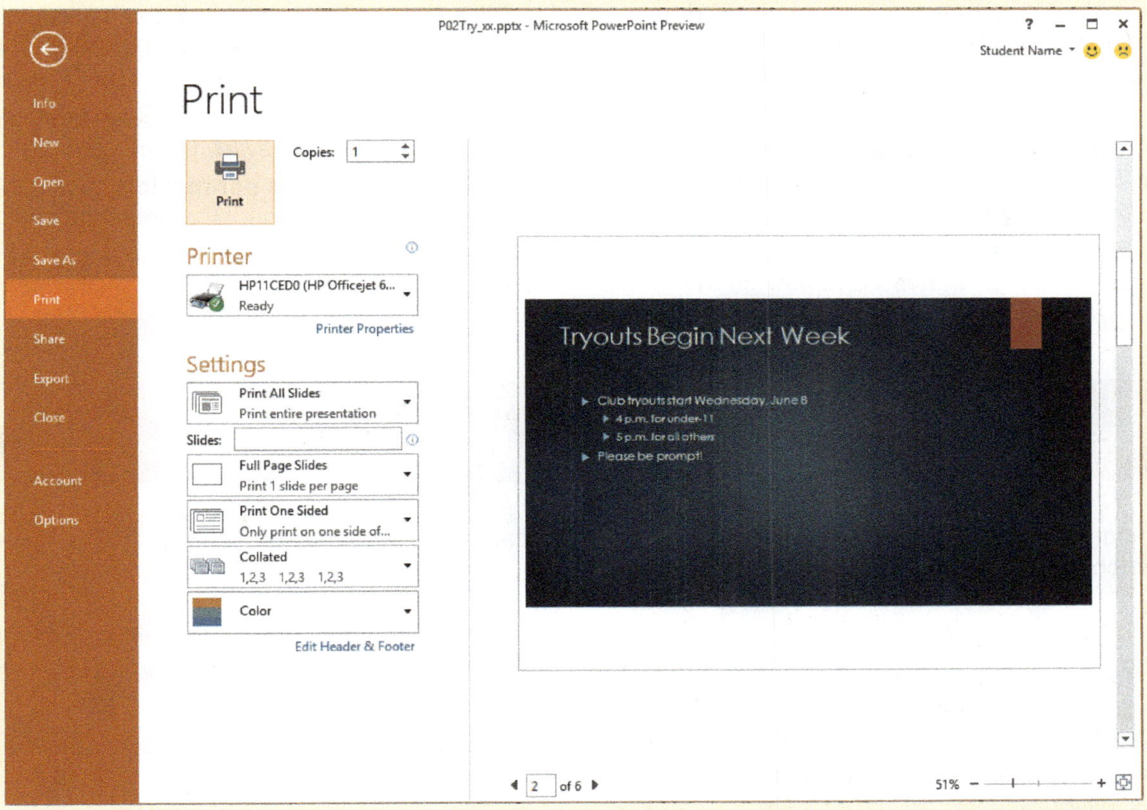

PowerPoint 2013, Windows 8, Microsoft Corporation

Lesson 2—Practice

In this project, you continue to work with the Wynnedale Medical Center presentation. You will add more content to the presentation using slides with different layouts.

DIRECTIONS

1. Start PowerPoint, if necessary, and open **P02Practice** from the data files for this lesson. Save the presentation as **P02Practice_xx** in the location where your teacher instructs you to store the files for this lesson.
2. Click on slide 3 to display it in the Slide pane.
3. On the HOME tab, click the **New Slide** drop-down arrow, then click **Two Content**.
4. Click in the title placeholder and type **Laser Eye Surgery Facts**.
5. Click in the left content placeholder and type the first bullet item, **LASIK is the most common refractive surgery**.
6. Press ENTER and then press TAB and type **LASIK corrects near-sightedness and astigmatism**.
7. Press ENTER and type the next bullet item, **Uncorrected vision may be 20/40 or better after surgery**.
8. Press ENTER and then press SHIFT + TAB to move back to a higher list level.
9. Type **Other options include PRK and LASEK**.
10. Click **HOME** > **Layout** > **Title and Content**.
11. Click **REVIEW** > **Spelling** to check spelling in the presentation, click Ignore or Change as needed, then click OK.
12. Click **Start From Beginning** on the Quick Access Toolbar to preview the presentation.
13. **With your teacher's permission,** click **FILE** > **Print**. Click **Print** to print the presentation.
14. Close the presentation, saving changes, and exit PowerPoint.

Lesson 2—Apply

In this project, you continue working with the Wynnedale Medical Center presentation. You add a slide, adjust list levels, and change slide layout.

DIRECTIONS

1. Start PowerPoint, if necessary, and open **P02Apply** from the data files for this lesson. Save the presentation as **P02Apply_xx** in the location where your teacher instructs you to store the files for this lesson.
2. Move to slide 2 and increase the list level of the last two bullet items to indent them.
3. Insert a new slide following slide 2 and then change the layout to Two Content.
4. Click in the title placeholder and type **A First Look at Laser Surgery**
5. Click in the left content placeholder and type the following items:

   Safe, fast, and reliable

   Covered by most insurance carriers

   The key to clear vision
6. Click in the right content placeholder and type the following items:

   Relative lack of pain

   Almost immediate results (within 24 hours)
7. Apply the **Ion Boardroom** theme to the presentation, and then move through the slides to see how the new theme has changed the appearance of slides. Your presentation should look like the one shown in Figure 2-1 on the next page.

8. Check the spelling and preview the presentation.
9. **With your teacher's permission,** print the presentation as handouts with 9 slides vertical.
10. Close the presentation, saving changes, and exit PowerPoint.

Figure 2-1

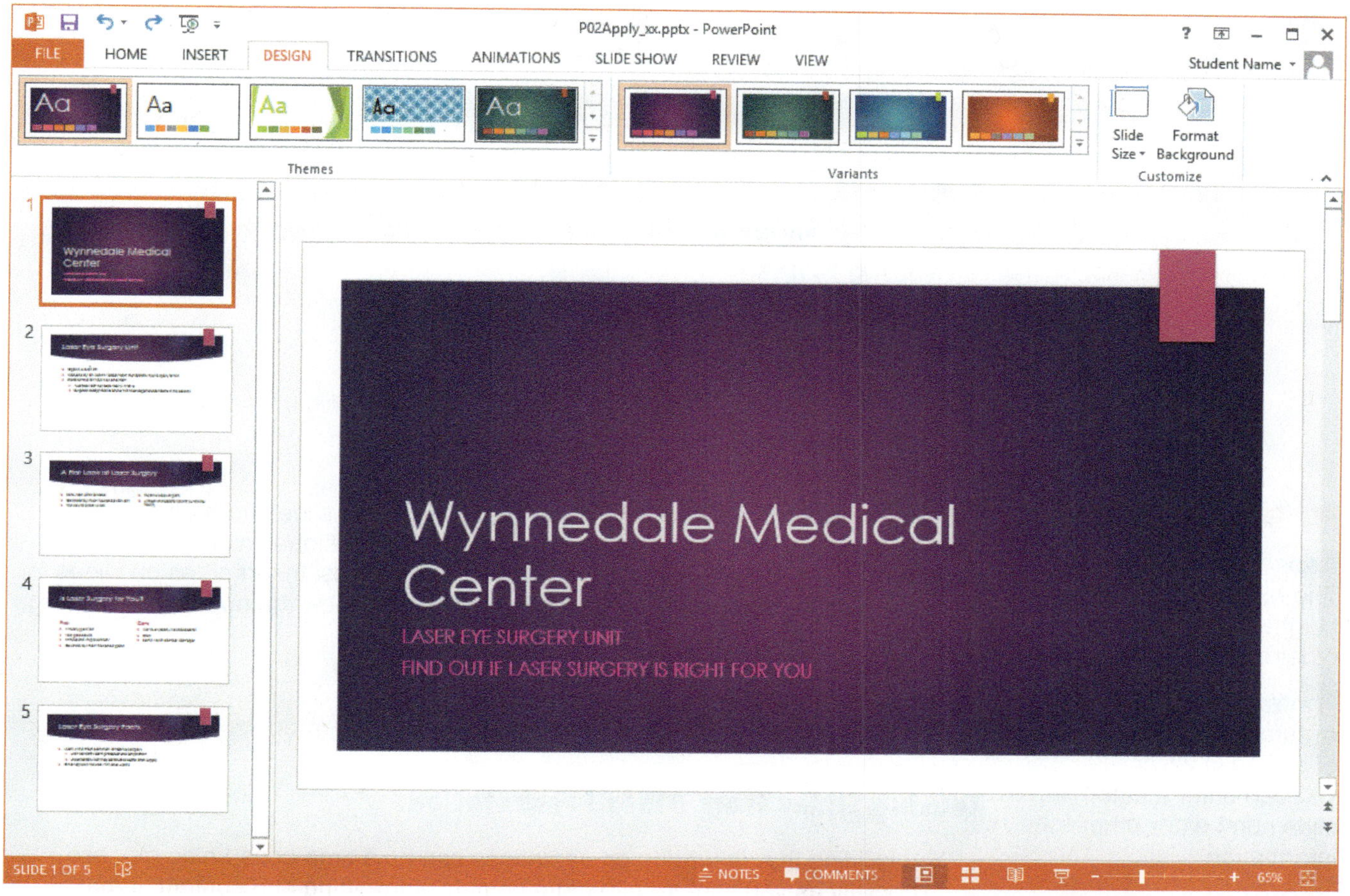

PowerPoint 2013, Windows 8, Microsoft Corporation

Lesson 3

Working with Headers, Footers, and Notes

➤ What You Will Learn

Reusing Slides from Other Presentations
Adding Notes
Changing Slide Size and Orientation
Inserting Headers and Footers
Working with Presentation Properties

Software Skills PowerPoint makes it easy to reuse slides from other presentations. Footers, dates, and numbers provide additional information on slides to help users navigate and work with presentations. Insert notes on slides for supplemental information you want to cover, and then view the notes in Notes Page view.

WORDS TO KNOW

Aspect ratio
The ratio of width to height in a screen or other output device.

Footer
An area at the bottom of a slide in which you can enter a date, slide number, or other information.

Header
An area at the top of a slide in which you can enter a date or other information that repeats for each page.

Landscape orientation
A slide or printout is wider than it is tall.

Portrait orientation
A slide or printout is taller than it is wide.

Properties
Categories of information about a presentation.

What You Can Learn

Reusing Slides from Other Presentations

- You will find that preparing presentations can be a time-consuming process, especially as you venture into more complex formatting and content. It makes sense to reuse slides whenever you can to save time.
- Borrowing slides from other presentations can also help to ensure consistency among presentations, an important consideration when you are working with a number of presentations for a company or organization.
- You can find the Reuse Slides command on the New Slide drop-down list. This command opens the Reuse Slides task pane where you can specify the presentation file to open. The slides are then displayed in the task pane. To see the content more clearly, rest the pointer on a slide in the current presentation. To insert a slide, simply click it.
- By default, slides you insert this way take on the formatting of the presentation they're inserted into (the destination presentation).
- If you want to retain the original formatting of the inserted slides, click the Keep source formatting check box at the bottom of the Reuse Slides task pane.

Try It! Reusing Slides from Other Presentations

1. Start PowerPoint, and open **P03TryA** from the data files for this lesson.
2. Save the presentation as **P03TryA_xx** in the location where your teacher instructs you to store the files for this lesson.
3. Click slide 4 in the Thumbnail pane to select it.
4. Click HOME > New Slide drop-down arrow, then click Reuse Slides.
5. In the Reuse Slides pane, click Browse and then click Browse File. Navigate to the location where the data files for this lesson are stored and open **P03TryB**. The slides from this presentation appear in the Reuse Slides pane, as shown in the figure at the right.
6. Click *June Calendar* to insert it into the destination presentation.

   ✓ *Note that the inserted slide takes on the theme and formatting of the destination presentation.*
7. Click on the remaining four slides in the Reuse Slides pane to insert them in the presentation.
8. Click the Close button × on the Reuse Slides pane to close the pane.
9. Save the **P03TryA_xx** file, and leave it open to use in the next Try It.

The Reuse Slides pane

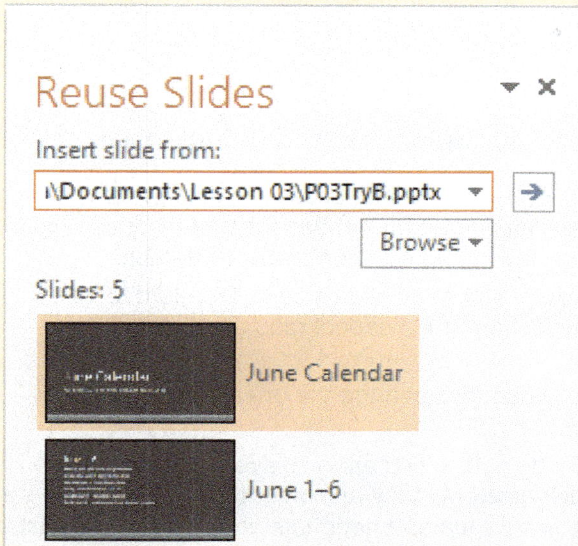

PowerPoint 2013, Windows 8, Microsoft Corporation

Adding Notes

- You can enter notes to which you want to refer during a presentation using either the Notes pane in Normal view or Notes Page view.
- Click the NOTES button in the status bar to display the Notes pane below the slide in the Slide pane.
- Use the Notes Page command on the VIEW tab to display the slides in Notes Page view. In this view, you can type notes in the Notes placeholder beneath the slide.
- You can preview or print slides in Notes Page layout to see the notes you entered below each slide.

Try It! Adding Notes

1. In the **P03TryA_xx** file, click slide 5 in the Thumbnail pane.
2. Click VIEW > Notes Page.
3. Click in the Notes placeholder and type **Tell them about what's coming up in June.**
4. Click VIEW > Normal, and then click NOTES on the status bar.
5. Press PG UP. Click in the Notes pane of slide 4 and type **Remind them that membership is free.**

(continued)

Try It! Adding Notes *(continued)*

6. Click the NOTES button to hide the Notes pane.
7. Click FILE > Print. Click Full Page Slides, then click Notes Pages in the Print Layout section of the gallery.
8. Click the Next Page arrow at the bottom of the Preview pane to see the next slide and its note.
9. Click the Back button to return to the presentation.
10. Save the **P03TryA_xx** file, and leave it open to use in the next Try It.

Changing Slide Size and Orientation

- In PowerPoint 2013, slides are displayed by default in Widescreen format because many output devices display the 16:9 **aspect ratio** by default.
- You can change slide size to Standard to view slides in the 4:3 aspect ratio used in previous versions of PowerPoint.
- You can also change the orientation of slide content.
- By default, slides are displayed in **landscape orientation**—they are wider than they are tall—and notes pages and handouts are displayed in **portrait orientation**—they are taller than they are wide.
- In some instances, you may want to reverse the usual orientation of slides to display them in portrait orientation.

✓ *If your presentation includes graphics, they may become distorted when orientation is changed.*

- You can change orientation in the Slide Size dialog box.
- Use this dialog box to select a size that will work best for a particular paper size, for 35mm slides, for overheads, or even for a custom size that you specify in the Width and Height boxes.
- When you change size or orientation, PowerPoint may display a dialog box that asks you if you want to maximize the size of the content or scale it to ensure it will fit in the new slide size.

Try It! Changing Slide Size and Orientation

1. In the **P03TryA_xx** file, click DESIGN > Slide Size and click Standard (4:3).
2. In the Microsoft PowerPoint dialog box, click the Maximize button. The slide layout changes to display content in the 4:3 aspect ratio.
3. Click DESIGN > Slide Size Custom Slide Size.
4. In the Slide Size dialog box, click Portrait in the Slides area, and then click OK.
5. In the Microsoft PowerPoint dialog box, click the Maximize button.
6. Scroll through the slides to see how the layout has changed to fit the portrait orientation.
7. Click DESIGN > Slide Size > Custom Slide Size.
8. Click the Slides sized for drop-down arrow and select Widescreen, and then select Landscape in the Slides area under Orientation. Click OK.
9. Click Ensure Fit.
10. Save the **P03TryA_xx** file, and leave it open to use in the next Try It.

Inserting Headers and Footers

- You can add several types of information that repeat for each slide to help organize or identify slides.
  - Use a slide **footer** to identify a presentation's topic, author, client, or other information.
  - Add the date and time to a slide footer so you can tell when the presentation was created or updated.
  - Include a slide number in the footer to identify the slide's position in the presentation.
- Use the Header and Footer dialog box to specify these options. Note that you can choose a fixed date or a date that updates each time the presentation is opened. You can also choose to not display the information on the title slide, apply the information only to the current slide, or apply it to all slides.
- If you are working with notes pages or handouts, you can use the options on the Notes and Handouts tab of the Header and Footer dialog box to add a **header** in addition to date and time, page number, and footer.

Try It! Inserting Headers and Footers

1. In the **P03TryA_xx** file, click INSERT > Header & Footer.

The Header and Footer dialog box

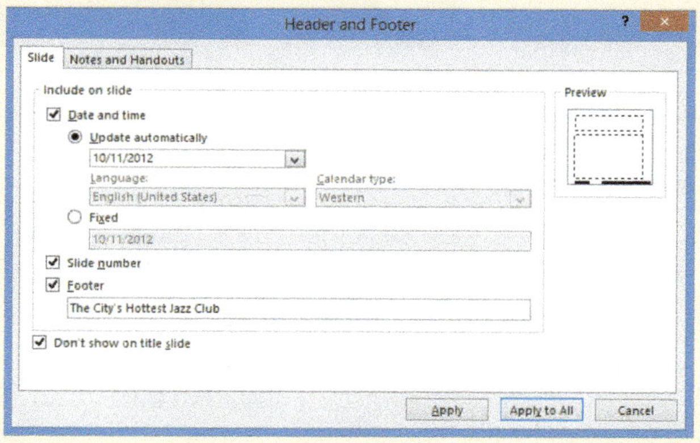

PowerPoint 2013, Windows 8, Microsoft Corporation

2. Click the Slide tab in the Header and Footer dialog box, if necessary, then click Date and time.
3. Click Slide number and Don't show on title slide.
4. Click Footer, and type **The City's Hottest Jazz Club**. The dialog box should look like the one shown in the illustration at the left.
5. Click the Notes and Handouts tab, then click Header and type **The City's Hottest Jazz Club**.
6. Click Apply to All. Click through the slides to view the footers.
7. On slide 5, click VIEW > Notes Page to view the notes page headers and footers.
8. Click VIEW > Normal to return to Normal view.
9. Save the **P03TryA_xx** file, and leave it open to use in the next Try It.

Working with Presentation Properties

- **Properties** are categories of information about a presentation, such as the name of the person who created the file, when the file was modified, and the file's size.
- Properties are stored with the presentation and display on the Info tab in the Backstage view.
- Some of a presentation's properties update automatically as you work with the file. You can also change properties to provide more information about the presentation.
- You can work with properties on the Info tab, in the Document Information Panel, or in the Properties dialog box.

Try It! Working with Presentation Properties

1. In the **P03TryA_xx** file, click FILE to display the Info tab in Backstage view.
2. In the Preview pane, under Properties, click the Title box and type **Embers Presentation**.
3. At the bottom of the properties list, click Show All Properties to see all the properties for the presentation.
4. Click the Properties drop-down arrow and click Show Document Panel. The panel opens above the Slide pane in Normal view.
5. In the Subject box, type **Information on Club**.
6. In the Status box, type **In progress**.
7. Click the Document Properties drop-down arrow and click Advanced Properties.
8. Click the Summary tab, and then click the Statistics tab.
9. Click OK, and then click the Close Document Information Panel button ×.
10. Close the **P03TryA_xx** file, saving changes, and exit PowerPoint.

Lesson 3—Practice

In this project, you will add existing slides to a new travel adventures presentation. You will add notes and footer information and change slide size and orientation.

DIRECTIONS

1. Start PowerPoint, if necessary, and open **P03PracticeA** from the data files for this lesson. Save the presentation as **P03PracticeA_xx** in the location where your teacher instructs you to store the files for this lesson.
2. Click on slide 3 to display it in the Slide pane.
3. Click **HOME** > **New Slide** drop-down arrow. Then click **Reuse Slides**.
4. In the Reuse Slides pane, click **Browse** and then click **Browse File**. Navigate to the location where the files for this lesson are stored and open **P03PracticeB**.
5. Click **Adventure Travel Packages** to insert it into the destination presentation.

   ✓ *Note that the inserted slide takes on the theme and formatting of the destination presentation.*
6. Click the **Close** button × on the Reuse Slides pane to close the pane.
7. Click slide 2, then click the **NOTES** button on the status bar to display the Notes pane.
8. Click in the Notes pane and type **Be sure to mention special group rates.**
9. Click **VIEW** > **Notes Page**, and then press PG DN to display slide 3.
10. Click in the Notes placeholder of slide 3 and type **Also tell them about special rates on the Web site.**
11. Click **VIEW** > **Normal**.
12. Click **INSERT** > **Header & Footer**.
13. Click the **Slide** tab in the Header and Footer dialog box, then click **Date and time**.
14. Click **Slide number** and **Don't show on title slide**.
15. Click **Footer** and type **Everywhere You Want to Go**. Click **Apply to All**.
16. Click **DESIGN** > **Slide Size** > **Standard (4:3)**, and then click **Maximize**.
17. Scroll through the slides to see the new layout.

18. Click **DESIGN** > **Slide Size** > **Widescreen**.
19. Click **REVIEW** > **Spelling** to check spelling in the presentation, then click **OK**.
20. Click **Start From Beginning** on the Quick Access Toolbar to preview the presentation.
21. **With your teacher's permission,** click **FILE** > **Print**. Select **Full Page Slides**, then click **Notes Pages**. Click **Color** and then click **Grayscale**. Then click **Print** to print the presentation.
22. Close the presentation, saving changes, and exit PowerPoint.

Lesson 3—Apply

In this project, you return to the Wynnedale Medical Center presentation. You reuse slides from another presentation, insert notes, add footers, and change the slide size.

DIRECTIONS

1. Start PowerPoint, if necessary, and open **P03ApplyA** from the data files for this lesson. Save the presentation as **P03ApplyA_xx** in the location where your teacher instructs you to store the files for this lesson.
2. Move to slide 4, and then choose to reuse slides from another presentation. Browse to **P03ApplyB**, and insert both slides from the presentation. Close the Reuse Slides pane.
3. Move to slide 5 and note that the picture overlaps the title area. Reapply the **Two-Content** layout.
4. Move to slide 6 and reapply the **Content with Caption** layout.
5. Add the following note to slide 5: **Compare surgery cost to the cost of glasses or contacts.** Add the following note to slide 6: **Make sure potential patients know that the surgery is painless.**
6. Add the following footers to all slides except for the title slide: **Date and time**, **Slide number**, and **Clear Vision in a Day** footer text.
7. Change the slide size to **Standard (4:3)** and ensure fit. Your presentation should look like the one in Figure 3-1 on the next page.
8. Check the spelling and then preview the presentation in Slide Show view.
9. **With your teacher's permission,** print the presentation.
10. Close the presentation, saving changes, and exit PowerPoint.

Figure 3-1

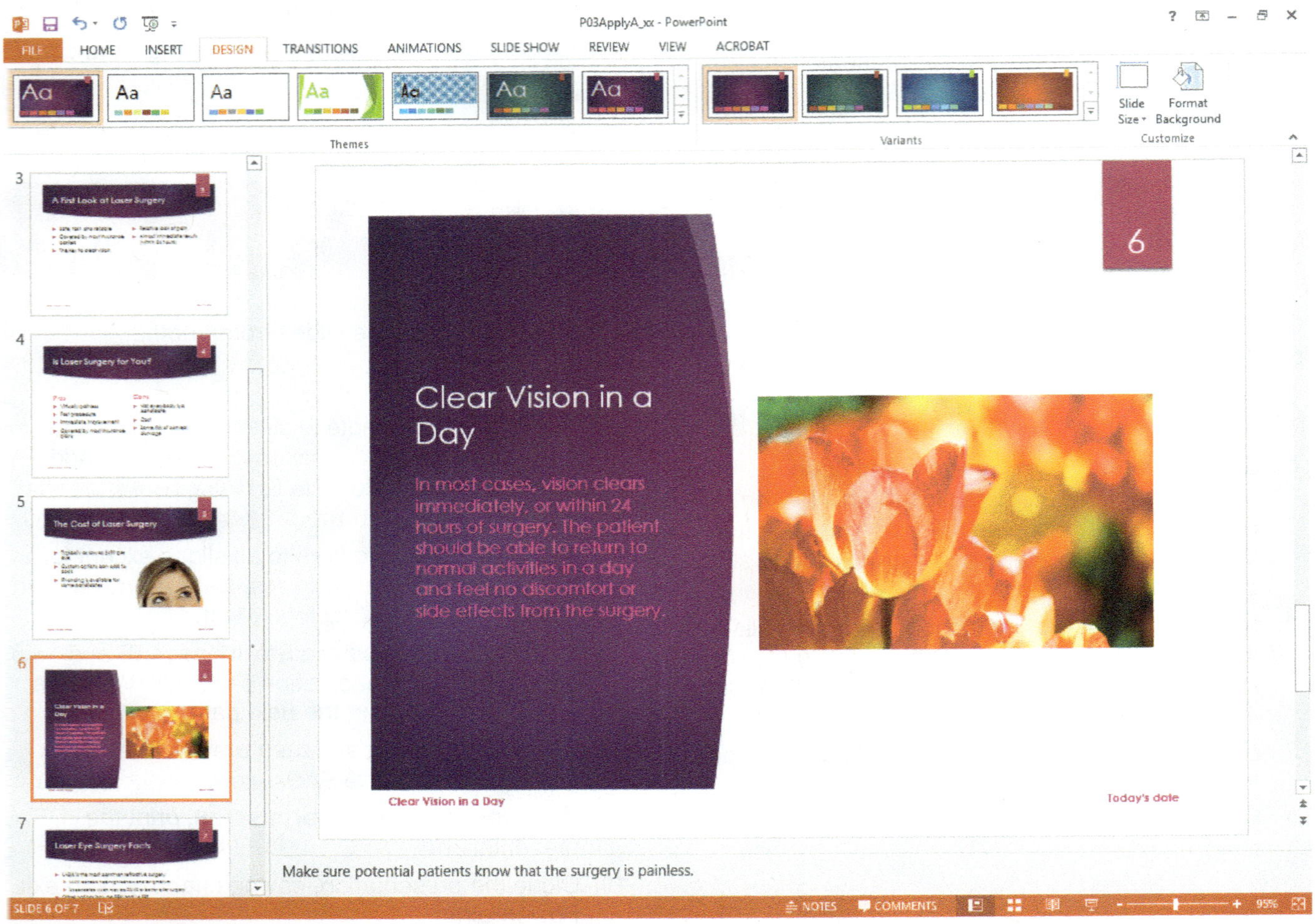

PowerPoint 2013, Windows 8, Microsoft Corporation

Lesson 4

Inserting and Formatting Pictures

➤ What You Will Learn

Inserting a Picture from a File
Formatting Pictures Using the PICTURE TOOLS FORMAT Tab
Formatting Pictures Using the Format Task Pane

Software Skills You can insert your own pictures in a presentation and then use tools on the PICTURE TOOLS FORMAT tab and the Format task pane to adjust the picture's appearance and apply special effects.

WORDS TO KNOW

Crop
Remove a portion of a picture that you don't want.

Scale
Specify a percentage of original size to enlarge or reduce the size of an object.

What You Can Do

Inserting a Picture from a File

- You can use your own pictures of specific locations, events, or people to illustrate your slides.
- You can scan your own pictures into the computer using a scanner. Using the scanner and computer, you can save the scanned image to the folder where you store your photos. If your picture is already in digital form, you only need to save it to the desired folder.
- Use the Pictures icon in any content placeholder or the Pictures button on the INSERT tab to place your own picture file on a slide. This command opens the Insert Picture dialog box so you can navigate to and select the picture you want to insert.

Try It! Inserting a Picture from a File

1. Start PowerPoint, and open **P04TryA** from the data files for this lesson.
2. Save the presentation as **P04TryA_xx** in the location where your teacher instructs you to store the files for this lesson.
3. Go to slide 2 and click the Pictures icon in the content placeholder.
4. Navigate to the location where files for this lesson are stored, select the **P04TryB_picture** image, then click Insert.
5. Press CTRL + M to add a new slide, and type **The Coast at Big Sur** in the title placeholder.
6. Click in the content placeholder, then click INSERT > Pictures. Navigate to the location where files for this lesson are stored, select the **P04TryC_picture** image, and then click Insert.
7. Save the **P04TryA_xx** file, and leave it open to use in the next Try It.

Formatting Pictures Using the PICTURE TOOLS FORMAT Tab

- Once you have inserted a picture, you can resize it by dragging a corner handle, or reposition it by dragging it to a new location.
- Use the tools on the PICTURE TOOLS FORMAT tab to modify and enhance a picture. Options on this tab allow you to create interesting and unusual picture effects as well as specify a precise size.
- Use the tools in the Adjust group to change brightness or contrast. You can also recolor a picture using the current theme colors or apply an artistic effect such as Paint Strokes or Marker.
- You can also use the Reset Picture option to remove any formatting or resizing to restore the picture to its original appearance.
- The Picture Styles group lets you apply a number of interesting styles to your pictures. You can also select border options or apply standard effects such as shadows or reflections.
- The Size group allows you to **crop** a picture to remove portions of the picture you don't need. You can restore the hidden portion of the picture by using the Crop tool again.
- The Size group also supplies width and height settings that allow you to precisely size a picture.
- You can quickly access picture styles and the Crop tool by right-clicking a picture to display shortcut formatting options.

Try It! Formatting Pictures Using the PICTURE TOOLS FORMAT Tab

1. In the **P04TryA_xx** file, click slide 2 and click the picture.
2. Click the upper-right corner handle and drag it up and to the right about 0.5" to enlarge the picture.
3. Click PICTURE TOOLS FORMAT > Corrections and then click the far-right image in the Sharpen/Soften row.
4. Click PICTURE TOOLS FORMAT > Color and select Saturation: 200% in the Color Saturation row.
5. Click PICTURE TOOLS FORMAT and select Soft Edge Rectangle from the Picture Styles gallery.
6. Click PICTURE TOOLS FORMAT > Crop to activate the crop tool. Click the bottom middle handle and drag it up to remove most of the trees from the picture.

(continued)

Try It! Formatting Pictures Using the PICTURE TOOLS FORMAT Tab *(continued)*

7. Click Crop again to complete the crop. Drag the picture down to center it vertically on the slide.

8. Click slide 3 and click the picture. Click PICTURE TOOLS FORMAT > Picture Effects > Soft Edges > 25 Point.

9. Click PICTURE TOOLS FORMAT > Artistic Effects, then select Glow Diffused.

10. Save the **P04TryA_xx** file, and leave it open to use in the next Try It.

Click and drag to move a picture on the slide

PowerPoint 2013, Windows 8, Microsoft Corporation

Formatting Pictures Using the Format Task Pane

- The galleries on the PICTURE TOOLS FORMAT tab allow you to easily apply standard formats to a picture. For more formatting options, use the Format task pane.
- You can display this task pane by clicking any Options command at the bottom of a format gallery, or by right-clicking the picture and selecting Format Picture.

  ✓ *If you have a picture selected, the task pane name is Format Picture. If you have a shape selected, the task pane name is Format Shape.*

- The Format Picture task pane (see Figure 4-1 on the next page) has four icons below the title you can use to display settings for fill and line, effects, size and properties, and picture adjustments.
- Clicking an icon displays a list of options in the task pane for making more detailed adjustments to the graphic than you can make with the PICTURE TOOLS FORMAT tab commands.
- Clicking the Size & Properties icon, for example, displays options not only for changing height and width, but also options to **scale** the picture to a percentage of its original size, rotate it, change its resolution, and position it precisely.
- Because it stays open as you work and allows you to switch among categories of options with the click of an icon, the Format task pane can be the most efficient way to format graphic objects.

Figure 4-1

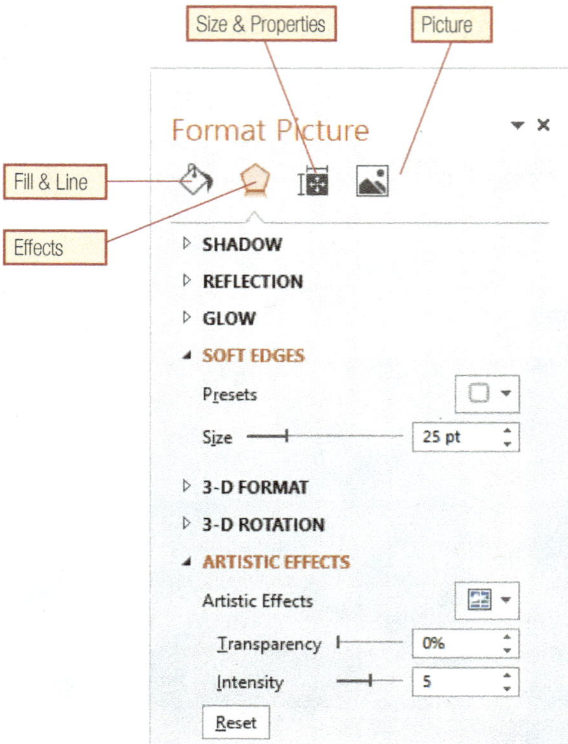

PowerPoint 2013, Windows 8, Microsoft Corporation

Try It! Formatting Pictures Using the Format Task Pane

1. In the **P04TryA_xx** file, click slide 2 and select the picture.
2. On the PICTURE TOOLS FORMAT tab, in the Adjust group, click the Reset Picture drop-down arrow and click Reset Picture & Size. The picture is uncropped and restored to its original formats.
3. Right-click the picture and click Format Picture to display the Format Picture task pane.
4. Click the Picture icon, and then click the PICTURE CORRECTIONS heading to display options for correcting the picture.
5. Drag the Contrast slider to the right until the Contrast box displays 30%.
6. Click the Size & Properties icon and click SIZE to expand options.
7. In the Height box, type **5.3**.
8. Click the down arrow in the Scale Height box to reduce the picture to 95% of its original size.

   ✓ *Notice that the Scale Width value changes at the same time to maintain the correct proportion of height to width.*
9. Expand the POSITION heading. Click in the Horizontal position box and type **5.3**. Click in the Vertical position box and type **1**.
10. Click the Effects icon and click the SHADOW heading to expand it.
11. Click the Presets button to display a gallery of shadow variations, and then click Offset Diagonal Bottom Left. Then drag the Distance slider to the right to increase the distance to 10 pt.
12. Close the Format Picture task pane.
13. Close the **P04TryA_xx** file, saving changes, and exit PowerPoint.

Lesson 4—Practice

A local environmental group, Planet Earth, has asked you to prepare a presentation they can show on Earth Day. In this project, you begin the presentation by inserting and formatting a picture.

DIRECTIONS

1. Start PowerPoint, if necessary, and open **P04PracticeA** from the data files for this lesson. Save the presentation as **P04PracticeA_xx** in the location where your teacher instructs you to store the files for this lesson.
2. Display slide 2 and click on the **Pictures** icon in the content placeholder to the right of the Preserving Planet Earth text.
3. Navigate to the location where files for this lesson are stored and select the **P04PracticeB_picture** image, then click **Insert**.
4. Click **PICTURE TOOLS FORMAT** > **Corrections** and then click the image to the right of the current image in Brightness and Contrast to increase the image brightness by 20%.

   ✓ *The current brightness/contrast setting has a light orange outline around it.*
5. Right-click the picture and click Format Picture to open the Format Picture task pane.
6. Click the **Picture** icon and expand PICTURE CORRECTIONS if necessary, and then drag the Contrast slider to the right to change the contrast to **25%**.
7. Expand the CROP heading in the Format Picture task pane, if necessary, and change the Crop position height to **3.75"**. Then close the Format Picture task pane.
8. On the **PICTURE TOOLS FORMAT** tab, type **3.9"** in the Height box.
9. Right-click the picture to display the shortcut options, click the **Picture Quick Styles** button, and click **Reflected Rounded Rectangle**.
10. Click **REVIEW** > **Spelling** to check spelling in the presentation, then click **OK**.
11. Click **Start From Beginning** on the Quick Access Toolbar to preview the presentation.
12. **With your teacher's permission,** click **FILE** > **Print**. Click **Print All Slides**, then select **Print Current Slide** and click **Print**.
13. Close the presentation, saving changes, and exit PowerPoint.

Lesson 4—Apply

In this project, you continue working on the Planet Earth presentation. You insert a second picture and format it with picture effects.

DIRECTIONS

1. Start PowerPoint, if necessary, and open **P04ApplyA** from the data files for this lesson. Save the presentation as **P04ApplyA_xx** in the location where your teacher instructs you to store the files for this lesson.
2. Insert the **P04ApplyB_picture** image in slide 3. Notice that the picture does not display entirely.
3. Display the Format Picture task pane, click the **Picture** icon, and display the Crop settings.
4. Change the Offset Y value to **1.3"**.
5. Recolor the image to **Aqua, Accent color 2 Dark**.
6. Apply the **Chalk Sketch** Artistic Effect to the image. Your slide should look like the one in Figure 4-2 on the next page.
7. Check the spelling and preview the presentation.
8. **With your teacher's permission,** print the presentation.
9. Close the presentation, saving changes, and exit PowerPoint.

Figure 4-2

PowerPoint 2013, Windows 8, Microsoft Corporation

Lesson 5

Formatting Text

➤ What You Will Learn

Finding and Replacing Text and Fonts in a Presentation
Selecting Text and Placeholders
Changing the Appearance of Text Using Fonts, Font Sizes, Styles, and Colors
Copying Text Formatting
Using Undo and Redo
Clearing Formatting

Software Skills Although themes and theme fonts are designed to produce a pleasing appearance, you may sometimes wish to modify the appearance of text by changing font, font style, size, or color. Use the Format Painter to copy formatting from one slide to another.

WORDS TO KNOW

Format Painter
A tool that lets you copy text formatting from one text selection and apply it to any other text in the presentation.

What You Can Do

Finding and Replacing Text and Fonts in a Presentation

- As with other Microsoft Office 2013 applications, you can search for specific text in a PowerPoint presentation and replace it with new text. You can use the Find and Replace buttons in the Editing group of the HOME tab to do this.
- You can also use the Replace Fonts command to find and replace text fonts throughout a presentation. Just indicate the font you want to replace, and the new font you want to use.

Try It! Finding and Replacing Text and Fonts in a Presentation

1. Start PowerPoint, and open **P05Try** from the data files for this lesson.
2. Save the presentation as **P05Try_xx** in the location where your teacher instructs you to store the files for this lesson.
3. Click HOME > Find and type **walkathon** in the Find dialog box. Click Find Next.
4. Click Replace and type **Walkathon** in the Replace with box in the Replace dialog box. Click Replace to change the selected text. Click Find Next to locate the instance of walkathon in the Notes pane, and then click Find Next again.
5. Click OK and then click Close.
6. Click HOME > Replace > Replace Fonts. Click the Replace drop-down arrow and select Tw Cen MT Condensed.
7. Click to select Calibri in the With list box, click Replace, then click Close. The font of the slide titles was replaced.
8. Save the **P05Try_xx** file, and leave it open to use in the next Try It.

Selecting Text and Placeholders

- Manipulating text in a presentation requires you to know some basics about selecting text and placeholders to ensure you are working efficiently.
- As in a word processing document, you can select text by dragging the insertion point over it, highlighting the selected text. You can also double-click a single word to select it.

✓ *If you are using a touch screen, double-tap text to select it.*

- As you are working with text in a placeholder, the placeholder displays a dashed line, sizing handles, and a rotation handle.
- You can also select the placeholder by clicking its outline with the four-headed pointer. The selected placeholder has a solid outline.
- While a placeholder is selected, any change you make using text tools will apply to all text in the placeholder.
- When you want to make a change to all text in a placeholder, it is speedier to select the placeholder rather than drag over the text to select it.

Try It! Selecting Text and Placeholders

1. In the **P05Try_xx** file, go to slide 2, then click and drag to select **Homeless** in the slide title. Note the dashed line, sizing handles and rotation handle shown in the following figure.

Placeholder tools with selected text

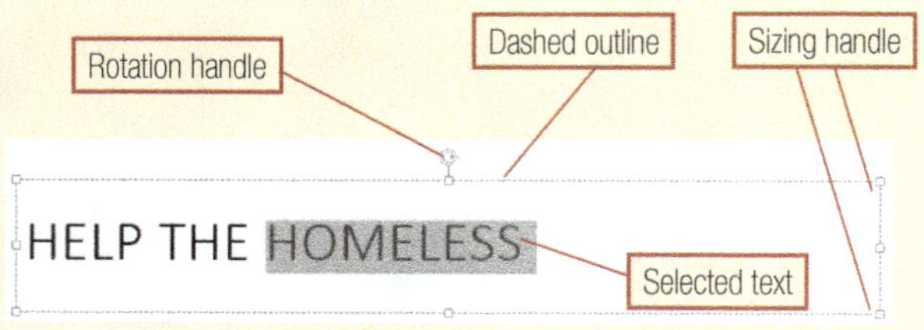

PowerPoint 2013, Windows 8, Microsoft Corporation

2. Click in the content placeholder, move the mouse pointer over the placeholder outline until it changes to a four-headed pointer, then click to select the slide content placeholder.
3. Double-click the word **homeless** in the second line of text to select it.
4. Move the mouse arrow slightly over the selected word to make the Mini toolbar appear. This toolbar can be used to change formatting of the selected text.
5. Save the **P05Try_xx** file, and leave it open to use in the next Try It.

Changing the Appearance of Text Using Fonts, Font Sizes, Styles, and Colors

- PowerPoint's themes guarantee a presentation with a sophisticated design, and that includes the appearance of text. You can, however, easily customize text appearance to emphasize it or to make your presentation more readable, interesting, or unique.
- Text appearance attributes include font family, size, color, style, and special effects. You can also change the case of text to control use of uppercase and lowercase letters.
- To change text attributes:
  - Select text or a placeholder and then use the options in the Font group on the HOME tab of the Ribbon. Commands in this group allow you to change font, font size, font style, and font color. You can also increase or decrease font size by set increments and clear formatting to restore default appearance.
  - Use the Mini toolbar that appears near selected text to modify text appearance as well as adjust paragraph features such as alignment, and indents.
- You can open the Font dialog box by clicking the Font group's dialog box launcher to change multiple attributes at one time and then apply them all at once.
- Note that effects such as superscript and subscript that are not available on Ribbon buttons are available in this dialog box.
- The Character Spacing option on the HOME tab and in the Font dialog box allows you to control the amount of space between characters from very tight to very loose, or you can set a specific spacing amount.

Try It! Changing the Appearance of Text Using Fonts, Font Sizes, Styles, and Colors

1. In the P05Try_xx file, display slide 5 and click the content placeholder.
2. Double-click Walkathon in the second line of text, then click the Font dialog box launcher. Click Equalize Character Height, then click OK.
3. Select the title placeholder. Click HOME > Font drop-down list, then click Tw Cen MT Condensed in the Theme Fonts section of the Font drop-down list.

   ✓ *Be sure you click the placeholder's border to display it as a solid line.*
4. Click HOME > Font Color and then select Brown, Accent 5 from the Theme Colors.
5. Click HOME > Text Shadow.
6. With the title placeholder still selected, click HOME > Character Spacing > Loose.
7. With the title placeholder still selected, click HOME > Font Size drop-down list > 66.
8. Save the P05Try_xx file, and leave it open to use in the next Try It.

Copying Text Formatting

- You can quickly copy and apply text formatting in PowerPoint by using the **Format Painter**.
- You can copy text and object formatting and apply it to one or multiple text blocks or objects.
- To copy formatting to multiple objects, double-click the Format Painter. Then click the button again to turn off the feature.

Try It! Copying Text Formatting

1. In the P05Try_xx file, click slide 5, if necessary, and click the title placeholder.
2. Click HOME > Format Painter .
3. Click the title placeholder in slide 4 to apply the formatting.
4. Save the P05Try_xx file, and leave it open to use in the next Try It.

Using Undo and Redo

- PowerPoint contains an Undo feature, as in other Microsoft Office applications, which reverses the most recent action or a whole series of previous actions.
- The Redo button allows you to redo actions after you undo them, if you change your mind.
- You can find the Undo and Redo buttons on the Quick Access Toolbar.

Try It! Using Undo and Redo

1. In the P05Try_xx file, click slide 4 and click Undo in the Quick Access Toolbar.
2. Now click Redo in the Quick Access Toolbar.
3. Click the Undo drop-down list arrow to see a list of the most recent actions you can undo. Click Text Shadow. Notice that all the subsequent actions are also undone.
4. Save the P05Try_xx file, and leave it open to use in the next Try It.

Clearing Formatting

- Use the Clear All Formatting button on the HOME tab to remove font formatting you have applied directly to text.
- You can also use the Reset button to clear formatting you have added to text and return the position, size, and formatting of the slide placeholders to the default settings.

Try It! Clearing Formatting

1. In the P05Try_xx file, go to slide 5.
2. Select the title placeholder and then in the Font group, click the Clear All Formatting button . All formats you applied to the title text are removed.

   ✓ *The font replacement, however, is not removed.*
3. Click Reset . Notice that the content placeholder formatting returns to the default settings, and the Equalize Character Height effect is removed from *Walkathon*.
4. Close the P05Try_xx file, saving changes, and exit PowerPoint.

Lesson 5—Practice

Whole Grains Bread, a company that sells fresh-baked breads and other bakery items at various locations around your area, wants you to help them create a presentation to display at a trade show. In this project, you explore ways to improve the appearance of text in the presentation.

DIRECTIONS

1. Start PowerPoint, if necessary, and open **P05Practice** from the data files for this lesson. Save the presentation as **P05Practice_xx** in the location where your teacher instructs you to store the files for this lesson.
2. Click **HOME** > **Find** and type **Breads, baguettes, and bagels** in the Find dialog box. Click **Find Next**.
3. Click **Replace** and type **Breads and baguettes** in the Replace with text box. Click **Replace All**.
4. Click **OK**. Click **Close**.
5. Click **HOME** > **Replace** > **Replace Fonts**. Click the **Replace** drop-down arrow and select **Century Gothic** from the list of fonts used in the presentation.
6. Click to select **Franklin Gothic Book** in the With list box, click **Replace**, then click **Close**.
7. Click to select slide 3, then select the title placeholder.
8. Click **HOME** > **Font** drop-down list, then click **Century Gothic (Headings)** in the Theme Fonts section of the Font drop-down list.
9. Click **HOME** > **Font Color** drop-down list and then select **Dark Red, Accent 1** from the Theme Colors.
10. Click **HOME** > **Character Spacing** > **Loose** and then click **HOME** > **Font Size** drop-down list > **40**. Click **HOME** > **Text Shadow** .
11. Double-click **HOME** > **Format Painter** . Click the title placeholder in slide 4. Use the Format Painter to apply the title placeholder formatting to all the remaining slides. Then click **Format Painter** again to turn off the feature.
12. Click slide 5 and click **Undo** in the Quick Access Toolbar. Then click **Redo** .
13. Click **Reset** , then click **Undo** . Your slide should look like the one shown in Figure 5-1.
14. Click **REVIEW** > **Spelling** to check spelling in the presentation, then click OK.
15. Preview your presentation in Slide Show view.
16. **With your teacher's permission,** click **FILE** > **Print**. Select **Print All Slides**, then click **Print** to print the presentation.
17. Close the presentation, saving changes, and exit PowerPoint.

Figure 5-1

Lesson 5—Apply

In this project, you work on a presentation that delivers information about acceptable use policies. You modify text formats to improve the presentation's appearance.

DIRECTIONS

1. Start PowerPoint, if necessary, and open **P05Apply** from the data files for this lesson. Save the presentation as **P05Apply_xx** in the location where your teacher instructs you to store the files for this lesson.
2. Replace the **Garamond** font with **Calibri** throughout the presentation.
3. Replace the word **teacher** with **instructor** throughout the presentation.

   ✓ *Be sure to check capitalization and punctuation throughout after replacing and correct as needed.*
4. On slide 2, change the title font to **40 point**. Change the font color to Theme Color **Red, Accent 2**, and apply the **Shadow** effect.
5. Copy this text formatting to the titles of all the slides in the presentation, except the title slide.
6. On slide 2, change the bullet list font to **22 point**. Change the font color to Theme Color **Olive Green, Accent 6**. On slide 6, copy the formatting to the first-level bullet only, not to the sub-bullets.
7. Copy this text formatting to the bullet lists on the remaining slides in the presentation, except the title slide.
8. On slide 6, format the sub-bullet font as **20 point, Olive Green, Accent 6**. Your slide should look like the one shown in Figure 5-2.
9. Check the spelling and preview the presentation.
10. **With your teacher's permission,** print the presentation.
11. Close the presentation, saving changes, and exit PowerPoint.

Figure 5-2

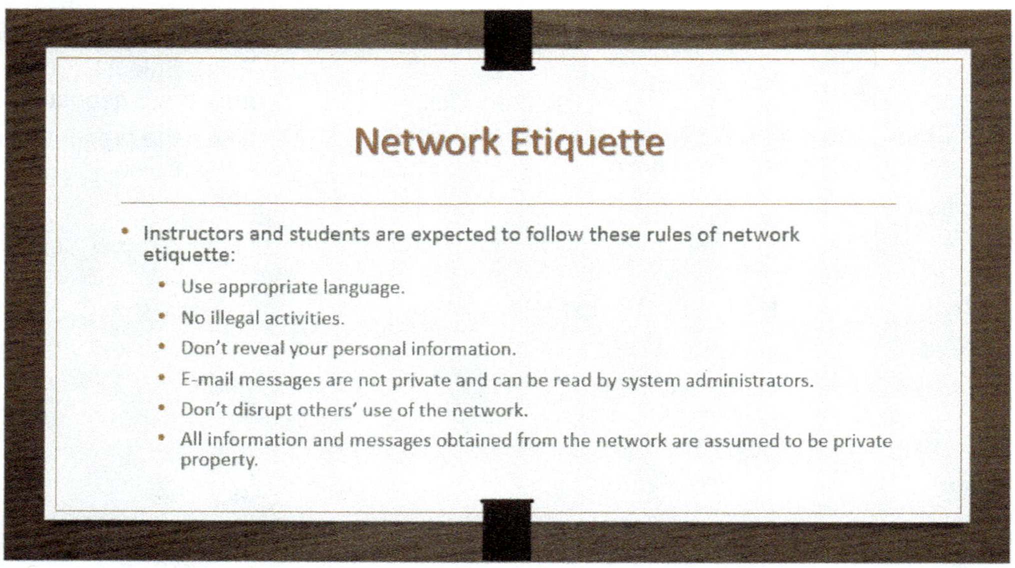

PowerPoint 2013, Windows 8, Microsoft Corporation

Lesson 6

Aligning Text

➤ What You Will Learn

Aligning Text
Adjusting Line Spacing
Adjusting Paragraph Spacing and Indents
Moving and Copying Text
Using AutoFit Options
Adjusting and Formatting Placeholders

Software Skills Other ways to modify the appearance of text on a slide include changing text alignment and tweaking paragraph spacing. Move or copy text from slide to slide just as you would in a document. You can also move, resize, copy, or delete any placeholder on a slide or any object on a slide.

WORDS TO KNOW

AutoFit
PowerPoint feature designed to reduce font size to fit text in the current placeholder.

What You Can Do

Aligning Text

- Themes control the alignment of text in placeholders. You can left-align, center, right-align, or justify text in any placeholder to add interest or enhance text appearance.
- You can change alignment of any paragraph of text in a text placeholder without affecting other paragraphs of text. In a title placeholder, however, changing alignment of one paragraph realigns all paragraphs in that placeholder.
- Use buttons in the Paragraph group on the HOME tab to align text. You can also use the Mini toolbar to apply left, center, or right alignment or use the Paragraph dialog box, discussed in the next section, to specify alignment.
- You can also click the Align Text button in the Paragraph group on the HOME tab to adjust the vertical alignment of text within a placeholder. Settings options are Top, Middle, and Bottom.

Try It! Aligning Text

1. Start PowerPoint, and open **P06TryA** from the data files for this lesson.
2. Save the presentation as **P06TryA_xx** in the location where your teacher instructs you to store the files for this lesson.
3. Go to slide 6 and click on the text placeholder below the slide title.
4. Click HOME > Align Left.
5. Click HOME > Justify.
6. Double-click on any word in the title placeholder, then move the arrow over the Mini toolbar and click Align Right.
7. Click HOME > Paragraph dialog box launcher. Click Centered in the Alignment drop-down list, then click OK.
8. Go to slide 3 and click on the text placeholder. Click HOME > Align Text > Middle.
9. Save the **P06TryA_xx** file, and leave it open to use in the next Try It.

Adjusting Line Spacing

- You can also change the spacing between lines of text in a placeholder.
- Use the Line Spacing button to apply line spacing options similar to those you would use in Word: 1.5, 2.0, and so on. Line spacing affects all lines of a paragraph.
- With the insertion point in a single paragraph in a placeholder, the new line spacing option applies only to that paragraph. To adjust line spacing for all items in a placeholder, select them or select the placeholder.
- From the Line Spacing drop-down list, you can click Line Spacing Options to open the Paragraph dialog box for more customized line spacing options.
- In the Paragraph dialog box, you can specify Single, Double, Exact, Multiple, or 1.5 lines of spacing.
- If you choose Exact or Multiple spacing, you can specify the exact amount of space you want between lines or the number of lines of space you want between lines by using the At text box in the Paragraph dialog box.

Try It! Adjusting Line Spacing

1. In the **P06TryA_xx** file, click slide 2 and click in the second line of text in the text placeholder.
2. Click HOME > Line Spacing > 2.0.
3. Click HOME > Line Spacing > 1.5.
4. Click HOME > Line Spacing > Line Spacing Options.
5. In the Paragraph dialog box, click Exactly in the Line Spacing drop-down list, then type **32** in the At text box and click OK.
6. Click in the third line of text in the text placeholder. Click HOME > Line Spacing, then move the mouse pointer over all the line spacing options to see the effect on the paragraph.
7. Move the arrow away from the drop-down list without changing the spacing.
8. Click to select the entire text placeholder. Click HOME > Paragraph dialog box launcher.
9. In the Paragraph dialog box, click Exactly in the Line Spacing drop-down list, then type **32** in the At text box and click OK.
10. Save the **P06TryA_xx** file, and leave it open to use in the next Try It.

Adjusting Paragraph Spacing and Indents

- Adjust paragraph spacing between bullets or other paragraphs to make text easier to read or to control space on a slide.
- For greater control over paragraph spacing, use the Paragraph dialog box. You can choose alignment and indention settings as well as specify a space before and/or after each paragraph and choose a line spacing option.

Try It! Adjusting Paragraph Spacing and Indents

1. In the **P06TryA_xx** file, click slide 2 and click the text placeholder to select it.
2. Click HOME > Paragraph dialog box launcher .
3. In the Paragraph dialog box, click in the Before text text box in the Indentation area and type **0.5"** to change the indentation.
4. Click in the By text box and type **0.5"** and click First line in the Indentation drop-down list.
5. Click in the Before text box in the Spacing area and type **10 pt**. Click OK.
6. Save the **P06TryA_xx** file, and leave it open to use in the next Try It.

Moving and Copying Text

- As you review a slide or presentation, you may rearrange the text to make it easier to follow.
- You can move text using drag-and-drop or cut-and-paste methods.
- Use the drag-and-drop method to move text to a nearby location, such as within the same placeholder or on the same slide.
- When you move text, a vertical line moves with the mouse to help you position the text.
- Use the cut-and-paste method to move text between two locations that are some distance apart, such as from one slide to another or from one presentation to another.

Try It! Moving and Copying Text

1. In the **P06TryA_xx** file, click slide 5 and select the text in the second line in the content placeholder.
2. Click and drag the text in the second line down below the next item, *Volunteer your services*.
3. Open the file **P06TryB** from the location where the files for this lesson are stored.
4. In the **P06TryA_xx** file, click slide 6, then click HOME > New Slide > Title and Content.
5. In the **P06TryB** file, click slide 1 and select the text in the title placeholder. Press CTRL + C.
6. Go to slide 7 of the **P06TryA_xx** file, click in the title placeholder, then press CTRL + V.
7. Save the **P06TryA_xx** file, and leave it open to use in the next Try It. Leave the **P06TryB** file open to use in the next Try It as well.

Using AutoFit Options

- If you enter more text than a placeholder can handle—such as a long slide title or a number of list entries—PowerPoint will by default use **AutoFit** to fit the text in the placeholder. AutoFit reduces font size or line spacing (or both) to fit the text into the placeholder.
- You can control AutoFit options using the AutoFit Options button that displays near the lower-left corner of a placeholder.

Try It! Using AutoFit Options

1. In the **P06TryB** file, click slide 1 and select all three bullets of text in the text placeholder. Press CTRL + C.
2. In the **P06TryA_xx** file, go to slide 7 and click in the text placeholder, then press CTRL + V.
3. In the **P06TryB** file, click slide 2 and select all four bullets of text in the text placeholder. Press CTRL + C.
4. In the **P06TryA_xx** file, go to slide 7 and click in the text placeholder after the three paragraphs of text you previously inserted, then press CTRL + V. Note that PowerPoint has used AutoFit to fit the text in the placeholder.
5. Click AutoFit Options > Change to Two Columns.
6. Click Undo to reverse the change.
7. Click AutoFit Options > Split Text Between Two Slides.

AutoFit to Two Columns

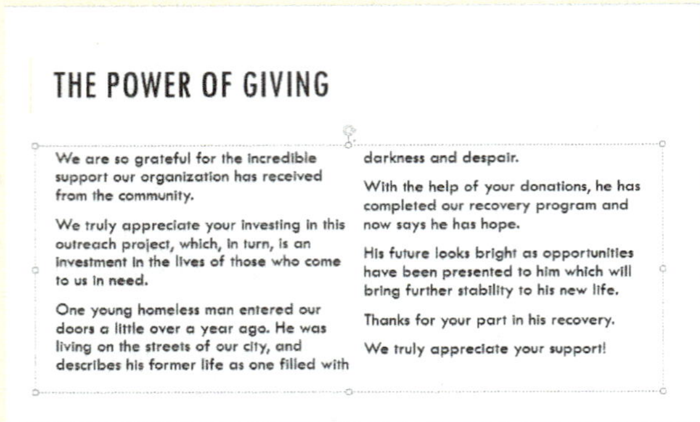

PowerPoint 2013, Windows 8, Microsoft Corporation

8. Save the **P06TryA_xx** file, and leave it open to use in the next Try It. Also leave the **P06TryB** file open to use in the next Try It.

Adjusting and Formatting Placeholders

- You can move or size any text or object placeholder to make room on the slide for other objects such as text boxes or images.
- You can also delete any placeholder to remove it from a slide, or copy a placeholder to use on another slide or in another presentation.
- To move, copy, size, or delete a placeholder and everything in it, select the placeholder so that its border becomes a solid line.
  - To move the placeholder, drag it by its border or use cut-and-paste to remove it from one slide and paste it on another.
  - To copy the placeholder, use copy-and-paste. A pasted placeholder appears in the same location on the new slide as on the original slide.
  - Delete a placeholder by simply pressing Delete while it is selected.
  - To resize a placeholder, drag one of the sizing handles at the corners and centers of the sides of the placeholder box.
- You can format a placeholder in various ways to add visual interest to a slide. Use a Quick Style, for example, to apply color and other effects to an entire placeholder.
- You can also apply a fill, outline, or other shape effect to a placeholder, using the DRAWING TOOLS FORMAT tab, the Format Shape task pane, or a right-click shortcut formatting option.

Try It! Adjusting and Formatting Placeholders

1. In the **P06TryA_xx** file, go to slide 8, if necessary, then click HOME > New Slide > Title and Content.
2. In the **P06TryB** file, go to slide 3 and click to select the title placeholder. Press CTRL + C.
3. In the **P06TryA_xx** file, go to slide 9, then click to select the title placeholder. Press CTRL + V.
4. Click the bottom center sizing handle and drag it up to resize the title placeholder.
5. In the **P06TryB** file, go to slide 3 and click to select the text placeholder. Press CTRL + C.
6. In the **P06TryA_xx** file, go to slide 9, then click to select the text placeholder. Press CTRL + V.
7. Click the right center sizing handle of the text placeholder and drag it left to the center of the slide to resize the text placeholder.
8. Go to slide 4 and click to select the text placeholder. Click the center top sizing handle of the text placeholder and drag it down slightly to move the text away from the title.
9. Click HOME > Quick Styles, then move the arrow over the various Quick Styles in the palette to see how they look in the text placeholder. Click on the Quick Style of your choice to apply it.
10. Right-click the title placeholder, and then click Format Shape on the shortcut menu to display the Format Shape task pane.
11. Click the LINE heading to expand it, click the Solid line option, click the Color drop-down arrow and select Orange, Accent 2, and then click the Width up arrow until the width is 2 pt.
12. Close the Format Shape task pane and deselect the placeholder to see the line format.
13. Save the **P06TryA_xx** file, and close the file. Close the **P06TryB** file without saving and exit PowerPoint.

Lesson 6—Practice

In this project, you work on the presentation for Wynnedale Medical Center by modifying list items, text alignment, text, and the position and size of placeholders.

DIRECTIONS

1. Start PowerPoint, if necessary, and open **P06PracticeA** from the data files for this lesson. Save the presentation as **P06PracticeA_xx** in the location where your teacher instructs you to store files for this lesson.
2. Go to slide 6 and click the text placeholder. Click **HOME** > **Align Left**.
3. Go to slide 5 and click the text placeholder. Click **HOME** > **Align Text** > **Top**.
4. Now click **HOME** > **Line Spacing** > **1.5**.
5. Go to slide 2 and click the text placeholder. Click **HOME** > **Line Spacing** > **1.5**.
6. Go to slide 6 and click the text placeholder. Click **HOME** > **Line Spacing** > **1.5**.
7. Go to slide 3 and click the left text placeholder. Click **HOME** > **Paragraph** dialog box launcher.
8. In the Paragraph dialog box, click in the **Before text** text box in the Indentation area and type **0.5"** to change the indentation.
9. Click in the **By** text box, type **0.3"**, and leave the indentation option set at Hanging. Click **OK**.

10. Click the right text placeholder. Click **HOME** > **Paragraph** dialog box launcher.
11. In the Paragraph dialog box, click in the **Before text** text box in the Indentation area and type **0.5"** to change the indentation.
12. Click in the **By** text box, type **0.3"**, and leave the indentation option set at Hanging. Click **OK**.
13. Go to slide 7 and click the picture. Drag the picture to align with the title placeholder at the left.

    ✓ *You will see a vertical dashed line when the picture aligns with the title. You learn about layout guides in Chapter 2.*

14. Click the center left sizing handle of the text placeholder and drag it to the right to resize the placeholder and display all text. Your slide should look similar to the one in Figure 6-1.
15. Click **FILE** > **Open** > **Computer** and navigate to the location where the files for this lesson are stored. Open **P06PracticeB**.
16. Select the text in the text placeholder. Press CTRL + C.
17. Go to slide 6 in the **P06PracticeA_xx** file, click after the last text bullet, press ENTER, then press CTRL + V.
18. Click to select the text placeholder, then click the bottom center sizing handle and drag it down to expand the text placeholder. PowerPoint AutoFits the text to the new placeholder size.
19. Select the text in the placeholder, then click **HOME** > **Line Spacing** > **1.0**.
20. Click **REVIEW** > **Spelling** to check spelling in the presentation.
21. Click **Start From Beginning** on the Quick Access Toolbar to preview the presentation.
22. **With your teacher's permission,** click **FILE** > **Print**. Select **Print All Slides**, then click **Print** to print the presentation.
23. Close the presentations, saving changes, and exit PowerPoint.

Figure 6-1

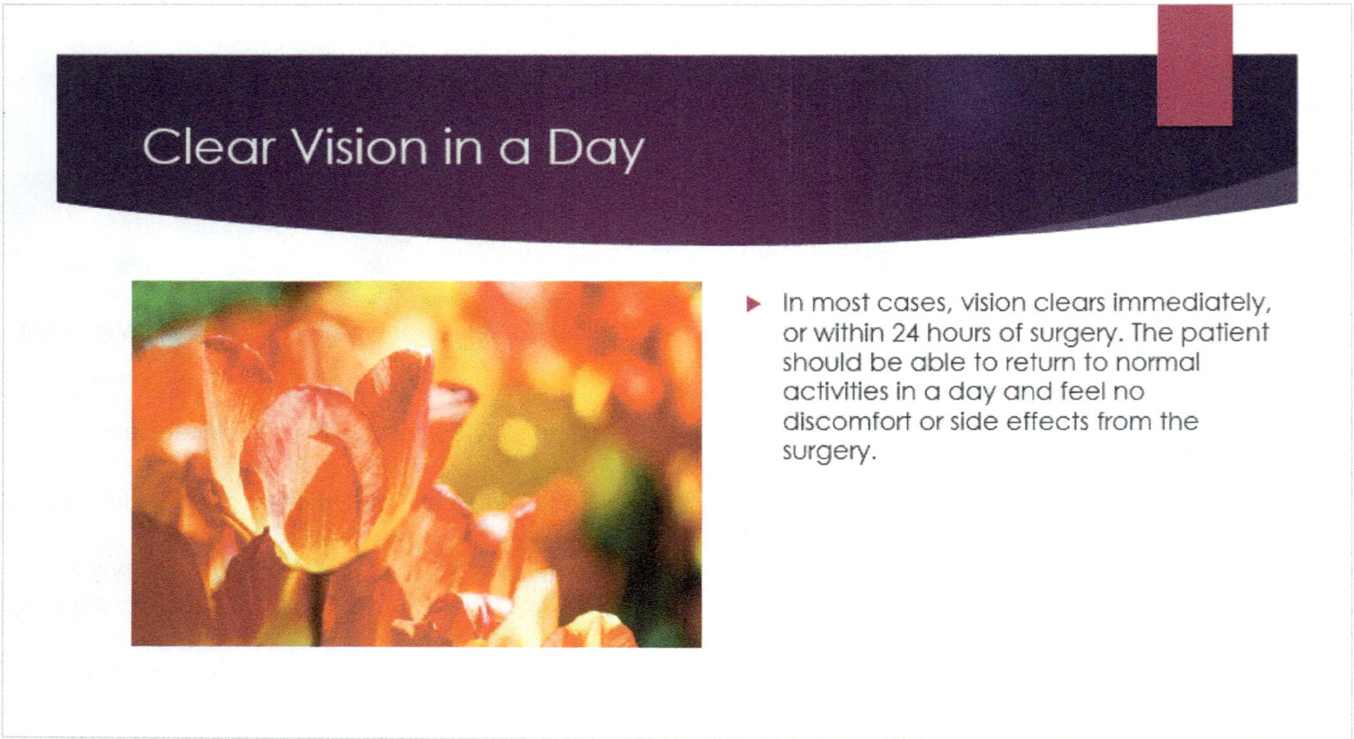

PowerPoint 2013, Windows 8, Microsoft Corporation

Lesson 6—Apply

In this project, you work with a presentation for Whole Grains Bread. You adjust paragraph and line spacing, copy and move text, adjust the size and position of placeholders, and format placeholders to add visual interest.

DIRECTIONS

1. Start PowerPoint, if necessary, and open **P06Apply** from the data files for this lesson. Save the presentation as **P06Apply_xx** in the location where your teacher instructs you to store the files for this lesson.
2. On slide 1, center the title and subtitle.
3. On slide 2, change the paragraph indent of the four bullet items under *Breads* and the three bullet items under *Sweet specialties* to: **0.55"** indentation before text.
4. On slide 3, position the insertion point after the first bullet item, press ENTER, and type **Franchises available**. Move the last bullet item on the slide to be the first bullet item.
5. On slide 4, copy the first item and paste it at the end of the list. Add an exclamation point at the end of the word *Quality* in the last item. Then change the word *Four* in the slide title to **Five**.
6. Change the line spacing for all items in the text placeholder to **1.5**.
7. On slide 5, delete the *Turbinado sugar* and *Gourmet sea salt* items and then drag the bottom of the placeholder upwards to redistribute the items so the *Fair trade* item is positioned in the right column. Your slide should look like the one shown in Figure 6-2.
8. On slide 6, select the empty text placeholder on top of the photo and delete it.
9. Select the photo and drag it to the right, to center it between the paragraph of text and the edge of the slide.
10. Right-align the text in the placeholder to the left of the photo.
11. Copy the subtitle placeholder from slide 1 and paste it on slide 6. Move it below the photo and resize the placeholder to be the same width as the photo. Click the **Bullets** button on the HOME tab to remove bullet formatting if necessary.
12. Apply a Quick Style to the placeholder. You may need to change the text color to make it stand out against the Quick Style formatting.
13. Select the placeholder that contains the paragraph of text to the left of the picture and adjust its size until it aligns at the bottom with the placeholder below the picture.
14. Display the Format Shape task pane, expand the FILL heading, and click the **Gradient fill** option. Then close the task pane.
15. Check the spelling and preview your presentation.
16. **With your teacher's permission,** print the presentation.
17. Close the presentation, saving changes, and exit PowerPoint.

Figure 6-2

Lesson 7

Displaying the Presentation Outline

➤ What You Will Learn

Displaying the Presentation Outline
Viewing a Presentation in Reading View
Viewing a Presentation in Grayscale or Black and White

WORDS TO KNOW

Grayscale
A way of displaying the current slide so that you can see how it will appear when printed on a black and white printer.

Software Skills Use PowerPoint views to work with the outline when doing detailed editing work and to view a finished presentation. You may want to view a presentation in black and white or grayscale to concentrate on text or see how the presentation would look printed on a black-only printer.

What You Can Do

Displaying the Presentation Outline

- It is sometimes easier to edit a presentation that has lots of text using the presentation outline.
- To display the outline, click Outline View on the VIEW tab.
- The outline of the presentation displays in the Thumbnail pane. You can cut, copy, and edit text here as you would within slide placeholders.
- To create a new slide in the outline, click to the right of the numbered slide icon and press ENTER.
- After typing the slide title, press ENTER and then TAB to begin typing list items.

Try It! Displaying the Presentation Outline

1. Start PowerPoint, and open **P07Try** from the data files for this lesson.
2. Save the presentation as **P07Try_xx** in the location where your teacher instructs you to store the files for this lesson.
3. Click VIEW > Outline View. The outline displays in the Thumbnail pane.

   ✓ *Note the slide icon to the right of the slide number in the Thumbnail pane. The active slide icon is orange.*

4. Read the presentation by scrolling through the outline using the scroll bar at the right of the Thumbnail pane.
5. Click at the end of each list item in the outline (not including the titles of the slides) and insert a period.

   ✓ *Note that the slide displayed in the Slide pane changes as you click on list items of subsequent slides. Outline view is good for this kind of detailed editing work.*

6. Save the **P07Try_xx** file, and leave it open to use in the next Try It.

Viewing a Presentation in Reading View

- Reading view can be used instead of full-screen Slide Show view to see how a presentation will appear when you deliver it to an audience.
- Reading view includes a simple control menu you can use to copy slides and move around the presentation.
- Reading view is also useful for someone who wants to display your presentation on his or her computer, rather than on a large screen with Slide Show view.

Try It! Viewing a Presentation in Reading View

1. In the **P07Try_xx** file, click Reading View on the status bar.
2. Click Next and Previous to scroll through the presentation.
3. Click Menu > Go to Slide > 4 Fair Use of Material.
4. Click Menu > Full Screen.
5. Click the left mouse button to advance to the next slide.
6. Right-click to display the shortcut menu, then click End Show.
7. Click Normal on the status bar to return to Normal view.
8. Save the **P07Try_xx** file, and leave it open to use in the next Try It.

Viewing a Presentation in Grayscale or Black and White

- If you plan on printing your presentation with a printer that has only black ink or toner, or you need to conserve colored inks, you may want to view the slides in a **grayscale** or black and white mode to see how the slides will look when printed.
- Click Grayscale on the VIEW tab to display a GRAYSCALE tab to the left of the HOME tab. This tab contains a variety of settings for viewing your slides in grayscale.
- Selecting Black and White on the VIEW tab displays the BLACK AND WHITE tab.
- Redisplay the presentation in color by clicking the Back To Color View button in either the GRAYSCALE or the BLACK AND WHITE tabs.

Try It! Viewing a Presentation in Grayscale or Black and White

1. In the P07Try_xx file, click VIEW > Normal to turn off Outline view and restore Normal view.
2. Click VIEW > Grayscale.
3. Click in the title of slide 1.
4. Click GRAYSCALE > Light Grayscale.
5. Click GRAYSCALE > Inverse Grayscale.
6. Click VIEW > Black and White.
7. Click BLACK AND WHITE > Black with Grayscale Fill.
8. Click BLACK AND WHITE > Back To Color View.
9. Close the P07Try_xx file, saving changes, and exit PowerPoint.

Lesson 7—Practice

In this project, you begin work on a presentation for a community aid organization. You edit text in Outline view and view the finished presentation in Reading view. You also display the presentation in grayscale to see how it will look when printed in one color.

DIRECTIONS

1. Start PowerPoint, if necessary, and open **P07Practice** from the data files for this lesson. Save the presentation as **P07Practice_xx** in the location where your teacher instructs you to store the files for this lesson.
2. Go to slide 1 and click **VIEW** > **Outline View**.
3. Click after *services* in the third bullet item of slide 4, then press ENTER.
4. In the new fourth bullet, delete **or** and capitalize the word **every** to start the new bullet item.

   ✓ *Note the changes as they appear in the slide displayed in the Slide pane.*

5. Delete the period at the end of the final bullet item.
6. Click **Reading View** on the status bar.
7. Click **Next** and **Previous** to scroll through the presentation.
8. Click **Menu** > **Go to Slide** > **3 Giving Can Mean...**.
9. Click **Menu** > **Full Screen**.
10. Click the left mouse button to advance to the next slide.
11. Right-click to display the shortcut menu, then click **End Show**.
12. If necessary, click **Normal** on the status bar, and then click **VIEW** > **Normal** to close the Outline view and to return to Normal view.
13. Go to slide 1 and click in the title placeholder.
14. Click **VIEW** > **Grayscale**. Click all of the options on the GRAYSCALE tab to see how the view changes.
15. Click **Back To Color View**.
16. Click **REVIEW** > **Spelling** to check spelling in the presentation. Click **OK**.
17. **With your teacher's permission,** click **FILE** > **Print**. Select **Print All Slides**, then click **Print** to print the presentation.
18. Close the presentation, saving changes, and exit PowerPoint.

Lesson 7—Apply

In this project, you work on a presentation for Voyager Travel Adventures. You work with the presentation outline to edit text, and then you preview the presentation using several different view options.

DIRECTIONS

1. Start PowerPoint, if necessary, and open **P07Apply** from the data files for this lesson. Save the presentation as **P07Apply_xx** in the location where your teacher instructs you to store files for this lesson.
2. Display the presentation in Outline view.
3. On slide 2, add the text shown in Figure 7-1.

   ✓ *You can press* ENTER *in the outline to enter a new bullet in the list, and press* TAB *to decrease the level of an item within the outline.*

4. View the presentation in Reading view, then return to Normal view.
5. View the presentation in black and white.
6. Check the spelling.
7. **With your teacher's permission,** print the presentation.
8. Close the presentation, saving changes, and exit PowerPoint.

Figure 7-1

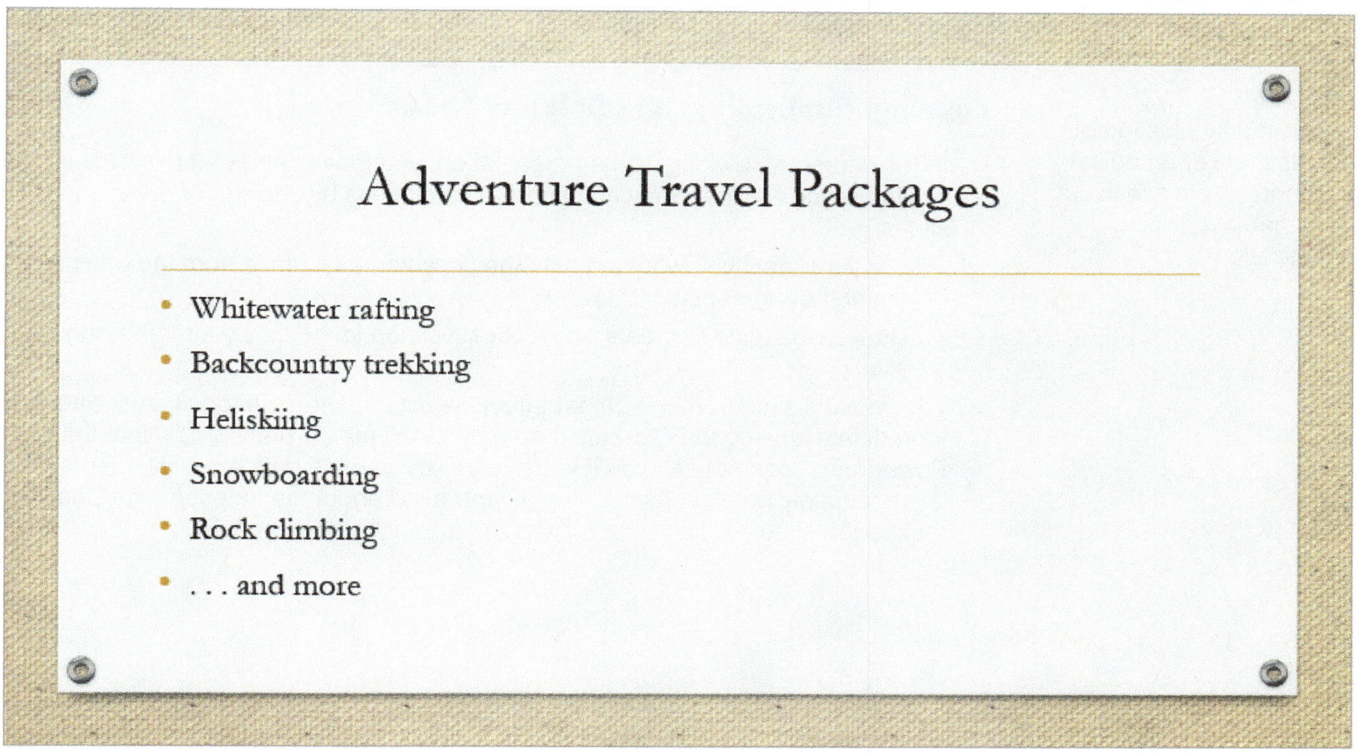

PowerPoint 2013, Windows 8, Microsoft Corporation

Lesson 8

Arranging Slides

➤ What You Will Learn

Copying, Duplicating, and Deleting Slides
Arranging Multiple PowerPoint Windows
Copying Slides from One Presentation to Another
Rearranging Slides

WORDS TO KNOW

Destination
The location or application in which you place an object that was originally in another location or application.

Source
The original location or application of an object you intent to place in another location or application.

Software Skills As you work on a presentation, you often need to copy or delete slides. You may sometimes need to view two presentations at the same time. You can arrange multiple PowerPoint windows to work with two presentations. Rearrange slides in either the Thumbnail pane or Slide Sorter view.

What You Can Do

Copying, Duplicating, and Deleting Slides

- In the course of working with a presentation, you may often need to create slides similar to one another. You can simplify this process by copying or duplicating slides.
  - Copy a slide if you want to paste the copy some distance from the original or in another presentation.
  - Duplicate a slide to create an identical version immediately after the original slide.
- To remove a slide from the presentation, select it in the Thumbnail pane and then delete it using the Cut button on the HOME tab, or press DEL. Note that PowerPoint does not ask you if you're sure you want to delete a slide—the slide is immediately deleted. If you change your mind about the deletion, use Undo to restore the slide.

Try It! Copying, Duplicating, and Deleting Slides

1. Start PowerPoint, and open **P08TryA** from the data files for this lesson.
2. Save the presentation as **P08TryA_xx** in the location where your teacher instructs you to store the files for this lesson.
3. Click slide 3.
4. Click HOME > Copy.
5. Click in the space between slides 4 and 5 in the Thumbnail pane, and then click Paste.

   ✓ *Note that a horizontal line appears in the space between the two slides when you click there.*
6. Click slide 8, then click HOME > Copy > Duplicate.
7. With slide 8 selected, click HOME > Cut.
8. Save the **P08TryA_xx** file, and leave it open to use in the next Try It.

Arranging Multiple PowerPoint Windows

- When you are working on a presentation, you may want to pull in content from another presentation.
- If you are not sure which slides you want to reuse, you may want to display the other presentation at the same time as your current presentation so you can easily work with the content of both presentations.
- Use commands in the Window group on the VIEW tab to open a new window showing your current presentation or arrange several open presentations side by side.
- Click the presentation you want to work with to make it active.
- To return to viewing only a single presentation, click its Maximize button.

Try It! Arranging Multiple PowerPoint Windows

1. In the **P08TryA_xx** file, click VIEW > New Window to open a new version of the current presentation. Note that the title bar designates the original presentation as **P08TryA_xx.pptx:1** and the new window as **P08TryA_xx.pptx:2**.
2. Click the Close button × for **P08TryA_xx.pptx:2**.
3. Open **P08TryB** from the data files for this lesson.
4. Click VIEW > Arrange All. The new presentation displays in the left half of the screen, and the original presentation displays in the right half of the screen.
5. Leave both presentations open for the next Try It.

Copying Slides from One Presentation to Another

- You can use the Copy and Paste commands to copy a slide from a **source** presentation to a **destination** presentation.
- As when copying within a presentation, you position the insertion point in the destination presentation where you want the slide from the source presentation to appear and then click Paste.
- If you have both presentations arranged onscreen, you can simply drag a slide from the source presentation to the destination presentation.
- As when you use the Reuse Slides command, slides you drag from a source presentation to a destination presentation will automatically display the theme of the destination presentation.

Try It! Copying Slides from One Presentation to Another

1. In the P08TryB file, click slide 2 in the Thumbnail pane, and click HOME > Copy.
2. In the P08TryA_xx file, click below slide 3 to position the horizontal line, and then click HOME > Paste.
3. Click the P08TryB file to make it active and click slide 3.
4. Drag the thumbnail for slide 3 to the P08TryA_xx file and drop it below slide 9.
5. Close the P08TryB file, and then click the P08TryA_xx file's Maximize button.
6. With slide 10 displayed, click HOME > Reset to restore the table to its proper place in this slide design.
7. Save the P08TryA_xx file, and leave it open to use in the next Try It.

Rearranging Slides

- Another task you must frequently undertake when working with slides is to rearrange them. Slide Sorter view is your best option for moving slides from one place in a presentation to another.
- Rearrange slides in Slide Sorter view by simply dragging a slide to a new location.
- You can also rearrange slides in the Thumbnail pane in Normal view, using the same dragging technique. This is an easy process in a presentation that has only a few slides, but for a large presentation, Slide Sorter view is the better choice because you can see more slides at a time without scrolling.

Try It! Rearranging Slides

1. In the P08TryA_xx file, click slide 5 in the Thumbnail pane and drag it above slide 2, so it becomes the second slide in the presentation.
2. Select slide 4 and press DEL.
3. Click the Slider Sorter view button in the status bar.
4. Click slide 6 and drag it to the position between slides 2 and 3.
5. Click slide 6 and press DEL.
6. Click slide 7 and drag it before slide 4.
7. Click slide 7 and drag it to follow slide 4.
8. Close the P08TryA_xx file, saving changes, and exit PowerPoint.

Lesson 8—Practice

In this project, you work on a presentation for Restoration Architecture, a local architecture firm. You will modify the presentation by copying slides within the presentation and from another presentation, and rearranging and deleting slides.

DIRECTIONS

1. Start PowerPoint, if necessary, and open **P08PracticeA** from the data files for this lesson. Save the presentation as **P08PracticeA_xx** in the location where your teacher instructs you to store the files for this lesson.
2. Click **Slide Sorter**, then click slide 11.
3. Click **HOME** > **Copy** > **Duplicate**.
4. Click and drag slide 12 before slide 5.
5. Click and drag slide 11 before slide 5.
6. Click **FILE** > **Open** and navigate to the location where the files for this Lesson are stored. Open **P08PracticeB**.
7. In the **P08PracticeB** file, click **VIEW** > **Arrange All**.
8. Hold the CTRL key down while you click to select slides 1, 2, and 3 in the Thumbnail pane.
9. Drag the three selected slides to **P08PracticeA_xx** and drop the slides to the right of slide 6.
10. Click the **P08PracticeB** file's Close button ×, and then click the **Maximize** button in the **P08PracticeA_xx** file.
11. Click slide 15, then press DEL. Your presentation should look like the one shown in Figure 8-1.
12. Preview the presentation to check the order of slides.
13. **With your teacher's permission,** click **FILE** > **Print**. Select **Full Page Slides** > **6 Slides Horizontal**, then click **Print** to print the presentation.
14. Close the presentation, saving changes, and exit PowerPoint.

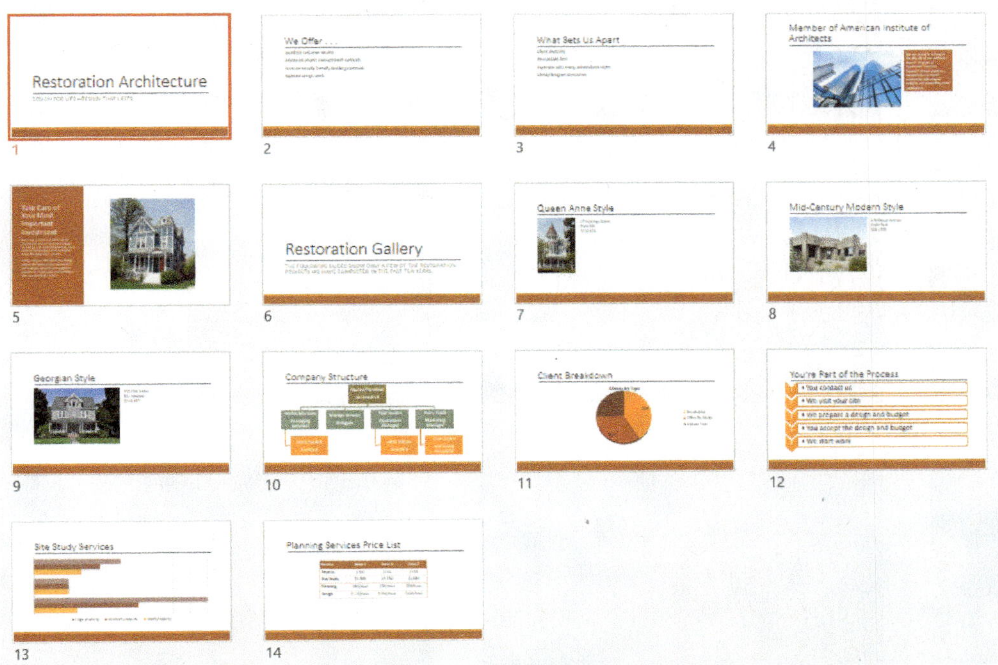

Figure 8-1

Lesson 8—Apply

In this project, you start on a strategic planning presentation. You copy and delete slides, and rearrange slides to improve the flow of information.

DIRECTIONS

1. Start PowerPoint, if necessary, and open **P08ApplyA** from the data files for this lesson. Save the presentation as **P08ApplyA_xx** in the location where your teacher instructs you to store the files for this lesson.
2. In the Thumbnail pane, move slide 2 to follow slide 3.
3. Change to Slide Sorter view.
4. Duplicate slide 4.
5. Double-click slide 5 to return to Normal view and change the title of slide 5 to **Additional Options**.
6. Open **P08ApplyB** and display it side by side with **P08ApplyA_xx**.
7. Drag the slide from **P08ApplyB** to follow slide 5 in **P08ApplyA_xx**.
8. Maximize **P08ApplyA_xx**. Change to Slide Sorter view again to view the sequence of the slides, which should look like that shown in Figure 8-2.
9. Check the spelling and preview the presentation.
10. **With your teacher's permission,** print the presentation.
11. Close both presentations, saving changes, and exit PowerPoint.

Figure 8-2

PowerPoint 2013, Windows 8, Microsoft Corporation

Lesson 9

Adding Slide Transitions

➤ What You Will Learn

Identifying Guidelines for Using Graphics, Fonts, and Special Effects in Presentations
Evaluating and Selecting Appropriate Sources of Information
Adding Slide Transitions
Controlling Slide Advance

Software Skills PowerPoint allows you to add transitions to make your slides more visually interesting during a presentation. After you set up the transitions, you can rehearse the show to make sure you have allowed enough time for the audience to view slide content.

WORDS TO KNOW

Advance slide timing
A setting that controls the amount of time a slide displays on the screen.

Transitions
The visual effects used when one slide moves off of the screen and another moves onto the screen.

What You Can Do

Identifying Guidelines for Using Graphics, Fonts, and Special Effects in Presentations

- When working with graphic information such as a PowerPoint presentation, keep in mind that you should avoid overloading a presentation with too many graphics, fonts, and special effects.
- Make sure all graphics you use, including images and shapes, fit with the color scheme of the slide or presentation, and serve a purpose for conveying your message.
- PowerPoint themes make it easy to provide visual interest with colors and fonts that are combined in a pleasing way. You can modify fonts to emphasize key information or provide additional visual appeal to a presentation.
- Make sure that all text stands out against placeholder backgrounds and is large enough to be readable. Also, make sure you're using text effects such as bold, italic, and underline in an appropriate way. And don't get too carried away with special effects such as drop shadows.
- PowerPoint also provides a wide variety of slide transitions and special effects to provide interest and movement as you present a slide show. Again, make sure that the effects you use are appropriate to the visual theme and the message of the presentation.
- In most cases, simpler, more subtle transition effects will prove to be most effective, and won't detract from the message you're delivering.

Evaluating and Selecting Appropriate Sources of Information

- When doing research for a project or presentation, it's important to evaluate and select appropriate sources of information, whether the source is print, electronic, video, or a person you interview.
- Use Internet search engines and bookmarks to locate and access information. Basic and advanced search techniques will help you pinpoint exactly what you need to find using search engines, directories, biographical dictionaries, and other research tools.
- Be sure to evaluate the accuracy and validity of the information you find by understanding the author's point of view, credentials, and any potential bias that might come as a result of his or her position.
- Finding information on the Internet often gives a source more credibility than it may deserve. It's important to be able to decide what is someone's opinion, and what is a fact backed up by research and data.
- As always, cite the sources of the information, and request permission to use if necessary.

Adding Slide Transitions

- PowerPoint provides **transitions** that you can use to make the slide show more interesting. You can apply transitions in either Normal view or Slide Sorter view using tools on the TRANSITIONS tab.
- The Transition to This Slide gallery offers almost 40 different transitions. Clicking a transition previews the transition on the current slide in either Normal or Slide Sorter view.
- The Transition to This Slide gallery organizes transition effects by Subtle, Exciting, and Dynamic Content.
- The TRANSITIONS tab offers several other important options. You can:
  - Choose an effect option to control the direction of the transition or how it appears.
  - Select a sound effect or sound clip to accompany the transition.
  - Choose a duration for the transition effect.
  - Choose how to advance slides: by clicking the mouse or automatically after a specific time lapse. This option is discussed further in the next section.
  - Apply settings to all slides at the same time.
  - After you have applied a transition, you can use the Preview button to review all effects you have applied to the slides.
- You can use multiple transitions in a presentation, or apply the same transition to all slides for a more formal presentation.

Try It! Adding Slide Transitions

1. Start PowerPoint, and open P09Try from the data files for this lesson.
2. Save the presentation as P09Try_xx in the location where your teacher instructs you to store the files for this lesson.
3. With slide 1 selected, click TRANSITIONS, then click Reveal.

   ✓ *Note that a star with lines appears to the left of the slide thumbnail in the Thumbnail pane to indicate a transition has been applied.*
4. Go to slide 2 and then click Fade from the Transition to This Slide gallery.
5. Go to slide 3, click the Transition to This Slide More button, and then click Flash from the Transition to This Slide gallery.
6. Go to slide 4, click the Transition to This Slide More button, and then click Random Bars from the Transition to This Slide gallery.
7. Go to slide 5, click the Transition to This Slide More button, and then click Ripple from the Exciting effects.
8. Go to slide 6, then click Fly Through from the Dynamic Content section of the Transition to This Slide gallery.

(continued)

Try It! **Adding Slide Transitions** *(continued)*

9 Go to slide 1, then click TRANSITIONS > preview. Click Slide Sorter, then click each slide and Preview the transition.

10 Double-click slide 1 to return to Normal view, then click Sound > Drum Roll. Click Apply To All.

11 Click SLIDE SHOW > From Beginning to view the transitions with the sound. Click to exit the slide show.

12 Try experimenting with the different Effect Options by clicking TRANSITION > Effect Options.

13 You can also try changing the duration of transitions by entering times in the Duration text box, or clicking the up or down arrows to increase or decrease the time.

14 Save the **P09Try_xx** file, and leave it open to use in the next Try It.

Controlling Slide Advance

- By default, you advance slides in a presentation manually by clicking the mouse button or a keyboard key. If you do not want to advance slides manually, you can have PowerPoint advance each slide automatically.
- **Advance slide timing** defines the amount of time a slide is on the screen before PowerPoint automatically advances to the next slide.
- You can set advance slide timing on the TRANSITIONS tab for individual slides or for all slides in a presentation. Set advance slide timing in seconds or minutes and seconds.
- Even if you set advance timings for your slides, you can also choose to advance a slide manually.
- The advance slide timing for each slide is indicated in Slide Sorter view by a number below the slide.

Try It! **Controlling Slide Advance**

1 In the **P09Try_xx** file, click Slide Sorter.

2 Click slide 1, then click TRANSITIONS > Advance Slide After and type 5.

3 Click Apply To All.

4 Click Sound > No Sound, then click Apply To All.

5 Click SLIDE SHOW > From Beginning to view the transitions without the sound. Click to exit the slide show.

6 Close the **P09Try_xx** file, saving changes, and exit PowerPoint.

Lesson 9—Practice

In this project, you continue to work on the presentation for the community aid organization by adding appropriate slide transitions.

DIRECTIONS

1. Start PowerPoint, if necessary, and open **P09Practice** from the data files for this lesson. Save the presentation as **P09Practice_xx** in the location where your teacher instructs you to store the files for this lesson.
2. Go to slide 1 and click **TRANSITIONS**, then click **Wipe** from the Transition to This Slide gallery.
3. Go to slide 2 and click **Wipe** from the Transition to This Slide gallery.
4. Go to slide 3 and click **Cover** from the Transition to This Slide gallery.
5. Go to slide 4 and click **Flip** from the Transition to This Slide gallery.
6. Go to slide 5 and click **Doors** from the Transition to This Slide gallery.
7. Go to slide 6 and click **Conveyor** from the Transition to This Slide gallery.
8. Go to slide 7 and click **Shape** from the Transition to This Slide gallery.
9. Go to slide 1, click **Slide Sorter**, then click the star below each slide to preview the transition.
10. Click **Normal**, go to slide 1, then click **Sound** > **Chime**.
11. Click **TRANSITIONS** > **Effect Options** > **From Left**.
12. Click **Advance Slide After**, then type **5** in the text box. Click **Apply To All**.
13. Click **SLIDE SHOW** > **From Beginning** to view the transitions. Click to exit the slide show.
14. **With your teacher's permission,** click **FILE** > **Print**. Select **Full Page Slides** > **6 Slides Horizontal**, then click **Print** to print the presentation.
15. Close the presentation, saving changes, and exit PowerPoint.

Lesson 9—Apply

In this project, you continue to work on the laser surgery unit presentation. You add slide transitions to give the slides more visual interest.

DIRECTIONS

1. Start PowerPoint, if necessary, and open **P09Apply** from the data files for this lesson. Save the presentation as **P09Apply_xx** in the location where your teacher instructs you to store the files for this lesson.
2. Apply several different slide transitions to the slides. View the slides in Slide Show view to see the transitions.
3. Apply the **Laser** sound to the first slide and the last slide.
4. Choose to advance all slides after 5 seconds.
5. View the presentation as a slide show, without clicking the mouse to advance each slide.
6. Check the spelling.
7. **With your teacher's permission,** print the presentation.
8. Close the presentation, saving changes, and exit PowerPoint.

End-of-Chapter Activities

➤ PowerPoint Chapter 1—Critical Thinking

Managing Computer Software and Maintenance

You work for Tech for All and have been asked to create a presentation that can be used to give clients a basic understanding of software and how to maintain a computer system. To complete this project, you will need to do research on the Internet and then create the presentation using the information you find.

You will need to locate information on the generally accepted categories of software—such as system software, programming software, and application software—and the uses of each type of software.

You will also need to locate information on how to maintain a computer system's software and hardware to keep the system working efficiently.

DIRECTIONS

1. Begin by doing your research on the Internet, evaluating each source as you explore its information to make sure the source is reputable and reliable. Take notes from your sources, recording the notes in a word processing document if desired.
2. When you have completed your research, create a storyboard for the presentation. You may sketch slide images on paper or use a word processing document to develop the storyboard.
3. Start a new presentation, and save it as **PCT01_xx** in the location where your teacher instructs you to store the files for this chapter.
4. Apply a theme and variant of your choice.
5. Insert the title **Managing Computer Software and Maintenance**, and in the subtitle placeholder, type **A Presentation by** and then insert your first and last name.
6. If necessary, use an AutoFit option to fit the title in the title placeholder.
7. Insert slides to record the information from your storyboard. Use different slide layouts as necessary to present your information clearly and in a visually appealing way.
8. If desired, use the Outline view to input your information. Adjust list levels as necessary to indicate items that are subordinate to other items.
9. Add notes to some slides to remind yourself of information you want to cover during the presentation.
10. Adjust font, font style, font size, and font color formatting as necessary to add visual interest to slides. You may also replace fonts on all slides if desired. Use the Format Painter to make sure formats are applied consistently throughout the presentation.
11. Adjust text alignment and line spacing as necessary. If text on any slides exceeds the depth of the content placeholder, use an AutoFit option to fit the text or divide it into columns or onto additional slides.
12. Adjust the position or size of placeholders, if necessary, and apply fill or line formatting to at least one placeholder in the presentation.
13. Insert the date and time, slide number, and an appropriate footer on all slides except the title slide.
14. Check spelling.
15. View the slides in Slide Sorter view and rearrange them as necessary.
16. Add slide transitions and an automatic advance timing to all slides.
17. Preview the presentation and then make any necessary corrections and adjustments.
18. Deliver the presentation to your class. Ask for comments on how the presentation could be improved.

19. After you have made all necessary corrections, view the presentation in Grayscale.
20. **With your teacher's permission**, print the presentation in Grayscale in Notes Page layout so you have a printed record of the notes you added to slides.
21. Close the presentation, saving changes, and exit PowerPoint.

➤ PowerPoint Chapter 1—Portfolio Builder

Franchise Sales Presentation

As a new sales manager for Whole Grains Bread, you have been asked by one of the sales representatives if you can help him spruce up his presentation for customers and potential franchisees. Follow the guidelines below to add stronger introductory slides to the presentation, additional photos and text formatting, as well as a new theme and transitions.

DIRECTIONS

1. Start PowerPoint, if necessary, and open **PPB01A** from the data files for this chapter. Save the presentation as **PPB01A_xx** in the location where your teacher instructs you to store the files for this chapter.
2. Apply a theme from the themes available on the DESIGN tab. Pick one that you think is appropriate for the audience. Change the variant if desired. Adjust placement of the objects on slide 4 if necessary, and reset slide 6 to move the table into its proper position.
3. Insert three new slides before slide 1. Make the first new slide a **Title** slide, the second new slide a **Two Content** slide, and the third new slide should be a **Title and Content** slide.
4. On slide 1, type **Whole Grains Bread** in the title placeholder. In the subtitle placeholder, enter **Fresh to You Each Day**.
5. On slide 2, type **A Variety of Baked Goods** in the title placeholder. In the left content placeholder, type the following bullets:
   - **Breads**
     - **Croissants**
     - **Bagels**
     - **Muffins**
     - **Rolls**
6. On slide 2, in the right content placeholder, type the following bullets:
   - **Sweet specialties**
     - **Pastries**
     - **Cookies**
     - **Cakes**
7. On slide 3, type **Fresh Is Best!** in the title placeholder. In the content placeholder, type the following bullets:
   - **Locally grown herbs**
   - **Whole grain flours**
   - **Fresh creamery butter**
   - **Free range eggs**
   - **Locally produced honey**
   - **Fair trade coffee and chocolate**
   - **Certified organic fruits and vegetables**
   - **Local and imported cheeses**
8. Change the title and text fonts throughout the presentation to a font, font size, and font color of your choice. Check all slides for text alignment and fit within placeholders after making the change.
9. Open **PPB01B** from the data files for this chapter.
10. Change the slide size of all slides in this presentation to **Widescreen**.
11. Arrange the two presentations side by side. Drag slide 1 from **PPB01B** to follow slide 8 of **PPB01A_xx**. Drag slides 2 and 3 from **PPB01B** to follow slide 4 of **PPB01A_xx**.
12. Close **PPB01B** without saving changes.

13. Find all instances of **Great Grains** and replace them with **Whole Grains**.
14. Insert **PPB01C_picture** on a slide of your choice; resize and position appropriately. Add picture styles and formatting to the photo you inserted and also to the photo on slide 9.
15. Change the footer to show only your full name.
16. Add a note to slide 8 that says **Remind seminar audiences that franchises are going fast!**
17. On slide 11, move the Soup information above the Sandwich information.
18. In Slide Sorter view, delete slide 10. Move slides 10 and 11 to follow slide 4. Move slide 9 in front of slide 4. Duplicate the new slide 4, and move the copy to the end of the presentation.
19. Add slide transitions, sounds, and timings of your choosing.
20. View the presentation in Reading View. After viewing each slide, make any necessary corrections or adjustments.
21. Check spelling, and, **with your instructor's permission,** print one copy of your presentation.
22. Deliver the presentation to your class.
23. Close the presentation, saving changes, and exit PowerPoint.

Chapter 2

(Courtesy Konstantin Chagin/Shutterstock)

Working with Lists and Graphics

Lesson 10
Working with Lists

- Applying or Removing Bullets
- Changing a Bulleted List to a Numbered List
- Modifying the Bulleted List Style

Lesson 11
Inserting Online Pictures

- Inserting Online Pictures
- Resizing and Positioning Online Pictures
- Formatting a Clip Art Illustration
- Removing the Background from a Picture

Lesson 12
Inserting Symbols and Text Boxes

- Inserting Symbols
- Inserting and Formatting a Text Box
- Using Multiple Columns in a Text Box

Lesson 13
Drawing and Formatting Shapes

- Using Rulers, Guides, and Gridlines
- Drawing Shapes
- Moving and Sizing Shapes
- Applying Fills and Outlines
- Picking Up a Color with the Eyedropper
- Applying Shape Effects and Styles
- Adding Text to Shapes

Lesson 14
Positioning and Grouping Shapes

- Stacking Objects
- Grouping Objects
- Combining Shapes to Create a New Shape
- Rotating and Flipping Objects
- Duplicating Objects
- Aligning and Distributing Objects

Lesson 15
Creating WordArt

- Understanding WordArt
- Applying WordArt Styles to Existing Text
- Inserting and Formatting WordArt

Lesson 16
Creating SmartArt Diagrams

- Creating a SmartArt Diagram
- Adding, Removing, and Resizing Shapes in a Diagram
- Reordering Diagram Content
- Changing the Diagram Type
- Changing the Color and Style of a Diagram
- Creating Picture-Based SmartArt

Lesson 17
Creating a Photo Album

- Creating a Photo Album
- Editing a Photo Album
- Adding Text and Captions
- Compressing Pictures

End-of-Chapter Activities

Lesson 10

Working with Lists

➤ What You Will Learn

Applying or Removing Bullets
Changing a Bulleted List to a Numbered List
Modifying the Bulleted List Style

WORDS TO KNOW

Picture bullet
A graphic specifically designed to be used as a bullet character.

Software Skills You can add or remove bullets from list items, or change a bullet character to customize a list style. You can also change any list to a numbered list when items should appear in a particular order.

What You Can Do

Applying or Removing Bullets

- In previous versions of PowerPoint, all list items were bulleted. In PowerPoint 2013, however, some themes format list items without bullets.
- When you want to customize the lists in a presentation, you may want to add bullets to list items that do not have them, or remove bullets from lists that do have them.
- You can apply or remove bullets from list items with the Bullets button on the HOME tab. This button is an on/off toggle for the Bullets feature.

✓ *The Bullets button also has a drop-down list for selecting a different bullet character. You will learn how to switch characters later in this lesson.*

Try It! Applying or Removing Bullets

1. Start PowerPoint, and open **P10TryA** from the data files for this lesson.
2. Save the presentation as **P10TryA_xx** in the location where your teacher instructs you to store the files for this lesson.
3. Display slide 2 and click in the third bullet item.
4. Click HOME > Bullets ☰ ▾. The bullet character is toggled off.
5. Click HOME > Bullets ☰ ▾. The bullet character is toggled back on again.
6. Save the **P10TryA_xx** file, and leave it open to use in the next Try It.

Changing a Bulleted List to a Numbered List

- Numbered lists are almost identical to bulleted ones except they use consecutive numbers rather than using the same character for each paragraph.
- Use a numbered list when the order of the items is significant, such as in step-by-step instructions.

✓ *Avoid using numbered lists when the order is not significant, because the audience may erroneously read significance into it.*

Try It! Changing a Bulleted List to a Numbered List

1. In the **P10TryA_xx** file, display slide 6.
2. Drag across the entire bulleted list to select it.

   OR

   Click to move the insertion point into the bulleted list and press CTRL + A to select all.
3. Click HOME > Numbering. The list becomes numbered.
4. Save the **P10TryA_xx** file, and leave it open to use in the next Try It.

Modifying the Bulleted List Style

- There are two ways of modifying a bulleted list's style. You can manually edit the individual paragraphs or lists that you want to specifically affect, or you can change the overall style for bulleted lists on the slide master.

✓ *You will work with the slide master in Chapter 4.*

- A wide variety of bullet characters are available, including symbols and pictures. You can select a bullet character from any font installed on your PC, or you can use any picture file to create **picture bullets**.
- Changes to the default bullet are made in the Bullets and Numbering dialog box.

Try It! Modifying the Bulleted List Style

1. In the **P10TryA_xx** file, display slide 2.
2. Click anywhere in the bulleted list and press CTRL + A to select all.
3. On the HOME tab, in the Paragraph group, click the down arrow on the Bullets button, opening its menu.
4. Click the small round bullets on the menu. The bullets change.
5. With the bulleted list still selected, click the down arrow on the Bullets button again.
6. Click Bullets and Numbering to open the Bullets and Numbering dialog box.
7. Click the Customize button. The Symbol dialog box opens.

Select a symbol

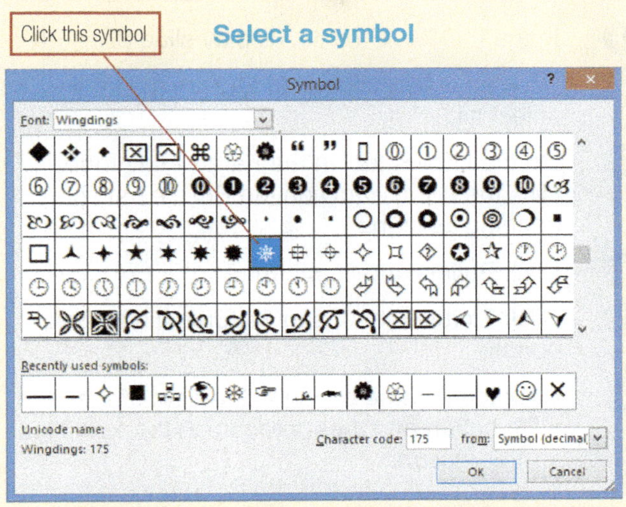

PowerPoint 2013, Windows 8, Microsoft Corporation

(continued)

Try It! Modifying the Bulleted List Style *(continued)*

8. If the Wingdings font is not already selected in the Font list, open the Font list and click Wingdings.

   ✓ *You can choose any character from any font as a bullet symbol. Wingdings is a font designed specifically for this purpose, but other fonts may have interesting bullet characters, too.*

9. Click a fancy star symbol in Symbol dialog box. and click OK.
10. Click the up increment arrow next to the Size text box to increase the size of the bullet to 110%.
11. Open the Color button's palette and click the Red, Accent 6 color from the theme colors.
12. Click OK. The bullets on the slide change.
13. Save the **P10TryA_xx** file, and leave it open to use in the next Try It.

Select a color

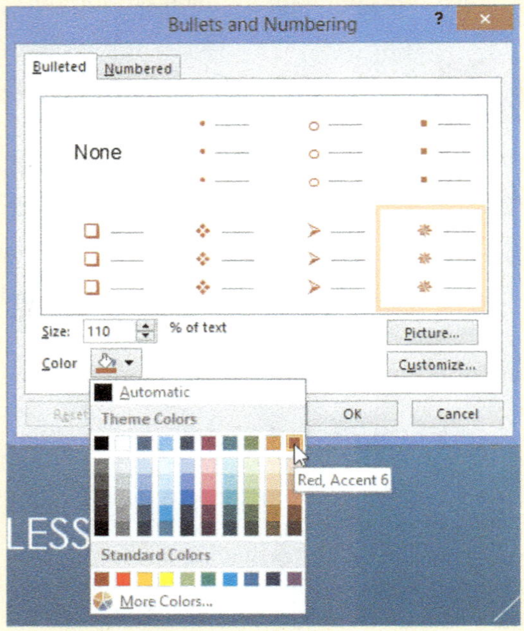

PowerPoint 2013, Windows 8, Microsoft Corporation

Try It! Using a Picture As a Bullet Character

1. In the **P10TryA_xx** file, display slide 3.
2. Click anywhere in the list and press CTRL + A to select all.
3. On the HOME tab, in the Paragraph group, click the down arrow on the Bullets button, opening its menu.
4. Click Bullets and Numbering.
5. Click Picture. The Insert Pictures dialog box opens.
6. Click the Browse button to the right of the From a file option and then navigate to the data files for this lesson.
7. Click **P10TryB_picture** and click Insert.
8. With the list still selected, click the down arrow on the Bullets button and click Bullets and Numbering.
9. Click the up increment arrow next to the Size box to change the bullet size to 100%. Click OK.
10. Close the **P10TryA_xx** file, saving changes, and exit PowerPoint.

Lesson 10—Practice

At Wynnedale Medical Center, the manager for whom you have created a presentation has commented that she does not like the bullet character in the draft presentation. You will apply several different bullet characters and customize them to give the manager options to choose among. You will also show her what list items would look like without bullets.

DIRECTIONS

1. Start PowerPoint, if necessary, and open **P10Practice** from the data files for this lesson.
2. Save the presentation as **P10Practice_xx** in the location where your teacher instructs you to store the files for this lesson.
3. Change the footer text on all slides (except the title slide) to your first and last name.
4. Click slide 2, select the first three bullet items, and then, on the HOME tab, click the drop-down arrow on the **Bullets** button.
5. Select the **Hollow Square Bullets** style.
6. Select the two subordinate bullet items, click the drop-down arrow on the **Bullets** button, and select **Filled Square Bullets**.
7. With the two subordinate bullet items still selected, click the drop-down arrow of the **Bullets** button and click **Bullets and Numbering**.
8. Click the up increment arrow to change the bullet size to 110% of text. Click the **Color** button and click **Red, Accent 3**. Click **OK**.
9. Display slide 4. Select the bullet items under Pros and click **HOME** > **Bullets** to turn off bullet formatting. Make the same change for the list under Cons.
10. Display slide 6, and then select all bullet items in the content placeholder.
11. Click **HOME** > **Bullets** > **Bullets and Numbering**.
12. Click **Customize**. The Symbol dialog box opens.
13. Open the Font drop-down list and click **Zapf Dingbats**.

    ✓ *If you do not have this font, choose Wingdings.*
14. Click a check mark symbol.
15. Click **OK** to close the Symbol dialog box.
16. Click **OK** to close the Bullets and Numbering dialog box.
17. Click slide 7, click the bullet item in the content placeholder, and click **Bullets** to turn off bullet formatting.
18. Preview the presentation to view the new bullet styles.
19. **With your teacher's permission**, print slide 2 of the presentation.

    ✓ *Refer to Lesson 2 in Chapter 1 for information on printing slides.*
20. Close the presentation, saving changes, and exit PowerPoint.

Lesson 10—Apply

The Wynnedale laser surgery presentation has a new look with a new theme. In this project, you will work with list formats to give your manager additional options to choose among.

DIRECTIONS

1. Start PowerPoint, if necessary, and open **P10ApplyA** from the data files for this lesson.
2. Save the presentation as **P10ApplyA_xx** in the location where your teacher instructs you to store the files for this lesson.
3. Replace the slide footer with your first and last names, displayed on all slides.
4. On slides 2 and 5, change the bullet character for the subordinate bullet items to **Hollow Round Bullets** in a color different from the current one.
5. On slide 4, apply the picture bullet **P10ApplyB_picture** to the lists beneath Pros and Cons. Your slide should look like Figure 10-1.
6. Close Master view.
7. Remove the bullet from the paragraph on slide 7.
8. Convert the bullet points on slide 6 to a numbered list, and then change the color of the numbers in the Bullets and Numbering dialog box.
9. Preview the presentation to view the new list formats.
10. **With your teacher's permission**, print the presentation as handouts (6 slides per page).
11. Close the presentation, saving changes, and exit PowerPoint.

Figure 10-1

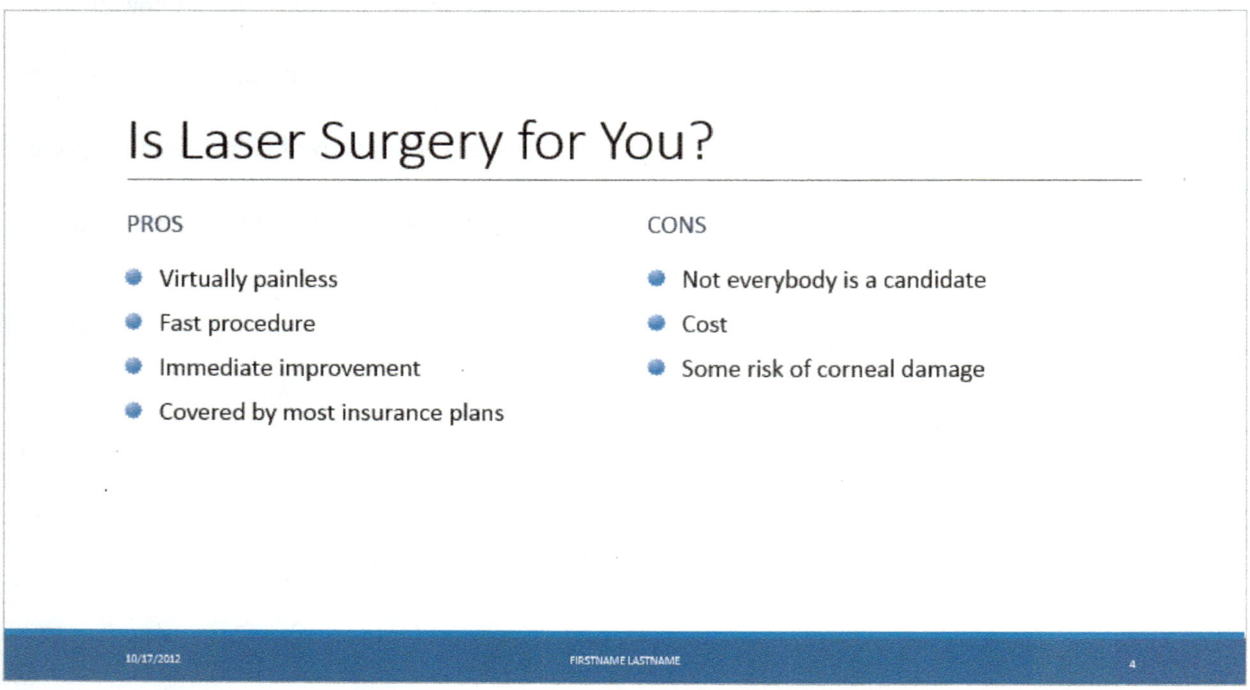

Lesson 11

Inserting Online Pictures

➤ What You Will Learn

Inserting Online Pictures
Resizing and Positioning Online Pictures
Formatting a Clip Art Illustration
Removing the Background from a Picture

Software Skills Clip art can be a tremendous asset to you as you create presentations. Your copy of PowerPoint includes free access to a huge library of ready-made drawings on Microsoft's Web site. You can access them through the Online Pictures feature in PowerPoint.

WORDS TO KNOW

Clip art
Generic, reusable drawings of common people, places, things, and concepts.

Keyword
A descriptive word attached to an image, used for searching and indexing the image library.

What You Can Do

Inserting Online Pictures

- **Clip art** can be used in any Office application, but it is especially suitable for PowerPoint because of the graphical focus of most slides.
- You use the Online Pictures command on the INSERT tab to open the Insert Pictures dialog box. Here you have options to use Bing to search the Web for an image, look on your OneDrive for images, or insert an image from Facebook or Flickr.

✓ *If you use Bing, be aware that you may find copyrighted pictures when you search. Do not insert copyrighted pictures in your slides without first determining whether you need permission to do so. You will be reminded when searching the Web with Bing that some search results are licensed.*

- You can find clip art by searching for specific **keywords**. Each clip art image has one or more keywords assigned to it that describe it. For example, a picture of a dog might include the keywords *dog, pup, canine, animal,* and *pet*.
- If the slide contains an open content placeholder, you can place the clip art using the Online Pictures button in the placeholder. You can also insert clip art on any slide without using a placeholder.
- Search results from your keywords display both photos and the illustrations that are usually called clip art. You do not have the option of searching only for clip art or only for photos.

Try It! Inserting Online Pictures

1. Start PowerPoint, and open **P11Try** from the data files for this lesson.
2. Save the presentation as **P11Try_xx** in the location where your teacher instructs you to store the files for this lesson.
3. Click slide 3 in the Thumbnail pane.
4. In the empty content placeholder, click the Online Pictures icon. The Insert Pictures dialog box opens.
5. In the text box to the right of Bing Image Search, type **helping hand** and click the Search button.
6. Scroll down to locate an image of clasped hands, and then click Insert. The clip appears in the placeholder.
7. Click slide 4 in the Thumbnail pane.
8. Click INSERT > Online Pictures to open the Insert Pictures dialog box.
9. Type **donation** in the search box and click Search.
10. Click Show all web results, click a jar of money similar to the one shown on the next page, and click Insert.
11. Save the **P11Try_xx** file, and leave it open to use in the next Try It.

Resizing and Positioning Online Pictures

- When you insert a clip art image in a placeholder, the placeholder determines the image's size and position.
- When you insert an image without a placeholder, the image appears in the center of the slide, at a default size.
- Resize and position an online image using the same options you learned in Lesson 4 when inserting pictures from files:
  - Resize an image by dragging a corner handle or by specifying an exact size using the Size controls on the PICTURE TOOLS FORMAT tab.
  - Position an image by dragging it to the desired location or by specifying an exact position using the Format Picture task pane.

Try It! Resizing and Positioning Online Pictures

1. In the **P11Try_xx** file, on slide 4, click the image to select it (if not already selected). Selection handles appear around it.
2. Click the upper-left corner handle and drag diagonally toward the lower-right of the image about 1" to resize the image.
3. Click PICTURE TOOLS FORMAT > Shape Height and type **4"**.
4. Drag the image to the right of the list items in the content placeholder.
5. Right-click the picture and click Format Picture to display the Format Picture task pane.
6. Click the Size & Properties icon, and click the POSITION heading to expand it.
7. Type **7"** in the Horizontal position box and **1.6"** in the Vertical position box. Close the Format Picture task pane.
8. Save the **P11Try_xx** file, and leave it open to use in the next Try It.

(continued)

Try It! Resizing and Positioning Online Pictures *(continued)*

Reposition the clip art on the slide

PowerPoint 2013, Windows 8, Microsoft Corporation

Formatting a Clip Art Illustration

- If you select an illustration rather than a photo from the Insert Picture search results, you can format the illustration in many of the same ways as a photo.
  - Resize and position an illustration using the same options as for a picture.
  - Use tools on the PICTURE TOOLS FORMAT tab to correct color or apply picture styles or effects.
- You can also ensure that the illustration blends well with your slide design by recoloring the image using the current theme colors.
- You can even make a color transparent to allow the theme background to become part of the image, for a more unified look.

Try It! Formatting a Clip Art Illustration

1. In the **P11Try_xx** file, display slide 5.
2. Click INSERT > Online Pictures to open the Insert Pictures dialog box.
3. In the Search box, type **family shelter** and click the Search button .
4. Locate an image that represents a family shelter and then click Insert.
5. Resize the image to 3.2" high, and position it in the upper-right corner of the slide.
6. Click PICTURE TOOLS FORMAT > Color , and choose Dark Purple, Accent color 2 Light in the bottom row of the Recolor gallery.
7. Click PICTURE TOOLS FORMAT > Color > Set Transparent Color.
8. Click the transparent color pointer on the background of the illustration. The background color is removed, allowing the slide background to appear in the illustration.
9. Save the **P11Try_xx** file, and leave it open to use in the next Try It.

Removing the Background from a Picture

- In some photos, the background detracts from the main image. Using a graphics program, you can cut out the part of the image you want to use.
- PowerPoint also provides this capability, so you can remove a photo's background without leaving PowerPoint.
- PowerPoint makes a guess about what part of the image is background and covers it with pink shading.
- You can fine-tune where the dividing lines are between the foreground and background of the image if PowerPoint does not guess them correctly.
- Use the Mark Areas to Keep tool to drag over parts of the image that should not be removed. Use the Mark Areas to Remove tool to drag over parts of the image you don't want.

Try It! Removing the Background from a Picture

1. In the **P11Try_xx** file, display slide 3.
2. Click the picture to select it, and then click PICTURE TOOLS FORMAT > Remove Background. Most of the image is covered with pink shading to indicate it will be removed.
3. Expand the selection area by dragging corner handles.
4. To keep the images of arms and hands from being removed, click BACKGROUND REMOVAL > Mark Areas to Keep.
5. The pointer changes to a pencil pointer. Drag the pointer along the areas you want to keep. PowerPoint removes the pink shading, indicating that this portion of the image will not be discarded.
6. Click Keep Changes ✓.
7. Close the **P11Try_xx** file, saving changes, and exit PowerPoint.

Lesson 11—Practice

In this project, you continue to work with the Wynnedale Medical Center presentation. You will select appropriate online images and insert them in the presentation to enhance its appearance.

DIRECTIONS

1. Start PowerPoint, if necessary, and open **P11Practice** from the data files for this lesson.
2. Save the presentation as **P11Practice_xx** in the location where your teacher instructs you to store the files for this lesson.
3. Change the slide footer to display your first and last name on all slides.
4. Click slide 2, and click **INSERT** > **Online Pictures**.
5. Click in the search box and type **eye chart**. Click the **Search** button.
6. Select a picture from the search results and click **Insert**. Then resize and drag the picture to place it to the right of the bulleted list.
7. Click slide 6 to display it.
8. Click the **Online Pictures** placeholder icon.
9. Click in the search box and type **dollar bill**. Click the **Search** button or press ENTER.
10. Click any of the found clips to insert it on the slide.

    ✓ *Try to find a clip that fits the content of the list as well as possible.*
11. Preview the presentation to see the new images in place.
12. **With your teacher's permission**, click **FILE** > **Print**. Select **Print All Slides**, and then click **Print** to print the presentation.
13. Close the presentation, saving changes, and exit PowerPoint.

Lesson 11—Apply

In this project, you continue to work with the Wynnedale presentation to add online images. You will also remove the background from an image.

DIRECTIONS

1. Start PowerPoint, if necessary, and open **P11Apply** from the data files for this lesson.
2. Save the presentation as **P11Apply_xx** in the location where your teacher instructs you to store the files for this lesson.
3. Change the footer to your first and last name.
4. Display slide 5 and use the keywords **woman glasses** to insert a picture similar to the one shown in Figure 11-1.
5. Size the clip art **4"** high, and move it to the lower right of the list.
6. Use Remove Background to begin the process of removing the background.
7. Adjust the outline inside the picture by dragging the corner handles to the edge of the picture, as shown in Figure 11-1, to identify more of the picture as foreground.
8. Mark areas to keep and remove as necessary.
9. Remove the picture background and adjust the size and position of the image as necessary to fit on the slide.
9. On slide 7, use the Online Pictures icon in the placeholder and the keywords **blue sky** to locate an appropriate image.
10. Preview the presentation and make any necessary corrections and adjustments.
11. **With your teacher's permission**, print the presentation as handouts, 6 slides per page.
12. Close the presentation, saving changes, and exit PowerPoint.

Figure 11-1

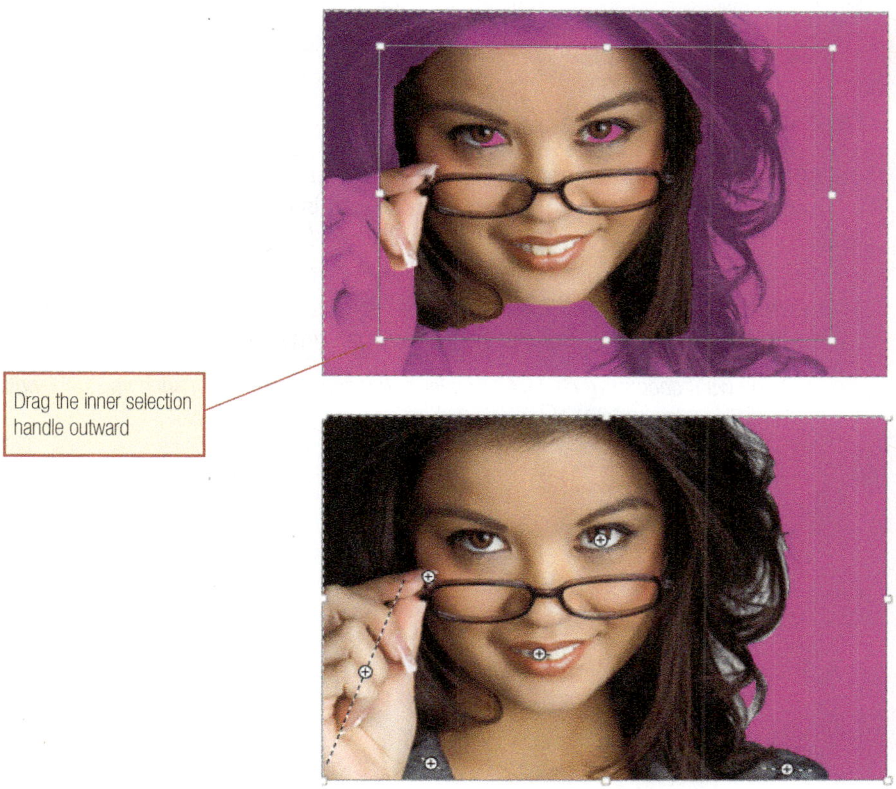

PowerPoint 2013, Windows 8, Microsoft Corporation

Lesson 12

Inserting Symbols and Text Boxes

➤ What You Will Learn

Inserting Symbols
Inserting and Formatting a Text Box
Using Multiple Columns in a Text Box

WORDS TO KNOW

Symbol
A typographical character that is neither a letter nor a number. Some symbols can be typed on a keyboard, and others must be inserted.

Text box
A non-placeholder container for text that you can position anywhere on a slide.

Software Skills Not all characters are available for insertion by typing on the keyboard. Some characters such as ® and © are available only as symbols. In this lesson, you will learn how to insert symbols in a presentation. You will also learn how to create text boxes that are not a part of a slide layout, and to format the text in multiple columns in a single text box.

What You Can Do

Inserting Symbols

- **Symbols** are characters that are neither alphabetic nor numeric. Most of them cannot be typed from the keyboard. Symbols can include decorative characters, foreign language characters, and mathematical or punctuation characters.
- You can insert symbols from the Symbols dialog box. You have a choice of fonts there. You can choose normal text, which uses the same font as the default used for list paragraphs in the presentation, or some other font.

  ✓ *If you want decorative characters instead, you can choose a font such as Zapf Dingbats or Wingdings, both of which are specifically designed for symbol use.*

Try It! Inserting Symbols

1. Start PowerPoint, and open **P12Try** from the data files for this lesson.
2. Save the presentation as **P12Try_xx** in the location where your teacher instructs you to store the files for this lesson.
3. Display slide 1, and click to place the insertion point immediately after the word *Giving* in the title.
4. Click INSERT > Symbol Ω. The Symbol dialog box opens.
5. If (normal text) does not appear in the Font box, open its drop-down list and select (normal text).
6. Scroll through the symbols, and click the TM (trademark) symbol.
7. Click Insert.
8. Click Close. The symbol appears in the title.
9. Save the **P12Try_xx** file, and leave it open to use in the next Try It.

The Symbol dialog box

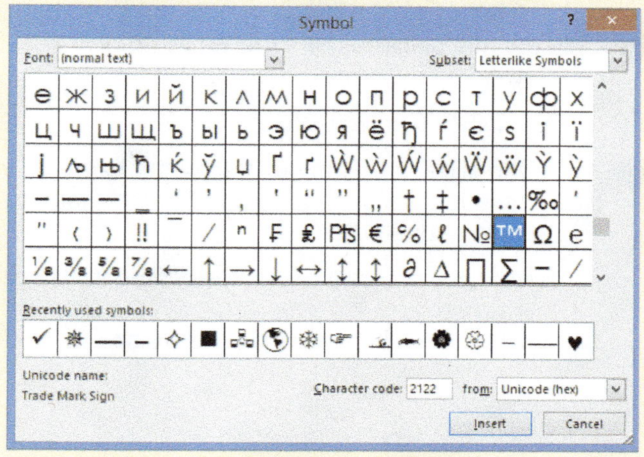

PowerPoint 2013, Windows 8, Microsoft Corporation

Inserting and Formatting a Text Box

- A **text box** is a container for text that you can position anywhere on a slide. It is not a placeholder, and not part of a slide layout. Like other slide objects, text boxes are inserted from the INSERT tab.
- There are two ways to use the Text Box tool. After clicking the Text Box button you can:
  - Click on the slide and start typing. This creates a text box in which the text does not wrap; the text box just keeps getting wider to accommodate your text.
  - Drag on the slide to define the size and shape of the text box, and then click inside it and start typing. This creates a text box in which text wraps to multiple lines automatically.
- You can resize a text box as you would any other object, by dragging the selection handles.
- You can format a text box as you would any other object. This includes adding a border, shading, and special effects. Use the tools in the Drawing group on the HOME tab, or use the DRAWING TOOLS FORMAT tab. You can also right-click the border of the text box and use the shortcut format tools, or display the Format Shape task pane to apply formats.

✓ *Lesson 13 covers object formatting in detail. The same basic formatting commands work for all types of objects, including drawn shapes and text boxes.*

- In addition to applying shape formats in the Format Shape task pane, you can display text options that allow you to control how the text appears in the text box (alignment, margins, and so on).

Try It! Inserting a Text Box

1. In the **P12Try_xx** file, in the Thumbnail pane, click between slides 6 and 7, and press ENTER, creating a new slide there.
2. With the new slide displayed, click HOME > Layout > Title Only.
3. In the title placeholder, type **What People Are Saying**.
4. Click INSERT > Text Box.
5. On the slide, drag the mouse pointer to create a box that is at least 4" wide and 3" high. Use the rulers to gauge size.

   ✓ *When you start typing, the height snaps back to the size of a single line of text at the default size. This is normal. The text box will expand vertically as you type.*

6. Type the text shown below. To manually insert a line break between the end of the quotation and the person's name, press SHIFT + ENTER.
7. Save the **P12Try_xx** file, and leave it open to use in the next Try It.

Type this text in the box

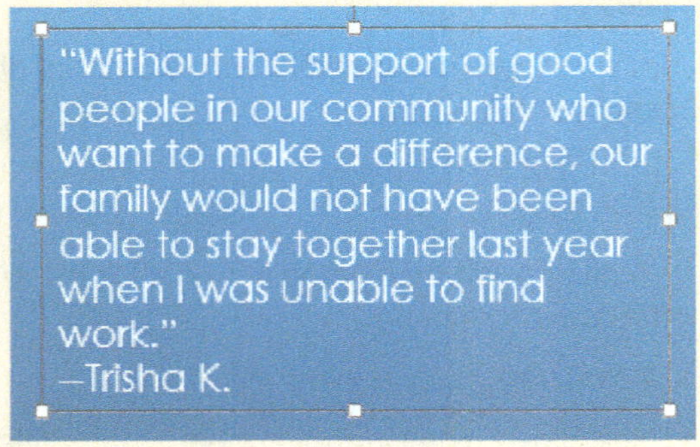

PowerPoint 2013, Windows 8, Microsoft Corporation

Try It! Formatting a Text Box

1. In the **P12Try_xx** file, click the outer border of the text box. This selects the box itself, and not the text inside.
2. On the DRAWING TOOLS FORMAT tab, click the More button in the Shape Styles group to open the Shape Styles gallery.
3. Click the second style in the bottom row of the Theme Styles section.
4. Click DRAWING TOOLS FORMAT > Edit Shape > Change Shape and click a rounded rectangle.
5. Right-click the text box and then click Format Shape to display the Format Shape task pane.
6. Click the Effects icon, expand the REFLECTION heading, click Presets, and click the first reflection type in the Reflection Variations section.
7. Expand the 3-D ROTATION heading, click Presets, and click the second sample in the first row of the Perspective section. When you are finished, the text box should look like that shown in the figure on the right. Close the Format Shape task pane.
8. Save the **P12Try_xx** file, and leave it open to use in the next Try It.

The formatted text box

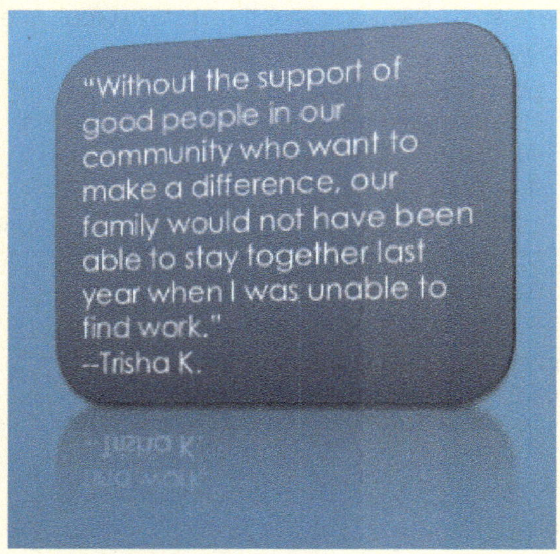

PowerPoint 2013, Windows 8, Microsoft Corporation

Using Multiple Columns in a Text Box

- You can place text in multiple columns in a single text box. This gives a different look than placing two text boxes side-by-side, and makes it easier to move text between columns after making edits.
- Use the Columns dialog box, accessed from the Columns drop-down list, to select the number of columns and space between them.

Try It! Using Multiple Columns in a Text Box

1. In the **P12Try_xx** file, click HOME > New Slide to create a new Title Only slide to become slide 8 in the presentation.
2. In the title placeholder, type **In the News**.
3. Click INSERT > Text Box.
4. On the slide, drag the mouse pointer to create a box that runs from the 4" mark on the horizontal ruler at the left to the 4" mark on the right.

   ✓ *The height you drag does not matter because PowerPoint will make the box as tall as needed for the content.*
5. Type the following paragraphs into the new text box:

   In a recent study at Purdue University, it was shown that the return on investment (ROI) for investing in job skills training programs for people living below the poverty line is approximately 5:1. That means for every one dollar invested, you can expect a return of five dollars.

   How is this money generated? When you train people who are currently receiving government assistance, they can get jobs and stop needing those payments. In addition, they begin paying income taxes, sales taxes, and property taxes as income rises and property is purchased.
6. Click HOME > Add or Remove Columns > Two Columns.
7. Click HOME > Add or Remove Columns > More Columns. The Columns dialog box opens.
8. In the Spacing text box, type **0.2"**.
9. Click OK.
10. Close the **P12Try_xx** file, saving changes, and exit PowerPoint.

The Columns dialog box

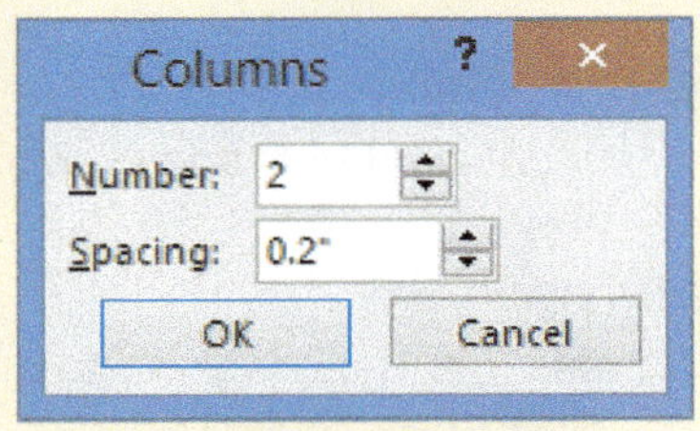

PowerPoint 2013, Windows 8, Microsoft Corporation

Lesson 12—Practice

In this project, you will add a copyright notice to the first slide of the Wynnedale presentation, break the text into columns, and format the text box.

DIRECTIONS

1. Start PowerPoint, if necessary, and open **P12Practice** from the data files for this lesson.
2. Save the presentation as **P12Practice_xx** in the location where your teacher instructs you to store the files for this lesson.
3. With slide 1 displayed, click **INSERT** > **Text Box**. Click at the top center of the slide and type your full name.
4. Click **INSERT** > **Text Box**.
5. Drag to create a 7" wide text box at the lower-right corner of the slide.
6. In the text box, type **Copyright** and press SPACEBAR once.
7. Click **INSERT** > **Symbol** Ω.
8. Click the Copyright symbol © and click **Insert**. Then click **Close**.
9. Press SPACEBAR again.
10. Type **2017**, press ENTER, type **Wynnedale Medical Group, LLC. All Rights Reserved.**
11. Press ENTER, and type **For information on how to obtain this presentation to show to your group, contact Wynnedale Medical Center.**
12. Press CTRL + A to select all the text in the text box.
13. On the **HOME** tab, in the Font group, open the **Size** drop-down list and click **10**.
14. Click **HOME** > **Add or Remove Columns** > **Two Columns**.
15. On the **DRAWING TOOLS FORMAT** tab, click in the **Shape Height** box and change the text box height to **0.6"**. Click in the **Shape Width** box and change the text box width to **6.7"**.
16. Right-click the border of the text box, click the **Shape Quick Styles** button, and click **Colored Fill - Plum, Accent 1**.
17. Adjust the position of the text box if necessary to fit exactly in the lower-right corner of the slide.
18. Click Slide Show on the status bar to preview your changes to slide 1. Then press ESC to end the slide show.
19. Close the presentation, saving changes, and exit PowerPoint.

Lesson 12—Apply

You continue to fine-tune the Wynnedale presentation. You will add customer testimonials to a page, using manually placed text boxes that you format in colorful ways.

DIRECTIONS

1. Start PowerPoint, if necessary, and open **P12Apply** from the data files for this lesson.
2. Save the presentation as **P12Apply_xx** in the location where your teacher instructs you to store the files for this lesson.
3. On slide 1, insert a text box at the top of the slide, and type your full name.
4. Move to slide 7 and create the text boxes shown in Figure 12-1 on the next page.
   a. Draw each text box and add the text shown in the figure. (You may need to change the font color initially to black to see what you are typing.)
   b. Italicize the names of the people and insert an em dash symbol to left of each name.
   c. On the **DRAWING TOOLS FORMAT** tab, use four different colors of presets from the bottom row of the Theme Styles section of the palette of Shape Styles.

5. Adjust the width and height of each text box as necessary to display the text attractively.
6. Move the text boxes on the slide as desired to create an interesting layout. Figure 12-1 shows one layout option.
7. Check the spelling and preview the slide in Slide Show view.
8. **With your teacher's permission**, print the presentation as handouts, six slides per page.
9. Close the presentation, saving changes, and exit PowerPoint.

Figure 12-1

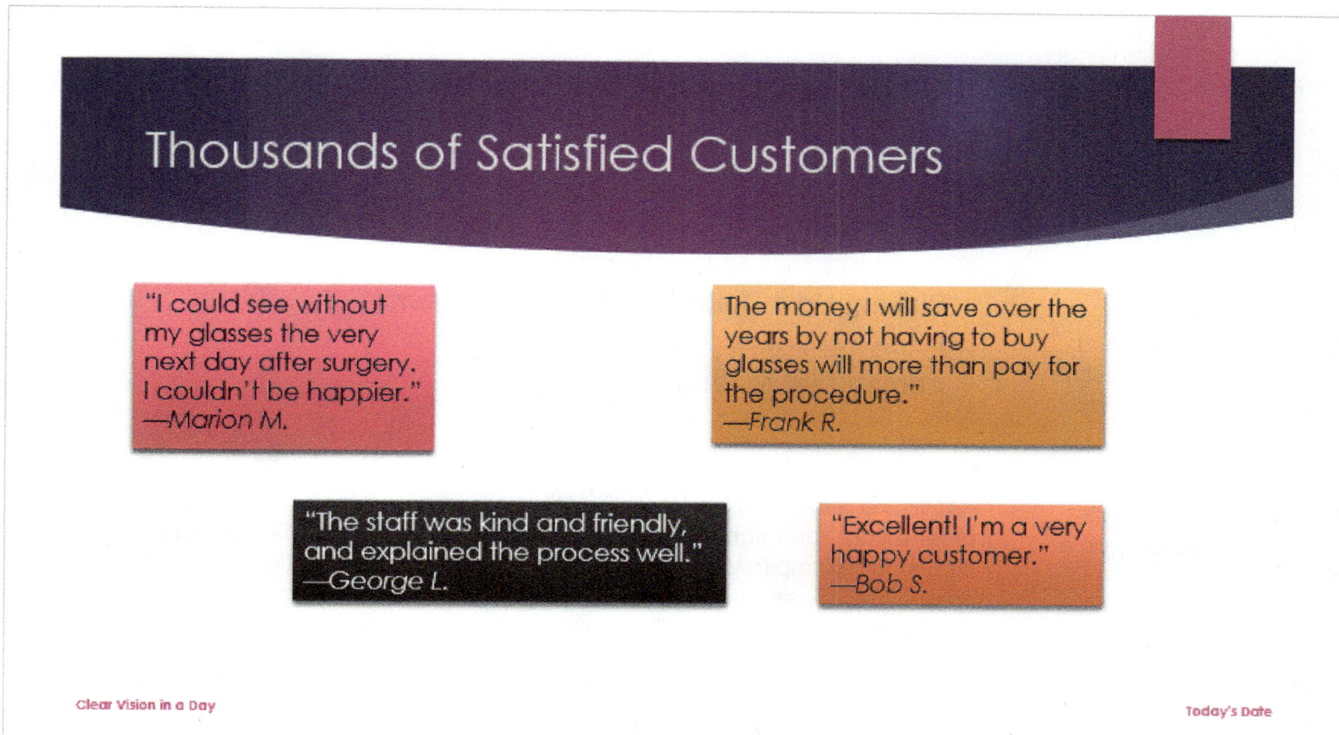

PowerPoint 2013, Windows 8, Microsoft Corporation

Lesson 13

Drawing and Formatting Shapes

➤ What You Will Learn

Using Rulers, Guides, and Gridlines
Drawing Shapes
Moving and Sizing Shapes
Applying Fills and Outlines
Picking Up a Color with the Eyedropper
Applying Shape Effects and Styles
Adding Text to Shapes

WORDS TO KNOW

Gridlines
A regular grid of dotted lines displayed on a slide to help arrange objects.

Guides
Nonprinting vertical and horizontal lines you can use to align objects on a slide.

Sample
Pick up a color from an object or slide background.

Shape effects
Special effects such as glow, shadow, 3D rotation, and soft edges applied to drawn shapes.

Shape styles
Preset combinations of shape effects that can be applied as a single formatting action.

Snap
To change position to align precisely with a gridline.

Software Skills Use PowerPoint's many drawing tools to help enhance a presentation. You might use rulers and guides or the grid to line up text or drawing objects, for example. Use shape tools to draw logos, illustrations, or other objects to add to slides. Then format shapes using fills, outlines, effects, and styles. Add text to a shape to use it as a visually interesting caption or label.

What You Can Do

Using Rulers, Guides, and Gridlines

- PowerPoint provides a vertical and horizontal ruler that you can show or hide at any time. Use the rulers to help you align objects on a slide.
- The ruler's origins (0 measurement on the ruler) change depending on whether you're using text or an object. The origin appears on the edge of the ruler when you're working with text and in the center point of the ruler when you're working with an object.
- As you move the mouse pointer, an indicator moves on each ruler showing your horizontal and vertical locations.
- **Guides** are alignment tools that help you line up objects and text. PowerPoint supplies one vertical and one horizontal guide that you can move and copy, as shown in Figure 13-1 on the next page.

- PowerPoint's **gridlines** display as a grid of dotted lines over the entire slide. Like guides, they can help you line up objects or position them attractively on the slide.
- By default, objects **snap** to the grid as they are drawn or positioned on the slide, even if the gridlines are not currently displayed. If you find you want to position an object more exactly, you can turn off the snapping feature or hold down ALT while dragging to temporarily disable the snapping feature.

Figure 13-1

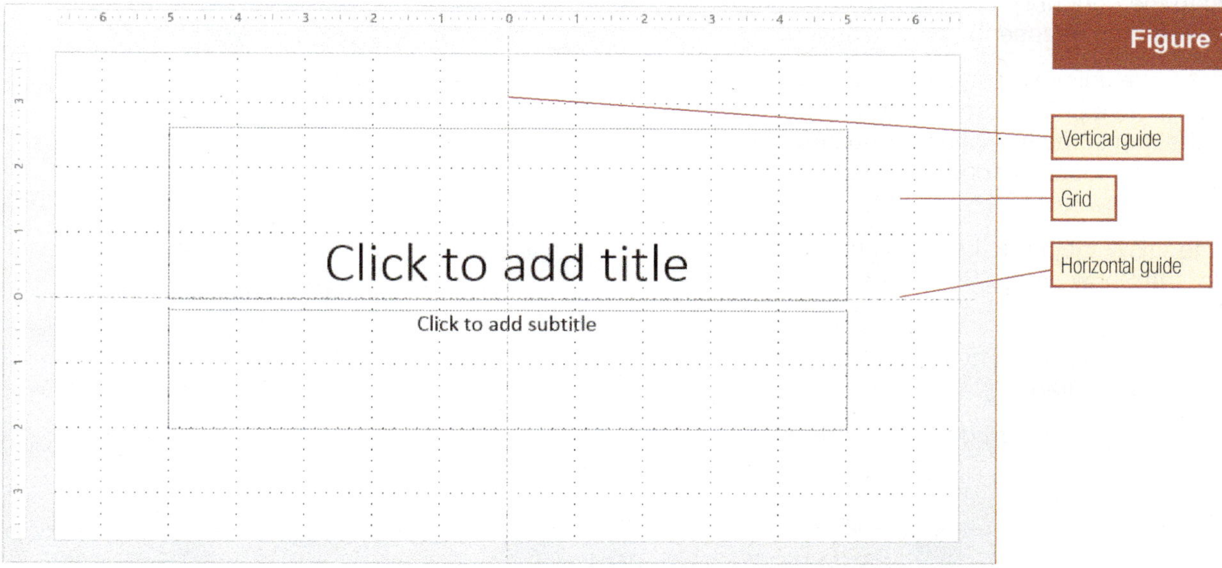

PowerPoint 2013, Windows 8, Microsoft Corporation

Try It! Turning on Rulers, Gridlines, and Guides

1. Start PowerPoint, and start a new blank presentation.
2. Save the presentation as **P13Try_xx** in the location where your teacher instructs you to store the files for this lesson.
3. Click the VIEW tab.
4. If the Ruler check box is not already marked, click to mark it.
5. If the Gridlines check box is not already marked, click to mark it.
6. If the Guides check box is not already marked, click to mark it.
7. Save the **P13Try_xx** file, and leave it open to use in the next Try It.

Try It! Adjusting Grid and Guide Settings

1. In the **P13Try_xx** file, position the mouse pointer over the dashed vertical guide and click and hold the left mouse button.

   ✓ *The mouse pointer changes to show 0.00.*

2. Drag to the right until the mouse pointer shows 1.50, and then release the mouse button.
3. Click on the guide you just moved, hold down the left mouse button, press CTRL, drag to the left until the mouse pointer shows 3.00, and then release the mouse button. You have copied the guide to a new location.
4. On the VIEW tab, click the dialog box launcher for the Show group. The Grid and Guides dialog box opens.
5. Click the Snap objects to grid check box if it is not already marked.
6. Open the Spacing drop-down list and click 1/16".
7. Click OK.
8. Save the **P13Try_xx** file, and leave it open to use in the next Try It.

The Grid and Guides dialog box

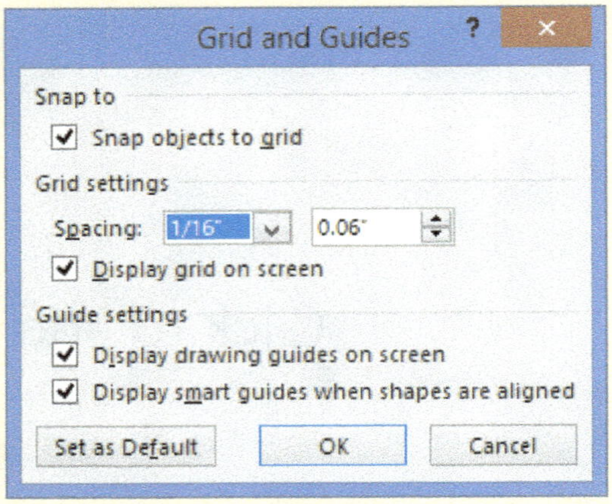

PowerPoint 2013, Windows 8, Microsoft Corporation

Drawing Shapes

- Use the shapes in the Shapes gallery to draw basic objects such as lines, rectangles, and circles as well as more complex shapes such as stars, banners, and block arrows.
- The Shapes gallery is available on the INSERT tab, as well as on the HOME tab, and on the DRAWING TOOLS FORMAT tab when a drawing object is selected.
- The Shapes gallery is divided into several sections that organize shapes of various kinds. Click a shape and then drag on the slide to draw it. You control the size as you draw.
- If you click on the slide instead of dragging, you get a default-sized shape.
- You can hold down SHIFT as you drag to constrain the shape to its original aspect ratio. If you draw an oval while holding down SHIFT, it's a perfect circle; if you draw a rectangle, it's a perfect square.

Try It! Drawing Shapes

1. In the **P13Try_xx** file, click HOME > Layout > Blank to switch to a blank layout with no placeholders.
2. Click INSERT > Shapes. In the Stars and Banners section, click the five-pointed star.
3. Hold down SHIFT and draw a star in the center of the slide, approximately 4" × 4".

   ✓ *Each square in the grid is 1".*

4. Click INSERT > Shapes. In the Basic Shapes section, click the oval.
5. Hold down SHIFT and draw a circle to the left of the star, approximately 3" in diameter.
6. With the circle still selected, click the Line shape in the gallery in the Insert Shapes group.
7. Hold down SHIFT and draw a straight horizontal line above the star.
8. Save the **P13Try_xx** file, and leave it open to use in the next Try It.

Moving and Sizing Shapes

- You can move, size, copy, and delete drawing objects just like any other PowerPoint object.
  - To move a shape, drag it.

    ✓ *You can also display the Format Shape task pane and use the Position settings in the Size & Properties settings.*
  - To size a shape, drag one of its selection handles.

    ✓ *You can also enter a precise height and width on the DRAWING TOOLS FORMAT tab, in the Size group, or on the Format Shape task pane.*
  - To delete a shape, select it and press DEL.
  - To nudge an object (move it in small increments), hold down CTRL while pressing an arrow key in the direction you want it to move.
- Some shapes also have one or more yellow resize handles that you can use to adjust the appearance of the shape.

Try It! Moving and Sizing Shapes

1. In the P13Try_xx file, click the circle to select it.
2. Hold down SHIFT and drag the shape's lower-right corner selection handle, to shrink the circle to approximately 2" in diameter.
3. On the DRAWING TOOLS FORMAT tab, click in the Shape Height box and type 2.5".
4. Click in the Shape Width box and type 2.5".
5. Drag the circle to the upper-right corner of the slide.
6. Right-click the circle and click Format Shape. The Format Shape task pane displays.
7. Click the Size & Properties icon, and click the POSITION heading to expand it.
8. In the Horizontal position box, type 0.5".
9. In the Vertical position box, type 0.5".
10. Close the Format Shape task pane.
11. Click INSERT > Shapes and in the Block Arrows section, click the Up Arrow shape.
12. Drag on the slide to place a block arrow to the right of the star, approximately 4" high and 2" wide.

    ✓ *Two yellow handles appear on it: one on the arrowhead and one on the arrow shaft.*
13. Drag the yellow handle on the arrowhead upward to change the shape of the arrowhead.
14. Drag the yellow handle on the arrow shaft to the right to change the width of the shaft.
15. Save the P13Try_xx file, and leave it open to use in the next Try It.

Modify the arrow by dragging the yellow handles

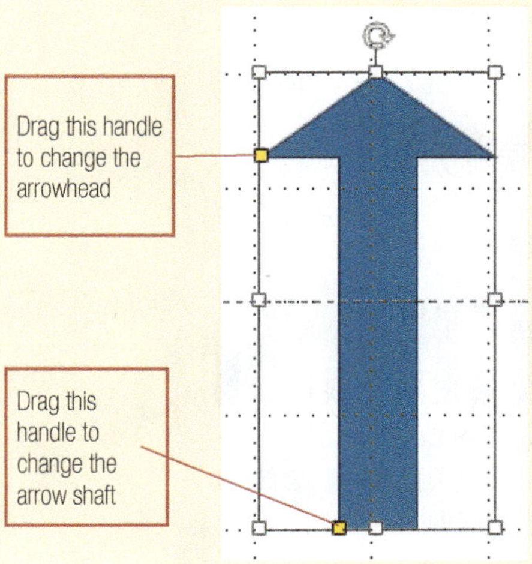

PowerPoint 2013, Windows 8, Microsoft Corporation

Applying Fills and Outlines

- By default, shapes are formatted with the current theme colors. The fill is the Accent 1 color in the theme (the fifth color), and the outline is a related color.
- On the DRAWING TOOLS FORMAT tab, you can use the Shape Fill and Shape Outline drop-down lists to format a shape differently from the default.
- You can also right-click the shape and use the Fill and Outline shortcut buttons, or choose Format Shape to open the Format Shape task pane, where a wider variety of formatting options are available.

Try It! Applying Fills and Outlines

1. In the **P13Try_xx** file, click the star to select it.
2. On the DRAWING TOOLS FORMAT tab, click the Shape Fill drop-down arrow, opening its menu.
3. Click the yellow square under Standard Colors.
4. Click the Shape Outline drop-down arrow, opening its menu.
5. Click More Outline Colors.
6. In the Colors dialog box, click the Standard tab.
7. Click an orange hexagon, and then click OK.
8. Right-click the star and click the Outline button.
9. Click Weight and then click 3 pt.
10. Right-click the horizontal line and click Format Shape on the shortcut menu to open the Format Shape task pane. Click the Fill & Line icon if necessary.
11. Click the LINE heading to expand it. Click the Width up arrow until the width is 5 pt, and then click the Dash type button, opening its menu. Choose the Square Dot dash style (the third style on the list).
12. Close the Format Shape task pane.
13. Save the **P13Try_xx** file, and leave it open to use in the next Try It.

Select a fill color

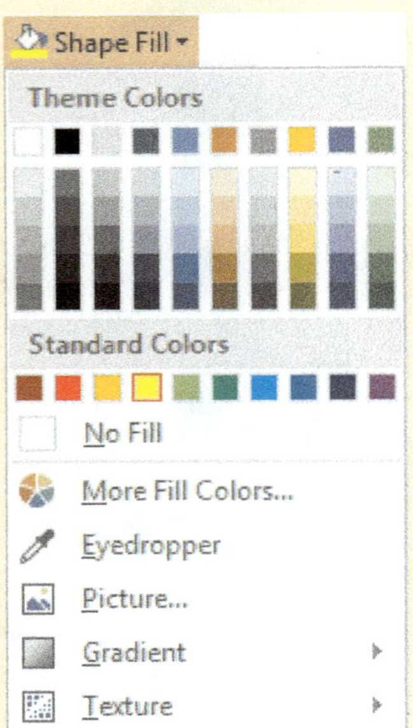

PowerPoint 2013, Windows 8, Microsoft Corporation

Select an outline color

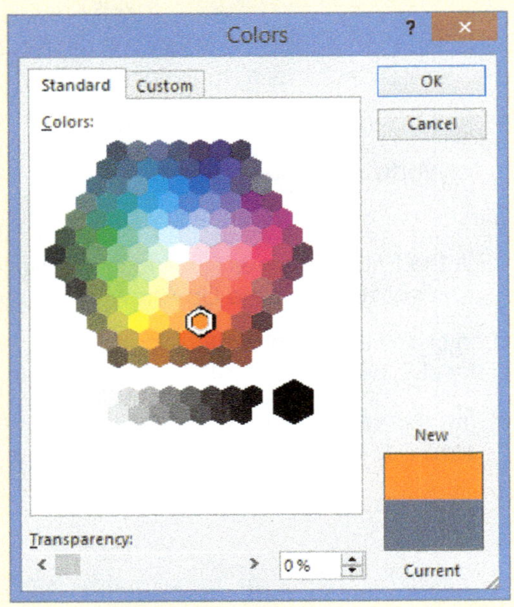

PowerPoint 2013, Windows 8, Microsoft Corporation

Picking Up a Color with the Eyedropper

- In PowerPoint 2013, you can use a new feature, the Eyedropper, to pick up a color from one object to use as the fill or outline color in another object.
- You can pick up a color from a photo or clip art illustration, for example, to fill a shape or placeholder. Using the Eyedropper to apply colors allows you to build unity among slide objects. Unity is one of the standard principles of design.
- As you move the Eyedropper over a slide and its contents, the Eyedropper **samples** the color under the pointer and shows you the exact color values using the RGB color mode.

✓ *RGB, or Red Green Blue, is the color mode used for images that appear onscreen, such as PowerPoint slide objects.*

Try It! Picking Up a Color with the Eyedropper

1. In the **P13Try_xx** file, click INSERT > Online Pictures.
2. In the Bing Image Search box, type **flowers** and click the Search button.
3. Select an illustration that contains a red flower and click Insert. Use the grid as a reference as you drag the upper-right corner handle to reduce the image to about 4.5" wide. Move the illustration to the lower-left corner of the slide.
4. Click the circle on the slide to select it and then click DRAWING TOOLS FORMAT > Shape Fill to display the Shape Fill menu.
5. Click Eyedropper. The pointer changes to the shape of an eyedropper, and a thumbnail attached to the pointer displays the color the Eyedropper is currently sampling.
6. Click anywhere on a red flower in the illustration with the Eyedropper. The circle fills with the same color.
7. With the circle still selected, click DRAWING TOOLS FORMAT > Shape Outline to display the Shape Outline menu.
8. Click Eyedropper, and then click on another color from the illustration, such as a leaf. Click DRAWING TOOLS FORMAT > Shape Outline > Weight > 6 pt.
9. Save the **P13Try_xx** file, and leave it open to use in the next Try It.

Applying Shape Effects and Styles

- **Shape effects** are special formatting options you can apply to PowerPoint objects. You have already used some of these effects in formatting pictures and text boxes.
- The available effects include shadows, reflections, soft edges, bevels, and 3D rotation. After opening the Shape Effects menu, you point to a submenu name and then click one of the presets from the submenu that appears.

✓ *The shape effect you choose does not affect the color or border of the object. However, some effects hide the shape's outline.*

- Each of the effect submenus has an Options command at the bottom that opens the Format Shape task pane with the corresponding options selected. For example, the Shadow Options command opens the task pane to the SHADOW settings.
- You have also previously applied **shape styles**, combinations of color, outline, and shape effects you add to an object with a single click.
- Shape styles automatically use the colors of the current theme. You can apply a shape style and then manually change the color if you like.

Try It! Applying Shape Effects and Styles

1. In the **P13Try_xx** file, click the circle to select it.
2. Click DRAWING TOOLS FORMAT > Shape Effects > Preset and click the second preset in the first row of the Presets section.
3. Click Shape Fill, click Eyedropper, and click another color from the illustration.

   ✓ *Notice that the effect remains, even though you have changed the color.*
4. Click Shape Effects > Bevel > Riblet (the second effect in the third row of the Bevel section).
5. Click the star to select it.
6. On the DRAWING TOOLS FORMAT tab, in the Shape Styles group, click the More button to open the Shape Styles gallery.
7. Click the style in the lower-right corner of the gallery.

   ✓ *Notice that the shape outline is removed because this shape style does not include an outline.*
8. Click the block arrow shape. Click the More button to open the Shape Styles gallery again.
9. Click the first style in the fourth row of the gallery.
10. Right-click the shape, click Format Shape to open the Format Shape task pane, click the Effects icon, and expand the GLOW heading.
11. Click the Presets button and then click Gold, 18 pt glow, Accent color 4.
12. Save the **P13Try_xx** file, and leave it open to use in the next Try It.

Adding Text to Shapes

- You can add text to any filled shape. Simply click on the shape and start typing. PowerPoint handles line length and text wrap. This allows you, in effect, to have any shape of text box you want, not just rectangular.
- You can edit and format text in a shape just as you would edit text in a text box. For a special effect, you can change text direction so that text reads from top to bottom or bottom to top.

Try It! Adding Text to a Shape and Rotating the Text

1. In the **P13Try_xx** file, click the block arrow to select it.
2. Type **Check out our specials**. The text appears in the shaft of the arrow, with only a few characters per line.
3. Right-click the block arrow and click Format Shape.
4. At the top of the Format Shape task pane, click TEXT OPTIONS.
5. Click the Textbox icon to display TEXT BOX settings.
6. Open the Text direction drop-down list and click Rotate all text 270°.
7. Close the task pane. The text now runs vertically in the shape.
8. Close the **P13Try_xx** file, saving changes, and exit PowerPoint.

Lesson 13—Practice

A friend who works for Kelly Greenery, a landscaping company, has asked you to create a presentation he can run at a garden show. You will begin work on the presentation by creating and formatting shapes on a slide to which you have already added a clip art photo.

DIRECTIONS

1. Start PowerPoint, if necessary, and open **P13Practice** from the data files for this lesson.
2. Save the presentation as **P13Practice_xx** in the location where your teacher instructs you to store the files for this lesson.
3. On slide 1, click **INSERT** > **Text Box** . Click at the bottom of the slide and type your full name.
4. On the VIEW tab, mark the **Guides** check box and the **Gridlines** check box, if necessary.
5. Display slide 2. Position the mouse pointer over the vertical guide, hold down the left mouse button, and drag to the left until the mouse pointer displays **1.75**.
6. With the mouse pointer still on the vertical guide, press CTRL and drag a copy of the vertical guide to the right until the mouse pointer displays **5.00**.
7. Click **INSERT** > **Shapes** . Click the Wave shape in the Stars and Banners section.
8. Drag on the slide above the tulips illustration to create a banner that extends from the left edge of the slide to the 1.75 guide you positioned in step 5.
9. Click **INSERT** > **Shapes** . Click the Up Arrow shape in the Block Arrows section.
10. Drag on the slide to the right of the tulips to create a block arrow from the bottom edge of the slide to the horizontal guide at the middle of the slide. The arrow should be about **2.3"** wide and **3.75"** tall.
11. Use the grid to draw an oval **5** inches wide and **3** inches high.
12. Position the shapes as follows:
    a. Move the block arrow so that its point is at the intersection of the left vertical guide and the horizontal guide.
    b. Move the oval so that its right edge snaps to the right vertical guide and it is vertically centered on the horizontal guide.
13. Change fill and outline formats as follows:
    a. Select the banner and click **DRAWING TOOLS FORMAT** > **Shape Fill** . Click **Eyedropper** and sample an area on one of the tulip leaves, as shown in Figure 13-2 on the next page.
    b. Right-click the oval, click the **Fill** shortcut button, and then click **Orange, Accent 2** from the theme colors.
    c. Right-click the block arrow and click **Format Shape** on the shortcut menu. Expand the **FILL** heading, click **Color** , and click **More Colors**. Click the Standard tab, and click the dark pink color that is second from the right in the third row from the bottom of the color chart. Click **OK**.
    d. With the block arrow still selected, click **LINE**, click Color and then click **Gold, Accent 4** from the theme colors. Click the **Width** up arrow until the width is **6 pt**.
14. Select the green banner and type **KELLY GREENERY**. Change the font to **Algerian** and the font size to **60**.
15. On the **DRAWING TOOLS FORMAT** tab, click **Shape Effects** > **Bevel** and click the first option in the first row, Circle.
16. Select the block arrow and type **TULIPS**. In the Format Shape task pane, click **TEXT OPTIONS**, click the **Textbox** icon , click the **Text direction** arrow, and click **Stacked**.
17. **With your teacher's permission**, print the slides.
18. Close the presentation, saving changes, and exit PowerPoint.

Figure 13-2

PowerPoint 2013, Windows 8, Microsoft Corporation

Lesson 13—Apply

In this project, you continue working on the Kelly Greenery presentation. You will adjust shape formats, add text to a shape, and insert a new shape with additional information.

DIRECTIONS

1. Start PowerPoint, if necessary, and open **P13Apply** from the data files for this lesson.
2. Save the presentation as **P13Apply_xx** in the location where your teacher instructs you to store the files for this lesson.
3. Create a text box at the bottom of slide 1 and type your name in it.
4. Turn off display of the gridlines and guides.
5. Remove the fill and the outline from the text box on slide 1.
6. On slide 2, make the following adjustments to the green banner shape:
   a. Drag upward on the adjustment handle near the upper-left corner of the object to make the shape less curvy.
   b. Resize it to be about 3" high and 5" wide and move it to the top of the slide.
   c. Use the Eyedropper to sample a different fill color, either a darker green or one of the other colors from the tulip picture.
   d. Left-align the text in the shape.
7. Boldface the text in the block arrow, change font color to black, and increase the font size as much as possible without having the text set in two columns.

   ✓ *Change Character Spacing to Very Tight to fit text at a larger font size.*
8. Apply a Glow effect to the block arrow. Click **More Glow Colors** on the Glow gallery and use the Eyedropper to sample a glow color from one of the tulip flowers.
9. Type the text **Buy Your Spring Bulbs Soon!** in the orange oval. Increase text size as much as possible while still fitting all words in the shape.

10. Insert a Down Arrow Callout shape above the orange oval and insert the text **On Sale Through October**.
11. Apply a fill color, outline color, effect, and/or style of your choosing, and adjust the font size as necessary. Figure 13-3 shows the completed slide.
12. **With your teacher's permission**, print the presentation.
13. Close the presentation, saving changes, and exit PowerPoint.

Figure 13-3

PowerPoint 2013, Windows 8, Microsoft Corporation

Lesson 14

Positioning and Grouping Shapes

➤ What You Will Learn

Stacking Objects
Grouping Objects
Combining Shapes to Create a New Shape
Rotating and Flipping Objects
Duplicating Objects
Aligning and Distributing Objects

WORDS TO KNOW

Group
To combine multiple shapes or other objects into a collective unit that can be controlled as a single object.

Rotate
Turn an object on a central axis to a new orientation.

Stack
To overlap objects, and control the order in which overlapping objects appear.

Software Skills Many of the drawings you create with the Shapes tools in PowerPoint will consist of multiple shapes that overlap each other. When a graphic consists of several pieces, you need to know how to combine and position them to make a cohesive whole.

What You Can Do

Stacking Objects

- As you create objects on a slide, they **stack** from the "back" (the first object created) to the "front" (the last object created). You can think of this process as a series of layers stacked on top of each other with an object on each layer.
- Use the DRAWING TOOLS FORMAT tab's arrangement tools to change an object's stack order:
  - Bring to Front and Send to Back move the object all the way to the top or bottom of the stack, respectively.
  - Bring Forward and Send Backward move an object back or forward one layer at a time.
- To make it easy to select objects for arranging or other manipulation, use the Selection pane. Access it from the DRAWING TOOLS FORMAT tab.
- The Selection pane shows all objects currently displayed on the slide. To select any object, click it in the Selection pane. You can also click on the visibility symbol (the open eye) to hide an object.

  ✓ *You can click on an object name to open the default name for editing and supply your own names for objects. Meaningful names for objects can also help you when you are creating animations for slide objects.*

Try It! Stacking Objects

1. Start PowerPoint, and open **P14Try** from the data files for this lesson.
2. Save the presentation as **P14Try_xx** in the location where your teacher instructs you to store the files for this lesson.
3. Click any of the shapes, and then click DRAWING TOOLS FORMAT > Selection Pane. The Selection pane opens.
4. In the Selection pane, click the eye symbol next to Oval 4. The circle disappears and the eye button changes to a blank. Click the blank button to make the circle reappear.
5. Click the circle to select it. Then hold down SHIFT and drag a corner selection handle on the circle to expand it so it is large enough to completely cover the star. Drag it to reposition it so it is directly over the star.
6. With the circle still selected, on the DRAWING TOOLS FORMAT tab, click the arrow to the right of the Send Backward button and click Send to Back.
7. Adjust the size and position of the circle so that the tips of the star barely touch the edges of the circle.
8. Click the pentagon, either on the slide or in the Selection pane.
9. Click the arrow to the right of the Bring Forward button and click Bring to Front.
10. Position the pentagon on top of the star, at its center.
11. Click DRAWING TOOLS FORMAT > Selection Pane to turn off the Selection pane. The design should look like that shown in the following figure.
12. Save the **P14Try_xx** file, and leave it open to use in the next Try It.

Select any object easily in this pane

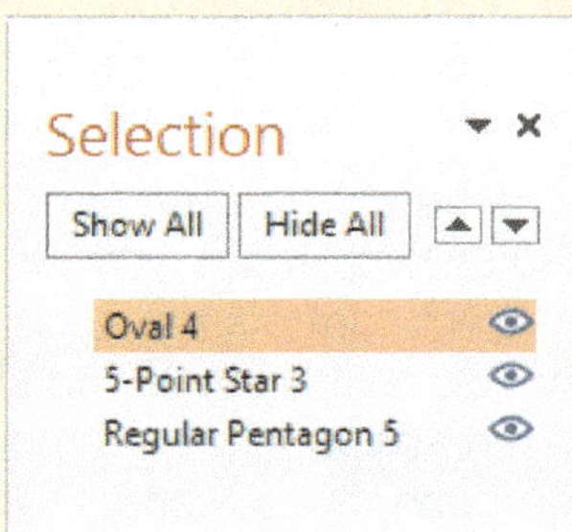

Arrange and stack the pieces of the design

Grouping Objects

- You can **group** the objects within a drawing so that they can be treated as a single object. Grouping objects makes them easier to copy, move, or resize.
- You can ungroup objects when you want to work with the objects individually again.
- Some changes can be made to the individual elements of a grouped object without ungrouping it, such as changing the colors.
- To select the objects to be grouped, you can hold down CTRL as you click on each one, or you can drag a lasso around all the objects to be included. To lasso a group, drag the mouse pointer to draw an imaginary box around the items.

Try It! Grouping Objects

1. In the **P14Try_xx** file, drag to lasso all the drawn shapes. Each one appears with its own selection handles.
2. Click DRAWING TOOLS FORMAT > Group > Group. The group now has a single set of selection handles.
3. Hold down SHIFT and drag the bottom-right corner of the shape inward to shrink it in size by 1".

   ✓ *All shapes are resized together because they are all part of the group.*
4. Click to select the object if it is not already selected.
5. Click DRAWING TOOLS FORMAT > Group > Ungroup. The shapes become ungrouped.
6. Save the **P14Try_xx** file, and leave it open to use in the next Try It.

Combining Shapes to Create a New Shape

- PowerPoint 2013 lets you combine shapes to create a new shape, in the same way you can merge shapes in sophisticated graphics programs.
- Merging differs from grouping in that the shapes used to create the combined object are transformed so that they cannot be separated back into their original shapes.

  ✓ *You can click Undo to reverse the joining process.*
- Select two or more shapes to merge, and then choose a merge option (see Figure 14-1):
  - Union joins all shapes into a single shape, with an outline that surrounds the entire merged shape.
  - Combine groups the shapes into a single object. Regions that overlap are removed from the combined shape to create empty spaces.
  - Fragment breaks the combined shapes into individual pieces that can be ungrouped and used separately.
  - Intersect removes all parts of the shapes except the area where they overlap.
  - Subtract removes one shape from the other shape where they overlap.
- When you merge shapes, it makes a difference to the final result which shape you select first. The first shape you select controls the action. If the shapes are different colors, the combined shape will be the color of the shape you selected first, and in a subtract operation, the second shape you select will be subtracted from the first one.

Figure 14-1

PowerPoint 2013, Windows 8, Microsoft Corporation

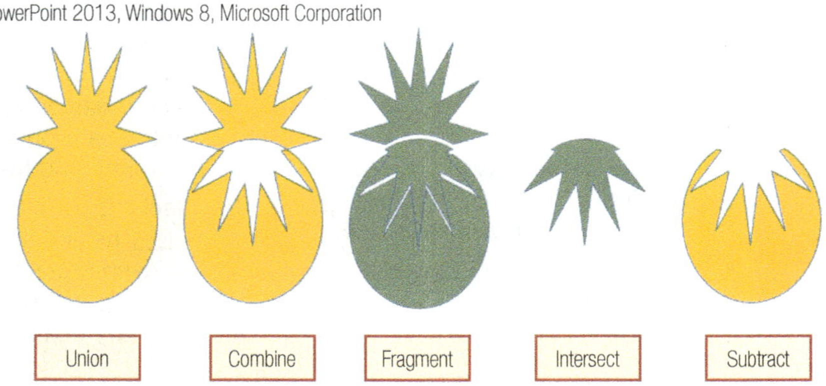

Try It! Combining Shapes to Create a New Shape

1. In the **P14Try_xx** file, on the HOME tab, click New Slide.
2. On slide 2, click INSERT > Shapes and select Heart from the Basic Shapes section.
3. Hold down [SHIFT] and drag to draw a heart about 5" high by 5" wide.
4. On the DRAWING TOOLS FORMAT tab, select a Rectangle shape from the Shapes gallery in the Insert Shapes group, hold down [SHIFT], and draw a square about 5" high. Move the square to overlap the bottom of the heart.
5. Right-click the square, click the Fill shortcut button, and select the Gold, Accent 4 fill.
6. With the gold square still selected, hold down [SHIFT] and click the blue heart, and then, in the Insert Shapes group, click Merge Shapes > Union. The two shapes are joined, and because the gold shape was selected first, the joined shape is gold.
7. Click Undo, and then, with the shapes still selected, click Merge Shapes > Subtract. The heart shape is removed, leaving the square with a chunk out of it that used to be the point of the heart.
8. Click Undo, and then deselect the shapes.
9. Select the blue heart, then the gold square, and click Merge Shapes > Fragment. Because you clicked the blue heart first, the new shape is blue.
10. Click outside the shape to deselect it, then click on the top of the heart and press [↑] five times to nudge this part of the shape away from the other parts.
11. Nudge the square bottom downward to move it away from the point of the heart.
12. Save the **P14Try_xx** file, and leave it open to use in the next Try It.

Fragment creates separate objects from combined shapes

PowerPoint 2013, Windows 8, Microsoft Corporation

Rotating and Flipping Objects

- When you **rotate** an object, you turn it on a central axis to a new orientation. You can rotate any PowerPoint object: shapes, pictures, text boxes, and placeholders.
- Drag a selected object's rotation handle, at the top center of the object, to rotate the object.

  ✓ *Hold down [SHIFT] while dragging to rotate in 15 degree increments.*

- You can also use a preset rotation such as Rotate Right 90° or Rotate Left 90° from the Rotate menu. Or click More Rotation Options to open the Format Shape task pane, where you can specify an exact degree of rotation.
- If a shape or other object is not facing the way you want it to, you can use the flip options on the Rotate menu.
- Flip Vertical switches the object from top to bottom, and Flip Horizontal switches the object from left to right.

Try It! Rotating and Flipping Objects

1. In the **P14Try_xx** file, display slide 1.
2. Click the star graphic to select it and display the rotation handle.
3. Drag the rotation handle to the right so that the top star point is pointing to about 2 o'clock on the blue oval.
4. On the DRAWING TOOLS FORMAT tab, click the Rotate drop-down arrow, and then click Rotate Left 90°.
5. Click the Rotate drop-down arrow, and then click More Rotation Options to display the Format Shape task pane.
6. In the Rotation box, select the current value and type **0**.
7. Select the polygon, click the Rotate drop-down arrow, and then click Flip Vertical.
8. Hold down SHIFT and drag the polygon's rotation handle to the left until it has returned to its original orientation. The Rotation box in the Format Shape task pane should read 180°. Close the Format Shape task pane.
9. Select all three objects on slide 1, click DRAWING TOOLS FORMAT > Group, and click Regroup.
10. Save the **P14Try_xx** file, and leave it open to use in the next Try It.

Duplicating Objects

- After drawing an object, you may want to duplicate it rather than drawing additional objects from scratch. For example, if you need three circles that are all exactly the same size, duplicating the first one twice ensures that they are identical.
- You can duplicate either with drag-and-drop, or with copy-and-paste.

Try It! Duplicating Objects

1. In the **P14Try_xx** file, select the object on slide 1, and on the DRAWING TOOLS FORMAT tab, enter a Height and Width of 2" each.

   ✓ *This makes the shape small enough that multiple copies of it will fit on the slide.*

2. Select the object and press CTRL + C. It is copied to the Clipboard.
3. Press CTRL + V. A copy is pasted on the slide.
4. Drag the copy to move it so it does not overlap the original.
5. Click the original object.
6. Hold down the CTRL key and drag the original to a different spot on the slide. It is copied there.

   ✓ *Now you have three copies of the shape, which you will use in the next Try It.*

7. Save the **P14Try_xx** file, and leave it open to use in the next Try It.

Aligning and Distributing Objects

- Sometimes it is important that the objects on a slide be precisely aligned, either with one another or with the slide itself.
- PowerPoint has several commands to help you accomplish this. You can use either commands from the DRAWING TOOLS FORMAT tab or use PowerPoint's new Smart Guides.
- The Align command aligns objects by their top, middle, bottom, right side, left side, or center. It can also be used to place one or more objects in relation to the slide itself. In Figure 14-2, the shapes are middle-aligned.
- On the Align button's menu is an Align to Slide command that is a toggle. When it is turned on, a check mark appears by it.
- When this command is on, the Align and Distribute commands apply to the object in relation to the slide, as well as in relation to the other selected objects.
- When this command is on, you can use Align or Distribute on a single object. When this command is off, the minimum number of selected objects to use Align is 2, and the minimum to use Distribute is 3.
- You can also use an Align menu command to distribute objects. Distributing equalizes space between objects. You can distribute objects either horizontally or vertically.
- PowerPoint 2013's new Smart Guides help you align and distribute objects by displaying onscreen guides that show you how objects are positioned relative to each other. (See Figure 14-2.)
- Smart Guides display as red dashed lines that appear when objects are moved near each other. A Smart Guide might display, for example, when the top of one object aligns with the top or bottom of another object, when objects align at their centers or middles, or when two objects align at their right or left sides.
- Smart Guides can also help you space objects evenly just by dragging. When you see the horizontal or vertical arrows between pairs of Smart Guides, the space between the objects is equal.

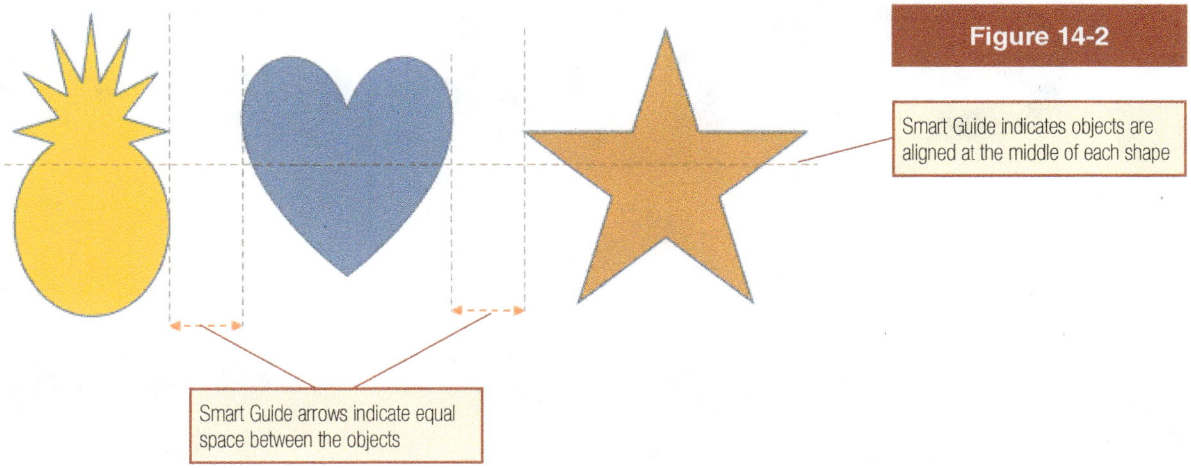

Figure 14-2

PowerPoint 2013, Windows 8, Microsoft Corporation

Try It! Aligning and Distributing Objects

1. In the **P14Try_xx** file, click the first object, click Align, and then click Align Middle. The object moves to the vertical middle of the slide.
2. Drag the second object until the Smart Guides indicate that the bottom of this object aligns with the top of the first object.
3. Click the first object, hold down SHIFT and click the third object, and then click Align > Align Bottom. Click anywhere on the slide to deselect both objects.
4. Click the third object, hold down CTRL, and drag a copy of the object to the right, using the Smart Guides to make sure the new object is aligned top and bottom with the third object.
5. Select all four objects, and then click Align > Distribute Horizontally.
6. Deselect all objects. Then, click the first object, hold down CTRL, and drag a copy to the left, keeping it aligned at the bottom with the other objects.
7. After you drop the copy, drag it horizontally back and forth until you see the Smart Guide arrows that show the space between all objects is the same.

   ✓ *If you do not have room on the slide to distribute all of the objects, move them closer together using the Smart Guides to make sure the space stays the same between all objects.*

8. Close the **P14Try_xx** file, saving changes, and exit PowerPoint.

Smart Guides show that all objects are equally spaced

PowerPoint 2013, Windows 8, Microsoft Corporation

Lesson 14—Practice

In this project, you continue working with the presentation for Kelly Greenery. You practice working with shapes and objects by stacking, grouping, rotating, duplicating, aligning, and distributing. You also begin work on a combined shape.

DIRECTIONS

1. Start PowerPoint, if necessary, and open **P14Practice** from the data files for this lesson.
2. Save the presentation as **P14Practice_xx** in the location where your teacher instructs you to store the files for this lesson.
3. On slide 1, insert a text box and type your first and last name.
4. With slide 1 displayed, select the light-brown rectangle and then, on the DRAWING TOOLS FORMAT tab, click **Selection Pane** to display the Selection pane.

5. Click the **Send Backward** arrow [▼] in the Selection pane until the rectangle is behind the title text.
6. In the Selection pane, click **Picture 10** and click the **Send Backward** arrow [▼] in the Selection pane until the leaf is behind the title text.
7. In the Selection pane, click **Picture 13** and click the **Bring Forward** arrow [▲] in the Selection pane until the leaf is in front of the light brown rectangle and behind the title text.
8. Rotate the light brown leaf in the lower-left corner of the slide by dragging its rotation handle to give it a different orientation.
9. Select the light orange leaf near the upper-left corner of the light-brown rectangle and then click **PICTURE TOOLS FORMAT** > **Rotate** > **Flip Vertical**. Close the Selection pane.
10. Display slide 3. Select the two clip art illustrations in the lower-left corner of the slide, and then click **PICTURE TOOLS FORMAT** > **Group** > **Group**.
11. With the group still selected, press CTRL + C, and then press CTRL + V four times to create four copies of the group.
12. Drag the last copied group to the right side of the slide, using the Smart Guides to make sure it is aligned at top and bottom with the original group.
13. Drag the other three groups to space them across the bottom of the slide, as shown in Figure 14-3.
14. Select all five objects, click **Align** > **Align Bottom**, and then click **Align** > **Distribute Horizontally**.
15. Click the group of two light gray triangles and drag them over the top of the pink oval, so that the group aligns with the oval at the top and the center.
16. With the group selected, click **DRAWING TOOLS FORMAT** > **Group** > **Ungroup**.
17. Select the pink oval and then select each gray triangle.
18. Click **DRAWING TOOLS FORMAT** > **Merge Shapes** > **Fragment**. The three shapes are broken into components.
19. Click outside the pink oval to deselect the shapes, click each of the four pieces that originally made up the triangles, and press DEL to delete these partial shapes. You should be left with the pink oval that now has a jagged top to represent a tulip flower, as shown in Figure 14-3.
20. **With your teacher's permission**, print slides 1 and 3.
21. Close the presentation, saving changes, and exit PowerPoint.

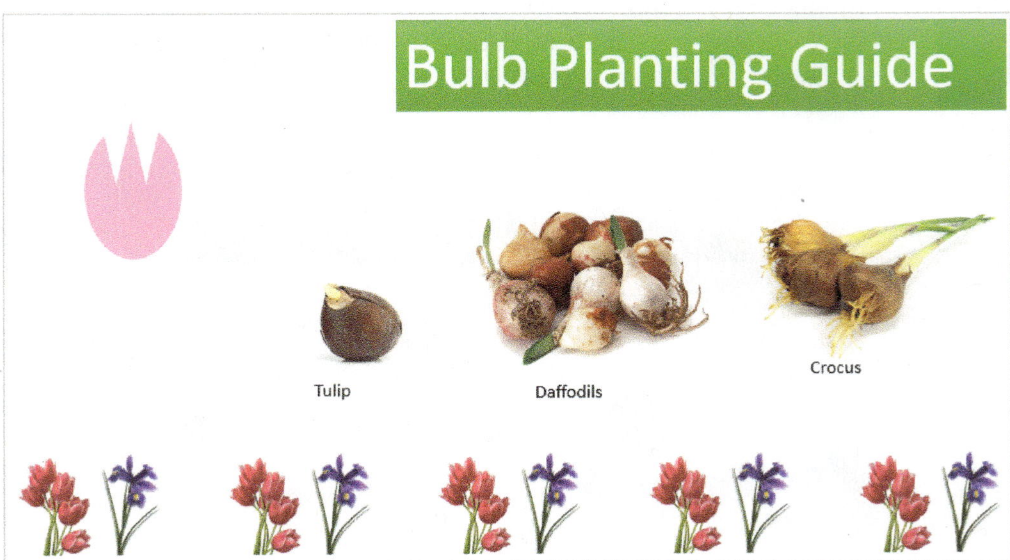

PowerPoint 2013, Windows 8, Microsoft Corporation

Figure 14-3

Lesson 14—Apply

In this project, you complete the Kelly Greenery presentation by combining shapes to create a stylized tulip, and further modifying and adjusting shapes and objects in the presentation.

DIRECTIONS

1. Start PowerPoint, if necessary, and open **P14Apply** from the data files for this lesson.
2. Save the presentation as **P14Apply_xx** in the location where your teacher instructs you to store the files for this lesson.
3. On slide 1, insert a text box and type your first and last name.
4. Display slide 3. Select the green jagged-topped tulip flower and the vertical blue stem and align them at the center.
5. Select the blue tulip leaf shape and rotate it about half an inch to the right, and then move it until the bottom tip of the leaf overlaps the bottom of the stem.
6. Select the flower, the stem, and then the leaf in that order and merge the shapes, using the Union option.
7. With the combined shape selected, apply the Perspective Diagonal Upper Right shadow shape effect.
8. Drag the title placeholder near the tulip shape and use the Smart Guide to align the placeholder with the top of the shape. Then use Align Center to center the placeholder on the slide.
9. With the placeholder still selected, copy and then paste the placeholder shape. Remove the text from the pasted shape.
10. Use the Eyedropper to fill the blank shape with the same green as the combined tulip shape, and then send the blank shape behind the original placeholder to create a shadow effect.
11. Flip the daffodil bulb picture horizontally, and then middle align the three bulb images.
12. Use the Smart Guides to center align each bulb's label with the bulb picture, and then align the labels at the bottom.
13. Group each bulb with its label, and then distribute the groups horizontally. Your finished slide should look similar to Figure 14-4.
14. **With your teacher's permission**, print slides 1 and 3.
15. Close the presentation, saving changes, and exit PowerPoint.

Figure 14-4

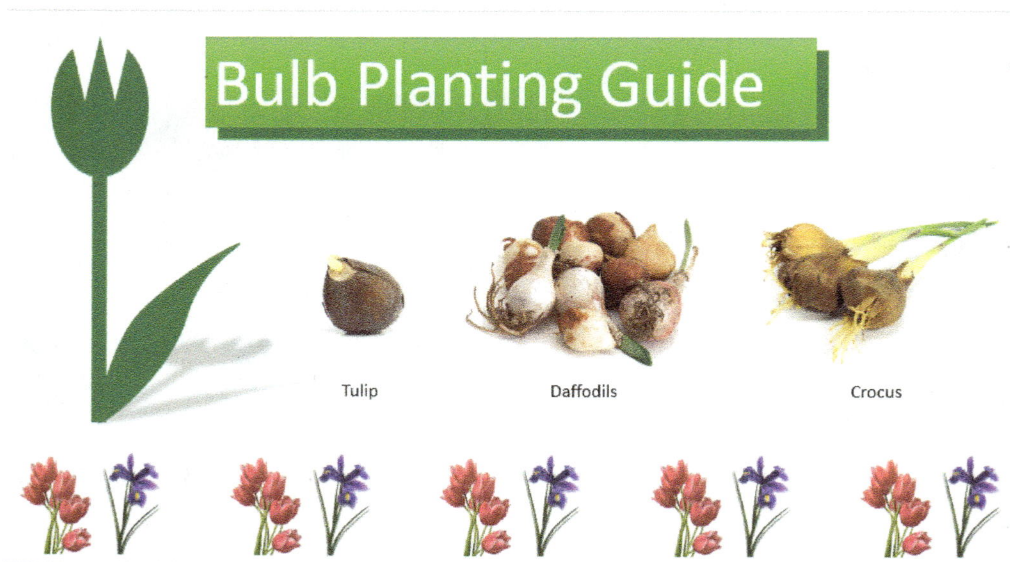

PowerPoint 2013, Windows 8, Microsoft Corporation

Lesson 15

Creating WordArt

➤ What You Will Learn

Understanding WordArt
Applying WordArt Styles to Existing Text
Inserting and Formatting WordArt

Software Skills WordArt enables you to apply special effects to text to make it appear more graphical. Using WordArt you can create logos and decorative text without a stand-alone graphics program.

WORDS TO KNOW

WordArt
Text that is formatted with graphical effects.

What You Can Do

Understanding WordArt

- Use **WordArt** to create a graphic from text. WordArt is useful whenever you want text to be both readable and decorative.
- WordArt is similar to drawn shapes in the ways you can format it. For example, you can apply a fill, an outline, and various formatting effects and styles to it. This formatting is the same as it is with shapes, which you learned about in the previous two lessons.
- The Transform command is unique to WordArt. It modifies the shape of the text to make it conform to a path. Figure 15-1 shows two Transform options applied to WordArt objects.

Figure 15-1

PowerPoint 2013, Windows 8, Microsoft Corporation

Applying WordArt Styles to Existing Text

- Any text can be easily turned into WordArt. Select any existing text, and then on the DRAWING TOOLS FORMAT tab, use the WordArt Styles group's commands and lists to select the effects that you want.

Try It! Applying WordArt Styles to Existing Text

1. Start a new blank presentation, and save it as **P15Try_xx** in the location where your teacher instructs you to store the files for this lesson.
2. Click HOME > Layout > Blank to change to a blank layout.
3. Click INSERT > Text Box.
4. Click on the slide, and type **Lowe Insurance**.
5. Press CTRL + A to select all the text.
6. Click the DRAWING TOOLS FORMAT tab.
7. Click the More button in the WordArt Styles group to open the WordArt Styles gallery.
8. Click the second style from the left in the second row from the top, Gradient Fill - Blue, Accent 1, Reflection.
9. Click the text box containing the WordArt.
10. Click the More button in the WordArt Styles group to open the WordArt Styles gallery.
11. Click Clear WordArt.
12. Save the **P15Try_xx** file, and leave it open to use in the next Try It.

Select a WordArt style

PowerPoint 2013, Windows 8, Microsoft Corporation

Inserting and Formatting WordArt

- You can also use the WordArt command to create a new WordArt object and then type the desired text in the object.
- Styles and colors available in the WordArt gallery depend on the current theme. If you change the theme after inserting WordArt, the colors and formatting will change to reflect the styles for the new theme.
- Use the tools in the WordArt Styles group to format the WordArt graphic by changing text fill and text outline and by applying text effects.
- You can also use the Format Shape task pane to modify WordArt formats.

Try It! Inserting WordArt

1. In the P15Try_xx file, click INSERT > WordArt . A palette of WordArt samples appears.

   ✓ *These samples are the same as the ones that appeared in the WordArt Styles list you saw in the preceding steps.*

2. Click the third sample in the fourth row.

   ✓ *A WordArt object appears, with generic text. The text is highlighted, so if you type something, it will be replaced.*

3. Type **Apex Industries**. Your text replaces the generic text.

4. Save the P15Try_xx file, and leave it open to use in the next Try It.

Try It! Formatting WordArt

1. In the P15Try_xx file, with the WordArt object selected, click DRAWING TOOLS FORMAT > Text Effects > Transform. A gallery of transformation options appears.

2. In the Warp section, click the first sample in the second row (Chevron Up).

3. Drag the pink handle at the left edge of the WordArt down as far as it will go.

   ✓ *The WordArt shape is further transformed.*

4. With the insertion point in the WordArt, press CTRL + A to select all the text.

   ✓ *If you do not select all the text, the formatting applies only to the word where the insertion point was.*

5. Click DRAWING TOOLS FORMAT > Text Fill . A palette of colors appears.

6. Click the Light Blue square in the Standard Colors section.

7. Click DRAWING TOOLS FORMAT > Text Outline . A palette of colors appears.

8. Click the Blue square in the Standard Colors section.

9. Click DRAWING TOOLS FORMAT > Text Outline .

10. Point to the Weight command. A submenu appears.

11. Click the solid 1½ point line.

12. Right-click the text and click Format Text Effects to open the Format Shape task pane with text options selected.

13. Click the SHADOW heading to expand it.

14. Click the Presets button, and then click the first shadow in the Perspective section.

15. Click DRAWING TOOLS FORMAT > Text Effects > Bevel.

16. Click the fourth sample in the third row of the Bevel section (Art Deco).

17. In the Format Shape task pane, click 3-D ROTATION, if necessary, to expand the options.

18. Click the Presets button, and then click the fourth sample in the second row of the Parallel section (Off Axis 2 Left). Close the Format Shape task pane.

19. Click away from the WordArt object to deselect it. It should look like the following figure.

20. Close the P15Try_xx file, saving changes, and exit PowerPoint.

The transformed WordArt object

PowerPoint 2013, Windows 8, Microsoft Corporation

The finished WordArt object

PowerPoint 2013, Windows 8, Microsoft Corporation

Lesson 15—Practice

In this project, you use WordArt to create a simple logo for Kelly Greenery.

DIRECTIONS

1. Start PowerPoint, if necessary, and open **P15Practice** from the data files for this lesson.
2. Save the presentation as **P15Practice_xx** in the location where your teacher instructs you to store the files for this lesson.
3. Click **INSERT** > **Text Box**. Click at the bottom of the slide and type your full name.
4. Click **INSERT** > **WordArt** and click the third sample in the second row.
5. Type **Kelly Greenery**.
6. Drag the WordArt so that the last letter overlaps the trunk of the tree graphic.
7. Press CTRL + A to select all the text.
8. Click **DRAWING TOOLS FORMAT** > **Text Fill** and click the Light Green square in the Standard Colors section.
9. Click **DRAWING TOOLS FORMAT** > **Text Outline** and click **No Outline**.
10. Click **DRAWING TOOLS FORMAT** > **Text Effects** > **Transform** and click the first sample in the fifth row of the Warp section (Wave 1).
11. Click the WordArt, hold down CTRL, and click the clip art.
12. Click **DRAWING TOOLS FORMAT** > **Group** > **Group**. Your slide should look like Figure 15-2.
13. **With your teacher's permission**, click **FILE** > **Print**. Select **Print All Slides**, and then click **Print** to print the presentation.
14. Close the presentation, saving changes, and exit PowerPoint.

Figure 15-2

Lesson 15—Apply

In this project, you use WordArt to create a different logo for Kelly Greenery.

DIRECTIONS

1. Start PowerPoint, if necessary, and open **P15Apply** from the data files for this lesson.
2. Save the presentation as **P15Apply_xx** in the location where your teacher instructs you to store the files for this lesson.
3. Insert a text box at the bottom of the slide, and type your full name in it.
4. Apply the Retrospect theme with the green variant to the presentation.
5. Insert WordArt that uses the fourth sample in the third row of the WordArt gallery.
6. Replace the placeholder text with **Kelly Greenery**.
7. Move the WordArt graphic above the oval picture, using Smart Guides to center the WordArt with the picture and align the bottom of the WordArt with the top of the picture.
8. Apply the **Arch Up** transformation from the Follow Path section of the **Text Effects** > **Transform** menu.
9. Use the Text Fill Eyedropper to pick up a green from the grass.
10. Use the Text Outline Eyedropper to pick up a yellow color from the flowers in the picture.
11. With the insertion point in the WordArt text, right-click and then click Format Text Effects. Expand the SHADOW effects if necessary, click the Color button, and click Lime, Accent 1 from the theme colors to change the shadow color. Close the Format Shape task pane.
12. Change the font size of the WordArt text to **66**.
13. Increase the height of the WordArt frame to **3"** and the width to **5.5"** and then position the WordArt so it is arched over the clip art.
14. **With your teacher's permission**, print one copy of the slide. The finished logo is shown in Figure 15-3.
15. Close the presentation, saving changes, and exit PowerPoint.

Figure 15-3

PowerPoint 2013, Windows 8, Microsoft Corporation

Lesson 16

Creating SmartArt Diagrams

What You Will Learn

Creating a SmartArt Diagram
Adding, Removing, and Resizing Shapes in a Diagram
Reordering Diagram Content
Changing the Diagram Type
Changing the Color and Style of a Diagram
Creating Picture-Based SmartArt

WORDS TO KNOW

SmartArt
Professionally designed graphics that organize and display information in various graphic types such as lists, processes, or hierarchical displays.

SmartArt style
The shading and texture effects on the shapes used in the diagram.

Software Skills SmartArt enables you to combine graphics with text to present information in a much more interesting and attractive layout than a plain bulleted list provides.

What You Can Do

Creating a SmartArt Diagram

- **SmartArt** is a tool that enables you to place text in graphical containers that make it more interesting to read. These container graphics are specially designed to arrange items in conceptually relevant ways, such as in an organization chart, cycle diagram, or pyramid.
- You can insert a SmartArt graphic in a content slide layout, or you can add it without a placeholder using the SmartArt button on the INSERT tab. You can also, if desired, convert a list to a SmartArt graphic.
- Each SmartArt diagram has a fly-out text pane where you can edit its content. Click the arrow button to the left of the diagram to open the text pane. You can also enter text by typing directly in the shapes. (See Figure 16-1 on the next page.) Click in a shape to position the insertion point, and then type the desired text. Move to the next text placeholder by clicking the mouse on the shape.
- If you already have the text you need for the SmartArt diagram in another form, such as in a Word document, you can copy the text and paste it directly in a SmartArt shape.
- The SmartArt layout determines how text appears and aligns in the shapes. You can, if desired, adjust alignment as you would any text.

Figure 16-1

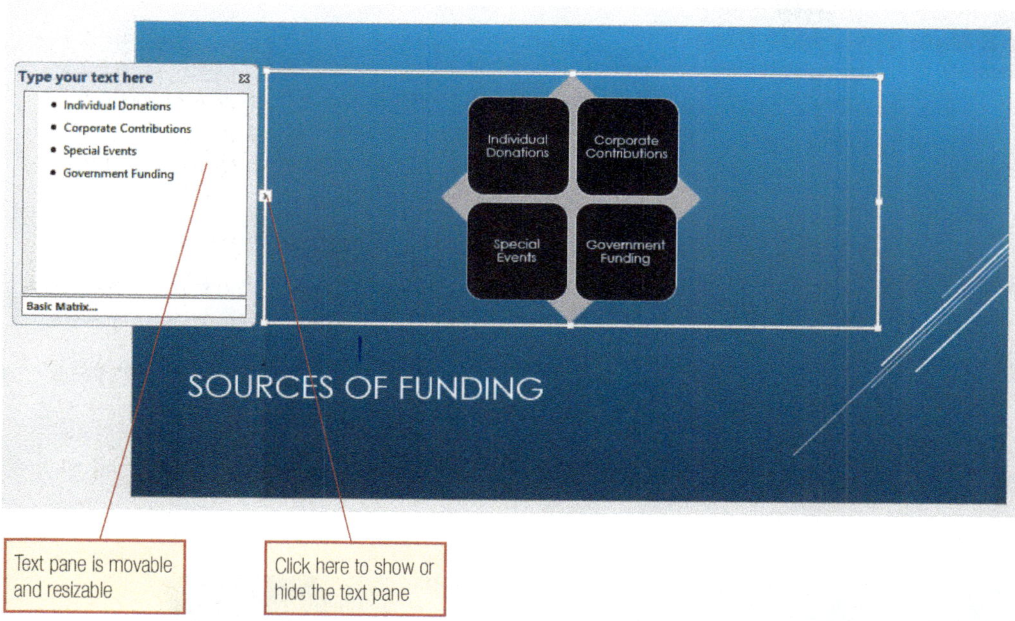

PowerPoint 2013, Windows 8, Microsoft Corporation

Try It! Converting a List to SmartArt

1. Start PowerPoint, and open **P16TryA** from the data files for this lesson.
2. Save the presentation as **P16TryA_xx** in the location where your teacher instructs you to store the files for this lesson.
3. Display slide 6. Click in the numbered list and press CTRL + A to select all the text.
4. Right-click the selected list and click Convert to SmartArt. A palette of samples appears.
5. Point to the Basic Timeline design (second design in the fourth row). The design is previewed behind the list.
6. Click the Continuous Block Process design (first design in the fourth row). The design is applied to the list.
7. Display slide 9. Click in the content area and press CTRL + A to select all the text.
8. Right-click the selected text and click Convert to SmartArt.
9. Click the Horizontal Bullet List (the first sample in the second row). The design is applied to the list.

   ✓ *Because this slide contained a multilevel bulleted list, the subordinate levels appear as bulleted lists within the main shapes.*
10. Save the **P16TryA_xx** file, and leave it open to use in the next Try It.

Try It! Inserting a New SmartArt Object

1. In the **P16TryA_xx** file, in the Thumbnail pane, click between slides 2 and 3 and press ENTER, inserting a new blank slide.
2. In the content area on the slide, click the Insert SmartArt Graphic icon. The Choose a SmartArt Graphic dialog box opens.
3. Click Matrix, and then click the Basic Matrix design (the first design).
4. Click OK. An empty diagram appears.
5. In the upper-left box, replace the [Text] placeholder with **Individual Donations**.
6. Replace the other three [Text] placeholders (going clockwise) with **Corporate Contributions**, **Government Funding**, and **Special Events**.

   ✓ *Notice that the text resizes automatically to fit.*
7. In the title placeholder at the bottom of the slide, type **SOURCES OF FUNDING**.
8. Save the **P16TryA_xx** file, and leave it open to use in the next Try It.

Fill in the placeholders on the new diagram

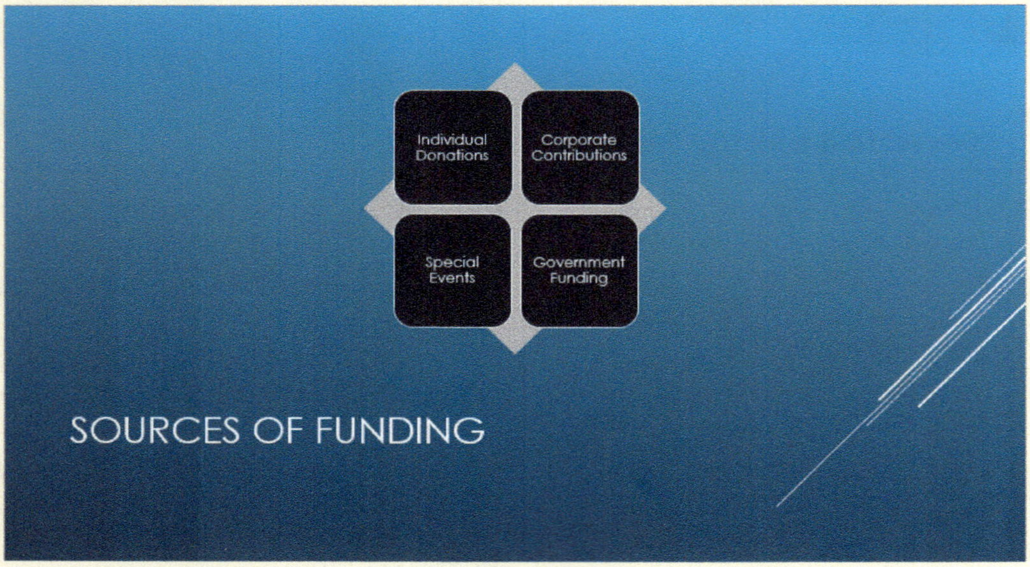

PowerPoint 2013, Windows 8, Microsoft Corporation

Adding, Removing, and Resizing Shapes in a Diagram

- Each diagram begins with a default number of shapes, but you can add or remove them as needed. Use the commands on the SMARTART TOOLS DESIGN tab.

  ✓ *There are some exceptions; some diagram types require a certain number of shapes in them. For such diagrams the Add Shape command is unavailable.*

- You can also resize each shape individually. Drag its selection handles to do so, just as you would any drawn shape. Instead of dragging, you can also use the Smaller or Larger buttons on the SMARTART TOOLS FORMAT tab.

Try It! Adding, Removing, and Resizing Shapes in a Diagram

1. In the **P16TryA_xx** file, on slide 7, select the last shape ("Follow up to assess progress").
2. Press DEL. The shape is removed and the other shapes resize to fill the space.
3. With the rightmost shape selected on the diagram on slide 7, click SMARTART TOOLS DESIGN > Add Shape. A new shape appears.

   ✓ *The Add Shape button has a down arrow you can click to choose where the new shape will be added, but you don't need it in these steps because you want the new shape in the default position, to the right of the selected shape.*
4. Click in the new shape and type the text that appeared in the deleted shape before ("Follow up to assess progress").
5. On slide 7, click the first rounded rectangle in the diagram to select it.
6. Hold down CTRL and click on each of the other rounded rectangles.
7. Position the mouse pointer on a top selection handle on any of the selected shapes and drag upward 0.5". The height of each of the rectangles changes equally.
8. Click SMARTART TOOLS FORMAT > Smaller. Then, click it again to make the shapes one more step smaller.
9. Save the **P16TryA_xx** file, and leave it open to use in the next Try It.

Reordering Diagram Content

- Even though each shape in a SmartArt diagram is individually movable, you should not drag shapes to reorder them in a SmartArt diagram, because it interrupts the automatic flow of the layout. Instead, you should use the reordering commands on the SMARTART TOOLS DESIGN tab.
- The Promote and Demote commands change the level of the text within the diagram hierarchy. This is like promoting and demoting list levels on a text-based layout.

Try It! Reordering Diagram Content

1. In the **P16TryA_xx** file, on slide 3, click the top left rounded rectangle to select it.
2. Click SMARTART TOOLS DESIGN > Move Down. The content of that shape is moved one position in the layout.

   ✓ *Notice that it moved to the right, and not literally down. In this case, down means to move it down in the flow one position, regardless of the direction of the flow. If the diagram's flow was top-to-bottom, moving "down" might even be up in the diagram.*
3. On slide 10, click in the *Get friends involved* bullet point in the second column.
4. Click SMARTART TOOLS DESIGN > Promote. That bullet point becomes a new shape.
5. Click SMARTART TOOLS DESIGN > Demote. The text goes back to being a bullet point in the second shape.
6. Click SMARTART TOOLS DESIGN > Right to Left. The diagram changes its flow direction, so that the right and left columns switch places.
7. Save the **P16TryA_xx** file, and leave it open to use in the next Try It.

Changing the Diagram Type

- There are many diagram types to choose from. If you don't like the diagram type you started with, you can easily switch to another.
- The diagram types are arranged in categories, but there is some overlap; some designs appear in more than one category.
- On the SMARTART TOOLS DESIGN tab, you can open a gallery of layouts and choose the one you want to apply to the diagram.

Try It! Changing the Diagram Type

1. In the **P16TryA_xx** file, click the SmartArt diagram on slide 10, if necessary.
2. On the SMARTART TOOLS DESIGN tab, in the Layouts group, click the More button to open the gallery of design samples.
3. Point at several different samples, and see previews of them on the slide, behind the open menu.
4. Click the Vertical Box List (last sample in the first row). The diagram changes to that layout.
5. Save the **P16TryA_xx** file, and leave it open to use in the next Try It.

Changing the Color and Style of a Diagram

- A SmartArt diagram's colors are determined by the color theme in use in the presentation. You can choose different combinations of those theme colors.
- **SmartArt style** refers to the shading and texture effects on the shapes used in the diagram. Some of the styles make the shapes look raised or shiny, for example.

Try It! Changing the Color and Style of a Diagram

1. In the **P16TryA_xx** file, click the SmartArt diagram on slide 10, if necessary.
2. On the SMARTART TOOLS DESIGN tab, click the More button in the SmartArt Styles group to open a gallery of style choices.
3. Click Polished (the first sample in the first row of the 3D section). It is applied to the diagram.
4. On slide 10, with the diagram still selected, click SMARTART TOOLS DESIGN > Change Colors . A palette of color presets appears.
5. Point to several of the presets, and see them previewed on the slide behind the open menu.
6. Click the fourth sample in the Colorful section. It is applied to the diagram.

   ✓ *The Colorful section's presets use a different color from the theme for each of the major shapes. Most of the other preset types stick to a single color.*
7. Save the **P16TryA_xx** file, and leave it open to use in the next Try It.

Creating Picture-Based SmartArt

- Some of the SmartArt layouts include picture placeholders. These are useful for providing small pieces of artwork, either to illustrate points being made in the text or as decoration.
- The main difference with this type of layout is that you have an extra step after inserting the SmartArt and typing the text—you must click each picture placeholder and select a picture to insert into it.
- In PowerPoint 2013, you can use the Picture Layout command on the PICTURE TOOLS FORMAT tab to convert any picture to a SmartArt graphic.

Try It! Creating Picture-Based SmartArt

1. In the **P16TryA_xx** file, on slide 5, select the picture and press DEL to remove the picture.
2. Select the bulleted list.
3. Right-click the bulleted list and click Convert to SmartArt > More SmartArt Graphics. The Choose a SmartArt Graphic dialog box opens.
4. Click the Picture category.
5. Click Picture Caption List (the third sample in the first row).
6. Click OK.
7. On the SmartArt diagram, double-click the Insert Picture from File icon in the leftmost picture placeholder. The Insert Pictures dialog box opens.
8. Next to From a file, click Browse and then navigate to the folder containing the files for this lesson.
9. Click **P16TryB_picture.jpg** and click Insert. The picture appears in the placeholder.
10. Using this same process, insert **P16TryC_picture.jpg** and **P16TryD_picture.jpg** in the other two placeholders on the slide.
11. Save the **P16TryA_xx** file, and leave it open to use in the next Try It.

Try It! Creating SmartArt from a Picture

1. In the **P16TryA_xx** file, display slide 11 and click the picture to select it.
2. Click the PICTURE TOOLS FORMAT tab, and then, in the Picture Styles group, click the Picture Layout button.
3. Click the Snapshot Picture List layout (the second from the right in the first row).
4. On the SMARTART TOOLS DESIGN tab, in the Create Graphic group, click the Text Pane button to display the Text pane.
5. Type **You Can Make a Difference**, and then press ENTER.
6. Click the Demote button, and then type the following entries, pressing ENTER after the first two items:
   People need help
   Organizations need volunteers
   Sign up today!
7. Close the Text pane. Click the outer border of the SmartArt diagram.
8. On the SMARTART TOOLS FORMAT tab, click the Size button, if necessary, and click in the Height box and type **4.8"**; click in the Width box and type **9.5"**.
9. Close the **P16TryA_xx** file, saving changes, and exit PowerPoint.

Picture used to create a SmartArt graphic

PowerPoint 2013, Windows 8, Microsoft Corporation

Lesson 16—Practice

In the Wynnedale Medical Center presentation, most of the information is presented in bulleted lists. In this project, you will convert two of those lists to SmartArt for a more interesting and graphical presentation.

DIRECTIONS

1. Start PowerPoint, if necessary, and open **P16Practice** from the data files for this lesson.
2. Save the presentation as **P16Practice_xx** in the location where your teacher instructs you to store the files for this lesson.
3. Display slide 1, and click **INSERT** > **Text Box**. Click at the top of the slide and type your full name.
4. On slide 4, click in the content area and press CTRL + A to select all.
5. Right-click the selection and point to **Convert to SmartArt**.
6. Click **More SmartArt Graphics**, and in the Choose a SmartArt Graphic dialog box, click the **Relationship** category.
7. Click the **Opposing Ideas** diagram and click **OK**.
8. On the **SMARTART TOOLS DESIGN** tab, click the **More** button in the SmartArt Styles group to open the SmartArt Styles gallery.
9. Click **Intense Effect** (the last sample in the Best Match for Document section).
10. Display slide 6, right-click in the list, and point to **Convert to SmartArt**.
11. Click **More SmartArt Graphics**, and then click the **Picture** category.
12. Click the **Vertical Picture List** diagram and then click **OK**.
13. Click in each of the picture placeholders and insert clip art pictures that relate to money.
14. On the SMARTART TOOLS DESIGN tab, click the **Change Colors** button, and select **Colorful Range - Accent Colors 3 to 4**. Then apply the **Intense Effect** SmartArt Style.
15. Preview the presentation to see the new diagrams in place.
16. **With your teacher's permission**, print one copy of the presentation as handouts, 6 slides per page.
17. Close the presentation, saving changes, and exit PowerPoint.

Lesson 16—Apply

In this project, you continue to work with the Wynnedale presentation. You convert several more lists to SmartArt graphics and then format them to add eye-catching visual interest.

DIRECTIONS

1. Start PowerPoint, if necessary, and open **P16Apply** from the data files for this lesson.
2. Save the presentation as **P16Apply_xx** in the location where your teacher instructs you to store the files for this lesson.
3. Place a text box containing your full name at the top of slide 1.
4. On slide 4, convert the bulleted list to the Vertical Block List SmartArt design.

   ✓ *You can determine a sample's name by hovering the mouse over it.*
5. Change the SmartArt Style to **Intense Effect**.
6. Change the colors to the first sample in the Colorful section of the color list. Figure 16-2 on the next page shows the finished slide.

7. On slide 5, change the colors for the SmartArt to the **Colored Fill** colors in the Accent 3 section of the color list.
8. On slide 9, convert the numbered list to the **Staggered Process** SmartArt.

   ✓ *You will need to open the Choose a SmartArt Graphic dialog box to find this design. After right-clicking the list, choose More SmartArt Graphics, and then look in the Process category.*
9. Change the colors for the diagram to the third sample in the Colorful section of the color list.
10. Change the SmartArt Style to **Polished** (the first sample in the 3D section of the SmartArt Styles gallery). Figure 16-3 shows the finished slide.
11. Preview the presentation, noticing how the SmartArt diagrams add more visual interest to the slides.
12. **With your teacher's permission**, print one copy of the presentation as handouts, 6 slides per page.
13. Close the presentation, saving changes, and exit PowerPoint.

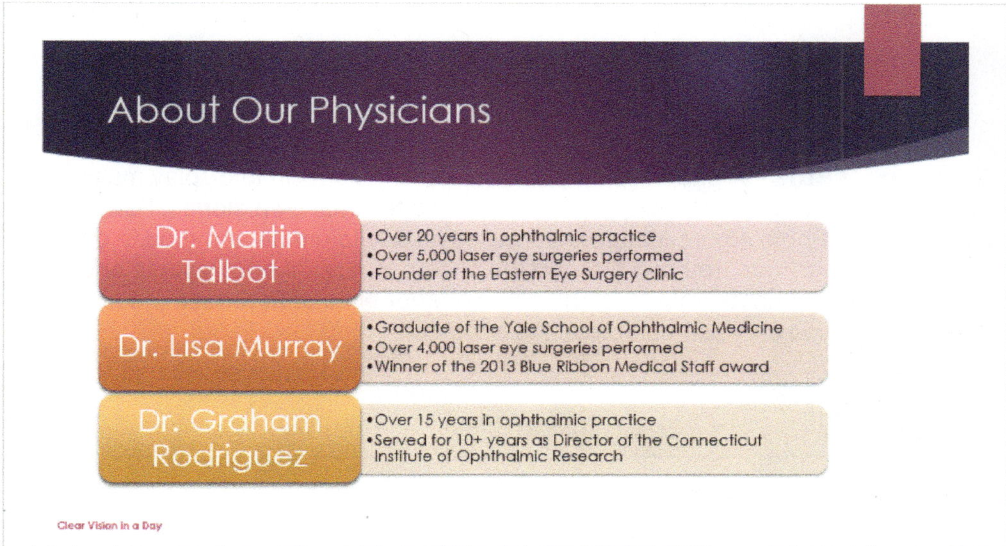

Figure 16-2

PowerPoint 2013, Windows 8, Microsoft Corporation

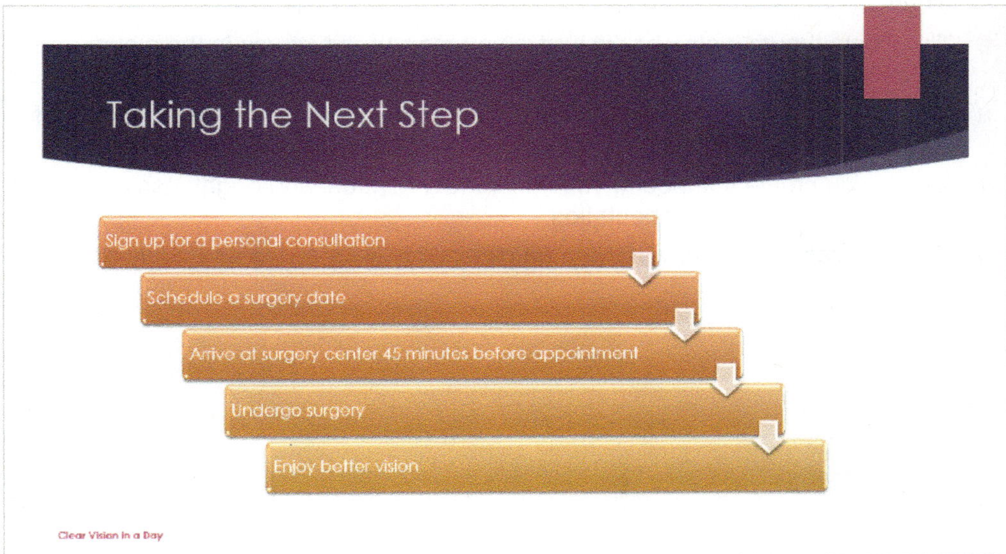

Figure 16-3

PowerPoint 2013, Windows 8, Microsoft Corporation

Lesson 17

Creating a Photo Album

➤ What You Will Learn

Creating a Photo Album
Editing a Photo Album
Adding Text and Captions
Compressing Pictures

WORDS TO KNOW

Photo album
A special type of presentation in which the main point is to display photos.

Resolution
The number of dots or pixels per linear unit of output.

Software Skills A photo album presentation enables you to display multiple photographs with very little text, to let the pictures tell their own stories. PowerPoint has a special Photo Album feature that makes it easy to create and modify photo albums in PowerPoint. You can arrange the photos in a number of layouts and apply enhancements such as frames, captions, and other effects. To reduce the size of a presentation, you can also compress the pictures.

What You Can Do

Creating a Photo Album

- A **photo album** presentation doesn't have placeholders for bulleted lists or other text; it is designed to efficiently display and organize photos.
- Use the Photo Album dialog box to import and arrange the pictures for the photo album.
- The Photo Album dialog box is where you rearrange pictures in the album and select settings for the way the pictures will display.
- Selected picture file names display in the Pictures in album list in the center of the dialog box. The currently selected picture displays in the Preview area.
- Before you create the album, you can correct contrast and brightness and rotate images to change their orientation.
- You can also choose how to arrange pictures on your slides and apply frame styles.

Try It! Creating a Photo Album

1. Start PowerPoint. Create a new, blank presentation.
2. Click INSERT > Photo Album. The Photo Album dialog box opens.
3. Click the File/Disk button. The Insert New Pictures dialog box opens.
4. Navigate to the location where data files for this lesson are stored and click **P17TryA_picture.jpg**.
5. Hold down the CTRL key and click **P17TryB_picture**, **P17TryC_picture**, **P17TryD_picture**, and **P17TryE_picture**.
6. Click Insert. The file names appear on the Pictures in album list.
7. Click the check box for **P17TryC_picture** on the list, and then click the Decrease Brightness button.
8. Open the Picture layout drop-down list and click 2 pictures.
9. Open the Frame shape drop-down list and click Rounded Rectangle.
10. Click Create. The photo album is created in a new presentation file.
11. On slide 1,change the subtitle to include your full name, if necessary.
12. Save the presentation as **P17Try_xx** in the location where your teacher instructs you to store the files for this lesson, and leave it open to use in the next Try It.

Editing a Photo Album

- You can edit an existing photo album by displaying it in Normal view and then clicking the down arrow on the Photo Album button. Choosing Edit Photo Album opens the Photo Album dialog box.
- You can adjust the order of pictures, add a picture, or remove a selected picture.
- You can also change the appearance of your album by changing the theme and variant to provide a different background for the pictures.
- After you make changes, click the Update button to apply your changes to the album.

Try It! Editing a Photo Album

1. In the **P17Try_xx** file, click INSERT > Photo Album down arrow.
2. Click Edit Photo Album.
3. Click the check box for the **P17TryE_picture** in the Pictures in album list.
4. Click the Move Up button four times to move it to the top of the list.
5. Clear the check mark from **P17TryE_picture**.
6. Click the check box for **P17TryA_picture** on the list, and click Remove to remove the item from the album.
7. Click the Frame shape down arrow and click Center Shadow Rectangle from the list.
8. Click the Browse button to the right of the Theme box. The Choose Theme dialog box displays.
9. Click Retrospect and click Select.
10. In the Edit Photo Album dialog box, click Update.
11. Save the **P17Try_xx** file, and leave it open to use in the next Try It.

(continued)

Try It! Editing a Photo Album *(continued)*

Use the Edit Photo Album dialog box to edit an album

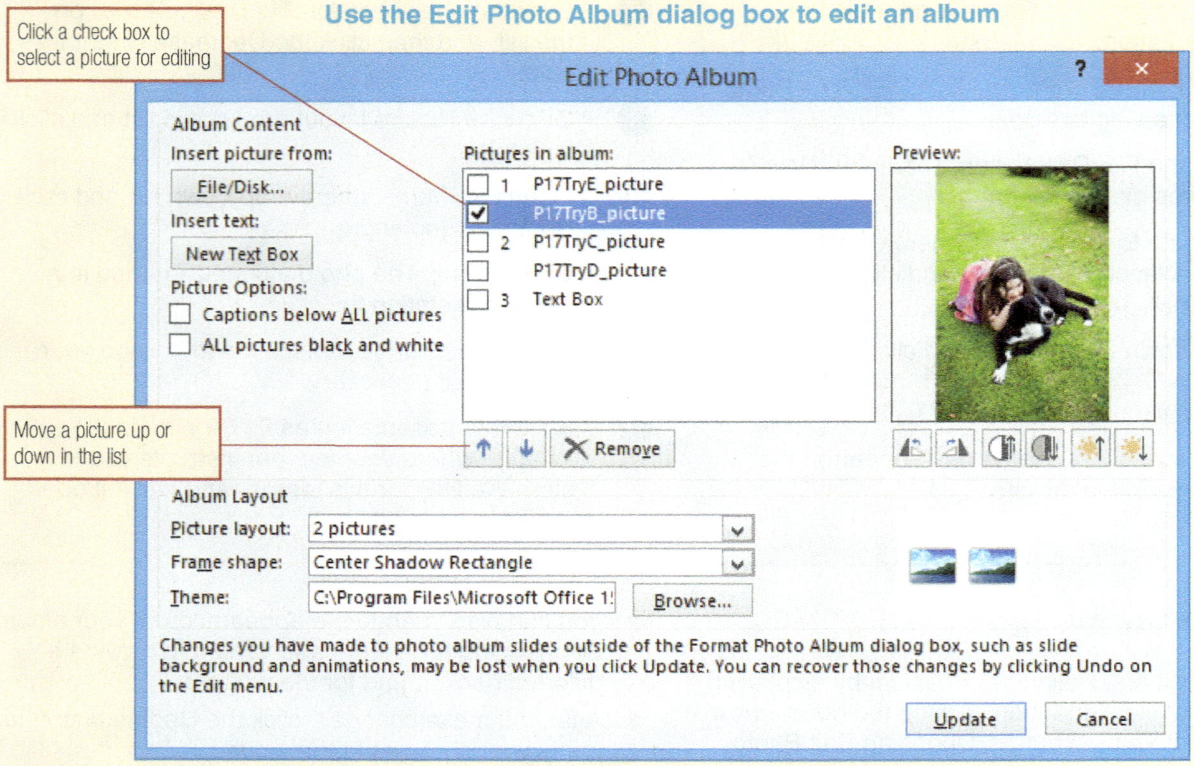

PowerPoint 2013, Windows 8, Microsoft Corporation

Adding Text and Captions

- A PowerPoint photo album is just like a physical photo album in that it is designed primarily to showcase images, but you also can add text in the form of captions or text boxes.
- The Picture Options check boxes in the Photo Album dialog box allow you to add a caption to each picture or transform all pictures to black and white.
- By default, PowerPoint uses a picture's file name as its caption, but you can replace these captions with more descriptive ones on the slides.
- You can choose to add a text box to the list of pictures. Text boxes display according to the current picture layout, at the same size as the pictures.
- PowerPoint might insert a text box placeholder for you, if you choose a layout that requires more images on a slide than you've included in your album. You can remove this text box placeholder if you don't need it, just as you would remove any picture.

Try It! Adding Text and Captions

1. In the **P17Try_xx** file, click the INSERT > Photo Album down arrow, and click Edit Photo Album.
2. In the Edit Photo Album dialog box, with the **P17TryE_picture** highlighted, click the New Text Box button in the Album Content area.

   ✓ *If the check box to the left of P17TryE_picture is selected, deselect it before you take the next step.*
3. Click the check boxes for Text Box and 4 Text Box, and then click Remove.
4. Select Captions below ALL Pictures.
5. Click Update and select slide 2.
6. Select the words *Text Box* on slide 2 and type **Friends for Life**.
7. Select the caption below the picture on slide 2.
8. Type **Two big smiles**.
9. Save the **P17Try_xx** file, and leave it open to use in the next Try It.

Compressing Pictures

- A photo album—or any presentation that contains pictures, movies, or sounds—can turn into a large file that may be a challenge to store or take extra time to open.
- To streamline a presentation's file size, use the Compress Pictures option on the PICTURE TOOLS FORMAT tab to open the Compress Pictures dialog box.
- By default, PowerPoint will compress all pictures in the presentation. If you want to compress only a single picture, click the Apply only to this picture check box.

✓ *Note that by default PowerPoint compresses pictures automatically when the file is saved.*

- The Target output settings allow you to choose a **resolution** appropriate for the way the pictures will be viewed. Measurements for the resolution are given in ppi, pixels per inch.
- Document resolution is chosen by default, but you can change the setting for screen or e-mail output.
- If you have cropped pictures to hide areas you don't want to see, you can also choose to delete the cropped portions of the pictures. Keep in mind, of course, you cannot go back and uncrop a picture if you have deleted the cropped areas.

Try It! Compressing Pictures

1. In the **P17Try_xx** file, click FILE > Info and note the size of the file in the Properties pane on the right of the window.
2. Click the Back button and select the picture on slide 2.
3. Click PICTURE TOOLS FORMAT > Compress Pictures.
4. Deselect Apply only to this picture in the Compression options area.
5. Select E-mail (96 ppi) in the Target output area.
6. Click OK.
7. Click FILE > Save and then click FILE > Info. Note that the file size in the Properties pane on the right of the window has been reduced significantly.
8. Close the **P17Try_xx** file, saving changes, and exit PowerPoint.

Compress Pictures dialog box

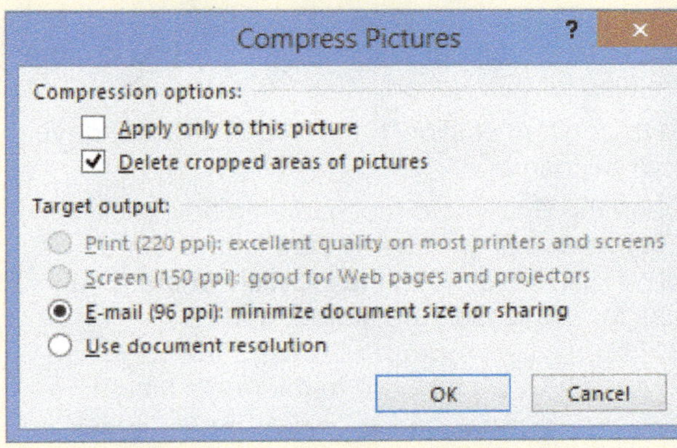

PowerPoint 2013, Windows 8, Microsoft Corporation

Lesson 17—Practice

Orchard School, a small private school in your area, has asked you to help create a photo album of pictures to market the school to local families. You will use the pictures you have been given so far to start the album.

DIRECTIONS

1. Start PowerPoint, if necessary. Create a new, blank presentation.
2. Click **INSERT** > **Photo Album**. The Photo Album dialog box opens.
3. Click the **File/Disk** button. The Insert New Pictures dialog box opens.
4. Navigate to the location where data files for this lesson are stored and click **P17PracticeA_picture.jpg**.
5. Hold down the CTRL key and click **P17PracticeB_picture.jpg**.
6. Click **Insert**.
7. Open the **Picture layout** drop-down list and click **1 picture**.
8. Click the **Browse** button next to the Theme text box.
9. Click the **Organic** theme, and click **Select**.
10. Click **Create**. A new presentation is created.
11. On slide 1, change the subtitle to your full name, if necessary.
12. Save the presentation as **P17Practice_xx** in the location where your teacher instructs you to store the files for this lesson.
13. Preview your presentation to see the album pictures in place.
14. **With your teacher's permission**, print one copy of the presentation as handouts, 6 slides per page.
15. Close the presentation, saving changes, and exit PowerPoint.

Lesson 17—Apply

In this project, you complete the photo album for Orchard School by adding more slides, modifying album formats, and finally compressing pictures so you can e-mail the album to your client.

DIRECTIONS

1. Start PowerPoint, if necessary, and open **P17ApplyA** from the data files for this lesson.
2. Save the presentation as **P17ApplyA_xx** in the location where your teacher instructs you to store the files for this lesson.
3. At the bottom of slide 1, insert a text box and type your full name.
4. Open the Edit Photo Album dialog box, click **P17PracticeB_picture** in the Pictures in album list, navigate to the location where data files for this lesson are stored, and add **P17ApplyB_picture.jpg** through **P17ApplyG_picture.jpg** to the photo album.
5. Move the **P17PracticeA_picture** photo to the bottom of the list.
6. Remove **P17ApplyF_picture**.
7. Choose a picture layout of 2 pictures per slide.
8. Change the frame shape to Soft Edge Rectangle.
9. Insert a text box after the last picture in the list.
10. Change the theme to Ion.
11. Update the photo album.
12. Click in the text box on slide 5 and type **We Grow Greatness!**
13. Compress all pictures and select E-mail resolution.
14. Preview your presentation to see the pictures in the album.
15. **With your teacher's permission**, print one copy of the presentation as handouts, 6 slides per page.
16. Close the presentation, saving changes, and exit PowerPoint.

End-of-Chapter Activities

➤ PowerPoint Chapter 2—Critical Thinking

Using the Internet Wisely

Your company, Tech for All, is frequently asked to provide information to students and businesspeople about how to use the Internet safely and intelligently. You have been asked to put together a presentation on smart, safe Internet use that can be delivered to a broad audience.

In this project, working alone or in teams, you will research several issues related to smart Internet use and create the presentation. You will include a minimum of 8 slides covering the following topics:

Understanding Internet addresses; evaluating Web site security and integrity; understanding information privacy and the pros and cons of using social media; using information technology ethically; explaining the legal and illegal use of the Internet and Internet content; and describing netiquette and how it applies to the use of e-mail, social networking, blogs, texting, and chatting.

DIRECTIONS

Content for Slide 1

1. Start a new presentation, and save it as **PCT02_xx** in the location where your teacher instructs you to store the files for this chapter.
2. Apply a theme and variant of your choice.
3. Insert the title **Using the Internet Wisely**, and in the subtitle placeholder, type **A Presentation by** and then insert your first and last name.
4. Adjust the size of the title to fit on one line, if necessary, and then apply WordArt styles and formatting of your choice.
5. Insert somewhere on slide 1 an online picture that relates to the Internet.
6. Format the picture:
   a. Crop the picture if necessary, and position it using Smart Guides to align it attractively with the title.
   b. Recolor the picture, or remove its background.
   c. Apply an artistic effect, if appropriate, or any other picture style or effect.
7. Tech for All often uses images of a lightning bolt striking a cloud as a symbol of bringing the light of knowledge to uncertainty. Create a logo for Tech for All as follows:
   a. Use lightning bolt and cloud shapes from the Shapes gallery to create the graphic portion of the logo. Rotate shapes if necessary and adjust sizes and positions so the bolt is striking the cloud.
   b. Apply fill and outline formats as desired, and apply shape effects to customize the shapes.
   c. Insert a text box that contains the text **Tech for All**. Format the text box with a Quick Style, then position it under the cloud graphic. Group all logo shapes, and position the logo in the lower-right corner of the slide.
8. Add a slide to the presentation with the title Sources. Use this slide to record the Web addresses of sites where you find information for the research you will be doing in the next part of the project.
9. Insert a footer that displays today's date, slide numbers, and your name on all slides except the title slide.

Completing the Presentation

1. **With your teacher's permission**, use the Internet to research the topics listed above. Use valid and reputable sites for your research, and copy site information to your Sources slide.
2. When your research is complete, organize your material into topics and plan how to use it in your presentation. You may use a storyboard if desired. Select slide layouts suitable for the type of information you find. Use numbered lists as appropriate. Use SmartArt diagrams to present some of the information in a more visual way. Add illustrations as desired, using online pictures or other graphics.
3. Each topic should be represented by at least one slide. Use additional slides to expand the topic as necessary.
4. Apply transitions to enhance the presentation's effectiveness.
5. Check spelling.
6. Preview the presentation and then make any necessary corrections and adjustments.
7. Deliver the presentation to your class. Ask for comments on how the presentation could be improved.
8. After making changes, print the presentation as handouts with 6 slides per page.
9. Close the presentation, saving changes, and exit PowerPoint.

➤ PowerPoint Chapter 2—Portfolio Builder

White River Restoration Project

The White River Restoration Society is recruiting new members to help with the cleanup and reforestation of some land they recently received as a donation. They have a basic presentation with all the text in it, but they need some graphics to make it more interesting. You will help them out by adding online pictures, shapes, SmartArt, and WordArt.

DIRECTIONS

1. Start PowerPoint, if necessary, and open **PPB02** from the data files for this chapter.
2. Save the presentation as **PPB02_xx** in the location where your teacher instructs you to store the files for this chapter.
3. At the bottom of slide 1, create a new text box and type the following:

   Copyright 2017 Friends of the White River – Student Name.
4. Insert a copyright symbol © after the word *Copyright*. Replace *Student Name* with your first and last name.
5. Format the text box as follows:
   - Format the text in the text box as 14-point and italic.
   - Apply a background fill to the text box that uses the palest shade of the light green theme color (the third color in the theme).
   - Align the text box at the horizontal center of the slide.
6. On slide 1, create a piece of WordArt with the text **White River Restoration Project**:
   - Start with the Dark Red filled sample (second sample in the first row).
   - Press ENTER after the word *River*, so the text appears on two lines.
   - Apply the **Arch Up** transformation (the first sample in the Follow Path section).
   - Size the WordArt to exactly **3"** high and **9"** wide.
   - Apply bold to the text, and then use Align Center to center the graphic on the slide.

7. On slide 1, create the logo shown in Illustration 2A:
   - Both shapes were drawn with the Shapes feature.
   - The pentagon is orange, and the banner is olive green.
   - Both have the **Preset 2** shape effect applied.
   - Type the text directly into the banner shape.
   - Group the shapes, and then use Smart Guides to center the group horizontally on the slide.
8. On slide 2, convert the bulleted list to the **Vertical Bullet List** SmartArt layout.
9. Apply the **Moderate Effect** SmartArt style to the SmartArt.
10. Change the color of the SmartArt to Colorful Range - Accent Colors 3 to 4.
11. On slide 4, in the empty content placeholder, insert an online picture of people canoeing on a river. Use Smart Guides to align the picture with the top of the bulleted text, if necessary.
12. From the **PICTURE TOOLS FORMAT** tab's **Picture Effects** menu, apply the Preset 5 settings to the canoe image.
13. On slide 5, in the empty content placeholder, insert an online picture that you find with the keywords **river pollution**. Align the picture with the top of the bulleted list to the right, and apply the same picture effect you applied on slide 4.
14. On slide 6, convert the bulleted list to a **Vertical Box List** SmartArt diagram.
15. On slide 7, remove the bullet characters from both paragraphs.
16. Preview the presentation, making any necessary adjustments, and then deliver the presentation to your class.
17. **With your instructor's permission**, print the presentation (6 slides per page).
18. Close the presentation, saving changes, and exit PowerPoint.

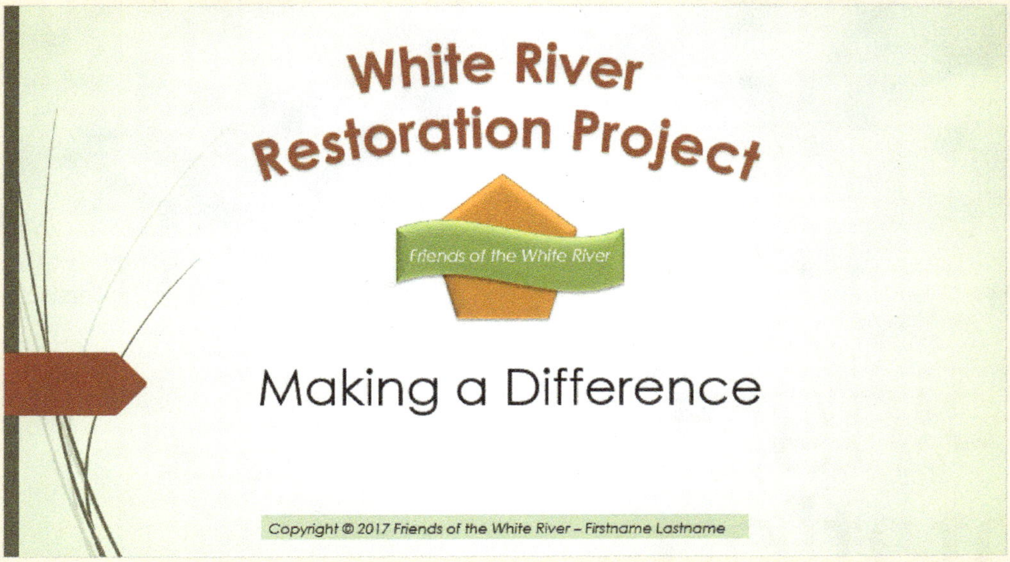

PowerPoint 2013, Windows 8, Microsoft Corporation

Illustration 2A

Chapter 3

(Courtesy Blend Images/Shutterstock)

Enhancing a Presentation

Lesson 18
Modifying a Theme

- Changing Background Style
- Changing Theme Colors
- Changing Theme Fonts
- Creating New Theme Fonts

Lesson 19
Modifying a Background

- Creating Slides from an Outline
- Hiding Background Graphics
- Applying a Background Fill Color
- Formatting a Slide Background with a Picture
- Resetting the Slide Background

Lesson 20
Animating Slide Objects

- Applying Animation Effects
- Setting Effect Options
- Changing the Order of Animation Effects
- Setting Animation Start and Timing Options
- Applying Animation Effects with Animation Painter
- Applying Animations to Objects, Charts, and Diagrams
- Changing or Removing an Animation

Lesson 21
Creating Multimedia Presentations

- Analyzing the Effectiveness of Multimedia Presentations
- Inserting a Video
- Modifying Video Appearance and Length
- Controlling a Video in a Presentation
- Inserting Sounds and Music

Lesson 22
Working with Tables

- Inserting a Table
- Formatting and Modifying a Table

Lesson 23
Working with Charts

- Inserting a Chart
- Formatting and Modifying a Chart

Lesson 24
Sharing a Presentation

- Packaging a Presentation for CD
- Presenting a Slide Show Online
- Creating a Video of a Presentation
- Publishing Slides

End-of-Chapter Activities

Lesson 18

Modifying a Theme

➤ What You Will Learn

Changing Background Style
Changing Theme Colors
Changing Theme Fonts
Creating New Theme Fonts

WORDS TO KNOW

Font
A set of characters with a specific size and style.

Software Skills You can change slide background style and theme colors and fonts to customize a presentation. You can also create new theme font combinations to easily apply in later presentations.

What You Can Do

Changing Background Style

- Each theme has a specific background color, and some have background graphics or other effects such as gradients—gradations from one color to another. Theme variants usually have the same graphics and background designs, but the base color may differ.
- To customize a theme, you can change the background style to one of the choices offered by the current theme, such as those shown in the Background Styles gallery. You display the Background Styles gallery from the Variants gallery on the DESIGN tab.
- Background styles use the current theme colors. You can apply a new style to all slides or to selected slides.
- As you rest your pointer on different background styles, the current slide shows what that background style will look like.
- If you want to make a more radical change to the background, click Format Background on the DESIGN tab to open the Format Background task pane where you can create a new background using a solid color, a gradient, a texture, or even a picture file.

Try It! Changing Background Style

1. Start PowerPoint, and open **P18Try** from the data files for this lesson.
2. Save the presentation as **P18Try_xx** in the location where your teacher instructs you to store the files for this lesson.
3. Select the words *Student Name* in the subtitle placeholder on slide 1 and type your name.
4. On the DESIGN tab, click the Variants More button and then click Background Styles.
5. Click Style 9 to apply it to all the slides in the presentation.
6. With slide 1 displayed, click the Variants More button, click Background Styles, and then right-click Style 10 in the gallery.
7. Click Apply to Selected Slides.
8. Save the **P18Try_xx** file, and leave it open to use in the next Try It.

Changing Theme Colors

- Each PowerPoint theme uses a palette of colors selected to work well together. Theme variants offer a different palette of colors. These colors are automatically applied to various elements in the presentation, such as the slide background, text, shape fills, and hyperlink text.
- To see different palettes of colors you can apply, click Colors on the Variants gallery. Some color palettes have theme names, such as Median and Slipstream, but most are organized in color families, such as Blue Green, Orange Red, or Violet.
- PowerPoint offers several ways to adjust theme colors:
  - If you like the layout and fonts of a particular theme but not its colors, you can choose a different color palette from the Colors gallery.
  - You can change one or more colors in the current theme to customize the theme.
- You modify theme colors in the Create New Theme Colors dialog box.
- Change a color by clicking the down arrow for a particular color to display a palette. Select a different tint or hue of a theme color, choose one of ten standard colors, or click More Colors to open the Colors dialog box and pick from all available colors.
- As soon as you change a theme color, the preview in the Create New Theme Colors dialog box also changes to show how your new color coordinates with the others in the theme.
- You can name a new color scheme and save it. It then displays in the Custom area at the top of the Theme Colors gallery. Custom colors are available to use with any theme.

✓ *You can delete custom theme colors by right-clicking the color palette set and selecting Delete.*

Try It! Changing Theme Colors

1. In the **P18Try_xx** file, select slide 2.
2. Click DESIGN > Variants > Colors to display the available color palettes.
3. Hover over several color themes. Live Preview shows you how the color theme will look on your slide.
4. Select the Slipstream theme.
5. Click DESIGN > Variants > Colors > Customize Colors.
6. In the Name box, type your name.
7. Click the down arrow for Accent 1.
8. Select Aqua, Followed Hyperlink, Darker 25% from the palette.

(continued)

Try It! Changing Theme Colors *(continued)*

9. Click Save.

10. Save the **P18Try_xx** file, and leave it open to use in the next Try It.

Create a new theme color

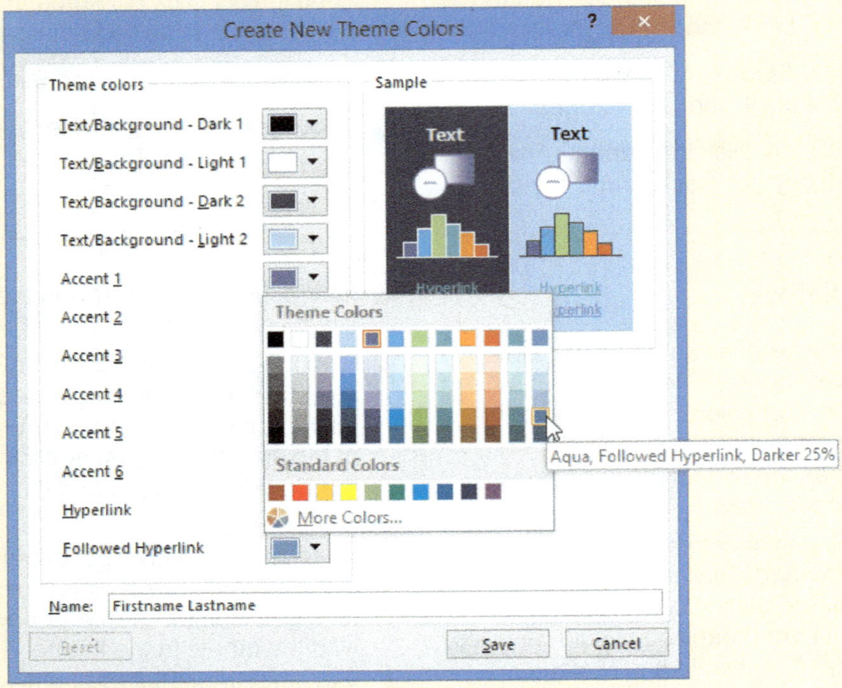

PowerPoint 2013, Windows 8, Microsoft Corporation

Changing Theme Fonts

- PowerPoint 2013 themes use a single **font** for all text on slides, including titles, lists, and text in text boxes.
- The Theme Fonts gallery lists other fonts you could use, organized by font name. Some choices on the Fonts gallery offer one font for headings and a different font for body text.

Try It! Changing Theme Fonts

1. In the **P18Try_xx** file, select slide 2.
2. Click DESIGN > Variants [▾] > Fonts [A].
3. Scroll through the available fonts.
4. Select Georgia.
5. Save the **P18Try_xx** file, and leave it open to use in the next Try It.

Creating New Theme Fonts

- If you do not find a font or set of fonts you like on the Fonts gallery, you can create your own theme fonts.
- Create new theme fonts in the Create New Theme Fonts dialog box. The Sample Preview window shows you the heading and body font as you select them.
- After you name your set of theme fonts, the set appears at the top of the Theme Fonts gallery in the Custom section.

✓ *You can delete custom theme fonts by right-clicking the font set and selecting Delete.*

Try It! Creating New Theme Fonts

1. In the **P18Try_xx** file, click DESIGN > Variants ▾ > Fonts A.
2. Click Customize Fonts.
3. Click the Heading font down arrow and select Tahoma.
4. Click the Body font down arrow and select Bookman Old Style.
5. Type your first and last name in the Name box, and then click Save.
6. Close the **P18Try_xx** file, saving changes, and exit PowerPoint.

Lesson 18—Practice

In this project, you work on a presentation for Medi-Ready Urgent Care. You want to explore how changing theme elements might improve the appearance of a presentation you have prepared for use at a community health and wellness event.

DIRECTIONS

1. Start PowerPoint, if necessary, and open **P18Practice** from the data files for this lesson.
2. Save the presentation as **P18Practice_xx** in the location where your teacher instructs you to store the files for this lesson.
3. Click at the end of the subtitle text, press ENTER, type **Presented by**, and then add your name.
4. Click **DESIGN** > **Variants** ▾ > **Fonts** A > **Franklin Gothic**.
5. Click **DESIGN** > **Variants** ▾ > **Background Styles**. The Background Styles gallery opens.
6. Select **Style 12** to apply the new background style to all slides.
7. Click **DESIGN** > **Variants** ▾ > **Colors** and select the **Yellow** theme colors.
8. Click **DESIGN** > **Variants** ▾ > **Colors** and click **Customize Colors**.
9. Click the **Accent 2** drop-down arrow and then click **Orange, Accent 2, Darker 25%**.
10. Type the name **Medi-Ready** in the Name box and click **Save**.
11. Scroll through all slides to see the changes.
12. **With your teacher's permission**, print slide 1. Your printout should look similar to Figure 18-1 on the next page.
13. Close the presentation, saving changes, and exit PowerPoint.

Figure 18-1

PowerPoint 2013, Windows 8, Microsoft Corporation

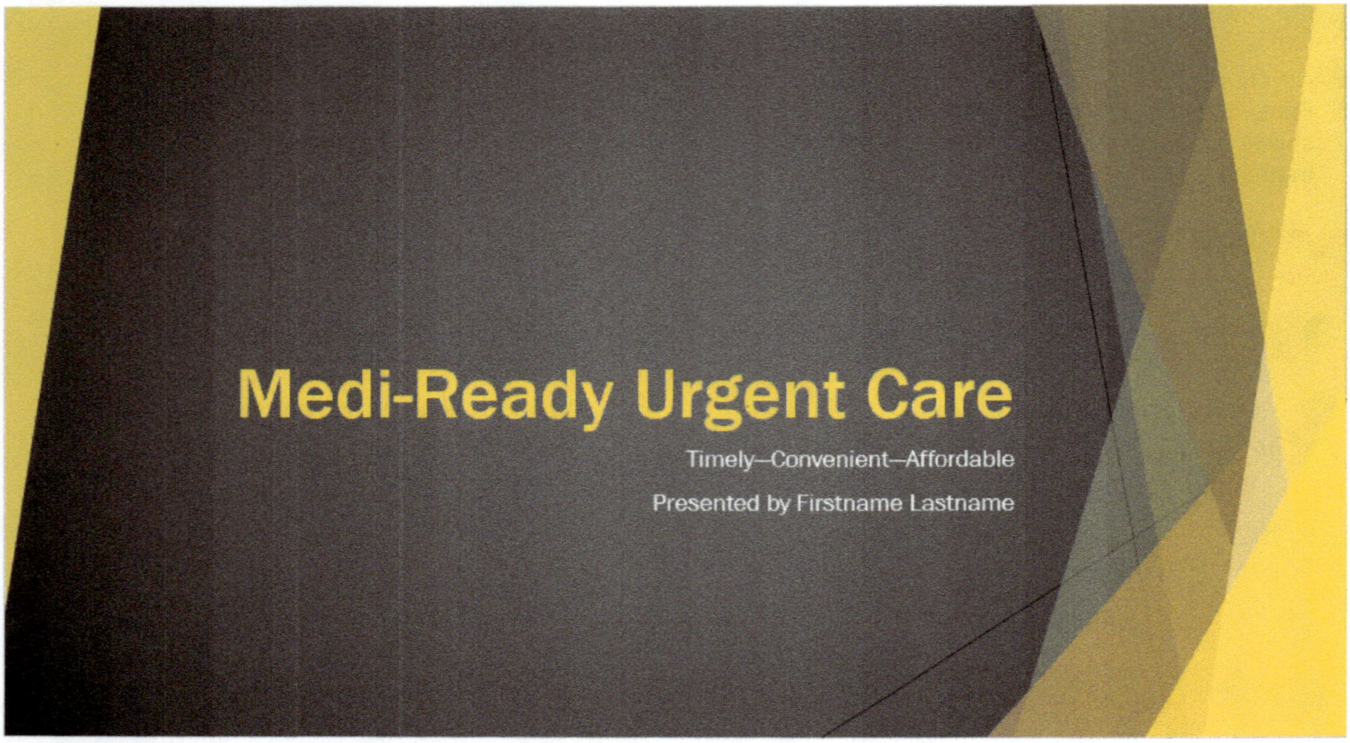

Lesson 18—Apply

In this project, you work with a different version of the Medi-Ready presentation. You customize theme fonts, adjust the background style, and apply new theme colors.

DIRECTIONS

1. Start PowerPoint, if necessary, and open **P18Apply** from the data files for this lesson.
2. Save the presentation as **P18Apply_xx** in the location where your teacher instructs you to store the files for this lesson.
3. Insert a text box on slide 1 that contains your first and last name, and format the text box with a shape style.
4. Apply the **Style 11** background style to all slides, and then apply **Style 9** to slide 1 only.
5. Change the theme colors to **Blue II**.
6. Customize the theme colors to change the Accent 2 color to **Dark Teal, Background 2, Lighter 60%**. Save the theme colors using your first and last name.
7. Create new theme fonts that use Calibri as the heading font and Bell MT as the body font. Save the theme fonts using your first and last name.
8. Preview the presentation to see the new theme formats in place.
9. **With your teacher's permission**, print all slides as handouts with 6 slides per page.
10. Delete any custom theme colors and fonts you created for this lesson.
11. Close the presentation, saving changes, and exit PowerPoint.

Lesson 19

Modifying a Background

➤ What You Will Learn

- Creating Slides from an Outline
- Hiding Background Graphics
- Applying a Background Fill Color
- Formatting a Slide Background with a Picture
- Resetting the Slide Background

Software Skills Word outlines can be readily imported to create slides. In some instances, you may want to hide the background graphics created as part of a theme. You can customize a slide background with a fill or a picture.

What You Can Do

Creating Slides from an Outline

- You can save time by reusing text created in other programs, such as Word, in your PowerPoint presentation.
- You can use Word to help you organize the contents of a presentation and then transfer that outline to PowerPoint.
- If you want to use a Word outline to create slides, you must format the text using Word styles that clearly indicate text levels.

  ✓ *For instance, text formatted with the Word Heading 1 style become slide titles. Text styled as Heading 2 or Heading 3 becomes bulleted items.*

- You have two options for using a Word outline to create slides:
  - You can simply open the Word document in PowerPoint to create the slides. Use this option to create a new presentation directly from outline content.
  - You can use the Slides from Outline command on the New Slide drop-down list to add slides to an existing presentation.

    ✓ *You cannot use this command unless a presentation is already open.*

- When a Word document is used to create a new presentation, the slides will display the same fonts and styles used in the document. These will not change even if a new theme or theme fonts are applied.
- If you want to change the fonts in a presentation created from an outline, you need to click the Reset button on the HOME tab.

✓ *You can also use this command to reverse changes made to slide layouts or themes.*

- The Reset function will delete the Word styles and apply the theme defaults for colors, fonts, and effects.

- Slides created from an outline may, in addition, be formatted with a layout called Title and Text. You can apply one of PowerPoint's default layouts such as Title and Content to make these slides more functional.

Figure 19-1

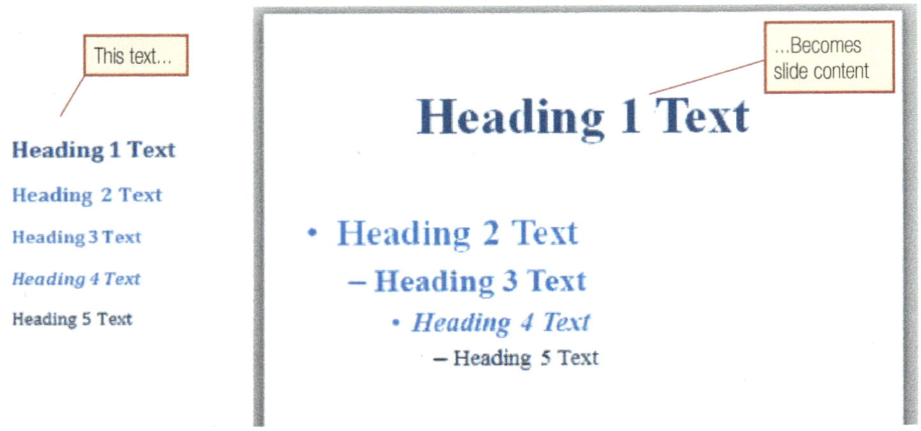

PowerPoint 2013, Windows 8, Microsoft Corporation

Try It! Creating Slides from an Outline

1. Start PowerPoint, click Open Other Presentations, and navigate to the location where the data files for this lesson are stored.
2. In the Open dialog box, click All PowerPoint Presentations and select All Files.
3. Select the Word document **P19TryA** and click Open.
4. Scroll through the presentation to see how the Word styles are applied to the slides.
5. Save the presentation as **P19TryA_xx** in the location where your teacher instructs you to store the files for this lesson.
6. Close the file.

Try It! Adding Slides from an Outline to an Existing Presentation

1. In PowerPoint, open **P19TryB** from the data files for this lesson.
2. Save the presentation as **P19TryB_xx** in the location where your teacher instructs you to store the files for this lesson.
3. Select slide 1 (the new slides will appear after this slide).
4. Click HOME > New Slide drop-down arrow.
5. Click Slides from Outline.
6. In the Insert Outline dialog box, navigate to the location where the data files for this lesson are stored and select **P19TryC**.
7. Click Insert.
8. Save the **P19TryB_xx** file, and leave it open to use in the next Try It.

Try It! Resetting a Slide

1. In the P19TryB_xx file, select slides 2–4 in the Thumbnail pane.
2. Click HOME > Reset.
3. Click HOME > Layout and click Title and Content.
4. Save the P19TryB_xx file, and leave it open to use in the next Try It.

Hiding Background Graphics

- Many themes include some type of graphics such as lines or shapes that form a part of the slide background.
- You can only select and modify theme background graphics in Slide Master view.

✓ *You will learn how to create and manipulate background graphics on slide masters in Lesson 25.*

- If you don't like these background graphics, you can hide them using the Format Background task pane.
- To open the Format Background task pane, click the Format Background button on the DESIGN tab.
- Remember that text colors are often chosen to contrast with the graphic background. If you hide the background graphic, the text colors might need to be changed so that they don't blend into the background.

Try It! Hiding Background Graphics

1. In the P19TryB_xx file, select slide 1.
2. Click DESIGN > Format Background to open the Format Background task pane.
3. Click the Hide background graphics check box in the FILL settings.
4. Save the P19TryB_xx file, and leave it open to use in the next Try It.

Applying a Background Fill Color

- Instead of changing the theme or variant in a presentation, you can change just the background color.
- You can apply a background fill color to one slide or to the entire presentation using the Format Background task pane.

Try It! Applying a Background Fill Color

1. In the P19TryB_xx file, click DESIGN > Format Background to display the Format Background task pane, if necessary.
2. With the Solid fill option selected, click the Color button.
3. Select Teal, Accent 6, Lighter 60%.
4. Click the Apply to All button at the bottom of the task pane.
5. Save the P19TryB_xx file, and leave it open to use in the next Try It.

(continued)

Try It! Applying a Background Fill Color *(continued)*

The Format Background dialog box

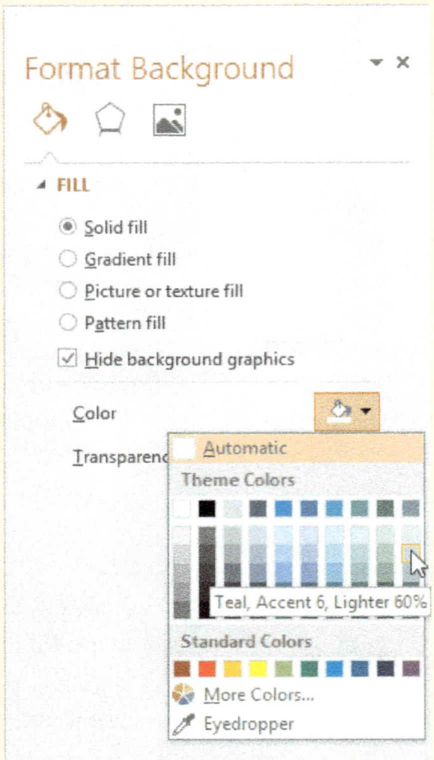

PowerPoint 2013, Windows 8, Microsoft Corporation

Formatting a Slide Background with a Picture

- Inserting a picture on your slide background adds interest and helps convey your message.
- You can format the background with a picture using the Format Background task pane.
- You can use online pictures or images stored on your system to add graphics to the slide background.

Try It! Formatting a Slide Background with a Picture

1. In the **P19TryB_xx** file, display slide 1, if necessary, and then click Format Background to display the Format Background task pane if it is not already open.
2. In the Format Background task pane, click Picture or texture fill.

   ✓ *Note that the background of the slide automatically changes to the first texture option.*
3. Click the Online button and type the keywords **helping hand** in the Bing Image Search box. Click the Search button.
4. Select the line drawing of clasping hands and click Insert.
5. Save the **P19TryB_xx** file, and leave it open to use in the next Try It.

Resetting the Slide Background

- Only changes made to individual slide backgrounds can be reset. If you apply a change to all the slides in a presentation, you cannot reverse the change using the Reset Background option.

✓ *You can, however, use the Undo button to reverse global changes.*

Try It! Resetting the Slide Background

1. In the P19TryB_xx file, with slide 1 displayed, click Format Background to display the Format Background task pane if it is not already open.
2. Click the Reset Background button at the bottom of the task pane. Notice that the slide background changes immediately to the solid color fill you applied to all slides.
3. Close the Format Background task pane.
4. Close the P19TryB_xx file, saving changes, and exit PowerPoint.

Lesson 19—Practice

Your client, Voyager Travel Adventures, has supplied you with files they want you to use in the presentation you're creating for them. You'll also add information on each slide to help identify and organize the presentation.

DIRECTIONS

1. Start PowerPoint, click **Open Other Presentations**, and navigate to the location where the data files for this lesson are stored.
2. In the Open dialog box, click **All PowerPoint Presentations** and select **All Files**.
3. Select the Word document **P19Practice** and click **Open**.
4. Save the presentation as **P19Practice_xx** in the location where your teacher instructs you to store the files for this lesson.
5. Click slide 1 in the Thumbnail pane, and then click CTRL + A to select all the slides.
6. Click **HOME** > **Reset**. Each slide will revert to the default formatting and placeholders.
7. Click slide 1, and then click **HOME** > **Layout** > **Title Slide**. Slide 1 changes to a Title Slide layout.
8. Select slides 2–4 in the Thumbnail pane, and then click **HOME** > **Layout** > **Title and Content**. Click slide 1.
9. On the **DESIGN** tab, click the **More** button to display the Themes gallery, and then click **Parallax**. The entire presentation changes to reflect the new Parallax theme.
10. Click **DESIGN** > **Format Background** > **Hide background graphics**. The graphics on the title slide disappear. Close the Format Background task pane.
11. Click **INSERT** > **Header & Footer**. The Header and Footer dialog box opens.
12. Select **Footer** and type your name. Click **Apply** to apply the footer to the title slide only.
13. Preview the presentation.
14. **With your teacher's permission**, print slide 1.
15. Close the presentation, saving changes, and exit PowerPoint.

Lesson 19—Apply

In this project, you add slides to another version of the Voyager presentation. You will modify slide backgrounds for a custom look.

DIRECTIONS

1. Start PowerPoint, if necessary, and open **P19ApplyA** from the data files for this lesson.
2. Save the presentation as **P19ApplyA_xx** in the location where your teacher instructs you to store the files for this lesson.
3. Insert the slides from the Word outline **P19ApplyB** at the end of the presentation and reset the slides.
4. Move slide 4 to be the first slide and apply Title Slide layout.
5. Apply the Title and Content layout to slides 5 and 6.
6. Move slide 5 to be slide 3.
7. Display slide 1. Use the Format Background task pane to change the background styles as follows:
   a. Click the Color button under the Gradient stops color bar and change the color to **White, Text 1**. Apply the change to all the slides.
   b. Use the file **P19ApplyC_picture.jpg** located in the data files for this lesson as a picture fill on the title slide.
   c. Hide the background graphics on slide 1.
   d. Change the font color of the slide title on slide 1 to Dark Blue, Background 2, Darker 25%.
8. Insert a date that updates automatically, slide numbers, and a footer that includes your name. Do not show this information on the title slide, but apply it to all other slides. Your presentation should look like Figure 19-2.
9. Spell check and preview the presentation.
10. **With your teacher's permission,** print the presentation as a 6 slides per page handout.
11. Close the presentation, saving changes, and exit PowerPoint.

Figure 19-2

PowerPoint 2013, Windows 8, Microsoft Corporation

Lesson 20

Animating Slide Objects

➤ What You Will Learn

Applying Animation Effects
Setting Effect Options
Changing the Order of Animation Effects
Setting Animation Start and Timing Options
Applying Animation Effects with Animation Painter
Applying Animations to Objects, Charts, and Diagrams
Changing or Removing an Animation

Software Skills PowerPoint allows you to add animations to make your slides more visually interesting during a presentation.

WORDS TO KNOW

Animate
To apply movement to text or an object to control its display during the presentation.

What You Can Do

Applying Animation Effects

- You can **animate** text and objects in a presentation to add interest or emphasize special points.
- Use the Animation gallery on the ANIMATIONS tab to apply animation effects organized in four categories: Entrance effects, Emphasis effects, Exit effects, and Motion Path effects.

Try It! Applying Animation Effects

1. Start PowerPoint, and open P20Try from the data files for this lesson.
2. Save the presentation as P20Try_xx in the location where your teacher instructs you to store the files for this lesson.
3. On slide 1, click the title placeholder.
4. On the ANIMATIONS tab, click the Animation More button and scroll down to see the Motion Paths effects.
5. Click Lines.
6. On slide 2, click the content placeholder.
7. On the ANIMATIONS tab, click the Fly In animation from the gallery.
8. Click the title placeholder.
9. On the ANIMATIONS tab, click Float In.
10. Save the P20Try_xx file, and leave it open to use in the next Try It.

Setting Effect Options

- The Effect Options button on the ANIMATIONS tab offers options for controlling the direction and sequence of the selected animation.
- Options on this gallery depend on the selected animation effect. You may have up to eight choices for the direction the animation will take.
- You can also select how the animation will control multiple objects. List items, for example, can be animated as one object or by paragraph, with each list item animated separately.

Try It! Setting Effect Options

1. In the **P20Try_xx** file, click the content placeholder on slide 2.
2. Click ANIMATIONS > Effect Options ↑.

   ✓ *The direction of the arrow on the button shows the direction selected most recently.*
3. Click From Left.
4. Click ANIMATIONS > Effect Options ↑.
5. Click By Paragraph if that option is not already selected.
6. Click the title placeholder on slide 2.
7. Click ANIMATIONS > Effect Options ↑ > Float Down.
8. Save the **P20Try_xx** file, and leave it open to use in the next Try It.

The Effect Options drop-down list

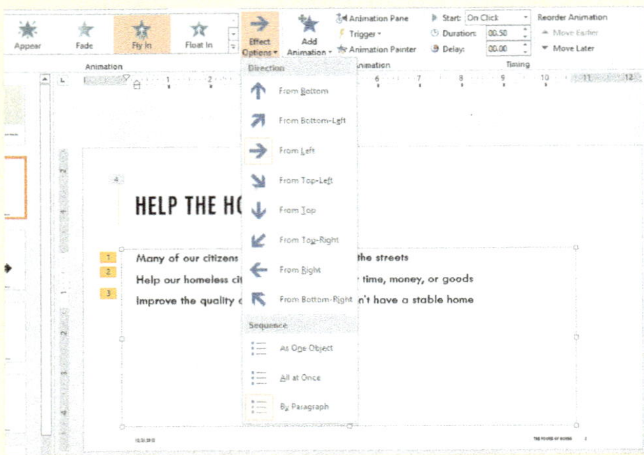

PowerPoint 2013, Windows 8, Microsoft Corporation

Changing the Order of Animation Effects

- If you want more control over animation effects, use the Animation Pane. The Animation Pane allows you to control the order in which animations occur as well as preview specific animation effects.
- When you add an effect, the object name and an effect symbol display in the Animation Pane. This list represents the order in which the effects take place when the slide is viewed.
- Each type of animation effect has its own symbol, such as a green star for entrance effects and a red star for exit effects.
- You can adjust the order in which effects take place using the up and down arrows near the top of the task pane.
- If the object you are animating has more than one line or part, such as a text content placeholder or a chart or diagram, a bar displays below the effect with a Click to expand contents arrow. Clicking the arrow displays all the parts of the object.
- Displaying the parts of the object allows you to animate each part with a different effect, or adjust the timing for the separate parts.
- When you have finished animating the parts, use the Click to hide contents arrow to collapse the effect and save room in the animation list.
- The Play button in the Animation Pane allows you to preview a selected animation to make sure it displays as you want it to.
- You can use the Preview button on the ANIMATIONS tab to preview all animations on a slide.

Try It! Changing the Order of Animation Effects

1. In the P20Try_xx file, on slide 2, click ANIMATIONS > Animation Pane.
2. In the Animation Pane, click Rectangle 1.
3. Click the up arrow near the top of the Animation Pane to move the title placeholder's animation effect above the content placeholder animation.
4. Click the content placeholder on the slide to select it, then click Effect Options and select From Bottom.
5. In the Animation Pane, click the Click to expand contents arrow in the bar below the Rectangle 2 item.
6. Click item 2 in the Animation Pane ("Many of our ...") and click the down arrow twice to move it to the bottom of the list.
7. Click item 3 and click the up arrow to move the item to the top of the list.
8. Click the Click to hide contents arrow to hide the list.
9. Click the Play Selected button in the Animation Pane to preview the selected animation.
10. Click ANIMATIONS > Preview Animations to preview all animations on the slide.
11. Save the P20Try_xx file, and leave it open to use in the next Try It.

Setting Animation Start and Timing Options

- The ANIMATIONS tab contains Start, Duration, and Delay options for controlling the timing of your animations.
  - The Start setting is On Click by default. You can adjust this setting to After Previous, to occur automatically after the previous event, or With Previous, to occur at the same time as the previous effect.
  - Use the Duration setting to adjust the speed of the animation.
  - Use the Delay setting to specify the amount of time that must elapse before the animation starts.
- Some animations allow you to change the way they start and end. By default, PowerPoint applies a smooth start and smooth end timing to avoid jerkiness in the animation.
- You can adjust start and end options in the effect options dialog box for the animation.

Try It! Setting Animation Start and Timing Options

1. In the P20Try_xx file, on slide 2, select effect 1 in the Animation Pane.
2. Click the Start drop-down arrow and click With Previous.
3. Click effect 1 (Rectangle 2), click the Start drop-down arrow, and click After Previous.
4. With the Rectangle 2 effect still selected, click the Duration up increment arrow until 02.00 displays.
5. With the Rectangle 2 effect still selected, click the Delay up increment arrow until 01.00 displays.
6. With the Rectangle 2 effect still selected, click the down arrow at the right side of the effect, and then click Effect Options.
7. Drag the Bounce end slider to about 0.7 sec, and then click OK.
8. Click ANIMATIONS > Preview Animations to preview changes to the animations on the slide.
9. Save the P20Try_xx file, and leave it open to use in the next Try It.

Applying Animation Effects with Animation Painter

- Creating just the right animation effect can be time-consuming. When you want to use the same animation effect on more than one slide, the best choice is to use the Animation Painter.
- Like the Format Painter, the Animation Painter duplicates the animation formatting from one placeholder to another.
- To copy the animation to another placeholder, select a placeholder that has the animation you want to use and click the Animation Painter button. Then, click the placeholder to which you want to apply it.
- To apply the animation to multiple placeholders, double-click the Animation Painter button after selecting your animation placeholder.

Try It! Applying Animation Effects with Animation Painter

1. In the **P20Try_xx** file, select the text placeholder on slide 2.
2. Double-click ANIMATIONS > Animation Painter.
3. Click slide 4 in the Thumbnail pane. Click the text placeholder.
4. Click slide 5 in the Thumbnail pane. Click the text placeholder.
5. Press ESC to turn off the Animation Painter.
6. Save the **P20Try_xx** file, and leave it open to use in the next Try It.

Applying Animations to Objects, Charts, and Diagrams

- Objects such as shapes and pictures, charts, and SmartArt diagrams can be animated using the same tools that you use to animate text. Animations can help you control the presentation of information in a chart or diagram to make it easier for your audience to understand each part of your data as you present it.
- Besides creating interesting entrance effects for objects, animations can be used to emphasize an object on a slide or to accompany an object's exit from a slide.

Try It! Applying Animations to Objects, Charts, and Diagrams

1. In the **P20Try_xx** file, click the grouped graphic on slide 3.
2. In the Animations gallery, click the More button and click Teeter in the Emphasis effects.
3. On slide 6, click the chart to select it, and then click Fade in the Animation gallery.
4. Click the Effect Options button and click By Element in Series.
5. Click the Preview Animations button to see how each bar in the chart displays separately for each series.
6. On slide 7, click the picture to select it and then click the More button in the Animation gallery to display all effects.
7. Click Wipe in the Exit effects category.
8. Save the **P20Try_xx** file, and leave it open to use in the next Try It.

Changing or Removing an Animation

- If you find that a particular animation option isn't giving you the effect you want, you can easily change the animation effect.
- You can also delete the effect entirely by selecting the item in the Animation Pane to display the effect options down arrow and choosing Remove from the drop-down menu.

Try It! **Changing or Removing an Animation**

1. In the **P20Try_xx** file, display slide 7 if necessary and click the picture to select it.
2. Click the Animation gallery More button to display all effects and click Fade in the Exit effects category.
3. Display slide 3 and click the Group 9 effect in the Animation Pane to select the effect.
4. Click the drop-down arrow to the right of the effect name, and then click Remove.
5. Preview all slides in the presentation to see the animation effects you have applied.
6. Close the **P20Try_xx** file, saving changes, and exit PowerPoint.

Lesson 20—Practice

In this project, you work with the Medi-Ready presentation to improve the slides by adding animations to content placeholders and objects.

DIRECTIONS

1. Start PowerPoint, if necessary, and open **P20Practice** from the data files for this lesson.
2. Save the presentation as **P20Practice_xx** in the location where your teacher instructs you to store the files for this lesson.
3. Click following the word *Affordable* in the subtitle on slide 1. Press ENTER, type **Presented by**, and then add your name.
4. Click the title placeholder on slide 1, click the **ANIMATIONS** tab, and click **Fade**.
5. Click **Start** and click **After Previous**.
6. Click the **Preview Animations** button to play the animations.
7. Click **Animation Pane** to open the Animation Pane, and then make these adjustments to the animations on slide 1:
   a. With the Title 1 animation effect selected, click the move up button to move the effect to the top of the list.
   b. Select the Subtitle 2 effect, click the Animation More button, and then click **Fly In**.
   c. Click the **Effect Options** button and click **From Left**, and then click **All at Once** in the Sequence section of the gallery.
8. Display slide 2 and click the picture to select it.
9. Click **ANIMATIONS** > **Fly In**.
10. Select the content placeholder on slide 2 and click **ANIMATIONS** > **Fly In**.
11. With the content placeholder still selected, make the following adjustments:
    a. Click **Effect Options** and click **By Paragraph**, if necessary.
    b. Click **Start** and click **With Previous**.
    c. Click the **Duration** up increment arrow to display **02.00**.
12. Click the Content Placeholder effect for the picture in the animation list, click **Start** and click **After Previous** and then click **Duration** up increment arrow to display **02.00**. Your slide should look like Figure 20-1 on the next page.

13. Display slide 5 and click the picture to select it.
14. Click the Animation More button to display the Animation gallery, and then click **Pulse** in the Emphasis category.
15. With the picture still selected, click **Start** and click **After Previous**.
16. With the picture still selected, click **ANIMATIONS** > **Animation Painter**, and then click on the picture on slide 6.
17. Close the Animation Pane and then preview your presentation to see the animation effects.
18. Close the presentation, saving changes, and exit PowerPoint.

Figure 20-1

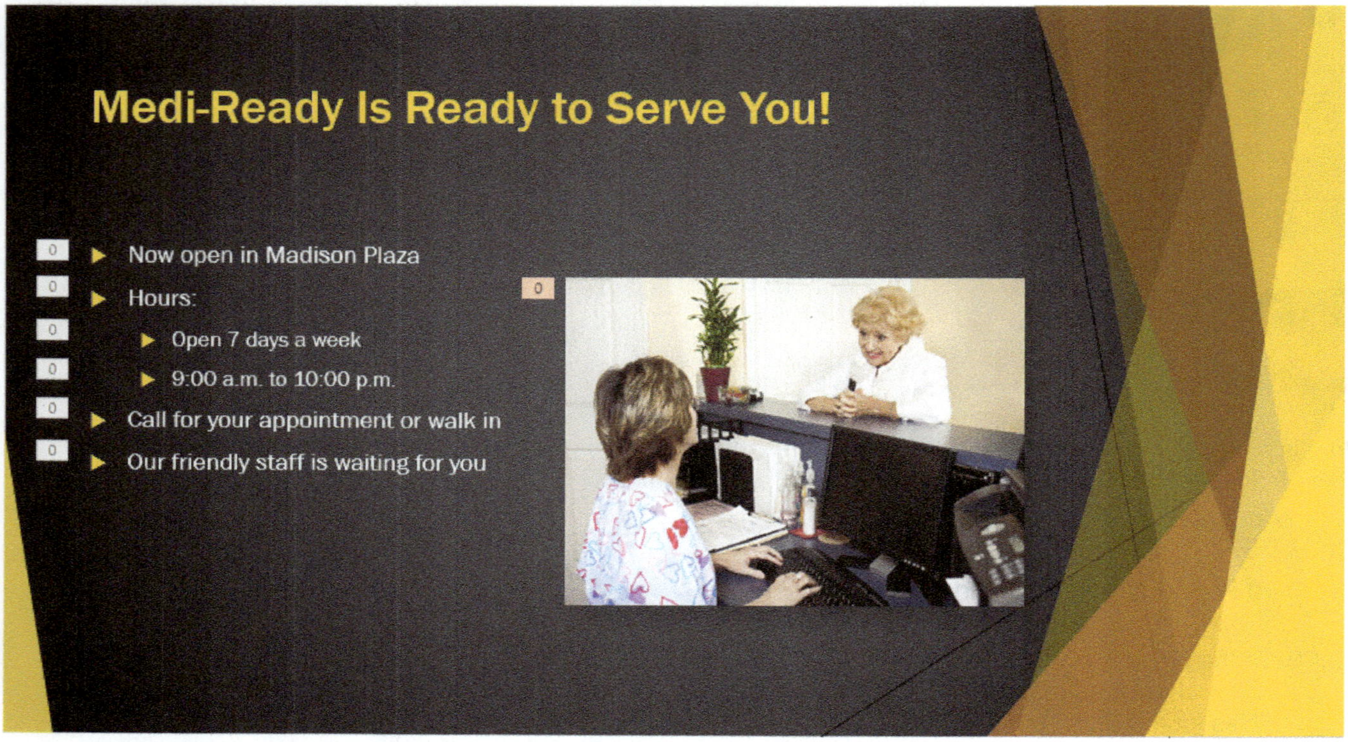

PowerPoint 2013, Windows 8, Microsoft Corporation

Lesson 20—Apply

In this project, you continue working with the Medi-Ready presentation. You will add more animations and modify existing ones to enhance the presentation's visual interest.

DIRECTIONS

1. Start PowerPoint, if necessary, and open **P20Apply** from the data files for this lesson.
2. Save the presentation as **P20Apply_xx** in the location where your teacher instructs you to store the files for this lesson.
3. Use the Animation Painter to copy the animation from the presentation title to the title placeholders on slides 2 through 6. Then adjust the order of animations if necessary so the title animation is first on all slides.
4. On slide 3, animate the SmartArt diagram with the **Wipe** animation effect, changing effect options to **From Left** and **One by One**. Change the Start to **After Previous** and the Duration to **02.00**.
5. Apply animations on slide 4 as follows:
   a. Animate the *Personal Injuries* placeholder to **Zoom** in **After Previous**.
   b. Animate the bullet list under *Personal Injuries* to **Fly In** from the left **After Previous**. Set a delay of **01.00**.
   c. Use the Animation Painter to copy the animation from *Personal Injuries* to *Illnesses*.
   d. Animate the bullet list under *Illnesses* in the same way as the left bullet list, changing the fly in direction for the bullets to **From Right**.
6. On slide 5, change the animation on the picture to **Fly In From Right**.
7. Animate the bulleted list on slide 5 to **Fly in** from left as one object.
8. On slide 5, adjust the order of animations so the picture animates at the same time as the bullet list. Make the same changes to the bullet list and the picture on slide 6.
9. On slide 7, apply the **Shapes** motion path effect to the WordArt graphic and have it start **After Previous**. Change the Smooth end setting for this effect to **0** sec.
10. Insert a text box on slide 1 with your name.
11. Watch the slideshow from start to finish, and then adjust any timings or effects to improve the presentation.
12. Close the presentation, saving changes, and exit PowerPoint.

Lesson 21

Creating Multimedia Presentations

➤ What You Will Learn

Analyzing the Effectiveness of Multimedia Presentations
Inserting a Video
Modifying Video Appearance and Length
Controlling a Video in a Presentation
Inserting Sounds and Music

Software Skills A multimedia presentation can engage an audience with video and sound or music clips. You can modify the way the video displays on the slide and control playback options for both video and sound.

What You Can Do

Analyzing the Effectiveness of Multimedia Presentations

- PowerPoint has many tools and features, but selecting the options that make your presentation effective depends on many factors, including the topic, the audience, and the purpose.
- Always consider your audience when creating a presentation. Research the audience's needs and knowledge level, and tailor the presentation to it.
- For example, a marketing presentation may be more effective if it uses lots of multimedia and animation effects, while a tutorial or training presentation may be more effective if it uses straightforward bullet text without distracting sounds and actions.
- Also consider how the presentation will be delivered. Not all presentations are delivered by a live narrator to a live audience.
  - Will it be printed? Select a light background and dark text for readability.
  - Will it be standalone? Include navigation tools for the viewer.
  - Will it run automatically in a loop? Keep it short so a viewer does not have to wait a long time for the presentation to begin anew.
  - Will it be delivered over the Internet? Make sure the audio is high quality.

- Follow general design guidelines when preparing a presentation. For example:
  - Apply a consistent theme to all slides. That means using the same font and color scheme throughout, and repeating elements such as bullets and backgrounds.
  - Limit bullet points to no more than five per slide.
  - Limit the number of fonts to one or two per slide.
  - Use contrasting colors when necessary to make text stand out. For example, use a dark background color such as dark green or blue and a light contrasting text color, such as yellow.
  - Avoid the use of pastels, which can be hard to read.
  - Make sure text is large enough so that even someone at the back of the room can read it. Text should be no smaller than 18 points and no larger than 48 points.
  - Use graphics such as tables, charts, and pictures to convey key points.
  - Make sure graphics are sized to fill the slide.
  - Use consistent transitions, sounds, and animations that enhance the presentation and do not distract from the content.
- Be clear about the message you are trying to convey. For example, if you are creating a marketing presentation, be clear about what you are trying to sell. If you are creating a training presentation, be clear about what you are teaching.
- Know your time limit based on your audience. Younger people have a shorter attention span, but most people will lose interest if the presentation goes on too long.
- An effective presentation has a logical progression:
  - Introduction in which you tell your audience what you are going to present.
  - Body in which you present the information.
  - Summary in which you tell your audience what you presented.
- Do not use slang, incorrect grammar, jargon, or abbreviations that your audience might not understand.
- Your role in the delivery of a live presentation is key. Dress appropriately, speak loudly and clearly, and make eye contact with your audience.
- You can assess a presentation's effectiveness by testing it on a practice audience. Ask for constructive criticism to help you improve.

Inserting a Video

- Insert a video file using the Insert Video button in a content placeholder or the Video button on the INSERT tab.
- You have several options for adding a video to your presentation:
  - Insert a video file saved in a format such as AVI or MPEG.
  - Insert a video you find with a search tool such as Bing.
  - Insert a video stored on your OneDrive.
  - Insert a video from the Web.
- By default, PowerPoint embeds the video file on the slide so it becomes part of the presentation. You can also choose to link the video to the presentation. Linking can reduce the size of the presentation.
- When you insert a video file or a video from the Web, the VIDEO TOOLS FORMAT and VIDEO TOOLS PLAYBACK tabs open. Use the tools on these tabs to modify the appearance of the video on the slide and to control playback options.

Try It! Inserting a Video from a File

1. Start PowerPoint, and open **P21TryA** from the data files for this lesson.
2. Save the presentation as **P21TryA_xx** in the location where your teacher instructs you to store the files for this lesson.
3. Select slide 4 and click the Insert Video icon in the content placeholder.

   OR

   Click INSERT > Video and then click Video on My PC.

(continued)

Try It! Inserting a Video from a File *(continued)*

4. If necessary, click Browse next to From a file. Navigate to the location where the data files for this lesson are stored and click **P21TryB_video**.
5. Click the down arrow on the Insert button and click Link to File. The video is now linked to the presentation.
6. Click Undo to remove the linked video.
7. Repeat steps 3 and 4 to navigate to the **P21TryB_video** file and select it.
8. Click Insert. The video is now embedded on the slide.
9. Save the **P21TryA_xx** file, and leave it open to use in the next Try It.

Insert a video from a file

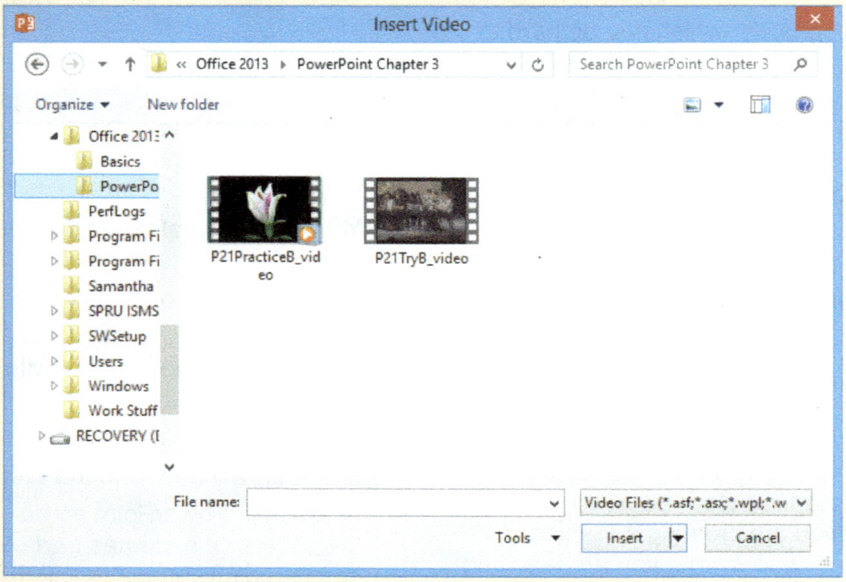

PowerPoint 2013, Windows 8, Microsoft Corporation

Modifying Video Appearance and Length

- You have a number of options for changing the way a video object displays on the slide.
  - You can crop the video to remove black margins at the left and right side of the object.
  - You can apply a video style to give the object a more finished look. Fine-tune the style by changing the style's effects, changing the shape of the video object, or changing the color of a frame if one is applied.
  - You can use the Color option to change the video's color. In addition to the most popular video color options—Black and White, Grayscale, Sepia, Washout—you can also choose to tint the video in 14 different variations, the same way you recolor a picture. Use More Variations to open a color palette for additional color options.
- You find these formatting options on the VIDEO TOOLS FORMAT tab. You can also display the Format Video task pane to make formatting tools available.
- You can use the Trim Video tool on the VIDEO TOOLS PLAYBACK tab to adjust the length of a video.
- In the Trim Video dialog box, you can drag start and end point markers to change where the video starts and ends. Or, set an exact start time in the Start Time box and an exact end time in the End Time box.

Try It! Modifying Video Appearance and Length

1. In the **P21TryA_xx** file, select the video on slide 4.
2. On the VIDEO TOOLS FORMAT tab, click the Crop button.
3. Drag the left cropping handle to the right to remove the black.
4. Drag the right cropping handle to the left to remove the black.
5. On the VIDEO TOOLS FORMAT tab, click the Crop button again to complete the crop.
6. With the video object still selected, on the VIDEO TOOLS FORMAT tab, click the More button to open the Video Styles gallery.
7. Move your mouse over several styles to see the live preview and then choose Drop Shadow Rectangle, the last option in the Subtle category.
8. Right-click the video object, and click Format Video to display the Format Video task pane.
9. Click the Recolor button and choose Grayscale. Close the Format Video task pane.
10. On the VIDEO TOOLS PLAYBACK tab, click Trim Video.
11. Drag the end point marker (the red marker at the right end of the timeline) to the left until the End Time box shows about 18 seconds. Click OK.
12. Save the **P21TryA_xx** file, and leave it open to use in the next Try It.

Drag the left cropping handle to the right

PowerPoint 2013, Windows 8, Microsoft Corporation

Controlling a Video in a Presentation

- Inserted video clips can be controlled using the standard play and pause controls on the bar beneath the video object.
- In addition to these controls, PowerPoint allows you to hide the movie during the presentation, play it full screen, loop it continuously, rewind it, change its arrangement relative to other objects, or scale it.

Try It! Previewing a Movie in Normal View

1. In the **P21TryA_xx** file, select the video on slide 4.
2. Click VIDEO TOOLS PLAYBACK > Play.

   OR

   Click the Play button below the video.
3. Watch for a few seconds and click VIDEO TOOLS PLAYBACK > Pause.

   OR

   Click the Pause button below the video.
4. Save the **P21TryA_xx** file, and leave it open to use in the next Try It.

Try It! Viewing a Video in a Slide Show

1. In the **P21TryA_xx** file, select slide 4, if necessary.
2. Click Slide Show on the status bar.
3. Hover your mouse over the video to display the Play button.
4. Click the Play button ▶.
5. Watch the video for a few seconds and then click the slide to progress to the next slide.
6. Press ESC.
7. Select the video on slide 4, if necessary, and click VIDEO TOOLS PLAYBACK > Start, and click Automatically.
8. Click Slide Show on the status bar. Notice that the video starts immediately.
9. Press ESC twice.
10. Save the **P21TryA_xx** file, and leave it open to use in the next Try It.

Inserting Sounds and Music

- You can add sound and music clips to your presentation to make it more interesting or to emphasize a slide. Your computer must have speakers and a sound card to play music or sounds during a presentation.
- Use the Audio button on the INSERT tab to choose what kind of sound to insert: a sound file from your system, or a sound that you record.
- As for video files, you can choose to link to a file on your system, rather than embed the audio file in the presentation.
- When you insert an audio clip, a sound icon displays on the slide. You can move this icon to a new location (or even off the slide) or resize it to make it less obtrusive.

  ✓ *The sound icon must appear on the slide if you intend to control a sound by clicking it during the presentation.*

- You can choose whether to play the sound automatically or when clicked. You can also choose to have the audio play across slides, so it continues as you progress through the presentation.
- Use the AUDIO TOOLS PLAYBACK tab to control sound options.

Try It! Inserting a Music File

1. In the **P21TryA_xx** file, select slide 5.
2. Click INSERT > Audio.
3. Click Audio on My PC.
4. In the Insert Audio dialog box, navigate to the location where the data files for this lesson are stored and select **P21TryC_audio.mid**.
5. Click Insert and drag the audio icon to the lower right of the slide.
6. On the AUDIO TOOLS PLAYBACK tab, click the Start down arrow, and click Automatically.
7. Save the **P21TryA_xx** file, and leave it open to use in the next Try It.

(continued)

Try It! Inserting a Music File *(continued)*

PowerPoint gives you complete control over audio clips

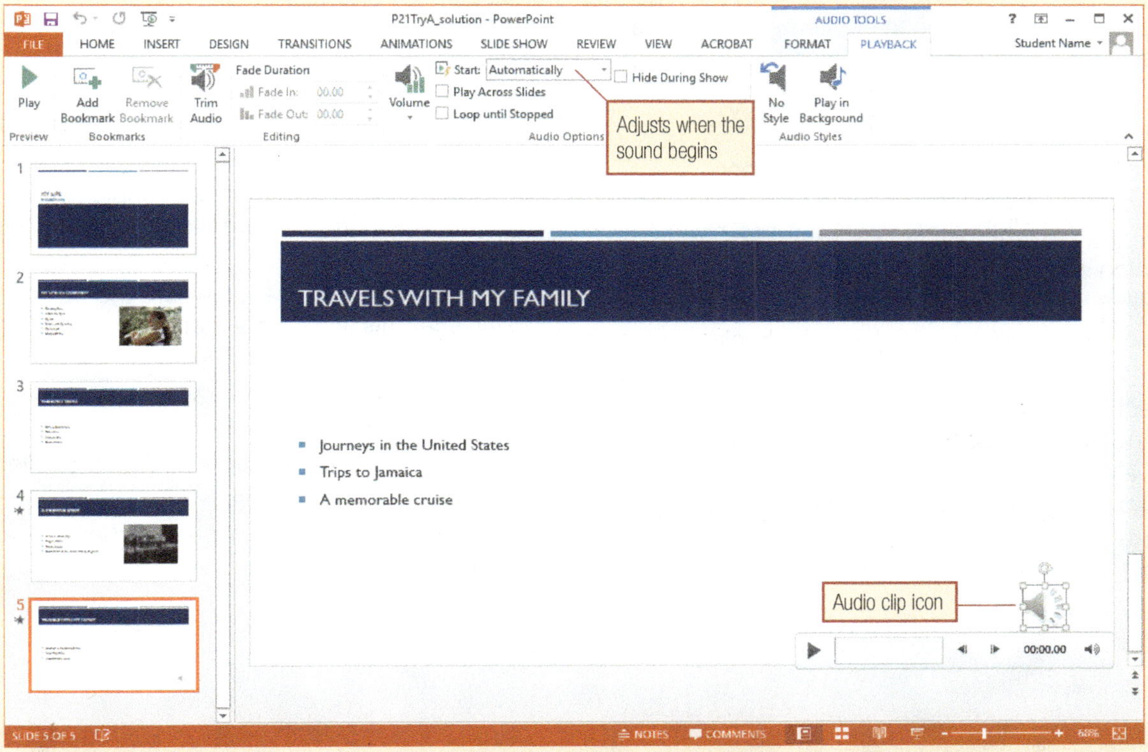

PowerPoint 2013, Windows 8, Microsoft Corporation

Try It! Recording a Sound on a Slide

1. In the **P21TryA_xx** file, select slide 1 and replace STUDENT NAME with your own first name and last name.
2. Click INSERT > Audio.
3. Select Record Audio.

   ✓ *You can complete these steps if your computer is equipped with a sound card, speakers, and microphone (attached, built-in, or separate webcam). PowerPoint presents a message if the feature cannot be performed; in that case, click OK in the message and skip to step 9.*

4. In the Record Sound dialog box, click in the Name box and type your first and last name.
5. Click the Record button and then substituting your own first and last name, speak, **"My Life presentation by Firstname Lastname."**
6. Press the Stop Recording button. Press the Play button to listen to your recording.
7. Repeat steps 5 and 6 if you want to start over, and then click OK. On slide 1, select the audio clip icon, if necessary.
8. On the AUDIO TOOLS PLAYBACK tab, click the Start down arrow and click Automatically.
9. Click SLIDE SHOW > From Beginning and watch the presentation.
10. Close the **P21TryA_xx** file, saving changes, and exit PowerPoint.

Lesson 21—Practice

Planet Earth has asked you to continue work on their Earth Day presentation. In this project, you add a video and a picture to a new presentation design to create a multimedia presentation.

DIRECTIONS

1. Start PowerPoint, if necessary, and open **P21PracticeA** from the data files for this lesson.
2. Save the presentation as **P21PracticeA_xx** in the location where your teacher instructs you to store the files for this lesson.
3. Select slide 1, click inside the subtitle placeholder, and type your name.
4. Select slide 2 and then click the **Insert Video** icon in the right placeholder. The Insert Video dialog box opens.
5. Click **Browse** and then navigate to the location where the data files for this lesson are stored and select **P21PracticeB_video.mov**.
6. Click **Insert**. The video appears in the placeholder, as shown in Figure 21-1.
7. Select slide 3 and in the placeholder, click the **Pictures** icon. The Insert Picture dialog box opens.
8. Navigate to the location where the data files for this lesson are stored and select **P21PracticeC_picture.jpg**.
9. Click **Insert**. The picture appears in the placeholder.
10. Preview the presentation, playing the video on slide 2.
11. Close the presentation, saving changes, and exit PowerPoint.

Figure 21-1

PowerPoint 2013, Windows 8, Microsoft Corporation

Lesson 21—Apply

In this project, you continue to work on the Planet Earth presentation. You format the video to improve the look of the presentation.

DIRECTIONS

1. Start PowerPoint, if necessary, and open **P21Apply** from the data files for this lesson.
2. Save the presentation as **P21Apply_xx** in the location where your teacher instructs you to store the files for this lesson.
3. Replace the text *Student Name* on the title slide with your name.
4. Modify the video clip on slide 2 as follows:
   a. Drag the video down so that the top of it is more or less aligned with the top of the SAVING THE EARTH text in the placeholder to the left of the video.
   b. Apply the **Simple Frame, White** video style to the video. Your slide should look like Figure 21-2.
   c. Set the video to start automatically.
   d. Trim the video so it starts about 1 second later.
   e. Preview the video in Normal view.
5. **With your teacher's permission**, print slide 2.
6. Close the presentation, saving changes, and exit PowerPoint.

Figure 21-2

PowerPoint 2013, Windows 8, Microsoft Corporation

Lesson 22

Working with Tables

➤ What You Will Learn

Inserting a Table
Formatting and Modifying a Table

Software Skills Use tables to organize data in a format that is easy to read and understand. Table formats enhance visual interest and also contribute to readability.

What You Can Do

Inserting a Table

- Use a table on a slide to organize information into rows and columns so it is easy for your audience to read and understand.
- You have two options for inserting a table on a slide:
  - Click the Insert Table icon in any content placeholder to display the Insert Table dialog box. After you select the number of columns and rows, the table structure appears on the slide in the content placeholder.
  - Click the Table button on the INSERT tab to display a grid that you can use to select rows and columns. As you drag the pointer, the table columns and rows appear on the slide.

    ✓ *If you use this option on a slide that does not have a content layout, you may have to move the table to position it properly on the slide.*

- Note that the Table menu also allows you to access the Insert Table dialog box, draw a table using the Draw Table tool, or insert an Excel worksheet to organize data.

Try It! Inserting a Table

1. Start PowerPoint and open **P22Try** from the data files for this lesson.
2. Save the presentation as **P22Try_xx** in the location where your teacher instructs you to store the files for this lesson.
3. Select slide 2 and click the Insert Table icon in the content placeholder.
4. Type 2 in the Number of columns scroll box.
5. Type 5 in the Number of rows scroll box.
6. Click OK.
7. Select slide 4.
8. Click INSERT > Table.
9. Drag the pointer over the grid or use arrow keys to select 5 columns and 3 rows.
10. Click or press ENTER to insert the table on the slide.
11. Save the **P22Try_xx** file, and leave it open to use in the next Try It.

Using the Insert Table icon to insert a table

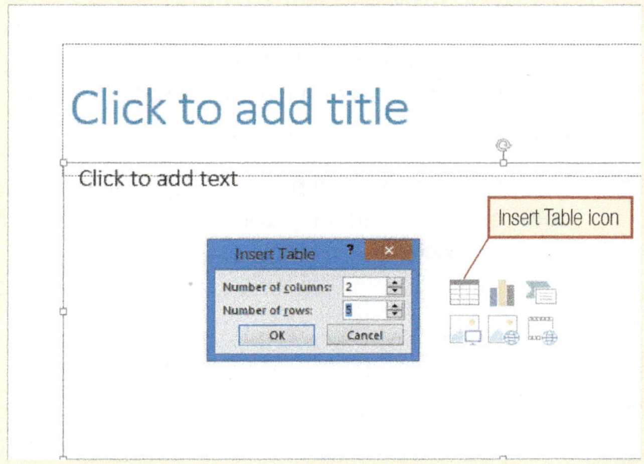

PowerPoint 2013, Windows 8, Microsoft Corporation

Using the Table Grid to insert a table

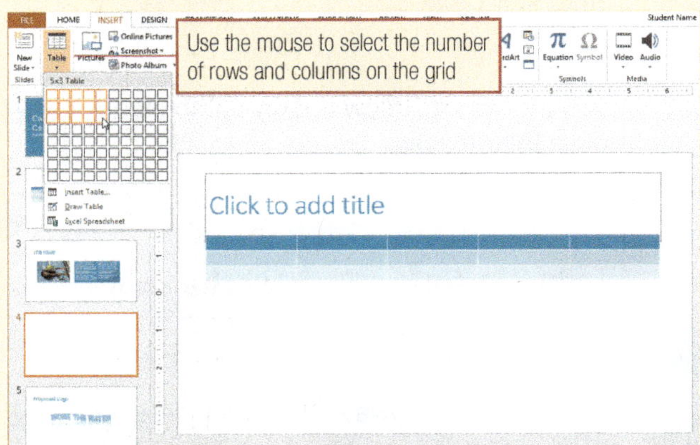

PowerPoint 2013, Windows 8, Microsoft Corporation

Formatting and Modifying a Table

- When a table appears on a slide, the TABLE TOOLS contextual tabs become active on the Ribbon.
- Use the TABLE TOOLS DESIGN tab to control formatting options, such as styles, shading, borders, and effects. You can also choose to emphasize specific parts of a table.
- Use the TABLE TOOLS LAYOUT tab to control the table structure, such as inserting or deleting rows and columns, merging or splitting cells, distributing rows or columns evenly, adjusting both horizontal and vertical alignment, changing text direction, and adjusting cell margins and table size.
- If you do not want to enter specific measurements for cells and table size, you can adjust rows, columns, or the table itself by dragging borders. You can also drag the entire table to reposition it on the slide if necessary.

Try It! Applying Table Formats

1. In the P22Try_xx file, click slide 2.
2. Click the table to select it.
3. Click TABLE TOOLS DESIGN > Table Styles More button to open the Table Styles gallery.
4. Click Medium Style 2 - Accent 6.
5. Select the entire table by dragging across all cells, or by clicking the table border. Click TABLE TOOLS DESIGN > Borders.
6. Select All Borders.
7. Click the Shading button and select a color, picture, gradient, or texture to fill table cells.
8. Click the Effects button and select from bevel, shadow, or reflection effects for the table.
9. Save the P22Try_xx file, and leave it open to use in the next Try It.

Try It! Inserting a Row or Column

1. In the P22Try_xx file, select slide 2.
2. Click one of the rows in the table to select it.
3. Click TABLE TOOLS LAYOUT > Insert Above.

   OR

   Click the Insert Below button to insert a row below the selected cell.
4. Click the Insert Left button to insert a column to the left of the selected cell.

   OR

   Click the Insert Right button to insert a column to the right of the selected cell.
5. Save the P22Try_xx file, and leave it open to use in the next Try It.

Try It! Deleting Part of the Table

1. In the P22Try_xx file, select slide 2.
2. Click one of the rows in the table to select it.
3. Click TABLE TOOLS LAYOUT > Delete.
4. Click Delete Rows to delete the selected row.
5. Click TABLE TOOLS LAYOUT > Delete.
6. Click Delete Columns to delete the selected column.
7. Save the P22Try_xx file, and leave it open to use in the next Try It.

Try It! Merging Table Cells

1. In the **P22Try_xx** file, type **Table Heading** in the first row of the table on slide 2.
2. Select the heading row by dragging across the cells. Click TABLE TOOLS LAYOUT > Merge Cells.
3. Click TABLE TOOLS LAYOUT > Center.
4. Save the **P22Try_xx** file, and leave it open to use in the next Try It.

Merging table cells

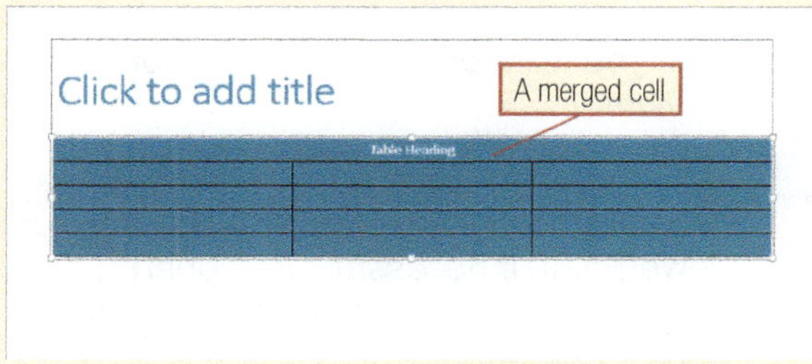

PowerPoint 2013, Windows 8, Microsoft Corporation

Try It! Distributing Rows Evenly

1. In the **P22Try_xx** file, select the third row in the table on slide 4.
2. Click TABLE TOOLS LAYOUT. In the Cell Size group, type **1** in the Height box.
3. Select the entire table, and click TABLE TOOLS LAYOUT > Distribute Rows.
4. Close the **P22Try_xx** file, saving changes, and exit PowerPoint.

Lesson 22—Practice

In this project, you work on a presentation for Restoration Architecture. You'll insert and format a table that lists planning services.

DIRECTIONS

1. Start PowerPoint, if necessary, and open **P22Practice** from the data files for this lesson.
2. Save the presentation as **P22Practice_xx** in the location where your teacher instructs you to store the files for this lesson.
3. Click the subtitle placeholder and move to the end of the text. Press ENTER three times and then type your name.
4. Click on slide 3 and then click **HOME** > **New Slide** drop-down arrow > **Title Only**. A new slide appears at the end of the presentation.
5. Click the title placeholder and type **PLANNING SERVICES** as the slide title.
6. Click outside the placeholder and click **INSERT** > **Table**.
7. Drag to create a table that is five rows and five columns.
8. Fill in the table with the text shown in Figure 22-1.
9. On the **TABLE TOOLS LAYOUT** tab, in the Table Size group, type **3** in the **Height** box. The table height is adjusted.
10. Click in the **Width** box and type **8.5**. The table width is adjusted. Drag the table to position it as shown in Figure 22-1.
11. **With your teacher's permission**, print the presentation.
12. Close the presentation, saving changes, and exit PowerPoint.

Figure 22-1

PowerPoint 2013, Windows 8, Microsoft Corporation

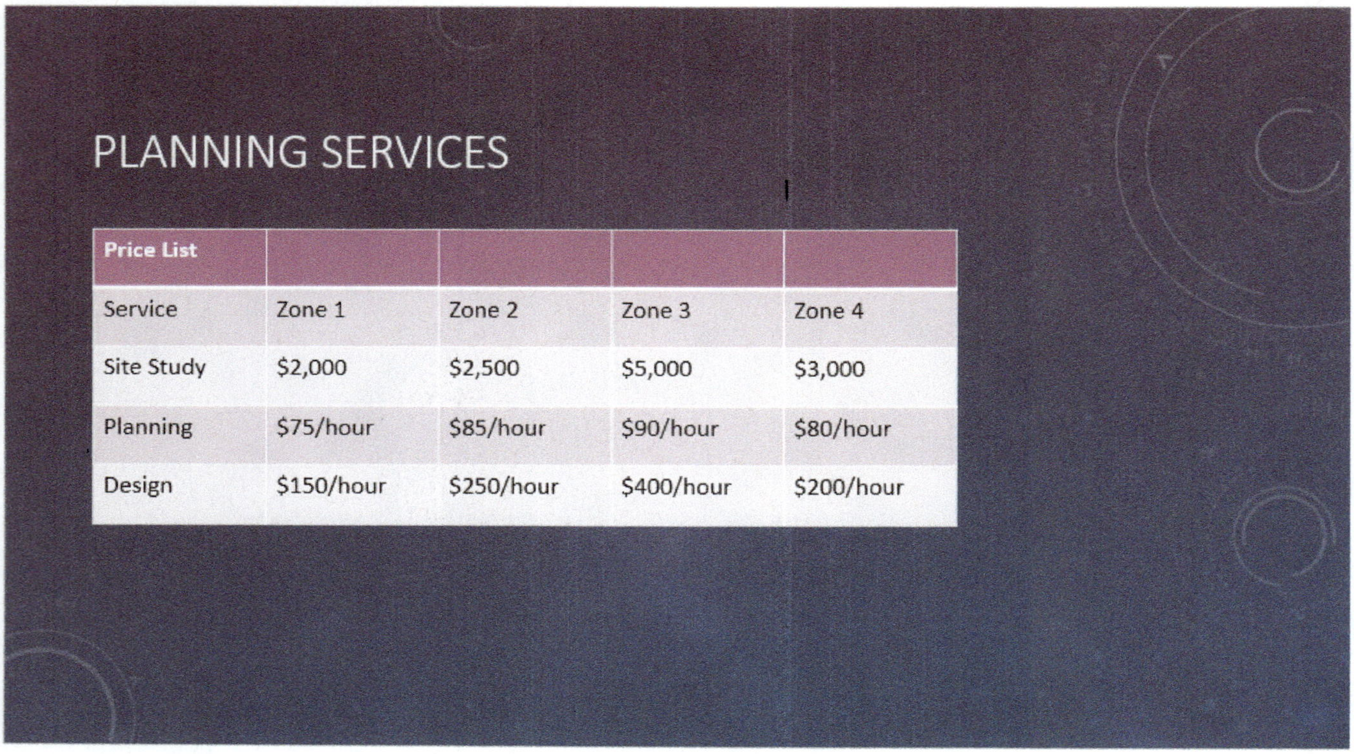

Lesson 22—Apply

In this project, you continue to work on the Restoration Architecture presentation. You edit the table you created in the last project to improve its appearance.

DIRECTIONS

1. Start PowerPoint, if necessary, and open **P22Apply** from the data files for this lesson.
2. Save the presentation as **P22Apply_xx** in the location where your teacher instructs you to store the files for this lesson.
3. You have decided to stop offering services for Zone 4. On slide 4, delete the *Zone 4* column in the table.
4. Use the TABLE TOOLS DESIGN tab to change the table style to **Themed Style 2 - Accent 5**. Apply All Borders to the table.
5. Center the entries in the last three columns, adjust column widths as desired, and position the table attractively on the slide.
6. Insert a row below the second row. Type the following:
   Permits $200 $350 $500
7. Merge the second, third, and fourth cell in the first row.
8. Select the first column and apply shading of Red, Accent 6, Darker 25%. Your slide should look like Figure 22-2.
9. Replace the text Student Name on the title slide with your name.
10. **With your teacher's permission**, print slide 4.
11. Close the presentation, saving changes, and exit PowerPoint.

Figure 22-2

PowerPoint 2013, Windows 8, Microsoft Corporation

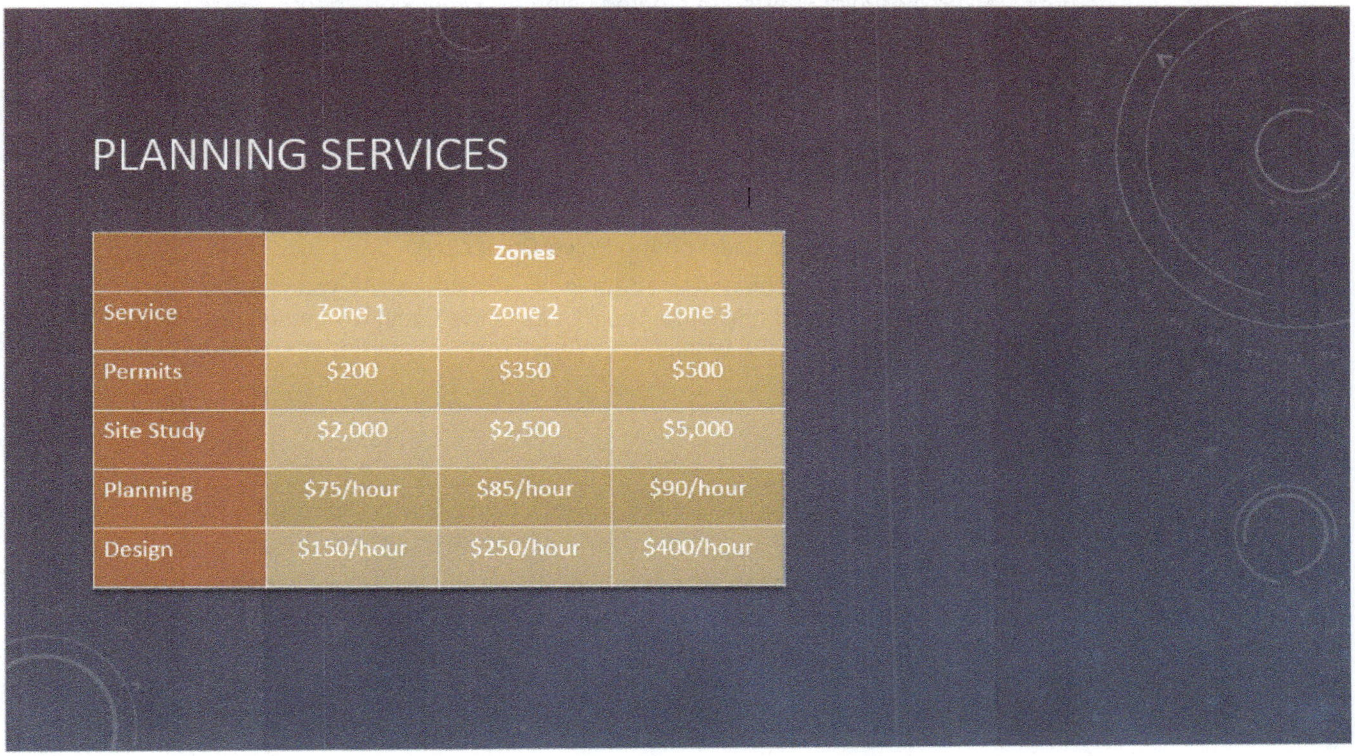

Lesson 23

Working with Charts

➤ What You Will Learn

Inserting a Chart
Formatting and Modifying a Chart

Software Skills Add charts to a presentation to illustrate data and other concepts in a graphical way that is easy to understand. Charts can be formatted or modified as needed to improve the display.

What You Can Do

Inserting a Chart

- You can add a chart to your presentation to illustrate data in an easy-to-understand format or to compare and contrast sets of data.
- PowerPoint charts are created using an Excel worksheet.
- The chart you create from the Excel worksheet is embedded on the PowerPoint slide. To work with a chart, you use the same tools you would use when working with a chart in Excel.
- You can insert a chart into a content slide layout or add it without a placeholder using the Chart button on the INSERT tab.
- When you insert a new chart, Excel displays a worksheet containing sample data above a sample chart on the PowerPoint slide.
- You can type replacement data in the worksheet. As you change the data, the chart adjusts on the slide. You can save the Excel worksheet data for the chart and then close the worksheet to work further with the chart on the slide.

Try It! **Inserting a Chart**

1. Start PowerPoint, and open **P23Try** from the data files for this lesson.
2. Save the presentation as **P23Try_xx** in the location where your teacher instructs you to store the files for this lesson.
3. Select slide 3 and click the Insert Chart icon in the content placeholder.

   OR

   Click INSERT > Chart .

(continued)

Try It! Inserting a Chart *(continued)*

4. Select the Clustered Column chart type and click OK.
5. The chart is inserted on the slide and Excel displays a worksheet with sample data above the chart.
6. Close the Excel data file.
7. Save the **P23Try_xx** file, and leave it open to use in the next Try It.

Sample data used to create a PowerPoint chart

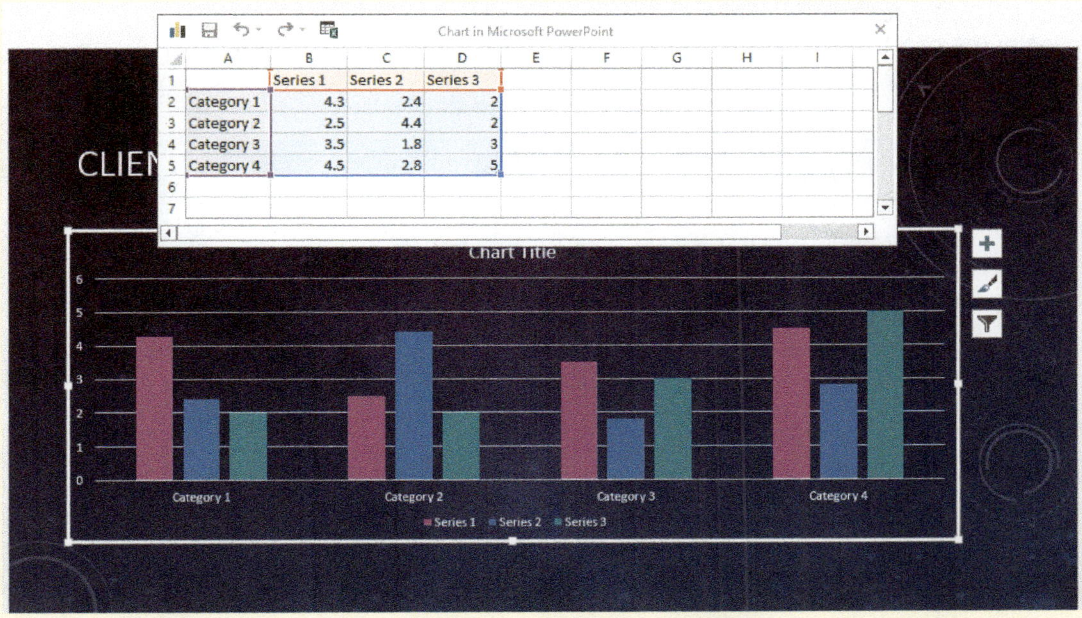

PowerPoint 2013, Windows 8, Microsoft Corporation

Formatting and Modifying a Chart

- When you click on a chart in PowerPoint, two content-specific tabs open on the Ribbon: CHART TOOLS DESIGN and CHART TOOLS LAYOUT.
- Use the tools on the CHART TOOLS DESIGN tab to modify the chart type and edit data. You can also select a new layout from the Quick Layout gallery, change the colors of the chart elements, or apply a chart style.
- You can choose from several chart types, including line, pie, bar, area, scatter, stock, surface, and radar.
- Use the tools on the CHART TOOLS FORMAT tab to apply special effects to the chart elements or insert a shape on the chart.
- A selected chart displays three buttons to the right of the chart selection border: the Chart Elements button, the Chart Styles button, and the Chart Filters button.
  - Click the Chart Elements button to see a pop-out list of chart elements you can apply to the chart by clicking check boxes. When you point to an element in the list, a right-pointing arrow displays that you can click to show additional formatting options. This list makes it easy to show, hide, or change the position of chart elements such as legends and titles.
  - Click the Chart Styles button to see a pop-out gallery of chart styles and color palettes to change the look of the chart.
  - Click the Chart Filters button to see a pop-out list of the chart's series and categories. You can choose to display specific data by selecting only the series and categories you want to see.
- You can see options for modifying a particular chart element by right-clicking the element on the chart to display a Format task pane for that element.
- You can move, copy, size, and delete a chart just like any other slide object.

Try It! Formatting and Modifying a Chart

1. In the **P23Try_xx** file, click the chart to select it, if necessary.
2. Click CHART TOOLS DESIGN > Change Chart Type .
3. Click Clustered Bar and click OK.
4. Click the Chart Styles button to the right of the chart to display the pop-out gallery of styles to the left of the chart.
5. In the STYLE list, click Style 3.
6. Click COLOR in the pop-out gallery, and then click Color 2 in the Colorful section.
7. Click the Chart Styles button to close the gallery.
8. Save the **P23Try_xx** file, and leave it open to use in the next Try It.

The Change Chart Type dialog box

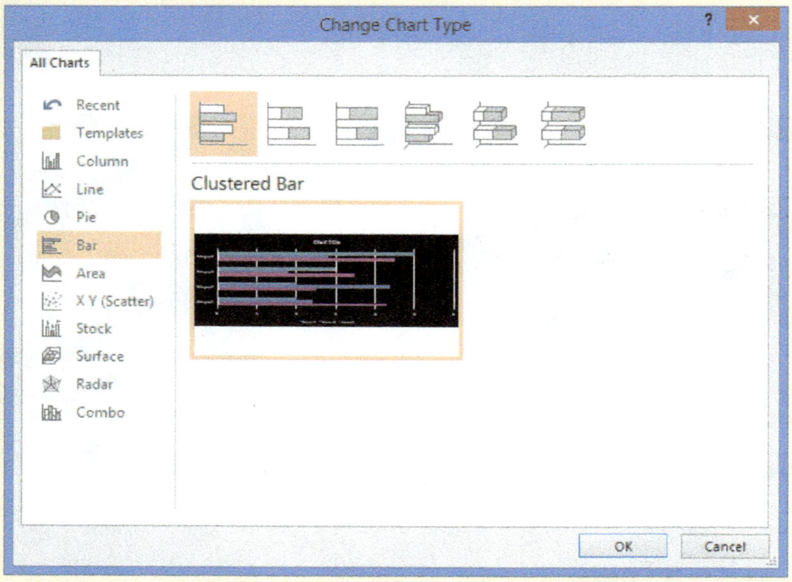

PowerPoint 2013, Windows 8, Microsoft Corporation

Try It! Editing the Excel Data

1. In the **P23Try_xx** file, click the chart to select it, if necessary.
2. Click CHART TOOLS DESIGN > Edit Data .
3. In the Excel data file, click cell A2.
4. Type **Project 1**, and press ENTER. Note that the change is immediately made in the chart as well.
5. Save the **P23Try_xx** file, and leave it open to use in the next Try It.

Try It! Switching Rows and Columns

1. Both the Excel worksheet and the P23Try_xx file should be open.
2. Click the chart to select it, and then, click CHART TOOLS DESIGN > Switch Row/ Column .
3. Close the Excel data file.
4. Save the P23Try_xx file, and leave it open to use in the next Try It.

Try It! Filtering Data in the Chart

1. In the P23Try_xx file, click the chart to select it, if necessary.
2. Click the Chart Filters button to the right of the chart to display the pop-out list of series and categories to the left of the chart.
3. Click in the Project 1 check box to clear the check mark.
4. Click Apply at the bottom of the pop-out list to remove the Project 1 entry.
5. Click the Chart Filters button again to close the pop-out list.
6. Save the P23Try_xx file, and leave it open to use in the next Try It.

Filtering data in the chart

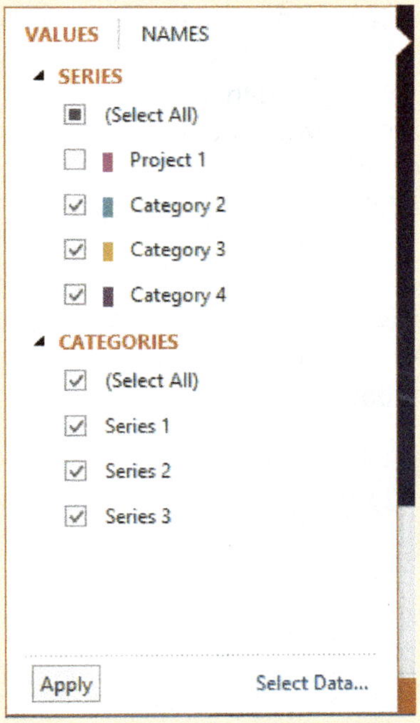

Try It! Changing Chart Layout

1. In the P23Try_xx file, click the chart to select it, if necessary.
2. Click the Chart Elements button to display the pop-out list of chart elements to the left of the chart.
3. Click the Chart Title check box to remove the check. The Chart Title is removed from the chart.
4. Click the Chart Elements button again to close the pop-out list.
5. Right-click the legend at the bottom of the chart and then click Format Legend on the shortcut menu to open the Format Legend task pane.
6. Select Right. Close the Format Legend task pane.
7. Close the P23Try_xx file, saving changes, and exit PowerPoint.

Lesson 23—Practice

In this project, you work on a presentation for the Campus Recreation Center. You insert a chart to show results of a usage survey.

DIRECTIONS

1. Start PowerPoint, if necessary, and open **P23Practice** from the data files for this lesson.
2. Save the presentation as **P23Practice_xx** in the location where your teacher instructs you to store the files for this lesson.
3. Click the subtitle placeholder and move to the end of the text. Press ENTER and then type your name.
4. Click on slide 3 and then click **HOME** > **New Slide** drop-down arrow > **Title and Content**. A new slide appears.
5. Click the title placeholder and type **Survey Results** as the slide title.
6. Click the **Insert Chart** icon in the content placeholder. The Insert Chart dialog box opens.
7. Select **3-D Clustered Column** and click **OK**. An Excel data file appears.
8. Replace the sample data with the data shown in Figure 23-1. Then close the Excel data file.
9. Click the chart to select it, if necessary, click **CHART TOOLS DESIGN** > **Quick Layout** , and click **Layout 3**.
10. Click the **Chart Styles** button to the right of the chart, click **COLOR**, and click the first palette under Monochromatic (Color 5). Click the **Chart Styles** button again to close the gallery.
11. Select the chart title and type **Visits per Week**.
12. Preview the entire presentation.
13. **With your teacher's permission**, print slide 4. It should look like that shown in Figure 23-2 on the next page.
14. Close the presentation, saving changes, and exit PowerPoint.

Figure 23-1

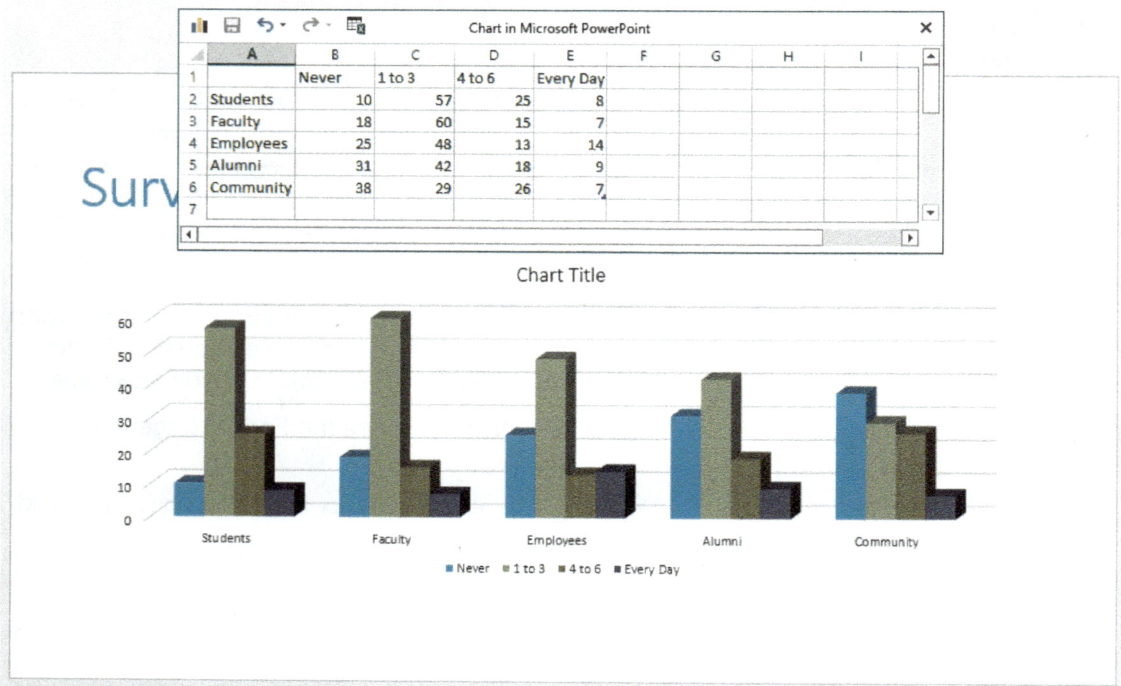

	Never	1 to 3	4 to 6	Every Day
Students	10	57	25	8
Faculty	18	60	15	7
Employees	25	48	13	14
Alumni	31	42	18	9
Community	38	29	26	7

Figure 23-2

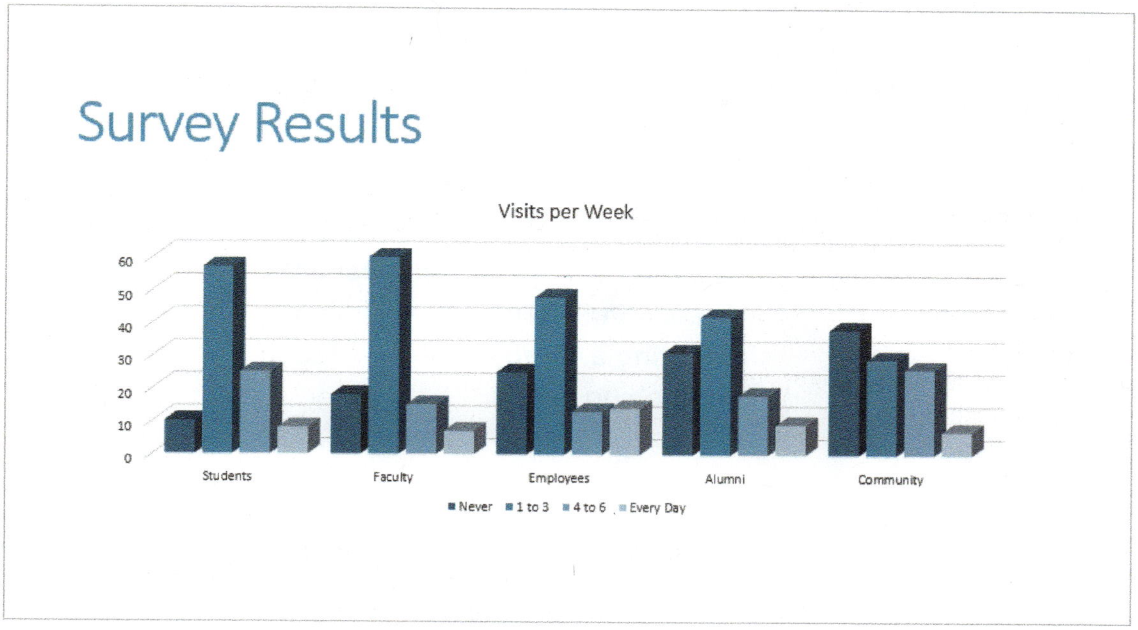

Lesson 23—Apply

In this project, you modify the chart you created in the last project. You change the chart type, adjust formats, and display new chart elements.

DIRECTIONS

1. Start PowerPoint, if necessary, and open **P23Apply** from the data files for this lesson.
2. Save the presentation as **P23Apply_xx** in the location where your teacher instructs you to store the files for this lesson.
3. On slide 4, change the appearance of the chart as follows:
   a. Change the chart type to **Clustered Column**.
   b. Click **Chart Elements** [+], point to **Gridlines**, and click the right-pointing arrow. Click **Primary Major Vertical** in the list of additional Gridline options.
4. Edit the Excel data as follows:
   a. Change the Students value for 1 to 3 to **47**.
   b. Change the Every Day value for Students to **18**.
5. Switch the rows and columns, and then close the Excel data file.
6. Change the color of the chart bars to **Color 1** in the Colorful category.
7. Filter the data to hide the Community series.
8. Add a slide footer to the presentation that includes your name and an automatically updating date on all slides.
9. Preview the presentation to see how your chart looks.
10. **With your teacher's permission**, print slide 4.
11. Close the presentation, saving changes, and exit PowerPoint.

Lesson 24

Sharing a Presentation

➤ What You Will Learn

Packaging a Presentation for CD
Presenting a Slide Show Online
Creating a Video of a Presentation
Publishing Slides

Software Skills You have a number of options for sharing a presentation with others. You can package the presentation materials on a CD. You can also create a video or use other output options, such as storing the presentation on OneDrive or saving the presentation as a PowerPoint Show.

What You Can Do

Packaging for CD

- Use the Package Presentation for CD feature when you want to run a slide show on another computer.
- When you package a presentation show, it automatically includes a link to download the PowerPoint Viewer, which allows the presentation to be viewed on a PC even if PowerPoint is not installed.

✓ *The recipient must be able to connect to the Internet to download the PowerPoint Viewer.*

- The Package Presentation for CD dialog box lets you control the process of packaging the presentation files and copying them to a folder or a CD.
- If you choose the folder option, you can store the presentation on removable media such as a flash drive that can be easier to transport than a CD.
- To see options for packaging the presentation's files, click the Options button in the Package Presentation for CD dialog box. By default, PowerPoint links all files used in the presentation, such as videos and images.
- PowerPoint will also embed the TrueType fonts used to create the text, so that even if the computer on which you will present the slides does not have the fonts, they will display correctly during the presentation.
- If your presentation includes images or media files such as videos or sounds, you should optimize and compress the media objects before you package the presentation. You can find these options on the Info tab.

Try It! Packaging for CD

1. Start PowerPoint, and open P24TryA from the data files for this lesson.
2. Save the presentation as P24TryA_xx in the location where your teacher instructs you to store the files for this lesson.
3. Click FILE > Info > Optimize Compatibility. When the optimization is complete, click Close.
4. Click Compress Media and then select Presentation Quality. When compression is complete, click Close.
5. Insert a recordable CD in the appropriate drive in the computer.
6. Click FILE > Export > Package Presentation for CD.
7. Click Package for CD.
8. In the Package for CD dialog box, type P24TryA_xx in the Name the CD box.
9. Click Options to see the items that will be included with the presentation, and then click OK.
10. Click Copy to CD.
11. When asked if you want to include linked files, click Yes.
12. Click No if asked if you want to copy the same files to another CD.
13. Click Close.

Try It! Copying to a Folder

1. In the P24TryA_xx presentation, click FILE > Export > Package Presentation for CD > Package for CD.
2. Type P24TryA_xx in the Name the CD box.
3. Click Copy to Folder.
4. Type P24TryA_xx in the folder name box.
5. Navigate to the folder where your teacher instructs you to store the files for this lesson and click Select.
6. Click OK and click Yes when prompted to copy linked files to the folder.
7. Close the File Explorer window that shows the files in the P24TryA_xx folder.
8. Click Close.

Presenting a Slide Show Online

- The Present Online feature allows you to share a presentation with others via the Internet.
- Use the Present Online option on the Share tab in the Backstage view or on the SLIDE SHOW tab.

  ✓ *You will need a Windows Live ID to present your slide show online. If you do not already have one, you can sign up for one for free.*

- Anyone who can access the Internet will be able to follow the provided link and view the presentation, even if they don't have PowerPoint 2013 installed on their PC.
- The Office Presentation Service will provide you with a URL that you can give to up to 50 people so they can watch the presentation.
- You will still control the presentation by starting and pausing the presentation as desired.

Try It! Presenting a Slide Show Online

1. In the **P24TryA_xx** file, click SLIDE SHOW > Present Online.

   OR

   Click FILE > Share > Present Online.

2. Click in the Enable remote viewers to download the presentation check box and then click CONNECT or Present Online.

The Present Online dialog box

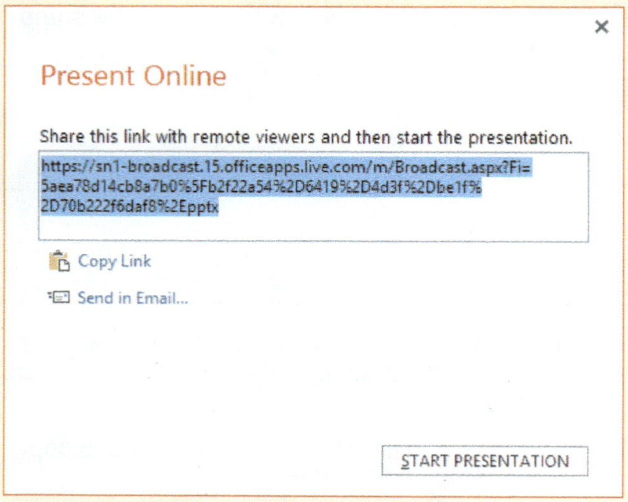

PowerPoint 2013, Windows 8, Microsoft Corporation

3. Click Send in Email, if you want to send the provided URL to your attendees using Outlook.

   OR

   Click Copy Link to send the URL to your attendees in a memo or any other format.

   When you open the document you plan to send to the attendees, press CTRL + V to paste the link.

4. Click START PRESENTATION when you and your attendees are ready to begin the presentation.
5. Advance through the presentation as you normally would. Your attendees will view the slide show through their browser window.
6. Click End Online Presentation on the PRESENT ONLINE tab.
7. Click End Online Presentation when warned that the remote viewers will be disconnected.
8. Leave the presentation open for the next Try It.

Creating a Video of a Presentation

- You can save your PowerPoint presentations as video that can be shared with others to be viewed on a PC or uploaded to the Internet.
- PowerPoint will save the presentation as an MP4 file, which can be uploaded to YouTube, Facebook, or other Web sites.
- When you save your presentation as a video, it can be played on any computer or DVD player that can handle the MP4 format.
- Your presentation video can include unique timings and narration, or you can set a specific number of seconds that each slide will be paused.

Try It! Creating a Video of a Presentation

1. In the **P24TryA_xx** file, click FILE > Export > Create a Video.
2. In the Create a Video pane, click Presentation Quality and then select the resolution you want to use.
3. Change the number of seconds that you want to spend on each slide to 6:00.

   ✓ *If you're unsure about the number of seconds to use, you can set the number of seconds and then click the second button (Don't Use Recorded Timings and Narrations) to see what it will look like.*

   OR

   Click Don't Use Recorded Timings and Narrations to see the options available.

   ✓ *This second button says Don't Use Recording Timings and Narrations because these items haven't been set yet. If you had already recording timings and narrations the button would say Use Recorded Timings and Narrations.*
4. Select Record Timings and Narration.
5. In the Record Slide Show dialog box, select one or both of the following:
   - Slide and animation timings
   - Narrations, ink, and laser pointer
6. Click Start Recording.

   ✓ *At this point, you would begin the process of recording your presentation. For more information refer to the Rehearsing Timings section in Lesson 28 on the CD that accompanies this book.*
7. Click Create Video.
8. Navigate to the location where your teacher instructs you to store the files for this lesson.

   ✓ *The file name box will have the same name that your PowerPoint presentation has. If you want to use a different name, select the name in the box and type a new name.*
9. Type the file name **P24TryB_xx**, and then click Save.
10. Save the **P24TryA_xx** file, and leave it open to use in the next Try It.

Saving a presentation as a video

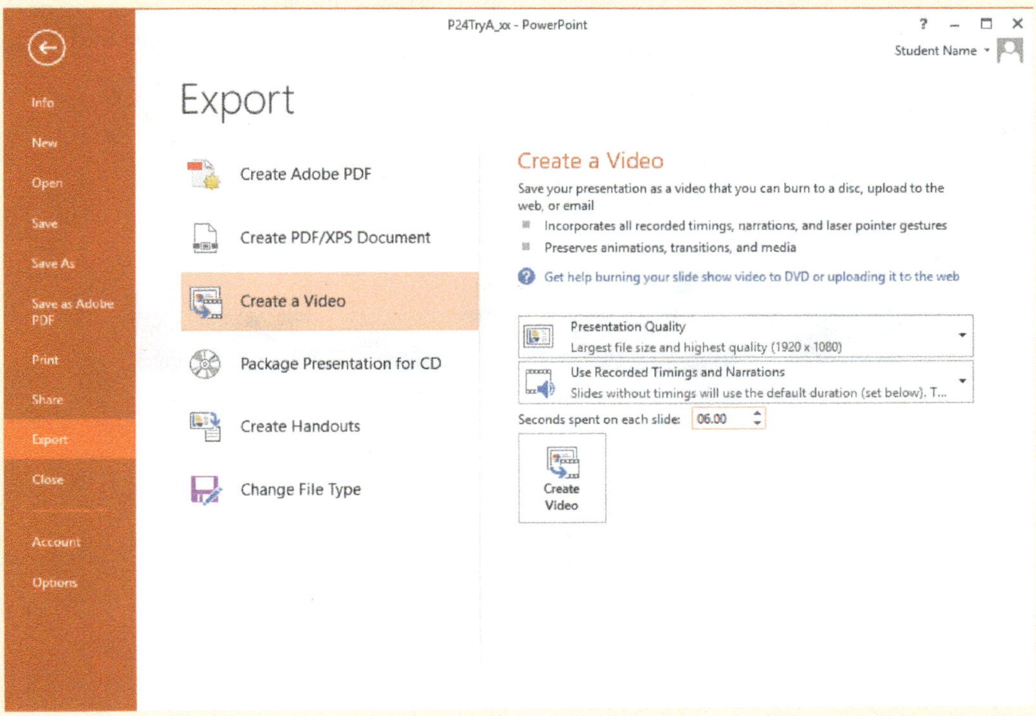

PowerPoint 2013, Windows 8, Microsoft Corporation

Publishing Slides

- You have other output options for a PowerPoint presentation.
- You can publish it to your Microsoft OneDrive site, where it can be viewed or edited online.
- You can save the presentation as a PowerPoint Show, which will open automatically in Slide Show view to save time.
- You can save the presentation to SharePoint, so that it is ready for collaboration.
- You can also set up a presentation to print on overhead transparencies, nonstandard paper sizes, or 35mm slides.
- You can export the presentation as a PDF or XPS document.
- You can export slides to Word handouts as an alternative to PowerPoint's built-in handout format.

Try It! Saving a Presentation on OneDrive

1. In the **P24TryA_xx** file, click FILE > Save As > OneDrive - Personal for your login e-mail address.
2. Click the Documents folder in the right pane to open the Save As dialog box.
3. Change the file name to **P24TryC_xx**, and then click Save. Try editing some of the slides online.
4. Close the **P24TryC_xx** file without saving, and leave PowerPoint open.

Try It! Viewing a Presentation on OneDrive

1. Start Internet Explorer and type **onedrive.live.com** in the address bar. Press ENTER.
2. In the Microsoft account box, type your Microsoft login e-mail address and click Sign in.
3. Press TAB and type your Microsoft account password.
4. Click Sign in. OneDrive opens in your browser.
5. Click the Documents folder to display the presentation you saved to OneDrive.
6. Click the presentation name to open it in the PowerPoint Online app.
7. Navigate through the slides using the next and previous arrows at the bottom of the window. Try making edits to some of the slides.
8. When you reach the end of the presentation, sign out of your OneDrive and close the browser.

Viewing the presentation in OneDrive

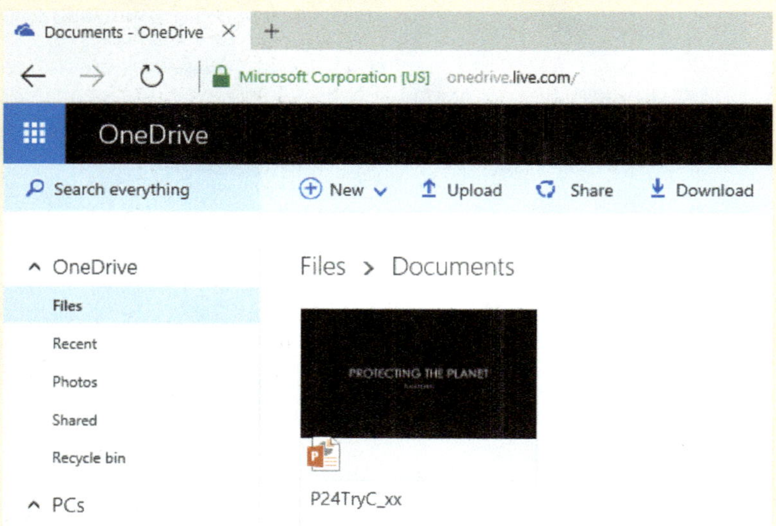

PowerPoint 2013, Windows 8, Microsoft Corporation

Try It! Saving a Presentation As a Show

1. In PowerPoint, click FILE > Open.
2. In the Recent Presentations list, click **P24TryA_xx**.
3. Click Save As > Browse and Navigate to the location where your teacher instructs you to store the files for this lesson.
4. Click the Save as type arrow, and click PowerPoint Show.
5. Type **P24TryD_xx**.
6. Click Save.
7. Close the file, and leave PowerPoint open.

Try It! Exporting a Presentation As a PDF

1. In PowerPoint, click FILE > Open.
2. In the Recent Presentations list, click **P24TryA_xx**.
3. Click FILE > Export > Create PDF/XPS Document.
4. Click Create PDF/XPS.
5. Navigate to the location where your teacher instructs you to store the files for this lesson.
6. Click the Save as type arrow, and click PDF (*.pdf), if necessary.
7. Type **P24TryE_xx**. in the File name box.
8. Click Publish. The presentation is saved and opens in a PDF viewer.
9. Browse and close the PDF file, and leave the **P24TryA_xx** file open in PowerPoint.

Try It! Exporting Handouts to a Word Document

1. With the **P24TryA_xx** file open in PowerPoint, click FILE > Export > Create Handouts.
2. Click Create Handouts.
3. In the Send to Microsoft Word dialog box, select Notes next to slides, or select a different page layout option.
4. Click Paste to paste the slides into Word. Click OK.
5. In Word, with the handouts displayed, click FILE > Save.
6. Navigate to the location where your teacher instructs you to store the files for this lesson.
7. Type **P24TryF_xx** in the File name box.
8. Click Save. You can print the handouts, if instructed, and then exit Word.
9. Close the **P24TryA_xx** file, and exit PowerPoint.

Lesson 24—Practice

The Campus Recreation Center is ready to start getting information out and wants to publish its presentation for several outlets. In this project, you create a video from the presentation slides.

DIRECTIONS

1. Start PowerPoint, if necessary, and open the **P24Practice** presentation from the data files for this lesson.
2. Click **FILE** > **Export** > **Create a Video**.
3. Click **Presentation Quality** and then click **Internet Quality**. The presentation video will have good clarity, but keep the file size small.
4. Click **Use Recorded Timings and Narrations** and then click **Preview Timings and Narration** to see how the presentation will look with the default 5:00 seconds spent on each slide.
5. Click the screen at the end of the slide show to return to the Create a Video options.
6. Type **6:00** in the Seconds spent on each slide box.
7. Click **Create Video**. The Save As dialog box opens.
8. Navigate to the location where your teacher instructs you to store the files for this lesson. Type **P24Practice_xx** in the File name text box, and then click **Save**, as shown in Figure 24-1.

   ✓ *Keep in mind that it will take several minutes for the video file to be completed.*

9. Close the presentation, and exit PowerPoint.
10. In File Explorer, navigate to the location where you stored the video and double-click it.
11. View the video, and, when it ends, close the Movies & TV window.

Figure 24-1

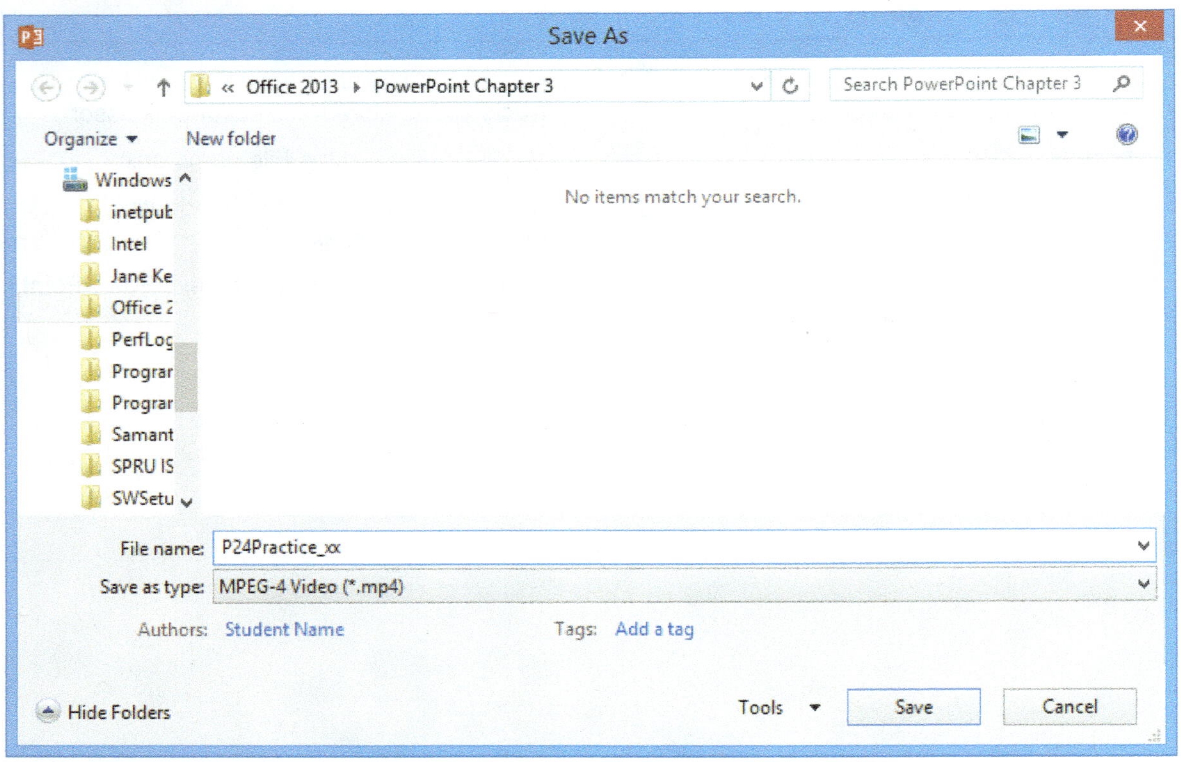

PowerPoint 2013, Windows 8, Microsoft Corporation

Lesson 24—Apply

You continue working with the Campus Recreation Center presentation. In this project, you will package the presentation on a CD or in a folder so that it can be transported to other locations.

DIRECTIONS

1. Start PowerPoint, if necessary, and open the **P24Apply** presentation from the data files for this lesson.
2. Save the presentation as **P24ApplyA_xx** in the location where your teacher instructs you to store the files for this lesson.
3. Package the presentation as follows:
   a. Name the CD folder in which to store the files **P24ApplyA_xx**.
   b. Display Options and choose to include linked files and embed TrueType fonts, if necessary.
   c. If you have the ability to copy to a CD, do so.
   d. If you cannot create a CD, then use Copy to Folder to save the folder where your teacher instructs you to store the files for this lesson.
4. Save the presentation as a PowerPoint Show with the name **P24ApplyB_xx**.
5. Navigate to the location where you stored the PowerPoint Show, double-click the file, and choose to view the show.
6. Close the file, saving changes, and exit PowerPoint.

End-of-Chapter Activities

➤ PowerPoint Chapter 3—Critical Thinking

Creating an Effective Presentation

As the office manager at the Michigan Avenue Athletic Club, you have found that many staff members deliver ineffective presentations. You decide to research techniques to make presentations more effective, and create a presentation about it to deliver at the next staff meeting.

DIRECTIONS

1. Use the Internet to research the topic "Creating an effective presentation in PowerPoint."
2. Start PowerPoint, and create a new presentation.
3. Save the presentation as **PCT03A_xx** in the location where your teacher instructs you to store the files for this chapter.
4. Apply the **View** theme to the presentation. Choose the variant with the orange vertical strip, and then hide background graphics on the title slide. Apply a different background style to the first slide only. Apply different theme colors and fonts if desired.
5. On slide 1, the title slide, enter the title **Effective Presentations** and the subtitle **Common Sense Rules for Delivering Your Message**.
6. Insert a footer that displays today's date and your name on all slides.
7. Add at least five slides to the presentation.
   a. Slide 2 should be an introduction.
   b. Slide 3 should be bullet points.
   c. Slide 4 should include a graphic.
   d. Slide 5 should be a conclusion or summary.
   e. Slide 6 should list your sources.
   f. You may choose to include additional slides between slide 4 and slide 5 to expand the topic, if necessary. Add graphics where they will enhance your message.
8. Apply transitions and animations to enhance the presentation's effectiveness.
9. If you have access to multimedia objects, insert them if they can enhance the presentation's effectiveness.
10. Save the presentation.
11. Preview the presentation to identify errors and problems, and assess how you might improve its effectiveness. For example, you might add slides so you can have fewer bullets per slide. You might adjust the font size or color to make it more readable. Save all changes.
12. Add notes to help you deliver the presentation.
13. Practice delivering the presentation, and then make changes to the presentation if necessary to improve its effectiveness. For example, you might want to make it longer or shorter, or change the timing for advancing between slides. Save changes.
14. Practice delivering the presentation again, until you are comfortable with it.
15. Deliver the presentation to your class.
16. Save the presentation as a PowerPoint Show with the name **PCT03B_xx**.
17. Navigate to the location where you stored the PowerPoint Show, double-click the file, and choose to view the show.
18. **With your teacher's permission**, print the presentation.
19. Close the presentation, saving changes, and exit PowerPoint.

➤ PowerPoint Chapter 3—Portfolio Builder

Enhancing a Presentation

The Marketing Manager of Restoration Architecture has asked you to take a recent presentation and improve its appearance to help get it ready for an upcoming event. You'll take advantage of your new skills to change the background, theme, colors, and fonts. You'll also add animations to the slides and change the chart and table. Finally, you'll create a video of the presentation.

DIRECTIONS

1. Start PowerPoint, and open **PPB03** from the data files for this chapter.
2. Save the presentation as **PPB03A_xx** in the location where your teacher instructs you to store the files for this chapter.
3. Change the theme colors to **Yellow**.
4. Change the background style for the title slide only to **Style 3**. Hide background graphics.
5. Change the font theme to **Gill Sans MT**.
6. Select the chart on slide 3 and change the chart type to **Pie**.
7. Change the chart style to **Style 7**.
8. Display the Chart Elements list and turn on Data Labels. Select **Outside End** for the data label position.
9. Change the colors in the chart to **Color 2**.
10. Right-click the dark gray chart area, click **Format Chart Area**, and then click No fill.
11. Select the table object on slide 5 and change its height to **3.5"** and the width to **8"**.
12. Center-align the table on the slide.
13. Change the table style to **Themed Style 2 - Accent 2**.
14. Select the WordArt graphic on slide 1 and change the WordArt style to **Fill - Orange, Accent 4, Soft Bevel**.
15. Add appropriate animations to text and objects.
16. Preview the presentation, and then make any necessary changes.
17. Deliver the presentation to your class.
18. Create a video of your presentation using the default resolution and timing settings. Save the video file as **PPB03B_xx** in the location where your teacher instructs you to store the files for this chapter. View the video.
19. Add a handout header and footer that includes a date that updates automatically and your name. Apply the footer to all.
20. **With your teacher's permission**, print a horizontal handouts page containing all the slides.
21. Close the presentation, saving changes, and exit PowerPoint.

Appendix A Computers and Software

Computer Basics

History and Purpose of Operating Systems

- An operating system (OS) is a set of instructions designed to work with a specific type of computer, such as a Dell® PC or a Macintosh® computer. The OS controls all the computer's functions. It also provides an interface, the on-screen tools you use to interact with the computer and your programs.
- The operating system manages the central processing unit (CPU) so that processing tasks are done properly, manages computer memory, manages files stored on the computer's disks, manages input and output devices, and loads application programs into memory.
- In 1984, Apple® became the first computer maker to offer a personal computer equipped with a graphical user interface (GUI). *Macintosh* names both the computer and its operating system.
- The DOS (Disk Operating System) operating system used in early personal computers was the basis for MS-DOS, Microsoft's first operating system. MS-DOS was eventually replaced in Microsoft computers by the Windows operating system, a GUI OS that has gone through multiple versions.
- UNIX was designed to work on powerful business and scientific computers. Later versions of UNIX have been developed to work on microcomputers, or personal computers.
- One of these versions of UNIX, a system called Linux, has become very popular. Linux works with an optional GUI and is very fast compared to other operating systems. It is also unique in that it is an open-source operating system, in which the source code (programming language) used to create it is available to the public.

Architecture of a Microcomputer System

- Microcomputer architecture refers to the hardware that makes up a typical computer system. Microcomputers generally have the following structure:
    - **Processing devices:** The *central processing unit*, or *CPU*, processes data. The CPU is a small, thin piece of silicon attached to a circuit board. The CPU is covered with tiny electrical circuits. By moving data along these circuits in specific ways, the CPU can calculate and compare data very quickly.
    - **Primary storage:** The computer's primary storage, called *random access memory*, or *RAM*, stores data and instructions while the computer is working in chips connected to the CPU. Data in RAM is lost when the computer is turned off.
    - **Secondary storage devices:** To provide storage for applications and files, most computers include secondary storage devices such as hard drives or DVD drives. These devices let you store data permanently—even when the computer is turned off.
    - **Peripherals:** Hardware that is separate but can be connected to the case is called a *peripheral*. Peripherals can include keyboards, mice, monitors, printers, scanners, and voice input devices. Peripherals are necessary to perform both input and output chores for the computer.

Figure A-1

Devices and peripherals connected to a computer system.

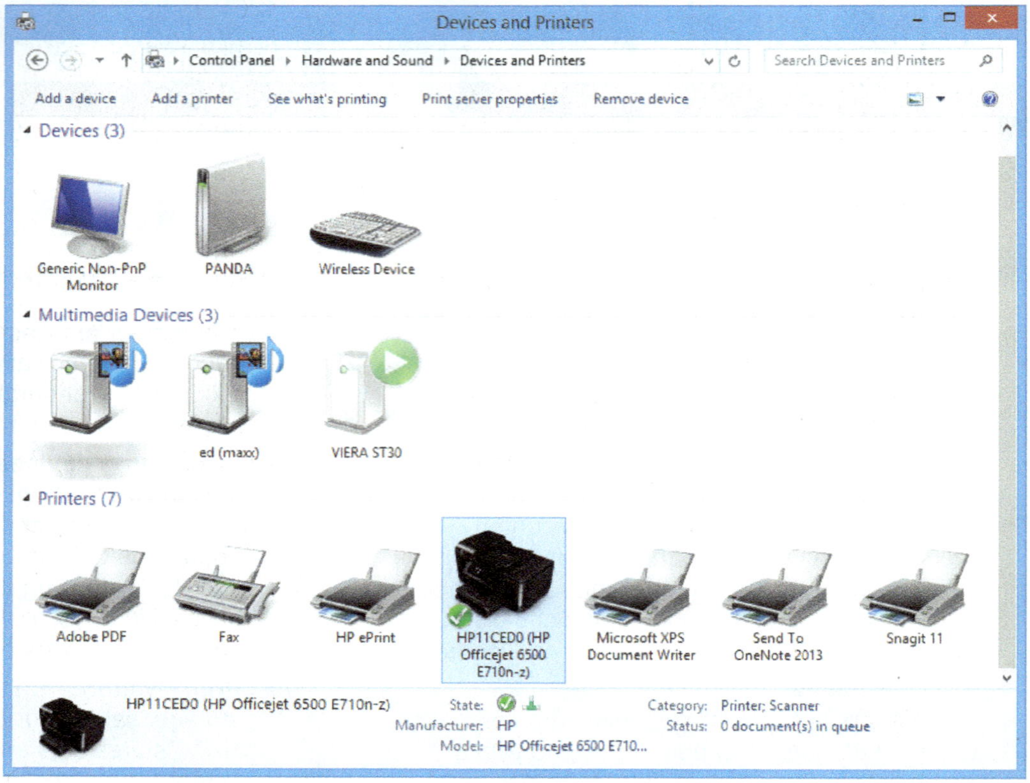

Understanding Software Applications and Software Upgrades

- Software includes all of the programs that tell a computer what to do and how to do it. Software is generally divided into two types: operating system software and application software.
- Application software performs a specific job or task. The most common types of application software include word processing software for writing letters and reports; spreadsheet software for calculations and numerical analysis; database software for storing and finding information; presentation software for creating slide shows; desktop publishing software for creating printer-ready publications such as brochures, newsletters, and invitations; browser software for navigating the Internet; and personal information manager (PIM) software for handling e-mail, schedules, tasks, and contacts.
- Other types of application software include programs for graphic design and manipulation, financial management packages, programs such as Java and Flash that allow you to create specialized content for Web pages, and even programs that allow you to write music.
- Most types of software undergo continuous review by their designers to identify performance problems and security issues, as well as to add new features and functionality. When software is changed by the vendor, the vendor issues an upgrade. Upgrades are usually handled by downloading revisions from the vendor. Some applications, such as operating systems, are configured to update automatically so users can always work with the most recent version.

Apply A-1

Several types of application software are listed in the *Understanding Software Applications and Software Upgrades* section. They include word processors, spreadsheets, databases, presentation graphics, telecommunications, and personal information managers. In this activity, you will learn more about application software.

DIRECTIONS

1. Using the Internet or other resources, prepare a report that evaluates, compares, and contrasts at least two types of application software that you may use based on their appropriateness for a task, licensing agreements, and available support.
2. As you work, take notes and keep track of your sources. Include a list of sources or bibliography with your report and format the bibliography using a standard reference style such as APA or MLA.
3. Evaluate the information you find and use it only if it is accurate, relevant, and valid.
4. Share your report with the class.

Internet Essentials

- The *Internet* is a network of networks. It connects everything from single computers to large networks. The Internet can even connect computers that run different operating systems. This ability to share information with almost any computer makes the Internet a powerful tool for communication.
- The *World Wide Web*, or *Web*, is one part of the Internet. The World Wide Web is a huge collection of documents linked by hypertext. Writers format documents and add the hyperlinks by using *HyperText Markup Language*, or *HTML*.

Connecting to the Internet

- Options for connecting to the Internet are based on availability, location, speed, and price. You can access the Internet using various types of phone lines (dial-up, DSL, or IDSN) or using cable or satellite technology. The resource you use to connect is called an *Internet service provider*, or *ISP*.
  - The least expensive way to get online is to use a dial-up connection between a standard phone line and a modem. These connections are called "dial-up" because your computer must connect to the Internet by using a telephone number to contact a server. Only 10 percent of households in the United States still use dial-up access.
  - Some Digital Subscriber Lines (DSL) require a special telephone line. Integrated Services Digital Network (ISDN) lines require a special ISDN adapter and modem. As a result, both services cost more than regular phone service. Furthermore, DSL and ISDN are not available in all areas.
  - Cable television companies offer Internet access through cable modems. This access is at speeds much faster than dial-up modems. You need a network card in your computer, a cable modem, and cable access. Satellite access is also very fast for downloading files to your computer, but it requires a phone line and a modem for sending files to outside users.
- Each computer that connects to the Internet has to be uniquely identified by a four-part number separated by periods called the *Internet Protocol (IP) address*. For example, the IP address for your computer might be 123.257.91.7. The administrator of the network to which your computer connects assigns your IP address.
- A *domain name* identifies one or more IP addresses and is used to locate information on the Internet. For example, an Internet server computer's domain name might be whitehouse.gov, but its numeric IP address might be 206.166.48.45. The domain name and the IP address are simply two ways to identify the same computer on the Internet.

- Every domain name has a suffix that tells which type of organization registered the name. The most common domains are .com (commercial), .edu (education), .org (nonprofit organizations), .gov (government), .mil (military), and .net (network organizations). These are called *top-level domains*.

How Browsers Work

- To access pages on the Web, users must use a Web browser. A *browser* is a software application designed to connect to and display pages from the Web.
- Browsers display Web pages in a graphical format that makes the content easy to understand. When you click a hyperlink (either a text link or an image), the Web browser retrieves and displays the document connected to that hyperlink. Every document has a unique address, called a *uniform resource locator (URL)*, which tells exactly where the document is located on the Internet. A hyperlink instructs the browser to go to the URL for that document.
- URLs give you all the information you need to know about connecting to a particular page, document, or other resource.
  - The first part of a URL specifies the protocol required to access the document. Web documents use http://, indicating that the file should be retrieved using hypertext transfer protocol (HTTP). Some URLs might have other protocols, such as ftp, which shows that the file should be retrieved with file transfer protocol. Another protocol, telnet, allows for access to remote computers.
  - The next part of a URL, such as www.fbi.gov, is the domain name of the server that stores the Web site. This part of the URL usually takes you to the site's home page.
  - The remainder of a URL, if any, defines the path to the document's location on the Web server. Like any computer, a Web server stores files in folders, so the path lists the folder and subfolders, if any, containing the desired document. Thus, a URL such as http://www.fbi.gov/employment/ identifies a folder named "employment" on the site's Web server.
  - At the end of a URL, you may see the name of a file—the specific Web resource for which you are looking. The resource may be an HTML document or a Web page, a video clip, a text file, or another type of resource. The file name extension identifies the type of resource.

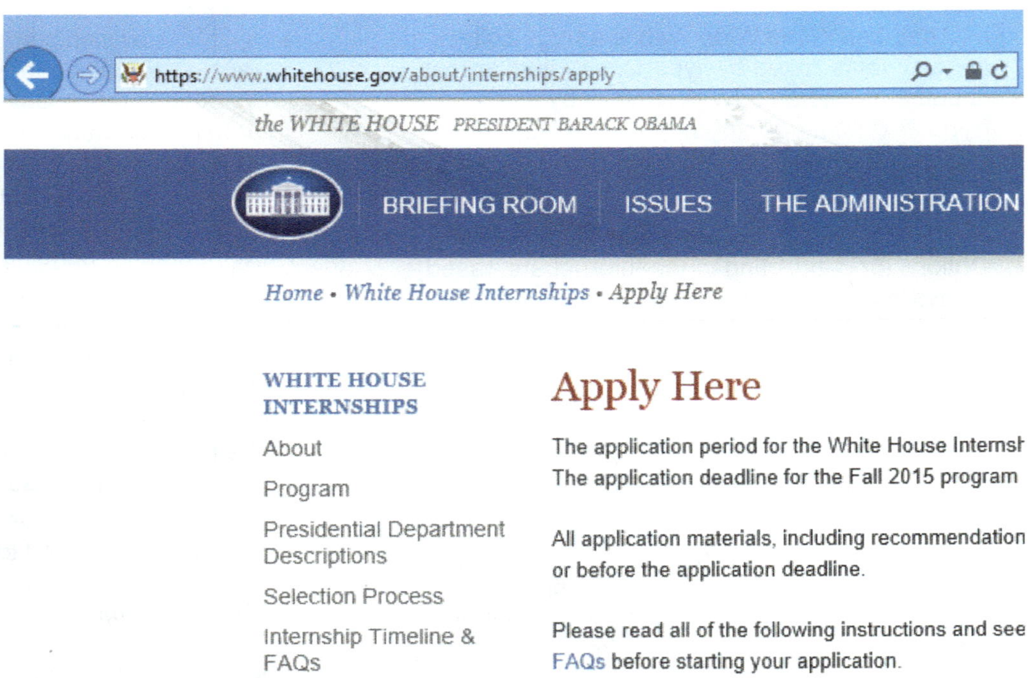

Figure A-2

The URL for this page at the White House Web site indicates the site is a secure site (the protocol is https) and has a government top-level domain (.gov). To reach this page, the user clicked a link for participation (about), then a link relating to internship information (internships), and finally a link to the Apply Here page (apply).

Working with a Browser

- Most Web browsers, including the popular Mozilla Firefox, Google Chrome, and Microsoft Internet Explorer, share some common features. By default, most browsers display Web pages in separate tabs so you can have more than one page open at a time. You can configure a browser's basic settings for your own needs by changing the default home page, for example, or adjusting the current zoom percentage.
- To keep track of Web pages you want to revisit, you can use a feature such as Favorites in Internet Explorer or Bookmarks in Google Chrome and Mozilla Firefox. Rather than retyping the URL, you can return to any bookmarked or favorite page by clicking its name in the list. You can delete a page from the Bookmark or Favorites list when you no longer need it. Browsers also track your browsing history. Display the History list to quickly find pages you visited in the past. Clear the History list to remove a record of sites you have visited.
- You can use your browser to access e-mail accounts if you do not subscribe to another mail client. Web mail accounts offer you access to your mail from any computer or mobile device and can be configured with appearance themes, custom folders, and information imported from other e-mail apps. You can import the contacts from your address book, for example, so you can easily sort mail according to who sent it.
- You can select different levels of security and privacy for your browser. For example, set a high security level to disable all Internet file downloads, or a high privacy level to block *cookies*—small files that store identification information—from being automatically stored on your computer. Most browsers include options for preventing tracking, so you do not leave a record of the sites you have visited.

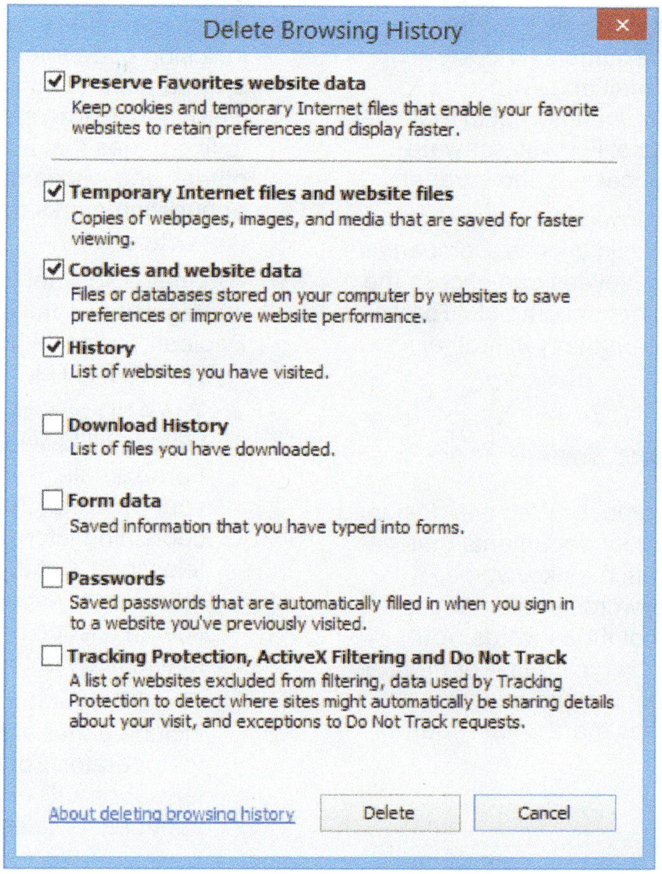

Figure A-3

Internet Explorer allows you to choose what information from your browsing sessions you want to keep.

Apply A-2

Being able to understand the information supplied in a URL will help you use the Web more efficiently. In this activity, you will apply what you have learned about URLs.

1. With your teacher's permission, use the Internet to locate a Web site with a URL that includes an international country code.
2. Copy the URL to a word-processing document.
3. Write a brief paragraph explaining the parts of the URL, including the country code.
4. Include a table in your document that lists country codes for at least ten countries, including the one you have already located.
5. Format the document and the table to improve visual appearance and reading comprehension.
6. Share your paragraph with a partner or the class.

Intranets and Extranets

- Rather than run all their operations and communications over the Internet, many companies, universities, and other organizations install intranets. An *intranet* is a private network that uses the same TCP/IP protocol as the Internet.
- Intranets offer many of the same services the Internet does, such as e-mail and Web sites. Intranets are different from the Internet in that they are not meant for public use. Firewall software prevents outsiders from accessing the intranet.
- An intranet can also be converted to an *extranet*, which allows for limited public access. Companies often use extranets so employees can access the network while they travel or telecommute. Extranets are also used to share information with other businesses.

Using Search Engines and Search Tools

- A *search engine* is a program or Web site designed to search the Web looking for documents that match specified criteria, such as keywords. Search engines index keywords in Web pages and maintain a database of those words. You can search for Web sites by typing one or more keywords in the search engine; the engine then displays a list of pages that contain your keyword(s).
- You can improve search effectiveness by using advanced search tools. For example, use an exact-phrase search by enclosing the text you want to find in quotation marks. Some search engines accept complete sentences in the form of a question, such as "How do hurricanes form?"
- Other advanced search tools include the use of inclusion operators (such as a plus sign) to find only pages that contain a match for all the specified words; exclusion operators (such as a minus sign) to find pages that contain certain words but not others; and wildcards—symbols such as asterisks or question marks that stand for one or more characters.
- You may also want to use Boolean search strategies to improve your searches. To conduct a Boolean search, type an operator such as AND, OR, or NOT to link the keywords in the search box.
  - The AND operator will result in pages that include all keywords connected by the operator. For example, if you use the word *telescope* as your keyword, the search engine will list pages containing information about every type of telescope. But if you are primarily interested in reflecting telescopes, you can use the Boolean search *telescope* AND *reflecting* to see pages that include both terms.
  - The OR operator will result in pages that include either of the keywords connected by the operator. For example, the search phrase *telescope* OR *microscope* will display pages about either telescopes or microscopes.

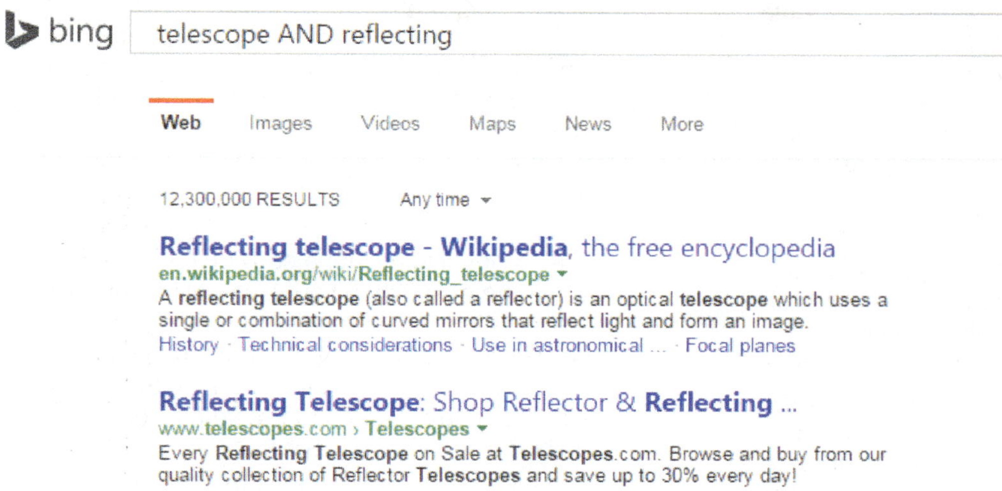

Figure A-4

A bing search using the Boolean operator AND finds pages for reflecting telescopes.

- The NOT operator excludes pages that might ordinarily be included in search results. The search phrase *tablet computers* NOT *iPad* would exclude iPad pages from the search results.

- Note that many search engines in wide use today do not necessarily follow Boolean search protocols because they use different algorithms to select and display search results. A search string such as *island resorts* NOT *Hilton Head* is likely to return a number of Hilton Head sites in a search engine such as Google or bing.

Using Web Tools to Display and Share Content

- The Internet makes it easy to share content using specialized tools for downloading and transferring content. File Transfer Protocol (FTP), for example, lets you transfer files from an FTP server to your computer in an operation called *downloading*. In *uploading*, you transfer files from the client to the server. Once you've stored a file on an FTP server, you can distribute the URL so that your friends can also download the file from the server.
- Telnet is an older protocol that lets users access files on remote computers. Telnet has largely been replaced by SSH and SSH2, which are encrypted and therefore more secure than telnet.
- The larger a file is, the more time it takes to travel over a network. File compression is a way of reducing file size so a file can travel more quickly over a network. If you are sending a large file, it is important to compress it. The most widely used compression software for a Windows system is WinZip®. Macintosh computers use a program called StuffIt™ to compress files and a utility called StuffIt Expander to decompress files.
- It's important to exercise caution when downloading files from the Internet, especially program files. Files are commonly used to transmit viruses. It's a good idea to check all downloaded files for viruses before saving them. You can also minimize the risk of getting a virus from a file by converting document files to PDF format. PDFs are less likely to contain viruses, and they can also be smaller than original document files.
- Many Web sites include mini programs called *plug-ins*. Plug-ins are embedded in a Web site to add a feature or function, such as a search engine or video player. One of the most well-known plug-ins is Adobe Flash Player. Plug-ins are complete programs and can even be installed on computers or other devices without a browser.

Internet Ethics

- How people use computers, including networks and e-mail, can affect other people. People who practice *ethics* behave morally. Ethical computer users respect others and make sure their actions do not harm anyone.
- One way you can act ethically is to follow your organization's *acceptable use policy*, or *AUP*. These policies identify the responsibilities of Internet use. They spell out certain rules of behavior and explain the consequences of breaking those rules.
- The federal government provides regulatory control over material you may find on the Internet. Copyright laws, the Fair Use Doctrine, and trademarks and patents should always be considered as part of ethical Internet behavior.
    - Copyright laws protect individuals and companies from the theft or misuse of their intellectual property, such as creative, literary, or artistic work. Copyright exists as soon as a work is created, but the creator can register it with the U.S. Copyright Office. It is a crime to copy this kind of work without the permission of the person who owns the copyright to it.
    - If the content is protected by copyright, you must have permission from the copyright holder to use the work. However, part of copyright law called the Fair Use Doctrine allows you to use a limited amount of copyrighted material without permission for educational purposes. For example, you can quote a few lines of a song or a passage from a book. Similarly, an author may issue a creative commons license allowing others to use the work.
    - Some intellectual property is protected by trademark or patent. A *trademark* is a symbol that indicates that a brand or brand name is legally protected and cannot be used by other businesses. A *patent* is the exclusive right to make, use, or sell a device or process. Many types of inventions can be patented.
- Two other ethical challenges may arise when using the Internet: software piracy and plagiarism.

Software Piracy

- ***Software piracy*** is the illegal copying of computer programs. It is estimated that about one-third of all software in use is pirated.
- Most programs that you buy are licensed only to the purchaser. In other words, it is illegal for you to copy such a program and give it to a friend. It is also illegal to accept a copy of software from someone else. When you use pirated software, you are violating U.S. copyright laws, and punishments can be serious: If you are convicted of copyright infringement, you can be fined up to $250,000 or sentenced to jail for up to five years—or you may be both fined *and* sentenced.
- Software piracy affects software publishers. They lose money when people use illegal copies of programs to avoid paying for legitimate copies.

Plagiarism

- If you do not cite your sources, you are guilty of *plagiarism*, which is the unauthorized use of another person's ideas or creative work without giving that person credit. Plagiarism is equivalent to stealing another person's work and passing it off as your own.
- The consequences of plagiarism can be quite significant. If you plagiarize work in school, you may have to redo the assignment or lose credit altogether. Your school may also take disciplinary actions, such as detention. In the professional world, the consequences of plagiarism are even more significant. A professional who plagiarizes work suffers a loss to his or her reputation and may face legal ramifications, such as a lawsuit.
- To avoid plagiarism you just need to properly cite your sources. You should insert a citation when you quote, summarize, or paraphrase someone else, use someone else's idea, or reference someone else's work. In a works cited section or footnote, you tell the reader the source of your credited information.

Apply A-3

In this activity, you will search the Internet to learn what types of information are protected by copyrights and what you legally can and cannot use. Then, you will use a word-processing program to make a top-ten list of facts about copyright laws.

1. Working with a partner and a table in which to record information, fill in one column with what you already know about copyright laws, creative commons, public domain, and open source regulations. Fill in another column with what you want to know.
2. **With your teacher's permission,** open your Web browser and navigate to a search engine.
3. Use the search engine to find information about copyright laws.
   a. Search for keywords from your table.
   b. Look for sites that explain what information you can and cannot use according to copyright laws.
   c. Research illegal acts such as software piracy, as well as patent and trademark infringement.
   d. Find sites that explain the consequences of violating these copyright laws in simple, easy to understand language.
4. Evaluate each site you visit for accuracy and validity.
5. Write down the source information about each Web page that you use.
6. **With your teacher's permission,** print relevant information from the Web sites you find most helpful. You may want to copy the information from the Web page into a word processing or notes program, along with the page's URL, and then print it.
7. Using your browser's History list, go back to one of the sites that explained the consequences of copyright violations. Mark the site as a favorite or bookmark it.
8. When you have finished your research, exit your Web browser.
9. Use your findings to write ten facts about copyright laws, creative commons, public domain, and open source regulations in a word processing document. Format the items as a numbered list.
10. Insert a page break after the last item in the numbered list. On the new page, insert a sources heading and format it appropriately.
11. On the next line, type a list of the Web sites or other sources you recorded, using a standard reference style such as MLA or APA. Format the sources in a smaller font size than the rest of the document text, and leave one blank line between sources. Remove all hyperlink formatting.
12. Proofread the document carefully. Check the spelling and grammar, and correct any errors.
13. Preview the document. Then, with your teacher's permission, print the document.
14. Close the document, saving all changes, and exit your word processing program.
15. As a class, brainstorm scenarios that do or do not violate copyright laws.

Networking and Emerging Technologies

Types of Networks and How They Work

- A computer network is two or more computers connected to one another to share resources such as files and equipment. Each computer has a network interface card that handles the flow of data to and from the computer. Computers may be connected with physical wires that carry data, or the network may be wireless, in which case the data travels through the air using microwave or radio wave technology.
- Networked computers that are near each other form a *local area network*, or *LAN*. A LAN might include all the computers in an office or a school; a home network could also be considered a LAN. Computers that are networked over an entire building, or in multiple locations, form a *wide area network*, or *WAN*.
- Two common types of network structure are peer-to-peer and client/server networks.
  - In a peer-to-peer (P2P) network, each computer is both a *client* and a *server*. Information can be shared equally from one computer to another; no specific computer controls the flow of information.
  - In a client/server network, one main computer or *server* controls access, permissions, and all aspects of network use. The server provides a directory, or list, of all resources available on the network. *Client* computers receive information from the server, usually requiring some form of security such as a user name and password to access the network.
- Networks are maintained by a *network administrator*. A network administrator may design, install, and monitor both the hardware and software required for the network. A network administrator also pays special attention to security to keep the network safe from trespassers and viruses.

Apply A-4

In this activity, you will explore more information about types of networks and how they are structured.

1. **With your teacher's permission,** conduct research in the library or on the Internet to find more details about different types of networks, including LANs, WANs, the Internet, and intranets.
2. Compare the advantages and disadvantages of peer-to-peer and client/server networks. If you can find illustrations of these network types, ask your teacher for permission to download and save them as files so you can use them in your report. Make sure to copy the source information for these images.
3. Explore the different operating capabilities of wired and wireless networks and the conditions under which they are appropriate.
4. Present your findings in a word processed document. Include in the document any images you were able to find to explain network architecture and functions.
5. Cite your sources of information and illustrations in MLA or APA format.
6. **With your teacher's permission,** print your report and share it with the class.

Benefits and Risks of Networked Computing

- People using a network can collaborate more easily than those working on standalone systems. Everyone on a network has the ability to access programs and data stored anywhere on the network. You might use an application such as Google Docs which is stored on a network rather than on your own computer, or you might print a document on a printer that is located on a different floor than your computer. Teams can function more efficiently when all members can access files from a network location.
- Networked computing also has risks. Anyone who is able to access the network, either legally using a password or illegally by hacking into the network, can gain access to sensitive files that might include financial or health data or proprietary company information. One of the most important tasks of a network administrator is to keep a network safe not only from careless users who may not follow internal security protocols but also from outside attackers determined to gain access to whatever is on the network.

Relationship between Computer Networks and Other Communications Networks

- "Communications network" used to refer to the widespread system of copper wiring that connected telephones throughout the world. Now copper wiring is being replaced by fiber-optic cables, strands of fiberglass that transmit digital data by pulses of light. These cables can carry large quantities of information, and they transmit data faster and more efficiently than copper wires.
- Fiber-optic cabling and wireless networks have made possible the same types of connectivity found with computer networks.
  - Wireless connections, or Wi-Fi, use radio waves to connect devices such as computers or cell phones.
  - Teleconferencing and videoconferencing rely on fast network connections and increased broadband width available with fiber-optic cabling.
  - "Telepresence" videoconferencing and virtual reality systems also rely on high-end computer networking to supply greater fidelity of motion and sound.

Communicating in the 21st Century

- Today's high-speed networks, both wired and wireless, are one contributor to the sophisticated ways people now communicate.
- Smart devices such as tablets, smartphones, and wearable technology rely on wireless communication options such as Wi-Fi and Bluetooth and communications satellites to supply information to the user at almost any location.
- Almost instant connectivity has had a tremendous impact on businesses around the world. A shopper can now use an online source to purchase almost anything, at any time of the day or night, on any day of the year. Corporations can form teams with members from widely separated locations who can collaborate by sharing information stored on the cloud, with deep savings in travel costs. Employees can telework, allowing businesses to function more efficiently in smaller office spaces. It is even possible for a surgeon in one city to control a robot to conduct an operation in a different city.
- Emerging technologies such as smart devices have driven a boom in consumer spending, because people are always eager to have the latest version of popular devices. As the science of nanotechnology becomes more widespread and cost-effective, the ability to manipulate matter at the atomic level may lead to ever more sophisticated computers and medical devices.

Figure A-5 Tablet PCs are a convenient way to keep in touch when you're traveling.

Apply A-5

In this activity, you will conduct research to learn about technology trends. Then, you will create a slide presentation to display your findings.

1. **With your teacher's permission,** open a Web browser and navigate to a search engine. Search for sites that offer information about technology trends and emerging technologies. Try to identify at least five trends. For example, you might research wireless networks, tablets, touch screens, smartphones, satellite technology, nanotechnology, or smart devices.
   a. Try searching for words or phrases such as *technology trends*, or use a Boolean search such as *Technology AND Trends*. Review each Web site you visit for accuracy and validity. When possible, find at least two sources for each fact. When you find a Web site with useful information, bookmark the site, or with your teacher's permission, print the pages. Check copyright guidelines to make sure you may legally use the content. When you have completed your research, close your Web browser.
   b. Record the information that you find. Include the name of each trend and a description.
   c. If you locate any images or photographs related to the trends, ask your teacher for permission to download and save them as files so you can use them in your presentation. Again, make sure you can use them legally.
   d. Record your source citation information.
2. With the information you have recorded, draw a storyboard to map a presentation of at least eleven slides. Use project- and time-management skills to be sure you complete the presentation by the due date.
3. Start your presentation program. Create a new presentation, and save it with an appropriate name in the location where your teacher tells you to store the files for this activity.
4. Apply a theme or design to the presentation.
5. Format the first slide to contain a title such as "What's New in the Computer World?" and a subtitle such as "Latest Technology Trends." Insert a footer on this slide only that reads "Prepared by [your full name]," along with today's date.
6. Develop your presentation, creating one or two slides for each trend you recorded. Select an appropriate slide layout, enter a title, and insert the content. Include a slide listing ways the trends and emerging technologies impact individuals and businesses. On another slide, create a chart that compares and contrasts the trends and technologies.
7. When you have finished creating your slides, proofread each one carefully with a partner or peer editor. Correct any errors in spelling, capitalization, punctuation, or usage.
8. View the slide show and make any changes that you think will improve the presentation value, or make the presentation more effective.
9. Add transitions and animations, and view the presentation again.
10. Add speaker's notes that you can refer to while delivering the presentation.
11. **With your teacher's permission,** print the notes pages for yourself, and print handouts with three slides per page for the class.
12. Rehearse the presentation.
13. Show your presentation to the class and respectfully watch the presentations of your classmates.
14. Close the presentation, saving all changes, and exit the presentation program.
15. As a class, discuss some of the more interesting trends you discovered during your research. What other new developments do you expect to see within the next ten years? In what new ways do you think computers and/or technology will be used in the future? How are these technology trends relevant to daily living, lifelong learning, and future careers?

Caring for a Computer System

Diagnosing and Troubleshooting Computer Problems

- When your computer is not working properly, you can use diagnosis and troubleshooting to identify and fix problems. Diagnosing includes steps for figuring out what is causing the problem, and troubleshooting involves solving the problem.
- You can solve many computer problems yourself by taking simple steps. For example, problems can occur when cables or wires become loose. When your monitor goes dark or your keyboard won't respond, turn the system off and check to make sure all cables are securely connected. Many computers are plugged in to a power strip. Make sure the power strip is on. If your wireless mouse or keyboard stops working, you may need to change the battery in the device.
- Many computer problems—such as a program freezing—can be solved by a simple reboot. When you reboot your computer, you turn it off and then on again. If your computer is unresponsive and you cannot reboot, you may be able to use a key combination to access a troubleshooting menu or restart the computer. On a Windows PC, you can press Ctrl + Alt + Delete.
- If programs do not work correctly, make sure you are running them on a compatible operating system, with at least the minimum operating criteria for the software. Also make sure you have the hardware required to run the software.
- You can often refer to documentation in a manual or online source for troubleshooting information. In addition, many systems come with built-in troubleshooter utilities. Usually these prompt you through a series of questions to diagnose the problem, and they may offer suggestions for action you should take.
- Steps for troubleshooting devices and peripherals are similar to troubleshooting the entire computer system. First, check the cables and connections. Second, turn the device off and then back on. If there is still a problem, you can look for a troubleshooter utility for the device in your operating system's Help program, or use a device management utility to check that the device is set up properly and that the driver software is installed and up to date. In Windows it is called Device Manager; on Mac systems, it is called Profile Manager.
- If a device stops working, you can update the driver, roll back the driver to a previous version, disable the driver, or uninstall and reinstall it.
- You can often use a utility to restore your system to the state it was in before it stopped working. Windows comes with a Restore utility. You select the date and time to which you want to revert, and Windows runs a program to restore that configuration. Changes that occurred since that date and time are undone, including new software installation or modified system settings.

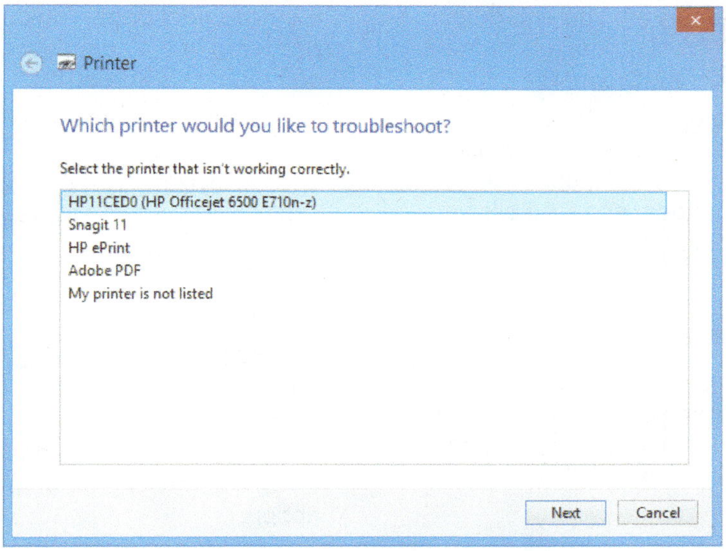

Figure A-6

A Windows 8 troubleshooting utility for solving printer problems.

- Some computers come with recovery CDs or DVDs that you insert into the appropriate drive before rebooting. You may then select from a menu of options for checking and repairing problems.

Software Security

- You can prevent many software problems by keeping your software secure.
- One of the simplest and most important methods of protecting data and keeping your computer running efficiently is to install and use an antivirus program or antimalware program to identify and remove viruses, spyware, and malware. These programs continually monitor your system for dangerous files. Once they find a virus, they delete it or at least quarantine it so it can do no harm.
- Simply installing an antivirus program is not enough to protect your computer. New viruses are created every day. Software publishers update their antivirus programs to defeat each new attack. You must update your version of the program to take advantage of these changes. Fortunately, the companies generally make it easy to download updates over the Internet.
- To protect yourself from viruses, follow these simple rules:
  - Install an antivirus program on your computer and keep the program up to date.
  - Always check files that you download from the Internet for viruses before saving them to your hard drive.
  - If your antivirus program can do so, set it to monitor incoming e-mail messages and to check files.
  - Always check the disks you borrow from someone else before using them on your computer.
- To help block unauthorized users from accessing your computer through a network, you can install and activate a firewall. A *firewall* is a program that restricts unauthorized access. Most operating systems, including Microsoft Windows, come with a firewall, and so do many antivirus programs.
- Backing up is simply creating a copy of the data on your hard drive that is stored separately in an offsite or remote location away from the hard drive. You can back up data manually or use a program that performs the backup automatically on a set schedule.

Advanced Word Processing Topics

Sharing Documents

- Word processing programs generally offer options for distributing content. In Microsoft Word, for example, you can create Web pages, send documents to others via e-mail attachment, output a document to a PDF or XPS file, post a document to a blog, or save it on your OneDrive.
- One good reason to share documents is to allow others to edit it in a team environment. Word offers several important collaboration tools, such as comments and tracked changes, and also allows the author to protect the document to allow only certain types of edits.

Inserting and Modifying Comments

- Insert a comment to annotate text, to communicate with readers, or to attach reminders or questions to a document. The command for inserting a comment is in the Comments group on the REVIEW tab of the ribbon.
- When you insert a comment, Word inserts comment marks around the word to the left of the current insertion point location, or around selected text. By default, each comment displays in a balloon in the markup area on the right side of the document page. You can also rest the mouse pointer over the comment marks to display the comment in a ScreenTip.
- Comment marks and comment balloons are color coded by reviewer.
- You can edit the text in a comment at any time. You can delete a single comment or you can delete all comments in a document.

Tracking Changes

- Word's Track Changes feature can be used to apply revision marks to all insertions, deletions, formatting changes, and ink annotations in a document. The commands for tracking changes are in the Tracking group on the REVIEW tab of the ribbon.

- By default, Word inserts a vertical line in the left margin of any changed line to indicate where revisions occur in the document.
- The way that revisions are marked onscreen depends on the selected Display for Review and Show Markup options.
- The Display for Review button provides four options:
    - Simple Markup displays the document with a red vertical line in the left margin of a line with a revision. Insertions, deletions, comments, and formatting changes display as they would look in the final document if the changes are accepted. This is the default option.
    - All Markup displays the document with all insertions, deletions, and comments marked. Formatting changes display as they look in the original document if the changes are accepted.
    - No Markup displays the document as it would look if all revisions are accepted.
    - Original displays the document as it would look if all revisions are rejected.
- Revisions are color coded by reviewer.

Protecting a Document

- You can protect a document from unauthorized changes by restricting the ability of others to make edits or apply formatting. To restrict formatting changes, you use options in the Formatting Restrictions dialog box to limit the ability of others to modify selected styles and apply direct formatting.
- To restrict editing changes, you may select from four options:
    - Tracked changes. Use this option to force edits to display using revision marks.
    - Comments. Use this option to allow others to enter comments without being able to edit document text.
    - Filling in forms. Use this option to allow changes in content controls only.
    - No changes (Read only). Use this option when you do not want to allow any changes at all.
- The options for setting restrictions are found in the Restrict Editing pane, which you can access using the Restrict Editing button on the DEVELOPER or REVIEW tab of the ribbon.

Figure A-7 Use comments and tracked changes to review a document.

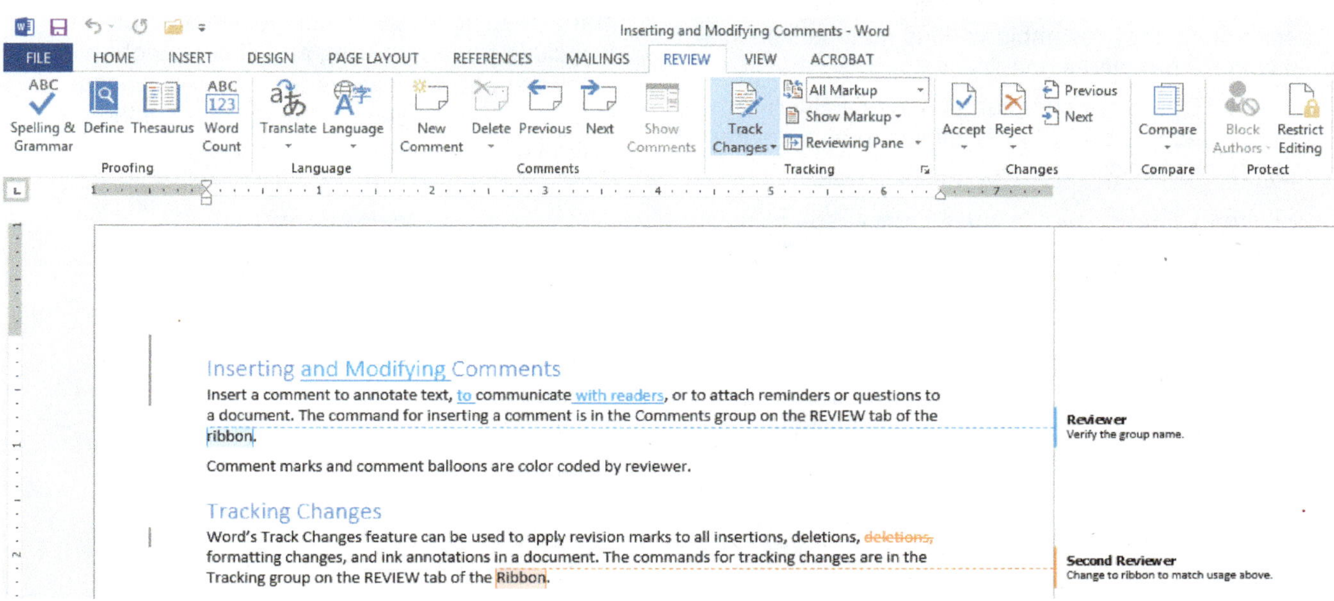

- When you open a protected document, the Restrict Editing pane displays information about the changes you may or may not make to the document.
- You can remove the protection to enable unlimited editing.
- Another way to protect a document is to assign a password or apply encryption. You can assign a password and encrypt a document at the same time using options on the Info tab in the Backstage view.

Inserting a Page Background and Hyperlinks

- You can format any Word document (or a Web page created with a Word document) with a page background and add hyperlinks to connect the document to other locations.
- By default, Word documents—including Web pages—have a plain white background. Add visual interest or create an effect by applying a color, pattern, fill effect, or picture to a document background.
- One of the fill effects available is gradient, which is a gradual blend from one color to another. Another effect is texture. Textures are small graphic files that repeat as many times as needed to fill the background; they resemble various materials such as wood, cloth, and stone.
- Use the Page Color command on the DESIGN tab to access colors and other fill effects to apply to the page background.
- Hyperlinks can be used to connect locations within a single document, to connect two documents, to connect a document to a Web page or e-mail address, or to point to a specific heading or bookmark within a document. Links can be created in any type of Word document.
- When you format text as a link, Word automatically applies the Hyperlink style, which by default uses a blue font and a solid underline, but may be different depending on the current theme. Once you click the link, the font color changes to indicate that the link has been used.
- Use the Hyperlink command on the INSERT tab to set up hyperlinks in a document.

Creating a Table of Contents

- Use the Table of Contents command on the REFERENCES tab to begin the process of inserting a table of contents. Word generates the table of contents based on paragraphs formatted with heading level styles. If there are no heading levels assigned, Word cannot generate the table of contents.
- You can select from a list of built-in table of contents styles or use options in the Table of Contents dialog box to manually create a customized table. For example, you can select how many heading levels to include, whether or not to include page numbers, and, if so, to right-align them and use tab leaders. You can also choose to format the headings in the table of contents as hyperlinks.

Figure A-8

Use the Table of Contents dialog box to choose the setup for your TOC.

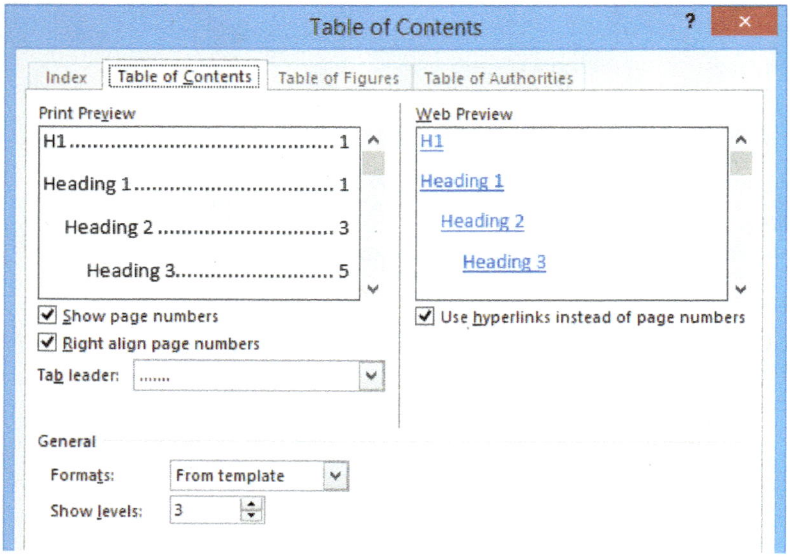

- If you make changes to text and headings in the document, you can update the table of contents to show new page numbers or contents entries.

Creating Macros

- To efficiently complete repetitive tasks, such as performing identical formatting chores in a number of documents, you can create a macro. A macro gathers a number of instructions into a single program that you can run with a single command. You will find the command to create a new macro on the VIEW tab in Word 2013.
- You create a macro by executing the steps you want to capture. Then you end the macro, storing it so that it can be used again.
- You may want to rehearse the steps you will use to create the macro before recording it because some tasks have to be done in a certain way during the recording process. You cannot use the mouse to select text, for example. Instead, you must use a keyboard combination to select text.
- When you start the process of creating a new macro, you assign it a name, choose a shortcut option for running the macro, and choose whether to store it in the current document or in the Normal template so it will be available for all documents based on that template.
- If you choose to store the macro in the current document, you must then save the document in the Word Macro-Enabled Document (*.docm) format. Trying to save the document as a regular Word document will result in Word's discarding the macro after you close the document.
- Run a macro by choosing it in the Macros dialog box, by clicking a button you create, or by pressing a key combination you assign.

Apply A-6

In this activity, you explore different word processing programs available for purchase or free download.

1. **With your teacher's permission,** use the Web to conduct research on different word processing programs.
2. Research both applications for purchase from vendors such as Microsoft and applications you can download or use for free, such as Google Docs.
3. Prepare a list of features by which to compare the applications. For example, what types of reviewing features does each application have? What options does each application have for saving documents in other formats and sharing documents with others?
4. Record your findings in a chart so you can compare and contrast the available features.
5. Select the program you think would be best for creating documents for business communication.
6. Explain your selection to a partner or to the class.

Advanced Presentation Topics

Design and Color Theory for Presentations

- When you use a presentation application such as PowerPoint 2013, some of the work of designing slides and selecting colors has already been done for you. PowerPoint design templates position titles, text, and other content according to standard design principles, including balance, emphasis, unity, and the use of white space.
- Each design template includes a palette of eight colors that are designed to work well together. These colors have been selected according to accepted principles of color theory: one color is used predominantly for the background of the slides, and then colors that may be complementary (opposite on the color wheel) or analogous (next to each other on the color wheel) are used for text and accents.
- If you want to design your own template, keep in mind the design and color principles used in the professionally designed templates. For example, make sure that the area you allow for content will balance the area used for the slide title. Do not crowd placeholders on the slide, leaving white space to make the content easy to understand. Use colors that do not clash with each other, as complementary colors often can, but include accent colors that will provide a welcome visual emphasis.

Finalizing and Packaging a Presentation

- Once you have completed the process of adding content to a presentation, you are ready to consider some final options, such as linking slides, rehearsing timings, and choosing how to package the presentation so you can deliver it elsewhere.

Figure A-9

In a PowerPoint theme, colors are preselected to provide choices of backgrounds and text and accent colors that work well together.

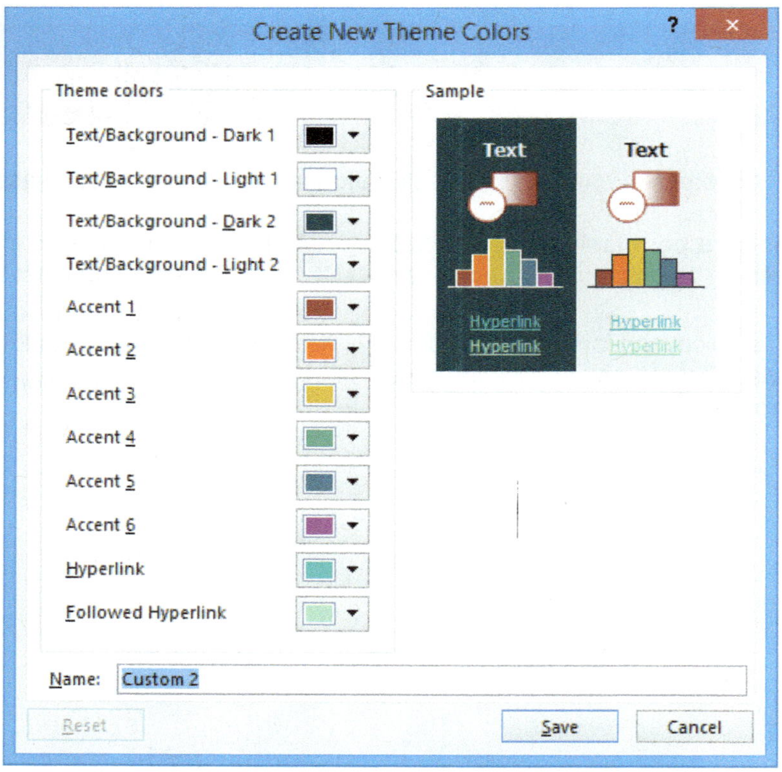

Linking Slides to Other Locations

- You can use hyperlinks to make it easy to navigate from place to place during the presentation.
- Use the Hyperlink button in the Links group on the INSERT tab to set up links from a slide to another slide, to a different presentation or document, to a Web site, or to an e-mail address. Use text for your link or use a shape, picture, or other graphic.
- The Insert Hyperlink dialog box allows you to select the target of the link—the slide that will display or the page that will open when the link is clicked.
- Links are active only in Slide Show view.

Rehearsing Timings

- You must decide at this point how the presentation will be delivered. Will you present each slide yourself, advancing the slides by mouse click at your own speed, or will you set up the show to be browsed at a kiosk, with the slides advancing automatically? If the slides are to advance automatically, you can rehearse slide timings to make sure you are allowing enough time for your audience to read each slide.
- Use the Rehearse Timings command on the SLIDE SHOW tab to start the presentation and display the Recording toolbar. As you view each slide, the timers show how much time you have spent on that slide as well as the total time elapsed for the show.
- You can use buttons on the Recording toolbar to pause and restart the show, and you can also repeat a slide if you find you need to start again.
- After you have finished viewing all slides, PowerPoint asks if you want to keep the slide timings. If you click Yes, these timings replace any other advance timings you have set.

Packaging and Creating Videos

- Use the Package Presentation for CD feature when you want to run a slide show on another computer.
- The Package for CD dialog box lets you control the process of packaging the presentation files and copying them to a folder or a CD.
- If you choose the folder option, you can store the presentation on removable media such as a flash drive that can be easier to transport than a CD.
- By default, PowerPoint links all files used in the presentation, such as videos and images. PowerPoint will also embed the fonts used to create the text, so that even if the computer on which you will present the slides does not have the fonts, they will display correctly during the presentation.
- You can also save your PowerPoint presentation as a video that can be shared with others to be viewed on a PC or uploaded to the Internet. PowerPoint will save the presentation as an MP4 file, which can be uploaded to YouTube, Facebook, or other Web sites.
- Your presentation video can include unique timings and narration, or you can set a specific number of seconds that each slide will be paused.

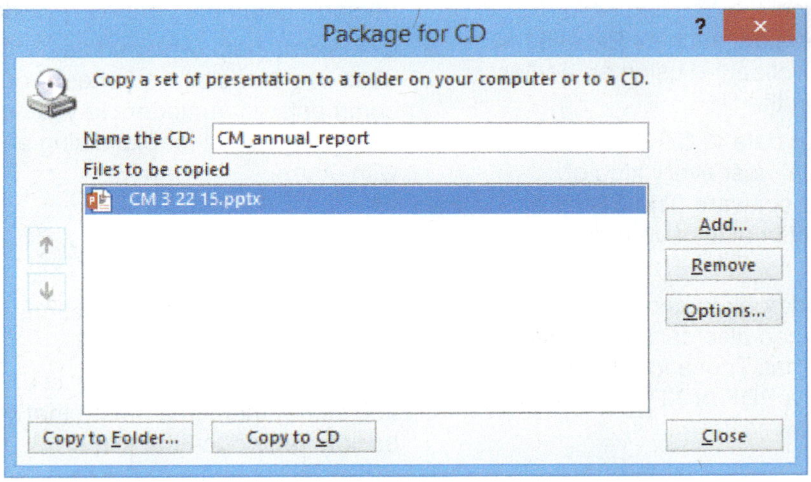

Figure A-10

Use the Package for CD dialog box to begin the process of packaging a slide show to present elsewhere.

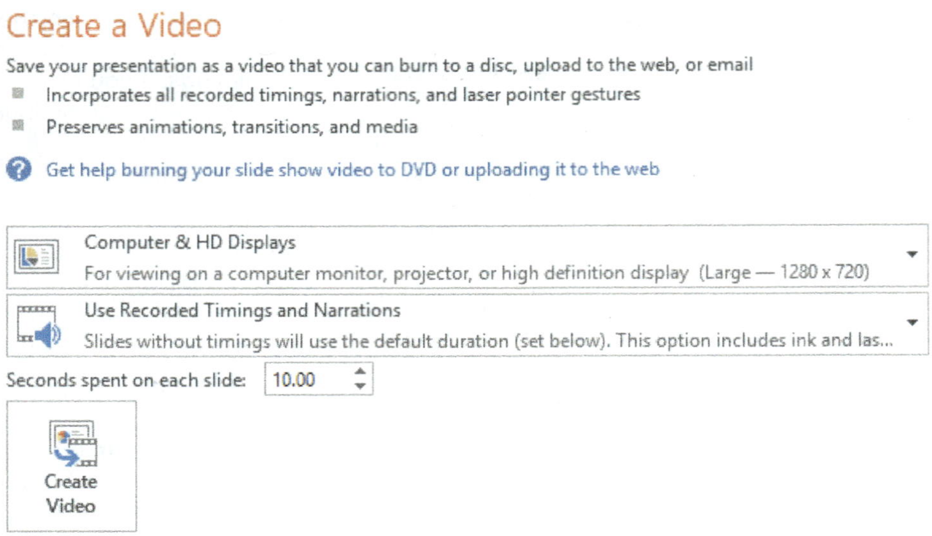

Figure A-11

Use the Create a Video option on the Export tab in Backstage view to create a PowerPoint video.

Advanced Spreadsheet Topics

Sharing Excel Worksheet Data

- One way to share worksheet data is to use the workbook as a data source in a mail merge operation. When you select a workbook during a word processing mail merge, you can select the desired worksheet and specify the worksheet's column headings as merge fields.
- Another way to share worksheet data is to simply send it to a colleague as an attachment to an e-mail message.
- When sharing worksheet data, you should consider whether the person you are sharing with has the capability to open the Excel file. You can save an Excel file to a previous version, such as Excel 97 – 2003 format, so that a colleague using an earlier version of Excel can open the file.
- You can also convert your data to CSV format, which is compatible with almost every kind of spreadsheet or database software. The CSV file format maintains the functionality of your data, but the formatting is lost.
- Besides converting a workbook to another spreadsheet format, you can also convert the file to PDF format and XPS format. These formats can be read by anyone who has a PDF or XPS reader, but the files cannot be edited.

Working with Comments

- You can attach a text note to a cell by using the New Comment button on the REVIEW tab. A red triangle appears in the upper-right corner of any cell with an attached comment.
- To display a comment, hover the mouse pointer on the cell containing the comment indicator (the red triangle). You can also display all comments on a worksheet using the Show All Comments command.
- Comments are marked with the user's name, so if more than one person works on a worksheet, each person's comments are easy to identify.
- Comments help explain data, formulas, and labels used in a complex worksheet. You can insert comments as reminders to yourself, but they are especially useful for explaining a worksheet shared with others.

Creating a Macro in Excel

- Create a macro to record actions that you intend to use for multiple worksheets.
- The macro recorder records every action you take and stores them in a macro that you can later play back to reproduce the steps.

- You can record a macro that includes steps such as typing text, selecting cells or cell ranges, clicking commands on the ribbon, and formatting cells, rows, or columns.
- The commands for recording, creating, and deleting macros are available on the DEVELOPER tab on the ribbon.
- When you record a macro, Excel records the actual addresses of the cells by default. For example, if the active cell happens to be cell D2 when you begin recording a macro that makes the active cell bold, the macro will always make cell D2 bold, regardless of the position of the active cell when you run that macro.
- You can also record a macro that will perform the recorded action on the cell or cell range selected before running the macro.
- You can name a macro to make it easier to reference. The first character of the macro name must be a letter. You can use letters, numbers, or underscore characters in the name of a macro; however, you cannot use spaces in a macro name.
- The default file extension for Excel 2013 is .xlsx. This file format cannot contain macros, by design, to avoid potential malware threats associated with macros.
- A workbook must be saved in .xlsm format in order to enable it to store macros.
- When you open a macro-enabled workbook, you can click Enable Content in the security warning notification to enable the macros.

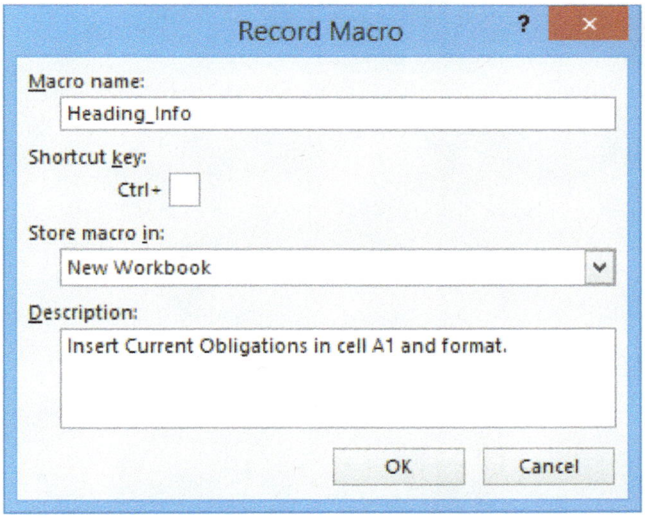

Figure A-12

Begin the process of creating a macro in the Record Macro dialog box.

Project Management Topics

Basic Project Management Concepts

- In order to successfully complete a project, it is important to use project management skills and techniques.
- Project management includes defining goals, developing a plan to achieve those goals, and then implementing the plan.
- It requires the ability to understand and employ concepts and tools such as:
    - Timeline—a graphic description of the events that will take place over time in a project.
    - Deadline—the date by which a project or a project phase should be completed.
    - Resource allocation—a plan for using available resources to complete a project.
    - Time management—controlling and organizing a schedule in order to accomplish tasks and meet responsibilities.
    - Delegation of tasks—distributing a project's responsibilities to appropriate staff members.
    - Collaboration—working with a team to complete a specific project.
- A well-managed project is completed on schedule and within budget, and achieves the stated goals.

Appendix B Web Topics

Working with Web Pages

Color Theory for Web Page Design

- As for presentation slide design, colors for Web pages should be selected according to accepted principles of color theory. Designers often select one of three basic color themes:
  - A triadic color theme uses three colors that are equidistant on the color wheel.
  - A complementary color theme uses colors that are opposite each other on the color wheel.
  - An analogous color theme uses colors that are next to each other on the color wheel.
- Another option is a monochromatic color theme, which uses one color along with tints or shades of that color.
- Color can be used to focus attention on a part of the page you want to emphasize, such as a box containing contact information or recent news. Generally speaking, bright colors draw attention while darker colors can lead to a more muted response from viewers.
- Color theory also assigns particular emotional responses to specific colors that a Web designer should be aware of. Red, for example, conveys power, passion, and importance. Green may be used to denote growth, stability, or an environmental approach.

Acquiring Graphics for Web Pages

- Web pages require images for visual interest. Images are generally saved in JPG format and may be acquired by scanning existing photos, taking pictures with a digital camera, or downloading images from reputable online sources such as stock photo vendors.
- You may also purchase images, both photos and clip art, on CD or DVD. This is a good way to acquire specialized images such as scrolls, symbols, or pictures that relate to particular topics.

Languages Used in Web Design

- Basic Web pages are constructed using HTML (Hypertext Markup Language) coding. This language is sufficient for placing text and graphics on a page.
- To simplify the process of storing and sharing data over different types of platforms, Web designers often use XML (eXtensible Markup Language).
- A designer may use DHTML (Dynamic HTML) to add interactivity and animation to a Web site. DHTML combines HTML with a scripting language such as JavaScript to run dynamic content after a Web page has loaded in a browser. Animation can also be added by embedding Flash objects in a Web page.
- Other high-level languages such as Python and Perl can be used to create Web site content. Perl is especially useful for processing large amounts of data for heavily used Web sites.
- You can learn more about computer programming from online tutorials and sites such as code.org.

Creating Personal and Business Web Pages

- Before you begin the process of creating Web content, you may find it helpful to create a storyboard of your Web site. A storyboard is a map or plan that defines the layout, organization, and navigational structure of the site.
- You have a number of options for creating your Web pages. For a simple Web site, you can enter HTML code directly into a text editor such as Notepad, or you can save a word processing document in HTML format. You can also use an HTML editor such as HomeSite™ or BBEdit™. These programs feature text editing and an easier way to add HTML tags.

- WYSIWYG Web page editors are sophisticated editing programs that let you create a page without entering tags yourself. (WYSIWYG stands for "What You See Is What You Get.") These applications are almost as easy to use as a word processor and feature many of the same kinds of editing and formatting tools. You set up the page to look the way you want, including graphics or hyperlinks, and the application automatically handles the HTML coding for you. Adobe® Dreamweaver® is an example of a program that automates the process of formatting documents for the Web. Microsoft Expression is a WYSIWYG editor you can download for free.
- Some WYSIWYG editors will also help you to create dynamic Web content such as rotating banners and rollover buttons using DHTML coding and work with XML content by creating XSLT (Extensible Stylesheet Language Transformations) pages.
- Create visual interest on your Web pages by adding graphics such as pictures, charts, illustrations, tables of data, or diagrams. To prevent your pages from being too static, and therefore dull, you can build in animation of various sorts. Include pictures that transition from one to another, menus that cascade, buttons that change appearance when you position the mouse over them or click on them, videos to deliver content visually, animated graphics such as those you can create using Flash, and so on.

Figure B-1 A Web editor such as Microsoft Expression lets you see the content as you build the code.

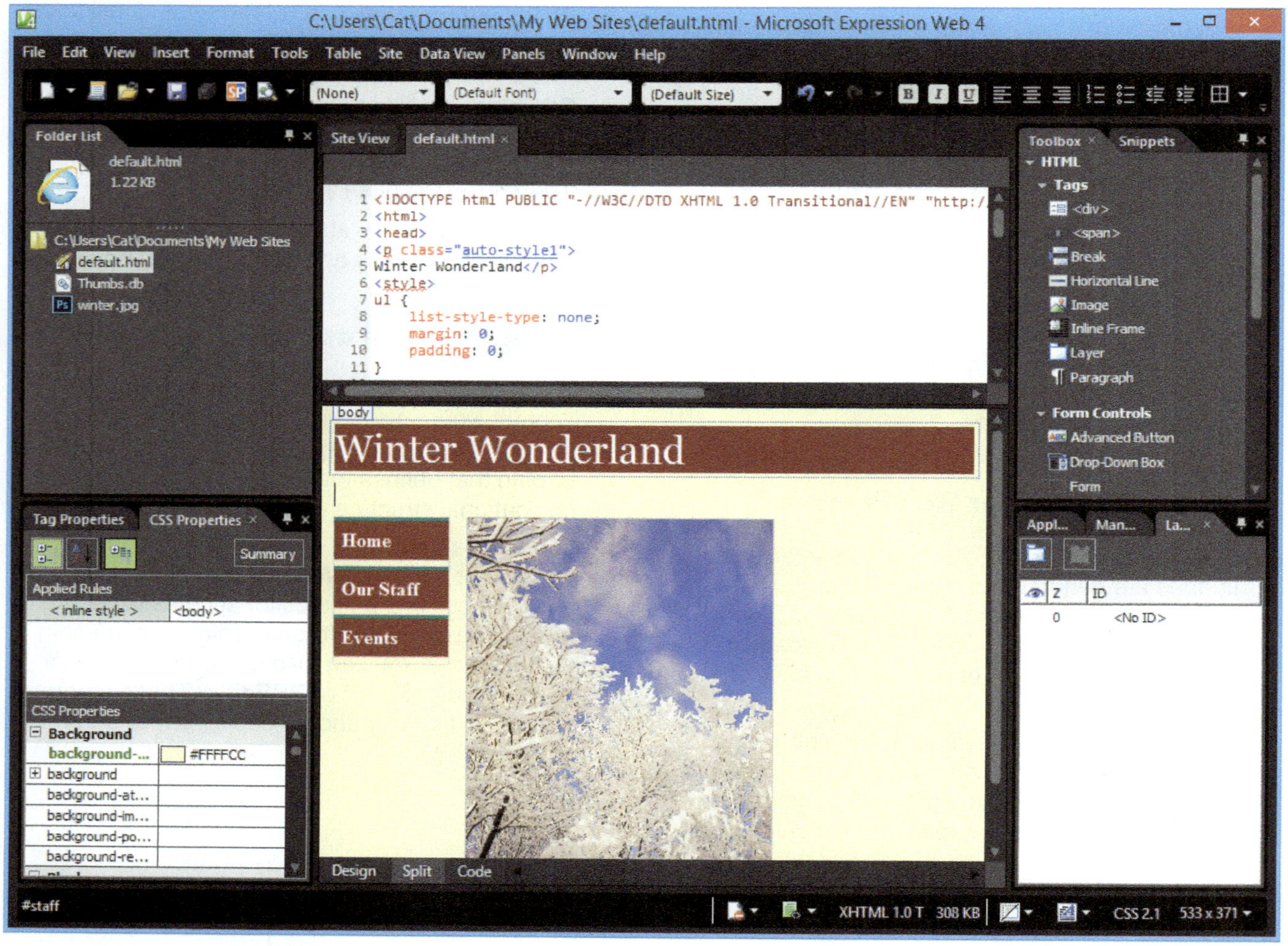

Apply B-1

In this activity, you have the opportunity to use what you have learned about Web page design to plan, design, and develop a Web site for a business. You can do these steps on your own, with a partner, or with a group.

1. First, decide which business you will create the Web site for. You may want to conduct online research to see how similar businesses have designed their Web sites.
2. Use storyboarding techniques to help you lay out the pages and plan how they will be linked.
3. Select the tools you will use to develop the site. For example, will you use HTML, DHTML, or XML editors? Will you need to convert from one to another?
4. Use the principles of design and color theory to make sure the pages in the Web site are consistent, appealing, and readable.
5. Acquire image files by scanning or saving a photo from a digital camera and insert one or more images on your pages.
6. If your Web page editor allows, try working with dynamic content using DHTML.
7. Publish your Web site to a host and invite comments from your peers.

Communicating on the Web

- There are a variety of ways to communicate with others online, ranging from instant messaging with friends to expressing yourself on social networking sites and blogs, and sharing photos and video clips.

Chatting and Messaging

- Internet Relay Chat (IRC) is an Internet service that enables users to join chat groups, called *channels*, and enter into live, or real-time, conversations. In addition to IRC channels, most ISPs offer chat forums as well. Chat channels can also be found within online video games.
- Every channel has a moderator who can remove a sender from the channel for any reason. The standards of behavior differ from channel to channel, so it is best to practice respectful online behavior.
- *Instant messaging* is when you send real-time messages to another Internet user. Instant messaging is like a chat room, except you get to choose your chat partners.

Photo and Video Sharing

- Photo and video sharing is using the Internet to send digital photos or video clips to another Internet user. These photos and videos can be shared privately or publicly on Web sites and apps, such as Instagram and YouTube.

Social Networking

- Sites such as Facebook and LinkedIn let you connect family, friends, and business colleagues by linking your own personal profile to those of others. Most social networking sites are free, although you have to register an account.
- On Facebook, as with other social networking sites, you can tailor your profile to add as much or as little personal information as possible, as well as uploading photos, posting messages, and linking to other sites.
- Twitter, another popular social networking site, lets you create 140-character messages, called "tweets," to keep others up to date on what you are doing or thinking about. You upload messages to the Twitter.com Web site, where they can be read by anyone who is interested.

- Take care to use social networking appropriately and responsibly. Remember that everything you do and say is online for others to see. Always think about what you are going to write before you post it. You do not want to post content that may embarrass you or hurt another's feelings.
- Tips such as the following can help to ensure that your social networking communications are safe ones.
    - Do not add just anyone as a "friend."
    - Check your settings.
    - Learn how to change your status to invisible, so others do not know you are online, or visible, so they do know you are online.
    - Remember that your posts and profiles can be easily tracked online. Don't write or post anything online that you would not want your grandparents or teachers to see or that you would not want posted about yourself.
    - Never give out private information such as your phone number or address.
    - Never agree to meet a new online friend in person.

Blogging

- A blog—or Weblog—is a type of Web page diary. People create blogs to share their thoughts and opinions.
- A blog is stored on a Web server, like a Web page, and the owner usually updates it on a regular basis. Anyone with access to the Internet can read the blog. Blogs are not restricted to only text. Photo blogs consist solely of digital photographs.
- Often, blogs provide a way for readers to comment on the blog content.

Using Collaborative Tools for File Sharing

- Collaborative software enables people work together more closely. With collaborative software, users can share calendars, work on a document together, or even hold meetings through the network. Collaborative software is also called groupware.
- Many Internet sites offer collaborative capability. Microsoft's OneDrive allows a user to post content and then invite other users to share those documents. Google also allows users to collaborate by sharing documents, worksheets, and slides. A user who shares content using these sites can specify whether a person can view only or view and edit content.

Using Listservers

- LISTSERVE is a commercial product that allows a person to e-mail content to an entire list of recipients at the same time. Such mailing lists are usually organized by common interest, and the members of the mailing list must often petition to join the list.
- Pushing content through a mailing list can be a very efficient way to communicate the same material to many interested recipients at the same time.

Figure B-2 An Internet site such as OneDrive allows you to share documents, music, and pictures with people you invite.

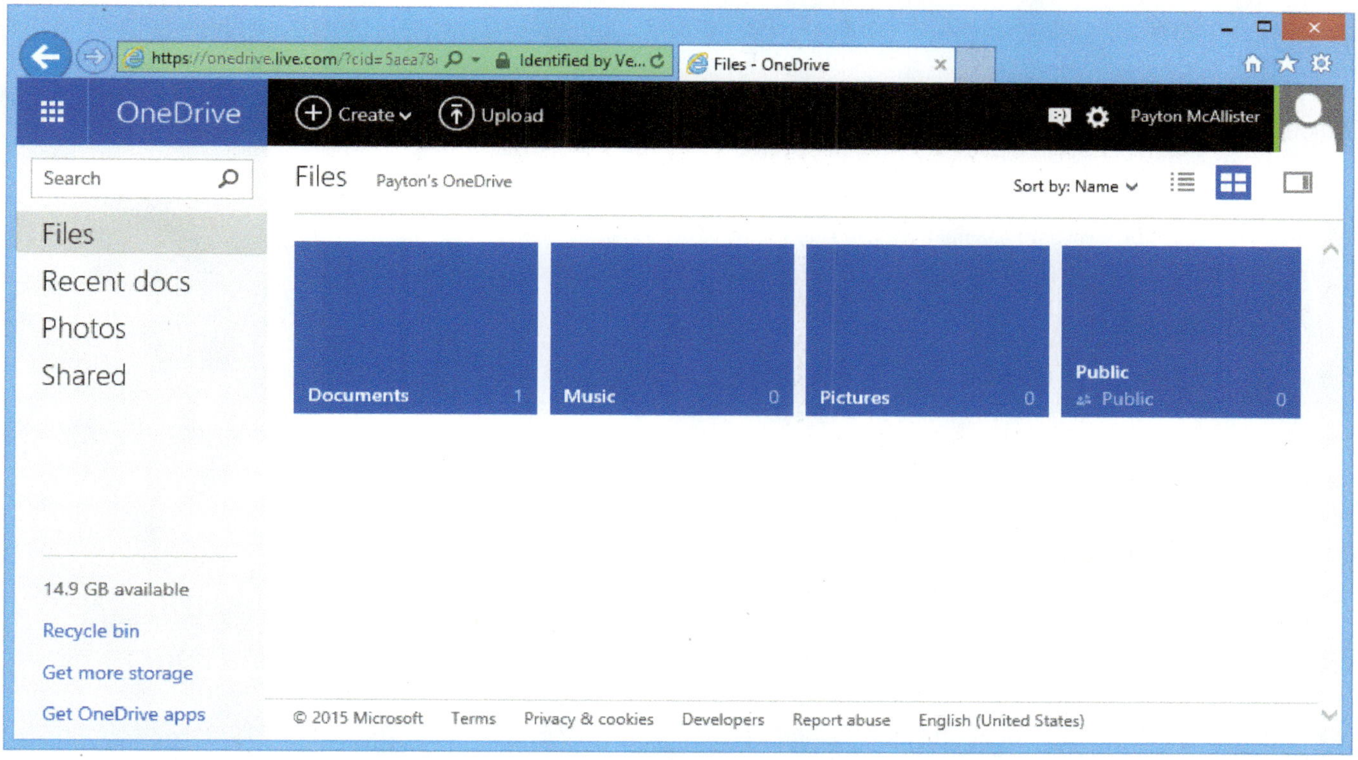

Appendix C Computers in Your Life

Managing Personal and Business Communications

Working with E-Mail

- E-mail, or electronic mail, allows people to send an unlimited number of messages quickly and easily to anyone with an e-mail address.

Create and Send Messages

- To compose a new message, click a button within the e-mail client. The client displays a form for you to complete. The form includes two main parts—the header, which includes places for entering the recipient(s) and the subject, and the body, which is where you type the message.
- Specify the message's recipient in the To line of the message form. Depending on your e-mail client's features, you may select someone's name from an address book. If you want to send a copy of the message to other recipients, you can add their names or addresses to the To line or place them in the Cc line.
- Next, fill in the Subject line. The Subject line gives the recipient an idea of the message's content and may help the recipient decide whether to open it or delete it. Add your message to the body of the form. Finally, click Send.
- If you do not want to send the message immediately, you can save it as a draft, then complete it later and send it.

Manage Signatures

- E-mail applications such as Microsoft Outlook allow you to create a signature that can be applied to every new message you send. You choose the wording for the signature, such as your name, department, e-mail address, and phone number. You can usually also apply font formatting to the signature. You may be able to create more than one signature, so that you can apply one to new work messages, another to replies to messages, and still another for informal communications.

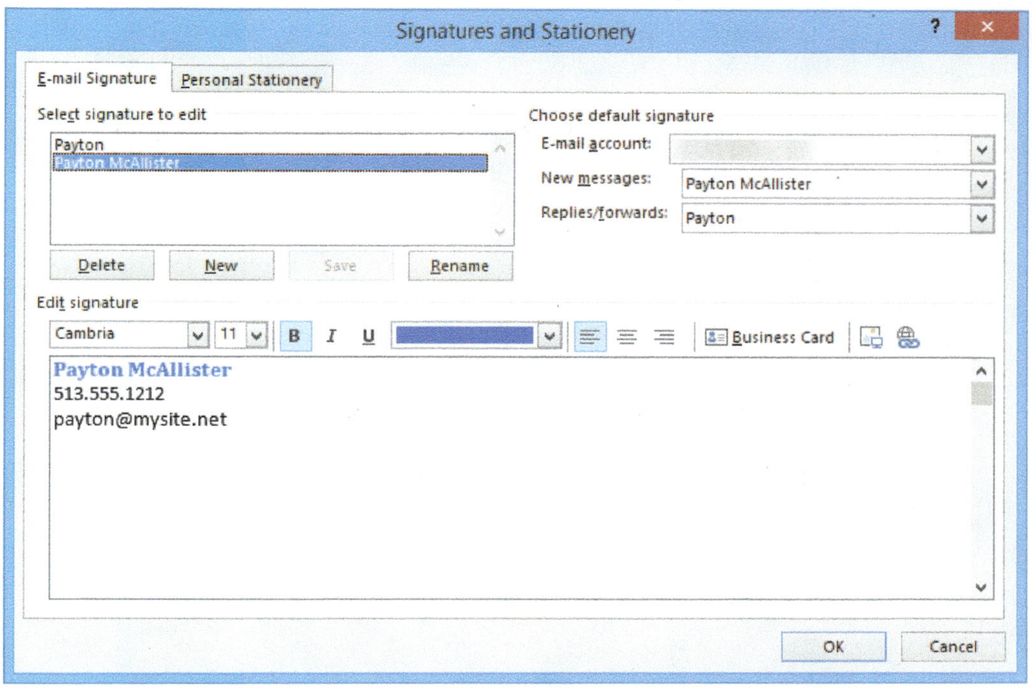

Figure C-1

Create signatures to add to new messages and replies or forwarded messages.

- If you do not specify that your signature will be applied to all new messages or replies, you can usually select your signature from a menu or ribbon tab button. You can edit or delete a signature at any time you want to stop using it.

Use Automated Messages

- When you are out of the office or otherwise not available, you can use an automatic reply, or "away" message to automatically send a reply to incoming messages. The reply can politely tell the sender that you are unavailable, and when you will be back. Some systems even let you customize an automatic reply for specific addresses.

Manage E-Mail

- E-mail applications provide a number of features to help you manage and organize your e-mail messages. Some programs allow you to display only unread messages, so that you can address them efficiently. You can create new folders in your application to store messages according to project or sender.
- Your application may also allow you to create rules or actions that make it easy to manage messages. For example, a rule could specify that all incoming messages from certain addresses will be stored in a specific folder, or that as soon as you click an action button, a message is moved to a particular folder.

Manage Junk Mail and Spam

- Spam is unwanted, or junk, e-mail messages and advertisements. Like physical junk mail, spam usually tries to sell something to the recipient. Some servers use technology to block "spammers" or automatically put spam in a "spam folder." Some e-mail clients provide special spam filters that users can configure to automatically delete junk mail.
- You can mark unwanted messages yourself as junk or spam so your program automatically delivers them to the junk or spam folder instead of to your inbox.
- It is worthwhile checking your spam folder regularly, because sometimes personal or important e-mail is mistakenly re-routed there. If you find a message that is not junk or spam, you can specify that the sender should be trusted and messages from that sender no longer be placed in the junk folder.

Set Message Sensitivity, Security, and Delivery Options

- Most programs let you set delivery options before sending a message. You may be able to select when you want a message to be sent, specify the level of importance or sensitivity, set security options such as encryption, and request a confirmation that a message has been opened or read.

Figure C-2

Specify importance, sensitivity, and delivery options for a message in the Properties dialog box.

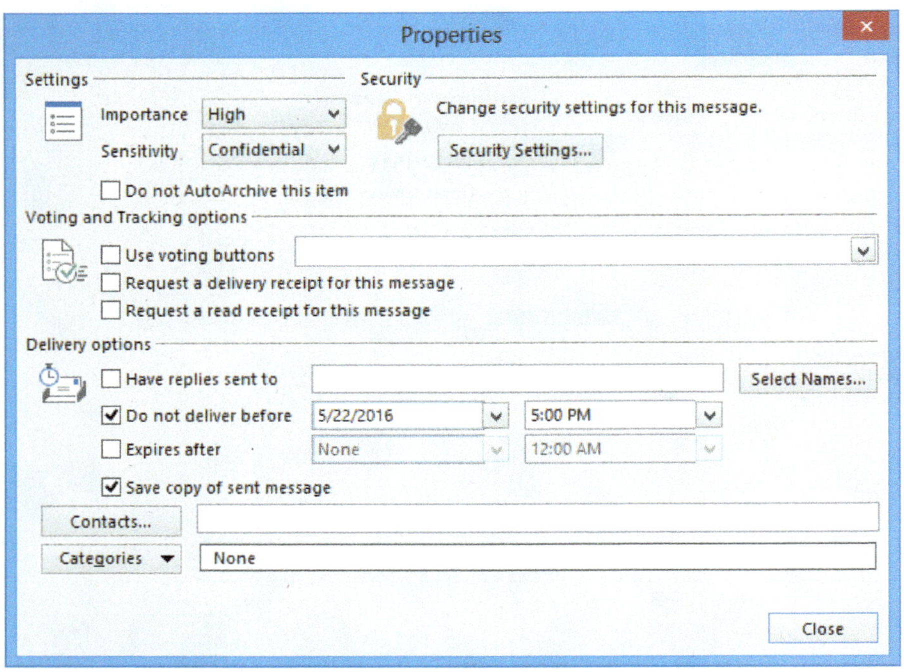

View Mailbox Details

- Most e-mail applications allow you to view current mailbox settings and customize them for your use. The Outlook Options dialog box, for example, gives you details on your settings for composing and receiving messages, formatting options, settings for receiving and forwarding messages, saving and sending messages, and tracking messages.
- You can also use a feature such as Mailbox Cleanup to view the current size of your mailbox folders, as well as to find items in your mailbox or archive messages and other items that are older than a specified date.

Working with Attachments

- E-mail also lets you attach files to a message. Anything sent with an e-mail message is called an attachment. Common attachments include word processing documents, spreadsheets, photos, artwork, and videos.
- You can add attachments by clicking a button and then clicking the name of the file you want to attach to the e-mail.
- When you receive a message with an attachment, you may be able to view it from within the message, using a preview utility. Or, you can save attachments to your computer so that you can verify the files are secure before you open them.

Organizing Your Life

Using a Digital Calendar to Set Up Meetings and Appointments

- Many communications programs such as Outlook include a calendar feature that you can use to schedule one-time and recurring events, meetings, and appointments. There are also stand-alone calendar programs and online calendars.
- To schedule a one-time event or appointment, you create the event and enter details such as the date, time, and location. The event or appointment displays on the calendar. You can even set a reminder to display on your screen to remind you. If an event or appointment will recur on a regular schedule, you can specify the interval that the item recurs, such as every Monday, or the fifth of every month, or even once a year.
- A meeting is similar to an appointment, but includes people other than yourself. When you set up a meeting, you supply details as for an appointment, and you can then send invitations by text message or e-mail to other people or contact groups that you want to attend the meeting and the program will keep track of their replies.
- Many Web sites maintain calendars of events. You can subscribe to these calendars and the Web site will send you notifications when an event is scheduled or changed.

Working with E-mail Contacts and Contact Groups

- E-mail programs provide you with an address book, where you can store the names and e-mail addresses of frequent e-mail contacts. You select a contact and then click a button to send a message to that person.
- You may be able to create group contact lists in your address book. If you and several friends are working on a project, you might create a contact group called Project and add the e-mail address of each project member to the contact group. This feature lets you send a message to all the contacts at once, saving you the time of typing each address separately.

Apply C-1

In this activity, you will work with some of Outlook 2013's basic features. You will need to have Outlook set up to send and receive e-mail messages.

1. Start Outlook 2013. On the HOME tab, click New Email to open a new message form. Create a message to yourself by typing your e-mail address in the To box, the subject **Test Message 1** in the Subject box, and a brief message in the body of the message form.
2. Click the Send button to send the message.
3. If you do not receive the message immediately in your Inbox, click the Send/Receive All Folders button on the HOME or SEND/RECEIVE tab.
4. View your message in the Reading Pane. Then click the Reply button above the message in the Reading Pane to open the reply area. Type a brief reply to the message and then click Send.
5. Click New Email to open another new message form. Address the message to yourself and add the subject line **See Attached**. Add an attachment to the message as follows:
    a. On the MESSAGE tab, click Attach File.
    b. In the Insert File dialog box, navigate to a location on your computer where you are storing files for this course, select a Word file, and click Insert.
    c. Type a brief description of the attached file in the message area.
    d. Click Send.
6. You should now have three messages in your Inbox. Click the first message, Test Message 1, to select it, and then click the Unread/Read button on the HOME tab to mark this message as read.
7. With the message still selected, click Delete on the HOME tab. Then click the Deleted Items or Trash folder to view the deleted message. Click the Inbox folder.
8. Create a signature as follows:
    a. Click the FILE menu and then click Options to open the Outlook Options dialog box.
    b. Click Mail in the left tab and then click the Signatures button.
    c. Click the New button and type a name for your new signature. Click OK.
    d. In the Edit signature area, type your name and any other information you want to include, such as your phone number or e-mail address.
    e. Use the formatting options to change font, font size, font style, and font color as desired.
    f. Click the Save button to store the signature.
    g. If necessary, click the down arrow for New messages and select your signature.
    h. Click OK twice.
9. Click New Email to open a new message. You signature should appear in the new message.
10. Address the message to yourself and add the subject line **Delay Delivery**. Add a message. Click the OPTIONS tab in the message and then click the More Options dialog box launcher to open the Properties dialog box. Change options as follows:
    a. Click the Importance down arrow and select High.
    b. Click the Sensitivity down arrow and select Confidential.
    c. Under Delivery options, click the Do not deliver before check box and set a time that is five minutes from now.
    d. Click Close and then click Send. Notice that your message is still in the Outbox.
11. While you are waiting for your delayed message to arrive, click the Junk E-mail folder to see if any messages have been sent there by your e-mail provider. Click Junk on the HOME tab, and then click Junk E-mail Options to see options for controlling junk mail. Click OK.
12. Click Calendar at the bottom of the window. Click on the calendar day that is a week from today and type appointment information, such as a doctor visit at 9:00 am. Click outside the appointment box to see the appointment on the calendar.

(continued)

Apply C-1 *(cont)*

13. Click on the calendar day that is a week from the appointment you set and then click New Meeting on the HOME tab. Set up the meeting as follows:
    a. Click in the To box and type the e-mail addresses of yourself and two of your classmates.
    b. Type the subject line **Board Meeting**.
    c. Type the location **Conference Room A**.
    d. Set the start time for 9:00 AM and the end time for 10:00 AM.
    e. Add a brief message and then click Send.
14. Click Mail to return to the mail window, and click Inbox if necessary. Your delayed message should have arrived, along with the meeting request. If you receive a meeting message from a classmate, reply to the message saying you will attend.
15. Click People at the bottom of the window to open Outlook contacts. If you do not have contacts already, use the New Contact button to open a form so you can enter contact information for several of your classmates.
16. Create a new contact group as follows:
    a. Click New Contact Group on the HOME tab and then type a name for a contact group.
    b. Click Add Members and then click From Outlook Contacts.
    c. Select each contact you want to include and then click the Members button at the bottom of the Select Members dialog box. Click OK.
    d. Click Save & Close.
17. Select the contact group name and then click Meeting on the HOME tab to send a meeting request to the members of the contact group.
18. Return to your Inbox, mark all messages as read, and delete all messages you created in this activity. Delete all appointments and meetings and close Outlook.

Comprehension and Communication Skills

Reading for Comprehension

- Throughout your personal and work life, you will need to demonstrate that you can read and comprehend many different types of content.
- Diagnosing or troubleshooting software issues, for example, may require you to consult various types of documentation. Documentation is typically available from the following sources:
    - Printed instructions that accompany the software or printed tutorials written either by the software vendor or a third party and available in libraries, online, or at bookstores.
    - Electronic help provided as part of the program or on a separate CD or DVD. Opening the program's Help menu lets you troubleshoot problems as they happen and find out how to perform certain operations or tasks.
    - Software documentation sometimes may be found on the software publisher's Web site. These sites often include answers to users' frequently asked questions (FAQs) and give other helpful hints. Web documentation can be updated quickly by the publisher and shared with users who need it.
    - Many software companies maintain an online knowledge base that users can search to find information and get help.

- As part of your school or work responsibilities, you may need to read material at various levels of technicality. Memos, letters, e-mail messages, magazine articles and the like may fall in the nontechnical range. Operational manuals and textbooks may be much more technical in scope.

Communicating Effectively

- Another important set of skills for personal and work life relates to communicating effectively with your peers and with supervisors and customers at your workplace. Communicating is how people connect with others. Communication prevents misunderstandings. It gives you a way to share ideas. It even makes it easier for you to appreciate and respect other people's opinions.
- At its most basic, communication is an exchange between a sender and a receiver. The sender transmits the message with a specific intent. The receiver interprets the message and responds.
- Effective communication is when the receiver interprets the message the way the sender intended. Ineffective communication is when the receiver misinterprets the message.
- Sometimes barriers get in the way of effective communication. When you recognize any potential communication barriers, you can take steps to overcome them—both when you listen and when you speak.
- Verbal communication is the exchange of messages by speaking or writing. Talking is usually a very effective form of verbal communication. When you speak clearly and use language the receiver understands, he or she almost always gets the message the way you intend it.
- Nonverbal communication helps put words into context. This form of communication includes visual messages that the receiver can see, such as a smile when you are talking. It also includes physical messages, such as a pat on the back.
- Active listening is an important part of effective communication. When you are an active listener, you pay attention to the speaker and make sure you hear and understand the message. Active listening is a sign of respect. It shows you are willing to communicate and that you care about the speaker and the message. When you listen actively, the other person is more likely to listen when you speak, too.

Apply C-2

In this activity, you will practice using effective communication skills with a partner.

1. Think of something you would like to tell your partner, then use verbal, nonverbal, and active listening techniques to deliver the message, and to receive the message delivered by your partner.
2. Would you use different methods to communicate with people in the workplace such as a co-worker, supervisor, or customer? What if there was a conflict?
3. Try the exercise again pretending to be in a work situation. Discuss the experience with the class.

Career Exploration and Planning

Researching Personal Skills and Aptitudes Relating to Jobs and Careers

- A *career* is a chosen field of work in which you try to advance over time by gaining responsibility and earning more money. Another word for career is occupation. A *job* is any activity you do in exchange for money or other payment. A job does not necessarily lead to advancement.
- The first step in identifying a career is self-assessment. That means taking a close, objective look at your interests, values, and abilities. You then use that information to select careers or career clusters to investigate further.
- Your interests tell what you like to do and what you do not like to do. They are the subjects or activities that attract your attention and that you enjoy doing or learning about. There are six general interest categories: the arts, business, crafts, office operations, science, and social. Knowing your interests helps you identify a career that you will find interesting.
- A value is the importance that you place on various elements in your life. Knowing what values you feel most strongly about helps you avoid compromising the things that are most important to you. Recognizing your values also helps you prioritize what matters most to you in a career. Money might be more important to you than leisure time. Working with people might be more important to you than what shift you work.
- An ability, or skill, is something you do well. You have many abilities. For example, you may work well with your hands, or you may be very good at mathematics. It is much more pleasant to work in an occupation that uses your abilities.
- There are fourteen general categories of abilities: artistic, clerical, interpersonal, language, leadership, manual, mathematical/numerical, musical/dramatic, organization, persuasive, scientific, social, visual, and technical/mechanical. You might have abilities in more than one category.

Using Career Resources to Research Occupations and Career Paths

- By conducting occupational research, you learn details about a career, including tasks performed, the job outlook, the education required, the working environment, and many other things. It requires time and effort to research the occupations that interest you and to prepare for a specific career. Remember, your efforts allow you to find a job that gives you satisfaction.
- Many resources are available to you for your research. A good way to get started is to interview individuals who are already working in an occupation that you are interested in.
- Another good resource is the Career Cluster information provided by the U.S. Department of Education. This system organizes careers into 16 clusters, listed below. The careers in each cluster are in related industries or business areas. Each cluster is organized into pathways. Each pathway leads to a set of specific careers. The careers in a cluster require a similar set of skills and the same core training and education. You can narrow your career search by identifying a cluster that interests you. You can investigate the career clusters and pathways at www.careertech.org.
    - Agriculture, Food & Natural Resources
    - Architecture & Construction
    - Arts, Audio/Video Technology & Communications
    - Business Management & Administration
    - Education & Training
    - Finance
    - Government & Public Administration
    - Health & Science
    - Hospitality & Tourism
    - Human Services
    - Information Technology
    - Law, Public Safety, Corrections & Security
    - Manufacturing
    - Marketing
    - Science, Technology, Engineering & Mathematics
    - Transportation, Distribution & Logistics

Demonstrating Job-Seeking Skills

- There is more to effective job seeking than simply preparing a good resume. As you have already learned, you can improve the chance your resume will be viewed by including a cover letter, and you can add to the impression you made in an interview by sending a thank-you letter.
- Additional skills that can tip the employment scales in your favor include mastering the process of filling out application forms, conducting a mock interview, and making a follow-up call.
- You may be required to fill out a job application either online or in person. Application forms require you to enter specific information about your education and past employment, including dates and locations. As with your resume, it is important to be truthful and accurate. If you have to fill out a hard copy application at a prospective place of employment, take with you all the information you are likely to need, and make sure you are dressed appropriately for that workplace.
- You can prepare yourself for the interview process by conducting a mock interview. In a mock interview, you engage in an interview with someone such as a career counselor that is as much as possible like a real interview. You should prepare to answer questions about your background and skills and present yourself as a real candidate for the job with appropriate dress and demeanor. Mock interviews are often videotaped so you can see what impression you made on the interviewer.
- After an interview, it is important to write a thank-you note to the employer to show your interest in the position. You should also be prepared to follow up with a phone call or e-mail.

Planning for Growth and Skill Development

- One way to begin the process of planning for personal growth and skill development is to create a personal academic plan. A personal academic plan helps you set goals for the things you want to accomplish in school. Some schools call it a personal career plan. Some things that you might put in your plan include:
  - Yearly academic goals
  - Assessment of your skills, knowledge, and experience
  - Assessment of factors that will contribute to your success
  - Assessment of factors that might interfere with your success
  - Basic skills assessment
- Some academic plans include a portfolio. A portfolio is a collection of information and documents that show the progress you make in school and in your career planning. It helps you stay on track to achieve your educational and career goals. A portfolio may be an actual folder that holds printed documents and other materials, or it may be electronic and stored on a computer. Some things to include in a portfolio are examples of achievement such as an essay you are proud of, and awards or certificates of accomplishment.
- Employability skills can generally be placed into two groups: hard skills and transferable skills. Employers often look for people with hard skills to fill specific jobs. For example, a software development company looks to hire people skilled at writing code. Transferable skills can be used on almost any job. They are called transferable skills because you can transfer them from one situation or career to another. The foundation skills you use to succeed in other areas of your life, such as decision-making and problem-solving, are transferable skills. You can practice and develop these skills in school, at work, and at home.
- Some computer skills are also transferable. There are very few jobs today that do not require basic computer use. If you have these basic skills, you can take them wherever you go:
  - Turn a computer on and start a program
  - Type on a computer keyboard without making many mistakes
  - Access the Internet and navigate from one location to another
  - Use a search engine to do basic Internet research
  - Write and send e-mail
- Growth and skill development can be a lifelong learning process. Lifelong learning means continually acquiring new knowledge and skills throughout the course of your life. Education and training are not limited to learning new skills for the workplace. You should consider educational opportunities to enrich your life at home, with friends, and in your community.
- Understanding and using technology can help you achieve lifelong learning. It provides access to online information and helps you stay informed about current events and other topics.

Impact of Local and Global Trends on Career Plans

- Employment trends influence the number of available jobs in a certain industry as well as where the jobs are. A trend is a general move in a certain direction. An employment trend is one way the job market is changing over time. Many factors influence employment trends, including economic factors and even cultural trends. For example, a shift from using personal computers to using smart phones impacts employment in the information technology industry.
- Technology itself has a strong influence on employment and job outlook. It creates new jobs, replaces old jobs, and changes the way some people perform their existing jobs. Understanding the function and use of technology in the modern workplace is an essential skill in many professions.
- A good source for information about employment trends is the Occupational Outlook Handbook, which is published by the U.S. Bureau of Labor Statistics. It describes more than 200 occupations, including responsibilities, working conditions, education requirements, salary ranges, and job outlook. Look it up at www.bls.gov/oco.
- Local and global trends can impact career plans and life goals in almost all career fields. You can use the Internet to monitor trends to help you stay prepared so you can adjust your plans and goals.

Building Community and Mentor Relationships

- Many companies pair new or younger employees with older, more experienced mentors. A mentor is someone who can provide career advice and guidance to help you achieve your career goals. Having a mentor is one way to build positive relationships in the workplace.
- As you make your way in a career, you will find that developing professional relationships with people and organizations in your community can be very rewarding. A cordial relationship with a local banker can be very helpful, for example, when you need money to expand your business.

Apply C-3

In this activity, you will use a personal assessment to identify a career that interests you and then record your personal career goals.

1. **With your teacher's permission,** use the Internet, library, or your school's guidance resources to learn more about that career, or interview someone who has that career.
2. Use these career resources to develop a list or database of businesses that hire people in that career and of opportunities for continuing education or workplace experience in that field.
3. Identify the education, job skills, and experience you will need to achieve your career goals.
4. Create a time line showing how you will achieve these goals, and present it to a partner or to the class.

Succeeding in the Workplace

Workplace Essentials

- Succeeding in a job or a career requires you to develop skills for working with your colleagues as well as your clients or customers. You can improve your chances for success by presenting a professional appearance and behaving in a professional manner with regard to the many aspects of business ethics with which you will come in contact. Keeping yourself and your workplace safe is another essential component of professionalism.

Customer Service

- An important part of the workplace environment is how a business treats its customers. Customer service is the way a business meets customer needs and wants. A happy customer will return; an unhappy customer will not. And many unhappy customers will post negative comments and reviews about the service, which will impact the business.
- If you interact with customers as part of your work responsibilities, your employer will expect you to behave in a polite and professional manner at all times. Even if you do not directly interact with customers, you will be expected to present yourself to co-workers and other businesses in a way that reflects positively on the company.

Appropriate Workplace Attire and Grooming

- Dress standards vary depending on the career that you choose. For example, you wouldn't expect your car mechanic to be wearing a suit and tie, and you wouldn't want your lawyer to be wearing grease-covered clothing.
- However, good grooming habits are required in all professions. The following are recommendations for maintaining a well-groomed, professional appearance:
  - Wear clothes that are clean, neat, and in good repair and wear clean and appropriate shoes.
  - Bathe daily, keep your hair neat and clean, and keep your nails clean.
  - Brush your teeth at least twice a day and floss daily. Use mouthwash or breath mints.
  - Keep makeup light and neutral and keep jewelry to a minimum.
  - Do not use perfume or cologne and use unscented deodorant.

Business Ethics

- Ethics are a set of beliefs about what is right and what is wrong. Work ethics are beliefs and behaviors about what is right and wrong in a work environment. Ethical behavior includes treating people with respect and also following the law. For example, taking home office supplies is not ethical—it's stealing. Employers value employees who behave ethically at work. It shows that you are honest and respectful, so others with trust and respect you in return.
- Behaving ethically at work also means following the company rules, regulations, and processes Usually, when you start a new job you are given an employee handbook. An employee handbook describes company policies and procedures, such as how to request vacation time, and the different benefits that are available. It should also list all rules and policies that you are expected to obey. These might include:
  - Maintaining confidentiality of information
  - Respecting copyrights and patents
  - Respecting co-workers' and customers' rights
- Ethics extends beyond the actions and behaviors of individual workers. It also applies to companies and organizations as a whole. A company that ignores the safety of workers, or hides information customers need to make an informed purchasing decision, is not behaving ethically.

Keeping the Workplace Safe

- In 1970, the federal government passed a law called the Occupational Safety and Health Act. This law requires all employers to provide a safe and healthful workplace. Workers must be provided with safe equipment, protective clothing when needed, and education about safety practices.

- The Occupational Safety and Health Administration (OSHA) was formed to inspect companies and enforce safety laws. Even so, more than 5,000 Americans die from on-the-job accidents every year. As a worker under the Occupational Safety and Health Act, you have the following rights and responsibilities:
    - Right to know. You have the right to know about hazards in your workplace, as well as the right to training to learn how to identify workplace hazards and what to do if there is an incident.
    - Right to refuse unsafe work. If you have reasonable grounds to believe the work you do or the piece of equipment you use is unsafe, you can stop work immediately. You cannot be laid off, suspended, or penalized for refusing unsafe work if you follow the proper procedures.
    - Responsibility to follow safety rules. It is your employer's responsibility to teach you the safety rules; it is your responsibility to follow the rules.
    - Responsibility to ask for training. If you feel that you need more training than your employer provides, it is your responsibility to ask for it.
    - Responsibility to speak up. It is your responsibility to report incidents and unsafe work practices as well as unsafe conditions.

Demonstrating a Professional Approach in the Workplace

- Professionalism, or work ethic, is the ability to show respect to everyone around you while you perform your responsibilities as best you can. It includes a basic set of personal qualities that make an employee successful. These qualities include:
    - Integrity
    - Courtesy
    - Honesty
    - Dependability
    - Punctuality
    - Responsibility
    - Cooperative
    - Positive attitude
    - Open-mindedness
    - Flexibility
- Professionalism also means you demonstrate positive work behaviors, such as regular attendance. A professional also maintains a clean and safe work environment, performs tasks effectively, shows initiative, and takes pride in his or her work accomplishments.

Index

A

G

H

I

J

K

L

M

Q